SIMESTER AND SULLIVAN'S CRIMINAL LAW

Simester and Sullivan's Criminal Law

Theory and Doctrine

Sixth Edition

AP SIMESTER
JR SPENCER
Findlay STARK
GR SULLIVAN
and
GJ VIRGO

·HART·
PUBLISHING

OXFORD AND PORTLAND, OREGON
2016

Hart Publishing

An imprint of Bloomsbury Publishing Plc

Hart Publishing Ltd
Kemp House
Chawley Park
Cumnor Hill
Oxford OX2 9PH
UK

Bloomsbury Publishing Plc
50 Bedford Square
London
WC1B 3DP
UK

www.hartpub.co.uk
www.bloomsbury.com

Published in North America (US and Canada) by
Hart Publishing
c/o International Specialized Book Services
920 NE 58th Avenue, Suite 300
Portland, OR 97213-3786
USA

www.isbs.com

HART PUBLISHING, the Hart/Stag logo, BLOOMSBURY and the
Diana logo are trademarks of Bloomsbury Publishing Plc

First published 2016

British Library Cataloguing-in-Publication Data

A catalogue record for this book is available from the British Library.

ISBN: PBK: 978-1-84946-722-3

Library of Congress Cataloging-in-Publication Data

Names: Simester, A. P., author. | Spencer, John R., 1946– author. | Stark, Findlay, author. |
Sullivan, G. R., author. | Virgo, Graham, author.

Title: Simester and Sullivan's Criminal law : theory and doctrine / A.P. Simester, J.R. Spencer,
F. Stark, G.R. Sullivan, and G.J. Virgo.

Other titles: Criminal law

Description: Sixth Edition. | Oxford [UK] ; Portland, Oregon : Hart Publishing, 2016. |
Includes bibliographical references and index.

Identifiers: LCCN 2016034354 (print) | LCCN 2016034955 (ebook) | ISBN 9781849467223
(pbk. : alk. paper) | ISBN 9781509912032 (Epub)

Subjects: LCSH: Criminal law—England.

Classification: LCC KD7869 .S56 2016 (print) | LCC KD7869 (ebook) | DDC 345.42—dc23

LC record available at https://lccn.loc.gov/2016034354

Typeset by Compuscript Ltd, Shannon
Printed and bound in Great Britain

PREFACE

Books, articles, and Law Commission reports may come and go. But there will always be crimes. There will always be a need for criminal law. And so there will always be a need for courts, and for secondary sources, to tell us what the law is; to tell us what is required of us; and to reassure us about what we need to do in order to circumnavigate the criminal justice system. Moreover, with the pace of change in English law nowadays, we need to be told not once but regularly.

Such lamentable truths bring us to the sixth edition. The criminal law never stops. As always, there are new legislative provisions to scrutinise and assess. A steady stream of appellate case law has added to, confirmed, or undermined existing principles. By and large, however, nothing truly radical or unpredictable has occurred since the last edition, save for the remarkable decisions delivered jointly by the Supreme Court and Privy Council in *Jogee* and *Ruddock* (2016). As many readers will be aware, these cases abolished the increasingly controversial adjunct to the principles of secondary liability known as the doctrine of 'joint enterprise'. The substance and effect of these decisions are of the utmost importance, conceptually and normatively, and are fully treated in this edition.

Equally remarkable is the way the Supreme Court/Privy Council went about the process of abolition. Binding appellate authorities were not finessed or reinterpreted. They were simply found to be 'wrong', when contrasted with the analysis of the relevant case law preferred by the Supreme Court, and thus abandoned. In a somewhat analogous spirit, shortly before we went to press the United Kingdom voted by referendum to leave the European Union. A source of criminal law of increasing importance has been the creation of substantive offences when necessary to give effectiveness to obligations imposed by EU law, particularly in the fields of consumer, employee, and investor protection. Though for the moment it lingers with us, that EU influence may fade into history. With it, and with abandonment of the codification programme, the criminal law of England and Wales is set to retain a distinctively Anglophone character, a melange of many statutes and countless cases, tempered to some extent (at least for now) by the European Convention for Human Rights.

Alongside our analysis of developments since the fifth edition, we have taken the opportunity to revise chapters on sexual offences, strict liability, and vicarious liability. Our discussion has been greatly enriched by the participation of Dr Findlay Stark. We welcome him warmly to this joint enterprise.

APS
JRS
GRS
GJV
July 2016

CONTENTS

CONTENTS

EXPANDED TABLE OF CONTENTS

ABBREVIATIONS

The following abbreviations for standard textbooks and statutory materials are used in the text and footnotes.

Ashworth, *Principles*	A. Ashworth and J. Horder, *Principles of Criminal Law* (Oxford: Oxford University Press, 7th ed., 2013)
ECHR	European Convention on Human Rights
Hart and Honoré	H.L.A. Hart and A.M. Honoré, *Causation in the Law* (Oxford: Oxford University Press, 2nd ed., 1985)
HRA 1998	Human Rights Act 1998
Model Penal Code	American Law Institute, *Model Penal Code* (Philadelphia: American Law Institute, Revised ed., 1985).
OAPA 1861	Offences Against the Person Act 1861
SOA 2003	Sexual Offences Act 2003
Smith and Hogan	D. Ormerod and K. Laird, *Smith and Hogan's Criminal Law* (Oxford: Oxford University Press, 14th ed., 2015)
Williams, *CLGP*	G. Williams, Criminal Law: The General Part (London: Stevens, 2nd ed., 1961)
Williams, *TBCL*	G. Williams, Textbook of Criminal Law (London: Stevens, 2nd ed., 1983)

TABLE OF CASES

TABLE OF LEGISLATION

United Kingdom

Australia

Belize

Canada

European Union

United States of America

TABLE OF INTERNATIONAL INSTRUMENTS

1

CRIMINAL LAW: DEFINITION AND AMBIT

The aim of this chapter is to introduce some of the theory that surrounds the criminal law: to explain why the criminal law matters, and to highlight the issues it raises. The chapter begins by considering the defining features of the criminal law, those which distinguish it from other varieties of law. Secondly, the ambit of criminal law is investigated—when is it apt to declare someone a criminal? The discussion in this chapter will lead on, in Chapter 2, to a discussion of the constitutional and Rule of Law principles that constrain the enactment and interpretation of criminal law; and later, in Chapter 16, to consideration of what sorts of actions properly attract criminal prohibitions.

§ 1.1 A search for definition

Like other types of law, the criminal law is a means by which the state participates in the ordering of its citizens' lives. Yet throughout the world, every society with a formal legal system distinguishes between criminal and civil law.[1] This raises a question about the scope of criminal law: what marks a law out as criminal rather than civil? One way of approaching that question is to look for a definition of the criminal law. Broadly speaking, a crime is an event that is prohibited by law, one which can be followed by a prosecution in criminal proceedings and, thereafter, by punishment on conviction:[2]

> "A crime must be defined by reference to the *legal* consequences of the act. We must distinguish, primarily, not between crimes and civil wrongs but between criminal and civil proceedings. A crime then becomes an act that is capable of being followed by criminal proceedings, having one of the types of outcome (punishment etc.) known to follow these proceedings."

Criminal law, in turn, is the variety of law that prohibits such crimes.

But to define criminal law only in these procedural terms fails to shed any light on a more fundamental problem: why does the distinction between criminal and other law matter? It is true that criminal prosecutions follow a different legal procedure from their civil counterparts. But if that is the sole difference, and there is no underlying reason for separating the two, drawing the distinction would be pointless.[3] We need to identify the distinguishing features that also justify treating crimes as a separate body of law.

---

[1] Robinson, "The Criminal–Civil Distinction and the Utility of Desert" (1996) 76 *Boston ULR* 201, 201–2.

[2] Williams, "The Definition of Crime" (1955) *CLP* 107, 123.

[3] Moreover there would be a problem explaining why the distinction is maintained in those countries which do not observe the procedural safeguards normally found in criminal law. See Robinson, "The Criminal–Civil Distinction and the Utility of Desert" (1996) 76 *Boston ULR* 201, 203.

(i) The harmful nature of the prohibited event

One suggestion might be that the harm proscribed by criminal law is greater in degree than that in the civil law, or is somehow public rather than private in nature. For example, across most if not all cultures, the criminal law contains provisions proscribing serious forms of violence and dishonesty. However, while it is true that prevention of harm is central to the criminal law, the distinctiveness of criminal wrongs cannot be captured by reference simply to the moral gravity of the wrongdoing and the importance of the interest being violated. For one thing, most harms are both public and private. The major oil spillage in Sydney harbour that gave rise to the *Wagon Mound* tort cases affected more than one person,[4] while by contrast an ordinary assault typically involves a single victim. Similarly, consider the situation where D plc has placed a large contract for the supply of raw materials with V Ltd. D is aware that without the contract, V would be forced to close with the loss of hundreds of jobs. If, despite this, D breaks the contract in order to obtain supplies from a cheaper overseas source, it commits no offence. Compare this case with the situation where a company fails to send its annual return to the Registrar of Companies within the time limits prescribed by the Companies Act 2006. It seems, therefore, that the events prohibited by criminal laws are not inherently distinguishable from those regulated by other sorts of law. Indeed, the same act can sometimes lead to both criminal and civil liability. If D takes V's car without V's consent, for example, he may be prosecuted for theft. He can also be sued in tort for conversion.

That said, there is intuitive appeal in the idea that criminal wrongs are typically more serious than their civil counterparts; sufficiently serious that, whether or not they also give rise to civil causes of action, the state feels constrained to step in and regulate them directly. This can be seen in the rule that a victim who forgives his attacker may discontinue his civil suit for damages, but cannot stop the prosecution of that attacker. Criminal offences are not merely a private matter. The public as a whole has an interest in their prevention and prosecution. Thus, according to Allen, behaviour is criminalised "because it consists in wrongdoing which directly and in serious degree threatens the security or well-being of society, and because it is not safe to leave it redressable only by compensation of the party injured".[5] Allen's remark is a useful pointer to why assaults are crimes while breaches of contract are not. Assault involves an interference with fundamental rights of the victim, rights which the State is perceived to have a duty to protect. By contrast, individuals are normally able to protect themselves against breach of contract, and can satisfactorily undo any damage suffered with the aid of the civil law.

Another possible basis for differentiating civil from criminal law is that criminal acts are those acts which are intrinsically morally wrong. (Such acts are sometimes called *mala in se*.) To some extent this is true of the more serious, stigmatic offences—assault, murder, and so

---

[4] *Overseas Tankship (UK) Ltd* v. *Morts Dock Engineering* [1961] AC 388; *Overseas Tankship (UK) Ltd* v. *Miller Steamship Co Pty* [1967] AC 617. Cf. public nuisance cases: *Halsey* v. *Esso Petroleum* [1961] 1 WLR 683.

[5] *Legal Duties and Other Essays in Jurisprudence* (1931) 233–4. Compare Coffee: "Characteristically, tort law prices, while criminal law prohibits". On this view, the criminal law should be invoked when the "price" of an action, that the defendant would have to pay in tortious damages, is insufficiently prohibitive. Coffee, "Does 'Unlawful' Mean 'Criminal'?: Reflections on the Disappearing Tort/Crime Distinction in American Law" (1991) 71 *Boston ULR* 193, 194.

forth.[6] But much of the modern criminal law involves prohibitions which constrain conduct which may be wrong only in the technical sense of breaching the terms of the prohibition (*mala prohibita*). Prohibitions of that kind are often in the public interest. For example, driving on the roads is safer overall because of speed limits. Yet there is little intrinsic moral difference, for instance, between driving safely at 70 miles per hour on the motorway and driving safely at 75; but the latter is an offence.[7] And conversely, lying may be immoral, but it is not *per se* a criminal act.

More generally, the sheer variety of conduct that has been designated a criminal wrong defies reduction to any "essential" minimum. One finds no unifying thread to the subject matter of the multifarious crimes known to England and Wales.[8] The criminal law has been used—indeed, overused—as a regulatory device, and consequently extends to conduct that can lack any inherent moral turpitude whatsoever, such as failing to notify the licensing authority of a change of address for one's driving licence, or omitting a required statement from a consumer credit contract. In this country, the fact that some particular action is criminal may reflect only a decision on the part of a regulatory body that the public interest requires resort to public means of suppression, and that the matter cannot be left to private redress or bargaining. Amongst the available public means of suppression, the criminal law is the most commonly employed coercive mechanism.

So there are limits to the extent to which we can safely elaborate upon our initial definition by reference to the things that criminal law prohibits. In part, this reflects the fact that criminal law engages with political and societal pressures which find expression in the form and content of the law. In Chapter 16, we shall discuss some of the reasons for the State to criminalise certain harms rather than others. But it should always be borne in mind that, in practice, criminal laws are characteristically deployed to control behaviour and events because there is perceived to be a societal, and political, interest in doing so.

(ii) Punishment

A second element of the preliminary definition given in § 1.1 was punishment. Perhaps the main distinction between criminal and civil law is that the criminal law licenses punishment whereas redress for civil law wrongs is predominantly compensation?

Punishment is an important facet of the criminal process. Indeed, it is an indispensable feature of criminal prohibitions. Parliament does not say, "Do not assault other people, *please*". That would not be a law at all. Rather, the law declares, "Do not assault other people, *or else* …". Of course, civil laws also specify sanctions. As Posner points out, however, the nature of the civil sanction differs from that found in criminal law. A defendant who is convicted of a crime will normally be imprisoned or fined. By contrast, someone who loses

---

[6] Cf. Gross, *A Theory of Criminal Justice* (1979) 13.

[7] A great deal of modern, statutory criminal law proscribes conduct that is not intrinsically problematic but which is suppressed for anticipatory or pre-emptive reasons. For a discussion and defence of such offences see Horder, "Harmless Wrongdoing and the Anticipatory Perspective on Criminalisation" in Sullivan and Dennis (eds.), *Seeking Security: Pre-empting the Commission of Criminal Harms* (2012) 79; a more critical discussion of such offences in the same volume is Simester, "Prophylactic Crimes", *ibid.*, 60. See also Chapter 16 below.

[8] See Ashworth, "Is the Criminal Law a Lost Cause?" (2000) 116 *LQR* 225.

a civil action faces perhaps an injunction, an order for specific performance, or a requirement to pay damages.

Posner argues that this difference reflects a crucial distinction between the functions of criminal and civil laws. In his opinion, the criminal law exists to impose punishments such as imprisonment in situations where tortious remedies are an insufficient deterrent.[9] But Posner's explanation is doubtful. Both criminal and tortious remedies can operate as deterrents. Each is likely to be regarded as unwelcome by a defendant, and indeed civil damages awards that compensate to the extent of the harm done often far exceed criminal fines in magnitude.

On the other hand, it is instructive to consider the reasons *apart from deterrence* which underlie the imposition of sanctions in these cases. In particular, whether or not they have deterrent effects, civil remedies are not normally regarded as punitive. Punishment involves more than simply imposing something unwelcome upon a defendant. A *punitive* sanction imposes hardship *because the recipient deserves it*.[10] Damages in a contract dispute, for instance, are a sanction; but ordinarily they are imposed without censure. It is not necessary to show that a defendant is at fault when he breaches his contractual obligations.

Punishment, by contrast, is imposed with censure as an integral aspect. It responds to the fact that the defendant has done something wrong.[11] Indeed, the level of sentence is one way in which a court signals the wrongfulness of the defendant's actions.[12] Of course, there are also fault-based actions in the law of tort. Nonetheless, damages for tort losses are normally compensatory, not punitive, and are understood as such. That is why one may usually insure against contractual or tortious damages, but not against criminal fines.[13]

Punishment, then, is one function of the criminal law. But punishment is not what is unique about crime. Indeed, punishment is not even a specifically legal phenomenon, let alone specifically the province of criminal law. We do not require a criminal conviction before punishing children or for a footballing foul,[14] and it is sometimes possible to obtain exemplary (or "punitive") damages in civil cases. One may be fined or even imprisoned for a civil contempt of court.[15] Conversely, neither is a conviction always accompanied by punitive sanctions. Sometimes offenders are discharged without receiving any sentence for their wrongdoing. Offenders may also be subject to confiscation orders,[16] or indeed to life

---

[9] Posner, "An Economic Theory of the Criminal Law" (1985) 85 *Col LR* 1193.

[10] Which is not to say that all defendants actually convicted of a criminal offence deserve punishment, particularly in the case of strict liability offences (below, § 1.2(ii)(c); Chapter 6). But it is to suggest that there is something morally problematic about imposing punitive sanctions upon defendants who do not deserve it.

[11] For discussion, see von Hirsch, *Censure and Sanctions* (1993).

[12] Cf. *Martineau* (1990) 79 CR (3d) 129, 138 (Lamer CJ): it is a "fundamental principle of a morally based system of law that those causing harm intentionally be punished more severely than those causing harm unintentionally".

[13] *Askey* v. *Golden Wine Co Ltd* [1948] 2 All ER 35; cf. *Clunis* v. *Camden and Islington Health Authority* [1998] QB 978.

[14] At the same time, criminal punishment is a distinctive variety of punishment in as much as its imposition is the responsibility of the community as a whole: Lamond, "What is a Crime" (2007) 27 *OJLS* 609, 614ff.

[15] On civil penalties more generally, see White, "Civil Penalties: Oxymoron, Chimera and Stealth Sanction" (2010) 126 *LQR* 593.

[16] Proceeds of Crime Act 2002. See Ulph, "Confiscation Orders, Human Rights, and Penal Measures" (2010) 126 *LQR* 251; Alldridge, "The Limits of Confiscation" [2011] *Crim LR* 827. The proportionality constraints on confiscation orders appear to be outer bounds rather than core determinants: *Waya* [2012] UKSC 51. For example, in *Varma* [2012] UKSC 42, the Supreme Court upheld the imposition of confiscation orders even in the context of a conditional discharge.

sentences or extended sentences of imprisonment for purposes of public safety rather than punishment.[17] This suggests that while punishment is an important facet of the criminal law, it is not its most distinctive feature.

(iii) Convictions

In addition to prohibition and punishment, a third aspect of the criminal process is the conviction itself—the type of verdict that the Court makes. Convictions are the most distinctive aspect of criminal law. In particular, while it also licenses the imposition of sanctions, a criminal conviction (at least for stigmatic offences) is regarded as a penalty *in its own right*, both by legal officials, such as judges, and by the public. This is because it has the effect of labelling the accused as a criminal.[18] A conviction makes a public, condemnatory statement about the defendant: that she is blameworthy for doing the prohibited action. It is, literally, a pronouncement that she is "guilty".[19] By contrast, civil judgments seem merely to pin the salient breach upon a defendant, without necessarily saying anything about her moral culpability. Thus, as we have noted, a claimant can sue for breach of contract without having to show fault by the defendant. The adverse civil verdict is made for the claimant's benefit and entails no formal public censure; the adverse criminal verdict is a pronouncement made on behalf of society and is a form of community condemnation.

This facet is not mentioned in the definition of criminal law that we proposed earlier. Rather, it is something that accompanies the procedural differences. Thus the essential distinction between criminal and civil law lies not so much in the operation as in the social significance of the criminal law—in the way criminal laws and convictions are understood. The criminal law has a communicative function which the civil law does not, and its judgments against the accused have a symbolic significance that civil judgments lack. They are a form of condemnation: a declaration that the accused did wrong. Public recognition of this fact can be seen in the relevance of the criminal law to applications for a visa, or for admission to practise as a lawyer, in which applicants are required to disclose any previous convictions. Or consider the difference between publicly denouncing someone as a "convicted criminal" and calling her a "tortfeasor".[20] The law exists in society, not in the abstract. Correspondingly, the law's labelling of a defendant as "criminal" imports all the resonance and social meaning of that term.

§ 1.2 Ambit

Three salient functions of criminal law emerge from the discussion so far. The first might be called *criminalisation*: the law sets out for citizens those things which must not be done.[21]

---

[17] Legal Aid, Sentencing and Punishment of Offenders Act 2012, part 5. These provisions replaced the life sentence and imprisonment for public protection scheme set down in ss. 224–36 of the Criminal Justice Act 2003 with a more moderate regime; which nonetheless imposes periods of imprisonment beyond retributivist desert.

[18] Chalmers and Leverick, "Fair Labelling in Criminal Law" (2008) 71 *MLR* 217.

[19] For extensive discussion of the communicative function of the criminal law, see Duff, *Punishment, Communication and Community* (2001).

[20] The former is certainly defamatory. Cf. *Carver* v. *Pierce*, an action for slander based on the words, "Thou art a thief, for thou hast stollen my dung" (1648) Sty 66, 82 ER 534.

[21] Or allowed to subsist: below, § 4.1(ii).

The second thing the law does is *convict* persons who are proved to have transgressed its prohibitions. Finally, it may *punish* those whom it convicts; and, more generally, the criminal law offers the prospect of punishment to reinforce its function of criminalisation.

The criminal law, then, is a powerful and condemnatory response by the State. It is also a bluntly coercive system, directed at controlling the behaviour of citizens. Criminalisation involves rules backed up by threats. In a sense, criminal law is the means by which the State forces citizens into complying with its injunctions.

When should the criminal law be invoked? No one, including the State, should coerce others without good reason. The constriction of people's conduct calls for justification, especially when it is accompanied by censorious and punitive treatment of those who do not comply. Unless there are compelling reasons, the criminal law should not be deployed by Parliament.

Nonetheless, sometimes the use of the criminal law *is* justified. Imagine the following scenario:

> One fine September morning, Jim is discovered dead in his home. His skull has been crushed by a blow inflicted with a heavy object. The police are called. Upon further investigation, they establish that he was murdered by his daughter, Alice, who killed him in order to receive her inheritance under his will.

Intuitively, most of us would regard this as a classic example of criminal wrongdoing. The reasons are twofold. First, what Alice has done is precisely the sort of activity that the State should prohibit. Murder is both harmful and wrong, and people ought to be protected against it. Secondly, Alice is clearly blameworthy, and deserving of censure for her actions. Thus she is precisely the sort of person who deserves the condemnation of a criminal conviction, as well as the punishment that a conviction exposes her to.

Alice's behaviour is a central case for the application of criminal law. It involves deliberate, culpable infliction of the sort of serious harm that the criminal law is meant to prevent. However, not every case is as clear as this. Suppose the following alternatives:

> Case I: Jim is discovered dead in his home. This time, the police establish that he died instantly after being struck by a vase. The vase was accidentally dislodged from the bookshelf by Barbara.

> Case II: During an argument, Clare insults Jim. Jim is deeply hurt by Clare's words.

It is much less obvious that the criminal law should intervene in these situations. In case I, Barbara has caused Jim's death, but there is no suggestion that she is at fault. Given this, it is inappropriate—indeed, wrong—to apply to her the sanctions of public condemnation and punishment. In case II, Clare has wronged Jim, and deserves censure. But not by the criminal law. Unlike murder, this is not the sort of behaviour that ordinarily should be prohibited by the Draconian technique of criminalisation.

In questioning when application of criminal law is legitimate, guidance may be had from the functions identified earlier. There are two dimensions to the operation of criminal law: *ex ante* and *ex post*. *Ex ante*, the law marks out actions that are prohibited, and warns citizens not to do those actions lest they be punished. *Ex post*, it censures (convicts) and punishes (sentences) persons who transgress its prohibitions. In the following pages, we investigate these two roles separately, and discuss some of the issues affecting when they should be invoked.

(i) *Criminalisation* ex ante

Why should some behaviour be criminalised, while other behaviour is permitted? The answer to that question is complex and somewhat fragmented. Prima facie, a legislature has the power to proscribe almost any sort of conduct.[22] Earlier, we pointed out that there is no obvious distinction between actions which are criminal and those which generate civil liability (§ 1.1(i)). When the legislature marks some action as criminal, however, it condemns it and rules it out as an acceptable option for citizens. A responsible legislature ought to take such drastic measures only if there are compelling reasons so to do.

There are a number of reasons to oppose the overuse of criminal law, but the most important of them is concern for individual *autonomy*. The need for tolerance, which underpins any liberal society, is grounded in autonomy. Prohibiting whatever is "wrongful" is likely to intrude much too far upon the liberties of citizens. This is not only to say that, in a liberal society, freedom of choice is to be fostered. It is also to claim that if the law is to respect the right of citizens to control their own lives, it should not deprive them of that control without good reason.

The criminal law stands in the way of free choice. It coerces people by threatening them with criminal liability unless they submit to its commands. Consequently, it circumscribes the individual's capacity to live her own life, in a manner that she herself dictates. By restricting the ways in which a person may shape her life, the law has the potential to prevent her from pursuing the goals and aspirations which matter to her.[23] Indirectly, the criminal law imposes the legislature's view and, on occasion, even a judge's view[24] of an acceptable life.

Individual freedom is valuable. Even though it is right, indeed necessary, to have criminal prohibitions, the fact that they restrict autonomy means we should be careful of overextending the reach of the criminal law, and of damaging the right of self-determination. Of course, if one considers each crime separately, most criminal prohibitions are unlikely to interfere with someone's freedom in any substantial, pervasive, or long-term sense. Outlawing arson still leaves us with a wide range of alternative activities. But the point about autonomy is more general than that. The effect of criminalisation must be assessed cumulatively, not in isolation. There are already thousands of things the State forbids. Autonomy requires us to have good reason before extending the reach of the criminal law.

None of this is to say that people ought to be allowed to disregard the interests of others, or that there is anything wrong with many of the criminal prohibitions we presently have. But it is a ground for the criminal law to beware of interfering more than the minimum necessary—a prima facie reason against the use of criminal sanctions. Bearing this in mind, once we have discussed various specific offences we will return to this issue in Chapter 16 and ask, what *should* the legislature prohibit through the criminal law? What sorts of considerations should a responsible legislator take into account when deciding whether to create a criminal offence?

---

[22] The Human Rights Act 1998 inhibits the passing of legislation which contravenes ECHR rights. In formal terms, however, the Act leaves parliamentary sovereignty intact. See further below, § 2.5.

[23] Raz, *The Morality of Freedom* (1986) 382.

[24] For a notorious example, see *DPP* v. *Shaw* [1961] AC 290; below, § 16.3.

(ii) **Ex post:** *censure*

Our search for definition fastened upon the pronouncement of guilt through conviction as the distinguishing mark of criminal law. This pronouncement connotes fault on the part of the criminal; a connotation that can be at variance with the facts, as when a blameless defendant is found guilty of a strict liability offence. When the Court finds an accused guilty of committing a crime, and purports to punish her through sentencing, there is a public implication that she is blameworthy. Of course, there are offences of a minor character (e.g. related to parking infringements) where this element of reproof may be relatively trivial—such offences are often characterised as not being "truly" criminal in nature. Paradigmatically, though, censure is inherent in criminal convictions.

(a) *The need for mens rea*

An institution which condemns and punishes people must take care to do so accurately. Being just matters. In particular, if a person is not to blame when something goes wrong, the censure of the criminal law is not appropriate—and if it is inflicted upon her, the public will tend to think that is because she is to blame. When the law labels a defendant as "criminal", it simply cannot avoid this implication. Consequently, it should not convict those for whom that implication is unjustified.

The grounds for wanting to avoid mislabelling defendants are twofold. First, it is unfair and unjust to stigmatise someone as a criminal when they do not deserve condemnation. Secondly, if the criminal law is seen regularly to make mistakes, it will lose its moral credibility. This, Robinson points out, will diminish its effectiveness as a tool of social control:[25]

> "The criminal law can also be more directly effective in increasing compliance with its commands. If it earns a reputation as a reliable statement of what the community perceives as condemnable and not condemnable, people are more likely to defer to its commands as morally authoritative.… A distribution of liability that the community perceives as doing justice enhances the criminal law's moral credibility; a distribution of liability that deviates from community perceptions of justice undermines it."

For these reasons, the criminal law ought not to convict people unless they are culpable for doing a prohibited action.[26] Therefore, in so far as possible, criminal offences should be structured so that there can be no conviction without fault. This is achieved by including within every criminal offence some element that reflects culpability.

Suppose the following example:

> Pam has killed Alex. Pam is a doctor, and Alex was one of her patients. Pam gave him a painkiller, to which he had an allergic reaction and died. Causing another's death is generally regarded as a very undesirable thing, and is at the heart of the crimes of murder and manslaughter. The police investigate. They establish that Pam's actions caused Alex's death, and conclude that she has committed a homicide.

---

[25] "The Criminal–Civil Distinction and the Utility of Desert" (1996) 76 *Boston ULR* 201, 212–13. Robinson's point is made about criminalisation, but applies in this context also.

[26] For an interesting debate which touches on this proposition, see Reiman and van den Haag, "On the Common Saying that it is Better that Ten Guilty Persons Escape than that One Innocent Suffer: Pro and Con" in Paul, Miller, and Paul (eds.), *Crime, Culpability, and Remedy* (1990) 226.

On these facts alone, is Pam therefore bad, or blameworthy? Should we convict her of murder? The answer is no. Alex may have been the one patient in a million who was unknowably allergic to the painkiller and died as a consequence. It is important not to kill people, but it does not follow from the fact that killing is undesirable, and normally prohibited, that someone should automatically be convicted or punished for causing another's death. In the criminal law, this principle is expressed by the maxim, *actus non facit reum nisi mens sit rea*:[27] an act does not make a man guilty unless his mind is (also) guilty. There must be *mens rea*—a guilty mind. The action must be done intentionally or recklessly, or wilfully or knowingly, or negligently, or with some other mental state because of which we can say that the defendant is culpable. In Kenny's words, "no external conduct, however serious or even fatal its consequences may have been, is ever punished unless it is produced by some form of *mens rea*".[28]

(b) Theories of culpability

The argument for having a mens rea element in criminal offences assumes that proof of mens rea establishes culpability. However, to what extent this is true is debated by criminal theorists.[29] Academics commonly argue over two accounts of when we may legitimately blame someone for her actions, which can only be sketched here. The first, which is reflected in the law regarding serious crimes, is sometimes called a "subjective" analysis: that culpability depends upon morally defective *choices*. We blame someone for choosing to do a wrong action—for instance, for choosing to set fire to the house. Conversely, fault is not made out unless someone *deliberately* does something bad.

The upshot of this approach is that the *actus non facit reum nisi mens sit rea* maxim transforms into a requirement that we should not convict without advertence. As will be seen in the chapter on mens rea, this would include such mental states as intention and recklessness. If Pam gave Alex the painkiller in order to kill him, we can blame her for causing his death because she intended to do so. Conversely, on the subjective account, it is perfectly reasonable for Pam to dose Alex if she is unaware that the medicine will kill him. Failing to take account of the risk of death is not something for which she can be blamed.[30]

---

[27] Coke, *Third Institute* (1641) 6, 107; an adaptation of the rubric, *reum non facit nisi mens rea*, found in the context of perjury in *Leges Henrici Primi* c. 5, § 28.

[28] *Outlines of Criminal Law* (2nd ed., 1904) 39. This proposition is subject to qualification in respect of strict liability (below, § 1.2(ii)(c) and Chapter 6). Note that the present claim is only that mens rea is *necessary* for culpability. Unfortunately, liability for an offence requiring mens rea is sometimes incurred notwithstanding the absence of moral fault: *Yip Chiu-Cheung* v. *R.* [1995] 1 AC 111, following *dicta* in *Kingston* [1995] 2 AC 355, 364–6. These cases are, however, somewhat unusual: where mens rea is present but moral fault is absent, this is usually recognised by the availability of defences. See below, § 1.2(ii)(d); Fletcher, *Rethinking Criminal Law* (1978) 511f, 799f.

[29] See, e.g., Hampton, "Mens Rea" in Paul, Miller, and Paul (eds.), *Crime, Culpability, and Remedy* (1990) 1 (also in (1990) 7 *Social Philosophy and Policy* 1); Bayles, "Character, Purpose and Criminal Responsibility" (1982) 1 *Law and Phil* 5; Arenella, "Character, Choice, and Moral Agency" in Paul, Miller, and Paul (eds.), *Crime, Culpability and Remedy* (1990) 59; Duff, "Choice, Character and Criminal Liability" (1993) 12 *Law and Phil* 345; Hart, "Negligence, Mens Rea, and Criminal Responsibility" in *Punishment and Responsibility* (1968) 136; Sullivan, "Making Excuses" in Simester and Smith (eds.), *Harm and Culpability* (1996) 131; Alexander and Ferzan, *Crime and Culpability: a Theory of Criminal Law* (2009); Moore and Hurd, "Punishing the Awkward, the Stupid, the Weak, and the Selfish: the Culpability of Negligence" (2011) 5 *Crim Law and Phil* 147; Simester, "A Disintegrated Theory of Culpability" in Baker and Horder (eds.), *The Sanctity of Life and the Criminal Law: The Legacy of Glanville Williams* (2013) 178.

[30] For an extended argument that culpability is a function of the act of choosing rather than the material consequences that may arise from choices, see Alexander and Ferzan, *ibid.*, esp. chaps. 2, 3, and 5.

The alternative account is "objective" in nature. It grounds fault in *conduct* rather than choices, arguing that an action attracts blame if it inflicts harm when a reasonable person would not have acted that way. Under the objective analysis, awareness of wrongdoing is not essential. If homicide is undesirable, then Pam has a reason not to do it whether or not she foresees the risk. Homicide does not become acceptable just because it is done inadvertently. Since it involves harm, not only does Pam have a moral (and, in this case, legal) duty not to do it, but she also has a duty to *take care* so that she does not do it inadvertently either. On this account, Pam may legitimately be convicted of a crime if she is unreasonably careless.

The objective view works best when explaining why someone may be blamed for negligence, and in giving substance to the idea of the "reasonable man". The "reasonable man" is archetypally a person of decent character. Thus if the defendant has failed to behave like a reasonable person, we may infer culpability, since her conduct has fallen short of reflecting that decent character.

These subjective and objective approaches are extreme alternatives, and middle ground is available. In the criminal law, inadvertent negligence *is* normally thought to be a standard of fault, but foresight of wrongdoing generally involves *greater* culpability. As we shall see in Chapter 5, adjudicating between the two approaches has not always been easy, particularly in the debate over subjective or objective interpretations of "recklessness", which is the minimum fault requirement for many stigmatic criminal offences. Suppose that David causes a fire in a house and is charged with reckless arson. Traditionally in the common law, "recklessness" has been interpreted to require some degree of actual foresight. So for David to be guilty he must have actually foreseen the risk of setting fire to the house when he did the act that caused it. Were he merely negligent (or even grossly so), he would have to be acquitted. Where that view is taken, the subjectivist holds sway. On the other hand, for two decades the law in England regarding this offence was objective:[31] David could be convicted of reckless arson even though he did not notice the risk, at least if the risk was an obvious one.

If fault is a prerequisite of criminal liability then it is easy to see why recklessness or other foresight-based mental states are so often required before a defendant can be convicted for his actions. Much more difficult are statutes that define an action to be an offence when it is done negligently. Indeed, subjectivists often argue that people should never be convicted for negligence.[32] We disagree, and it seems to us that one may fairly be blamed for an unreasonable failure to take care; though no doubt the criminalisation of such cases ought to be sparing. But whether one adopts a subjective or objective stance, and whatever one's views regarding the culpability of negligence, one thing is clear. Without at least some form of fault, a defendant should not be convicted of a crime. For the most part, this proposition is reflected in English criminal law where, in the absence of recklessness about the harm (or, in some cases, of negligence), a defendant must generally be acquitted of any serious criminal offence.

---

[31] *Caldwell* [1982] AC 341. The decision in *Caldwell* was eventually reversed by *G* [2003] UKHL 50, [2004] 1 AC 1034, which restored the law to a subjective test. See below, § 5.2.

[32] Below, § 5.5(iv).

(c) Regulatory offences

What, then, of strict liability? There are many crimes for which the prosecution need not prove any element of fault before the defendant may be convicted. In these offences, the defendant's liability is said to be "strict", and the actus non fit reum maxim is said not to apply. For example, under the Environmental Permitting (England and Wales) Regulations 2010 a defendant may be convicted for discharging polluting matter into controlled waters if the prosecution shows merely that he caused the pollutant to be discharged.[33] There is no need to prove that the defendant's involvement was a culpable one.

We deal with strict liability offences more fully in Chapter 6. For now, two observations may be made. The first is that, as we shall see, the courts in some common-law jurisdictions have moved to base "strict" liability on a presumption of fault—where culpability on the part of the defendant is presumed, but may be rebutted. If D can prove that the harm was not at all his fault, he will be acquitted. Thus the essential difference, in other countries, between offences of strict liability and those of negligence is the burden of proof. Arguably, for some minor offences it may be appropriate for that burden to rest upon the defendant rather than the prosecution; and it is to be regretted that English courts have rejected this possibility, which would substantially have ameliorated the harshness of strict liability in this country.[34]

The fact that strict liability offences are often minor raises a second point. Strict liability offences tend not to involve the same level of public censure as serious crimes. A parking offence, for example, comprises an altogether different order of wrongdoing from murder. This is not to deny that traffic offences and their like are part of the criminal law, although perhaps they should not be.[35] But most people distinguish in ordinary life between minor, regulatory-type offences and "true" crimes, and the element of public condemnation is and should be conveyed only by a conviction of the latter type. The difference in social significance is illustrated by the question we mentioned earlier, commonly found in visa and employment applications, about an applicant's criminal record. It is not a request that is intended to elicit disclosure of minor infractions such as parking infringements. To the extent that English law restricts strict liability to minor offences (and it does not do so invariably)[36], its use is therefore somewhat less objectionable.

---

[33] Regulation 38(1). Cf. *Alphacell Ltd* v. *Woodward* [1972] AC 824, considering the predecessor offence under s. 85 of the Water Resources Act 1991.

[34] There remains, hopefully, the prospect of legislative reform: the Law Commission has proposed that a due diligence defence be provided for strict liability offences: LCCP No. 195, *Criminal Liability in Regulatory Contexts* (2010) para. 6.95.

[35] According to Robinson, "[s]erious deterrent sanctions can and ought to be imposed [for regulatory violations] but they can as easily and effectively be imposed under an administrative system distinct from criminal law that carries a noncriminal label, such as 'violation'": "The Criminal–Civil Distinction and the Utility of Desert" (1996) 76 *Boston ULR* 201, 214. Cf. Mann's proposal for a separate system of justice to deal with such minor crimes, in "Punitive Civil Sanctions: The Middle Ground Between Criminal and Civil Law" (1992) 101 *Yale LJ* 1795. No such distinction exists in English law: cf. Reid, "Strict Liability: Some Principles for Parliament" (2008) *Stat LR* 173. Notably, however, Part 3 of the Regulatory Enforcement and Sanctions Act 2008 empowers ministers to make orders that authorise regulatory bodies to impose civil fines in lieu of criminal prosecutions: a bypass mechanism that allows for practical "civilisation" of many regulatory crimes. For an illuminating contrast with France and Germany, see Spencer and Pedain, "Approaches to Strict and Constructive Liability in Continental Criminal Law" in Simester (ed.), *Appraising Strict Liability* (2005) 237.

[36] See, e.g., the child sex offences proscribed by ss. 5–8 of the Sexual Offences Act 2003; below, § 12.11.

(d) Allowing defences

The medical homicide example (§ 1.2(ii)(a)), in which Pam kills Alex, illustrates one way in which the defendant may be absolved of fault when a prohibited consequence occurs. Her answer is that, although she killed Alex, it was an accident. She neither intended his death, nor was she negligent in bringing it about: she lacked mens rea. Sometimes, however, a person may not be culpable even though she harms another person deliberately. For example:

> Ian is a policeman in the Armed Offenders squad. He is standing outside a bank when a robbery occurs. John, who is one of the robbers, comes out of the bank and runs toward him, pointing a gun. In order to protect himself, Ian shoots and injures John.

Prima facie, this is a crime. Ian cannot claim that he shot John by accident. Nevertheless, Ian is not to blame. His action, we would say, is *justified*, and he does not deserve to be convicted of any crime.

In order to deal with this sort of case, the law recognises a number of general defences, under which the defendant may acknowledge that he did an otherwise prohibited act and yet escape conviction. Examples of these justificatory defences are self-defence, prevention of crime, and defence of property. In effect such defences allege that, although D's conduct was harmful and normally unlawful, his conduct was nevertheless appropriate in the circumstances.[37] They claim that the defendant's conduct was the right (or an acceptable) thing to do, and so was not deserving of censure. As such, justifications are generalised: they involve judgements about the situation which apply to all the participants; so, e.g., John is not entitled to resist Ian's justified use of force.

There are other predicaments where inflicting harm can be defensible on a more restricted basis. In these cases a person may choose to do something wrong, i.e. unjustified, but we may nevertheless think her insufficiently blameworthy to warrant the censure of the criminal law. For example:

> Susan is arrested after taking part in the bombing of a Government building. She drove the car in which the bombers, a gang of terrorists, had made their escape. After her arrest, it is discovered that she did so only because the terrorists had threatened to kill her otherwise.

In this type of case, Susan's conduct may not be justified, and other people would be entitled to try to stop her. Nevertheless her culpability is lessened by the fact that she was coerced. Thus she has an *excuse*. The rationale for allowing excusatory defences is that advanced by H.L.A. Hart: "unless a man has the capacity and a fair opportunity or chance to alter his behaviour to the law its penalties ought not to be applied to him".[38] Susan's wrongdoing was deliberate, but understandable. By admitting compulsion as a defence,[39] the criminal law acknowledges that Susan did not have a genuine and fair opportunity to choose not to

---

[37] Indeed one may say of such cases that no prohibited harm occurred. Thus A.T.H. Smith remarks, "[w]here the defendant's conduct can fairly be described as coming within the terms of the proscribed activity, an offence has, prima facie, been committed: liability will ensue unless he advances some explanation of his conduct which shows that it was justified, in which case there is no actus reus": "On Actus Reus and Mens Rea" in Glazebrook (ed.), *Reshaping the Criminal Law* (1978) 95, 97.

[38] "Punishment and the Elimination of Responsibility" in *Punishment and Responsibility* (1968) 158, 181.

[39] Subject to restrictions: below, Chapter 20.

break the law. We may have no reason to praise her. But she does not warrant the penalties of the criminal law, because she is below the threshold of blameworthiness that is appropriate to criminal liability.

(e) Accountability

So far in § 1.2, we have argued that the criminal law should convict only people who are culpable when a prohibited event occurs, and that events should be prohibited only when they are sufficiently harmful to override considerations such as the need to protect the autonomy of citizens. There is, however, a further requirement to be met before the criminal law may convict someone of a crime: accountability. Recall the example with which we began this discussion:

> One fine September morning, Jim is discovered dead in his home. His skull has been crushed by a blow inflicted with a heavy object. The police are called. Upon investigation, they establish that he was murdered by his daughter, Alice, who killed him in order to receive her inheritance under his will.

This, as we said earlier, is a plain case. But it is not just the fact that Alice is culpable which licenses her conviction. Culpability, by itself, is insufficient. Suppose that Jim's brother, David, had suspected Alice might try to murder Jim and had done nothing to warn him? David may be blameworthy, but ought we to prosecute him? Certainly not for homicide, at any rate. The difference between David and Alice is that only Alice is legally accountable, or *responsible*, for Jim's death. Only Alice has performed an action that caused Jim's death. Because he is not legally responsible, there is simply no point in prosecuting David, however much we may disapprove of his conduct.[40]

Although a great range of differing conduct can be subjected to criminal sanction, the process of finding guilt and pronouncing a conviction entails certain limits on the boundaries of criminalisation. The finding of guilt on which the conviction is based assumes a degree of accountability for something done or omitted to be done. Unless one subscribes to some extreme version of Calvinism or other doctrine of the damned, guilt is not a state of being, a natural property. Guilt can be generated only in respect of something additional to what the defendant is; something for which he is accountable. Otherwise, the "presumption of innocence" is meaningless. Consider, for example, a nation-state where the government is following a policy of expelling all citizens who are not members of the dominant ethnic group. Acting through civil law process, such a State could pass legislation confiscating the property of minority citizens and impose various forms of disability in terms of profession, marriage, etc., in ways all too familiar. But it would be incoherent for the State to make it a crime simply to be a member of a minority racial grouping; there would be nothing on which the conviction could be based.[41]

The constraint may be ineffective in practice. Where the political environment is so extreme that a State is willing to create an offence simply of being a member of less favoured

---

[40] Or, as Lord Esher MR put it, "[a] man is entitled to be as negligent as he pleases towards the whole world if he owes no duty to them": *Le Lievre* v. *Gould* [1893] 1 QB 491, 497.

[41] See further Sullivan, "Conduct and Proof of Conduct: Two Necessary Conditions for the Imposition of Criminal Liability" in Kaikobad and Bohlander (eds.), *International Law and Power: Perspectives on Legal Order and Justice* (2009) 235.

groups, it is quite likely the judges of that State would be unreceptive to the argument sketched here. But in countries with a judiciary prepared to judge in good faith, the need for accountability—for something additional to one's state of being—should properly limit the scope of criminalisation. This should have been required in the notorious case of *Larsonneur*,[42] a decision castigated by Jerome Hall as the "acme of strict injustice!"[43] On what can be ascertained from the available law reports, D, in circumstances wholly beyond her control, was brought from the country then known as Eire into police custody in the United Kingdom. Once here, she was charged with being an alien (she was French) who was in the United Kingdom without permission to land. With an excessively literal inter-pretation of the legislation in question, the Divisional Court upheld the trial conviction. Lord Hewart ruled that the circumstances of her entry and continuing confinement were "perfectly immaterial". It was enough, said the Court, that she was present in the United Kingdom without permission. In substance then, she was convicted solely for being French. But that, in our submission, is not enough.

Even at the level of principle, the argument from incoherence is narrow. It would be per-fectly coherent, however unconscionable, for the nation-state described above to make it a crime for members of a minority group to give birth to children. Neither does the argument rule out what are known as *status*, or *situational*, offences, such as being an illegal immi-grant or a parent of a child of compulsory school age who is not regularly attending school. If it can be shown that there were acts or omissions for which D is responsible and by which D could have avoided the proscribed status, then the accountability requirement is satis-fied. Translated into criminal law doctrine, this condition is embodied in a requirement of *voluntariness*, which is discussed in § 4.3. Where one's status is involuntary, it cannot legiti-mately be a criminal offence simply to be what one *is*. The criminal law is concerned with the acts, omissions and, on occasion, the acquired status of human beings. It takes human beings as its starting point and then asks what they are accountable *for*.

In addition to the requirement of voluntariness, the need for accountability can raise other difficult issues. Suppose a further variation on the death of Jim:

> Case III: Jim is discovered dead in his home. The police establish that he died after being struck by a vase which fell accidentally from the bookshelf. However, his daugh-ter, Edith, had observed the scene and deliberately failed to summon an ambulance in time to save him.

This is very similar to Alice's case, except for one aspect: our complaint here is not about what Edith did, but about what she *failed* or *omitted* to do. Another way of expressing the difference might be to say that, unlike Alice, Edith did not *cause* Jim's death.[44] Either way, however, because of that distinction, criminal liability does not necessarily follow.

The issues of omission and causation will be discussed in more detail in Chapter 4, but it is important to note that these, too, are crucial matters affecting the range and intrusive-ness of the criminal law. Prohibiting an omission is not like prohibiting an action. When the law prevents Ian from (say) punching Bob, it leaves him with plenty of options and rules out only one. Ian is free to choose what to do or not do instead. By contrast, when the law

---

[42] (1933) 149 LT 542. The case is discussed further below, § 4.1(ii)(a).
[43] *General Principles of Criminal Law* (2nd ed., 1960) 329 n. 14.
[44] Cf. Moore, *Act and Crime* (1993) 267–78. But the law may disagree: see below, § 4.2(iv)(a).

proscribes an omission, it tells him exactly what to do. If Jim is dying, Edith *must* rescue him—she is not free to choose what to do or not do instead. One option is *required*, and all the other options are ruled out. Thus liability for omissions is much more likely to impinge upon individual autonomy and freedom of action.

In a liberal community, the concern with autonomy is fundamental.[45] If the law is to acknowledge and respect individuals as independent members of society, then it must judge them according to their own actions, and not those of others. The process of shaping and controlling a person's life should be left to that person, and would be undermined were citizens constantly forced to assume responsibility for events they do not bring about.[46] For this reason, it is a guiding principle of the law that defendants are liable according to what *they* do, not what others do and they might prevent;[47] correspondingly, they should be left free to live their own lives and pursue their own goals without having legal duties to act or intervene constantly thrust upon them, unanticipated, unpredictable, and unwanted, because of the actions of others. This is why there is no general duty to prevent crime,[48] and why principles of accountability are so important.[49]

Implicit in this reasoning, however, is that omissions are special not because they deny culpability, but because of the implications of their proscription for individual freedom. Thus they are not ruled out *tout court*. In practice, a criminal law duty to intervene is imposed, if at all, only when the defendant has a special connection to the harm—for example, when the defendant is the victim's parent.[50] But even that need not be true. Sometimes an altruistic reason for a stranger to get involved may justify the extension of responsibility. Suppose that Ian, a passer-by, sees a child drowning in a paddling pool. He can rescue the child at no risk to himself. In this situation, for Ian not to intervene would be monstrous. Although English criminal law does not at the moment criminalise such cases, it might justifiably do so, depending upon such factors as the seriousness of the impending harm and the degrees of risk and inconvenience involved in averting it. In many other jurisdictions, it is a crime not to rescue someone in peril when doing so involves no personal danger.[51]

Similarly, the criminal law need not always require D's behaviour to *cause* a specified consequence. For example, the law of secondary liability recognises the responsibility of those who do not themselves perpetrate a crime, but are nevertheless parties to its commission.[52]

---

[45] Above, § 1.2(i).

[46] Thus *Hart and Honoré* lxxx–xi: "respect for ourselves and others as distinct persons would be much weakened, if not dissolved, if we could not think of ourselves as the separate authors of the changes we make in the world". For further discussion, see below, § 4.1(i).

[47] To a degree, criminal liability as an accomplice to another's crime may be seen as a qualification to this principle. However, proof of complicity by D in P's crime requires proof of an actus reus and mens rea personal to D: see below, Chapter 7. There is also some limited use of vicarious liability, discussed in Chapter 8.

[48] Cf. *Coney* (1882) 8 QBD 534, 557–8; *Clarkson* [1971] 3 All ER 344, 347.

[49] There is a pragmatic side to accountability. If a swimmer drowns, the law cannot afford to prosecute every person on the beach. More generally, the State could not possibly contemplate prosecuting everyone who might have prevented it each time a prohibited harm occurs. So the general principle against liability for omissions has a realistic air about it as well as a philosophical justification.

[50] See below, § 4.1(i)(b). There can also be something to be said for offences, separate from homicide, of failing to take reasonable steps to safeguard the lives of others. For instance, members of households must take reasonable steps to safeguard the lives of children or vulnerable adults who reside in the household: Domestic Violence, Crimes and Victims Act 2004, s. 5.

[51] See Ashworth, "The Scope of Criminal Liability for Omissions" (1989) 105 *LQR* 424.

[52] Below, Chapter 7.

Suppose, for example, that David plans to kill Tony. Knowing this, Rebecca lends David her gun. Rebecca is a participant in Tony's murder, and his death may be attributed to her as a secondary party. The point here is that Rebecca does not cause Tony's death.[53] (David would have killed him anyway, using someone else's gun.) But she is not like a mere bystander, who can claim that David's action has nothing to do with her; that it is none of her business. Instead, she has involved herself in the murder, and *made* it her business. Thus, although it is David who kills Tony, Rebecca shares in the responsibility for his death.

Like liability for omissions, secondary liability involves an extension of the criminal law beyond the core cases of wrongdoing. As such, it involves a greater intrusion upon people's freedom of action: not only may D not strike V, he may not do anything to help someone else strike V either, a much greater limitation upon what he is left free to do. This raises difficult questions of policy: if Rebecca is a shopkeeper, should she refuse to sell matches to David if she suspects or believes he has an illicit purpose? Secondary liability has the potential to force individuals to police the actions of others, and squarely raises issues of autonomy once more.[54] It is a hard question how far such extensions of responsibility should go, since, like vicarious liability,[55] they can have the effect of imposing liability largely on the basis of the defendant's status rather than his behaviour. Yet, once again, accountability is not ruled out *tout court*.

(iii) Ex post: *sanction*

Although punishment is not a constitutive element of the criminal conviction and lies outside the scope of this text, one cannot overlook its salience in the criminal process. If we were to dismantle punishment and its forbidding infrastructure, much of the *raison drêtre* of the criminal law would go with it. Despite its importance, however, the question *why* we punish remains a matter of perennial and irresolvable dispute and has given rise to a vast and challenging literature.[56] In the following paragraphs, we can only sketch the major competing punishment theories, as any attempt to enter the debate would not do it justice.

The common starting point is to require grounds which justify the imposition of punishment on a candidate individual. One should always be sure that the legal verdict which licenses punishment is well founded, a restraint with implications for criminal procedure and evidence. If we can be sure of the facts for the instant case, one group of theorists,

---

[53] See, e.g., *Hart and Honoré* 51ff, 363ff; J.C. Smith, "Aid, Abet, Counsel, or Procure" in Glazebrook (ed.), *Reshaping the Criminal Law* (1978) 120, 131–4.

[54] Particularly in cases of complicit liability for omissions, which may arise when the secondary party has some form of control over the wrongdoer. See for example *Du Cros* v. *Lambourne* [1907] 1 KB 40, in which the passenger in a car was convicted of being a party to dangerous driving, on the basis that he owned the car and failed to exercise his right of control over the driver's actions. The case is further discussed below, § 7.4(iii).

[55] The doctrine of vicarious liability provides a second route with which a causal requirement may be bypassed. However, vicarious liability is normally to be avoided in criminal law, since it arises out of a more general relationship between the defendant and the actual perpetrator of a wrong, and so is not specific to the wrongful action; consequently the defendant risks being convicted of a crime for which he is not morally responsible. As a rule, "*Qui peccat per alium peccat per se* is not a maxim of criminal law": *Tesco Supermarkets Ltd* v. *Nattrass* [1972] AC 153, 199 (Lord Diplock). See further below, § 8.2.

[56] For excellent accounts of questions of punishment and sentence see Ashworth, *Sentencing and Justice* (5th ed., 2015), Duff and Garland (eds.), *A Reader on Punishment* (1994) and von Hirsch and Ashworth (eds.), *Principles of Sentencing: Readings on Theory and Policy* (2nd ed., 1998).

commonly known as retributivists, would then ask whether punishment is *deserved*.[57] Desert is a function of the moral quality of the conduct; if it is bad (i.e. wrongful and culpable), a measure of hard treatment may be dispensed, the measure dependent on how bad that conduct is.[58] Once the grounds of desert are present, punishment ceases to be problematic. Indeed, it becomes something that ought to be imposed, a required response to the moral imbalance that the malefactor has caused. A consistent retributivist will confine punishment to wrongdoing and will typically (though not necessarily) find culpability in the mental state of the person to be punished rather than the consequences of her actions.[59] Consistent retributivism would entail a criminal law more scrupulous about finding fault sufficient to allow just punishment.

Retributivism is contrasted with utilitarianism, a species of consequentialism which asserts that any instance of punishment is justified only if the welfare of society is advanced. For a utilitarian, the pain of the person to be punished is a disutility, a diminution in the quantum of general welfare. Accordingly, pain should be inflicted only if it entails net gains in welfare across society: the institution of state punishment must produce overall benefi-cent effects. The particular effect that utilitarians most commonly seek from punishment is general deterrence, i.e. that without hard treatment of offenders there would be more offending and less welfare overall.[60] As the term "consequentialism" implies, the moral character of a defendant's action is determined primarily by its results. A death remains a death whether it ensues from a brutal killing or a blameless accident. Many attempts have been made to demonstrate that blame and desert matter to utilitarianism,[61] but the rela-tionship is, at best, a contingent one.[62] There is no reason, internal to utilitarianism, why a legal system should differentiate deliberate killings from accidental deaths. If it could be demonstrated that an unvarying penalty of life imprisonment for anyone who causes death in whatever circumstances would radically diminish the number of untimely deaths, then a utilitarian has reason to endorse that practice. The only permissible objections in conse-quentialist terms to such indiscriminate hard treatment must be made in terms of its cost to net social utility. Indeed, consequentialism need not imply a system of criminal law. Other forms of deterrence may be more efficient tools for social control.

Consequentialism and retributivism are incompatible theories. That, of course, does not preclude individuals, even judges, from using consequentialist and retributivist justifica-tions at one and the same time, as when D is sent to prison for a very long time "because you deserve it and because it will deter others of like mind"—an example of belt and braces rather than contradiction. In terms of English sentencing policy, the retributivist approach reached its apogee with the Criminal Justice Act of 1991, whereby proportionality became the primary criterion for deciding penalties. By 1993, concern with the impact of this approach, particularly in the area of fines on motorists, had become politically salient and

---

[57] A classic account is von Hirsch, *Doing Justice* (1976).

[58] On evaluating the gravity of wrongdoing see von Hirsch, *Censure and Sanctions* (1993) chap. 4.

[59] A stimulating example is Ashworth, "Taking the Consequences" in Shute, Gardner and Horder (eds.), *Action and Value in Criminal Law* (1993) 107. We discuss problems of moral luck further in § 6.5 below.

[60] This claim is, of course, an empirical matter. Even if it is true in general terms, there is disagreement whether increasing punishment levels for a particular offences will reduce the incidence of their commission. For a survey of the literature, see von Hirsch et al., *Criminal Deterrence and Sentencing Severity* (1999).

[61] Hart, *Punishment and Responsibility* (1968) chaps. 1, 7.

[62] See Wootton, *Crime and the Criminal Law* (2nd ed., 1981).

the then Criminal Justice Act 1993 and Crime (Sentences) Act 1997 departed significantly from the "just deserts" rationale in sentencing.[63] Prior convictions are once again a significant aggravating feature in sentencing decisions, following a shift of emphasis from the moral deserts of the crime at hand toward law-and-order considerations of the offender's general dangerousness. The Criminal Justice Act 2003 further widened the range of sentencing factors by stipulating five explicit principles underlying sentencing: as well as a retributive punishment principle and a consequentialist goal of crime reduction through deterrence, the three additional principles are reform and rehabilitation of criminals; public protection (itself a crime-reduction principle); and reparation.[64] Part 5 of the Legal Aid, Sentencing and Punishment of Offenders Act 2012 permits the imprisonment of offenders beyond retributivist limits, in the interests of public protection.[65] Proportionality, thus, is no longer primary. It is no coincidence that rates of incarceration in England and Wales remain at a high level even though general crime rates have fallen.

Some theorists, most notably H.L.A. Hart,[66] have argued for a composite theory of criminal responsibility and punishment, expressed in terms of a distinction between the "general justifying aim" of the criminal law on the one hand and the principles of criminal responsibility and just punishment on the other. For Hart, the general purpose of the criminal law was consequentialist: to deter anti-social conduct. However, this goal is properly inhibited by reference to issues of blame and proportion when adjudicating guilt and passing sentence. The inhibition is necessary to ensure fairness and to maximise autonomy. Although Hart argued for his composite theory with incomparable elegance, the predominating if not the exclusive element within it would appear to be retributivism. To be sure, utilitarianism is given the task of determining which conduct will be punished. Yet retributivism would generate many of the same primary norms and it is retributivism which resolves who will be punished and how much punishment will be meted.[67] For the moment, however, the role of retributivism as a limiting principle in a consequentialist matrix is on the wane in England and Wales.

§ 1.3 The structure of a criminal offence

The discussion in this chapter has practical implications for criminal offences. We have characterised the criminal law as a system of prohibition and censure. Correspondingly, the main elements of crimes are twofold, harm and fault. The first of these is primarily an

---

[63] For an account of the background to the 1991 Act and the move away from its principles, see Koffman, "The Rise and Fall of Proportionality: The failure of the Criminal Justice Act 1991" [2006] *Crim LR* 281.

[64] Reparation is given greater salience by s. 63 of the Legal Aid, Sentencing and Punishment of Offenders Act 2012, which provides that a court must consider whether to make a compensation order whenever it is empowered to do so.

[65] The legislation does, however, ameliorate the more draconian public protection sentences formerly allowed by ss. 224–36 and schedules 15 and 15A of the Criminal Justice Act 2003.

[66] *Punishment and Responsibility* (1968) chaps. 1, 7. Compare Simester and von Hirsch, *Crimes, Harms and Wrongs: On the Principles of Criminalisation* (2011) chap. 1.

[67] See the critique of Hart's "mixed theory" by Galligan, "The Return to Retribution in Penal Theory" in Tapper (ed.), *Crime, Proof and Punishment* (1981) 144.

external element:[68] an event or conduct which causes the harm that the law is designed to prevent. For example, the external element in murder is the killing of one human being by another.[69] This external element is known as the *actus reus* of the offence. It sets out the physical thing that must happen before the criminal law can be invoked, and will be discussed in detail in Chapter 4.

Generally, the actus reus is not enough by itself to constitute an offence. In § 1.2(ii)(a) we discussed the example of Pam, a doctor, who killed Alex by injecting him with a painkiller to which he was allergic. Pam has done the actus reus of a murder. But if Alex's allergy was unknowable, then Pam is not to blame, and should not be convicted. Alex's death is simply a tragic accident. The need for fault in an offence gives us the second element, which is known as *mens rea*. This is what might be termed the "mental" element—the guilty mind, such as the intention, knowledge, or recklessness, of the defendant with respect to the actus reus. Mens rea is the subject of Chapter 5.

Like the actus reus, the mens rea varies for each offence. In some crimes, intention or recklessness will be required before D can be convicted, while in others negligence or some other fault element may suffice. An example will help to illustrate. Imagine that Tom has been charged with an offence against section 15(1) of the Forgery and Counterfeiting Act 1981. He recently purchased a toaster from the local shop, paying for it in £10 notes. However, it later turns out that the notes are not genuine, as both Tom and the shopkeeper had thought, but very high quality forgeries. The relevant section provides as follows:

15. Offences of passing etc. counterfeit notes and coins.

(1) It is an offence for a person—

(a)   to pass or tender as genuine any thing which is, and which he knows or believes to be, a counterfeit of a currency note or of a protected coin....

In this crime, the actus reus is passing or tendering as genuine money which is in fact counterfeit. The mens rea of the crime is knowing or believing that the money is counterfeit. On the facts given, Tom will not be guilty of passing counterfeit notes since he lacks the mens rea required for an offence against section 15(1).

Sometimes the mens rea can be present without the actus reus. Suppose instead that Tom found the notes on the street and believed that they were counterfeit, but that they were actually genuine. In this case Tom does not commit the offence of passing forged notes, because the actus reus is missing.[70]

(i) Defences: a separate element

The examples above illustrate that both specified parts of the offence, the actus reus and the mens rea, must be proved before there is any question of D's being guilty of a crime. Even if both parts are proved, however, there might still be a defence available, and so we have a third basic element of every crime: the absence of a valid defence.

---

[68] Although it may not be entirely external. Sometimes actions acquire a harmful or criminal character only when done with a particular mental state. For illustrative discussion of this point, see Horder, "Crimes of Ulterior Intent" in Simester and Smith (eds.), *Harm and Culpability* (1996) 153; see also below, § 5.3.

[69] Below, Chapter 10.

[70] Cf. *Deller* (1952) 36 Cr App R 184.

Suppose, for example, that Tom had indeed known the notes were counterfeit, but had been forced to make the purchase because he had been accosted outside the store by two men who had supplied the notes and "asked" him to buy the toaster, while wielding a shotgun suggestively. Tom has performed the actus reus of section 15(1), with the required mens rea. So we can say that he has committed a *prima facie offence*. Despite this, he will not be convicted since he has a further defence of duress or compulsion.

The word "defence" can sometimes be misleading, because it tends to be used by lawyers to describe any reason why the defendant should be acquitted. Thus if the defendant has an alibi, he will rely on this for his defence. More precisely, however, an alibi is not a defence but rather a denial that there was a prima facie offence at all. If the alibi is accepted, it means that the defendant did not do the actus reus. Similarly, automatism is not so much a defence as a denial of voluntariness, and as such a denial of responsibility for the actus reus. Duress and self-defence, by contrast, deny neither actus reus nor mens rea, but rather seek to defend the commission of a prima facie offence by reference to events not contemplated in the actus reus.[71]

Normally, defences reside at large in the common law, and are not expressly set out as part of each offence. Similarly, they are treated in separate chapters of this text. This is because defences are normally of general application to all crimes, unless expressly or impliedly excluded by the statute which creates a particular crime. The fact that defences make up a third element was accepted by Lord Wilberforce in *Lynch*. Duress, he stated:[72]

"is something which is superimposed on the other ingredients which by themselves would make up an offence, i.e. on the act and the intention. *Coactus volui* sums up the combination: the victim completes the act and knows that he is doing so; but the addition of the element of duress prevents the law from treating what he has done as a crime."

In case it is helpful, we represent this relationship by the following diagram:

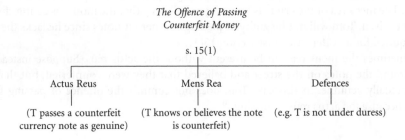

The Offence of Passing
Counterfeit Money

s. 15(1)

Actus Reus	Mens Rea	Defences
(T passes a counterfeit currency note as genuine)	(T knows or believes the note is counterfeit)	(e.g. T is not under duress)

---

[71] Cf. A.T.H. Smith, "On Actus Reus and Mens Rea" in Glazebrook (ed.), *Reshaping the Criminal Law* (1978) 95, 97ff; Simester, "Mistakes in Defence" (1992) 12 *OJLS* 295, 295–6.
[72] [1975] AC 653, 679–80.

2

THE RULE OF LAW AND THE EUROPEAN CONVENTION

It is temptingly easy for a government to misuse the criminal justice system as a convenient means of social ordering. The criminal law, in seeking to secure benefits (including security)[1] to society at large, can be a major threat of *in*security for any individual charged with the commission of a crime. Indeed, in some respects the criminal justice system constitutes this country's most potent peacetime threat to the civil rights of those citizens suspected of and prosecuted for crimes. Accordingly, society, while endeavouring to control and reduce criminal conduct, must be sensitive to the rights and legitimate expectations of those charged with crime.

Central to the protection of those rights and expectations is the Rule of Law, which demands that those under the State's control should be dealt with by fixed and knowable law, and not according to the untrammelled discretion of State (including judicial) officials. As such, the Rule of Law embodies a cluster of legal values, including certainty, clarity, and prospectivity. These values have at their heart not merely the constitutional premise that government should operate under the law, but also the ideal that citizens should be able successfully to live within the law, by deriving guidance from the law itself.[2] As Gardner summarises that ambition,[3]

> "the law must be such that those subject to it can reliably be guided by it, either to avoid violating it or to build the legal consequences of having violated it into their thinking about what future actions may be open to them. People must be able to find out what the law is and to factor it into their practical deliberations. The law must avoid taking people by surprise...."

This view, in turn, requires that the criminal law must be an organised, ascertainable, system of legal rules—and not *ad hoc* responses to the conduct of individuals.

The Rule of Law exists, first and foremost, at the level of principle. It comprises values to which the law should aspire, and to which legislators and judges should pay heed when enacting and interpreting law.[4] It is not a legally mandatory doctrine in its own right, save in so far as it operates as an informing principle of statutory interpretation.[5] However, with

---

[1] See Ramsay, *The Insecurity State: Vulnerable Autonomy and the Right to Security in the Criminal Law* (2012).

[2] See Raz, *The Authority of Law* (2nd ed., 2009) chap. 11; Colvin, "Criminal Law and the Rule of Law" in Fitzgerald (ed.), *Crime, Justice and Codification* (1986) 125.

[3] Introduction to Hart, *Punishment and Responsibility* (2nd ed., 2008) xxxvi.

[4] Cf. *Codification of the Criminal Law* Law Com. No. 143 (1985) para. 1.3, where making the criminal law "more accessible, comprehensible, consistent and certain" was regarded as the aim of codification.

[5] An illustration of its role in statutory interpretation may be seen in Lord Steyn's assertion in *B (a minor)* v. *DPP* [2000] AC 428, 470 that "in the absence of express words or a truly necessary implication, Parliament must be presumed to legislate on the assumption that the principle of legality will supplement the text".

the enactment of the Human Rights Act (HRA) 1998, which provides for the direct applicability of parts of the European Convention on Human Rights and Fundamental Freedoms (ECHR), many of the principles associated with the Rule of Law have independent constitutional significance. In this chapter, we will explore the significance of those principles for the criminal law. More generally, we will consider the impact of the ECHR upon English criminal law.

§ 2.1 No conviction without criminalisation

The first limiting principle is inherent in the definition of criminal law offered at the beginning of Chapter 1: that a crime involves, among other things, an event prohibited by law.[6] This implies that nobody should be convicted of a criminal offence unless what was done is, in law, a crime. *Nullum crimen sine lege*, the maxim goes: no crime without law.[7] Suppose, for example, that Jane is a visitor from another country where adultery is a criminal offence. While in Wales she has an affair with a married man. Even though she believes that in law she is committing a crime, she cannot be convicted of any offence, since adultery is not illegal under English and Welsh criminal law.[8] A similar situation arises where D assumes facts which would make his conduct criminal under an existing offence, but his assumption is wrong. Consider the case of *Deller*:[9] the defendant sold a car, stating as he did so that it was free of encumbrances (meaning that Deller could deal with the property as he pleased). In fact, he thought the car was encumbered, because he had earlier mortgaged it to a finance company. Deller was charged with obtaining the proceeds of the car sale under false pretences. The earlier mortgage was, however, apparently invalid, and hence the car *was* unencumbered. By chance, Deller's pretence was not false. He could not be convicted of the offence charged because he had not satisfied its legal definition.[10]

§ 2.2 Retrospective crimes

A corollary of the *nullum crimen* principle is that there should be no retrospective criminalisation, whereby citizens might be convicted on the basis of conduct which was not, *when they did it*, an offence. In such cases, it is not enough that the relevant law is to hand at the time of the trial. It would still be true that at the time of D's conduct he committed no applicable crime. Remedying the legal deficiency by passing a retrospective law, which deemed the offence into existence at the time of its commission, would be to subvert, rather than uphold, the Rule of Law. Particularly given the dramatic implications of criminal penalties for the lives of individuals, criminal liability is not the sort of nasty surprise that should be sprung on citizens *ex post facto*.

---

[6] Above, § 1.1.

[7] Sometimes called the principle of *legality*, especially in the United States. See Hall, *General Principles of Criminal Law* (2nd ed., 1960) chap. 2.

[8] Cf. *Taaffe* [1984] AC 539.

[9] (1952) 36 Cr App R 184.

[10] Deller could nowadays be convicted of (at least) an attempted fraud by false representation. See below, § 15.3.

A contrast might usefully be drawn here with changes in rules of criminal evidence and procedure. Suppose that D's alleged indecent assault, committed against V in 1970, comes to light in 2016. The rules regarding the admissibility of a number of types of evidence (importantly, hearsay and bad character) have changed markedly in the intervening 46 years.[11] D will not have planned his life in 1970 around the existing rules on hearsay and bad character; the rules of evidence are not meant to guide the conduct of citizens living under the criminal law. D thus has no legitimate complaint if his trial in 2016 uses current rules of evidence to assess whether he committed an offence in 1970. If, however, the court were to go further, and apply 2016 standards of indecency to establish that D had perpetrated the actus reus of indecent assault in 1970, matters might be different. If what D did was not indecent by 1970s' standards, but was indecent by the standards of 2016, D has a legitimate complaint should the later understanding of indecency be adopted.[12] The guidance offered by the concept of indecency (a key part of establishing the precise wrongfulness of D's conduct) would be frustrated if, *at the time of acting*, D could only guess at what might one day be perceived to be indecent. Citizens should not be put in such situations when the criminal law is in play.

We have argued that it is important to optimise the transparency and efficacy of the substantive criminal law by stating its rules clearly in advance. Failure to do so undermines the entire operation of the law, as a system of rules designed to guide society's behaviour. When interpreting criminal statutes, the common law contains a presumption against retrospective crimes. Although the presumption may be overridden by the express terms of a legislative enactment,[13] it provides a signal protection against that possibility. Moreover, were Parliament expressly to override that presumption, it would also be in clear contravention of Article 7 of the ECHR, which plainly interdicts retroactive criminal law and retroactive increases in the penalties for existing crimes.[14] As things stand, both at common law and under the terms of the HRA 1998, courts are required to accept Parliament's will (subject to the tensions and contradictions described below, in § 2.5). Nonetheless, the incorporation of Article 7 via the HRA 1998 should at least ensure that English courts will, in the absence of the clearest language, be loath to interpret a newly created crime, or a statutory increase in penalty, as having retrospective effect. In addition, both the common law presumption and Article 7 may act as a warning sign: any finding that they are overridden involves public acknowledgement that a part of the criminal law transgresses the Rule of Law and contravenes one of the defendant's basic human rights.

---

[11] See Criminal Justice Act 2003, pt. 11.

[12] The prosecution argued that 2015 standards of indecency should be applied to offending spanning the 1980s to the 2000s in *CPS* v. *Fox*, Westminster Magistrates' Court, 15 December 2015. The Chief Magistrate refused to do so, without expressly citing Art 7, on the basis that subsequent changes in attitudes towards touching could not retrospectively make past actions criminal. The prosecution made the valid point that this (surely right) approach could nevertheless lead to problems in prosecuting cases of historical sexual offending. Granted, it is difficult to fathom how a juror born in 1997 can reach a meaningful decision about whether conduct in 1968 was indecent by the standards of the time.

[13] *Waddington* v. *Miah* [1974] 1 WLR 683 (HL); *Deery* [1977] Crim LR 550 (CA); *Sutcliffe-Williams and Gaskell* [1983] Crim LR 255 (CA).

[14] On the importance of the principle that penalties should be reasonably predictable, see *Camilleri* v. *Malta* (2013) 57 EHRR 32. Note, however, that the defendant will not necessarily win an appeal against sentence on the ground that, when he is finally sentenced for "historical" offending, the sentence is higher than would have been given had the trial proceeded at the time of the offending. A troubling example is *R* v. *Bell* [2015] EWCA Crim 1426, [2016] 1 WLR 1.

At common law, the courts formerly also had the power to create offences: indeed, this is the foundation of many of the oldest crimes—including murder, which remains undefined by legislation. By the twentieth century, however, the power was exercised less frequently and more controversially, since it involves a retrospective deployment of the criminal sanction. In *Shaw* v. *DPP*,[15] for example, the defendant was charged with conspiring to corrupt public morals—an offence that had not existed until he was indicted for it. (Another view is that the offence had fallen into desuetude and was resurrected.) The House of Lords upheld the validity of the indictment. *Whether or not* the defendant's actions were covered by an existing law, the courts were said to have residual power to criminalise his conduct. The decision led to an outcry, especially among lawyers and academics.[16] It is now accepted that the courts no longer have the power to create new offences,[17] or indeed to abolish old ones.[18] The authority to create or repeal offences nowadays lies solely with Parliament:[19]

> "an important democratic principle in this country [is] that it is for those representing the people of the country in Parliament, not the executive and not the judges, to decide what conduct should be treated as lying so far outside the bounds of what is acceptable in our society as to attract criminal penalties."

In principle, the courts do not even have the power to *widen* existing offences, in order to criminalise conduct that previously was permitted.[20] Nevertheless, as the European Court of Human Rights (European Court) has observed,[21]

> "However clearly drafted a legal provision may be, in any system of law, including criminal law, there is an inevitable element of judicial interpretation. There will always be a need for elucidation of doubtful points and for adaptation to changing circumstances. Indeed, in the United Kingdom, as in the other Convention States, the progressive development of the criminal law through judicial lawmaking is a well-entrenched and necessary part of legal tradition. Article 7 of the Convention cannot be read as outlawing the gradual clarification of the rules of criminal liability through judicial interpretation from case to case, provided that the resulting development is consistent with the essence of the offence and could reasonably be foreseen."

There is a clear tension between the evolutionary nature of the common law and the interpretive role of judges generally, and the *nullum crimen* principle. In *R*,[22] for example, the House of Lords abolished an exemption in the common law crime of rape, which had

---

[15] [1962] AC 220.
[16] *Shaw* is objectionable on a second count: it is also discussed in § 16.3, with respect to criminalising *immoral* activity. See generally Goodhart, "The *Shaw* Case: The Law and Public Morals" (1961) 77 LQR 560; Note (1962) 75 Harv LR 1652; Smith, "Judicial Law Making in the Criminal Law" (1984) 100 LQR 46.
[17] *Knuller (Publishing, Printing and Promotions) Ltd* v. *DPP* [1973] AC 435; *DPP* v. *Withers* [1975] AC 842.
[18] *Rimmington and Goldstein* [2005] UKHL 63, [2006] 1 AC 459.
[19] *Jones et al.* [2006] UKHL 16, [2007] 1 AC 136, para. 29 (Lord Bingham). See also paras. 60–2 (Lord Hoffmann). The House rejected the direct incorporation without legislation of new international law crimes into the domestic law of England and Wales.
[20] *Withers* [1975] AC 842, 863 (Lord Simon); *Rimmington and Goldstein* [2005] UKHL 63, [2006] 1 AC 459, para. 33 (Lord Bingham). Nonetheless, the House of Lords held in *Rimmington* that the common law offence of public nuisance did not breach Art. 7, if confined to well-established instances of the offence and not used to evade time limits and sentencing restrictions on more specific statutory offences.
[21] *SW* v. *UK* (1995) 21 EHRR 363, para. 36.
[22] [1992] 1 AC 599.

meant that a husband could not be convicted of raping his wife. While that change is to be welcomed as a matter of social and legal policy, the manner in which it was achieved is more controversial, since it led to R's being convicted on the basis of conduct that was apparently immune from the charge of rape when it was performed.[23]

Moreover, the decision of the European Court in *SW* v. *UK*[24] shows just how delicate the balance may be between acceptable evolution of common law principles and illegitimate lawmaking. On appeal from *R*, the Court found that there was no breach of Article 7 when the House of Lords ruled against a husband's immunity in rape. There would have been the clearest breach of Article 7[25] if the House of Lords had acknowledged a current, legally valid, immunity but had decided that it was no longer acceptable and would therefore be abolished. To ensure Article 7 compatibility, the following view must be taken of the House of Lords' decision in *R*: instead of abolishing the exemption, their Lordships ruled that the claim for immunity was unfounded in law. On this view, they cast their ruling in the form of a finding that, *by the time of the defendant's actions*, the historical immunity for spouses was no longer part of the law. This may seem close to sophistry, but it is a vital distinction when understanding Article 7. The House of Lords determined that the better view of the law, *at the time of the appellant's conduct*, was that the immunity had gone. Ascertaining the best view of the current state of the law is not a matter of majority prediction, even if the majority is drawn from an expert community of criminal lawyers. The best view consists of the most cogent and intellectually convincing resolution of the issues to be adjudicated by the court hearing the case.

Their Lordships' dissection of the legal and social grounds of the immunity, together with their demonstration of the incoherence and instability of recent case law, which had reluctantly conceded the immunity but, at the same time, had sought to evade its consequences, was the strongest indication available that the day of the immunity was done. Indeed, the European Court of Human Rights concluded that the decision by the House of Lords in *R* was predictable. Strictly, however, predictability is not the point. (It is a separate Rule of Law value, considered in § 2.3.) What blocks a claim of retrospective criminalisation here is a demonstration that the defendant's case was decided on the basis of what the law was *at the time* of the defendant's conduct. The best judgments are not always predictable; Dworkin's perfect judge, Hercules, may surprise everyone, but still get it right.[26] Prior to the decision in *R*, most criminal lawyers would have assumed with justification that the husband's immunity in rape was circumscribed but extant. But, on the understanding of the case presented above, the reasoning of the House of Lords demonstrates this assumption was incorrect *at the time it was made*. Accordingly, as the European Court found, there was no breach of the *nullum crimen* principle or of Article 7.

Unfortunately it is all too easy for a court fixated on the brute merits of a case to shun an analysis of what the law was *at the time of the alleged offence* and slip into plain retroactivity. *R* was decided in 1991. Subsequently, in *C*,[27] a different defendant was convicted in 2002 of

---

[23] See Giles, "Judicial Law-making in the Criminal Courts: The Case of Marital Rape" [1992] *Crim LR* 907.

[24] (1995) 21 EHRR 363.

[25] Subject to the possibility that the husband's action fell within the exception created by Art. 7(2), noted below in the text.

[26] See Dworkin, *Law's Empire* (1986) ch. 7.

[27] [2004] EWCA Crim 292, [2004] 1 WLR 2098.

raping his wife *in 1970*. Upholding the conviction, the Court of Appeal expressed itself in the following blunt terms:[28]

> "We need not discuss either the 'declaratory' theory of the effect of judicial decision relating to the development of the common law, nor whether by its decision, the House of Lords was retrospectively creating a new offence where none existed before. The stark fact is that R was convicted.... The decision applied to events that had already taken place, as well as those in the future."

This approach effectively abdicates the judicial task. What matters when consulting precedents is not just whether a previous defendant was convicted, but the reasons why. In effect, the Court of Appeal's analysis implies that *any* development in the law might be applied retrospectively. While an overly literal reading of the declaratory theory of judicial decision-making might support this view, such a reading sits badly with the Rule of Law, and with the incorporation of Article 7 into English Law. Given the acknowledgement of the spouse's exemption in appellate cases between 1970 and 1991,[29] it is tolerably clear that the Lords' conclusion regarding what the law was in 1991 was not applicable in 1970. The Court of Appeal in *C* asserted, without offering any relevant (and quite a lot of irrelevant) evidence to support its claim, that a solicitor consulted in 1970 would have advised any client that "he might be liable for rape".[30] Even if that were true (which is surely doubtful), it misses the constitutional point that this is not just a matter of predictability of *future* developments in the criminal law. Lord Bingham saw the distinction in *Rimmington and Goldstein*:[31]

> "There are *two* guiding principles: no one should be punished under a law unless it is sufficiently clear and certain to enable him to know what conduct is forbidden before he does it; and no one should be punished for any act which was not clearly and ascertainably punishable when the act was done."

The first principle concerns fair warning (discussed in the next section). The second principle expresses the *nullum crimen* idea: even if retrospective criminalisation through a later development of the law is predictable, it is still wrong. It would have been preferable for the Court of Appeal to acknowledge the revisionary nature of its ruling in *C*, but defend it as an isolated exception—hence specific to rape—on the grounds of the Article 7(2) exception, which allows for retrospective conviction where a person's act "was criminal according to the general principles of law recognised by civilised nations".

§ 2.3 Fair warning

Apart from its constitutional implications, we have noted that the most important reason for requiring criminal offences to be created prospectively is that failure to do so undermines predictability in the law. In *Shaw v. DPP* (discussed above), the enterprising Mr Shaw had been assured by his lawyer that his proposed publication, *The Ladies' Directory* (a directory of prostitutes), passed muster in legal terms. Yet the House of Lords found that Shaw, with

---

[28] *Ibid.*, para. 22.
[29] E.g. *Steele* (1977) 65 Cr App R 22; *Sharples* [1990] Crim LR 198 (CA).
[30] [2004] EWCA Crim 292, [2004] 1 WLR 2098, para. 19.
[31] [2005] UKHL 63, [2006] 1 AC 459, para. 33 (emphasis added).

others, had conspired to corrupt public morality. If even competent legal advice cannot predict the unlawfulness of a defendant's conduct, his attempt to live within the law is no easy task.

The importance of security from prosecution by way of surprise was forcefully recognised by the House of Lords in *R (Purdy)* v. *DPP*.[32] D wished to assist his terminally ill partner to travel to Switzerland so that she could receive skilled assistance in ending her life. All members of the Appellate Committee considered that what D proposed to do contravened English criminal law.[33] Yet Article 8 of the ECHR (concerning the right to private life) was held to require the Director of Public Prosecutions to make public the criteria he would use when resolving whether to prosecute in cases of this kind, so as to provide *ex ante* guidance to D, V and other persons faced with similar circumstances.[34] Of course, the facts of *Purdy* are very particular. But if it is the case that persons whose conduct seems in clear breach of law may be *legally* entitled to information relating to the chances of prosecution, in terms of due process, the case for protecting persons seeking to conform their conduct to law in cases of legal uncertainty seems stronger.

It is important to notice that, in *Shaw*, predictability was threatened not just because the offence was created retrospectively. Suppose that the House resurrected rather than invented this species of conspiracy, and that the principle against retroactivity was not breached. Either way, the nebulous terms of the offence leave to speculation what kinds of thing one must not conspire to do. Similarly, even if the view of the European Court that *R* involved no retrospective criminalisation were accepted, the decision remains problematic because of its element of surprise.

This shows that non-retroactive legislation is not the only standard set by the Rule of Law, and that the need for predictability has more general implications. The criminal law is not there solely to tell police and judges what to do *after* someone offends, but also to tell citizens what not to do *in advance*. As such, it is not enough for there to be a law in place before people can commit a crime. They should also be told about it:[35]

> "Respect for law, which is the most cogent force in prompting orderly conduct in a civilised community, is weakened, if men are punished for acts which according to the general consensus of opinion they were justified in believing to be morally right *and in accordance with law*."

That is the reason why non-publication or unavailability of a statutory instrument may be a defence, if a person is charged with a crime under that instrument while incapable of knowing about its existence.[36] It also explains why the increasing complexity and obscurity

---

[32] [2009] UKHL 45, [2010] 1 AC 345.

[33] Either as assisting suicide contrary to s. 2 of the Suicide Act 1961 or, controversially, complicity in murder.

[34] At the time of the proceedings in *Purdy*, to public knowledge there had been over 150 similar cases, none of which had been prosecuted. All that the Director had said publicly was that it should not be assumed that prosecutions would not be brought in such cases. The House of Lords unanimously decided that this uncertainty surrounding prosecution entailed failure of the "quality of law" test required by the ECHR jurisprudence for a lawful interference with the right to respect for private and family life under Art. 8. For further discussion see below, § 18.2(ii)(a).

[35] *State* v. *O'Neil* 126 NW 454, 456 (1910) (emphasis added). See, further: Brett, "Mistake of Law as a Criminal Defence" (1966) 5 *MULR* 179; Ashworth, "Ignorance of the Criminal Law, and Duties to Avoid It" (2011) 74 *MLR* 1.

[36] *Grant* v. *Borg* [1982] 1 WLR 638 (HL); *Burns* v. *Nowell* (1880) 5 QBD 444 (CA); *Lim Chin Aik* v. *R.* [1963] AC 160 (PC); *Golden-Brown* v. *Hunt* (1972) 19 Fed LR 438; *Catholique* (1980) 49 CCC (2d) 65.

of domestic law is a major threat to basic principles of legal justice. Matters are made worse, particularly in the area of regulatory criminal law, by the sheer volume of primary and secondary legislation and the piecemeal additions made regularly to it.[37] Furthermore, although legislation passed by the UK Parliament is now routinely placed online, it is not always updated when amended by subsequent legislation.

The Rule of Law mandates that people should be governed by concrete rules that are ascertainable and certain,[38] and which minimise the opportunity for officials to wield arbitrary power.[39] This requires both that the rule be stated in advance, and also that it be stated clearly.[40] Clarity is essential if citizens are to have *fair warning* that by their prospective actions they are in danger of incurring a criminal sanction.[41] If individuals understand the law, they will be able properly to decide what to do in light of the guidance that the law is meant to provide. Only then can the law act as the deterrent it is intended to be. And only then do citizens have a fair opportunity to steer themselves clear of criminal liability.

Once again, however, fair warning is a Rule of Law aspiration that is not always achieved in practice. Prior to the House of Lords decision in *Ireland*,[42] English criminal lawyers would not generally have predicted that the menace of silent phone calls would be curbed by including them within the definition of assault. Before the decision in *R* (above), it was widely assumed that a cohabiting husband was immune from the charge of raping his wife. Nonetheless, the House found the immunity to be ungrounded in law.

Still, both decisions predate the coming into effect of the Human Rights Act 1998,[43] and the courts must nowadays take account of the ECHR. In *Kokkinakis* v. *Greece*, the European Court spoke of the principle that:[44]

> "the criminal law must not be extensively construed to the accused's detriment, for instance by analogy; it follows from this that an offence must be clearly defined in law. This condition is satisfied where the individual can know from the wording of the relevant provision and, if need be, with the assistance of the courts' interpretation of it, what acts and omissions will make him liable."

---

[37] Something about which the courts are rightly worried, when neither they nor the enforcement authorities can be sure whether they have to hand the current version of the law: see the extraordinary case of *Chambers* [2008] EWCA Crim 2467.

[38] Raz, *The Authority of Law* (2nd ed., 1999) 214–6.

[39] Cf. *R. (on the application of Gillan)* v. *Commissioner of Police of the Metropolis* [2006] UKHL 12, [2006] 2 AC 307, para. 75 (Lord Brown), regarding the "in accordance with the law" provision of Art. 8(2) of the ECHR. See, also, *Gillan and Quinton* v. *UK* (2010) 50 EHRR 45, paras. 76–7.

[40] Distinctions are sometimes drawn between different types of clarity: see Stark, "'It's Only Words': On Meaning and *Mens Rea*" (2013) 72 *CLJ* 155, 164–6.

[41] See the discussion in *Misra and Srivastava* [2004] EWCA Crim 2375, [2005] 1 Cr App R 21, paras. 29–34. Compare, in the United States, *Papachristou* v. *City of Jacksonville* 405 US 156, 162 (1972) (vagrancy ordinance void for vagueness). Fair warning is also relevant to inadvertence-based liability, e.g., for negligence. It is one reason why criminal liability for serious crimes should normally be confined to (subjectively) reckless or intentional wrongdoing. This is because if there were widespread exposure to State interference for inadvertent wrongdoing, then it would be much harder for citizens to plan and get on with their lives, without fearing the unforeseen disruption that facing criminal charges entails. See, e.g., Hart, *Punishment and Responsibility* (2nd ed., 2008) 181–2. However, this argument is not insuperable. To the extent that the Rule of Law enjoins unpredictable interference by the State, liability for negligence is reasonably predictable. Moreover, unless negligence liability is no deterrent, the argument prima facie deprives victims of protection from similarly unlooked-for intrusions by other citizens.

[42] [1998] AC 147; below, § 11.2(i)(b).

[43] Below, § 2.5.

[44] (1994) 17 EHRR 397, 423. Cf. *G* v. *Federal Republic of Germany* (1989) 60 DR 252, 262; *Gillan and Quinton* v. *UK* (2010) 50 EHRR 45, para. 76.

The passage makes clear that judicial creativity and interpretation—the legitimate principles of which are considered in Chapter 3—can be reviewed under the terms of Article 7. As the European Court has emphasised, even where there are policy grounds favouring an expansive interpretation, they are secondary to the principle that criminal offences must be unambiguously defined:[45]

> "More specifically ... the principle that a provision of the criminal law may not be applied extensively to the detriment of the defendant, which is the corollary of the principle of legality in relation to crime and punishment and more generally of the principle of legal certainty, precludes bringing criminal proceedings in respect of conduct not clearly defined as culpable by law. That principle, which is one of the general legal principles underlying the constitutional traditions common to the Member States, has also been enshrined in various international treaties, in particular in Article 7 of the Convention for the Protection of Human Rights and Fundamental Freedoms ..."

The importance of this passage has been acknowledged in the House of Lords.[46] The principle it espouses has led the Strasbourg Court to hold that the power of an English or Welsh court to bind over (i.e. require, on pain of penalty) persons to "be of good behaviour" was incompatible with the ECHR, because the prescribed standard was too imprecise.[47] But it remains uncertain how far the constraints of Article 7 are being observed: "conduct likely to provoke a breach of the peace", for example, has been held to be sufficiently certain.[48]

One consideration in these decisions was whether the imprecision was offset by reference to other, more objective, offence elements.[49] Beyond that, however, there is little guidance regarding what factors will be taken into account when reviewing interpretive decisions for compliance. *If* conduct has been engaged in on the reasonable assumption that it was lawful, that should count as a factor to be considered by a court. But it may be that the *kind* of conduct at issue should properly influence a court. Hence, if the objection is one of fair warning rather than a constitutional one of retrospective criminalisation, the decision in *R* is defensible, perhaps, on the footing that R's conduct did constitute a crime when done by anyone else, and that the reasons for criminalisation apply just as forcefully to a husband as to anyone else. It should have made no difference had R received an assurance from a lawyer, immediately prior to making his wife submit to intercourse by drawing a knife, that in legal terms he would not be committing rape. That is not, of course, to say that courts may craft new law in order to catch husbands who treat wives in that fashion. It is merely to say that in considering what the current law is, the fact that the defendant thought it was different has less weight in a context where the defendant's act breached in the most fundamental

---

[45] *Procura della Republica* v. *X* [1996] ECR I-6609, para. 25. See too *Sunday Times* v. *UK* (1979) 2 EHRR 245, para. 49.

[46] *R (on the application of Junttan Oy)* v. *Bristol Magistrates' Court* [2003] UKHL 55, [2004] 2 All ER 555, para. 21 (Lord Nicholls, dissenting).

[47] *Hashman and Harrup* v. *United Kingdom* (1999) 30 EHRR 241. See, further, Ashworth, "Preventive Orders and the Rule of Law" in Baker and Horder (eds.), *The Sanctity of Life and the Criminal Law* (2013) 45.

[48] *Steel* v. *UK* (1999) 28 EHRR 603. An instructive example is the common law offence of cheating, cogently criticised by Ormerod, "Cheating the Public Revenue" [1998] *Crim LR* 627, but held to be compatible with the ECHR in *Pattni* [2001] Crim LR 570 (CC).

[49] Cf. *Hashman and Harrup* v. *United Kingdom* (2000) 30 EHRR 241, where dishonesty offences were distinguished (at para. 39) on the basis that the element of dishonesty "is but one element of a more comprehensive definition of the prescribed behaviour". Similarly, breach of the peace—understood as conduct "the natural consequences of which would be to provoke others to violence"—was distinguished (para. 38) because it is defined "by reference to its effects".

way his wife's rights to bodily integrity and sexual autonomy. By contrast, if the owner of a factory has done his best to comply with health and safety law and has received professional assurance that he has done enough, this should be recognised when determining whether he has provided a safe system of work "so far as is reasonably practicable".[50]

It is for Parliament to make law and, although judicial interpretation of law may properly be purposive,[51] current legal resources cannot always be stretched to cover the conduct in question. The Rule of Law requires a system of legal ordering, not *ad hoc* responses to the conduct of individuals. As such, it is particularly important in the criminal law to identify where the law and the jurisdiction of judges runs out. We have seen that, in the past, judges have gone beyond that point in order to criminalise conduct they disapproved of even in cases where the policy arguments for criminalisation were not clear cut. That is contrary to adjudication under law. The incorporation of Article 7 enhances the already compelling case against such judicial activism.

(i) Use of evaluative concepts

We have argued that a legal system should seek to provide as much guidance and predictability as it can. Realism is required, however, when deciding what degree of certainty is attainable in particular laws. Explicitness is necessarily compromised in offences that involve vague and open-ended concepts such as "unreasonable" and "fraudulent". Similarly, if we drive a car we know, or should know, that we must drive with "due care and attention".[52] The phrase sets a standard for a myriad of driving contexts and inevitably must leave an ultimate assessment to the Court. The phrase gives no more than open-ended guidance, and further glosses on it, such as driving that "falls below what would be expected of a competent and careful driver",[53] hardly help matters. The degree of error or inattention that will turn us into criminals cannot be stated with exactitude. If the criminal law is to involve itself with standards of safety, which surely it must, it cannot give a rigid specification of the circumstances under which criminal liability will follow.

At the same time, both legislature and judiciary should be cautious about the deployment and interpretation of such expressions. Consider, for example, the imposition of negligence-based criminal liability, through offences which are typically couched in terms of the "unreasonableness" of the defendant's behaviour. The touchstone, be it "unreasonable" or "negligent", is not susceptible of accurate or formal definition. What is "reasonable"? Nowhere does the law say, and to some extent the individual must judge the law's standard for himself, and take the risk that a court might later disagree with him.[54] Such gambles ought to be minimised,[55] and where possible these discretionary terms should be replaced by more concrete definitions of what counts as illegal, and what as legitimate.

---

[50] Health and Safety at Work etc. Act 1974, s. 2.

[51] See below, § 3.1(ii).

[52] Road Traffic Act 1988, s. 3.

[53] Road Traffic Act 1988, s. 3ZA.

[54] Indeed, the judge should not even provide guidance to the jury concerning the ordinary meaning of language used in a statute—which is a matter of fact, not law. See *Brutus* v. *Cozens* [1973] AC 854, 861–2 (Lord Reid); cf. *Stephens and Mujuru* [2007] EWCA Crim 1249, [2007] 2 Cr App R 26.

[55] "A statute which either forbids or requires the doing of an act in terms so vague that men of common intelligence must necessarily guess at its meaning and differ as to its application, violates the first essential of due process

This reservation should not be overstated, and it cannot be claimed that such terms deprive individuals of advance warning altogether. The defendant's judgement is not purely a guess: words such as "reasonable" are not meaningless.[56] We understand them, and know how to apply the implicit judgements they import. The use of broad evaluative terms such as "negligent" and "fraudulent" may well provide an acceptable level of guidance where there is a high degree of social consensus about appropriate behaviour in the area of activity under regulation. One may assume that degree of necessary consensus, for instance, in matters of road safety; accordingly a requirement to drive with due care and attention may tell us all we really need to know. Furthermore, extra-legal guidance, such as that found in the *Highway Code*, can go some way to solidifying consensus regarding what is considered to be "due care and attention" or the standard of the "competent and careful driver".

Moreover, evaluative standards are useful. Terms like "reasonable" and "dangerous" give the law flexibility to deal with cases that a legislator might not foresee. It is too much to expect a statute to list every single mode of negligent homicide, and meaningful (if open) terms like "unreasonable" save us from being straitjacketed by a rigid specification of the circumstances under which criminal liability will or will not follow. This much has been accepted by the Strasbourg Court, which has observed that "[t]he need to avoid excessive rigidity and to keep pace with changing circumstances means that many laws are inevitably couched in terms which, to a greater or lesser extent, are vague …".[57] Indeed, without such flexibility, the law would be unfair and incomplete. There will always be matters which require regulation, but where a degree of imprecision is inevitable. Over many years, for example, the courts sought a legal definition of when an act was sufficiently close to the commission of a crime to constitute an attempt to commit that crime. Various tests were tried; all were unsatisfactory. Nowadays the jury is simply asked whether D's act was "more than merely preparatory" to committing the full offence.[58]

Nonetheless, evaluative terms *are* imprecise, and for that reason, at least in serious crimes, they should normally be used only sparingly and for clear cases of wrongdoing. This is one justification of the common law's requirement that negligence be "gross" before one may be guilty of manslaughter:[59] it is not merely that D's culpability is greater, but also that we can be surer D is culpable.[60] Sometimes, the imprecision is such that these terms ought not to be used at all. It is doubtful whether there is a sufficient degree of consensus about the acceptable contents of literature, plays, and film to render the standard "tendency to deprave and corrupt", employed in obscenity law,[61] a sufficient guide to producers and

of law": *Conally v. General Construction Company* 269 US 385, 391 (1926). Cf. Rawls, *A Theory of Justice* (revised ed., 1999) 210: "if the precept of no crime without a law is violated, say by statutes being vague and imprecise, what we are at liberty to do is likewise vague and imprecise".

[56] Lucas, "The Philosophy of the Reasonable Man" (1963) 13 *Phil Qtrly* 97.

[57] *Kokkinakis* v. *Greece* (1994) 17 EHRR 397, para. 40; citing *Müller and Others* v. *Switzerland* (1991) 13 EHRR 212, para. 29. The Court noted that potential vagueness of an offence may be ameliorated once the surrounding case law is taken into account.

[58] See below, § 9.4(i).

[59] See below, § 10.6(ii). The use of gross negligence as a culpability standard for manslaughter was held compatible with Article 7 in *Misra* [2004] EWCA Crim 2375, [2005] 1 Cr App R 21.

[60] An interesting discussion is Horder, "Gross Negligence and Criminal Culpability" (1997) 47 *U Toronto LJ* 495.

[61] Obscene Publications Act 1959, s. 1(1). This statutory test differs from that applicable to "obscene" items sent in the post, which are regulated by the Postal Services Act 2000, s. 85(3). The test of "obscenity" in the post is simply that of the word's ordinary meaning, and may include anything that is shocking, lewd, or indecent: *Kirk*

publishers operating in those fields. If a government wishes to maintain a regulatory presence there, it is better that it regulates by description, expressly identifying those things which are not to be produced, published, or possessed. For instance, it is an offence to possess extreme pornography: an image is extreme if it is "grossly offensive, disgusting or otherwise obscene"; but it *also* must be a realistic depiction of various more specific activities.[62]

Alas, the ECHR seems unlikely to introduce greater rigour into this area. In *Handyside* v. *UK*,[63] a case resolved by the European Court, the applicant complained that the offence of obscenity in the Obscene Publications Acts 1959–1964 "was so far-reaching and imprecise that it might be applied almost without limit". Under that legislation, items which have a tendency "to deprave and corrupt" are obscene unless they are redeemed by some scientific, educational, literary, or artistic merit.[64] In the absence of a societal consensus on what constitutes obscenity, what kinds of sexual or violent material could be published was essentially a matter of guesswork about how the particular jury empanelled for the case would respond to the items with which they were presented. Despite this, the European Court dismissed the applicant's Article 7 argument, stating that "the requirement of certainty in the law cannot mean that the concrete facts giving rise to criminal liability should be set out in the statute concerned".[65] It was enough that the court was provided with a text, a general definition, which it could amplify and make concrete on a case-by-case basis. This glosses the fact that the formula, "to deprave and corrupt" normally involves a finding of fact. It is not subject to judicial amplification and explication; there are merely the *ad hoc* verdicts of different juries.

§ 2.4 Fair labelling

We have seen that the *ex ante* guidance the law is meant to provide requires it to be clearly stated. However, there is another reason for expecting clarity in criminal offences. When a crime occurs, justice must not only be done, it must be seen to be done. The law needs precision in order to identify exactly what offence the wrongdoer has committed. If he is publicly convicted of "murder", D should *be* a murderer and not a parking offender. At the same time, neither would it be satisfactory for the law simply to label all convicted offenders unspecifically as "criminals", for that would equate the convictions of rapists with those of pickpockets. The criminal law speaks to society as well as wrongdoers when it convicts them, and it should communicate its judgment with precision, by accurately naming

[2006] EWCA Crim 725. Yet that standard, too, may be thought rather nebulous; especially since its application is a matter for the jury. Indeed, even in judicial hands the application of evaluative terms may vary. Thus, in *Collins* v. *DPP* [2006] UKHL 40, [2006] 1 WLR 2223, the House of Lords saw fit to overturn a finding by Leicestershire Justices that certain racist telephone messages sent by D were "offensive" but not "grossly offensive". Apparently a reasonable person—but not the Justices—*would* have found the messages to be grossly offensive. Such variation *ipso facto* suggests the need for more detailed legislative guidance.

[62] Such as of sexual interference with a human corpse. See Criminal Justice and Immigration Act 2008, s. 63.
[63] (1979-80) 1 EHRR 737.
[64] Obscene Publications Act 1959, s. 4.
[65] Council of Europe, *European Convention on Human Rights, Year: 1974* (1976) 290.

the crime of which they are convicted. This requirement is known as the principle of fair labelling.[66]

The need for fair labelling is one reason why we should not merge the separate offences of murder and manslaughter into a single crime of unlawful homicide, as was suggested by Lord Kilbrandon in *Hyam*;[67] nor combine arson and vandalism into a single crime of criminal damage, as was once proposed by the Law Commission.[68] In the eyes of society, such offences involve distinct types of wrongdoing, and the communicative function of the law would be impaired were the law to blur these differences.[69]

Underlying this objection is the point that different offences may criminalise *actions* which have differing social significance, and not just *outcomes*. So, for example, it would be a mistake to assimilate vandalism with negligent damage to property. Even though the harm to property is the same, vandalism expresses a certain sort of contempt for society and the victim that negligent damage does not. If the criminal law were not to distinguish the two, a conviction would be potentially misleading.[70]

The law must make clear what sort of criminal each offender is—what the conviction is *for*. It should communicate this to the defendant, so that he may know exactly what he has done wrong and why he is being punished, in order that his punishment appears meaningful to him, not just an arbitrary harsh treatment. It should also communicate to the victim that her interests were wrongfully set back by the defendant's conduct, and that the State denounces that misconduct. In addition, the law should communicate the crime to the public, so that it too may understand the nature of his transgression. The public record matters. While an employer may have few qualms about hiring a convicted fraudster as an orderly in a children's hospital, it would be an entirely different matter to contemplate employing someone who has been convicted of offences related to paedophilia.

§ 2.5 The European Convention on Human Rights

The impact of the European Convention on Human Rights (ECHR) and the Human Rights Act 1998 (HRA 1998) on substantive criminal law has been mentioned already in passing. This section discusses the role of the ECHR and HRA 1998 in more detail.

The United Kingdom was one of the original parties to the ECHR.[71] States which contract into the ECHR are obliged to secure the enjoyment of Convention rights for their

---

[66] Ashworth, "The Elasticity of *Mens Rea*" in Tapper (ed.), *Crime, Proof and Punishment* (1981) 45, 53–6; Williams, "Convictions and Fair Labelling" (1983) 42 *CLJ* 85; Mitchell, "Multiple Wrongdoing and Offence Structure: A Plea for Consistency and Fair Labelling" (2001) 64 *MLR* 393, 398–400; Chalmers and Leverick, "Fair Labelling in Criminal Law" (2008) 71 *MLR* 217; Tadros, "Fair Labelling and Social Solidarity" in Zedner and Roberts (eds.), *Principles and Values in Criminal Law and Criminal Justice* (2012) 67.

[67] [1975] AC 55, 98. For defence of a unitary offence of homicide, see Blom-Cooper and Morris, *With Malice Aforethought* (2004).

[68] *Malicious Damage*, Working Paper No. 23 (1969) para. 22.

[69] See Gardner, "Rationality and the Rule of Law in Offences Against the Person" (1994) 53 *CLJ* 502, 504–6, 512–20.

[70] See further below, § 16.6(ii).

[71] On the law of the Convention generally, consult Harris, O'Boyle, and Warbrick, *Law of the European Convention on Human Rights* (3rd ed., 2014). For consideration of the Convention in the context of criminal law, evidence, and procedure see Emmerson, Ashworth, and Macdonald, *Human Rights and Criminal Justice* (3rd ed., 2012).

citizens. Usually, this will require ensuring that State and public officials do not conduct themselves in a manner inimical to Convention rights. Sometimes, however, positive action may be required; including the creation, amendment, or enforcement of criminal offences.[72] If a country is found to be in breach of one or more Articles of the ECHR, it incurs a treaty obligation to bring its law and practices into step with Convention requirements. Alleged breaches of the Convention are adjudicated on by the European Court of Human Rights (European Court), which sits in Strasbourg. Since 1966, the United Kingdom has allowed individuals to take cases to the Court. On a variety of occasions the European Court has found against the United Kingdom. A significant number of these adverse judgments concern matters of criminal procedure, criminal law, and sentencing.[73]

Consequently, the HRA 1998, which requires all public authorities (including courts) to act compatibly with Convention obligations,[74] is of direct concern to all criminal lawyers.[75] The Act enables the defence or the prosecution to raise Convention arguments in any criminal proceedings, whether before the local magistrates or the Supreme Court. Should those arguments be found wanting by the English courts, a disappointed individual retains the opportunity to persuade the European Court of the merits of her case by making an application directly to it.[76] From a criminal lawyer's perspective, claims that human rights have been violated are most likely to arise in the contexts of procedure, evidence, and sentencing. Significantly, Article 6 of the ECHR, which guarantees the right to a fair trial and a presumption of innocence, has been construed as having no bearing on the fairness of the substantive law to be applied at the trial.[77] There is no explicit right to a fair substantive criminal law.[78] But this does not mean that the substantive criminal law is immune

---

[72] See Ashworth, *Positive Obligations in Criminal Law* (2013), chap. 8; Lazarus, "Positive Obligations and Criminal Justice: Duties to Protect or Coerce?" in Zedner and Roberts (eds.), *Principles and Values in Criminal Law and Criminal Justice* (2012) 135.

[73] Significant decisions involving findings against the United Kingdom include *McCann and others* v. *UK* (1996) 21 EHRR 97 (permissible force in the prevention of crime); *Tynne, Wilson and Gunnell* v. *UK* (1991) 13 EHRR 666 (discretionary life-sentencing); *Saunders* v. *United Kingdom* (1997) 23 EHRR 313 (compulsory powers of questioning); *Vinter* v. *United Kingdom* [2014] Crim LR 81 ("whole life" sentences).

[74] HRA 1998, s. 6. For general discussion of the HRA 1998 see Wade, "The United Kingdom's Bill of Rights" in Cambridge Centre for Public Law, *Constitutional Reform in the United Kingdom: Practice and Principles* (1998) 61; Bamforth, "The Application of the Human Rights Act 1998 to Public Authorities and Private Bodies" (1999) 58 *CLJ* 159.

[75] For discussion of the HRA 1998 in the context of criminal law see Cambridge Centre for Public Law, *The Human Rights Act and the Criminal and Regulatory Process* (1999); Smith, "The Human Rights Act and the Criminal Lawyer: The Constitutional Context" [1999] *Crim LR* 251; Arden, "Criminal Law at the Crossroads: The Impact on Human Rights from the Law Commission's Perspective and the Need for a Code" [1999] *Crim LR* 439; Buxton, "The Human Rights Act and the Substantive Criminal Law" [2000] *Crim LR* 331; Ashworth, "The Human Rights Act and the Substantive Criminal Law: A Non-minimalist View" [2000] *Crim LR* 564; Ashworth, "A Decade of Human Rights in Criminal Justice" [2014] *Crim LR* 325.

[76] The passing of the HRA 1998 is without prejudice to a right of individual petition to the European Court. However, Art. 35 of the Convention requires that domestic remedies be exhausted before the matter is raised at Strasbourg. Thus Convention rights must first be asserted in the courts of England and Wales.

[77] *Concannon* [2002] Crim LR 213 (CA); *Z* v. *UK* (2002) 34 EHRR 3; *G* [2008] UKHL 37, [2009] 1 AC 92; *G* v. *UK* (2011) 53 EHRR SE25; *Barnfather* v. *London Borough of Islington and Secretary of State for Education and Skills* [2003] EWHC 418 (Admin), [2003] 1 WLR 2318.

[78] Cf. Tadros, "A Human Right to a Fair Criminal Law" in Chalmers, Leverick and Farmer (eds.), *Essays in Criminal Law in Honour of Sir Gerald Gordon* (2010) 103.

from scrutiny under the Convention: successful challenges to English criminal offences and defences have been made at Strasbourg.[79]

The following sections offer a brief account of those Convention Articles most directly affecting the substantive criminal law. More lengthy consideration will be given to particular human rights issues throughout this work where relevant to the subject matter under discussion. First, however, it is necessary to present an overview of the HRA 1998, in order that the manner and extent to which Convention arguments may be put in the context of criminal proceedings is understood properly.

(i) The Human Rights Act 1998—the framework

At the outset, it should be noted that the HRA 1998 does not elevate the European Convention of Human Rights into a form of higher, fundamental law against which the validity of all other primary legislation may be tested, and those laws invalidated if found wanting. Instead, the Act obliges courts to interpret legislation, whenever the legislation was passed, "so far as possible … in a way which is compatible with the Convention Rights".[80] If there remains any incompatibility which cannot be erased by interpretation, the High Court and appellate courts (the Court of Appeal and the Supreme Court) may make a *declaration of incompatibility* under section 4 of the HRA 1998. Section 4(6) of the HRA 1998 nevertheless provides that a declaration of incompatibility does not affect the validity, continuing operation, or enforcement of any incompatible legislation.[81]

No explicit provision is made in the HRA 1998 for cases of incompatibility between the common law and the Convention. One example of a likely incompatibility is the common law defence of insanity, which, at present, is arguably too broad in treating as insane persons who suffer from conditions such as epilepsy and diabetes.[82] Some writers have suggested that this practice contravenes Article 5, which ensures the right to liberty and security of the person.[83] Additionally, it has been claimed that placing the burden of proof on D to prove the elements of the defence contravenes the presumption of innocence guaranteed by Article 6(2).[84]

Suppose that a Crown Court judge is persuaded that an insanity verdict in respect of D will contravene Article 5 or Article 6(2). Can she disregard English precedents of the highest authority that require such a verdict in D's case? It has been argued that in this

---

[79] Notably in *McCann and others* v. *UK* (1996) 21 EHRR 97; *A* v. *UK* (1998) 27 EHRR 611; *Dudgeon* v. *UK* (1982) 4 EHRR 149.

[80] HRA 1998, s. 3(1). For arguments about how English courts should use the interpretive power conferred by s. 3 see Gearty, "Reconciling Parliamentary Democracy and Human Rights" (2002) 118 *LQR* 248 and Phillipson, "(Mis-)Reading Section 3 of the Human Rights Act" (2003) 119 *LQR* 183.

[81] See, too, HRA 1998, s. 3(2)(b). Subordinate legislation, on the other hand, is likely to be invalid to the extent of any incompatibility with Convention rights: cf. s. 3(2)(c).

[82] See below, § 19.1(iii).

[83] See Sutherland and Gearty, "Insanity and the European Court of Human Rights" [1992] *Crim LR* 418; Baker, "Human Rights, *McNaghten* and the 1991 Act" [1994] *Crim LR* 84; below, § 19.1(iii). In other respects, the defence is also arguably too narrow, allowing the conviction of some persons in contravention of Art. 3 (interdicting, in addition to torture, "inhuman or degrading treatment or punishment").

[84] See Law Commission, *Insanity and Automatism: A Discussion Paper* (2013) paras. 8.20–1 (critiquing *H* v. *UK* App. No. 15023/89).

situation she *must* now override previous authority. Section 6 of the HRA 1998 imposes a duty on public authorities to act compatibly with Convention rights. It has been argued that in light of that section, courts—being public bodies—must hand down judgments which are Convention-compatible, unless precluded from doing so by the clear terms of a statute or other primary legislation. On that view, the statutory duty under section 6 obliges courts of whatever stature to override any common law authority at odds with the Convention, however high and long-standing that authority may be.[85] (As will be seen in Chapter 19, however, the courts have not impugned the validity of the authorities on insanity.)

It seems that the duty of public authorities to act compatibly with Convention may be displaced in circumstances where the United Kingdom is obliged under general international law to act in a manner incompatible with a Convention right. In *Al-Jedda*,[86] V claimed that he had been unlawfully detained in Iraq, contrary to Article 5 of the ECHR, by the UK military. Normally the acts of UK soldiers are subject to the ECHR wherever they occur.[87] However, in this case they acted under the authority of Security Council resolutions which required the detention of V for "imperative reasons of security". The House of Lords accorded primacy to the UN Charter, and its scheme for binding resolutions, over the ECHR.

(a) The power to reinterpret

Although, as we have noted, the 1998 Act does not confer upon courts the power to invalidate statutes, judges should do what they can to render statutes compatible with the Convention. The injunction "so far as it is possible to do so"[88] indicates both the limits placed on the interpretive process and the extent of the judicial effort that must be made to achieve compatibility. Where a statutory provision potentially contravenes Convention rights, interpretation is no longer solely a matter of divining the intention of Parliament regarding the meaning of that provision, but instead one of rendering the provision compatible with the relevant Convention rights (if at all possible). The decision of the House of Lords in *Lambert*[89] illustrates the potential reach of this new power of interpretation. The case concerned a "reverse burden" of proof: to avoid a conviction for possession of a drug with intent to supply, D was required to prove that he did not know, suspect or have reason to suspect that he possessed a controlled drug. By a majority of 4:1, the House of Lords decided that the presumption of innocence enshrined in Article 6(2) of the Convention implied that the word "prove" must be interpreted in future as imposing an *evidential* rather than a legal/persuasive burden on D. (In other words, the defendant simply had to *raise evidence* of his lack of knowledge or suspicion, rather than *prove* it on the balance of

---

[85] For an opinion to this effect see HL Debs., 24 Nov. 1998, col. 783 (Lord Chancellor). For a narrower view of the effect of s. 6, see Kentridge, "The Incorporation of the European Convention on Human Rights" in Cambridge Centre for Public Law, *Constitutional Reform in the United Kingdom: Practice and Principles* (1998) 69. See also Phillipson, "The Human Rights Act, 'Horizontal Effect' and the Common Law: a Bang or a Whimper?" (1999) 62 *MLR* 824.

[86] [2007] UKHL 58, [2008] 1 AC 332.

[87] The relevant authorities are surveyed in *R (Al-Saadoon and Others)* v. *Secretary of State for Defence* [2015] EWHC 715 (Admin), [2015] 3 WLR 503.

[88] HRA 1998, s. 3.

[89] [2001] UKHL 37, [2002] 2 AC 545.

probabilities.)[90] This interpretation of the word "prove" is a remarkable feat of interpretation, notwithstanding the strong terms of section 3(1) of the HRA 1998.

Should courts go even further and "read in" words into statutory provisions in order to ensure compliance with the Convention? Writing extra-judicially about the likely effect of the incorporated Convention on the criminal law, Arden LJ entertained as a serious possibility the reading in of words to statutory provisions in order to achieve compatibility.[91] She envisaged, for example, that courts might "write in" due diligence defences for strict liability offences to avoid convictions which otherwise would violate Article 3 (inhuman or degrading treatment or punishment). Save for one Court of Appeal decision reversed by the House of Lords,[92] the courts have refrained from explicit rewriting of statutes. None the less, they have made decisions going well beyond the canons of interpretation existing prior to the HRA 1998.[93] In *A (No. 2)*,[94] the House of Lords arguably went beyond even the broadest conception of interpretation and into the realm of overriding the statutory text under consideration. In the past, defendants in sexual offence trials have sought to dredge up the complainant's sexual history in an effort to cast doubt on the complainant's credibility.[95] Concern about this practice, and with conviction rates in contested rape trials, led Parliament to place restrictions on the extent to which the complainant in a sexual offence case could be questioned about his or her previous sexual history.[96] The House of Lords found these restrictions to be in contravention of the guarantee of fair trial provided by Article 6 of the ECHR, in so far as they sometimes made it impossible for the defendant to mount a credible defence (where, for instance, the previous sexual history evidence concerned acts involving both the defendant and the complainant).[97] Not even the extended power of interpretation allowed by section 3 of the HRA 1998 could massage the language of the relevant provisions into a form compatible with Article 6. Instead of making a declaration of incompatibility, however, the judgment of the House of Lords requires trial judges to allow cross-examination of V's previous sexual history if necessary to ensure a fair trial, notwithstanding the clear statutory language disallowing the line of questioning.

Given subsequent cases, the approach to sections 3 and 4 of the HRA 1998 in *A (No. 2)* may be regarded as misguided. In *A (No. 2)*, a declaration of incompatibility was taken to be a thing of very last resort, to be avoided if at all possible.[98] By contrast, in *R (Anderson)* v.

---

[90] The distinction between evidential and legal burdens is returned to below, § 3.2.

[91] "Criminal Law at the Crossroads: the Impact on Human Rights from the Law Commission's Perspective and the Need for a Code" [1999] *Crim LR* 439, 447–51. See also Hooper, "The Impact of the Human Rights Act on Judicial Decision-making" [1998] *EHRLR* 676.

[92] *Re W and B; Re W (Care Plan)* [2001] EWCA Civ 757, [2001] 2 FLR 582, reversed in *Re S (Minors) (Care order: implementation of care plan); Re W (Minors) (Care order: adequacy of care plan)* [2002] UKHL 10, [2002] 2 AC 291.

[93] Perhaps the most notable example is *Ghaidan* v. *Godin-Mendoza* [2004] UKHL 30, [2004] 2 AC 557, where the statutory phrase "husband and wife" was interpreted to include same-sex couples.

[94] [2001] UKHL 25, [2002] 1 AC 45.

[95] For discussion by the Canadian Supreme Court of the myths associated with such evidence, see *Seaboyer* [1991] 2 SCR 577.

[96] Youth Justice and Criminal Evidence Act 1999, ss. 41–3.

[97] Cf. *Martin* [2004] EWCA Crim 916, [2004] 2 Cr App R 22.

[98] Cf. *Sheldrake* v. *DPP; Attorney-General's Reference (No. 4 of 2002)* [2004] UKHL 43, [2005] 1 AC 264; *Ghaidan* v. *Godin-Mendoza* [2004] UKHL 30, [2004] 2 AC 557.

Secretary of State for the Home Department,[99] the House of Lords straightforwardly made a declaration of incompatibility, after resolving that the statutory provision empowering the Home Secretary to fix the time in prison to be spent by persons serving a mandatory life sentence could not be interpreted in a manner compatible with Article 6. This latter decision comports better with the scheme of the HRA 1998.

Although the HRA 1998 provides for new principles of interpretation, they presumably ought to be exercised in a manner compatible with the sovereignty of Parliament. This same point about the sovereignty of Parliament can, however, be used to support an expansive use of section 3 to interpret criminal legislation beyond the text of the statute. According to Lord Bingham in *Attorney-General's Reference (No. 4 of 2002)*:[100]

> "It was argued for the Attorney General that [the contested provision, section 11(2) of the Terrorism Act 2000] could not be read down under section 3 of the [HRA 1998] so as to impose an evidential rather than a legal burden if (contrary to his submissions) the subsection were held to infringe, impermissibly, the presumption of innocence. He submitted that if the presumption of innocence were found to be infringed, a declaration of incompatibility should be made. I cannot accept this submission.... In my opinion, reading down section 11(2) so as to impose an evidential instead of a legal burden falls well within the interpretative principles discussed above.... Such was not the intention of Parliament when enacting the 2000 Act, but it was the intention of Parliament when enacting section 3 of the [HRA 1998]."

In other words, the interpretation inconsistent with Parliament's intention in the 2000 Act is, in fact, mandated by Parliament's intention as expressed in 1998, and so observes the sovereignty of Parliament. The problem with this sleight-of-hand analysis, as all students of Constitutional law will recognise, is that parliamentary sovereignty requires that, where the intentions of Parliament conflict in domestic legislation, the later expression is to be preferred. It is submitted that the possibility of compatible (re)interpretations contemplated in the HRA 1998 extends only to reasonable interpretations of the legislative will, and not to far-fetched but "possible" readings, particularly when such "readings" take the form of re-writings of the legislative text (such as in *A (No. 2)*). The existence of House of Lords and Supreme Court cases where declarations of incompatibility have been made[101] shows that there are boundaries to the realm of the "possible".

(b) Reviewing legislation "on the face"

The emphasis of the HRA 1998 on interpreting domestic legislation in a manner compatible with the ECHR indicates that the form of review is likely to be "on the face" (a term familiar in US constitutional jurisprudence). That is to say, the reviewing court will look at the impugned statutory provision and evaluate whether the provision, across the range of its likely applications, is compatible with the ECHR. By contrast, there is a form of review known as "as applied". Under the latter approach, the issue to be resolved is whether the pro-

---

[99] [2002] UKHL 46, [2003] 1 AC 837. See, further, the declarations of incompatibility in *Bellinger* v. *Bellinger* [2003] UKHL 21, [2003] 2 AC 467; *A* v. *Home Secretary* [2004] UKHL 56, [2005] 2 AC 68.

[100] *Sheldrake* v. *DPP*; *Attorney-General's Reference (No. 4 of 2002)* [2004] UKHL 43, [2005] 1 AC 264, para. 53.

[101] E.g. *R (Anderson)* v. *Secretary of State for the Home Department* [2002] UKHL 46, [2003] 1 AC 837; *Bellinger* v. *Bellinger* [2003] UKHL 21, [2003] 2 AC 467; *R (T)* v. *Chief Constable of Greater Manchester Police and Others* [2014] UKSC 35, [2015] AC 49.

vision being challenged contravened the complainant's Convention rights *on a particular occasion.*

In its own jurisprudence the European Court takes the "as applied" approach, with its emphasis on whether the rights of the particular applicant have been breached.[102] Yet certain of its decisions are stated in such broad terms as, in effect, to impugn the provision under scrutiny in general terms. For example, in *Saunders* v. *UK*,[103] the European Court found that the use, at trial, of evidence obtained from the defendant under powers of compulsory questioning was objectionable *per se* and therefore a breach of Article 6(1) (the right to a fair trial). This apparently amounted to the imposition of a *general* limitation, i.e. one not particular to the case.[104] By contrast, in *Salabiaku* v. *France*,[105] where a reverse burden of proof was under challenge, the European Court—while remarking that reverse burdens were matters for concern and proper issues for judicial scrutiny—found against the appellant on the ground that he had suffered no unfairness in the particular circumstances of the case.

What of the approach in English courts? In *R.* v. *Director of Public Prosecutions, ex p Kebilene*,[106] the Divisional Court found certain reverse burdens of proof contained in the Prevention of Terrorism Act 1989 to be in "flagrant" breach of Article 6(2) (which guarantees the presumption of innocence). The finding of the Court was based entirely on the terms of the legislation, i.e. on its face: the Court did not consider whether the particular defendants might have suffered any unfairness. Although, on further appeal,[107] the House of Lords decided the case on different grounds, Lords Hope and Hobhouse each demurred from the Divisional Court's approach and indicated that the effect upon the defendants of applying the reverse burden would be relevant matters for consideration. Lord Hobhouse spoke of a necessity "to examine each case on its merits" and "to examine whether the relevant provision has in fact resulted in an injustice to the complainant".[108] This case-specific approach is visible in other decisions.[109] If it were to be adopted generally, the impact of the HRA 1998 on the content of domestic legislation would be considerably diminished—and significantly less predictable. The more general perspective adopted by the Divisional Court and contemplated by Lord Steyn's majority judgment in *Kebilene* better comports with the framework of the HRA 1998.[110] Indeed, in subsequent appeals concerning whether reverse

---

[102] See, e.g., *Austin* v. *UK* (2012) 55 EHRR 14.

[103] (1997) 23 EHRR 313.

[104] Cf. *O'Halloran* v. *UK* (2008) 46 EHRR 21.

[105] (1988) 13 EHRR 379.

[106] [1999] 3 WLR 175.

[107] [2000] 2 AC 326.

[108] *Ibid.*, 397.

[109] See, e.g., *Beghal* v. *DPP* [2015] UKSC 49, [2016] AC 88 (considering the specific facts to determine the compatibility of the power to, *inter alia*, detain persons, in ports and at borders, for questioning without reasonable suspicion of involvement in terrorism under Terrorism Act 2000, sched. 7). See, too, *R (Miranda) v Secretary of State for the Home Department* [2016] EWCA Civ 6 [2016] 1 WLR 1505.

[110] It is understandable that the European Court adopts the "as applied" approach. It is not a constitutional court for Europe with power to strike down the laws of States party to the ECHR. In order to have standing the applicant before the European Court must, typically, be a "victim", seeking vindication for wrongs actually endured. Thus the Court will be required to consider whether, *in that particular case*, there was a violation of the applicant's rights under the Convention. By contrast, in domestic law under the HRA 1998, there need be no determination that the defendant's rights are violated. Convention questions can arise as collateral issues in criminal trials, without the same requirement of standing. In that context, the appropriate focus is the condition of English law in terms of its compatibility with the ECHR. This supports the generalist approach of the Divisional

legal burdens within particular offences are in breach of Article 6(2),[111] their Lordships have focused on how such a legal burden will affect trials for the relevant offence *in general*, rather than on the impact of the reverse burden upon the particular appellant's trial. This seems right: it would be odd (and inimical to clarity and consistency in practice) to conclude that a particular statutory offence imposes a reverse legal burden on some defendants and not on others.

That said, whether the applicant's rights have been contravened should not be overlooked when assessing in general terms the Convention compatibility of a legislative provision. In *R (Denby Collins) v. Secretary of State for Justice*,[112] the applicant argued that the law relating to the use of self-defence by householders against trespassers present in their home was not compliant with Article 2 (right to life) of the Convention. The applicant had entered D's house as a trespasser and had been caused serious and permanent brain damage when D restrained him for six minutes in a headlock. A prosecution was not brought against D because the CPS took the view that while the force that D used was arguably disproportionate, householders were entitled to use disproportionate force against trespassers provided the force was not grossly disproportionate.[113] The Divisional Court disagreed: under the householder legislation, "disproportionate" but permissible force would still have to be force that was reasonable in the circumstances. Force that was unreasonable in the circumstances was not protected by the statute. On that basis, the applicant's contention that the legislation contravened Article 2 failed. What went unexplored was whether the force that D used against the applicant was, despite its magnitude, reasonable in the circumstances.[114]

The *Kebilene* litigation illustrates how the application of the HRA 1998 can give rise to differences of judicial opinion. The Divisional Court was convinced that the relevant provisions of the Prevention of Terrorism Act 1989 were incompatible with the ECHR[115]

Court and of the majority judgment in the House of Lords in *Kebilene*, and is assumed by the framework of the HRA 1998 itself.

[111] *Lambert* [2001] UKHL 37, [2002] 2 AC 545; *Johnstone* [2003] UKHL 28, [2003] 1 WLR 1736, paras. 44–54 (Lord Nicholls). In *Sheldrake v. DPP; Attorney-General's Reference (No. 4 of 2002)* [2004] UKHL 43, [2005] 1 AC 264, para. 21, it was said by Lord Bingham that "[t]he justifiability of any infringement of the presumption of innocence cannot be resolved by any rule of thumb, but on examination of all the facts and circumstances of the particular provision as applied in the particular case". But this assertion needs to be understood in light of the subsequent discussion by his Lordship, which emphasises the generic facts and circumstances of the offence provision, rather than those of the particular defendant (see, especially, paras. 26 and 30). The point is that courts must examine each provision afresh, rather than the circumstances of each individual defendant affected that provision.

[112] [2016] EWHC 33 (Admin) [2016] 2 WLR 1303.

[113] The decision not to prosecute was based on an interpretation of s. 76(5A) of the Criminal Justice and Immigration Act 2008 which has been widely understood to allow householders to use any degree of force, falling short of grossly disproportionate force, in defending themselves and others lawfully present in their house.

[114] The parties to the litigation had agreed that the facts as assumed by the CPS were correct. Hence there was a basis for reviewing whether, on these agreed facts, the force to which D resorted was reasonable in the circumstances. If D's use of force was excessive, then the failure to prosecute would fall short of what is required of the state under Art 2, which requires active steps to enforce the applicable law on its part to protect persons under its jurisdiction from life threatening force that is not "absolutely necessary": the leading case is *Osman v. UK* (1998) 2 EHRR 245.

[115] Lord Bingham CJ reasoned, convincingly, that a reverse burden of proof on a matter central to the wrongdoing alleged against D (i.e. possession of items to be used in connection with terrorism, where the burden of proof was placed on D to show that the items were not used in connection with terrorism once a reasonable suspicion was established by the prosecution), was directly at odds with the presumption of innocence guaranteed by Art. 6(2). See further below, § 2.5(iii).

and that, as a consequence, any conviction of the defendants would ultimately, assuredly, be quashed on appeal. By contrast, the House of Lords, reversing the Divisional Court, reasoned that even if there were a "flagrant" breach of the ECHR, it does not follow that an appeal would succeed. A more likely outcome, pursuant to section 4 of the HRA 1998, would be a declaration of incompatibility. In any event, their Lordships were not convinced that the provisions under challenge *would* contravene Article 6(2). Lord Steyn, with whom Lords Slynn and Cooke agreed, thought it a distinct possibility that, under the interpretative requirement imposed by section 3 of the HRA 1998, reverse burdens of proof would in future be read as creating merely an evidential burden on a defendant to adduce some evidence, rather than a legal burden to prove the relevant matter on the balance of probabilities. This last possibility has, in fact, sometimes been the outcome in subsequent cases.[116]

It is worth noting, in closing, that the law reform process is also influenced by the ECHR. Under the HRA 1998, a minister in charge of a Bill must inform Parliament whether he is able to make a statement that the provisions of the Bill are compatible with the ECHR.[117] This usefully ensures that the civil servants and drafters who prepare legislation must consider ECHR questions. Notably, the Law Commission also now pays close attention to ECHR issues when formulating reform proposals.

(ii) The interpretation of Convention rights

In determining the compatibility of statutory provisions and common law with the requirements of the ECHR, some degree of particularity is required concerning the effect and ambit of the various Articles of the ECHR. The terms of the ECHR, an awkward blend of the general and the particular, do not always render the content of the relevant rights self-evident. Additionally, when determining a question that arises in connection with an ECHR right, a court must take into account the decisions and judgments of various bodies, in particular the European Court, if the court is of the opinion they are relevant to the proceedings.[118]

These interpretive sources are not binding; they are things to be taken into account. The ECHR has been described by the European Court as "a living instrument",[119] responsive to social and moral change. Accordingly, decisions and opinions of earlier periods may have little or no weight. For instance, early decisions of the European Commission of Human Rights had found that proscriptions of forms of homosexuality were compatible with the ECHR whereas, more recently, the Commission found that stipulating different ages of consent for heterosexual and homosexuals contravened both Article 8 (respect for private life) and Article 14 (principle of non-discrimination).[120]

The ECHR is an international treaty. As such, it is not a constitutional Bill of Rights but an undertaking by party States to observe acceptable standards of human rights in their

---

[116] For discussion of burdens of proof see below, §§ 2.5(iii) and 3.2.
[117] Section 19.
[118] HRA 1998, s. 2. In addition to decisions of the European Court, earlier opinions and decisions of the European Commission on Human Rights and decisions of the Committee of Ministers should also be taken into account.
[119] *Tyrer* v. *UK* (1979–80) 2 EHRR 1.
[120] *Sutherland and Morris* v. *UK* (1996) 22 EHRR CD22.

respective jurisdictions.[121] In the light of this, courts, when exercising the jurisdiction instituted by the HRA 1998, should not derogate from the baseline standards clearly set by the European Court. The European Court authoritatively sets the minimum terms for compliance. However, it does not follow that, when construing the ECHR in a domestic context, English courts should go no further to protect rights than does the European Court. In its jurisprudence the European Court has applied a "margin of appreciation",[122] particularly in cases involving Article 10 (freedom of expression) and Article 11 (freedom of assembly and association). This margin recognises that uniform standards cannot be imposed by an international court on States with different histories and sensitivities. Yet no such restraint is required when judges address human rights issues for their own society.[123] If, say, an English judge were to take the view that freedom of speech requires a more robust defence than is found in European Court jurisprudence, she is free to give a fuller effect to the terms of Article 10.[124] That said, a degree of deference is due to the legislative will of a democratically elected Parliament, and where an issue is finely balanced, courts should not be too astute to find that legislation breaches the ECHR. Determining whether or not a legislative provision breaches an Article of the Convention may require consideration of the doctrine of proportionality—is the legislation under consideration a proportionate response in combating the social mischief or advancing the social policy with which the legislation is concerned? Some degree of diminution in the enjoyment of Convention-protected rights may be an acceptable price for gains in welfare or efficiency and there may well be trade-offs to be made between different Convention-protected rights.[125]

When determining whether a breach of the ECHR has occurred, certain rights are guarded more jealously than others. Articles 2 (the right to life), 3 (the right not to be subjected to torture, inhuman or degrading treatment and punishment), and 7 (no retrospective penal law) cannot be derogated from, even in times of war or dire emergency. All the other Articles of the ECHR may be derogated from in such circumstances.[126] When the extremities of war and national emergency do not obtain, however, the possibility of derogation does not imply that these other Articles have lesser weight. Article 6 (fair trial, including the presumption of innocence) in particular has been expansively interpreted.[127]

---

[121] See Harris, O'Boyle, and Warbrick, *Law of the European Convention on Human Rights* (3rd ed., 2014) 10–3.

[122] *Ibid.*, 14–7.

[123] In *Kebilene* [2000] 2 AC 326, 380–1, Lord Hope considered that the margin of appreciation doctrine would not be available to English judges when interpreting the convention. Of course, as Lord Hope recognised, many Convention questions will be matters of broad evaluation affected by matters of national culture and subject-matter even in the absence of that doctrine.

[124] It may be noted that s. 12 of the HRA 1998 makes particular reference to freedom of expression, but only in contexts where the court is considering whether to grant any relief.

[125] The doctrine of proportionality does not come into play unless the right is expressed in qualified terms. Some Convention rights are absolute, for example the right not to be tortured or subjected to inhuman or degrading treatment (Art. 3). As put by Lord Clyde in *de Freitas* v. *Permanent Secretary of Ministry of Agriculture, Fisheries, Lands and Housing* [1999] 1 AC 69, 80 (PC), whether encroachment on a Convention right is a proportionate legislative response requires consideration of "whether: (i) the legislative objective is sufficiently important to justify limiting a fundamental right; (ii) the measures designed to meet the legislative objective are rationally connected to it; and (iii) the means used to impair the right or freedom are no more than is necessary to accomplish the objective". Cf. *R (Daly)* v. *Secretary of State for Home Department* [2001] UKHL 26, [2001] 2 AC 532, para. 27 (Lord Steyn).

[126] Article 15.

[127] Harris, O'Boyle, and Warbrick, *Law of the European Convention on Human Rights* (3rd ed., 2014) chap. 6.

Apart from drastic circumstances permitting derogation, a Convention right may alternatively be restricted by rulings about its scope. It is fair to say that Article 3 provides an unconditional right: if conduct amounts to torture, or to inhuman or degrading treatment or punishment, it will violate Article 3 whatever the circumstances. However, in respect of Articles 2 and 7, while non-derogation status underlines the importance of the right at issue, it does not preclude argument about the nature and ambit of these rights. For instance, the uncertain state of the English law of obscenity, and judicial abolition of the husband's immunity in rape, arguably, in each case, involved breaches of Article 7, yet the European Court ruled otherwise.[128] Questions concerned with abortions have been raised under Article 2 and, in that context, the European Court has applied the margin of appreciation doctrine in light of the considerable differences in the laws of the contracting States.[129] Additionally, even in cases that fall, prima facie, within the general scope of an Article right, exceptions may sometimes be justified. In the case of certain Articles, for instance Articles 8 (the right to private life) and 9 (freedom of thought and religion), the declaration of the right in the ECHR is followed by a statement of the circumstances in which that right may be justifiably interfered with.[130]

(iii) The ECHR and the substantive criminal law

The ECHR is capable of affecting significantly the substantive criminal law, although some of that capacity remains latent. It may be helpful to list, non-exhaustively, areas of criminal law where, in principle, the ECHR has the potential to have an impact:[131]

Article 2 (right to life): self-defence; force used in the prevention of crime and to make arrests; abortion; assisted suicide and euthanasia.

Article 3 (right not to be subjected to torture or inhuman or degrading treatment and punishment): offences against the person arising from staff (mis)conduct in prison, military and mental health establishments; offences of strict liability, especially 'status' offences; defence of parental chastisement.

Article 5 (right to liberty and security of person): insanity defence; offences against the person in prison, military and mental health establishments.

Article 6 (right to fair hearing and presumption of innocence): offences of strict liability (but see below); reverse burdens of proof; entrapment.

Article 7 (right not to be convicted under retroactive law): offences of dishonesty with broad and vague conduct elements; common law assault; offences of corrupting public morality and of outraging public decency; Protection from Harassment Act 1997.

---

[128] *Handyside* v. *UK* (1979–80) 1 EHRR 737 (obscenity); *SW* v. *UK* (1996) 21 EHRR 363 (marital rape).

[129] "National laws on abortion differ considerably … in such a delicate area the contracting states must have a certain discretion": *H* v. *Norway* App. No. 7004/90 (1992).

[130] Arguably, the distinction drawn in Convention jurisprudence between disputes over the scope of an Article right and over exceptions to that right is spurious. On questions of coherence and uncertainty in Convention jurisprudence generally, see McHarg, "Reconciling Human Rights and the Public Interest: Conceptual Problems and Doctrinal Uncertainty in the Jurisprudence of the European Court of Human Rights" (1999) 62 *MLR* 671.

[131] See Ashworth, "The European Convention and Criminal Law" in Cambridge Centre for Public Law, *The Human Rights Act and the Criminal and Regulatory Process* (1999) 37.

Article 8 (right to respect for private life): definition of sexual offences; limits of consent to sexual acts; limits of consent to physical injury; ambit of Protection from Harassment Act 1997; "lifestyle" offences: sections 77–80 of the Criminal Justice and Public Order Act 1994; Proceeds of Crime Act 2002 (onus to prove provenance of funds).

Article 10 (right to freedom of expression): obscenity, and other offensive conduct;[132] harassment and hate crimes; criminal libel; contempt of court; Official Secrets Act 1989; incitement to disaffection.

Article 11 (right to freedom of assembly and association): Criminal Justice & Public Order Act 1994 (control of demonstrations and processions), breach of the peace.

These opportunities for raising Convention issues during criminal trials will not be further developed here. Some are mentioned in later chapters, as appropriate.

While it is also addressed in § 3.2 below, it is worth making particular mention here of the burden of proof, which is a pervasive and important issue that straddles the divides between evidential, procedural, and substantive law.[133] Reverse burdens of proof are commonplace in English law[134] and there will, therefore, be many occasions on which to raise this issue. Broadly, if a *legal* burden of proof is placed on a defendant, she will have to prove the relevant matter (e.g. that she lacked a certain piece of knowledge) on the balance of probabilities. If the defendant faces a mere *evidential* burden, she will simply have to adduce some evidence of the relevant matter. As we noted above, the majority of the House of Lords in *Kebilene*[135] anticipated that reverse burdens may, under the HRA 1998, be interpreted as imposing merely an evidential burden and not a legal burden on the accused. Yet one might think there are further possibilities. As Lord Rodger noted in the case of *Sheldrake*, there is something paradoxical in the existing jurisprudence on reverse legal burdens of proof. As noted above, there is no right to a fair criminal law; arguments about reverse burdens of proof are arguments about *the procedure* for establishing offences, not the definitions of those offences. This raises the following possibility. Assume there is an offence of, say, knowingly selling food which does not comply with food safety standards. Assume it to be a serious offence with a maximum sentence of, say, 10 years' imprisonment. If the legal burden were placed on D to prove that he did not know that the food which was sold was non-compliant, the courts could (consistent with section 3 of the HRA 1998) "read down" the legal burden to an evidential one. It would now suffice for D to raise the possibility that he did not know; he would no longer be required to *prove* that matter on the balance of probabilities. What if Parliament were to respond to this judicial finding by dropping *any* reference to knowledge and making it an offence simply to sell food, even inadvertently, that is non-compliant with safety standards? Would this then remove any potential to present an Article 6 argument about the compatibility of the offence with the Convention? Is it a sufficient response to say that there are no Article 6 presumption-of-innocence implications

---

[132] Including threatening, abusive, or insulting conduct falling within s. 5 of the Public Order Act 1986: see the cases discussed in Bailin, "Criminalising Free Speech?" [2011] *Crim LR* 705.

[133] For excellent analysis of the impact of the ECHR on reverse burdens of proof see Dennis, "Reverse Onuses and the Presumption of Innocence: In Search of Principle" [2005] *Crim LR* 901.

[134] Blake and Ashworth, "The Presumption of Innocence in English Criminal Law" [1996] *Crim LR* 306.

[135] [2000] 2 AC 326; above, § 2.5(i). Burdens of proof are discussed further below, § 3.2.

because no reverse burden of proof is employed?[136] Some academics have argued that it should be insufficient, an answer that potentially would open up the field of strict liability offences for ECHR scrutiny.[137] However, the House of Lords has foreclosed the application of Article 6 to matters of procedural rather than substantive fairness. Thus, reversing the burden to prove some offence element may violate Article 6, but eliminating that element altogether from the offence does not.[138]

A final point worth noting here is that the taking of Convention points is not restricted to the defence. In *A v. UK*,[139] the physical chastisement of children was found to be inhuman and degrading treatment, and thus in breach of Article 3. Clearly, if D is charged with assaulting his son following an act of parental discipline, the prosecution will be entitled to raise the issue of the State's duty to uphold Article 3 in response to D's claim that his conduct was "reasonable chastisement" within the terms of English law. Similarly, it has been argued that English law is too lax in allowing law enforcement officials exemption from criminal liability on the basis of a belief in the necessity to use fatal force even in cases where that belief was unreasonable.[140] It is arguable that allowing such latitude to officials contravenes Article 2 (right to life).[141]

The interrelationship of the ECHR and English substantive criminal law is an ongoing project. Sometimes it requires accommodation of Convention jurisprudence to the specific context of national law.[142] More often, the required accommodation is the other way around. While they are still sometimes missed,[143] Convention-based arguments are now a familiar feature of our criminal law, at least for the moment.[144]

---

[136] The offence in English law of selling food that is non-compliant with safety standards (Food Safety Act 1990, s. 8) is an offence of strict liability with a maximum penalty of two years' imprisonment. The strict nature of the offence is mitigated by the provision of a due diligence defence with a reverse onus on D (s. 21). From the perspective of effective regulation of a problematic industry, one may hope the offence will withstand Convention scrutiny. However, there are some offences of strict liability that carry high terms of imprisonment and are not mitigated by any due diligence defence: e.g. unlawful possession of a firearm as interpreted in *Howells* [1977] QB 614, and rape of a child under 13 as interpreted in *G* [2008] UKHL 37, [2009] 1 AC 92. Such offences are much more difficult to justify. See below, chapter 6.

[137] See, e.g. Tadros and Tierney, "The Presumption of Innocence and the Human Rights Act" (2004) 67 *MLR* 402; Tadros, "The Ideal of the Presumption of Innocence" (2014) 8 *Criminal Law and Philosophy* 449. Contrast Roberts, "Strict Liability and the Presumption of Innocence" in Simester (ed.), *Appraising Strict Liability* (2005) 151.

[138] *G* [2008] UKHL 37, [2009] 1 AC 92 (rape of a child under 13, contrary to s. 5 of the Sexual Offences Act 2003), confirmed (in the context of that offence) in *G v. UK* (2011) 53 EHRR SE25.

[139] (1999) 27 EHRR 611. See, further, *R (Williamson) v. Secretary of State for Education and Employment* [2005] UKHL 15, [2005] 2 AC 246.

[140] Leverick, *Killing in Self-defence* (2006) chap. 10. Cf. Smith, "The Use of Public or Private Defence and Article 2" [2002] *Crim LR* 958.

[141] For further discussion see below, § 21.2(ix).

[142] Cf. *Al-Khawaja and Tahery v. UK* (2012) 54 EHRR 23, para. 146.

[143] As in *Smith* [2012] EWCA Crim 398, [2012] 1 WLR 3368 (private communication of obscene material).

[144] The current Conservative government made a manifesto pledge to repeal the HRA 1998 and replace it with a British Bill of Rights. It is unclear at the time of writing whether this will result in concrete proposals being laid before Parliament and, if so, what form they might take.

3

INTERPRETATION AND PROOF

§ 3.1 Statutory interpretation

In Chapter 2 we saw how the Rule of Law embodies values such as fair warning—values which are proper aspirations for the criminal law, now partly cast in justiciable form by the European Convention on Human Rights (ECHR) and the Human Rights Act (HRA) 1998. However, neither the Rule of Law nor the ECHR supports demands for unattainable measures of predictability and certainty. A degree of imprecision is inherent in the enterprise of legal ordering. Statutes are necessarily expressed in general terms, and must be interpreted and applied to particular cases. The agent of this process is the court.[1]

In practice, the judicial task is more substantial than it need be. While legislators cannot be expected to foresee every variant case that might arise when they create an offence, the standard of draftsmanship in this jurisdiction is such that offences frequently omit to specify quite obvious matters, such as what (if any) mental element an offence requires, on whom the burden of proof lies, and whether omissions as well as acts are within the conduct proscribed. Moreover, some fundamental aspects of the criminal law, such as causation, are untouched by statute. Consequently, the role of judges is pivotal and powerful.

One way of observing the rights and expectations of citizens under the Rule of Law is for judges to show proper restraint when interpreting the rules of the criminal law. In the civil law—say, a case involving the law of restitution—a judgment may earn praise for the way it reconceptualises the grounds of restitution, thereby vindicating new restitutionary claims. Similar creativity in the criminal law is generally to be avoided, since the scope for condemnation and punishment might thereby be enlarged.[2] In Chapter 2 we noted the remark by the European Court of Human Rights (European Court) that "the criminal law must not be extensively construed to an accused's detriment, for instance by analogy".[3] This need for restraint means that interpreting a criminal statute should involve determining its meaning

---

[1] For general discussion, see Ashworth, "Interpreting Criminal Statutes: A Crisis of Legality?" (1991) 107 *LQR* 419; MacCormick and Summers (eds.), *Interpreting Statutes: A Comparative Study* (1991); Kremnitzer, "Interpretation in Criminal Law" (1986) 21 *Israel LR* 358; Jeffries, "Legality, Vagueness, and the Construction of Penal Statutes" (1985) 71 *Va LR* 189; Hall, "Strict or Liberal Construction of Penal Statutes" (1935) 48 *Harv LR* 748.

[2] Cf. Dworkin, *Taking Rights Seriously* (1977) 100: by contrast with "standard civil cases, when the ruling assumption is that one of the parties has a right to win ... [t]he accused in a criminal case has a right to a decision in his favour if he is innocent, but the state has no parallel right to a conviction if he is guilty. The court may therefore find in favour of the accused, in some hard case testing rules of evidence, for example, on an argument of policy that does not suppose that the accused has any right to be acquitted." Different considerations may apply when enlarging the scope of defences: below, § 22.3.

[3] *Kokkinakis v. Greece* (1994) 17 EHRR 397, para. 52. See above, § 2.3.

in a non-expansive way. Before examining the interpretation of criminal laws, however, it is useful to sketch a backdrop by commenting first upon the sources of the criminal law.

(i) The sources of the criminal law

Until the nineteenth century, the definition of crimes and the rules of criminal responsibility evolved and were developed by judges on a case-by-case basis. Also influential were writers of authority—the institutional writers—most notably Blackstone, Coke, East, Foster, Hale, and Hawkins. Today, English criminal law is no longer predominantly the result of judicial creativity, but is primarily enacted through parliamentary statutes and subordinate regulations. There are, it seems, over 10,000 different criminal offences on the statute books,[4] by far the most important source of criminal law.[5] This corpus of statutory law reflects, as Glazebrook puts it, "two centuries of draftsmanship of very uneven quality ... the product of changing views of morality and of when and how penal measures should be used in the hope of protecting the community against the violent, the lustful, the avaricious, the selfish and the careless".[6]

Historically, the authority of any criminal law introduced through secondary regulations had to derive from a parliamentary statute. However, under section 2(2) of the European Communities Act 1972, the UK executive also has a general authority to create new criminal offences where the creation of such offences is made necessary by any European Union legislation.[7] Nowadays, offences are quite frequently introduced through subordinate regulation,[8] especially in order to give effect to European law.[9]

The predominance of statutory and regulatory law should not obscure the creative role of the judiciary. Statutes have to be interpreted and, as we have mentioned, the poor draftsmanship to which Glazebrook alludes commonly includes failures to specify the burden of proof or even the mens rea requirement in an offence. Perforce, such fundamental issues have to be resolved by judicial interpretation. Even where there is a degree of specificity—

---

[4] Herring, *Criminal Law Statutes* (2012) x. Obtaining an accurate figure on the number of criminal offences in existence is difficult. See Chalmers and Leverick, "Quantifying Criminalization" in Duff *et al.* (eds.), *Criminalization: The Political Morality of the Criminal Law* (2015) 54; Chalmers, "'Frenzied Law Making': Overcriminalization by Numbers" (2014) 67 *CLP* 483; Chalmers and Leverick, "Tracking the Creation of Criminal Offences" [2013] *Crim LR* 543.

[5] The proliferation of statutory offences is sometimes presented as a modern problem, but see Chalmers, Leverick and Shaw, "Is Formal Criminalization Really on the Rise? Evidence from the 1950s" [2015] *Crim LR* 177.

[6] Glazebrook, *Blackstone's Statutes on Criminal Law* (9th ed., 1999) xiii. Cf. McBain, "Abolishing Obsolete Legislation on Crimes and Criminal Procedure" (2011) 31 *LS* 96.

[7] This power cannot be used to create any new offence punishable by more than two years' imprisonment when tried on indictment (with further reduced maxima when tried summarily): European Communities Act 1972, sched. 2, para. 1.

[8] The Law Commission rightly expressed concern about this trend, and its expansionist potential, in *Criminal Liability in Regulatory Contexts* LCCP No. 195 (2010) paras. 3.144–3.158. The Commission suggested provisionally that "criminal offences should be created and (other than in relation to minor details) amended only through primary legislation" (para. 3.158). This proposal has not, to date, been taken forward.

[9] See, e.g., the Consumer Protection from Unfair Trading Regulations 2008 (SI 2008 No. 1277). Some offences and defences designed to comply with EU Directives are introduced through Acts of Parliament. See, e.g., Modern Slavery Act 2015, s. 45, intended to implement the EU Directive on Human Trafficking (Directive 2011/36/EU), para. 14.

e.g. where the offence in question states that intention or recklessness by D is required—in the absence of stipulative definitions for those terms, the judges must resolve their meaning.[10] Moreover, it is still the case that some significant offences, including murder, manslaughter, and assault, remain in large part common law offences. General doctrines affecting criminal liability, such as complicity and causation, remain largely unaffected by statute and new statutory crimes must be received and absorbed into this common law background.

Even among nations with a common law background, this approach is unusual. An influential strand in Enlightenment political theory was the conviction that the organs of representative democracy should be more influential than unelected judges in the creation and administration of the criminal law. To that end, criminal codes were promulgated, both here and elsewhere, in the hope that they would stipulate with clarity the content of crimes and the conditions of liability, reducing the role of the judge to that of an agent executing the will of the legislature. These hopes were optimistic, yet by no means wholly unfounded, and the vast majority of developed countries now have criminal codes. Codification passed England and Wales by. From time to time, efforts have been made to remedy the situation. The Law Commission, for example, once published a Draft Criminal Code Bill,[11] but neither that draft code nor any future draft is likely to be enacted for England and Wales in the foreseeable future. The political will for codification is simply not there. Indeed, the Law Commission for England and Wales has abandoned the project to codify the criminal law all at once, in favour of a more piecemeal and progressive approach to reform.[12]

Modernisation of English criminal law is long overdue. Certain statutes, such as the vitally important Offences against the Person Act 1861, are riddled with uncertainty and unhelpful overlaps and duplication.[13] Yet reform and rationalisation should not be at the expense of abolishing offences that constitute a valuable cultural endowment. A Law Commission draft bill, usefully updating the law of criminal damage, made no provision for an offence of arson.[14] Understandably, in the legislation that ensued, Parliament reinstituted the offence[15]—"arson" is an evocative term which should not be lost.[16] The same applies to "robbery", rightly preserved in the Theft Act 1968 as a form of acquisitive violence and not merely retained as an aggravating feature of a general offence of theft. At the same time, the past decade has seen an enormous quantity of legislation relating to the criminal law passed without regard for structure and guiding principles.[17] The role of the judges will be a powerful one for the foreseeable future.

---

[10] See Stark, "'It's Only Words': On Meaning and *Mens Rea*" (2013) 72 *CLJ* 155.

[11] *A Criminal Code for England and Wales* LC No. 177 (1989).

[12] See *Tenth Programme of Law Reform* LC No. 311 (2008) para. 1.6: "Rather than specifically referring to codification as the intended outcome … [we will seek] to undertake projects to simplify the criminal law…. We see this work as the necessary precursor to any attempts to codify the criminal law." See, further, Dennis, "The Law Commission and the Criminal Law: Reflections on the Codification Project" in Dyson, Lee and Stark (eds.), *Fifty Years of the Law Commissions: The Dynamics of Law Reform* (2016) 108.

[13] An illuminating discussion is *Reform of Offences against the Person* HC 555 (2015).

[14] See *Malicious Damage*, Working Paper No. 23 (1969) paras. 22, 66.

[15] Criminal Damage Act 1971, s. 1(3).

[16] Cf. the discussion of fair labelling, above, § 2.4.

[17] This is not a problem limited to England and Wales. See, e.g., Husak, *Overcriminalization: The Limits of the Criminal Law* (2007).

(ii) The interpretation of criminal statutes

It is not possible in a text of this nature to provide more than an overview of the relevant principles regarding the interpretation of criminal statutes. When questions about the meaning of an offence arise, there are three main steps for a court to take.

(a) Ordinary meaning

In the first instance, the interpretation of a criminal statute need not differ in technique from the interpretation of any other statute. Modern statutory interpretation should first take the form of ascertaining the *ordinary meaning in context*.[18] The reference to context is particularly important. It is a feature of language that meaning is not merely lexical, but also depends on the surrounding words and the purpose of the writer. A crucial issue in one famous criminal trial was the meaning of "Let him have it, Chris".[19] Was this an injunction to hand over or to fire a gun? The latter, thought the jury, and a life as well as an argument was lost. Such uncertainties are not confined to vernacular speech. For example, the former section 20(2) of the Theft Act 1968 enacted an offence *inter alia* of procuring, by deception, another person to indorse a valuable security.[20] On one meaning, to "indorse" something is to express approval of it. But it was quite clear, both from the lexical context (execution of a valuable security) and the purpose of the offence, that the intended meaning was to assign by writing.

When determining the ordinary meaning of a provision, the judge may be addressing a text of considerable age, such as the Offences against the Person Act 1861. Should the judge interpret the statutory wording by reference to its meaning in 1861, or should current usage dictate the understanding of the statute? It may be that the matter is resolved by previous authority—an appellate case in, say, 1937 may have interpreted the term in a manner clearly applicable to the instant case. But what if there is no such authority? Then it seems the meaning the term bears in present-day English is to be applied, even if it is a meaning clearly not contemplated by the legislature back in 1861. As it was put by the House of Lords in *Burstow*,[21] criminal statutes "are always speaking" and the speech is of the present day.[22] Accordingly the court in construing the expression "actual bodily harm" for the purposes of section 47 of the OAPA 1861 (assault occasioning actual bodily harm) was able to conclude that psychiatric injury was a form of bodily harm.

Even the best-drafted statute can require interpretive decisions by the court. If grammatical context as well as lexical meaning is addressed, one meaning will usually emerge as clearly the best suited to express the purposes of the statute or the relevant part thereof. Where it does so, there can be no objection, even in the case of a criminal statute, to an interpretative choice that goes against the defendant. When one interpretation of a statutory provision is tenable and preferable to any competing interpretation, there is nothing

---

[18] Cf. Bell and Engle, *Cross on Statutory Interpretation* (3rd ed., 1995) 31–3, chap. 3.

[19] The case of Derek Bentley, who was convicted of murder as an accessory and sentenced to death. Bentley received a posthumous pardon and his conviction was eventually quashed: *Bentley*, Court of Appeal, 30 July 1998.

[20] Repealed by Fraud Act 2006, sched. 3.

[21] [1998] AC 147.

[22] See too *K* [2001] UKHL 41, [2002] 1 AC 462; *R (on the application of Smeaton)* v. *Secretary of State for Health* [2002] EWHC 610 (Admin).

particular about the interpretation of criminal statutes. The "ordinary meaning in context" prevails.

(b) Legislative background

Sometimes the meaning of a provision cannot be determined within the four corners of the statute itself. In such cases, the courts have limited powers to consider the legislative background of an Act in order to ascertain the intention of Parliament. An illustration of this process is *A-G's Reference (No. 1 of 1988)*,[23] where determining the "ordinary meaning in context" left the Court with a choice between two meanings, each of which was "ordinary". In the course of a consultation with a merchant bank, D had been informed on confidential terms that X plc was to be the subject of a takeover bid. D acquired shares in X plc in anticipation of the inevitable rise in the share price. This acquisition would have constituted an offence against insider trading legislation, provided D had "obtained" the information. Had D "obtained" inside information? At trial, he argued successfully that he had not, on the basis that the *Oxford English Dictionary* gave "to acquire by endeavour" as the primary meaning of the term. There had been no effort made to obtain this information; he had merely been informed of it while seeking a banker's advice. If this interpretation were to succeed, the offence of insider dealing would be confined to those who actively seek out inside information in order to deal. However, the legislative history and the overall scheme of the Companies Securities (Insider Dealing) Act 1985 was strongly suggestive that chance recipients of insider information were within the scheme of the Act where the informant was a corporate "insider" (as the merchant bank clearly was). Accordingly, the House of Lords adopted "to get, to come by", the secondary meaning of "obtained" allowed by the *OED*, as the meaning which was to prevail.

While the history of a statute can certainly be considered as part of the legislative background that can aid interpretation, there are restrictions on the extent to which parliamentary debates can be investigated, at least in the context of criminal law. The well-known case of *Pepper* v. *Hart*[24] recognised an exceptional and limited permission for judges to seek resolution of ambiguity in a statute by reference to statements made by sponsors of the preceding bill, even in favour of an interpretation which confirmed settled and reasonable expectations. In *Thet* v. *DPP*, Lord Phillips CJ nevertheless questioned[25]

> "the use of *Pepper v Hart* [1993] AC 593 in the context of a criminal prosecution. [Counsel for the Prosecution] was not able to refer the court to any case in which *Pepper v Hart* has been used in that context. If a criminal statute is ambiguous, I would question whether it is appropriate by the use of *Pepper v Hart* to extend the ambit of the statute so as to impose criminal liability upon a defendant where, in the absence of the parliamentary material, the court would not do so. It seems to me at least arguable that if a criminal statute is ambiguous, the defendant should have the benefit of the ambiguity."

---

[23] [1989] AC 971.

[24] [1993] AC 593. In terms of the Rule of Law, consultation of such sources as Hansard is unobjectionable provided the source is adequately made available to the public, so that potential defendants have fair warning of its import. See Evans, *Statutory Interpretation: Problems of Communication* (1988) 289.

[25] [2006] EWHC 2701 (Admin), [2007] 1 WLR 2022, para. 15. See, too, *Massey* v. *Boulden* [2002] EWCA Civ 1634, [2003] 1 WLR 1792, paras. 18–9.

For a time, it appeared that these comments pertained only to use of parliamentary materials by the prosecution, i.e. to *extend* the criminal law. Hence Lord Phillips CJ subsequently qualified his remarks in *Tabnak*: "In this case it is the defendant who seeks to apply *Pepper* v. *Hart* in a criminal process and those comments [in *Thet*] may not have the same force".[26] This prosecution/defence-based distinction is consistent with other areas of the criminal law, but is difficult to square with Lord Phillips' opinion in the further case of *JTB*.[27]

In *JTB*, the question to be resolved was whether the defence of *doli incapax* remained an available defence. If the defence was available then, in addition to any relevant mens rea requirements, for any defendant between the ages of 10 and 14, the prosecution would be required to prove the defendant's awareness that his conduct was wrong (should this issue be raised by the defendant). Formerly, there was a rebuttable presumption that such defendants were incapable of knowing right from wrong. This *presumption* (of *doli incapax*) was clearly abolished by section 34 of the Crime and Disorder Act 1998, but section 34 said nothing about *the defence* itself. None the less, Lord Phillips concluded that the statute's effect was to abolish the defence as well as the presumption. Invoking *Pepper* v. *Hart*, his Lordship perused the parliamentary debates on the bill that led to the 1998 Act and convinced himself that the sponsors of the bill used the term *doli incapax* to refer to the defence as well as the presumption. On that basis, Lord Phillips declared that section 34 had abolished the defence. This is a troubling application of *Pepper* v. *Hart*, particularly in the context of a provision that went against the interests of a defendant.[28] In effect, Lord Phillips invoked *Pepper* v. *Hart* to subvert the plain language of a statute, to the benefit of the prosecution. This is clearly problematic, and the distinction in *Thet* v. *DPP* between prosecution and defence use of parliamentary debates should not lightly be disregarded.

Whether or not the legislative history is consulted, even for the benefit of the defendant, often depends upon the inclination of judges. In the notorious case of *Caldwell*,[29] to which we return in Chapter 5, Lord Diplock conceded that there was an issue of interpretation in respect of the meaning to be given to the mens rea term, "reckless". He resolved the issue by recourse to "ordinary" English, which informed him that the term comprehended not only defendants who perceived the likely consequences of their conduct, but also defendants who failed to give thought to the obvious risks involved in that conduct. He signally failed to consider a Law Commission report that stated, unequivocally, that only defendants who actually perceived the consequences of their conduct were to be found reckless in cases of criminal damage.[30] Parliament had not intended to adopt a distinct understanding of recklessness when passing the Criminal Damage Act 1971.[31] Similarly, in *Khan*,[32] resort to a Law Commission report would have informed the Court of Appeal that their decision about the meaning of "intent" for the crime of attempt was contrary to the meaning envisaged

---

[26] [2007] EWCA Crim 380, [2007] 1 WLR 1317, para. 17.
[27] [2009] UKHL 20, [2009] 1 AC 1310.
[28] Bennion, "Mens Rea and Defendants below the Age of Discretion" [2009] *Crim LR* 757, 766–8.
[29] [1982] AC 341.
[30] *Report on Offences of Damage to Property* LC No. 29 (1970) para. 44.
[31] The decision in *Caldwell* was departed from by the House of Lords in *G* [2003] UKHL 50, [2004] 1 AC 1034. In *G*, their Lordships paid careful attention to Parliament's intention: see paras. 12–13, 29 (Lord Bingham), 47–50 (Lord Steyn), and 63–4 (Lord Bridge).
[32] [1990] 1 WLR 813 (CA). Discussed below, § 9.3(iii)(b).

by the Commission when proposing the clause subsequently adopted, unamended, by Parliament.[33]

The decisions in *Caldwell* and *Khan* are, unfortunately, only two of many instances of expansive interpretation of statutory offences unsupported by judicial examination of the policy and legislative history of the offence interpreted. One may even find different approaches in the same case. In *Gomez*,[34] the minority in the House of Lords consulted the report of the Criminal Law Revision Committee which had formulated the provisions under review in that case, namely sections 1 and 15 of the Theft Act 1968. The consultation resolved any doubts: on the facts of the case there could have been a conviction under section 15 for obtaining property by deception but there was no theft within the terms of section 1. Untroubled by an engagement with the legislative history, the majority found that there had been a theft, reducing, as Sir John Smith put it, "the *actus reus* of theft almost to vanishing point".[35]

(c) Constitutional, EU and international law presumptions

Thirdly, where alternative interpretations are available, an interpretation is to be preferred that conforms to the Rule of Law presumption of legality and against retrospectivity,[36] and to the requirements of the ECHR. In general, as we saw in Chapter 2, these presumptions do not override parliamentary legislation: they can be rebutted by the explicit and ineluctable language of a statute—which is why a declaration of incompatibility is available to the courts.[37]

In the case of laws emanating directly or indirectly from the European Union (which, it must be remembered, the British public has recently voted to leave), we must make a distinction between laws authorised by the treaties which constitute the European Community and laws which derive from the framework arrangements, which were instigated outside the legal matrix constituted by the treaties.[38] In the case of laws authorised by the treaties themselves, the direct effect of many of these laws entails precedence over domestic law. Where a rule of English criminal law conflicts with an EU directly applicable law, the latter prevails.[39] The domestic law is disapplied and no conviction can ensue.[40]

In the case of EU framework laws (where these apply to the UK), there is a presumption that domestic law within the EU is compatible with any relevant EU instruments; thus domestic courts within the EU are obliged to interpret offences, *in so far as is possible*, so as to conform with EU requirements.[41] The proviso reflects the fact that, should the domestic

---

[33] *Attempt, and Impossibility in Relation to Attempt, Conspiracy and Incitement* LC No. 102 (1980) paras. 2.11–8.

[34] *DPP* v. *Gomez* [1993] AC 442. Discussed in detail below, § 13.6(ii).

[35] Commentary at [1993] Crim LR 304, 306.

[36] Cf. *B (a minor)* v. *DPP* [2000] 2 AC 428, 470 (Lord Steyn).

[37] Above, § 2.5(i).

[38] Following the coming into force of the Lisbon Treaty, EU criminal law instruments will take the form of Directive or, possibly, Regulations.

[39] For a survey of EU criminal law developments, see Spencer, "EU Criminal Law" in Barnard and Peers (eds), *European Union* Law (2014) 751. More generally, see Mitsilegas, *EU Criminal Law* (2nd ed., 2016).

[40] Baker, "Taking European Criminal Law Seriously" [1998] *Crim LR* 361. Cf. *Pubblico Ministero* v. *Tullio Ratti* [1979] ECR 1629; *IB* v. *R.* [2009] EWCA Crim 2575, [2010] 1 Cr App R 16.

[41] *Pupino* Case C-105/03 (16 June 2005), [2006] QB 83 (ECJ).

legislation not admit of an EU-law-compliant interpretation, the will of the domestic Parliament prevails, at least in domestic courts.[42]

So, too, for international law. Where there is ambiguity in an offence, the terms of any relevant treaty conventions, and no doubt other sources of international law, can be considered as interpretive aids. Thus there is a rebuttable presumption that domestic law complies with the nation's international obligations:[43]

> "where there is a relevant treaty or ratified convention courts when free to do so will interpret statutory provisions in such a way as to comply with the United Kingdom's international obligations, but that cannot be done when the statutory words are clear, and were enacted in full knowledge of the Convention obligations."

So international law cannot effect the repeal of domestic crimes, although it may influence the construction of our substantive law. Under certain circumstances our international obligations can, however, have a procedural impact, and it may be an abuse of process (leading to the permanent cessation of proceedings) to prosecute defendants for conduct that the State was obliged under international law not to criminalise.[44]

Conversely, international criminal law does not directly create crimes in domestic law—they must be imported by specific legislation. Thus, under section 51 of the International Criminal Court Act 2001, it is an offence under domestic law to commit genocide, a crime against humanity or a war crime. Other crimes recognised by international law, such as the crime of aggression, are not offences in England and Wales.[45]

(d) Strict construction

Finally if, after examining the statutory context and background (including the presumptions and obligations mentioned in the foregoing section), there is still some uncertainty about which interpretation is preferable, then the court should give the benefit of that uncertainty to the defendant: "If a penal provision is reasonably capable of two interpretations, that interpretation which is most favourable to the accused must be adopted."[46]

This is a presumption of strict construction of criminal statutes. It is justified primarily by the requirement to give fair warning,[47] which implies that ambiguity in offences should not be construed so as to generate unpredictable criminal liability; statutes should not require citizens to guess at their meaning, and so should be construed against imposing liability upon a defendant who reasonably could have thought that she was within the terms of the law.

---

[42] See further Peers, *EU Justice and Home Affairs Law* (4th ed., 2016). It is noteworthy that, as of December 2014, the European Court of Justice has full jurisdiction over EU criminal law matters.

[43] *Navabi* [2005] EWCA Crim 2865, para. 28; cf. *R (Pepushi)* v. *CPS* [2004] EWHC 798 (Admin), para. 33.

[44] *Asfaw* [2008] UKHL 31, [2008] 1 AC 1061; *L* [2013] EWCA Crim 991, [2014] 1 All ER 113 (on which, see Spencer, "International Law, People Trafficking and the Power to Stay Proceedings for Abuse of Process" (2014) 73 *CLJ* 11).

[45] *Jones* [2006] UKHL 16, [2007] 1 AC 136.

[46] *Sweet* v. *Parsley* [1970] AC 132, 149 (Lord Reid). Cf. *Passmore* [2007] EWCA Crim 2053, [2008] 1 Cr App R 12, para. 18: "It is a well established principle that if a penal statute is reasonably open to rival constructions it should be construed in the defendant's favour."

[47] Above, § 2.3.

Fair warning is not the entire rationale for the presumption of strict construction. Its origins are to be found in judicial interpretations *in favorem vitae* ("in favour of life") in times where the number of capital offences was very large:[48] a particularly sharp version of more general values of parsimony in punishment. As such, the presumption argues for judicial restraint when interpreting not only offences but also defences (and not merely justificatory defences, such as self-defence and necessity, which may guide conduct). Altering the scope of defences alters the scope of criminal liability too. Accordingly, it is debatable whether Hughes LJ was correct to dismiss the relevance of strict construction when ruling on the ambit of the defence of diminished responsibility;[49] particularly when citing in support the controversial decision of the House of Lords in *JTB*,[50] where, as noted in § 3.1(ii)(b), the reading of a legislative provision which the Appellate Committee considered tenable was rejected in favour of abolishing the presumption of *doli incapax* for children aged between ten and fourteen.

The principle of strict interpretation does not require that *any* measure of doubt over the meaning of a statute should be construed in the defendant's favour. The strict construction principle is a default rule, one to rely on if the meaning of the statute cannot be ascertained by other standard techniques. In the past, the principle of strict construction has sometimes been read as entailing that the benefit of *any* favourable interpretation which passes a minimal threshold of plausibility must always be given to the defendant.[51] Yet, as Lord Reid recognised in *DPP v. Ottewell*,[52] this extreme approach is untenable. A lexically possible meaning should not be adopted if the statutory context makes clear that an alternative interpretation is best suited to the purposes of the statute:[53]

> "The Court of Appeal (Criminal Division) refer to the well-established principle that in doubtful cases a penal provision ought to be given that interpretation which is least unfavourable to the accused. I would never seek to diminish in any way the importance of that principle within its proper sphere. But it only applies where after full inquiry and consideration one is left in real doubt. It is not enough that the provision is ambiguous in the sense that it is capable of having two meanings. The imprecision of the English language (and, so far as I am aware, of any other language) is such that it is extremely difficult to draft any provision which is not ambiguous in that sense. This section is clearly ambiguous in that sense: the Court of Appeal (Criminal Division) attach one meaning to it, and your Lordships are attaching a different meaning to it. But if, after full consideration, your Lordships are satisfied, as I am, that the latter is the meaning which Parliament must have intended the words to convey, then this principle does not prevent us from giving effect to our conclusions."

As a subsidiary principle, then, strict construction is and should be retained in modern criminal law.[54] Nonetheless, it is fair to say that the courts have come to treat the rule of

---

[48] *CLGP*, 586–92.

[49] *Dowds* [2012] EWCA Crim 281, [2012] 1 WLR 2576, para. 36.

[50] [2009] UKHL 20, [2009] 1 AC 1310.

[51] E.g. *Harris* (1836) 7 C & P 446, 173 ER 198.

[52] [1970] AC 642; cf. *Tuck & Sons v. Priester* (1887) 19 QBD 629, 638, where Lord Esher MR required that the favourable alternative must be a "reasonable construction".

[53] *DPP v. Ottewell* [1970] AC 642, 649.

[54] Not merely in England and Wales: *Barker* (1983) 153 CLR 338, 350 (Murphy J).

strict construction as one of "last resort",[55] and sometimes have failed to apply it even in a case where it was appropriate. As Glanville Williams observes:[56]

> "The courts cannot manufacture statutes as they manufacture precedents, but they can 'interpret' them. They can cut them down, or expand them. Courts still pay lip-service to the ancient principle that in case of doubt a criminal statute is to be 'strictly construed' in favour of the defendant; but the principle is rarely applied in practice, if there are social reasons for convicting. Indeed, we may make bold to say that the looser the defendant's conduct, the more loosely the judges construe the statute designed to control him."

Indeed.[57] Sometimes, the Rule of Law is displaced by the discretionary rule of individual judges. In *Gomez*,[58] for example, D was convicted of theft, contrary to section 1 of the Theft Act 1968, by "appropriating" property that he had deceived V into giving him. The conduct was a plain case of obtaining by deception, contrary to section 15 of the same Act. The House of Lords upheld D's conviction for theft, notwithstanding that the "appropriation" was authorised by V and rested upon a construction that wrenched the crime of theft away from (i) a reasonable alternative meaning more favourable to D,[59] which was also (ii) its intended meaning,[60] and (iii) had been unequivocally embraced in an earlier decision by the House of Lords.[61] The problem arose only because D had been charged, incompetently, with theft rather than obtaining by deception. Their Lordships therefore had the alternatives of acquitting altogether a man obviously guilty of the offence under section 15, or of distorting the law of theft. Convicting one dishonest person was, apparently, more important.

Sometimes, then, the courts disregard the principle of strict construction in cases to which it ought to apply. But when they do so, they go wrong. The principle *is* a part of English law, where it operates as a residual doctrine of construction in the way we have described. Moreover, it *ought* not to be ignored. The principle is an important means of upholding the Rule of Law, by making sure that the defendant has fair warning of the scope of the relevant offence, and that (in a case like *Gomez*, where D was plainly guilty of something else)[62] his wrongdoing is fairly labelled. If, after considering the context and legislative history, a criminal prohibition is reasonably capable of being interpreted in two different ways, it is wrong not to give the defendant the benefit of the doubt. Indeed, as was suggested in Chapter 2, in our view the principle is mandated by Article 7 of the ECHR.[63] A strict approach to construction helps to prevent criminal liability from coming as a surprise to defendants. It ensures that the scope of an offence extends only to those cases where its application,

---

[55] *R (on the application of Junttan Oy)* v. *Bristol Magistrates' Court* [2003] UKHL 55, [2004] 2 All ER 555, para. 84 (Lord Steyn): "If it has a role to play it is as a rule of last resort: it is only to be applied if all other grounds of determining legislative intent have failed."

[56] *TBCL* 12. Cf. Smith, "Codification of the Criminal Law" (1987) 2 *Denning LJ* 137, 143–4.

[57] Compare, e.g., *Duncalf* [1979] 1 WLR 918; *Delgado* [1984] 1 WLR 89; *R (on the application of Junttan Oy)* v. *Bristol Magistrates' Court* [2003] UKHL 55, [2004] 2 All ER 555, para. 84 (Lord Steyn): "In the present context there is at stake a cogent countervailing legal policy: the protection of health and safety at work is of overriding importance."

[58] *DPP* v. *Gomez* [1993] AC 442, discussed in detail below, § 13.6(ii).

[59] Compare *Hinks* [2001] 2 AC 241, where, unlike *Gomez*, D would otherwise have committed no offence at all.

[60] Cf. the dissent in *Gomez* by Lord Lowry.

[61] *Morris* [1984] AC 320.

[62] See Shute and Horder, "Thieving and Deceiving: What is the Difference?" (1993) 56 *MLR* 548.

[63] See above, §§ 2.2–3.

ex ante, was clear and predictable. If this approach results in unwanted acquittals, then it is open to Parliament to remedy the problem by amending the relevant law.

(e) Summary

We have argued that the correct approach to statutory interpretation is first to seek the ordinary meaning in context. Where the meaning of a phrase emerges clearly from the context and purpose of the statute, that meaning should be adopted even though it goes against the defendant. Otherwise, if the meaning is not apparent from the Act or the relevant part of the Act, a review of the legislative history should be undertaken. Relevant constitutional presumptions, EU and international laws should also be considered. If, at the end of that process, the interpretation of the provision remains a matter of reasonable dispute, the benefit of the doubt should be given to the defendant. In practice, as we noted above, the approach argued for here is sometimes vulnerable to judges minded to override interpretive uncertainty in the interests of crime-control. Such vulnerability is unfortunate. Compromising the Rule of Law for the sake of short-term policy objectives is improper adjudication.

(f) The obvious drafting error?

The above states the correct general approach to interpreting criminal statutes. There is apparently one exception—although, in our view, it involves a regrettable compromise of the Rule of Law. The exception concerns the correction of an "obvious drafting error", as in *R (on the application of the CPS)* v. *Bow Street Magistrates Court and others*.[64] In that case, the defendants were charged with possessing a false passport on 4 April 2006, formerly an offence under section 5 of the Forgery and Counterfeiting Act 1981.[65] Section 44(2) of the short-lived Identity Cards Act 2006, which came into force on 30 March 2006,[66] repealed the relevant offence under the 1981 Act. It was intended that the 1981 offences would be replaced by corresponding provisions in sections 25 and 26 of the new 2006 Act, but those new provisions had not themselves come into force by 4 April 2006, because there had not yet been any commencement order. Section 44(3) of the 2006 Act suspended the coming into force of most of that Act, although not of section 44 itself:

> This Act (apart from this section and sections 36 and 38) shall come into force on such day as the Secretary of State may by order appoint; and different days may be appointed for different purposes.

There was certainly a slip-up here. By section 44(3), section 44(2) came into force on 30 March 2006 to repeal the offence charged under the 1981 Act; but the replacement offences did not come into force on the same date. The Divisional Court ruled that the statute could be corrected. Section 44(3) was interpreted to read as follows:[67]

> This Act (apart from this section, *other than subsection (2) hereof*, and sections 36 and 38) shall come into force on such day as the Secretary of State may by order appoint; and different days may be appointed for different purposes.

---

[64] [2006] EWHC 1763 (Admin), [2007] 1 WLR 291.
[65] See, now, Identity Documents Act 2010, ss. 4, 6.
[66] The 2006 Act was itself repealed in its entirety by s. 1 of the Identity Documents Act 2010.
[67] See *ibid.*, para. 44.

It seems that there are three criteria which must be met before such a corrective intervention can be made. The criteria are laid down by the House of Lords in *Inco Europe Ltd and others* v. *First Choice Distribution (a Firm) and Others*:[68]

> "This power is confined to plain cases of drafting mistakes. The courts are ever mindful that their constitutional role in this field is interpretative. They must abstain from any course which might have the appearance of judicial legislation. A statute is expressed in language approved and enacted by the legislature. So the courts exercise considerable caution before adding or omitting or substituting words. Before interpreting a statute in this way the court must be abundantly sure of three matters: (1) the intended purpose of the statute or provision in question; (2) that by inadvertence the draftsman and Parliament failed to give effect to that purpose in the provision in question; and (3) the substance of the provision Parliament would have made, although not necessarily the precise words Parliament would have used, had the error in the Bill been noticed."

No doubt those criteria were met in the present case. But *Inco Europe* was a civil case, not criminal, and the House of Lords had emphasised this point:[69]

> "Sometimes, even when these conditions are met, the court may find itself inhibited from interpreting the statutory provision in accordance with what it is satisfied was the underlying intention of Parliament. The alteration in language may be too far-reaching.... Or the subject matter may call for a strict interpretation of the statutory language, as in penal legislation. None of these considerations apply in the present case. Here, the court is able to give effect to a construction of the statute which accords with the intention of the legislature."

In construing the Identity Cards Act 2006 in the manner it did, the Divisional Court in *R (on the application of the CPS)* v. *Bow Street Magistrates Court and Others* wrongly discounted this qualification.[70] Civil law contains no direct equivalent of the *nullum crimen* rule (discussed earlier in §§ 2.1–2). In the criminal law, it is not appropriate to read words into a statute to create an offence that, on the clear meaning of the statute when applying the correct approach outlined on the pages above, does not exist.[71] The "obvious error" rule in *Inco Europe* should be confined to the civil law.

(iii) Interpretation and development of common law offences

Contrasts are frequently made between statutory interpretation, on the one hand, and the creation and development of the common law. Despite the importance of statutory law for vast tracts of English law, statutes, it is claimed, do not become part of a general body of

---

[68] [2000] 1 WLR 586, 592 (Lord Nicholls).

[69] *Ibid.*, 592–3.

[70] The Court dealt with the point by opining that the novel construction of s. 44(3) of the 2006 Act did "not inflict any detriment or greater detriment" upon any of the defendants or any other person, because it merely continued the existing law until its replacement by the new provisions, and that no increase in penalty was involved at any stage ([2006] EWHC 1763 (Admin), [2007] 1 WLR 291, paras. 47–8). But of course it did: the interposition of words created an offence where there was otherwise none.

[71] Compare the approach taken in some cases involving defective indictments: "Technicality is always distasteful when it appears to contradict the merits of a case. But the duty of the court is to apply the law, which is sometimes technical, and it may be thought that if the state exercises its coercive power to put a citizen on trial for serious crime a certain degree of formality is not out of place." *Clarke and McDaid* [2008] UKHL 8, [2008] 1 WLR 338, para. 17 (Lord Bingham).

law, organically linked to the other statutory and common law norms that already occupy the relevant legal domain. Each statute remains a thing apart, to be interpreted within its own four corners and legislative history and not to be used as a means of extrapolation and analogy for the treatment of issues that do not arise under the statute itself. By contrast, the common law is said to be an entity which subsumes its constituent parts, thereby allowing ideas developed in one branch of common law to be deployed freely in other branches should cognate issues arise. The self-confident and conscious development of common law rules and doctrines finds no counterpart in statutory interpretation.[72]

Although that account risks parody, it contains a core of truth: for the civil law. The criminal law is different. The criminal branch of the common law is essentially a realm apart.[73] It has not been integrated with contract and property; or even, to any significant extent, with the law of tort. In the criminal law, a comparison between statutory interpretation and the development and interpretation of common law crimes reveals parallel tendencies toward expansive interpretation, usually done in the interests of crime control. One point of difference is that the common law has contained rules of such breadth and imprecision that expansive interpretation frequently was not required. In effect, the common law was there ready and waiting to rubber-stamp a prosecutor's decision to proceed.

Perhaps the best illustration of the flexibility of common law crimes is the common-law version of conspiracy—an agreement between two or more persons to effect some unlawful purpose.[74] Left to judicial devices, "unlawful" was allowed free rein and led to the criminalisation of many actions which, if done by individuals acting alone, would not have been criminal. This freedom was exercised to large and controversial effect,[75] and at the price of the Rule of Law, until finally limited by the Criminal Law Act of 1977. Even so, "elasticity" was not completely forsworn. Common law conspiracies to defraud,[76] to corrupt public morality, and to outrage public decency were retained by the 1977 Act pending their replacement by narrower, statutory offences. These forms of conspiracy are still in rude health, although it is now accepted that their expansion, if any, should be by marginal steps only.[77]

A similar example is the former catch-all offence of "public mischief". In Manley,[78] a prosecution was launched against D for deliberately wasting police time. In the absence of

---

[72] See the classic article by Pound, "Common Law and Legislation" (1907) 21 Harv LR 383. The contrast still retains substance but statutes are no longer treated so circumspectly as formerly they were. As Atiyah has demonstrated ("Common Law and Statute Law" (1985) 48 MLR 1), statutes may be used by judges as sources of analogy and policy for legal development generally, though this tends to occur on a haphazard, ad hoc, basis.

[73] "The miserable history of crime in England can be shortly told. There is no achievement to trace. Nothing worthwhile was created." With these words, Milsom introduces a chapter in which he demonstrates, by contrast with the rest of the common law, the impoverished development and lack of resources of the law of crime: Historical Foundations of the Common Law (2nd ed., 1981) 403.

[74] Wright, Law of Criminal Conspiracies and Agreements (1873) 63–5.

[75] Kamara v. DPP [1974] AC 104, 109.

[76] Below, § 15.9. Remarkably the Fraud Act 2006, which creates a general fraud offence, does not abolish common law conspiracy to defraud. We can assume that this protean and widely prosecuted offence will be with us for the indefinite future, though it will apparently no longer be extended to criminalise novel forms of activity: Norris v. USA [2008] UKHL 16, [2008] 1 AC 920.

[77] "If the ambit of a common law offence is to be enlarged, it 'must be done step by step on a case by case basis and not with one large leap'" Rimmington and Goldstein [2005] UKHL 63, [2006] 1 AC 459, para. 33 (Lord Bingham), citing Clark (Mark) [2003] EWCA Crim 991, [2003] 2 Cr App R 23, para. 13. In the specific context of common law conspiracy to defraud, see Norris v. USA [2008] UKHL 16, [2008] 1 AC 920; below, § 15.9(iii)(a).

[78] [1933] 1 KB 529.

anything more suitable to hand, the Court of Criminal Appeal approved the trial judge's resurrection of the offence, a "public mischief" being anything injurious to the public interest. It is perhaps needless to emphasise the extent to which such an offence undermines any aspiration to fair warning[79] in the criminal law. Happily, the offence was infrequently resorted to and eventually consigned to legal history by the House of Lords in *DPP* v. *Withers*.[80]

Whatever criticisms may be made of modern parliaments, it is doubtful whether offences based on phrases so nebulous, extensible, and threatening[81] as "public mischief" or "corrupting public morality" would survive the modern legislative process. Yet even modern parliaments seem disinclined to abolish established, widely phrased offences.[82] In a modern democracy, judges should not be allowed to help themselves to such untrammelled power. Yet we have seen that the phrasing of modern statutes is not always a sufficient constraint on judicial activism,[83] and it seems the internal resources of the criminal law are an insufficient bulwark.

The need for restraint is pressing. Judicial activism is visible in relatively recent cases, for example the decision of the House of Lords in *Ireland*.[84] For hundreds of years, an assault required the threat of imminent violence; that is, the threat of some immediate, unwanted bodily contact. Remarkably, the House found that this condition could be satisfied in a case involving silent phone calls, despite the caller's being miles away from his victim. As we will see in Chapter 11, the reasoning of the House does not convince. Also remarkably, this decision was reached despite the fact that such conduct would (in subsequent cases) have been caught by sections 1 and 2 of the Protection from Harassment Act 1997. Yet the House reached its interpretation not merely to avoid an acquittal in the instant case. It also considered that the penalties provided by the new Act were insufficient and that recourse to the greater penalties provided by the sanctions for aggravated assaults was required. Accordingly, their Lordships decided to customise centuries of common law in order to circumnavigate the new Act. Such judicial activism is undesirable in the context of the criminal law.

Judicial activism is a little less problematic when it results in a radical cut-back of criminal liability, which seems likely in the context of accessories following the revision of joint enterprise doctrine by the Supreme Court in *Jogee*.[85] When there is a joint enterprise to commit just one crime, as when P and S agree to burgle the house of V, and burglary is the only crime committed, the fact of joint enterprise does not affect the application of the normal rules relating to complicity. But, if in the course of the burglary, P should kill V with the mens rea for murder, S too was, at least prior to the decision in *Jogee*, also guilty of

---

[79] And fair labelling: above, § 2.4.

[80] [1975] AC 842.

[81] Potentially, such phrases permit criminalisation on the basis of immorality rather than harm or offence: see below, § 16.3.

[82] As can be seen in the omission by the Fraud Act 2006 to abolish common law conspiracy to defraud, when reforming the law of fraud. See below, § 15.1.

[83] Though the *existence* of a statutory offence may displace its common-law antecedent: *Rimmington and Goldstein* [2005] UKHL 63, [2006] 1 AC 459, para. 30. The interpretation of common-law offences is also subject to EU and international law norms that constrain the construction of statutes: above, § 3.1(ii)(c).

[84] [1998] AC 147. See above, § 2.3; below, § 11.2(i)(c).

[85] *Jogee*; *Ruddock* [2016] UKSC 8; [2016] UKSC 8, [2016] 2 WLR 681. See below, § 7.5.

murder provided that he had foreseen a possibility of P's collateral offence (i.e. that P would deliberately inflict serious violence on V).

For the Supreme Court in *Jogee*, the law that allowed S to be convicted of murder on this basis was simply "wrong" and should not be applied in any future case. This "error" was made first by the Privy Council,[86] then in two unanimous decisions by the appellate committee of the House of Lords,[87] and accepted in an earlier Supreme Court decision.[88] But it was not an error in terms of precedent. There was no binding authority that barred the adoption of foresight of possibility as the culpability for offences collateral to the joint enterprise. Those earlier decisions, that is to say, were not *per incuriam*. The zeal of the Supreme Court to correct them should properly be restricted to such findings or to formal invocations of the power contained in its Practice Directions to depart from previous decisions of the Supreme Court and the House of Lords.[89] *Jogee* may be activism in a good cause, but it is radical activism none the less.

§ 3.2 The burden of proving actus reus and mens rea

In Chapter 1, we argued that convicting an innocent person would be seriously to defame him. Punishing him, of course, compounds the wrong. Because criminal liability is so serious, every citizen has the right not to have the State inflict such liability on him unless he is, in fact, guilty. That right is fundamental: it is profoundly wrong for the State to mistreat an innocent person, and to do so breaches one of the keystones of an individual's relationship with the State.

So when the State brands someone a criminal, it needs to be sure that it is right—or at least, in the absence of omniscience and unlimited resources, as sure as it can be.[90] For that reason, there is a basic presumption in English law that the defendant in a trial is innocent until proved guilty. The presumption is also codified in Article 6(2) of the ECHR, which provides that a person "charged with a criminal offence shall be presumed innocent until proved guilty according to the law". In the words of the European Court of Human Rights:[91]

> "Paragraph 2 embodies the principle of the presumption of innocence. It requires, *inter alia*, that when carrying out their duties, the members of a court should not start with the preconceived idea that the accused has committed the offence charged; the burden of proof is on the prosecution, and any doubt should benefit the accused. It also follows that it is for the prosecution to inform the accused of the case that will be made against him, so that he may prepare and present his defence accordingly, and to adduce evidence sufficient to convict him."

---

[86] *Chan Wing-Siu* [1985] AC 168.

[87] *Powell and English* [1999] 1 AC 1; *Rahman* [2008] UKHL 45.

[88] *Gnango* [2011] UKSC 59.

[89] Direction 3.1.3 states that that the terms of the Supreme Court's power to depart from its own decisions and from decisions of the House of Lords will be on the same terms as previously employed by the House of Lords when it empowered itself to depart from its own decisions: Practice Statement (Judicial Precedent) [1966] 1 WLR 1234; cf. *Austin v. Mayor and Burgesses of the London Borough of Southwark* [2010] UKSC 28 paras. 24–5. It is worth noting that Direction 3.1.3 requires appellants to give notice if they are to ask the Supreme Court to depart from any of its own decisions or from decisions of the House of Lords so that an enlarged panel of Justices may be convened. No such panel was convened in *Jogee*.

[90] Cf. the judgment of Brennan J in *Re Winship* 397 US 358 (1970).

[91] *Barberà, Messegué and Jabardo v. Spain* (1989) 11 EHRR 360, para. 77.

None of this is novel. The presumption of innocence predates the ECHR, and has been a part of English common law at least since *Woolmington* v. *DPP*.[92] In *Woolmington*, a murder case, the trial judge had relied on earlier authorities to direct the jury that, once the prosecution had proved that the defendant had killed the deceased, mens rea could be presumed and it was up to the defendant to "satisfy" the jury either that mens rea (the intention to kill or cause serious harm) was absent and the killing had been accidental, or that the killing had been justified (for instance, by self-defence). On this view, the prosecution had to prove only the actus reus, and the burden then lay on the defendant to prove either the lack of mens rea or the existence of a defence. Not so, said the House of Lords:[93]

> "Throughout the web of the English Criminal Law one golden thread is always to be seen, that it is the duty of the prosecution to prove the prisoner's guilt.... If, at the end of and on the whole of the case, there is a reasonable doubt, created by the evidence given by either the prosecution or the prisoner, as to whether the prisoner killed the deceased with a malicious intention, the prosecution has not made out the case and the prisoner is entitled to an acquittal. No matter what the charge or where the trial, the principle that the prosecution must prove the guilt of the prisoner is part of the common law of England and no attempt to whittle it down can be entertained."

It was not for the defendant to demonstrate that the actus reus was an accident; the prosecution must establish mens rea beyond reasonable doubt.

The effect of *Woolmington* may be summarised in the following steps:

(i)　　The prosecution has the *legal (or "persuasive") burden* to bring evidence which prima facie proves all actus reus and mens rea elements of the offence *beyond reasonable doubt*.

(ii)　　Once the prosecution has done so, it is then open to the defendant either to raise a reasonable doubt about the evidence the prosecution has brought, or to point to some further evidence which raises a doubt whether the prosecution's evidence is in fact sufficient to prove both actus reus[94] and mens rea beyond reasonable doubt.

(iii)　Alternatively, if the prosecution proves both actus reus and mens rea, the defendant has an *evidential burden* to raise any evidence which suggests the possible availability of a defence (e.g. that the actus reus was done in self-defence).[95] If he does so, or if the evidence introduced by the prosecution does so,[96] then the

---

[92] [1935] AC 462.

[93] [1935] AC 462, 481–2 (Viscount Sankey LC). See also *Mancini* v. *DPP* [1942] AC 1, 11–2 (Viscount Simon LC).

[94] This includes claims of involuntariness or automatism: *Bratty* v. *A-G for Northern Ireland* [1963] AC 386, 406–7 (Viscount Kilmuir LC), 413–14 (Lord Denning). See below, § 4.3(iv).

[95] *Lobell* [1957] 1 QB 547, 551 (self-defence); *Gill* [1963] 2 All ER 688, 691 (duress). The evidentiary burden to introduce defences differs from the option to refute evidence of actus reus or mens rea in step (ii). The latter is sometimes called a *tactical burden* on the defendant (referring to the tactical imperative to combat the prosecution's evidence that the offence elements are present). The difference is that, where there is an evidential burden on D to suggest (e.g.) a defence, its absence will be *presumed* by the court unless D discharges that burden. By contrast, a tactical burden involves no presumption. Thus, D may choose not to respond to the prosecution's evidence of actus reus and mens rea, and simply hope that the jury is not convinced by it.

[96] Thus the defence must be considered even if the defendant has not raised it himself: *Palmer* v. *R.* [1971] AC 814, 823 (Lord Morris) (PC); *Wheeler* [1967] 1 WLR 1531, 1533–4 (CA); *Hamand* (1986) 82 Cr App R 65. The same principle applies to partial defences to murder: *Coutts* [2006] UKHL 39, [2006] 1 WLR 2154, para. 14.

prosecution assumes the *legal* burden of proving beyond reasonable doubt that the relevant defence is not available in this case.[97] These propositions apply to common law defences with the exception of insanity; there is also an exception for statutory defences. We will consider these exceptions below.

The defendant does *not* have to prove that he is innocent.[98] The jury[99] may think that he is untrustworthy, and be unconvinced by his story. But, save in the exceptional cases of insanity and statutory defences, if the jury thinks there is a reasonable possibility that he is not guilty of the crime charged, the defendant must be acquitted. As the Privy Council put it, in *Jayasena v. R.*, "the only burden laid upon the accused in this respect is to collect from the evidence enough material to make it possible for a reasonable jury to acquit".[100]

In practical terms, the effect of the *Woolmington* approach is that a defendant need not collaborate in his own conviction; however strong the grounds of suspicion against him he need not give any account of himself or in any other way assist the prosecution to make its case. As such, the presumption of innocence is an essential counterpart to the defendant's right of non-self-incrimination.[101]

The "beyond reasonable doubt" standard is, thus, crucial to protecting citizens from unjust conviction.[102] It means that the jury must be *sure* that the defendant committed the offence,[103] and acquit if there is a realistic or genuine doubt about the defendant's guilt, although not if the doubt is only vague or fanciful.[104] Such a high standard is needed for the State to be sufficiently sure that it is imposing criminal liability accurately. It is not enough that the defendant "very likely", or even "probably", did the crime; otherwise there would be too many cases of error and consequent miscarriages of justice, which would endanger public confidence in and support for the criminal justice system. The possibility of error is all the greater when it is also remembered that the State typically has far greater resources with which to conduct a prosecution than the defendant has with which to defend himself. In addition, the high standard of proof acts as a constraint upon the decision to prosecute. Without the presumption of innocence, those who make that decision would have an immense and potentially oppressive power to disrupt the lives of citizens.

---

[97] *Lobell* [1957] 1 QB 547 (CA); *Gill* [1963] 2 All ER 688 (CA); *Chan Kau v. R* [1955] AC 206, 211 (PC); *Mancini v. DPP* [1942] AC 1.

[98] Perversely, if the defendant is convicted, and that conviction is later quashed, he will have to prove *beyond reasonable doubt* that he was innocent if he wishes to be compensated: Criminal Justice Act 1988, s. 133; Bailin and Craven, "Compensation for Miscarriages of Justice—Who Now Qualifies?" [2014] *Crim LR* 511.

[99] The finder of fact is the jury in serious cases tried on indictment—the same principles will, however, apply where the defendant is tried summarily in the Magistrates' Court. For the sake of clarity, reference will only be made to "the jury" in the text below.

[100] [1970] AC 618, 623 (Lord Devlin).

[101] It should be noted that s. 35 of the Criminal Justice and Public Order Act 1994 allows the jury to draw "adverse inferences" from the defendant's failure to give evidence at his trial. This provision places some pressure on defendants to forfeit the privilege against self-incrimination and give evidence at trial.

[102] This may be a more stringent standard than that required by Art. 6(2) of the ECHR, which demands evidence "sufficiently strong in the eyes of the law to establish his guilt": *Austria v. Italy* 6 YB 740, 784 (1963).

[103] In practice, the requirement of being "sure" is used in directions to the jury, in preference to the language of "beyond reasonable doubt".

[104] *Miller v. Minister of Pensions* [1947] 2 All ER 372, 373 (DC).

(i) Exceptions

(a) Statutory exceptions

It is not uncommon for a statute to modify the normal burden of proof, "reversing" it so that it is placed on the defendant. An example of this is the offence of child abduction contrary to section 2 of the Child Abduction Act 1984. Subsection (3) provides a defence, *inter alia*, if the defendant proves "that, at the time of the alleged offence, he believed that the child had attained the age of sixteen". In this case, once the prosecution has proved the other elements of an offence against section 2, the defendant has a legal (and not merely evidential) burden to prove that the conditions of the defence exist. In all such cases, the defendant must prove that such a belief existed to the civil standard of the balance of probabilities.[105] It must, in other words, be more likely than not that he held such a belief.

This is not a textbook on evidence. However, for the reasons given in the last section, statutory exceptions of this sort are generally to be deplored.[106] Effectively, they reverse the presumption of innocence, and replace it with a presumption of criminality, whereby the defendant is to be convicted of a crime unless she exculpates herself. As such, they expose the defendant to conviction for a crime without the prosecution being required, at any stage, to lead evidence which proves the *entire* basis for her guilt beyond reasonable doubt. There *may* be occasions when it is apt to require the defendant, in respect of matters that lie peculiarly within her knowledge, to suggest reasons why she should not be convicted.[107] But rather like the tort doctrine of *res ipsa loquitur*, this is a principle to be sparingly used and only if the prosecution has established a prima facie case of wrongdoing.[108] Moreover, even then the desired result can usually be achieved by imposing an *evidential* burden to introduce defences upon the defendant, without requiring her to discharge the full legal burden of persuading the court on the balance of probabilities that she is innocent. The defendant should not, on any occasion, be required to prove her innocence to such a standard.

Be that as it may, statutory reversal of the burden of proof occurs quite frequently, and not always expressly.[109] One situation where the burden of proof is generally reversed by implication is in respect of any exonerating circumstances provided for by the statute creating the offence. Where the offence is tried summarily before a Magistrates' Court, section 101 of the Magistrates' Courts Act 1980 provides that the burden of proving any "exception, exemption, proviso, excuse or qualification" shall fall upon the defendant (as always in such cases, to the balance of probabilities).[110] Extending that, the House of Lords held in *Hunt*[111]

---

[105] *Carr-Briant* [1943] KB 607 (CA). The defendant is *never* required to prove a matter in a criminal trial beyond reasonable doubt.

[106] See, e.g., Roberts, "Taking the Burden of Proof Seriously" [1995] *Crim LR* 783; Jeffries and Stephan, "Defenses, Presumptions and Burden of Proof in Criminal Law" (1979) 88 *Yale LJ* 1325.

[107] Cf. *Jayasena v. R.* [1970] AC 618, 626–7 (PC). See also the discussion of (and reservations about) strict liability, below, chapter 6.

[108] Cf. Dennis, "Reverse Onuses and the Presumption of Innocence: In Search of Principle" [2005] *Crim LR* 901. Dennis argues that legal burdens should be imposed on defendants only where the prosecution has established a case of *prima facie* morally blameworthy behaviour.

[109] *Hunt* [1987] AC 352, 374 (Lord Griffiths), 379–80 (Lord Ackner). See the survey by Ashworth and Blake, "The Presumption of Innocence in English Criminal Law" [1996] *Crim LR* 306.

[110] *Hunt* [1987] AC 352, 385 (Lord Ackner).

[111] *Ibid*; confirming that particular aspect of *Edwards* [1975] QB 27 (CA). See Smith, "The Presumption of Innocence" (1987) 38 *NILQ* 223.

that the same rule exists at common law, applicable to indictable offences as well as to summary proceedings.[112]

Following *Hunt*, the default position is that the defendant must prove statutory defences on the balance of probabilities, even if the relevant statute does not expressly say that this is the case. By contrast, in common law defences such as self-defence and duress (but not insanity) the defendant bears only an evidential burden, and the existence of the defence must then be negated beyond reasonable doubt by the prosecution.

The merits of this default position regarding statutory defences may be doubted. It is not always clear what constitutes an aspect of the offence and what constitutes an "exception, exemption, proviso, excuse or qualification". Suppose an (imaginary) statute were to be enacted prohibiting assaults, where "assault" were defined as "the application of force without consent or some other lawful excuse". Is the victim's absence of consent an ingredient of the offence definition, or is consent an "exception, exemption, proviso, excuse or qualification"? There is no easy answer, and the guidance available from the cases is limited[113]—so limited, indeed, that an Australian judge once remarked that "judges are inclined eventually to assert that a case falls on one side of the line or the other without really being able to assign reasons for their view".[114] Given the implications of the categorisation being made, this is a thoroughly unsatisfactory state of affairs.

The discussion so far suggests that a legal burden will, by default, be placed on the defendant in a wide variety of contexts. Is this approach compatible with the European Convention, particularly Article 6(2), which declares that "Everyone charged with a criminal offence shall be presumed innocent until proved guilty according to law"? In *Lingens* v. *Austria*[115] the European Court ruled that imposing a legal burden on the defendant does not necessarily contravene Article 6(2). Similarly, statutory presumptions of fact, where the burden of rebuttal falls on the accused, have been held consistent with Article 6(2), provided the presumption operates "within reasonable limits which take into account the importance of what is at stake and maintain the rights of the defence".[116] The need for "reasonable limits" does, at least, offer hope that in extreme cases the imposition of a legal burden on the defendant will be disallowed by Article 6(2). But it seems the case would have to be extreme. In *Salabiaku* v. *France*,[117] D had been found in possession of drugs in the "green" channel (i.e. the route taken by those without imported goods to declare) at Paris airport. He was charged with the serious, imprisonable offence of drugs smuggling. Under French law, smuggling was presumed from the fact of possession in such circumstances unless D

---

[112] Note that the rule did not apply to claims of reasonable excuse for breaching an anti-social behaviour order (*Charles* [2009] EWCA Crim 1570, [2010] 1 WLR 644) or a restraining order made under s. 5 of the Harassment Act 1997 (*Evans (Dorothy Gertrude)* [2004] EWCA Crim 3102, [2005] 1 WLR 1435).

[113] See *Hunt* [1987] AC 352, 374 (Lord Griffiths); *Nimmo* v. *Alexander Cowan & Sons Ltd* [1968] AC 107, 135 (Lord Pearson). A useful discussion of this aspect of *Hunt* is Orchard, "The Golden Thread—Somewhat Frayed" (1988) 6 *Otago LR* 615, 624–8.

[114] *Francis* v. *Flood* [1978] 1 NSWLR 113, 119 (Sheppard J).

[115] (1982) 4 EHRR 373.

[116] *Salabiaku* v. *France* (1991) 13 EHRR 379; cf. *X* v. *UK* No. 5124/71, 42 CD 135 (1972). In *Duhs* v. *Sweden* No. 12995/87, 67 DR 204 (1990), the Court held that imposition of a parking fine on the basis of car ownership was within such reasonable limits, and hence was permissible. See also *A-G of Hong Kong* v. *Lee Kwong-Kut* [1993] AC 951 (PC) (in the context of the Hong Kong Bill of Rights); *Vasquez* v. *R* [1994] 1 WLR 1304 (PC) (constitution of Belize).

[117] (1991) 13 EHRR 379.

could establish to the satisfaction of the court that he was unaware of the nature of the items possessed. The Court found that this presumption did not contravene Article 6(2). Similar findings have been made in respect of a presumption that D, a company director, was guilty of an offence if the offence has been proved against his company,[118] and in respect of a presumption that D was living off immoral earnings if it is proved that D was cohabiting with a prostitute.[119]

Fortunately, a series of House of Lords decisions has established a somewhat less permissive attitude to reverse *legal* burdens.[120] While there is no universal bar to reverse legal burdens, and each offence must be considered on its merits,[121] on some occasions at least a reverse legal burden has been ruled incompatible with Article 6(2). An example is *Lambert*,[122] where, in order to avoid conviction for an offence of drug trafficking under section 5 of the Misuse of Drugs Act 1971, D was required to "prove" that he neither knew, nor suspected, nor had reason to know or suspect, that the substance in his possession was a controlled drug. As a matter of simple interpretation, the use of the word "prove" suggests that Parliament intended to impose a *legal* burden on a defendant charged with the section 5 offence. By a majority of 4:1, the House of Lords decided that, notwithstanding the public interest in prohibiting the trade in illegal drugs, to impose a legal burden on a defendant was a disproportionate legislative response and, consequently, a breach of Article 6(2). It was held that, within the interpretive possibilities allowed for by section 3 of the HRA 1998, the requirement to "prove" lack of knowledge, suspicion, etc., could be reinterpreted to require D merely to raise the possibility that he neither knew nor suspected—merely an evidential burden and not a legal burden. A notable feature of the decision was a refusal to rely upon any formal distinction between definitional elements of an offence and matters of defence when determining the acceptability of a reverse burden. What mattered was whether D would be found guilty of an offence unless he could prove the particular matter in dispute.

In so far as the various decisions by their Lordships can be distilled,[123] it seems that the proper approach to the issue of reverse legal burdens is as follows. Where, on ordinary techniques of statutory interpretation (above, § 3.1), a particular piece of legislation imposes expressly or by implication a legal burden on the defendant, the court must then enquire whether doing so is an unjustifiable infringement of the presumption of innocence in Article 6(2).[124] In establishing whether an unjustifiable infringement has occurred, the court will ask whether imposing the reverse legal burden is a proportionate response to whatever aim the statute is pursuing. Where a reverse legal burden is disproportionate, the presumption of innocence is unjustifiably infringed. In such circumstances, the court must,

---

[118] *G* v. *Malta* No. 16641/90 (1991).

[119] *X* v. *UK* No. 5124/71, 42 CD 135 (1972).

[120] *R.* v. *DPP, ex p. Kebilene* [2000] 2 AC 326; *Lambert* [2001] UKHL 37, [2002] 2 AC 545; *Johnstone* [2003] UKHL 28, [2003] 1 WLR 1736; *Sheldrake* v. *DPP*; *Attorney-General's Reference (No. 4 of 2002)* [2004] UKHL 43, [2005] 1 AC 264.

[121] *Lambert* [2001] UKHL 37, [2002] 2 AC 545, paras. 34 (Lord Steyn), 152 (Lord Clyde); *Sheldrake* v. *DPP*; *Attorney-General's Reference (No. 4 of 2002)* [2004] UKHL 43, [2005] 1 AC 264, para. 21 (Lord Bingham).

[122] [2001] UKHL 37, [2002] 2 AC 545.

[123] See, in particular, the valuable discussion by Dennis, "Reverse Onuses and the Presumption of Innocence: In Search of Principle" [2005] *Crim LR* 901.

[124] The placing of an evidential burden on the defendant does not infringe Art. 6(2).

if possible, reinterpret the legislative provision so as to impose an *evidential* burden.[125] If such an interpretation is precluded by the terms of the legislation, a declaration of incompatibility with the ECHR should be made.[126] Typically, the courts have found it possible to "read down" legislation so as to impose only an evidential burden on the defendant. Resort to a declaration of incompatibility has not yet proved necessary.

When considering whether a reverse legal burden is proportionate, one should balance, on the one hand, society's interest in the effective suppression of the social mischief with which the offence is concerned (and the associated practicalities of proof and enforcement) and, on the other hand, D's right to a fair trial. When weighing up these two competing interests, the courts have emphasised the importance of the seriousness of the offence at issue (usually marked by the severity of the maximum sentence), the relative ease of proof for one party or the other in relation to the element at issue, and the likely risk that the reverse legal burden creates of convicting innocent defendants.

However, the extent to which these considerations are capable of supplying adequate general guidance for future cases has rightly been doubted.[127] The assessments of proportionality in cases to date have been rather *ad hoc*, and it is worth observing that, in the main, reverse legal burdens have been upheld—even in the context of imprisonable offences.[128] In *Williams*,[129] for example, D was charged with the unlawful possession of an imitation firearm that was readily convertible into a firearm.[130] It is a defence to the charge for D "to show that he did not know and had no reason to suspect that the imitation firearm was so constructed or adapted as to be readily converted into a firearm".[131] The use of the word "show" suggested that Parliament intended to place a legal burden on the defendant, and the Court of Appeal refused to construe the provision as imposing an evidential burden. The Court considered that the public interest in suppressing the possession of firearms made the derogation from the presumption of innocence necessary and proportionate.

It was reasoning of this kind that consistently upheld comparable reverse legal burdens in drug possession cases until the intervention of the House of Lords in *Lambert*. It would be very much in the interests of justice and consistency if the Supreme Court were to resolve more general principles when adjudicating upon reverse burdens. Indeed, it is submitted that the primary general principle should be that, for stigmatic crimes involving proof of culpability and a potential sentence of imprisonment, reverse probative burdens should *always* be reduced to evidential burdens.[132] Support for a more assertive approach to the

---

[125] Using the procedure outlined in HRA 1998, s. 3; see above, § 2.5(i).

[126] HRA 1998, s. 4.

[127] By Ashworth, in the commentary on *Sheldrake v. DPP* [2005] Crim LR 218. See also Ashworth, "Four Threats to the Presumption of Innocence" (2006) 10 *Evidence and Proof* 241, 257–70.

[128] See, for example, *Chargot Ltd* [2008] UKHL 73, [2009] 1 WLR 1 (up to two years' imprisonment and an unlimited fine). The interpretation in *Chargot* of ss. 2–3 of the Health and Safety at Work etc. Act 1974 is difficult to reconcile with *Porter* [2008] EWCA Crim 1271 and is criticised in Spencer, "Criminal Liability for Accidental Death: Back to the Middle Ages?" (2009) 68 *CLJ* 263.

[129] [2012] EWCA Crim 2162, [2013] 1 WLR 1200.

[130] Contrary to Firearms Act 1968, s. 5(1).

[131] Firearms Act 1982, s. 1(5).

[132] The hostility to reverse burden provisions evinced in decisions such as *Lambert* [2001] UKHL 37, [2002] 2 AC 545 gives some support for such a general principle. See, further, Williams, "The Logic of 'Exceptions'" (1988) 47 *CLJ* 261.

presumption of innocence can be found in the important sentencing case of *Newton*[133] and its associated jurisprudence. At the sentencing stage, any disputed fact unfavourable to D must be proved beyond reasonable doubt.[134] This fundamental principle of criminal justice is even more in point when the grounds of liability are contested at trial.

It would also be helpful if the European Court were to denounce reverse legal burdens, rather than adhering to *Salabiaku*'s vague "reasonable limits" test. It is instructive to compare the attitude towards reverse legal burdens with that taken towards self-incrimination. In *Funke* v. *France*,[135] the Court ruled that answers obtained from D in relation to his tax affairs under statutory powers of compulsion could not be put before the judge at his subsequent criminal trial for tax evasion. A decision to the same effect was reached in *Saunders* v. *UK*,[136] in respect of answers obtained under compulsory powers of questioning allowed under companies legislation. These decisions sit uneasily beside the relaxed attitude exhibited by the Court to the reversal of the burden of proof. The protection against self-incrimination is rendered largely meaningless if there is a presumption of guilt, whereby the prosecution need not prove guilt at all and it falls to the defendant to demonstrate his innocence.

It is worth noting another important statutory incursion upon the principle that the defendant is not required to prove her innocence. Section 34 of the Criminal Justice and Public Order Act 1994 permits the finding that a defendant failed to mention some fact during police questioning, a fact that she later relies upon in her defence at trial, to be used as the basis of an "adverse inference" against her. Likewise, section 35 of the same Act allows (subject to narrow exceptions) the defendant's failure to give evidence at her trial to be put to similar use.[137] As Ashworth has remarked, "if there is to be a presumption that a person is innocent until proved guilty by the prosecution, there appears to be some inconsistency in holding that the defendant can through his or her silence supply an element in that case".[138] The practical effect of modifying a defendant's right to silence is partially to reallocate the burden of proof. For this and other reasons,[139] the provisions of the Criminal Justice and Public Order Act 1994 remain profoundly controversial, even though their broad compatibility with Article 6 has been recognised by the European Court.[140]

---

[133] (1983) 77 Cr App R 13.

[134] However, reverse burdens concerning D's assets have been allowed in the context of post-conviction confiscation orders, which are regarded as part of the sentencing process—even though the orders are supported by substantial terms of imprisonment upon default. Cf. *Phillips* v. *UK* (2001) 11 BHRC 280; *Grayson and Barnham* v. *UK* (2009) 48 EHRR 30.

[135] [1993] 1 CMLR 897.

[136] (1997) 23 EHRR 313. Cf. *O'Halloran* v. *UK* (2008) 46 EHRR 21.

[137] Other provisions in the 1994 Act allow similar adverse inferences to be drawn in different circumstances. See Owusu-Bempah, "Silence in Suspicious Circumstances" [2014] *Crim LR* 126.

[138] *The Criminal Process: An Evaluative Study* (2nd ed., 1998) 96. Cf. *Funke, Cremieux and Miailhe* v. *France* [1993] 1 CMLR 897. For further criticism of the 1994 Act's provisions, see Jackson, "Curtailing the Right to Silence: Lessons from Northern Ireland" [1991] *Crim LR* 404; Galligan, "The Right to Silence Reconsidered" (1988) 41 *CLP* 69; Dennis, "The Criminal Justice and Public Order Act 1994: The Evidence Provisions" [1995] *Crim LR* 4; Birch, "Suffering in Silence: A Cost—Benefit Analysis of Section 34 of the Criminal Justice and Public Order Act 1994" [1999] *Crim LR* 769; Dennis, "Silence in the Police Station: The Marginalisation of Section 34" [2002] *Crim LR* 25.

[139] E.g. the suspect's right to privacy and her privilege against self-incrimination.

[140] See, e.g., *Murray* v. *UK* (1996) 22 EHRR 29. The UK has on occasion lost cases concerning the 1994 Act at Strasbourg, but typically on the basis of the trial judge's defective explanation of the adverse inference provisions, rather than the provisions themselves. See, e.g., *Beckles* v. *UK* (2003) 36 EHRR 13.

(b) The common law exception: insanity

A second situation in which the legal burden can be on the defendant concerns the defence of insanity. The common law makes a default presumption of sanity.[141] Once again, if she wants to rely on the defence, the defendant must prove it on the balance of probabilities. This is an incongruous anomaly, given that the defendant bears only an evidential burden in respect of other general defences, and that the consequence of proving insanity may be compulsory detention.[142] A similar rule applies to the statutory defence of diminished responsibility.[143] Note, however, that the need for a defendant to show insanity or diminished responsibility arises only if the prosecution can prove the actus reus (and, in diminished responsibility, the mens rea) beyond reasonable doubt in the normal way. Insanity is discussed in detail in § 19.1; diminished responsibility is considered in § 19.2.

(c) Strict liability

Strict liability is discussed in Chapter 6. To anticipate the discussion there, in offences of strict liability, the prosecution is relieved of the burden of proving mens rea in relation to one or more aspects of the actus reus. The House of Lords and the European Court have both held that strict liability offences, of which there are many in English criminal law, are not prohibited by Article 6(2).[144] Typically, the use of strict liability is regarded as a matter of substantive rather than procedural criminal law, even though (as we shall see) a standard rationale for imposing strict liability is convenience of proof for prosecutors. It is a false dichotomy. Strict liability has the capacity almost entirely to circumvent the values protected by the presumption of innocence.[145]

(ii) The "golden thread": somewhat frayed?[146]

At the time, the decision in *Woolmington* was delivered with great rhetorical flourish. Viscount Sankey LC described the burden of proof always falls upon the prosecution as "the one golden thread always to be seen throughout the web of the English criminal law".[147] However, even then it was recognised that insanity was a common law exception, and that

---

[141] Cf. *M'Naghten* (1843) 10 Cl & F 200, 210, 8 ER 718, 722; *Woolmington* v. *DPP* [1935] AC 462, 475 (Viscount Sankey LC).

[142] For excellent discussion, see Jones, "Insanity, Automatism, and the Burden of Proof on the Accused" (1995) 111 *LQR* 475.

[143] Homicide Act 1957, s. 2(2). An unsuccessful challenge to the compatibility of this provision with Art. 6 was made in *Foye* [2013] EWCA Crim 475.

[144] *G* [2008] UKHL 37, [2009] 1 AC 92; *G* v. *UK* (2011) 53 EHRR SE25; *Salabiaku* v. *France* (1991) 13 EHRR 379.

[145] For discussion of whether the presumption of innocence does have necessary implications for the imposition of strict liability, see Ashworth, "Four Threats to the Presumption of Innocence" (2006) 10 *Evidence and Proof* 241; Sullivan, "Strict Liability for Criminal Offences in England and Wales following Incorporation into English Law of the European Convention on Human Rights" in Simester (ed.), *Appraising Strict Liability* (2005) 195; Tadros and Tierney, "The Presumption of Innocence and the Human Rights Act" (2004) 67 *MLR* 404, 422–4; and, *contra*, Roberts, "Strict Liability and the Presumption of Innocence: An Exposé of Functionalist Assumptions" in Simester (ed.), *Appraising Strict Liability* (2005) 151.

[146] Orchard, above n 113.

[147] See the quotation above, in the text, at § 3.2.

Parliament might legislate other exceptions, seemingly without limitation. Article 6(2) of the European Convention has not, to date, generated strict limits on the legislature's power to place legal burdens of proof (to the balance of probabilities) on defendants. On many occasions, the presumption of innocence has been ruled by the European Court and the English courts to be compatible with imposing a legal burden of proof on the defendant. There is a multitude of statutory provisions where legal burdens are placed, expressly or by implication, on the defendant. In an illuminating study published in 1996, Blake and Ashworth found that, in 40 per cent of offences triable before the Crown Court, a burden of proof on one or more issues was imposed on the defendant.[148] The authors discovered little that was systematic about the allocation of burdens of proof; it tended to be happenstance, with similar proof issues allocated differently under different statutes. There is no reason to suspect that the position has improved since then.

Still, the situation is not hopeless. The clear iteration of a presumption of innocence in Article 6(2), combined with decisions such as *Lambert* and the restrictive approach sometimes displayed by the ECHR to self-incrimination,[149] may one day prompt a better shielding of the presumption of innocence (even if not yet). It cannot be satisfactory, particularly for serious crimes, that D must prove facts crucial to the maintenance of her innocence. This objection is exacerbated by the unsystematic treatment, noted by Ashworth and Blake, of very similar exculpatory factors in different offences. Moreover, the random variation they describe is not just a matter of statutory stipulation. It is not uncommon, for example, for a defendant charged with murder to plead in the alternative the defences of loss of control and diminished responsibility. As we shall see,[150] as the law stands it may be very difficult to determine whether particular evidence will give rise to one or other of these defences; it may be too that the evidence will satisfy the differing criteria for each of these defences. But the burden of proof does not reflect these similarities. With loss of control, the evidence need only be *suggestive* of the defence: if it is, the prosecution (*à la Woolmington*) must negate the defence beyond reasonable doubt.[151] By contrast, the defendant has the onus of establishing the defence of diminished responsibility on the balance of probabilities.[152] Not only is this confusing for juries dealing with the same evidence under different heads of defence: it is unsustainable as a matter of principle.

---

[148] "The Presumption of Innocence in English Criminal Law" [1996] *Crim LR* 306.

[149] Above, § 3.2(i)(a).

[150] Below, §§ 10.5, 19.2.

[151] Coroners and Justice Act 2009, s. 54(5). The question of how much evidence is required to suggest loss of control has proved controversial: see, e.g., *Gurpinar and Kojo-Smith* [2015] EWCA Crim 178, [2015] 1 WLR 3442.

[152] Homicide Act 1957, s. 2(2).

4

THE ACTUS REUS

In Chapter 1 we discussed some of the reasons why a person cannot and should not be guilty of a crime unless both (a) he has caused or is otherwise responsible for the external event prohibited by law—the actus reus—and (b) he had the required mental state (as specified for the particular crime) with respect to that external event—the mens rea. If D kills V, she may have brought about the actus reus of murder, but it does not follow that she has committed any offence. When the doctor gives a painkiller to her patient, who turns out to be unknowably allergic to it, she may kill that patient: but it is an accident, and no criminal liability will follow. The mens rea is missing. Conversely, if she administers the drug intending it to kill him, and he dies of an unrelated heart attack, she does not murder him.[1] The actus reus is missing. In the next two chapters, we investigate the orthodox general principles of criminal law regarding these two elements. It is convenient to begin here with the actus reus.

For the purposes of identifying the constituent elements of an offence, it is conventional to identify the actus reus of a crime with that part of the definition which does not refer to the defendant's mental state.[2] The actus reus can usefully be divided into three types of ingredient: behaviour, consequences, and circumstances. Often the circumstances or consequences surrounding something the defendant does are relevant to her wrongdoing, and so the offence does not just turn on D's behaviour. It is an essential part of our concept of murder, for instance, that someone dies. Thus the victim's death—a consequence—is a constitutive part of the actus reus of murder. Such offences are sometimes called "result crimes",[3] because they cannot be committed unless the defendant's actions cause the specified result or consequence actually to occur.

An example of a crime requiring *circumstances* is bigamy, which involves D's going through a marriage ceremony (the behaviour) while being married to someone else (the circumstance). It is important to realise that, since specification of the actus reus of each offence differs, there is no requirement that all three types of ingredient be present in the actus reus of each offence. Hence the actus reus of murder—i.e. the killing of one person by another—requires that there be (i) some (unspecified) behaviour on the part of the defendant with (ii) the consequence that another person dies. By contrast, the actus reus of rape is made out if there is (i) behaviour (sexual intercourse) by the defendant with the victim,

---

[1] *White* [1910] 2 KB 124.

[2] This division of crimes into actus reus and mens rea elements is a helpful expository device but not an analytical necessity. Sometimes, moreover, it is not easy to divide a crime in this way. For instance, as we will see in § 5.6(iv), whether D is in "possession" of something may depend both on her physical conduct and on her understandings about that conduct.

[3] The term is from Gordon, *Criminal Law of Scotland* (2nd ed., 1978) 61.

in (ii) circumstances where the victim does not consent to it. No further consequence is necessary.

§ 4.1 The behaviour element

Normally, the actus reus doctrine requires an action of some sort: something *done* by the defendant. This is not always obvious. It might sometimes appear as though result crimes such as murder could be specified solely by reference to the consequence, and without the actus reus containing any behavioural element. Thus it is the outcome which is emphasised in Kenny's definition of actus reus: "such result of human conduct as the law seeks to prevent".[4] And consider, for instance, the crime of murder. Surely it is the result, death, which is central to that crime? V's death is the harmful result that, as Kenny puts it, the law seeks to prevent. Without that death, murder is not and cannot be committed. The relevant harm has not occurred.

But the view that it is only the consequence or result that matters is not quite right. The law is not concerned with deaths *per se*, but rather with deaths that other people and, exceptionally, companies and other organisations[5] bring about. The actus reus is causing death, not death itself. The result *is* important: it helps to mark out what type of wrongdoing the law is concerned with. Indeed, it is the nature of the result, rather than of the behaviour which causes it, that gives homicide its special moral and social significance. Murder is murder whether done by knife or poison, and this is why the behaviour element of the actus reus is unspecific. But it exists all the same.

On the other hand, it is possible for an actus reus to consist *only* of behaviour. This is especially true of inchoate crimes, such as encouraging or assisting another to commit a crime, where there is no requirement that the encouragement or assistance be effective.[6] Crimes of this type are sometimes termed "conduct crimes", since the actus reus requires proof only of specified conduct by the defendant and does not specify any particular circumstances or consequences.

(i) Behaviour and omissions

Where behaviour is an element of the actus reus, standard legal doctrine stipulates that the behaviour requirement is a requirement of positive action by the defendant. Except occasionally, an omission will not do. Thus it is a crime for D deliberately to drown V, but no crime for D gleefully to stand on the beach and watch while his enemy, V, is caught in the tide and drowns nearby.[7]

---

[4] Turner, *Kenny's Outlines of Criminal Law* (19th ed., 1965) 17.

[5] The Corporate Manslaughter and Homicide Act 2007 creates the offence of corporate manslaughter which only companies and some other organisations such as the NHS and the Prison Service can commit.

[6] Below, Chapter 9. Other examples include the offence of false accounting (contrary to s. 17 of the Theft Act 1968), the actus reus of which can be committed merely by omitting to disclose a material particular in a document: cf. *Lancaster* [2010] EWCA Crim 370.

[7] Cf. Stephen, *Digest of the Criminal Law* (4th ed., 1887) Art. 212. Other writing includes Hughes, "Criminal Omissions" (1958) 67 *Yale LJ* 590; Glazebrook, "Criminal Omissions: The Duty Requirement in Offences Against the Person" (1960) 76 *LQR* 386; Ashworth, "The Scope of Criminal Liability for Omissions" (1989) 105 *LQR* 424; Alexander, "Criminal Liability for Omissions: An Inventory of Issues" in Simester and Shute (eds.), *Criminal Law*

This standard doctrine in fact comprises two rules. First, behaviour specified in an actus reus can prima facie be satisfied only by a positive act on the part of the defendant, and not by the defendant's omission. Secondly, there are certain exceptions to the first, prima facie rule. These exceptions usually arise when the defendant has a *duty* to intervene and prevent the prohibited harm from occurring, whereupon his failure to do so counts as an omission satisfying the behavioural element of that actus reus. The first rule is general in nature: the exceptions, and the duties on which they are based, are specific and confined.

In the above approach the criminal law resembles the civil law, which is generally averse to imposing liability for omissions,[8] and is willing to do so only in special cases where the reasons in favour are strong enough to override that aversion. The distinction between misfeasance and non-feasance is deeply embedded in the common law. Civil law duties to intervene are dependent upon, for example, the defendant's having created the risk[9] or in some other way having assumed responsibility for it.[10] Similarly, an omission to reject a contractual offer cannot constitute its acceptance.[11] Silence is no representation in the tort of deceit;[12] neither is it *per se* a misrepresentation when negotiating a contract.[13]

(a) Why omissions are special

One might, of course, accept that the law often does distinguish between acts and omissions, but still ask why that distinction *should* make any practical difference to criminal liability. There are various reasons. One is based upon considerations of autonomy. We value living in a society where citizens are respected as individuals—where they are free to live their own lives and pursue their own priorities without having their choices determined by legal duties to act or intervene. The prohibition of omissions is far more intrusive upon individuals' autonomy and freedom than is the prohibition of acts, which is why the systematic imposition of (criminal or civil) liability for failures to act is to be resisted.[14]

Theory: Doctrines of the General Part (2000) 121; Ashworth, "Public Duties and Criminal Omissions: Some Unresolved Questions" [2011] *J Commonwealth Criminal Law* 1.

[8] *Per* Lord Keith in *Yuen Kun-Yeu* v. *A-G of Hong Kong* [1988] AC 175, 192, there is no liability in negligence "on the part of one who sees another about to walk over a cliff with his head in the air, and forbears to shout a warning". Cf. *Ancell* v. *McDermott* [1993] 4 All ER 355; *Alexandrou* v. *Oxford* [1993] 4 All ER 328; *Hill* v. *Chief Constable of West Yorkshire* [1989] AC 53; *Curran* v. *Northern Ireland Housing Association Ltd* [1987] AC 718; *East Suffolk Catchment Board* v. *Kent* [1941] AC 74; *Gautret* v. *Egerton* (1867) LR 2 CP 371, 375.

[9] *Johnson* v. *Rea* [1961] 1 WLR 1400.

[10] E.g. *Dorset Yacht Co* v. *Home Office* [1970] AC 1004; *Barnett* v. *Chelsea and Kensington Hospital Management Committee* [1969] 1 QB 428.

[11] *Felthouse* v. *Bindley* (1862) 11 CB (NS) 869, 142 ER 1037; cf. *The Leonidas* [1985] 2 All ER 796; *The Santa Clara* [1995] 3 All ER 971.

[12] *Peek* v. *Gurney* (1873) LR 6 HL 377, 392, 403; *Arkwright* v. *Newbold* (1881) 17 Ch D 301, 318; *Banque Keyser Ullman* v. *Skandia* [1990] 1 QB 665.

[13] *Fox* v. *Mackreth* (1788) 2 Cox Eq Cas 320, 321; *Keates* v. *Lord Cadogan* (1851) 10 CB 591, 138 ER 234; *Bell* v. *Lever Bros Ltd* [1932] AC 161, 227.

[14] See, very generally, Simester, "Why Omissions Are Special" (1995) 1 *Legal Theory* 311; also the earlier discussion in §§ 1.2(i)(b), 1.2(ii)(e). There is philosophical controversy whether the act–omission distinction, of and by itself, is morally significant. Nonetheless, it is worth observing that acts usually manifest a greater level of hostility than do omissions, and we tend to feel very differently about killers than about non-savers. Omissions are often incidental to the defendant's practical deliberations—they disclose a different and lesser fault, of limited imagination or empathy, rather than malice.

This is not to suggest that there should never be liability for omissions. Those writers who advocate a criminal law duty of easy rescue, for example, have at least an arguable case.[15] Rather, the present argument is that liability for omissions should be exceptional, and not as widespread as liability for actions. At any moment in time, the number of positive actions we are doing is very small. But the number of things we are failing to do is enormous. This is because there are very few ways in which one can do an action, whereas the number of ways in which one can fail to do something is much greater. For example, while D is not saving the drowning swimmer she may be walking, reading a book, swimming herself, playing cricket, etc. But she is unlikely to be able to do these things while she *is* saving the swimmer. The burden the law imposes when it prohibits a person from doing something is therefore lighter and less intrusive than when it orders that person to act. Enforced forbearance involves the sacrifice of fewer options, and is more likely to leave the defendant with a chance of conforming to law without significant disruption. "Compare being banished to Liechtenstein with being banished from Liechtenstein."[16] Or, in a more apposite example, compare being prohibited from drowning the other swimmers when sunbathing at a beach to being required to save (or, indeed, drown) them. Wholesale liability for omissions would force us constantly to interrupt our own actions and plans in order to prevent outcomes that are brought about by others: to become, in effect, our brothers' keepers. It would be incompatible with a country's ambition to be a liberal State.

A second consideration is that if prohibited omissions involve the sacrifice of more options, then they are also likely to require a greater sacrifice of our own interests. If D buys a piece of furniture for his home, why is he not held responsible for the lives that money would save in, say, Ethiopia? One factor is our widespread acceptance that people are to some extent entitled to prefer their own interests, and the interests of those near to them, above the interests of others. A mother who gives her own child pocket-money warrants no reproof when she does not do the same for the child next door. Of course, such a view may be no more than a moral mistake. But if so, it is an inescapable feature of our society, and the law must bow to its almost universal acceptance. Moreover, given that individuals exist in different and specific situations, they are typically better placed to assess and contribute to their own lives, and to the lives of those they know, than to the lives of strangers. These points help to explain examples where someone does not save starving children in foreign countries: they limit the extent to which the needs of strangers take precedence over and mandate the sacrifice of our own plans and interests. We cannot do everything, and it would be absurd to expect us to try. When we make decisions, we are entitled to acknowledge that our own lives, and the lives of people we are close to, are important to us. So, even apart from questions of autonomy, the law's presumption against penalising omissions can be justified as a simple and workable means by which the law can recognise the priority individuals are entitled to accord to the conduct of their own lives.

---

[15] See, especially, Ashworth, *Positive Obligations in Criminal Law* (2013).

[16] Bennett, "Morality and Consequences" in McMurrin (ed.), *The Tanner Lectures in Human Values* (1981) 47, 78; cf. Bennett, *The Act Itself* (1995) 92. A similar principle applies in the context of false imprisonment: *Bird* v. *Jones* (1845) 7 QB 742.

(b) The exceptions

Case 1: Specific statutory and common law offences.
Many statutes now contain offences which expressly impose liability for an omission.[17] Often these are offences which can *only* be committed by omission, such as failing to provide a breath specimen,[18] or failing to file an annual return as required by the Companies Act 2006. Similarly, section 1(2)(a) of the Children and Young Persons Act 1933 requires persons to supply legally dependent children with adequate food, clothing, medical aid, and lodging; an offence is committed when D fails to discharge that duty. The common law also knows some, though very few, offences specifically of omission. Perhaps the most significant of these is the refusal to assist a police officer when called upon to aid in restoring the peace.[19]

The above offences involve specific reference to a behavioural element on the part of the defendant. A second variety of statutory crime which can be done, indirectly, by omission is that where the actus reus names no behavioural element at all, and requires only proof of certain events or circumstances. (This type of offence is discussed below, in § 4.1(b).) Characteristically, offences of the latter sort are an indirect imposition of liability for D's omission to prevent the specified event or outcome occurring. Of course, in these cases liability will also lie for bringing the outcome about by a positive act. But no such act is *required*.

It merits emphasis that, where an offence criminalises D's omission to prevent something, the courts generally import a requirement that the defendant had the ability or power to stop the relevant outcome from occurring.[20] This kind of restriction, which is grounded in the broader requirement of voluntariness, will be considered further in § 4.3(ii).

Case 2: Duties imposed on persons in a special relationship to the victim.
Sometimes, even without a specific offence, the law holds that considerations such as autonomy and self-interest are outweighed. This occurs when the defendant is found to be under a more general legal duty, such as the duty of parents to their children. A stranger can stand by and watch a child starve or drown. But that child's parent cannot.

The law does not normally require us to be guardians of the interests of others. But parents already *are* the guardians of their children, and are responsible for their welfare. The law does no more than reflect that by imposing a legal duty upon parents to intervene on behalf of their children. To some extent these duties now have parallels in statute: we noted in the last section that the Children and Young Persons Act 1933 requires legally dependent children to be supplied with adequate food and other necessaries. However, that Act merely creates a particular and confined offence. The common law duties of parents are wider ranging than this, and prima facie apply to any offence (unless excluded: below, § 4.1(i)(c)).

---

[17] Even in the context of homicide: s. 5(1) of the Domestic Violence, Crime and Victims Act 2004 (causing or allowing the death of a child or vulnerable adult).

[18] Contrary to s. 6 of the Road Traffic Act 1988. Cf. *Raymond Parry* v. *Department for Work and Pensions* [2005] EWHC 1486 (Admin) (failing to disclose employment when in receipt of an incapacity benefit).

[19] *Brown* (1841) Car & M 314, 174 ER 522; Nicholson, "The Citizen's Duty to Assist the Police" [1992] *Crim LR* 611. It is also a common law offence of misconduct in a public office for a police constable to refuse to perform his duty to preserve the Queen's peace: *Dytham* [1979] QB 722; *A-G's Reference (No. 3 of 2003)* [2004] EWCA Crim 868, [2005] QB 73.

[20] See, e.g., *Tilley* [2009] EWCA Crim 1426, paras. 37–9; citing *Crabtree* v. *Fern Spinning Co. Limited* (1901) 85 LT 549, 552 (in the context of "allowing").

Thus a parent's failure to effect an easy rescue of her child would count as the actus reus of murder even though it is scarcely a failure to supply necessaries.[21] And more generally, it is submitted that a parent who willingly permits another to assault his child (when he can prevent this happening) is himself guilty of an assault.[22]

So a parent has a duty to rescue his child from harm. But is this so if the child is 30? Where the child is no longer dependent upon her parents, a special relationship still exists between them, but it no longer involves the same commitment to responsibility for the child's welfare.[23] The latter is surely the more important feature. In the old cases governing the relationship of master to apprentice, the duty of care is said to arise from the master's assumption of responsibility and the apprentice's dependence, so that it was necessary to allege the apprentice was of tender years: "[t]here is a clear distinction between treatment of this sort to a child and to an adult".[24] Similarly, it is submitted, parents do not ordinarily owe legal duties to rescue their adult children.[25] Neither do children owe such duties to their parents.[26] This is not to deny that people have moral obligations to their relatives. But it is quite a different matter to hold them criminally liable for failing to discharge those obligations.

The view that, rather than the closeness of their emotional or other relationship, it is D's responsibility for V's welfare that is the decisive feature is consistent with the case law regarding legal duties owed toward someone who is in the defendant's care. In *Stone and Dobinson*,[27] S and his mistress D (both of limited understanding) were held to have assumed responsibility for the care of S's sister when allowing her to lodge with them and making some efforts to assist her while she stayed with them. The sister died from a combination of anorexia nervosa and their incompetent neglect. *Both* were convicted of manslaughter, irrespective of the fact that only S was related to V.[28] The family relationship did not of

[21] *Handley* (1874) 13 Cox CC 79; *White* (1871) 12 Cox CC 83, 86 (Blackburn J).

[22] Cf. *Emery* (1993) 14 Cr App R (S) 394 (cruelty); *Russell* [1933] VLR 59 (manslaughter); *Commonwealth* v. *Howard* 402 A 2d 674 (1979) (manslaughter). On the particular question whether assault can be committed by omission, see also the discussion below, § 4.1(i)(c). The parent would in any case be guilty as a secondary party: below, § 7.4(iii).

[23] Compare s. 1 of the Children and Young Persons Act 1933, the application of which terminates when the child reaches the age of 16 years.

[24] *Ridley* (1811) 2 Camp 650, 652, 170 ER 1282, 1283; *Friend* (1802) Russ & Ry 20, 168 ER 662. See also *Charlotte Smith* (1865) 10 Cox CC 82 (servant).

[25] *Smith* (1826) 2 C & P 449, 172 ER 203; *Shepherd* (1862) 9 Cox CC 123; *contra Chattaway* (1922) 17 Cr App R 7.

[26] Nor do adult children owe such duties to their half-sisters, even if living in the same house and where the half-sister is a minor: *Evans* [2009] EWCA Crim 650, [2009] 1 WLR 1999. However, courts may be astute in circumstances such as *Evans* (which involved drug taking and a drug-related death in the family home) to find a duty of care on other grounds. The half-sister was found guilty of manslaughter of her sibling: see further Case 5 below, and § 10.6(ii)(a).

[27] [1977] QB 354. Arguably, the Court's finding of an assumed responsibility was doubtful on the facts; see Ashworth, "The Scope of Criminal Liability for Omissions" (1989) 105 *LQR* 424, 443. Strikingly, the ineffectual efforts of the defendants to help V played the dual role of establishing a duty of care and providing evidence of its breach. The case is also unsatisfactory on the question of causation: did the neglect make any difference? Whether V, a person with an extreme eating disorder, could have been helped by anyone was a matter not addressed. Additionally, it is problematic on the question of gross negligence (given the couple's intellectual limitations—compare the discussion of *Elliott* v. *C* [1983] 2 All ER 1005, below, § 5.5(ii)). See also Ashworth, "Public Duties and Criminal Omissions: Some Unresolved Questions" [2011] *J Commonwealth Criminal Law* 1, 6–13.

[28] Cf. *R.* v. *West London Coroner, ex p. Gray* [1987] 2 All ER 129; *Condé* (1867) 10 Cox 547; *Instan* [1893] 1 QB 450; *Marriott* (1838) 8 C & P 425, 173 ER 559; *Nicholls* (1874) 13 Cox CC 75; *Bubb* (1841) 4 Cox CC 455.

itself impose any duties upon them; they were not obliged to let her stay with them nor to offer any other form of help. What mattered is that they voluntarily assumed a duty of care toward her.

Also consistent is *Smith*,[29] in which the Court of Appeal assumed that the institution of marriage does not itself generate a duty of care between spouses, although an assumption of responsibility for the welfare of one's spouse or partner will readily be inferred, particularly where the parties are cohabiting.[30] If this is right,[31] the Australian decision of *Russell* would not be followed here: R's estranged wife had drowned herself and their sons while R was present, whereupon R was convicted of the manslaughter not only of the sons but also of the wife.[32] By implication, a mutual obligation to protect would not extend to the partners in a merely casual sexual relationship.[33]

Case 3: Duties imposed on persons assuming a particular responsibility.
The cases discussed so far have been concerned with duties arising from a wide-ranging and unspecific responsibility for another's welfare. Such duties tend to be general in nature, with the result that the criminal law treats omissions like actions for most purposes. A more complex relationship is that between a doctor and her patient.[34] This duty is a confined one—a doctor on her way home may drive past the scene of an accident without attracting criminal liability for doing so. The duty applies only to the patients in her care. In such cases, injury resulting from the doctor's failure to provide proper care is regarded by the criminal law just as if it were brought about by an act of improper treatment.

Even to her patients, however, the doctor's duty is not all-encompassing. She may not kill by positive act, but it appears that she may withdraw care, with judicial approval, from a patient in a persistent vegetative state.[35] The duty is not to keep the patient alive, but to make reasonable efforts to do so, consonant with proper medical practice,[36] and only in so far as doing so is in the patient's best interests.[37]

See Williams, "Criminal Omissions—The Conventional View" (1991) 107 *LQR* 86, 90. A valuable and wide-ranging discussion may be found in the Australian case of *Taktak* (1988) 14 NSWLR 226.

[29] [1979] Crim LR 251. This decision throws doubt on the assertion made by Horder and McGowan, "Manslaughter by Causing Another's Suicide" [2006] *Crim LR* 1035, 1044, that "[t]here is no doubt that a duty of care exists between spouses". The authors cite the case of *Hood* [2003] EWCA Crim 2772, which in our view illustrates that an assumption of a duty of care between spouses will be readily inferred but not that a duty of care arises from marital status *per se*.

[30] E.g. where D is the sole carer for his disabled wife, as in *Hood* [2003] EWCA Crim 2772, [2004] 1 Cr App R (S) 73.

[31] *Contra Plummer* (1844) 1 C & K 600, 174 ER 954 (estranged spouse).

[32] [1933] VLR 59 (McArthur J dissenting).

[33] Cf. *People* v. *Beardsley* 113 NW 1128 (1907); discussed by Hughes, "Criminal Omissions" (1958) 67 *Yale LJ* 590, 624. See also *Lewis* v. *CPS* [2002] EWHC Crim 1049, where the Court upheld a refusal to prosecute after D left his intoxicated friend asleep in an unlocked car during a very hot day, with the result that the friend died.

[34] For another example of role-based responsibility, see *Curtis* (1885) 15 Cox CC 746 (duty of a local authority officer to provide medical assistance to a destitute person).

[35] *Airedale NHS Trust* v. *Bland* [1993] AC 789. See also the note by Finnis, "*Bland*: Crossing the Rubicon?" (1993) 109 *LQR* 329.

[36] Cf. *TBCL* 236.

[37] *Airedale NHS Trust* v. *Bland* [1993] AC 789, 868–9 (Lord Goff); *R (Burke)* v. *GMC* [2004] EWHC 1879 (Admin). See also the difficult cases involving the degree of care owed by doctors to handicapped neonates: *Arthur* (1981) 12 B Med LR 1; *Re B* (1981) [1990] 3 All ER 927; *Re F* [1990] 2 AC 1.

Another source of specific criminal law duties is civil law obligations. The classic case is *Pittwood*.[38] D had been employed by a railway company to keep the gate at a level crossing. He went to lunch forgetting to close the gate. A haycart subsequently entered the crossing and was struck by a train. D was convicted of manslaughter. It is not clear whether D's duty depended upon his having been hired to discharge a duty to the public that was owed by his employers,[39] or was grounded on the fact that he was hired to protect other people and that they were likely to be injured by his dereliction. The latter seems to have been the rationale adopted by Wright J,[40] but there is reason to support the former view. Consider a hypothetical case in which D, a nurse, has signed a contract that contains a term requiring her to intervene and save people at large—that is, even when off duty and away from the hospital. In such a case, D's failure to rescue someone when at the beach may be a breach of contract, but surely would not be a criminal offence.

Case 4: The continuing act doctrine.
Sometimes a defendant brings about an actus reus without mens rea but then, while the harmful consequences continue, intentionally omits to remedy or discontinue them. In such cases the "continuing act" doctrine may be applied, and liability imposed without the need to find a legal duty owed by the defendant.[41] In *Fagan* v. *Metropolitan Police Commissioner*,[42] F accidentally drove onto a policeman's foot. When apprised of his action, he refused to move the car. He was convicted of assault on the basis that his refusal to remove the vehicle amounted to a continuation of the original (positive) act of battery,[43] and was not a mere omission. Hence it could satisfy the actus reus requirement.

A similar case is *Kaitamaki*.[44] D had sexual intercourse with V without her consent. D's evidence was that he became aware V was not consenting only after penetration had occurred. However, he did not then withdraw from intercourse. The trial judge directed the jury that "if, having realised she is not willing, he continues with the act of intercourse, it then becomes rape". On appeal, the correctness of the direction was affirmed by the Privy Council.

Case 5: Duties imposed on persons with a special relationship to the harm.
In *Miller*,[45] a trespasser set fire to his mattress with a cigarette while sleeping. He awoke to find the mattress smouldering. Without taking any steps to extinguish the fire, he simply

---

[38] (1902) 19 TLR 37. See also *Hughes* (1857) Dears & B 248, 169 ER 996; approved in *Roberts* [1942] 1 All ER 187, 192; *Kelly* v. *The King* [1923] VLR 704, 708 (reversed on a different ground in 32 CLR 509).

[39] Compare *Smith* (1869) 11 Cox CC 210, where a watchman who deserted his post was held not liable for manslaughter because his employer has no duty to provide a watchman; also *Singh (Gurphal)* [1999] Crim LR 582 where D, who was in charge of a lodging house while the landlord was away, was held to owe a duty of care to the tenant such that both D and the landlord were guilty of manslaughter when a faulty gas fire caused the tenant's death by carbon monoxide poisoning. The decision in *Smith* is criticised by J.W.C. Turner in Kenny's *Outlines of Criminal Law* (17th ed., 1958) 169.

[40] "The man was paid to keep the gate shut and protect the public…. A man might incur criminal liability from a duty arising out of contract": (1902) 19 TLR 37, 38.

[41] Compare, in contract, the law governing a representation which later becomes false but where the change of circumstances is not disclosed: *With* v. *O'Flanagan* [1936] Ch 575 ("continuing representation").

[42] [1969] 1 QB 439.

[43] Which had not itself been an assault because F lacked mens rea at that time.

[44] [1985] AC 147. See also *Cooper and Schaub* [1994] Crim LR 531.

[45] [1983] 2 AC 161; see J.C. Smith [1982] *Crim LR* 526; Williams (letter to the editor) [1982] *Crim LR* 773.

moved to the next room and went to sleep. The house itself caught fire, and he was charged with arson. Although the Court of Appeal upheld his conviction on the basis of a continuing act, the House of Lords took a different approach. It acknowledged that the arson had been committed by M's knowing omission to deal with the fire, and held that this omission could satisfy the actus reus requirement because M's unintentional starting of the fire *created* a legal duty. The duty is "to take measures that lie within one's power to counteract a danger that one has oneself created".[46] The relevant sorts of "danger" are those which threaten an interest protected by the criminal law—thus the duty arises where, unless D intervenes, his earlier (positive) act will bring about the prohibited harm.[47]

Note that a defendant's subsequent failure to prevent the risk will not by itself constitute an offence—it must be accompanied by such other elements of the offence as are required, e.g. mens rea. Neither does *Miller* generate any duty to undo a crime that has already occurred;[48] merely to intercept the self-created risk of a harm that lies in the future.

It is important to distinguish the basis of liability in *Miller* from the continuing act doctrine (above). The approach taken in *Miller* is generally to be preferred, and indeed *Fagan* can itself be explained as a case where D created the harm and therefore had a duty to counteract that harm.[49] Nonetheless, it is sometimes necessary to rely on the continuing act doctrine. Because *Miller* imposes liability for an omission, it is inapplicable to those offences that cannot be committed by omission,[50] i.e. where the terms of the offence exclude liability for omissions. Offences of this type are the subject of the next section.

The doctrine in *Miller* is based on D's own causation of the actus reus, and it should be restricted to that basis. Even so, the Court of Appeal has sought—dubiously—to expand the scope of the *Miller* duty. In *Evans*,[51] D, the half-sister of V, lived together with their mother. D bought heroin for V, who injected herself with it and became ill. D and her mother decided not to seek medical help for fear that they may all "get into trouble". V subsequently died. On these facts, D's conviction for manslaughter was upheld on the basis of her (grossly negligent) failure to aid V once she became ill.

The extension from *Miller* is as follows.[52] In *Miller*, D had caused ("created") the risk which he later failed to abate. In *Evans*, D did not *cause* the risk: as the House of Lords has

---

[46] [1983] 2 AC 161, 176.

[47] Compare also *Santana-Bermudez* [2003] EWHC 2908 (Admin), [2004] Crim LR 471. (D lied to a police officer, before being searched, that there were no needles on him. During the search, the officer was pricked by a needle in D's pocket; a risk that D had created.) For an extension of this type of case see *Speck* [1977] 2 All ER 859, in which D was convicted of gross indecency because he passively allowed an 8-year-old girl to touch him indecently.

[48] This is the explanation of *Ahmad* (1987) 84 Cr App R 64.

[49] Where necessary, however, the two cases can be distinguished, since (unlike *Miller*) in *Fagan* the actus reus had already occurred by the time D acquired *mens rea*.

[50] Indeed, this restriction was considered in *Fagan* [1969] 1 QB 439, 444 itself to apply to the offence of assault: "a mere omission to act cannot amount to an assault". See also § 4.1(i)(c) below; also § 11.2(i)(b). Surprisingly, this point was not considered in *Santana-Bermudez* [2003] EWHC 2908 (Admin), [2004] Crim LR 471.

[51] [2009] EWCA Crim 650, [2009] 1 WLR 1999; discussed by Williams, "Gross Negligence Manslaughter and Duty of Care in 'Drugs' Cases: R. v Evans" [2009] *Crim LR* 631.

[52] There is one other difference: recklessness toward the risk (at that time interpreted as *Caldwell* recklessness) was required of D in *Miller*, whereas in *Evans* the Court held that the application of the duty requires only that D ought to have been aware of the risk. However, this difference is not part of the *Miller* doctrine itself. It is explained by the different mens rea requirements of the offences charged: arson requires proof of recklessness, whereas gross negligence suffices for manslaughter.

made abundantly clear,[53] causal responsibility lay with V herself, when she freely and deliberately injected herself with the heroin that D supplied. According to the Court of Appeal,
however, Miller-type duties can now arise "when a person has created *or contributed* to the
creation of a state of affairs ...".[54]

The extension should be doubted. What kind of non-causal contribution to the danger
is required? What about another person, E, who may introduce D (or V) to the heroin
dealer? Or F, who lends money to buy the drugs? What about a vendor of alcohol, when he
sees the buyer in a drunken altercation? Or a driver who leaves his intoxicated friend sleeping in the car on a hot day, never to awake?[55] All kinds of background acts of facilitation
could now underpin potential criminal-law duties. Part of the point of causation doctrines,
which we will consider in § 4.2, is to restrict the ambit of criminal responsibility when
things go wrong. *Evans* is a plain attempt to evade the scope of those doctrines. In our view,
it represents an illegitimate extension of the otherwise sound principle in *Miller*. It is to be
hoped that the decision in *Evans* will, *at most*, be confined to cases where D has materially
contributed to and then intentionally failed to prevent the consequences of a risk arising
from intervention by the victim.[56] This revised version of the *Miller* doctrine is no more
than a device to evade the problem that arises when D helps P to inflict *self*-harm rather
than harm to a third person. Because self-harm is not generally a crime, secondary liability
usually does not apply and D cannot be convicted of complicity in P's offence.[57] But general
principles of responsibility should not be invented on an *ad hoc* basis to deal with specific
problems such as this.

(c) Statutory restrictions: offences that cannot be committed by omission

Some offences exclude liability for omissions by specifying the particular type of behaviour
that is required. For example, section 32 of the OAPA 1861 makes it an offence (*inter alia*) to
"put or throw" objects onto a railway. It would seem that this manner of behaving can only
be done by a positive act. Similarly, the actus reus of rape requires active sexual intercourse
with, including penetration of, the victim; an omission cannot suffice.[58]

In these offences, liability for omissions is restricted because the behavioural element
of the actus reus has been specified quite precisely by statute. Conversely, omission-based
liability should normally be possible where an offence has an unspecific behaviour element,
and its actus reus is defined mainly by reference to consequences or circumstances. An
example of this is murder, for which, in essence, the actus reus requires the causing of one
person's death by another.[59]

---

[53] *Kennedy (No. 2)* [2007] UKHL 38, [2008] 1 AC 269; below, § 4.2(iii)(b) (Principle 1).

[54] [2009] EWCA Crim 650, [2009] 1 WLR 1999, para. 31.

[55] Cf. *Lewin v. CPS* [2002] EWHC Crim 1049, where the decision not to prosecute was upheld: "the young man
who was left in the unlocked car was an adult, not a small child or dog" (para. 24).

[56] Note that it must *also* be proved that the subsequent omission to intervene was a cause of death, in that, but
for D's omission, V would not have died: below, § 4.1(i)(d). This point was not discussed at all by the Court of
Appeal in *Evans* [2009] EWCA Crim 650, [2009] 1 WLR 1999.

[57] Below, Chapter 7, esp. § 7.6(i).

[58] Sections 1, 44 Sexual Offences Act 1956. See also the offence of throwing missiles, contrary to the Football
(Offences) Act 1991, s. 2.

[59] Cf. *Dyson* [1908] 2 KB 454, 457; below, Chapter 10.

Homicide is a clear case. It is settled law that culpable homicide can be committed by omission.[60] But what about other offences? An assault by battery, for example, requires *inter alia* the unlawful application of force to another person.[61] Can this be done by omission? The traditional view is no,[62] but there is contradictory authority on the matter.[63] Consider the following example proposed by Smith and Hogan:[64]

> "It is generally said that D must have done some act and that it is not enough that he stood still and obstructed V's passage like an inanimate object. But suppose D is sitting at the corner of a corridor with his legs stretched across it. He hears V running down the corridor and deliberately remains still with the intention that V, on turning the corner, shall fall over his legs. Why should this not be a battery? It would be if D had put out his legs with the intention of tripping up V."

Glanville Williams, however, was doubtful. In his view, the example put by Smith and Hogan:[65]

> "is a case of special type. The man presumably committed an act when he put his foot there in the first place, though initially it was without wrongful intent. When he later failed to remove his foot, with the requisite mental element, he became guilty of an assault under the rule [in *Miller*]."[66]

According to Williams, assault cannot be committed by a pure omission:[67]

> "if a person merely stands stock still, being 'entirely passive like a door or a wall' as it was put in one case, it is not an assault, however inconvenient his presence at that particular spot may have been…."

With respect to Williams, the example cannot be analysed as a *Miller*-type situation, unless P was already running down the corridor when D (without mens rea) stretched out his legs. The case proposed by Smith and Hogan should not normally be a battery. However, this is not, *contra* Williams, because assault cannot be committed by omission. Rather, it is for the reasons given earlier, in § 4.1(i): that a stranger generally does not owe duties to act. By contrast, consider a case where the duty *is* owed. It seems implausible to say that a parent who intentionally trips his child in the way Smith and Hogan describe cannot be convicted of assault. He certainly ought to be. It is submitted that where an offence is unspecific as to the manner of behaviour required, it should be possible to commit that offence by omission. The mere fact that an offence is defined in terms of "action", as such, should not be determinative.[68] This is especially since positive action is the default requirement of offences with a behavioural element anyway—the entire sphere of omissions liability is predicated on an exception from that requirement.

---

[60] Cf. *Gibbins and Proctor* (1918) 13 Cr App R 134.
[61] Below, Chapter 11.
[62] *Fagan* [1969] 1 QB 439, 444.
[63] *Santana-Bermudez* [2003] EWHC 2908 (Admin), [2004] Crim LR 471; *Speck* [1977] 2 All ER 859.
[64] *Smith and Hogan* § 17.1.5.
[65] "What Should the Code Do about Omissions?" (1987) 7 *LS* 92, 116.
[66] See above, § 4.1(i)(b) (Case 5).
[67] *TBCL*, 179; citing *Innes* v. *Wylie* (1844) 1 C & K 257, 263, 174 ER 800, 803 (Lord Denman CJ).
[68] *Speck* [1977] 2 All ER 859. Although it sometimes is: *Ahmad* (1986) 84 Cr App R 64 (in the context of the Protection from Eviction Act 1977).

Sometimes, as we have seen, the action requirement *is* excluded by linguistic considerations. It would be unfair to convict a defendant for conduct the statutory language clearly excludes.[69] But such instances are and should be rare. There is no judicial compunction about saying that a parent can kill a child by failing to feed it,[70] and it is submitted that linguistic conventions unreflective of valid moral principles or distinctions should normally not pre-empt the possibility of liability for omissions.

If such harms as "killing", "obstructing",[71] "harassing",[72] cheating,[73] and "falsely imprisoning"[74] can be done by omission, and if the difference between various offences over whether one can be convicted for an omission is not to be arbitrary and piecemeal, then a coherent general approach should be taken. Unless the legislature has demonstrated a contrary intention by specifying the particular manner of behaviour in which the offence must be committed, a criminal offence should be capable of being committed by omission. This is the only approach capable of producing predictable and consistent rather than random law. Any concern over the width of that approach should be tempered by the knowledge that the defendant would have to be under a legal duty to act, and that mens rea would still have to be proved.[75]

As was noted in the previous section, even if omission-based liability is excluded by the terms of the offence, a conviction may still be obtained under the continuing act doctrine (above). Suppose that D and V are having consensual sexual intercourse, and that sexual connection has already occurred. During intercourse, V withdraws her consent. D, however, remains in a state of sexual connection with V. His failure to withdraw is a continuation of the original act of having sexual intercourse with V. Since it is no longer consensual, he commits the actus reus of rape.[76]

(d) Omissions and consequences: causation

One problem that arises for omissions is whether or not they can be said to "cause" things. Characteristically, what is significant about omissions is that they fail to prevent *other* factors from bringing about the harm. If D watches from the beach while V drowns, a post mortem will conclude that V's death was caused by drowning. D merely failed to intervene: can she truly be said to have caused V's death? We shall consider this question more fully in § 4.2(iv), when we discuss causation. But it is clear that in the law omissions can be causes. If D could have saved V (and we must be sure of that beyond reasonable doubt), then her

---

[69] See the fair warning discussion in § 2.3. For this reason, Williams argues in a letter to the editor of the *Criminal Law Review* that "the courts should not create liability for omissions without statutory authority. Verbs used in defining offences and prima facie implying active conduct should not be stretched by interpretation to include omissions": [1982] *Crim LR* 773. See also his "Criminal Omissions—The Conventional View" (1991) 107 *LQR* 86, 87–9; "What should the Code do about Omissions?" (1987) 7 *LS* 92, 94–5.

[70] And for other examples, see *Shama* [1990] 2 All ER 602; *Firth* (1990) 91 Cr App R 217.

[71] *Stunt v. Bolton* [1972] RTR 435; *Gully v. Smith* (1883) 12 QBD 121.

[72] *Yuthiwattana* (1984) 80 Cr App R 55.

[73] *Mavji* [1987] 2 All ER 758; *Tonner* [1985] 1 All ER 807.

[74] *TBCL* 179; *Smith and Hogan* 571.

[75] The requirement for mens rea, in particular, seems to meet Williams's concern that "it would be unfair to describe a slack and ineffective tenant who lets the premises burn as an arsonist": *TBCL* 152.

[76] *Kaitamaki* [1985] AC 147; *Cooper and Schaub* [1994] Crim LR 531. These decisions are now entrenched in legislation by s. 79(2) of the Sexual Offences Act 2003.

failure to do so was *a* reason why V drowned. And if D had a legal duty to save her, then that failure will be a cause of death in law.

(e) Distinguishing acts from omissions

Given that, as we have seen, there is normally no liability for omissions, it is important to be able to distinguish acts from omissions in order to decide whether a defendant's behaviour counts as one or the other. Unfortunately, the line between them is not easily drawn:[77]

> "If a doctor is keeping a patient alive by cranking the handle of a machine and he stops, this looks like a clear case of omission. So too, if the machine is electrically operated but switches itself off every 24 hours and the doctor deliberately does not restart it. Switching off a functioning machine looks like an act; but is it any different in substance from the first two cases? On the other hand, is it any different from cutting the high-wire on which a tight-rope walker is balancing (which is an act, if ever there was one)? Is the ending of a programme of dialysis an omission, while switching off a ventilator is an act? Is the discontinuance of a drip feed, which is keeping a patient alive, by withdrawing the tube from his body an act and failure to replace an emptied bag an omission? In theory, it might be possible to distinguish between these cases, but it seems offensive if liability for homicide is so heavily dependent on such very fine distinctions of this kind; but it appears to be so."

Why is switching off a ventilator an act, and failing to (re)start it an omission? The difference seems to be that the former *requires* certain bodily movements, whereas the latter does not. Switching the ventilator off can be done in only one way,[78] but failing to switch the ventilator on (or off) can be done while doing any number of things—one might be talking to the nurse, reading a journal, taking a walk, booking dinner at a restaurant, etc. Similarly, cranking the handle of a machine and cutting the high-wire are actions because they require very specific behaviour by D: "not cranking the handle" and "not replacing the emptied bag" are not specific about D's behaviour at all.

As we saw earlier, this difference is an important facet of the rationale for separating omissions from acts when it comes to criminalisation. Prohibiting omissions rules out many more options than does prohibiting acts. If D is enjoined by law not to strike V, that leaves him with plenty of freedom for legal movement of his arm, not to mention the rest of his body. But if D is *required* to strike V (i.e. prohibited from omitting to do so) then his freedom of movement is severely curtailed. His options are down to one.

The difference is legally irrelevant, however, where the defendant is held responsible for the actus reus through the existence of a legal duty. With this in mind, we should reconsider Smith and Hogan's remark that "it seems offensive if liability for homicide depends on such very fine distinctions of this kind; but it appears to be so". The obvious response is that liability does not *just* depend on the act/omission distinction, but also on the issue in each case whether D is under a duty to intervene. What the examples do suggest, though, is that one might be doubtful of the judicial reasoning in life-and-death medical cases. In *Airedale*

---

[77] *Smith and Hogan* § 4.4.2.4. See, in respect of the examples, Williams, *TBCL* 236–7; Kennedy, "Switching Off Life Support Machines: The Legal Implications" [1977] *Crim LR* 443; Beynon, "Doctors as Murderers" [1982] *Crim LR* 17. A helpful overview of academic discussion in this area is McGee, "Finding a Way Through the Ethical and Legal Maze: Withdrawal of Medical Treatment and Euthanasia" [2005] *Medical LR* 357.

[78] Or, at most, in only a few ways.

NHS Trust v. *Bland*,[79] B had been in a persistent vegetative state for 3½ years without medical hope of improvement. Having obtained parental consent, the hospital applied for a declaration that it would be lawful to discontinue artificial feeding and hydration, with the intention that B should be allowed to die. The House of Lords upheld the declaration. Their Lordships affirmed that for the doctors to bring about B's death by lethal injection or suchlike would be murder,[80] but reasoned that (i) what was proposed was an omission rather than an act, and (ii) the legal duty of the doctors did not extend to prolonging treatment of a patient when it was no longer in his best interests to do so.[81]

The difficulty with this reasoning is that ceasing treatment normally involves switching off a ventilator or other life-support machine. Notwithstanding that the House of Lords explicitly countenanced this step,[82] it is an act, not an omission. An intruder who does such a thing commits murder, even though she has no legal duty to save the patient's life. The true explanation of these cases must surely be that there is a limited justification available to doctors, in certain circumstances, to take some quite specific measures toward ending life. Those measures can include particular acts as well as omissions; although the permissible scope of such measures remains, of course, a matter of intense and shifting ethical debate.[83]

(ii) Crimes with no (explicit) behaviour element

Some academic writers have suggested that there can be no criminal liability without a "voluntary act" on the part of the defendant; meaning by this that there must be (i) a behavioural element specified in every actus reus, which (ii) must be done "voluntarily" by the defendant.[84] For the most part, the second aspect of this suggestion seems right (see below, § 4.3). The first claim, however, is less plausible.

It is certainly true that crimes such as murder, rape, and assault—with which ordinary citizens are most familiar, and which have the greatest moral resonance—are crimes which require wrong*doing*, and necessarily involve some behaviour (whether act or omission) by the defendant. But many other crimes stipulate no behavioural element on the part of the defendant. These are offences which penalise a defendant on the basis of the situation in which she finds herself. It is the circumstances themselves which make up the harm that the criminal law is designed to address, and so it is possible to specify the actus reus of these crimes solely by reference to those circumstances.

---

[79] [1993] AC 789. See Keown, "Restoring Moral and Intellectual Shape to the Law after *Bland*" (1997) 113 *LQR* 481.

[80] A conclusion endorsed in *R (on the application of Nicklinson)* v. *Ministry of Justice* [2014] UKSC 38, [2015] 1 AC 657.

[81] [1993] AC 789, 868–9 (Lord Goff). Compare *Re A (Children)* [2001] Fam 147, where surgical intervention was ruled to be a positive act. Cf. MacEwan, "Murder by Design: The Feel-good Factor and the Criminal Law" [2001] *Medical LR* 246.

[82] [1993] AC 789, 866 (Lord Goff), 881–2 (Lord Browne-Wilkinson).

[83] Contrast the decisions in *R (on the application of Pretty)* [2001] UKHL 61, [2002] 1 AC 800 and *Re B* [2002] EWHC 429, [2002] 2 All ER 449.

[84] E.g. Stephen, *A History of the Criminal Law of England* (1883) vol. II, 97; Cross and Jones, *An Introduction to Criminal Law* (3rd ed., 1953) 32; Turner, *Kenny's Outlines of Criminal Law* (17th ed., 1958) 26–7; O'Connor and Fairall, *Criminal Defences* (2nd ed., 1988) 2, 6–7; Moore, *Act and Crime* (1993) chap. 2. The claim made is normally, in fact, even stronger: that there must be a positive (and voluntary) act by the defendant specified in every actus reus. The phrasing in the text is designed to allow for omissions.

For convenience, we can divide offences of this sort into two main types: crimes where the actus reus specifies only the occurrence of some state of affairs; and crimes of possession.

(a) Crimes involving states of affairs

Sometimes known as crimes of "situational liability",[85] these are crimes where the actus reus is simply an event or circumstance that is in some way connected to the defendant. An example is provided by section 3(1) of the Prevention of Oil Pollution Act 1971:

> If any oil to which section 1 of this Act applies, or any mixture containing such oil, is discharged into any part of the sea (a) from a pipe-line ... then, subject to the following provisions of this Act, the owner of the pipe-line ... shall be guilty of an offence....

Here the actus reus of the offence is apparently complete without the need to prove any act or omission on the part of the defendant.[86]

Of course, it is not enough for a defendant to be criminally liable for an offence just because something bad happens—e.g. because a pipe-line leaks oil into the sea. The defendant must in some way be connected to, and responsible for, the actus reus. Normally this connection is through his having a particular status, or relationship, with respect to that actus reus. If a pipe-line discharges oil, it is the pipe-line's *owner* who is picked out for attention by the criminal law, and not, for instance, every person living or sailing nearby. Situational offences are in this respect similar to offences of omission, in that they raise the problem of attribution to defendants, discussed earlier (§ 1.2(ii)(e)). The potential for over-broad criminalisation means that there is a need on the part of the legislator to contain liability by specifying only defendants who are responsible for, and in a position to control, the prohibited situation.

The requirement for a particular status or relationship is typically found in another type of situational liability, being the vicarious criminal liability sometimes imposed on employers for the acts of their employees. Vicarious liability is dealt with further in Chapter 8.[87] A third form of connection may be seen in the notorious case of *Larsonneur*.[88] In that case, L was convicted of being found in the United Kingdom when permission for her to enter the country had previously been refused. It was, however, undisputed that the only reason for her being back on UK soil was that she had been brought there against her will by the police. In convicting her of a situational liability offence, the law has picked out Larsonneur because it was she to whom the actus reus happened, and not because of anything she did.[89]

Larsonneur has been widely criticised, and rightly so.[90] But the proper reason for criticising it is less clear. One problem with the case is that the language used in many situational offences appears not to require any mens rea or fault element on the part of the defendant,

---

[85] Glazebrook, "Situational Liability" in Glazebrook (ed.), *Reshaping the Criminal Law* (1978) 108; Cohen, "The 'Actus Reus' and Offences of 'Situation'" (1972) 7 *Israel LR* 186. Crimes of this sort are sometimes ruled unconstitutional in the United States: *Robinson* v. *California* 370 US 660 (1962) (being addicted to narcotics); *Papachristou* v. *City of Jacksonville* 405 US 156 (1972) (being a vagrant).

[86] Limited defences are, however, provided by ss. 3(1) and 6 of the same Act.

[87] See also above, § 1.2(ii)(e).

[88] (1933) 149 LT 542.

[89] Though see Lanham, "Larsonneur Revisited" [1976] *Crim LR* 276, who suggests the possibility of prior fault.

[90] E.g. Hall, *GPCL* 329, n. 14; Williams, *CLGP* 11; Howard, *Strict Responsibility* (1963) 47.

and thereby imposes what is known as *strict liability*. This is an important criticism, and we shall return to it in § 6.3. But that has not been the only ground of opposition. Ashworth, for instance, once disapproved of "defining an offence in a way that seems to require no act by the defendant as a basis for liability".[91] The objection was that, quite apart from there being no mens rea element, there is no behavioural requirement in the actus reus. However, this is not a valid objection. There is nothing inherently defective or unjust about an offence that contains no behaviour element.

To see this, *Larsonneur* may be contrasted with the New Zealand case of *Finau* v. *Department of Labour*,[92] where F was prosecuted under the Immigration Act 1964 for remaining in New Zealand after the expiry of her visitor's permit. The Court of Appeal upheld F's appeal against conviction on the basis that it had been impossible for her to leave the country, owing to her pregnancy and the consequent refusal of any airline to carry her.

The result in the New Zealand case demonstrates that there need be no injustice, and there is nothing intrinsically wrong, in criminalising states of affairs, so long as the class of potential defendants is clearly identified. However, what *Finau* does is to make clear a further requirement under New Zealand law: that the defendant could have done something about it. The actus reus, although it specifies no act or omission, must still have been *voluntary*. It is the failure of English law to observe *this* requirement which seems to us the main problem with *Larsonneur*, and the reason why the decision in that case is so objectionable.[93]

At the level of theory, two points emerge from this comparison between the jurisdictions. First, where, by contrast with the facts of *Larsonneur*, the defendant *could* have prevented the actus reus from occurring, then situational liability operates, in effect, just like liability for voluntary omissions. Indirectly, it involves the defendant being prosecuted for her failure or omission to prevent the actus reus from happening.[94]

Conversely, it is submitted that, unless there is a requirement of voluntariness, situational offences are at odds with the deepest presuppositions of the criminal law. The very notion of a trial, of a plea, assumes putative answerability for something. One is not answerable for a state of affairs (e.g. having red hair), and it should not be the actus reus of an offence, unless one is able to avoid that state of affairs (e.g. by shaving one's head or dyeing the hair another colour).

---

[91] *Principles of Criminal Law* (2nd ed., 1995) 105. The discussion of *Larsonneur* has been modified in later editions, withdrawing the phrasing quoted here.

[92] [1984] 2 NZLR 396; also with *Martin* v. *State of Alabama* (1944) 17 So 2d 427. Contrast the approach of the House of Lords in *Porter* v. *Honey* [1988] 3 All ER 1045, which sought to exculpate a blameless defendant through techniques of statutory interpretation, rather than by reference to impossibility: see below, § 4.3(ii)(b).

[93] For an argument that to convict D on facts such as *Larsonneur* contravenes D's right to a fair trial guaranteed by Art 6(1) of the European Convention for Human Rights, see Sullivan, "Strict Liability and the ECHR" in Simester (ed.), *Appraising Strict Liability* (2005) 195, 207–10. An argument that a conviction in such circumstances breaches the presumption of innocence guaranteed by Art 6(2) of the Convention failed, however, in *Barnfather* v. *London Borough of Islington Education Authority* [2003] EWHC Admin 418. The literal and intransigent approach of English law to the frequently prosecuted parental truanting offence is vividly exemplified by *Hampshire County Council* v. *E* [2007] EWHC 2584 (Admin), where duress was rejected as a defence on the ground that the behaviour element of the offence was perpetrated by the child rather than the parent. For a comparison of English and New Zealand judicial approaches to offences of this kind, see Sullivan, "Parents and their Truanting Children: an English Lesson in Liability Without Responsibility" (2010) 12 *Otago LR* 285.

[94] An illustrative New Zealand case of this sort is *Tifaga* v. *Department of Labour* [1980] 2 NZLR 235. There D *was* convicted of overstaying, following the termination of his temporary entry permit, because his inability to leave the country was due to his own failure to retain sufficient funds to do so.

Turning to matters of doctrine, it is clear that English law admits the existence of situational offences, where there is no formal necessity to prove an act or omission by the defendant. However, in light of cases such as *Larsonneur*,[95] it appears that situational offences do not incorporate a defence of involuntariness. We consider this point in detail below (§§ 4.3(ii), 6.2(i)).

(b) Crimes of possession

Possessory offences are a creation of statute. They are not found in the common law.[96] There are a number of such offences especially relating to controlled drugs, and to weapons or tools of crime.[97] According to section 5(2) of the Misuse of Drugs Act 1971, for example, "it is an offence for a person to have a controlled drug in his possession". The offence makes no reference to the defendant's conduct.

Characteristically, possession is criminalised as a convenient substitute for the harm that is really objected to, being the *use* of the thing possessed.[98] Criminalisation at the earlier stage both simplifies evidential issues and makes an offence out of behaviour which might otherwise not even count as an *attempt* to do the ultimate crime contemplated. Thus, if offences of this sort did not exist, the police would not be able to intervene at an early stage to prevent many crimes without the prospective offender's escaping the clutches of the criminal law. It is undesirable as well as wasteful of resources that they should have to wait until the contraband is actually used before making an arrest.[99]

In crimes of possession, there is no formal requirement for an act or omission by the defendant.[100] No doubt D put the crowbar in his car before heading out to commit a burglary, but the offence of going equipped for stealing requires only that he *has* it.[101] So far as

---

[95] A later case to similar effect is *Winzar* v. *Chief Constable of Kent, The Times*, 28 March 1983. D, who had been brought to hospital but found merely to be drunk, was subsequently removed by the police to their car parked on the road outside; whereupon he was charged with being found drunk on the highway. His conviction was upheld by the Divisional Court. Contrast *Winzar* with decisions in other jurisdictions: *O'Sullivan* v. *Fisher* [1954] SASR 33; *Palmer-Brown* v. *Police* [1985] 1 NZLR 365.

[96] Compare, e.g., *Heath* (1810) Russ & Ry 184, 168 ER 750; *Dugdale* v. *R.* (1853) 1 E & B 435, 118 ER 499.

[97] E.g. s. 25 of the Theft Act 1968 (going equipped for stealing); s. 1 of the Firearms Act 1968.

[98] Alternatively, the wrong is sometimes in the *making* of the thing, as in the possession of indecent photographs of children contrary to s. 160(1) of the Criminal Justice Act 1988 (the making of such photographs itself being a criminal offence under s. 17(1) of the Protection of Children Act 1978).

[99] For criticism of this rationale, see Ashworth, *Positive Obligations in the Criminal Law* (2013) chap. 6; Fletcher, *Rethinking Criminal Law* (1978) 197–205. Dubber makes a powerful case for seeing possession offences as a paradigm control mechanism for reinforcing state authority: "The Possession Paradigm: The Special Part and the Police Power Model of the Criminal Process" in Duff and Greed (eds.), *Defining Crimes: Essays on the Special Part of the Criminal Law* (2005) 91.

[100] It is otherwise in the United States; § 2.01(4) of the Model Penal Code states that possession is established "if the possessor knowingly procured or received the thing possessed or was aware of his control thereof for a sufficient period to have been able to terminate his possession".

[101] Theft Act 1968, s. 25. The physical nature of the possession requirement varies for different offences. Under s. 25, it is necessary to show that D "has with him" the instrument of theft, burglary, etc.; which requires personal possession, either upon one's person or in one's car nearby: cf. *Doukas* [1978] 1 All ER 1061; *McCalla* (1988) 87 Cr App R 372, 378. By contrast, it will ordinarily be enough for possession that the prohibited item is held by a third party on behalf of D: *Kelt* [1977] 1 WLR 1365; *Sullivan* v. *Earl of Caithness* [1976] QB 966. In the case of drugs, the physical element of possession will be established if the substance is present at a place which is subject to D's dominion or control: *Lewis* (1987) 87 Cr App R 270.

proving the actus reus is concerned, it does not matter how that situation came about.[102] Nonetheless, like offences of situational liability, possessory offences can normally be thought of as having an implicit behavioural element, albeit one that the prosecution need not prove. In effect, criminalisation of D's possession of the crowbar may be treated as imposing an indirect liability, either for the act of obtaining the crowbar (i.e. acquiring possession) or for the omission by D to dispose of it.[103]

So possession and situational offences contain no formal requirement for proof of a behavioural element on the part of the defendant. Despite this, criminal convictions in these cases can usually be explained in terms of an implicit act or omission by the defendant. Recognition of this implicit element helps to explain some of the more difficult cases where D did not obtain the prohibited item by dint of his own efforts. Suppose that D is stopped while in his car, and is found to have with him a package containing cannabis. He claims, however, that he had nothing to do with the presence of the package in his car, and that it had been placed there by a friend. While that claim would suggest that D is not responsible—and therefore should not be criminally liable[104]—for the fact that the cannabis is in his possession, the law may still be justified in imposing criminal liability because of his voluntary failure to dispose of the item. The difficult cases for this analysis occur when D's possession (whether by acquisition or non-disposal) is *involuntary*. We shall return to this issue in § 4.3(ii).

§ 4.2 Consequences: the need for causation

Not all consequences involve persons. For example, the sudden arrival of a very large meteor is thought to have caused the extinction of dinosaurs; and the collapse of many of San Francisco's buildings in 1906 occurred because of an earthquake rather than by human hand. But for the purposes of the criminal law, consequences are those circumstances, events, or states of affairs which are the result of (i.e. *caused* by) the defendant's behaviour. Thus, whenever a consequence, such as death, is specified as part of the actus reus of an offence, the prosecution must prove both that the consequence occurred and that the defendant's behaviour caused that consequence.

This does not mean that D must in any immediate physical sense cause the consequence. A post-disaster inquiry may find that D was in flagrant breach of his duty in failing to pass on a flood warning to the emergency services of the devastated city. The flooding is the most direct physical cause of the deaths by drowning; but, in law, D's behaviour will also be regarded as *one* of the causes of the deaths of those who would have been saved had he done his duty. It is enough that there is *a* causal link from D's behaviour to the consequence.

The requirement of causation is fundamental to our understanding of the actus reus in criminal law. Suppose, for example, that V dies. The result, death, is an element of the actus

---

[102] Moreover, the mode of acquisition may be relevant to mens rea. In particular, the possibility of inadvertent possession is usually excluded by the mens rea requirement of knowledge that the courts have held is implicit in the word "possess". Cf. *Cugullere* [1961] 1 2 All ER 343; *Warner v. Metropolitan Police Comr* [1969] 2 AC 256; below, §§ 4.3(ii)(c), 5.6(ii).

[103] Cf. Williams, *CLGP* 8; Husak, *Philosophy of the Criminal Law* (1987) 12; Moore, *Act and Crime* (1993) 21; *Porter* [2006] EWCA Crim 560, [2006] 1 WLR 2633 (rendering electronic images irretrievable, at least to D).

[104] Cf. § 1.2(ii)ff; also below, § 4.3.

reus of murder. But normally it would be wrong to hold someone guilty of murder who does not cause V's death. Imagine B is a bystander who happens to be standing beside V when, suddenly, D rushes up to V and stabs him fatally. Here our criminal law takes a very individualistic approach, emphasising the distinctive responsibility of citizens for their own actions. Thus the law does not prosecute D's parents, who brought D up in such a way that he was not adequately instilled with the values that would have stopped him from killing V. Neither would it hold B guilty of murder even if B had, in fact, been planning to kill V himself, and had delightedly stood aside upon perceiving D's murderous intentions.[105] In short, there is no doctrine of collective social responsibility in our criminal law. This reflects the nature of our society. Even in team games, such as a football match, the newspaper statistics record the names of those who scored goals. Of course, other approaches are possible.[106] At one time, it was the practice in Greece to hold the entire city punishable for the crimes of its leaders. Similarly, the Chinese doctrine of *lian-tsua* would result in a whole family or village being punished for the wrongdoing of one of its members. But these are not the ways of liberal democracies. Moreover, to impose criminal liability upon someone for the actions of others would not only be out of step with public perceptions, but would also substantially restrict individual liberty.[107]

(i) The rule of thumb

The starting, and frequently finishing, point of any causation problem is the "but for" or *sine qua non* test: would the consequence specified in the actus reus have occurred *but for* the defendant's behaviour? If it would not have occurred except for the defendant's acting as he did, then prima facie his behaviour caused that consequence. Conversely, if it would have occurred anyway, that is a reason to deny the existence of causation (and consequently to refrain from holding the defendant criminally liable for the occurrence of the actus reus).

Suppose, for example, that a doctor injects his patient with a painkiller, and the patient subsequently dies. Whether or not the doctor is guilty of manslaughter or murder depends upon a number of factors, but he definitely commits neither unless injecting the painkiller caused that patient's death. If the patient would have died when she did whether or not the doctor had injected her (e.g. of an unrelated heart attack), then the *but for* test is not satisfied and we have grounds for saying that the doctor's actions did not cause her death.[108] Conversely, if it can be proved that (subject to a *de minimis* exception)[109] she would not have died when she did without the doctor's intervention, then prima facie he killed her.[110]

Most of the time, the *sine qua non* test will, in the absence of any unusual circumstances, be a reasonable indicator of causation. But it is important to realise that *but for* causation is

---

[105] B may, however, become guilty of murder if he manifests his delight in a manner which is intended to encourage D. Not all liability for outcomes is predicated on the *defendant*'s having caused the outcome; he may be held responsible for the consequence of someone else's actions as a secondary party. See below, Chapter 7.

[106] See, e.g., Fauconnet, *La Responsabilité: Étude de Sociologie* (1920).

[107] Cf. the argument against liability for omissions, above, § 4.1(i)(a); also the discussion in Chapter 1.

[108] Cf. *Master* [2007] EWCA Crim 142, where D stabbed V 11 times, aggravating a condition of deep-vein thrombosis from which she died. Although the pre-existing condition might have killed V anyway, D's acts were held to have accelerated her death significantly. Hence causation was established.

[109] Below, § 4.2(ii)(a).

[110] Cf. *Dalloway* (1847) 2 Cox CC 273; *White* [1910] 2 KB 124.

just an indicator, and not a substitute for true legal causation.[111] Suppose, for instance, that D invites V to meet her for lunch. Unfortunately, while driving to their rendezvous, V's car is hit by a runaway lorry, the brakes of which have failed. But for D's inviting V to lunch, the accident would not have occurred. Yet in law D did not cause the accident: she was not responsible for the brake failure. The *but for* test also misdirects in *Hensler*.[112] D sent V a begging letter in which he misrepresented his plight. V was not deceived, but nevertheless sent D some money. On these facts, although V would not have sent the money but for D's letter, D could not be convicted of obtaining by false pretences, because the false pretence had not caused D to send the money.[113]

So the presence of *but for* causation does not necessarily mean that there is true legal causation.[114] Conversely, the absence of *but for* causation does not imply an absence of true legal causation either. Suppose this time that D sets fire to V's house, rasing it. It turns out, however, that there was a faulty electrical circuit in the house that was about to overheat and cause a similar fire. We cannot say that, but for D's conduct, V's house would not have burned down. Yet despite this, it *is* D who causes the damage by the fire he set. Similarly, imagine that D strikes V, causing him to fall to the ground and strike his head. The head injury is fatal. It is revealed in the subsequent post-mortem that, at the time of his death, V was suffering from a pulmonary embolism that was about to rupture and which would have killed him instantly. Again we are unable to say that, but for D's conduct, V would not have died. Yet D's action causes V's death.

The difficulty arises because so-called *but for* "causation" *is not in itself a form of causation at all.* Rather, it is a formula which merely expresses a certain sort of relationship between two things: that, in the circumstances, it was impossible for the second event (the "consequence") to happen without the first action (the "cause") having occurred. What really matters in the law is not whether there is a logical *but for* relationship between the defendant's behaviour and the prohibited consequence, but *why* (or why not). It is only by investigating that further question that we can decide whether there is a true causal relationship *at law*.

(ii) Causation in law

Some causal relationships are very mechanical, and present no problems for the law. This sort of causation occurs when the action leads to the relevant consequence through the ordinary workings of physics, biochemistry, and the like. Thus the connection between D's knocking over the tumbler and its watery contents pouring out is a simple mechanical one; the consequence follows straightforwardly given the existence of gravity and the fluidity of

---

[111] Cf. *L* [2010] EWCA Crim 1249, para. 9 ("the defendant's driving must have played a part not simply in creating the occasion for the fatal accident, i.e. causation in the 'but for' sense, but in bringing it about"); *Hughes* [2013] UKSC 56, [2013] 1 WLR 2461, para. 23, This is old common law: "It must have been the *causa causans*; it is not enough that it may have been the *causa sine qua non.*' *Emperor* v. *Omkar Rampratap* (1902) 4 Bom LR 679, 682.

[112] (1870) 11 Cox CC 570.

[113] D was, however, convicted of an attempt to obtain by false pretences. Compare *Mills* (1857) 1 Dears & Bell 205, 169 ER 978. If similar facts arose today, D would be guilty of fraud by false representation, *per* s. 2 of the Fraud Act 2006. It is enough for that offence to make a false or misleading statement with a view to gain or causing loss: no actual gain or loss need occur. See below, § 15.3.

[114] However, as will be seen in § 4.2(iv) below, *but for* causation remains important as a causative test for omissions.

the liquid inside, without the intervention of subsequent events. The connection between D's shooting V and V's consequential death is normally just as straightforward, something that a pathologist might be able to discuss in technical terms.

The real difficulties arise when there are other actions, or events of nature, which *also* play a role in bringing about the relevant consequence. Consider, for example, the facts in *Pittwood*,[115] where D failed to close the gate at a railway crossing, with the result that a cart entered the crossing and was hit by a train. One can say, of this case, that the arrival of the train was itself a causal factor in the accident. Yet we can still agree that D's negligence caused the crash. Why?

It is not possible to give a definitive analysis of the principles of causation here.[116] But over the next few pages a number of guiding principles will be suggested. Perhaps the most important point to remember during the discussion which follows is that, while causation frequently depends upon physical, mechanical, relationships between actions and outcomes (such as the relationship that D's firing a gun may bear to V's death a moment later), causation is also and very often a function of moral and policy evaluations about D's responsibility for an event. When we state that Pittwood's dereliction "caused" an accident, we are articulating a view that his behaviour was responsible for that accident. In other words, the ascription of causation in *Pittwood* is not so much a *prerequisite* of his being held responsible as it is an expression of the moral *conclusion* that, through his behaviour, he is responsible, and legally answerable, for the accident that resulted. The moral considerations underlying that conclusion find legal expression in the guiding principles outlined below.

(a) Significant (i.e. non-negligible) cause

Whatever other causes play a role in bringing the actus reus about, the first requirement is that D's behaviour must contribute in some significant way to its occurrence. In *White*,[117] W gave his mother poison. Before it could take effect, however, she died of an unrelated heart attack. W was guilty of an attempted murder. But he did not commit murder because the poison played no role in his mother's death.

The contribution that D makes must be more than insignificant or *de minimis*.[118] If a doctor takes a blood sample from a patient who is dying from gunshot wounds, the additional loss of blood for the sample may further weaken the patient and hasten death by a few moments. But the doctor's role in the patient's death is, in this context, causally insignificant, and the law will impute the death solely to the gunshot wounds.[119]

---

[115] (1902) 19 TLR 37.

[116] The classic work is *Hart and Honoré*. See also Kadish, *Blame and Punishment* (1987) chap. 8; Williams, *TBCL* chap. 14. For more philosophical discussion, see Honoré, "Necessary and Sufficient Conditions in Tort Law" in Owen (ed.), *Philosophical Foundations of Tort Law* (1995) 363; Mackie, "Causes and Conditions" in Sosa (ed.), *Causation and Conditionals* (1975) 15; Moore, *Causation and Responsibility* (2009).

[117] [1910] 2 KB 124.

[118] See *Cato* [1976] 1 All ER 260, 265–6.

[119] Cf. *Adams* [1957] Crim LR 365. The direction to the jury by Devlin J is reproduced in Arlidge, "The Trial of Dr David Moor" [2000] *Crim LR* 31, 34–5. Where the role of the doctor is not causally insignificant, the doctor may require a defence of necessity: cf. *Re A (Children)* [2001] Fam 147; below, § 21.3.

However, the defendant's contribution need only be *significant*.[120] It need not be substantial. In *Hennigan*,[121] for example, it was ruled wrong to direct a jury that D was not liable if less than one-fifth to blame for the actus reus. Certainly, D's behaviour need not be the main cause of death. It is enough that her conduct plays a part which is not "minute or negligible",[122] not "insubstantial", or not "insignificant".[123]

(b) Causal salience

As well as making a "not insignificant" contribution, D's causal role must also be *salient*. Suppose that D is driving to work at a speed in excess of the speed limit. He slows to the correct speed in advance of an intersection, but is involved in an accident on the intersection with another car. If he had not been speeding he would not have arrived at the intersection when he did, and the accident would not have occurred. But his speeding is not a cause of the accident. Its only role was to ensure that D was present in a particular place at a particular time, and this in no way affected the likelihood of an accident occurring. The risk would have been just as great had he arrived later;[124] indeed, neither would the accident have happened if his speed had been even *more* excessive. A slightly different example is put by Hart and Honoré:[125]

> "If it is negligent of the defendant to hand a child a loaded gun, and the child drops the gun on his foot and injures it, the injury to the foot is not within the risk (shooting) that made it negligent to hand the child the loaded gun. It is also true that the aspect of the defendant's conduct which made it negligent, the fact that the gun was loaded, was not causally relevant to the injury, since that fact did not significantly increase the gun's weight."

Here D, by giving the gun to the child at all (whether loaded or not), played a causal role in V's subsequent injury. But the reasons why D is at fault—which concern the risk that the child will discharge the gun—are in no way salient to the injury that V sustains.

Salience is frequently in point in cases of manslaughter, whether by gross negligence or by an unlawful and dangerous act. In each case, it must be the conduct constituting the gross negligence or the unlawful and dangerous act that caused death. Conversely, it is impermissible for the Crown to prove gross negligence by reference to conduct, even grossly culpable conduct, that is not causatively salient to the fatality. In the New Zealand case of *Fenton*,[126] for example, D had caused the death of a passenger in the utility vehicle he was driving when he failed to exercise reasonable care to avoid danger to human life, by conduct that established ordinary negligence. It was held that further failings which were merely part of the background to the accident (in this case, the vehicle's lack of a warrant of fitness and registration, the appellant's failure to wear a seatbelt, and the fact he had

---

[120] *Kennedy (No. 2)* [2007] UKHL 38, [2008] 1 AC 269, para. 7; citing *Cato* [1976] 1 All ER 260, 265–6. For the application of this standard test in the context of omissions, see § 4.2(iv).

[121] [1971] 3 All ER 133. Cf. *Garforth* [1954] Crim LR 936.

[122] *Williams* [2010] EWCA Crim 2552, [2011] 1 WLR 588, paras. 33–6; *L* [2010] EWCA Crim 1249, para. 9 (not "negligible").

[123] *Cato* [1976] 1 All ER 260, 265–6; *Cheshire* [1991] 3 All ER 670, 677.

[124] Cf. *Berry* v. *Borough of Sugar Notch* 43 Atl 240 (Pa) (1899); *Hart and Honoré* 168–70; Williams, *TBCL* § 16.7.

[125] *Hart and Honoré* lxiii. Cf. *Wrigley* (1829) 1 Lew CC 171, 168 ER 1001; *Gorris* v. *Scott* (1874) LR 9 Ex 125; Fleming, *The Law of Torts* (7th ed., 1987) 174.

[126] [2003] 3 NZLR 439, especially para. 14.

converted the vehicle without the owner's permission), were inadmissible to prove gross negligence causing death. Similarly, in *Carey*,[127] the defendants were convicted of affray and of manslaughter by unlawful and dangerous act, after a confrontation in which one of them punched V. Subsequently V, a seemingly healthy 15-year-old girl, died from unexpected ventricular fibrillation triggered, apparently, by her flight. The Court of Appeal quashed the manslaughter convictions. The punch, which was certainly an unlawful and dangerous act, was not the cause of death. Even if the *affray* was a cause of death, on the other hand, in the view of the Court it was not itself dangerous.[128]

(c) Multiple causes

A further principle is that there may be multiple causes. In *Pittwood*,[129] both the arrival of the train and the defendant's failure to close the gate were causes of the accident. This may be true even when more than one person is at fault.[130] Suppose that D shoots V who is taken to hospital. While in hospital, V is attended to by E, an inexperienced doctor who negligently fails to recognise the true extent of her injuries. V dies because those injuries are improperly left untreated. In this case, the actions of both D and E cause V's death, and (depending on mens rea considerations) both D and E may be guilty of homicide-related offences. Similarly, if both A and B simultaneously shoot C fatally through the heart, and C dies instantly, then both A and B kill him; even though we cannot say "but for" each shot, C would not have died.[131] It is enough that the actus reus or consequence can be attributed to the defendant's conduct as *a*, not *the*, cause. The general test when there are multiple causes is whether the defendant's contribution was, by the time the consequence came about, still a "significant and operating cause".[132] If so, then it is irrelevant whether that same consequence can also be attributed to other defendants.[133]

Moreover, when multiple causes are concurrently at work, there is no requirement that a defendant's conduct must have been sufficient to cause the prohibited outcome by itself.[134] As we shall see on the following pages, there are many cases where the actus reus occurs only in conjunction with a pre-existing condition,[135] or because of the contribution of a third party[136] or of the victim himself.[137] An example of this is the case of *National Rivers Authority* v. *Yorkshire Water Services*,[138] where the defendant company was charged with causing noxious matter to enter a river. The company regularly and legitimately discharged treated sewage into the river. One night, however, somebody covertly introduced a

---

[127] [2006] EWCA Crim 17.

[128] *Ibid.*, para. 37. "Dangerous" here is a technical term within the meaning of unlawful act manslaughter: see below, § 10.6(i)(d).

[129] (1902) 19 TLR 37; above, § 4.1(i)(b) (Case 3).

[130] Cf. *Benge* (1865) 4 F & F 504, 176 ER 665.

[131] *Jones* v. *Commonwealth* (1955) 281 SW 2d 920, 922–3. From a moral and legal perspective, no other conclusion is possible, even though this type of case presents difficulty for philosophical accounts of causation.

[132] Usually "substantial and operating"—cf. *Smith* [1959] 2 QB 35, 42–3; but see above, § 4.2(ii)(a). The test for omissions works differently: see § 4.2(iv).

[133] Cf. *Haines* (1847) 2 Car & K 368, 175 ER 152; *Malcherek* [1981] 2 All ER 422; *Blaue* [1975] 3 All ER 446.

[134] Cf. *Warburton* [2006] EWCA Crim 627, paras. 21–23.

[135] E.g. *Master* [2007] EWCA Crim 142 (deep-vein thrombosis); below, § 4.2(iii)(a).

[136] E.g. *Pagett* (1983) 76 Cr App R 279; below, § 4.2(iii)(b).

[137] E.g. *Roberts* (1971) 56 Cr App R 95; below, § 4.2(iii)(e).

[138] [1994] 4 All ER 274; reversed on another ground by the House of Lords, [1995] 1 All ER 225.

prohibited substance into the sewer, with the result that when the sewage was discharged, the prohibited material also entered the river. On appeal, the Divisional Court reversed the Crown Court and held that the defendant *had* caused the noxious substance to enter the river: the fact that a stranger also caused the pollution was "neither here nor there".[139] This seems correct. Although the defendant did not cause the sewage to become polluted, it did cause the contents of the sewer to enter the river. It was, of course, blameless in doing so; but that is another matter.[140] Where, as here, the pollution occurs only because of the cumulative actions of defendant and vandal, *both* may be said to have caused the harm. Once again, the general test is the same: whether the particular defendant's own conduct was a significant contributor in bringing about the actus reus.

(iii) Intervening causes

In such cases as *Pittwood* and *National Rivers Authority* v. *Yorkshire Water Services*, the other causal factors operated in tandem with D's conduct to bring about the prohibited harm. Sometimes, however, D's contribution is followed by an action by someone else, or a coincidental event, that is the more immediate (or "proximate") cause of death and which displaces D's causal responsibility for the actus reus. A good example of this is the case of *White*, mentioned earlier.[141] Suppose that in the normal course of events the poison D gave his mother would have caused her death.[142] Nonetheless, it was a subsequent, unrelated, heart attack that killed her. The occurrence of the heart attack supervened over the effects of D's conduct and pre-empted his causal responsibility for her death.

Where the later event displaces D's responsibility in this way, it is often called a *novus actus interveniens*. A *novus actus* is an action or event which "intervenes" to "break the causal chain" leading from D to the eventual harm. Where the prohibited consequence is attributable to a *novus actus*, D is not criminally liable for bringing about that consequence. His behaviour is no longer a significant and operating cause.

We look now at the main types of intervening causes in more detail.

(a) Natural events

Where the other causal factors involve natural events rather than persons, the basic rule is that causation is attributed to the defendant *unless* the intervening natural event was not reasonably foreseeable. Another way of putting this test, in the language preferred by Lord Hoffmann, is to say that an intervening natural event is a *novus actus interveniens* only if its occurrence is "something extraordinary" rather than an ordinary occurrence or ordinary

---

[139] [1994] 4 All ER 274, 279–80.

[140] The case should be distinguished from *National Rivers Authority* v. *Wright Engineering Ltd* [1994] 4 All ER 281. In that case D used a tank to store oil near a brook. Vandals opened a tap on the tank, with the result that the oil flowed into the brook. D was acquitted of causing a noxious substance to enter the brook—again, correctly. This is a clear case of *novus actus interveniens*, discussed below, § 4.2(iii)ff. By contrast, in *Yorkshire Water Services*, the vandal's intervention occurred prior to the company's processing and discharging the effluent. The distinction is not, of course, one that tracks culpability.

[141] Above, § 4.2(ii)(a).

[142] In fact, although D probably thought otherwise, it appears that the quantity given was insufficient to cause death, save perhaps as part of a cumulative dose.

fact of life.[143] A number of overseas cases have usefully illustrated this point. In *Hart*,[144] D assaulted V, leaving her lying unconscious on a beach below the high-water mark. V was subsequently drowned by the incoming tide. The New Zealand Court of Appeal held that D had caused the death of the victim. It is thought that D would not have killed her had V been left lying above the high-water mark and had only drowned because of a freak tidal wave.[145]

The idea here is that the further cause is not merely a coincidence. Rather, it is the sort of risk that is created or increased by D's initial actions; and the prospect of the prohibited consequence coming about by that further means is one of the reasons we might sensibly give when stating why D should not act as he does.[146] Thus in cases such as *Gowans and Hillman*,[147] where D inflicted serious injuries upon V, sending him into coma and thereby making V susceptible to serious infection which V later contracted and from which he died, it was held that D's conduct, in rendering V especially vulnerable to the further, immediate cause of death, was a sufficient cause for the death to be attributable to D. A contrasting case with different result is *Bush* v. *Commonwealth*.[148] In that case D shot V, who subsequently died of scarlet fever, transmitted to him in hospital by the surgeon who operated on the bullet wound. D was acquitted of unlawful homicide. His attack on V did not substantially increase the risk of V's contracting scarlet fever; neither was that risk a significant reason why we would think D's initial actions wrong. A different view might have been taken if D had succumbed to an infection characteristically associated with his injuries.

There are three important exceptions to the general rule that unforeseeable or extraordinary events are capable of breaking the causal chain linking defendant to eventual outcome.

Exception 1: Pre-existing conditions.
For the purpose of analysing causal paths,[149] *pre-existing* natural conditions or vulnerabilities in the victim—"egg-shell skulls"—are treated in law as baselines: "defendants must take [the condition of] their victims as they find them".[150] In *Master*,[151] for example, D inflicted a number of stab wounds upon V, aggravating an existing condition of deep-vein thrombosis. In turn, this triggered a pulmonary embolism, from which she died. D was rightly held to have caused V's death.

---

[143] *Environment Agency* v. *Empress Car Co. (Abertillery) Ltd.* [1999] 2 AC 22, 34–6. Provided it is borne in mind that what must be foreseeable is events of the same *type*, rather than the *particular* intervening event, and that it must be foreseeable to an ordinary person rather than the particular defendant, these alternative ways of phrasing the causation test involve little practical difference.

[144] [1986] 2 NZLR 408. See also *Hallett* [1969] SASR 141; *Phillips* [1971] ALR 740; *Hill* [1953] NZLR 688, 694–5.

[145] Perkins, "The Law of Homicide" (1946) 36 *J Crim L & Crim* 391, 393–4.

[146] Cf. the requirement for salience, above, § 4.2(ii)(b).

[147] [2003] EWCA Crim 3935. Cf. *Forrest* (1886) 20 SASR 78; *D* [2003] EWCA Crim 2772, [2004] 1 Cr App R (S) 73, para. 6.

[148] (1880) 78 Ky 268.

[149] As opposed to analysing mens rea, where the foreseeability of V's condition will be relevant at least to any finding of negligence (or, in the context of manslaughter, to any finding that D's act was dangerous: *Carey, Cyeol and Foster* [2006] EWCA Crim 17).

[150] *Blaue* [1975] 3 All ER 446, 450. However, this rule does not apply to actions by the victim: see below, §§ 4.2(iii)(e), 4.2(iv)(b).

[151] [2007] EWCA Crim 142; cf. *JM and SM* [2012] EWCA Crim 2293.

Exception 2: Concurrent causes.

The outcome in *Bush* v. *Commonwealth* would have been different if the fever had caused death only *in conjunction with* the fact that V was weakened by the wound D had inflicted. The latter would be a case of multiple concurrent causes, rather than of *novus actus*, since the original injury would still be making an ongoing (operating) contribution to V's death.

Exception 3: Intended effects.

Finally, a coincidental or fortuitous and unforeseeable route involving natural events will not normally be a *novus actus* when the ultimate result was *intended* by the defendant.[152] For example:

> D shoots at V on a mountainside, meaning to kill him. She misses, but the noise of her shot triggers an avalanche in which V is swept away and killed. D is guilty of murder. She has brought about the intended result, and cannot escape responsibility by pointing to the unexpected causal detour of the means that she herself initiated.

This exception is sometimes described as a rule that "intended consequences are never too remote". It is preferable not to characterise the exception in that way, and indeed to do so would be inaccurate. For example, D's intended contribution to an outcome may be superceded by the *novus actus* of a third party.[153] It is to that possibility that we now turn.

(b) Human beings

In some respects, there are similarities between the causal status of natural events and the intervening actions of third parties. If D stabs V, and V later dies, D is nevertheless not causally responsible if it turns out that V dies because the ambulance within which he was being carried to hospital was crushed by a runaway lorry. Neither does D kill V if, after being fatally wounded and left for dead, V is chanced upon by his old enemy T, who shoots V, killing him instantly.[154] In these situations, the unforeseeable intervention of another breaks the causal chain between D's contribution and the eventual outcome. However, there are also significant differences between the attribution of causation where there are intervening natural events and that where there are intervening actions by other persons. In the former case, as we have seen, the main test is one of "ordinariness" or reasonable foreseeability. In the latter, this is only one aspect of a more complex enquiry.

At a very generalised level, there are three main principles guiding causation when a third person intervenes.

Principle 1: Free, deliberate, and informed human interventions.

First is the proposition that T's intervention which causes the actus reus will normally be a *novus actus*, and will absolve D of responsibility, when that intervention is "free, deliberate and informed".[155] This occurs when T *knowingly* intervenes to bring about the prohibited outcome, without her choice to do so being induced, fettered or constrained by the situation

---

[152] E.g. *Anon* ("The Harlot's Case"), Crompton's Justice 24, discussed in *TBCL* 389; *Michael* (1840) 9 C & P 356, 173 ER 867 (where the intervention was by another person); *Demirian* [1989] VR 97, 113–14 (approved in *Royall* v. *R* (1991) 172 CLR 378, 392, 400, 411, 452 (HCA).

[153] The rule would also be subject to a salience requirement regarding unexpected interventions: § 4.2(ii)(b).

[154] Cf. *State* v. *Wood* (1881) 53 Vt 558; *Evans and Gardner* [1976] VR 523, 527–8. See below, § 4.2(iii)(b) (Case 2).

[155] *Pagett* (1983) 76 Cr App R 279, 288–9; *Latif* [1996] 1 WLR 104, 115 (HL).

D has created. In that situation T assumes full responsibility for the outcome, displacing or pre-empting its attribution to D. The legal correctness of this principle was resoundingly confirmed by the House of Lords in *Kennedy (No. 2)*:[156]

> "The criminal law generally assumes the existence of free will. The law recognises certain exceptions, in the case of the young, those who for any reason are not fully responsible for their actions, and the vulnerable, and it acknowledges situations of duress and necessity, as also of deception and mistake. But, generally speaking, informed adults of sound mind are treated as autonomous beings able to make their own decisions how they will act, and none of the exceptions is relied on as possibly applicable in this case. Thus D is not to be treated as causing V to act in a certain way if V makes a voluntary and informed decision to act in that way rather than another."

In *Kennedy*, D had prepared a heroin mixture for V in a syringe which he then gave to V. V injected himself with the heroin and subsequently died. D was convicted of manslaughter. On appeal,[157] the House quashed D's conviction on the ground that D had not caused V's death. Even though D had played a part in the events leading to V's death, there was an intervening act by another, V himself, who had self-administered the injection. The intervention by V was free, deliberate, and informed; as such, it was a novus actus, absolving D of causal responsibility for the homicide.

The rationale for this principle is ably expressed by Glanville Williams:[158]

> "Underlying this rule there is, undoubtedly, a philosophical attitude. Moralists and lawyers regard the individual's will as the autonomous prime cause of his behaviour. What a person does (if he has reached adult years, is of sound mind and is not acting under mistake, intimidation or similar pressure) is his own responsibility, and is not regarded as having been caused by other people. An intervening act of this kind, therefore, breaks the causal connection that would otherwise have been perceived between previous acts and the forbidden consequence."

Very often T's knowing intercession will not meet those criteria. The doctor's intervention in treating V is not free or unconstrained, but rather is a justified response to the need for treatment that D has engendered. This point can be stated more generally: T's participation in begetting the actus reus is insufficiently free, and *cannot* be a *novus actus*, when it is justified or excused by the demands of the situation that D's conduct has placed her in. While T's conduct may itself be a cause of the harm, it is not an independent cause; rather, in law, it has the status of being itself a consequence of D's wrongdoing. Thus, instead of T's

---

[156] [2007] UKHL 38, [2008] 1 AC 269, para. 14; reversing [2005] EWCA Crim 685, [2005] 1 WLR 2159. But not in Scotland: *MacAngus and Kane* v. *HM Advocate* [2009] HCJAC 8.

[157] In fact, this was D's second appeal. The first saw his conviction upheld: see [1999] Crim LR 65. However, following uncertainty in the subsequent case law, the case was referred back to the Court of Appeal for reconsideration by the UK Criminal Cases Review Commission: [2005] EWCA Crim 685, [2005] 1 WLR 2159. For critical analysis of that court's decision, see the third edition of this work, § 4.2(iii)(d) (Case 2).

[158] *TBCL* 391. Notice that this autonomy-based principle rests upon moral rather than conceptual argument; while endorsed here, it has not been adopted universally. See, e.g., Spencer and Brajeux, "Criminal Liability for Negligence—A Lesson from Across the Channel?" (2010) 59 *ICLQ* 1, 12–13. It seems the position is now also different in Canada, if the unsatisfactory decision in *Maybin* 2012 SCC 24, [2012] 2 SCR 30 is to be believed. In that case, two brothers who started a fight in a bar were said to be causally responsible for the subsequent violence inflicted on V by a bouncer—seemingly on the basis that their actions had "set the tone" for what followed. The decision fails (in paras. 45–59) to recognise the genuinely distinctive nature of the free, deliberate, and informed principle.

becoming fully (and exclusively) responsible for the eventual outcome, D remains at least partly responsible for that intervention by T, and for its effects.

Neither will T's input be "free, deliberate and informed" when T is ignorant of the relevant facts. In this sort of case, T's contribution to the harm is an inadvertent one. Her role may be innocent or accidental, but need not be, and may instead be negligent. Either way, there is no deliberate choice by T to bring the harm about, and so she cannot be said to assume full responsibility for that harm to the exclusion of D. The same is in principle true where T lacks the capacity to make informed decisions, being (say) a child or while suffering psychiatric injury.[159]

Principle 2: Other human interventions.
The second main principle applies where, because of ignorance or other reasons, T's intervention does not meet the "free, deliberate and informed" criteria. In that case the third-party intervention is, in effect, no different from a natural event. Thus it is subject to the further tests that govern intervention by a natural event. In particular, it can only count as a *novus actus* if its occurrence was independent of D's wrongdoing and was not reasonably foreseeable.[160] One new factor in examining this issue will be T's culpability for her conduct: if the harm occurred only following T's gross negligence, it is less likely to be reasonably foreseeable and the sort of risk which provides a reason why D should not have acted as he did in the first place.[161]

Principle 3: Concurrent causes.
As with any intervening cause, whether natural or human, a third principle also applies: that even if the intervention was independent of D and unforeseeable, it will be no more than a concurrent cause if D's contribution is still playing a direct, contributory role at the time the harm eventually occurs. This is a straightforward application of the proposition that there can be multiple causes of an outcome.[162]

In the following subsections, we will consider these rather abstract principles in the more practical context of the leading cases, and in light of judicial *dicta*.

Case 1: Foreseeable and innocent interventions.
Cases where another's intervention does not break the causal chain occur in a variety of ways. In some of the most dramatic examples, D will still be ascribed with causal

---

[159] Cf., in tort, *Corr v. IBC Vehicles Ltd* [2008] UKHL 13, [2008] 1 AC 884. In *D* [2006] EWCA Crim 1139, [2006] 2 Cr App R 24, para. 8, the Court of Appeal noted that "subject to evidence and argument on the critical issue of causation, unlawful violence on an individual with a fragile and vulnerable personality, which is proved to be a material cause of death (even if the result of suicide) would at least arguably, be capable of amounting to manslaughter". It may be in some cases that suicide by the victim is, alternatively, a reasonably foreseeable (or, as Horder and McGowan prefer, "natural") reaction to the defendant's wrong. See below, § 4.2(iii)(e); also Horder and McGowan, "Manslaughter by Causing Another's Suicide" [2006] *Crim LR* 1035, 1039ff.

[160] Or, in Lord Hoffmann's phrasing, if its occurrence was "extraordinary": above, § 4.2(iii)(a). In *Girdler* [2009] EWCA Crim 2666, [2010] RTR 28, para. 43, the Court accepted that the language of reasonable foreseeability was apt "for a lawyer", but thought that a jury could more helpfully be asked whether the subsequent events "could sensibly have been anticipated".

[161] Above, § 4.2(iii)(a). Less likely, but not impossible: cf. *Benge* (1865) 1 F & F 504, 176 ER 665, where a railway accident occurred only because the risk created by D's negligence was not counteracted when others also failed to observe proper procedures. See further below, § 4.2(iii)(b) (Case 3).

[162] See above, § 4.2(ii)(c). Cf. *Hennigan* [1971] 3 All ER 133.

responsibility if the contribution of the other party is both predictable (i.e. reasonably fore-seeable) and itself innocent.

A famous case of this variety is *Michael*.[163] D wished to murder her illegitimate child, who was in the care of a foster-mother. She gave a bottle of poison to the foster-mother, tell-ing her it was medicine and instructing her to administer it to the baby. The foster-mother decided not to give the medicine and put it on the mantelpiece. Some days later the foster-mother's own five-year-old child removed the bottle and administered a fatal dose to the child. D was convicted of murder.[164]

The events in *Michael* involved the input of a young child, undoubtedly an innocent for the purposes of legal responsibility. But they would be treated no differently by the law if T were an adult whose foreseeable intervention was inadvertent and blameless. Suppose, for example, that an altercation occurs between D and V on the pavement of a busy city street. D pushes V, who stumbles onto the road and is run over and killed by a passing car.[165] In such a case, the intervention of the car (unintended by its driver) could not be regarded as a *novus actus*, and D would properly be treated as having caused V's death.

By contrast, the innocent intervention will be regarded as a *novus actus* where it is unforeseeable. In *Martin*,[166] D was held not to have caused death after he offered his child a sip of an alcoholic drink, whereupon the child seized and consumed the entire drink. Similarly, the example in the last paragraph may be compared with a situation in which D assaults V, leaving her unconscious in a quiet and well-lit street. Prima facie, he should not be held responsible for V's death if, subsequently, she is run over by a driver who had ample opportunity to avoid her.[167]

Where T's actions are not inadvertent but instead justified or excused because of the situation D has created, T will effectively be counted as an innocent intervener. T's interven-tion is itself a consequence of D's actions rather than an independent (i.e. free, deliberate, and informed) cause. This will frequently be the correct analysis regarding the effects of justified medical treatment given in response to injuries D inflicts.[168] Perhaps the most graphic case of this type, however, is *Pagett*,[169] in which the defendant holed up in a build-ing, then emerged firing at police and using his hostage as a human shield. The police returned fire in the dark, killing the hostage. The consequence, that the police would—quite understandably—return fire, and so kill the girl, was an entirely foreseeable upshot of what the defendant did, and so could not break the chain of causation which led from his behav-iour to the hostage's death.

It was said in *Pagett* that the policeman's reaction in returning fire was instinctive and "involuntary". But it need not be involuntary. It was enough that the reaction was a reason-able response, justifiable in terms either of self-defence or the execution of a legal duty.

---

[163] (1840) 9 C & P 356, 173 ER 867; see also *Tessymond* (1828) 1 Lew CC 169, 168 ER 1000.

[164] It is thought that T's intervention was reasonably foreseeable. (See *TBCL* 394.) However, even if it were unforeseeable and extraordinary, D's conviction can be justified on the basis that, T's intervention being innocent, it should be treated like a natural event and the rule about intended consequences applied. See above, § 4.2(iii)(a).

[165] *Fleeting* [1977] 1 NZLR 343.

[166] (1827) 3 C & P 211, 172 ER 390.

[167] *Knutsen* [1963] Qd R 157.

[168] The difficult cases are where the treatment is itself misjudged. See further below, § 4.2(iii)(b) (Case 3) and the analysis of *Cheshire* in § 4.2(iv)(c).

[169] (1983) 76 Cr App R 279.

Either way, it is not sufficiently "free" to usurp the defendant's causal responsibility for the eventual consequences.[170]

An extension of the decision in *Pagett* may be seen in the tort case of *Scott v. Shepherd*.[171] D threw a lighted squib into the market house, where it landed beside T. T, in order to protect himself, threw the squib across the warehouse. It landed beside R, who in turn also threw the squib away, such that it struck P and exploded, blinding P in one eye. D was held to have caused P's injury, on principles that were said in the case to be analogous to those applying in the criminal law.[172] From the point of view of the criminal law, this seems to be right. The case is slightly different from *Pagett*, in that T's (and R's) reaction involved necessity rather than self-defence, and was excusable rather than justifiable. But it was reasonably foreseeable, and moreover one for which T could not be blamed—a response induced by the circumstances that D himself had generated. Thus T's reaction is allowed to be a mistake,[173] and unjustified, provided it is a reasonable or understandable response made in the heat or emergency of the moment.

One other case worth mention is *Martin*.[174] Intending to cause confusion and terror, D put out the gaslights on a staircase to the exit of a theatre, and placed an iron bar across the exit doorway. In the subsequent panic, a number of persons were seriously injured. D's conviction for inflicting grievous bodily harm was affirmed on appeal. Again, rightly so. The immediate cause of injury was no doubt the stampeding of the audience. Yet the behaviour of the audience was hardly "free, deliberate, and informed". Rather, it was a foreseeable and understandable consequence of the panic induced by D.

Case 2: Foreseeable and intentional interventions.
The cases above illustrate the general rule that, where the intervention is both innocent and foreseeable, it will not normally suffice to break the causal chain linking the defendant to the actus reus. But what if the third party's free intervention is foreseeable, yet not innocent or blameless? Here things get a little more complicated. The reason for this is the importance of individual autonomy and responsibility in the law. A person's actions are not usually regarded as caused by others, and the law stipulates that a defendant is responsible for her own actions but is normally not responsible for the wrongdoing of a third party even if it was foreseeable, and would not have occurred but for the defendant's contribution. So if D inflicts serious injuries upon V during a mugging, and another assailant later chances upon and shoots V (killing him instantly), then D does not cause death even if it was foreseeable[175] that another person might subsequently kill V. Similarly, the result in

---

[170] A dubious extension of *Pagett* may be seen in *Gnango* [2011] UKSC 59, [2012] 1 AC 827. Without any justification or excuse, P and S exchanged gunfire. P aimed his shot at S but missed. Instead, the bullet hit and killed V, an innocent passer-by. S was held to be guilty of V's murder as either accomplice or principal, *inter alia* on the ground that, by firing at P, he caused P to return fire. For a trenchant critique, see Buxton, "Being an Accessory to One's Own Murder" [2012] *Crim LR* 275. See also Sullivan "Accessories and Principals after *Gnango*" in Reed and Bohlander (eds.), *Participation in Crime: Domestic and Comparative Perspectives* (2013) 25.

[171] (1773) 2 Bl W 892, 96 ER 525. Cf. *Tomars* [1978] 2 NZLR 505; *Madison v. State* 234 Ind 517, 130 NE 2d 35 (1955).

[172] (1773) 2 Bl W 892, 899, 96 ER 525, 528 (De Grey CJ).

[173] Cf. *McKechnie* (1992) 94 Cr App R 51, 58.

[174] (1881) 8 QBD 54. See also the cases involving interventions by the victim: below, § 4.2(iii)(e).

[175] Or even made "likely" by D's actions: *Dalby* [1982] 1 All ER 916. As Glanville Williams states, "[t]he fact that [D's] own conduct, rightful or wrongful, provided the background for a subsequent voluntary act by another does

Michael[176] would have been different if T had been a mature adult who knew the details of D's plans when she administered the poison to D's baby.[177]

Where the third party's wrongful intervention is itself intentional, something other than causation is required before the outcome can *also* be ascribed to the original actor-defendant. Characteristically, the extra ingredient is supplied when the third party's intervention is in some way induced or underwritten by the defendant. In these cases, D's liability is predicated on a derivative, or secondary party basis, rather than upon causation.[178] Thus when D deliberately incites or assists T to commit a crime, D too will be criminally liable alongside T for its commission. Secondary liability is dealt with separately in Chapter 7.

Sometimes an intervention to bring about the actus reus may be intentional without necessarily being culpable. As we saw in the preceding section, where this occurs because of a justification or excuse arising from D's conduct, T is treated as if his were an innocent intervention. However, where T's intervention is intentional, free, and unconstrained by justificatory or excusatory circumstances, it will usually break the causal link between defendant and outcome. In *Latif*,[179] D was charged, *inter alia*, with importing a controlled drug. The drug was in fact brought into the country by a customs officer with full knowledge of the contents of the packages he carried. The House of Lords held that the officer's voluntary and knowing intervention relieved D of causal responsibility for importation of the drugs, and that the most he could be convicted of was an attempt to commit the offence.[180]

Case 3: Foreseeable and culpable interventions.
Normally, when there is no *intentional* wrongdoing by the intervener, it is less likely—but not impossible—that the culpable intervention will break the causal link between D and the eventual outcome.[181] This is because, as was stated at the beginning of § 4.2(iii)(b), T cannot be said to have assumed a full responsibility for the effects of her intervention.[182] Nonetheless, it is still possible for T's conduct to disrupt the causal path joining D with the actus reus.[183] For example, where V is injured by D, but killed in an accident en route to hospital, the fact that the accident was unintended by T is no bar to an application of the

---

not make him responsible for it. What he does may be a but-for cause of the injurious act, but he did not do it": "*Finis* for *Novus Actus*?" (1989) 48 *CLJ* 391.

[176] Above, § 4.2(iii)(b) (Case 1).
[177] Compare *Hilton* (1838) 2 Lew CC 214, 168 ER 1132, where a stranger's intervention was a *novus actus*, with *Lowe* (1850) 3 Car & Kir 123, 175 ER 489, where the intermediary was an "ignorant boy" and D was not absolved of responsibility. Cf. *People* v. *Elder* 100 Mich 515, 59 NW 237 (1894); *Commonwealth* v. *Root* 403 Pa 571, 170 A 2d 310 (1961).
[178] Cf. G. Fletcher, *Rethinking Criminal Law* (1978) 582.
[179] [1996] 1 WLR 104. To similar effect is *Tse Hung-Lit* [1986] AC 876. For another, extraordinary, example, see *People* v. *Campbell* 124 Mich App 333, 335 NW 2d 27 (1983).
[180] It is possible that the officer's intervention could be regarded as culpable since the House of Lords treated him as having committed an offence himself. But this was not required in *Horsey* (1862) 3 F & F 287, 176 ER 129.
[181] Cf. *Benge* (1865) 4 F & F 504, 176 ER 665.
[182] Cf. V's death in *Winter* [2010] EWCA Crim 1474. In that case, the defendants stored fireworks in a manner contrary to regulations. A fire broke out, leading to an explosion, in which T (a fireman, carrying out his duties properly) and V (a media awareness officer employed by the fire service, who continued filming after he had been ordered to move back) were killed. T's death is straightforwardly analogous to the situation of the police officers in *Pagett* (Case 1 above). However, the defendants were rightly convicted also for the manslaughter of V.
[183] E.g. *Ledger* (1862) 2 F & F 857, 175 ER 1319.

novus actus doctrine and denial of D's responsibility. The most instructive legal examples of this variety arise in a medical context, where D inflicts injuries upon V the extent of which are at least exacerbated by the medical treatment V subsequently receives.

A case where "palpably" bad medical treatment was held to cause death to the exclusion of D's original actions is *Jordan*.[184] In that case the defendant had stabbed V, who was admitted to hospital and died eight days later. On appeal, evidence was admitted to show that when he died, the original injury had substantially healed. V's death was in fact caused by his allergic reaction to the antibiotic he was given in hospital and by the intravenous administration of too much liquid. Moreover, the antibiotic was introduced to prevent infection only after he had shown he was intolerant of it. The Court of Criminal Appeal, in quashing Jordan's conviction, held that the grossly negligent[185] medical treatment broke the causal link between the stabbing and V's death.

While we submit that *Jordan* was rightly decided, it must be regarded as a very unusual case, distinguished by its rather extreme facts. Acknowledging this, the Court was "disposed to accept it as law that death resulting from any normal treatment employed to deal with a felonious injury may be regarded as caused by the felonious injury".[186] Thus where death results from normal treatment applied to the injury, then both the treatment and the injury are causes of death and the treatment does not break the chain of causation from the original injury to death.

Even if the intervening treatment is abnormal, however, it will not necessarily count as a *novus actus*. In *Smith*,[187] V was stabbed by P with a bayonet. His lung was pierced, but this injury went unrecognised by those who attended to him. He was dropped twice on the way to the medical reception station. There the medical officer failed to diagnose the seriousness of the situation and gave the wrong treatment, which very likely increased the risk of death.[188] On appeal, it was held that where the original injury is still an operating and significant[189] cause of death, then—regardless of other contributing causes—the death can still be attributed to the defendant. It is only if the original wound is merely a *historical setting* for the second injury (here, the treatment), which is then the major operating cause of death, that there can be a break in the causal chain. By contrast with the facts in *Jordan*, in *Smith* the stab wound and consequent haemorrhage were still immediate medical factors explaining V's death.

There appear, therefore, to be two conditions which must be satisfied before the intervening behaviour can supersede the defendant's causal role. Loosely stated:

(I)   The original harm inflicted by D must no longer be contributing to the occurrence of the eventual result (i.e. as a concurrent cause).

This condition applies even if T's wrongdoing is intentional. For example, if D inflicts a non-fatal stab wound upon V, then D (as well as T) causes V's death if T later also stabs V and the loss of blood from both wounds is a contributing factor bringing about V's

---

[184] (1956) 40 Cr App R 152.

[185] See Williams, "Causation in Homicide" [1957] *Crim LR* 429.

[186] (1956) 40 Cr App R 152, 157.

[187] [1959] 2 QB 35.

[188] Indeed, it was said in evidence at the trial that V's chances of recovery were 75 per cent given proper treatment.

[189] "Substantial" in the speech of Lord Parker CJ [1959] 2 QB 35, 42–3. But see above, § 4.2(ii)(a).

death.[190] Contrast this example with the example mentioned earlier, where D stabs V and T later chances upon V and shoots her, killing her instantly. In that case T and not D causes V's death.

The second condition is as follows:

(II)   The relevant intervention by T must be independent (i.e. not itself a consequence) of the original wrongdoing by D.

This condition is conveniently illustrated by the New Zealand case of *Kirikiri*.[191] In that case, V was the victim of a serious assault by D, which caused structural damage to her face. At the hospital where she was first treated, a temporary tracheostomy was performed in order to assist her breathing. She was then transferred to another hospital for reconstructive surgery, which was to take place four days later and was not essential to save her life. Before surgery, however, the inserted tracheal tube slipped. Attempts to replace it failed and V died. The High Court held, on a pre-trial motion, that there was "ample evidence" on these facts for a jury to hold that D caused V's death. This seems right. The immediate cause of death was the failure of the tracheostomy and of the surgeons' attempts to repair it. But the tracheostomy itself was a medically appropriate response, made necessary by the injuries D had inflicted upon V. D might therefore be regarded as causally responsible for the (necessitous, appropriate) intervention that, in turn, led to V's death.

It may be helpful to illustrate the different legal character of the causal sequences in these cases with diagrams. In *Jordan*, the conduct of the doctor amounted to a *novus actus* independent of D's actions:

Jordan: D —→ stabs V —| T —→ injects antibiotics —→V dies

By contrast, in *Kirikiri* the doctor's intervention was a direct response to the injuries D had inflicted, and thus could be treated as a consequence of D's actions:

Kirikiri: D —→ attacks V —→ T performs tracheostomy —→ V dies

In *Smith*, the doctor's conduct made an independent contribution to V's death. But the stab wound inflicted by D remained a concurrent, operating cause of death:

Smith: D ————→ stabs V ————————⌐
                                                                                      └—→ V dies
               T —→ exacerbates wounds ————⌐

One important factor in determining whether the medical intervention counts as a consequence for the purposes of condition II will be the extent to which that treatment is negligent. "Palpably" wrong—i.e. grossly negligent—treatment is obviously not a consequential intervention falling within condition II. (As *Smith* illustrates, the question whether it is a

---

[190]   This may be the best explanation of *Dear* [1996] Crim LR 595.
[191]   [1982] 2 NZLR 648. Condition II is also crucial to the explanation of *Cheshire* [1991] 3 All ER 670, the most important recent case on medical interventions. However, because of the complexity of that case its analysis is deferred to the end of our discussion of causation, in § 4.2(iv)(c). For present purposes, *Kirikiri* provides the better illustration.

novus actus interveniens will then depend upon condition I.) On the other hand, reasonable, even if ultimately incorrect and harmful, treatment *is* a consequence.[192] However, the status of treatment which is negligent, but not grossly negligent, is unclear. Authority on this question is both *obiter* and inconsistent.[193] It is submitted that, by analogy with the principles stated in § 4.2(iii)(b) above (Case 1) and § 4.2(iii)(e) below, medically erroneous treatment that is neither reasonable nor reasonably foreseeable should count as independent action within condition II.

(c) Distinction from the innocent agent doctrine

Sometimes persons bring about outcomes deliberately through the agency of another person. If D gives V's daughter a lethal draught of poison, telling her it is for V's cold, and the daughter administers the poison to V, D is guilty of murder as if he had administered the poison himself.[194] Similarly, D may be convicted of importing prohibited drugs even though the means of conveyance was an airline.[195] The doctrine of innocent agency renders the intervening participant the mere instrument of D, enabling courts to find that D has committed the offence as a principal offender.

Discussion of this doctrine belongs in Chapter 7, on secondary parties. It is mentioned here in order to distinguish it from the causation question that arises upon an innocent third party's intervention. Innocent agency requires that D knowingly uses T as his agent to bring about the prohibited result. Thus *Michael*, where a child later and independently administered the poison that D had instructed V's nurse to give to V, is not a suitable case for application of the doctrine.

Innocent agency and causal principles nonetheless share some common ground. Like causation, innocent agency requires that T should be ignorant of the true nature of her actions. Where this is not so, and T is aware that her conduct constitutes an actus reus, responsibility for her actions and their result cannot then be imputed back to D.

(d) Two special cases of intervention: pollution and driving

There are two controversial lines of decisions governing third-party interventions, which we discuss here as special cases which may be difficult to reconcile with cases from other domains.

Case 1: Pollution and other environmental crimes.
The first line of cases begins with the decision by the House of Lords in *Environmental Agency* v. *Empress Car Co. (Abertillery) Ltd.*[196] In that case, D had attached a tap to a diesel tank in its yard. The tap overrode existing barriers designed to contain spillage from the tank, meaning that it was possible for overflows from the tap to drain into the nearby river. On 20 March 1995 the tap was opened by an unknown person, with the result that the

---

[192] *McKechnie* (1992) 94 Cr App R 51, 58; *Kirikiri* [1982] 2 NZLR 648.
[193] For a survey of the case law, see *Hart and Honoré* 352ff. The more recent case of *McKechnie* (1992) 94 Cr App R 51 suggests a standard of simple negligence.
[194] *Anon* (1634) Kel 53, 84 ER 1079.
[195] *White* v. *Ridley* (1978) 140 CLR 342.
[196] [1999] 2 AC 22.

entire contents of the tank were drained and flowed into the river. D was convicted of "causing polluting matter to enter controlled waters",[197] a conviction that was affirmed by the House of Lords.

The leading judgment, given by Lord Hoffmann, contains a number of useful statements of principle.[198] But it is, in one respect, profoundly unsatisfactory. Apparently, the intervention of the third party was free, deliberate, informed, and indeed malicious. Prima facie, therefore, it was a *novus actus*. But Lord Hoffmann accorded no special status to such interventions and failed to distinguish informed acts by third persons from acts which are either uninformed or unfree, or indeed from interventions of nature. "By parity of reasoning",[199] the same test was said to apply to all:

> "The true common sense distinction is, in my view, between acts and events which, although not necessarily foreseeable in the particular case,[200] are in the generality a normal and familiar fact of life, and acts or events which are abnormal and extraordinary."

The main effect of this conclusion is to assimilate interventions by third parties with interventions by natural events, thereby extending the appropriate test of the latter (discussed in § 4.2(iii)(a)) also to the former. Hence a normal or foreseeable intervention, even if fully informed and deliberate, would not break the chain of causation linking D to the ultimate outcome.

This holding is contrary to both principle and law. At the level of principle, it is unexplained how D's lawful storage of oil on its land had any causal effect. V may lawfully park his car in a street. D may come along and vandalise the vehicle. V inadvertently gives D the opportunity to cause criminal damage but his parking of his car was not a cause of its being damaged. If the physical location of the car is regarded as a cause of the damage, all other features of the environment which made it possible for D to damage it should be regarded too as causes of the damage. The same reasoning applies to D's storage of the oil in *Empress*. The winnowing out of such factors is, in part, accomplished by the long-standing precept of causation rules in the criminal law that a person is responsible for his own autonomous actions and not for those of others. As Williams puts it, "[w]hat a person does … is his own responsibility, and is not regarded as having been caused by other people".[201] Otherwise, D's criminal liability for causing an actus reus would not be under his own control, but would instead be subject to the autonomous choice of someone else. Giving other citizens the power to render D guilty of a crime not only disempowers D and undermines

---

[197] Contrary to s. 85(1) of the Water Resources Act 1991.

[198] E.g. [1999] 2 AC 22, 29 f, 30e–31b.

[199] [1999] 2 AC 22, 33d, 35d.

[200] Thus his Lordship eschews the language of "foreseeability" in favour of "ordinariness", although the distinction is unlikely to be of great practical significance. See above, § 4.2(iii)(a).

[201] *TBCL* 391; the passage is quoted more fully above, § 4.2(iii)(b). Cf. *Hart and Honoré* 364–5. Certain jurisdictions take the view that conduct, while remaining free, deliberate, and informed, can be causally influenced by the interventions of other human agents as when, say, P resolves to kill V as a result of being offered £10,000 by D to do so. In Germany, for instance, D would be regarded as "the principal behind the principal" in the murder of V: Fletcher, *Rethinking Criminal Law* (1978) 657ff. Whatever the merits of this less restricted approach, it cannot suddenly be adopted *ad hoc* for England and Wales at the cost of a major disruption in settled doctrine and resulting uncertainty, particularly in the area of parties to crimes. In English and Wales, such a case is properly handled within the law of complicity.

his autonomy, but is also contrary to the importance attached in modern English law to an individual's separate identity and responsibility.[202]

The dealer who sells T a gun does not shoot V. T does. It may sometimes be appropriate to criminalise the dealer's actions, but not on the basis of causation. Similarly, in the present case, D did not pollute the river. T did. It was possible for the legislature to make D responsible for that outcome by stipulating vicarious or situational liability; but the legislation did not do that. The statute requires causation by the *defendant*, in the normal way. The House of Lords trampled upon a fundamental precept of criminal law.

Bad principle, then. Bad law, too. The decision is inconsistent with the reasoning in such decisions as *Latif*,[203] *Hilton*,[204] and *Dalby*,[205] mentioned earlier.[206] Glanville Williams's conclusion on *Dalby* holds just as aptly for *Empress*:[207]

> "The fact that [D's] own conduct, rightful or wrongful, provided the background for a subsequent voluntary act by another does not make him responsible for it. What he does may be a but-for cause of the injurious act, but he did not do it."

In *Empress*, D's storage of oil provided no more than the opportunity for T's vandalous act. Were it otherwise, the law of complicity would be largely redundant. One who assists another to commit a crime could be held to have caused the prohibited harm, and so be convicted of the crime as a principal. Lord Hoffmann's analysis virtually demolishes the need for liability of secondary parties. Yet the decision in *Empress* purports to follow law. Unfortunately, in the face of extensive criminal law precedent to the contrary, the only unequivocal authority Lord Hoffmann cited for his conclusion was a tort case.[208] Moreover, his Lordship placed great weight on the statement attributed to Lord Wilberforce in *Alphacell* v. *Woodward* that "the *deliberate* act of a third party does not necessarily negative causal connection".[209] But Lord Wilberforce did not use the word "deliberate". During his speech in *Alphacell* v. *Woodward*, Lord Wilberforce had, *obiter*, merely rejected the proposition that "in every case the act of a third party necessarily interrupts the chain of causation"; a warranted rejection that provides no support whatsoever for the reasoning in *Empress*. So: bad principle, bad law, and bad reasoning.

Be that as it may, the decision was confirmed by the House of Lords in *Kennedy (No. 2)*, though only in the particular context of interpreting and applying "a statutory provision imposing strict criminal liability on those who cause pollution of controlled waters".[210] Thus this line of authority appears to be confined to the sphere of regulatory offences, and

---

[202] Cf. the principle of personal responsibility argued for in Simester, "The Mental Element in Complicity" [2006] 122 *LQR* 578, 580–1.

[203] [1996] 1 All ER 353; also *Tse Hung-Lit* [1986] AC 876.

[204] (1838) 2 Lew CC 214, 168 ER 1132.

[205] [1982] 1 All ER 916.

[206] Above, § 4.2(iii)(b). See also *People* v. *Elder* 100 Mich 515, 59 NW 237 (1894); *Commonwealth* v. *Root* 403 Pa 571, 170 A 2d 310 (1961); *People* v. *Campbell* 124 Mich App 333, 335 NW 2d 27 (1983); *Horsey* (1862) 3 F & F 287, 176 ER 129. *Empress* is also inconsistent with *Impress (Worcester) Ltd* v. *Rees* [1971] 2 All ER 357, which Lord Hoffmann asserted was wrongly decided, notwithstanding that the result in that case had been endorsed by the House of Lords in *Alphacell* v. *Woodward* [1972] AC 824, 835 (Lord Wilberforce) 847 (Lord Salmon).

[207] "*Finis* for *Novus Actus*?" (1989) 48 *CLJ* 391; above, n. 161.

[208] *Stansbie* v. *Troman* [1948] 2 KB 48.

[209] *Empress* [1999] 2 AC 22, 33c. See *Alphacell* v. *Woodward* [1972] AC 824, 835.

[210] [2007] UKHL 38, [2008] 1 AC 269, paras. 15–16.

in particular those governing pollution and, perhaps, other environmental wrongs.[211] That is, in our view, a desirable restriction,[212] albeit one that remains sensitive to the practical difficulties of enforcing environmental crimes.

Case 2: Being in control of a car involved in an accident?
Section 3ZB of the Road Traffic Act 1988[213] establishes a crime of causing death by driving when the driver happens to be uninsured, unlicensed, or disqualified. Under the clear terms of the statute, there is no need for the illegal circumstance of D's being unlicensed/uninsured/disqualified to be causally related to the death.[214] In terms of causation, section 3ZB requires only that D cause death *by driving a car on the road*.

Initially even that requirement was liberally interpreted. In *Williams*,[215] for example, W lacked both insurance and a licence. He was otherwise driving lawfully and within the speed limit when the victim, L, suddenly stepped in front of his car, about three feet away. W was unable to stop in time, and L was killed. In the subsequent case of *Hughes*,[216] MH, who was uninsured, was driving at a safe speed on the correct side of the road. V was driving in the opposite direction, exhausted from overwork and disoriented by a cocktail of drugs. After weaving erratically across both sides of the road, V finally veered across the carriageway, collided with H, and died. In terms of civil law, the victim in each case was entirely responsible for the accident. Neither defendant was at fault.[217] Yet both defendants were ruled by the Court of Appeal to have caused death by their driving, and as such to have committed the section 3ZB offence.

Indeed, the Court of Appeal was prepared to hold (in *Hughes*) that "if [V] had ploughed into the respondent's van whilst stationary in a queue of traffic or at a traffic light, the respondent, it could be said, would have caused the death of [V] by driving a motor vehicle".[218] But in the context of causation, that is to confuse driving with presence,[219] and it is to confuse true legal causation with so-called "but for" causation. As was argued in § 4.2(i), the "but for" test is a red herring. It is only an indicator and not a true test of causation in these contexts. D's *presence* was an ingredient in the accident, to be sure, but it

[211] In *Natural England* v. *Day* [2014] EWCA Crim 2683, [2015] 1 Cr App R (S) 53, para. 23, the Court of Appeal did not decide the point but noted that "we see strong arguments for following the approach in *Empress Car*" in relation to the Wildlife and Countryside Act 1981.
[212] Even then, however, the analysis will permit some extraordinary conclusions: see, e.g., *RL and JF* [2008] EWCA Crim 1970, [2009] 1 Cr App R 16, where the *members* of an unincorporated golf club were said to be criminally liable for the same offence as in *Empress*, after an underground pipe supplying oil to the club boiler was fractured when work was done on the ground above by independent building contractors. The Court did not even trouble to enquire whether the intervention was extraordinary, as *Empress* requires (above, § 4.2(iii)(a)). Presumably, if vandals are considered by the judiciary to be an everyday intervener, a fortiori clumsy builders. (And, in Canada, homicidal bouncers: *Maybin* 2012 SCC 24, [2012] 2 SCR 30.)
[213] As amended by the Road Safety Act 2006. The offence carries a maximum sentence of two years' imprisonment.
[214] Thus the offence is a morally illegitimate example of constructive liability: below, § 6.5. See further Hirst, "Causing Death by Driving and Other Offences" [2008] *Crim LR* 339.
[215] [2010] EWCA Crim 2552.
[216] [2013] UKSC 56, [2013] 1 WLR 2461; *sub nom MH* [2011] EWCA Crim 1508.
[217] Cf. *MH* [2011] EWCA Crim 1508, para. 22.
[218] *Ibid.*, para. 44.
[219] No doubt it is appropriate to regard D as "driving" while stationary on the highway for the purpose of offences like driving with excess blood alcohol; but that legitimate interpretation does not obviate the need to prove causation in offences such as s. 3ZB.

does not follow that D's *driving* was a non-negligible cause. Suppose that Jim was walking from his home to the shops when Kevin, who was drunk, lost control of his car, mounted the pavement, and collided with Jim. If Jim died, no one would seriously suggest that Jim's walking is a cause of his own death. But he was there and, on the logic of the Court of Appeal, it did.

Fortunately, this line of objection was accepted by the Supreme Court, which observed that a but-for relationship is not to be equated with common-law causation. The Court noted that section 3ZB contains no explicit abrogation of normal causal requirements, and emphasised that any such abrogation would require particular legislative clarity in the context of a serious homicide offence.[220]

Moreover, in an important ruling, the Supreme Court went on to hold that V's death must be connected to something objectively wrong about D's driving: "Juries should thus be directed that it is not necessary for the Crown to prove careless or inconsiderate driving, but that there must be something open to proper criticism in the driving of the defendant, beyond the mere presence of the vehicle on the road, and which contributed in some more than minimal way to the death."[221] In effect, the Court generalised a common-law requirement of causal salience,[222] notwithstanding that the section 3ZB was drafted in terms that contained no such requirement. On this analysis, causation requirements in the criminal law are intimately bound up with fault.

The Supreme Court's decision is understandable in the context of a strict liability offence, but it goes too far. When Brandon Lee died tragically during filming of *The Crow*, after an error in preparing the prop gun, it was actor Michael Massee who pulled the trigger. Massee's act was *a* cause of Lee's death despite his lack of fault. The firing of the bullet caused death, and pulling the trigger was a cause of that. By contrast, the "common sense"[223] principle espoused in *Hughes* would lead us to conclude that Massee did not do an act that caused Lee's death. That conclusion should be rejected.

Be that as it may, the fault-based principle in *Hughes* is an appropriate one to apply in the context of offences, like section 3ZB, that contain aggravating consequence elements for which liability is strict. The extent to which the principle is applicable outside that context, and is generalisable to offences beyond the driving context, remains to be seen.[224] As the Supreme Court itself confirmed, causation requirements are very much offence-specific.[225] But their Lordships certainly did not go so far as the Court of Appeal in *Williams*, which had specifically invoked Lord Hoffmann's claim in *Environmental Agency* v. *Empress Car Co.*

---

[220] *Hughes* [2013] UKSC 56, [2013] 1 WLR 2461, paras. 26–8.

[221] *Ibid.*, para. 33.

[222] Above, § 4.2(ii)(b).

[223] *Hughes* [2013] UKSC 56, [2013] 1 WLR 2461, para.32.

[224] *Hughes* was affirmed in *Taylor* [2016] UKSC 5, [2016] 1 WLR 500, in the context of a prosecution for aggravated vehicle taking—i.e. where injury or damage is caused—under s. 12A of the Theft Act 1968. In substance, however, the decision in *Taylor* turned on the Court's finding that s. 12A was not to be construed as imposing strict liability with respect to the aggravating circumstances, rather than on its making a finding of causation premised upon fault. In *Natural England* v. *Day* [2014] EWCA Crim 2683, [2015] 1 Cr App R (S) 53, para. 23, the Court of Appeal declined counsel's invitation to extend the approach in *Hughes* to environmental offences. While the Court did not decide the point, it considered there were "strong arguments", in the environmental context, for retaining the approach taken in *Environmental Agency* v. *Empress Car Co. (Abertillery) Ltd* [1999] 2 AC 22. (See Case 1 above in this subsection.)

[225] *Ibid.*, para. 20.

(Abertillery) Ltd that "one cannot give a common sense answer to a question of causation for the purpose of attributing responsibility under some rule without knowing the purpose and scope of the rule".[226] Effectively, the Court of Appeal had suggested that that there are no general principles of causation: there is only the interpretation of causal responsibility requirements for specific crimes. By contrast, the Supreme Court accepted that there established doctrines of causation which are prima facie of general application. Rightly so. The requirements of causation may differ somewhat across legal contexts, but causation doctrine does have some core content. That's what makes it causation.

(e) The victim

What about cases where the intervention is by V himself, rather than by a third party? The general rule is that the consequences of V's intervention are attributable to D provided that:

1. V's conduct is in reaction to D's wrongdoing; and
2. V's reaction was a reasonably foreseeable possibility.

In *Roberts*,[227] the defendant made sexual advances to V while driving a car. V leapt out of the moving vehicle and suffered resulting injuries. D's conviction for assault occasioning actual bodily harm was upheld by the Court of Appeal, which asked whether the injury was "the natural result of what the alleged assailant said and did, in the sense that it was something that could reasonably have been foreseen as the consequence of what he was saying or doing?"[228] The same principle is capable of explaining the American case of *People* v. *Lewis*,[229] in which V, who was dying painfully from a gunshot wound, committed suicide by cutting his throat. D was held to have caused V's death.[230] It would be otherwise, however, if V had killed himself not in reaction to the suffering that D had inflicted,[231] but rather in order to shield D or, indeed, in an attempt to make D liable for a homicide offence.

The second requirement, of reasonable foreseeability, may not be met where the victim's reaction is disproportionate. Although it is sometimes said that "the victim must be taken as he is found",[232] in *People* v. *Lewis* D would not have been guilty of murder if the wound had merely been painful rather than dangerous and, knowing this, V had taken his life only in order to escape pain.[233] In general, V's reaction will not be a *novus actus* where it is "in the

---

[226] [1999] 2 AC 22, 29; *Williams* [2010] EWCA Crim 2552, para. 32.

[227] (1971) 56 Cr App R 95. Other cases include *Lewis* [2010] EWCA Crim 151, paras. 25, 39-41; *Marjoram* [2000] Crim LR 372; *DPP* v. *Daley* [1980] AC 237; *Williams and Davies* [1992] 1 WLR 380; *Pitts* (1842) Car & M 284, 174 ER 509; *Halliday* [1886–90] All ER 1028, (1889) 61 LT 701. See Elliott, "Frightening a Person into Injuring Himself" [1974] *Crim* LR 15.

[228] (1971) 56 Cr App R 95, 102.

[229] 124 Cal 551, 57 P 470 (1898).

[230] Although the *ratio* of the decision was multiple causes (that V died from loss of blood from the combined wounds), the court would have been prepared to decide the case on this ground if the facts had been clear regarding D's motive for cutting his own throat. See also *State* v. *Angelina* 73 WVa 146, 80 SE 141 (1913); *Jones* v. *State* 220 Ind 384, 43 NE 2d 1017 (1942); *Stephenson* v. *State* 205 Ind 141, 179 NE 633 (1932) (torture).

[231] Cf. *D* [2006] EWCA 1139, [2006] 2 Cr App R 24, where the history of abuse may be capable in principle of explaining why V's suicide was a "natural" or intelligible response, taken in circumstances where V's choices are limited by the D's acts of oppression. See the discussion by Horder and McGowan, "Manslaughter by Causing Another's Suicide" [2006] *Crim LR* 1035, 1039–43.

[232] E.g. *Blaue* [1975] 3 All ER 446, 450; below, § 4.2(iv)(b).

[233] *Pace* the *obiter dicta* in *D* [2006] EWCA Crim 1139; [2006] 2 Cr App R 24, where it is suggested that a minor assault on a person with a fragile and vulnerable personality (thus not a sufficiently free intervener), who then

foreseeable range",[234] and is not "daft".[235] This remains so even if that reaction is negligent or unlawful.[236]

As is the case with third-party interventions, the possibility of a victim's contribution being a *novus actus interveniens* remains subject to the proviso that the original harm inflicted by D must no longer be contributing to the occurrence of the eventual result. In *Wall*,[237] the defendant (a colonial governor) sentenced V to an illegal flogging of some 800 lashes. V died from the punishment. It appeared that V had drunk alcohol after the flogging, which may well have accelerated his death. If so, however, it did so in combination with the effects of the flogging, and so would have been no more than an accompanying rather than overriding causal factor. The defendant therefore remained causally responsible for V's death.

(f) Summary of approach to intervening causes

It is impossible to be precise and comprehensive about the principles governing the attribution of causation. The rich detail of the cases defies reduction to a list of simple rules: sometimes when confronting new situations, the best technique may be simply to argue by analogy to one or more decided cases. Nonetheless, at the risk of oversimplication we offer the following general guidelines to causation problems where there are intervening causes.

Begin by considering whether D's original act is still making an ongoing contribution, in its own right, to the prohibited result at the time that result occurs (e.g. where V dies after losing blood from D's wound as well as T's). If so, then regardless of the other interventions, D's act is a concurrent cause of the result (§ 4.2(ii)(c)) and the causal chain is not broken by any *novus actus interveniens*. The analysis is concluded.

If the conclusion is not determined by that first step, it then becomes necessary to enquire whether D's original act is a cause of the prohibited result *through the medium of* T's intervention. This question is approached as follows.

First, assuming T is a human agent, consider whether T's intervention is free, deliberate, and informed (§ 4.2(iii)(b)). If it meets these criteria in full, then, regardless of its predictability, T's intervention is a *novus actus interveniens* that breaks the causal chain between D's original act and the prohibited result. *Pace Empress* (§ 4.2(iii)(d)), D is absolved of causal responsibility and the analysis is concluded.

Alternatively, if T is not a human agent (§ 4.2(iii)(a)) or the intervention was not free, deliberate, and informed, consider whether that intervention was reasonably foreseeable, as opposed to unforeseeable and extraordinary. If the former, then it may be expected not to sever the causal chain linking D's original act to the prohibited result; if the latter, then the intervention is a *novus actus interveniens*.

---

committed suicide, might be capable of constituting manslaughter. At least in most such cases, deliberate suicide would not be "in the foreseeable range".

[234] *Corbett* [1996] Crim LR 594 (CA); *pace Dear* [1996] Crim LR 595 (CA). It is submitted that the former case is to be preferred on this point, being consistent with existing case law (see, e.g., the cases cited in n. 157 above).

[235] *Roberts* (1971) 56 Cr App R 95, 102.

[236] Cf. *Walker* (1824) 1 C & P 320, 171 ER 1213; *Swindall and Osborne* (1846) 2 Car & Kir 230, 2 Cox CC 141, 175 ER 95.

[237] (1802) 28 St Tr 51, 145. See also *Flynn* (1867) 16 WR 319 (Ir); *Mubila* [1956] SA 31.

(iv) Omissions

(a) As causes

It is sometimes suggested that omissions cannot be causes.[238] This idea is founded on the notion that non-events, like failures to intercede and rescue a drowning victim, cannot bring things about: they are merely failures to prevent. To some extent this is true. If D watches without intervening while in a position to save V, her causal contribution to D's death is not of the same order as that when D herself holds V's head under water. One thing that is distinctive about omissions is that they do not initiate causal processes. Instead, they permit other causal processes to bring about the harm.

As such, omissions are distinctive in as much as they describe events that did *not* happen. Nonetheless, neither ordinary language nor the law has much compunction about attributing causal responsibility to omissions. Both within and outside the courtroom, it is acceptable to say that the railway gatekeeper's failure in *Pittwood*[239] to close the gate before the train came through caused the resulting accident. By contrast, it would be misleading just to state that the train's arrival caused the accident, although that was also a causal factor. We tend to reserve the language of causation for those factors which are most relevant to our explanations.

All this reflects the point made earlier in § 4.2(ii), that causation in law is rarely a simple mechanical issue. Rather, it is intimately connected with the process of ascribing *responsibility* for the actus reus. Active intervention, while an obvious means of "causing" harm in the mechanical sense, is not the only way of being involved in bringing that harm about. In law, responsibility for the consequences of omissions involves a twofold test. D is normally held legally responsible for the consequences of an omission when (i) he has a duty to prevent those consequences from occurring (considered earlier in § 4.1(i)(b)), and (ii) his omission to intervene made a difference: that is, *if he had intervened, his intervention would have made a difference*. Part (ii) is the causal test.[240] For omissions, because of their counterfactual nature, it is usually satisfied by proof of "but for" causation. In other words, D's omission causes an outcome if, but for that omission by D, the outcome would not have occurred.[241] If there is a reasonable possibility that it might have resulted anyway, then D's omission might have made no difference and D cannot be held causally responsible for that outcome. As an example:

> Suppose that D, a doctor, does not notice that V has stopped breathing and fails to give him artificial respiration. She cannot be held causally responsible for his death unless it can be shown that V would have survived if D had discharged her duty to intervene and artificially respirate him.

---

[238] E.g. Moore, *Act and Crime* (1993) 267–78; Moore, *Causation and Responsibility* (2009) 444ff. For discussion, see Hughes, "Criminal Omissions" (1958) 67 *Yale LJ* 590, 627–31; Husak, *Philosophy of Criminal Law* (1987) chap. 6; Leavens, "A Causative Approach to Omissions" (1988) 76 *Cal LR* 547; Beynon, "Causation, Omissions and Complicity" [1987] *Crim LR* 539. Fletcher, "On the Moral Irrelevance of Bodily Movements" (1994) 142 *U Pa L Rev* 1443; Hart and Honoré 38; Fletcher, *Rethinking Criminal Law* (1978) 589ff.

[239] (1902) 19 TLR 37. Cf. the discussion in *Hart and Honoré* 32ff; also Feinberg, *Harm to Others* (1984) 172ff.

[240] *Quaere* whether this requirement was overlooked in *Stone and Dobinson* [1977] QB 354.

[241] *Morby* (1882) 8 QBD 571; *Barnett v. Chelsea and Kensington Hospital Mgmt Cttee* [1969] 1 QB 428.

A similar example is *Dalloway*,[242] in which D was driving a cart without retaining a proper grip on the reins. A young child ran out in front of the cart and was struck and killed. It was ruled that D might be convicted of manslaughter only if it were proved that, had D been using the reins correctly, the child would have been saved.

Note that the prosecution must show, beyond reasonable doubt, that D's intervention *would*—not *might*—have made a difference. This rule is made clear in *Morby*, the facts of which were as follows:[243]

> D's child, aged 8, died of smallpox. Owing to D's religious beliefs, he obtained no medical aid for his son. At trial, it was established that proper medical treatment might have saved or prolonged the child's life, and would certainly have increased his chances of survival; but it could not definitely be said that treatment would have made any difference. It might have been of no avail.

On these facts, the Court for Crown Cases Reserved held unanimously that D's conviction could not be sustained. In this respect the stringency of the causal test for omissions matches that for acts: it must positively be proved that D's conduct *did* cause death, not that it may have done. In the context of *Morby*, this requires the prosecution to prove beyond reasonable doubt that if D had called for medical assistance V *would*, not may, have survived.

It is worth emphasising that even where it can be shown that D's omission is a "but for" cause of the harm, the omission will not be a legal cause if a *novus actus* intervenes. It is also subject to the requirement of salience.[244] Suppose, for example, that Alice makes a luncheon appointment with James. Later she discovers that she will not be free on the day they have arranged. Unfortunately, she discourteously fails to telephone James and cancel the appointment. While en route to the restaurant, James is killed in an automobile accident. If Alice had remembered to cancel, James would have eaten lunch at his office. Thus, but for Alice's omission, James would not have died. In this situation, however, Alice's omission is not a cause of death.

(b) As interventions

The general rule is that, while an omission by a third party can be a causal factor, it cannot be a *novus actus interveniens*. Where D omits to prevent harm, his omission may be a legal cause of that harm, but it is normally a *concurrent* cause; that is, alongside those causal processes that the omission has failed to prevent. To illustrate:

> Suppose that D stabs V, who is admitted to hospital with substantial loss of blood and in urgent need of a blood transfusion to save her life. Apart from the loss of blood, V's injuries are not life-threatening. T, the doctor who attends V, recognises that she needs a blood transfusion and prepares to give her one. While waiting for the blood to arrive, he goes to check on another patient. Unfortunately, he is distracted by a conversation with the patient and forgets to return and administer the transfusion to V. V dies from the loss of blood. Had the transfusion been performed, she would have survived.

---

[242] (1847) 2 Cox CC 273.
[243] (1882) 8 QBD 571. See Williams, "What Should the Code Do about Omissions?" (1987) 7 *LS* 92, 106.
[244] Above, § 4.2(ii)(b).

In this case, *both* D and T cause V's death. Diagrammatically, their actions are multiple concurrent causes:

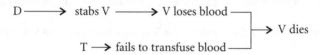

T's omission is not a *novus actus* that intervenes to break the causal chain from D's conduct to V's death. The whole reason why T's omission is causally significant is that it *fails to break* the causal sequence from D's action's to V's death. Indeed, we fault T and hold him (as well as D) liable for V's death precisely because he should have intervened and broken that chain before it reached its fatal culmination.

The proposition that an omission normally does not break a pre-existing causal chain is the proper explanation of *Blaue*.[245] In that case V was stabbed, and was admitted to hospital having lost a large quantity of blood. She was a Jehovah's Witness, and refused the blood transfusion that was necessary to save her life. Consequently, the following day she died. D was convicted of her manslaughter. He appealed, contending that V's refusal to have a blood transfusion had broken the causal chain between the stabbing and V's death.

While it was accepted by the Crown that V's refusal to have a transfusion was *a* cause of her death, the Court of Appeal quite rightly ruled, using an analogy with *Smith*,[246] that the original wound inflicted by D was still an operating cause of death. However, faced with the submission by D's counsel that V's decision was an unreasonable one, the Court responded that:[247]

> "It has long been the policy of the law that those who use violence on other people must take their victims as they find them. This in our judgment means the whole man, not just the physical man. It does not lie in the mouth of the assailant to say that his victim's religious beliefs which inhibited him from accepting certain kinds of treatment were unreasonable."

As a general proposition, this is not valid law. Cases such as *Roberts*, discussed in § 4.2(iii)(e), establish that an intervening reaction by V *does* break the chain of causation where it is not a reasonably foreseeable possibility—or, as was said in that case, where the reaction is "so daft" that it is really V's own voluntary act.[248] This means that D does not have to take his victim however he finds her, but only in so far as her reaction is a reasonably foreseeable or understandable one.

Suppose, then, that V's refusal of a transfusion *was* "daft", and not a sensible or foreseeable possibility (this was not decided by the Court). Prima facie, on the authority of *Roberts* and similar cases, this would then be a *novus actus* for which D was not responsible. In *Blaue*, however, the difference from those other cases was that V's intervening conduct involved not an act but an omission.[249] Thus, while it played a causal role in bringing about her death, and was a factor (unlike *Roberts*) for which D was not responsible, it did not break the causal chain from the stabbing to V's death. D's appeal, in effect, was that by her

---

[245] [1975] 3 All ER 446; also of *Holland* (1841) 2 Mood & R 351, 174 ER 313.
[246] See above, § 4.2(iii)(b) (Case 3).
[247] [1975] 3 All ER 446, 450.
[248] (1971) 56 Cr App R 95, 102.
[249] More precisely, an action (refusal) whose causal role depends upon an omission (non-transfusion).

refusing to break the causal sequence D had set in motion, V broke the chain of causation. But an omission cannot, by itself, do that.[250]

The difference between the two cases can be illustrated, once again, with causal diagrams:

Roberts: D ⟶ frightens V ⟶ V jumps from car ⟶ V is injured

Blaue: D ⟶ stabs V ⟶ V loses blood ⟶
                                                    ⟶ V dies
               V ⟶ refuses transfusion of blood ⟶

(c) Two case studies

By way of conclusion, it may be helpful to consider two more complex examples. One case that combines both omissions and the issue of medical interventions is *McKechnie*.[251] The facts of the case were as follows:

> D attacked V, inflicting serious head injuries. V was taken, deeply unconscious, to hospital, where he was discovered to be suffering from a duodenal ulcer which required surgery. However, the attending doctors decided not to operate on the ulcer. This decision was taken because, in the doctors' view, administration of the necessary anaesthesia to someone with such extensive head injuries could be fatal. A month later, the ulcer burst, and V died without having regained consciousness.

On these facts, D's conviction for manslaughter was upheld by the Court of Appeal. How should the question of causation be analysed? One cause of V's death is, of course, the ulcer. But another, concurrent, causal factor is the doctors' omission to operate: if it had been safe to operate, there was no doubt but that the ulcer would have been removed.[252] What is therefore crucial to D's liability is whether the omission to operate, which *was* a cause of death, can be said in turn to be a consequence of D's actions in inflicting the head injuries upon V. And it seems clear enough that it was. The doctors' decision not to operate was made precisely because of the injuries D inflicted. Moreover, although expert testimony at trial conflicted over whether it was *possible* to proceed with the operation without endangering V's life, there was no dispute that the decision was a reasonable one to take. Hence it was not a *novus actus interveniens*. We may represent the causal analysis as follows:

McKechnie:

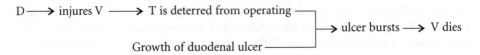

D ⟶ injures V ⟶ T is deterred from operating ⟶
                                                      ⟶ ulcer bursts ⟶ V dies
               Growth of duodenal ulcer ⟶

---

[250] *Contra Hart and Honoré* 361. Occasionally, an omission may be a *novus actus* when *combined* with a positive intervention: e.g. when the railway gatekeeper fails to close the gate, causing the ambulance taking V to hospital to be hit by a train. The gatekeeper causes V's death, not V's original assailant.

[251] (1992) 94 Cr App R 51.

[252] *Ibid.*, 57.

We are also in a position now to consider the difficult case of *Cheshire*.[253] The relevant facts of the case were as follows:

> In early December 1987, D shot V in the leg and stomach. V was taken to hospital where his injuries were operated on and he was then transferred to the intensive care unit. He developed respiratory problems and in mid-December a tracheotomy tube was inserted into his windpipe, where it remained for some four weeks. In early February his condition began to improve, and it appears that by this time the injuries inflicted by D's bullets had ceased to threaten his life. Unfortunately, he then began to develop breathing difficulties. These arose because his windpipe had narrowed near the site of the tracheotomy—a rare but known side-effect of tracheotomies. The medical staff negligently failed to diagnose the cause of the breathing difficulties, and V died in mid-February.

The Court of Appeal upheld D's conviction for murder, and properly so. Both D and V's doctors caused V's death. The key point is that the tracheotomy and subsequent complication occurred without negligence by the doctors. Thus there is no disruption of the causal chain between D's act of shooting V and the narrowing of V's windpipe. This being so, the question then becomes whether the doctors' subsequent negligence is a *novus actus interveniens* that breaks the causal chain between the narrowing of the windpipe and V's death. And the answer to that question is no—because it constitutes an omission. The complaint against the doctors is that they *failed* to prevent the (natural, albeit rare) complication from causing death. Diagrammatically:

Cheshire:

D ⟶ injures V ⟶ T performs tracheotomy ⟶ windpipe narrows ⟶ ⟶ V dies

T(2) ⟶ fails to rectify windpipe ⟶

§ 4.3 The requirement of voluntariness

It is a fundamental requirement of the criminal law that D cannot be held liable for the occurrence of an actus reus unless he was *responsible* for it: unless its occurrence can in some way be attributed to D.

We noted in Chapter 1 that when an actus reus occurs (e.g. Jim is murdered), the criminal law begins with every member of society as a potential defendant.[254] The legal criteria that define responsibility for an actus reus also help to tell us which members of society are suitable defendants. Suppose that while investigating Jim's death, the police learn that his daughter Alice had secretly wished him dead because she stood to gain from his will. Despite her desires, the need for responsibility means that Alice is not guilty of murder unless she actually played some role in bringing about his death.

In respect of consequences, responsibility is established by showing causation. The police may conclude that although Alice wanted Jim's death, she did not cause it. Hence she did not murder Jim. More generally, causation is necessary to establish a link between D's

---

[253] [1991] 3 All ER 670.
[254] See §§ 1.2(ii)(e), 7.1.

behaviour and the prohibited consequences. If an actus reus includes specification of such consequences (e.g. a person's death), the prosecution must prove causation in order to show that D's behaviour was responsible for that consequence, as part of showing that the actus reus as a whole can be attributed to D.

However, before she can be criminally liable the defendant must also be responsible for the *behaviour* element of the actus reus. This requirement is met when her behaviour is voluntary. Suppose that Alice did in fact cause Jim's death, but that she did so while suffering an epileptic seizure, during which her movements caused a heavy object to fall and crush Jim. Alice's behaviour, which causes Jim's death, is not voluntary. She is not responsible for his death, and cannot be convicted of murder.

Very often, acquittal in these circumstances need not be based upon involuntariness. Crimes such as murder require proof of some mental element on the part of the defendant, i.e. proof of some form of mens rea.[255] In most cases, murder itself cannot be committed unless D intends to kill or cause serious injury.[256] Thus, even though Alice's behaviour may have caused death, she lacks the mental element required to be guilty of murder. She lacks mens rea.

But it is important to emphasise that involuntariness is *not* merely a denial of intention, or of other forms of mens rea, or even a denial of fault in general.[257] Alice does not claim that she killed Jim by *accident*. Her denial is much more profound. It is a claim that the movements of her body which caused Jim's death do not belong to Alice as a reasoning person. It is, as such, a denial of responsibility for the actus reus itself.

This deserves elaboration. As part of our conception of what it is to be a human being, we look for a link between an agent's deliberations and the consequent movements (or non-movements) of her body. Not all movements of one's body can be identified with the person whose body it is that moves. When the doctor tests Simon's reflexes by tapping him on the knee, the swinging of his leg cannot be attributed to Simon. It is merely an event in the history of his body, rather like the lurching of passengers standing in a crowded bus. These are not actions that a person is answerable for doing. They are things that happen to him, over which he has no control, and for which he is not responsible. So it is with Alice in the example above. Her behaviour is part of her body's history, but is not attributable to her as a reasoning person. It is not produced by any exercise of the capacities that identify Alice as a moral agent. In the words of H.L.A. Hart:[258]

> "What is missing in these cases appears to most people as a vital link between mind and body; and both the ordinary man and the lawyer might well insist on this by saying that in these cases there is not 'really' a human action at all and certainly nothing for which anyone should be made criminally responsible however 'strict' legal responsibility might be."

(i) Involuntary behaviour

In general, D's deliberative control over her behaviour can be lost or impaired in two ways. First, D's normal capacity to reason about her behaviour may be suppressed because of

---

[255] Below, Chapter 5.
[256] Below, Chapter 10.
[257] For useful discussion of this point, see Patient, "Some Remarks about the Element of Voluntariness in Offences of Absolute Liability" [1968] *Crim LR* 23.
[258] Hart, "Acts of Will and Responsibility" in *Punishment and Responsibility* (1968) 90, 107.

an impaired consciousness. Alternatively, even if D is able to reason normally about her actions, she may have lost physical control over the movements of her body. In either case, her actions are not responsive to reason. They are "movements of the body which occurred though the agent had no reason for moving his body in that way".[259]

(a) Loss of physical control

Imagine the following assault:

> Deborah is standing between Vicky and Tanya. Suddenly, Tanya grasps Deborah's arm and forces it into Vicky's midriff. Tanya is more powerful than Deborah, and Deborah has no chance to resist her. Vicky is winded.

In this situation, Deborah does not commit an assault on Vicky, because her arm movement is involuntary.[260] The movement does not occur under her control, and she cannot prevent its occurrence. Thus she is not responsible for the actus reus which eventuates. (Indeed, it is Tanya who assaults Vicky, using Deborah's arm.) Comparable instances are where D's arm strikes V as the result of a reflex movement or a muscular convulsion or spasm.[261]

(b) Impaired consciousness

It has also been held that if D, while driving, were to be stunned by a blow and rendered incapable of controlling his car, his consequent failure to give way to a pedestrian at a pedestrian crossing would be involuntary and not subject to criminal liability.[262] An analogous situation is sleepwalking. In *Hughes*, a woman had got out of bed during the night and had gone to the kitchen "to peel potatoes", whence she had taken a knife and returned to the bedroom to stab her husband. She was acquitted of wounding with intent.[263]

Sleepwalking is an instructive case, because D's behaviour in this state may well be purposive,[264] and exhibit many outward signs of intentionality. Glanville Williams makes this point vividly:[265]

> "The sleep-walker does not always proceed as the cartoonists imagine him, with eyes tightly closed and arms outstretched. His eyes may be open and he may appear to be in perfect control. He will open a door and turn a corner, walk downstairs, open a drawer, take out a carving-knife, and return to the bedroom where his wife is asleep. But after waking up he will not remember his deed (except sometimes as a dream). Although his acts have a certain purpose (indeed, he may have an understandable reason for killing his wife), it is the purpose of a dream-state. He is not acting with his normal conscious mind."

When Lady Macbeth is observed "washing" her hands at night,[266] her movements are hardly random or uncontrolled. They exude purpose. Her actions are, in some sense, a

---

[259] The definition of involuntariness proposed by Hart, *Punishment and Responsibility* (1968) 255–6.

[260] *Farduto* (1912) 10 DLR 669, 673; compare *O'Sullivan v. Fisher* [1954] SASR 33, 39–40.

[261] *Bratty v. A-G for Northern Ireland* [1963] AC 386, 409.

[262] *Hill v. Baxter* [1958] 1 QB 277, 282–3, 286; *Burns v. Bidder* [1967] 2 QB 227, 36; *Kay v. Butterworth* (1945) 61 TLR 452, 453; *Spurge* [1961] 2 QB 205; *Bell* [1984] 3 All ER 842, 846.

[263] Reported in *The Times*, 3 May 1978, p. 5. Cf. *Bratty v. A-G for Northern Ireland* [1963] AC 386, 403, 409; *Carpenter, The Times*, 14 October 1976; *Carter* [1959] VR 105; *Fain v. Commonwealth* (1879) 39 Am Rep 213. Seemingly, the case should have been regarded as one of insane automatism: below, §18.1(ii)(c).

[264] Compare also *Charlson* [1955] 1 All ER 859.

[265] TBCL 665.

[266] *Macbeth*, Act V, scene i.

subintentional product of her unconscious or subconscious mind. Certainly they are not mere reflex movements. But the control that Lady Macbeth has over them is in no way a conscious control—indeed, she is incapable of acting intentionally at all. Her "acts" are, in law, involuntary.

In the criminal law, these forms of involuntary behaviour are known as automatism. Like Lady Macbeth, the defendant may be unconscious or semi-conscious when she does the actus reus. Where this is so, and her actions are the product of a sufficiently impaired consciousness, those actions are described as automatic. However, as the assault example involving Deborah, Tanya, and Vicky shows, automatism predicated upon unconsciousness or impaired consciousness is not *required* for the defendant to be absolved of responsibility for her behaviour. Whether she was conscious or unconscious, what is essential to the denial of responsibility for a defendant's involuntary behaviour is that *she was unable deliberatively to control that behaviour and to prevent it from occurring.*

In most cases, there will be a connection between consciousness and control: the greater the degree of consciousness a defendant has, the greater the degree of conscious or deliberative control she will have over her actions. This raises a further question. Where D's claim of involuntariness is based upon automatism and an impaired consciousness, must D have lost *all* conscious control over her limbs?

Historically, the law has been unclear. The leading case is *A-G's Reference (No. 2 of 1992)*, and it sets a very high standard indeed. In that case, D was charged with causing death by reckless driving. He had steered his truck onto the hard shoulder of the motorway and then into a stationary vehicle. At the time, D had been driving for six of the past 12 hours. The defence adduced evidence that D had entered a condition known as "driving without awareness", in which a driver's ability to avoid a collision was negated because repetitive stimuli experienced during long motorway journeys induced a trance-like state in which the focal point for forward vision gradually came nearer and nearer until the driver was focusing just ahead of his windscreen. The Court of Appeal held that such evidence could not support a defence of automatism. In the Court's words, "the defence of automatism requires a total destruction of voluntary control on the defendant's part. Impaired, reduced, or partial control is not enough."[267] By contrast, someone driving without awareness "retains some control. He would be able to steer the vehicle and usually to react and return to full awareness when confronted by significant stimuli".[268] The Court observed that although "very little" may intrude upon the driver's consciousness, he is not entirely (just "largely") unaware of steering or of the road ahead.[269]

This standard accords with that in the earlier case of *Watmore v. Jenkins*, where automatism was said to connote no "wider or looser concept than involuntary movement of the body or limbs".[270] Similarly, in *Broome v. Perkins*, the contrast between normal and automatic driving was described as follows:[271]

> "When driving a motor vehicle, the driver's conscious mind receives signals from his eyes and ears, decides on the appropriate course of action as a result of those signals, and gives directions

---

[267] [1994] QB 91, 105.
[268] *Ibid.*
[269] *Ibid*, 102.
[270] [1962] 2 QB 572, 586.
[271] (1987) 85 Cr App R 321, 332.

to the limbs to control the vehicle. When a person's actions are involuntary and automatic his mind is not controlling or directing his limbs."

On this footing, the defendant Perkins was convicted of driving without due care and attention, even though in a hypoglycaemic state. Since his erratic driving manifested reaction to stimuli (e.g. veering away from another vehicle, braking behind traffic), his mind must, at least from time to time, have been in control of his limbs. During those periods he was driving, and therefore, in the view of the Divisional Court, the offence was made out. On a similar rationale, the defendant in *Watmore* v. *Jenkins* was convicted of dangerous driving when in a hypoglycaemic state.[272]

These decisions are somewhat rigid in their approach, and are difficult to reconcile with an earlier body of cases not involving driving offences. In *Charlson*,[273] D was charged with causing grievous bodily harm to his 10-year-old son, whom he had suddenly struck on the head with a mallet and then defenestrated. D may well have been suffering from a cerebral tumour, which would render him liable to an outburst of impulsive violence over which he had no control. On these facts, D was permitted to raise a defence of automatism (and found not guilty) even though he could recall hitting V on the head. Similarly, in *Quick*, on a charge of assault D was allowed to raise automatism consequent upon hypoglycaemia, notwithstanding that his condition was one of semi-consciousness.[274] It is hard to see how the same condition, hypoglycaemia, may ground a claim of automatism in *Quick* but not in *Watmore* v. *Jenkins* or *Broome* v. *Perkins*.

In principle, *Charlson* and *Quick* are to be preferred. There seems no reason to require that D be altogether unconscious.[275] Indeed, what is striking about the driving cases is the simplistic approach of the courts. No middle ground is acknowledged: in which D may not be fully unconscious, yet may have no conscious control over his actions. His limbs may respond to subconscious commands, but not to reason. And in the absence of deliberative control, D cannot be regarded as a moral agent with respect to his behaviour. Blaming judgements are inappropriate.[276]

Until quite recently, it seemed that the more Draconian[277] cases on this matter were restricted to contexts involving driving offences. However, in *Coley*,[278] the Court of Appeal followed *Watmore* v. *Jenkins* and *A-G's Reference*, and insisted—in the context of an attempted murder charge—that the state of automatism was confined to agents afflicted with "a complete destruction of voluntary control". Strictly speaking, the point was not tested in that case, since the jury had found that D had the mens rea for murder and so

---

[272] *Isitt* (1977) 67 Cr App R 44 may be thought of as a similar authority, in that D's claim of hysterical fugue did not forestall his conviction for dangerous driving. However, on the facts his conduct appears to have involved action for a purpose—merely without moral inhibition (see at 48–9).

[273] [1955] 1 All ER 859. Strictly speaking, since D was suffering from an "internal" disorder, the case should be regarded as one of *insane* automatism: below, §§ 4.3(i)(d), 18.1(ii)(c).

[274] [1973] QB 910, 916b.

[275] The possibility of semi-conscious automatism appears to have been accepted also in *Stripp* (1978) 69 Cr App R 318, 320–1; cf. *Toner* (1991) 93 Cr App R 382; *Carter* [1959] VR 105, 108–9.

[276] Except where the involuntariness arises from D's prior fault: below, § 4.3(iii).

[277] Cf. *Clarke* [2009] EWCA Crim 921, [2010] 1 Cr App R (S) 26, in which a diabetic driver was sentenced to imprisonment for dangerous driving causing death despite, it seems, impeccable management of his condition: Rumbold and Wasik. "Diabetic Drivers, Hypoglycaemic Unawareness, and Automatism" [2011] *Crim LR* 863.

[278] [2013] EWCA Crim 223, para. 22. Hughes LJ also pointed to the defendant's prior fault in taking a large quantity of strong cannabis, without noticing that attempted murder is a specific intent offence.

was not automatic (albeit that he was under the influence of strong cannabis). Yet the decision suggests, at least for now, that the current law on automatism may be stringent in the extreme.

That would be unfortunate. In this context it is helpful to consider *Bratty* v. *Attorney-General for Northern Ireland*, in which Lord Denning stated:[279]

> "No act is punishable if it is done involuntarily: and an involuntary act in this context—some people nowadays prefer to speak of it as 'automatism'—means an act which is done by the muscles without any control of the mind, such as a spasm, a reflex action or a convulsion; or an act done by a person who is not conscious of what he is doing, such as an act done whilst suffering from concussion or whilst sleep-walking."

At first blush, this passage may seem to contemplate only situations where there is a complete loss of consciousness. However, Lord Denning's definition is asserted in order to draw a contrast, later in the same judgment, with an act that the accused merely cannot remember, or which "is unintentional or its consequences merely foreseen". Understood in this context, there is no suggestion that his Lordship intended to equate involuntariness with unconsciousness; indeed concussion, expressly included in the definition, is a clear case where behaviour is not consciously but at some lower level *willed*. Moreover, the judgment goes on to discuss, without reservation on this point, the direction given in *Charlson*;[280] in which (as we saw) D's actions were not only conscious but remembered. The conclusion is inescapable that his Lordship envisaged the conscious, reasoning control of the mind as what must be lacking in automatism.[281]

Moreover, as we noted earlier, at the level of principle this analysis seems correct. What counts is the inability *deliberatively* to control one's conduct—that one's movements are not responsive to a capacity to reason and deliberate about one's conduct. Obviously, where the defendant is altogether unconscious her reasoning capacities will be inactive. But a defendant need *not* be unconscious before those capacities may be suppressed or inoperative. A hypnotised patient who carries out the instructions of the hypnotist must be able to comprehend and implement those instructions at some level of consciousness. Yet he lacks capacity to deliberate about what actions to take or his reasons for taking them. He is an automaton, and is not responsible for his behaviour.[282]

Apart from sleepwalking and hypnotism, standard cases of semi-conscious conduct which are capable of qualifying as automatic and involuntary behaviour include acts done while in a state of concussion,[283] dissociation,[284] and advanced stages of hypoglycaemia.[285] In each of these instances, a loss of the capacity deliberatively to control D's behaviour will mean that he cannot be held criminally responsible for his actions and their consequences.

---

[279] [1963] AC 386, 409. See also the judgment of Viscount Kilmuir LC, at 401, 527.

[280] [1955] 1 All ER 859; see *Bratty* [1963] AC 386, 411. (Lord Denning thought, however, that case should have been regarded as insane rather than sane automatism. See above, n. 243.)

[281] A conclusion reached by the New Zealand Court of Appeal in *Burr* [1969] NZLR 736, 744–5 (North P), when considering the same passage.

[282] For interesting discussion, see Williams, "The Actus Reus of Dr Caligari" (1994) 142 *U Pa L Rev* 1661, 1667f.

[283] Cf. *Bratty* v. *A-G for Northern Ireland* [1963] AC 386, 403; *Quick* [1973] QB 910, 918, 920–2.

[284] Cf. *Toner* (1991) 93 Cr App R 382; *T* [1990] Crim LR 256; *Rabey* (1980) 15 CR (3d) 225.

[285] *Quick* [1973] QB 910.

(c) Imperfect deliberative capacity?

Although the above cases show that semi-conscious action can be automatic, they all involve a *complete* loss of deliberative control. It must be emphasised, on the other hand, that where D does in fact form an intention to commit a crime, then however clouded and confused D's awareness may have been, automatism is excluded. Responsibility for behaviour is not denied merely because D's deliberative faculties are "confused"[286] or "not working in top gear".[287] "Not thinking clearly" implies that D is still thinking about his actions, even if not very well. He is still exercising some deliberative control over his conduct, and cannot claim that his conduct was involuntary—it is a far cry from this state to one in which D is not reasoning at all. Rather than automatism, the appropriate defence (if applicable) is one of absence of mens rea. An instructive case is *Kingston*, the facts of which were as follows:[288]

> D was invited to a flat for ostensibly innocent purposes. While there, he was given coffee laced with disinhibiting drugs. He was then taken into a bedroom where a 15-year-old boy lay, also drugged, on a bed. D touched the boy sexually, and was subsequently charged with an indecent assault. His conviction was upheld by the House of Lords.

It is quite likely that D would not have acted as he did had he not (unknown to him) ingested the drugs, which may well have affected his judgement by freeing him of his usual self-restraint. But a disinhibited intent is still an intent, and the explanation cannot amount to a denial of responsibility for D. He acts for reasons—albeit perhaps not reasons that would normally motivate him—and thus is not automatic.[289] More generally, it is no defence that D acted upon an *irresistible impulse*, if he knew what he was doing and acted intentionally.[290] An impulsive action is conscious and intentional—it is action for a reason, not action uncontrolled by reason.

(d) Insane automatism

Whenever a defendant's involuntariness is found to be due to automatism, the court must then determine whether it is to be classified as *sane* or *insane* automatism. This classification depends upon the cause of the automatism. Where the defendant loses consciousness as a result of a blow on the head, for example, his behaviour will be regarded as occurring in a state of sane automatism.[291] By contrast, behaviour occurring during an epileptic fit will be exculpated on the footing of insane automatism.

The test for differentiating these types of automatism will be discussed in Chapter 19, when we consider the defence of insanity. The importance of the distinction is that sane

---

[286] Cf. *Poole* [2003] EWCA Crim 1219, [2013] All ER (D) 448 (Mar), para. 6.

[287] *Isitt* (1977) 67 Cr App R 44, 48.

[288] [1995] 2 AC 355.

[289] Cf. *Isitt* (1977) 67 Cr App R 44, 49; *A-G for South Australia* v. *Brown* [1960] AC 432; *Bratty* v. *A-G or Northern Ireland* [1963] AC 386, 409; *HM Advocate* v. *Kidd* [1960] SLT 82. A similar analysis would apply to provocation; D's provoked intention is still an intention. Thus the defence functions as an excuse rather than as a denial of voluntariness. See below, § 10.5. For an argument that Kingston might deserve an excusatory defence, see Sullivan, "Making Excuses" in Simester and Smith (eds.), *Harm and Culpability* (1996) 131.

[290] *Bratty* v. *A-G for Northern Ireland* [1963] AC 386, 409; *A-G for South Australia* v. *Brown* [1960] AC 432; cf. *Dodd* (1974) 7 SASR 151, 157; *Burr* [1969] NZLR 736, 750.

[291] Cf. *Foye* [2013] EWCA Crim 475, para. 34: automatism "may well involve no abnormality of the mind at all".

automatism operates as a straightforward denial of voluntariness and thus leads to an outright acquittal. By contrast, insane automatism is treated in law as a species of insanity, for which there is a special verdict and a different burden of proof upon the defendant.

(ii) Omissions, states of affairs, and possession

So far we have considered involuntariness in the context of positive actions by a defendant. However, we saw earlier in this chapter (§ 4.1) that not every actus reus requires a positive action. For example, if D stands by while her child drowns in the bath, her omission to save him is prima facie the actus reus of culpable homicide.[292]

Obviously, the involuntariness of omissions cannot be explained in the same way as actions. It would be odd indeed to talk of a reflex or convulsive omission. Nonetheless, even for omissions the criminal law in general requires that D must be responsible for her behaviour before she commits the actus reus of a crime. D's omission is involuntary, and her responsibility for the actus reus is negated, when she fails to discharge a duty to intervene because it was *impossible* for her to do so. There is extensive authority for this proposition.[293] As Sir William Scott put the point, in *The Generous*:[294]

> "But the law itself, and the administration of it, must yield to that to which everything must bend—to necessity. The law, in its most positive and peremptory injunctions, is understood to disclaim, as it does in its general aphorisms, all intention of compelling them to impossibilities; and the administration of law must adopt that general exception in the consideration of all particular cases."

That general exception was adopted in *Bamber*,[295] where a landowner charged with non-repair of a highway across his land was absolved of liability on the ground that repair of the highway was impossible:[296]

> "Both the road which the defendant is charged with liability to repair, and the land over which it passes, are washed away by the sea. To restore the road, as he is required to do, he must create a part of the earth anew.... But here all the materials of which a road could be made have been swept away by the act of God. Under those circumstances can the defendant be liable for not repairing the road? We want an authority for such a proposition; and none has been found."

In the context of an offence more familiar to students, suppose the following example:

> After an earthquake, D observes that his daughter is suffocating under a pile of rubble. D fails to rescue her because he is pinned beneath some collapsed masonry from which he cannot escape. D is not responsible for failing to rescue his daughter, and cannot be attributed with the actus reus of a homicide.

---

[292] Above, § 4.1(i)(a) (Case 2).
[293] *Stockdale v. Coulson* [1974] 3 All ER 154; *Brown* (1841) Car & M 314, 318, 174 ER 522, 524 ("without any physical impossibility" a proviso); *Mary Hogan* (1851) 2 Den 277, 169 ER 504; *Burns v. Bidder* [1967] 2 QB 227; *Vann* (1851) Cox CC 379. A valuable discussion is Smart, "Criminal Responsibility for Failing to Do the Impossible" (1987) 103 *LQR* 532. See also Williams, *CLGP* 746–8.
[294] (1812) 2 Dods 322, 323, 165 ER 1501.
[295] (1843) 5 QB 279, 114 ER 1254.
[296] *Ibid.*, 287, 1257.

This is true even if, for some reason, D had wanted his daughter dead, and would not have rescued her had it been possible to do so.[297]

In such cases, where a defendant would not have complied with the law even if possible, it is sometimes important to distinguish between involuntary *behaviour* and unavoidable *consequences*. In the earthquake example, D has no control over his behaviour. But imagine the following case:

> E is sunbathing on the beach when he observes his young daughter entering the sea and starting to swim in shallow water. Unfortunately, she encounters difficulties and is caught in an outgoing tide. E does not lift a finger to help, despite her cries to him, and watches as she is swept out to sea and drowned.

E may be able to deny responsibility for his daughter's death on the basis of *causation*. In a prosecution for murder or manslaughter, the prosecution must prove that E's omission to intervene caused his daughter's death. If in fact there was a riptide, and E would have been unable to save her anyway, then he is not responsible for the fatal consequence and cannot be convicted of a homicide offence.

The difference between this case and the earthquake example is that E denies responsibility for a *consequence* of his omission, on the basis of causation, while D denies responsibility for his *behaviour*, on the basis of involuntariness. Either way, a vital element of the actus reus of homicide is missing. But unlike D, E may still be criminally liable for any relevant offence where consequences are not part of the actus reus,[298] including an *attempt*. Because E's behaviour was not involuntary, it is capable in principle of constituting the actus reus of an attempted murder.[299] (Whether he would be convicted then depends upon questions of mens rea and proximity.) By contrast, it is impossible for D even to attempt a rescue. Therefore he cannot be held responsible for failing to do so.

(a) Omission cases that derogate from principle

In *Stockdale* v. *Coulson* it was said that "nobody ought to be prosecuted for that which it is impossible to do".[300] Similarly, in *Burns* v. *Nowell*:[301]

> "before a continuous act or proceeding, not originally unlawful, can be treated as unlawful by reason of the passing of an Act of Parliament, ... a reasonable time must be allowed for its discontinuance...."

At the level of principle, these sentiments endorse a defence of impossibility in ringing terms. Yet there are cases where such a defence has not been allowed. In *Davey* v. *Towle*,[302] for example, the driver of a car was not excused for failing to produce a test certificate, even though it was impossible for him to do so because the car owner was unable or unwilling to produce the certificate. Such cases should be regarded as exceptional. Derogation from the

---

[297] Cf. *Starri* v. *SA Police* (1995) 80 A Crim R 197.

[298] Compare *Brown* (1841) Car & M 314, 318, 174 ER 522, 524.

[299] Subject to the language of the Criminal Attempts Act 1981, which prima facie requires an "act": below, § 9.3(ii)(c).

[300] [1974] 3 All ER 154, 157.

[301] (1880) 5 QBD 444, 454.

[302] [1973] RTR 328. Cf. *Strowger* v. *John* [1974] RTR 124; *Pilgram* v. *Dean* [1974] 2 All ER 751.

principle *lex non cogit ad impossibilia* is not to be encouraged: it is both morally undesirable and inconsistent with a significant body of case law.[303]

It may be that the exceptional cases such as *Davey* v. *Towle* can be explained, and therefore confined. They all involve strict liability offences—especially driving offences—where the defendant chose to engage in a specialist, risk-creating activity, and thereby brought himself within the scope of the relevant criminal law duty. Moreover, the defendant had an opportunity, before doing so (e.g. commencing to drive), to ensure that he had the ability to comply with the law.[304] In such circumstances, it may be reasonable to expect the onus to lie on the defendant to make sure in advance that he has the wherewithal to comply with the law. Failure to do so would then count as a species of antecedent fault: discussed below, § 4.3(iii).

An additional consideration is that, in *Davey* v. *Towle*, to permit D to shelter behind the recalcitrance of the car owner would undermine the effectiveness and purpose of the offence itself. Provided there is the possibility of ensuring compliance in advance, this would seem a legitimate reason for excluding a defence of impossibility at the time of the infraction. Where, however, the features identified here do not apply, it is submitted that the general rule is that impossibility is a defence to crimes of omission.

(b) States of affairs

In principle, the test of responsibility for crimes which specify no behavioural element, and which criminalise states of affairs, ought to be similar to the impossibility test for crimes of omission. This follows from the point made earlier (in § 4.1(ii)(a)) that such offences, while formally needing no proof of particular behaviour by the defendant, can be seen as indirectly imposing liability for a defendant's omission to prevent the actus reus from occurring.

Unfortunately, English courts have not acknowledged this point as a matter of universal principle. Rather, it appears to be incorporated only as a matter of statutory construction. The leading modern decision is *Robinson-Pierre*.[305] D owned a pit bull terrier, a breed that is classified as "dangerous" within the meaning of the Dangerous Dogs Act 1991. Early one morning, police officers executed a search warrant at D's house by breaking down the door without warning and charging into the house. D's dog was locked inside the house at the time. Unsurprisingly, it went berserk, chasing the officers out of the house and continuing to attack and injure them on the street. D was charged with an offence, under section 3 of the 1991 Act, of being the owner of a dog which caused injury while dangerously out of control in a public place.

The Court of Appeal quashed D's conviction. While section 3 created an offence of strict liability, nonetheless it was to be presumed that the offence "requires proof by the prosecution of an act or omission of the defendant (with or without fault) that to some (more than minimal) degree caused or permitted the prohibited state of affairs to come about."[306]

---

[303] See the cases cited above, n. 258.

[304] Compare *Strowger* v. *John* [1974] RTR 124, 130, where, on a charge of failing to display a vehicle excise licence (which had fallen off the windscreen), Lord Widgery CJ observed that it might be different if a stranger had broken into the car and removed the licence without the defendant's knowledge.

[305] [2013] EWCA Crim 2396, [2014] 1 WLR 2638.

[306] *Ibid.*, para. 42.

A general presumption of this sort is to be welcomed. It is important to emphasise, however, that the voluntariness requirement is presumed *as a matter of statutory interpretation*. Thus it can be excluded by the terms of the statute creating the offence:[307]

> "we have no doubt that the supremacy of Parliament embraces the power to create 'state of affairs' offences in which no causative link between the prohibited state of affairs and the defendant need be established. The legal issue is not, in our view, whether in principle such offences can be created but whether in any particular enactment Parliament intended to create one."

In practice, where the offence specifies no explicit behavioural element at all, the courts have very often regarded such claims as legally irrelevant.

It need not be so. In *Dr Bonham's Case*, Coke CJ spoke words of great power:[308]

> "when an Act of Parliament is against common right and reason, or repugnant, *or impossible to be performed*, the common law will controul it...."

The defence of impossibility, it may be observed, has venerable spiritual heritage: a law that demands the impossible surely is against common right and reason, warranting an exception. Consistently with this, Lord Uthwatt commented in 1948 that a driver who failed to accord precedence at a pedestrian crossing "has, subject only to the application of the principle *Lex non cogit ad impossibilia*, broken the regulation".[309] Yet in 1988 such grand sentiments were nowhere to be found in the Court of Appeal. In *Porter* v. *Honey*[310] D, an estate agent, was prosecuted for displaying a "for sale" board on a property at a time when a second board was also displayed. D had erected the board at a time when no other board was displayed, and prima facie committed an offence only when (unknown to D) a competing estate agent erected a second "for sale" board on the same property. Faced with this situation, the House of Lords succeeded in exculpating D only by a convoluted (and far-fetched) exercise in statutory reinterpretation. The moral poverty of this technique was captured, without irony, by Lord Griffiths' first words:

> "the question for your Lordships is whether on the true construction of the relevant legislation an estate agent who lawfully places a 'for sale' board on a property should be held to have committed a criminal offence because another estate agent unlawfully and without the knowledge or consent of the first estate agent places a second 'for sale' board on the same property. I suggest that any layman would not hesitate to answer, 'No, Parliament cannot have intended such an unjust and absurd result'. Unfortunately, the legislation poses a more difficult problem of construction for the lawyer...."

This "interpretive", rather than general principle-based, approach has had a significant impact upon situational crimes. In English law, by contrast with other jurisdictions,[311] there is no general defence of impossibility to crimes that impose liability purely for a state of affairs. Authority for this proposition includes *Larsonneur*,[312] discussed earlier, and a

---

[307] *Ibid.*, para. 38.

[308] 8 Co Rep 113b, 118a, 77 ER 646, 652. Coke CJ's words must now be read in light of the doctrine of parliamentary sovereignty. But there is nothing in that doctrine that prevents recognition of a common law defence of impossibility.

[309] *London Passenger Transport Board* v. *Upson* [1949] AC 155.

[310] [1988] 3 All ER 1045. Compare *Leicester* v. *Pearson* [1952] 2 QB 668.

[311] See, e.g., *O'Sullivan* v. *Fisher* [1954] SASR 33; *Finau* v. *Dept of Labour* [1984] 2 NZLR 396.

[312] (1933) 149 LT 542; above, § 4.1(ii)(a).

number of other cases.[313] In *Larsonneur*, it will be recalled, D was brought into the United Kingdom against her will by the police, and consequently convicted of "being found" in the country when permission for her to enter had previously been refused. A similar case is *Winzar v. Chief Constable of Kent*.[314] D, who had been brought to hospital but found merely to be drunk, was later removed by the police to their car parked on the road outside. He was then charged with being found drunk on a highway, and his conviction was upheld by the Divisional Court. "Being found", it was held, refers only to the perceptions or actions of the finder and not to any conduct by the defendant. Given the language used in the statute, the fact that the defendant's involvement was involuntary was said therefore to be immaterial.

Since the defendants were said to be guilty of offences in these cases, presumably the policemen involved should have been charged with procuring. So far as responsibility for the offence is concerned, its commission in each case was brought about by the police and had nothing to do with the defendant.[315] Yet it was the defendant who was convicted. Cases such as *Larsonneur* and *Winzar* show a lack of regard for fundamental principles of humanity and justice.[316]

Fortunately, *Robinson-Pierre* points towards a more sympathetic construction of situational offences in the future. Unlike in *Larsonneur* and *Winzar*, the Court in that case was astute to the point that D's dog had only got out into public space because of the unforeseen intervention of a third party. To that extent, the decision is in line with the interpretation of other offences that criminalise D's failure to prevent another person from doing something wrongful: for example, the offence of dishonestly allowing another person (T), who is in receipt of a social security benefit, to refrain from disclosing a change in circumstance that affects T's entitlement to the benefit.[317] In such cases the courts are more likely to read in a requirement that D had the ability to prevent T's wrongful conduct.[318] Underlying this greater willingness, like the decision in *Porter v. Honey* above, is an implicit Rule of Law constraint: that D's liability should not normally lie in the hands of another person, who has the power independently of D's conduct to make D guilty of a crime.[319] It is one thing to say that D failed to prevent harm; it is quite another to say that, although D could do nothing about it, someone else deliberately made of her a criminal.

(c) Involuntary possession

Like situational offences, criminal possession (e.g. of an instrument of burglary[320] or of a controlled drug)[321] can be established without proving any behaviour by D (above,

---

[313] Cf. *Hawkins v. Holmes* [1974] RTR 436; *Duck v. Peacock* [1949] 1 All ER 318; *Crump v. Gilmore* [1970] Crim LR 28; *Smedleys Ltd v. Breed* [1974] AC 839; also the cases mentioned above, n. 267.

[314] *The Times*, 28 March 1983.

[315] Subject to the argument by Lanham, "Larsonneur Revisited" [1976] *Crim LR*, that *Larsonneur* involved prior fault; a rationale not, however, relied upon in the Court's decision.

[316] For a consideration of the potential impact of the European Convention of Human Rights on such cases, see Sullivan, "Strict Liability for Criminal Offences in England and Wales following Incorporation into English Law of the European Convention on Human Rights" in Simester (ed.), *Appraising Strict Liability* (2005) 195.

[317] Contrary to s. 111A(1B) of the Social Security Administration Act 1992.

[318] Cf. *Tilley* [2009] EWCA Crim 1426, paras. 37–9; *Crabtree v. Fern Spinning Co. Limited* (1901) 85 LT 549, 552.

[319] See Simester, "The Mental Element in Complicity" (2006) 122 *LQR* 578, 580–1.

[320] Theft Act 1968, s. 25.

[321] Misuse of Drugs Act 1971, s. 5.

§ 4.1(ii)(b)). The physical element of "being in possession" is a state of affairs in which D has control, with or without custody,[322] of the prohibited item. It is usually sufficient for the actus reus to show that the item is at a location where it is subject to D's power of control.[323]

As it happens, most offences of possession are unlikely to raise issues of involuntariness, since they generally require proof of a mental element in addition to proof of the actus reus. Thus, according to Lord Morris in *Warner v. Metropolitan Police Commissioner*, possession involves "being *knowingly* in control of a thing in circumstances which have involved an opportunity (whether availed of or not) to learn or discover, at least in a general way, what the thing is".[324] We will consider mens rea issues surrounding possession below, in § 5.6(ii). For present purposes, suppose that D is asleep when another person places controlled drugs in her hand. There is no need to address the question of voluntariness, since D lacks the knowledge required to constitute possession of the drugs.[325]

As we shall see in Chapter 5, the view that "possession" has an embedded mental element has been criticised. If that criticism were to be accepted by the courts, the question of involuntary possession would become more important. However, it is possible to construct situations in which, even if Lord Morris is right, one may involuntarily be in possession:

> Imagine that D acquires possession of controlled drugs but not by means of his own voluntary actions—for example, if a visitor to his house leaves the drugs behind when she departs. D may not be responsible for acquiring possession, but normally he is still responsible for *being* in possession because he fails to divest himself of the drugs. Suppose further, however, that D knows that he has been left the drugs yet happens to be bed-ridden through illness and is thus unable to dispose of them.

It is submitted that, by analogy with offences involving omissions, D should not be held responsible for the actus reus and his involuntary possession should not be attributed to him for the purposes of criminal liability. Indirect authority for this proposition may be inferred from the reasoning of the House of Lords in *Warner*. Presumably the reason Lord Morris required an opportunity to discover possession is in order that the defendant should have the chance to divest himself of contraband unknowingly acquired. It would seem both harsh and unlikely that, the instant some stranger thrusts a package into D's arms while D is out walking, he should be held criminally responsible for possession before he has had even the chance to drop it.[326]

(d) Distinction between impossibility and ignorance of duty

Impossibility amounting to involuntariness should be distinguished from situations where D is reasonably unaware of the existence of facts that trigger a duty to act in a

---

[322] Cf. *Kelt* [1977] 1 WLR 1365; *Sullivan v. Earl of Caithness* [1976] QB 966 (item held on behalf of D by third party). In some offences control without the availability of imminent custody may not suffice: *Lester* (1955) 39 Cr App R 157.

[323] At least in respect of drugs: *Lewis* (1987) 87 Cr App R 270.

[324] [1969] 2 AC 256, 289.

[325] See, e.g., the hypothetical case posed by Parker LCJ in *Lockyer v. Gibb* [1967] 2 QB 243, 248; discussed by the House of Lords in *Warner v. Metropolitan Police Comr* [1969] 2 AC 256, 282, 286, 300, 303, 311; below, § 5.6(ii). In addition, even if it were held that D "possessed" the drugs, she would have a defence of justified ignorance under s. 28 of the Misuse of Drugs Act 1971.

[326] Compare *Wright* (1975) 62 Cr App R 169.

certain manner. For example, one does not, apparently, commit an offence of remaining in Singapore when one's presence there becomes unlawful pursuant to an unpublished law.[327] Exculpation in such cases does not depend upon any claim of involuntariness, but rather upon the source and reasonableness of D's ignorance of law or fact. It is thus a matter for particular defences.

(iii) Involuntariness: responsibility by antecedent fault

Sometimes, even though the actus reus occurs involuntarily, D may still be held criminally responsible. One way in which this may occur is through vicarious liability, which is discussed below in Chapter 8. Leaving that possibility aside, however, D may also be liable for an offence if his involuntariness, and in turn the actus reus, was the consequence of earlier conduct by D in respect of which D was at fault.[328] There are three main situations in which this can occur.

(a) Intoxication

The first is voluntary intoxication. Suppose that D drinks himself into a stupor, and then commits an assault. Even if the court accepts his claim that the assault occurred while D was an automaton, it will not negate his criminal responsibility for the actus reus. In such circumstances, the presence of intoxication has two roles. First, it precludes the claim of involuntariness. Secondly, it is constitutive of certain mens rea states, including recklessness (the mens rea element in assault). A helpful illustration is provided by *Lipman*, the facts of which were as follows:[329]

> L and his female friend, V, took a quantity of LSD while in V's flat. During the hallucination which followed, L suffocated V by cramming bed sheet into her mouth. He believed when he did so that he was fighting snakes while descending to the centre of the earth.

L's behaviour while hallucinating is analogous to sleepwalking. It did not occur under his conscious or deliberative control. However, the automatism was self-induced, and moreover induced by D's own fault in becoming intoxicated. His claim to be exculpated on the basis of automatism was therefore refused, and L was convicted of manslaughter.[330]

The legal ramifications of intoxication will be explored further below, in Chapter 18. It is worth mentioning here, however, that English law on this point is out of line with that prevailing in other common law jurisdictions; where, unless one of the two further exceptions (below, § 4.3(iii)(b)–(c)) applied, automatism would be available and L would not be convicted.[331] The reasoning in other jurisdictions is as follows. Even though L is responsible

---

[327] *Lim Chin Aik* v. *R.* [1963] AC 160. Cf. *Harding* v. *Price* [1948] 1 KB 695 (failing to report an accident when D did not know it had occurred); *Hampson* v. *Powell* [1970] 1 All ER 929, 931; *Hardcastle* v. *Bielby* [1892] 1 QB 709; *Simons* v. *Rhodes and Son Ltd* [1956] 1 WLR 642; *Belling* v. *O'Sullivan* [1950] SASR 43. See below, § 18.2(iii).

[328] See Finkelstein, "Involuntary Crimes, Voluntarily Committed" in Shute and Simester (eds.), *Criminal Law Theory: Doctrines of the General Part* (2000) 143; Robinson, "Causing the Conditions of One's Own Defense: A Study in the Limits of the Criminal Law Doctrine" (1985) 71 *Virginia LR* 1.

[329] [1970] 1 QB 152.

[330] Approved in *DPP* v. *Majewski* [1977] AC 443. See MacKay, "Intoxication as a Factor in Automatism" [1982] *Crim LR* 146; Horder, "Pleading Involuntary Lack of Capacity" [1993] *CLJ* 298, 304ff.

[331] *O'Connor* (1980) 146 CLR 64; *Martin* (1984) 51 ALR 540; *Kamipeli* [1975] 2 NZLR 610; *Cottle* [1958] NZLR 999, 1002, 1007 (Gresson P); *Daviault* (1994) 118 DLR (4th) 469; Orchard, "Surviving without Majewski—A View from Down Under" [1993] *Crim LR* 426.

for his automatism, becoming automatic is not a criminal offence. It does *not* follow that he is responsible for the further consequences of his automatism. Before that can be the case, L must have the required mens rea not merely in respect of becoming automatic, but also in respect of those further consequences which make up the actus reus. Thus if an offence requires proof that the defendant foresaw the actus reus, the claim of automatism or involuntariness denies responsibility unless she actually foresaw the possibility of her incapacity *and* the resulting offence.[332]

Ignoring such reasoning, English courts have focused on public policy concerns surrounding the inherent dangerousness of the defendant's conduct, and generally impose strict liability for the consequences of voluntary intoxication.

(b) Recklessness

The doctrine by which voluntary intoxication overrides a defence of automatism operates only if the intoxication is self-induced through D's taking alcohol or non-soporific drugs (such as LSD). Thus it does not apply in a case such as *Bailey*[333] where D, a diabetic, failed to take sufficient food after a normal dose of insulin and lapsed into automatism. Similarly, the doctrine does not apply if D's automatism arises from taking valium, a sedative.[334]

The distinction appears to be that, in the latter cases, the substance that induces automatism is not one with generally recognised tendencies to produce aggressive, dangerous behaviour. Consequently, the public policy considerations that underlie decisions such as *Lipman* are less pressing, and there is no need to regard the defendant as being "on notice" of the dangerous consequences of his becoming intoxicated.

Where the defendant's automatism is not self-induced by alcohol or non-soporific drugs, the test is different. The defendant may rely upon his involuntariness as a defence *unless* he actually foresaw the risk of his behaviour becoming "aggressive, unpredictable and uncontrolled with the result that he may cause some injury to others".[335] The standard of prior fault required is known as subjective *recklessness*, which is discussed further in the chapter on mens rea (below, § 5.2).

(c) Antecedent actus reus

In each of the above situations, the actus reus occurs while the defendant is automatic, and the defendant is simply precluded in law from claiming that automatism to exculpate herself. A third alternative for prosecutors is to show that the behavioural element of the actus reus occurred *before* the defendant became automatic. One such case arises where D falls asleep while driving and then has an accident. Although D's driving was involuntary

---

[332] *O'Connor* (1980) 146 CLR 64, 73 (Barwick CJ), 103 (Stephen J); cf. *Egan* (1897) 23 VLR 159; *Sione* v. *Labour Dept* [1972] NZLR 278; *Ryan* (1967) 121 CLR 205. In these other jurisdictions, Lipman might have been convicted of manslaughter if the risk of killing someone while under the influence of LSD were such as to make his taking the drug "grossly negligent". (For discussion of the mens rea element in manslaughter see below, § 10.6.)

[333] [1983] 2 All ER 503.

[334] *Hardie* [1984] 3 All ER 848.

[335] *Bailey* [1983] 2 All ER 503, 507, overruling the earlier decision in *Quick* [1973] QB 910, 922, where it was said that automatism would not be available where its onset "could have been reasonably foreseen as a result of either doing, or omitting to do something, as, for example, taking alcohol against medical advice after using certain prescribed drugs, or failing to have regular meals while taking insulin". See generally Ashworth, "Reason, Logic and Criminal Liability" (1975) 91 *LQR* 102, 106–9; Robinson, "Causing the Conditions of One's Own Defence: A Study in the Limits of Theory in Criminal Law Doctrine" (1985) 71 *Va LR* 1.

at the time of the collision, he will be guilty of careless driving at the earlier time when he continued to drive despite feeling sleepy.[336] Indeed, D will have committed the offence even if no accident should occur.

Another example may be the phenomenon sometimes called "Dutch courage": where D, intending to murder V, drinks himself into a stupor *in order* to perpetrate the killing.[337] The ordinary rule governing intoxication (above, § 4.3(iii)(a)) will make D guilty of man-slaughter, but is not sufficient to make him guilty of murder, since the mental element required for murder is intention rather than recklessness. Nonetheless, it is arguable that his conduct in becoming drunk is itself a cause of death, and therefore constitutes the actus reus of murder. Hence, rather than focusing upon D's actions while automatic, his responsi-bility will be based upon his earlier conduct, which caused the prohibited harm, and which was itself accompanied by the fault element required for the crime.

To illustrate this type of analysis, consider the following facts:[338]

> D attempts to rob a jeweller's shop. He threatens those in the shop by pointing a loaded and cocked gun at them with his finger on the trigger. V, the shopkeeper, then springs at him. D is jolted back against the door, causing his finger to depress the trigger involuntarily. V is killed when the gun goes off, and D is charged with murder.

In such a case, D commits homicide. Even if the immediate cause of death is an involun-tary act by D, that is not a *novus actus interveniens*; his actions leading up to that point, in threatening V and other people in the shop by pointing a gun at them with his finger on the trigger, are (also) a cause of death.[339] Thus D's earlier conduct, rather than the firing of the gun itself, is the actus reus of murder.

(d) Strict liability offences?

For the sake of clarity, special mention should be made of offences that do not require proof of mens rea. Such offences, involving what is known as strict or absolute liability, are considered in Chapter 6. Unless one of the foregoing exceptions applies, it is submitted that because voluntariness is fundamental to D's responsibility for the actus reus, and not merely relevant to mens rea, in principle its absence will still result in there being no crimi-nal liability for D's conduct:[340]

> "When a man is charged with dangerous driving, it is no defence for him to say, however truly, 'I did not mean to drive dangerously.' There is said to be an absolute prohibition against that offence, whether he had a guilty mind or not, see *Hill* v. *Baxter*[341] by Lord Goddard CJ. But even though it is absolutely prohibited, nevertheless he has a defence if he can show that it was

---

[336] *Kay* v. *Butterworth* (1945) 173 LT 191; *Spurge* [1961] 2 QB 205; below, § 5.8(i)(c)–(d). Cf. *Jiminez* v. *The Queen* (1992) 173 CLR 572.

[337] *A-G for Northern Ireland* v. *Gallagher* [1963] AC 349, 382 (Lord Denning).

[338] Taken from *Wickliffe* [1987] 1 NZLR 55, 60, where the approach suggested here was accepted as a possible analysis by the New Zealand Court of Appeal; also by the Australian High Court in *Ryan* v. *R.* (1967) 121 CLR 205, 218–19, 231, 233, 239; cf. Elliott, "Responsibility for Involuntary Acts: Ryan v The Queen" (1968) 41 *ALJ* 497. See also the commentary on *Burke* [1987] Crim LR 480, 484.

[339] See also the discussion of causation earlier in this chapter, § 4.2(iii)ff.

[340] *Bratty* v. *A-G for Northern Ireland* [1963] AC 386, 409–10. Cf. *Hill* v. *Baxter* [1958] 1 QB 277; *O'Connor* (1980) 146 CLR 64; Williams, "Absolute Liability in Traffic Offences" [1967] *Crim LR* 142 and 194, 199ff.

[341] [1958] 1 QB 277, 282.

an involuntary act in the sense that he was unconscious at the time and did not know what he was doing, see *H.M. Advocate v. Ritchie*,[342] *Reg. v. Minor*[343] and *Cooper v. McKenna, Ex parte Cooper*.[344]"

The exception, as we saw earlier, is in respect of pure situational offences, which the courts in cases such as *Larsonneur*[345] have construed as imposing criminal liability notwithstanding that it may be impossible to prevent the actus reus from occurring.

It is also worth noting that some offences impose strict liability only for a part of the actus reus, and require mens rea for other parts of the offence. The famous strict liability case of *Woodrow*[346] is a convenient example. D was convicted of possessing adulterated tobacco, even though he did not know it was adulterated. The offence was held to impose strict liability in respect of the fact that the tobacco was adulterated. But there was no suggestion that liability in respect of the *possession* was also strict. Had someone put the tobacco in his hand while D was sleeping, then involuntariness would have precluded liability in the normal way.[347]

(e) Evidential issues

A claim of involuntariness or automatism is often described by lawyers as a "defence". In terms of substantive legal doctrine, it is not. It is a denial of the actus reus, rather than a plea that the defendant's actions were justified or excused. As such, it is for the prosecution to prove voluntariness on the part of the defendant alongside the rest of the actus reus. So far as the burden of proof is concerned, however, automatism is like a defence. In practice, there is a presumption of deliberative capacity to control one's actions, and voluntariness will become an issue only if there is evidence which genuinely raises the issue.[348] Thus, if the defendant wishes to deny responsibility on this basis, she must point to credible evidence that supports her claim. It is said that "blackout is one of the first refuges of a guilty conscience".[349] In general, since it is so easily feigned, the defendant's testimony of automatism will not be accepted unless it is buttressed by relevant evidence of surrounding circumstances or medical conditions.[350]

---

[342] [1926] SC(J) 45.
[343] (1955) 15 WWR (NS) 433.
[344] [1960] QLR 406.
[345] Above, § 4.3(ii)(d).
[346] (1846) 15 M & W 404.
[347] See above, § 4.3(ii)(e).
[348] *Bratty v. A-G for Northern Ireland* [1963] AC 386, 406–7, 413, 416–17. Similarly for impossibility: cf. *Bailey* [1983] 1 WLR 760, 765–6. For further discussion of the burden of proof, see above, § 3.2.
[349] *Cooper v. McKenna* [1960] Qd R 406, 419 (Stable J); *Bratty v. A-G for Northern Ireland* [1963] AC 386, 413–14 (Lord Denning).
[350] *Cook v. Atchison* [1968] Crim LR 266; cf. *Hill v. Baxter* [1958] 1 QB 277; *Stripp* (1978) 69 Cr App R 318; contrast *Budd* [1962] Crim LR 49.

5

MENS REA

The mens rea of a crime is, generally speaking, that part of the offence which refers to the defendant's mental state. Consider, for example, section 15(1) of the Forgery and Counterfeiting Act 1981:

> It is an offence for a person—
>
> (a) to pass or tender as genuine any thing which is, and which he knows or believes to be, a counterfeit of a currency note or of a protected coin. ...

When Tom is charged with an offence of passing a counterfeit note under section 15(1)(a), the offence may be established only if Tom *knew or believed that the "note" was counterfeit*. The italicised part of the last sentence is the mens rea requirement.

In the case of section 15(1)(a), the mental element is fairly straightforward. But it is possible for an offence to contain a variety of actus reus elements for which the corresponding mens rea requirements differ. One such offence is section 3 of the Criminal Damage Act 1971, which provides, in part, that:

> A person who has anything in his custody or under his control intending without lawful excuse to use it ...
>
> (b) to destroy or damage his own ... property in a way which he knows is likely to endanger the life of some other person;
>
> shall be guilty of an offence.

There are two parts to the mens rea for this offence. A defendant must (i) have *intended* to use the item in question to damage his own property, and (ii) have *known* that doing so was likely to endanger another person's life.

Although mens rea is often regarded as the requirement that the defendant have a "guilty mind", and is taken to contain the fault elements of each offence, in fact the mens rea elements serve a number of functions,[1] and it is in practice a rather technical area of law. For a prosecutor, mens rea requires her to establish only that the defendant had the specified mental state toward the actus reus which is required for that crime. In particular, proof that the defendant has the requisite mens rea of an offence does not mean that she must know her conduct is illegal,[2] or wrong. Similarly, a laudable motive which prompts the defendant to commit an offence is no defence. In *Smith*,[3] for instance, the defendant offered

---

[1] Chan and Simester, "Four Functions of Mens Rea" (2011) 70 *CLJ* 381.
[2] See below, § 18.2 (ignorance of law).
[3] [1960] 2 QB 423.

a bribe to the town mayor. He did so in order to expose the mayor as corrupt. Despite his good motive, he was convicted of offering a bribe to a public servant since he had intentionally (the mens rea) offered the bribe (the actus reus). At that stage the offence was complete, and his motive could not help him.[4]

There are three steps to be taken in establishing whether a defendant has mens rea. The first step is to determine what mens rea standard is required in respect of each separate element of the actus reus. The second is to interpret the criteria of those mens rea element(s). Third is the factual question: did the defendant in fact act with the mens rea element(s) required?

The present chapter is concerned with the second of those steps; its purpose is to explain the main types of mens rea which the law might require. There are in fact a great variety of possible mens rea states, including purpose, intention, recklessness, wilfulness, knowledge, belief, suspicion, reasonable cause to believe, maliciousness, fraudulence, dishonesty, corruptness, and negligence. However, in this chapter we will confine our discussion to the most common, and most important, types of fault element.

§ 5.1 Intention

The central, and usually the most grave, case of wrongdoing occurs when the defendant's crime is intentional.[5] Both in law and in society at large, praise and blame are most obviously incurred for conduct that a person intends: D attracts greater censure if she deliberately breaks V's vase than if she carelessly drops it. For the majority of offences, it is not necessary to prove that the actus reus was intended, since recklessness will normally suffice for a conviction. (Intention will therefore often be most relevant at the sentencing stage.) But this is not always so—murder, for example, requires an intention to kill or cause grievous bodily harm; recklessness will not suffice. Other offences requiring proof of an intent include theft, burglary, wounding with intent, conspiracy, and attempt. There are other important reasons for distinguishing intention from recklessness, and we shall return to these later.

There is normally no need for an elaborate definition of intention in order to decide whether an actus reus was intended. A few exceptional situations may present difficulty, but

---

[4] The decision does not sit well with *Clarke* (1984) 80 Cr App R 344, which holds that a citizen has a defence if acting honestly and solely to reveal crime and recover its proceeds. However, the view that mens rea means no more than the mental element for the offence is endorsed in *Hinklin* (1868) LR 3 QB 360, 370–2; *Yip Chiu-Cheung* [1995] 1 AC 111; *Kingston* [1995] 2 AC 355; also *Dodman* [1998] 2 Cr App Rep 338 (C-MAC). This approach, which disconnects a finding of mens rea from the presence of fault, is appropriate only if a suitable range of defences is available. See above, § 1.2(ii); also Brett, *Inquiry into Criminal Guilt* (1960).

[5] See, e.g., Smith, "Intention in Criminal Law" (1974) 27 *CLP* 93; White, "Intention, Purpose, Foresight and Desire" (1976) 92 *LQR* 569; Buzzard, "'Intent'" [1978] *Crim LR* 5; Smith, "'Intent': A Reply" [1978] *Crim LR* 14; Duff, "The Obscure Intentions of the House of Lords" [1986] *Crim LR* 771; Williams, "Oblique Intention" (1987) 46 *CLJ* 417; Buxton, "Some Simple Thoughts on Intention" [1988] *Crim LR* 484; Duff, "Intentions Legal and Philosophical" (1989) 9 *OJLS* 76; Smith, "A Note on 'Intention'" [1990] *Crim LR* 85; Simester and Chan, "Intention Thus Far" [1997] *Crim LR* 704; Norrie, "After *Woollin*" [1999] *Crim LR* 532; Kaveny, "Inferring Intention from Foresight" (2004) 120 *LQR* 81; Moore, "Intention as a Marker of Moral Culpability and Legal Punishability" in Duff and Green (eds.), *Philosophical Foundations of Criminal Law* (2011) 179; Duff, "Intention Revisited" in Baker and Horder (eds.), *The Sanctity of Life and the Criminal Law* (2013) 148.

usually the analysis will be intuitively obvious: "[t]he general legal opinion is that 'intention' cannot be satisfactorily defined and does not need a definition, since everybody knows what it means".[6] Nonetheless, the fact that some cases are difficult means that we do sometimes need guidelines about what intention means. The legal territory of intention comprises two alternative categories. D may be found to have intended the actus reus if:

(I)   D *intended* the actus reus in the ordinary, core sense of "intention"; or

(II)   D recognised that the actus reus was a *virtually certain* consequence of his actions.

The first case, (I), is the standard or core variety and largely reflects the ordinary language meaning of "intention". In this paradigm case, D tries (seeks, attempts) to bring about the relevant outcome. For whatever reason, he wants or needs to bring about that outcome, and that is why he acts as he does. By contrast, in the virtual certainty case, (II), D does not act in order to bring about the intended outcome. He acts for other reasons. However, he knows that the actus reus is a virtually certain consequence of his actions. Though that is not what he is trying to bring about, it is a practically inevitable concomitant.

In the following sections, we will elaborate upon these definitions. In §§ 5.1(i)–(iii), the paradigm category of intention (I) will be discussed. The virtual certainty case (II) is considered in § 5.1(iv).

(i) Ways of speaking about intention (in its core sense)

As a starting point, it may be helpful to consider how "intention" has been paraphrased by judges and academic writers. In *Cunliffe* v. *Goodman*, Lord Asquith stated that intention "connotes a state of affairs which the party 'intending' ... does more than merely contemplate: it connotes a state of affairs which, on the contrary, he decides, so far as in him lies, to bring about".[7] In other words, D generally intends an outcome if it is something that he decides, or seeks, to bring about.[8] Additionally, it seems clear that D intends a result if he acts with the *purpose*,[9] or object, of bringing it about. In Smith and Hogan's useful example:[10]

> "If D has resolved to kill V and he fires a loaded gun at him with the object of doing so, he intends to kill. It is immaterial that he is aware that he is a poor shot, that V is nearly out of range and that his chances of success are small. It is sufficient that killing is his object or purpose: that he acts in order to kill."

At the heart of this approach is a recognition that D intends to kill P if he means to bring about P's death by his actions—if he acts with the aim, object, or purpose of killing P.[11]

---

[6] Williams, *TBCL* 74. *Per* Lord Bridge, in *Moloney* [1985] AC 905, 926, "[t]he golden rule should be that ... the judge should avoid any elaboration or paraphrase of what is meant by intent, and leave it to the jury's good sense to decide whether the accused acted with the necessary intent". Cf. *Belfon* [1976] 3 All ER 46 (CA); *Nedrick* [1986] 1 WLR 1025, 1027 (CA).

[7] [1950] 2 KB 237, 253.

[8] Cf. *Mohan* [1976] 1 QB 1, 11 (CA); *Pearman* (1984) 80 Cr App R 259 (CA).

[9] *Burke* [1991] 1 AC 135, 147 (HL).

[10] *Smith and Hogan* § 5.2.1.

[11] Cf. *Gollins* v. *Gollins* [1964] AC 644, 663 (Lord Reid); *DPP* v. *Smith* [1961] AC 290, 327 (Viscount Kilmuir LC); *Hyam* v. *DPP* [1975] AC 55, 79 (Lord Hailsham).

Antony Duff has built on this idea. Suppose that D fires a gun knowing that P is nearby, and we are trying to decide whether he intended to kill P. Duff argues that if D aims to cause P's death by his actions, then we can say that D *attempts* to kill P.[12] Furthermore, an attempt can be either a success or a failure. Therefore, Duff shows, one feature of intention is that a defendant who intends (aims, tries, attempts) to kill P would regard himself as having "failed" in some sense if P does not die.[13] By contrast, if he does not intend P's death, then he would not think he had failed if P survives. So this is another way of testing whether D intended P's death.

An illustration of Duff's argument is provided by the case of *Hyam*.[14] D had poured petrol through the letterbox of V's house and set fire to the petrol, intending only to frighten V but realising her actions risked causing death. Duff remarks:[15]

> "Mrs Hyam intended to set fire to Mrs Booth's house; her action would have failed had the house not caught fire…. She intended thereby to frighten Mrs Booth: had the fire not frightened Mrs Booth, her action (though successful as one of 'setting fire to the house') would have failed as one of 'frightening Mrs Booth'. But she did not intend to cause death or injury: though she foresaw death or injury as a likely effect of her action, her action would not have been a failure had no one been killed or injured; death or injury were foreseen side-effects, not intended effects, of her action."

By frightening Mrs Booth, the defendant would have succeeded in her purpose; her actions would not have been a failure if no one had died, since it was no part of her purpose to kill. Neither, we would say, was she trying to kill anyone. Thus the deaths were not intended (at least not in the core sense).

(ii) A formal definition of intention in its core sense

The differences noted above between intended and unintended actions can also be set out in terms of means, ends, and side-effects. Things done as means or ends are intended; side-effects are not.[16] In *Hyam*, D set fire to the house as a means of frightening Mrs Booth. Hence, both setting fire to the house and frightening Mrs Booth were intended. But the ensuing fatalities were neither a means nor an end. They were side-effects of her actions, and as such unintended.

Ideas of means, ends, and purpose point to a more formal way of thinking about intention. The purposes or ends for which one acts are the reasons *why* one acts. They motivate and explain one's action. Intention embraces both these and the intermediate steps (the means) that one undertakes in order to achieve those ends. Formally, we can capture the central cases of intention as follows. D intends to do an action (or to bring about some consequence) if:

---

[12] This point was made by the Court of Appeal in *Moloney*, *The Times*, 22 December 1983 (May LJ); see *Moloney* [1985] AC 905, 919 (Lord Bridge). Compare also *Walker* (1989) 90 Cr App R 226, 230: "'[t]rying to kill' is synonymous with purpose. It has never been suggested that a man does not intend what he is trying to achieve."

[13] Duff, *Intention, Agency and Criminal Liability* (1990) 61–3. See now his *Criminal Attempts* (1996) chap. 1.

[14] [1975] AC 55.

[15] Duff, *Intention, Agency and Criminal Liability* (1990) 61.

[16] Finnis, "Intention and Side-effects" in Frey and Morris (eds.), *Liability and Responsibility* (1991) 32. See also Williams, "Oblique Intention" (1987) 46 *CLJ* 417, 421.

(a)   He *wants* to do that action (or to bring about that consequence), or
(b)   He *believes* it is possible for him to achieve something he wants by doing that action (or by bringing about that consequence); and
(c)   He behaves as he does *because*[17] of his desire in (a) or his belief in (b).

Notice that nothing in this definition requires that D should believe the action or consequence is probable, highly likely, or anything more than merely possible. This is shown by Smith and Hogan's example cited earlier, where D attempts to kill P despite the chances of doing so being small. The combination of (a) with (c) covers actions which are done as ends:

(a)   He *wants* to do that action (or to bring about that consequence); and
(c)   He behaves as he does *because* of that desire.

Mrs Hyam wanted to frighten Mrs Booth, and she set fire to the house because she wanted to frighten her. Therefore she intended to frighten Mrs Booth. Her desire to frighten, which is the desire contemplated in (a) above, is often termed the defendant's *motive*. But it is important to recognise that a desire, or motive, is not enough by itself to establish intention. Often people want things which they never set out to achieve. If D stands to inherit from his mother's will, he may have a reason for wanting her death. But the mere wish that another person were deceased is not an intention to kill that person: "intention is something quite different from motive or desire".[18] Distinguishing between desire and intention here is (c), the requirement that the defendant act because of that motive. A motive is irrelevant to intention unless it is also *why* D did the actus reus.

On the other hand, desire is not an essential component of intention.[19] Often, we bring things about not because we want them, but because they are a *means* to something else (that we do want).[20] The parent who punishes a child for misbehaving may do so regretfully, believing it to be her only option and wishing very much that there were something else she could do; yet she intends to punish him all the same.[21] What she wants (say) is to deter her child from behaving that way again, and she punishes him in order to achieve that aim. But she does not desire his punishment, at least not for its own sake. This sort of case, where the actus reus is done as a means to an end, is captured by the combination of (b) with (c):

(b)   He *believes* it is possible for him to achieve something he wants by doing that action (or by bringing about that consequence); and
(c)   He behaves as he does *because* of that belief.

---

[17] Or, at least *in part because*. We consider the possibility of multiple intentions below, in § 5.1(vi).

[18] *Per* Lord Bridge in *Moloney* [1985] AC 905, 926. Cf. *Hales* [2005] EWCA Crim 1118, para. 28.

[19] Cf. *Mohan* [1976] QB 1, 11 (James LJ): intention is "a decision to bring about, in so far as it lies within the accused's power, the commission of the offence ... no matter whether the accused desired that consequence of his act or not".

[20] See *Hyam* [1974] 2 All ER 41, 74 (Lord Hailsham): intention includes "the means as well as the end"; also Williams, *CLGP* §16. This point is seen clearly in *Hales* [2005] EWCA Crim 1118, para. 28: "The Crown's position was that [D] was prepared to kill in order to escape. It may not have been a gratuitous killing in the sense that the motive was a desire to kill. The motive was that the officer was in the way and that the appellant Hales was prepared to kill in order to escape. That is not a situation which requires any different direction from the conventional one on intent."

[21] Compare *Lang* v. *Lang* [1955] AC 402, 428–9.

In *Smith*,[22] D believed that by bribing the mayor he would be able to expose him. This was why he acted as he did. Therefore he intended to bribe[23] the official, even though his ultimate aim was to expose him. It may be helpful to show D's reasoning with a diagram:

$$Smith: \qquad S \longrightarrow \text{bribe mayor}_{Means} \longrightarrow \text{expose corruption}_{End}$$

Similarly, Mrs Hyam believed that by setting fire to the house she would be able to frighten Mrs Booth. That was why she acted as she did. Therefore she intended to set fire to the house:

$$Hyam: \qquad H \longrightarrow \text{set fire to house}_{Means} \longrightarrow \text{frighten V}_{End}$$

$$\text{kill V}_{Side\text{-}effect}$$

But as this diagram shows, it was no part of her intentions to kill V or do grievous bodily harm to her.

In practice, of course, looking at the defendant's desires and beliefs is an indispensible aid in helping us to ascertain her intentions. Even in (b), the case of doing something as a means to an end, there must be a motive in the background. And although it does not matter in principle what that background motive is, often it will be important for evidential purposes. "To prove the intention, you may show the motive, and this is a link in the chain of evidence."[24]

(iii) *Foresight of consequences is not enough*

The key ingredient of any account of intention is (c), that the defendant acts because of her desire or belief. Without it, there cannot be intention. If D foresees an outcome, and indeed welcomes it, but that outcome nonetheless plays no part in her decision to act, then she does not intend it.[25] The outcome is, for D, incidental. Mrs Hyam foresaw the possibility of killing Mrs Booth, but she did not set fire to the house because of her belief that doing so might bring about Mrs Booth's death. Hence, although she was reckless,[26] she did not intend to kill. Similarly, a judge who awards compensatory damages against a defendant may realise that, in so doing, he might cause the bankruptcy of the defendant, but that has nothing to do with why he awards the damages. The bankruptcy is no more than a foreseen but unintended side-effect.

The law has not always been clear on this point. In *Hardy* v. *Motor Insurers' Bureau*, for instance, it was said of the accused that "he must have foreseen, when he did the act, that it would in all probability injure the other person. Therefore he had the intent to injure

---

[22] [1960] 2 QB 423. See above, § 5.

[23] Or, more accurately, to "corrupt" the official. In fact s. 1(2) of the Public Bodies Corrupt Practices Act 1889 requires that the defendant act "corruptly". The Court interpreted this to mean only that he must intend to induce a corrupt bargain. See above, n. 3; Shyllon, "The Corruption of 'Corruptly'" [1969] *Crim LR* 250.

[24] *Heeson* (1878) 14 Cox CC 40, 44 (Lush J).

[25] A point made by Kenny, "Intention and Purpose in Law" in Summers (ed.), *Essays in Legal Philosophy* (1968) 146, 155.

[26] Below, § 5.2.

the other person."[27] And in *Jakac*, the Supreme Court of Victoria was of similar mind: if the defendant "knew what the consequences were likely to be, and with that knowledge he deliberately did the act and if the consequences in fact did follow, he must be taken to intend them".[28] Indeed, in 1960 the House of Lords in *DPP* v. *Smith* simply presumed (*inter alia*) that Jim Smith intended whatever he foresaw.[29] The House of Lords later divided on this question in *Hyam*. Although Lord Hailsham declared it "clear that 'intention' is clearly to be distinguished alike from 'desire' and from foresight of the probable consequences",[30] his Lordship's view does not reflect a consensus. Viscount Dilhorne, for instance, remarked that if someone does an act "knowing when he does it that it is highly probable that griev-ous bodily harm will result, I think that most people would say and be justified in saying that whatever other intentions he may have had as well, he at least intended grievous bod-ily harm".[31] Indeed, Lord Diplock felt able, following *Hyam*, to hold that the law was now "well-settled":[32]

> "Where intention to produce a particular result was a necessary element of an offence, no distinction was to be drawn in law between the state of mind of one who did an act because he desired it to produce that particular result and the state of mind of one who, when he did the act, was aware that it was likely to produce that result but was prepared to take the risk that it might do so."

More recently, however, the distinction between intention and mere foresight has been accepted by the House of Lords. The key cases are *Moloney*[33] and *Hancock and Shankland*.[34] In *Moloney*, the defendant was charged with murder after shooting his stepfather during a drunken game. It was not clear that, when he pulled the trigger, he realised the gun was pointing at the victim. His conviction was quashed because the trial judge was ruled to have misdirected the jury in stating:[35]

> "a man intends the consequence of his voluntary act (a) when he desires it to happen, whether or not he foresees that it probably will happen, and (b) when he foresees that it will happen, whether he desires it or not."

Contrast that direction (which was based upon *Hyam*) with the view of Lord Bridge, who was "firmly of opinion that foresight of consequences, as an element bearing on the issue

---

[27] [1964] 2 QB 745, 764 (Pearson LJ); see also at 758 (Lord Denning MR). Cf. Lord Diplock's definition of "purpose" in *Chandler* v. *DPP* [1964] AC 763, 805 to "designate those objects which he knows will probably be achieved by the act, whether he wants them or not".

[28] [1961] VR 367, 371. Cf. Saunders, *Mozley & Whitley's Law Dictionary* (9th ed., 1977) 175: "a person who contemplates any result, as not unlikely to follow from a deliberate act of his own, may be said to intend that result, whether he desire it or not".

[29] [1961] AC 290. Cf. Viscount Kilmuir LC, at 326: "the test of what a reasonable man would contemplate as the probable result of his acts, and, therefore, would intend". The reference to the reasonable man was highly controversial in that it implied (wrongly) that the test for intention was objective rather than subjective: see now below, § 5.1(x); also *Ward* [1956] 1 QB 351; Kenny, "Intention and Purpose in Law" in Summers (ed.), *Essays in Legal Philosophy* (1968) 146.

[30] [1975] AC 55, 74.

[31] *Ibid.*, 82.

[32] *Lemon* [1979] AC 617, 638. See also a similar dictum in *Hyam* [1975] AC 55, 86.

[33] [1985] AC 905.

[34] [1986] AC 455.

[35] [1985] AC 905, 917.

of intention in murder, or indeed any other crime of specific intent, belongs, not to the substantive law, but to the law of evidence".[36]

Strictly speaking, Lord Bridge's remarks were *obiter dicta*,[37] since the decisive factor in the decision was that D apparently did not think about the risk of death at all,[38] and the case was therefore not one of foresight.[39] Fortunately, the point was not *obiter* in *Hancock and Shankland*. In that case the defendants, miners who were on strike, pushed concrete blocks off a bridge onto the motorway below. The blocks struck a taxi ferrying another miner to work. The taxi driver was killed. The defendants, it appears, recognised the dangerousness of their actions but claimed they intended only to frighten the miner and prevent him from going to work, but not to harm anyone. Their convictions for murder were quashed. As Lord Scarman put it, "foresight does not necessarily imply the existence of intention".[40] This rule has since been reiterated by the Court of Appeal in *Nedrick*[41] and *Matthews*,[42] and by the House of Lords in *Woollin*.[43] It may safely be regarded as now prevailing.[44]

(iv) Virtually certain consequences: the second category of intention

Mere foresight of a consequence, then, does not establish an intention. But one question is still unresolved: what if the consequence is foreseen not merely as possible, but as *certain* to occur—does "intention" include such a case? Consider the following example used by a number of philosophers. V, a fat man, is trapped in the mouth of a cave. The waters in the cave are rapidly rising, and the cave will soon be flooded. The trapped man is immovable, and is preventing the escape and survival of his fellow spelæologists. The only way of unblocking the exit is by blowing him up with a stick of dynamite. Can they do so without intending his death?[45] The case can be represented as follows:

$$\textit{Spelæologist}: \quad S \longrightarrow \text{blow up V} \longrightarrow \text{escape and survive}$$
$$\| \quad \|$$
$$\text{kill V}$$

---

[36] *Ibid.*, 928.

[37] Cf. *ibid.*, 920; *Hancock* [1986] AC 455, 460 (CA), [1986] AC 455, 468 (HL).

[38] See *Moloney* [1985] AC 905, 920B–D. Their Lordships must have overlooked the jury's finding that D foresaw death or grievous bodily harm.

[39] Thus, strictly, the decision rules only that inadvertence forecloses intention—contra *DPP* v. *Smith* [1961] AC 290. Apart from being undone by s. 8 of the Criminal Justice Act 1967, *DPP* v. *Smith* itself was effectively overruled by the Privy Council in *Frankland and Moore* v. *R.* [1987] AC 576.

[40] [1986] 1 AC 455, 472.

[41] [1986] 1 WLR 1025.

[42] [2003] EWCA Crim 192, [2003] 2 Cr App R 30.

[43] [1999] 1 AC 82.

[44] In the *Law Quarterly Review*, Lord Goff concludes that "after the journey through *Smith*, *Hyam*, *Moloney* and *Hancock*, the law is really back where it was…. Foresight of consequences is not the same as intent, but is material from which the jury may, having regard to the circumstances of the case, infer that the defendant really had the relevant intent": "The Mental Element in the Crime of Murder" (1988) 104 *LQR* 30, 41.

[45] For philosophical discussion of the case see Geddes, "On the Intrinsic Wrongness of Killing Innocent People" (1973) 33 *Analysis* 93; Duff, "Intentionally Killing the Innocent" (1973) 34 *Analysis* 16; Finnis, "The Rights and Wrongs of Abortion: a Reply to Judith Jarvis Thomson" (1973) 2 *Philosophy and Public Affairs* 117; Hanink, "Some Light on Double Effect" (1975) 35 *Analysis* 147.

As this example illustrates, some consequences which are not themselves sought (as either means or end) are nevertheless much too close to the intended effects to be separated off as mere side-effects. V's colleagues would be delighted if they could blow him up, and free themselves, without killing V. But they cannot. It is a certainty that V will die.

This kind of case is regarded as a second variety of intention by the Law Commission, amongst others:[46]

> "(1) A person should be taken to intend a result if he or she acts in order to bring it about.
> (2) In cases where the judge believes that justice may not be done unless an expanded understanding of intention is given, the jury should be directed as follows: an intention to bring about a result may be found if it is shown that the defendant thought that the result was a virtually certain consequence of his or her action."

Limb (2) captures the case of the spelæologists. The language of virtual certainty reflects the need for something more than just foresight that the result is likely or possible; the latter would be a case of recklessness.

In the past, the courts have been equivocal about this type of case. Although Lord Hailsham did not think that "foresight as such of a high degree of probability is at all the same thing as intention",[47] he nevertheless stated explicitly that intention includes not only those things done as ends or means but also "the inseparable consequences of the end as well as the means". The extension is supported by reference to an example developed by Glanville Williams:[48]

> "suppose that a villain of the deepest dye blows up an aircraft in flight with a time-bomb, merely for the purpose of collecting on insurance. It is not his aim to cause the people on board to perish, but he knows that success in his scheme will inevitably involve their deaths as a side-effect."

According to Lord Hailsham, "if any passengers are killed he is guilty of murder, as their death will be a moral certainty if he carries out his intention".[49] In *Moloney*, Lord Bridge, too, accepted that there may be cases where things which are seemingly not sought as ends or means should be analysed as cases of intention:[50]

> "A man who, at London Airport, boards a plane which he knows to be bound for Manchester, clearly intends to travel to Manchester, even though Manchester is the last place he wants to be and his motive for boarding the plane is simply to escape pursuit.... By boarding the Manchester plane, the man conclusively demonstrates his intention to go there, because it is a moral certainty that that is where he will arrive."

In such a case the law would say that the "morally certain" consequence is intended. But the basis on which it does so is unclear.[51] There are two main alternatives: either there

---

[46] Law Com. No. 304, *Murder, Manslaughter and Infanticide* (2006) 3.27. For earlier proposals, see *A New Homicide Act for England and Wales?* LCCP No. 177 (2006) 4.3; and see the discussion in Part 4 generally. See too Law Com. No. 218 7.1–7.14 and Law Com. No. 122 (1992) 5.4–5.11.

[47] *Hyam* [1975] AC 55, 77.

[48] "Oblique Intention" (1987) 46 *CLJ* 417, 423; cf. his earlier *The Mental Element in Crime* (1965) 34–5. For discussion of these types of cases and the surrounding literature, see Pedain, "Intention and the Terrorist Example" [2004] *Crim LR* 284. More generally, see also Kugler, *Direct and Oblique Intention in the Criminal Law* (2002).

[49] *Hyam* [1975] AC 55, 74.

[50] *Moloney* [1985] AC 905, 926.

[51] Duff, *Intention, Agency and Criminal Liability* (1990) 21–2; also Duff, "The Obscure Intentions of the House of Lords" [1986] *Crim LR* 771.

is, *by definition*, a second category of (indirect) intention involving morally certain consequences,[52] or there is not and moral certainty is simply evidence of an intention in its core sense. In the latter case, there is no second category of intention: foresight of a moral certainty is no more than a ground for inferring that the consequence was (directly) intended,[53] and the inference may be rebutted by other evidence.

There is something to be said for thinking the link is merely evidential, and that there is no second category. Even consequences that are certain to occur may appear not to be intended. If D drinks a bottle of whiskey one evening, he may be sure that he will get a hangover in the morning, but he does not drink the whiskey with the intention of having a hangover.[54] Support for this position is found in decisions subsequent to *Moloney*, where the courts frequently tended to read Lord Bridge's remarks as pertaining to evidential matters. In *Nedrick*, Lord Lane CJ held that "if the jury are satisfied that at the material time the defendant recognised that death or serious harm would be virtually certain (barring some unforeseen intervention) to result from his voluntary act, then that is a fact from which they may find it easy to infer that he intended to kill or do serious bodily harm".[55] Writing extra-judicially in 1987, Lord Goff condemned the extension of intention to embrace moral certainty as "illegitimate".[56]

If Lord Lane and Lord Goff are right, then the explanation of cases like the flight to Manchester has nothing to do with moral certainty. Rather, it is that the fugitive intentionally travels to Manchester as a *means* of leaving London. This is consistent with the account of intention stated earlier, in § 5.1(ii):

Traveller :   T ————→ go to Manchester ————→ leave London

But this answer does not help to deal with the spelæologists, or with the insurance-bombing case proposed by Glanville Williams, where the deaths of the airline passengers are clearly not a means to anything. Despite this, it does seem that the passengers' deaths are so intimately bound up with the villain's intended actions as to be inseparable, and it would be wrong to call them mere side-effects. It appears, therefore, that there is a special category of intention, which falls outside the standard definition given in § 5.1(ii). This second category arises where the defendant recognises that the additional effect is inseparable from those which he intends. A useful definition of this type of case is the rule proposed by H.L.A. Hart: a foreseen outcome is to be regarded as intended when it "is so immediately and invariably connected with the action done that the suggestion that the action might not have that outcome would by ordinary standards be regarded as absurd, or such as only a mentally abnormal person would seriously entertain".[57] These outcomes are intended even

---

[52] Cf. Lord Bridge in *Moloney* [1985] AC 905, 925: an overwhelming probability "will *suffice to establish* the necessary intent" (emphasis added). Compare also the use of "conclusively" in the quotation above at n. 49.

[53] Cf. *Nedrick* [1986] 1 WLR 1025, 1029: where D realises that a consequence is inevitable, "the inference *may* be irresistible that he intended that result" (emphasis added).

[54] Duff, *Intention, Agency and Criminal Liability* (1990) 89–90. The temporal delay seems to be important in how we tend to think about examples of this kind.

[55] [1986] 1 WLR 1025. See also the judgment by Lord Scarman in *Hancock*, above at n. 39.

[56] "The Mental Element in the Crime of Murder" (1988) 104 *LQR* 30, 59.

[57] "Intention and Punishment" in *Punishment and Responsibility* (1968) 113, 120. Hart continues, "the connexion between action and outcome seems therefore to be not merely contingent but rather to be conceptual". See

though D is not trying or aiming to bring them about. They represent a supplementary category to the core definition of intention stated in § 5.1(ii).

The law accommodates these supplementary cases with a special (albeit imprecise) rule. In *Woollin*,[58] D had lost his temper and thrown his three-month-old son against a hard surface. The child's skull fractured and death ensued. In D's trial for murder, the prosecution expressly disavowed that D had intended (in the core sense) his son's death or serious injury. His conviction implies, therefore, that foreseeing a result as a virtual certainty is, in law, an alternative category of intention, and not just evidence from which to infer the core definition of intention. On appeal,[59] Lord Steyn accepted this and explicitly rejected the language of inference. Distilled from his judgment, his Lordship asserts that:[60]

> "in the rare cases where the [standard] direction that it is for the jury simply to decide whether the defendant intended to kill or to do serious bodily harm is not enough, the jury should be directed that they are not entitled to *find* the necessary intention, unless they feel sure that death or serious bodily harm was a virtual certainty (barring some unforeseen intervention) as a result of the defendant's actions and that the defendant appreciated that such was the case."

There are, therefore, two types of intention. First, the normal, core variety is that defined in § 5.1(ii): where an outcome is sought directly by D (because he wants it for its own sake or as a means to something else). Secondly, there are outcomes which, in D's eyes, are so closely bound to normally intended outcomes that they are virtually certain to occur alongside. They may also be regarded as (indirectly) intended.

Cases requiring a *Woollin* direction are rare. Normally, as Lord Steyn said, the jury should consider only the core sense of intention.[61] The *Woollin* decision gives the prosecution an alternative way of proving that an outcome was intended; it is supplementary to, and not a substitute for, intention in the core sense.[62]

However, while clarifying the independent status of this second legal category of intention, *Woollin* does leave its definition not fully unresolved. Lord Steyn's model direction is expressed in negative terms: "the jury should be directed that they are not entitled to find the necessary intention, unless they feel sure that death or serious bodily harm was a virtual certainty". This suggests that, although foresight of virtual certainty is *necessary* before the alternative category of intention is satisfied, it may not always be *sufficient*.[63] It seems

---

further Simester, "Moral Certainty, and the Boundaries of Intention" (1996) 16 *OJLS* 445. This is a tighter connection (as with respect it ought to be) than that required by the Canadian Supreme Court in *Chartrand* (1994) 116 DLR (4th) 207, 225–30.

[58] [1999] 1 AC 82 (HL).

[59] Ultimately, D's conviction was quashed and a conviction for manslaughter substituted, because the trial judge had misdirected the jury on the alternative limb by requiring only that D foresaw a "substantial risk" (rather than virtual certainty) of serious injury or death.

[60] [1999] 1 AC 82, 96.

[61] Cf. *Phillips* [2004] EWCA Crim 112, para. 10; *Allen* [2005] EWCA Crim 1344.

[62] *MD* [2004] EWCA Crim 1391, [2004] All ER (D) 11, para. 29: "*Woollin* is designed to help the prosecution to fill a gap in the rare circumstances in which a defendant does an act which caused the death without the purpose of killing or causing serious injury, but in circumstances where death or serious bodily harm had been a virtual certainty (barring some unforeseen intervention) as a result of the defendant's actions and the defendant had appreciated that such was the case".

[63] Hence the Court of Appeal was right to judge, in *Matthews* [2003] EWCA Crim 192; [2003] 2 Cr App R 30, para. 43, that "the law has not yet reached a definition of intent in murder in terms of appreciation of a virtual certainty". Foresight of virtual certainty is not the same thing as (indirect) intention, but rather a basis on which it may be found.

that, where there is virtual certainty, the jury is permitted to conclude that the defendant intended the outcome and, absent any special considerations, the jury should normally so conclude;[64] but they are entitled not to find intention should there be such considerations.[65] For example, a doctor may know that by injecting a terminally ill patient with the morphine necessary to dull pain, incidentally it is virtually certain that she will shorten the patient's life. The doctor does not aim to shorten the patient's life, and does not intend his death in the core sense. In such a case, notwithstanding that it is a virtually certain side-effect, the jury may well conclude that she does not intend his death, even indirectly.[66] This approach to indirect intention thus confers an element of discretion upon the jury.[67]

(a) Objective and subjective virtual certainty?

There is another oddity about the *Woollin* direction. Lord Steyn requires not only that the defendant *think* the outcome is virtually certain; it must also in fact *be* virtually certain. Arguably, however, it is only the former that counts.[68] Intention is a measure of the agent's perceptions and mental state, and should be unaffected by facts of which the agent is unaware. Suppose that D is a fugitive. She accelerates her car toward a policeman who is blocking her escape. The fugitive, let us say, wishes only to escape but thinks it is virtually certain that, by knocking over the policeman, she will cause grievous bodily harm. In fact, there is a 20 per cent chance in such collisions that the victim will not be seriously injured; but D does not know this and, as it happens, the policeman is severely hurt. In our view, D should be held to have intended the injury.[69]

(b) Definitions and evidence

What, then, is the role of evidential inference? Where the prosecution seeks to prove that D (directly) intended the actus reus under the standard definition, foresight of a probability is evidence from which that intention may be *inferred*. Notice, however, that reference to probability forms no part of that standard definition (given in § 5.1(ii)). In terms of the

---

[64] Compare, e.g., the analysis of the events in *Matthews*, *ibid.*, para. 46: "If the jury were sure that the appellants appreciated the virtual certainty of Jonathan's death when they threw him from the bridge and also that they then had no intention of saving him from such death, it is impossible to see how the jury could not have found that the appellants intended Jonathan to die".

[65] In its Consultation Paper on homicide, the Law Commission discusses one such case invented by Lord Goff, in which D takes a virtually certain risk of killing or injuring his children by defenestrating them during a house fire, because that is the only chance of saving them: LCCP No. 177, *A New Homicide Act for England and Wales?* (2006) para. 4.21. Clearly, in this situation, the intent is to save rather than to take life. Cf. *Emperor* v. *Dhirajia* AIR 1940 All 486, where D jumped down a well with her baby in order to escape her violent husband.

[66] For a discussion of cases that contain *dicta* to this effect, see Ashworth, "Criminal Liability in a Medical Context: The Treatment of Good Intentions" in Simester and Smith (eds.), *Harm and Culpability* (1996) 173. Cf. *Re A (Children)* [2001] Fam 147, 251–2 (Robert Walker LJ).

[67] A result that has found favour with the Law Commission: Law Com. No. 304, *Murder, Manslaughter and Infanticide* (2006) 3.20–3.26. For critical discussion, see Tadros, "The Homicide Ladder" (2006) 69 *MLR* 601.

[68] The former is certainly necessary. It is not sufficient that the outcome *be* virtually certain; D must recognise this. Cf. *Stringer* [2008] EWCA Crim 1222, [2008] All ER (D) 102, paras. 35–6. As *Stringer* goes on to observe (at para. 38), however, the fact that an outcome is virtually certain may also support the inference that D *appreciated* it was virtually certain.

[69] Cf. Simester, "Moral Certainty, and the Boundaries of Intention" (1996) 16 *OJLS* 445, 465–6. As the quotation in the text at § 5.1(iv) shows, the Law Commission agrees: Law Com. No. 304, *Murder, Manslaughter and Infanticide* (2006) 3.27.

paradigm type of intention, there is no reason to require virtual certainty before inferring (direct) intent. If D aims a pistol at V and pulls the trigger, it may not be virtually certain, or even very likely, that V will die—perhaps it is a difficult shot—yet we would normally infer that D's intention was to kill; that he was trying to kill.[70] The connection between (standard, direct) intention and foresight of probability is purely evidential.

On the other hand, the connection between foresight of probability and the virtually certain category of intention is not even evidential. It is non-existent. Without foresight of an outcome that D perceives to be virtually certain, the second category of (indirect) intention is simply not in play.

(v) Intention and circumstances

The account of intention we have given so far needs qualification when applied to any circumstances which form a part of the actus reus. This is best seen by means of an example. Rape can only be committed by D's having sexual intercourse with V without her consent. The circumstance, that V does not consent, is part of the actus reus of the offence. There are two ways in which D's mental state regarding V's non-consent can satisfy the demands of intention. The plain case occurs where D rapes V by intentionally having sexual intercourse with her, *hoping or desiring* that she does not consent. In this case D intends "sexual intercourse without consent" in its full sense, because it is part of his purpose not merely to have sexual intercourse with V, but to have it without her consent. Duff's test of failure shows this clearly:[71] D would regard himself as having "failed" if V did in fact consent to having sexual intercourse with him.

Although the clearest sort of case, this is the less common variety of intention where circumstances are at issue, and probably occurs only rarely. More often, rape is intentional when D is aware that V does not consent, yet neither intends nor hopes (and does not care) that V is not consenting. In this situation, D intends to have "sexual intercourse without consent", because he intends to have sexual intercourse *believing* that V does not consent.

So there are two ways of showing that an actus reus is intended when it involves circumstances. The first is by showing that the behaviour and consequences are intended, and that D hopes the circumstances are present. The second is by showing that the behaviour and consequences are intended, and that D believes the circumstances are present. What does "believing" mean in this context? In our view "believing" has the same meaning as "knowing", with one exception. We consider the meaning of knowledge below,[72] but in essence what is required is that the defendant hold a positive belief, amounting to an acceptance, that the circumstance exists.

The one difference, in law, between knowledge and belief is that a belief need not be correct. The defendant may believe something wrongly, but she cannot "know" something

---

[70] Cf. *MD* [2004] EWCA Crim 1391, [2004] All ER (D) 11, para. 29: "*Woollin* is not designed to make the prosecution's task more difficult. Many murderers whose purpose was to kill or cause serious injury would escape conviction for murder if the jury was given only a *Woollin* direction. The man who kills another with a gun would be able to escape liability for murder if he could show that he was such a bad shot that death or serious bodily harm was not a virtual certainty or that the defendant had thought that death or serious bodily harm was not a virtual certainty."

[71] Above, § 5.1(i).

[72] See § 5.4.

that is false. Usually the difference will not matter very much. For example, if D wrongly believes that V does *not* consent to sexual intercourse, when in fact she does consent, then regardless of his mens rea he cannot commit rape, because the actus reus is missing. But sometimes it will still be important to establish whether D has mens rea, since even without the actus reus he might nonetheless be guilty of an attempt. In this example, his false belief that V does not consent will be sufficient to help constitute an intention for the purposes of attempted rape.[73]

(vi) Multiple intentions

Very often, a person has more than one reason for acting as he does. By cooking dinner, John might intend not only to assuage his hunger, but also to use up the contents of the fridge, as well as surprise and please his flatmates. All three results are intended. The mere fact that a defendant can point to some other result that he was also trying to achieve does not mean that he cannot have intended the actus reus. It is no answer for a newspaper that deliberately publishes *sub judice* material to say that it was really trying to increase its circulation. Ignoring extraneous intentions, the criminal law focuses only on the actus reus; and asks, whatever else he intended, did D intend that *actus*?

(vii) "With intent" or "ulterior intent" crimes

Sometimes the intentional doing of an actus reus is not itself an offence, and becomes criminal only when done for some further purpose. For example, if D carries a crowbar in his bag he does nothing wrong; but if he carries the crowbar with intent to use it in a burglary, he is guilty of an offence.[74] Crimes of this sort require what is often called an "ulterior intent".[75] The main feature of such crimes is that they specify, as part of the mens rea, an intent to do something that is not part of the actus reus. In the example above, the actus reus is simple possession of the crowbar—it does not matter whether the crowbar is actually used in a burglary.[76] This is why such crimes are said to involve "ulterior" intent: because the eventual intention is ulterior to the actus reus.

In other respects, however, these crimes are no different from crimes of ordinary intent. In particular, where a crime specifies an ulterior intent as part of the mens rea, it seems clear that mere foresight of the further consequence will not do. The crime can be committed only if the defendant intends that consequence.[77] This is the explanation of the controversial case of *Steane*.[78] Steane had been compelled, through concern for the safety of his

---

[73] The claim here is merely that knowledge or belief satisfies the demands of intention. It is a further question (taken up in Chapter 9) whether, with respect to circumstances, intention is *required* to establish the mens rea of attempt offences. The cases of *Khan* [1990] 1 WLR 813 (CA) and *A-G's Reference (No. 3 of 1992)* [1994] 1 WLR 409 (CA) have suggested otherwise. Fortunately, the reasoning in those cases is specific to attempts, and does not carry over to substantive offences.

[74] Theft Act 1968, s. 25. Cf. *Ellames* [1974] 1 WLR 1391; *Hargreaves* [1985] Crim LR 243.

[75] See generally Horder, "Crimes of Ulterior Intent" in Simester and Smith (eds.), *Harm and Culpability* (1996) 153.

[76] Cf. *Rodley* (1913) 9 Cr App R 69, 76.

[77] *Belfon* [1976] 3 All ER 46, 49.

[78] [1947] KB 997. See, e.g., Williams, "Oblique Intention" (1987) 46 *CLJ* 417, 428.

family, to make broadcasts on behalf of the Germans during the Second World War. He was prosecuted under English wartime regulations for doing an act likely to assist the enemy (the actus reus), "with intent to assist the enemy". The Court of Criminal Appeal quashed his conviction for lack of mens rea, and rightly so. Although in making the broadcasts Steane had done an act likely to assist the enemy, the prosecution had failed to prove that he intended thereby to assist the enemy (i.e. that assisting the enemy was a part of his purposes in broadcasting). It is important to emphasise that the mens rea required is ulterior to the actus reus. The actus reus is *"any act likely* to assist the enemy", and does not involve proof that the defendant in fact did assist the enemy. The mens rea is an intent "to assist the enemy"; which goes beyond the actus reus. Steane intended to make the broadcasts, but his ulterior intent in so doing had been to protect his family. It would be otherwise if the foreseen further consequence were "morally certain" to accompany his intended actions; in which case they too would be intended.[79]

(viii) Conditional intent

Sometimes a person is willing to commit a crime but her actions will not necessarily result in one. For example, if a thief makes off with a handbag, meaning to keep the contents, she steals those contents only if there are any. In this situation, her intention to take the contents is conditional upon there being anything to steal. Such cases are not uncommon in the criminal law, especially in the context of offences involving an ulterior intent. The general rule is that an intention to do or bring about something only if particular conditions hold is in law, an intention. Thus a burglar who enters a flat with intent to steal a television set provided there be a set to steal, intends to steal.[80]

(ix) No presumption of intention

Proving mens rea is often difficult. It is impossible to look directly into the minds of defendants in order to know whether they had mens rea at the time of the offence. Usually, if the defendant does not himself confess to having it, the prosecution will be put to proving the relevant state of mind through supporting evidence, e.g. of the defendant's actions before, during, and after the actus reus occurred. Suppose that D is found to have shot V. If there is evidence that D planned the shooting in advance, this may be admissible to support the allegation that D's actions were intentional. The same is true if it is shown that D took careful aim at V's heart before pulling the trigger. In this case, proof by the prosecution that the prohibited harm (i.e. V's death) was a natural consequence of D's actions will support the inference that D intended it. Similarly, proof that the defendant foresaw the outcome (e.g. because D knew the gun was loaded) may also help to support such a conclusion. Inferences of this variety depend upon a recognition that there is no reasonable interpretation of the evidence other than that the defendant had mens rea.

---

[79] See above, § 5.1(iv); also *Chartrand* (1994) 116 DLR (4th) 207, 225–30.

[80] *A-G's References (Nos. 1 and 2 of 1979)* [1980] QB 180 (noted [1979] Crim LR 585), distinguishing and confining *Husseyn* (1977) 67 Cr App R 131n; *Walkington* [1979] 2 All ER 716, noted [1979] Crim LR 526; *Buckingham* (1976) 63 Cr App R 159. See Campbell, "Conditional Intention" (1982) 2 *LS* 77.

But such inferences are a matter of evidence only. They are neither irrebuttable, nor are they substantive rules of criminal law. Intention is a subjective concept, and any inference made from the evidence is *not* a presumption. Where the prosecution is obliged to prove mens rea, it must do so beyond reasonable doubt. Supporting evidence, e.g. of foresight, is simply a part of what the prosecution may show in order to convince the court that, in light of all the evidence,[81] it may safely conclude, beyond reasonable doubt, that D had the required mens rea.

It was not always so. In *DPP* v. *Smith*,[82] the House of Lords held there was an irrebuttable presumption in law that a person intends the reasonably foreseeable consequences of his acts. Fortunately, this highly controversial decision has been reversed by section 8 of the Criminal Justice Act 1967. In any offence requiring the prosecution to prove mens rea on the part of the defendant, section 8 provides that the court:

(a)   shall not be bound in law to infer that he intended or foresaw a result of his actions by reason only of its being a natural and probable consequence of those actions; but

(b)   shall decide whether he did intend or foresee that result by reference to all the evidence, drawing such inferences from the evidence as appear proper in the circumstances.

The section does not, alas, offer a definition of "intention"—hence the difficulties seen earlier in this chapter. Its only role is to govern, and restrict, evidential rules of inference.

§ 5.2 Recklessness

Often people cause injury without intending to—that is, without acting in order to do so. The doctor who injects her patient with a painkiller may unintentionally kill him, if the patient proves to be allergic to the drug that she injects. But the fact that an injury is unintended does not mean that the person who causes it is blameless; the doctor may have been aware of the risk of injury, a risk that she nevertheless chose to run. In such cases, we would say, she foresaw (but did not intend) the harm.

Not every case of foresight amounts to recklessness. In order for a defendant to be reckless, the risk that she chooses to run must also be an unreasonable one.[83] Although in practice this issue does not often arise, the qualification is important. It means that anaesthetists, who knowingly undertake a slight risk that the patient will have a fatal allergic reaction when anaesthetised before an operation, are not necessarily guilty of reckless homicide when the patient dies. The question of what is reasonable is an objective question, and it is not an issue of whether the defendant thought the risk was reasonable; rather, it is a question whether an ordinary and prudent person would have been prepared to take that risk. To this extent defendants cannot be permitted to judge what is right for themselves.

There are a number of factors for the law to consider when deciding whether a particular risk was reasonable. These include the probability of the risk occurring, and the nature and gravity of the harm being risked. Driving at 30 mph on a busy road may be reasonable;

---

[81] Cf. *Hales* [2005] EWCA Crim 1118, [2005] All ER (D) 371, para. 17: "The jury has to put all the circumstances together, leaving out nothing of potential relevance".

[82] [1961] AC 290. The decision was treated as wrongly decided by the Privy Council in *Frankland* v. *R.* [1987] AC 576.

[83] Cf. *Renouf* [1986] 2 All ER 449.

driving at 50 may not be, because of the increased risk of accidents and the more serious injuries that are likely to ensue should there be a crash. Against these considerations should be balanced the value and likelihood of achieving what the defendant was trying to do while running that risk. A high-risk surgical operation may be justifiable when it is done as a last resort or in an emergency to save the patient's life. But the risks involved may not be acceptable if less dangerous alternatives are available, or if the purpose of the operation is trivial, or if reasonable steps are not taken to reduce those risks.

One point that should be made here is that the incorporation of a standard of reasonableness means that there is no need for a separate "threshold" criterion of probability or likelihood. Obviously, if a risk is thought to be minimal or only an "outside chance", running that risk is likely to be unobjectionable. But even a very slight risk can be enough for recklessness if the harm being risked is serious enough and the act concerned has no social value. A game of "Russian roulette" would be reckless even if the chances of being killed were thought to be only one in 200.[84] In such cases, it may be necessary to abandon an activity altogether if the defendant cannot eliminate the risk entirely. One example of this is provided by *Chief Constable of Avon and Somerset Constabulary* v. *Shimmen*.[85] D, a martial arts expert, was demonstrating his skill to friends by kicking close to a window without intending to break it. This experiment in controlled risk-taking failed: he smashed the window. Even though he thought he had "eliminated as much risk as possible", he was nevertheless guilty of reckless criminal damage since he had chosen to run the slight and unjustifiable risk which remained. Conversely, there may be a very substantial risk of injury or death in certain "last resort" surgical operations, but those operations are not necessarily unreasonable when undertaken.

There are two definitions of recklessness known to English law: "subjective" or *Cunningham* recklessness, and "objective" or *Caldwell* recklessness. Of the two, subjective recklessness is the standard variety. Formally, under the subjective definition, D acts recklessly if:

(a)   He believes his conduct will give rise to a risk of harm; and
(b)   It is unreasonable for D to run the risk that he foresees.[86]

The main difference between intention and (subjective) recklessness is that while in both cases the defendant must foresee the possibility of realising the actus reus, in recklessness he need not seek or be motivated to bring it about. However, while this subjective definition currently dominates the law, some decisions for a time suggested that element (a), actual foresight of the risk, should not always be required and that an objective definition of recklessness should be adopted. We consider this issue in the next section.

(i) The need for foresight

Traditionally, the leading case to require that there be actual foresight before a defendant can be considered reckless is *Cunningham*.[87] In that case, D interfered with the coin-operated

---

[84] Cf. *Vehicle Inspectorate* v. *Nuttall* [1999] 1 WLR 629, 636. Indeed, whether an outcome is sufficiently probable to be, in law, "likely" also depends on the gravity of the outcome at risk: *Whitehouse* [2000] Crim LR 172.

[85] (1987) 84 Cr App R 7.

[86] There is no further requirement that the risk be obvious and significant: *Brady* [2006] EWCA Crim 2413.

[87] [1957] 2 QB 396. Cf. *Briggs* [1977] 1 All ER 475, 477; *Stephenson* [1979] QB 695, 1203; *Mullins* [1980] Crim LR 37; *Flack* v. *Hunt* [1980] Crim LR 44.

gas meter in an unoccupied house in order to steal money from it. The gas escaped, seeped into an adjoining house, and endangered the life of a person living there. Upon his appeal against conviction for maliciously administering a noxious thing so as to endanger life,[88] the Court of Criminal Appeal held that "malice" required either intention or recklessness. Recklessness would be present if "the accused has foreseen that the particular kind of harm might be done, and yet has gone on to take the risk of it".[89]

On this view, failing to think about a risk is not a ground of criminal culpability. An illustration of this principle is found in *Stephenson*,[90] where D lit a fire in order to warm himself while sheltering in a haystack, and was charged with reckless arson after the haystack itself caught fire and was destroyed. Stephenson's conviction was quashed on appeal because (as he suffered from schizophrenia) he might not have been aware of the risk to the haystack.[91]

On the other hand, the law as stated in *Cunningham* does not entitle a defendant deliberately to close her mind to an obvious risk when she is aware of the risk but does not think about it because she does not care. In *Parker*,[92] D slammed down a public telephone receiver with such force that he broke it. The Court rejected his defence that he had been too enraged to think about the risk. The inherent association of his violent action with its consequence meant that he could be taken to have appreciated the risk without the awareness of that risk being at the forefront of his mind, and without the need for sober or careful deliberation in advance.

The inference made in *Parker* must arise clearly from the facts if it is to be properly drawn.[93] In *Briggs*,[94] D took hold of the door handle to V's car and tried to open the door, apparently with a normal arm movement. The handle broke. On appeal, the Court of Appeal quashed D's conviction for misdirection. The trial judge had failed to instruct the jury that, in order to be held reckless, D must have given thought to the risk of damaging the door handle; it was possible that D had not done so.

Unlike in *Parker*, the risk created by the defendant in *Briggs* was not so inherent in his actions that it was inevitable that D had appreciated it. *Briggs* reinforces the point that there must be awareness of the risk at some level of the defendant's consciousness before he can be found reckless.

(a) An alternative, objective version of recklessness

The above states the established position after *Cunningham*. In 1981 the House of Lords invented a second version of recklessness in *Metropolitan Police Commissioner* v. *Caldwell*[95]

---

[88] Contrary to the OAPA 1861, s. 23.

[89] [1957] 2 QB 396, 399. Quoting with approval from Turner, *Kenny's Outlines of Criminal Law* (16th ed., 1952) 186.

[90] [1979] QB 695.

[91] Note that on these facts, D might properly have been obliged to plead insanity. (Contrast, however, *Harris* [2013] EWCA Crim 223, where D was allowed to explain his lack of awareness that setting fire to his house endangered the lives of others on the basis of his mental disorder.) See further below, Chapter 19.

[92] [1977] 2 All ER 37.

[93] Indeed, it is arguable that the inference was inappropriate in *Parker* itself. As such the decision by the Court of Appeal may be a precursor of *Caldwell*, discussed below in the next subsection. If so, however, the approach in *Parker* is narrower than that taken by the House of Lords in *Caldwell*; it would justify inferring recklessness only where D "deliberately closes his mind" to obvious consequences because he is "in a self-induced state of temper", or for a similarly discreditable reason. See [1977] 2 All ER 37, 40.

[94] [1977] 1 All ER 475.

[95] [1982] AC 341.

and the companion case of *Lawrence*.[96] In *Caldwell*, the defendant set fire to a hotel while intoxicated. He was charged, *inter alia*, with an offence against section 1(1) of the Criminal Damage Act 1971, which makes it an offence to damage another's property "being reckless as to whether any such property would be destroyed or damaged". The House of Lords held that a defendant is reckless in law if:[97]

> "(1) he does an act which in fact creates an obvious [and serious][98] risk that property would be destroyed or damaged and (2) when he does the act he either has not given any thought to the possibility of there being any such risk or has recognised that there was some risk involved and has nonetheless gone on to do it."

The essence of the decision was to create a second category of recklessness in criminal law. In addition to the cases of actual foresight covered by *Cunningham*, the defendant would also be treated as reckless if he failed to think of a risk when that risk was a glaring one. In effect, the *Caldwell* definition of recklessness embraces both advertent wrongdoing and gross negligence.[99]

(b) The predominance of subjective recklessness

The extension of recklessness proposed in *Caldwell* was always controversial.[100] Although the decision exercised a considerable influence over English criminal law during the 1980s,[101] its importance quickly diminished, to the point that its application came to be restricted to the offence in *Caldwell* itself (criminal damage and its variants), and to a few other statutory offences.[102] Eventually, in *G*,[103] the House of Lords overruled the application of objective recklessness even to criminal damage, reversing the very decision in *Caldwell*. Advertent recklessness is, once more, the dominant—perhaps even the only—form.

In *G*, two children aged 11 and 12 had stolen away camping without their parents' permission. During the night they entered the back yard of a Co-op shop, where they found some bundles of newspapers. After opening the newspapers, they set fire to some of them and threw them under a wheelie-bin in the yard. The defendant children then left the yard without putting out the fire. Subsequently, the fire spread to the bin and to the adjacent shop, causing approximately £1 million worth of damage. The defendants apparently expected the newspapers to burn themselves out on the concrete floor of the yard, and did not foresee the risk of the fire spreading to the building. At trial, following a *Caldwell* direction, they were convicted of reckless arson, a conviction upheld by the Court of Appeal. The House of Lords, however, quashed the convictions. *Caldwell* was overruled: it was held to have

---

[96] [1982] AC 510. Cf. also *Miller* [1983] 2 AC 161.

[97] [1982] AC 341, 354.

[98] Interpolated in *Lawrence* [1982] AC 510, 527. The requirement of obviousness does not apply where the risk is in fact foreseen: *Reid* [1992] 3 All ER 673, 691.

[99] See below, § 5.5(iv). Cf. *Adomako* [1995] 1 AC 171, 187, 189 (Lord Mackay).

[100] See, e.g., Smith [1981] Crim LR 393, 410; Williams, "Recklessness Redefined" [1981] *CLJ* 252; Syrota, "A Radical Change in the Law of Recklessness?" [1982] *Crim LR* 97; Duff, "Professor Williams and Conditional Subjectivism" [1982] *CLJ* 273; Williams, "The Unresolved Problem of Recklessness" (1988) 8 *LS* 74.

[101] Contrast other jurisdictions, where *Caldwell* generally failed to take hold: *Smith* (1982) 7 A Crim R 437; *Sansregret v. R.* (1985) 17 DLR (4th) 577; *Harney* [1987] 2 NZLR 576.

[102] E.g. *Large v. Mainprize* [1989] Crim LR 213.

[103] [2003] UKHL 50; [2004] 1 AC 1034.

misinterpreted Parliament's intention when enacting the Criminal Damage Act 1971. More generally, the objective test of recklessness established in *Caldwell* was labelled "unjust".

Technically, *G* is a decision on the mental element of criminal damage. It therefore remains possible in theory that, in some future context, the courts will interpret a specific statutory requirement of recklessness as entailing *Caldwell* and not *Cunningham* recklessness. Indeed, this possibility was left open by Lords Bingham and Rodger in *G*.[104]

But it is prima facie desirable that the courts should interpret core terms like "recklessness" in a consistent fashion,[105] and the likelihood that courts will ever adopt *Caldwell* recklessness in a statutory interpretation exercise is surely now remote; notwithstanding that there are some ordinary-language senses of "recklessness" which are not subjective (below, § 5.2(ii)). Moreover, while the actual decision in *G* concerns the meaning of recklessness in the context of the Criminal Damage Act 1971, the principles it lays down are general in nature.[106] Unless the statute expressly or by necessary implication precludes it,[107] the fault element for criminal offences should normally be subjective. As the House of Lords itself acknowledged in *G*, convictions of serious crimes should not normally be visited on the inadvertent. In the absence of compelling reasons, such as a clear legislative indication, we should not ordinarily make criminals of those who act without any intent or awareness of wrongdoing, since they may not be sufficiently blameworthy to warrant conviction or punishment:[108]

> "But it is not clearly blameworthy to do something involving a risk of injury to another if … one genuinely does not perceive the risk. Such a person may fairly be accused of stupidity or lack of imagination, but neither of those failings should expose him to conviction of serious crime or the risk of punishment."

Indeed, especially where the defendant suffers from limitations of age, intellect, or the like, to apply the *Caldwell* standard would be manifestly unfair, since it could lead to the conviction of persons, including children, who lacked even the *capacity* to appreciate risks that would be obvious to ordinary adults:[109]

> "It is neither moral nor just to convict a defendant (least of all a child) on the strength of what someone else would have apprehended if the defendant himself had no such apprehension. Nor, the defendant having been convicted, is the problem cured by imposition of a nominal penalty."

We concur. The justification of *Caldwell*, according to Lord Diplock, was that inadvertence to an obvious risk frequently is just as blameworthy as choosing to run a risk which is foreseen, and so should be treated the same way. There is some force in this: it is an unattractive

---

[104] *Ibid.*, paras. 28 (Lord Bingham) and 69 (Lord Rodger).

[105] An argument made by Stark, "It's Only Words: On Meaning and Mens Rea" (2013) 72 *CLJ* 155.

[106] Cf. *A-G's Reference (No. 3 of 2003)* [2004] EWCA Crim 868, [2005] QB 73, para. 12; *Brady* [2006] EWCA Crim 2413, para. 15; *Mbagwu* [2007] EWCA Crim 1068, para. 20.

[107] An argument along these lines is advanced by Cartwright in the context of some consumer offences: "Corporate Criminal Liability: Models of Intervention and Liability in Consumer Law", Appendix B of LCCP No. 195, *Criminal Liability in Regulatory Contexts* (2010) paras. B16–17.

[108] *G* [2003] UKHL 50; [2004] 1 AC 1034, para. 32 (Lord Bingham); see also para. 55 (Lord Steyn).

[109] *Ibid.*, para. 33 (Lord Bingham); cf. paras. 52–4 (Lord Steyn). The House rejected a modified test, of whether the risk would have been obvious to one with *the defendant's* capacities: *ibid.*, paras. 37–8 (Lord Bingham). See further below, § 5.5(ii).

option to acquit a defendant who did not consider the risks because he was too drunk, too temperamental, or too uncaring a person to bother thinking about them.[110] But, as we shall see in § 5.2(iv), there are already special rules in place which deal with intoxication. Moreover, a question might be asked whether the moral equation constructed by Lord Diplock will always (or almost always) hold—which ought to be the case before a court makes such a comprehensive extension. In particular, it seems harsh to treat as reckless those whose inadvertence was due to preoccupation or distraction,[111] and who may be utterly horrified when they recognise the consequences of their actions. It is even more harsh to equate with advertent recklessness the actions of those who were *incapable* of perceiving the risk.[112]

(ii) Recklessness with respect to the behaviour element, rather than circumstances or consequences

The plausibility of an objective approach in cases involving reckless driving, such as *Lawrence*,[113] rests upon a distinction that we drew in Chapter 4.[114] In *Lawrence*, the actus reus of the offence was concerned only with D's *behaviour* (i.e. with his reckless driving). By contrast, in many other offences D's behaviour alone is not sufficient to establish the actus reus. There must be an additional element, e.g. that the victim is not consenting, or that she dies. Where an offence involves *circumstances* and *consequences*, it is natural for a lawyer to think of recklessness as a mens rea term, requiring advertence to the specific circumstance or consequence named in that offence. For example, to commit a reckless homicide one has to foresee the possibility of death ensuing. But matters are different when the actus reus is concerned only with the behaviour of the defendant. In an offence of reckless driving the court did not ask, "Was the defendant aware of the possibility that she might be driving a car?" Rather, what counted was whether the *manner* of her behaviour was sufficiently dangerous—not what she thought about that behaviour. "Reckless", in this context, qualifies the nature of the behaviour that is needed for the offence. Hence, it is an actus reus term. One might, for example, drive in a reckless manner (the *actus*) deliberately (the *mens*).[115] Where recklessness refers to the manner of D's behaviour, the case for an objective interpretation is therefore stronger.

(iii) Recklessness and circumstances

Just as with consequences, recklessness as to circumstances requires that the defendant acts believing that there is a possibility, or risk, that the circumstance might exist. This is sometimes called "reckless knowledge", but the term is a misleading one, since "knowledge" as

---

[110] Cf. Lord Goff in *Reid* [1992] 3 All ER 673, 687ff. This seems to have been the thinking underlying *Parker* (above, § 5.2(i)).

[111] Cf. Griew, "Reckless Damage and Reckless Driving: Living with *Caldwell* and *Lawrence*" [1981] *Crim LR* 743, 747; in tort, *West Ky. Tel. Co. v. Pharis* 25 Ky LR 1838 (1904).

[112] As, following *Caldwell*, was done in *Elliott* v. *C (a minor)* [1983] 1 WLR 939; discussed further below, § 5.5(ii).

[113] Above, § 5.2(i)(a).

[114] See §§ 4, 4.1.

[115] Winslade, "Brady on Recklessness" (1972) 33 *Analysis* 31.

such is not needed, and it will be enough if the defendant merely recognises that the circumstance *may* exist.

The definition just stated is derived from general principles. Recklessness requires that the defendant be aware of the possibility that the actus reus, as a whole, may occur. Hence it requires the defendant to be aware that each element of that actus reus may be present, including circumstances. A useful illustration of this is the offence of assault. One requirement of that offence is the victim's lack of consent. The mens rea for this element is recklessness.[116] Thus the defendant cannot be guilty if he believes that his victim consents, and may only be convicted if he goes ahead recognising that she may not be consenting. As Lord Bingham put it in *G*, a person is reckless with respect to a circumstance "when he is aware of a risk that it exists or will exist".[117]

The difference between recklessness and intention can be shown by the following example. If D has sexual intercourse with V recognising (but not caring) that she may not be consenting, then if V does not consent D commits a reckless rape. On the other hand, if D has sexual intercourse *believing* positively that V does not consent, he rapes her intentionally. (In either case D commits the offence of rape.)[118]

The above states the law in principle. Sometimes, however, this definition leads to difficulties where the defendant acts without giving thought to attendant circumstances. This may occur, for example, where D indecently touches another person but claims it did not occur to him that she might not consent. What if D did not think about the possibility because he did not care, and would have gone ahead anyway? Should he be acquitted? In order to deal with such situations, the courts have suggested two alternative ways of finding recklessness by the defendant.

The first suggested extension is that a defendant may be held reckless about a circumstance, such as non-consent, if he was indifferent to, or could not care less about, whether the victim was consenting. The validity of this extension is doubtful. Its genesis seems to be the references to indifference found in *Lawrence*. It has been endorsed in a number of decisions, for example *Kimber*, where in the Court of Appeal's words, D's "attitude to [V] was one of indifference to her feelings and wishes. This state of mind is aptly described in the colloquial expression, 'couldn't care less'. In law this is recklessness."[119] But if that proposition was ever correct, it is not now. *Caldwell*, as we have noted, is no longer good law. Mens rea is not normally concerned with the *attitudes* of defendants; it is concerned with what they intended, knew, and did not know. This is why a worthy attitude, or a good motive, is no defence under the criminal law.[120] It is also why, under the *Cunningham* approach to

---

[116] Cf. *C* [1992] Crim LR 642 (indecent assault).

[117] [2003] UKHL 50; [2004] 1 AC 1034, para. 41, quoting from the proposed clause 18(c) in *A Draft Code for England and Wales* Law. Com. No. 177 (1989).

[118] Whether D's recklessness would be sufficient for him to be convicted of an attempt (if V in fact does consent) is discussed below, in Chapter 9.

[119] [1983] 1 WLR 1118, 1123. Cf. *Pigg* [1982] 2 All ER 591 (reversed on different ground [1983] 1 All ER 56); *Millard* [1987] Crim LR 393; *Khan* [1990] 1 WLR 813 (CA); *Paine* [1998] 1 Cr App R 36. Compare, in Australia, *Tolmie* (1995) 37 NSWLR 660; *Kitchener* (1993) 29 NSWLR 696; *Vehicle Inspectorate v. Nuttall* [1999] 1 WLR 629, 636. The approach in *Tolmie* was endorsed by Callinan J in *Banditt v. R.* [2005] HCA 80, para. 86, but not by the majority, which favoured a subjective test: see paras. 20, 25, 33–6.

[120] Cf. *Smith* [1960] 2 QB 423; above, §§ 5, 5.1(ii). For the rule that a positive attitude, of hoping the actus reus would not happen, supplies no defence, see *Crabbe* (1985) 156 CLR 464, 470.

recklessness, defendants are not to be convicted merely on the basis of an unworthy attitude or bad motive, e.g. for indifference. Correspondingly, the law should not be concerned to enquire *why* D failed to foresee a risk, and whether it was because he did not care or exhibited some other indifferent attitude.[121] Such fine nuances have no practical place in the law.

The second extension to traditional recklessness is more plausible, and is almost certainly part of current law. On this test, D will be held reckless about a circumstantial element in an offence *unless* he has a positive belief that the circumstance is lacking. Thus, if D deliberately and indecently touches V, it is an indecent assault unless he believes that V consents. More generally, where recklessness about non-consent is required to establish mens rea, it suffices *either* if D recognised V might not be consenting, *or* if D did *not* believe that she was consenting. This test was accepted by the House of Lords in *B (a minor)* v. *DPP*.[122] In effect, the prosecution need prove only that D lacked a genuine belief that V consented, without having to prove, in addition, that he believed there was a risk that she did not consent. This formulation of recklessness will not convict defendants who wrongly assume that V consents, but will catch those who proceed to harm V without believing they have V's agreement. The advantage of this test is that (like *Cunningham*) its focus is restricted to D's cognitive beliefs, whereas the test suggested in *Kimber* requires consideration of D's attitude. Moreover, *Kimber* itself also falls within this second category.

(iv) Intoxication and the presumption of recklessness

In general, there is no presumption of recklessness, and the prosecution is obliged to prove recklessness without the assistance of irrebuttable inferences.[123] As always, the prosecution may rely on evidential inferences in the normal way: for example, the fact that D took precautions, say by wearing fire-resistant clothing when dealing with flammable materials, may be relied on to suggest that he recognised his conduct was dangerous. However, there is no rule of substantive law by which the defendant is deemed to have foreseen a consequence merely because it was likely or obvious.[124]

This generalisation is subject to one exception. If the defendant fails to foresee a risk because he was voluntarily intoxicated, he may be treated, in law, as having foreseen that risk.[125] Voluntary intoxication can lead, as a matter of law, to a finding of recklessness— including *Cunningham* recklessness. The legal significance of intoxication will be discussed in more detail below, in Chapter 18.

---

[121] Moreover, as Norrie points out, there are different kinds of indifferent attitude: "Between Orthodox Subjectivism and Moral Contextualism: Intention and the Consultation Paper" [2006] *Crim LR* 486, 492–3. Thus the objection is compounded by ambiguity about *which* standard to apply.

[122] [2000] 2 AC 428, 459 (Lord Mackay), 466 (Lord Nicholls). Cf. *K* [2002] 1 AC 462, 471 (Lord Bingham), 479 (Lord Hobhouse); also *Satnam and Kewal Singh* (1983) 78 Cr App R 149. Contrast, however, the quotation from Lord Bingham in *G* [2003] UKHL 50, [2004] 1 AC 1034, para. 41, in the text above at n. 113.

[123] See s. 8 of the Criminal Justice Act 1967; above, § 5.1(ix).

[124] *Caldwell* [1982] AC 341, discussed earlier in § 5.2(i), is not such a decision; rather, it holds that for the objective variety of recklessness actual foresight by the defendant is not a required element.

[125] *Bennett* [1995] Crim LR 877.

§ 5.3 Why distinguish intention from recklessness?

In practice, recklessness satisfies the mens rea requirement in most crimes. This raises an obvious question: why bother discussing a separate category of intention at all? There are three reasons for doing so. First, some actions can only be done intentionally. For example, a person attempts to harm another only if he intends to do so. It would be a misuse of language to describe a knowing risk-taker as "attempting" to inflict harm.

Often this linguistic difference reflects a moral distinction,[126] because the presence of intention can alter the very nature of what is done. As Glanville Williams once pointed out, "[t]he act constituting a crime may in some circumstances be objectively innocent, and take its criminal colouring entirely from the intent with which it is done".[127] It was the defendant's intention which changed the action from simple assault to indecent assault in *Court*,[128] a case where D spanked a young girl on the seat of her shorts. He was convicted of indecent assault because he had not done so in order to administer discipline, but rather for sexual gratification—his intention made the behaviour "indecent".[129] Similarly, the difference between negligent appropriation of property and theft lies not merely in the degree of culpability but also in the nature of the action itself (even though the physical harm may be the same). Theft cannot fully be defined in terms of its consequence because the action itself expresses a certain sort of contempt for property rights, and for the victim, which the mere appropriation of property does not.

The second rationale for distinguishing intention from recklessness is that, as we have seen, recklessness is established only if the defendant risked doing the actus reus *unreasonably*. By contrast, there is no condition of unreasonableness attaching to intention. Neither is there a general defence known to the criminal law of reasonable action.[130]

The third ground also involves defences, which is a topic we have not yet discussed. As the law presently stands, in order to claim a defence such as self-defence, the defendant must *intend* to defend himself when he does the actus reus. This point is illustrated by the well-known case of *Dadson*,[131] in which a policeman shot and wounded a thief who was stealing wood. It was then, as now, an offence intentionally to shoot another, and both the actus reus and mens rea were made out in Dadson's case. However, the thief was in fact a felon, and a defence existed at that time to the effect that the policeman would be justified in shooting to prevent the escape of a felon. The difficulty was that the policeman had not realised that the person he was shooting was a felon. Hence, although he intended to shoot V, he did not intend to use this justification: i.e. to prevent the escape of a felon. Therefore, the Court ruled, he was not entitled to claim the defence, and he was convicted.[132]

---

[126] See, e.g., Duff, "Attempted Homicide" (1995) 1 *Legal Theory* 149; Horder, "Crimes of Ulterior Intent" in Simester and Smith (eds.), *Harm and Culpability* (1996) 153.

[127] *CLGP* 22. See also Lynch, "The Mental Element in the Actus Reus" (1982) 98 *LQR* 109.

[128] [1989] AC 28; discussed in Sullivan, "The Need for a Crime of Sexual Assault" [1989] *Crim LR* 331.

[129] *Per* Lord Ackner (at 230), "[t]o decide whether or not right-minded persons might think that the assault was indecent, the following factors were clearly relevant: the relationship of the defendant to this victim …, how had the defendant come to embark on this conduct and *why* was he behaving in this way?"

[130] Cf. *Yip Chiu-cheung v. R.* [1995] 1 AC 111. For a discussion of this point in the context of medical necessity, see Ashworth, "Criminal Liability in a Medical Context: the Treatment of Good Intentions" in Simester and Smith (eds.), *Harm and Culpability* (1996) 173.

[131] (1850) 4 Cox CC 358.

[132] See also *Thain* [1985] NI 457; Sullivan, "Bad Thoughts and Bad Acts" [1990] *Crim LR* 559; Hogan, "The *Dadson* Principle" [1989] *Crim LR* 679.

§ 5.4 Knowledge

Where an offence is formulated so as to require that the defendant act "knowing" that some circumstance exists, this demands a positive (and correct)[133] belief on the part of the defendant that the relevant circumstance does indeed exist.[134] Legally speaking, "knowledge means true belief".[135] If Tom purchases goods suspecting they may well be stolen, he commits no offence of handling stolen goods because he does not "know" that they are stolen—he merely suspects they are.[136] Belief or knowledge that a circumstance *may* obtain, which would be sufficient for recklessness, is not knowledge that it does obtain. Hence it is inadequate to satisfy the mens rea of any offence which requires knowledge or intention that some circumstance exists.[137] In this respect "knowledge" of circumstances is the cognitive cousin of intention, rather than recklessness.

What is not necessary, however, is that the defendant should think that the relevant circumstance exists with provable certainty. In law, it is sufficient that the defendant accepts, or assumes, and has no serious doubt, at the time he acts, that the circumstance is present.[138] Hence if Tom refrains from investigating further whether or not the goods are indeed stolen, and goes ahead with the purchase believing that they may well be, he is not guilty of handling. It is not enough for him to believe there is a possibility or likelihood that they are stolen.[139] But if, despite the fact that he has not actually seen proof of another's ownership, he accepts the vendor's disclosure to him that the goods are purloined, then he handles them when he goes ahead with the purchase.

(i) Wilful blindness

The situation where Tom realises there is a chance the goods are stolen, yet deliberately refrains from checking his suspicion, raises the issue of "wilful blindness". Cases of wilful blindness often appear to fall between the mens rea alternatives (i) recklessness as to the circumstance ("reckless knowledge"), and (ii) (actual) knowledge, which satisfies intention. One alternative is straightforward. *Every* case where a defendant realises or suspects the circumstance might exist and refrains from investigating further is a case of reckless knowledge (i). Even without further investigation, the defendant knows already that there is a risk that the circumstance is present. So if the mens rea of an offence requires only recklessness, then the defendant may be convicted.[140]

Finding actual knowledge is more difficult. In some cases of deliberate non-inquiry by a defendant, the court will invoke what is known as the "doctrine" of wilful blindness.

---

[133] *US* v. *Dynar* (1977) 147 DLR 4th 399, 424.

[134] See generally Shute, "Knowledge and Belief in the Criminal Law" and Sullivan, "Knowledge, Belief and Culpability" in Shute and Simester (eds.), *Criminal Law Theory: Doctrines of the General Part* (2002) 184 and 207 respectively.

[135] *Saik* [2006] UKHL 18, [2007] 1 AC 18, para. 26. Cf. *Montila* [2004] UKHL 50, [2004] 1 WLR 3141.

[136] *Grainge* [1974] 1 All ER 928 (CA). In law, a "suspicion" involves believing there is a genuine possibility that the circumstance exists: *Da Silva* [2006] EWCA Crim 1654, [2007] 1 WLR 303, para. 16.

[137] *Hall* (1985) 81 Cr App R 260 (CA); *Ismael* [1977] Crim LR 557.

[138] Cf. Smith, noting *Charles* [1977] Crim LR 615, 620: "doubts are inconsistent with belief"—at least if those doubts are serious ones. See the interesting discussion by Griew, "Consistency, Communication and Codification—Reflections on Two Mens Rea Words" in Glazebrook (ed.), *Reshaping the Criminal Law* (1978) 57, 69ff.

[139] *Griffiths* (1974) 60 Cr App R 14 (CA); *Woods* [1969] 1 QB 447 (CCA).

[140] Above, § 5.2(iii).

This doctrine applies where the defendant intentionally chooses not to inquire whether something is true because he has no real doubt what the answer is going to be. Its effect is to attribute knowledge of the circumstance to the defendant. In other words, where the wilful blindness doctrine applies, the law will treat the defendant as having actual knowledge (ii), and not merely the reckless knowledge that he otherwise would have.

The conditions under which the doctrine applies are not capable of being stated precisely.[141] Broadly speaking, if there is an obvious way of finding something out and the defendant deliberately shuts his eyes to a risk by failing to find out, he will not be permitted to exculpate himself by claiming that he did not know the truth. Wilful blindness covers the case where D "deliberately refrained from making inquiries the results of which he might not care to have".[142] Or, as the House of Lords stated in *Westminster CC* v. *Croyalgrange Ltd*:[143]

> "it is always open to the tribunal of fact, when knowledge on the part of a defendant is required to be proved, to base a finding of knowledge on evidence that the defendant had deliberately shut his eyes to the obvious or refrained from enquiry because he suspected the truth but did not want to have his suspicion confirmed."

On the other hand, wilful blindness cannot be invoked just because D *should* have inquired into the facts,[144] or even if he suspected the truth;[145] otherwise knowledge would effectively be indistinguishable from recklessness. However, the line between recklessness and wilful blindness is a fine one. It appears that the defendant is wilfully blind in two situations. The first is if he shuts his eyes and fails to enquire because he is virtually certain what the answer will be.[146] This approach squares with the test once proposed by the Law Commission:[147]

> "The standard test of knowledge is—Did the person whose conduct is in issue either know of the relevant circumstances or have no substantial doubt of their existence?"

Alternatively, the wilful blindness doctrine will also apply if the means of knowledge are easily to hand, and D realises the likely truth of a matter but refrains from enquiry *in order* not to know. In such circumstances, although D in fact lacks knowledge there are clear normative grounds for inculpation. This type of case is helpfully elucidated by the judgment of Lord Sumner in *The Zamora*:[148]

> "There are two senses in which a man is said not to know something because he does not want to know it. A thing may be troublesome to learn, and the knowledge of it, when acquired, may

---

[141] See Wasik and Thompson, "Turning a Blind Eye as Constituting Mens Rea" (1981) 32 *NILQ* 328; *CLGP* § 57; Lanham, "Wilful Blindness and the Criminal Law" (1985) 9 *Crim LJ* 261; Ryan, "Reckless Transmission of HIV: Knowledge and Culpability" [2006] *Crim LR* 981, 984–9.

[142] *Roper* v. *Taylor's Central Garages Ltd* [1951] 2 TLR 284, 288, quoting from *Evans* v. *Dell* [1937] 1 All ER 349, 353.

[143] *Westminster CC* v. *Croyalgrange Ltd* [1986] 2 All ER 353, 359.

[144] Sometimes, perhaps misleadingly, called "constructive knowledge", but not to be assimilated with knowledge: cf. *Flintshire County Council* v. *Reynolds* [2006] EWHC 195 (Admin), para. 17, citing Devlin J's judgment in *Roper* v. *Taylor's Central Garages Ltd* [1951] 2 TLR 284.

[145] *Griffiths* (1974) 60 Cr App R 14; *Court* [1954] Crim LR 622; *Havard* (1914) 11 Cr App R 2. Cf. *Saik* [2006] UKHL 18, [2007] 1 AC 18, paras. 32 (Lord Nicholls), 78 (Lord Hope), and 120 (Lord Brown).

[146] E.g. *Ross* v. *Moss* [1965] 2 QB 396.

[147] Draft Criminal Liability (Mental Element) Bill, Law Com. No. 89 (1978) cl. 3(1). This is a more demanding test than that finally endorsed by the Law Commission: Law Com. No. 177, *A Criminal Code for England and Wales* (1989) cl. 18(a).

[148] [1921] 1 AC 801, 812. See *Borthwick-Norton* v. *Romney Warwick Estates Ltd* [1950] 1 All ER 362, 365–6; *Redgate* v. *Haynes* (1876) LR 1 QB 89; *Somerset* v. *Wade* [1894] 1 QB 574. Cf. *Sansregret* v. *R.* [1985] 1 SCR 570, 584–6; *Barbeau* (1996) 110 CCC (3d) 69, 92–5 (Que CA).

be uninteresting or distasteful. To refuse to know any more about the subject or anything at all is then a wilful but a real ignorance. On the other hand, a man is said not to know because he does not want to know, where the substance of the thing is borne in upon his mind with a conviction that full details or precise proofs may be dangerous, because they may embarrass his denials or compromise his protests. In such a case he flatters himself that where ignorance is safe, 'tis folly to be wise, but there he is wrong, for he has been put upon notice and his further ignorance … is a mere affectation and disguise."

It should be emphasised that wilful blindness is a doctrine of substantive rather than evidential law. It imputes knowledge to the defendant for legal purposes where there is not, in fact, such knowledge. Even if the doctrine does not apply, however, there remains the further possibility that a jury may *infer* actual knowledge on the part of the defendant (i.e. that in fact he accepted the truth and had no serious doubt), from evidence that D recognised the likely circumstances and made no further enquiry.[149] Nonetheless, proof of the latter does not constitute proof of the former.

§ 5.5 Negligence

Unlike such mens rea varieties as recklessness, intention, and knowledge, negligence does not presuppose any particular state of mind on the part of the defendant. It is, however, a standard that reflects fault on the part of the defendant, and so it is appropriately discussed alongside the other mens rea categories. The main feature distinguishing negligence from the categories we have mentioned so far is that, in negligence, there is no requirement that the defendant foresee the risk that the actus reus might occur. Sometimes we blame people precisely because they have *failed* to think about something—because they were careless or thoughtless. It is this sort of case that is captured by negligence.

(i) The test for negligence

Even though negligence permits the finding of fault for inadvertent wrongdoing, it does not actually matter whether the defendant attends to or contemplates the risks. As Glanville Williams asserts, "the essential question, at any rate for legal purposes, is whether it was reasonable for you to go ahead with your conduct in the circumstances".[150] Of course, normally one who foresees and runs an unreasonable risk will be reckless as well as negligent. Negligence does not, however, *require* inadvertence. This is for two reasons. The first is that in the criminal law, the lesser fault standard incorporates the greater. A defendant should not be able to exculpate herself by pleading that her actions were reckless or intentional rather than negligent. It follows that where negligence is enough for criminal liability, then, *a fortiori*, there is liability for intention or recklessness.

The second reason is that, as we mentioned earlier, a defendant can foresee the actus reus without being reckless, yet may still be negligent. For example, an anaesthetist who recognises there is a slight risk of killing his patient is not normally reckless. But if he has unknowingly miscalculated the dose, then he is negligent even though not reckless.

---

[149] *Smith (Albert)* (1976) 64 Cr App R 217.
[150] Williams in Fitzpatrick and Williams, "Carelessness, Indifference and Recklessness: Two Replies" (1962) 25 *MLR* 49, 57.

Recklessness involves an objective assessment of running the subjectively perceived risk. Negligence involves an objective assessment of running an objectively recognisable risk.[151]

So the emphasis is on the unreasonableness of the defendant's behaviour. Formally, the defendant is negligent if a reasonable person in the same circumstances (a) would have been aware of the risks of doing the actus reus and (b) would not have run those risks. It does not matter if the defendant herself was unaware of the risks. What counts is that her behaviour falls short of the standard of conduct that we would expect of a reasonable person—that she failed to take reasonable precautions against the harm specified in the actus reus.

(a) Ordinary or gross negligence?

The criminal law knows two types of negligence: ordinary negligence and gross negligence. One example of an offence requiring ordinary negligence is that of driving without due care and attention, contrary to section 3 of the Road Traffic Act 1988.[152] D commits an offence by making an error while driving that a reasonably prudent and skilful driver would not make;[153] in other words, by driving in a manner which involves a risk of harm that the reasonable man would regard as unjustifiable. A standard of ordinary negligence may also be imported by the requirement that D exhibit "due diligence", for example in section 21 of the Food Safety Act 1990. Alternatively, there may be a direct reference to the reasonableness of D's mental state: in rape, for instance, it is sufficient that D "does not reasonably believe" that his victim consents.[154] In these cases, it is enough that D has failed to exercise a reasonable level of care in exercising the required diligence or considering whether V has consented.

Sometimes, however, the mens rea of an offence cannot be satisfied by anything less than gross negligence. For example, the Road Traffic Act 1988 also contains the offence of dangerous driving, which is committed by a defendant if:[155]

(a)   the way he drives falls far below what would be expected of a competent and careful driver, and

(b)   it would be obvious to a competent and careful driver that driving in that way would be dangerous.

The standard is that of gross rather than ordinary negligence. While the difference between the two is a matter of degree and judgement in each case, broadly speaking, negligence will be gross if the defendant's conduct not merely fails to meet the standard set by the reasonable man test, but falls short of that standard by a considerable margin—i.e. if the defendant's conduct is not merely unreasonable, but *very* unreasonable:[156]

> "in order to establish criminal liability the facts must be such that, in the opinion of the jury, the negligence of the accused went beyond a mere matter of compensation between subjects and showed such disregard for the life and safety of others as to amount to a crime against the State and conduct deserving punishment."

---

[151] Although this proposition will be qualified below, in § 5.5(ii).

[152] Cf. Gas Act 1995, sched. 2 para. 10.

[153] *Simpson* v. *Peat* [1952] 2 QB 24, 27.

[154] Sexual Offences Act 2003, s. 1; below, Chapter 12.

[155] Section 2A.

[156] *Bateman* (1925) 19 Cr App R 8, 11.

It may be negligent to drive around a particular bend at 50 mph; if so, it is grossly negligent to do so at 80 mph. Hart puts the test another way: "[n]egligence is gross if the precautions to be taken against harm are very simple, such as persons who are but poorly endowed with physical and mental capacities can easily take".[157]

At common law, a conviction for manslaughter may be predicated on gross negligence. One example is provided by *Adomako*.[158] D, an anaesthetist, was attending an operation when the tube supplying oxygen to the patient became dislodged. D failed to notice the signs of disconnection, in consequence of which the patient, some nine minutes later, suffered cardiac arrest and subsequently died. D was convicted of manslaughter, on the footing that his failure to notice and remedy the problem was a gross dereliction of the standard of care that may reasonably be expected from a competent anaesthetist.

(b) Emergency

One of the features of *Adomako* was that the situation was urgent: the defendant, in his own testimony, stated that "after things went wrong I think I did panic a bit".[159] The test of negligence has sometimes been criticised for being insensitive to circumstances, and for assessing emergency judgements in the cold light of the courtroom. Jeremy Horder has argued that in such situations we should not demand clinical accuracy, and that legitimate emotions such as fear and compassion, which sometimes lead us to make mistakes, are not properly allowed for by the orthodox test of negligence.[160] But this underestimates the legal test. We usually excuse a prima facie "negligent" mistake because it was not unreasonable *in the circumstances*. Although the evaluation of a defendant's conduct is done in a courtroom, in each case it must be done in the light of the defendant's particular circumstances and of normal social and personal values—including those of compassion and self-preservation. This is why it is sometimes reasonable to react precipitously.[161] The law does make allowance for emergencies: as Holmes J once noted, "detached reflection cannot be demanded in the presence of an uplifted knife".[162] A nice illustration of this principle is given in *Simpson v. Peat*:[163]

> "Suppose a driver is confronted with a sudden emergency through no fault of his own; in an endeavour to avert a collision he swerves to his right—it is shown that had he swerved to the left the accident would not have happened: that is being wise after the event and, if the driver was in fact exercising the degree of care and attention which a reasonably prudent driver would exercise, he ought not to be convicted, even though another and perhaps more highly skilled driver would have acted differently."

Horder claims that negligence in such cases "is not culpable". But if it is not culpable, this will be because it is not negligence at all.

---

[157] "Negligence, *Mens Rea*, and Criminal Responsibility" in *Punishment and Responsibility* (1968) 136, 149.

[158] [1995] 1 AC 171.

[159] [1995] 1 AC 171, 182.

[160] "Cognition, Emotion and Criminal Culpability" (1990) 106 *LQR* 469, 482. Compare Glanville Williams, "Offences and Defences" (1982) 2 *LS* 233, 242. See also Merry and McCall-Smith, *Errors, Medicine and the Law* (2001) 58–64.

[161] As Bernard Williams notes: *Ethics and the Limits of Philosophy* (1985) 185. See Horder, "Cognition, Emotion and Criminal Culpability" (1990) 106 *LQR* 469, 481.

[162] *Brown* v. *US* 256 US 335, 343 (1921). More prosaically, see *Wood* v. *Richards* (1977) 65 Cr App R 300; also Williams, *TBCL* 90.

[163] [1952] 2 QB 24, 28.

(ii) Abnormal defendants—does the reasonable man share any of their characteristics?

The tests of negligence that we have identified seem at first blush to be objective. We complain of the defendant's *conduct*, and decide that she was negligent simply by determining that her conduct does not match a standard of behaviour that would have been acceptable in the circumstances. However, if negligence is truly a measure of culpability, there would seem to be a problem with this approach. In other categories of mens rea, the defendant is blameworthy because she *knowingly* does the wrong thing—not merely because her behaviour is wrong. But that ground of fault cannot apply here. In negligence, the law says that the defendant *should* have done whatever the reasonable man would have done: but why? Why should the defendant be regarded as blameworthy, and attract the odium of criminal culpability, just because her behaviour causes some harm that she did not foresee?

The law's response is to assume that the reasonable man test incorporates the requirements of blame. If the defendant's conduct is objectively unreasonable, then it manifests a failing on the part of the defendant for which she may properly be blamed. Putting things the other way around, had she not been deserving of blame, her behaviour would not have failed the reasonable man test.

Most of the time this is a satisfactory answer. For example, if D had been a properly attentive and caring parent, she would not have left her child unattended by the swimming pool—we may hold her negligent, and blame her, for doing so where a reasonable parent would not. And the fact that D was not a naturally caring parent is no excuse. But not every case is so straightforward. What if D is in some way abnormal? Suppose, for example, that D fails to observe a child climbing into the pool. A normal person would have seen the child. Is D negligent? Perhaps not, if it turns out that D is blind. The example suggests that, although the reasonable man test is mostly independent of the particular defendant, it is not entirely so. We do not expect D to behave as if she were sighted, but rather as a reasonable blind person would.

Generally speaking, the law states that behaviour is negligent if it involves a failure to exercise that "care and caution which a reasonable and prudent person ordinarily would exercise under like conditions or circumstances",[164] But what exactly is meant by the "reasonable and prudent person"? The illustration above suggests that we do not replace the defendant altogether with objective characteristics, otherwise the youngest child would receive no allowance for immaturity[165] and the blind would be expected to see.[166] *Smith and Hogan*, however, considers it to be orthodoxy that where D has less capacity for foresight than the reasonable person, this will not generally help him.[167] Similarly, asked

---

[164] *Cordas* v. *Peerless Transportation Co* 27 NYS 2d 198, 4 Am LR 2d 147 (1941).

[165] An allowance that is made under current law: *R (on the application of The Royal Society for the Prevention of Cruelty to Animals)* v. *C* [2006] EWHC 1069 (Admin), [2006] 170 JP 463. Cf., in tort, Gray, "The Standard of Care for Children Revisited" (1980) 45 *Mo LR* 597; Shulman, "The Standard of Care Required of Children" (1928) 37 *Yale LJ* 618. See e.g. *McHale* v. *Watson* (1966) 115 CLR 199; *Yorkton Agricultural Assoc* v. *Morley* (1967) 66 DLR (2d) 37. Compare *DPP* v. *Camplin* [1978] AC 705, 718 (provocation).

[166] Compare, in tort law, *Bernard* v. *Russell* 164 A 2d 577 (1960); *Keith* v. *Worcester St R.R.* 82 NE 680 (1907); *Balcom* v. *City of Independence* 160 NW 305 (1921). See Weisiger, "Negligence of the Physically Infirm" (1946) 24 *NCLR* 187; James, "The Qualities of the Reasonable Man in Negligence Cases" (1951) 16 *Missouri LR* 1, 17ff; Lowry, "The Blind and the Law of Tort" (1972) 20 *Chittys LJ* 253.

[167] *Smith and Hogan* § 6.1.2.2.

"what if the defendant is substandard in abilities?", Williams responds, "the reasonable man is not imagined to be substandard in intelligence or foresight".[168]

It will be clear that we disagree. The test is mostly objective, but it can, if properly and sensitively applied, be in part, subjective. As a minimum, the test should comprise a reasonable person of the same age and gender as the defendant's, to the extent such matters are relevant;[169] for these are not abnormalities of any sort. Beyond this, in our view the reasonable man should be endowed with any peculiar physical characteristic of the defendant—including sight and hearing.[170] If his colleague's electrocution could have been avoided simply by throwing the mains switch, D is not negligent if he fails to do so because he is a paraplegic. Similarly, it would be bizarre to require a blind person to see, or even to behave as if sighted. She ought to behave like a reasonable blind person.[171]

Sometimes this can work against the defendant. If she has additional *knowledge*, over and above that which a reasonable man would possess, then she will be held to the standard of that extra knowledge.[172] Thus a driver with exceptionally good vision would be expected to avoid the cyclist she notices ahead of her even if drivers with normal vision would not see that cyclist in time. And a professional, acting in a professional capacity,[173] will be judged by the standard of a reasonably skilful and competent practitioner;[174] not by the standard of a layman.

In what other ways is the reasonable man test to be influenced by facts about the particular defendant? Often, we can accommodate the defendant's personal situation by asking what a reasonable man, *in the circumstances of the defendant*, would have perceived (and done). Within that rubric, the reasonable man may be taken to have the same levels of training, experience and knowledge that are possessed by the defendant herself. In *Price*,[175] for example, in the context of a prosecution under the Armed Forces Act 2006, the Court of Appeal held that D's conduct was to be measured against that of a reasonable serviceman with D's (lack of) training, knowledge and experience. The Court's approach sets the standard of a reasonable person who is placed in the same position as the defendant. Moreover, it remains fundamentally objective, in as much as it takes no cognisance of the defendant's own lack of skill,[176] or indeed of her above-average skill.[177]

---

[168] *TBCL* 94.

[169] *R (on the application of The Royal Society for the Prevention of Cruelty to Animals)* v. *C* [2006] EWHC 1069 (Admin), [2006] 170 JP 463. See too Ashworth, *Positive Obligations in the Criminal Law* (2013) 193–4.

[170] Cf. *S.A. Ambulance* v. *Waldheim* (1948) 77 CLR 215.

[171] *Smith and Hogan* asserts (§ 6.1.2.2) that "it is doubtful that the courts would entertain such a radical qualification of the objective standard" as to accommodate "characteristics such as age, hearing, sight, cognitive capacity, etc." The difficult case of intellectual limitations is discussed below. But the claim that, say, a blind person would be expected by the law to see is a serious error, both morally and legally. It is not true even in tort: see n. 166 above.

[172] Cf. *Lamb* [1967] 2 QB 981; *Haynes* v. *Swain* [1975] RTR 40 (DC); *Gossett* (1993) 105 DLR (4th) 681, 694–6; Road Traffic Act 1988, s. 3ZA(3).

[173] This constraint may not apply in tort: *McComiskey* v. *McDermott* [1974] IR 75.

[174] *Bateman* (1925) 19 Cr App R 8, 12–13; *Adomako* [1995] 1 AC 171, 188. As will be noted in the next paragraph, the standard is also sensitive to D's level of training and experience.

[175] *Price* [2014] EWCA Crim 229.

[176] *Ibid.*

[177] *Bannister* [2009] EWCA Crim 1571. As was noted in the previous paragraph, where D is acting in a professional capacity she will be held to the average standard of skills expected from a reasonably competent practitioner. This applies even if D's own abilities are *above* that average: hence the rule for skills differs from that for knowledge.

Price involves a specialist field of activity. In that sense, it resembles other specialist activities such as, say, operating a crane. It could hardly be an answer for D to say, "I'm sorry, but I am just a bad crane operator." To permit such a response would undermine the law's regulatory role. Thus we can summarise the position for professionals or other specialists as follows: the specialist, acting in a specialist capacity, is held to the standard of a reasonably competent specialist with D's level of training and experience, blessed with any additional knowledge that D happens to have.

Yet does that mean we should disregard the defendant's own capacities *altogether*, even in non-specialist activities? In order to answer that question, consider why we would expect the apparently "objective" standard in negligence to be affected by a defendant's physical limitations. The reason is that to convict a blind person for failing to see would be wrong and unfair. The blind do not deserve blame for failing to see. This, it is submitted, is the right way to approach the question of objectivity in negligence. The reasonable man test should be subjective to the extent that the defendant's shortcomings do not disclose fault. In particular, apart from physical limitations there is one other failing for which an abnormal defendant should not be blamed: intelligence. Consider the facts of *Elliott* v. *C (a minor)*.[178] C, a 14-year-old girl of low intelligence, had wandered away from home and spent the night outdoors without sleep before ending up in a garden shed. There she found some white spirit, which she poured onto the floor and ignited by dropping lighted matches on it. The shed was destroyed in the ensuing fire. Although someone of normal intelligence would no doubt have appreciated the risk of burning down the shed, it was found as a fact that the risk would not have been obvious to one of her limited capacities.[179] Under the objective test of recklessness prevailing at the time, C was convicted of criminal damage.[180] But this seems to us highly problematic. It is submitted that to regard her even as having destroyed the shed *negligently* would be wrong.

That having been said, however, it is not clear whether the criminal law currently makes any allowance for low intelligence when assessing negligence. Academic argument favours taking account of personal incapacities. H.L.A. Hart proposed a general precondition for criminal liability of the form, "*could* the accused, given his mental and physical capacities have taken [the required] precautions?"[181] Although the Canadian Supreme Court has approved a similar requirement,[182] there is *obiter dicta* from the High Court of Australia endorsing an objective test, one that disregards individual capacities.[183] In England there is little relevant legal authority. The suggestion of a test like Hart's may be found in *Hudson*,[184] where the defendant was charged with having sexual intercourse with a defective woman.[185] It is a defence to this charge that the defendant "does not know and has no reason to suspect

---

[178] [1983] 1 WLR 939.

[179] *Ibid.*, 945 ("in the circumstances this risk [that the shed would be destroyed] would not have been obvious to her or appreciated by her if she had given thought to the matter").

[180] By application of the *Caldwell* definition of recklessness, now reversed by the House of Lords in G: above, § 5.2(i)(a)–(b).

[181] "Negligence, Mens Rea and Criminal Responsibility" in *Punishment and Responsibility* (1968) 136, 154. See also Simester, "Can Negligence be Culpable?" in Horder (ed.), *Oxford Essays in Jurisprudence* (Fourth Series, 2000) 85.

[182] *Creighton* (1993) 105 DLR (4th) 632.

[183] *Lavender* [2005] HCA 37, para. 128 (Kirby J).

[184] [1966] 1 QB 448. See also *Hardie* [1985] 1 WLR 64.

[185] Contrary to the Sexual Offences Act 1956, s. 7.

her to be a defective". In adjudicating the defence, the court was prepared to consider the limitations of the particular defendant:[186]

> "There may be cases, of which this is not one, where there is evidence before the jury that the accused himself is a person of limited intelligence, or possibly suffering from some handicap which would prevent him from appreciating the state of affairs which an ordinary man might realise."

Contra, subjective allowances are impliedly excluded by *Elliott* v. *C*[187] (above), where C was held to have acted recklessly on the *Caldwell* standard because the risk was obvious to a normal adult. An objective standard of negligence has also been applied in the context of causing unnecessary suffering to animals and failing to ensure their welfare,[188] notwithstanding that (as in *Elliott*) the offences were imprisonable. The Court of Appeal also excluded the defendant's schizophrenia in *C (Sean Peter)*,[189] when determining whether, under section 1(2) of the Protection from Harassment Act 1997, a reasonable person would think that threatening letters sent by the defendant to his local MP amounted to harassment. Similarly, in *Braham*, delusional beliefs arising from a schizophrenic disorder were excluded, *obiter*, from the range of reasonable beliefs in consent under section 1 of the Sexual Offences Act 2003: "A delusional belief in consent, if entertained, would be by definition irrational and thus *un*reasonable, not reasonable".[190]

Notably, however, the Court of Appeal in *Braham* restricted its analysis to cases where the defendant's belief was irrational, arising from delusional personality disorders and the like. By contrast:[191]

> "It does not follow that there will not be cases in which the personality or abilities of the defendant may be relevant to whether his positive belief in consent was reasonable. It may be that cases could arise in which the reasonableness of such belief depends on the reading by the defendant of subtle social signals, and in which his impaired ability to do so is relevant to the reasonableness of his belief. We do not attempt exhaustively to foresee the circumstances which might arise in which a belief might be held which is not in any sense irrational, even though most people would not have held it. Whether (for example) a particular defendant of less than ordinary intelligence or with demonstrated inability to recognise behavioural cues might be such a case, or whether his belief ought properly to be characterised as unreasonable, must await a decision on specific facts. It is possible, we think, that beliefs generated by such factors may not properly be described as irrational and might be judged by a jury not to be unreasonable on their particular facts. But once a belief could be judged reasonable only by a process which labelled a plainly irrational belief as reasonable, it is clear that it cannot be open to the jury so to determine without stepping outside the Act."

---

[186] [1966] 1 QB 448, 455.

[187] [1983] 1 WLR 939, above, § 5.2(i); also *R (Stephen)* (1984) 79 Cr App R 334; *Stone and Dobinson* [1977] QB 354; *Ward* [1956] 1 QB 351.

[188] Contrary to ss. 4 and 9 of the Animal Welfare Act 2006: *R. (Gray)* v. *The Crown Court Aylesbury* [2013] EWHC 500 (Admin).

[189] [2001] EWCA Crim 1251; [2001] Crim LR 845. See also below, § 11.8. The decision is perhaps explicable on policy grounds specific to the statute (at paras. 18–19): "The conduct at which the Act is aimed, and from which it seeks to provide protection, is particularly likely to be conduct pursued by those of obsessive or otherwise unusual psychological make-up and very frequently by those suffering from an identifiable mental illness…. We are satisfied that to give the Act the construction for which [counsel] contends would be to remove from its protection a very large number of victims and indeed to run the risk of significantly thwarting the purpose of the Act."

[190] *Braham* [2013] EWCA Crim 3, para. 35.

[191] *Ibid.*, para. 41.

The question awaits definitive resolution by the Supreme Court. Nonetheless, there are signs of a more compassionate approach in House of Lords decisions. Lord McKay suggests in *Adomako* that gross negligence involves conduct so bad that it may be characterised as reckless "in the ordinary connotation of that word";[192] in *Elliott* v. *C*, C was certainly not "reckless" in ordinary language. There are also *dicta* in *Reid* to the effect that fault should be assessed by reference to the capacities of the particular defendant: Lord Keith makes it clear that a defendant should not be liable where his inadvertence is owing to "some condition not involving fault on his part",[193] while Lord Goff refers to "illness or shock",[194] and Lord Browne-Wilkinson to "sudden disability".[195] Subsequently, in *G*, the House of Lords was plainly hostile to the unfairness of convicting of arson "a defendant (least of all a child) on the strength of what someone else would have apprehended".[196] In Lord Steyn's view:[197]

> "it is contrary to art 40(1) [of the United Nations Convention on the Rights of the Child] to ignore in a crime punishable by life imprisonment, or detention during Her Majesty's pleasure, the age of a child in judging whether the mental element has been satisfied.... If it is wrong to ignore the special characteristics of children in the context of recklessness under s 1 of the 1971 [Criminal Damage] Act, an adult who suffers from a lack of mental capacity or a relevant personality disorder may be entitled to the same standard of justice. Recognising the special characteristics of children and mentally disabled people goes some way towards reducing the scope of s 1 of the 1971 Act for producing unjust results which are inherent in the objective mould into which the *Caldwell* analysis forced recklessness."

There remains room, therefore, for some optimism that ultimately the approach of the Court of Criminal Appeal in *Hudson* will prevail, at least in the context of low intelligence.

(iii) Negligence with respect to behaviour rather than consequences or circumstances

As with recklessness, negligence sometimes operates like an actus reus term. It does so when it qualifies the *behavioural* element in the actus reus, as opposed to elements of consequence or circumstance. So, for example, in an offence of careless driving the carelessness—i.e. negligence—of the driving is not a mens rea term meaning that a reasonable person would (and the defendant should) have realised that he was driving. Rather, it is effectively an actus reus term: meaning that the defendant was driving in a *manner* that fell short of the standard a reasonable person would set. Thus careless driving is a different type of negligence offence from negligent rape, where the law's concern is not so much with the manner of the defendant's action as with the fact that it was done at all.

Most of the time the difference will not be important, since even as a mens rea term negligence is assessed by reference to the defendant's conduct. However, it seems that the

---

[192] [1995] 1 AC 171, 187. See the note by Gardner (1995) 111 *LQR* 22, 23–4.
[193] [1992] 3 All ER 673, 675c. But D's paranoid schizophrenia was disregarded by the Court of Appeal in *Colohan* [2001] Crim LR 845, when determining whether D ought to have known that his conduct amounted to harassment contrary to s. 1 of the Protection from Harassment Act 1997. On the other hand, it was said in *Khan* [2009] EWCA Crim 2, [2009] 1 WLR 2036, para. 33 that the defendant's own vulnerability may be allowed for when determining what can reasonably be expected of *that* defendant in the context of a charge under s. 5(1) of the Domestic Violence, Crime and Victims Act 2004 of allowing the death of a vulnerable adult.
[194] [1992] 3 All ER 673, 690J.
[195] *Ibid.*, 696F.
[196] [2003] UKHL 50, [2004] 1 AC 1034, para. 33 (Lord Bingham).
[197] *Ibid.*, paras. 53–4.

subjective elements of the reasonable man test may not apply when negligence is operating as an actus reus standard. Hence in *McCrone* v. *Riding* it was said that the standard of care in driving:[198]

> "is an objective standard, impersonal and universal, fixed in relation to the safety of other users of the highway. It is in no way related to the degree of proficiency or degree of experience to be attained by the individual driver."

In other words, it is irrelevant to assessment of the quality of D's driving that D is a driver of below-average ability, or indeed of above-average ability.[199] This sets an even more stringent standard than the demands made of specialists when negligence operates as a mens rea term: in those cases, account can be taken of D's own levels of training and experience.[200] As we noted in § 5.5(ii), part of the justification for imposing impersonal standards lies in the need for the law to discharge its regulatory functions when governing specialist activities. In the context of driving, the even more objective, actus reus standard also helps to establish a co-operative regime that other drivers can rely upon. Driving is a voluntary activity, and those who engage in it may be thought to hold themselves out to their fellow drivers as being reasonably competent to do so.

(iv) The place of negligence

A number of writers have argued that people should never be subject to criminal liability on the basis of negligence,[201] and that its place lies properly in the arena of torts and compensation rather than of crimes and punishment. There is force in this argument, since it would normally be harsh to equate those who do wrong inadvertently with others who break the law intentionally or recklessly. There can also be concerns about fair warning in negligence offences.[202] The person who inadvertently does harm might well have refrained from doing so, had she only realised the risk. But the fact that negligence is often not as bad as recklessness or intention does not mean that it is not culpable at all,[203] or that it is never serious enough to warrant criminalisation. Baker's example is instructive:[204]

> "Carelessly handling loaded firearms in a crowded area, or speeding through a school zone at lunch hour oblivious to the dangers to others because one is absorbed in an interesting

---

[198]   [1938] 1 All ER 157, 158. See too *Gosney* [1971] 2 QB 674, 680; *Preston Justices, ex p Lyons* [1982] RTR 173; Wasik, "A Learner's Careless Driving" [1982] *Crim LR* 411.

[199]   *Bannister* [2009] EWCA Crim 1571.

[200]   *Price* [2014] EWCA Crim 229; above, § 5.5(ii).

[201]   Hall, "Negligent Behaviour Should be Excluded from Penal Liability" (1963) 63 *Columbia LR* 632; Turner, "The Mental Element in Crimes at Common Law" in Radzinowicz and Turner (eds.), *The Modern Approach to Criminal Law* (1948) 195, 207–11; Hall, *General Principles of Criminal Law* (2nd ed., 1960) 138. Hart's refutation of Turner's argument is convincing: "Negligence, *Mens Rea*, and Criminal Responsibility" in *Punishment and Responsibility* (1968) 136. More recently, see Alexander and Ferzan, *Crime and Culpability: a Theory of Criminal Law* (2009); Moore and Hurd, "Punishing the Awkward, the Stupid, the Weak, and the Selfish: the Culpability of Negligence" (2011) 5 *Crim Law and Phil* 147.

[202]   See, e.g., Gardner, 'Wrongs and Faults' in Simester (ed.), *Appraising Strict Liability* (2005) 51, 69–72; discussed in Chan and Simester, "Four Functions of Mens Rea" (2011) 70 *CLJ* 381, 390–3.

[203]   See, e.g., the discussion of negligence in Simester, "A Disintegrated Theory of Culpability" in Baker and Horder (eds.), *The Sanctity of Life and the Criminal Law* (2013) 178, 190–7.

[204]   Baker, "Mens Rea, Negligence and Criminal Law Reform" (1987) 6 *Law and Phil* 53, 81; see too Leipold, "A Case for Criminal Negligence" (2010) 29 *Law and Phil* 455. In *Principles* § 5.5(d), Ashworth posits the following

conversation, is more culpable … than deliberately taking a $0.50 store item without payment or than many other knowing offences against property."

Sometimes, one who knowingly takes the risk of a minor crime is not so deserving of a criminal sanction as another who carelessly risks serious harm. It would be wrong for the criminal law only ever to convict in the former case.

Such instances are properly exceptional, and normally the law is reluctant to inflict serious criminal (rather than civil) sanctions upon people who have merely been negligent. Nonetheless, it would be a mistake to discount the significance of negligence. Quite apart from setting a key mens rea standard for manslaughter and various statutory offences (especially in the context of specialist activities),[205] it remains very important in the context of defences, both common law and statutory. For example, duress is available only if the defendant's reaction is reasonable, while in many health and safety offences the defendant may be exculpated if found to have taken reasonable precautions.[206]

§ 5.6 Other mens rea states

We have mentioned that there is a variety of other mens rea terms used in the criminal law. Some of these, such as "dishonestly", occur primarily in the context of property crimes such as theft, and will be explored in some detail when we come to look at the specific offences.[207]

(i) "With a view to"

The phrase, "with a view to", introduces a form of ulterior intention. A person does X with a view to Y when Y supplies one of the reasons why she does X.[208] Foresight that Y is likely to occur is insufficient.[209] On the other hand, it is not necessary that Y be the ultimate motive, or even the dominant objective, behind the doing of X.[210] It is enough that it be *one* of the objectives or intentions with which X is done.

As such, the phrase is cognate to intention rather than recklessness, and overlaps considerably with "with an intention to". It goes beyond intention, however, in that there is no requirement for any crystallized intention to be formed by D. It is enough if, for example, X is done *in case* Y will later be sought. Thus the phrase is apt to capture preparatory conduct such as taking certain preliminary steps (X) in readiness for the possibility of later pursuing an unlawful objective (Y).

---

example: "D, a shooting champion, fires at a target, knowing that there is a slight risk that the bullet will ricochet and injure a spectator, which it does; E, who rarely handles guns, is invited to participate in a shooting party and fires wildly into bushes, failing to consider the possibility of others being there, and one is injured. Is D manifestly more culpable than E?"

[205] Perhaps most notably in the context of sexual offences: below, Chapter 12.

[206] See ss. 2 and 3 of the Health and Safety at Work Act 1974, read together with s. 40 (placing the burden of proof on the defendant).

[207] Below, Chapter 13.

[208] *Dooley* [2005] EWCA Crim 3093, [2006] Crim LR 544, para. 14.

[209] Whether this holds if Y is seen as virtually certain was left open in *Dooley, ibid.*, para. 17.

[210] Cf. *J. Lyons and Sons v. Wilkins* [1899] 1 Ch 255, 269; *Bevans* (1988) 87 Cr App R 64.

(ii) Wilfulness

Historically, the case law regarding this term was inconsistent.[211] Fortunately, its meaning has been clarified over time, beginning with the House of Lords decision in *Sheppard*.[212] The defendants in that case were charged with wilfully neglecting their young child.[213] They had failed to ensure adequate medical care for the child, but apparently had not realised how ill he was. At trial, the judge directed the jury that wilful neglect was established if a reasonable parent would have appreciated the danger to the child in the same circumstances. On appeal, the House of Lords quashed the defendants' conviction. Wilfulness, it was held, requires either a deliberate decision to neglect the child, by refraining from calling a doctor when it is known that a doctor is needed; or a failure to call the doctor because the defendant does not care whether the child may need a medical examination. In essence, this meant that wilfulness is an alternative term for objective (i.e. *Caldwell*) recklessness, and is satisfied if the defendant either consciously disregards the child's needs or ignores those needs because he is indifferent to the child's welfare.

The link between wilfulness and objective recklessness was perhaps not surprising in a decision handed down only a few months before *Caldwell* itself. More recently, however, wilfulness has become restricted to situations where the defendant actually foresees the prohibited outcome. In *A-G's Reference (No. 3 of 2003)*, the Court of Appeal asserted that the principles behind the rejection of *Caldwell* in *G* applied to wilfulness too:[214]

> "We do not accept the submission that *Sheppard* imposes a lower duty on the prosecution than does G. Indeed, we do not accept the submission that, in the present context, there is any material difference between them and, in our view, the approach to recklessness in G can be incorporated into a direction on wilfulness in relation to this offence."

Subsequent decisions confirm that wilfulness now requires intention or subjective recklessness.[215] Indeed, support for the subjectivist reading can be found in *Sheppard* itself, where, according to Lord Keith:[216]

> "The primary meaning of 'wilful' is 'deliberate'. So a parent who knows that his child needs medical care and deliberately, that is by conscious decision, refrains from calling a doctor, is guilty under the subsection. As a matter of general principle, recklessness is to be equiparated with deliberation."

Lord Keith's analogy with deliberateness does, however, raise a question. Recklessness, we saw earlier, requires that the actus reus be an unreasonable risk. Is it possible that "wilfully",

---

[211] Andrews, "Wilfulness: A Lesson in Ambiguity" (1981) 1 *LS* 303, 315ff.

[212] [1981] AC 394.

[213] The context was therefore one of omission rather than positive act. But the reasoning did not turn on this distinction, and it seems that nothing is to be made of it: *Daniels* [2008] EWCA Crim 2360, [2009] Crim LR 280, paras. 15, 21.

[214] [2004] EWCA Crim 868, [2005] QB 73, para. 27. See above, § 5.2(i)(b).

[215] *Emma W* [2006] EWCA Crim 2723; *D* [2008] EWCA Crim 2360; *Turbill* [2013] EWCA Crim 1422. Some earlier case law also supports a subjective interpretation of wilfulness, including *Holroyd* (1841) 2 M & Rob 339, 174 ER 308; *Eaton v. Cobb* [1950] 1 All ER 1016; *Bullock v. Turnbull* [1952] 2 Lloyd's Rep 303; *Wilmott v. Attack* [1977] QB 498; *Ostler v. Elliott* [1980] Crim LR 584. Contrast *Cotterill v. Penn* [1936] 1 KB 53, rightly criticised by Andrews, "Wilfulness: A Lesson in Ambiguity" (1981) 1 *LS* 303, 316–17; *McPherson* [1980] Crim LR 654, criticised by Williams, [1981] *Crim LR* 796.

[216] [1981] AC 394, 418.

like "deliberately", imports no such requirement? If so, a surgeon who carries out a risky yet medically justified operation might be said to injure her patient willfully, even though she is not reckless. It is submitted, however, that in the context of the criminal law "wilfully" should bear the more restricted meaning, i.e. of subjective recklessness. The defendant who, without intending the actus reus, takes a reasonable risk of bringing that actus about should not be regarded as having brought it about wilfully.

(iii) Malice

Many older statutes use the term "maliciously" when specifying crimes. Section 48 of the Malicious Damage Act 1861, for instance, provides that "whosoever shall unlawfully and maliciously cut away, cast adrift, remove, alter, deface, sink, or destroy ... any boat, buoy, buoy rope, perch, or mark used or intended for the guidance of seamen" commits an offence imprisonable for up to seven years. It is settled law that "maliciously" comprises intention or *Cunningham* recklessness.[217] Inadvertence, even *Caldwell* recklessness, will not do. On the other hand, there is no requirement that D's actions must be accompanied by "malice" in the ordinary sense of that term (i.e. by animosity or spite).[218] Foresight or intention is sufficient.

One special case is section 20 of the OAPA 1861, which provides that "whosoever shall unlawfully and maliciously wound or inflict any grievous bodily harm upon any other person" commits an offence. Although it is clear that "maliciously" in section 20 requires subjective foresight, the courts have held that D need only foresee the prospect of *some* bodily harm, and need not foresee a wounding or grievous bodily harm.[219] The rule makes a crucial part of the offence—the occurrence of an injury more serious than mere bodily harm—effectively a matter of strict liability. Quite apart from distorting the meaning of "maliciously", such a departure from principle[220] is particularly undesirable in the context of a serious crime like that in section 20. Fortunately, the definition of maliciousness has not suffered from similar judicial creativity when appearing in other offences.

(iv) Possession

Although primarily an actus reus term,[221] "possession" typically imports into the offence a concomitant mental ingredient. The leading decision, at least in the context of drug offences, is *Warner*.[222] D was convicted of unauthorised possession of a controlled drug,

---

[217] *Cunningham* [1957] 2 QB 396, 399; *Savage; Parmenter* [1991] 4 All ER 698, 721; *CLGP* § 30; Turner, *Kenny's Outlines of Criminal Law* (16th ed., 1952) 186.

[218] *Solanke* [1969] 3 All ER 1383. Neither is it required that the risk foreseen be "obvious and significant": *Brady* [2006] EWCA Crim 2413.

[219] *Mowatt* [1968] 1 QB 421; *Savage; Parmenter* [1992] 1 AC 699; *Rushworth* (1992) 95 Cr App R 252. The offence is discussed in detail below, § 11.5.

[220] Cf. "the ordinary principle that, where it is required that an offence should have been knowingly committed, the requisite knowledge must embrace all the elements of the offence": *Westminster City Council v. Croyalgrange Ltd* [1985] 1 All ER 740, 744 (DC); affd [1986] 2 All ER 353 (HL).

[221] Above, § 4.1(ii)(b).

[222] [1969] 2 AC 256; cf. *McNamara* (1988) 87 Cr App R 246. Amongst earlier cases, see *Southern* (1821) R & R 444, 168 ER 889; *Woodrow* (1846) 15 M & W 404, 153 ER 907; *Pearson* (1908) 1 Cr App R 79.

contrary to section 1 of the then Misuse of Drugs Act 1964, after being found with a box containing 20,000 amphetamine tablets. He claimed that he had thought the box contained scent. The House of Lords upheld his conviction. Although a *ratio decidendi* is difficult to distil from the judgments, it appears a majority of their Lordships were prepared to accept that the mens rea of possession requires only that D should know he is in possession of *something*, provided the something he thinks he possesses is not completely different from the thing he actually has. D need not know the precise nature of the material he possesses. Thus, if D had thought the box was empty, he would not have been in possession of its contents—yet since, on the facts, he thought it contained scent, he had sufficient mens rea to be in possession of the drugs (because scent, apparently, is not sufficiently different from drugs). Lord Pearce summarised the law as follows:[223]

> "I think that the term 'possession' is satisfied by a knowledge only of the existence of the thing itself and not its qualities, and that ignorance or mistake as to its qualities is not an excuse. This would comply with the general understanding of the word 'possess'. Though I reasonably believe the tablet which I possess to be aspirin, yet if they turn out to be heroin I am in possession of heroin tablets. This would be so I think even if I believed them to be sweets."

Where the contraband is not in a container, the rule is the same. Suppose that a stranger plants a cannabis cigarette in D's handbag or car, without D's knowledge. According to *Warner*, D would lack the mental element required to be in possession of the cannabis: "if someone surreptitiously puts something into my pocket, I am not in possession of it until I know it is there".[224]

The rule stated here is subject to certain qualifications. First, even though D does not realise he is in physical possession of something, he will nevertheless be in legal possession if he invited receipt of the thing. In *Peastol*,[225] D ordered a delivery of amphetamines, which arrived in the post. He was held to be in possession of the drugs as soon as the envelope was delivered through the letter box, even though he was not yet aware it had arrived.

Secondly, certain passages in *Warner* suggest that as well as knowing one is in possession of something, one must also have had a right or opportunity to discover the nature of that thing, e.g. (in *Warner* itself) by opening the box. Lord Morris characterised possession as "being knowingly in control of a thing in circumstances which have involved an opportunity (whether availed of or not) to learn or to discover, at least in a general way, what the thing is".[226] This additional requirement became redundant when the Misuse of Drugs Act 1971, section 28, enacted a defence that the defendant neither believed, suspected, nor had reason to suspect that the thing in his possession was a controlled drug; it was abandoned by the Court of Appeal in *McNamara*.[227] However, in *Lewis*[228] the requirement was

---

[223] [1969] 2 AC 256, 305. Lord Pearce's subsequent qualification, that "it would be otherwise if I believed them to be something of a wholly different nature", is hard to justify and has not been observed in subsequent cases: *Marriott* [1971] 1 All ER 595; *McNamara* (1988) 87 Cr App R 246, noted [1988] *Crim LR* 440, (1988) 34 *MLR* 582.

[224] [1969] 2 AC 256, 299 (Lord Guest). Cf. *ibid.*, 305 (Lord Pearce); *Ashton-Rickardt* [1978] 1 All ER 173; *Irving* [1970] Crim LR 642; *Cugullere* [1961] 2 All ER 343 ("having with him an offensive weapon").

[225] (1978) 69 Cr App R 203.

[226] [1969] 2 AC 256, 289.

[227] (1988) 87 Cr App R 246.

[228] (1987) 87 Cr App R 270, criticised [1988] Crim LR 517. An instructive contrast is the language of the otherwise wide-ranging Terrorism Act 2000, s. 57(3): possession is established if the relevant article was either on any premises at the same time as the accused or on premises of which the accused was the occupier or which he

resurrected, not as a necessary (i.e. exculpatory) condition of possession, but as a sufficient (i.e. inculpatory) one. The Court of Appeal held in that case that the sole tenant of a house may be in possession of drugs found there even though he visited the house infrequently and did not know they were on the premises, provided he had an opportunity to find out they were present. The decision is unfortunate and should not be followed. It seriously mis-construes Lord Morris's words by turning a dual requirement, for knowledge of the thing's being within his physical custody (whatever it might be) *and* opportunity to discover its nature, into *alternative* inculpatory tests, of knowledge *or* opportunity to discover the drug.

By now, it may be apparent that *Warner* is a deeply problematic decision. Unfortu-nately, the section under which D was charged contained no explicit mens rea require-ment. With the exception of Lord Reid, who was prepared to imply a requirement for mens rea into the offence as a whole, their Lordships therefore saw themselves as constrained to choose between the options of making drug possession a no-fault, strict liability, offence or implying a mental ingredient into the term "possession" itself. The House resorted to a fic-tional, artificial, construction rather than face squarely the true root of the difficulty, i.e. the absence of an express mens rea element in the statute. Smith's comment encapsulates the problem nicely:[229]

> "The difficulty arises because possession has become the criterion of guilt, yet possession is a neutral concept, not involving blame or fault. We shrink from saying that the lady with the shopping basket is in possession of the packet slipped in without her knowledge because it contains controlled drugs. If it were a box of chocolates dropped in by a friend as a birthday present, would any of the judges in *Warner* have hesitated to hold that she was in possession of it? If it were removed by a thief would they have had any doubt that it was stolen from her … ? Of course not. So far as the question of possession is concerned, there should be no distinction between the drugs and the chocolates. If the House in *Warner* had followed the lead of Lord Reid, these difficulties would have been largely if not entirely avoided…."

One clear limitation, at least, on the scope of possession is helpfully articulated in *Kousar*,[230] a valuable counterweight to *Lewis*. D's husband was a market trader who sold counterfeit goods, a large quantity of which were stored in the loft of the matrimonial home. D's con-viction under the Trade Marks Act 1994 was quashed. The goods belonged to her husband and were not joint property. Therefore, although D may have known about and acquiesced in their storage, and may have had the *ability* to control the stored goods, what is necessary for her, as well as her husband, to have possession is that she *exercises* control (or otherwise has personal possession or custody of them). Knowledge is not enough:[231]

> "In the course of argument some discussion was engendered about the normal domestic situ-ation: is a husband or wife to be regarded as in joint possession of items in that house which are in fact the property of the other spouse? Is a husband to be regarded as in possession of clothing and cosmetics, for example, of which his wife is both the owner and the possessor? We venture to suggest that that concept is quite inappropriate. One is not in possession of one's spouse's personal property in that sense. The term 'permission' has been used, that she

habitually used otherwise than as a member of the public *unless* he did not know of its presence on the premises or he had no control over it.

---

[229] [1988] *Crim LR* 519.
[230] [2009] EWCA Crim 139, [2009] 2 Cr App R 5.
[231] *Ibid*, para. 18.

permitted this property to be in the house. Permission may be something more than an acquiescence but even then is not in our judgment sufficient to render the permittor a person in possession of the goods. In the field of drugs offences, there is a specific offence of permitting premises to be used for certain activities but there is no equivalent in the legislation with which we are concerned. A finding of being able to exercise a measure of control, which is the basis upon which this issue was in due course left to the jury, is not the same as a finding that she did exercise control."

The decision emphasises a long-established point,[232] that merely knowing another person possesses the relevant goods does not suffice to make one personally in possession.

§ 5.7 Transferred mens rea

It is a general rule that, if the defendant does an actus reus with the required mens rea (and without being able to plead any relevant defence), she is guilty of an offence even though the occurrence of the actus reus may be unexpected in a way which is immaterial to the definition.[233] To illustrate:

> Suppose that Duncan takes aim at Tom with intent to kill him, and pulls the trigger. Just as Duncan shoots, however, Tom bends down to pick a flower. Duncan's shot misses Tom and hits Bill, who was standing behind Tom. Bill is killed instantly. In this situation Duncan is guilty of murdering Bill, notwithstanding that he did not foresee that possible outcome. The actus reus of murder is to kill a *person*.[234] Thus, although Duncan intended to kill Tom rather than Bill, he had the mens rea for murder since he intended to kill a *person*; the identity of that person is immaterial to the definition of the offence.

The doctrine of "transferred malice", as it is popularly known, is not confined to murder.[235] Neither is it a doctrine merely of transferred *intention*. Imagine, this time, that Jane bears a grudge against Daniel. She throws a stone at the brickwork of his house, No. 6 King Street. She recognises that the stone may break one of Daniel's windows, although she does not intend it to do so. As it happens, the stone misses the windows of No. 6 but ricochets off the brickwork and breaks Pat's window at No. 8. Jane's recklessness is sufficient mens rea for the crime of damaging property,[236] and is transferrable to the (otherwise unanticipated) result: damage to *Pat's* property.

---

[232] See, e.g., *Searle* [1971] Crim LR 592 (CA).

[233] For critical discussion, see Ashworth, "Transferred Malice and Punishment for Unforeseen Consequences" in Glazebrook (ed.), *Reshaping the Criminal Law* (1978) 77; Ashworth, "The Elasticity of Mens Rea" in Tapper (ed.), *Crime, Proof and Punishment* (1981) 45; Williams, "Convictions and Fair Labelling" [1983] *CLJ* 85; Horder, "Transferred Malice and the Remoteness of Unexpected Outcomes from Intentions" [2006] *Crim LR* 383; Bohlander, "Transferred Malice and Transferred Defenses: A Critique of the Traditional Doctrine and Arguments for a Change in Paradigm" (2010) 13 *New Criminal LR* 555; Eldar, "The Limits of Transferred Malice" (2012) 32 *OJLS* 633. More abstract treatments include Husak, "Transferred Intent" (1996) 10 *Notre Dame Journal of Legal Ethics and Public Policy* 65; also Dillof, "Transferred Intent: an Enquiry into the Nature of Criminal Culpability" [1998] *Buffalo Crim LR* 501.

[234] *Gore* (1611) 9 Co Rep 81, 77 ER 853; *A-G's Reference (No. 3 of 1994)* [1996] 2 All ER 10; *Hopwood* (1913) 8 Cr App R 143.

[235] E.g. *Mitchell* [1983] QB 741 (unlawful act manslaughter); *Gross* (1913) 77 JP 352 (voluntary manslaughter); *Latimer* (1886) 17 QBD 359 (wounding); *McCullum* (1973) 57 Cr App R 645 (handling stolen goods).

[236] Criminal Damage Act 1971, s. 1(1).

However, transferred malice does not operate when the divergence between actus reus and mens rea *is* relevant to the definition of the offence. In general, it is not possible to convict someone on the basis of an actus reus for one offence accompanied by the mens rea for a different offence. If Jane were to throw a stone at Daniel and miss but inadvertently break his window, she is not guilty of criminal damage (unless she foresaw a risk to the window when throwing the stone at Daniel).[237] Her intent to injure Daniel does not satisfy the mens rea requirement for damage to property.

When malice is transferred, so also are defences.[238] Imagine one last variant: Duncan attempts to shoot Tom only because Tom is attacking him and Duncan is in immediate peril of his life. He misses and unexpectedly kills Bill. Duncan's intention may be transferred, but so too is his claim of self-defence. He is not guilty of murder.[239]

Although the transferred malice doctrine has been criticised,[240] in its modern incarnation (i.e. as stated here) the doctrine is unobjectionable. Indeed, it is not really a doctrine at all—merely a particular type of immaterial variation. The causal miscarriage of D's actions in transferred malice cases has exactly the same legal status as, for example, cases of immaterial mistake. If Ian steals a cheap painting because he thinks it is a valuable Constable, he has the mens rea (and commits the actus reus) of theft since the specific identity of the property stolen forms no necessary part of the offence definition. It is enough that he takes "property belonging to another", whether or not that property is of great value.[241] Transferred malice cases are governed by the same principle: D's actions cause an outcome that is in some way unexpected,[242] but not in a way relevant to the offence definition.[243]

(i) "Incompatible" or "remote" transfers where the offence elements are satisfied?

Lord Mustill has observed of transferring mens rea that "to make any sense of this process there must, as it seems to me, be some compatibility between the original intention and the

---

[237] Compare *Pembliton* (1874) LR 2 CCC 119; *Taaffe* [1984] AC 539. (Jane could, of course, have been convicted straightforwardly if she had foreseen the risk of breaking the window.) Compare however *Ellis and Street* (1986) 84 Cr App R 235, which pays lip service to the principle that the actus reus and mens rea must correspond, but at the same time subverts that fundamental requirement for the sake of enforcement convenience.

[238] The same would apply to the infanticide example discussed by Eldar, "The Limits of Transferred Malice" (2012) 32 *OJLS* 633, 642.

[239] Cf. *Gross* (1913) 77 JP 352 (provocation). Note that the transfer of a defence will not necessarily preclude liability for an independent offence. It may, for example, have been grossly negligent to shoot at Tom because of the risk of hitting Bill.

[240] See, e.g., *A-G's Reference (No. 3 of 1994)* [1998] AC 245, 259–62 (Lord Mustill); below, § 10.2(i)(a).

[241] Cf. *Wrigley* [1957] Crim LR 57.

[242] A proviso: transferred malice is unproblematic only if causal principles are properly observed. This explains the otherwise troubling case of *Heigho* 18 Idaho 566 (1910), discussed in Williams, *TBCL* 181 n. 1. In that case, D assaulted W, and an onlooker died of fright. D was convicted of the manslaughter of W. It is submitted the conviction was wrong; D was not causally responsible for the onlooker's death. Horder disagrees with this view ("Transferred Malice and the Remoteness of Unexpected Outcomes from Intentions" [2006] *Crim LR* 383, 389–90),' but one of the criteria of causal responsibility here is that the intervening event be reasonably foreseeable: above, § 4.2(iii)(a)–(b).

[243] Cf. *Wrigley* [1957] Crim LR 57. This analysis would allow variations where the greater incorporates the lesser, as in Ashworth's example of an assault committed while intending to wound: discussed by Eldar, "The Limits of Transferred Malice" (2012) 32 *OJLS* 633, 641. Yet Eldar would go beyond that, contending that mens rea may genuinely be transferred if the difference in what actually happened was *morally* immaterial and was reasonably foreseeable. Perhaps, then, we might contemplate liability for offence X where D commits the actus reus of offence X, with the mens rea for offence Y, *and the two offences criminalise (in different actus reus forms) the same wrong*. Such pairs of offences are surely, hopefully, rare! Moreover, as we noted in § 2.1, even then there is a constitutional-law difficulty about extending liability to cases falling outside the definition of an offence.

actual occurrence, and this is, indeed, what one finds in the cases".[244] We have suggested above that the need for compatibility is satisfied when the variation is immaterial to the definition of the offence. However, Jeremy Horder has suggested an additional limitation, which would sometimes prevent the transfer of mens rea even though the mens rea and actus reus elements are present. In his view, an outcome is too "remote" for mens rea to be transferred if (i) the victim was not the intended victim and (ii) the victim was killed in an unexpected way, in a manner unforeseen by the defendant.[245] Thus consider the following example:

> D shoots at V1, intending to kill him. The bullet misses, but enters a factory behind V1. There, it strikes an electrical transformer, causing the transformer to explode. The explosion kills a factory worker, V2.

There is general agreement that the intention to kill V1 cannot be transferred to any charge of criminal damage involving the unanticipated explosion. At the same time, on the transferred mens rea analysis we have set out, D is straightforwardly guilty of murder, since by her act she intended to, and did, kill a human being. However, if we were to accept Horder's limiting principle of "remoteness" or "incompatibility", it seems that D would not be convicted of murder but, rather, of the attempted murder of V1 and of the manslaughter of V2.[246]

In our view, such a limiting principle should be rejected. First, it promotes uncertainty. When is the manner in which an outcome is caused sufficiently different and unexpected to count as incompatible? One might think that causation doctrines already have this in hand, but Horder's principle is meant to apply *after* causal responsibility for V2's death is established. It is undesirable to compound the complexity of the enquiry into D's guilt, since the criteria of any additional limitation do not seem susceptible of clear enunciation. Moreover, the moral case for a limitation seems unmeritorious. Suppose that the unexpected explosion had, in fact, killed V1. Convicting D of murder is then straightforward. Why should it make all the difference that it was V2 instead who died? Both are human beings. All the elements of the offence are present. As was observed in *Mitchell*, "the criminality of the doer of the act is precisely the same whether it is A or B who dies".[247] To convict D of unlawful-act manslaughter, on the basis of an attempted murder causing death, is an unnecessary sophistication.

§ 5.8 Concurrence

As a general rule, the actus reus and mens rea of a crime must coincide in time. That is, the behavioural and circumstantial elements of the actus reus must occur at the same time

---

[244] *A-G's Reference (No. 3 of 1994)* [1998] AC 245, 262.

[245] "Transferred Malice and the Remoteness of Unexpected Outcomes from Intentions" [2006] *Crim LR* 383, 388–9.

[246] In this he aligns himself with Ashworth: "Transferred Malice and Punishment for Unforeseen Consequences" in Glazebrook (ed.), *Reshaping the Criminal Law* (1978) 77.

[247] [1983] QB 741, 748. The same objection applies to Eldar's argument for a limitation of (reasonable) foreseeability: "The Limits of Transferred Malice" (2012) 32 *OJLS* 633, 649ff. Suppose that D sets out to damage T's property. In an unforeseeable circumstance, it is V's property that she harms. Although Eldar suggests (at 657) that circumstantial variations may be different from consequential ones, there seems no merit in the distinction.

as the mens rea requirements are satisfied. Unless there is a moment in time, a *scintilla temporis*, at which these elements are all present, the crime is not committed.[248] Consider the following illustration:

> D is an assassin who has been hired to kill V. One evening she drives over to V's house in order to shoot him when he comes home. On the way, however, she is involved in an accident when she collides with a cyclist who has suddenly cut in front of her car. Upon getting out of the car, D recognises that the cyclist is V. Thinking V is unconscious but alive, she shoots him through the heart. V, however, was already dead as a result of the accident.

D has not murdered V. Although she may have caused his death (the actus reus) by driving into him, when she did so she did not have a present intention to kill. Later, when she shot V, she had the mens rea for murder but her behaviour did not cause his death, so could not constitute the actus reus. Thus there is no moment in time at which both the actus reus and mens rea of murder are present.

Neither can an antecedent mens rea be added to a subsequent actus reus in order to support a conviction. For example:

> D takes a new umbrella to the law library one morning. When she departs, she cannot remember exactly what her umbrella looked like. Seeing an attractive umbrella in the stand, she decides to take and keep that one instead—not realising that it is in fact her own umbrella. Later, she begins to feel guilty. She returns to the law library, and replaces the attractive umbrella. In its place, she takes with her a different umbrella which she mistakenly thinks is the one she originally came with.

When D first leaves the library, she attempts to steal an umbrella but fails to do so because the one she takes is her own. She has the mens rea for theft but does not commit the actus reus.[249] Later, when she departs for a second time, she commits the actus reus of theft by taking another person's umbrella, but does so innocently—without an "intention of permanently depriving the other".[250] There is no moment in time at which all elements of the definition of theft are co-existent.

A striking illustration of this principle is supplied by *Wright*.[251] D was charged with possessing a Class B drug with intent to supply. At the time of his arrest, the many cannabis plants in his possession were too immature to qualify as a Class B drug within the meaning of section 5(3) of the Misuse of Drugs Act 1971. Since D's intended supply related to the harvested end-product and not to the immature plants, there was no temporal concurrence and his conviction was quashed.

Where the actus reus includes consequences, the requirement for concurrence applies to the behavioural element rather than its consequence. If D deliberately poisons V, and V takes some hours to die, the fact that D repents in the meantime will not absolve her of murder.[252] Conversely, if D is driving and accidentally hits a cyclist, the fact that she realises

---

[248] *Fowler v. Padget* (1798) 7 Term Rep 509, 101 ER 1103.
[249] The umbrella is not property belonging to another: Theft Act 1968, s. 1(1).
[250] Theft Act 1968, s. 1(1).
[251] [2011] EWCA Crim 1180.
[252] Cf. *Jakeman* (1982) 76 Cr App R 223.

the cyclist is V, her enemy, and rejoices while he is dying of his injuries will not make her guilty of a homicide offence. For the purposes of concurrence, the actus reus has already occurred.

Although concurrence is a standard requirement for offences involving mens rea, there are some situations where the need for concurrence does not operate or can be circumnavigated.[253] We consider these below.

(i) Circumventing the concurrence requirement

(a) Fresh acts, continuing acts, and subsequent omissions

Where an actus reus by D precedes his having mens rea, one technique available to the prosecutor is to show another, later, occurrence of the actus reus which coincides with D's mens rea—i.e. to look for a different moment in time at which the offence can be proved to have occurred.

A standard, if unusual, case of this would be where D does a second positive act which also brings about the actus reus. Suppose, in the days when tort actions died with the plaintiff,[254] that while driving D accidentally runs over V. V, fatally injured, lies dying. D is uninsured and, panicking, she backs up hoping thereby to avoid tortious liability. If the further injuries D inflicts by reversing over V play any causal role by accelerating V's death then D becomes guilty of murder, on the basis of the second and not the first incident.

Absent a fresh causative act by the defendant, the prosecution may try instead to show a *continuing* act: that the actus reus, although initiated by D without mens rea, is still occurring or being perpetrated by D at a later moment when D now has the required mens rea. This type of case is discussed in § 4.1(i)(b).[255] It is exemplified by *Fagan* v. *Metropolitan Police Commissioner*,[256] in which D accidentally stopped his car on a policeman's foot. That itself was no assault, since D did not yet have mens rea. However, when he deliberately refrained from moving his car, an assault was established. There was an ongoing application of force to the policeman by D (the actus reus), which was now accompanied by mens rea.[257]

Alternatively, the prosecution can try to bring its case within the ambit of *Miller*.[258] In this situation, a subsequent omission to prevent harm may constitute the actus reus if it amounts to a failure to prevent a danger that D has himself created by his earlier actions. *Miller* is discussed further in § 4.1(i)(b).[259]

(b) The complex single transaction

The law is different when the actus reus of an offence occurs *after* D has mens rea. Here it will sometimes be possible to convict D on the basis that the particular act that caused harm

---

[253] Marston, "Contemporaneity of Act and Intention in Crimes" (1970) 86 *LQR* 208. See also White, "The Identity and Time of the Actus Reus" [1977] *Crim LR* 148.

[254] Winfield, "Death as Affecting Liability in Tort" (1929) 29 *Col L Rev* 239.

[255] See Case 4.

[256] [1969] 1 QB 439.

[257] See also *Kaitamaki* v. *R.* [1985] AC 147; *Cooper and Schaub* [1994] Crim LR 531.

[258] [1983] 2 AC 161.

[259] See Case 5.

was part of a larger, complex series of actions which should be viewed as a whole, where D has mens rea at some earlier point during that "transaction".

The classic case is *Thabo Meli* v. *R*.[260] In that case, four defendants conspired to kill V and dispose of his body. In accordance with their plan, they struck V on the head (with intent thereby to kill him). Thinking him dead, they rolled him over a cliff. In fact, V was not killed by the blow and died from exposure suffered after falling down the cliff. Prima facie, the act of disposal, which caused V's death, was unaccompanied by the mens rea for murder since the defendants believed he was already dead. Nonetheless, the Privy Council upheld their convictions for murder. Rather than slicing up the events of the killing into component moments of time and then looking for a single moment at which actus reus and mens rea coincide:[261]

> "It appears to their Lordships impossible to divide up what was really one series of acts in this way. There is no doubt that the accused set out to do all these acts in order to achieve their plan, and as parts of their plan; and it is much too refined a ground of judgment to say that, because they were under a misapprehension at one stage and thought that their guilty purpose was achieved before, in fact, it was achieved, therefore they are to escape the penalties of the law."

It is hard to disagree with this decision, which represents a genuine exception to the concurrence requirement.[262] The defendants did exactly what they planned to do, and brought about exactly the result they had intended. The fact that the manner in which their success occurred was unexpected seems no ground for exculpation.

As the quotation above emphasises, the actions of the defendants were deliberate and pursuant to a preconceived plan. However, these elements of preplanning and intent have not been required in subsequent cases. In *Church*[263] the defendant knocked the victim unconscious during a fight and, mistakenly believing he had killed her, threw her into a river where she drowned. His conviction for manslaughter was upheld. Similarly, in *Le Brun*,[264] D, in an argument with his wife, knocked her unconscious and, while attempting to drag her body away, dropped and killed her. On appeal, the trial judge was held correctly to have directed the jury that they could convict D of murder or manslaughter (depending on the intention with which he first struck his wife) if D had accidentally dropped her while either attempting to move her to her home against her known wishes, and/or attempting to dispose of the body or cover up the assault. In such circumstances, English law holds that the sequence of wrongful acts by the defendant may be regarded as elements of a single episode of unlawful conduct,[265] where the transaction as a whole incorporates both mens rea and actus reus elements of a crime.

---

[260] [1954] 1 All ER 373.

[261] *Ibid.*, 374.

[262] It is worth noting, however, that the case could have been decided on a more straightforward causation basis, to be discussed in § 5.8(i)(c). The same could be said of *Church*, considered below in the next paragraph. Arguably, *Le Brun* (also considered below) is the only case where the one transaction analysis was actually needed.

[263] [1966] 1 QB 59.

[264] [1991] 4 All ER 673. See also *Moore and Dorn* [1975] Crim LR 229; *A-G's Reference (No. 4 of 1980)* [1981] 2 All ER 617. For discussion, see Sullivan, "Cause and the Contemporaneity of *Actus Reus* and *Mens Rea*" [1993] CLJ 487, 495–9.

[265] Contrast some other jurisdictions: *Ramsay* [1967] NZLR 1005; *Chiswibo* 1960 (2) SA 714; *Shorty* [1950] SR 280; *Khandu* (1890) ILR 15 Bom 194.

Le Brun does suggest one limitation to the *Thabo Meli* principle. The Court of Appeal appeared to acquiesce in the trial judge's direction that:[266]

> "if the fatal injury had happened in the course of ... well-intentioned efforts to help her, he would be guilty neither of murder nor manslaughter ... the distinction I am drawing [is] between as it were an extension or a furtherance or a continuation of the unlawful conduct and a different tack where whatever he has done to her before he is trying his best to help or comfort her even if in a misguided way."

According to Lord Lane CJ, "the judge was drawing a sharp distinction between actions by the appellant which were designed to help his wife and actions which were not so designed". This suggests the *Thabo Meli* doctrine will apply only where the ongoing actions are still tainted by D's unlawful purpose, so that there is a moral congruence between D's earlier culpability and his subsequent conduct.[267] Had D dropped his wife while carrying her to hospital, his doing so would have been a separate incident, divisible from the earlier, unlawful transaction.

(c) A causation approach

Where the defendant's mens rea precedes the action that most obviously constitutes the actus reus, another way of circumventing concurrence difficulties is to show that some earlier action by the defendant, done at the time when he had mens rea, was *also* a cause of the prohibited harm. The clearest illustrations of this approach are to be found in overseas cases. In *McKinnon*,[268] D assaulted V and knocked him unconscious. D then manhandled V, apparently causing an accidental nose-bleed, before leaving V lying on the ground and running off. While V was lying unconscious, the blood from his nose entered his lungs and he suffocated. The New Zealand Court of Appeal upheld D's conviction for murder. Although D may not have had the required mens rea when he caused the injury to V's nose, he did have mens rea when he struck V and knocked him unconscious. Moreover, the Court ruled, D's striking V was a contributory cause of his death, in combination with the nose-bleed, since it rendered V unable to deal with the bleeding. Thus there was no need to invoke a series-of-acts analysis, of the sort found in *Thabo Meli*, since there was already a *scintilla temporis* at which both an actus reus and the mens rea of murder were present.

Indeed, it is arguable that *Thabo Meli* could itself have been decided on a causation basis.[269] On this approach, the *Thabo Meli* doctrine would still be necessary in some cases, but only where the second event was overwhelmingly the cause of death, and amounted to a *novus actus interveniens* (e.g. where V is killed instantly by the impact after he is thrown over a cliff).[270] Conversely, the causation analysis will be necessary in situations where *Thabo Meli* cannot apply, for example because D's second intervention was innocent and well-meaning, or where the intervention is by a stranger rather than by D.

---

[266] [1991] 1 QB 61.

[267] Another illustration is the Singaporean case of *Muhammad Radi* v. *PP* [1994] 2 SLR 146, where D's follow-up conduct involved an attempt to conceal the evidence.

[268] [1980] 2 NZLR 31. Compare *S* v. *Masilela* 1968 (2) SA 558. For discussion of multiple causes see above, § 4.2(ii)(c).

[269] Adams, "Homicide and the Supposed Corpse" (1968) 1 *Otago LR* 278, 287; Marston, "Contemporaneity of Act and Intention in Crimes" (1970) 86 *LQR* 208, 218–19; *McKinnon* [1980] 2 NZLR 31, 36–7.

[270] Compare *Le Brun* [1992] 1 QB 61.

(d) Involuntariness and antecedent fault

If D perpetrates an actus reus while in an automatic state, normally the concurrence requirement will not be satisfied. Exceptionally, however, it may be possible to convict D, on the basis that his automatism is a consequence of his own earlier actions which occurred at a time when he had the mens rea for the offence. This type of case is discussed more fully in § 4.3(iii). Suppose, for example, that David is a diabetic. One day he deliberately takes insulin without eating any food. He does this in the hope of reducing himself into a semi-conscious state, where he knows that he is likely to become violent and assault his flatmate whom he does not like. Should his plan be successful, David will be guilty of an intentional assault, notwithstanding his automatism at the time the assault occurs.

Sometimes the offence may be proved without reference to the defendant's subsequent, involuntary conduct. In *Kay* v. *Butterworth*,[271] D fell asleep while driving and collided with soldiers marching on the road. He was convicted of careless driving, but not because he drove into the soldiers. (At that time he was asleep and his behaviour was involuntary.) Rather, the offence was complete when he continued to drive while drowsy—that, in itself, was careless driving. Indeed, D would have committed the offence even if he had not run into the soldiers.[272] Glanville Williams illustrates this point in a lucid example:[273]

> "When, for example, a driver proceeds along Church Lane in a sleepy condition, and falls asleep at the wheel just before entering High Street, where he is involved in an accident, he cannot be convicted of careless driving in High Street, because in contemplation of law he did not 'drive' in High Street, and it makes no difference that his involuntary accident in High Street was the result of his own previous fault. He can, indeed, be convicted of careless driving, but this must be laid as having taken place in Church Lane, when the driver was undoubtedly 'driving'."

The offence occurs in Church Lane.

---

[271] (1945) 61 TLR 452. Cf. *Moses* v. *Winder* [1980] Crim LR 232. For a rather more dramatic example, see *People* v. *Decina* 2 NY 2d 133 (1956).

[272] *Spurge* [1961] 2 QB 205, 210.

[273] *TBCL* 682. Obviously, this analysis works only if the time-frame for commission of the actus reus is sufficiently elastic, and not tied to a particular incident. Contrast *Burns* v. *Bidder* [1967] 2 QB 227 (failing to accord precedence at a pedestrian crossing).

6

STRICT AND CONSTRUCTIVE LIABILITY

We argued in Chapter 1 that serious criminal offences, where considerable public stigma attaches to a conviction, should always stipulate some form of mens rea that must be proved in relation to the actus reus before the defendant may be convicted. Such a scheme helps to avoid inflicting "the disgrace of criminality"[1] upon defendants who are not at fault when harm occurs. However, not every offence against the criminal law involves the sort of public condemnation that is implicit in a conviction for theft or homicide. A parking offence, for example, involves little or no stigma, so the need for mens rea with regard to the actus reus is not as pressing.[2] In recognition of this fact, there are many offences of a regulatory nature which lack a mens rea ingredient with regard to one or more elements of the actus reus.[3] These offences involve strict *liability*.[4] Strict liability is sometimes called absolute *liability* in England and Wales, but—due to the fact that a distinction between these terms is recognised elsewhere in the Anglo-American world[5]—that terminology will be eschewed in this chapter.

To see strict liability in action, consider *Pharmaceutical Society of Great Britain* v. *Storkwain Ltd*.[6] There, the defendant chemists were convicted of selling controlled medicines without prescription even though they neither knew nor had reason to suspect that the "prescriptions" they filled were forgeries. No mens rea element was required with regard to that aspect of the actus reus. This does not mean that the offence contains no mens rea element at all. It had to be shown that D intended to sell controlled medicines. In principle, if a chemist were to pick up the wrong packet, and hand over controlled medicines thinking they were headache tablets, he could not be convicted should his mistake vitiate the contract of sale. Other cases can be analysed similarly. In 1846, a dealer was held in *Woodrow*[7]

---

[1] *Warner* v. *Metropolitan Police Commissioner* [1969] 2 AC 256, 272 (Lord Reid).

[2] Cf. "acts not criminal in any real sense": *Sherras* v. *De Rutzen* [1895] 1 QB 918, 922 (Wright J).

[3] See Reid, "Strict Liability: Some Principles for Parliament" (2008) 29 *Statute LR* 173; Simester (ed.), *Appraising Strict Liability* (2005); Horder, "Strict Liability, Statutory Construction, and the Spirit of Liberty" (2002) 118 *LQR* 458; Richardson, "Strict Liability for Regulatory Crime: The Empirical Research" [1987] *Crim LR* 295; Leigh, *Strict and Vicarious Liability: A Study in Adminstrative Criminal Law* (1982); Howard, *Strict Responsibility* (1963); Kadish, "Some Observations on the Use of Criminal Sanctions in Enforcing Economic Regulations" (1963) 30 *U Chicago LR* 423; Sayre, "Public Welfare Offenses" (1933) 33 *Col LR* 55.

[4] This definition of strict liability—found in Smith and Hogan, *Criminal Law* (4th ed., 1978) 79—was endorsed in *Lemon* [1979] AC 617, 656 (Lord Edmund-Davies).

[5] See below, § 6.4.

[6] [1986] 1 WLR 903 (HL). See too *Harrow London BC* v. *Shah* [2000] 1 WLR 83 (DC).

[7] (1846) 15 M & W 404, 153 ER 907. The case is said to be the first to impose strict liability, although doubt is cast on this view by Singer, "The Resurgence of Mens Rea: III—The Rise and Fall of Strict Criminal Liability" (1989) 30 *Boston College LR* 337, 340–45.

to be guilty of possessing adulterated tobacco even though he had no ground for suspecting the tobacco was adulterated, and could only have discovered it to be so by a chemical analysis that it would be unreasonable to expect of dealers (thus the dealer was not even *negligent* with regard to the nature of the tobacco). The sale itself would have to be intentional, but no fault was required with regard to the adulteration of the tobacco. Similarly, in *Lundy* v. *Le Cocq*,[8] D was convicted of selling intoxicating liquor to a drunken person, contrary to section 13 of the Licensing Act 1872, which provided that "if any licensed person ... sells any intoxicating liquor to any drunken person, he shall be liable to a penalty". Although D neither knew nor had reason to suspect the buyer was drunk, the Divisional Court held that no mens rea was required with regard to that element of the actus reus. An intentional sale of intoxicating liquor to a person who was, in fact, drunk was enough to secure liability.

Strict liability is a controversial (though common) element of modern criminal law statutes, and there is a presumption that mens rea is required as to each and every aspect of the actus reus. This presumption, and the factors that can overcome it in relation to a particular criminal offence, are considered in § 6.1. The relationship between strict liability and defences will then be considered in § 6.2, before the more general question of whether strict liability should be used in the criminal law is covered in § 6.3. As this is an area where opinions differ around the Anglo-American world, § 6.4 considers comparative approaches to the issue of strict liability. Finally, § 6.5 discusses the concept of "constructive liability", which is at times difficult to distinguish from strict liability, but can be—in theory—a defensible part of the criminal law.

§ 6.1 Recognition of strict liability in a statutory offence

With isolated exceptions, strict liability offences are a creation of statute rather than the common law.[9] The opportunity to impose strict liability generally arises from the fact that criminal legislation may be silent regarding the mens rea element(s) pertaining to each element of the actus reus, leaving it to the courts either to imply a mens rea requirement or to interpret the offence as one involving strict liability. Originally, the courts recognised a principle that in such cases mens rea was to be implied as to each element of the actus reus: "Acts of Parliament are to be so construed, as no man that is innocent, or free from injury or wrong, be by a literal construction punished or endamaged."[10] Although operation of the principle could be overridden by Parliament itself, the legislation would have to be clear on the point:[11]

> "it is contrary to the whole established law of England (unless the legislation on the subject has clearly enacted it), to say that a person can be guilty of a crime in England without a wrongful intent—without an attempt to do that which the law has forbidden."

---

[8] (1884) 13 QBD 207.

[9] The common law exceptions included an employer's liability for public nuisance and the former crime of criminal libel (abolished by the Coroners and Justice Act 2009, s. 73). Common law contempt of court, once thought to be a matter of strict liability, is now said, *obiter*, to require mens rea: *Yousaf* v. *Luton Crown Court* [2006] EWCA Crim 469, para. 19.

[10] *Margate Pier Co* v. *Hannam* (1819) 3 B & Ald 266, 270, 106 ER 661, 663 (Abbott CJ), quoting Lord Coke; cf. *Tolson* (1889) 23 QBD 168, 187 (Stephen J).

[11] *Attorney-General* v. *Bradlaugh* (1885) 14 QBD 667, 689 (Brett MR); cf. *Chisholm* v. *Doulton* (1889) 22 QBD 736, 741 (Cave J).

Extensive authority can be found in support of this proposition, which applied even to summary offences.[12] Indeed, as we shall see, it remains the point of departure for courts when determining whether a particular statute creates an offence of strict liability or one requiring mens rea as to every aspect of the actus reus.[13] But the presumption of mens rea is not always decisive, and the courts are often willing to read statutes without implying a mens rea requirement as to every aspect of the actus reus.

The seeds of this willingness were sown during the later part of the nineteenth century, when strict liability offences tried summarily in magistrates' courts began to emerge as a convenient and—compared with creating special administrative or industrial courts—an inexpensive means of dealing with rapidly changing social and industrial practices.[14] Most often they owe their existence to a perception that the need to protect the public from harm might on occasion justify convicting people of criminal offences even where they were not necessarily at fault;[15] especially, though not invariably, where the harm involved resulted from a specialised activity, one which might naturally lend itself to control by regulatory rather than "truly criminal" prohibitions. Even the enforcement of such offences tends to be distinctive. They are frequently the responsibility not of the police, but by specialist agencies created to monitor and control the effects of particular types of activity such as pollution and industrial safety. Habits of prosecution differ also. In practice, it appears that while prosecution is a typical response of the police to breaches of the law, regulatory agencies by contrast tend to prosecute only for recurring or very serious breaches of the law. Characteristically, in the hands of regulatory agencies, the fact that an offence imposes strict liability operates as an important background consideration in compliance negotiations.[16]

The discussion of mens rea and strict liability has so far concentrated on defining the leading terms. But a further question arises every time we consider a particular offence. *Which* mens rea state is required to satisfy *that* offence? The answer varies from offence to offence. For assault, recklessness about the apprehension of immediate unlawful violence will suffice.[17] For murder, an intention to kill or cause grievous bodily harm is required.[18] Driving while disqualified, by contrast, is an offence of strict liability: no fault as to the fact of disqualification need be proved.[19] Often the answer to the question of what type of mens

---

[12] E.g. *Fowler v. Padget* (1798) 7 Term Rep 509, 101 ER 1103; *Hearne v. Garton and Stone* (1859) 2 El & El 66, 121 ER 26; *Batting v. Bristol and Exeter Ry Co* (1860) 3 LT 665; *Sleep* (1861) L & C 44, 169 ER 1296; *Core v. James* (1871–2) LR 7 QB 135; *Sherras v. de Rutzen* [1895] 1 QB 918; *Paul v. Hargreaves* [1908] 2 KB 289.

[13] An exception found in some contexts is where an aspect of the actus reus is evaluative. This point is discussed in § 6.1(ii)(d) below.

[14] See, e.g., Carson, "Symbolic and Instrumental Dimensions of Early Factory Legislation" in Hood (ed.), *Crime, Criminology and Public Policy* (1974) 107; Carson, "The Conventionalisation of Early Factory Crime" (1979) 7 *Int J Soc Law* 37.

[15] Cf. *Hobbs v. Winchester Corporation* [1910] 2 KB 471, 484 (Kennedy LJ): "the natural inference from the statute and its object is that the peril to the butcher from innocently selling unsound meat is deemed by the legislature to be much less than the peril to the public which would follow from the necessity in each case of proving a *mens rea*".

[16] See, e.g., Hawkins, *Law as Last Resort* (2003); Hutter, *The Reasonable Arm of the Law?* (1988); Hawkins, *Environment and Enforcement* (1984); Reiss, "Selecting Strategies of Social Control over Organizational Life" in Hawkins and Thomas (eds.), *Enforcing Regulation* (1984) 25. But the discretionary nature of prosecutions in such instances is not without Rule of Law problems: Simester, "Is Strict Liability Always Wrong?" in Simester (ed.), *Appraising Strict Liability* (2005) 21, 32–3.

[17] *Spratt* [1990] 1 WLR 1073 (CA); *Parmenter* [1992] 1 AC 699.

[18] *Cunningham* [1982] AC 566.

[19] See below, n. 21.

rea is required with regard to each element of the actus reus will be found straightforwardly in the explicit words of the statute that creates the offence. For example, section 2 of the Explosive Substances Act 1883 makes it an offence "maliciously" to cause an explosion likely to endanger life or property: the offence cannot be committed inadvertently of such potential consequences.[20] But, frequently, a statute will specify only the actus reus elements, and be silent regarding whether a form of mens rea is required as to each element, and—if so—*what* variety of mens rea will do. In such instances the courts must decide whether an offence involves strict liability.

The first point to consider is whether the mens rea standard has been settled by judicial precedent. As noted above, the offence of driving while disqualified has been held to impose strict liability with regard to the fact of disqualification.[21] Unless the offence becomes altered by legislation,[22] there would seem to be no reason for another court to reconsider the question in the future.

If the mens rea standard for the offence is not settled by statute or case law, the court will have to make a fresh decision. The guiding principles (to the extent that these exist) affecting that decision are stated in the following subsections. By way of introduction, however, it is helpful to quote from the Privy Council's summary of those principles in *Gammon Ltd* v. *A-G of Hong Kong*:[23]

> "In their Lordships' opinion, the law relevant to this appeal may be stated in the following propositions …: (1) there is a presumption of law that mens rea is required before a person can be held guilty of a criminal offence; (2) the presumption is particularly strong where the offence is 'truly criminal' in character; (3) the presumption applies to statutory offences, and can be displaced only if this is clearly or by necessary implication the effect of the statute; (4) the only situation in which the presumption can be displaced is where the statute is concerned with an issue of social concern, and public safety is such an issue; (5) mens rea stands unless it an also be shown that the creation of strict liability will be effective to promote the objects of the statute by encouraging greater vigilance to prevent the commission of the prohibited act."

As will be seen, establishing what, if any, mens rea is required with regard to an element of the actus reus is often far from easy.

(i) The initial presumption

The basic presumption from which one starts is that mens rea is required for every element of the actus reus. It should be emphasised that the presumption of mens rea generally imports intention or recklessness (or, as appropriate, knowledge or belief). Thus in *Sweet* v. *Parsley*, the House of Lords regarded itself as able to choose only between strict liability and advertent mens rea (in that case, knowledge).[24] Negligence is not, apparently, on the common-law table.

---

[20] Malice incorporates both intention and "subjective" recklessness: *Cunningham* [1957] 2 QB 396 (CA).

[21] See *Bowsher* [1973] RTR 202 (CA); *Miller* [1975] 1 WLR 1222 (CA).

[22] The offence, formerly contained in Road Traffic Act 1972, s. 99, was re-enacted by Road Traffic Act 1988, s. 103, without substantive change.

[23] [1985] AC 1, 14.

[24] Cf. Lord Diplock's discussion of negligence and duties of care in [1970] AC 132, 162–5. See Devlin's discussion of this point in *Samples of Lawmaking* (1962) 67–82. For a suggestion that due diligence (i.e. no-negligence)

This presumption of mens rea has in the past been controversial.[25] Its place has nevertheless been secured by the House of Lords in two leading decisions on strict liability, *Sweet* v. *Parsley*[26] and *B* v. *DPP*.[27] In *Sweet* v. *Parsley*, a schoolteacher was prosecuted for "being concerned in the management of premises used for the purpose of smoking cannabis".[28] She had sublet her farmhouse to a group of students who, without her knowledge, smoked cannabis there. Even though the terms of the statute prima facie were satisfied—she was concerned in the management of the premises, and cannabis was smoked there—the House of Lords quashed her conviction. Knowledge that cannabis was being smoked on the premises, albeit unstated, was an element of the offence:[29]

> "there has for centuries been a presumption that Parliament did not intend to make criminals of persons who were in no way blameworthy in what they did. This means that, whenever a section is silent as to mens rea there is a presumption that, in order to give effect to the will of Parliament, we must read in words appropriate to require mens rea."

The justification for this starting-point rests in the issues discussed in Chapter 1 and in § 3.2. According to Lord Diplock:[30]

> "the mere fact that Parliament has made the conduct a criminal offence gives rise to *some* implication about the mental element of the conduct proscribed.... This implication stems from the principle that it is contrary to a rational and civilised criminal code, such as Parliament must be presumed to have intended, to penalise one who has performed his duty as a citizen to ascertain what acts are prohibited by law (ignorantia juris non excusat) and has taken all proper care to inform himself of any facts which would make his conduct lawful."

Parliament normally does not, and indeed should not, intend to make criminals of those who are not blameworthy regarding the actus reus, and do not warrant that label. Thus, according to Lord Reid in Sweet v. Parsley:[31]

> "it is a universal principle that if a penal provision is reasonably capable of two interpretations, that interpretation which is most favourable to the accused must be adopted."

B v. *DPP*[32] strengthens the presumption of mens rea even further. During a bus journey B, a boy aged 15, persistently requested a 13-year-old girl to perform oral sex on him. He was charged with the (now-repealed) offence of inciting a girl under 14 to commit an act of gross indecency, contrary to section 1(1) of the Indecency with Children Act 1960. B claimed that he had honestly believed that the girl was over 14. However, the Youth Court

---

defences may be "read in" to comply with Art. 3 of the ECHR, see Arden, "Criminal Law at the Crossroads: The Impact on Human Rights from the Law Commission's Perspective and the Need for a Code" [1999] *Crim LR* 439, 450. Contrast, however, *Salabiaku* v. *France* (1991) 13 EHRR 379.

[25] E.g. "in construing a modern statute this presumption as to *mens rea* does not exist": *Hobbs* v. *Winchester Corporation* [1910] 2 KB 471, 483 (Kennedy LJ); *St Margaret's Trust Ltd* [1958] 1 WLR 522 (CA). Cf. *Brent* v. *Wood* (1946) 175 LT 306, 307 (Lord Goddard CJ) (DC); *Harding* v. *Price* [1948] 1 KB 695, 700–1 (Lord Goddard CJ) (CA); *Reynolds* v. *G.H. Austin and Sons* [1951] 2 KB 135 (DC).

[26] [1970] AC 132.

[27] [2000] 2 AC 428.

[28] Contrary to s. 5(b) of the (now superseded) Dangerous Drugs Act 1965.

[29] [1970] AC 132, 148 (Lord Reid).

[30] *Ibid.*, 162–3. See also at 153 (Lord Morris).

[31] *Ibid.*, 149.

[32] [2000] 2 AC 428.

justices ruled, following the leading early case of *Prince*,[33] that the offence was one of strict liability in respect of the victim's age, and that therefore his state of mind concerning her age was irrelevant. B appealed ultimately to the House of Lords, arguing that since the Act did not specify a mens rea requirement, the common law presumption that mens rea was necessary should apply; and that, since he had thought the girl was over 14, he lacked the intent, knowledge or recklessness presumptively required.

The House of Lords allowed B's appeal.[34] It ruled that the common-law presumption of mens rea applied to section 1(1) of the 1960 Act:[35]

> "In these circumstances the starting point for a court is the established common law presumption that a mental element, traditionally labelled mens rea, is an essential ingredient unless Parliament has indicated a contrary intention either expressly or by necessary implication. The common law presumes that, unless Parliament indicated otherwise, the appropriate mental element is an unexpressed ingredient of every statutory offence."

The presumption is only to be overridden, according to their Lordships, if there is a *necessary* implication that Parliament intended the offence to be strict:[36]

> "[T]he test is not whether it is a reasonable implication that the statute rules out mens rea as a constituent part of the crime–the test is whether it is a *necessary* implication."

As will be seen, this strict test is not always applied to the letter. Frequently, the courts have ruled that the only reasonable construction of regulatory offences is that they are intended to be of strict liability, and they remain willing to do so notwithstanding *B* v. *DPP*.[37] But, at least for serious crimes, *B* v. *DPP* sets down an important marker in the law of strict liability (although not, alas, in the new law of sexual offences).[38] In *K*,[39] decided shortly afterwards, the defendant, aged 26, indecently assaulted V contrary to (the now repealed) section 14 of the Sexual Offences Act 1956. V was aged 14, and by section 14(2) of the 1956 Act a girl under the age of 16 could not in law consent to an indecent assault. However, K believed that V was aged 16: she had told him so. The Court of Appeal upheld K's conviction, refusing to overrule previous decisions that liability is strict as to age in the offence of indecent assault.[40] This decision is not inconsistent with *B* v. *DPP*. In *K*, the Court of Appeal rightly

---

[33] (1875) LR 2 CCR 154. In *Prince*, D was convicted of an offence against s. 55 of the OAPA 1861,which enacted that "whosoever shall unlawfully take … any unmarried girl, being under the age of sixteen years, out of the possession and against the will of her father or mother … shall be guilty of a misdemeanour". D did exactly that, but reasonably believed the girl's age was 18. The Court for Crown Cases Reserved held that the age of the girl was a matter of strict liability, so that D's belief was irrelevant. Notwithstanding that *Prince* was a leading decision for 125 years, its authority must be regarded as doubtful in light of *B* v. *DPP*.

[34] For criticism of the decision, see Horder, "How Culpability Can, and Cannot, be Denied in Under-age Sex Crimes" [2001] *Crim LR* 15; Glazebrook, "How Old Did You Think She Was?" (2001) 60 *CLJ* 26.

[35] [2000] 2 AC 428, 460 (Lord Nicholls), citing the passage from Lord Reid's judgment (above in the text) in *Sweet* v. *Parsley* [1970] AC 132, 148–9.

[36] [2000] 2 AC 428, 481 (Lord Hutton: emphasis in original). This requirement was said to be fulfilled only if such a reading is "compellingly clear" (according to Lord Nicholls, with whom Lord Irvine agreed), "sufficiently clear" (per Lord Steyn), or "necessary" (Lord Hutton, whose speech Lord Steyn also endorsed; see, also, Lord Mackay's opinion).

[37] See, e.g., *Muhamad* [2002] EWCA Crim 1856, [2003] QB 1031 (materially contributing to insolvency by gambling); *Hart* v. *Anglian Water Services Ltd* [2003] EWCA Crim 2243, [2004] 1 Cr App R (S) 62 (causing a discharge of effluent); *Matudi* [2003] EWCA Crim 697, [2003] EHLR 13 (importing contrabanded animal products); *G* [2008] UKHL 37, [2009] 1 AC 92 (rape of a child under 13; below, § 12.11(i)).

[38] As we see below, the Sexual Offences Act 2003 subsequently introduced a regime of designedly strict liability offences with respect to sexual offences involving children aged under 13 years.

[39] [2001] UKHL 41, [2002] 1 AC 462.

[40] *K* [2001] 1 Cr App R 35.

started with a presumption that the offence in section 14 required mens rea as to all ele-ments, but was led by various factors (in particular, the statutory history) to conclude that the presumption was overridden in respect of age where the victim was under 16, and that Parliament had intended that particular element of the offence to be one of strict liability.

Despite this, the House of Lords overruled the Court of Appeal. Notwithstanding the history, it was not a *necessary* implication of the legislation that, in respect of V's age, the offence was one of strict liability. Given the strength of the arguments in favour of the view that section 14 imposed strict liability (indeed, as Lord Millett noted, that was clearly Par-liament's intention), their Lordships' decision in *K* signals clearly that, in serious criminal offences, the courts will strive to uphold the presumption in favour of mens rea.[41]

K reinforces the strength of the presumption of mens rea as a principle of statutory interpretation in the context of the criminal law. At the same time, it remains merely a pre-sumption under English law and not a fundamental constitutional right. The presumption of mens rea is simply a point of departure, and can be outweighed by other factors. Even imprisonable offences have on occasion been held to be of strict liability.[42]

That this is so is demonstrated by *G*,[43] where a presumption of mens rea in the offence of rape of a child, contrary to section 5 of the Sexual Offences Act 2003, was—rightly, if regrettably, as a matter of statutory interpretation—excluded altogether by the intention of Parliament as manifested in the scheme of the statute.[44] Unfortunately, the courts in *G* went on to rule further that this interpretation was consistent with Article 6(2) of the ECHR.[45] The imposition of strict liability is still a matter of interpretation, rather than a question of the defendant's right to a fair trial.

In ascertaining whether the presumption of mens rea will be overcome in relation to one or more elements of a criminal offence, the courts have emphasised the importance of a number of factors.[46] These factors—which interact, and can exist in tension, with each another—are considered in the following sections.

(ii) Factor 1: The nature of the offence

(a) The nature of the offence in general

The first, and perhaps most important, concern is whether the offence is "serious" or "truly criminal", as opposed to a "quasi-criminal",[47] "public welfare", or "regulatory" offence.[48]

---

[41] Compare *Kumar* [2004] EWCA Crim 3207, [2005] 1 WLR 1352, where the Court of Appeal cited both *B* and *K* in ruling that, in the former offence of buggery contrary to s. 12 of the Sexual Offences Act 1956, a mens rea requirement with respect to the victim's age had been neither expressly nor necessarily excluded by the legislation.

[42] E.g. *Gammon Ltd* v. *A-G of Hong Kong* [1985] AC 1 (PC); *Howells* [1977] QB 614 (CA).

[43] [2008] UKHL 37, [2009] 1 AC 92.

[44] Below, § 12.11(i).

[45] A ruling confirmed (in the context of that offence) in *G* v. *UK* (2011) 53 EHRR SE25. Cf. *Deyemi and Edwards* [2007] EWCA Crim 2060, [2008] 1 Cr App R 25, paras. 26–7; *O'Riordan* v. *DPP* [2005] EWHC 1240 (Admin). Contrast the law in Canada, at least where the offence imports the possibility of imprisonment (including in the event of failure to pay a fine): *Reference re Section 94(2) of the Motor Vehicle Act* [1985] 2 SCR 486; *Pontes* [1995] 3 SCR 44.

[46] An illustrative discussion, in the context of unlawful low flying contrary to Air Force Act 1951, s. 51, is *Jackson* [2006] EWCA Crim 2380, [2007] 1 WLR 1035.

[47] *Pearks, Gunston & Tee Ltd* v. *Ward* [1902] 2 KB 1, 11 (Channell J). Cf. *London Borough of Harrow* v. *Shah* [2001] 1 WLR 83, 89 ("not truly criminal in character" *per* Mitchell J) (DC).

[48] Strict liability offences are typically "founded on collective convenience rather than moral imperatives": *Taylor* [2016] UKSC 5, [2016] 1 WLR 500 para. 26 (Lord Sumption).

At the heart of this (sometimes very difficult) question is the nature of the mischief the offence is designed to suppress. Very obviously, an offence will be of the truly criminal variety, and require a mens rea element for each element of the actus reus, when it prohibits an activity that is, in itself, overtly wrongful (e.g. murder, assault, and the like).[49] In these cases the activity may occasion moral condemnation even without being criminalised, and a conviction is therefore likely to attract a substantial level of moral stigma. By contrast, where conviction for the offence is likely to occasion little or no public stigma (as in the case of a parking infringement), the courts will be more willing to impose strict liability. Such instances are said to fall within the "class of acts … which are not criminal in any real sense, but are acts which in the public interest are prohibited under a penalty".[50]

(b) Specialist activities

More problematic are cases where the defendant's activity is not necessarily or inherently wrongful, but becomes the actus reus of an offence when done in a particular manner. Such offences often involve strict liability. Driving a vehicle may be a legitimate activity, but driving a vehicle without insurance is a strict liability offence—the defendant does not need to know, or even be reckless, about his lack of insurance.[51] Factors relevant to the assessment of such offences include whether the offence is directed at regulating trades, activities, and the like, especially those which involve specialist skills and those for which one must be licensed. Where this is the case, it is more likely to be treated as a public welfare offence, i.e. as one that regulates and controls excesses in an otherwise acceptable practice, and strict liability is more likely to be imposed.

The fact that the activity is a specialist one also increases the probability that its regulation will involve strict liability. One reason for this is that the use of strict liability simplifies prosecutions, a factor that is especially salient when the defendant may be expected to know far better than the prosecutor what went wrong and how it could have been prevented. In such circumstances, it may be unreasonable to suppose that the prosecutor will be able to acquire sufficiently accurate knowledge of the workings of the defendant's business organisation to prove mens rea for each element of the actus reus. As Lord Salmon commented in *Alphacell Ltd* v. *Woodward*, on a charge brought under a now-repealed offence under the Rivers (Prevention of Pollution) Act 1951:[52]

> "If … no conviction could be obtained under the 1951 Act unless the prosecution could discharge the often impossible onus of proving that the pollution was caused intentionally or negligently, a great deal of pollution would go unpunished and undeterred to the relief of many riparian factory owners."

This reasoning is reinforced (at least in the eyes of the courts) by the fact that regulation of a voluntary specialist activity does not lead to the conviction of citizens for doing ordinary things without being on notice that their conduct was in danger of breaching the criminal

---

[49] Note, however, that murder does not require mens rea as to the causing of death: an intention to cause grievous bodily harm will suffice. Murder is an example of constructive liability, discussed in § 6.5 below.

[50] *Sherras* v. *De Rutzen* [1895] 1 QB 918, 922 (Wright J).

[51] Road Traffic Act 1988, s. 143(2); *Tapsell* v. *Maslen* [1967] Crim LR 53 (DC).

[52] [1972] AC 824. Cf. *Woodrow* (1846) 15 M & W 404, 417, 153 ER 907, 913 (Parke B).

law. Concerns about fair warning[53] are thus less pressing where the defendant may be said to some extent to have assumed the risks of liability by voluntarily bringing herself within the particular sphere of operation of a regulatory law. In *Hobbs* v. *Winchester Corporation*, for example, a butcher suing for compensation in respect of unsound meat that had been destroyed was held to have been in default, and so barred from recovering, even though he had no reasonable means of discovering the condition of the meat:[54]

> "the policy of the Act is this: that if a man chooses for profit to engage in a business which involves offering for sale of that which may be deadly or injurious to health he must take that risk, and that it is not a sufficient defence for anyone who chooses to embark on such a business to say 'I could not have discovered the disease unless I had an analyst on the premises.'"

A similar point was made in *Sweet* v. *Parsley* by Lord Diplock:[55]

> "Where penal provisions are of general application to the conduct of ordinary citizens in the course of their every day life, the presumption is that the standard of care required of them in informing themselves of facts which would make their conduct unlawful, is that of the familiar common law duty of care. But where the subject-matter of a statute is the regulation of a particular activity involving potential danger to public health, safety or morals, in which citizens have a choice whether they participate or not, the court may feel driven to infer an intention of Parliament to impose, by penal sanctions, a higher duty of care on those who choose to participate."

Whether this is a *good* argument for imposing strict liability will be considered below, in § 6.3. For the moment it is sufficient to note that some judges think it is, and we may anticipate a greater willingness to find strict liability where the statute governs a specialist activity.

(c) The danger posed by the relevant conduct

As Lord Diplock contemplates in the quotation above, the likelihood that strict liability will be read into an offence is also increased if the activities it regulates have a tendency to endanger sections of the public[56] or, in recent times, the environment.[57] Obvious places for such laws are regulations governing the quality of food products,[58] the distribution of drugs,[59] and safety on the road[60] or in the workplace. An important instance of the last type is *Gammon (Hong Kong) Ltd* v. *A-G for Hong Kong*.[61] Following the collapse of construction

---

[53] See above, § 2.3.

[54] [1910] 2 KB 471, 484–85 (Kennedy LJ).

[55] [1970] AC 132, 163. One interesting philosophical discussion which makes a point of this type is Honoré, "Responsibility and Luck: The Moral Basis of Strict Liability" (1988) 104 *LQR* 530.

[56] Or, it seems, the economy: *St Margaret's Trust Ltd* [1958] 1 WLR 522, 527 (CA): "[t]he present generation has witnessed the collapse of the currency in other countries and the consequent chaos, misery and widespread ruin".

[57] Cf. *Alphacell Ltd* v. *Woodward* [1972] AC 824, 848 ("many rivers which are now filthy would become filthier still and many rivers which are now clean would lose their cleanliness" *per* Lord Salmon); *Kirkland* v. *Robinson* [1987] Crim LR 643 (DC). This approach is still adopted, notwithstanding the fact that environmental offences now involve significant social stigma.

[58] Especially prior to the introduction of a statutory "due diligence" defence in Food Safety Act 1990, s. 21. Cf. *Lim Chin Aik* [1963] AC 160, 174 (PC); *CLGP* 218–227.

[59] *Pharmaceutical Society of Great Britain* v. *Storkwain Ltd* [1986] 1 WLR 903 (HL); *Warner* v. *Metropolitan Police Commissioner* [1969] 2 AC 256.

[60] *Bowsher* [1973] RTR 202 (CA); *Reynolds* v. *GH Austin & Sons* [1951] 2 KB 135 (DC).

[61] [1985] AC 1 (PC).

work on a building site, the defendants responsible for the site were charged with deviating in a material way from the approved plan, contrary to local construction regulations. The offence carried a substantial fine and possible imprisonment for up to three years. Noting that the presumption of mens rea is "particularly strong" in such circumstances, since the offence did appear to be "truly criminal" in character, the Privy Council nonetheless advised that the offence was one of strict liability. Lord Scarman highlighted the importance of the danger that the offence sought to guard against: "the only situation in which the presumption can be displaced is where the statute is concerned with an issue of social concern, and public safety is such an issue".[62]

Lord Scarman went on to describe an additional condition that should be met: efficacy. Overriding the presumption of mens rea should not be done simply as a matter of convenience—something more substantial must be gained by doing so:[63]

> "Even where a statute is concerned with such an issue [of social concern], the presumption of mens rea stands unless it can also be shown that the creation of strict liability will be effective to promote the objects of the statute by encouraging greater vigilance to prevent the commission of the prohibited act."

(d) Legal assessment of the defendant's conduct

Another factor relevant to strict liability is that, if one element of the actus reus involves the arbitrary drawing of a line over such matters as time, quantity, or size, mens rea may be less likely to be required in respect of it. The most obvious case is a speeding offence, where the difference between 30 and 31 m.p.h. may have a significance that is purely the result of law.[64] It would be indulgent to require knowledge of one's speed in such cases, and in the absence of a default negligence standard, strict liability becomes the leading alternative.

Sometimes the law will not draw determinative lines, but will rather seek to evaluate the defendant's conduct with regard to criteria such as "reasonableness". If an element of the actus reus involves the legal assessment of certain facts, then the defendant need possess only whatever mens rea is required regarding the facts themselves. She need not be aware of the legal assessment itself,[65] which is a legal conclusion in the nature of a value judgement that the defendant is not permitted to second-guess.[66] For example, it is not determinative whether, in the circumstances as she perceived them, a defendant believed she was using "*reasonable* force" in self-defence: it is for the court to decide whether the force she used

---

[62] Ibid., 14.

[63] Ibid. Cf. Lim Chin Aik [1963] AC 160, 175 (PC); Sweet v. Parsley [1970] AC 132, 163 (Lord Diplock); Reynolds v. GH Austin & Sons [1951] 2 KB 135, 150 (Devlin J) (DC).

[64] This principle does not apply to age, at least in the context of sexual offences—where V's age has independent moral significance: B v. DPP [2000] 2 AC 428.

[65] A notable exception is "dishonesty", where the defendant must be aware that her conduct would be considered "dishonest" by the standards of reasonable and honest people: Ghosh [1982] QB 1053; § 13.8(iv), below.

[66] As in Doring [2002] EWCA Crim 1695, [2003] 1 Cr App R 9 (being concerned in the management of a company while being an undisclosed bankrupt). D had been involved in the publicity, promotion, and design activities of the company, but had neither hired nor fired staff and made no financial decisions or contracts for the company. Apparently, D believed that in doing so she was not directly or indirectly managing the company. The Court of Appeal upheld her conviction, ruling that it was a matter of strict liability whether her acts, objectively understood, amounted to being concerned in the management of the company. Cf. Lemon and Gay News Ltd [1979] AC 617 (whether a statement is "calculated to outrage the feelings of Christians"); also the discussion of evaluative terms, above, § 2.3(i). But compare the dissent on this point by Barwick CJ in Iannella v. French (1968) 119 CLR 84, 97.

was reasonable.[67] (Indeed, sometimes a failure to recognise the status of one's actions—e.g. that the force one uses is excessive—may itself disclose culpability.)[68] The presence of a legal assessment within the actus reus raises conflicting concerns between the need to prevent individuals from undermining the law's values, and the need to give them fair warning of the criminal implications of their conduct. We will return to this issue in the discussion of ignorance of law.[69]

(e) The severity of punishment

In asking whether an offence requires mens rea for each element of the actus reus, the range and severity of punishments prescribed upon conviction should be taken into account. In *Gammon*, for example, the fact that the maximum penalty for the offence was a substantial fine and imprisonment for three years was said by the Privy Council to be a "formidable point"[70] militating against strict liability. The severity of punishment might inform the court about the nature of the offence: the potential for imprisonment is often a clear indication that an offence is "truly criminal" rather than merely "regulatory" in character, and in such cases the presumption of mens rea normally should not be displaced.

It seems, however, that the courts do not regard the mere prospect of imprisonment as enough to make a crime "serious". In *Muhamad*,[71] the offence of materially contributing to one's insolvency by gambling, contrary to a now repealed offence under the Insolvency Act 1986, was held to involve strict liability notwithstanding the maximum sentence of two years' imprisonment. In the view of Dyson LJ, doing so:[72]

> "The starting point, therefore, is to determine how serious an offence is created by section 362(1)(a), and accordingly how much weight, if any, should be attached to the presumption. Some weight must undoubtedly be given to the presumption, but in our judgment it can be readily displaced. As we have said, the maximum sentence indicates that Parliament considered this to be an offence of some significance, but not one of the utmost seriousness. This is not surprising. We do not believe that great stigma attaches to a conviction of this offence."

It is not clear why an offence must be of "the utmost seriousness" if the presumption of mens rea is not to be readily displaced. There is much to be said for the approach adopted in the Model Penal Code, which asserts that the possibility of imprisonment for any term should be a conclusive reason against imposing strict liability.[73] Nonetheless, the English courts and the Privy Council have ruled some quite substantial maximum sentences to be consistent with the imposition of strict liability, after taking into account such considerations as the interest (e.g. public safety) being protected.[74] These include the offence in

---

[67] *Williams (Gladstone)* [1987] 3 All ER 411 (CA); *Clegg* [1995] 1 AC 482; *Owino* [1996] 2 Cr App R 128; *DPP* v. *Braun* [1999] Crim LR 416 (DC); Criminal Justice and Immigration Act 2008, s. 76. See, further, below, § 21.2(ii).

[68] For brief discussion of this point, see Simester, "Is Strict Liability Always Wrong?" in Simester (ed.), *Appraising Strict Liability* (2005) 21, 42–4.

[69] Below, § 18.2.

[70] [1985] AC 1, 17.

[71] [2002] EWCA Crim 1856, [2003] QB 1031, para. 16.

[72] *Ibid.* Cf. *Lim Chin Aik* [1963] AC 160, 175 (PC).

[73] § 6.02(4). Cf., in Canada, *Reference re Section 94(2) of the Motor Vehicle Act* [1985] 2 SCR 486.

[74] E.g. *R. v. Wells Street Magistrates' Court and Martin, ex p Westminster City Council* [1986] 1 WLR 1046 (DC); *Pharmaceutical Society of Great Britain v. Storkwain Ltd* [1986] 1 WLR 903 (HL); *Howells* [1977] QB 614 (CA). Indeed, English courts have even imposed strict liability in crimes attracting a *mandatory* minimum term of imprisonment, such as Firearms Act 1968, s. 5: see, e.g., *Zahid* [2010] EWCA Crim 2158.

Gammon itself, where the Privy Council, immediately after acknowledging the severity of the maximum penalties, continued with a "but": "there is nothing inconsistent with the purpose of the Ordinance in imposing severe penalties for offences of strict liability".[75]

One may ask whether the Privy Council has missed the point. The mere fact that strict liability is "not inconsistent" with the purpose of the statute is hardly a reason to impose it, and in no way meets the objection that in *Gammon* the maximum penalties were severe, which points towards the "truly criminal" nature of the offence. Neither does the logic in *Gammon* conform to the requirement—now laid down in *B* v. *DPP*[76]—that the imposition of strict liability must be a *necessary implication* of the statute, and not merely *consistent* with it. It is to be hoped that *B* v. *DPP* will make decisions such as *Gammon* rarer in the future.

That having been said, the potential for heavy penalties in an offence gives rise to a tension. Severe sanctions generally give the offence a criminal character, yet they may also reflect the fact that the subject matter of the offence—the social danger or harm involved— is itself substantial, a factor (as seen above) weighing in favour of strict liability. The type of offence most suitable for strict liability would involve substantial ultimate public harm or inconvenience (whether directly or cumulatively), and relatively little stigma for an individual offence. This may occur, for example, in certain road traffic offences. Similarly, the offence in *Alphacell Ltd* v. *Woodward*[77] of causing polluted material to enter a stream, which carried a low maximum penalty, was also relatively well suited to strict liability; especially in 1972, when pollution offences tended to be regarded as "acts not criminal in any real sense".[78] It is clear from the foregoing discussion that in practice the courts have extended their recognition of strict liability well beyond these examples. Moreover, attitudes change. Destruction and despoliation of the natural environment is now a very salient concern and acts degrading and threatening an environment would now readily be regarded as "truly criminal". On the face of it, that would give greater weight to the presumption in favour of mens rea for environmental offences, a move not likely to be favoured by anyone committed to optimum enforcement of environmental law.

(iii) Factor 2: The language of the legislation

Sometimes, rather than being presumed or explicit, or established by the judicial history, the legislature's intent to include or exclude a mens rea requirement can be *implied* directly from the words or scheme of the statute. This may occur in a number of ways.[79]

First, a verb specifying part of the actus reus may import a mental element. An example of this is "possession", the meaning of which was discussed in § 5.6(iv). According to the House of Lords,[80] D is not in possession of an article unless she is *aware* that she possesses

---

[75] [1985] AC 1, 17.

[76] [2000] 2 AC 428; above, § 6.1(i).

[77] [1972] AC 824.

[78] *Sherras* v. *De Rutzen* [1895] 1 QB 918, 922 (Wright J).

[79] Cf. Manchester, "Knowledge, Due Diligence and Strict Liability in Regulatory Offences" [2006] *Crim LR* 213, 216–19, 223–7.

[80] *Warner* v. *Metropolitan Police Commissioner* [1969] 2 AC 256.

something.[81] Similarly, it has been held that "permitting" another to use a vehicle when equipped with defective brakes can only be done knowingly. As a matter of ordinary language, the Divisional Court said, permitting "in our opinion, at once imports a state of mind".[82] Thus it is impossible, at least in that offence, to "permit" inadvertently.[83] A similar argument can be made in respect of "allowing".[84]

(iv) Factor 3: The scheme of the legislation

A third factor in establishing whether an offence involves strict liability is the scheme of the statute. Some of the earliest strict liability cases turned on this point. In *Betts v. Armstead*[85] the defendant was charged with selling adulterated bread, contrary to section 6 of the Sale of Food and Drugs Act 1875. He was apparently unaware the loaf was adulterated; nonetheless, he was convicted, since under section 5 an absence of knowledge had expressly been made a defence to offences enacted by sections 2–4, but not to section 6.

The validity of this type of inference was, however, subsequently doubted by Lord Goddard CJ,[86] since verbal distinctions of this sort may arise from the consolidation of earlier statutes without thematic revision, the vagaries of parliamentary amendment, or even imperfect draftsmanship. The present situation appears to be that linguistic difference between sections is a factor that may be taken into account, but is not itself decisive:[87]

> "It is also firmly established that the fact that other sections of the Act expressly require *mens rea*, for example because they contain the word 'knowingly', is not itself sufficient to justify a decision that a section which is silent as to *mens rea* creates an absolute offence."

Similarly, some offences have a defence of non-negligence (due diligence) attached to them.[88] Such a defence would be otiose if the offence were to require proof of full mens rea. Section 21 of the Food Safety Act 1990, for example, provides, in respect of offences created by sections 1–20 of the Act, that "it shall ... be a defence for the person charged to prove that he took all reasonable precautions and exercised all due diligence to avoid the commission of the offence". By implication, the offences enacted in those preceding sections are otherwise of strict liability. This type of statutory "due diligence" defence is now a common feature of regulatory offences.[89]

---

[81] Although she need not be aware of the item's character; to that extent, therefore, a possession offence which specifies no further mens rea element can be regarded, in substance, as an offence of strict liability.

[82] *James & Son Ltd v. Smee* [1955] 1 QB 78, 91 (Parker J).

[83] Although the same may not hold for other offences: *DPP v. Fisher* [1992] RTR 93 (DC) (permitting a vehicle to be used without insurance a strict liability offence). The meaning of "permit" appears to depend on the context and may vary across offences: contrast, e.g., *Vehicle Inspectorate v. Nuttall* [1999] 1 WLR 629 (HL); *Brock and Wyner* [2001] 1 WLR 1159 (CA).

[84] Edwards, *Mens Rea in Statutory Offences* (1955) 162–3. Cf. also *CPS v. M* [2009] EWCA Crim 2615, [2011] 1 WLR 822 ("throwing" held to import mens rea).

[85] (1888) 20 QBD 771. Cf. *Parker v. Alder* [1899] 1 QB 20; *Fitzpatrick v. Kelly* (1873) LR 8 QB 337.

[86] *Lines v. Hersom* [1951] 2 KB 682, 686–7 (DC).

[87] *Sweet v. Parsley* [1970] AC 132, 149 (Lord Reid). This factor will be particularly weak if the statute is a consolidation of previous statutes passed at different times: cf. *K* [2002] 1 AC 462, 467 (Lord Bingham).

[88] See Parry, "Judicial Approaches to Due Diligence" [1995] *Crim LR* 695.

[89] See, e.g., Simester and Roberts, "Strict Liability in UK Regulation" in Macrory, *Regulatory Justice: Sanctioning in a post-Hampton World* (2006) annex E.

The difference is more likely to be decisive, however, where the relevant statute was drawn up as a coherent regime, especially where the legislature has created parallel pairs of offences only one of which specifies a mens rea requirement. An example is the Sexual Offences Act 2003, which—as Chapter 12 explains—aims to set out a coherent body of sexual offences. Differences in the drafting of sections of the 2003 Act can therefore help to uncover strict liability. Consider section 9, which creates an offence of "sexual activity with a child". Section 9 provides that, if the child is between 13 and 15 years of age, the defendant must be proved not to have reasonably believed that the child was over 16: a negligence-based standard. If the child is under 13, however, no fault element is mentioned. It can be assumed that Parliament intended to draw a distinction between cases involving 13- to 15-year-olds (where fault is required) and children under 13 (where no fault is required). Further support for this proposition can be taken from the offence under section 5 ("rape of a child under 13"). Again, no fault element is mentioned with regard to the age of the child, and it has been held that Parliament intended this to engage strict liability.[90] It would be odd, in a statute enacted so recently and with aspirations of consistency, for Parliament to have intended strict liability in section 5, and then—with the same wording in the parallel part of section 9—intended there to be a requirement of fault. This example demonstrates both how internal reasoning (within section 9) and analogical reasoning (from section 5) can help uncover whether a particular offence within a coherent statute involves strict liability.

(v) The ability of others to affect D's liability?

One further factor, which has been recognised elsewhere, has not to date been invoked expressly by the English courts. In overseas jurisdictions, it has sometimes been said that if strict liability is to be imposed at all, it should be done only in offences that are set out in the clearest terms, so that it is possible for a defendant to know in advance what are the boundaries of the offence: "When there is absolute liability there ought to be absolute certainty as to the ingredients of the offence so that the offender cannot say that he was unable beforehand to conduct himself so as to avoid the offence".[91] As part of this general approach, the New Zealand courts have been reluctant to ascribe absolute liability in cases where the defendant's activity is affected by what others are doing. Thus, in *Jackson v. Attorney-General*,[92] the High Court held that one reason for not imposing absolute liability for the (former) offence of possessing cannabis in a prison cell, contrary to section 32 of the Penal Institutions Act 1954 (NZ), was that imposition of absolute liability would tend to encourage inmates to take retribution against another inmate by placing cannabis or other drugs in the other's cell.[93]

---

[90] *G* [2008] UKHL 37, [2009] 1 AC 92.

[91] *Re Wairarapa Election Petition* [1988] 2 NZLR 74, 117.

[92] [2006] 2 NZLR 534, 542.

[93] Compare, too, *Police v. Creedon* [1976] 1 NZLR 571, 573, a prosecution for failing to yield the right of way at an intersection, where the Court of Appeal emphasised the importance of the fact that "the regulation requires a driver of a motor vehicle to take a specific course of action if, and only if, something else is being done by someone else". By contrast with (say) failing to stop at an intersection governed by a stop sign, the offence in *Creedon* does "not impose an omnipresent and unvarying obligation" (*ibid.*, 574). Its uncertain boundaries were said therefore to militate against strict liability.

The potential for third parties to bring D within the scope of an offence should not normally be accompanied by strict liability on the part of the defendant.[94] These considerations, which involve principles applicable to the common law generally, deserve also to be given weight by English courts when determining whether a particular offence imposes strict liability.

§ 6.2 The availability of common law defences

If an offence is found to involve strict liability, this can impact upon the arguments available to D. Obviously, unless a specific statutory defence has been created, D may plead neither absence of mens rea nor absence of fault when charged with a strict liability offence. It appears that D may still, however, plead common law defences. There appears to be nothing, even in the older case law on strict liability, to foreclose such defences as duress. Moreover, there is modern appellate authority expressly recognising that duress, whether by threats or circumstances, is available as a defence to the strict liability offence of driving while disqualified.[95] Defences such as duress, necessity, and self-defence therefore seem to be available. We saw in Chapter 4 that the same is true for automatism and involuntariness.[96]

The position is less clear regarding insanity. In principle, this defence should also be available to strict liability offences. In *DPP* v. *H*, McCowan LJ nevertheless stated that:[97]

> "The [insanity] defence is based on the absence of mens rea, but none is required for the offence of driving with an excess of alcohol. Hence the defence of insanity has no relevance to such a charge as it is an offence of strict liability."

This is simply wrong. Insanity, in law, is not based on the absence of mens rea. It is a much more profound denial of the defendant's moral agency; of his moral responsibility for the actus reus.[98] As we shall see in the chapter on insanity (Chapter 19), the defence comes in two main forms: either as (effectively) insane automatism or as incapacity to recognise the wrongness of one's act. Regarding the first variety: automatism—whether sane or insane—is not merely a denial of mens rea, as a matter either of law or of principle. It is clearly established that automatism is a general defence to strict liability as well as other offences, and there is Court of Appeal authority that this includes insane automatism[99]—which, at the level

---

[94] Cf. *Re Wairarapa Election Petition* [1988] 2 NZLR 74, 117. For related discussion of this point, see Simester, "The Mental Element in Complicity" (2006) 122 *LQR* 578, 580–1.

[95] *Martin* [1989] 1 All ER 652 (CA); though see *Cichon* v. *DPP*, noted and criticised at [1994] Crim LR 918 (DC). Neither was the defence doubted (except on the facts) in *DPP* v. *Mullally* [2006] EWHC 3448 (Admin), [2006] All ER (D) 49. See, further, *Pipe* v. *DPP* [2012] EWHC 1821 (Admin); [2012] All ER (D) 238 (duress of circumstances a defence to speeding). Canadian authority supports the availability of such defences as a general proposition: *Cancoil Thermal Corp and Parkinson* (1986) 27 CCC (3d) 295, 301–2; *Walker* (1979) 48 CCC (2d) 126, 134–5; *Kennedy* (1972) 7 CCC (2d) 42; *Breau* (1959) 125 CCC 84. There is a brief discussion of these questions in Sayre, "Public Welfare Offences" (1933) 33 *Col LR* 55, 75–8.

[96] Above, § 4.3(i).

[97] [1997] 1 WLR 1406, 1409 (DC). Cf. *R.* v. *Horseferry Road Magistrates' Court, ex parte K* [1997] QB 23 (DC), and see the criticism of *DPP* v. *H* in Ward, "Magistrates, Insanity and the Common Law" [1997] *Crim LR* 796, 800–2.

[98] Simester, "On Justifications and Excuses" in Zedner and Roberts (eds.), *Principles and Values in Criminal Law and Criminal Justice* (2012) 95, 96–7.

[99] *Hennessy* [1989] 1 WLR 287 (CA); *Isitt* (1978) 67 Cr App R 44 (CA); cf. *Hill* v. *Baxter* [1958] 1 QB 277, 283 (Lord Goddard CJ), 285–6 (Devlin J) (DC).

of principle, is surely right. There is no reason to distinguish sane from insane automatism for the purposes of strict liability. Regarding the second variety of insanity: there is no denial of mens rea at all. The defendant *has* mens rea, and is simply incapable of recognising that his actions (of which he is aware) are wrong. It is therefore impossible for insanity to be "based on the absence of mens rea". McCowan LJ's analysis contains a fundamental error.

The nature of the insanity defence will be further discussed in Chapter 19. So far as strict liability offences are concerned, it suffices to say there is dubious Divisional Court authority that insanity is not available as a defence—and to hope that the decision, which is contrary to principle, will be overruled by a more senior court.

(i) Exception for situational offences

In Chapter 4, during the discussion of involuntariness, a distinction was drawn between state-of affairs offences and other types of offences, e.g. those involving an act or omission by the defendant. As we saw in § 4.3(ii)(b), it appears that automatism and impossibility are not available to offences that comprise purely a state of affairs, and which make no reference to the defendant's behaviour. It may be that the same is true for other common law defences such as duress. If so, then although duress seems generally to be available for strict liability offences, it would not be available when the particular strict liability offence criminalises a pure state of affairs. The point appears to be undecided.[100]

A second distinction reinforces this possibility. In those strict liability cases where a common law defence has been recognised, the offence has always been a mixed one, containing a strict liability element together with one or more actus reus elements for which mens rea is required. However, where the offence is mixed, defences such as duress will be available anyway, since they can attach in respect of the components that require mens rea. By contrast, strict liability offences which criminalise states of affairs *simpliciter* are likely to contain no mens rea element whatsoever. There is no case of this type in which a common law defence has been allowed, and *obiter* authority to the contrary. In the context of the strict liability crime of being a parent of a child who fails to attend school regularly,[101] Richards LJ was most sceptical:[102]

> "I am reluctant to decide this point on the basis of a late short argument from one side and without the benefit of contrary submissions. I have to say, for my part, that I am very doubtful whether the terms of s 444(1) admit of the possibility of a defence of duress of circumstances at all. The subsection looks not to the conduct of the parent or even to the parent's failure to act, but simply to whether the child has failed to attend regularly at school and whether the defendant is the parent of that child. There is no obvious scope for a defence that the parent acted or failed to act by reason of some necessity or duress of circumstances. In my view, this was not the kind of offence that Rose LJ can have had in mind when formulating his broad proposition in *R v Abdul-Hussain and Others* [1999] Crim LR 570 as to the cases in which the defence is available. In *Abdul-Hussain* he went on to say that:
>
> 'Imminent peril of death or serious injury to the defendant or those to whom the defendant had responsibility is an essential element in the defence and that the perils operated on the

---

[100] In this respect, *Larsonneur* (1934) 24 Cr App R 74 is authority only that *lawful* compulsion by another would be no defence.

[101] Contrary to the Education Act 1996, s. 444(1).

[102] *Hampshire County Council* v. *E* [2007] EWHC 2584 (Admin), [2008] ELR 260, paras. 10–11.

mind of the defendant at the time that he commenced the otherwise criminal act so as to overbear his will.'

That reference to the will being overborne reinforces my concern about the availability of the defence in the context of a strict liability offence of this nature."

Nonetheless, in our view the legal and moral case for excepting situational offences should be rejected. For one thing, it is founded on a category error, a false assimilation of defences with mens rea. Especially given the technical nature of mens rea requirements,[103] the two are quite separate kinds of liability element. Secondly, as will be seen in Chapter 20, duress is *not* a refutation of "will"—rather, it explains why D (reasonably) made the choice *that D wilfully made*. Thirdly, and most importantly, there is no moral basis for drawing a distinction that deprives situational liability offences, as opposed to other strict liability crimes, of access to the common-law defences. As we noted earlier,[104] situational liability is simply a convenient and indirect way of imposing liability for D's failure to prevent the "situation"—i.e., the actus reus—from occurring. If the offence had been phrased in terms of that failure to prevent, the defences would be available.

§ 6.3 The justification of strict liability

Like it or not, strict liability appears to be well entrenched in our legal system. Indeed, studies have suggested that approximately half of all offences involve at least one strict liability element.[105] But is it ever *morally* right to impose strict liability for a criminal offence? Without a mens rea requirement, strict liability inevitably licenses the conviction of the blameless. Can doing so ever be justified?

In the following sections, we argue that the answer is "no": strict liability should be replaced with a requirement that the prosecution proves at least negligence with regard to the relevant actus reus element, or—if that is unrealistic—strict liability offences should systematically allow for "due diligence" (i.e. no negligence) defences, with a legal burden being placed on the defendant.

(i) The need for public protection

The first argument that is often given for abandoning a mens rea requirement with regard to one or more aspects of the actus reus is that protection of the public sometimes requires a high standard of care on the part of those who undertake risk-creating activities.[106] Proper care needs to be taken by such persons, and without strict liability the careless will be able to transfer the considerable costs of their foolishness to the rest of society, without having any serious incentive to reduce or eliminate those risks. The threat of strict criminal liability supplies a motive for persons in risk-generating activities to adopt precautions,

---

[103] Above, chap. 5.

[104] Above, §§ 4.1(ii)(a), 4.3(ii)(b).

[105] Ashworth and Blake, "The Presumption of Innocence in English Criminal Law" [1996] *Crim LR* 306; JUSTICE, *Breaking the Rules* (1980).

[106] For an elaboration of the assumption of risk argument, see Honoré, "Responsibility and Luck: The Moral Basis of Strict Liability" (1988) 104 *LQR* 530.

which might not otherwise be taken, in order to ensure that unforeseen mishaps and errors are eliminated.[107] Lady Wootton's writing is a useful example of this type of argument:[108]

> "If the law says that certain things are not to be done, it is illogical to confine this prohibition to occasions on which they are done from malice aforethought; for at least the material consequences of an action, and the reasons for prohibiting it are the same whether it is the result of sinister malicious plotting, of negligence, or of sheer accident.... [I]n the modern world ... as much and more damage is done by negligence, or by indifference to the welfare or safety of others, as by deliberate wickedness."

In practice, such deterrence-based reasoning seems to be reflected in the law, since, as we have observed already, regulatory offences are often found where there is a need to protect the public from risks created by industrial and other specialist activities. Particularly where the harmful impact of the actus reus is severe and widespread, the law has reason to provide incentives through criminalisation for persons not only to refrain from advertent wrongdoing, but also to take care against inadvertent harms.

Two responses are available to this argument. First, it is unclear why *criminal* rather than civil sanctions should be used to regulate the activities involved and deter risk-takers. Even if private individuals cannot pursue a claim for damages, it may be open to the State, by legislative reform, to pursue miscreants through an administrative system of regulations that applies a standard of strict liability without the accompanying connotations of a criminal conviction—a welcome move that has been contemplated by the Cabinet Office.[109] Arguably, as things stand now, the moral authority of the criminal law is being undermined by the extension of liability to what are, in essence, mere regulatory violations.[110]

Against this response it may be noted that the description, "mere regulatory violations", somewhat underplays the vital public protection role that construction standards, work-safety standards, pollution standards, etc., discharge. Setting up a new system to try these matters as civil infractions rather than crimes would, admittedly, be a major task, and might be seen as downgrading the importance of effective regulation. There is little evidence that the proliferation of regulatory crimes has blunted the distinction between doing wrong and getting something wrong.

Yet, even if an alternative system to deal with such activities is rejected, it is unclear why we should prefer strict liability to negligence. It is true that regulatory offences seek to deter those entering into specialist activities from inflicting harm upon others, and by criminalising negligence such offences may help to deter the careless and indifferent and not merely the malicious or wicked. But strict liability goes beyond that, by criminalising accidents and reasonable conduct. This goes further than is necessary or desirable.

---

[107] R. v. *City of Sault Ste. Marie* [1978] 2 SCR 1299, 1310–1311. Cf. the criterion of efficacy, above, § 6.1(ii)(c).

[108] *Crime and the Criminal Law* (2nd ed., 1981) 46, 50. The claim of illogicality is, incidentally, false. Sometimes the presence of mens rea is crucial to the wrongfulness of what is done: cf. above, § 5.3. Wootton's argument therefore applies only to those harms whose nature is independent of the mens rea with which they are caused, and which (as such) are sufficiently severe to warrant criminalisation.

[109] Macrory, *Regulatory Justice: Sanctioning in a Post-Hampton World* (2006). The Macrory Review recommended introducing a complementary regime of Monetary Administrative Penalties, using strict liability to enforce regulatory breaches outside the criminal law.

[110] Compare Robinson, "The Criminal–Civil Distinction and the Utility of Desert" (1996) 76 *Boston ULR* 201, 212–14.

It is foolish for the law to demand that defendants do more than what is reasonable,[111] and there is no evidence that strict liability is a more effective deterrent than mens rea or negligence offences.[112] The effect of demanding the unreasonable, through strict liability, is to force a defendant either to desist from the risk-creating activity altogether, or to persist and accept that he must run all risks, however esoteric and unlikely, of the prohibited harm occurring, and incur the ensuing conviction if disaster occurs.[113] The first option cannot be taken seriously. It is surely not the intention of the law to discourage people from entering into productive activity altogether. The nation's economy would not last very long if that were the outcome. Rather, the aim of regulatory laws must be to discourage people from entering into an activity (or from executing it in a manner) which creates *unreasonable* risks of the unwanted harm occurring. But *that* aim can be achieved by imposing negligence liability. Strict liability forces the blameless defendant to become a gratuitous risk-taker, subject to a criminal legal lottery over which he has no reasonable control. If he is unlucky, he will be convicted. A lottery is no basis on which to conduct the nation's criminal law. Such a Draconian system, moreover, is likely to promote cynicism and disrespect for the law among innocent people who are labelled criminal "offenders" by their conviction.

(ii) The distinction between "real" crimes and quasi-criminal offences

Another point about the deterrence, or public protection, argument for strict liability is that it cannot possibly succeed by itself. The public needs also to be protected from assaults, damage to property, and the like, yet these are not strict liability offences; they require proof of mens rea in the ordinary way.[114] The difference, it is said, is that assault is a "true" crime, conviction for which entails serious social stigma—hence the need for a higher standard of fault, which partially overrides the deterrence argument—whereas regulatory offences control "quasi-" (i.e. not truly) criminal actions.[115] This leads to a second argument in favour of strict liability: that it is legitimate to use it when the offence under consideration is not "truly criminal".

---

[111] *Pace* Lord Salmon: strict liability "encourages riparian factory owners not only to take reasonable steps to prevent pollution but to do everything possible to ensure that they do not cause it": *Alphacell Ltd* v. *Woodward* [1972] AC 824, 848–9. See also Donovan J, in *St Margaret's Trust Ltd* [1958] 1 WLR 522, 527 (CA): "[t]here would be little point in enacting that no one should breach the defences against a flood, and at the same time excusing any one who did it innocently".

[112] See Jackson, "*Storkwain*: A Case Study in Strict liability and Self-Regulation" [1991] *Crim LR* 892; Richardson, "Strict Liability for Regulatory Crime: The Empirical Research" [1987] *Crim LR* 295; Baldwin, "Why Rules Don't Work" (1990) 53 *MLR* 321; Hall, *General Principles of Criminal Law* (2nd ed., 1960) 344–7. In terms of economic incentives, it is possible that strict liability may lead to reduced rather than increased deterrence: Simester, "Is Strict Liability Always Wrong?" in Simester (ed.), *Appraising Strict Liability* (2005) 21, 30–1.

[113] Cf. Lord Sumption's point that strict liability should be imposed only where practical steps against the occurrence of the actus reus can realistically be taken: *Taylor* [2016] UKSC 6, [2016] 1 WLR 500, para. 26.

[114] Cf. Mannheim, "Mens Rea in German and English Criminal Law" (1936) 18 *J Comp Leg* 78, 90: "the number of larcenies committed, e.g., is also very great; nevertheless, nobody would suggest that acts of larceny should be punished when committed without mens rea".

[115] See above, § 6.1(ii); see also the interesting discussion by Lamond, "What is a Crime?" (2007) 27 *OJLS* 609, esp. 629–631, where he suggests that strict liability can sometimes perform a valuable role in co-ordinating behaviour so as to minimise risk.

As noted above, in the context of strict liability both the House of Lords and the Privy Council have recognised a distinction between "truly criminal" and "regulatory" offences.[116] Danger nevertheless lies in the fact that, if a defendant's interests are to be subordinated to those of the general public in "regulatory" offences, the line between such offences and "true" crimes is not always easy to draw.[117] We have seen already (§ 6.1) that categorising offences is a difficult exercise, involving conflicting factors whose force is not readily quantified. Indeed, the courts have sometimes imposed strict liability for offences that are punishable by imprisonment;[118] surely an *indicium* of serious rather than minor transgression?[119] If a clear distinction between "regulatory" and "truly criminal" offences cannot be drawn, or if that distinction fails to capture the public imagination, then the arguments[120] for retaining the presumption of innocence—and for always requiring proof of mens rea—are much harder to surmount.

Furthermore, it may be responded that transgressors for so-called "regulatory" crimes still suffer the rigours of the criminal process, with associated costs and loss of time, not to mention the fact of a conviction and a criminal record. And—once again—if the conviction is a trivial consideration, why make the wrongdoing a criminal rather than civil or administrative matter? A regime of civil sanctions would help safeguard the moral force of the criminal law.[121] "When it becomes respectable to be convicted, the vitality of the criminal law has been sapped."[122]

(iii) The practicalities of proof and the need for efficiency

Another argument frequently wheeled out in support of strict liability concerns the practicalities of proof. Very often, the activities controlled by regulatory offences involve the commercial behaviour of corporations rather than the private conduct of individuals. Strict liability seems particularly useful where the offence is directed toward controlling the activity of corporations. There are three reasons for this. First, corporate convictions do not normally involve the same level of stigma as do those attaching to individuals, nor the same practical implications. Secondly, corporate activity is characteristically on a larger scale than that by individuals, and correspondingly creates greater levels of social threat. Finally, and most importantly for present purposes, the proof of mens rea (particularly subjective mens rea) presents special difficulty in the context of corporate bodies, since there

---

[116] *Sweet* v. *Parsley* [1970] AC 132, 149 (Lord Reid), 163 (Lord Diplock); *Alphacell Ltd* v. *Woodward* [1972] AC 824, 839 (Viscount Dilhorne), 848 (Lord Salmon); *Gammon (Hong Kong) Ltd* v. *A-G for Hong Kong* [1985] AC 1, 12–14.

[117] *Woolmington* v. *DPP* [1935] AC 462, 481; compare *Mancini* v. *DPP* [1942] AC 1, 11 (Viscount Simon LC); Orchard, "The Judicial Categorisation of Offences" (1983) 2 *Canterbury LR* 81, 94.

[118] Above, § 6.1(ii)(e).

[119] It is worth noting that the US Model Penal Code eschews such a possibility, asserting that the possibility of imprisonment should be a conclusive reason against imposing strict liability: § 6.02(4), though a contrary statute would not be unconstitutional: *US* v. *Freed* 401 US 601 (1971).

[120] See above, §§ 3.2, 3.2(i)(a).

[121] Progress has been made in this direction with the passing of the Regulatory Enforcement and Sanctions Act 2008, though we have a long way to go before we match the sophistication of French and German regimes: see Spencer and Pedain, "Approaches to Strict and Constructive Liability in Continental Criminal Law" in Simester (ed.), *Appraising Strict Liability* (2005) 237.

[122] Sayre, "The Present Significance of *Mens Rea* in the Criminal Law" in Pound (ed.), *Harvard Legal Essays* (1934) 399, 409.

may be no one person who can be identified as the agent when a corporation acts.[123] Strict liability, by contrast, is much more easily applied to companies and the like, since it can be administered without reference to the defendant's mental state, or even its negligence. Administration of justice would be more expensive and greatly slowed if the prosecution were put to proving fault—even negligence—in respect of every element of a minor offence before the court. This is especially true in areas regulated by public welfare offences, where the defendant may be far better placed to understand the nature of her own specialist activity, and thus to prevent the occurrence of harm, than is the prosecutor to learn the nature of the defendant's activity in order to prove fault; all the more so in the case of activities (and transgressions) by large and complex corporations.

Admittedly, regulatory enforcement needs to be done efficiently—a government cannot afford to spend large amounts of money on prosecutions, especially where the offences involved are common and individually involve no serious harm or even any harm at all. (Where substantial harm does ensue for individual transgressions, the prosecution should in any event be for a more serious crime involving mens rea and greater penalties.) Moreover, individual offences that involve no serious stigma can protect against a cumulative harm that may be very substantial indeed. These costs of controlling economic activity are, in truth, part of the costs of carrying on that activity, and it therefore makes some economic sense that the burden of criminal penalties should be borne as a form of production expense by those who voluntarily initiate risk-creating activities.[124]

Again, however, negligence would seem to fit the bill better than strict liability. Negligence can be established with relative ease compared to subjective mens rea elements, in as much as it need not involve proving the state of mind of a controlling officer. Negligence is measured, typically, in terms of conduct.[125] It is, of course, true that even that form of negligence obliges the prosecution to establish behaviour by the employee that can be attributed to the company—but the same constraint applies to strict liability.

More generally, there is a profound moral problem with the efficacy argument: it presents an issue of *procedural* convenience as a reason to change *substantive* law. The better answer, surely, is to change the procedure: by reversing the burden of proof.[126] This approach has been taken elsewhere in the Commonwealth, where "strict liability" offences require the prosecution to prove the actus reus beyond reasonable doubt, whereupon the defendant may exculpate himself by proving absence of fault (i.e. a "no-negligence" defence) on the balance of probabilities. Moreover, the question whether the defendant is at fault in a strict liability offence will still be relevant to any common-law defence and, in particular, to sentencing. Indeed, fault is likely to be relevant even to the decision to prosecute.[127] In light of

---

[123] On the need for such identification in most cases of corporate criminal liability, see below, § 8.2(iii)(b).

[124] "In the case of a minor pollution ... a comparatively nominal fine will no doubt be imposed. This may be regarded as a not unfair hazard of carrying on a business which may cause pollution on the banks of a river": *Alphacell Ltd* v. *Woodward* [1972] AC 824, 848 (Lord Salmon).

[125] This is not always the case. Negligence sometimes attaches to a defendant's beliefs, as in the main non-consensual sexual offences—see below, § 12.5.

[126] See, however, *Lambert* [2001] UKHL 37, [2002] 2 AC 545, where, in the context of the application of the HRA 1998 to s. 28 of the Misuse of Drugs Act 1971, the House of Lords interpreted a reverse burden of proof as imposing only an *evidential* and not a legal/persuasive burden. For discussion of this and other impacts of the HRA 1998 upon strict liability, see above, §§ 2.5(i), 2.5(iii), 3.2(i)(a).

[127] Richardson, Ogus, and Burrows, *Policing Pollution: A Study of Regulation and Enforcement* (1982); Hutter, *The Reasonable Arm of the Law: The Law Enforcement Procedures of Environmental Health Officers* (1988); *Smedleys*

this, it seems that the evidence may as well be heard straightforwardly before conviction.[128] The judge certainly cannot pass sentence without deciding whether the offence was committed knowingly, negligently, or blamelessly,[129] and will, if the facts are disputed, in any case have to hold a further hearing to determine them.[130] Given the advantage the defendant may have, of familiarity with the nature of his specialist activity, it is arguable that, as well as being more efficient, shifting the burden of proof may also result in better justice, and be more compatible in spirit with Article 6(2) of the European Convention (which guarantees the presumption of innocence).[131]

In summary, it is doubtful whether there are any significant advantages to be gained from the device of strict liability, and significant moral costs. It is wrong to convict the innocent. To do so is a misuse of criminal law, the most condemnatory institution available to society. If someone does not deserve to be convicted, then they should not be. To convict innocent people violates this most basic tenet of criminal liability.[132] It also arguably breaches the requirement for fair warning. Although citizens can know the activities to which strict liability attaches (assuming they have been publicised adequately, etc.), citizens have no way of predicting reliably when they may be about to incur criminal liability; too much is left to chance.[133] No doubt the public need to be protected from the harms that regulatory offences are designed to prevent. But the public need to be protected, too, from random liability. Either the prosecution should be required to prove at least negligence as to each element of the actus reus, or the defendant should be afforded the opportunity to prove the absence of negligence in order to secure an acquittal.

§ 6.4 Taking the middle ground: strict liability in the Commonwealth

In parts of the Commonwealth, a distinction is drawn between the terms "strict liability" and "absolute liability". In "strict liability" offences, the prosecution is required to prove the actus reus but, in relation to one or more elements of the actus reus, there is no mens rea element to prove. Nonetheless, the defendant can prove absence of fault in order to escape liability. In essence, the offences are negligence-based, but with a reversed burden of proof, such as the one argued for in the previous section. "Absolute liability", by contrast, refers to what in England is known as "strict liability". There is no need to prove fault in relation to

---

Ltd v. *Breed* [1974] AC 839, 856 (Viscount Dilhorne); *James & Son* v. *Smee* [1955] 1 QB 78, 93 (Parker J) (DC). Compare *Hart* v. *Bex* [1957] Crim LR 622 (DC), where the Court convicted but thought that a prosecution should not have been brought.

[128] As things stand, such evidence is inadmissible and its introduction may lead to the quashing of D's conviction of a strict liability offence, because of its potentially prejudicial effect: cf. *Sandhu* [1997] Crim LR 288 (CA). Some of the difficulty this generates may be observed in *Hill* [1997] 2 Cr App R (S) 243.

[129] See, e.g., *Smedleys Ltd* v. *Breed* [1974] AC 839, 857 (Viscount Dilhorne); *Lester* (1976) 63 Cr App R 144. Compare *Attorney-General's References (Nos. 74 and 83 of 2007)* [2007] EWCA Crim 2550, [2008] 1 Cr App Rep (S) 110. In one case (*Fenn*) following conviction of rape of a child under 13, contrary to s. 5(1) of the SOA 2003, it was regarded as relevant to the sentence that V had "ostensibly consented" and that his appearance was "significantly older than 13".

[130] See *Newton* (1983) 77 Cr App R 13.

[131] See above, § 3.2.

[132] See above, § 1.2(ii)(a).

[133] Cf. above, § 2.3.

at least one part of the actus reus, and the defendant cannot claim an absence of fault in his own defence.

In the leading case of *R. v. City of Sault Ste Marie*,[134] the Supreme Court of Canada decided that although mens rea need not be an essential ingredient of an offence, an alternative to absolute liability was nonetheless possible: there might be a defence available of "total absence of fault", the onus of proof for which would lie on the defendant. This third category, which the Court named strict liability, was characterised as follows:[135]

> "the doing of the prohibited act *prima facie* imports the offence, leaving it open to the accused to avoid liability by proving that he took all reasonable care. This involves consideration of what a reasonable man would have done in the circumstances. The defence will be available if the accused reasonably believed in a mistaken set of facts which, if true, would render the act or omission innocent, or if he took all reasonable steps to avoid the particular event."

The Supreme Court thus claimed a middle ground that the House of Lords denied itself in *Sweet v. Parsley*.[136] Indeed, the Supreme Court of Canada went further and held that regulatory offences, if they were not found to require proof of full mens rea, should presumptively involve "strict" rather than "absolute" liability.[137] Absolute liability is now a rare phenomenon in Canada and other Commonwealth jurisdictions, such as New Zealand: as a matter of principle, it should be applied only if imposed by the legislation "in clear terms or by necessary implication".[138]

The Law Commission has itself advocated that the English courts should have a general power to apply a defence of due diligence when a statutory offence is silent about mens rea.[139] That would, of course, now require legislative reform. Yet why did the House of Lords reject the possibility of a negligence-based middle ground? The answer is that, although a "halfway house" between mens rea and "absolute" liability was looked upon favourably by many of their Lordships in *Sweet v. Parsley*,[140] the House regarded the imposition of a persuasive burden of proof upon the defendant as inconsistent with *Woolmington*. In *Woolmington*, Viscount Sankey LC had said that, saving insanity and express statutory exceptions, the prosecution was required to prove guilt "no matter what the charge or where the trial".[141] The objection raised by the House is not merely of technical precedent: the Commonwealth version of strict liability contravenes the fundamental principle espoused in *Woolmington* that the prosecution must prove the whole of its case, and it is not for the defendant to prove his innocence. The irony of this is surely obvious, even if lost upon their

---

[134] [1978] 2 SCR 1299 (water pollution). See, for analysis, Hutchinson, "*Sault Ste. Marie*, Mens Rea and the Halfway House: Public Welfare Offences Get a Home of Their Own" (1979) 17 *Osgoode Hall LJ* 415.

[135] [1978] 2 SCR 1299, 1326. Compare, in Australia, *Proudman v. Dayman* (1941) 67 CLR 536, 540 (Dixon J); Howard, "Strict Responsibility in the High Court of Australia" (1960) 76 *LQR* 547. See also Brett, "Strict Responsibility: Possible Solutions" (1974) 37 *MLR* 417; Orchard, "The Defence of Absence of Fault in Australasia and Canada" in Smith (ed.), *Criminal Law: Essays in Honour of J.C. Smith* (1987) 114.

[136] [1970] AC 132; above, § 6.1(i).

[137] [1978] 2 SCR 1299, 1326. The policy reasons for preferring strict liability are stated at 1311–12.

[138] *Millar v. MOT* [1986] 1 NZLR 660, 668 (CA).

[139] *Criminal Liability in Regulatory Contexts* LCCP No. 195 (2010) Part 6.

[140] [1970] AC 132, 150 (Lord Reid), 158 (Lord Pearce), 164 (Lord Diplock).

[141] [1935] AC 462, 481; above, § 3.2. Cf. *Mancini v. DPP* [1942] AC 1, 11: the rule is "of general application in all charges under the criminal law".

Lordships.[142] *Woolmington* is, and was meant to be, a bastion for the defendant, a fortress against conviction of the innocent. How extraordinary that, in *Sweet v. Parsley*, it led to an "absolute" liability doctrine whereby the innocent defendant is denied even the *opportunity* to exculpate himself.

It is, moreover, not clear that the English view of strict liability was genuinely entailed by the precedent set by *Woolmington*. First, the point made by the Supreme Court in *Sault Ste Marie*, that *Woolmington* was concerned with "criminal offences in the true sense" and not with regulatory offences,[143] has much force. There is no reason to suppose that Viscount Sankey intended or even envisaged the implication later drawn from his words. Secondly, if it comes to judicial creativity, the House of Lords has more recently shown little compunction about trampling upon *Woolmington* in *Hunt*, when (as we saw earlier) it ruled that the defendant bears the onus of proving any statutory exceptions to an offence, even where the statute does not expressly impose that burden.[144] Finally, if *Woolmington* really does foreclose the Commonwealth version of strict liability, alternatives were available. In particular, a defence of absence of fault where the *evidential* (rather than persuasive) burden lies on the defendant is certainly consistent with *Woolmington* (and the European Convention), and was favoured by Lord Diplock in *Sweet v. Parsley*.[145] But the House preferred to impose a knowledge requirement in that case, and foreclosed the option of developing an approach to strict liability such as that embraced in *Sault St Marie*. Although they achieved justice in *Sweet v. Parsley*, the Lords' refusal to engage with due diligence defences leaves English law looking extremely harsh when compared with some of its Commonwealth equivalents.

§ 6.5 The correspondence principle, moral luck, and constructive liability

This chapter has outlined a number of objections to strict liability. One such objection concerns the fact that strict liability leads to the imposition of criminal liability based on luck: the defendant has, in respect of the relevant aspect(s) of the actus reus, entered a punishment lottery. Even if she exercises reasonable care to avoid the occurrence of the relevant part(s) of the actus reus, she can still be convicted.

This objection to strict liability needs to be probed further, because there is a closely related species of criminal liability—constructive liability—that is not always so susceptible to this argument about luck. Constructive liability is difficult to define precisely (and the courts have never defined it). Like strict liability, it exists where the prosecution is relieved of the burden of proving that the defendant was at fault with regard to an element of the actus reus. By contrast to strict liability, however, constructive liability arises in two parts: a gateway wrong, and an aggravating part. The actus reus of the gateway wrong has a corresponding mens rea requirement, while the aggravating part is a matter of strict liability.[146]

---

[142] Not, however, upon others: *R. v. City of Sault Ste Marie* [1978] 2 SCR 1299, 1316; *Millar v. MOT* [1986] 1 NZLR 660, 666; Cooke, *Turning Points of the Common Law* (1997) 47.

[143] [1978] 2 SCR 1299, 1316; cf. *Civil Aviation Dept v. MacKenzie* [1983] NZLR 78, 84.

[144] Above, § 3.2(i)(b).

[145] [1970] AC 132, 164. More accurately, the defence was said to be one of "honest and reasonable belief in a state of affairs which, had it existed, would have made his act innocent" (in effect, an absence of fault). Lord Diplock's preference was subsequently adopted by the New Zealand Court of Appeal in *Strawbridge* [1970] NZLR 909, but that decision is now superseded: *Millar v. MOT* [1986] 1 NZLR 660, 668.

[146] Simester, "Intoxication is Never a Defence" [2009] *Crim LR* 3, 7.

Moreover, at least in legitimate versions of constructive liability, the risk of that further, constructive-liability part will be connected (in ways explored below) to the defendant's gateway wrong. Consider the offence of murder: D need not intend (or even foresee a risk of) killing V—an intention to cause serious injury ("GBH") suffices.[147] Although no mens rea element need be proved formally with regard to V's death, D must be at fault in relation to a closely related matter (the causing of GBH). Moreover, depending on how stringently GBH is interpreted, death may be a foreseeable consequence of D's intended attack. On that footing, we think that "GBH murder" can be a defensible instance of constructive liability; but our argument does not support all forms of constructive liability. In order to differentiate between acceptable and unacceptable uses of constructive liability, it is necessary to consider what has become known as the "correspondence principle".

(i) The correspondence principle

In § 5.8, we discussed a requirement of *concurrence*: that the actus reus and mens rea of an offence must coincide in time. The concurrence requirement reflects a more general principle, of *correspondence*, in criminal law. Loosely stated, the standard version of the correspondence principle maintains that for every offence there should be mens rea elements relating to the whole of the actus reus, and that all of these elements must simultaneously be satisfied before the offence is committed.

The correspondence principle has an ancient pedigree.[148] As long ago as 1798 Lord Kenyon described it as "a principle of natural justice, and of our law, that *actus non facit reum nisi mens sit rea*. The intent and the act must both concur to constitute the crime."[149] Before that, references to the principle may be found in Bracton and Coke. According to Bracton, for example:[150]

> "For take away the will and every act will be indifferent, because it is your intent which gives meaning to your act, and a crime is not committed unless an intent to injure exists; neither is a theft committed without the intention to steal."

Certainly in the centuries after Coke,[151] these early sentiments had become so entrenched in the common law that mens rea could properly be described as "one of the fundamental requisites of criminality".[152] "The general rule of English law is, that no crime can be committed unless there is mens rea."[153] Criminal conviction, therefore, required something more than the mere occurrence of harm. Subject to limited exceptions whose genesis, we have observed, lay in the nineteenth century,[154] strict liability would not do.

---

[147] *Cunningham* [1982] AC 566.

[148] Cf. Horder, "Two Histories and Four Hidden Principles of Mens Rea" (1997) 113 *LQR* 95.

[149] *Fowler* v. *Padget* (1798) 7 Term Rep 509, 101 ER 1103.

[150] *De Legibus et Consuetudinibus Angliae*, 101b. Cf. Coke, *Third Institute* (1641) 6, 107.

[151] For discussion see Sayre, "*Mens Rea*" (1932) 45 *Harv LR* 974.

[152] Sayre, "The Present Significance of Mens Rea in the Criminal Law" in Pound (ed.), *Harvard Legal Essays* (1934) 399, 399.

[153] *Williamson* v. *Norris* [1899] 1 QB 7, 14 (Lord Russell).

[154] "It is true that there are cases where the Legislature in its wisdom has declared that, in the particular class of cases dealt with, a man is to be treated as guilty of the offence in question, although he has not acted with

Understood in this way, the principle of correspondence is a limited ethical principle, one that recognises that criminal liability should depend not only upon a person's acts but also upon her moral culpability (as indicated by the presence of mens rea) with respect to those acts. However, some writers have claimed a larger role for the correspondence principle. They defend what may be termed a "rigid version" of the principle.[155] According to the rigid version, for *every* actus reus element there should be a corresponding mens rea element, every one of which should simultaneously be satisfied before the offence is committed. Thus, according to Ashworth:[156]

> "if the conduct element of a crime is 'causing serious injury', the principle of correspondence demands that the fault element should be intention or recklessness as to causing serious injury, and not intention or recklessness as to some lesser harm such as a mere assault. Another example, as we shall see, is the law of murder: in English law a person may be convicted of murder if he either intended to kill or intended to cause grievous bodily harm. However, the latter species of fault breaches the principle of correspondence: the fault element does not correspond with the conduct element (which is, causing death), and so a person is liable to conviction for a higher crime than contemplated."

Another offence that violates the rigid version of the correspondence principle is section 1 of the Road Traffic Act 1988, causing death by dangerous driving. Once the preliminary offence of dangerous driving is committed,[157] liability for the greater offence in section 1 becomes a matter of strict liability, because the only difference in the definitions of these two offences is whether D causes someone's death; and that is an actus reus element for which no additional mens rea element is required.

Offences of this sort—where there is, so to speak, a "gateway offence"[158] coupled with strict liability for some further event—are said to impose constructive liability. In many such offences, the further event involves a death. For example, one well-known constructive liability offence is manslaughter by an unlawful act. If D commits a gateway offence which creates a reasonably foreseeable risk of some injury to another person, D becomes guilty of manslaughter should her gateway conduct happen to cause someone's death.[159] This form of manslaughter contains no mens rea ingredient referring to the crucial actus reus element, death. Similarly, once the driving is dangerous, liability for the greater, homicide-based offence in section 1 of the Road Traffic Act 1988 becomes a matter of strict liability. Again, the only difference is that D causes someone's death; and that is an actus reus element for which no additional mens rea element is required.

Constructive liability of the type seen here breaches the correspondence principle, at least in its rigid form. But is constructive liability necessarily a bad thing, or is slavish

---

negligence, and had no guilty mind. There are several such cases, but they form an exception to the general rule of law": *ibid.*

[155] There are, in fact, multiple versions of the correspondence principle: see Tadros, *Criminal Responsibility* (2005) 93–5.

[156] *Principles* 75. See Horder, "A Critique of the Correspondence Principle in Criminal Law" [1995] *Crim LR* 759; Mitchell, "In Defence of a Principle of Correspondence" [1999] *Crim LR* 195; Horder, "Questioning the Correspondence Principle—A Reply" [1999] *Crim LR* 206.

[157] Road Traffic Act 1988, s. 2. We take it that, like the sister offence (in s. 2B) of causing death by careless, or inconsiderate, driving, this is an implicit negligence offence: see above, § 5.5(iii).

[158] Cf. Horder, "Reconsidering Psychic Assault" [1998] *Crim LR* 392, 402–3.

[159] Below, § 10.6(ii). See especially the critique in § 10.6(ii)(f).

adherence to the correspondence principle overrated? The answer, surely, is a bit of both. The rigid version of the correspondence principle is not and never has been a part of the criminal law.[160] On the other hand, the case for the standard version of the correspondence principle is much stronger. The maxim *actus non facit reum nisi mens sit rea* is rightly a venerable one because we want convictions for causing harm to be a matter of culpability and not of luck. We have seen that strict liability is objectionable because it exposes defendants to convictions purely on the basis of luck rather than fault. Is constructive liability vulnerable to the same objection? Sometimes, but not always. To defend this answer, and to discriminate between cases of legitimate and illegitimate use of constructive liability, we must first address the problem of moral luck.

(ii) Moral luck

Luck is integral to the criminal law. If D shoots at V and misses, for example, the most she can be guilty of is attempted murder. If V dies, D becomes liable for murder; a different conviction with different penal consequences. Yet, once D has pulled the trigger, the outcome is a matter of luck. "We never do more than move our bodies: the rest is up to nature."[161]

The problem is as follows. Luck, it may be thought, is involuntary—the antithesis of control. And culpability, surely, should be dependent upon control rather than luck. As Nagel puts it:[162]

"Prior to reflection it is intuitively plausible that people cannot be morally assessed for what is not their fault, or for what is due to factors beyond their control. [Moral] judgment is different from the evaluation of something as a good or bad thing, or state of affairs. The latter may be present in addition to moral judgment, but when we blame someone for his actions we are not merely saying it is bad that they happened, or bad that he exists: we are judging *him*, saying he is bad.... Without being able to explain exactly why, we feel that the appropriateness of moral assessment is easily undermined by the discovery that the act or attribute, no matter how good or bad, is not under the person's control."

If that is so, there is an obvious difficulty because outcomes—harms—unavoidably involve luck. Nagel continues:[163]

"Whether we succeed or fail in what we try to do nearly always depends to some extent on factors beyond our control. This is true of murder, altruism, revolution, the sacrifice of certain interests for the sake of others—almost any morally important act. What has been done, and what is morally judged, is partly determined by other factors. However jewel-like[164] the good will may be in its own right, there is a morally significant difference between rescuing

---

[160] Gardner, "Rationality and the Rule of Law in Offences Against the Person" (1994) 53 *CLJ* 502, 509.

[161] Davidson, *Essays on Actions and Events* (1980) 59. Cf. Ashworth, "Taking the Consequences" in Shute, Gardner and Horder (eds.), *Action and Value in Criminal Law* (1993) 107.

[162] *Mortal Questions* (1979) 25. See Honoré, "Responsibility and Luck: The Moral Basis of Strict Liability" (1989) 104 *LQR* 530; Mandil, "Chance, Freedom and Criminal Liability" (1987) 87 *Cal LR* 125; André, "Nagel, Williams and Moral Luck" (1983) 43 *Analysis* 202; Williams, "Moral Luck" in *Moral Luck* (1981) 20; Schulhofer, "Harm and Punishment: A Critique of Emphasis on the Results of Conduct in the Criminal Law" (1974) 122 *U Pa LR* 1497; Smith, "The Element of Chance in Criminal Liability" [1971] *Crim LR* 63.

[163] *Mortal Questions* (1979) 25.

[164] A reference to Kant, *Groundwork of the Metaphysics of Morals* (1785) § 1: if "only the good will were to remain ... then, like a jewel, it would still shine by itself, as something that has its full worth in itself".

someone from a burning building and dropping him from a twelfth-storey window while trying to rescue him. Similarly, there is a morally significant difference between reckless driving and manslaughter. But whether a reckless driver hits a pedestrian depends on the presence of the pedestrian at the point where he recklessly passes a red light."

And that, we have noted, is a matter of luck.

Ashworth, amongst others, has used this type of point to oppose segregating attempt liability: where the difference is merely down to luck, a failed attempt to kill ought to be punished just as severely as if it had succeeded, and vice versa.[165] On Ashworth's view, any substantive offence, such as murder, is analogous to a constructive liability offence: the gateway crime committed by D is attempted murder, and what elevates D's crime to murder is (like dangerous driving causing death) merely the actus reus element of causing death—for which no additional mens rea element is required.

It is not possible, in a book of this nature, to answer these objections in full; here, we can only sketch a defence of moral luck in the criminal law. The key point is that in causing death by dangerous driving, like in murder, death is not *merely* a matter of luck. To see this, consider the following example proposed by Smith:[166]

> "the daughter of a business executive has been assigned a science project of investigating the distribution of blood-types within the population. To assist her, the executive asks his secretary to survey the office staff and prepare a report on their blood-types by noon. Instead of carrying out this request, the secretary reads a spy novel. At 11:45 a co-worker suffers massive bleeding as a result of an office accident. Paramedics arrive, and could start a transfusion immediately if the workers' blood-type were known. Unfortunately he is unconscious, cannot provide this information, and so dies before the transfusion can be started. Had the secretary followed her boss's orders, she would have known the worker's blood-type and his life would have been saved. Her failure to obtain this information is both objectively wrong *and* culpable, and it led to her inability to save her co-worker's life. But [there is] no inclination to say that the secretary is to blame for the co-worker's death."

Contrast Smith's example, moreover, with a different type of case:

> Edgar is driving through a village at a speed 20 miles per hour in excess of the speed limit. Unexpectedly he loses control of his car, mounts the pavement, and kills Allan, who had been walking quietly toward the corner shop in order to buy a newspaper.

Driving through the village at such excessive speed is, we may conclude, dangerous driving. As such, Edgar commits the offence of causing death by dangerous driving notwithstanding that he does not foresee Allan's death. As noted earlier, the offence imposes constructive liability. But there is nothing wrong with that. Certainly it is, in one sense, a matter of luck that Allan was killed. But the luck is not random or unrelated in the way it was for Smith's delinquent secretary. Here, the possibility of this type of outcome forms part of the very reason why dangerous driving is wrongful—and itself criminalised.

---

[165] "Criminal Attempts and the Role of Resulting Harm" (1988) 19 *Rutgers LJ* 725; "Belief, Intent, and Criminal Liability" in Eekelaar and Bell (eds.), *Oxford Essays in Jurisprudence* (3rd Series, 1987) 1. The argument is restricted to "complete" rather than "incomplete" attempts: cf. Duff, "Subjectivism, Objectivism and Criminal Attempts" in Simester and Smith (eds.), *Harm and Culpability* (1996) 19. For an interesting discussion of these issues see Lewis, "The Punishment that Leaves Something to Chance" (1989) 18 *Phil & Pub Aff* 53. See also below, § 9.3(vi).

[166] "Culpable Ignorance" (1983) 92 *The Philosophical Review* 543, 550–51.

A comparison between Edgar's case and Smith's delinquent secretary example highlights the importance of distinguishing between two types of luck: intrinsic and extrinsic.[167] The secretary is not blameworthy for the coworker's death because that risk was *extrinsic* to her culpability. Such risks affect the outcome, and perhaps affect our retrospective judgements about what D *did*, but they are not the relevant factors when deciding, *in advance*, what D should do. By contrast, in Edgar's case, the risk of death was *intrinsic* to his culpability: it formed part of the reason why, even *ex ante*, Edgar's behaviour was wrong. The same can be said of "GBH murder" cases: the risk of killing a person is *intrinsic* to D's culpability in intentionally causing serious injury to V. Mounting such attacks is to be avoided, in part, *because* they can easily result in an unintended fatality. The risk of death is one reason not to intentionally cause someone serious harm.

Ashworth and Nagel are right to observe that many factors affecting an outcome are beyond our control. But this does not imply that the outcome itself is beyond our control. It is only *given* D's behaviour that the outcome is—thereafter—beyond her control. D does have control over the outcome; she exercises that control *through* her behaviour. It is D's dangerous driving, or her pulling the trigger, or her intentionally causing V serious harm, that brings the uncontrolled factors into play, and makes the luck relevant. Where that luck is intrinsic, there seems no difficulty about holding D responsible and culpable for the outcome.[168] Constructive liability is defensible in such circumstances.

Moreover, constructive liability is consistent with the Rule of Law. Where such offences are predicated on intrinsic luck, they do not defeat the desire to give fair warning in criminal law.[169] Indeed, D may be regarded as already warned, since she has committed the gateway crime (e.g. causing GBH) with mens rea;[170] and the intrinsic luck forms part of the rationale for blaming D and regarding that gateway crime as wrong.[171]

At the same time, such constructive liability advances the goal of representative labelling in the law.[172] If D intentionally shoots and kills V, we do not reprove the attack and, separately, regret V's death. No: we reprove the murder. It does not sufficiently describe D's act to say that she attempted to murder V. She murdered him. Similarly, it would be incomplete and therefore inaccurate to describe Edgar's conduct merely as dangerous driving.

---

[167] Williams, *Moral Luck* (1981) 25–6. This distinction supports a better analysis of Horder's gun-cleaning example than the author himself offers: "A Critique of the Correspondence Principle in Criminal Law" [1995] *Crim LR* 759, 764. Suppose I clean my gun outside *in order* to upset V. Although my deliberate wrong changes my normative position, it does not does not do so with respect to extrinsic risks such as an accidental discharge that causes V's death by shock. The distinction also takes our account outside the version of "moderate constructivism" critiqued by Ashworth, "A Change of Normative Position: Determining the Contours of Culpability in Criminal Law" (2008) 11 *New Criminal LR* 232. Ashworth himself associates *Simester and Sullivan* with moderate constructivism (*ibid.*, 241), rather oddly quoting not from the present section but from the discussion of joint enterprise in Chapter 7.

[168] Our concern here is primarily with the issue of liability rather than punishment. Simons rightly observes that, even if liability is appropriate, quantifying the amount of deserved punishment in constructive liability cases remains a deep problem: "Is Strict Criminal Liability in the Grading of Offences Consistent with Retributive Desert?" (2012) 32 *OJLS* 445.

[169] Discussed above, § 2.3.

[170] See Gardner, "Rationality and the Rule of Law in Offences Against the Person" (1994) 53 *CLJ* 502, 521–3.

[171] This further point presupposes that the goal of giving potential offenders fair warning of their crimes does not always require advertence by defendants to the actus reus. Crimes of negligence are capable, on this view, of giving fair warning.

[172] Above, § 2.4.

Even where the mens rea for two offences is the same, fair labelling in the criminal law is constrained by harm. Why are reckless endangerment by dangerous driving, attempts to kill, and the like wrongful? The answer is not because they involve any direct (e.g. physical) harm to the victim, but because D wrongfully manipulates, subordinates, attacks, or endangers V's interests and autonomy. But when an attempt succeeds, when dangerous driving kills, or when serious bodily harm results in a fatality, the harm is rather different. V is dead. Only by acknowledging that fact can the criminal law adequately communicate what D has done.

To be clear, some offences under English law push the boundaries of constructive liability too far, because they pay insufficient attention to the distinction between intrinsic and extrinsic luck. One example is the offence of manslaughter by an unlawful act. As we noted above, and will see in Chapter 10, if D commits a crime (with mens rea) which creates a reasonably foreseeable risk of *some* harm to V, D becomes guilty of manslaughter should his gateway crime in fact cause V's death. This form of manslaughter contains no mens rea ingredient referring to the key actus reus element, death. The difficulty with imposing homicide-based liability in such circumstances is that the defendant's initial criminal act might not be prohibited because of its close relationship with death, but merely because of a connection with *some* physical harm. Consider a case where D throws a brick through V's window, intending to break it, and disaster (not to mention the brick) strikes. Should V die as a result of being hit, D will be liable for manslaughter. True, there must have been *some* foreseeable risk of injury as a consequence of D's action; that risk supplies one reason not to perpetrate criminal damage. But it did not supply the reason why criminal damage is wrong—far less the risk that someone would die. The link between risks of death and the wrongfulness of criminal damage is an extrinsic one. This is a reason why the offence of unlawful act manslaughter should be reformed.[173]

---

[173] Below, § 10.6(i)(f).

7

SECONDARY PARTICIPATION

§ 7.1 The possibility of derivative liability

In Chapter 1, we considered the following example:[1]

> One fine September morning, Jim is discovered dead in his home. His skull has been
> crushed by a blow inflicted with a heavy object. The police are called. Upon investiga-
> tion, they establish that he was murdered by his daughter, Alice, who killed him in
> order to receive her inheritance under his will.

This, as we said earlier, is a paradigm case of criminal wrongdoing by Alice, involving
deliberate, culpable infliction of the sort of serious harm that the criminal law seeks to
prevent. Alice is precisely the sort of person who deserves the condemnation of a criminal
conviction. But she may not be the only person culpable in respect of Jim's death. Imagine
the following additional details:

> During the course of their investigation, the police unearth a number of related facts.
> Frank, Jim's cousin, had learned by accident of Alice's plan to murder Jim, but had
> done nothing because he, too, stood to inherit under the will. Alice had planned the
> murder with the help of Gertrude, whom she had consulted about possible methods
> of carrying out the killing. The baseball bat that Alice eventually used belongs to
> Harry, who lent it to Alice for the purpose.

When an offence is committed it is not only the immediate perpetrator of the actus reus
who may incur criminal liability. Others may also be held accountable by the criminal law.
Usually, this will occur when those others have participated in the commission of the crime,
albeit without directly perpetrating the actus reus.[2] Such persons, when they are held to be
criminally accountable, are said to be *parties* to the offence.

The difficult questions, for both theory and doctrine in criminal law, are *when* and *why*
persons other than the perpetrator of a crime should be held liable, along with the perpetrator, for the offence itself. Theoretically, when Jim dies every legally competent person
within the jurisdiction is a potential defendant, yet it is inappropriate to regard every member of society as involved in the crime that Alice commits. But how do we narrow the field
in a principled way? In short, when a crime occurs, who are the suitable defendants?

---

[1] Above, § 1.2 and, especially, § 1.2(ii)(e).
[2] Note, however, occasional suggestions of a causal approach to participants' liability in the case law and literature, the logic of which threatens to undermine this proposition—and in turn, much of the rationale for secondary
liability. See below, § 7.7(i).

In Chapter 4 we considered the criminal law's doctrines of omissions and causation, which play a vital role in identifying those persons who may be ascribed with legal responsibility for committing a crime. Because of the law regarding omissions, for example, Frank will not be held responsible for Jim's death. On the other hand, these are not the only doctrines of responsibility in criminal law. Gertrude and Harry did not cause Jim's death: Alice's action was free and unconstrained.[3] Nonetheless they, as well as Alice, will be held guilty of Jim's murder.

In this and the following chapter, we consider the doctrines by which a defendant may be held responsible for a crime she does not herself commit.[4] There are two main ways in which this may occur. The first gives rise to *secondary liability*. Although they did not perpetrate the crime, Gertrude and Harry have participated in Jim's murder by rendering aid and encouragement to Alice. Hence, they are known as secondary parties to the murder and are guilty of the offence alongside Alice. The second doctrine of responsibility occurs when a person is held responsible, at large, for the various acts of another person. This is known as *vicarious liability* and is much more common in civil than in criminal law. For example, an employer may sometimes be sued in tort for the damage its employee causes to P's property, but cannot itself be prosecuted for vandalism.

Both forms of liability are *derivative*. The defendant is indirectly held responsible for a crime committed by another and, as such, her liability is dependent upon the criminal actions of that other person. If no crime is committed, there is generally nothing of a criminal character that can be secondarily or vicariously attributed to the defendant.[5] As was noted in § 1.2(ii)(e), and will be seen below, the fact that liability is derived from the crime of another raises difficult questions of principle and policy. The level of involvement required to make D guilty when P commits a crime must balance the consideration that D is often just as culpable as P (and indeed sometimes more culpable), even though it was not D who pulled the trigger, against the difficulty that derivative liability casts the net of guilt well beyond the direct infliction of criminal harms, to catch ostensibly innocent conduct such as lending (or selling)[6] Alice a baseball bat or even sitting as a passenger in a car.[7] It is for this reason that the mens rea requirements of secondary liability, in particular, are generally more complex than those for the underlying offence.

For similar reasons, vicarious liability is normally to be avoided altogether in criminal law, since it arises simply out of a pre-existing relationship between the defendant and the actual perpetrator of a crime, and so is not specific to the crime or to any conduct by D relevant to that crime. It follows that D risks being convicted of a crime to which he has not contributed and for which he is in no way at fault. As Chapter 1 argued, that would be an undesirable outcome, especially in the context of stigmatic crimes. Consequently, it

---

[3] See above, § 4.2ff. Their assistance need not even be a *sine qua non* of the crime—Alice, we may suppose, would have received the same advice and aid from others had Gertrude and Harry been unavailable or unwilling.

[4] A classic discussion is Sayre, "Criminal Responsibility for the Acts of Another" (1930) 43 *Harv LR* 678. Other American writings include Perkins, "Parties to Crime" (1941) 89 *U Pa LR* 581; Dressler, "Reassessing the Theoretical Underpinnings of Accomplice Liability: New Solutions to an Old Problem" (1985) 37 *Hastings LJ* 91.

[5] Kadish, *Blame and Punishment* (1987) 146ff. This proposition is subject to certain exceptions, e.g. where S has procured P to do the actus reus of an offence without mens rea, or under duress: see below, § 7.6(ii).

[6] Cf. *NCB* v. *Gamble* [1959] 1 QB 11. See, e.g., Duff, "'Can I Help You?' Accessorial Liability and the Intention to Assist" (1990) 10 *LS* 165; Williams, "Complicity, Purpose and the Draft Code" [1990] *Crim LR* 4.

[7] E.g. *Du Cros* v. *Lambourne* [1907] 1 KB 40; below, § 7.4(iii).

will be seen in Chapter 8 that vicarious liability is not a general doctrine of the criminal law, being normally restricted to statutory regulatory offences and imposed only when it is found that Parliament must have intended it.

In the second part of Chapter 8, we will turn our attention to the liability of corporations. Although corporations are sometimes credited with a legal capacity to act, or omit, and to commit crimes directly, as will be seen, corporate liability often is to be explained as a specialised variety of vicarious liability.

§ 7.2 Modes of participation

The law recognises two main varieties of participation in a crime. For convenience, we begin with a summary. Participation in an offence may occur in the following ways:

(i)   As principal (the person who carries out the offence); or

(ii)   As secondary party who assists or encourages the offence—by aiding, abetting, counselling, or procuring the commission of that offence.

Suppose that D commits an assault by hitting V during an argument. In this case, D acts as the *principal*—the person who actually commits the crime. In general, D will be a principal offender if he personally fulfils the actus reus and mens rea requirements of the crime.

Alternatively, the crime itself may be done by P, but S may be involved as a *secondary party*. Secondary parties are those persons whose role in giving assistance or encouragement to P is sufficient to make them also participants in and guilty of the crime committed by the principal, notwithstanding that they do not themselves satisfy the actus reus and mens rea elements of the crime. *Per* section 8 of the Accessories and Abettors Act 1861, as amended by the Criminal Law Act 1977:

> Whosoever shall aid, abet, counsel or procure the commission of any indictable offence,[8] whether the same be an offence at common law or by virtue of any Act passed or to be passed, shall be liable to be tried, indicted, and punished as a principal offender.

A secondary party should be distinguished from a person who assists someone else (who may be either a principal or secondary party) who has committed an offence *after* the crime has been completed. Such a person does not participate in the crime itself, and his liability is not for the original crime committed, but instead arises independently as an offence under section 4 of the Criminal Law Act 1967.[9] By contrast, participation by a party to the offence must occur before that offence is completed.[10]

---

[8] Similar rules apply to summary trials: Magistrates' Courts Act 1980, s. 44.

[9] See Williams, "Evading Justice" [1975] *Crim LR* 430. This rule differs from the common law, which was repealed by the Criminal Law Act 1967. At common law, whenever D subsequently gave assistance to any person committing or party to a felony, which assistance tended to and had the object of enabling that person to avoid arrest, trial, or conviction, D also became a party to the original felony and did not commit an independent offence.

[10] *King* (1817) Russ & Ry 332, 168 ER 830; *Stally* [1959] 3 All ER 814. In the case of a continuing offence, such as rape (cf. Sexual Offences Act 2003, s. 79(2); *Kaitamaki* [1985] AC 147), the participation may occur after commencement of the offence but must happen before its completion (i.e. prior to withdrawal by the rapist): *Mok Wei Tak v. R.* [1990] 2 AC 333 (PC); *Mayberry* [1973] Qd R 211.

A secondary party should also be distinguished from someone who commits an inchoate offence by assisting or encouraging a crime. A person who encourages another person to commit a crime may, by giving that encouragement, commit the inchoate offence (as a principal); and, should the encouraged crime ultimately be perpetrated, become guilty of that crime too (as a secondary party). But the inchoate offence involves a separate conviction under the Serious Crime Act 2007.[11] It is committed as principal, and it is committed whether or not the encouraged crime later occurs. By contrast, the conviction of a secondary party is *for the principal's crime*; it is derived from one person's participation in the crime actually committed by another.

The formal distinction between principals and secondary offenders is now of little practical significance when it comes to the verdict, because each is deemed to be guilty of the full offence. Thus it will not affect his resulting conviction for, say, murder, whether D himself killed another person or was simply a secondary party. Indeed, it can be very difficult on the facts of some cases to differentiate between principals and secondary parties,[12] and under current law the form of charge need not specify the nature of D's participation, but may simply allege guilt.[13] This practice is somewhat in tension with the ECHR, as Article 6(1) has been held to require that an offender should be able to understand clearly the basis on which she is convicted.[14] The full ramifications of that ruling for English law remain to be seen.[15]

Certainly, differentiation between principals and secondary parties is still to be found in the case law. One reason for this is that the distinction is still crucial to the operation of section 8 itself. If D was not a principal, the enquiry whether D was a secondary party will depend in part upon the existence of a principal who did perpetrate the offence,[16] and will take a different form—with a different actus reus and different mens rea—from the enquiry into the principal's liability. The elements of the principal's liability are specific to each offence: in murder, for example, the prosecution must prove an intent to kill or inflict grievous bodily injury (Chapter 10), while strict liability offences require no proof of mens rea on the part of a principal (Chapter 6). By contrast, for both types of offence the elements of secondary liability are the same; they are as set out in this chapter *whatever* the main offence.

The difference between principals and secondary parties matters for at least two other reasons. First, some offences are defined so that certain participants are excluded from liability, either because only a named class of persons may commit the offence as a principal

---

[11] See below, § 7.7 and, for a detailed analysis of assistance and encouragement as inchoate offences, § 9.2.

[12] See, e.g., *Swindall and Osborne* (1846) 2 C & K 230, 175 ER 95; *Du Cros* v. *Lambourne* [1907] 1 KB 40.

[13] A practice that is said to be compatible with Art. 6(3)(a) of the ECHR: *Mercer* [2001] All ER (D) 187. However, it is desirable wherever possible for the prosecution to specify the form of participation when laying the charge: *DPP for Northern Ireland* v. *Maxwell* [1978] 3 All ER 1140, 1142.

[14] *Taxquet* v. *Belgium* [2009] ECHR 2279, [2010] ECHR 1806.

[15] The practice was thought compatible with Art. 6 in *Mercer* [2001] EWCA Crim 638, [2001] All ER (D) 187 and *Concannon* [2002] Crim LR 213; but see Ashworth, "A Decade of Human Rights in Criminal Justice" [2014] Crim LR 325, 327. The Scottish system of jury trial was said to pass muster in *Judge* v. *UK* (App no 35863/10) (2011) 52 EHRR SE17, especially in light of other features (details in the indictment; directions by the judge; the right to appeal for a miscarriage of justice) that conveyed information to the defendant despite the lack of reasons for the jury verdict itself. Whether that bill of health would extend to a case where D's participatory basis went unspecified remains to be seen.

[16] There must *be* a principal, even if unidentified: cf. the commentary to *Bristow* [2013] EWCA Crim 1540, [2014] Crim LR 457, 461.

or (more rarely) because the possibility of secondary participation is excluded.[17] Secondly, there is no vicarious liability for the acts of secondary parties.[18]

§ 7.3 The principal

Before considering the varieties of secondary participation falling within section 8, it is necessary to make some observations regarding the participation of principal offenders. First, there may be more than one principal offender. If P and Q assault V by jointly raining blows on him, they are each principals. If V dies from the combination of blows, they will each be guilty of manslaughter or murder.[19] There are two ways in which multiple defendants may be held to be principals. First, each may separately satisfy all the required ingredients of the relevant offence. In the above example, P and Q are each independently guilty of an assault. Alternatively, each may separately satisfy *some* part of the actus reus for the offence where their actions, in combination, fulfil the complete actus reus requirement and each has the requisite mens rea. The latter is a true case of joint principals, in that it is sufficient for liability that each party does a part of the actus reus.[20]

Note, however, that there must be *some* contribution to the occurrence of the actus reus before one can be held to have committed the offence as a principal.[21] Thus, if S and P attack C in concert yet it is a particular blow by P that causes death independent of the effect of the earlier blows by S, then S cannot be convicted of murder as a principal and must be convicted as a secondary party. While the outcome may be the same (both are convicted of murder), the importance of this is that the actus reus and mens rea elements required to be proved in order to convict S as a secondary party are different from those required to convict P.

(i) Innocent agents

Sometimes the actus reus is not perpetrated personally by the defendant, but instead P arranges for it to be brought about by T, who is unaware of the significance of his actions. Where the defendant deliberately[22] *uses* an "innocent agent" to bring about the actus reus, the participation of the intervening actor is disregarded and the law treats the defendant as the principal.[23] Conceptually, it is as if P "stands in the shoes" of the innocent agent.

---

[17] See below, § 7.6(iv).

[18] *Ferguson* v. *Weaving* [1951] 1 KB 814.

[19] Cf. *Langman* v. *Valentine* [1952] 2 All ER 803 (joint drivers).

[20] E.g. *Bingley* (1821) Russ & Ry 446 (each forged part of a banknote); *Cornwall* (1730) 2 Str 881, 93 ER 914 (breaking and entering). See Lanham, "Complicity, Concert and Conspiracy" (1980) 4 *Crim LJ* 276.

[21] "The essential ingredient for joint principal offending is a contribution to the cause of the actus reus. If this is absent, the fact that there is a common purpose … cannot transform the offending into joint principal liability." *Gnango* [2011] UKSC 59, [2012] AC 827, para. 129 (Lord Kerr).

[22] Exceptionally, an actus reus brought about by an innocent agent may also be attributed to D if it resulted from D's negligence, when negligence is sufficient to establish mens rea: *Tessymond* (1828) 1 Lewin 169.

[23] For discussion, see Alldridge, "The Doctrine of Innocent Agency" (1990) 2 *Crim L Forum* 45; Williams, "Innocent Agency and Causation" (1992) 3 *Crim L Forum* 289; Alldridge, "Common Sense, Innocent Agency, and Causation" (1992) 3 *Crim L Forum* 299. By contrast, secondary liability is thought to depend upon the existence of a principal offender: a striking illustration is *Demirian* [1989] VR 97. This requirement is considered below, § 7.6(i).

An example is when the host at a party gives a waiter a glass of wine to take out to the victim, when only the host knows that the wine contains poison. Although the waiter gives the victim poison, he is merely an innocent agent and it is the host who is the perpetrator of the crime.[24]

The doctrine of innocent agency does not apply if the intervening agent is herself guilty of the offence; consequently, it is normally inapplicable to strict liability offences.[25] Further, it may only be invoked, and the agent can only be categorised as an *innocent* agent, either if she does not know that she is committing the actus reus or if she lacks criminal capacity, in particular through being insane[26] or an infant.[27]

There are also some crimes for which the doctrine is excluded altogether because, by the very nature of those crimes, direct perpetration of the crime is required of the principal offender. This will depend upon the interpretation of each particular offence, but in general such cases are of two types.

First, innocent agency is more likely to be excluded where the essence of the crime is specified *behaviour* by the criminal, rather than the bringing about of some *consequence*.[28] In bigamy, for example, it seems impossible to say that P has gone through a ceremony of marriage with V (the actus reus) when he has procured T to do so. The same is true for rape (notwithstanding the contrary decision in *Cogan and Leak*)[29], and for crimes such as careless driving[30] and driving with excess alcohol.[31] The doctrine of innocent agency operates only where it is possible for P to fulfil the elements of the actus reus by the instrument of some other person. That is straightforwardly done where the actus reus does not specify particular behaviour by the defendant. For example, in murder, which requires the causing of another's death, it is apt to view P as having killed V herself, even though she in fact procures the waiter to deliver the poison.[32] It is rather less easy to treat P as having done the actus reus personally when the gist of the wrong is T's actual conduct, rather than its consequence.

However, while the distinction may seem clear enough in principle, the question whether the conduct element of a particular offence requires P's direct, personal involvement can involve fine—indeed, seemingly arbitrary—distinctions. For instance, it is apparently

[24] Cf. *Anon* (1634) Kel 53, 84 ER 1079; *Johnson* (1805) 7 East 65, 103 ER 26; *Butcher* (1858) Bell 6, 169 ER 1145; *Butt* (1884) 15 Cox CC 56; *White* v. *Ridley* (1978) 140 CLR 342.

[25] Where, despite her innocence, the intervening agent is guilty of an offence, D should be convicted as a secondary party: *A-G's Reference (No. 1 of 1975)* [1975] QB 773; below, § 7.4(i)(d).

[26] *Tyler* (1838) 8 C & P 616, 173 ER 643—notwithstanding that the insane "innocent agent" in that case was the ringleader!

[27] *Manley* (1844) 1 Cox CC 104; *Mazeau* (1840) 9 C & P 676, 173 ER 1006.

[28] See the distinction made between behavioural, circumstantial, and consequential elements of the actus reus, above, § 4.

[29] [1976] QB 217; see the commentary in [1975] *Crim LR* 584. *Cogan and Leak* was followed by the Victorian Court of Appeal in *Hewitt* (1996) 84 A Crim R 440, but should now be explained on the basis of procurement: below, § 7.6(ii)(b).

[30] *Thornton* v. *Mitchell* [1940] 1 All ER 339, considered in *CLGP* § 129 n. 11. Cf. *Millward* [1994] Crim LR 527. Both cases are discussed in the text below, §§ 7.6(i), 7.6(ii)(b).

[31] Cf. *A-G's Reference (No. 1 of 1975)* [1975] QB 773, in which D secretly laced P's drink. (Note that the offence in that case was held to be one of strict liability, and that P was therefore guilty of committing the offence as a principal, notwithstanding his "innocence". D, in turn, was a secondary party.)

[32] Cf. *Butt* (1884) 15 Cox CC 56 (D guilty as principal of falsifying his employer's accounts by making a false statement to the employer's innocent bookkeeper).

possible to "enter" premises as a burglar through the agency of another;[33] but one cannot "buy" liquor on licensed premises unless personally present on those premises.[34] Thus the range of offences to which the innocent agent doctrine applies is somewhat uncertain.

Secondly, innocent agency is also excluded if P is not a member of the class of persons eligible to commit the offence as a principal. A typical example is an offence that can only be committed by a licensee. A useful illustration of this sort of offence, though not one involving innocent agency, is *Morris v. Tolman*:[35]

> D obtained a licence to use his vehicle on the highway. S, his employee, then used the vehicle for a purpose not covered by the licence. It was a statutory offence for the licensee to use the vehicle outside the terms of the licence.

On these facts, no offence was committed by either P or S. P had not used the vehicle himself (hence no actus reus by P). S had used the vehicle, but could not be guilty of the offence since he was not the licensee (hence no actus reus by S).

Suppose, instead, that by a trick S procures P, the innocent licensee, to use the vehicle outside the terms of the licence. Because he is not the licensee, S is incapable of committing the offence personally; therefore the innocent agency doctrine cannot apply and he cannot be convicted as principal. A crime will be committed in such cases only if the main offence is one of strict liability; in which case P is himself guilty as principal and S, in turn, is guilty as a secondary party who procures the offence.

(ii) Law Commission proposals

In its report on *Participation in Crime*, the Law Commission proposed to simplify and extend the doctrine of innocent agency. Summarising the proposals in the Commission's own terms,[36]

> "[S] would be liable for an offence as a principal offender if he or she intentionally caused P, an innocent agent, to commit the conduct element of an offence but P does not commit the offence because P:
> (1)   is under the age of 10 years;
> (2)   has a defence of insanity; or
> (3)   acts without the fault required to be convicted of the offence…."

The effect of the proposed statutory regime would have been to abolish the limitations we have noted at common law, where personal conduct by P is required to commit the offence, as in bigamy, or where only a limited class of persons can commit the offence as principal and where S is not within that class.[37] A simplification of this sort would have

---

[33] Hale 1 PC 555 (1736). Cf. *Brisac* (1803) 4 East 164, 102 ER 792 (conspiracy to cheat). By contrast, in *Pratt v. Martin* [1911] 2 KB 90, D was held not to have effected "entry" within the meaning of the Game Act 1831, s. 30, when he sent a dog onto land.

[34] Hence, in *Woby v. B and O* [1986] Crim LR 183, the two defendant minors, who had sent an adult into an off-licence to buy lager on their behalf, were ruled not to be guilty of "buying intoxicating liquor on licensed premises, being aged under 18 years" since they were not on the premises when they did so.

[35] [1923] 1 KB 166.

[36] Law Com. No. 305 (2007), para. 1.52.

[37] *Ibid.*, para. 4.9.

been welcome. The proposed regime would go beyond that, however, in as much as it would permit the conviction of S where P is *not* an innocent agent but acted with a lesser degree of mens rea than S envisaged and so is guilty of a lesser offence. In that situation, the proposals would make S guilty of the more serious offence.

Additionally, in order to secure the conviction of S in a case where the innocent agency doctrine is unavailable because the offence is one of strict liability (and so P is herself guilty of the offence), the Commission suggested the enactment of a distinct crime of "causing a no-fault offence".[38] It is questionable whether these further innovations are either necessary or desirable.[39] Moreover, the proposed mens rea requirements, which echo the proposals for secondary participation generally, are highly problematic.[40] Be that as it may, the recommendations have not been adopted by the legislature.

§ 7.4 Secondary parties who assist or encourage crime

Section 8 applies to persons who involve themselves in a crime by giving assistance or encouragement to its commission. The section mentions four varieties of conduct counting as secondary participation: aiding, abetting, counselling, and procuring. These are also standard categories of participation recognised at common law.[41] Because, as we shall see, the categories overlap, it appears that they include the actus reus of virtually any form of assistance, encouragement, or contribution toward a crime by the principal.

Historically, there was a fifth variety of secondary participation, sometimes called "joint enterprise", which arises through S's forming a *common unlawful purpose* with the principal. Following the now-leading Supreme Court decision in *Jogee*,[42] liability based on a common purpose is abolished. (This former ground of liability is outlined in § 7.5 below.)

(i) The conduct element

Although section 8 identifies four types of conduct constituting participation, it is not necessary in the charge to specify which type of conduct is relied on, and all four verbs may also be used together.[43] Indeed, to some extent the overlap in meanings between the words makes this a sensible practice,[44] and it is slightly artificial to analyse the terms as independent, alternative, actus reus elements. (The overlap is such that the Law Commission has proposed a simplification, by replacing the traditional language with "assisting or

---

[38] *Ibid.*, paras. 4.28–4.37; Draft Bill, cl. 5. This supplementary offence would be necessitated by the Law Commission's further proposal to reduce the forms of participation to assistance and encouragement, thereby removing the procurement route to conviction in such cases.

[39] For critical discussion, see Taylor, "Procuring, Causation, Innocent Agency and the Law Commission" [2008] *Crim LR* 32.

[40] Below, § 7.7.

[41] *Benford v. Sims* [1898] 2 QB 641.

[42] *Jogee* [2016] UKSC 8; *Ruddock* [2016] UKPC 7, [2016] 2 WLR 681.

[43] *Ferguson v. Weaving* [1951] KB 814.

[44] Albeit not a desirable one in cases where the evidence allows the particular form of participation to be specified: *Maxwell* [1978] 3 All ER 1140; *Gaughan* [1990] Crim LR 880.

encouraging".)[45] Nonetheless, each word has a different meaning,[46] and makes a particular contribution to the scope of participation covered by section 8. They will therefore be examined separately.

(a) Aiding

S aids P by assisting, helping, or giving material support to P in the commission of a crime.[47] There must be actual assistance: merely trying to help is not enough.[48] If S, knowing that P is going to rob a bank, plans to lend P her gun, she does not aid the offence if her car breaks down on the way over to P's house and P leaves to commit the robbery before S arrives. On the other hand, the assistance need not be substantial. If T acts as lookout for P during the bank robbery, he is a party to the robbery even should there be no need to give a warning.[49]

It is no longer necessary that the assistance should take place at the scene of the offence.[50] Traditionally, the common law divided secondary parties into two groups. Aiders and abettors were said to be "principals in the second degree", and distinguished from counsellors and procurers—"accessories before the fact"—by their actual or constructive presence *at the time* the offence is committed.[51] The division is now only of historical interest, and it seems that the requirement of presence for aiders and abettors, and conversely the requirement of absence for counsellors and procurers, has also disappeared.[52] This seems to follow from the Court of Appeal's instruction in *A-G's Reference (No. 1 of 1975)*[53] that the four terms are, in so far as possible, to be interpreted according to their ordinary meanings.

Neither is it required that the principal should be aware of the assistance, provided she is in fact assisted.[54] Suppose that P plans a robbery, intending to use her gun. The day before

---

[45]   Law Com. No. 305, *Participation in Crime* (2007) paras. 3.9–3.10. This move would necessitate separate provision for certain instances of procurement where S causes P to commit an offence: *ibid.*, part 4; above, § 7.3(ii).

[46]   As was pointed out by Lord Widgery CJ in *A-G's Reference (No. 1 of 1975)* [1975] 1 QB 773, 779. The Chief Justice's view is a departure from traditional learning (cf. criticism by Smith, "Aid, Abet, Counsel, or Procure" in Glazebrook (ed.), *Reshaping the Criminal Law* (1978) 120, 125). It is submitted that the modern view is now to be preferred, given that traditional distinctions between aiders and abetters (present at the time of the offence) and counsellors and procurers (accessories before the fact) is no longer of legal effect. See below, § 7.4(i)(a).

[47]   E.g. *Bainbridge* [1960] 1 QB 129 (supplying oxygen cutting equipment for use in a burglary); *Stansfeld & Co v. Andrews* (1909) 22 Cox 84 (supplying beer for illegal sale).

[48]   See Smith, "Secondary Participation and Inchoate Offences" in Tapper (ed.), *Crime, Proof and Punishment* (1981) 21, 36–9. Cf. *A-G v. Able* [1984] 1 QB 795, 812 (Woolf J): no offence unless the reader "was assisted or encouraged by so reading the booklet to take or attempt to take his own life, otherwise the alleged offender cannot be guilty of more than an attempt". Note that there is no general offence of attempting to aid another to commit a crime: Criminal Law Act 1977, s. 1(4)(b).

[49]   "The assistance given, however, need not contribute to the criminal result in the sense that but for it the result would not have ensued. It is quite sufficient if it facilitated a result that would have transpired without it": *State v. Tally* 102 Ala 25, 15 So 722 (1894). Cf. *Gogerly* (1818) R & R 343, 168 ER 836.

[50]   *Blakely* v. *DPP* [1991] RTR 405, 411; *Thambiah* v. *R.* [1966] AC 37 (PC).

[51]   *Ferguson* v. *Weaving* [1951] 1 KB 814, 819; *Bowker* v. *Premier Drug Co* [1928] 1 KB 217. "Constructive" presence tended to be interpreted broadly. It included any assistance rendered while the offence was being carried out, even if such assistance was from afar—compare *State* v. *Tally* 102 Ala 25, 15 So 722 (1894); as well as being near enough to render assistance if called upon, cf. *Betts* (1930) 22 Cr App R 148. For discussion, see Smith, "Aid, Abet, Counsel, or Procure" in Glazebrook (ed.), *Reshaping the Criminal Law* (1978) 120, 125f; *CLGP* § 120.

[52]   Compare *A-G v. Able* [1984] 1 QB 795, where advice given in advance was regarded as within the scope of aiding and abetting, with *Bainbridge* [1960] 1 QB 129, where it was treated as counselling or procuring.

[53]   [1975] QB 773, 779 (Lord Widgery CJ).

[54]   Cf. *Fury* [2006] EWCA Crim 1258, para. 15; *Kupferberg* (1918) 13 Cr App R 166, 168. *Per* Turner, *Russell on Crime* (12th ed., 1964) 147, "it is quite possible for a complete stranger to be guilty of aiding and abetting a crime

the robbery takes place, S notices that P's gun is missing from its drawer. Without telling P, he places his own gun, a similar model, in the drawer for P to use instead. P carries out the robbery using S's gun. In this case S has aided P and is a party to the robbery even though P is ignorant of S's contribution. A well-known illustration is the American case of *State* v. *Tally*.[55] Judge Tally, whose brothers-in-law were pursuing and planning to kill V, prevented a third party from warning V of the danger, thereby making it easier for the pursuers to kill V. Tally was guilty of aiding murder, notwithstanding that his brothers-in-law were unaware of the assistance.[56]

(b) Abetting

In terms of its dictionary definition, "to abet" means to incite by aid, to instigate, or to encourage. In practice, because of its overlap with the other forms of participation in section 8, abetment is typically associated with encouragement.[57] Even so, there is extensive overlap with other forms of participation in crime. For example, in cases where S is alleged to "assist" P by offering support (e.g. as a lookout) on which P relies, the reliance itself may be sufficient encouragement for P to be abetted, whether or not any assistance is in fact provided. Similarly, encouragement of P to commit an offence is likely also to constitute counselling.[58]

Whether S's actions constitute encouragement is always a question of fact,[59] and there are no specified forms of qualifying behaviour. The encouragement may be by words[60] or conduct—nodding one's head in endorsement of a crime may be just as effective as a verbal indication of agreement. Indeed, mere presence may constitute abetment where that presence supplies an incentive to the principal to go ahead. For example, in *Coney*[61] it was said that attendance at an illegal prizefight might be evidence of abetting battery by the fighters, since, as Mathew J observed:[62]

> "The chief incentive to the wretched combatants to fight on until (as happens too often) dreadful injuries have been inflicted and life endangered or sacrificed, is the presence of spectators watching with keen interest every incident of the fight."

---

committed by a principal offender who does not even know that he is being aided". This passage was approved by Martin JA in *Hobart* v. *R.* (1982) 25 CR (3d) 214, 236 (Ont CA).

[55] 102 Ala 25, 15 So 722 (1894).

[56] See also *Larkins* v. *Police* [1987] 2 NZLR 282, where S spontaneously decided to act as lookout during a robbery. *Per* Eichelbaum J (at 290), "the appellant's action in providing the principal offenders with, as counsel put it, an extra pair of eyes was at least evidence of actual assistance regardless whether those offenders were aware of its availability".

[57] Cf. *Clarkson* [1971] 3 All ER 344.

[58] In fact, at common law the main difference between abetting and counselling was merely the timing of the encouragement. If it occurred prior to the crime, S would be an "accessory before the fact" (counsellor or procurer) rather than a "principal in the second degree" (abettor or aider). See, e.g., the discussion in *A-G* v. *Able* [1984] QB 795, 809.

[59] *Stringer* [2011] EWCA Crim 1396, [2012] QB 160, para. 51.

[60] *Royce* (1767) 4 Burr 2073, 2082, 98 ER 81, 86.

[61] (1882) 8 QBD 534.

[62] *Ibid.*, 544 (dissenting).

Simply by watching, S may encourage the fighters. (Although, as we shall see below, the mens rea requirement means that S must also *intend* this result.[63]) Similarly, joining P in a chase after V could amount to encouraging P's use of violence against V when they caught up with him.[64]

However, such cases are exceptional, because it is necessary to show that S did *in fact* communicate encouragement to P.[65] A good illustration of this principle is *Clarkson*.[66] Two soldiers, hearing noises emanating from a room at their barracks, entered the room where they found other soldiers raping a young woman. The two remained in the room to watch. Apparently, they neither did nor said anything, either to encourage or discourage continuance of the rape. The Court of Appeal quashed their convictions for aiding and abetting, because the Judge-advocate had not clearly stated that it must be proved the appellants intended to and did encourage commission of the crime. While the Court acknowledged it was possible that the rapists *might* in fact have received encouragement from the appellants' presence,[67] that encouragement had to be proved. Mere presence *which does not by itself encourage* is insufficient: "[t]here must be an intention to encourage; and there must also be encouragement in fact".[68] Edmund Davies J, giving the judgment of the Court of Criminal Appeal in *Allan*, stated the point as follows:[69]

> "In our judgment, before a jury can properly convict an accused person of being a principal in the second degree to an affray, they must be convinced by the evidence that, at the very least, he by some means or other encouraged the participants. To hold otherwise would be, in effect, as counsel for the appellants rightly expressed it, to convict a man on his thoughts, unaccompanied by any physical act other than the fact of his mere presence."

In practice, therefore, the inference of encouragement will usually require something further, such as proof of some additional action by S (e.g. words or gestures) or of a particular circumstance that implies support,[70] for example that P and S are members of the same gang or that S's presence is pursuant to some prior arrangement.[71] Alternatively, as in

---

[63] It is submitted that this point was not taken sufficiently seriously by the Supreme Court in the bizarre case of *Gnango* [2011] UKSC 59, [2012] 1 AC 827. S and P engaged in a (perhaps spontaneous) shoot-out, during which V, a passer-by, was killed by one of P's stray bullets. Upholding S's conviction, the Court reasoned (*inter alia*) that S encouraged P to fire the shot (at S) that killed V. But did S intend to encourage P in this way? For criticism, see Buxton, "Being an Accessory to One's Own Murder" [2012] *Crim LR* 275, 276–8; Sullivan, "Accessories and Principals after *Gnango*" in Reed and Bohlander (eds.), *Participation in Crime: Domestic and Comparative Perspectives* (2013) 37, 43–6.

[64] *Stringer* [2011] EWCA Crim 1396, [2012] QB 160.

[65] "It is, however, important to make clear to juries that mere approval of (ie 'assent' to, or 'concurrence' in) the offence by a bystander who gives no assistance, does not without more amount to aiding." *Robinson* [2011] UKPC 3, para. 14. Cf. *Coney* (1882) 8 QBD 534; *Young* (1838) 8 C & P 644, 173 ER 655; *Atkinson* (1869) 11 Cox CC 330; below, §§ 7.4(ii), (iii).

[66] [1971] 3 All ER 344.

[67] *Ibid.*, 347a.

[68] *Ibid.*, 348. Cf. *Smith* v. *Baker* [1971] RTR 350. (S, a passenger, does not abet driving without insurance merely by sitting in the car. For cases where S also owns the car, see below, § 7.3(iii).)

[69] [1965] 1 QB 130, 138.

[70] See also *Wilcox* v. *Jeffery* [1951] 1 All ER 464, where S attended a concert by Coleman Hawkins in his capacity as a jazz critic and, further, paid a fee to attend. The concert was unlawful since Hawkins was an American who did not have a work permit. S was held to have abetted P's contravention of the Aliens Order 1920: "his presence and his payment to go there was an encouragement" (at 466 *per* Lord Goddard CJ).

[71] E.g. *Smith* v. *Reynolds* [1986] *Crim LR* 559 (presence pursuant to a prior agreement).

Coney (above), it may be sufficient that S is part of a group offering encouragement, and that P is aware of the group's behaviour, albeit unaware of S's individual conduct.

Indeed, there could even be situations where the presence of a particular individual—say, a trusted confidant or a superior officer—reassures and encourages P's commission of a crime. This is not to say that their *mere* presence constitutes abetment: it does not.[72] But the additional consideration that, say, S is someone in whom P places great faith may suffice to establish the required encouragement, and the question remains one of fact for each case.

By contrast with aid, which can be rendered to P without P's knowledge (above, § 7.4(i)(a)), it is essential that the encouragement be communicated successfully to P. There cannot be "encouragement in fact" by S unless P knows of it. Suppose, for example, that S knows P intends to commit a robbery. S posts a letter to P in which she encourages P to commit the robbery, but the letter is never delivered. On these facts alone, S cannot be a party to the robbery because her encouragement, although offered, is not received by P.[73]

This point, which applies also to incitement and counselling, is considered further below (§ 7.4(ii)). But it is important to emphasise that the requirement, that S's encouragement be communicated to P, is not a requirement that the encouragement had any effect upon P, by inducing him to commit the offence. It is unnecessary to show that P would not have offended but for the encouragement, or even that P was in any way influenced by it. P must be aware of his being encouraged (the encouragement must be communicated), but it need not make a difference.[74]

(c) Counselling

"Counselling" has two varieties of meaning. First, it includes the provision of advice or information,[75] though such conduct may also amount to aiding or abetting.[76] Alternatively, counselling may contemplate "urging" someone to commit an offence[77]—in which sense the overlap is with abetting and, to a lesser extent, procuring. In this second context, counselling may also constitute the inchoate offence of incitement (below, § 9.1).

(d) Procuring

By contrast with the other varieties of secondary participation, procurement of an offence requires that the secondary party deliberately *induces* or *influences* the principal to commit the offence. Therefore the requisite connection between S and the commission of the

---

[72] As was emphasised in *Willett* [2010] EWCA Crim 1620 (brother).

[73] Cf. *Stringer* [2011] EWCA Crim 1396, [2012] QB 160, para. 49.

[74] Cf. *Wilcox* v. *Jeffery* [1951] 1 All ER 464. This proposition appears to be accepted in *Stringer* [2011] EWCA Crim 1396, [2012] QB 160, paras. 49–50. Although the Court states that such encouragement will be "treated" as "materially contributing to the commission of the offence", there is no need to prove a material contribution as such.

[75] A classic example is *Baker* (1909) 28 NZLR 536, where S wrote to P with advice how to break into a safe using explosives. The case is criticised by Williams, *CLGP* § 125, but only on the issue of mens rea.

[76] Cf. *A-G* v. *Able* [1984] QB 795, 809, where it was noted that "[i]gnorance how to commit suicide must by itself be a deterrent.... The contents of the booklet provide information as to methods which are less likely to result in an unsuccessful attempt. This assistance must encourage some readers to commit or attempt to commit suicide."

[77] *Calhaem* [1985] QB 808; cf. *Stuart* v. *R.* (1976) 134 CLR 426.

offence must be rather stronger than for aiding, abetting, or counselling. By contrast with those other terms, which require only that S play some part in the crime:[78]

> "To procure means to produce by endeavour. You procure a thing by setting out to see that it happens and taking the appropriate steps to produce that happening."

Thus the perpetration of the principal crime must in some sense be a consequence of the procurement by S.[79] However, S's contribution need not be a decisive or *sine qua non* ingredient of the decision by P to commit the offence: it is enough that the procurement was influential. Even if there were other reasons why, without S's contribution, P might have chosen to commit the offence anyway, that does not matter. Provided that S's conduct in fact played some part in influencing P, S will be guilty of procurement.[80]

Normally, procurement by S will take the form of persuasion, inducement, or threats. Sometimes, however, the causation element of a procurement may operate without influencing P's reasons; indeed, P may be entirely ignorant of S's role. In cases where an offence can be committed without mens rea, and the innocent agent doctrine does not apply,[81] S may become a secondary party to an offence by causing P to commit it. In *A-G's Reference (No. 1 of 1975)* [82] S secretly laced the drinks of P, who was subsequently convicted of driving with excess alcohol (a strict liability offence). S was guilty of procuring the offence.

(ii) The need for a connection

Secondary liability is derived from S's *involvement* in the principal offence, and not merely her attempt to become involved. It follows that S's conduct must somehow be connected to the commission of the offence by P. As we have seen, in the case of aiding this requirement is manifested by the need to demonstrate that assistance of some sort *was in fact* provided to P; in the case of procuring, it is reflected in the need to show a link of influence or inducement between S's conduct and perpetration of the offence. A link must also exist for abetting and counselling. Although causation need not be shown (otherwise S would normally be a principal),[83] a sufficient degree of connection between S's conduct and the actus reus

---

[78] *A-G's Reference (No. 1 of 1975)* [1975] QB 773. See also *Millward* [1994] Crim LR 527; *Beck* [1985] 1 WLR 22; *Reed* [1982] Crim LR 819; *Broadfoot* [1976] 3 All ER 753; *Bryce* [2004] EWCA Crim 1231.

[79] See the summary by Smith, "Aid, Abet, Counsel, or Procure" in Glazebrook (ed.), *Reshaping the Criminal Law* (1978) 120, 134.

[80] For a civil law illustration see *Barton v. Armstrong* [1976] AC 104, 121 (execution of deed voidable for duress, even though P had other reasons to execute the deed apart from D's threat): "the illegitimate means used was a reason (not the reason, nor the predominant reason nor the clinching reason) why the complainant acted as he did. We are also prepared to accept that a decisive answer is not obtainable by asking the question whether the contract would have been made even if there had been no threats because, even if the answer to this question is affirmative, that does not prove that the contract was not made because of the threats."

[81] Above, § 7.3(i).

[82] [1975] QB 773. The decision has considerable untapped potential for the liability of hosts and publicans: see below, § 7.4(iv)(a).

[83] Cf. the discussion in *Luffman and Briscoe* [2008] EWCA Crim 1739. The Court of Appeal retreats on this point in *Stringer* [2011] EWCA Crim 1396, [2012] QB 160, paras. 47ff, from its earlier suggestion in *Mendez v. R* [2010] EWCA Crim 516, [2011] QB 876, para. 18 that "secondary liability is founded on a principle of causation". Gardner argues for a causal relationship but in a very attenuated sense rarely encountered in legal discourse: "Complicity and Causality" (2007) 1 *Crim L & Phil* 127. Cf. Sullivan, "First Degree Murder and Complicity" (2007) 1 *Crim L & Phil* 271.

of P's offence must be proved. It must be established by the prosecution that the principal *received* encouragement, urging, or advice, before S's conduct may count as participation falling within section 8.[84]

This point is fundamental to the nature of secondary participation. Derivative liability is *not* a form of inchoate liability. Liability is not based on S's act of encouragement (for example) *per se*, as it is in inchoate offences such as incitement. Rather, it is derived from S's *participation in* the offence perpetrated by P. If P is not aware of the encouragement, urging, or advice, S necessarily fails to participate in the commission of the offence. In such a case, S cannot be a party to its commission.

The result is the same if the encouragement was so long ago that P has forgotten about it by the time she resolves to commit the offence, in which case S will not be a party to the offence.[85] This type of "forgotten advice" case is covered by a further *connection-based* requirement, suggested in the extraordinary case of *Calhaem*:[86] P must not only be aware of S's encouragement (for example), but he must also act in accordance with, or within the scope of,[87] the endorsement provided by S's encouragement. The Court of Appeal provided the following illustration:[88]

> "For example, if the principal offender happened to be involved in a football riot in the course of which he laid about him with a weapon of some sort and killed someone who, unknown to him, was the person whom he had been counselled to kill, he would not, in our view, have been acting within the scope of his authority; he would have been acting outside it, albeit what he had done was what he had been counselled to do."

This is not to require that the encouragement, counselling, etc., actually "made a difference" in influencing P to commit the offence. As Woolf J stated in *A-G v. Able*, "it does not make any difference that the person [counselled] would have tried to commit suicide anyway".[89] P must have received and been aware of, say, encouragement by S, but the encouragement need not have played any further role.

(iii) Omissions

S may aid or abet an offence by omission.[90] Most obviously, this may occur where S's failure to discharge a legal duty assists P to commit an offence: for example, when the security guard at a warehouse deliberately fails to lock a door, intending that P may readily gain entry into the building and steal some of the goods stored inside.

---

[84] *Clarkson* [1971] 3 All ER 344 (abetting); *Calhaem* [1985] QB 808 (counselling). Cf. Smith, "Aid, Abet, Counsel, or Procure" in Glazebrook (ed.), *Reshaping the Criminal Law* (1978) 120, 131–4.

[85] Cf. *A-G v. Able* [1984] 1 QB 795.

[86] [1985] QB 808. S had hired P to murder her rival V. It was said that P, after having second thoughts, had decided not to kill V but went to V's house in order to act out a pretence so that both S and V would think an attempt had been made to kill V. However, after V screamed, P apparently went "berserk" and killed V by hitting her several times with a hammer. On these facts, the Court of Appeal upheld S's conviction for counselling murder.

[87] See also the discussion in § 7.4(iv)(c) (Other variations within a type).

[88] *Ibid.*, 813. The connection is "a matter of fact and degree": *Jogee* [2016] UKSC 8; *Ruddock* [2016] UKPC 7, para. 12.

[89] *A-G v. Able* [1984] 1 QB 795, 812.

[90] Sullivan, "Conduct and Complicity: Liability Based on Omission and Risk" (2008) 39 *Cambrian LR* 687.

Rather more problematic are cases where a person is held liable as a party for omitting to interfere and prevent an offence when she has a duty to do so and/or a power of control over the principal or the victim, together with an opportunity to exercise that duty or power.[91] Standard examples of this variety of abetment are said to occur if a parent permits another to commit an offence against her child, or if the owner of a car, while sitting in the passenger seat, permits the driver to break the law. However, these are not the same type of case.

Consider, first, the case where S, a parent, permits another to inflict fatal injuries upon his child when he is in a position to prevent the assault from taking place. It is sometimes suggested that such a person would be party to a culpable homicide if, by not intervening, S encouraged (and—the mens rea element—intended to encourage) the principal offender.[92] As far as secondary liability is concerned, this seems to understate the position. It is submitted that where S has (i) a legal duty and (ii) the present ability[93] to prevent V's death, his failure to do so, *in itself*, constitutes *aiding*, and not merely evidence of encouragement.[94] (Hence there would be no need to show an additional intention thereby to encourage P's crime.) The case is analogous to that of the warehouse security guard (above); in both examples, the conduct would be aiding whether or not P knew of the decision by S to refrain from performing his duty.[95]

Indeed, arguably S is not merely a secondary party; he may be independently guilty as a principal. Provided his intervention would have been causally efficacious in preventing the actus reus from occurring, it seems open to conclude that death results from his culpable failure to discharge his duty as a parent to intervene,[96] in which case this is a plain case of direct liability for murder or manslaughter resulting from his omission to perform a legal duty.[97]

At the other end of the scale is the case where S, a stranger, chances upon the commission of a crime and remains to watch. As we have noted already, such facts by themselves are insufficient to make S a party to the crime. This point is illustrated by *Clarkson*,[98] which was discussed in § 7.4(i)(b). Two soldiers entered a room where a rape was taking place.

---

[91] The duty or power is not sufficient by itself; it must be proved that S had an opportunity to intervene: *Webster* [2006] EWCA Crim 415, [2006] 2 Cr App R 6, paras. 27–9.

[92] E.g. *Foreman and Ford* [1988] Crim LR 677 (police officer); *Witika* (1991) 7 CRNZ 621(CA); *Nixon* (1990) 57 CCC (3d) 97, 109–10; cf. *Witika* [1993] 2 NZLR 424 (CA). For discussion, see Finn, "Culpable Non-Intervention: Reconsidering the Basis for Party Liability by Omission" (1994) 18 *Crim LJ* 90.

[93] Cf. *Webster* [2006] EWCA Crim 314, [2006] 2 Cr App R 6; *Tilley* [2009] EWCA Crim 1426, [2010] 1 WLR 605 ("allows").

[94] This appears to be the analysis in *Russell* [1933] VLR 59, 66 (Cussen ACJ), 76 (Mann J) (Vic SC); *Popen* (1981) 60 CCC (2d) 232 (Ont CA). Cf. *Rubie v. Faulkner* [1940] 1 KB 571; *Russell and Russell* (1987) 85 Cr App R 388.

[95] Although in *Russell* [1933] VLR 59, 67, Cussen ACJ suggests the spouse must have known of S's acquiescence. R's wife drowned herself and their sons in R's presence, wherefore R was convicted of manslaughter. See above, § 4.1(i)(b) (Case 2).

[96] This would require analysis of the case as involving concurrent causes (i.e. P's action and S's omission), rather than a novus actus by P. Yet such an approach seems plausible, provided that S is able to prevent P's conduct.

[97] See the judgment of McArthur J in *Russell* [1933] VLR 59. The existence of such a duty is discussed above, § 4.1(i)(b) (Case 2). The failure of household member to prevent a child's death may also be an offence, committed directly as principal, of causing or allowing the death of a child or vulnerable adult, contrary to s. 5 of The Domestic Violence, Crime and Victims Act 2004. See below, § 10.8.

[98] [1971] 3 All ER 344.

They stayed to observe the events, purportedly without either encouraging or discouraging commission of the offence. The Court of Appeal quashed their convictions for aiding and abetting. In the absence of actual and intended encouragement, their failure to intervene attracted no criminal liability, since they were under no duty to intervene.

The difficult case arises when S is not under a duty but has a specific legal power to control P's activity. Consider the facts of *Du Cros* v. *Lambourne*.[99] S was the owner of a car that had been driven dangerously, but it was not clear whether S or his companion, P, was driving at the time. Nonetheless, S was convicted of being a party to dangerous driving, it being irrelevant whether he was principal or abettor. If P was driving, S had the legal power as owner to direct the manner in which P drove; his acquiescence in the manner of P's driving was therefore held to constitute abetment of the offence of dangerous driving.

Du Cros v. *Lambourne* was regarded by the Court of Appeal in *Webster* as authority that failure by S to exercise a legal *power* (not duty) of control over P's activity may be, without more, constitutive of secondary participation in crime:[100]

> "*Du Cros v Lambourne* [1907] 1 KB 40 establishes that a defendant might be convicted of aiding abetting dangerous driving if the driver drives dangerously in the owner's presence and with the owner's consent and approval. The owner was in control and ought to have prevented or attempted to prevent the driver driving in a dangerous manner."

In other words, there is no need to show that S's non-intervention actually assisted or encouraged P. However, the judgments in *Du Cros* are in fact equivocal on the point,[101] and the point was *obiter* in *Webster*, where it was not established that the owner-passenger had any opportunity to intervene. Moreover, in *Cassady* v. *Reg. Morris Transport Ltd* it was held that an employer's failure to forbid an offence by its employee was merely *evidence* (and not constitutive) of encouragement.[102] Thus, strictly speaking, it remains open for a defendant to argue that where D has a mere power, not only must there be a failure to intervene, but the non-intervention must in fact encourage (and be intended to encourage) P in her commission of the offence.[103] Support for that conclusion can also be found in a number of possession cases, usually involving drugs or counterfeit goods. Suppose that D lives with E, who keeps contraband on the premises. While a cohabitee may well have a power to demand that contraband be removed from the shared premises, the courts have required more than the mere power to establish either that D herself jointly possesses the goods (i.e. commits the offence as principal) or that she aids and abets E to do so. Thus D must do

---

[99] [1907] 1 KB 40. See generally on this topic Smith, *A Modern Treatise on the Law of Criminal Complicity* (1991) 39ff.

[100] *Webster* [2006] EWCA Crim 415, [2006] 2 Cr App R 6, para. 28.

[101] Darling J appears to have regarded non-intervention as abetment *per se* ([1907] 1 KB 40, 46–7); Lord Alverstone CJ, with whom Ridley J agreed, refused to "attempt to lay down any general rule or principle, but having regard to these findings of fact, it is, in my opinion, impossible to say that there was in this case no evidence of aiding and abetting" (at 46). It appears that in *Webster* the matter was not subject to argument from counsel.

[102] [1975] RTR 470. Cf. *Duxley* v. *Gilmore* (1959) 123 JP 331, but contrast *Ferguson* v. *Weaving* [1951] 1 KB 814, 819; *Thomas* v. *Lindop* [1950] 1 All ER 966, 968.

[103] Cf. *Martin* [2010] EWCA Crim 1450, para. 32 ("D intended to assist or encourage P to drive in this manner and D did in fact by his presence and failure to intervene encourage P to drive dangerously").

something *more* than simply acquiesce. Sir John Smith's commentary to *McNamara* help-fully summarises the position:[104]

> "The evidence must be sufficient to satisfy a jury either that each party was in possession … or that someone [else] was and the defendant not only knew that he was but also assisted or encouraged him."

Hence in *Bland*,[105] where D was living with a drug-dealer, her conviction as an accomplice was quashed notwithstanding that she knew of his activities.

In any event, the gulf between specific power and duty is easily bridged. Where S has a supervisory role, e.g. as the instructor of a learner-driver, it seems clear that a mere omis-sion to intervene is sufficient to establish liability as a secondary party, and that the instruc-tor is under a *duty* (and does not merely have a right) to intervene and prevent a dangerous manoeuvre by the learner-driver.[106] And in *Tuck* v. *Robson*,[107] a public house licensee was held to have assisted others in drinking after hours through "passive assistance", which the Court defined as "presence with no steps being taken to enforce his right either to eject the customers or at any rate to revoke their licence to be on the premises".[108] The decision is problematic: although the Court relied upon the publican's "right" (i.e. power) and did not use the language of duties, the decision effectively imposes a duty on the publican to revoke his customers' licence. Seemingly, that duty rests on nothing other than the existence of a corresponding power.

In light of these cases, it appears that the current law regarding omissions is as follows:

(i)   If S has a *legal duty* to prevent an offence (e.g. in the case of a parent to protect his child), then a failure by S to take reasonable steps to intervene *in itself* constitutes the actus reus of aiding and abetting. (Indeed, if causation can be established, S may be guilty as a principal.)

(ii) If S has neither a duty nor a particular power, then he must intend by his non-intervention to encourage P, and, in fact, his inaction must also communicate encouragement to P.

(iii) If S has a specific power of control over P, but no particular legal duty, it seems that the position is the same as in (i): a failure by S to take reasonable steps to intervene *in itself* constitutes the actus reus of aiding and abetting.

That said, the matter is finely balanced. If, in future, *Cassady* v. *Reg. Morris Transport Ltd* came to be seen as representing the better view, the position of those such as the owner-passenger in (iii) would be identical in law to that in (ii), i.e. the owner-passenger would be in the same legal position as the onlookers to the rape in *Clarkson*, or the casual spectators at the prizefight in *Coney*.[109] (Of course, in that event the existence of a power of control

---

[104] [1998] Crim LR 278; a summary endorsed in *Kousar* [2009] EWCA Crim 139, [2009] 2 Cr App R 5, para. 16, where D was charged as a principal; above, § 5.6(iv).

[105] (1987) 151 JP 857, [1988] Crim LR 41.

[106] *Rubie* v. *Faulkner* [1940] 1 KB 571, 575: "[f]or him to refrain from doing anything when he could see that an unlawful act was about to be done, and his duty was to prevent an unlawful act if he could, was for him to aid and abet". See also *Harris* [1964] Crim LR 54; Wasik, "A Learner's Careless Driving" [1982] *Crim LR* 411; Lanham, "Drivers, Control, and Accomplices" [1982] *Crim LR* 419.

[107] [1970] 1 All ER 1171.

[108] *Ibid.*, 1175.

[109] (1882) 8 QBD 534.

would remain potentially relevant to an allegation that, by her acquiescence, S *in fact* encouraged P. Even though, under the approach in *Cassady* v. *Reg. Morris Transport Ltd*, it would not constitute abetment in law, known acquiescence by an authoritative figure could still be the "something further" that supports the inference of encouragement required for such cases.[110])

There are arguments in favour of *Cassady*, arguments strong enough to convince the Law Commission.[111] To impose liability in such cases is, effectively, to extend criminal liability for omissions. As we saw in § 4.1, the law is reluctant to impose liability for omissions, and for good reason. Forcing persons to intervene and regulate the actions of others (e.g. requiring property-owners to police the actions of users) substantially widens the scope of criminal responsibility for wrongdoing and, in turn, risks intruding severely upon the autonomy of citizens.[112] This point is particularly significant when one takes into account the fact that *everyone* has a power to control the criminal activities of others, by virtue of section 3(1) of the Criminal Law Act 1967.[113] If a mere power were sufficient to make S an accomplice, then anyone, stranger or friend, who is in position to intervene to prevent a crime would become an accessory to that crime. *That*, surely, cannot be allowed, since it would entirely subvert the policy of the law against generally criminalising omissions.

On the other hand, in the difficult case, S is not a mere stranger, a passer-by who stumbles upon a crime that she is under no duty to prevent. An important distinction can be drawn between the background general power to prevent crimes, under section 3(1) of the Criminal Law Act 1967, and the more specific powers of control at issue in cases such as *Du Cros* v. *Lambourne*: it is only in the latter cases that S is entitled to control P's activity *whether or not* an offence is being committed. Although there is no general obligation to prevent crime,[114] it seems reasonable to conclude that those with specific legal powers to prevent a crime *do* contribute to—hence, participate in—the wrongdoing by refraining from exercising their authority and, thus, permitting that crime to occur.

As with active forms of secondary participation, the omission to intervene must occur at a time when S also has the requisite mens rea—i.e., as we see below, knowledge of the essential matters of P's crime. In the specific context of omissions, however, it is worth re-emphasising that S's knowledge must arise at a point when she has an opportunity to intervene. Mere knowledge of P's misconduct is not enough if it is too late for S to prevent it.

(iv) Mens rea for participation by assistance or encouragement

The mens rea for secondary participation (by aiding, abetting, counselling, or procuring) is intention: S must intend to participate in (help; encourage; procure) the crime committed by P.[115] Stated in this way, the fault element appears straightforward. However, it is in fact

---

[110]   Above, § 7.4(i)(b).

[111]   Law Com. No. 305, *Participation in Crime* (2007) paras. 3.39–41, citing the second edition of this book.

[112]   For elaboration of this argument, see above, §§ 4.1(i)(a), 1.2(i)(b), 1.2(ii)(e). See also Bronitt, "Defending *Giorgianni*—Part Two: New Solutions for Old Problems in Complicity" (1993) 17 *Crim LJ* 305, 310–11.

[113]   "A person may use such force as is reasonable in the circumstances in the prevention of crime, or in effecting or assisting in the lawful arrest of offenders or suspected offenders or of persons unlawfully at large."

[114]   Cf. *Allan* [1965] 1 QB 130.

[115]   *Jogee* [2016] UKSC 8; *Ruddock* [2016] UKPC 7, [2016] 2 WLR 681, para. 9. See generally Dennis, "The Mental Element for Accessories" in P. Smith (ed.), *Criminal Law: Essays in Honour of J.C. Smith* (1987) 40;

quite complex, because the mens rea element must relate to two different matters: S's own conduct, in assisting or encouraging P, and the fact that P's actions are criminal in nature. We may summarise the mens rea requirement as follows:

(i)   S must intend his own contribution (i.e. to aid, abet, counsel, or procure P); and

(ii) S must appreciate the nature of P's actions. That is, S must know about the "essential matters" relating to P's actions which make those actions an offence.

(a) S's own contribution: the intention to aid, abet, counsel or procure

Although section 8 itself is silent on the question of mens rea, it is clear that the essence of aiding and abetting is intentional help or encouragement. This means that not only must S intend her actions, but she must also act with the intent thereby to aid, abet, counsel, or procure P's conduct.[116] (Moreover, this requirement counts as a specific intention requirement for the purposes of the voluntary intoxication rules.[117])

The criteria of intention are considered above, in § 5.1. In the context of secondary parties, there is no requirement for S to desire that P commit the offence she aids (abets, etc.). It is the *assistance* or the *encouragement*, not the ultimate crime, that must be intended by S.[118] Consider, for example, the following facts, which are based on *Cafferata v. Wilson*:[119]

> Stephen is a firearms wholesaler. He sells a firearm to Pamela, a general shopkeeper. Stephen knows that Pamela will re-sell the firearm in her shop, and that Pamela does not have a licence to deal in firearms. Stephen does not sell the firearm to Pamela because he wants her to resell it, but rather because he wants the money that Pamela is prepared to pay for it.

The claim that Stephen does not want or intend Pamela to resell the firearm is irrelevant. It may be characterised as a claim about Stephen's motive, or ultimate purpose, which is of course to make money. But what matters is whether he intended to assist Pamela. The answer to that question is, yes: Stephen intended to provide Pamela with an ingredient essential to the selling of a firearm. It is this facilitation, not the ultimate offence, that must be intended; whether that aid is itself rendered for the further purpose of bringing about the offence is simply beside the point. Indeed, any requirement that the *offence* must be intended would deprive secondary liability of much of its current scope.

K. J. M. Smith, *A Modern Treatise on Criminal Complicity* (1991) part II; Sullivan, "Intent, Purpose and Complicity" [1988] *Crim LR* 641; Dennis, "Intention and Complicity: A Reply" [1988] *Crim LR* 649.

[116] For criticism of the Supreme Court's failure to consider this requirement in *Gnango* [2011] UKSC 59, [2012] 1 AC 827, see Buxton, "Being an Accessory to One's Own Murder" [2012] *Crim LR* 275, 276–8.

[117] *McNamara* [2009] EWCA Crim 2530; below, § 18.3.

[118] See *Bryce* [2004] EWCA Crim 1231, at [61], citing this proposition from the first edition. Cf. *National Coal Board* v. *Gamble* [1959] 1 QB 11, 23; *Lynch* v. *DPP for Northern Ireland* [1975] AC 653, 678; *A-G* v. *Able* [1984] 1 QB 795; *Clarke* (1984) 80 Cr App R 344; *Jogee* [2016] UKSC 8; *Ruddock* [2016] UKPC 7, [2016] 2 WLR 681, para. 10. Note that the connection is necessarily tighter in cases of participation by procurement. S must similarly be proved to have intended his act of procurement; however, because procurement requires a causal contribution that influences or induces P to commit the crime, it follows that S must intend to help bring it about that P will commit the crime itself. For this reason, it was said in *A-G's Reference (No. 1 of 1975)* [1975] QB 773, 779 that, by contrast with aiding, abetting, or counselling, procuring an offence requires an "endeavour" or "setting out" to cause the commission of the offence.

[119] [1936] 3 All ER 149.

On the other hand, the help must be *intended*. Recklessness is insufficient.[120] Thus it would not be enough for secondary liability that S merely thinks it is likely P may be assisted. Suppose, for example, the following variation:

> Susan is an auctioneer of various goods. She sells an unlabelled box of goods to Peter, a wholesaler. Because the goods are in bond, she is unsure (i.e. reckless) whether the goods are toy pistols or real guns. Susan knows that Peter does not have a licence to deal in firearms.

On these facts, Susan lacks the mens rea for secondary participation because she is merely reckless whether Peter is assisted or encouraged.

S's own contribution: the intention to procure.
In respect of S's intending her own contribution, procurement is a special case. By contrast with assistance and encouragement, the connection is necessarily tighter. S must still be proved to have intended her act of procurement. However, because procurement requires a contribution that actually influences or induces P to commit the crime, it follows that S must intend to help bring it about that P will commit the crime itself. For this reason, it was said by the Court of Appeal in *A-G's Reference (No. 1 of 1975)* [121] that, unlike aiding, abetting, inciting, or counselling, procuring an offence requires an "endeavour" or "setting out" to cause the commission of the offence.[122]

An exception for duress or necessity?
Suppose that S aids P for some further reason, such as out of fear. This may, of course, give rise to a supervening defence of duress or necessity. Sometimes, however, the courts have treated such circumstances as vitiating S's intent to aid. In *Gillick*,[123] the House of Lords appeared to hold that a doctor who gives contraceptive advice or treatment to a girl aged under 16 years for clinical reasons, while recognising that this would facilitate acts of unlawful sexual intercourse, would lack the intent to aid and abet unlawful sexual intercourse. Similarly, in *Fretwell*,[124] S reluctantly supplied an abortifacient to a woman who had threatened to kill herself should S not do so. Although S hoped P would not take the drug, she did so and died. S was held not liable for murder as an accessory (to the crime of *felo de se*, or "self-murder") because he was "unwilling that the woman should take the poison".[125]

---

[120] *Scott* (1978) 68 Cr App R 164 (suspicion not enough).

[121] [1975] QB 773, 779 (CA).

[122] This point went unconsidered in *Jogee* [2016] UKSC 8; *Ruddock* [2016] UKPC 7, [2016] 2 WLR 681, where the distinctive character of procurement was not in issue.

[123] *Gillick* v. *West Norfolk and Wisbech Area Health Authority* [1986] AC 112 (HL), adopting Woolf J's views on the criminal law aspects of the case (which was brought as a civil action for a declaration) at [1984] QB 581, 589 (QBD). Cf. *Janaway* v. *Salford Health Authority* [1989] AC 537, 550–1 (Slade LJ), 558 (Stocker LJ), CA; contrast at 572 (Lord Keith), 572–3 (Lord Lowry), HL. For general discussion, see Ashworth, "Criminal Liability in a Medical Context: The Treatment of Good Intentions" in Simester and Smith (eds.), *Harm and Culpability* (1996) 173; J.C. Smith, *Justification and Excuse in the Criminal Law* (1989) 64–70; Spencer, "Trying to Help Another Person Commit a Crime" in P. Smith (ed.), *Criminal Law: Essays in Honour of J.C. Smith* (1987) 148.

[124] (1862) Le & Ca 161, 169 ER 1345. *Per* Woolf J, in *A-G* v. *Able* [1984] 1 QB 795, *Fretwell* should be regarded as "confined to its own facts".

[125] (1862) Le & Ca 161, 164, 169 ER 1345, 1346.

The analysis in these decisions is understandable—Fretwell, in particular, faced the death penalty—but problematic. Notwithstanding the language of the judgments, in both cases the aid *is* intended by S. Like the example of Susan and Peter above, in both *Fretwell* and *Gillick* S may hope that P will not ultimately engage in the criminal conduct. Nonetheless, S's own help is intended: it is reluctant, justified, and deliberate. Moreover, as we have seen, the benevolent further purpose of S is irrelevant to the question whether S has mens rea. Contrast the analysis in *Lynch* v. *DPP for Northern Ireland* where, under duress, S drove P to a garage where P planned to murder a policeman. According to Lord Morris:[126]

> "If in the present case the jury were satisfied that the car was driven towards the garage in pursuance of a murderous plan and that the appellant knew that was the plan and intentionally drove the car in execution of that plan he could be held to have aided and abetted even though he regretted the plan or indeed was horrified by it."

The better approach in cases such as *Fretwell* and *Lynch* is to accept that S has the mens rea to aid and abet, but to allow S a defence based on duress or necessity. This is precisely the view taken by Lord Morris in *Lynch*. His Lordship continued:[127]

> "But if that intention and all that he did only came about because of the compulsion of duress of the nature that I have described he would, in my view, have a defence."

The decisions in *Fretwell* and *Gillick* were constrained from taking such an enlightened approach by the fact that, at the time, it was thought that the defences of duress and necessity did not cover those cases.[128] It is to be hoped that the fiction of denying an intent by S will not be required in future and that, in particular, the scope of the necessity defence will ultimately be accepted as embracing such instances of *bona fide* medical treatment.

An exception for performance of a duty?

Consider the following facts, which occurred in *National Coal Board* v. *Gamble*:[129]

> S (the National Coal Board) sold P's employer a large quantity of coal. P, a lorry driver, was despatched to collect some of the coal. Once loaded, the lorry was weighed before leaving the colliery. S's employee, the weighbridge clerk, realised the load exceeded that permitted to be carried on the highway. He drew P's attention to the illegality. P said that he was prepared to take the risk of being caught, whereupon the clerk issued P with a weighbridge ticket. The weighbridge clerk's function in issuing the ticket to P was to record how much coal had been taken, in order that S could then charge the buyer for that amount of coal, and also to pass title in the coal to the buyer.

On these facts, it was held by a majority of the Divisional Court[130] that S, through its servant, was an accessory to the offence committed by P. In handing over the ticket and passing title to the coal, S aided P by enabling the lorry to depart from the colliery with the coal (and thereby to commit an offence). The fact that the clerk was motivated only by considerations of accounting was irrelevant to the question whether he intended that aid.

---

[126] [1975] AC 653, 678.

[127] *Ibid*. Cf. Hibbert (1995) 99 CCC (3d) 193. Note that duress is no longer available as a defence to participation in murder: below, § 20.1(i)(d).

[128] For discussion of the current scope of these defences, see below, §§ 20.1, 21.3.

[129] [1959] 1 QB 11. See Duff, "'Can I Help You?' Accessorial Liability and the Intention to Assist" (1990) 10 *LS* 165; Williams, "Complicity, Purpose and the Draft Code" [1990] *Crim LR* 4.

[130] Lord Goddard CJ and Devlin J, Slade J dissenting.

In the majority judgments, a great deal was made of the fact that ownership of the coal had not passed before the clerk handed over the weighbridge ticket. Implicit in this is the proposition that if P already owns some item possessed by S, then by handing the item over S merely performs her legal duty to deliver up possession to P; she does not aid or abet P to commit an offence with that item. Regard the facts of *Lomas*:[131]

> S has possession of a jemmy, which she borrowed from P. S knows that P is a professional burglar. P asks for return of the jemmy and S gives it to him. P then uses the jemmy to commit a burglary.

S was held not to be a party to P's crime. Properly so, observed Devlin J in *NCB* v. *Gamble*:[132]

> "In a sense a man who gives up to a criminal a weapon which the latter has a right to demand from him aids in the commission of the crime as much as if he sold or lent the article, but this has never been held to be aiding in law.... In the transfer of property there must be either a physical delivery or a positive act of assent to a taking. But a man who hands over to another his own property on demand, although he may physically be performing a positive act, in law is only refraining from detinue. Thus in law the former act is one of assistance voluntarily given and the latter is only a failure to prevent the commission of a crime by means of forcible detention."

By contrast, the act of a shopkeeper who knows P's criminal purpose before selling P the jemmy would be an act "of assistance voluntarily given":[133]

> "If one man deliberately sells to another a gun to be used for murdering a third, he may be indifferent about whether the third man lives or dies and interested only in the cash profit to be made out of the sale, but he can still be an aider and abettor. To hold otherwise would be to negative the rule that mens rea is a matter of intent only and does not depend on desire or motive."

Prima facie, then, the law after *NCB* v. *Gamble* is as follows. S intentionally aids P to commit a crime when he intentionally provides material assistance (e.g. by handing over an instrument of burglary) *except* when P has a legal right to receive that assistance from S and S renders the assistance only because he owes a legal duty to do so.

Unfortunately, this summary of the law involves a false distinction. The underlying rationale identified by Devlin J is spurious. Whether or not P owns the jemmy, he is aided when S gives it to him, because he now has possession when before he did not. In both cases (i.e. owned and unowned), the aid itself is intended. The fact that the jemmy belongs to P is relevant, once again, only to motive.

Neither does P's ownership establish a legal duty on S to hand over the jemmy. While there is normally a civil law duty on bailees-at-will to return borrowed property upon demand, it is defeated by the duty not to commit a crime. Just as it is "incumbent on a court of equity to act by such rule as tends most to discountenance the crime",[134] so it is that the rules of the civil law must always be subject to exception whenever they would tend to

---

[131] (1913) 9 Cr App R 220; discussed in *Bullock* [1955] 1 All ER 15.
[132] [1959] 1 QB 11, 20.
[133] *Ibid.*, 23.
[134] *Bridgman* v. *Green* (1855) 2 Ves Sen 627, 628, 28 ER 399. Cf. *Amicable Society* v. *Bolland* (1830) 4 Bligh (NS) 194, 211, 5 ER 70; *Re Estate of Crippen, decd.* [1911] P 108, 112; Smith, "Civil Law Concepts in the Criminal Law" [1972B] *CLJ* 197, 208–11.

undermine the criminal law. This point was recognised by Parker LCJ in *Garrett* v. *Arthur Churchill (Glass) Ltd*:[135]

> "albeit there was a legal duty in ordinary circumstances to hand over the goblet to the owners once the agency was determined, I do not think that an action would lie for breach of that duty if the handing over would constitute the offence of being knowingly concerned in its exportation."

The inevitable conclusion must be that, in terms of legal principle, ownership makes no difference. Assuming in each case that S knows the essential matters of P's offence, there is no distinction to be drawn between the situation in *Lomas* and that in *NCB* v. *Gamble*. Both cases, moreover, are inseparable from the case of a shopkeeper who sells a jemmy to P knowing his purpose. Notwithstanding the distinction laid down in *NCB* v. *Gamble*, in principle all three situations ought to result in the same outcome: the conviction of S.

Civil liberties and the interests of victims.
Accordingly, liability for complicity is a real possibility for persons who are merely performing the routines of their jobs or trades. Given this possibility, it is important to consider whether, morally speaking, an exception *ought* to be allowed in such cases as those of the weighbridge clerk, the bailee, and/or the shopkeeper? Williams argues that, at least in the case of the shopkeeper, there should be an exception:[136]

> "From the point of view of policy the question is one of some complexity. On the one side are the policy of repressing crime, and the difficulty of distinguishing between the merchant who knowingly assists a crime and the ordinary accessory before the fact. On the other side stand the undesirability of giving too great an extension to the criminal law, and the inconvenience to legitimate trade of requiring a merchant to concern himself with the affairs of his customers.... It is submitted that ... the seller of an ordinary marketable commodity is not his buyer's keeper in criminal law unless he is specifically made so by statute. Any other rule would be too wide an extension of criminal responsibility."

Williams suggests that the exception should be confined to sellers of "an ordinary marketable commodity". Some American states have a general exception for shopkeepers, provided it is not the *purpose* of the seller to assist the buyer's offence.[137] In respect of bailment cases like *Lomas*, a further possibility would be to create an exception covering those who return property to its owner, provided that it is not S's purpose thereby to assist the owner to commit a crime, and that the contemplated crime is not a serious one (say, a crime triable only on indictment).[138]

In our view, the criminal law should take priority over the civil law in this matter. Sometimes, where criminal and civil law overlap, the criminal law must perforce follow the civil law, e.g. where it is the civil law that defines the relevant harm. An example is the law of theft; where property rights, the interests being safeguarded by the criminal law, are a creature of civil law.[139] But complicity is not like theft. When S hands P a weapon, P is aided, and the victim's rights are put at risk, equally *whoever* of them owns it.

---

[135] [1970] 1 QB 92, 99. To similar effect, see *K Ltd* v. *National Westminster Bank* [2006] EWCA Civ 1039, [2007] 1 WLR 311, para. 10; below, § 9.2(iii)(b).

[136] *CLGP* § 124.

[137] Cf. Model Penal Code, § 2.06(3).

[138] Williams, "Obedience to Law as a Crime" (1990) 53 *MLR* 445; Sullivan, "The Law Commission Consultation Paper on Complicity: Fault Elements and Joint Enterprise" [1994] *Crim LR* 252.

[139] For discussion of this proposition, and of derogations from it by the courts, see below, Chapter 13.

The argument against our view is a strong one. Williams highlights the inconvenience to shopkeepers if they are required to concern themselves with the affairs of their customers. A similar point may be made regarding ordinary citizens who return the belongings of others. It is important that persons engaging in ordinary activities should be able to perform those activities—i.e. to live their lives—without being harassed by the criminal law, especially if the harassment requires them to modify their own activities because of the plans and conduct of others, and not because of anything they have done themselves. It is significant that the duty not to help P arises out of P's intentions, and not from S's conduct or plans. Thus, as Williams objects (in the context of the weighbridge operator's case):[140]

> "It seems a strong thing to hold that a man who is simply pursuing his ordinary and lawful vocation, and takes no special steps to assist illegalities, becomes involved as a third party to a crime committed by the customer merely because he realises that his customer will be enabled by what he himself does to commit a crime."

Consider also the case of *A-G's Reference (No. 1 of 1975)*,[141] mentioned earlier, in which S was convicted of procuring P to drive with excess alcohol after secretly lacing P's drinks. Although P was ignorant of S's actions in that case, one possible implication of the decision is that publicans—and, indeed, generous hosts at a dinner party—could be regarded as aiding and abetting whenever their customers or guests then drive home drunk.[142] Williams's objection may be extended to these cases too, and one should hesitate before allowing the criminal law to reach so far into the ordinary commercial and private activities of citizens.

Nonetheless, while Williams's reasoning is powerful, it is not in our view conclusive. These are not cases where S stands by passively and omits to prevent P's crime. S *actively and intentionally helps* P to commit that crime. Indeed, S's aid may even be an indispensable feature of P's wrongdoing.[143] The rights of victims not to be burgled, assaulted, etc. mean that it is sometimes necessary to curtail the liberty of citizens to intervene and assist criminals, as well as the liberty of shopkeepers to sell goods to anyone at will. Those rights should prevail here. Moreover, the intrusive implications of this position for the lives of citizens are not as great as they may seem. S's duty is not to refuse aid to those suspected of having a criminal purpose; as will be seen below, the duty arises only if S *knows or believes* that a crime will be committed.[144] Thus S is not required to police the actions of P. She does not have to enquire into P's purpose; neither must she take active steps, either to stop P or to inform the police. She is simply not free to assist P deliberately when she realises that P plans to commit a crime.

There is room for compromise, one which balances individual liberty against the need to prevent crime. The potential intrusiveness of criminal liability for ordinary activities—including the activities of bailees otherwise mandated by the civil law—would be reduced

---

[140] *TBCL* 342.

[141] [1975] QB 773; above, § 7.4(i)(d).

[142] Williams, *TBCL* 338–41. Widgery LCJ refers to the question of hosts in the case itself, and argues that they are unaffected by the decision, since where the provision of alcohol is overt rather than by lacing, guests make up their own minds whether or not to take drink—hence, no procurement by the host. Unfortunately, this reasoning is unconvincing since it applies only to the case of secondary participation by procurement; and not to aiding, abetting, or counselling, which lack a requirement of causation: above, § 7.4(i)(d).

[143] Cf. *NCB v. Gamble* [1959] 1 QB 11.

[144] For discussion of the trade-off between a stringent mens rea requirement and the reach of criminalisation, see Simester, "The Mental Element in Complicity" (2006) 122 *LQR* 578, 591–2.

by excluding party liability for persons who assist or encourage summary offences.[145] A similar step has already been taken in respect of attempts liability,[146] and there seems little reason not to carry the logic over to complicity.[147] Apart from fostering individual autonomy, such a move would give due recognition to the seriousness of the underlying offence and the interests being protected by that offence, while avoiding the uncertainties of "balance of evils" or "reasonable conduct" defence[148] in these difficult cases.

(b) P's criminal conduct: S must have knowledge of essential matters

Sometimes, S offers assistance or encouragement *in order that* doing so will facilitate some criminal act by P, without being certain what P actually means to do. Of such a case, we can say straightforwardly that S (directly) intends to aid or abet P's (potential) crime. However, most of the time S has no particular intent concerning what P will do. In those cases, it suffices that she intends to help or encourage P, *knowing* what it is that P will do: this is a case of oblique (or virtually certain) intent to aid or abet P. The classic statement of this latter requirement is to be found in *Johnson v. Youden*, where it was said that:[149]

> "Before a person can be convicted of aiding and abetting the commission of an offence he must at least know the essential matters which constitute that offence."

Two issues arise from this traditional requirement: (i) is "knowledge" by S really required or is foresight of a risk sufficient, and (ii) what "essential matters" of an offence must S know about?

The meaning of "knowledge" is considered earlier, in § 5.4: S must accept, or assume, and have no substantial doubt that the relevant facts are true. There must be actual knowledge: it is not enough that S *ought* to have known the facts.[150] Neither is it sufficient if S suspects that they may well be true, even if accompanied by a negligent[151] or reckless failure to enquire into the facts;[152] although in the more extreme case of wilful blindness, S will be treated as having knowledge.[153]

As we shall see, *Johnson v. Youden* is still good law. Thus the requirement for knowledge would exclude from liability a person who renders assistance to P believing that P may be about to commit a crime but not knowing that he will. Mere belief in the possible existence

---

[145] Cf. *TBCL* 343; Spencer, "Trying to Help Another Person Commit a Crime" in P. Smith (ed.), *Criminal Law: Essays in Honour of J.C. Smith* (1987) 148, 162.

[146] Below, § 9.3(ii)(a).

[147] Cf. *NCB v. Gamble* [1959] 1 QB 11, 20 ("except in the case of a felony" *per* Devlin J).

[148] A defence of acting reasonably is now available to the inchoate offences of assisting or encouraging crime: Serious Crime Act 2007, s. 50; below, § 9.2(iii)(b). Given the dilution of the mens rea requirement with respect to P's conduct (foresight of probability: below, § 7.4(iv)(b)), were such a defence to be available for aiding and abetting, the better way to implement it would surely be by treating that mens rea requirement now as one of recklessness.

[149] [1950] 1 KB 544, 546.

[150] *Webster* [2006] EWCA Crim 415, para. 25.

[151] Cf. *Callow v. Tillstone* (1900) 64 JP 823.

[152] *Bainbridge* [1960] 1 QB 129, 134; *DPP for Northern Ireland v. Maxwell* [1978] 3 All ER 1140, 1146–8.

[153] *Antonelli* (1905) 70 JP 4. The doctrine of wilful blindness is examined above, § 5.4(i).

of a set of facts is the stuff of recklessness, not intention.[154] Consider the following variant of an example used in section § 7.4(iv)(a):

> S is a firearms wholesaler. He sells a firearm to P, a general shopkeeper. S knows that P does not have a licence to deal in firearms. S does not sell the firearm to P because he wants her to resell it, but rather because he wants the money that P is prepared to pay for it. However, (this time) S is unsure whether P intends to resell the firearm in her shop or to keep the firearm for her own use. In fact, P does resell the firearm.

On these facts, S is merely reckless about whether P will resell the firearm. Assuming S does not satisfy the criteria of wilful blindness,[155] he does not *know* the firearm will be resold. As such, according to the criteria laid down in *Johnson* v. *Youden*, S is innocent of secondary participation in P's crime.

The requirement of knowledge has been adopted expressly in numerous cases,[156] and has received the endorsement of the House of Lords.[157] However, for a while its importance was doubted. In its 1993 Consultation Paper on *Assisting and Encouraging Crime*, the Law Commission suggested that notwithstanding the dicta in *Johnson* v. *Youden*, whenever a case has turned on the point, recklessness has been sufficient to convict the accessory:[158]

> "there is no case which rejects the awareness of a mere possibility of the commission of the principal offence as a ground of accessorial liability, and at least some authority that seems to support that analysis."

One such authority appears to be *Carter* v. *Richardson*,[159] where S was supervising P, a learner driver, who was driving with excess alcohol. Even though it was impossible for S to know precisely P's blood-alcohol level, S was convicted of aiding and abetting the offence committed by P. On a case stated, the Divisional Court held that "it was sufficient if the defendant was aware that the principal offender had consumed excessive alcohol even though the precise amount had not been determined";[160] a test satisfied, Lord Widgery CJ continued, if S "*knew* that [P] had been drinking to such an extent that it was *probable* that his blood alcohol content was over the limit".[161] The first statement is unobjectionable. However, it seems that the second quotation pitches the standard lower than "knowledge" in that, prima facie, it does not require S to have a settled belief, or no substantial doubt, that P's blood alcohol content was over the limit. To the extent that this is so, the test shades into (subjective)[162] recklessness.[163]

---

[154] See above, §§ 5.2(iii), 5.4.

[155] Above, § 5.4(i).

[156] E.g. *Ackroyds Air Travel Ltd* v. *DPP* [1950] 1 All ER 933; *Thomas* v. *Lindop* [1950] 1 All ER 966; *Ferguson* v. *Weaving* [1951] 1 KB 814; *Smith* v. *Jenner* [1968] Crim LR 99; *Patel* [1970] Crim LR 274. Compare *Webster* [2006] EWCA Crim 415, para. 21; *Martin* [2010] EWCA Crim 1450, [2011] RTR 4, para. 35.

[157] *Churchill* [1967] 2 AC 224, 236–7; *Maxwell* v. *DPP for Northern Ireland* [1978] 3 All ER 1140. Cf. the decision by the High Court of Australia in *Giorgianni* v. *R.* (1984) 156 CLR 473.

[158] Consultation Paper No. 131 (1993) para. 2.58. The Law Commission's final Report prefers a requirement that S intend (directly or obliquely) that P will commit the offence: *Participating in Crime* Law Com. No. 305 (2007).

[159] [1974] RTR 314. Contrast *Tinsley* [1963] Crim LR 520.

[160] [1974] RTR 314, 318 (Lord Widgery CJ).

[161] *Ibid.* (emphasis added).

[162] Objective or *Caldwell*-recklessness is insufficient: *Blakely and Sutton* v. *DPP* [1991] RTR 405.

[163] It is not clear that, on the facts of *Carter* v. *Richardson*, the Court needed to go so far as this. The case seems better analysed as a situation where (given, e.g., S's awareness of P's behaviour and of the amount of alcohol consumed by P) the court could readily infer from the facts of the case that S had no substantial doubt that, whatever

Subsequent decisions of the Court of Appeal have also supported the proposition that foresight of the probable existence of the essential matters of P's crime satisfies the mens rea requirement of aiding and abetting. Such a standard was endorsed by the Court of Appeal in *Rook*,[164] where contemplation or foresight of the crime "as a real or serious risk" was said to suffice; in *Reardon*,[165] where foresight by S of the "strong possibility" of P's crime was sufficient; and in *Bryce*,[166] where (following *Rook*) a "real or substantial risk" would do. Although the (*obiter*) reasoning in those cases was open to criticism,[167] for a period this position came to be regarded as orthodox.

In a welcome return to principle, however, the law stated in *Johnson* v. *Youden* was re-established by the Supreme Court and Privy Council in *Jogee*:[168]

> "the mental element in assisting or encouraging is an intention to assist or encourage the commission of the crime and this requires knowledge of any existing facts necessary for it to be criminal."

The Court cited a number of leading cases in support of this position,[169] besides endorsing *Johnson* v. *Youden* itself.[170] Disappointingly, it did so without reference to the contrary body of case law that had built up in decisions such as *Rook*, *Reardon*, and *Bryce*. Yet the Supreme Court's decision seems right in principle. As we saw in § 5.1(v), "intending" to do some action requires an intention with respect to the *behavioural* and *consequential* elements of that action, but is generally satisfied by knowledge or settled belief (with no significant doubt) regarding the action's *circumstance* elements. The same distinction applies here. S's intention to assist or encourage P's crime is established if she intends her own contribution, knowing what P will do—the latter is, from S's perspective, a circumstance element that accompanies and need not be brought about by S's behaviour.

The merits of requiring less than knowledge.
Still, perhaps a broadening of the law on this point is desirable? An argument for the merits of requiring less than knowledge might be summarised as follows:

> Why should knowledge (or settled belief) be necessary for there to be an intention to help or encourage P? No doubt S should be required to know of any relevant circumstance where knowledge is required of P. But it does *not* follow that recklessness should be insufficient for S's liability when it suffices for P's. Otherwise, S would escape liability in many cases where she willingly assists P to commit a crime, and has the same mens rea, i.e. recklessness, toward that crime as has P; and there is no merit in that. Surely S has crossed the threshold justifying conviction, both in terms of her culpability and her conduct?

the precise blood-alcohol measurement, it was in excess of the permitted level. Indeed, S had originally pretended he himself was the driver, presumably for this very reason. Cf. *Crampton* v. *Fish* [1970] Crim LR 235, where "the evidence was apparently so overwhelming that no reasonable magistrate could fail to be satisfied of the accused's knowledge".

164 [1993] 1 WLR 1005, 1009–10.
165 [1999] Crim LR 392 (CA).
166 [2004] EWCA Crim 1231, para. 71.
167 See Simester, "The Mental Element in Complicity" (2006) 122 *LQR* 578, 583–8.
168 *Jogee* [2016] UKSC 8; *Ruddock* [2016] UKPC 7, [2016] 2 WLR 681, para. 9.
169 *National Coal Board* v. *Gamble* [1959] 1 QB 11; *Attorney-General* v. *Able* [1984] QB 795; *Gillick* v. *West Norfolk and Wisbech Area Health Authority* [1986] AC 112; *Director of Public Prosecutions for Northern Ireland* v. *Maxwell* [1978] 1 WLR 1350.
170 *Jogee* [2016] UKSC 8; *Ruddock* [2016] UKPC 7, [2016] 2 WLR 681, para. 16.

Despite the attractiveness of this argument, in our view the relaxation of the requirement for "knowledge" into one of foresight, let alone foresight of a mere possibility, should be avoided.[171] The basis of secondary liability is different from that of a principal. There is no suggestion that the secondary party actually commits the offence himself or that he satisfies the actus reus requirements of the relevant crime. The actus reus element of secondary participation is entirely independent of the actus reus of the principal offence. This being so, there seems no reason why the mens rea requirement for participation should be determined by that principal offence.

Moreover, derivative liability of any variety involves widening the net of the criminal law beyond those who actually perpetrate offences: not only may S not strike V, she may not do anything to help anyone else strike V either.[172] Because of this widening, the grounds of derivative liability ought correspondingly to be constricted, in order to prevent excessive criminalisation of conduct that does not itself cause a criminal harm. If something less than knowledge were required, the legitimate activities of people like shopkeepers, trading in products with potentially illicit usages, could be significantly compromised. It is one thing to convict a shopkeeper of selling a baseball bat or kitchen knife that she *knows* will be used in a criminal assault. It is quite another to convict her just because she foresees that risk.[173] Computer sellers, who know there is a real risk their hardware will be used to pirate music, would be forced out of business. More generally, over-criminalisation through weakening the mens rea requirement has the potential to lead, in turn, to a disproportionate intrusion upon the freedoms of citizens who do not themselves commit crimes. Respectable citizens such as shopkeepers should not be obliged to stop trading, on pain of risking convictions, whenever they realise that P may put his purchases to criminal use.[174] The same goes for ordinary citizens going about their everyday activities, just because they realise there is a *risk* some miscreant will exploit what they do.

Future facts?
In *Webster*, S allowed P to drive S's car, which P then drove dangerously. The Court of Appeal drew a distinction between present and future facts. It opined that, where P's conduct lay in the future, in order to establish S's aiding and abetting of P's dangerous driving the prosecution must prove that S "foresaw that [P] was *likely* to drive in a dangerous manner".[175] Alternatively, if S had *not* foreseen that likelihood when allowing P to take the wheel, the Court noted that it would be open to establish that S abetted P, by allowing P to remain at the wheel while P was actually driving dangerously. In that situation, where S's

---

[171] See Simester, "The Mental Element in Complicity" (2006) 122 *LQR* 578, 588–92.

[172] Above, § 1.2(ii)(e).

[173] See the discussion of *National Coal Board* v. *Gamble* [1959] 1 QB 11 and related cases, above, § 7.4(iv)(a).

[174] One compromise possibility, discussed in the fifth edition of this work, might be to moderate the traditional requirement for knowledge to one of *recklessness*. Since recklessness is only established when the risk taken by the defendant is unreasonable, this may help to keep reasonable conduct by shopkeepers and the like outside the scope of the criminal law; they are not obliged to stop trading, on pain of risking convictions, *whenever* they realise that P may put his purchases to criminal use. Even that compromise would, however, significantly impinge upon the liberties of law-abiding persons to conduct their day-to-day activities, and tend to make them legal risk-takers; all the more so given the likely assumption, once P has actually committed a crime aided by S, that a jury would retrospectively adjudge that risk an unreasonable one.

[175] [2006] EWCA Crim 415, para. 26 (emphasis added).

abetment occurred *at the time* P's conduct was occurring, the Court asserted that S must *know* the essential matters of P's crime:[176]

> "In pursuance of this second approach, we conclude that the prosecution had to prove that [S] knew that [P] was, by virtue of the speed the vehicle was travelling, driving dangerously at a time when there was an opportunity to intervene."

The latter position is now uncontroversial. But is foresight of likelihood sufficient for *future* facts? An analogous distinction, between knowledge of present facts and beliefs about future ones, has been drawn in New Zealand, where a lesser degree of confidence suffices for the latter.[177] One might, then, seek to defend the a foresight requirement in England and Wales on the ground that it is impossible to "know" future facts.[178] As it happens, that ground is dubious; it does seem possible for one to know about a future event: to know, for instance, that the sun will rise tomorrow.[179] But more importantly, there is no *legal* difficulty here. As we noted earlier in this section, a requirement of knowledge is—as always[180]—satisfied whenever S holds a settled belief, with no substantial doubt, that the fact exists or, in the case of future facts, will exist. So the distinction drawn in *Webster* between present and future facts is unnecessary.

Uncertainty about future facts is, however, no barrier to S's liability where the aid or encouragement is directly (rather than obliquely) intended. Characteristically, such cases involve a conditional form of intention. Suppose that S lends P a knife in order to help P to kill V, *should V be found*. As the Supreme Court made clear in *Jogee*,[181] if V is indeed killed, S will be complicit in the murder.

Strict liability offences.
One implication of the analysis above is that an intention to assist or encourage, and foresight of essential matters, is still required notwithstanding that the principal offence may be one of negligence or even strict liability. The classic authority for this proposition is *Callow* v. *Tillstone*.[182] In that case, P, a butcher, was convicted of the strict liability offence of exposing unsound meat for sale. P had offered the meat for sale only after asking S, a veterinary surgeon, to examine the meat and certify whether it was sound. S had performed the examination negligently, and wrongly certified the meat as sound. Despite his negligence, S's conviction for abetting the offence by P was quashed. S did not know the meat was unsound.

The result in *Callow* v. *Tillstone* seems odd. P, who lacked fault, was convicted while S, whose fault induced the offence, was acquitted. Once again, however, it is important to note that, unlike P, S did not commit the actus reus of any offence. (The doctrine of innocent

---

[176] *Ibid.*, para. 29. Cf. *Martin* [2010] EWCA Crim 1450, [2011] RTR 4.

[177] *Cooper* v. *MOT* [1991] 2 NZLR 693: knowledge is required with respect to present facts, but knowledge of the probable existence of future (or otherwise unknowable) facts suffices.

[178] Something that seems to have troubled Lord Nicholls in *Saik* [2006] UKHL 18, [2007] 1 AC 18, para. 20. Cf. *Bryce* [2004] EWCA Crim 1231, para. 49.

[179] See on this point Shute, "Knowledge and Belief in the Criminal Law" and Sullivan, "Knowledge, Belief and Culpability" in Shute and Simester (eds.), *Criminal Law Theory: Doctrines of the General Part* (2002) 184, 186–7 and 207, 214–15 respectively.

[180] Above, § 5.4.

[181] *Jogee* [2016] UKSC 8; *Ruddock* [2016] UKPC 7, [2016] 2 WLR 681, paras. 92-95. See also below in this section (What count as essential matters in murder and manslaughter?).

[182] (1900) 64 JP 823. See also below, § 7.4(iv)(c) (Constructive liability elements of P's crime).

agency was ruled out by the fact that S fell outside the class of persons who could commit that offence.) The anomalous-looking outcome in the case should be attributed not to the law governing secondary parties, but rather to the morally indefensible phenomenon of strict liability for principals.

(c) P's criminal conduct: what "essential matters" must S know about?

It is also a difficult question what aspects of P's crime count as "essential matters",[183] such that they must be recognised by S. The following propositions may be asserted.

First, S must appreciate that P intends or contemplates doing actions which constitute the actus reus of an offence, although S need not recognise that those actions in fact constitute an offence.[184] Secondly, S need not know all the details of the proposed offence, such as the time or place of its commission.[185] However, mere knowledge that "something illegal" is intended by P is not enough. S must know either:

(i)   the *type* of offence intended (and eventually committed) by P; or

(ii)   that P would commit any one of a number of offences, the "list" of which includes the type of offence that eventually was committed.

The leading cases are *Bainbridge*[186] and *Maxwell*.[187] In *Bainbridge*, S supplied oxygen-cutting equipment to P, who later used it to break into the Midland Bank at Stoke Newington. S claimed that he had suspected P wanted the equipment for some illegal purpose (e.g. to break up stolen goods), but had not known it would be used to break into a bank, let alone the Midland Bank at Stoke Newington. While his claim failed on the evidence, the Court of Criminal Appeal ruled that, on those facts, S would have lacked mens rea. His knowledge that he was aiding "some illegal venture" would be insufficient:[188] he had to know what *type* of crime would be committed by P. On the other hand, S need only appreciate the type and not the details. It was sufficient that S knew P intended to break and enter, and steal. S did not have to know the particulars of the plan, e.g. that the target was a particular bank in Stoke Newington.

In general, a crime is of different type when it has different essential elements. S will not be liable for those variations by P which take P's conduct outside the types of crime that S knew P may commit. Another way of putting this is to say that it is not enough to prove that S knew about the essential matters of crime X (say) when the charge is complicity in crime Y and the two crimes have different essential elements. In such a case, the prosecution must prove that S knew about *all* the essential elements of crime Y.

---

[183] An "essential matters" approach is effectively endorsed in *Jogee* [2016] UKSC 8; *Ruddock* [2016] UKPC 7, [2016] 2 WLR 681, para. 9: "the mental element in assisting or encouraging is an intention to assist or encourage the commission of the crime and this requires knowledge of any existing facts *necessary for it to be criminal*." And in para. 16: "an intention to assist or encourage the commission of an offence requires knowledge by D2 of any facts *necessary to give the principal's conduct or intended conduct its criminal character*." (Emphases added.) Cf. para. 99 ("necessary for it to be a prohibited act"). See also the discussion of constructive liability offences below in this section.

[184] *Johnson* v. *Youden* [1950] 1 KB 544, 546: "[h]e need not actually know that an offence has been committed, because he may not know that the facts constitute an offence and ignorance of the law is not a defence".

[185] *Bainbridge* [1960] 1 QB 129; *Bullock* [1955] 1 All ER 15; cf. *Lomas* [1913] 9 Cr App R 220.

[186] [1960] 1 QB 129.

[187] [1978] 3 All ER 1140.

[188] [1960] 1 QB 129, 133; *Scott* (1978) 68 Cr App R 164; *Patel* [1970] Crim LR 274.

An example may be helpful. Suppose that S is charged with aiding and abetting a burglary.[189] S had encouraged P to steal V's wallet, but had not anticipated that P would steal the wallet from V's house. In such a case, it would be a misdirection for the trial judge to state that S need not know that P proposed to steal from the house. Trespassory entry into a building is an essential element of the offence of burglary; indeed, it is the distinguishing feature of that offence. It follows that burglary cannot be regarded as being the same *type* of offence as simple theft. S can only be convicted as a party to burglary if, as well as knowing that P contemplated a theft, he also realised that P contemplated doing so within a building.

Bainbridge, decided in 1959, establishes alternative (i) above. In 1978, the House of Lords in *DPP for Northern Ireland* v. *Maxwell*[190] extended the reasoning in *Bainbridge* to cover alternative (ii). S was a member of the UVF, a terrorist organisation. One night he was called upon to drive a car guiding other UVF members to a public house. He did so knowing that a terrorist attack was planned, though uncertain whether the attack was to be perpetrated by bomb, gun, or other means. In fact, the attack was carried out using a bomb. S was guilty of aiding two offences against the Explosive Substances Act 1883, since these offences were within the range of types of crime that S contemplated P would commit. According to Lord Scarman, the accessory:[191]

> "may have in contemplation only one [type of][192] offence, or several; and the several which he contemplates he may see as alternatives. An accessory who leaves it to his principal to choose is liable, provided always the choice is made from the range of offences from which the accessory contemplates the choice will be made. Although the court's formulation of the principle goes further than [*Bainbridge*], it is a sound development of the law and in no way inconsistent."

Thus S would instead have been guilty of murder if, alternatively, P had killed the publican by shooting him. Conversely, and odd as it might seem, S would not have been liable had the principals entered the pub and stolen a bottle of whiskey—notwithstanding that the latter offence is so much lesser than those actually contemplated by S.[193]

Mens rea of the principal.
P's mens rea is also an essential matter. S must know that P will do the actus reus with the level of mens rea required for it to amount to an offence.[194] S cannot abet murder, for example, if S recognises that P is about to kill V negligently,[195] since negligence is insufficient mens rea for P to be guilty of murder. Similarly, if P's offence requires proof of an ulterior intention, S must be aware of that intent by P.[196] To illustrate: on a charge of abetting

---

[189] Contrary to s. 9 of the Theft Act 1968; below, § 14.4. Cf. *Barnard* (1980) 70 Cr App R 28 (D's agreement to a theft did not establish his liability for conspiracy to rob); below, § 9.3(ii)(b) (Case 1).

[190] [1978] 3 All ER 1140; endorsed in *Jogee* [2016] UKSC 8; *Ruddock* [2016] UKPC 7, [2016] 2 WLR 681, paras. 15–16.

[191] [1978] 3 All ER 1151 (Lord Scarman).

[192] The insertion is an implication of *Bainbridge*.

[193] It is an interesting question why the correspondence principle (above, § 6.5) is observed even when, as here, D is prepared to do an actus reus more heinous (albeit of a different type) than he in fact does. The point perhaps deserves closer attention than it has yet received in the literature.

[194] Cf. *A, B, C and D* v. *R.* [2010] EWCA Crim 1622, [2011] QB 841.

[195] *Cruse* (1838) 8 C & P 541, 173 ER 610; *Quick* [1973] QB 910, 923; Dennis, "The Mental Element for Accessories" in P. Smith (ed.), *Criminal Law: Essays in Honour of J.C. Smith* (1987) 40, 46–7, 55.

[196] *DPP for Northern Ireland* v. *Maxwell* [1978] 3 All ER 1140.

possession of a controlled drug with intent to supply,[197] S would have to know not only about P's possession, but also about her intent to supply the drug to another.[198]

Constructive liability elements of P's crime.
Many offences contain a mixture of actus reus elements where, for some of those elements, the prosecution must prove mens rea on the part of the principal and, for other actus reus elements, no mens rea is required. In the context of secondary liability, where no mens rea going to such consequences need be proved against P, neither need any mens rea in respect of those consequences be proved against S. Effectively, those strict-liability consequences are not regarded as part of the essential matters of P's conduct that S must contemplate. For example, S need not anticipate the consequence (death) in order to abet the offence of "dangerous driving causing death". For the purposes of secondary participation, only the dangerous driving counts as an essential element.[199] Similarly, if S aids or abets P to inflict a common assault upon V, and V dies, both S and P are guilty of manslaughter even though neither may have contemplated the prospect of V's death. P is guilty because causing death by an unlawful act satisfies the required elements of manslaughter as a principal;[200] upon proof of the criminal assault, death is a constructive liability element. Correspondingly, death is not an "essential matter" and S need not contemplate V's death for the purposes of secondary liability.[201] Thus V's death need be anticipated by neither P nor S.

This doctrine sits poorly with cases such as *Callow v. Tillstone*,[202] discussed earlier. Where P, a butcher, was convicted of the strict liability offence of exposing unsound meat for sale, S—a veterinary surgeon—who had negligently certified the meat as sound, was ruled not to be an accessory because he did not know the meat was unsound. Yet the unsoundness of the meat was a matter of strict liability for P: why, then, must S know about it?

There are two possible ways of distinguishing cases such as *Callow v. Tillstone*. The first, less satisfactory basis is that what was at issue in that case was a circumstance element (that the meat was unsound), whereas in dangerous driving causing death and other constructive homicide offences the aggravating feature is a *consequence* element (death). But that would require, in the context of unlawful-act manslaughter, that S must recognise the dangerousness of P's unlawful act, which is contrary to current law. More plausibly, what is key in these constructive liability offences is that S knowingly abets or assists P to *do a prohibited act*, and the relevant strict liability element (death) is merely an aggravating feature. The latter analysis comports with the position taken in *Jogee*:[203]

> "Where the offence charged does not require mens rea, the only mens rea required of the secondary party is that he intended to encourage or assist the perpetrator to do the prohibited act, with knowledge of any facts and circumstances necessary for it to be a prohibited act: *National Coal Board v Gamble*."

---

[197] Contrary to s. 5(3) of the Misuse of Drugs Act 1971.

[198] Cf. *Samuels* [1985] 1 NZLR 350.

[199] *Robert Millar (Contractors) Ltd* [1970] 2 QB 54; *Harris* [1964] Crim LR 54. This point was left open by the Court in *Martin* [2010] EWCA Crim 1450, but it is submitted that the applicable legal principle is a settled one, albeit it is more familiar in the context of unlawful-act manslaughter. See the note by Cunningham, "Complicating Complicity: Aiding and Abetting Causing Death by Dangerous Driving in *R v Martin*" (2011) 74 *MLR* 767.

[200] See below, Chapter 10.

[201] *Creamer* [1966] 1 QB 72; *Buck* (1960) 44 Cr App R 213; *Baldessare* (1930) 22 Cr App R 70; *Reid* (1976) 62 Cr App R 109; *Swindall and Osborne* (1846) 2 C & K 230, 175 ER 95.

[202] (1900) 64 JP 823; above, § 7.4(iv)(b) (Strict liability offences).

[203] *Jogee* [2016] UKSC 8; *Ruddock* [2016] UKPC 7, [2016] 2 WLR 681, para. 99.

What counts, then, is whether S has intentionally assisted or encouraged "a prohibited act": the unlawful act in manslaughter cases; the intentional infliction of (at least) grievous bodily harm in murder; or the dangerous driving in causing death by dangerous driving. In principle, this approach is not restricted to consequence elements.[204] For example, the offence of assaulting a constable, contrary to section 89 of the Police Act 1996, imposes strict liability with respect to the fact that the victim is a constable.[205] It would seem to follow that S participates in the section 89 offence by intentionally assisting or encouraging P to commit an assault on any person who—however unexpectedly—turns out to be a constable.

What count as essential matters in murder and manslaughter?
It may be worth explicating the foregoing law, concerning what elements count as essential, in the specific context of murder and manslaughter. In murder, S must intend to aid or abet at least grievous bodily harm. The intention may be conditional, in as much as S recognises the need may not arise, provided he intends his participation if necessary. As it was put in *Jogee*:[206]

> "If D2 joins with a group which he realises is out to cause serious injury, the jury may well infer that *he intended to encourage or assist the deliberate infliction of serious bodily injury* and/ or intended that that should happen if necessary. In that case, if D1 acts with intent to cause serious bodily injury and death results, D1 and D2 will each be guilty of murder."

In unlawful-act manslaughter,[207] only the unlawful act counts as an essential matter for the purposes of secondary liability:[208]

> "If a person is a party to a violent attack on another, without an intent to assist in the causing of death or really serious harm, but the violence escalates and results in death, he will be not guilty of murder but guilty of manslaughter. So also if he participates by encouragement or assistance in any other unlawful act which all sober and reasonable people would realise carried the risk of some harm (not necessarily serious) to another, and death in fact results.... The test is objective."

The position is different for manslaughter predicated on gross negligence rather than on an independently unlawful act. In that situation, both the death and P's gross negligence count as essential matters, because they constitute the very basis of P's liability; whereas for unlawful-act manslaughter it is the unlawful act that generates P's culpability for the homicide offence.

Other variations within a type.
For the most part, variations *within* a type will not affect secondary liability. Suppose that P plans to set fire to V's house. Knowing the details of the plan, S helps P by giving him

[204] Cf. the element of dangerousness in the context of unlawful-act manslaughter, which S need not foresee: *Jogee* [2016] UKSC 8; *Ruddock* [2016] UKPC 7, [2016] 2 WLR 681, para. 96.
[205] *Forbes and Webb* (1865) 10 Cox CC 362; *Maxwell* (1909) 2 Cr App R 26; *Mark* [1961] Crim LR 173.
[206] *Jogee* [2016] UKSC 8; *Ruddock* [2016] UKPC 7, [2016] 2 WLR 681, para. 95 (emphasis added).
[207] Below, § 10.6(i).
[208] *Jogee* [2016] UKSC 8; *Ruddock* [2016] UKPC 7, [2016] 2 WLR 681, para. 96, citing *Church* [1965] 1 QB 59; *DPP v. Newbury* [1977] AC 500; *F(J) & E(N)* [2015] EWCA Crim 351, [2015] 2 Cr App R 5. See also below, § 10.6(i)(d).

V's address. P goes to the house, then changes his mind and instead sets fire to V's car.[209] Is S guilty of arson? Yes. As cases like *Bainbridge* establish, incidental variations of detail such as time and place are immaterial since they do not alter the type of crime committed by P (and assisted by S). Therefore, because P commits the same offence (arson) either way, S's liability is normally unaffected by this variation.

The exception is if S's assistance or encouragement is directed specifically to the aspect of P's offence that was varied. In such cases, even though that aspect be immaterial to P's guilt, it becomes essential to S's complicity. For example:

> S counsels P to murder a particular person, V. P, having set out to kill V, then changes his mind and decides instead to kill W. S is not a party to the murder of W.[210]

It is otherwise if the identity of the victim to be killed—or the identity of the property to be fired, in our earlier example—were of no particular relevance to S's intervention. Thus, for instance, if P were to receive S's help with obtaining a weapon in order to kill someone ("as it happens, X"), S would still be liable when Y is shot instead.

At first glance, although this states the law, the law looks somewhat odd. Since the difference between shooting V and shooting W is immaterial to the definition of murder, the variation would seem to be covered by the doctrine of transferred malice.[211] It is murder of any human being, and participation therein, that the law criminalises; not murder of a particular person. In principle, since the identity of the victim does not matter to P's liability for murder, prima facie neither should it make a difference to the liability of S.

Notwithstanding its apparent oddity, however, the exception is defensible on the basis of the *Calhaem* principle: that P must act within the scope of the encouragement.[212] As such, it is submitted that the rule applies to encouragement rather than assistance; a distinction that is consistent with the case law. Assistance should always be covered by the transferred malice doctrine, but encouragement (say) to murder V can be expressed in such confined terms that it does not encourage murder generally, i.e. of anyone else; in which case the *Calhaem* principle may appropriately displace S's liability.[213] (In such a case, S would in any event be exposed to a conviction for the inchoate offence of assisting or encouraging crime.[214])

The oddity is anyway avoided, and S remains liable, if the variation is unintentional. Suppose that P does not change his mind, and carries out his attempt to shoot V. Unfortunately, he mistakes W for V and kills W. Here, the transferred malice doctrine applies to S as well as P, and both S and P are guilty of murdering W.[215]

---

[209] The facts of *Dunning and Graham* (unreported, Preston Crown Court, Dec. 1985), discussed in *Smith and Hogan* 204.

[210] *Saunders and Archer* (1573) 2 Plowd 473, 75 ER 706; *Leahy* [1985] Crim LR 99; *S v. Robinson* 1968 (1) SA 666; Hawkins, 2 PC ch. 29, §§ 20, 21; Foster, *Crown Law* 369; Stephen, *Digest* art. 43. For criticism of this rule, see Smith, *A Modern Treatise on the Law of Criminal Complicity* (1991) 200ff; Clarkson, "Complicity, *Powell* and Manslaughter" [1998] *Crim LR* 556, 559.

[211] Above, § 5.7.

[212] Above, § 7.4(ii).

[213] This distinction would support S's conviction in *Reardon* [1999] Crim LR 392.

[214] Below, § 9.2.

[215] Hawkins, 2 PC ch. 29, § 22; Foster, *Crown Law* 370; Stephen, *Digest* art. 41.

§ 7.5 Secondary parties pursuant to common unlawful purpose ("joint enterprise")

In § 7.4, we considered the standard forms of secondary participation; those which are mentioned expressly by section 8 of the Accessories and Abettors Act 1861.[216] In these standard cases, liability is established on the basis that S assists or encourages the principal by aiding, abetting, counselling, or procuring the relevant offence. As an accessory, S knows the essential facts of the offence charged and she intends to assist or encourage P in committing that offence.

Prior to its abolition in *Jogee*,[217] a second form of participation was known to the common law: where S and P embark on a *common purpose* to commit a crime. If that crime is actually committed by P during their venture, S too is guilty of it.

Common-purpose liability was an ancient form of secondary participation.[218] In its most basic form, sometimes described as the "plain vanilla" variety of joint enterprise,[219] it was uncontroversial and added nothing to aiding and abetting, which we considered in § 7.4 above. The standard forms of complicity are expressed by reference to a single offence: i.e. the offence that is deliberately aided or encouraged by S and which ultimately is committed by P. By forming a common purpose with P to commit that offence, S effectively abets it.[220]

What was much more controversial, however, was the twin-crime scenario of common-purpose liability, which gave rise to what was sometimes called "parasitic accessory liability".[221] This more complicated scenario involved *two* offences: an offence (A) that was the subject of a common purpose between S and P,[222] and a further offence (B) then committed by P alone. The secondary party need not have specifically assisted or encouraged offence B to become liable for its commission. He became a party to the offence if he foresaw that its commission was a possible consequence of proceeding with the original plan to commit some different crime (A); even though he may not have intended or even been directly involved in the commission of that further, or "collateral", offence (B) that was perpetrated by P. For example:

> P and S agree to commit a burglary. Together they break into V's home. In the course of the burglary, P is challenged by V whom he attacks and injures. S does not participate physically in the assault. However, S knew that P has a propensity toward violence, and realised that P might well assault the occupier of the house were they to be confronted. S is guilty, with P, of assault occasioning actual bodily harm.

It mattered not that S did not intend that an assault should be committed; nor that S was uncertain whether the assault would occur; nor that S did not intend to help or encourage

---

[216] Set out in the text above, § 7.2.

[217] *Jogee* [2016] UKSC 8; *Ruddock* [2016] UKPC 7, [2016] 2 WLR 681, para. 99.

[218] For discussion of some of the older cases, see Smith, *A Modern Treatise on the Law of Criminal Complicity* (1991) chap. 8.

[219] *Brown and Isaac* v. *The State* [2003] UKPC 10, para. 13 (Lord Hoffman).

[220] Unless, of course, P commits it outside the scope of that abetment: above, § 7.4(ii).

[221] *Gnango* [2011] UKSC 59, [2012] 1 AC 827, paras. 42–3, 94–6. The phrase is attributable to Smith, "Criminal Liability of Accessories: Law and Law Reform" (1997) 113 *LQR* 453.

[222] Note there is no requirement in joint enterprise liability for offence B that offence A must successfully be perpetrated. Obviously, if it is perpetrated by P, joint enterprise liability would also apply, although S will normally be liable anyway for the offence on standard principles of abetment.

its commission. Liability arose because S participated in a criminal enterprise with P, pursuant to which P has committed a further, "collateral", offence which S foresaw might occur. In simple terms, we might say that the parties set out to commit one crime and become liable for a different one. The difference between the two varieties of secondary participation, in so far as the conduct element is concerned, is that there was *no need to show specifically that S assisted or encouraged the second offence*.

As the burglary example illustrates, the idea of a common purpose has a strong affinity with the inchoate offence of conspiracy. The elements of this more complicated, twin-crime form of participation were as follows:[223]

(i) S and P jointly embark on the commission of crime A.

(ii) S foresees that, in the course of the joint enterprise to commit crime A, P may commit crime B (with the requisite mens rea for that crime).

(iii) P commits crime B.

(iv) The commission of crime B occurs as an incident of the joint enterprise, and not in a manner that is fundamentally different from the possibility foreseen by S.

(v) P's commission of crime B occurs at a point in time when the joint enterprise is still ongoing, and S has not withdrawn from it.

If these requirements were met, then in addition to any liability S may have had for conspiracy to commit a crime, and as a (principal or secondary) party to crime A, S became liable as a party to crime B. Indeed, where S and P formed a common purpose to commit a crime, S potentially became liable for any offence that she contemplated might be committed by P in furtherance of that purpose.

Notwithstanding its endorsement in multiple decisions by our most senior courts,[224] in the wake of *Jogee*, common purpose is no longer a distinct basis of secondary liability. The Supreme Court in *Jogee* rejected those earlier decisions, but not by invoking superior authority. Indeed, there was no binding authority that barred twin crime scenarios at common law. Those earlier decisions were not *per incuriam*. Rather, they were rejected because the Court in *Jogee* considered their reasoning to be wanting. Overruling those earlier decisions is constitutionally possible, but requires reference to the power contained in the Court's Practice Directions to depart from previous decisions of the Supreme Court and the House of Lords.[225] No such reference occurred in *Jogee*.

Constitutional worries aside, the main implications of abolishing common-purpose liability are outlined below.

(i) The main doctrinal differences

Formerly, the actus reus requirements of common-purpose-based liability differed in twin-crime scenarios from those applying to participation by assistance or encouragement. In

---

[223] For a fuller discussion, see § 7.5 of the previous edition of this work.

[224] Including *Chan Wing-Siu* [1985] AC 168 (PC); *Hui Chi-Ming* v. *R* [1992] 1 AC 34 (PC); *Powell; English* [1999] 1 AC 1 (HL); *Rahman* [2008] UKHL 45, [2009] 1 AC 129. Cf. *Gnango* [2011] UKSC 59, [2012] 1 AC 827, paras. 42–3 (Lords Phillips and Judge, Lord Wilson concurring) and 94–6 (Lord Dyson), where the Supreme Court upheld secondary liability on the basis of aiding and abetting while rejecting what their Lordships called "parasitic accessory liability" on the facts; thus distinguishing the two bases.

[225] Direction 3.1.3; cf. Practice Statement (Judicial Precedent) [1966] 1 WLR 1234.

the "plain vanilla", single-crime scenario,[226] the shared purpose necessarily constituted abetment of crime A. In a twin-crime situation, however, it did not. It was settled law that S may form a common purpose to commit crime A while opposing crime B; and that liability for crime B nonetheless could follow. It followed without S's having assisted or encouraged crime B, the crime for which S could be convicted.[227] Suppose S participates in a burglary knowing P has both a knife and a propensity for violence. S, however, makes it clear to P that she is opposed to his using the knife. If P, confronted during the burglary, stabs his victim, the stabbing is foreseen but unauthorised. In such cases, the courts held, S was a party to the stabbing,[228] notwithstanding that she did not aid or abet it.

The mens rea requirement also differed. As *Jogee* itself has clarified, liability for aiding or abetting any crime requires knowledge of the essential facts of that crime.[229] By contrast, the law applicable to twin-crime scenarios clearly required only that S foresaw the possibility[230] that P *might* commit the relevant "collateral" crime (with mens rea). In *Powell*,[231] for example, S1 and S2 went with P to buy drugs from V, a drug dealer. Before the transaction could take place, the dealer was shot dead using a gun carried by P. S1 and S2 knew that P was armed, and had realised P might use the gun to kill or inflict grievous bodily injury on V. On these facts the House upheld their convictions for murder. Notwithstanding that the mens rea for murder as principal is *intention* to kill or inflict grievous bodily injury, it was sufficient if secondary parties to a joint unlawful enterprise *foresaw* that murder by P was possible. In so holding, their Lordships followed the lead taken in a number of decisions by the Court of Appeal and Privy Council.[232]

(ii) The underlying structural and normative differences

The twin-crime scenario was fundamentally structurally different from ordinary aiding and abetting. In cases of aiding and abetting, and now for all forms of complicity post-*Jogee*, S's liability for any crime by P is considered purely in terms of her involvement in and mental state regarding that particular crime.[233] S directly participates in each crime by her intended act of aiding or abetting that very crime. The wrong which makes S responsible for each crime is that deliberate assistance or encouragement: it is her act of directly connecting herself with P's crime. In common-purpose cases, the wrong was the agreement

---

[226] *Brown and Isaac* v. *The State* [2003] UKPC 10, para. 13 (Lord Hoffman).

[227] Toulson LJ finesses this point in *Mendez* v. *R* [2010] EWCA Crim 516, [2011] QB 876, para. 36, suggesting that "by going along with P in the criminal venture knowing that P may commit murder, D encourages or assists P to place himself in the position where that may occur". But that is obviously not the same thing as encouraging or assisting the murder itself.

[228] *Powell; English* [1999] 1 AC 1, 19–20; *Hui Chi-Ming* v. *R.* [1992] 1 AC 34, 53; *Hyde* [1991] 1 QB 134, 139. Cf. *Rahman* [2008] UKHL 45, [2009] 1 AC 129, para. 36 (Lord Rodger); also *Day* [2001] Crim LR 984, where S's conviction was upheld because he foresaw that P might kick V in the head, notwithstanding that apparently he did not approve of it.

[229] *Jogee* [2016] UKSC 8; *Ruddock* [2016] UKPC 7, [2016] 2 WLR 681, paras. 9, 16, 99; above, § 7.4(iv).

[230] Not probability: cf. *Powell; English* [1999] 1 AC 1, 14 (Lord Steyn), 30–1 (Lord Hutton).

[231] *Ibid.*

[232] *Smith (Wesley)* [1963] 3 All ER 597 (CCA); *Anderson and Morris* [1966] 2 QB 110 (CCA); *Chan Wing-siu* v. *R* [1985] AC 168 (PC); *Hui Chi-ming* v. *R* [1992] 1 AC 34 (PC). See Smith, "Criminal Liability of Accessories: Law and Law Reform" (1997) 113 *LQR* 453.

[233] Although, of course, crime A may be committed on more than one occasion; as when P uses the jemmy supplied by S to commit several burglaries.

or confederacy.[234] The agreement (to commit crime A) opened a wider door to liability; it exposed S to conviction for any foreseen crimes B, C, and D, committed by P in the course of executing the agreement. As such, S's connection to crime B was *indirect*. It operated only because of the agreement to commit crime A.

It is important to recognise that aiding, abetting, counselling, and procuring are not doctrines that operate as ends in themselves. They exist as channels via which the law sets aside the normal limitations of autonomy, individual responsibility, and causation doctrines in order to ascribe one person with responsibility for a crime committed by another. There is no in-principle objection, therefore, to the law's recognising complementary doctrines where a similar rationale for extending responsibility applies.[235] Common-purpose liability presents just that situation.

Even so, we should ask, *why* should the agreement or confederacy make such a difference?[236] Clearly, the law regarded the common unlawful purpose as an aggravating factor, such that S became liable to be convicted of crimes to which she had not actually contributed.

There is little discussion of the normative merits in *Jogee* itself. However, the Court worried that common-purpose liability imported "the striking anomaly of requiring a lower mental threshold for guilt in the case of the accessory than in the case of the principal."[237] Yet there is no *a priori* reason why S and P should have identical mens rea requirements. The basis of P's liability is different: he is liable because he satisfies the actus reus and mens rea requirements of the relevant crime. S was liable because she satisfies the actus reus and mens rea requirements of common-purpose liability (and note that this meant she must foresee not only the prospect of P's acts, but also that they will be done with mens rea; it is not enough even to foresee, say, the possibility of death). Since the actus reus requirements are different, logic does not compel the mens rea requirements to be the same. Quite the opposite: even after *Jogee*, S still does not have to possess the "same" mens rea as P to be convicted of murder. Suppose that S gives P a crowbar, intending that this will assist P in intentionally causing grievous bodily harm to V. S does not need to intend that grievous bodily harm be caused to V. So S's mens rea is different from P's, yet S too is a murderer.

Of course, opinions may differ on, say, whether foresight of death or grievous bodily harm is sufficient culpability for convicting *anyone* of murder. But the key normative question here is not whether S is identically, or even *equally*, guilty as P. What counts is whether S is *sufficiently* culpable to be held responsible for P's crime.

---

[234] Compare the American rule that one who enters into a conspiracy thereby becomes liable for every reasonably foreseeable crime committed by his co-conspirators in furtherance of the conspiracy: *Pinkerton v. United States* 328 US 640 (1946); Johnson, "The Unnecessary Crime of Conspiracy" (1973) 61 *Calif LR* 1137, 1146ff. The (overbroad) rule is not found in the Model Penal Code (see § 2.06).

[235] Admittedly, a pragmatic consideration is whether to do so would over-complicate the law and associated jury directions: cf. *Clayton* [2006] HCA 58, paras. 113–17 (Kirby J, dissenting). On the other hand, common purpose doctrine offers real practical gains in overcoming the evidential difficulties, where there is concerted action, of distinguishing between the contributions made by individual actors and of establishing precisely what part was taken by each member of the combination.

[236] In particular, the free use—overuse—of common-purpose liability in spontaneous group-fight cases had meant that, in practice, individuals peripherally associated with such events could be convicted more or less just for being there. But that should not have been happening. It ought to have been crucially important to prove, positively, the existence of a *shared* unlawful purpose—a conspiracy—on the part of S.

[237] *Jogee* [2016] UKSC 8; *Ruddock* [2016] UKPC 7, [2016] 2 WLR 681, para. 85.

In turn, the answer to that question depends on how much significance is given to the fact that S's common purpose was *unlawful*. Arguably, it is S's commitment to a common unlawful purpose that adds the crucial extra normative ingredient, justifying the law's requiring only that S must foresee the possibility of P's crime. This is an entirely different basis from aiding and abetting, where S's actions need not be in themselves wrongful. Lending P (an adult) a knife is unproblematic *until* we know that P's plans for its use are wrongful. What makes S's actions the stuff of criminal law, in other words, is her mens rea with respect to P's conduct. In turn, that is why we should be wary of criminalising aiding and abetting by someone who merely foresees a risk of P's criminality. As we observed in § 7.4(iv), relaxing the stringent mens rea requirements for aiding and abetting would reduce an ordinary citizen's freedom to do things that may happen to help others to commit crimes. It seems most undesirable to hold someone liable for doing something otherwise ordinary and lawful—say, selling a knife or a baseball bat—merely because she realised it was *possible* that P may have a crime in mind. No case has ever held this. It would mean a massive expansion of the criminal law into the lives of private citizens. Perhaps this increased scope of criminalisation would be justified, although that is doubtful. Certainly, however, the implications of such a rule for ordinary citizens needed to be more carefully considered before the distinction between aiding/abetting and common-purpose liability was so blithely abandoned in *Jogee*: because one probable effect of abandoning that distinction is to increase the pressure to dilute those mens rea requirements for aiding and abetting.[238]

The same worry does not apply to the pursuit of common unlawful purposes—to conspiracies acted out.[239] By entering into a common unlawful purpose S becomes, through her own deliberate choice, a participant in a group action to commit a crime.[240] Moreover, her new status has moral significance: she allies herself with the conduct of the other members of the group in a way that the mere aider or abettor, who remains an independent character throughout the episode, does not.[241] The law has a particular hostility to criminal groups. As with the inchoate crime of conspiracy, the rationale is partly one of dangerousness: "Experience has shown that joint criminal enterprises only too readily escalate into the commission of greater offences."[242] Criminal associations are dangerous. They present a threat to public safety that ordinary criminal prohibitions, addressed to individual actors,

---

[238] As *Jogee* itself confirmed, those requirements involve proof of intention and/or knowledge by S: above, § 7.4(iv).

[239] Simester, "The Mental Element in Complicity" (2006) 122 LQR 578, 592–600; an argument accepted by the High Court of Australia: *Clayton v. R* [2006] HCA 58, para. 20.

[240] In *Clayton* [2006] HCA 58, para. 107, Kirby J (dissenting) rejects this argument: "The law may indeed dislike anti-social activities, particularly where they result in death. But a rational and just legal system will dislike such activities equally, whether the conduct charged is prosecuted as an offence of acting in concert or of aiding and abetting others in carrying out the group activity." (See also Sullivan, "Complicity for First Degree Murder and Complicity in an Unlawful Killing" [2006] *Crim LR* 502, 509–10.) Yet the point being made here in the text is that S's activity is not merely anti-social but independently criminal. By contrast, aiding and abetting need involve no otherwise criminal conduct; it is S's intention to aid, abet, etc. that turns her otherwise lawful conduct into the stuff of criminality. Hence a rational legal system may distinguish between the two, especially with respect to the mens rea requirement.

[241] In "Joint Criminal Enterprise" (2010) 73 *Modern LR* 578, 599, Krebs worries that the sharing of an unlawful purpose would make S guilty of crimes that P does alone. Not so: P's crime needed to be an incident of his pursuing their common purpose, a purpose in which S must be a participant.

[242] *Powell; English* [1999] 1 AC 1, 14 (Lord Steyn); cf. *Rahman* [2007] EWCA Crim 342, para. 61; Marshall, Webb and Tilley, *Rationalisation of Current Research on Guns, Gangs and other Weapons: Phase 1* (2005) § 3.4.

do not entirely address. Moreover, the danger is not just of an immediately physical nature. A group is a form of society, and a group constituted by a joint unlawful enterprise is a form of society that has set itself against the law and order of society at large. Individuals offending alone do not do this. Thus concerted wrongdoing imports additional and special reasons for the law to intervene. It is regrettable that English law no longer accommodates those reasons.

§ 7.6 General principles applying to all secondary parties

Secondary liability is subject to certain general doctrines governing the nature of the link required between the participant's actions and the commission of the offence to which she is party. These doctrines are discussed below.

(i) Liability is normally dependent on commission of the offence

As we have observed already, and unlike inchoate crimes of assisting and encouraging crime and conspiracy, the forms of secondary participation liability are derivative and not themselves offences. Rather, they involve S in being ascribed with legal responsibility for the offence that P commits. It follows that, subject to certain exceptions, S may only be attributed with that offence *if it actually is committed.*[243] For example:

> S urges P to shoot V, a common enemy. P purchases a gun, but before he has the opportunity to purchase any ammunition the gun dealer becomes suspicious and alerts the police, who cancel P's gun licence and confiscate the weapon.

S is guilty of the inchoate offence of encouragement to commit a crime, but since P does not actually commit the crime, S cannot be a party to murder.[244] In these standard examples, there can be no secondary liability because there is no actus reus by the principal.[245] Consider the facts of *Thornton* v. *Mitchell:*[246]

> S, a bus conductor, negligently directed the bus driver to reverse. Two pedestrians were in consequence hit by the bus. However, the driver was acquitted of careless driving, since he had quite properly relied upon the instructions of the conductor.

In these circumstances, S was acquitted of aiding and abetting the offence of careless driving. There was no actus reus by the bus driver—he had not been driving carelessly[247]—and thus no criminal conduct from which S's liability might derive.

---

[243] *A, B, C and D* [2010] EWCA Crim 1622, [2011] QB 841, para. 37; cf. *Rahman* [2008] UKHL 45, [2009] 1 AC 129, para. 21 (Lord Bingham).

[244] Cf. *Demirian* [1989] VR 97; Lanham, "Primary and Derivative Criminal Liability: An Australian Perspective" [2000] *Crim LR* 707.

[245] A proposition confirmed, if confirmation be needed, in *Kenning* [2008] EWCA Crim 1534, [2009] Crim LR 37, para. 26.

[246] [1940] 1 All ER 339. See also *Loukes* [1996] Crim LR 341; Taylor, "Complicity and Excuses" [1983] *Crim LR* 656. In *Pickford* [1995] QB 203, 213 the Court of Appeal noted, *obiter*, that S could not be convicted of aiding an abetting an offence by P if P was not a member of the class of persons who, in law, could commit the offence.

[247] For explanation, see above, § 5.5(iii).

(ii) Exceptions: secondary liability without the primary offence

The case is straightforward where P does not commit an actus reus at all. However, there are certain circumstances where something less than the full offence by P is required. The first occurs when P commits the actus reus of the offence, but is not criminally responsible for doing so because of infancy or insanity. To illustrate, consider the following facts from the Australian case of *Schultz v. Pettitt*:[248]

> D allowed P, his five-year-old daughter, to operate a power boat. P pushed the throttle too far and the boat ploughed into another boat. D was charged with carelessly operating the boat.

Prima facie, P has operated the boat carelessly. However, as we shall see in Chapter 19, P could not be convicted because of her infancy. Therefore, no offence was committed by P. Despite this, Cox J would have been willing to uphold D's conviction as a secondary party. This analysis seems right in principle.[249]

English law recognises at least two further exceptions to the requirement that P be guilty of an offence, although the scope of these exceptions is not fully settled. We consider them in the following subsections.

(a) When S is responsible for P's excuse

The first exception is for other possible defences, apart from infancy and insanity, that P may claim but which do not negate S's liability as a party. There is at least one such general defence:[250] that of duress, when S is the source of the duress. In *Bourne*,[251] S forced his wife to have sexual connection with an animal. S was convicted of abetting her to commit buggery notwithstanding that it was assumed his wife, had she been charged with the same offence, would have been acquitted owing to the availability of a defence of duress.[252] It appears that this defence operates only as a personal excuse. Similar reasoning would not, therefore, carry over to situations where (for example) P acted in justifying self-defence.[253]

(b) When S procures P to act without mens rea

The second exception arises when P does the actus reus of an offence but lacks mens rea.[254] In limited circumstances, S may be liable as a secondary party when she procures P to

---

[248] (1980) 25 SASR 427. Note that the innocent agency doctrine was held not to apply: see §§ 7.3(i), 7.6(ii)(b).

[249] As it happened, this ground for upholding the conviction failed on the facts, because the father apparently lacked the mens rea required for secondary participation.

[250] And see also below, § 7.6(iii).

[251] (1952) 36 Cr App R 125. See Edwards, "Duress and Aiding and Abetting" (1953) 69 *LQR* 227; Cross, "Duress and Aiding and Abetting (A Reply)" (1953) 69 *LQR* 354.

[252] Compare *Howe* [1987] AC 417, 458, where Lord Mackay highlighted the fact that duress involved a "reason special to [P] himself". Note that this was not the reasoning used by the Court in *Bourne* itself: see below, n. 280, and accompanying discussion in § 7.6(ii)(b) of the limitations of such reasoning. The best explanation of *Bourne* is that highlighted by Lord Mackay and adopted here. For discussion of the distinction between justification and excuse see below, § 17.2.

[253] Strictly, the appropriate defence would have been coercion, a special, extended, variety of the duress defence, formerly available to wives who committed crimes in the presence of their husbands. See below, § 20.2.

[254] Cf. *DPP v. K and B* [1997] 1 Cr App R 36, in which two girls, B and K, used threats of violence to order V to have sexual intercourse with P, an unknown boy apparently under 14 years of age. Note, however, that the analysis in that case is flawed. The Divisional Court treated P as lacking mens rea on the basis of the *doli incapax* presumption (*ibid.*, 42). This was wrong: the *doli incapax* presumption is not against mens rea but against

commit the actus reus of an offence for which P lacks mens rea. In *Cogan and Leak*,[255] P had sexual intercourse with S's wife, apparently believing (on the basis of what S told him) that the wife was consenting. On appeal, P's conviction for rape was quashed, but S's conviction was upheld. The main ground for upholding his conviction was said to be that P was an innocent agent through whom S had acted as a principal in committing the offence. However, that analysis is problematic, in so far as rape is one of a number of offences that cannot be committed through an innocent agent.[256]

Alternatively, the Court of Appeal reasoned that S was guilty of procuring rape, since even though P could not be convicted, S's wife had "clearly" been raped: "Cogan had sexual intercourse with her without her consent. The fact that Cogan was innocent of rape because he believed that she was consenting does not affect the position that she was raped."[257]

This, with respect, is misconceived. Rape is not an absolute liability crime, constituted simply by its actus reus. The fact that P lacked mens rea under the then-prevailing law[258] means that, for the purposes of the criminal law (and by contrast with ordinary language), no rape occurred.[259] Nonetheless, S's conviction seems a just result. If so, the better analysis seems to be that, where S *procures* P to commit the actus reus of an offence without mens rea, S may be convicted of procuring that offence. The Court of Appeal subsequently accepted this account in *Millward*,[260] the facts of which were as follows:

> S instructed P, his employee, to drive S's tractor on the highway. The tractor was in a defective condition, and by driving it on the highway P (the Court assumed[261]) committed the actus reus of reckless driving. S knew, and P did not know, that the vehicle was unroadworthy. While on the highway, the tractor's condition caused an accident, killing the passenger of another car.

On these facts, P was acquitted of causing death by reckless driving but S was convicted as a party to the offence. The Court of Appeal upheld S's conviction explicitly on the basis that he had procured commission of the actus reus by P.

The propriety of this exception to the rule that P must be guilty of the offence has been doubted,[262] but its place in English law seems secure.[263] In any event, such cases will be

---

P's having the capacity to distinguish right from wrong (below, § 19.4(ii)). It is therefore a denial of criminal responsibility, like insanity and the irrebuttable presumption of *doli incapax* for infants below 10 years of age. For criticism, see the commentary at [1997] Crim LR 121.

[255] [1976] QB 217.

[256] See above, § 7.3(i). This common-law limitation upon the scope of rape is preserved in s. 1 of the Sexual Offences Act 2003; below, § 12.6.

[257] *Cogan and Leak* [1976] QB 217, 223.

[258] More recently, the mens rea requirement in rape has been modified by the Sexual Offences Act 2003, and it is likely that P would now be found guilty. See below, § 12.5.

[259] A similar example of this reasoning appears in *Bourne* (1952) 36 Cr App R 125, discussed in the previous section (see especially n. 272). Lord Goddard asserted (at 128) that the fact that P would have been acquitted of buggery presented no impediment to S's conviction for complicity because "that [P] could have set up duress ... means that she admits that she has committed the crime but prays to be excused from punishment". Yet an acquittal would mean that she committed no crime.

[260] [1994] Crim LR 527; see also *Wheelhouse* [1994] Crim LR 756.

[261] Erroneously. In fact, the case was like *Thornton* v. *Mitchell*, discussed above in § 7.6(i), where no actus reus occurred. Cf. the acceptance of this criticism of *Millward* by Smith, in his discussion of *Loukes* [1996] *Crim LR* 341, 343.

[262] See, e.g., Kadish, "Complicity, Cause and Blame" in *Essays in the Criminal Law* (1987) 135, 180; Law Com. No. 305, *Participation in Crime* (2007) para. 2.16.

[263] The Law Commission's own preference is to deal with such cases by an extended statutory doctrine of innocent agency (§ 7.3(i) above) together with a specific new offence of causing another to commit a strict liability crime. See Law Com. No. 305, *Participation in Crime* (2007) part 4.

rare, since whenever the actus reus involves consequences, S may normally be convicted as a principal offender (either on the basis of having caused the actus reus personally or by means of the innocent agent doctrine).

(iii) Conviction for different offences with the same actus reus

A variant situation arises when there are two offences constituted by the same actus reus, and differentiated only by degree of culpability. The leading example of this is murder and manslaughter. Suppose, for instance, the following situation:

> S lends P a cosh, which he knows P plans to use to in order to assault V. S knows that the blow may cause V's death, but believes P intends only to knock V out and does not mean to kill him. In this, however, S is mistaken. P intends to kill V. Unfortunately, although P hits V no harder than agreed, she succeeds in her aim of killing him.

In cases of this sort, S and P need not be convicted of the same offence. Where P is guilty of murder, it is possible to convict S only of manslaughter, provided P's acts are within the scope of the assistance or encouragement lent by S.[264] This issue, amongst others, arose in Yemoh,[265] the relevant facts of which were as follows:

> S joined with others in an attack on V, during the course of which V was fatally stabbed. By implication of the jury finding,[266] S realised that P might use a knife to cause injury, but may not have realised that P intended to kill.

On these facts, the Court of Appeal upheld S's conviction for manslaughter.

The rationale for S's lesser conviction in such cases is that S's participation was done with the intention of assisting or encouraging P whose proposed conduct was such that, were V to die, P would be guilty of manslaughter; in circumstances where, ultimately, P performed the envisaged conduct with sufficient mens rea for murder.[267]

The fact that these two offences share the same actus reus means that any incursion upon the principle that S's liability is derivative upon P's is minimal. Indeed, manslaughter may be regarded as a lesser included offence within murder. Moreover, arguably the jury has a constitutional power on a charge of murder (improperly) to return a verdict of manslaughter, even though the jury is satisfied that every element necessary to constitute the crime of murder has been established.[268]

---

[264] Above, § 7.4(ii). If outside that scope, S is generally entitled to a complete acquittal in respect of P's crime.

[265] [2009] EWCA Crim 930, [2009] Crim LR 888.

[266] Ibid., para. 124.

[267] Cf. Gilmour [2000] 2 Cr App R 407; Murtagh and Kennedy [1955] Crim LR 315.

[268] See, e.g., Gammage v. R. (1969) 122 CLR 444, 450–1, 453, 460, 463, 465 (HCA). English courts have not determined the point authoritatively, but in Shipley (1784) 4 Doug KB 73, 178, 99 ER 774, 828, Ashurst J drew a distinction similar to that accepted by the Australian High Court in Gammage: "I admit the jury have the power of finding a verdict against the law, and so they have of finding a verdict against the evidence, but I deny that they have a right to do so". In Meany (1862) L & C 213, 216, 169 ER 1368, 1370, Pollock CB noted that the judge "is not bound to receive their verdict unless they insist upon his doing so". A manslaughter verdict contrary to direction has been accepted, reluctantly, by the judge in at least one case, noted (1942) 86 Sol LJ 251; see also Soanes [1948] 1 All ER 289, 290 (infanticide); Clement v. Blunt (1623) 2 Rolle 460, 81 ER 916. In Smith, The Times, 14 January 1804 (discussed by Williams, "Homicide and the Supernatural" (1949) 65 LQR 491, 500–3), however, the Court refused to receive the jury's first verdict of manslaughter, and sent the jury back out with a direction to convict of murder or acquit; see also Snelling, "The Alternative Verdict of Manslaughter" (1958) 32 ALJ 137.

However, the reverse is not true, and it does not follow from the above that S may be convicted of murder if the principal party is guilty only of manslaughter. Imagine the following example:

> S encourages P to punch V. S knows, and P does not, that V has an "egg-shell skull", and she hopes that the blow will cause V's death. P strikes V, killing him.

P is guilty of manslaughter. But is S guilty of murder, or only of manslaughter? In *Richards*,[269] the Court of Appeal first suggested that S can only be guilty of manslaughter. The facts of that case were as follows:

> S hired P1 and P2 to beat up V, her husband, badly enough to hospitalise him for a month. P1 and P2 then attacked V and inflicted a minor but no serious wound. The principals were acquitted of wounding with intent to cause grievous bodily harm and convicted instead of unlawful wounding, a lesser offence. S was convicted of wounding with intent to cause grievous bodily harm.

The Court of Appeal quashed S's conviction, and substituted a conviction for unlawful wounding. However, the decision has been powerfully criticised,[270] and was disapproved by both the Court of Appeal and the House of Lords in *Howe*.[271] It appears, therefore, that under current law S may be found guilty of the greater offence (e.g. murder) even though, because of lack of mens rea, P is guilty of only of the lesser offence (e.g. manslaughter).

It may be the law, but does the position after *Howe* accord with principle? One might worry that, on the view taken in *Howe*, the accomplice's liability can no longer derive from the principal's crime—it is driven more by the accomplice's personal culpability than by his participation in the principal's crime.

Certainly, P has acted without the mens rea for the more serious offence of murder. Prior to *Howe* the only permitted exception in such cases (i.e. where S may be convicted despite P's lacking mens rea) was restricted to situations in which S has actively procured the actus reus through P;[272] and that is a special case, justified by analogy with the doctrine of innocent agency. The exception approved in *Howe* can claim no such analogy.

Nonetheless, there are reasons why S should be convicted of murder. It is misleading to present murder and manslaughter as independent offences. Although the wrong in each is not *precisely* the same (there are some reasons against killing someone deliberately which do not apply to killing someone inadvertently, and vice versa), the core of the wrong is identical. The dominant rationale for each offence is the protection of life. Indeed, it is generally appropriate to think of manslaughter as an alternative rather than separate charge, available when the mens rea of murder cannot be proved or when the defendant has some limited defence such as loss of control. Arguably therefore, it is wrong to characterise the theory underlying the *dicta* in *Howe* as a matter of culpability triumphing over

---

[269] [1974] QB 776.

[270] E.g. [1974] Crim LR 96; Smith, "Aid, Abet, Counsel, or Procure" in Glazebrook (ed.), *Reshaping the Criminal Law* (1978) 120, 128–30; *TBCL* § 15.18. Contrast Kadish, "Complicity, Cause and Blame" in *Blame and Punishment* (1987) 135, 184–6.

[271] [1987] AC 417 (HL), *sub nom. Burke* [1986] QB 626, 641–2 (CA).

[272] Above, § 7.6(ii)(c). Where S's participation is by procurement, it may even be possible in such cases to convict her as principal on ordinary principles of causation. See Alldridge, "The Doctrine of Innocent Agency" (1990) 2 *Crim L Forum* 45, 61ff.

the principles of derivative liability; in the context of derivation, these offences should not be regarded as separate.

As we observed in § 7.5(ii), the principles of derivative liability do not have a life of their own. They exist only for a further purpose: to supplement ordinary actus reus doctrines (governing omissions, causation, etc.) by identifying other persons who are answerable when a criminal wrong is done. Once we consider this underlying rationale, it becomes apparent that S *can* be attributed with responsibility for the actus reus of murder in these cases. At least arguably, the underlying function of derivative liability doctrines is properly served by the ruling in *Howe*.

In any event, there is one further, uncontroversial, exception. Consistent with the case of duress above (§ 7.6(ii)(a)), it arises when there is a personal excusatory defence available to P. Culpable homicide admits of palliative defences: especially, for loss of control, diminished responsibility,[273] suicide pacts,[274] and infanticide.[275] Where such a defence is open to the principal, the secondary party's liability for murder (or manslaughter, in the case of infanticide) will not be correspondingly reduced.

(iv) *Limitations on secondary liability*

(a) *The Tyrrell principle*

The common law contains a limited exemption from secondary liability for victims of crime. The exemption arises in respect of offences that exist for the *protection* of a certain class of person, i.e. persons who are regarded by the statute as victims rather than co-offenders. Such persons are treated as incapable of participating in crimes against themselves. The leading case is *Tyrrell*, where it was held that D, a girl under the age of 16 years, could not be convicted of abetting unlawful sexual intercourse with herself, because the Act that created the offence "was passed for the purpose of protecting women and girls against themselves".[276] However, the common law principle espoused in *Tyrrell* is of limited scope,[277] and its application may be doubtful in areas other than offences against young persons and persons suffering from a disability. Indeed, its place even in sexual offences involving the young is now uncertain, following enactment of the Sexual Offences Act 2003. That Act, while not explicitly excluding the *Tyrrell* principle,[278] frequently fails to identify with consistency or clarity whether its various offences are designed to protect particular

---

[273] Cf. Homicide Act 1957, s. 2(4).

[274] Homicide Act 1957, s. 4(1).

[275] Infanticide Act 1938, s. 1(1).

[276] [1894] 1 QB 710, 712 (Lord Coleridge CJ). See also *Whitehouse* [1977] QB 868; *Pickford* [1995] 1 Cr App R 420, 428; *Congdon* [1990] NLJR 1221. However, while these three cases were decided on the basis of the *Tyrrell* principle, they are better analysed as falling within the next type of exceptions (§ 7.6(iv)(b)), where liability is excluded as a matter of statutory interpretation. See Williams, "Victims and Other Exempt Parties in Crime" (1990) 10 *LS* 245, 249–50.

[277] Williams, "Victims and Other Exempt Parties in Crime" (1990) 10 *LS* 245; Hogan, "Victims as Parties to Crime" [1962] *Crim LR* 683; Williams, "Victims as Parties to Crimes—A Further Comment" [1964] *Crim LR* 686; Heydon, "The Corroboration of Accomplices" [1973] *Crim LR* 264, 274.

[278] See s. 73(3), which preserves existing exceptions to complicity liability.

classes of persons, and allows that young persons can commit many of the Act's offences even as principals.[279] Consequently, we must await future rulings about which, if any, of its offences remain subject to the common law exception.[280]

The possibility of applying the *Tyrrell* principle depends on the purpose of the relevant legislation, and arises only if the statute is directed toward protecting an identified class of persons.[281] There is certainly no *general* exception for victims of crime.[282] Thus if, for example, in the course of a sadomasochistic episode S asks P to inflict injury on him, it appears that both P and S commit an offence of assault occasioning actual bodily harm contrary to section 47 of the Offences Against the Person Act 1861, since that offence protects the public at large.[283]

(b) Specific legislation

Quite apart from situations where the policy of a statute invokes the *Tyrrell* principle, the relevant primary offence may also be defined by legislation in such a way that it delimits the class of persons who may commit that offence. In such instances, secondary participation is excluded except in so far as such participants qualify within the class stipulated by the primary offence. One example of a statutory restriction on the range of secondary participants was suggested, *obiter*, by Lord Parker CJ in *Carmichael & Sons Ltd* v. *Cottle*.[284] The Chief Justice observed that, in the context of regulations prohibiting the use or causing or permitting of use of a defective vehicle on the road, since "normally, 'using' is applicable to the actual driver" it may follow that:

> "when the words used are 'using or causing or permitting [to be used]', there is no room for the application of the principle in regard to aiders and abettors. The statute in other words itself provides the alternatives, and, if a person is to be charged as an aider and abettor or an accessory, he should be so charged, and under these provisions should be specifically charged with causing or permitting the user."

However, such cases are rare. More commonly, the statute may define a class of persons who may commit the offence *as a principal*, without restricting the class of persons who may be guilty of the offence as a secondary party.[285] A good example is the offence of rape,

---

[279] Below, Chapter 12.

[280] Bohlander, "The Sexual Offences Act 2003 and the *Tyrrell* Principle—Criminalising the Victims" [2005] *Crim LR* 701.

[281] Cf. *Gnango* [2011] UKSC 59, [2012] 1 AC 827, paras. 17–18, 48–9. A similar restriction is favoured by the Law Commission: Law Com. No. 305, *Participation in Crime* (2007) paras. 5.24–5.39.

[282] *Wright's Case* (1603) 1 Co. Lit. 127a: D agreed to cut off V's hand so that V could beg more effectively. Both D and V were convicted of mayhem.

[283] Cf. *Brown* [1994] 1 AC 212. Interestingly, since the rhetoric of the majority judgments in that case emphasises the paternalistic aspect of not allowing the masochist legally to consent to violence perpetrated by the sadist, arguably it follows that the masochist ought to be treated as a victim falling within the protected class to which the *Tyrrell* principle applies. It is legal moralism, not paternalism, that indicts the masochist.

[284] [1971] RTR 11, 14. Cf. *Crawford* v. *Haughton* [1972] WLR 572 (DC); *Farr* [1982] Crim LR 745. Arguably, *Sockett* (1908) 72 JP 428 should have been treated as such a case: see *TBCL* § 15.15 n. 11. S, who was not pregnant, was convicted of aiding and abetting P to use an instrument on S with intent to procure a miscarriage; even though the statute made it no offence for someone not pregnant to use such an instrument on herself, so that S fell outside the class of persons who could commit the offence as principal.

[285] Cf. the actual decision in *Sockett, ibid.*; also *Mok Wei Tak* v. *R.* [1990] 2 AC 333; Heydon, "The Corroboration of Accomplices" [1973] *Crim LR* 264, 271.

which can only be committed by a male.[286] This criterion means that a female cannot commit rape as a principal. But she may nonetheless aid and abet a rape committed by someone else.[287]

(c) Law enforcement

One exception of uncertain scope is law enforcement.[288] Suppose that S is a police officer (or indeed a private individual) who assists P to commit a crime in order to gather evidence against P. Is S too guilty of the crime? The answer appears to depend on the nature of S's participation. Consider first the case where S instigates the crime herself. According to the House of Lords in *Sang*, in that case S has no defence:[289]

> "I would now refer to what is, I believe and hope, the unusual case in which a dishonest police-man, anxious to improve his detection record, tries very hard with the help of an *agent provocateur* to induce a young man with no criminal tendencies to commit a serious crime, and ultimately the young man succumbs to the inducement.... The policeman and the informer who acted together in inciting him to commit the crime should ... both be prosecuted and suitably punished."

(So too, added their Lordships, should the young man.[290]) By contrast, where P has instigated the offence and S then participates solely in order to trap P, or to prevent the offence from coming to fruition,[291] S appears to be exempted from liability as a secondary party even though he may satisfy the actus reus and mens rea elements required for liability. According to the Court of Appeal in *Birtles*:[292]

> "It is one thing for the police to make use of information concerning an offence that is already laid on. In such a case the police are clearly entitled, and indeed it is their duty, to mitigate the consequences of the proposed offence, for example, to protect the proposed victim, and to that end it may be perfectly proper for them to encourage the informer to take part in the offence or for the police officer himself to do so. But it is quite another thing, and something of which this court thoroughly disapproves, to use an informer to encourage another to commit an offence or indeed an offence of a more serious character, which he would not otherwise commit."

There is difficult middle ground.[293] In *Williams* v. *DPP*,[294] police officers exposed cartons of cigarettes, apparently unguarded, in the back of a van parked in the street; then prosecuted P after he helped himself to some of them. While there is much to be said for allowing the police to use temptation-based methods to trap criminals, such cases do present difficulties for complicity law. The Divisional Court in *Williams* stated that the police had

---

[286] Sexual Offences Act 2003, s. 1 (penetration of vagina, anus, or mouth "with his penis") Cf. § 12.6.

[287] See *Ram* (1893) 17 Cox CC 609.

[288] The Law Commission has recommended a somewhat complex statutory defence of acting to prevent an offence or to limit harm, provided that S's conduct is reasonable in the circumstances: Law Com. No. 305, *Participating in Crime* (2007) paras. 5.10–5.23.

[289] [1980] AC 402 (Lord Salmon).

[290] See further the discussion of entrapment: below, § 20.4.

[291] As in *Gillick* v. *West Norfolk and Wisbech Area Health Authority* [1986] AC 112. Such cases are, perhaps, better dealt with under the rubric of necessity: see below, § 21.3.

[292] [1969] 2 All ER 1131n, 1132 (Lord Parker CJ). Cf. *Bainbridge* [1991] Crim LR 535; *Clarke* (1984) 80 Cr App R 344; *McEvilly* (1973) 60 Cr App R 150; *McCann* (1971) 56 Cr App R 359.

[293] See Ashworth, "Testing Fidelity to Legal Values: Official Involvement and Criminal Justice" in Shute and Simester (eds.), *Criminal Law: Doctrines of the General Part* (2002) 299.

[294] (1993) 98 Cr App R 209.

not aided or abetted P's crime; yet it is arguable that they did so. Provision of the "bait" constituted an essential ingredient of the crime, not to mention encouragement. Perhaps there is a subtle distinction to be drawn between "instigation" and mere "temptation"; a distinction favourably construed where S's motive is law enforcement. It is impossible, in a text of this nature, to resolve the many difficulties raised by these cases. Suffice it to note, however, that the judgment in *Birtles* is very difficult to reconcile with decisions such as *Yip Chiu-Cheung* v. *R.*,[295] where an undercover police officer (who was not charged) was said by the Privy Council to be a co-conspirator with D to export heroin, even though the officer had entered into the conspiracy solely in order to expose the operation. A look behind the judgments is revealing. By ruling the officer a conspirator in *Yip*, their Lordships secured D's conviction for conspiracy. By ruling the officer a non-participant in *Birtles*, the Court of Appeal freed him from the rules constraining evidence given by accomplices, so that his evidence against D did not need corroboration. Making law for ulterior purposes like these, it must be said, is a recipe for bad law.

(v) Secondary liability and inchoate offences

We have observed that secondary participation is not *per se* a crime. Its doctrines do not create offences. They operate as a conduit to S's responsibility for some other form of criminal wrongdoing. Therefore, since secondary participation is not an offence, it follows that S cannot commit the inchoate crime of attempting to be a party to an offence.[296] (By contrast, it is possible to attempt to commit the distinct, inchoate offences of assisting or encouraging crime.[297]) If there were ever any doubt about attempted participation at common law, it has been resolved by section 1(4)(b) of the Criminal Attempts Act 1981, which expressly excludes aiding, abetting, counselling, and procuring from the ambit of the crime of attempting to commit an offence.[298]

Similarly, neither may one commit an offence of conspiring to aid and abet. Although the question had been left open by the House of Lords in *Hollinshead*,[299] the position has been confirmed more recently by the Court of Appeal,[300] and may for now be regarded as settled.

Conceptually, the view that there can be no inchoate offence of attempted participation in crime seems right. If S has failed to participate in a crime, she has no connection with it and should not be convicted. Her conduct is, one might say, too remote from manifest criminality to warrant the attention of the criminal law—attention that would be tantamount to punishing for little more than wrongful thoughts.[301] Conversely, however,

---

[295] [1995] 1 AC 111; below, § 9.3(iv). Cf. *Latif* [1996] 1 ALL ER 353; above, § 4.2(iii)(b) (Case 2).

[296] Smith, "Secondary Participation and Inchoate Offences" in Tapper (ed.), *Crime, Proof and Punishment* (1981) 21. See also Spencer, "Trying to Help Another Person Commit a Crime" in P. Smith (ed.), *Criminal Law: Essays in Honour of J.C. Smith* (1987) 148; below, § 7.7. Contrast the Model Penal Code, § 2.06(3)(a)(ii).

[297] Below, § 9.2(i)(d) (Inchoate offences).

[298] Cf. *Dunnington* [1984] QB 472.

[299] *Hollinshead* [1985] AC 975 (HL).

[300] *Kenning* [2008] EWCA Crim 1534; endorsing the Court's own conclusion in *Hollinshead* [1985] 1 All ER 850, 857–8 (CA).

[301] Per Fletcher, *Rethinking Criminal Law* (1978) 680–1: "there is no social wrong in acting to aid the crime of another, unless the aid actually furthers the criminal objective".

the inchoate offences *are* offences in themselves, independent of the further crime that is attempted or conspired toward. Therefore, S may be a party to (aid, abet, etc.) an attempt[302] or a conspiracy[303] by P to commit an offence.

An exception to the general rule that there is no inchoate liability for participation arises if assistance or encouragement is itself made a substantive offence by legislation. In *McShane*,[304] D visited her mother in hospital where they discussed the possibility of the mother's suicide. D was convicted of attempting to counsel or procure her mother's suicide. She appealed on the ground that no such offence was known to law. However, the Court of Appeal dismissed the appeal. The relevant substantive offence at that time was enacted by section 2(1) of the Suicide Act 1961 in the following terms:

> A person who aids, abets, counsels or procures the suicide of another, or an attempt by another to commit suicide, shall be liable on conviction to imprisonment for a term not exceeding 14 years.

Under this section, the counselling or procuring was not a secondary form of participation in some further offence; it constituted an offence in its own right. Consequently, there could be an inchoate offence of attempting to commit an offence against that section, and D was rightly convicted of attempting to counsel or procure another's suicide.[305]

In 2007, the government generalised this last technique, by making assisting or encouraging crime an inchoate offence *in its own right*, independently of the perpetration of the principal's crime. Under sections 44–6 of the Serious Crime Act, one who (say) encourages P to commit a murder becomes, herself, immediately guilty of an inchoate offence of *encouraging or assisting crime*. The new offences are inchoate, in that S's guilt does not depend on the occurrence of the substantive crime; and the conviction is for an offence under one of sections 44–6, not for a homicide offence. Thus these new offences are complementary to, and do not displace, secondary liability. If, subsequently, P then carries out the crime as encouraged, complicity doctrines would operate to make S guilty of *murder*. These new inchoate offences are noted further in § 7.7. They are considered in detail in Chapter 9.

(vi) Withdrawal

When perpetrating the principal offence, P cannot undo his crime. Once the elements of the offence are concurrently satisfied, the offence is committed and cannot be "uncommitted". By contrast, secondary participation *can* be undone. S may withdraw her participation, although she must do so before the crime is committed:[306]

> "A person who unequivocally withdraws from the joint enterprise before the moment of the actual commission of the crime by the principal ... should not be liable for that crime, although his acts before withdrawing may render him liable for other offences."

---

[302] *Hapgood* v. *Wyatt* (1870) LR 1 CCR 221, 11 Cox CC 471; *Clayton* (1843) 1 C & K 128, 174 ER 743. Cf. *Mackie* [1957] NZLR 669 (CA).

[303] *Anderson* (1984) 80 Cr App R 64; cf. *McNamara (No. 1)* (1981) 56 CCC (2d) 193.

[304] (1977) 66 Cr App R 97.

[305] The relevant substantive offence would now be encouraging or assisting suicide, contrary to s. 59 of the Coroners and Justice Act 2009—an offence which cannot be attempted. See below, § 10.9(ii).

[306] *O'Flaherty* [2004] 2 Cr App R 20, para. 58.

Withdrawal, however, is not easy. Repentance is insufficient.[307] The participation must not merely be discontinued. It must be countermanded.[308]

(a) Withdrawal from abetment by a common purpose

Where S has participated simply by joining in a common purpose to commit a crime, without giving specific assistance or encouragement, the common purpose may generally be abandoned by S's communicating his withdrawal in an unequivocal and timely way. This may become particularly important if, having agreed to participate in a criminal enterprise (crime A), S realises *subsequently* that P may go beyond what was agreed and perpetrate some further crime (crime B): for example, if, in the course of burgling a house, S suddenly realises that her companion is armed with a knife and may use it on anyone found in the house. S can avoid liability for crime B by then withdrawing from the joint enterprise before crime B is committed.

A helpful statement of the criteria for withdrawing from a common unlawful purpose is found in the Canadian case of *Whitehouse*:[309]

> "where practical and reasonable there must be timely communication of the intention to abandon the common purpose from those who wish to dissociate themselves from the contemplated crime to those who decide to continue in it."

The emphasis here is on effective manifestation of the withdrawal. As the Court of Appeal put the matter in *O'Flaherty*,[310]

> "To disengage from an incident a person must do enough to demonstrate that he or she is withdrawing from the joint enterprise. This is ultimately a question of fact and degree for the jury."

The notice of withdrawal, whether made by words or actions,[311] must be "unequivocal";[312] a perfunctory disclaimer is likely to be insufficient,[313] as is merely leaving the scene[314] or simply not turning up.[315] It must also be timely, occurring before the crime is committed, and perhaps before its commission is even commenced.[316]

There is no general requirement that S must, in addition to withdrawing unequivocally, also take reasonable steps to prevent P from committing the offence.[317] However, where the

---

[307] *Croft* [1944] 1 KB 295; *Becerra and Cooper* (1976) 62 Cr App R 212; Hale, 1 PC 618.

[308] Compare the Law Commission's report, which describes withdrawal in terms of "negating" the effect of S's participation: Law Com. No. 305, *Participating in Crime* (2007) paras. 3.60ff.

[309] [1941] 1 DLR 683, 685; see also *Henderson* v. *R.* [1949] 2 DLR 121. The statement is approved by English authorities: *Becerra and Cooper* (1976) 62 Cr App R 212; *Whitefield* (1983) 79 Cr App R 36; *Rook* [1993] 2 All ER 955. For discussion of the common law and recommendations for reform see K.J.M. Smith, "Withdrawal in Complicity: A Restatement of Principles" [2001] *Crim LR* 769.

[310] [2004] 2 Cr App R 20, para. 60.

[311] E.g., by S's action of quitting the company he has joined: *Hyde* (1672) 1 Hale PC 537; *Foster, Crown Law* 354; *Edmeades* (1828) 3 C & P 390, 392, 172 ER 469, 470. *Hyde* and *Foster* are endorsed in *Jogee* [2016] UKSC 8; *Ruddock* [2016] UKPC 7, [2016] 2 WLR 681, para. 13, suggesting that the law on this point has not changed.

[312] *Rook* [1993] WLR 1005, 1012; *Baker* [1994] Crim LR 444.

[313] Cf. *Fletcher* [1962] Crim LR 551.

[314] *Becerra and Cooper* (1976) 62 Cr App R 212.

[315] *Goodspeed* (1911) 6 Cr App R 133; *Rook* [1993] 62 All ER 955.

[316] A possibility raised in *Perman* [1996] 1 Cr App R 24, 34.

[317] *O'Flaherty* [2004] 2 Cr App R 20, paras. 60–1. Compare, however, *Gallant* [2008] EWCA Crim 1111, para. 14, where the Court took note of the fact that S was the instigator of the attack: "In those circumstances, assuming that the attack started as a joint enterprise, he clearly would have had to do more than merely walk away in order to

situation is such that communication of withdrawal to the other parties is impossible or impractical, withdrawal may alternatively be effected by taking steps to prevent the commission of the offence, e.g. by warning the victim or the police.[318] There may come a point when events are so far advanced that efficacious withdrawal by S is impossible.[319]

In principle, the common purpose could simply come to an end. Thus it is sometimes alleged by S that, whereas she participated (say) in an attack on V, that attack had finished and V was later killed in a separate attack by P and/or others. While each case will depend on its facts, such a conclusion is likely to be rare.[320]

It is worth re-emphasising that, even where the common purpose ends, or withdrawal is effected by S, it will not preclude liability if the actus reus of P's crime occurs prior to that withdrawal. In *Campbell (André)*,[321] S engaged in a joint attack with P and others upon V. Subsequently, P continued the assault on the other side of the road. While their common purpose may by then have come to an end, S's conviction was upheld on the alternative basis that the events during the earlier attack were themselves a contributing (concurrent) cause of death.

(b) Withdrawal from assistance or encouragement

When S has provided specific assistance or encouragement toward the commission of a crime, countermanding that participation is more onerous. Mere cessation of further participatory activity will be insufficient.[322] Withdrawal may only be effected by taking steps to counteract the effect of his previous actions. What steps are sufficient will, it seems, depend upon the circumstances and upon the extent of S's prior participation: the greater the involvement, the more S must do to withdraw.[323] Encouragement can normally be undone by an express statement to the opposite effect.[324] However, if material assistance has been rendered, there may have to be some form of physical intervention to impede the crime. For example, S may have to try to recover the knife loaned to P or attempt to protect the victim, perhaps even by restraining P physically.[325] Advice or counsel, on the other hand, cannot as such be undone, but may be countermanded by attempts to dissuade P from proceeding with the crime. In *Grundy*,[326] S had provided P1 and P2 with information about premises

---

demonstrate that he was withdrawing from any further participation". This more onerous standard may be justified on the basis that, as well as withdrawing from the common purpose, an instigator needs also to countermand the encouragement given: § 7.6(vi)(b).

[318] *Becerra and Cooper* (1976) 62 Cr App R 212. Cf. Lanham, "Accomplices and Withdrawal" (1981) 97 *LQR* 575, 580ff; *Eldredge v. United States* (1932) 62 F 2d 449; *Commonwealth v. Huber* (1958) 15 D & C 2d 726.

[319] As appears to have occurred in *White v. Ridley* (1978) 140 CLR 342.

[320] See, e.g., *Mitchell* [2008] EWCA Crim 2552, where the appellant's convictions were upheld.

[321] [2009] EWCA Crim 50.

[322] *Johnson and Jones* (1841) Car & M 218, 174 ER 479.

[323] Australian case law requires that S take "all reasonable steps" to undo the impact of his participation: *Menniti* [1985] 1 Qd R 520, noted at (1986) 10 *Crim LJ* 236; *Wilton* (1993) 64 A Crim R 359. The proposition that S must seek to "neutralise" the effect of previous assistance was left undecided by the Court of Appeal in *Rook* [1993] 2 All ER 955, 962–3, but seems implicit in *Becerra and Cooper* (1976) 62 Cr App R 212, 219: where S handed over the knife to P, "something vastly different and vastly more effective" than an announced departure was required to constitute withdrawal.

[324] *Saunders and Archer* (1573) 2 Plowd 473, 75 ER 706. Cf. *Croft* [1944] KB 295; *Rook* [1993] 1 WLR 1005.

[325] *Becerra and Cooper* (1976) 62 Cr App R 212; *Baker* [1994] Crim LR 444.

[326] [1977] Crim LR 543; cf. *Whitefield* (1984) 79 Cr App R 36.

they were planning to burgle. Two weeks before the burglary was to be committed, however, S apparently had a change of heart and thereafter had been trying to stop the principals from carrying out their plan. The Court of Appeal ruled that the trial judge had erred by refusing to leave S's defence of withdrawal to the jury.

§ 7.7 Do we need complicity?

Should the day ever arrive when England and Wales join with the rest of the civilised world in codifying their criminal law, Peter Glazebrook has suggested that we might dispense with doctrines of complicity.[327] Glazebrook would simply specify the various modes of involvement in crimes—i.e. modes by which one may become guilty of committing a crime—without drawing a formal distinction between principals and accessories. More recently, Michael Moore has argued that derivative liability is at odds with the fundamental principle that criminal liability should be based on findings of *personal* responsibility for one's own acts and omissions.[328] To be sure, the effects of one's conduct on the conduct of others can be taken into account, but only in terms of what one is personally responsible for. It should be added that, in terms of causal theory, Moore contends that it is perfectly possible to hold that something done by S can be a cause of something voluntarily done by P, such as when P kills V because he has been paid to do so by S.[329] On that relaxed view of causation in inter-personal relations, much of the territory currently covered by complicity could be re-mapped as forms of direct liability.

It is certainly possible to express a person's involvement in wrongs that are perpetrated by others without resorting to a formal notion of complicity, as the law on joint tortfeasors demonstrates. Removing the labels, however, may not dissolve the reasons that begat them. Even on Glazebrook's draft provisions,[330] helping and encouraging crime are only modes of committing an offence *if* some other person (let us call her the "principal") actually commits that offence. So the liability of the helper or encourager is dependent. Moreover, the actus reus of offending by helping will necessarily differ from the actus reus of offending by committing (i.e. as principal). It looks as if distinct principles will still be needed in order to identify separately those who independently commit the offence and those who commit it only by helping or encouraging another.

Parliament has, however, gone even further than Glazebrook's proposal, and has chosen to supplement the law of complicity with three inchoate offences of assisting and encouraging crime, contrary to sections 44–46 of the Serious Crime Act 2007.[331] S's liability

---

[327] "Structuring the Criminal Code: Functional Approaches to Complicity, Incomplete Offences and General Offences" in Simester and Smith (eds.), *Harm and Culpability* (1996) 195.

[328] *Causation and Responsibility: An Essay in Law, Morals and Metaphysics* (2009) chap. 13. See also Sullivan, "Doing Without Complicity" [2012] *J Commonwealth Criminal Law* 199.

[329] *Ibid.*, chs. 11, 12.

[330] "Structuring the Criminal Code: Functional Approaches to Complicity, Incomplete Offences and General Offences" in Simester and Smith (eds.), *Harm and Culpability* (1996) 195, 211–12.

[331] Below, § 9.2. Cf. Law Com. No. 300, *Inchoate Liability for Assisting and Encouraging Crime* (2006). When these offences were first contemplated by the Law Commission, they were intended to replace rather than supplement complicity: LCCP No. 131 (1993). See Sullivan, "Inchoate Liability for Assisting and Encouraging Crime— The Law Commission Report" [2006] *Crim LR* 1047.

for these inchoate offences is constituted by her own actions and intentions, and arises independently of whether the relevant substantive offence is, ultimately, committed by P. The attraction of such a proposal is that, like any inchoate offence, it would reduce the element of luck in S's conviction. The point is made by Spencer:[332]

> "If you commit the crime I knew you intended with my help to commit, I am likely to be an accessory, but if you do not, I may well commit no offence at all…. This is very strange. In either case, I have done all that I have to do to incur criminal liability. It is no fault of mine—or to be accurate, it is not due to any lack of fault on my part—that the crime was never committed. If my behaviour was bad enough to punish where you actually made use of the help I gave you, it was surely bad enough to punish where I fully expected you to use it but you got caught before you had the chance."

The existence of these new offences is likely to take some of the pressure off the law of complicity, with its controversial and uncertain boundaries, since alternative convictions are now likely to be available under the wide ambit of the Serious Crime Act, with a potential maximum sentence corresponding to that of the principal's offence (even where that offence is ultimately not committed).

At the same time, there remains a place for complicity doctrine. The inchoate offences generate a stand-alone conviction under the Serious Crime Act. By contrast, secondary liability generates a conviction *for the principal offence*. If S supplies an automatic weapon to P for the purpose of murdering V, a conviction of murder may better represent her criminality than one of "intentionally encouraging or assisting an offence".

Admittedly, one upshot of preserving complicity liability is the phenomenon to which Spencer and presumably subjectivists such as Ashworth[333] would object: that S's liability becomes a matter of moral luck. So far as S is concerned, it is no more than luck that determines whether he is guilty of burglary as a secondary party or escapes scot-free. S has made a complete attempt to aid P's offence. Therefore, the subjectivists would say, he *deserves* to be convicted.

The issue of moral luck was considered earlier, in § 6.5(ii). Suffice it to say here that moral luck of this variety is an indispensable aspect both of ordinary life and of the criminal law. It establishes what action D *does*, and therefore what D is guilty *for doing*. Correspondingly, convicting S for complicity in a particular crime captures the moral quality of the events in which S was involved better than would her conviction for an inchoate offence.[334] The difference between being convicted, say, for attempted murder and for murder may be a matter of luck (e.g. whether D's shot misses; whether the bomb fails to explode). But it matters nonetheless. So too in secondary participation. Moreover, the luck is not random. The defendant *makes* his guilt a matter of luck, by attempting to kill or by attempting to aid another's crime. If other areas of the criminal law are properly subject to moral luck, so too is secondary liability.

---

[332] Trying to Help Another Person Commit a Crime" in P. Smith (ed.), *Criminal Law: Essays in Honour of J.C. Smith* (1987) 148, 148.

[333] Cf. Ashworth, "Taking the Consequences" in Shute, Gardner, and Horder (eds.), *Action and Value in Criminal Law* (1993) 107.

[334] For a valuable general discussion of these questions, see Kadish, "Complicity, Cause and Blame" in *Blame and Punishment* (1987) 135.

(i) A causation analysis?

An even more radical suggestion would be to extend the "causal" analysis of complicity, identified by K.J.M. Smith.[335] Smith suggests that complicity liability is best understood as resting on a causal basis, i.e. that S is liable because of her causal contribution to the crime that P commits. Of course, to adopt that analysis would require a much wider notion of causation than is usually employed by the criminal law, yet it would still be implausible.[336] Even the most generous and broad version of causation is absent in some cases of secondary liability—at least, absent in any sense that leaves causation a meaningful concept. S abets P to offend, for instance, by communicating encouragement to P, whether or not the encouragement makes any difference to P.[337] A person may be sufficiently involved in the crime of another to merit condemnation and punishment without that involvement creating any causal ripples.

Nonetheless, it is worth noting that the case law has sometimes suggested just such a widening of causation, of the sort that Smith's analysis would require. In *Empress*,[338] D was charged with causing a pollutant to enter the nearby river.[339] D had removed a protective device which would otherwise have contained overflows from the drum in which the pollutant was contained. Subsequently, an unknown person (T) opened the tap on the drum, whereupon the contents poured out and overflowed into the river. D's conviction was upheld by the House of Lords. T also caused the pollution, but his act was not a *novus actus* because, according to Lord Hoffmann, it was not "extraordinary":[340]

> "If the defendant did something which produced a situation in which the polluting matter could escape but a necessary condition of the actual escape which happened was also the act of a third party or a natural event, the justices should consider whether that act or event should be regarded as a normal fact of life or something extraordinary. If it was in the general run of things a matter of ordinary occurrence, it will not negative the causal effect of the defendant's acts, even if it was not foreseeable that it would happen to that particular defendant or take that particular form. If it can be regarded as something extraordinary, it will be open to the justices to hold that the defendant did not cause the pollution."

With respect to his Lordship, if this were a correct statement of the criminal law on causation, it would undermine almost entirely the need for complicity liability. The action of P will virtually never count as extraordinary where it is aided or abetted by S, and so will not count as a *novus actus*. Therefore it would almost always be possible to convict S as a principal for the crime that P commits.

Fortunately, as we saw when discussing *Empress* in § 4.2(iii)(d), the passage quoted is not a correct statement of the law. Notwithstanding Lord Hoffmann's purported denial, T's action was a *novus actus*. It was free, deliberate, and informed,[341] and meets all the criteria

---

[335] *A Modern Treatise on the Law of Criminal Complicity* (1991).

[336] A causal analysis is rejected, for instance, by Smith, "Aid, Abet, Counsel, or Procure" in Glazebrook (ed.), *Reshaping the Criminal Law* (1978) 120; also *Hart and Honoré* 377–88.

[337] See, e.g., *Wilcox v. Jeffery* [1951] 1 All ER 464; above, §§ 7.4(i)(b), 7.4(ii).

[338] *Empress Car Co (Abertillery) Ltd v. National Rivers Authority* [1999] 2 AC 22.

[339] Contrary to the then s. 85(1) of the Water Resources Act 1991.

[340] [1999] 2 AC 22, 36.

[341] *Kennedy (No. 2)* [2007] UKHL 38, [2008] 1 AC 269; *Pagett* (1983) 76 Cr App R 279, 288–9.

of a fresh intervening act outlined in § 4.2(iii)(b). The reasoning in *Empress* is inconsistent with the case law discussed in that section;[342] it is, quite simply, wrong. The decision is to be restricted to its specific statutory context.[343]

The core of Lord Hoffmann's error is his likening of deliberate intervening acts *by persons* to the interventions of nature. They are not the same, and are not governed by the same rules. Lord Hoffmann has correctly stated the relevant test for whether a natural event[344] (or a third party's action which is not free, deliberate, and informed)[345] counts as a *novus actus*. However, when T's intervention is free, deliberate, and informed, it breaks existing chains of causation *whether or not* it is predictable, foreseeable, or ordinary.

The rationale for distinguishing human from natural intervention was discussed in § 4.2(iii)(b). In the context of secondary liability, recall the example with which we began this chapter:

> One fine September morning, Jim is discovered dead in his home. His skull has been crushed by a blow inflicted with a heavy object. The police are called. Upon investigation, they establish that he was murdered by his daughter, Alice, who killed him in order to receive her inheritance under his will. The baseball bat that Alice used to murder Jim belongs to Harry, who lent it to Alice for the purpose.

It matters who killed Jim. Alice did, not Harry. Neither was it a joint murder. Without special causal rules of some form for intervening human agents, we would be forced to say that both Harry and Alice caused Jim's death. But to do so would disregard the claim Harry and Alice each has to be treated as a separate, human, moral agent.

Why is secondary liability special? The answer is that, normally, liability ought to depend on a person's own intentions and actions. Rightly, the law is profoundly reluctant to put one person's criminal liability at the mercy of another person's deliberate choice. This is true as a general proposition. Consider, for example, the question posed once by *Smith and Hogan* in the context of liability for omissions:[346]

> "It is generally said that D must have done some act and that it is not enough that he stood still and obstructed V's passage like an inanimate object. But suppose D is sitting at the corner of a corridor with his legs stretched across it. He hears V running down the corridor and deliberately remains still with the intention that V, on turning the corner, shall fall over his legs. Why should this not be a battery? It would be if D had put out his legs with the intention of tripping up V."

But if D has a duty to remove his leg, then P is granted a power to put D under that duty, simply by running toward him. The law that facilitates this has become a tool by which P may subject D's will to his own. More generally, under a legal system of this sort, D's choices and liability would be governed not merely by his own goals and values but equally by the whims of others.

So, too, principles of causation and secondary liability. Free, deliberate, and informed interventions by third parties have a distinctive causal status because we do not want T to

---

[342] E.g. *Latif* [1996] 1 ALL ER 353, noted in §§ 4.2(iii)(b) (Case 2).
[343] *Kennedy (No. 2)* [2007] UKHL 38, [2008] 1 AC 269, paras. 15–16; above, § 4.2(iii)(d).
[344] Above, § 4.2(iii)(a).
[345] Above, § 4.2(iii)(b).
[346] Above, § 4.1(i)(c).

have the power to choose that D shall become guilty of a crime.[347] Complicity liability is a special case. The aider or abettor places her liability in the hands of P deliberately by her actions, and cannot complain when responsibility for P's crime is attributed also to her. However, S does not commit the offence as a principal, in the way that causation-based approaches to her liability may suggest. It *is* a special case, properly constituted by actus reus and mens rea elements that are quite distinct from those applying to the principal.

---

[347] Cf. Simester, "The Mental Element in Complicity" (2006) 122 *LQR* 578, 580–1.

8

VICARIOUS AND CORPORATE LIABILITY

§ 8.1 Vicarious liability

Vicarious liability involves attributing to the defendant the conduct and state of mind possessed by another person. For instance, tort law imposes extensive liability upon employers for torts committed by employees in the course of their employment;[1] and, more recently, even for those akin to employees.[2] The criminal law contains nothing like the general doctrine of vicarious liability found in tort law.[3] This difference is unsurprising. The law of negligence, the mainstay of tort, aims predominantly to provide compensation for injury. It may well be unjust to an injured party for a judgment debt against the employee to go unsatisfied because of the employee's lack of means. Thus the employer (who presumably will have the required means, or suitable insurance) is held liable to the injured party as well. There is no equivalent pressure to forge a general doctrine of vicarious liability in the criminal law. The traditional concern of the criminal law is thus with individuals who commit or participate in crimes.[4]

The judicial disinclination to create a general, common law doctrine of vicarious criminal liability is clearly visible in the well-known case of *Huggins*.[5] D, the governor of a prison, was charged with aiding and abetting E, a warder, to murder V, a prisoner who had died on account of E's mistreatment. D was open to considerable criticism in the manner in which he discharged his office. Yet D had not caused E's death, nor had he ordered or encouraged

---

[1] See Atiyah, *Vicarious Liability* (1969); Giliker, *Vicarious Liability in Tort* (2013).

[2] In a series of decisions: *JGE v. Trustees of the Portsmouth Roman Catholic Diocesan Trust* [2012] EWCA Civ 938, [2013] QB 722; *Various Claimants v. Catholic Child Welfare Society and the Brothers of the Christian Schools* [2012] UKSC 56, [2013] 1 AC 1; *Cox v. Ministry of Justice* [2016] UKSC 10, [2016] 2 WLR 806. See Morgan, "Vicarious Liability on the Move" (2013) 129 *LQR* 139; Lord Hope, "Tailoring the Law on Vicarious Liability" (2013) 129 *LQR* 514.

[3] On vicarious criminal liability generally, see Glazebrook, "Situational Liability" in Glazebrook (ed.), *Reshaping the Criminal Law* (1978) 108; Leigh, *Strict and Vicarious Liability: A Study in Administrative Criminal Law* (1982); *CLGP* chap. 7. In *R v. Chief Constable of Northumbria v. Newcastle Magistrates Court* [2010] EWHC 935 (Admin), the Divisional Court confirmed that there was no general doctrine of vicarious liability for criminal offences at common law.

[4] For critiques of the criminal law's preoccupation with individuals and its presuppositions of liability see Norrie, *Crime, Reason and History* (3rd ed., 2014) chaps. 2, 3; Wells, *Corporations and Criminal Responsibility* (2nd ed., 2001) chap. 3; Norrie, "'Simulacra of Morality?' Beyond the Ideal/Actual Antinomies of Criminal Justice" in Duff (ed.), *Philosophy and the Criminal Law* (1998) 101.

[5] (1730) 2 Str 883, 93 ER 915.

E's mistreatment of V. In the absence of such personal involvement, D could not be liable for V's murder:[6]

> "It is not a point to be disputed … that in criminal cases the principal is not answerable for the act of the deputy, as he is in civil cases; they must each answer for their own acts and stand or fall by their own behaviour."

Despite this statement of general principle, it is perhaps inaccurate to state that there is *no* doctrine at all of criminal vicarious liability at common law. One example[7] of such liability is found in the crime of public nuisance, where some authorities suggest that an employer may be liable for the act of an employee despite the lack of any instruction or knowledge in respect of the employee's act.[8] The authorities are not, however, univocal on the extent to which vicarious liability is possible in relation to public nuisance.[9] Furthermore, public nuisance is an anomalous crime, which in some respects has more affinity with the law of tort than the law of crime.[10]

The position with regard to statutory offences is slightly more certain. There, it seems that there are now four ways in which vicarious or quasi-vicarious liability may arise:

(i) By express legislation.

(ii) Where the employee/agent's actions are, in civil law, the actions of the employer/ principal (e.g. selling or possessing something in the course of employment). Properly, this is not an instance of vicarious liability, since it requires no attribution of another person's actus reus to the defendant. It may, however, be described loosely as generating vicarious liability, in the sense that D's liability is triggered by the conduct of another person. These cases generally involve offences of strict liability.

(iii) By the delegation doctrine. This arises where a licence is awarded to a named individual to manage a property or activity within the terms of that licence. Should the individual to whom the licence is awarded delegate the performance of the terms of the licence to another person then, in matters relevant to the licence, the conduct *and state of mind* of the other person is attributed to the delegator.[11]

(iv) Finally, there is a fourth, anomalous, category of cases where vicarious liability for acts of employees has been imposed without delegation.

In the following sections, we consider the defensibility of each of these categories of vicarious liability.

---

[6] (1730) 2 Str 883, 93 ER 915, 885 (Str), 917 (ER).

[7] At one time, the offence of criminal libel imposed vicarious liability on owners of newspapers for libels published by employees without requiring proof of any knowledge or instruction on the part of the proprietor: *Walter* (1799) 3 Esp 21, 170 ER 524; *Gutch, Fisher and Alexander* (1829) Mood & M 432, 173 ER 1214. The crime was abolished by Coroners and Justice Act 2009, s. 73 (in force 12 Jan 2010).

[8] *Stephens* (1865–6) LR 1 QB 702. The decision in *Stephens* is limited carefully: the court was anxious to avoid disturbing "the general rule that a principal is not answerable for the act of his agent" (at 709). See, also, *Medley* (1834) 6 C & P 292, [1824–34] All ER Rep 123.

[9] See, e.g., *Chilsholm* v. *Doulton* (1889) LR 22 QBD 736.

[10] In *Stephens* (1865–6) LR 1 QB 702, the proceedings were said to be civil "in substance" (708).

[11] *Allen* v. *Whitehead* [1930] 1 KB 211; *Mullins* v. *Collins* (1874) LR 9 QB 292.

(i) Express legislation

There is nothing to prevent Parliament from explicitly imposing vicarious liability, and sometimes this is done. For example, Parliament has deemed D the perpetrator of certain minor traffic offences by conclusively presuming him to be the driver of a vehicle at the material time if he is the owner of that vehicle, a form of vicarious liability that even extends to companies.[12]

(ii) When the act of an employee/agent is that of the employer/principal

There is a group of cases which are sometimes said to involve vicarious liability but which, on ultimate analysis, are cases of *strict* liability. Unfortunately, as we discussed in Chapter 6, English law quite often allows conviction without the need to establish mens rea on the part of D as to every aspect of the actus reus. The unfairness of strict liability can be exacerbated when the trigger for liability is a third party's conduct. Consider the offence of being the parent of a child of compulsory school age who fails to attend regularly at school.[13] In *Crump* v. *Gilmore*,[14] the Divisional Court confirmed the conviction of D, the parent of E, where E made too few appearances at school. The court took the offence to be one of strict liability, and therefore it was irrelevant that D neither knew nor had reason to know of E's sporadic school attendances.[15] Accordingly, D's liability was attributable to E's conduct but it was not truly vicarious; she was *directly* responsible on the basis of her involuntary acquisition of a particular status.[16] It is not unnatural to perceive such liability as vicarious, because D's liability arises out of the conduct of a third party. Legally, however, D's liability is imposed directly.

A similar analysis applies where D Ltd, a company, sells food not complying with food safety standards and thereby contravenes section 8 of the Food Safety Act 1990. Since the offence is strict in this regard, liability ensues if it can be proved the seller sold non-compliant food; there is no need to demonstrate any form of knowledge, recklessness, or negligence by anyone.[17] D Ltd sells food each time one of its shop assistants makes a sale to a customer and, if the food is non-compliant, D commits the offence. This situation is often described as an instance of vicarious liability, with liability imposed on the company in respect of the act of its assistant. But, structurally, the facts may be analysed in the same

---

[12] Road Traffic Offenders Act 1988, s. 64(5). See, further, Highways Act 1980, s. 168.

[13] Formerly Education Act 1944, s. 39(1); now Education Act 1996, s. 444(1). For critical discussion of the line of authority imposing this extreme form of strict liability, see Horder, "Whose Values Should Determine when Liability Is Strict?" in Simester (ed.), *Appraising Strict Liability* (2005) 105; Sullivan, "Parents and Their Truanting Children: An English Lesson in Liability without Responsibility" (2010) 12 *Otago LR* 285.

[14] [1970] Crim LR 28.

[15] In *Barnfather* v. *London Borough of Islington and Secretary of State for Education and Skills* [2003] EWHC 418 (Admin), D argued that to convict parents who were blameless with respect to their child's truanting contravened the presumption of innocence guaranteed by Art. 6(2) of the ECHR. The argument failed on the basis that the presumption of innocence does not engage with the elements of criminal liability, but merely with proof of those elements. It failed despite the recognition by Elias J (paras. 50–7) that parents would then be convicted of this stigmatic offence, with its implications of irresponsible parenting, in circumstances where securing regular attendance of their child at school was for practical purposes impossible.

[16] See the discussion in Glazebrook, "Situational Liability" in Glazebrook (ed.), *Reshaping the Criminal Law* (1978) 108, 108–14.

[17] Although s. 21 of the Act provides for a defence of due diligence with a reverse burden of proof.

manner as the facts of *Crump* v. *Gilmore*. Each time a sale is made by an assistant to a customer, the company, as legal owner of the item sold, is selling to the customer. Thus the company commits the offence *directly*. An illustration is *Coppen* v. *Moore (No. 2)*,[18] where a shop assistant sold food under a false description to a customer. The sale, in the legal sense of the term, was made by D, the employer and owner of the goods sold. The employer "was the seller, although not the actual salesman".[19] Consequently, since the offence of selling goods under a false trade description did not require any form of knowledge, recklessness, or negligence with regard to the falsity to be proved against D, liability was established against him on proof that the assistant intentionally sold the item and a false description had been given of it.

That this is not a case of true vicarious liability can be demonstrated by a contrasting example of a selling offence requiring proof of mens rea. Consider, for instance, the old offence of selling intoxicating liquor to an under-age person.[20] Here D, the owner of the liquor (and the licensee), made a sale each time liquor was sold by one of his employees; but D would only have been liable for the offence if *he* knew that the customer was under-age (direct personal liability), or if he had delegated the running of the licensed premises to the employee who then knowingly sold intoxicating liquor to an under-age customer (a case of true vicarious liability, as explained in the next section).

A difficult point is raised where the employee acts outside the scope of guidance given by the employer. In *Coppen* v. *Moore*, the employer had expressly instructed his employees to describe the ham as "breakfast ham", rather than a regional ham. An employee sold the meat as a regional ham. The employer's express instructions did not prevent liability from being imposed upon him, for it was still *he* who (in law) had made the sale. What is clear, however, is that where an employee does something she has *no* right to do, liability will not be imposed upon the employer. In *Adams* v. *Camfoni*,[21] it was held that a master was not liable when a servant boy, who had no authority to do so, supplied his master's liquor to a customer out of hours. Similarly, if a cleaner, lacking any authority to do so, opens a hotel bar outside the legal hours and sells liquor to customers, the licensee will not be liable.[22] The cleaner's acts are clearly outside the scope of his employment or any implicit permission from the licensee who employs him. Not so with the employee in *Coppen* v. *Moore*, who was acting closely enough to the manner in which he was employed to act.

(iii) Delegation

Vicarious liability based on the principle of delegation is a judicial creation made in response to a perceived legislative deficiency.[23] Suppose that, pursuant to legislation, a licence is granted to a named person of presumed good character. Typically, the legislation will be silent about the legal position if the licence holder devolves responsibility for compliance with the terms of that licence to someone else. Of course, if the legislation allows

---

[18] [1898] 2 QB 306.
[19] *Ibid.*, 313 (Lord Russell).
[20] See, now, Licensing Act 2003, s. 146 (no knowledge of the purchaser's age is required).
[21] [1929] 1 KB 95.
[22] See *Jull* v. *Treanor* (1896) 14 NZLR 513.
[23] See, generally, Pace, "Delegation: A Doctrine in Search of a Definition" [1982] *Crim LR* 627.

criminal liability for breaches of the licence terms to be imposed on the delegate, enforcing such offences is possible notwithstanding the fact of delegation.[24] Frequently, however, the only person who may commit the offence is the licensee. For instance, section 44 of the Metropolitan Police Act 1839 states that it is an offence for:

> "every person who shall have or keep any house, shop, room or place of public resort within the metropolitan police district wherein … refreshments of any kind shall be sold … and who shall knowingly permit or suffer prostitutes or persons of notoriously bad character to meet together and remain therein."

It will be noted that the persons who may commit offences under this provision are the owner, tenant, or keeper of a house, shop, room, or place of public resort. Prima facie, it must be a person within that class who *knowingly* permits or suffers prostitutes, etc. Accordingly, in the leading case of *Allen* v. *Whitehead*,[25] when D, the occupier and licensee of a café, was charged with an offence under section 44, he defended himself on the basis that, as an occasional visitor to his own café, he was unaware that his manager (E) was allowing prostitutes to remain on the premises. Indeed, D had instructed E not to allow this to happen and had arranged for notices to be placed in the café warning prostitutes off. Confirming D's conviction, Lord Hewart CJ held that, if D had delegated to E the conduct of the café, "knowledge in the manager was knowledge in the keeper of the house". Were it otherwise, the Chief Justice reasoned, "this statute would be rendered nugatory".[26] In short, *Allen* v. *Whitehead* is best understood as being a decision based on the practicalities of enforcement, and the belief that licencees should not be able to evade their responsibilities by delegating duties to someone else.

In so ruling, Lord Hewart CJ confirmed a line of authority to the same effect that, though varying in expression and emphasis, can best be explained as imposing vicarious liability based on a delegation principle. This line of authority was reviewed by the House of Lords in *Vane* v. *Yiannopoullos*,[27] where E, a waitress employed by D, knowingly sold drinks to customers who were not ordering a meal, in contravention of the terms of D's licence. Once again, D had not encouraged or known about E's behaviour. The Lords did not accept the delegation principle enthusiastically. Lords Reid, Evershed and Morris suggested that the delegation principle was a judicial gloss designed to respond to the practicalities of enforcement,[28] whilst Lord Donovan opined that difficulties in convicting licence holders should be resolved by Parliament, not the courts.[29] Lord Hodson expressed no view on the legitimacy of the delegation principle. As it happens, all these opinions were *obiter* since it was found on the facts that no delegation had occurred: D, the licensee, remained on the premises, albeit on the upper floor of his restaurant, while E served the drinks two floors below. Their Lordships took the view that a delegation required a *total* devolvement to someone else of responsibility for keeping to the terms of the licence. This was not the

---

[24] For instance, the Licensing Act 2003, which repeals much but not all of the previous licensing legislation, creates offences relating to the sale of alcohol on licensed premises which can be committed by bar staff as well as the licensee, removing the need to resort to the delegation principle to enforce the terms of the licence.

[25] [1930] 1 KB 211.

[26] *Ibid.*, 220.

[27] [1965] AC 486.

[28] *Ibid.*, 496 (Lord Reid), 500, 504 (Lord Evershed), 507 (Lord Morris).

[29] *Ibid.*, 512.

case here. D was involved in the running of his business, even if he could not be every-where at once. Accordingly, he had not contravened the terms of his licence because he was unaware of the illicit sales by E. Only if he had *totally* delegated management to E would E's knowledge have been attributed to him.

This approach to delegation has been attacked.[30] It has been regarded as paradoxical that, if D is miles away, she should be fixed with knowledge on the basis of delegation, but can evade the attribution of her employee's knowledge when she is much closer to the action. But there is no paradox. Let us accept, if only for the moment, the legitimacy of vicarious criminal liability based on delegation. It follows that where D, the licence holder, remains involved in the management of the licensed premises, it is entirely appropriate that his criminal liability be determined by reference to D's own culpability: if liability requires knowledge, he must be proved to have knowledge. By contrast, if he accepts the obliga-tions of a licence by becoming a licence holder, but leaves it to another person to ensure compliance with its terms, there need be no inconsistency in fixing the licence holder with the delegate's knowledge. D has assumed the risk. That said, such reasoning will not always resolve liabilities fairly. D may take great care in appointing his delegate but be fixed with any knowledge the delegate acquires. Contrast E, who remains on the premises but manages them very slackly. The knowledge of his employees cannot be imputed to him. It cannot be said, therefore, that the delegation principle ensures an even-handed pattern of enforce-ment of licence conditions.

Given the potential harshness of the doctrine of vicarious liability by delegation, it is unsurprising that it has come under attack in the courtroom as well as in the literature. In *Winson*,[31] defence counsel argued that, given the division of opinion amongst their Lordships in *Vane* concerning the propriety of the doctrine, the Court of Appeal was free to reject this body of law. The Court of Appeal demurred, ruling that vicarious liability based on delegation was too firmly established to have been unsettled by the *obiter* doubts expressed in *Vane*. Further, the Court opined that the doctrine was justified by the need to prevent a licensee from evading her responsibilities by delegating them to another.[32] As long as the relevant statute can be construed consistently with the doctrine of delegation, then vicarious liability remains a possibility.[33]

At the same time, the Court of Appeal in *Winson* emphasised that only a *complete* delegation of the principal's legal duties would trigger the doctrine. Similar sentiments were expressed by their Lordships in *Vane*.[34] Even the most conscientious of persons can-not be attending to their legal responsibilities at all hours. If D has gone to bed to sleep, or has left her post to pick up her children from school, she will not normally have made a complete delegation of her responsibilities to someone else, even if she leaves a deputy in charge *pro tem*. Ultimate authority and recourse will remain with her. In *Bradshaw* v. *Ewart-James*,[35] for example, it was held that a ship's master had not delegated his responsibilities as

---

[30] Pace, "Delegation: A Doctrine in Search of a Definition" [1982] *Crim LR* 627, 629, 636.
[31] [1969] 1 QB 371 (CA).
[32] *Ibid.*, 382.
[33] See, further, *St Regis Paper Company Ltd* [2011] EWCA Crim 2527, [2012] 1 Cr App R 14, para. 28.
[34] [1965] AC 486, 497 (Lord Reid), 504–5 (Lord Evershed), 510–11 (Lord Hodson).
[35] [1983] QB 671 (DC).

master when he took himself off to bed leaving the first mate with temporary responsibility for the vessel. Such temporary delegations are not enough for vicarious criminal liability to arise. Only a complete delegation of authority will suffice.[36]

From the above discussion, two principles can be developed. First, the delegation approach will be employed only where the statutory provision would otherwise be impractical to enforce. Secondly, the delegation principle will only be applied where there was a total delegation of authority from D to another person. These principles cast significant doubt on the correctness of the decision of the Divisional Court in *Howker v. Robinson*.[37] In that case, D's conviction for knowingly selling alcohol to a person under the age of 18 was upheld. The sale was made by E, an employee who served in the lounge bar. At the time of the sale, D was in the public bar. The first problem is that the offence in question was an offence not exclusive to licensees; it could also be committed by employees, undermining the "rendered nugatory" rationale of vicarious liability discussed above. It is useful to contrast *Howker* with the case of *Qureshi*,[38] where D, a landlord, was charged with interfering with the peace and comfort of a residential occupier.[39] The acts complained of were done by members of D's family rather than by D. Since the offence can be committed by the landlord or an "agent" of the landlord, the Court of Appeal nevertheless ruled that the offence was committed by D's agents, precluding any possibility of vicarious liability for the offence on the part of D.[40] A similar approach should have been adopted in *Howker*.

The second difficulty with *Howker* is that the magistrates had made a finding of fact that there had been a delegation of authority to E in respect of the lounge bar, which the Divisional Court refused to disturb on the ground that the finding was not plainly unreasonable. Yet it clearly emerges from *Vane* and *Winson* that, as a matter of law, the delegation principle will come into play only if D has *completely* devolved to another his obligation to ensure that the terms of the licence are complied with. There seems to have been no evidence of that in *Howker*. D was serving in the public bar while E was in the lounge bar, but there was nothing in the facts to suggest that the lounge bar was in any sense E's "domain" where he enjoyed a managerial authority. D could not be everywhere; E was just a barman. *Howker* is wrong and should not be followed.

(iv) Anomalous cases of liability for an employee's act

We turn now to consider other, anomalous, cases in which an employer has been found liable for the conduct of an employee. In straightforward cases such as selling or possession there can be no objection to attributing an actus reus to D. Activities like "selling" and "possessing" are, in law, technical terms. They are legally constructed activities whose application is determined by the civil law. Thus it comes as no surprise that, legally, one can sell or possess through the instrumentality of others. The injustice, if any, does not arise from

---

[36] For further discussion of *Bradshaw*, see Warbrick and Sullivan, "Ship Routeing Schemes and the Criminal Liability of the Master" [1984] *LMCLQ* 23.

[37] [1973] QB 178.

[38] [2011] EWCA Crim 1584, [2012] 1 WLR 694.

[39] Contrary to s. 1(3A) of the Protection from Eviction Act 1977.

[40] Of course, D might have been liable as a secondary party to his agent's offence, but that was not argued by the prosecution.

the way in which the actus reus is established, but instead from the fact that liability may be imposed on proof of actus reus alone.

The picture changes where the actus reus is not a technical legal act, but seemingly something that requires personal conduct on the part of D. That necessary element of liability is missing if the conduct proved was the conduct of someone else. If D is charged as a principal offender with a driving offence, she can quite properly complain if the driving in question was the driving of E and not her own. The courts have therefore required the driving to be by D if she is to be convicted as a principal offender of a driving offence.[41]

Unfortunately, the courts have not always adopted this sensible approach. In *James & Son Ltd v. Smee*,[42] D, a company, claimed that "using" a vehicle required the same degree of personal involvement as driving a vehicle. A company employee had used a vehicle with defective brakes in the course of his employment. The condition of the brakes was not known to the defendant company. The company was charged under the Motor Vehicles (Construction and Use) Regulations 1951 with "using or causing or permitting to be used … a motor vehicle which did not comply with [these] regulations". The company conceded that it may have "caused" or "permitted" the vehicle to be used, but liability could not be imposed under those heads because, under the statute, proof of causing or permitting a vehicle to be used in a defective condition required proof that D was aware of the condition of the vehicle. Nonetheless, the Divisional Court imposed liability on the company for "using" the vehicle.[43] That term, as the court interpreted it, simply required the vehicle to be used by an employee in the course of employment and did not require any knowledge, on the part of the company, of the state of the vehicle. In its statutory context, this would appear a strained interpretation. The juxtaposition of the term "using" as an alternative to "causing or permitting to be used" is strongly suggestive that a personal physical act (D himself/itself using) is being contrasted with a permitting or causing of the same physical act (of using by another person). Be that as it may, the Divisional Court considered that a use of the vehicle by an employee in the course of employment was also a use by the employer.

The decision in *James & Son Ltd v. Smee* appears to be confined to the employer–employee relationship. It has been held that the owner of a vehicle does not "use" it when he lends it to a friend,[44] nor when it is taken by a stranger.[45] This suggests that *James & Son Ltd v. Smee* is a case of true vicarious liability (outside the sphere of managerial delegation). It is a case of an attributed actus reus, not an example of an actus reus requirement that can be fulfilled by the conduct of someone other than the defendant.

An even starker example of this phenomenon is *Slatcher v. George Mence Smith Ltd*,[46] where the "act" of an employee was taken, in law, to be the "act" of the employer. One could not imagine a word more redolent of personal involvement than "act". In the pungent

---

[41] *Richmond London Borough Council v. Pinn & Wheeler Ltd* [1989] RTR 354 (DC).
[42] [1955] 1 QB 78 (DC).
[43] See, too, *Evans v. Dell* [1937] 1 All ER 349 (DC).
[44] *Crawford v. Haughton* [1972] 1 WLR 572 (DC).
[45] *Strutt v. Cliff* [1911] 1 KB 1 (DC).
[46] [1951] 2 KB 631 (DC). In a prosecution under s. 2 of the Merchandise Marks Act 1887, D was entitled to a defence (per s. 2(2)(c)) if he could establish "that otherwise he had acted innocently". The Divisional Court disallowed the defence because, although D personally had acted innocently, its employee had not. See also *Sopp v. Long* [1970] 1 QB 518 (DC) ("caused").

words of Glanville Williams, "a mere statement of this decision is sufficient to show that something must have gone wrong with the reasoning".[47]

It is also worth noting here that it can be said that, as a result of the decision of the House of Lords in *Environmental Agency* v. *Empress Car Co. (Abertillery) Ltd*,[48] in substance the scope of unacknowledged vicarious liability has been extended even beyond employees. Recall that the defendant company was found to have "caused" pollution to a river when the immediate cause of the pollution was the act of an unknown intruder who had turned the tap of the oil tank sited on the company's land. We will not rehearse again here our criticisms of the finding that the mere presence of oil on the company's land was a cause of the pollution. It suffices to say that, if those criticisms are well founded, then in substance the company was made vicariously liable for the intruder's act. Such a finding is deeply unsettling, in the absence of any prior relationship between D and the person whose conduct is to be attributed to her/it.

(v) Summary

To summarise, we have argued that the occurrence of true vicarious liability is confined to statutes which expressly impose such liability and to situations where a duty of compliance with the requirements of a licence or other regulatory regime has been delegated, and vicarious liability is required to ensure the practical enforcement of the relevant statutory provision. There are some cases of strict liability which may be described as cases of vicarious liability, but these merely demonstrate that certain activities, such as selling or possessing, can be done through the agency of others. By contrast, other verbs imply personal involvement. A company, for instance, can sell a car through a salesperson but does not itself "use" or "drive" a car when a company car is used or driven by a company employee.

However, even in cases where the actus reus seemingly requires personal agency, D has sometimes been held vicariously liable without there being any finding of delegation. Decisions such as *James & Son Ltd* v. *Smee* have attributed to D the actus reus of an offence which requires personal involvement even though D was not personally involved. Such cases involve a form of vicarious liability because an activity such as, say, driving can only be *attributed* to a person who was not in fact driving. This last form of vicarious criminal liability is *ad hoc* and unacknowledged even when imposed. We contend that it ought not to exist as part of English criminal law.

(vi) Reform

In its Draft Criminal Code, the Law Commission provided no statutory version of the delegation principle. Under the Code, if vicarious liability is to be imposed, it must be done so expressly.[49] This change would have been welcome. The judicial creation of the delegation principle is an undiscriminating way of enforcing the duties of licensees. As we have acknowledged, there is some reason to discriminate between cases where D retains a

---

[47] *CLGP* 222–3.
[48] [1999] 2 AC 22; discussed above, § 4.2(iii)(d).
[49] *A Criminal Code for England and Wales*, Law Com. No. 177 (1989) cl. 29.

responsibility for complying with the terms of the licence and cases where he wholly delegates the discharging of his duties to another person. Yet it is an unsatisfactory distinction. As noted above, D1 may remain on his premises, manage his business inattentively, and take no care in the discharge of his legal duties. Conversely, D2 may take particular care in appointing a delegate and have good reason to think that the appointed person will be scrupulous in her observance of the delegated duties. Yet the former case is treated more indulgently than the latter.

The Law Commission scrutinised the delegation principle in a 2010 consultation paper.[50] It proposed there that criminal liability based on the fact of delegation, without more, should be abolished. In its place should be an offence of failing to prevent an offence by a person to whom the running of the business has been delegated.[51] The proposal is influenced by the offence of failure of a commercial organisation to prevent bribery done on its behalf.[52] Under that offence, the commercial organisation incurs liability if its failure to prevent bribery reflects an omission to have adequate procedures to prevent persons associated with the organisation from committing bribery offences on its behalf. Although the culpability for this offence is of a lower order than the culpability for bribery itself, at least some form of managerial failure is required. If applied generally, this technique would therefore represent an improvement on present liability based upon the mere fact of delegation.

§ 8.2 Corporate liability[53]

(i) The justification of corporate liability

Since the mid-nineteenth century, it has been established that companies may commit crimes of strict liability.[54] Unless there is a clear legislative intent to the contrary,[55] the word "person" in legislation includes "a body of persons corporate or unincorporate".[56] Where no culpability is required in the definition of the offence, the fact that a company is, in law, a separate "person" distinct from its directors, employees, and shareholders presents no

---

[50] *Criminal Liability in Regulatory Contexts* LCCP No. 195 (2010) part 7. At the time of writing, some aspects of the Commission's proposals have been implemented through Government guidance to departments. The other aspects of the project have been placed on hold until a project on corporate liability can be undertaken.

[51] *Ibid.*, para. 7.58.

[52] Bribery Act 2010, s. 7. See Sullivan, "The Bribery Act 2010—An Overview" [2011] *Crim LR* 87, 95–6, 98; Gentle, "The Corporate Offence" [2011] *Crim LR* 101.

[53] Wells, "Corporate Criminal Liability: A Ten Year Review" [2014] *Crim LR* 849; Pieth and Ivory (eds.), *Corporate Criminal Liability: Emergence, Convergence and Risk* (2011); List and Pettit, *Group Agency: the Possibility, Design and Status of Corporate Agents* (2011); Gobert and Punch, *Rethinking Corporate Crime* (2003); Wells, *Corporations and Criminal Responsibility* (2nd ed., 2001); Clarkson, "Kicking Corporate Bodies and Damning Their Souls" (1996) 59 *MLR* 557; Sullivan, "The Attribution of Culpability to Limited Companies" (1996) 55 *CLJ* 515; Sullivan, "Expressing Corporate Guilt" (1995) 15 *OJLS* 281; Gobert, "Corporate Criminality: New Crimes for the Times" [1994] *Crim LR* 722; Fisse and Braithwaite, *Corporations, Crime and Accountability* (1993).

[54] *Birmingham and Gloucester Railway Co.* (1842) 3 QB 223, 114 ER 492.

[55] For discussion of whether a contrary statutory intention exists in the context of harassment, contrary to s. 2(1) of the Protection from Harassment Act 1997, see *Kosar v. Bank of Scotland plc T/A Halifax* [2011] EWHC 1050 (Admin).

[56] A "person" is, unless a contrary statutory intention is apparent, presumed to include a corporation: Interpretation Act 1978, Sch 1, pt 1.

barrier to the imposition of criminal liability. For example, environmental legislation may require that the carbon levels of smoke emissions must not exceed a given level, a matter of strict liability.[57] If the smoke emissions of a factory owned by D plc should exceed permitted levels, then D plc, as owner of the factory, will be liable straightforwardly for the offence. Historically, there was a view that companies, by virtue of their artificial nature, were incapable of being guilty of any crime because guilt was perceived to be exclusively a human property.[58] That view did not survive long into the era of industrialisation and the advent of the joint-stock company. The application of regulatory law to limited companies is now almost completely uncontroversial. It is arguable whether such regulation should ever take the form of strict liability, but hardly anyone objects specifically to the fact that *companies* are held liable for such offences. Indeed, given the overwhelming predominance of the limited company in industrial, transport, and commercial activity,[59] corporate liability is essential for the efficacy of any legislation concerned with pollution, health, safety, and trading standards.

Nonetheless, some writers have queried the need for any form of corporate criminal liability, even with respect to regulatory law.[60] It has been objected that the fines paid by the company ultimately will be borne by the shareholders who are not, in any sense, responsible for the offence. However, this stance overlooks the nature of an investment as a shareholder in a limited company. An investment on the terms of limited liability is a legally created privilege, and the terms on which sums of capital can be aggregated and deployed have, from the controversial inception of limited companies, been a matter of continuing legislative scrutiny and revision. The funds of limited companies are subject to a host of different financial constraints imposed in (what is taken to be) the public interest. Investments must be made on the assumption that companies will not seek illegitimate competitive advantages by non-compliance with regulatory law. From that perspective, there is no difference in principle between fines and other forms of financial exaction (e.g. by a regulator for underperformance on agreed targets). The impact of fines on investors, arising from non-compliance with law, is merely one of a large number of investment risks. In our view, it is not enough to punish the individuals responsible for breaching regulations. In fairness to those companies which commit resources to meet their legal obligations, companies found in breach should be fined at least to the extent necessary to correct any competitive advantage gained thereby.

In principle, then, corporations should be capable of being held criminally liable. The next sections explain how, practically, such liability is imposed under English law.

(ii) Crimes of strict liability

For crimes of strict liability, the artificial personality of a limited company poses few conceptual difficulties in imposing corporate liability. In a limited sense all corporate

---

[57] Clean Air Act 1993, s. 2.

[58] In the famous words of Edward, First Baron Thurlow, a company has "no soul to be damned and no body to be kicked": Mencken, *A New Dictionary of Quotations* (1942) 223.

[59] As of November 2015, there are over three million incorporated companies in England and Wales: Companies House, *Statistical Release: Incorporated Companies in the United Kingdom—November 2015* (2015).

[60] See, e.g., the view of the former authors of Smith and Hogan, *Criminal Law* (10th ed., 2002) 207: "the necessity for corporate criminal liability awaits demonstration". This statement does not appear in subsequent editions.

liability can be spoken of as vicarious liability, because corporate conduct is ultimately referable to some form of human conduct.[61] When the corporately owned factory chimney belches pollution, it does so as a product of a set of acts and omissions by human agents. In legal terms, however, companies will commit offences of strict liability directly: the company, of itself, will fulfil the offence specifications of regulatory crimes (in terms of selling, leasing, possessing, using, etc.) if done in the course of business of the company. This type of case is discussed in more detail above, in § 8.1(ii).

(iii) Crimes of mens rea

(a) The policy issue: how is corporate culpability possible?

For crimes where forms of mens rea are required—defrauding the revenue, acting dishonestly when appropriating property belonging to another with an intent permanently to deprive, killing V by an act of gross negligence, etc.—some legal means of attributing the requisite mens rea to the company is required. This raises a potential issue. The view might be taken that "culpability", in the non-legal sense of the term, is an entirely human property; something that a corporation, with its inherently artificial form, cannot possess.[62] Acceptance of that view leads to two possible approaches to corporate liability for crimes of mens rea. On the first view, any question of companies becoming responsible for what may be termed "culpability crimes" is regarded as a mistake. On the second view, corporate liability for such crimes is allowed, but it is recognised that the attribution of culpability to companies is a matter of form rather than substance (for companies cannot *really* be culpable). This fiction is engaged in in order to secure whatever consequentialist returns may be had. On this second approach (the approach by and large taken by English law), the conduct and state of mind of an individual is attributed to the company, thus becoming *corporate* conduct and a *corporate* state of mind (while remaining also, for legal purposes, the conduct and state of mind of the given individual). So, to take defrauding the Revenue as an example, if E, an employee of D plc, submits a dishonest tax return by misrepresenting D plc's income in the course of his employment with D plc, it may be possible to attribute E's conduct and culpability to D plc, allowing both D plc and E to be convicted of tax fraud.[63] In so doing, the law does not claim that D plc *actually* itself exhibited culpability.

A radically different approach is in order if the view is taken, as increasingly it is, that companies are culpability-bearing agents in their own right, manifesting an inherently *corporate* agency and culpability not reducible to a matter of human agency. If corporations *as corporations* can possess intentionality, concoct schemes to injure or defraud, etc., then rules and doctrines must be crafted to capture (in a forensically manageable way) this form of culpability.

In the next sections, we will consider how liability for crimes of mens rea is imposed on companies in English law, noting its traditional adoption of the view that corporations themselves cannot commit crimes (and so human agents' conduct and culpability must

---

[61] Although this claim may be disputed, a matter to be discussed below, § 8.2(v)(d).

[62] Wolf, "The Legal and Moral Responsibility of Organisations" in Pennock and Chapman (eds.), *Criminal Justice* (1985) 267.

[63] *DPP* v. *Kent and Sussex Contractors, Limited* [1944] KB 146 (DC).

be ascribed to the corporation) and its more recent moves in the direction of recognising corporate fault as a distinct conceptual possibility.

(b) Attributing culpability to limited companies: the doctrine of identification

The idea that forms the basis of the identification doctrine is a simple one. The identification doctrine, sometimes known as the *alter ego* or "directing mind" principle, takes the conduct and state of mind of certain high-ranking corporate officials to be the conduct and state of mind of the company itself. If, for example, a company director, of sufficient stature to be regarded as a corporate *alter ego*, were to form a dishonest intent in the course of transacting company business, so too his company would possess the same dishonest intent.

This anthropomorphic doctrine first surfaced in the civil case of *Lennards Carrying Co Ltd* v. *Asiatic Petroleum Ltd*,[64] where the defendants were being sued by plaintiff cargo-owners for the loss of cargo caused by the unseaworthiness of the vessel managed by the defendants. Under applicable legislation, the defendant's liability in damages would be capped unless it could be proved that the loss was attributable to the defendant's "fault". As interpreted by Lord Haldane for the Privy Council, "fault" required personal fault on the part of *Lennards*, the company that managed the ship on behalf of the owners. This fault was supplied by Mr Lennard, the managing director of Lennards, who was aware of the condition of the vessel yet permitted it to be taken to sea. According to Lord Haldane:[65]

> "Mr Lennard was the directing mind of the company ... his action was the action of the company itself ... [his] fault is not merely that of a servant or agent for whom the company is liable upon the footing *respondent superior* but somebody for whom the company is liable because his action is the very action of the company itself."

This identification of high-ranking officials with the company itself was adopted into the criminal law in the cases of *DPP* v. *Kent and Sussex Contractors*,[66] *ICR Haulage Ltd*,[67] and *Moore* v. *Bressler*,[68] where companies were held liable (for intending to deceive the Revenue and for conspiracy to defraud) after the court in each case identified the culpable states of mind of corporate officials with their companies. The decision in *Moore* is particularly noteworthy because of the flexible manner in which the identification doctrine was applied: the tax returns that implicated the company were made by a company secretary and a branch sales manager. However, as we shall see, there is reason to think that such flexibility would no longer be utilised.[69]

Over time, the identification doctrine became well embedded into both civil and criminal law, and an increasingly liberal approach was taken to the question of which corporate officials could be identified with the company.[70] This liberality was checked by the House

---

[64] [1915] AC 705.
[65] *Ibid.*, 713, 714.
[66] [1944] KB 146 (DC).
[67] [1944] KB 551 (CA).
[68] [1944] 2 All ER 515 (DC).
[69] In *St Regis Paper Co. Ltd* [2011] EWCA Crim 2527, [2012] 1 Cr App R 14, the decision in *Moore* was reviewed sceptically.
[70] E.g. *The Lady Gwendolen* [1965] 3 WLR 91 (CA).

of Lords decision in *Tesco Supermarkets Ltd* v. *Nattrass*,[71] where it was ruled that only individuals at the apex of the corporate hierarchy could be identified with the company. Lord Diplock took a rigid and formal approach to this question: only officials granted plenary authority (i.e. the power to take decisions) over a company's affairs in the articles of association (basically, the company's constitution) could be so identified. For him, that would include the board of directors making decisions on behalf of the company, together with the chief executive and, possibly, any other executive possessing a plenary authority for the activity at issue in a particular case.[72] Lord Reid, too, required a plenary authority, but was prepared to look at substance as well as form. He did not make a grant of authority in the articles of association a precondition for identification.[73]

The narrowness of the identification doctrine post-*Tesco Supermarkets Ltd* v. *Nattrass* is exemplified by the decision in *Redfern*.[74] There, Dunlop (Europe) Ltd was charged with knowingly exporting combat equipment to Iran in contravention of an embargo that formed part of agreed sanctions. The facts of the matter were known to the European sales manager, but he was considered insufficiently important in Dunlop's scheme of things to be identified with the company. Similarly, in *P&O Ferries (Dover) Ltd*,[75] where P&O Ltd were charged with manslaughter following the Zeebrugge ferry disaster, the ship's master was ruled not to be sufficiently senior to be identified with the company.

The one thing to be said in favour of the doctrine of identification is that, provided it is confined to the very top echelon of corporate officials, the operation of the doctrine allows a fair measure of predictability. Lord Diplock, in *Tesco*, reasoned that this exclusive focus on top management was integral to the very nature of the doctrine.[76] He insisted that it involved a form of *direct* corporate responsibility in contradistinction to vicarious liability. As the doctrine identifies the very state of mind of the company itself, that entity is to be located solely at the top—the very "brains" of the company in Lord Denning's quaint idiom.[77] Yet scrutiny of the way that the doctrine works reveals it, in substance, to be very close to vicarious liability. The company's culpability is a derivative of human culpability. Within the doctrine's own terms, a finding that the company possessed the mens rea for an offence may only be made if some decision-making organ or individual of sufficient seniority possessed the mens rea for the offence. This narrowness is the doctrine's major limitation in terms of obtaining corporate convictions.

(c) Vicarious corporate liability

The narrowness of the identification doctrine prevents effective prosecutions for offences involving mens rea. The forms of vicarious liability mentioned earlier in this chapter did little to help matters.

Until comparatively recently, it would have been accurate to say that vicarious liability in its full sense was not imposed on companies in the sphere of criminal law. To be

---

[71] [1972] AC 153.
[72] *Ibid.*, 199.
[73] *Ibid.*, 171.
[74] (1992) 13 Cr App R (S) 709.
[75] (1991) 93 Cr App R 72.
[76] [1972] AC 153, 199–200.
[77] *Bolton (Engineering) Co Ltd* v. *Graham & Sons* [1957] 1 QB 159, 172 (CA).

sure, any employee selling, using, possessing, etc., in the course of employment might incriminate a company for a strict liability offence. But for a mens rea offence, identification was required.[78] In *Tesco Supermarkets plc v. Brent LBC*,[79] an issue arose concerning whether Tesco "knew or had reasonable cause to believe" that a hirer of a restricted video was under the age of 18; a matter of culpability which, according to Professor Sir John Smith, had to be resolved under the terms of the identification doctrine.[80] However, the Divisional Court confirmed the company's conviction, ruling that the state of mind of the checkout assistant could be identified with Tesco. Staughton LJ blithely distinguished the earlier *Tesco* decision on the basis that it concerned a provision in a different statute. The House of Lords took a similar line in *Director General of Fair Trading v. Pioneer Concrete (UK) Ltd*,[81] finding that the knowledge and conduct of a company's sales force sufficed to place the company in contempt of court.

These, and other decisions, may give the impression that identification was—due to its limitations—in the process of being supplanted by vicarious liability. Yet prospects of an orderly demise were confounded by the House of Lords decision in *Seaboard Offshore Ltd v. Secretary of State for Transport*,[82] where a company was charged with failing to take reasonable steps to secure maritime safety. The human fault lay with a company engineer, who allowed the ship to sail despite an inadequate inspection of the engines. One might expect that, in a regulatory offence concerned with safety standards, vicarious liability might be imposed. Instead, identification was the principle applied, entailing an acquittal of the company on the ground that the engineer was insufficiently senior to generate criminal liability for the company. Consequently, there is now considerable confusion over the appropriate rule of attribution to employ when resolving corporate liability for a regulatory offence that requires proof of some form of culpability.

(d) A middle road

This uncertainty in the law was directly addressed by Lord Hoffmann in the Privy Council case of *Meridian Global Funds Management Asia Ltd v. Securities Commission*.[83] Conducting a broad review of previous authority, Lord Hoffmann concluded that there is no general theory of attribution in the matter of assigning culpability to companies. Instead, there are specific rules of attribution tailored for the terms and policies of the statutory or common law offence at issue in particular cases. What were previously thought to be leading cases on the theory of attribution—*Tesco Supermarkets Ltd* and *Asiatic Petroleum Ltd*—were thus downgraded by Lord Hoffmann to authorities dealing with specific statutory provisions.[84] For him, the way to proceed in determining a question of corporate criminal liability is, first, to resolve whether the offence in question is an offence that may be committed by a company. If it is, one then moves on to consider the level in the corporate hierarchy where

---

[78] Cf. *Mousell Brothers, Limited v. London and North Western Railway Company* [1917] 2 KB 836 (DC).

[79] [1993] 1 WLR 1037 (DC).

[80] [1993] Crim LR 624, 626.

[81] [1995] 1 AC 456.

[82] [1994] 1 WLR 541.

[83] [1995] 2 AC 500.

[84] Trade Descriptions Act 1968 (*Tesco*); Merchant Shipping Act 1894 (*Asiatic Petroleum*).

culpability should be located in order best to give expression to the terms and policy of the offence under consideration.[85]

According to the *Meridian* analysis, the identification doctrine on the one hand and vicarious liability on the other are the two polar extremes of a range of different rules of attribution. One must allow this as a theoretical possibility. Yet the fact is that, of the rules of attribution on offer, the choices made have been confined to either identification or vicarious liability. The case law does not disclose a spectrum of choices but only two. It is not difficult to understand why choices made to date divide into these two possibilities. If uppermost in a court's mind is the need for an effective law that maximises deterrence of companies, the broad-based inculpation offered by vicarious liability becomes attractive. Thus, in *Meridian* itself, the issue was whether the company "knew" that it had acquired a shareholding in another company.[86] The knowledge of a fund manager of insufficient status to be identified with the company was, nonetheless, found to be knowledge attributable to the company. The Privy Council advised that the statutory policy informing the offence—the need for prompt disclosure of acquisitions to provide transparency in securities markets—required the imposition of vicarious liability.[87]

Militating against a wholesale adoption of vicarious liability is the concern to be fair to companies and to their constituencies. The more serious the offence, the greater the potential for damage to corporate reputation and the more compelling the value of fairness. Restraint in the imposition of corporate liability for serious offences has been expressed, until now, by insisting on the applicability of the identification doctrine. *Post Meridian*, we must now allow the possibility of some *via media* between vicarious liability and identification. To date there has been no experiment along those lines. The decision in *Attorney-General's Reference (No. 2 of 1999)*,[88] which rigidly confirms that the doctrine of identification is the rule of attribution for corporate manslaughter, is not a good augury for a more flexible approach—at least, not in the area of serious, stigmatic criminal offences. Indeed, the more recent decision of the Court of Appeal in *St Regis Paper Co. Ltd* [89] is an example of a rigid approach to proof of mens rea even in the context of regulatory offences. The company was charged with "intentionally making a false entry" as to the amount of solids it was discharging into a river. The record keeper was the company's waste disposal manager, the person who supervised the company's discharge of waste products. The doctrine of identification was applied and, under its strictures, the waste disposal manager was found to be an insufficiently senior officer for the purposes of identification—he was too far down the chain of decision-making in the company. Lord Hoffman's judgment in *Meridian* formed the basis of the prosecution's argument for a more flexible approach; but his Lordship's judgment, despite its range and depth, was taken to be no more than authority on the legislative provisions at issue in that case.[90] Unfortunately, the question of how criminal liability might be attributed to a company is now to be addressed on a case-by-case basis.

---

[85] [1995] 2 AC 500, 507.
[86] Securities Amendment Act 1988 (New Zealand), s. 20(4)(e).
[87] [1995] 2 AC 500, 511.
[88] [2000] QB 796 (CA).
[89] [2011] EWCA Crim 2527, [2012] 1 Cr App R 14.
[90] *Ibid*, para. 22.

(iv) Summary: the current law

Any summary of the current law of corporate criminal liability must, inevitably, be tentative:

(i)   If an offence is of a regulatory nature, makes no reference to mens rea, and concerns activities which can straightforwardly be attributed to companies ("selling", "possession", "polluting", etc.), corporate liability will be a simple exercise in the imposition of strict liability.

(ii)   Recalling the earlier general discussion of vicarious liability, vicarious liability will be imposed for mens rea offences concerned with compliance with the terms of a licence should it be found that the company has completely delegated to another the task of compliance with its duties. This follows on ordinary vicarious liability principles, applicable to corporate and individual defendants alike.

(iii)   Even in the absence of total delegation, mens rea may be attributed to a company on the basis of vicarious corporate liability if the offence concerns retail regulation (*Tesco Supermarkets* v. *Brent*)[91] or market regulation (*Meridian*).[92]

(iv)   In the light of *Seaboard Offshore*[93] and *St Regis*,[94] it cannot be assumed that vicarious liability will always be the rule of attribution for corporate defendants, even where the offence is of a regulatory nature. As the *Seaboard* and *St Regis* decisions show, if a regulatory offence requires mens rea, the identification doctrine can be chosen as the rule of attribution. There is a depressing lack of theory and system in the matter of regulatory crimes requiring proof of mens rea. The identification doctrine may be departed from, but only as a matter of *ad hoc* statutory interpretation.

This summary leaves the question of when, if ever, the doctrine of identification will be put aside where serious, stigmatic criminal offences are involved. Recall that, in *Pioneer Concrete*,[95] the House of Lords found companies to be in contempt of court on the basis of vicarious liability. Contempt is a matter of grave reputational consequence and may give rise to unlimited fines. But its nature is too anomalous to warrant any general conclusions. In recent cases where serious crimes have been charged, including manslaughter, identification has remained the basis of attribution.[96] In *Meridian*, Lord Hoffmann particularly warned against assuming that anything in his judgment had any implications for corporate manslaughter;[97] a warning corroborated by the decision in *Attorney-General's Reference (No. 2 of 1999)*,[98] which confirmed identification as the rule of attribution for corporate manslaughter in the context of a prosecution following a large-scale rail crash. It may well be the case that identification will remain the principal, perhaps even the sole, basis of attribution of culpability for serious, stigmatic crimes. It is simply not clear.

---

[91] [1993] 1 WLR 1037 (DC).
[92] [1995] 2 AC 500.
[93] [1994] 1 WLR 541 (HL).
[94] [2011] EWCA Crim 2527, [2012] 1 Cr App R 14.
[95] [1995] 1 AC 456.
[96] See, e.g., *H M Coroner for East Kent* (1989) 88 Cr App R 10; *P & O Ferries (Dover) Ltd* (1991) 93 Cr App R 72; *Great Western Trains Co* (unreported: Central Criminal Court, Scott Baker J, 30 June 1999).
[97] [1995] 2 AC 500, 512.
[98] [2000] QB 796 (CA).

(v) Reform: new conceptions of corporate action and responsibility

The previous sections have outlined the sorry state of the law on corporate criminal liability in England and Wales. There is a growing strand of opinion that the unsatisfactory state of the law regarding corporate criminal liability is in large part explained by a failure to ask the right questions. To date in English law, the approach has been to ask questions first about the culpability of *individuals* associated with companies, and then to ask further questions concerning how the culpability of these individuals has implications for the culpability of their companies. To proceed in this way, it may be argued, overlooks the crucial fact that there is such a thing as genuine corporate agency and, in turn, corporate culpability—a free-standing culpability that need not be derived from the faults of individuals associated with the company.[99] Indeed, it has been asserted that corporate culpability may be present even if no one associated individual has been in any degree at fault.[100] Two attempts to capture this form of culpability will now be examined. This is of more than academic interest because, as will be seen, there have been proposals for England and Wales to attempt to formulate a "corporate" corporate criminal liability. There have also been legislative measures that appear to move in somewhat new directions.

(a) Reactive fault

"Reactive fault" is a proposal of Professors Fisse and Braithwaite for a new basis of corporate liability.[101] They are committed to the view that companies, in moral terms, amount to something more than the sum of the individuals associated with them, that something important is lost if corporate conduct is represented exclusively as a function of human conduct.[102] This perspective forms the backdrop of their proposal; they do not, however, try to devise a new regime that gives direct expression to an intrinsically corporate form of culpability. Their proposal dispenses entirely with the need to establish culpability at the time of the actus reus. The fault of the company is to be found in terms of its reaction, or lack of reaction, to the commission of the actus reus.[103] In their words:[104]

> "Reactive fault [is an] … unreasonable corporate failure to devise and undertake satisfactory preventative or corrective measures in response to the commission of the actus reus of the offence."

---

[99] French, *Collective and Corporate Responsibility* (1984) esp. 30–65. French law appears to claim that the structure and practice of decision-making in companies may constitute a distinctive form of corporate intentionality which is not reducible to the mental states, past and present, of human agents associated with companies. For a view that French is offering merely a semantic account of the agency of companies see Ouyang and Shiner, "Organizations and Agency" (1995) 1 *Legal Theory* 283.

[100] Dan-Cohen, *Rights, Persons and Organisations: A Legal Theory for Bureaucratic Society* (1986) chap. 3.

[101] See Fisse and Braithwaite, *Corporations, Crime and Accountability* (1993); Fisse and Braithwaite, "The Allocation of Responsibility for Corporate Crime: Individualism, Collectivism and Accountability" (1988) 11 *Sydney LR* 468. Cf. French, "Fishing the Red Herrings out of a Sea of Moral Responsibility" in LePore and McLaughlin (eds.), *Actions and Events: Perspectives on the Philosophy of Donald Davidson* (1985) 73.

[102] Fisse and Braithwaite, *Corporations, Crime and Accountability* (1993) chap. 2.

[103] It should be noted that one factor telling in favour of the prosecution of a corporation is that "[t]he company had been previously subject to warning, sanctions or criminal charges and had nonetheless failed to take adequate action to prevent future unlawful conduct, or had continued to engage in the conduct". Against prosecution is a "genuinely proactive approach adopted by the corporate management team when the offending is brought to their notice, involving self-reporting and remedial actions, including the compensation of victims": CPS, *Corporate Prosecutions*, available at http://www.cps.gov.uk/legal/a_to_c/corporate_prosecutions/.

[104] Fisse and Braithwaite, *Corporations, Crime and Accountability* (1993) 48.

Finding culpability from acts, omissions, and states of mind which arise *after* the commission of the actus reus is a radical departure from the norm. Yet we would not have left
behind the appraisal of the conduct of human beings. Let us assume that the actus reus
is the death of a worker caused, say, during the course of building activities undertaken
by D Ltd. There would, of course, have to be an initial investigation of the death-causing
incident. There would follow an examination of what could and should have been done to
make the working practices of D Ltd safer for the future. It is hard to see how the conduct of
individuals associated with D Ltd would not form a key element at the trial. There are other,
allied, problems. What charge would be brought against D Ltd? Would it (could it) depend
on the degree of reactive fault found to be present? How would it be determined whether
the degree of reactive fault proved against D Ltd merited a conviction for manslaughter?
If the jury brought in a verdict of manslaughter against D Ltd, what would be the position
of individuals associated with D Ltd whose conduct was found to be wanting? Would there
be a possibility of complicity charges and, if so, on what conceptual basis? If such charges
are not to be brought, would and should any civil law consequences follow for individuals
closely associated with the guilty verdict against the company?

   The adoption of reactive fault would signal an enormous change in corporate liability.
Deaths or injuries occurring in the context of manufacturing, construction, mining, air,
rail and sea transport activities, road accidents involving corporately owned vehicles, etc.,
potentially involve serious criminal liability on the part of companies. The issues arising
at trial would not turn on the culpability at the time of a particular incident but instead
would require a review of corporate safety and other procedures within an open-ended
time frame.[105] The prosecutorial and forensic burden would be enormous. Reactive fault is
an untenable basis for corporate liability.

(b) The theory of aggregation

Under this theory,[106] the faults of any two or more persons associated with the company
may be aggregated and attributed *in toto* to the company. A judgement then has to be made
as to whether the totality of this consolidated fault constitutes, for the company, the culpability required for the offence. If one or more of the associated individuals possessed in full
the culpability the offence requires, the aggregation theory will not, in that particular application, extend beyond vicarious liability. The theory comes into its own when it cannot be
said of any associated individual that she possessed the culpability the offence requires. If,
for example, a company is charged with manslaughter by gross negligence, it may be that
none of its directors or employees can be shown individually to have been grossly negligent
but, nonetheless, two or more individuals are open collectively to criticism in relation to
the incident which caused the death of V. The question then is whether the sum of these
criticisms constitutes gross negligence on the part of the company. This theory can attain
some degree of metaphysical coherence only if one assumes that the company has the moral

---

[105] The efficacy and acceptability of trial by jury comes under increasing pressure the more protracted and
complex the issue to be resolved, as is evidenced by the difficulties experienced in effectively prosecuting serious
fraud. See Sullivan, "The Particularity of Serious Fraud" in Birks (ed.), *Pressing Problems in the Law: Vol. 1—
Criminal Justice and Human Rights* (1995) 99, 102–3.

[106] Discussed by Wells, *Corporations and Criminal Responsibility* (2nd ed., 2001) 156.

and agency properties of a real person, absorbing, over time and space, the faults of those associated with it. In that sense, the theory of aggregation is a theory genuinely concerned with *corporate* guilt.

The theory of aggregation can be seen as potentially more efficacious in securing convictions against corporations than the identification doctrine. If we confine our attention to charges of corporate manslaughter, by 2005 there had been only 34 prosecutions for manslaughter brought against companies, with no convictions against companies of any size or complexity.[107] Successful prosecutions have been confined to small companies where the top management ran the company in a "hands on" manner. In any larger company, it is exceedingly unlikely that an official of sufficient stature to count as an *alter ego* of the company would be found grossly negligent in respect of particular safety matters. The failed *P&O* ("a [company] infected with the disease of sloppiness")[108] prosecution demonstrates that. Notwithstanding increasing public concern with corporate safety standards through the 1980s and 1990s, the Court of Appeal confirmed in *Attorney-General's Reference (No. 2 of 1999)*[109] that liability for gross negligence manslaughter could only be imposed on a company under the principle of identification.

The legislature's response to this difficulty endorses, to an extent, the theory of aggregation.[110] Aggregation is an element in the scheme of liability for the offence of corporate manslaughter, created by the Corporate Manslaughter and Homicide Act 2007. The specifics of this offence will be examined below.[111] For now we should note that a company will be liable for corporate manslaughter if it causes a person's death as a consequence of a gross breach of a relevant duty of care.[112] A gross breach of a duty of care will be established if "the conduct of [the organisation] falls far below what can reasonably be expected of the organisation in the circumstances".[113] In resolving that issue, the jury may consider the conduct of the entirety of the workforce, the safety policies and practices of the company, and any failures to comply with health and safety legislation.[114] However, a full version of aggregation is not adopted by the 2007 Act. Although the elements just referred to must be weighed when determining whether the company's conduct in relation to causing V's death fell far below what should have been reasonably expected, the organisation will be guilty of the offence only if the way in which its activities are managed or organised by its senior management was a "substantial element" in the breach of the duty of care.[115] The 2007 Act thus in reality represents "an uneasy no man's land between competing approaches to corporate criminal liability".[116]

Even in this modified form, however, one may have reservations about the implications for individuals of the aggregation approach. The practical implementation of that approach will inevitably be linked to criticisms made against the company's personnel.

---

[107] Home Office, *Corporate Manslaughter: The Government's Draft Bill for Reform* Cm. 6497 (2005).

[108] *Report of Court No. 8074* (HMSO, 1987) para. 14.1 ("Sheen Report").

[109] [2000] QB 796 (CA).

[110] The 2007 Act also contains elements of the organisational approach discussed in the next section.

[111] See below, § 10.6(iii).

[112] Corporate Manslaughter and Corporate Homicide Act 2007, s. 1.

[113] *Ibid.*, s. 1(4)(b).

[114] Section 8.

[115] Section 1(3).

[116] Wells, "Corporate Criminal Liability: A Ten Year Review" [2014] *Crim LR* 849, 865. Norrie, *Crime, Reason and History: A Critical Introduction to Criminal Law* (3rd ed., 2014) 125–6.

Persons connected with the company who have been subjected to criticism at public trials will be closely linked to any guilty verdict sustained by the company, with possible adverse legal consequences, at least at civil law.[117] There is a danger that they will be tainted with the stigma of a homicide offence without any necessary proof of their *personal* culpability commensurate with a serious criminal offence.[118] Given the relatively small number of successful prosecutions for corporate manslaughter to date,[119] it is not clear how much of a concern this is in practice.

(c) The organisational model

An alternative conception of corporate fault can be premised on a corporation's structures— i.e. its policies and practices.[120] For instance, in dealing with the Zeebrugge ferry disaster, the question for an organisational fault proponent would not be whether P&O's senior management was reckless (the identification doctrine), or whether awareness of risk can be aggregated through the consideration of various actors within the corporation (the aggregation approach). Rather, the question would be whether "the corporation can be blamed because its system, its operating policies, displayed a reckless attitude to safety".[121]

Such an organisational approach has been adopted in the Australian Capital Territory.[122] There, alongside the identification doctrine, sit alternative modes of corporate fault that involve "proving that a corporate culture existed within the corporation that directed, encouraged, tolerated or led to noncompliance with the … law" or "proving that the corporation failed to create and maintain a corporate culture requiring compliance with the contravened law". This culture-based approach is similar to Wells' organisational model, but has not yet been adopted expressly in England and Wales (even if aspects of it are visible in the offence of corporate manslaughter).[123] This is fortunate. The corporate culture model is inherently vague, despite Wells' best efforts to explain it in terms that would satisfy the requirements of the Rule of Law.

(d) The future of corporate liability

On one view, the Corporate Manslaughter and Corporate Homicide Act 2007 (which covers "organisations", which is a wider concept than "corporation")[124] breaks new

---

[117] The Act confines criminal liability to organisations. Individuals cannot be criminally liable for corporate manslaughter either as principals or accessories: s. 18.

[118] Interestingly, it appears that public attitudes towards *work-related* deaths are perhaps less punitive than those regarding fatalities in other contexts: Almond, "Public Perceptions of Work-related Fatality Cases: Reaching the Outer Limits of 'Populist Punitiveness'?" (2008) 48 *Brit J Criminology* 448.

[119] The Act came into force on 6 April 2008. For a survey of cases under the old and new regime, see Wells, "Corporate Criminal Liability: A Ten Year Review" [2014] *Crim LR* 849, 860–2.

[120] Wells, *Corporations and Criminal Responsibility* (2nd ed., 2001) chap. 8.

[121] *Ibid.*, 158.

[122] Criminal Code 2002, s. 51. See, too, Criminal Code Act 1995 (which applies to federal criminal law in Australia).

[123] Cf. Bribery Act 2010, s. 7(2): "it is a defence for [a commercial organisation] to prove that [it] had in place adequate procedures designed to prevent persons associated with [it] from" committing an offence of bribery for the benefit of the commercial organisation.

[124] The Corporate Manslaughter and Homicide Act 2007 takes organisational culpability beyond companies, which are of course legal persons in their own right. The Act includes within the purview of the corporate manslaughter offence non-corporate entities such as partnerships, health trusts, prisons, and the emergency services.

conceptual ground. We now have an offence where the grounds of corporate liability for a serious offence are not dependent on establishing that any individual associated with the company possessed the culpability for the crime.

For those who favour this development, and indeed in going further in the aggregation or organisational fault direction, the question is whether this idea of aggregation or organisational culpability can be implemented for other crimes. That may prove difficult. Corporate manslaughter has a close affinity with manslaughter by gross negligence and, whatever the reservations expressed above, the negligence standard—which is assessed primarily by reference to a defendant's conduct—is well adapted to a holistic appraisal of the company's performance in safety matters. Many other serious offences have states of mind such as intent, dishonesty, or recklessness as definitional elements. Posing questions relating to general corporate performance would less clearly capture these states of mind. Attributing intentionality and other states of mind to a company directly, without any mediation through the intentions and states of mind of persons connected with it, would require full adoption of the view that companies are, sufficient unto themselves, moral agents or "intelligent machines".

This seems an unlikely prospect. In line with English traditions of empiricism is the assertion of Lord Hoffman that "there is no such thing as the company itself, no ding an sich".[125] The traditional view of English company law is that companies are inherently and exclusively *legal* regimes with no transcendent reality beyond the merely legal realm.[126] That view of companies fits well with a rejection of the claim that human agency may be submerged and transmuted by social and bureaucratic structures. Instead, one may assert that companies, in terms of their activities and planning, depend on human agency and are not, in terms of conduct and states of mind, some form of non-human sentient creature.[127] This perspective does not need to deny the force of corporate culture on behavioural patterns. It merely insists that those cultures emanate from the interactions, past and present, of human beings.[128]

On this view, the gateway to corporate liability lies through the conduct and states of mind of persons connected with the company. If it is thought right to convict companies for serious offences on a broader front than is currently the case, the most straightforward way of doing this would be to convict companies on the basis of vicarious liability. It may be objected that this would be too undiscriminating: why, it might be asked, should, say, a reputable insurance company be found guilty of fraud by false pretences because one of its sales force on a particular occasion made false and dishonest statements when selling a

---

One may note too an increasing willingness on the part of the judiciary to interpret regulatory statutes in a manner that imposes criminal liability on non-corporate entities, such as partnerships and unincorporated associations: e.g. *Stevenson and Sons* (a partnership) [2008] EWCA Crim 273, [2008] 2 Cr App R 14; *L(R) and F(J)* [2008] EWCA Crim 1970, [2009] 1 Cr App R 16 (golf club organised as an unincorporated association).

[125] *Meridian Global Funds Management Asia Ltd* v. *Securities Commission* [1995] 2 AC 500, 507 (*sic*). In Kantian philosophy, *Ding an sich* refers to a thing that has not been mediated through perception or conceptualisation.

[126] Hart, "Definition and Theory in Jurisprudence" (1954) 70 *LQR* 37.

[127] A perspective identified as "methodological individualism": Popper, *The Poverty of Historicism* (1957); Watkins, "Historical Explanation in the Social Sciences" (1957) 8 *British Journal for the Philosophy of Science* 104.

[128] For an account which accepts methodological individualism but which emphasises the formative influence of group and social structures in creating forms of "collective intentionality" see Searle, *The Construction of Social Reality* (1995).

policy to a customer? This objection has considerable force. Vicarious liability would be far more acceptable if companies were allowed a due diligence defence.[129] In the insurance company example, the company should be exonerated if it could demonstrate that its recruiting, training, and monitoring practices emphasised and supported honesty in sales and penalised dishonesty.

Even if more inventive approaches are not adopted in England and Wales, something should be done to clarify the mechanisms for establishing corporate liability for offences involving mens rea. In 2010, the Law Commission proposed that Parliament should expressly state what the rule of attribution was if an offence was intended to apply to companies and that for the meantime courts should not assume that the doctrine of identification was the predominant principle.[130] Alas, this sensible proposal has not been taken forward. As noted above, the Court of Appeal in *St Regis Paper Company Ltd*[131] was of the view that, for any offence involving proof of culpability, there was a strong presumption that the identification doctrine provided the applicable rule of attribution. It seems unlikely that, following the piecemeal development of specific offences targeting bribery and corporate manslaughter, a general restatement of the law on corporate liability is now possible or likely.[132] This is a shame.

One final point, in closing, concerns punishment. If companies are regularly to be convicted for serious offences, it is necessary to consider what forms of sanction are appropriate. It should be uncontroversial that companies, by way of fines, should be stripped of any illicit gains and of any quantifiable competitive advantage attributable to the crimes and breaches of regulation occurring in the course of their activities. But what level of sanction beyond that? There is an intractable tension between imposing monetary penalties aimed at deterrence[133] and avoiding adverse consequences for employees, creditors, and shareholders not implicated in the wrongdoing. If the company is forced into liquidation, a valuable source of employment and goods and services may be lost. Adaptation of monetary penalties such as the "equity" fine and non-monetary alternatives such as corporate probation have been suggested but are fraught with difficulty in both theory and practice.[134] These problems have yet to be resolved. Corporate punishment, like corporate liability, remains a rich source of philosophical and economic challenges.[135]

---

[129] Cf. Bribery Act 2010, s. 7. The Law Commission put out for consultation a recommendation that a due diligence defence be provided in respect of all regulatory strict liability, offences: *Criminal Liability in Regulatory Contexts*, LCCP No. 195 (2010) para. 6.95. There is much to be said for extending this proposal to corporate liability for any offence, including mens rea offences, thereby allowing a company to demonstrate that the offence was committed on the initiative of an individual employee rather than a by-product of the company's policies and practices.

[130] *Criminal Liability in Regulatory Contexts*, LCCP No. 195 (2010) para. 5.110.

[131] [2011] EWCA Crim 2527, [2012] 1 Cr App R 14.

[132] *Criminal Liability in Regulatory Contexts*, LCCP No. 195 (2010) para 5.91; above n 50.

[133] And fines should, in principle, be large enough to encourage management and shareholders to ensure future compliance: *Thames Water Utilities Ltd* [2015] EWCA Crim 960, [2015] 1 WLR 4411.

[134] For discussion of the forms of sanction that may be deployed against companies see Wells, *Corporations and Criminal Responsibility* (2nd ed., 2001) 31–9, 165–8; Coffee, "No Soul to Damn: No Body to Kick: An Unscandalized Inquiry into the Problem of Corporate Punishment" (1981) 79 *Michigan LR* 386.

[135] See Lederman, "Models for Imposing Corporate Criminal Liability: From Adaptation and Imitation towards Aggregation and the Search for Self-identity" (2001) 4 *Buffalo Crim LR* 641 for a thoughtful account of theorising in the area.

9

THE INCHOATE OFFENCES

The offences of encouragement, assistance, conspiracy, and attempt are known as the inchoate offences because liability for these crimes may arise before, or even without, the commission of any substantive offence.[1] The essentials of these offences are clear. D will be liable for encouraging theft as soon as he urges P to steal property from V. D will be liable for assisting theft as soon as she tells P where V's property is located. D and P will be liable for a conspiracy to commit theft the moment P agrees with D that he should steal from V. P will be guilty of attempted theft from V if and when, intending to steal from V, she does anything that comes sufficiently close to appropriating property from V.

The virtue of inchoate offences is that they permit the lawful restraint and arrest of aspirant criminals prior to the realisation of any concrete harm.[2] If D, lacking any justification or excuse, were to shoot at V with an intent to kill her, it is a matter of great relief should the bullet miss V and harmlessly fall to the ground. Yet it would be a remarkably indulgent system of criminal law that allowed the absence of concrete harm to preclude any criminal liability of D. From a consequentialist perspective, D's liability for attempted murder is justified by society's need to restrain and deter dangerous people. Provided there was a clear and present danger of the violation of a protected interest of any innocent person, the use of restraining and punitive measures against D is justified. Indeed, to subject an innocent person to an unwarranted risk of death may properly be considered *in itself* to constitute the harmful violation of a protected interest.

From a retributivist position, moreover, many "desert" theorists would maintain that a person who tries to do harm but fails to achieve her objective is, in terms of culpability, not materially different from the person who tries and succeeds.[3] Further, even theorists who insist that the occurrence of harm does have moral significance (i.e. that it matters to D's culpability whether she succeeds or fails) would not question the restraint and punishment of a person who has unequivocally tried to harm another; they merely dispute whether failure should be penalised as heavily as success.[4]

---

[1] The terms "substantive offence", "full offence", and "principal offence" will be used in this chapter to denote the crime that is the objective of the encourager, assister, conspirator, or attemptor.

[2] Despite the evident utility of these offences, they have been criticised for their potential to punish conduct too remote from the realisation of any concrete harm. Some of these criticisms will be addressed later in this chapter. For a general critical survey, see Husak, "The Nature and Justifiability of Nonconsummate Offences" (1995) 37 *Arizona LR* 151.

[3] Ashworth, "Criminal Attempts and the Role of Resulting Harm under the Code and in the Common Law" (1988) 19 *Rutgers LJ* 725.

[4] Duff, *Criminal Attempts* (1996) chap. 4. For further discussion and references, see below, § 9.4(vi).

The consequentialist and retributivist justifications for inchoate offences are most graphically demonstrated when, as in our shooting example, D has done everything that he intends to do in his attempt to harm V. In that case, D's attempt is complete. The appropriateness, however, of penalising conduct which is of a more preliminary nature is controversial. For instance, there has been considerable debate as to whether agreeing with another to commit a crime at some future date warrants criminalisation.[5] In the United States, certain jurisdictions and federal law require, before liability for conspiracy may arise, that at least one overt act in pursuance of the criminal objective be carried out by a party to the agreement.[6] In England and Wales, however, conspiracy is well entrenched without proof of any overt act and permits restraint well before the commission of the substantive offence. The legitimacy of having a crime of conspiracy has been considered by the Law Commission, which concluded that it is justifiable to have an offence founded on the making of an agreement without the need to prove that anything was done in pursuance of the objective, since the relevant culpability can be inferred from the fact that the agreement was made.[7] Indeed, a policy of early intervention is not confined to inchoate crimes. Many substantive offences, particularly those which proscribe possession of such things as guns, explosives, and drugs, are designed indirectly to prevent future harms.[8]

§ 9.1 Incitement

The common law offence of incitement was first recognised in *Higgins*,[9] where D urged or persuaded others to perpetrate crimes. This offence was committed at the point when D had successfully communicated with P.[10]

Although there was some uncertainty about the interpretation of the crime of incitement, especially concerning the relevant mens rea, the offence was generally workable and acceptable. There was, however, a significant gap in the law[11] where a person sought to assist the commission of a crime but did not communicate to anybody a desire that the offence should be committed. If the substantive offence was committed, D could be convicted as an accessory; however, if no substantive offence was committed, D could not be guilty of any offence. So, if D placed poison in a drink knowing that P would administer that drink to V but P tripped and spilled the drink before it could be administered, D would not be guilty of a crime. D could not be an accessory to administration of the poison, since

---

[5] Johnson, "The Unnecessary Crime of Conspiracy" (1973) 61 *Cal LR* 1137; Marcus, "Criminal Conspiracy Law: Time to Turn Back from an Ever Expanding, Ever More Troubling Area" (1992) 1 *William and Mary Bill of Rights J* 1.

[6] Perkins and Boyce, *Criminal Law* (3rd ed., 1982) 685–7.

[7] Law Com. No. 318, *Conspiracy and Attempts* (2009) para. 2.33. See also LCCP No. 183, *Conspiracy and Attempts* (2007) para. 2.33.

[8] To this category, one might add crimes involving the proscription of conduct associated with drink-driving, and forms of sexual conduct and obscenity, which are frequently justified by reference to the ultimate impact that such conduct may have on the social order. The link between the proscribed activities and such generalised further or underlying harm may be tenuous. For discussion of the role of remote harms in the creation of criminal offences, see Simester and von Hirsch, *Crimes, Harms, and Wrongs* (2011) chaps. 5–6.

[9] (1801) 2 East 5, 102 ER 269.

[10] *Banks* (1873) 12 Cox CC.

[11] Identified by Spencer, "Trying to Help Another Person Commit a Crime" in Smith (ed.), *Criminal Law: Essays in Honour of J. C. Smith* (1987).

accessorial liability turns on the substantive offence being committed. D could not be guilty of an attempt, since her actions were not sufficiently proximate to the commission of the substantive offence. D could not be guilty of a conspiracy, since there had been no agreement with P. D could not be guilty of incitement, since there had been no communication with P. The absence of criminal liability in such a case is difficult to justify in terms of culpability and social defence.

The Law Commission[12] considered this to be a major gap in the law and recommended the creation of a new inchoate offence of assisting the commission of a crime and replacing the common law offence of incitement with a new inchoate offence of encouraging crime. These recommendations were rapidly enacted in the Serious Crime Act 2007, albeit in a different form from that recommended by the Law Commission. Section 59 of that statute abolished the common law offence of incitement. It does not follow, however, that crimes of incitement no longer exist in English law, since a number of statutory offences use the language of inciting crimes, or similar language. For example, there are various incitement offences within the Sexual Offences Act 2003, including inciting a child under 13 to engage in sexual activity.[13] Further, section 4 of the Offences Against the Person Act 1861 criminalises the solicitation, encouragement, persuasion, or proposal of murder;[14] the Incitement to Disaffection Act 1934 creates an offence of endeavouring to seduce members of the armed forces from their duty or allegiance; and the Terrorism Act 2006, section 1(2) creates an offence of encouraging or inducing terrorism.

§ 9.2 Encouraging and assisting a crime

Part 2 of the Serious Crime Act 2007 creates new inchoate offences of assisting and encouraging a crime.[15] Although this statutory scheme purported to implement the recommendations of the Law Commission,[16] the eventual scheme is very different from that which had been recommended, involving the creation of three offences in an unnecessarily prolix and complex way. Each of these offences requires that D perform an act which is capable of encouraging or assisting the commission of a substantive offence. They are distinguished by their mens rea requirements. D's conduct becomes an offence when he acts:

(i)   with intent to encourage or assist the commission of the substantive offence (section 44);

(ii)   believing that the substantive offence will be committed and that the act will encourage or assist its commission (section 45); or

---

[12] Law Com. No. 300, *Inchoate Liability for Assisting and Encouraging Crime* (2006).

[13] Sexual Offences Act 2003, s. 8. See *Jones* [2007] EWCA Crim 1118, [2008] QB 460 (no specific child needs to be identified).

[14] The Law Commission has recommended that there is still a need for this offence, despite the general inchoate offences of assisting and encouraging crime, because the solicitation offence may be needed where D has incited groups or advice to kill is only intended to be followed in certain circumstances. The Law Commission recommends that this offence be called "encouraging murder": Law Com. No. 316, *Reform of Offences Against the Person* (2015).

[15] Spencer and Virgo, "Encouraging and Assisting Crime: Legislate in Haste, Repent at Leisure" [2008] 9 *Arch. News* 7; Ormerod and Fortson, "Serious Crime Act 2007: The Part 2 Offences" [2009] *Crim LR* 389.

[16] Law Com. No. 300, *Inchoate Liability for Assisting and Encouraging Crime* (2006).

(iii) where the act is capable of encouraging or assisting the commission of one or more of a number of principal offences, believing that one or more of those offences will be committed and that his act will encourage or assist one or more of them (section 46).

Each of these inchoate offences can be committed even though the substantive offence is not committed,[17] and even though there has been no effective encouragement or assistance of P, who might have had no idea that D has done any act of encouragement or assistance. The maximum penalty for D who is convicted of one of these statutory inchoate offences will be the same as for the anticipated substantive offence,[18] save that the penalty for encouraging or assisting murder may be life imprisonment rather than a mandatory life sentence.[19] These new statutory inchoate offences expand the ambit of inchoate liability significantly. It is sufficient that D does an act which is capable of encouraging or assisting a substantive offence, without needing to prove that it assisted or encouraged P in any way, so the identification of any relevant potential harm becomes increasingly difficult to discern. The fact that one's unsuccessful attempt to get another to commit a crime is sufficient in itself for criminal liability has not escaped criticism before, on the grounds of the remoteness of D's conduct from the commission of any substantive offence.[20] In creating new offences of encouraging and assisting crime, Parliament clearly considered that this form of liability is not too remote from the commission of a substantive offence to prevent D from being convicted.

Further, this legislative regime is inherently complex and overlaps substantially with existing criminal liability, notably conspiracy and accessorial liability. Many parties to a conspiracy will have encouraged the commission of a crime and so could be convicted of the encouragement offence. Similarly, D, who successfully assists the substantive offence to be committed, could be convicted either of assistance or as an accessory.

For a significant time after Part 2 of the Serious Crime Act 2007 was brought into force, the offences were rarely charged. Following riots in England in August 2011, the crimes of assisting and encouraging proved to be particularly significant. The fact that some defendants, who placed messages on social media encouraging riot and other offences, were convicted of the encouraging offence and received sentences of four years' imprisonment,[21] shows that these offences can have a very significant role to play in the criminal justice system. The Court of Appeal recognised that "the abuse of modern technology for criminal purposes extends to and includes incitement of very many people by a single step".[22] The offences may also have a significant role to play in relation to serious organised crime in

---

[17] Serious Crime Act 2007, s. 49(1). D can also be convicted of one of the statutory inchoate offences if it can be proved that she must have committed either the inchoate offence or the relevant substantive offence as principal, but not as accessory, but it is not proved which offence she committed: *Ibid.*, s. 56.

[18] Or the anticipated substantive offence with the longest maximum term if s. 46 applies: *ibid.*, s. 58(4)–(7).

[19] *Ibid.*, s. 58.

[20] For a critique of the old offence of incitement see Robbins, "Double Inchoate Crimes" (1989) 26 *Harv J Legis* 1. Robbins argues that incitement essentially penalised attempts to conspire and, consequently, targeted conduct too remote from the principal offence. There is some force in his critique, and more so in respect of the new statutory inchoate offences.

[21] See *Blackshaw et al* [2011] EWCA Crim 2312, [2012] 1 WLR 1126.

[22] *Ibid.*, para. 73.

dealing with the background figures who organise the criminal activities of others,[23] and in relation to activities relating to terrorism. There are, however, few reported cases relating to the encouragement and assistance offences.[24]

(i) Actus reus

(a) Encouragement

Encouragement is not defined comprehensively by the Serious Crime Act 2007, so it is appropriate to assume that the cases which defined the actus reus of the common law offence of incitement remain relevant to the interpretation of the actus reus of the new statutory offence. The essence of encouragement is consequently some communication or gesture on the part of D which might persuade, induce, or influence P to commit a crime. It is not necessary for D's encouragement to have any effect on the intentions or conduct of others. It is consequently immaterial if, as in *DPP* v. *Armstrong*,[25] P is an undercover police officer who is not influenced by D's encouragement. The target of the encouragement may be either a particular individual or people generally—as when D addresses a meeting or writes a newspaper article.[26]

Whether D's conduct is capable of encouraging a crime may require some careful analysis of the context of the particular act. Encouragement was found to be present, for purposes of the crime of incitement, in *Invicta Plastics* v. *Clare*,[27] where D, a company, advertised in a motoring magazine a device, "Radatec", which indicated the presence of a police radar device monitoring traffic. It is illegal for private persons to install such devices.[28] Pictorial detail in the advertisement illustrated the utility of "Radatec" in avoiding detection for speeding. The company was endeavouring to persuade motorists to acquire the device in order to assist purchasers to contravene the laws against speeding and so the Divisional Court confirmed D's conviction for inciting the commission of offences. In *Marlow*,[29] D was convicted of incitement on the basis of publishing instructions on the growing of cannabis, something which clearly might encourage others to follow suit.[30]

A rather more dubious decision is *Goldman*,[31] where D was held to have incited E by responding positively to an advertisement placed by E which offered the sale of indecent photographs of children. That E's advertisement constituted encouragement is not in doubt. D's role, however, seems to have been confined to that of a willing recipient of E's criminal services. D's encouragement allegedly took the form of "arousing [E's] cupidity",

---

[23] *Sadique (No 2)* [2013] EWCA Crim 1150, [2014] 1 WLR 986.

[24] With most cases involving sentencing issues relating to the offences. See, for example, *McCaffery* [2014] EWCA Crim 2550; *Bell* [2014] EWCA Crim 1660.

[25] [2000] Crim LR 379.

[26] *Most* (1881) 7 QBD 244. See also *Jones* [2007] EWCA Crim 1118, [2008] QB 460.

[27] [1976] RTR 251.

[28] Wireless Telegraphy Act 1949, s. 1(1).

[29] [1997] Crim LR 897 (CA).

[30] A challenge against the decision in *Marlow* on the ground that it contravened D's right to freedom of expression guaranteed by Art. 10 ECHR was held by the European Court to be inadmissible on the ground that the derogation from that freedom was in pursuit of the legitimate aim of suppressing the foreseeable commission of crimes: [2001] EHRLR 444.

[31] [2001] Crim LR 822.

yet D did nothing more than show himself to be a purchaser of E's child pornography. It would be perverse to think that we, say, encourage the sale of a sweater by Marks & Spencer when we present the item for payment. On the facts of *Goldman*, the crucial element of inducement or persuasion appears to be missing. It is difficult to overlook the fact that the Court of Appeal's rather strained analysis enabled D to be found criminally liable for conduct in England in respect of seeking to access child pornography supplied from overseas. An understandable zeal to curb this vile trade seems to have distorted the natural meaning of encouraging a crime. The same impetus may explain *O'Shea* v. *Coventry Magistrates' Court*,[32] where D had accessed internet sites featuring child pornography. He was charged with inciting P, who ran the site, to distribute indecent photographs of children. D's defence was that he had incited no one, merely downloaded images from his computer. The Divisional Court confirmed D's conviction on the basis that, by accessing the site, D would have encouraged P to maintain the site. It seems that no evidence was required that P was aware that D had visited the site. This stretches any reasonable conception of encouragement to its limits and beyond. Today, the preferable way of dealing with defendants such as Goldman and O'Shea is to treat them as assisting the substantive crime to be committed, in the sense of facilitating P's criminal conduct. Without buyers, the child pornographer cannot sell his illegal wares. The artificial extension of the meaning of encouragement in these cases might consequently be explained on the basis that an inchoate offence of assistance did not exist until the enactment of the Serious Crime Act 2007.

Lord Denning, when determining the scope of the statutory offence of incitement to racial hatred in *Race Relations Board* v. *Applin*,[33] considered that threats as well as encouragement and persuasion fell within the legal conception of incitement.[34] That encouragement includes threatening or putting pressure on another to commit an offence is specifically recognised by the Serious Crime Act 2007.[35] Although, as a matter of ordinary language, we would not describe coercion or threats as "encouragement", to confine that word to its ordinary meaning in this context would be perverse. Take a case where D seeks to persuade her employee P to commit an offence within the course of his employment. If she offers a rise in salary by way of inducement, she unequivocally encourages the offence. The same must surely follow if she uses the stick of redundancy rather than the carrot of financial reward. Threats are a mode of influence, and it is conduct which seeks to induce and influence the commission of crimes that constitutes the legal conception of encouragement.

D's attitude or motivation may be relevant to the identification of encouragement. For instance, P may ask D whether V, P's wife, is still seeing E. D answers truthfully that she is, although D is aware that this information may lead to P's killing V. If D simply felt constrained to tell P the truth, no encouragement of murder arises. Contrast the case where D seeks P out to impart this information in order to deceive P into thinking that V is seeing E; depending on D's mens rea, this could constitute the crime of encouragement.

The encouragement of P can be indirect,[36] so the crime can be committed if D gives a letter to X with the instruction that she should pass it to P and the letter encourages P to kill V.

---

[32] CO/6342/2003.
[33] [1973] QB 815.
[34] *Ibid.*, 827.
[35] Serious Crime Act 2007, s. 65(1).
[36] *Ibid.*, s. 66.

(b) Assistance

Assistance is not defined by the Serious Crime Act 2007, so its interpretation will be a matter for the courts, presumably with reference to the interpretation of aiding in accessorial liability.[37] The essence of assistance is conduct which can be considered to make it easier for the substantive offence to be committed. As with encouragement, it is possible to provide assistance indirectly,[38] so, for example, if D gives to X the combination number for V's safe and asks X to pass this on to P, who is intending to steal from the safe, the necessary act of assistance can be established.

(c) An act capable of encouraging or assisting

Whereas the common law offence of incitement would only be committed where D communicated persuasion or pressure to P, and this continues to be the case for the statutory incitement offences, the offences of encouragement and assistance are committed once D has done any act which is capable of encouraging or assisting the crime to be committed. Presumably, this need not be a substantial act, and neither will it be necessary to establish any communication or interaction with P. In *Banks*,[39] D's letter to P advising P to kill V was intercepted in the post. D was convicted of attempting to incite, but today this would be sufficient to constitute the crime of encouragement, because sending such a letter is capable of encouraging P. Although it would not be necessary to show that the letter had been received by P, presumably it would be required to show that the letter had been posted, this being the act performed by D which is capable of encouraging the crime. Although this act would not have encouraged P until P had read the letter, the focus of the actus reus is on D's act and its capability rather than on its actual effect, so the posting would be sufficient. The earlier act of writing the letter might also be analysed as constituting an act which is capable of encouraging the crime; but, since D must do further acts, including posting it, before this capability can be realized, the preferable view is that this is not a sufficient act. D might instead be guilty of attempting to encourage a crime, but that would require the writing of the letter to be considered a more than merely preparatory act towards the commission of the encouragement offence.[40]

The notion of an act which is capable of assisting or encouraging a crime is fraught with ambiguity, since there is no reference to any notion of remoteness within the statute. The courts will undoubtedly be required to impose some remoteness limitation to make sense of the provision: ideally, that D has performed the last act which is capable of encouraging or assisting the crime without D's having to perform any other acts.

The relevant act can include a course of conduct[41] and also the taking of steps which reduce the possibility of proceedings being brought in respect of the substantive offence.[42] So, for example, D would be guilty of assisting theft if she tripped up a police officer who was chasing a thief from the scene of the crime, although only because the act of theft would

---

[37] See above, § 7.4(i)(a).
[38] Serious Crime Act 2007, s. 66.
[39] (1873) 12 Cox CC 393.
[40] See below, § 9.4(i)(c).
[41] Serious Crime Act 2007, s. 67.
[42] *Ibid.*, s. 65(2)(a).

be continuing.[43] D could not be regarded as assisting or encouraging an offence once the substantive offence has been completed. Further, an act which is capable of assisting or encouraging a crime includes an omission where D has failed to take reasonable steps to discharge a duty to act.[44] So, for example, D, a security guard, who fails to switch on a burglar alarm with the intent to assist a burglary, will have assisted by the failure to act.

(d) The conduct encouraged or assisted

Substantive offences.
D will be guilty if the conduct he encourages or assists would constitute any offence on the part of P: save that the crime of corporate manslaughter[45] cannot be encouraged or assisted; the offence contrary to section 44 cannot be committed in respect of encouraging or assisting suicide;[46] and the offences contrary to sections 45 and 46 cannot be committed in respect of certain substantive offences.[47]

At common law, the offence of incitement could only be committed if the conduct D encouraged involved the commission of an offence by P in the capacity of a principal offender.[48] There is no such limitation in respect of the new statutory inchoate offences, so it is possible to assist or encourage P to do something which will involve P's liability as an accessory.

Inchoate offences.
Logically, there is nothing to preclude bringing a charge of encouragement or assistance in respect of another inchoate offence (e.g. D's encouraging T to encourage P to commit an offence or to conspire with X to commit an offence). Reservations may be had, however, about criminalising conduct which can be considered too remote from the commission of a substantive offence. In the context of encouraging or assisting inchoate offences, Parliament has given only partial effect to these reservations.

The inchoate offence of assisting or encouraging a crime with intent that the crime be committed, contrary to section 44, can be committed in respect of any inchoate offence including itself. So it is possible for D1 to assist or encourage D2 to assist or encourage P to commit a substantive offence, but only if D2 has done the act which is capable of assisting or encouraging the substantive offence;[49] or for D1 to assist or encourage D2 to conspire with X; or for D1 to assist or encourage D2 to attempt an offence, so long as, in each case, D1 intends D2 to assist, encourage, conspire to commit, or attempt the substantive offence. For example, suppose that D1 urges D2 to attend a clandestine meeting of terrorists and advocate the immediate resumption of a bombing strategy. For reasons of security, D1 instructs D2 to leave immediately after he has addressed the meeting and on no account to enter into any conversation with any of the other parties. D1 will have encouraged D2 to encourage the others to commit a terrorist offence. Alternatively, D1 may require D2 to

---

[43] See below, § 13.6(iv).
[44] Serious Crime Act 2007, s. 65(2)(b).
[45] Corporate Manslaughter and Corporate Homicide Act 2007, s. 18(1A).
[46] Serious Crime Act 2007, s. 51(A).
[47] Listed in sched. 3.
[48] *Bodin* [1979] Crim LR 176.
[49] Serious Crime Act 2007, s. 66.

make calls on individual terrorists and obtain their respective agreements to resume bombing activities. D1 will be guilty of encouraging a conspiracy to be made. Similarly, suppose that D1 orders D2 to enter V's bedroom at night and shoot V in his bed. D1 knows that V is already dead; she wants the unwitting D2 to shoot a bullet into V's corpse to obfuscate the true cause of death. D2 would be guilty of attempted murder. D1, with her knowledge of the true facts, should be guilty of encouraging attempted murder. She would not be guilty of encouraging murder, since she was aware that murder was impossible and therefore she was not seeking, through the agency of D2, to bring about that crime. Nonetheless, she was encouraging conduct which would constitute attempted murder on D2's part, and a conviction for encouraging D2's attempt appropriately reflects her culpability.[50]

It is not, however, possible to commit the inchoate offences contrary to sections 45 and 46 (involving assisting and encouraging believing that one or more substantive offences will be committed), in respect of any of the inchoate offences.[51] Consequently, where the mens rea in respect of the principal offence is one of belief rather than intent that the offence will be committed, the remoteness from the commission of the substantive offence negates liability.

(e) Encouraging or assisting an actus reus

In our discussion of the liability of accomplices, we saw that the perpetration of a mere actus reus by P may sometimes ground a charge of complicity against D.[52] Recall that if, say, D persuades P to have intercourse with V by alleging that V's genuine protestations will be feigned, D may yet be an accomplice to rape even if P is acquitted of the substantive offence because of lack of proof of mens rea.[53] D's conviction as an accomplice to rape is appropriate because D has procured the occurrence of the harm associated with commission of the substantive offence. This reasoning carries over to the inchoate offences of encouragement and assistance. On the facts above, D may be guilty of encouraging rape as soon as he urges or persuades P to have intercourse with V, whether or not P goes on to rape V, because the harm of rape, i.e. non-consensual sexual activity, is still being sought through D's actions. D's persuasion is certainly capable of encouraging the offence of rape, although liability will turn on whether D had the appropriate mens rea for the encouragement offence.[54]

For the common law offence of incitement there had to be encouragement of what in law constituted an actus reus. In C,[55] D incited P, a boy of 12, to sodomise him. At the time of the event there was a conclusive presumption of law that a boy under the age of 13 was incapable of sexual intercourse.[56] It followed from this presumption that any act of sodomy by P would not constitute an offence on his part and the Court of Appeal reluctantly held

---

[50] *Hapgood* (1870) LR 1 CCR 221 indicates that D1 would also be liable as a secondary party to D2's attempt. See further Smith, "Secondary Participation and Inchoate Offences" in Tapper (ed.), *Crime, Proof and Punishment* (1981) 21, 26–7.

[51] Serious Crime Act 2007, s. 49(5).

[52] Above, § 7.6(ii)(b).

[53] Although this is now unlikely under the Sexual Offences Act 2003, because the relevant mens rea is absence of a reasonable belief in consent.

[54] See below, § 9.2(ii).

[55] [2005] EWCA Crim 2827, [2006] 1 Cr App R 20.

[56] Now repealed by the Criminal Justice Act 1993.

that this entailed the failure of the charge of incitement to sodomy made against D. Of course, in a physical sense, an act of anal intercourse did occur when P penetrated D. But in a legal sense, P was incapable of doing that which he actually did, so that the actus reus of the substantive offence could not have occurred.

(f) Future crimes

It is immaterial that the crime D encourages or assists will become possible only at some time in the future. For example, D will be liable for encouragement if he urges the killing, at birth, of a baby yet to be born[57] or the receiving of goods yet to be stolen.[58]

(ii) Mens rea

The mens rea for the offences of assisting and encouraging is complex. First, it is presumably necessary to establish that D intended to do the act which is capable of encouraging or assisting P. Secondly, it is necessary to consider D's mens rea in respect of P's offence which D is assisting or encouraging.

The second requirement is the complicated one. There are three alternative ways of satisfying it. In straightforward cases, either intention or belief will suffice, depending on the particular inchoate offence with which D is charged.

(a) Intention

The section 44 offence will be committed where D intends to encourage or assist the commission of an offence. It is not possible to assume that D had the necessary intent merely because encouragement or assistance of an offence was a foreseeable consequence of her act.[59] It is unclear whether the effect of this provision is simply that it is not possible to assume intention because encouragement or assistance of an offence was objectively foreseeable, or that subjective recklessness is not sufficient evidence of intent, both of which would appear to be obvious; or whether it also means that oblique intent, involving foresight of a virtually certain consequence, does not constitute an intent for purposes of this offence. The latter would seem to be the more appropriate interpretation of the provision, especially because the case where D foresees (but does not intend) the assistance or encouragement of a substantive crime, as virtually certain or otherwise, is impliedly excluded from section 44 by the high standard of foresight (that the offence *will* occur) in sections 45 and 46.

(b) Belief

The offence contrary to sections 45 will be committed where D believes that the substantive offence will be committed and he also believes that his act will encourage or assist that offence. It is not sufficient that D believes that the offence might be committed. D will have

---

[57] *Banks* (1873) 12 Cox CC 393.
[58] *McDonough* (1962) 47 Cr App R 37.
[59] Serious Crime Act 2007, s. 44(2).

the relevant mens rea even if he believes that an offence will be committed only if certain conditions are met.[60]

(c) Believing that one or more offence may be committed

The section 46 offence applies in situations where D believes that his act *might* encourage or assist a number of offences to be committed and that his act *will* encourage or assist one or more of those offences, but he has no belief as to which. It is not sufficient that D believes *only* that one or more of the offences *may* be committed.

Section 46 is needed to ensure that D should not be acquitted of assisting or encouraging a crime simply because his act might assist or encourage multiple offences (rather than just one specific offence), at least where he has the appropriate mens rea in respect of those offences.[61] The operation of this offence is illustrated by *Blackshaw et al.*,[62] where one defendant had posted messages on Facebook encouraging people to meet at a particular location and time generally to wreak havoc in a town. The defendant was convicted of the Section 46 offence even though he believed that a number of different offences might be committed, including riot, burglary, and criminal damage, it being sufficient that he believed that one of those offences would be committed.

The operation of section 46 was considered by the Court of Appeal in *Sadique (No.1)*,[63] where D had been charged with assisting in the supply of Class A and/or Class B drugs by supplying various chemical cutting agents. The key issue in that case was whether the section 46 offence was incompatible with Article 7 of the ECHR on the ground that it was too vague and uncertain. In confirming its compatibility, the Court of Appeal sought to make sense of the offence; but in doing so made the offence effectively redundant. The Court examined the mens rea for the section 46 offence. The section states that D must believe that one of more of the offences which are capable of being encouraged or assisted by his act *will* be committed. But does this mean that D must believe that each identified offence will be committed, or is it sufficient that he contemplates that each of the offences *may* be committed, as long as he believes that one of those offences *will* be committed, even though he is not sure which one? The Court of Appeal in *Sadique (No. 1)* considered the first interpretation to be the correct one and consequently that, when D was charged with an offence contrary to section 46, each offence which his act was capable of encouraging or assisting (which was identified as the "reference offence"), must be charged as a separate offence. It followed that, if D contemplated a variety of offences which were capable of being assisted or encouraged by his act but was unsure which offence would be committed, he could not be guilty of the section 46 offence nor of any other offence under the Serious Crime Act. The decision in *Sadique (No. 1)* had one further implication. According to the Court of Appeal, D would only be guilty of each count under section 46 if he believed both that the particular reference offence would be committed and that his act would encourage that offence. But this is also what must be proved for the section 45 offence. (Indeed, the Serious

---

[60] *Ibid.*, s. 49(7).

[61] A similar result is obtained in the law of complicity. See *DPP for Northern Ireland* v. *Maxwell* [1978] 1 WLR 1350.

[62] [2011] EWCA Crim 2312, [2012] 1 WLR 1126.

[63] [2011] EWCA Crim 2872, [2012] 1 WLR 1700. See Virgo, "Encouraging or Assisting More Than One Offence" (2012) 2 *Arch Rev* 6; "Part 2 of the Serious Crime Act 2007—Enough Is Enough" (2013) 3 *Arch Rev* 7.

Crime Act states that, where a person's act is capable of encouraging or assisting a number of offences, the section 45 offence applies separately in respect of each offence which D believes will be encouraged or assisted.)[64] It follows that section 46 was rendered effectively redundant by *Sadique (No 1)*.

Such a decision was unconvincing, both as regards the interpretation of the statute and the reach of the Serious Crime Act 2007. This was subsequently confirmed by the Court of Appeal in *Sadique (No. 2)*,[65] which rejected the analysis of *Sadique (No. 1)* and confirmed that the section 46 offence required D to believe that *one or more* of the offences which are capable of being committed *will* be committed, but this perceived inevitability of commission is not required in respect of *each* offence. This is emphasised by the fact that section 46(1)(b)(i) adds in parentheses, "(but has no belief as to which)" offence will be committed. Further, as regards the requirement that D believes that his act will encourage or assist one or more of the offences which are capable of being encouraged or assisted, it is specifically recognised[66] that it is immaterial whether he believes that a particular offence will be assisted or encouraged, it consequently being sufficient that D believes that *an* offence will be assisted or encouraged.[67] In addition, section 46(3) makes specific provision for the charging of an offence contrary to section 46. The indictment must specify the reference offences which are capable of being assisted or encouraged by D's act. This need not be a comprehensive list of all the possible offences which could be assisted or encouraged, but just those which are identified for the purposes of the charge.[68] Nothing is stated about each of the reference offences being identified in separate counts. Consequently, section 46 creates a single offence and not a number of individual offences depending on the number of reference offences which are identified. It followed that, on the facts of *Sadique*, D would be guilty of a section 46 offence in supplying chemical cutting agents if he believed that the chemicals would be used to supply drugs but was not sure whether these would be Class A or Class B, but would be one of them.

It might be thought that this interpretation of section 46 creates a problem for sentencing. If D is convicted of the single section 46 offence, what will be the maximum sentence where he believes that one of the range of offences will be committed but has no belief as to the commission of any specific offence? However, reinforcing the interpretation adopted in *Sadique (No. 2)*, this question is answered specifically by section 58(4)–(7), the effect of which is that, where the defendant is convicted under section 46 by reference to more than one offence, the maximum prison sentence is that of the reference offence which has the longest term.[69] Admittedly, this has the potential to generate harsh results. Suppose that D lends P a jemmy. D thinks that P will use it to commit burglary, assault, or murder, but is not sure which. Since D contemplates that P might use the jemmy to commit murder, and since this is the most serious offence contemplated, D is liable to life imprisonment. Whilst this is a shocking result, it is one that is explicitly acknowledged

---

[64] Serious Crime Act 2007, s. 49(2)(b).

[65] [2013] EWCA Crim 1150; [2014] 1 WLR 986. See Stark, "Encouraging or Assisting Clarity?" [2013] *CLJ* 497; [2014] *Crim LR* 61; Virgo, "Making Sense of Section 46 of the Serious Crime Act 2007" (2013) 7 *Arch Rev* 4.

[66] Serious Crime Act 2007, s. 46(2).

[67] Which can include a lesser included offence of an offence specified in the indictment: *ibid.*, s. 57(2), (3).

[68] *Ibid.*, s. 46(3)(b).

[69] Where one of the reference offences is murder, the maximum term is life imprisonment: Serious Crime Act 2007, s. 58(5).

by the Serious Crime Act 2007, where one of the reference offences is murder.[70] Note, however, that this is only the maximum sentence; the trial judge will undoubtedly exercise appropriate discretion when sentencing. Moreover, it must not be forgotten that D has willingly provided P with a jemmy contemplating that she might commit murder. D has done all that he can to assist P in her criminal enterprise: D's conduct is certainly wrongful, and it is of a kind that section 46 was intended to prohibit. Indeed, if P does commit murder, D would be subject to the mandatory life sentence as an accessory, but only, after *Jogee*,[71] if D intended this; whereas, for section 46, it is sufficient that D foresaw that murder might be committed but believed that another offence would be committed. It is most undesirable that D can be convicted of an inchoate offence relating to murder with less culpability than is required for accessorial liability. But this is a consequence of the draconian approach to inchoate offences expressed by Parliament in the Serious Crime Act, and of the failure of the Supreme Court to appreciate the disconnect created in *Jogee* between accessorial and inchoate liability.

Despite this, the decision of the Court of Appeal in *Sadique (No. 2)* does, at least, affirm that section 46 applies as was intended, as a result of which it is possible to convict D of assisting or encouraging more than one offence so long as he believes that at least one of the reference offences will be committed, even though he has no belief as to which one will be committed.

(d) Intention or belief relating only to the behaviour element of the offence

Where it is not possible to prove an intention to encourage or assist a specific offence for section 44 or a belief that an offence will be committed for either section 45 or 46, it may be possible to convict D of assisting or encouraging if he only intended to encourage or assist the doing of an "act" which would amount to the commission of the crime for the purposes of section 44,[72] or believed that P would do the act amounting to the crime and that D's act would encourage or assist P's act, for section 45,[73] or one or more acts for the purposes of section 46.[74]

The notion of an "act" is widely defined to include a failure to act, the continuation of an act which has already begun, and an attempt to do an act.[75] In other words, rather than proving an intention or a belief in respect of the commission of a crime by P, it may be sufficient to prove that D only intended to encourage or assist the behaviour element of P's crime, or believed that this element would be committed. In such a case it is necessary to prove additional mens rea elements concerning: (i) the consequences or circumstances of P's behaviour, to the extent that they form part of the actus reus of P's substantive offence; and (ii) P's mens rea for the substantive offence. These need to be considered separately.

---

[70] Serious Crime Act 2007, s. 58(5).

[71] *Jogee* [2016] UKSC 8; *Ruddock* [2016] UKPC 7, [2016] 2 WLR 681.

[72] *Ibid.*, s. 47(2).

[73] *Ibid.*, s. 47(3).

[74] *Ibid.*, s. 47(4).

[75] *Ibid.*, s. 47(8). The language of s. 47(8) does at least seem to preclude liability for assisting or encouraging situational crimes which have no behaviour element at all: above, § 4.1(ii)(a).

Circumstances and consequences of P's anticipated crime.
Where the substantive offence requires proof of particular circumstances or consequences or both, it is necessary to prove that D believed[76] or was reckless[77] as to whether the act would be done in those circumstances or with those consequences. So, to be guilty of encouraging murder contrary to section 44 where D does not intend to encourage that specific crime, it must be shown that D had intended to encourage the doing of an act which he believed would result in death or thought that it might have that consequence. For example, in *Attorney-General's Reference (No. 39 of 2011)*,[78] D had been convicted of intentionally encouraging aggravated criminal damage, for which it had to be proved that D intended arson to be committed in circumstances where P would be reckless about whether life was endangered, the latter element was, in effect, treated as a circumstance of the substantive offence, although it is better treated as an ulterior mens rea element.[79]

Mens rea in offences requiring proof of fault.
If the substantive offence is one which requires proof of fault, it will be necessary to prove an additional fault element on the part of D,[80] being:[81]

(i)   a belief that the act would be done with the requisite mens rea for the substantive offence; or

(ii)   recklessness as to whether P would have the relevant mens rea for the substantive offence; or

(iii) D's state of mind was such that, had he committed the act, he would have the appropriate mens rea for that substantive offence.[82]

So, if D does not intend to encourage P to commit murder but intends to encourage P to do an act which he believed or suspected might cause V's death, D could be convicted of encouraging murder contrary to section 44, but only if one of the three additional mens rea elements is proved, namely: a belief that P would intend to kill or cause serious injury; recklessness as to whether P would have such mens rea;[83] or, if D had done the act himself, he would have intended to kill or cause serious injury.

These requirements have no application where the substantive offence is one of strict liability, in which case D's mens rea need only relate to his own act and to P's actus reus and section 47(5)(a) is not engaged. Where the substantive offence does require proof of fault, section 47(5)(a) may influence the offence which D will have assisted or encouraged. Thus, if D does not intend P to commit murder but intends to encourage P to do an act which, D realises, might cause V's death,[84] that may be sufficient for D to be convicted of

---

[76] Intention or belief suffices for the s. 44 offence: Serious Crime Act 2007, s. 47(7).

[77] *Ibid.*, s. 47(5)(b).

[78] [2011] EWCA Crim 2617.

[79] Child, "The Structure, Coherence and Limits of Inchoate Liability: The New *Ulterior* Element" (2014) 34 *LS* 537. See further below, § 9.4.(iii)(c).

[80] And not the other party: *Sadique (No. 1)* [2011] EWCA Crim 2872, [2012] 1 WLR 1700, para. 64.

[81] Serious Crime Act 2007, s. 47(5)(a).

[82] Or for one of them, if charged under section 46: *ibid.*, s. 48(2).

[83] That recklessness might be sufficient mens rea for the s. 44 offence was not appreciated by the Supreme Court in *Jogee* [2016] UKSC 8, [2016] 2 WLR 651 where Lords Hughes and Toulson said, at para. 86, "that Parliament has provided that foresight is not sufficient mens rea for the offence of intentionally encouraging or assisting another to commit an offence". In the light of s. 47(5)(a), this is incorrect.

[84] Serious Crime Act 2007, s. 47(5)(b)(ii).

encouraging murder provided that D foresaw a risk that P might act with intent to kill or cause serious injury (option ii). Alternatively, it may be sufficient for D to be convicted of encouraging manslaughter provided that, were D himself to do the act he intends P will do, that would be grossly negligent (option iii).

While section 47 is described in the statute as a provision concerning the proof of sections 44–6, subsection (5) radically expands the ambit of these offences. Sections 44–6 have a requirement that D intends or believes that he will encourage or assist P *to commit an offence*; but that requirement is immediately dispensed with in section 47, since D could be guilty of one of the inchoate offences if he only intends or believes that P will do the act which amounts to the commission of the offence.

(d) Application of the mens rea provisions

The implications of these absurdly complex provisions can best be appreciated with reference to some hypothetical examples.

D offers P a necklace which D has stolen. D believes that P knows the necklace to be stolen, but in fact P believes that D acquired it honestly. In such circumstances, D will clearly be guilty of assisting P to handle stolen goods contrary to section 45. This is because D believes that P will commit the substantive offence of handling due to his belief as to her knowledge of the provenance of the jewellery and his act of giving her the jewellery will assist her to commit the crime. Being an inchoate offence, it is irrelevant that P's lack of knowledge or belief as to the provenance of the jewellery means that she will not be guilty of the substantive offence.

If, however, D believes that P thinks that D has acquired the necklace honestly, it might be assumed that D cannot be guilty of assisting the crime of handling stolen goods contrary to section 45 because he does not believe that his act will assist her to commit the offence. But, since D does believe that his act will assist P to commit the act of the substantive offence, namely to handle goods, it is necessary to consider section 47(5). D does believe that the relevant circumstance of the substantive offence, namely that the goods are stolen, will be satisfied, this being a circumstance which D must believe or suspect.[85] D does not, however, believe or suspect that P will have the mens rea for the substantive offence. But, if D committed the actus reus of the substantive offence himself, he would have the mens rea for that crime since he knows that the necklace is stolen.[86] Consequently he will be guilty of assisting P to handle stolen goods contrary to section 45.

If D encourages P to beat up V and intends that P will do so, D could be guilty of encouraging murder contrary to section 44 if she (i) believes or is reckless as to whether V might die,[87] this being the relevant consequence of the substantive offence; and (ii) believes or is reckless that P would have the relevant mens rea for murder, or, if D did the act of beating up V herself, she would have intended to kill V or to cause him serious injury. Similarly, D would assist murder contrary to section 44 if D supplied P with a poisoned drink intending P to do the act of administering the drink to V and D (i) foresaw that V might die and (ii) believed that P would intend to kill or cause serious injury, or suspected that P might

---

[85] *Ibid.*, s. 47(5)(b).
[86] *Ibid.*, s. 47(5)(a).
[87] *Ibid.*, s. 47(5)(b).

kill with this fault, or, had D himself supplied V with the drink, D would have had the necessary mens rea for murder. In both cases D could therefore be convicted of encouraging or assisting murder, for which a sentence of life imprisonment is potentially available, even though D did not intend or believe that P would commit murder.

Further, if D encourages P to have sex with D's wife, V, knowing that V will not consent to have sex with P, whether D is guilty of encouraging P to commit rape involves a convoluted analysis of D's mens rea. If it is assumed, for the sake of argument, that D thinks that P will have non-consensual sex with V but P will reasonably believe that V is consenting to sex, D will not intend or believe that rape will be committed. But, since rape is an offence requiring proof of fault (namely that the defendant did not reasonably believe that the victim consented), section 47(5)(a) is engaged. Since D does not believe or suspect that P would have no reasonable belief in V's consent, the question then is whether, were D to have sex with V, he would not reasonably believe that V was consenting. But if D had sex with his wife he would presumably believe on reasonable grounds that she was consenting, and indeed she probably would consent to have sex with him, so the offence would not be made out.

Apart from the tortuous path which needs to be followed through the statutory provisions to reach such conclusions, which makes jury directions very difficult, the fact that D could be convicted of an inchoate offence relating to a serious crime, even though D does not contemplate that the substantive offence would be committed by P, means that the ambit of inchoate criminal liability is far removed from the commission of any substantive offence. The ambit of criminal liability has been extended here far beyond its legitimate limits.

(iii) Defences

(a) Withdrawal?

Since the inchoate offences of assistance and encouragement are complete at the point when D has done the act which is capable of encouraging or assisting the crime, in principle any countermanding or withdrawal of her initial encouragement or assistance by D should count, at most, as mitigation but cannot undo the crime she has already committed. In the cognate sphere of complicity, if D counsels P to commit an offence but then, prior to the commission of that offence, effectively revokes her earlier counselling or contacts an appropriate person in authority, she will no longer be a party to the offence if P goes on to commit it.[88] No such defence of revocation or withdrawal applies to the offences of encouragement and assistance, but should it have been made available? Encouragement and counselling are not precisely parallel. D will not be an accomplice until the principal commits the substantive offence, whereas encouragement is complete once D has done the act which is capable of encouraging a crime. Yet the counsellor and the encourager are very much alike. In each case, all the elements of liability personal to D are present as soon as the encouragement is given. The public policy considerations that allow a withdrawal defence where the charge is one of complicity also seem germane to a charge of encouragement, and also of assistance. Furthermore, it will undermine the policy behind the withdrawal defence in complicity if

---

[88] See the discussion above, § 7.6(vi).

the prosecution could obviate it by charging encouragement or assistance on the same facts. In our view, the encourager or assister should have been allowed a defence if, prior to the commission of the offence encouraged or assisted, she countermanded encouragement or assistance of the crime to the person she encouraged or assisted, or informed an appropriate authority (such as the police) of the details of her conduct.

(b) Acting reasonably

Section 50 of the Serious Crime Act 2007 recognises a defence of acting reasonably. This defence takes two forms:

(i) where D knew that certain circumstances existed and it was reasonable for D to act as she did in those circumstances;[89] and

(ii) where D reasonably believed certain circumstances to exist and it was reasonable for D to act as he did in the circumstances as he believed them to be.[90]

The second version will be relevant where D is mistaken as to the circumstances, though her mistake must be a reasonable one. Various factors are identified to determine whether D had acted reasonably, including the seriousness of the anticipated offence; the purposes for which D was acting, which would presumably include preventing a crime; and any authority by which D claims to have been acting, such as through being a police officer. The defence is tested at the time of acting, so the fact that D subsequently may have acted reasonably cannot be taken into account. Consequently, the defence cannot be interpreted to incorporate a defence of withdrawal.

The potential application of the defence can be illustrated with reference to the facts of *Shaw*,[91] which concerned the old common law offence of incitement. D incited P and other fellow employees to commit thefts against their employer. D's motivation, apparently, was to bring deficiencies in the firm's security system to the notice of the employer. It was held that D's motivation was incompatible with liability for incitement to steal. Yet what P was persuaded by D to do was clearly theft,[92] and D was aware of all the material circumstances which rendered P's conduct theft. For conspiracy, the Privy Council in *Yip Chiu-Cheung* assumed that D would commit a serious drugs offence even though his sole motivation in importing drugs was to expose the activities of drug traffickers.[93] The approach of English law, though not beyond criticism,[94] is that mens rea may be present even though D's conduct may lack moral culpability; indeed, it may be present even if his conduct merits praise. The decision in *Shaw* cannot be reconciled with this stance; there are no particular features of inchoate offences which argue for a different approach. Accordingly, *Shaw* should be regarded as wrongly decided. At the very least it has been regarded as authoritative only in terms of the wording of the charge: in *DPP* v. *Armstrong*,[95] the decision in *Shaw* was given guarded approval because D was charged with *dishonestly* inciting P to commit theft. The

---

[89] Serious Crime Act 2007, s. 50(1).
[90] *Ibid.*, s. 50(2).
[91] [1994] Crim LR 365.
[92] Note that P, unlike D, was dishonest since he was unaware of D's reason for encouraging the thefts.
[93] [1995] 1 AC 111.
[94] See above, § 1.2(ii); § 5.
[95] [2000] Crim LR 379 (QBD).

reference to dishonesty in the charge was otiose, since dishonesty was not a constituent element of incitement. If the facts of *Shaw* arose today and D was charged with encouraging theft, he would probably not have a defence of acting reasonably. Although he may reasonably have believed that there were deficiencies in the employer's security system, his actions in encouraging theft were seemingly not reasonable: the anticipated offence was serious, he was not acting to prevent a crime, and he was not acting under any particular authority.

This reasonableness defence is unsatisfactory in a variety of ways,[96] most notably because the burden of proof is placed on D and because its application depends on the vagueness of what is "reasonable". For example, if D is a shop assistant who sells a knife to P, whom she believes will use it to commit murder, so the section 45 offence is engaged, is it possible to conclude that she acted reasonably in selling the knife to P, bearing in mind that she was under a contractual obligation to her employer to do so? In assessing the reasonableness of D's conduct, it is necessary to have regard to the seriousness of the crime that she believes P will commit, but is it relevant that she was employed to sell the knife; is this a relevant purpose? In *K Ltd* v. *National Westminster Bank plc*,[97] in the context of the distinct crime of facilitating the use or control of criminal property, it was recognised that D had no defence that he contractually obliged to use the property. Similar reasoning would mean that D would have no defence to encouraging or assisting a crime when selling a knife to P.

The "reasonableness defence" is certainly inadequate if it is being used as a sop to counteract the breadth of liability for the inchoate offences. Bearing in mind the detailed complexity of the definition of mens rea for the inchoate offences, it is unacceptable that the statutory defence has been left so vague. It is inevitable that the courts will at some point be required to set limits on the defence and to identify more detailed principles against which the notion of reasonableness can be assessed.

(c) Victims

D will have a defence if she would be the victim of the substantive offence that she assists or encourages,[98] provided that the relevant substantive offence is a "protective offence" in that it exists wholly or partly for the protection of a particular category of people and that D falls within that category. It follows that D, a child, who encourages or assists P, an adult, to commit a sex offence against D, will not be guilty of assisting or encouraging that crime. The offence exists to protect D and it would be an odd form of protection to then convict D of assisting or encouraging it.

The defence is a statutory parallel to the so-called *Tyrrell* exception at common law to complicity liability.[99] However, as with its common law counterpart, the determination whether an offence is a protective offence, and whether D falls within the protected category, will not always be clear. This was considered by the Supreme Court in *Gnango*,[100] as regards complicity, but will be significant to the inchoate offences as well. Lords Phillips and Judge[101]

---

[96] See Ormerod and Forston, "Serious Crime Act 2007: The Part 2 Offences" [2009] *Crim LR* 389, 411.

[97] [2006] EWCA Civ 1039, [2007] 1 WLR 311; see also above, § 7.4(iv)(a) (An exception for performance of a duty?).

[98] Serious Crime Act 2007, s. 51.

[99] Described above, § 7.6(iv)(a).

[100] [2011] UKSC 59, [2012] 1 AC 827.

[101] *Ibid.*, para. 52.

described section 51 as giving a "limited exemption" from liability. They considered that masochists, who have consented to be injured by sadists,[102] could be convicted of aiding and abetting the infliction of injuries on themselves. It would follow that the masochists could also be guilty of encouraging the injuries on themselves, because they would not fall within the statutory exception, since the offence of inflicting injuries does not exist to protect masochists. It might, however, be different if D was a child or was suffering from a psychiatric condition when encouraging P to commit a harmful assault against him, since then it might be appropriate to characterise the offence as protective.

(d) The future of Part 2 of the Serious Crime Act 2007

The intentions behind the enactment of Part 2 of the Serious Crime Act were good. Since the common law offence of incitement did not extend to conduct which purported to assist a crime, there was a gap in the law which needed to be plugged. The significance of this is illustrated by the conviction secured in *Sadique (No. 2)*[103] for assisting the supply of drugs, which could not have been prosecuted before Part 2 of the Serious Crime Act was enacted. If a statutory offence of assisting was to be created, it was entirely appropriate to codify the crime of incitement at the same time, to ensure consistency between the two offences. But, whereas the common law offence of incitement could be expressed very simply, and was a body of law about which there was little uncertainty, that is not true of the offences which replaced it. Whilst those offences can be considered to have plugged a gap in the law, they cannot be considered to have done so successfully. The key point of principle relating to the legitimacy of Part 2 of the Serious Crime Act 2007 relates to the appropriate formulation of criminal legislation, which needs to be certain, clear, and readily explicable. The success of a new criminal offence should not be judged simply by the intellectual satisfaction derived from providing solutions to unlikely problems. The application of the law in the real world by the police, prosecutors, judges, and legal advisers must be considered as well. Judged in this way, Part 2 is not fit for purpose. Further, the growing disconnect between the breadth of inchoate liability and the restrictive interpretation of accessorial liability, especially following the decision of the Supreme Court in *Jogee*,[104] is a cause of particular concern, especially since this might mean that prosecutors prefer to prosecute D for the inchoate offence of assisting or encouraging despite the commission of the substantive offence.

The real problem with Part 2 of the Serious Crime Act 2007 is that it is seeking to do far too much, by providing for a wide variety of different circumstances and resulting in the criminalisation of conduct artificially. Where, for example, D encourages P to handle goods in circumstances where D knows that the goods are stolen, D should only be guilty of encouraging the offence if she knows or believes that P will commit it. What is required is radical, but simple, reform. Part 2 of the Act needs to be replaced with one new offence of encouraging or assisting another to commit an offence, knowing or believing that the other would commit that offence. Provision would also need to be made for the situation where D knows or believes that one offence from a list of offences will be committed, but is not sure which. Whilst the coverage of these new provisions would not be quite as wide as the

---

[102] As in *Brown* [1994] 1 AC 212. See below, § 21.1.
[103] [2013] EWCA Crim 1150; [2014] 1 WLR 986.
[104] *Jogee* [2016] UKSC 8; *Ruddock* [2016] UKSC 7, [2016] 2 WLR 681. See above, § 7.4(iv)(b)–(c).

existing offences in Part 2, that is no bad thing; moreover, it would facilitate greater consistency between inchoate and accessorial liability, thereby helping to ensure that the inchoate offences of assistance and encouragement were fit for purpose.

§ 9.3 Conspiracy

Conspiracy is predominantly a statutory offence, defined by section 1 of the Criminal Law Act 1977. The essence of statutory conspiracy is an agreement between two or more people which, if carried out in accordance with the intentions of the parties, will result in the commission of a statutory or common law crime by at least one of the parties to the agreement.

Apart from statutory conspiracy, there are also some forms of conspiracy surviving at common law. Prior to the enactment of the Criminal Law Act 1977, the Law Commission examined the common law of conspiracy and prepared a Bill which, with some significant alterations by Parliament, became the substance of the 1977 Act.[105] The aspiration of the Law Commission, echoed in ministerial statements, was ultimately to replace entirely common law conspiracy by a statutory offence. However, at the time the Act was passed, abolition in its entirety of common law conspiracy was not regarded as a feasible option.[106] Three heads of common law conspiracy were felt to be indispensable until new offences, as yet unresolved, were created to replace them. The common law conspiracies retained were (i) to outrage public decency; (ii) to corrupt public morality; and (iii) to defraud. Accordingly, common law conspiracy, to this diminished extent, still exists.[107]

These three heads of common law conspiracy were retained, as it was unclear to what extent they criminalise agreements to carry out conduct that would not be criminal if done by an individual acting alone. Statutory conspiracy is confined to agreements to commit crimes that individuals can commit when acting alone. Rightly or otherwise, it was the opinion of Parliament at the time that provision for common law conspiracy was required in these three areas, even if that required penalising conduct which would not be criminal but for the presence of a conspiracy. However, since the enactment of the 1977 Act, *Gibson*[108] has resolved that conduct outraging public decency constitutes a substantive offence in its own right, which can be committed by an individual acting alone. Accordingly, an agreement to outrage public decency will now fall within the ambit of statutory conspiracy.[109] The position in respect of corrupting public morality is less clear, but is probably the same as for outraging public decency.[110] Consequently these offences are now covered by statutory conspiracy and will not be further considered here.

By contrast, in the case of conspiracy to defraud, it is incontrovertibly the case that forms of dishonest conduct which would not otherwise be criminal are rendered criminal only

---

[105] Law Com. No. 76, *Conspiracy and Criminal Law Reform* (1976).

[106] HL Vol. 379, col. 206 (Lord Harris of Greenwich).

[107] Criminal Law Act 1977, s. 5.

[108] [1990] 2 QB 619 (CA).

[109] Under the terms of s. 5(3) of the Criminal Law Act 1977, if there is a substantive offence of outraging public decency, as now appears to be the case, an agreement to commit that offence must be charged as a statutory conspiracy, falling within s. 1 of the Act, and may not be charged as a common law conspiracy.

[110] In *Shaw* v. *DPP* [1962] AC 220, the Court of Criminal Appeal held that there was a substantive offence of corrupting public morality. However, the House of Lords confirmed the appellant's conviction for conspiracy to corrupt public morality and did not go on to confirm whether or not there was a substantive offence.

by virtue of the common law conspiracy.[111] This form of conspiracy, which is of enormous breadth, is frequently resorted to, particularly in the sphere of large-scale commercial fraud. Moreover, it seems that this last vestige of common law conspiracy is to be retained on a permanent basis. It was widely anticipated that the Fraud Act 2006 would abolish the offence, but the Government has not done so, fearful, it seems, of leaving gaps in the coverage of dishonest conduct.[112] The offence will be considered in detail below, in the context of property offences.[113] In this chapter, we will examine the elements of statutory conspiracy. Unfortunately, as we shall see, the Criminal Law Act 1977 does not provide clear answers to many of the points of interpretation that arise.[114] It may consequently be necessary sometimes to refer to pre-Act common law authority to assist with the resolution of difficulties of interpretation.

(i) Statutory conspiracy—definition and ambit

(a) Indictable and summary offences

Section 1 of the Criminal Law Act 1977 provides that:

> if a person agrees with any other person or persons that a course of conduct will be pursued which, if the agreement is carried out in accordance with their intentions, either—
> (a)   will necessarily amount to or involve the commission of any offence or offences by one or more parties to the agreement, or
> (b)   would do so but for the existence of facts which render the commission of the offence or any offences impossible,
> he is guilty of conspiracy to commit the offence or offences in question.

At the core of statutory conspiracy is an agreement between two or more persons which will necessarily involve the commission of an offence by one or more of the parties should the agreement be carried out in accordance with their intentions. The offence may be common law or statutory, indictable or summary.

Formerly, any conspiracy charged under the Criminal Law Act 1977 had to involve an agreement to commit an offence that was triable within England and Wales.[115] An agreement made in Birmingham to rob a bank in Brussels has never been indictable under the terms of section 1. However, such an agreement will now constitute a conspiracy triable in England and Wales under the subsequently interpolated section 1A.[116] In remarkably broad

---

[111] Conduct which clearly falls within the ambit of a substantive offence involving dishonesty, such as theft, will almost invariably fall within the ambit of conspiracy to defraud if two or more persons are involved. Section 12 of the Criminal Justice Act 1987, resolving an interpretative conflict that had arisen over the effect of s. 5(2) of the Criminal Law Act 1977, provides that in such circumstances the conduct may be charged as either a statutory conspiracy or a common law conspiracy. Contrast s. 5(3) of the Criminal Law Act 1977, which clearly provides that if corrupting public morality, or outraging public decency, constitute substantive offences, only a charge of statutory conspiracy may be brought in respect of any agreement to commit such offences.

[112] Ormerod, "The Fraud Act 2006: Criminalising Lying?" [2007] *Crim LR* 193, 194.

[113] § 15.9.

[114] See Smith, "Conspiracy under the Criminal Law Act 1977" [1977] *Crim LR* 598 and 638 for a remarkably prescient discussion of the interpretative difficulties that have arisen.

[115] Criminal Law Act 1977, s. 1(4); *Board of Trade v. Owen* [1957] AC 602.

[116] Criminal Justice (Terrorism and Conspiracy) Act 1998, s. 5.

terms, section 1A of the Criminal Law Act 1977 turns agreements to contravene the laws of foreign states into conspiracies under English law. This amendment is a reaction to the international dimensions of some forms of modern criminal activity. It will be discussed in more detail below (§ 9.6), when we address the issue of jurisdiction over inchoate offences.

(b) Inchoate offences

The phrase "commission of any offence" employed in section 1 of the Criminal Law Act 1977 is perfectly apt to cover inchoate offences. Accordingly it is possible to conspire to commit the inchoate offences of assisting or encouraging a crime contrary to Part 2 of the Serious Crime Act 2007. This would be relevant, for example, on facts similar to *Invicta Plastics* v. *Clare*.[117] Managers of the company would be guilty of conspiracy to encourage believing that the substantive offence will be committed when they agreed the specifics of the "Radatec" advertisement that, when published, constituted an encouragement to motorists to commit offences under the Wireless Telegraphy Act 1949. One implication of this is that the reach of the criminal law will extend far back from the point of commission of the substantive offence. Serious doubts may be entertained on the propriety of such charges for conduct so remote from the substantive crime,[118] yet there appears to be no legal impediment to such a prosecution.

Similarly, in principle there are no legal difficulties precluding charges of conspiracy to conspire or conspiracy to attempt. However, such charges will rarely be apt. It is hard to envisage a conspiracy to conspire which is not, more straightforwardly, a conspiracy to commit a substantive offence. Likewise, a conspiracy to attempt will be a conspiracy to commit the substantive offence, save for some very rare cases where D is aware that it is impossible to commit the substantive offence.[119]

(c) Secondary liability

"Commission of any offence" is a term appropriate to acts of perpetration of a crime but is unsuited to convey complicity in the offence of another. An agreement between and *confined* to D and E to assist the commission of an offence by P will consequently not constitute a statutory conspiracy on the part of D and E.[120] The fact that section 1 of the Criminal Law Act 1977 contemplates that only "*one* or more parties to the agreement" may commit the agreed crime strengthens this view. Further, even if all the acts are performed as the conspirators have agreed, no offence will be committed unless the principal, who is not party to the conspiracy, commits the substantive offence, and there is no certainty that she will do so; consequently the conspirators' agreed course of conduct will not *necessarily* amount to an offence as section 1(1) of the Criminal Law Act 1977 requires. Of course, if D and E agree, for example, to assist P in the commission of burglary and P is party to that

---

[117] [1976] RTR 251; above, § 9.2(i)(a).

[118] For critical discussion, see Johnson, "The Unnecessary Crime of Conspiracy" (1973) 61 *California LR* 1137; Marcus, "Criminal Conspiracy Law: Time to Turn Back from an Ever Expanding, Ever More Troubling Area" (1992) 1 *William and Mary Bill of Rights J* 1.

[119] See the discussion above, § 9.2(i)(d) (encouragement and assistance offences); the example given there could be adapted to conspiracy.

[120] *Kenning* [2008] EWCA Crim 1534, [2009] QB 221. See also *Dang* [2014] EWCA Crim 348.

agreement, this will constitute a conspiracy on the part of all of them to commit burglary. However, where D and E agree to assist the commission of an offence by P, where P is not party to the agreement, it is possible to convict D and E of a conspiracy to commit the inchoate offence of assisting a crime, intending or believing that the substantive offence will be committed.

(ii) The agreement

(a) Conspiracy as collaboration

Agreement[121] is the essence of conspiracy; in the terms of section 1 of the Criminal Law Act 1977, it is required that D "agrees with any other person or persons that a course of conduct shall be pursued". Yet the term must be regarded with some caution, particularly by lawyers familiar with the concept of agreement as used in other areas of law, such as contract. It is not enough that D and E agree a course of conduct which necessarily involves the commission of an offence. The commission of that offence must constitute a project that they have in common; their agreement must be indicative of a collaboration to achieve that end.

The collaborative nature of the agreement necessary for a criminal conspiracy was usefully highlighted by the Court of Appeal in Mehta,[122] where Toulson LJ recognised the following propositions:

"1. A conspiracy requires that the parties to it have a common unlawful purpose or design.
2. A common design means a shared design. It is not the same as similar but separate designs."

The Criminal Law Act 1977 provides no definition of agreement.[123] Accordingly, we may assume that the Act intends no change from the common law regarding the nature of the agreement required for conspiracy. The Canadian case of Sokoloski[124] provides a useful illustration of an agreement directed at criminal activity which falls short of a criminal conspiracy. D and E arranged a rendezvous at which D could hand over drugs to E in exchange for cash. The selling of drugs by D constituted the crime of drug-trafficking on his part. E was charged with conspiracy with D to traffic in drugs. On appeal, it was held that there was no drug-trafficking conspiracy between D and E. Selling drugs for cash was D's project, and his alone. The fact that E agreed arrangements with D which enabled D to sell drugs did not alter the fact that E's role in these arrangements was that of a buyer of drugs, an activity which did not constitute drug trafficking. But for this limitation on the kind of agreement required for conspiracy, all manner of consumption of illegal services could be brought within the net of conspiracy.[125]

---

[121] Orchard, "Agreement in Criminal Conspiracy" [1974] Crim LR 297, 335; Marcus, "The Criminal Agreement in Theory and in Practice" (1977) 65 Geo LJ 925; Jarvis and Bisgrove, "The Use and Abuse of Conspiracy" [2014] Crim LR 261.
[122] [2012] EWCA Crim 2824, para. 36. See also Ardalan [1972] 2 All ER 257, 261; Shillam [2013] EWCA Crim 160, para. 19 (Toulson LJ).
[123] The Law Commission has recommended that a conspiracy should be defined as involving an agreement between at least two people to engage in the conduct element of an offence and, where relevant, to bring about the consequences of that offence: Law Com. No. 318, Conspiracy and Attempts (2009) para. 2.45.
[124] [1977] 2 SCR 523.
[125] But see the criticism of just such a development in the law of encouragement above, § 9.2(i)(a).

The core requirement of a common purpose between the conspirators was further emphasised in *Mehta*,[126] where Toulson LJ said:

"In criminal law (as in civil law) there may be an umbrella agreement pursuant to which the parties enter into any further agreements which may include parties who are not parties to the umbrella agreement. So, A and B may enter into an umbrella agreement pursuant to which they enter into a further agreement between A, B and C, and a further agreement between A, B and D, and so on. In that example, C and D will not be conspirators with each other."

This requirement of commonality of purpose was signally lacking in the much-criticised case of *Meyrick and Ribuffi*.[127] D and E separately owned nightclubs occupying adjacent premises. Each acting on his own initiative, D and E paid bribes to the same police officer in return for non-enforcement of the licensing laws in respect of their own premises. Notwithstanding the lack of any personal communication between D and E regarding the bribes, a verdict of conspiracy to corrupt was reached on the basis that "each well knew what the other was doing".[128] *Griffiths*[129] provides a useful contrast with *Meyrick*. In *Griffiths*, the defendants were all farmers who purchased lime from the same supplier. The supplier had instructed the defendants in various ways of dishonestly obtaining subsidies from the Ministry of Agriculture. The Court of Appeal found that, while individual defendants may have been aware that fellow defendants were acting on the instructions of the same supplier to similar fraudulent effect, this did not, of itself, make them conspirators: each was engaging in fraudulent conduct in the course of his own affairs. *Meyrick* was "explained" in *Griffiths* on the basis of the proximity of the respective premises. Why should that matter? If D and E, both shoplifters, should notice what the other is doing, that would not make for a conspiracy to steal, however close together they stood. *Meyrick* should be regarded as wrong, both in light of the decision in *Griffiths* and by reference to the statement of general principle in *Mehta* (quoted above) of a shared design. The essence of liability for conspiracy in such cases was summarised by Toulson LJ in *Shillam*:[130]

"although each conspirator need not necessarily know of the identity or even the existence of all the other conspirators, there must be shared criminal purpose of design in which all have joined, rather than merely similar or parallel ones."

In *Griffiths* the criminal designs were parallel rather than joint.

If the purpose of the conspirators is narrower than what the prosecution alleged, it is possible to convict them of a narrow conspiracy, the smaller purpose being included in the larger. As Toulson LJ recognised in *Mehta*:[131]

"Conspiracy requires a common design, but it is not a bed of Procrustes whose minimum dimensions are fixed by the prosecution's initial measurements."

So, for example, if A and B are charged with a conspiracy to rob but it can only be established that they conspired to steal, they should be convicted of a conspiracy to commit

---

[126] [2012] EWCA Crim 2824, para. 36. See *D* [2009] EWCA Crim 584.
[127] (1929) 21 Cr App R 94.
[128] *Ibid.*, 102.
[129] (1965) 49 Cr App R 279.
[130] [2013] EWCA Crim 160, para. 20.
[131] [2012] EWCA Crim 2824, para. 45.

the lesser offence.[132] Similarly, if A, B and C are charged with conspiracy to import drugs illegally in years 1, 2 and 3 and the evidence leaves the jury unsure as to whether A was party to such a conspiracy but there is evidence that B and C agreed to import drugs in years 2 and 3, then B and C should be convicted of that conspiracy.[133]

The existence of a common purpose may be questioned when D's role is merely to supply some weapon or other object to be used in the commission of the offence. If D agrees with E that V should be killed and volunteers to provide a weapon, clearly he is E's partner in the project of killing V. By contrast, that appears not to be the case where D supplies a weapon to E for cash, aware that E intends to use the weapon to kill V but without agreeing with E that V should be killed. In *Gemmell*,[134] the Court of Appeal of New Zealand held that, where D knows that other persons have agreed to commit a crime but he is not a party to their agreement, if he does certain acts intended to assist the commission of the crime he does not become a party to the conspiracy. *Gemmell* lays down the correct approach. No doubt D is a secondary party to the substantive offence, if and when it is committed, but he is not involved in the conspiracy. If the substantive offence is not committed, D can instead be convicted of assisting the commission of the offence intending or believing that it will be committed contrary to sections 44 or 45 of the Serious Crime Act 2007.

(b) Differences between the parties over what has been agreed

To what extent can it be said that D and E have reached agreement on a course of conduct when the evidence reveals differences between them as to the content of their agreement? Two situations must be distinguished: (i) where D and E have different offences in mind; and (ii) where the differences between D and E do not preclude an agreement to commit the same offence.

Case 1: Different offences in mind.
In *Barnard*,[135] E and F (and others) agreed to commit robbery. D agreed to assist them, but he thought the scheme was to commit the less serious offence of theft. The Court of Appeal ruled that D was not guilty of conspiracy to rob; an intention to agree to the lesser offence of theft was not equivalent to an intention to agree to commit robbery. In *Patel*,[136] Woolf LJ considered, *obiter*, the converse situation; he instanced circumstances where D took himself to be agreeing to the importation of heroin, whereas his fellow conspirators planned to import cannabis, a lesser offence. Given that the offences were of the same type, Woolf LJ took the view that the greater implied the lesser and D could not disassociate himself from the conspiracy merely because the crime to be committed was less serious than the offence he had contemplated. Woolf LJ's view receives support from *dicta* of the Court of Appeal in *Taylor (Robert John)*,[137] where the Court ruled that an agreement to import Class B drugs would not encompass the importation of Class A drugs. However, the converse did not apply: if D agreed to import Class A drugs he would be liable for a conspiracy to import Class B drugs if that was what his co-conspirators had agreed to.

---

[132] By virtue of section 6(3) of the Criminal Law Act 1967.
[133] See *Mehta* [2012] EWCA Crim 2824, para. 43.
[134] [1985] 2 NZLR 740.
[135] (1980) 70 Cr App R 28.
[136] Unreported, 7 August 1991 (CA). Transcript 89/4351/51.
[137] [2002] Crim LR 205.

In terms of policy, the conclusion is entirely reasonable if the matter is assessed from the perspective of D's culpability; he has demonstrated his preparedness to do something that was cognate with, yet even more serious than, the crime his fellow conspirators had in mind. The problem with this culpability-driven approach, however, is that in purely conceptual terms it blurs the lines between actus reus (the agreement) and mens rea (the intention to commit a particular crime). In strict terms, the presence of agreement should first be established objectively and one should then move on to determine whether the mens rea of each party is consonant with the objectively established agreement.

In *Barnard*, the conduct of the parties, assessed objectively, amounted to formation of a conspiracy to rob, a conspiracy to which D was a party. The actus reus of conspiracy—agreement—was present. The reason D was not guilty of the offence was that he lacked mens rea; a readiness to thieve was not equivalent to a willingness to rob. Likewise, in the situation discussed by Woolf LJ in *Patel*, there was a conspiracy to import cannabis which D had, by his actions, joined; unlike Barnard, D would be guilty of conspiracy to import cannabis, since an intent to import heroin was sufficient mens rea for the smuggling offence with which he was charged.[138] In some cases, however, differences between the parties may preclude the formation of an agreement if an objective approach is taken. Suppose that D and E agree to import drugs; D assumes the agreement concerns a consignment of heroin, a Class A drug, whereas E has in mind a consignment of cannabis, a Class B drug. It may be that, objectively, one view of their agreement is more reasonable than the other; on the evidence, a court may find that this was a conspiracy to import heroin or it was a conspiracy to import cannabis, as the case may be. In that case, there will be an objective act of agreement ascribable to both parties and their ultimate liability will hinge on their respective states of mind and whether it suffices for liability for the crime each, respectively, had in mind to commit. Alternatively, their actions may be considered to be genuinely ambiguous, so that both views of the agreement are plausible. If the presence of agreement is to be judged objectively, then in this case there is none to be found.

Understandably, a criminal court may be reluctant to reach such a conclusion as it would involve the acquittal of persons who had demonstrated a commitment to perpetrate crimes. There would be a natural temptation to reason that each defendant is to be judged from his own, subjective, perspective; even if, in the light of their differing perspectives, there is no agreement in the strict contractual sense. A less strict approach would, in our example, enable a court to find D guilty of conspiracy to import heroin and E guilty of conspiracy to import cannabis. Both parties have the mens rea for importation contrary to section 170 of the Customs and Excise Management Act 1979, and no great injustice is done if they are convicted of conspiracy to commit the offence, provided the punishment that each party receives is appropriate to his mens rea.

Case 2: Same offence in mind.
In *Broad*,[139] D and E agreed to manufacture drugs. D believed their agreement was to produce heroin, whereas E thought they had arranged to produce cocaine. The Court

---

[138] Importation of a controlled drug contravenes s. 170 of the Customs and Excise Management Act 1979. As interpreted, the mens rea for the offence is awareness that some form of contraband is being imported even though penalties vary markedly (potentially life imprisonment for importing a Class A drug) according to the objects actually imported: *Taafe* [1984] AC 539.

[139] [1997] Crim LR 666.

of Appeal held the difference to be immaterial: on either view of the agreement, the objective would constitute the same offence, i.e. production of a Class A drug. *Broad* should be read as settling a general principle to the effect that differences over the content of their agreement between the parties do not vitiate any agreement between them if the respective course of conduct that each party contemplates will result in the commission of the same offence.

Professor Sir John Smith, however, queried the generality of *Broad*.[140] He contrasted the facts of that case with a hypothetical situation where D takes himself to be agreeing with E to murder V and is subsequently horrified to learn that the victim E intends is W. Smith suggests that differences regarding the kind of Class A drug are immaterial, but the identity of the victim is a matter of substance. On that view, D would not be liable for conspiracy to murder. This conclusion may be doubted. The mens rea for murder takes no account of the identity of the victim. In the terms of section 1 of the Criminal Law Act 1977, D had agreed a course of conduct which "will necessarily amount to or involve the commission of [an] offence". Accordingly, differences between the parties as to the particulars of their agreement should not preclude liability for conspiracy if, notwithstanding those differences, the parties have agreed to commit the same offence. If, on account of such differences, there are variations in the moral standing of the respective defendants, normally they can be taken into account at the sentencing stage.

(c) Conditional agreements

The parties must conclude an agreement before liability for conspiracy can arise. This means that, if D makes the resolution of certain matters a precondition to final agreement,[141] there is no conspiracy; as in *Walker*,[142] where D agreed in principle to robbery but then withdrew because of unresolved differences between himself and the other parties on how the robbery was to be carried out. The Court of Appeal quashed D's conviction for conspiracy, reasoning that he had not concluded a final agreement with the other parties because his conditions for joining their criminal project had not been met.

If, however, the parties have unequivocally agreed a criminal project, liability arises at that point. Such liability is unaffected by its being contingent on future events. In *O'Hadhmaill*,[143] the defendants, members of the IRA, resolved to carry out a bombing campaign. They agreed not to give effect to this project unless and until the IRA abandoned a ceasefire policy. In confirming the defendants' convictions for conspiracy to cause explosions, the Court of Appeal held that this condition did not preclude the formation of an agreement on a course of conduct which, in the words of section 1 of the Criminal Law Act 1977, "if carried out in accordance with their intentions … will necessarily amount to or involve the commission of any offence". The agreement was in no sense equivocal. It was the intention of the parties to carry it out should a particular state of affairs arise. *O'Hadhmaill* is salutary. Practically all future projects will be subject to implicit conditions. For instance, suppose D and E agree to rob a bank. They are asked by some third party what they will do should they find the bank surrounded by armed police at the time they propose to rob it.

---

[140] *Ibid.*, 668.
[141] Broderick, "Conditional Objectives of Conspiracies" (1985) 94 *Yale LJ* 895.
[142] [1962] Crim LR 458.
[143] [1996] Crim LR 509.

A reply that they would then abandon their scheme in no way alters the fact that they have unequivocally agreed to rob a bank.

The reasoning in *O'Hadhmaill* clearly applies where the project of D and E is intrinsically criminal, e.g. to cause explosions or to rob banks. According to dicta in *Reed*,[144] such reasoning does not extend to situations where D and E conceive an objective which may be realised lawfully but agree to act in a criminal manner should that prove necessary in order to attain their goal. The following example was given in *Reed*:[145]

> "A and B agree to drive from London to Edinburgh in a time which can be achieved without exceeding the speed limits, but only if the traffic which they encounter is exceptionally light. Their agreement will not necessarily involve the commission of any offence, even if it is carried out in accordance with their intentions, and they do arrive from London to Edinburgh in the stated time."

Apparently, conditional agreements of that description fall outside the ambit of statutory conspiracy. This conclusion rests on a questionable interpretation of the phrase, "course of conduct" which appears in section 1 of the Criminal Law Act 1977; the matter will be dealt with more fully below, in § 9.3(iii), when we examine the meaning of that phrase.

(d) The sufficiency of agreement

Liability for conspiracy arises as soon as a course of conduct is agreed which is sufficiently specific to identify the crime(s) that would be committed should the agreement be carried out. Consequently, conduct which is very remote from the commission of a substantive offence may constitute a conspiracy. Suppose D and E agree to hire themselves out as "contract killers". From that point, they are parties to a conspiracy to murder notwithstanding that vital matters such as clients, victims, and rates of payment have yet to be resolved. In certain jurisdictions, there is a further requirement for an overt act done in pursuit of the agreed criminal objective before liability in conspiracy can arise. This has much to commend it. The overt act is evidence that the agreement is a serious one and constitutes a real social threat. Moreover, such a requirement has the potential to lessen reliance on confessions as a mode of proof. The overt act requirement has not, however, been received into English law to date and its introduction has not been proposed by any law reform agency.

In principle, once liability for conspiracy has arisen, it cannot be undone through any voluntary revocation of the agreement by all the parties to it or, in terms of the liability of specific individuals, through any voluntary withdrawal by a party to the agreement. In *Walker*,[146] D's conviction for conspiracy was quashed on the basis that he withdrew from negotiations with other parties *prior* to reaching an agreement with them; the Court of Appeal indicated, *obiter*, that had the point of agreement already been reached, a subsequent voluntary withdrawal would have provided at most mitigation of sentence and not a defence. As we have seen, a voluntary withdrawal defence is allowed for accomplices.[147] Although the conceptual bases of conspiracy and complicity differ—conspiracy is a form of direct liability which arises at the point of agreement; complicity is a form of derivative

---

[144] [1982] Crim LR 819 (CA).
[145] *Ibid.*, 820.
[146] [1962] Crim LR 458.
[147] Above, § 7.6(vi).

liability which arises on the commission of a substantive offence by another person—providing an incentive to withdraw from a criminal project prior to the commission of the substantive offence is equally in point for conspiracy. Moreover, many accomplices will be parties to a conspiracy made with the principal offender. In terms of policy, it seems inconsistent to allow D a defence of voluntary withdrawal in respect of a complicity charge yet to impose liability upon D as a conspirator. Currently, providing a defence of voluntary revocation and withdrawal for alleged conspirators would be within the competence of a trial judge, there being no binding appellate authority disallowing such a defence. Such a defence has not, however, been created for the crimes of assisting and encouraging.[148]

(iii) The "course of conduct"

Under the terms of section 1(1) of the Criminal Law Act 1977, the parties must agree that:

> a course of conduct shall be pursued which, if the agreement is carried out in accordance with their intentions, … will necessarily amount to or involve the commission of any offence or offences.

On the face of it, this statutory requirement is straightforward: it demands proof of what it was the parties had agreed to do and proof that doing what had been agreed would *necessarily* have involved the commission of one or more crimes by at least one party to the agreement. Unfortunately, the position is not as straightforward as it should be. Interpretative difficulties have arisen over the phrase, "course of conduct". Two areas of ambiguity will be discussed: (i) how broadly or narrowly should the phrase be construed? and (ii) how many courses of conduct may a particular episode of conduct contain?

(a) A broad or narrow construction?

At its broadest, "course of conduct" may be construed as including any acts or omissions the parties propose to do and any consequences that will arise from the perpetration of those acts or omissions. At its narrowest, the reference to conduct could be read as signifying simply the acts or omissions the parties propose without reference to ensuing consequences. The broad interpretation is most consistent with the language of the Act and the rationale of conspiracy. The Act speaks of a "course of conduct … carried out *in accordance with their intentions*", which seems to imply that the consequences the parties intend to bring about are to be included within the expression, "course of conduct". Suppose that D and E agree to tamper with the brakes of V's car with the intention that it should crash and V be killed. That agreement is, surely, a conspiracy to murder, a judgment confirmed if "course of conduct" includes the results that D and E intend their conduct to achieve. If that is the correct interpretation of the phrase, then the course of conduct they have agreed, "will *necessarily* amount to or involve the commission of [an] offence". However, if the narrow interpretation prevails and the course of conduct that D and E have agreed is confined to the physical interference with the brakes of the car, it cannot be said that their conduct will necessarily cause the death of V. V might survive any ensuing crash, the tampering might prove ineffective, and so on. The narrow interpretation attains a measure of plausibility from the fact

---

[148] Above, § 9.2.(iii)(a).

that it is common practice to break down the elements of "result" crimes into a tripartite division of conduct elements, circumstance elements, and consequence elements; where the "conduct" element encompasses only the physical movements of D.[149] But that is merely done for the purposes of exposition and in no sense determines the correct interpretation of section 1(1). In ordinary English speech, it is perfectly permissible to describe the same incident in a manner whereby D's conduct includes consequential results (as in "D killed V by shooting him") or in a manner which separates D's conduct from its consequence (as in "D fired a gun at V causing V to die").[150] Therefore, in terms of the wording of the Act and an effective law of conspiracy, the broader interpretation should be adopted so that the conduct of the parties is taken to include the intended consequences of their agreed acts and omissions. There is no theory of language nor legal principle which precludes this interpretation.

Unfortunately, the approach argued for here is contrary to the approach of the House of Lords in *Nock*.[151] That case involved common law conspiracy, on which the Criminal Law Act has no bearing. Lord Scarman, however, adverted to the defining elements of statutory conspiracy and regarded them as an effective summary of the common law position for conspiracies where the objective of the conspiracy was the commission of a crime. D and E had attempted to produce cocaine from a set of materials which, unknown to them, did not contain any coca-base, rendering their project impossible. Lord Scarman construed the phrase "course of conduct" as a reference to what D and E physically proposed to do, i.e. to apply certain chemical procedures to the material they had. The consequence they intended to bring about from applying these procedures was not, itself, to be taken as part of their course of conduct; it was the objective of their agreed course of conduct but was not part of it.[152] Accordingly, D and E were not parties to a conspiracy to produce cocaine because the implementation of what they had agreed would not "necessarily" involve the commission of a crime.

The actual decision in *Nock* was reversed by an amendment of the Criminal Law Act 1977. It now suffices that an offence would have been committed, "but for the existence of facts which render the commission of the offence … impossible".[153] Lord Scarman's reasoning has therefore been displaced for cases of impossibility. Seemingly, however, it remains in place for cases where attainable objectives are pursued by ineffectual means. On this view, D and E would now be conspirators on the original facts of *Nock* but not in circumstances, say, where it was *possible* to manufacture cocaine from the materials D and E possessed but not by the method they agreed to use.

This conclusion is so perverse that one is tempted peremptorily to reject it. However, if the interpretation we have argued for—that the course of conduct includes the consequences the parties intend to achieve—is correct, the amendment to the Act for the case of impossibility was unnecessary. Under our preferred interpretation, a course of conduct includes intended consequences and it is thus irrelevant whether those consequences are possible or impossible of attainment.

---

[149] See above, § 4.

[150] Feinberg describes this as the "accordion effect": "Action and Responsibility" in Black (ed.), *Philosophy in America* (1965) 134.

[151] [1978] AC 979.

[152] *Ibid.*, 995–6, 998.

[153] Section 1(1)(b) of the Criminal Law Act 1977, as amended by the Criminal Attempts Act 1981.

Lord Scarman's analysis in *Nock* may be contrasted with the decision of the Court of Appeal in *Bolton*.[154] The latter case concerned a dishonest scheme agreed between D and E to obtain a mortgage advance from a building society. They anticipated that they would receive the advance by way of a cheque, a valuable security, but, because of changes in the society's payments system, they received the advance by way of electronic transfer, a method that did not involve the creation of a valuable security. It was held that they had conspired to procure the execution of a valuable security as their expectation of receiving a cheque was to be regarded as part of the "course of conduct" they had agreed. Unfortunately, Lord Scarman's contrary analysis of this phrase was not considered by the Court of Appeal. Recall that, although Lord Scarman construed the terms of the Act, he was taking the Act as a guide to the common law. His Lordship's reading of section 1(1) is of only persuasive authority, but the analysis in *Bolton* is to be preferred. Further, the amendment of the Criminal Law Act 1977 relating to cases of impossibility should be treated as being intended to remove the long-standing common law defence of impossibility to the crime of statutory conspiracy. It should not be regarded as confirming Lord Scarman's analysis by way of creating a special exemption to it.

(b) How many courses of conduct?

Suppose that D and E agree, say, to commit a burglary and contingently agree also to commit some further offence, such as murder, should they encounter opposition in the course of the burglary. It may be asked how many conspiracies arise in these cases. Clearly, in our example, there is a conspiracy to commit burglary. Is there an additional conspiracy to commit murder? If we characterise their agreement as an agreement involving but one agreed course of conduct—to commit burglary—then there is no conspiracy to murder. They may successfully conclude the burglary without necessarily committing murder. However, it is possible to separate the strands of their overall agreement: an agreement to burgle and an agreement to murder on a particular eventuality. Linguistically, it is perfectly apt to regard them as two separate agreements to pursue two different courses of conduct. It is true that their project is burglary rather than murder: the murder, if it should occur, would be but a means to an end. But that has no bearing on the wrongfulness of agreeing to murder someone. *O'Hadhmaill*[155] decides that it is no answer to a charge of conspiracy that the implementation of an agreement was subject to a condition which may not be fulfilled, provided the parties have unequivocally agreed to pursue a criminal course of conduct should the terms of the condition be fulfilled. It is submitted that the better view is that in such circumstances there are as many separate courses of conduct as there are crimes the parties have unequivocally agreed to commit. This conclusion is supported by *A-G's Reference (No. 4 of 2003)*,[156] where the Court of Appeal was sympathetic to the view that, if D and others agree to steal a particular item and resolve that should it be necessary they will commit burglary or robbery to get it, there are conspiracies for theft, burglary, and robbery.

---

[154] (1992) 94 Cr App R 74.
[155] [1966] Crim LR 509.
[156] [2004] EWCA Crim 1944, [2005] 1 WLR 1574.

Recall, however, our discussion of the "driving to Edinburgh" example put by Lord Lane in *Reed*.[157] Lord Lane took the view that if the objective of D and E—arriving in Edinburgh in time, say, for lunch—could be achieved by driving within speed limits, their agreement to exceed those limits, should need arise, did not constitute a conspiracy to exceed statutory limits. Their course of conduct could reach a successful conclusion without necessarily involving the commission of a crime. His view appears to be that courses of conduct are identified by reference to the ultimate objective of the parties and to any means employed to attain that objective which are intrinsically necessary and not merely contingently necessary. On that view, the Edinburgh agreement takes in lunching and driving to lunch, two separate courses of conduct, but not speeding to lunch.

Employing a distinction between intrinsically necessary means and contingently necessary means to delimit the ambit of conspiracy entails some fine distinctions. Suppose that D and E agree to obtain money from V. They agree to try first to obtain the money by a hard-luck story; should that not succeed they agree to kill V and then take his money. Here the distinction between intrinsically necessary means and contingently necessary means does not apply. They contemplate the possibility of having to try two means to the same end, plan A and plan B. Surely there is a conspiracy to defraud *and* a conspiracy to murder? Distinguishing between situations such as the lunch in Edinburgh scenario and the money plot is too refined for the practical concerns of the criminal law. It is submitted that, in the spirit of the decision in *O'Hadhmaill*, if the parties have unequivocally agreed to commit an offence should a particular eventuality arise, they have agreed "a course of conduct shall be pursued which … will necessarily … involve the commission of an offence". The dictum to the contrary of Lord Lane in *Reed* should not be followed.

(iv) The mens rea of conspiracy

There is an element of contrivance in subdividing the constituents of conspiracy into sections dealing with actus reus—the agreement—on the one hand, and mens rea on the other. After all, agreement, the meeting of minds, involves a mental operation. That said, the presence of a consensus does not exhaust what is required by way of a mental element for this offence. Agreements operate on the surface of things and the fact of agreement may coexist with secret reservations or betrayals that one or more of the parties may have in mind. For example, suppose D and E agree to meet later that night in order to carry out a burglary at the house of V. D has no intention of showing up. He agrees with E because he is disinclined to admit that he lacks the courage to commit burglary. E, on the other hand, is an undercover policeman who plans to arrest D before the burglary is committed. If neither D nor E is guilty of conspiracy, as is likely the case, it will be because each lacks mens rea, rather than because no agreement had been formed.

(a) Intention to carry out the course of conduct agreed

Section 1 of the Criminal Law Act 1977 refers to an agreement, "carried out in accordance with the intentions of [the parties]". This indicates that liability in conspiracy is predicated on the intention of the parties to carry out their agreement. The requirement for this form

---

[157] [1982] Crim LR 819 (CA). See above, § 9.3(ii)(c).

of intention is a matter of implication rather than express stipulation. The Law Commission recommended that there should be express stipulation on the matter. It drafted the following provision:[158]

> "both he and the other person or persons with whom he agrees must intend to bring about any consequence which is an element of that offence, even where the offence in question may be committed without that consequence actually being intended by the person committing it."

In the debates on the Bill that became the Criminal Law Act 1977, this provision was rejected on the ground of excessive complexity. Nonetheless, the Lord Chancellor, when agreeing to the deletion of the clause, stated that what is now section 1 of the Criminal Law Act 1977 required "full intention and knowledge before conspiracy can be established".[159]

This legislative history needs to be borne in mind[160] when considering the implications of the House of Lords decision in *Anderson*.[161] Seemingly, a unanimous House decided that an intention to carry out the agreed course of conduct was not a defining element of conspiracy. It sufficed that D had agreed a criminal project with others and intended to play his assigned part in it; nothing else was required. In particular, the prosecution need not establish that D intended that the agreement be carried through to completion.

The ruling in *Anderson* was novel. Previously, it had never been suggested, let alone decided, that an intention to realise the objective of the conspiracy was not essential to liability as a conspirator.[162] The elements of liability will, of course, be the same for each conspirator. Consequently, *Anderson* raises the possibility of liability for conspiracy in circumstances where none of the parties to a particular agreement intends that it be carried out. So radical is this interpretation, and so out of accord with the legislative history of statutory conspiracy and the history of conspiracy generally, that it is necessary to examine the facts of *Anderson* to see if any limitations or special considerations can be brought to bear on the ambit of the decision:

> The appellant D had been a prisoner, along with E and F. E and F conceived a plan to effect the escape from prison of G. D agreed with E and F to help effect G's escape and undertook that when he, D, was released from prison he would procure some diamond cutting equipment and arrange for it to be smuggled into the prison. D sought to defend himself from liability for conspiracy on the basis that his sole interest in this venture was to make some money from selling the equipment to E and F. He claimed that he envisaged no prospect that E and F would succeed in their plan.

There was no necessity for the House to revamp the mental element of conspiracy in order to sustain D's conviction for the offence. D had entered into an agreement with E and F, the object of which was to bring about the escape of G. D's role was not as a mere supplier of materials; he was part of the plot to spring G. The plot was a real one in the sense that

---

[158] Law Com. No. 76, *Conspiracy and Criminal Law Reform* (1976); Law Com. No. 177, *A Criminal Code for England and Wales* (1989) cl. 1(3). The Law Commission has now recommended that a specific statutory provision is required which states that a conspirator must intend that both the conduct and consequence elements of the substantive offence should be brought about: Law Com. No. 318, *Conspiracy and Attempts* (2009) para. 2.56.

[159] HL Debs, vol. 379, col. 55.

[160] Including reference to Ministerial statements to Parliament, pursuant to *Pepper* v. *Hart* [1993] AC 593.

[161] [1986] AC 27.

[162] In *Thomson* (1965) 50 Cr App R 1, for example, the Court of Criminal Appeal had ruled that to be guilty of conspiracy a person must not only agree a criminal project but also intend that the project be carried out.

D knew that E and F would try to put it into effect. Not infrequently, a party will join a conspiracy in circumstances where it is not envisaged that he will take any part in the commission of the substantive offence. For such a party, his "intent" that the substantive offence be carried out is constituted by the knowledge that his co-conspirators intend to do so. In *Anderson*, D knew that E and F intended to carry out the substantive offence, and he assisted that project. He did not intend to frustrate their scheme by, say, reporting them to the relevant authorities. That he thought nothing or little of E and F's prospects of success would seem neither here nor there. His conviction was perfectly in accord with the orthodox understanding of the mental element in conspiracy. Any reference to his ultimate motive (i.e. to make money) was irrelevant: the House of Lords simply confused D's motive with his intent.

An appreciation that the innovative approach of the House of Lords was unnecessary, for the decision in *Anderson* increases one's confidence in the validity and authority of several appellate decisions and dicta which subsequently have sought to minimise the effects of that decision.

One such case is *McPhillips*,[163] where Lowry LCJ, giving judgment for the Court of Appeal of Northern Ireland, ruled that section 1(1) of the Criminal Law Act 1977 required an intention on the part of a conspirator that the object of the conspiracy be carried out. Accordingly, D was not liable for conspiracy to murder in *McPhillips* because he intended to alert the relevant authorities prior to the explosion of the bomb he and his partners had set. Lord Lowry distinguished the decision in *Anderson* on the basis that, on the facts of that case, D had had no intention of frustrating the plans of his fellow conspirators to effect the escape of a prisoner. The facts of the respective cases do differ in the manner indicated by his Lordship. Yet if one were to remain faithful to the decision in *Anderson*, it is unclear why this factual difference should be of any consequence. By becoming a party to an agreement to murder and intending to play a part (indeed playing a part) in carrying out the agreement, the appellant in *McPhillips* fulfilled the requirements for liability in conspiracy as set down by Lord Bridge in *Anderson*.

In other cases, too, Lord Bridge's requirements have not been taken as either a necessary or a sufficient basis for liability in conspiracy. In *Edwards*,[164] the Court of Appeal ruled that D could incur liability for conspiracy to supply amphetamine only if he intended that amphetamine be supplied. No reference to *Anderson* was made in the judgment. In *Yip Chiu-Cheung*, again without reference to *Anderson*, Lord Griffiths in the Privy Council stated that "the crime of conspiracy requires an agreement between two or more persons to commit an unlawful act with the intention of carrying it out. *It is the intention to carry out the crime* that constitutes the mens rea of the offence."[165] Finally, in *Saik*,[166] Lord Nicholls recognised, albeit *obiter* and without reference to *Anderson*, that conspirators must intend to do the act which is prohibited by the substantive offence.

Of course, this post-*Anderson* case law, comprising, as it does, a decision of the Court of Appeal of Northern Ireland, a *per incuriam* decision of the Court of Appeal, dicta of the Privy Council, and even an *obiter dictum* from the House of Lords, cannot overturn

---

[163] [1989] NI 360.
[164] [1991] Crim LR 45.
[165] [1995] 1 AC 111, 118 (PC) (emphasis added). See too *Harvey* [1999] Crim LR 70.
[166] [2006] UKHL 18, [2007] 1 AC 18, para. 4.

an unequivocal ruling of the House of Lords. Yet, in estimating the future influence of the *Anderson* ruling, it is pertinent to recall our previous discussion of the legislative history of statutory conspiracy. That history clearly indicates that it was not the intention of Parliament, when enacting section 1(1) of the Criminal Law Act 1977, to dispense with the venerable requirement of an intention to carry out the agreement; section 1(1) was understood to require such an intention. Furthermore, as will be seen below, section 1(2) requires proof of intent or knowledge with respect to any circumstances necessary for the commission of the substantive offence. It would have been quite bizarre for Parliament to insist on full mens rea as to circumstance elements of the substantive offence while, at the same time, dispensing with mens rea as to any consequence element required to establish the substantive offence. Finally, as we have already argued, if the nature of the intention required for the crime of conspiracy had been properly analysed by the House of Lords in *Anderson*, the appellant's conviction could have been sustained without recourse to the legal innovations to which the House resorted. Accordingly, it is submitted, with some confidence, that to be a guilty party to a conspiracy, D must intend that the course of conduct that the parties have agreed should be carried out in circumstances which would necessarily amount to the commission of an offence by at least one of the parties to the agreement.

(b) Intention and foresight of certainty

Where the substantive offence is the very object of the conspiracy, mens rea is straightforward. Assuredly, there will be a conspiracy to murder where D and E agree to firebomb V's house with the objective of killing V. Suppose, however, that D and E conceive of a plan to set fire to a house, occupied by V, in order to make a fraudulent insurance claim for destruction of the building. They appreciate the life-threatening potential of their projected conduct, yet the prospect of death or injury to V is not a motivating factor in the making of their agreement. From the perspective of potential conspiracy charges, there are obvious charges in relation to their fraudulent objective and there is also a conspiracy to commit arson, since arson is an intended means to their fraudulent end. Assume that it can be proved that D and E contemplate the death of V as a virtual certainty if the course of conduct they have agreed is carried out according to their intentions. Can we say that their agreement is, also, a conspiracy to murder?

English criminal law consistently, though not invariably, permits inferences of intent to be drawn with respect to side-effects which are the virtually certain outcome of D's conduct, if D foresaw the outcome as virtually certain.[167] At common law, the conflation of intent with foresight of virtually certain consequences has been carried over to conspiracy. For example, in *Cooke*,[168] D and other railway employees were found guilty of conspiracy to defraud British Rail on the basis that, in scheming to sell their own food and drink to British Rail customers, they intended to cause loss to their employer. Of course, it was no part of D's purpose to cause loss; that was merely the inevitable concomitant of making such gains. It may well be that the same analysis will be made in the context of statutory conspiracy.[169]

---

[167] See above, § 5.1(iv).
[168] [1986] AC 909.
[169] Cf. *Walker* (1989) 90 Cr App R 226, where a similar analysis was adopted in respect of statutory attempt.

Should that prove to be the case, then in our house-burning example D and E would be liable for conspiracy to murder.

Intention, as always, must be distinguished from motive. In *Yip Chiu-Cheung*,[170] it was the view of the Privy Council that D would incur liability for conspiracy to import drugs to Sydney from Hong Kong if he intended that the agreement be carried out, notwithstanding his secret role as an undercover police officer and his desire to bring his fellow conspirators to justice. If, however, he had planned to secure the arrest of the others prior to the implementation of the agreement he would not have been guilty of conspiracy, since he would have lacked an intention to carry out the agreement. In either of those scenarios, the timing of any arrests may depend on contingencies which would have no bearing on the moral quality of D's conduct. Despite this, English courts regard mens rea as a technical legal description of D's state of mind which need not necessarily involve any culpability on the part of D.[171] Accordingly, the analysis in *Yip* represents current English law.[172]

(c) Intention to take some part in carrying out the agreement

As we have discussed, the decision in *Anderson* sought to dispense with the requirement of an intent that the agreement be carried out. According to Lord Bridge, the relevant intent to be established is simply an intent by D to take some part in carrying out the agreement:[173]

> "But, beyond the mere fact of agreement, the necessary mens rea of the crime is, in my opinion, established if, and only if, it is shown that the accused, when he entered into the agreement, intended to play some part in the agreed course of conduct in furtherance of the criminal purpose which the agreed course of conduct was intended to achieve. Nothing less will suffice; nothing more is required."

Prior to *Anderson*, a requirement that D must intend to play some part in carrying out the agreement was unknown to English law. From the origin of the offence until the present time, liability for conspiracy has been founded on the fact of agreement.[174] Suppose, for the moment, we take *Anderson* at face value and accept that the requirement of an intention to play some part in implementing the agreement is a part of English law. It appears that D, for instance, would no longer be liable for conspiracy to murder if he induced E and F to agree to kill V by offering a financial incentive.[175] D's conduct would have brought about an agreement to kill to which she was a party but, assuming the validity of *Anderson*, she cannot incur liability for conspiracy unless she intended to play some part in implementing this agreement.

What does "taking some part" require by way of conduct? In our agreement-to-murder example from the last paragraph, it would be enough, by analogy with the facts

---

[170] [1995] 1 AC 111.

[171] See also the discussion earlier, § 5.

[172] In *Somchai Liangsiriprasert* v. *US Government* (1991) 92 Cr App R 77, 82 the Privy Council had left open the question whether law enforcement officials should be given dispensation to enter conspiracies in order to frustrate criminal objectives, but *Yip Chiu-Cheung* suggests no such dispensation will be given. For valuable discussion of the issues of principle and policy in condoning illegal actions in the interests of law enforcement see Ashworth, "Testing Fidelity to Legal Values: Official Involvement and Criminal Justice" in Shute and Simester (eds.), *Criminal Law Theory: Doctrines of the General Part* (2002) 299.

[173] [1986] AC 27, 39.

[174] *Poulterer's Case* (1611) 9 Co Rep 55b, 77 ER 813; *Starling* (1664) 1 Sid 174, 82 ER 1039.

[175] Although D could be convicted of encouraging murder contrary to the Serious Crime Act 2007; above, § 9.2.

of *Anderson*, for D to provide some practical assistance to E and F, such as providing them with a weapon. Presumably, it would also suffice if D, say, informed E and F of V's whereabouts. But, if D had no active role to play in implementing the agreement, he would not be liable for conspiracy. Yet surely one can be party to an agreement—and thus a member of a conspiracy—without being allocated an active role in its implementation? The test in *Anderson* apportions liability on the basis of differences that are irrelevant to the gist of conspiracy. The gist of conspiracy is the entry into the agreement.

With that in mind, the approach of the Court of Appeal in *Siracusa*[176] is to be welcomed. D had recruited and agreed with E and others that offences be committed in contravention of section 170(2)(b) of the Customs and Excise Management Act 1979. It could not be proved against him that he intended to play an active part in implementing this agreement. O'Connor LJ confirmed his conviction for conspiracy on the basis that his "intention to participate in the furtherance of the criminal purpose is … established by his failure to stop the unlawful activity. Lord Bridge's dictum does not require anything more".[177] On O'Connor LJ's approach, D, in our agreement-to-kill example, would intend to play some part in carrying out the agreement should she fail to report their agreement to the police or take some similar steps.

O'Connor LJ's analysis is artificial: not preventing an offence is hardly "playing a part" in its commission. But the artificiality is forced by the need to pay lip-service to *Anderson*. It would labour the obvious to say anything more than that O'Connor LJ is departing from the view of the law held by Lord Bridge under the guise of complying with it. As Lord Bridge's conception of the mental element in conspiracy is so novel, so strange, and so destructive of the rationale of conspiracy, O'Connor LJ's "interpretation" of Lord Bridge should prevail.

(d) Intention and knowledge as to facts or circumstances necessary for the commission of the offence

Section 1(2) of the Criminal Law Act 1977 provides:

> Where liability for any offence may be incurred without knowledge on the part of the person committing it of any particular fact or circumstance necessary for the commission of the offence, a person shall nevertheless not be guilty of conspiracy to commit that offence by virtue of subsection (1) above unless he and at least one other party to the agreement intend or know that that fact or circumstance shall or will exist at the time when the conduct constituting the offence is to take place.

Section 1(2) is the only provision of the Act which deals explicitly with the mens rea requirements for conspiracy. Ostensibly, its terms are of limited effect. It deals with the situation where liability for the substantive offence may be incurred without knowledge on the part of D of any particular fact or circumstance necessary for the commission of the offence; for example, where the substantive offence is one of strict liability. If a conspiracy charge relating to an agreement to commit an offence of strict liability is brought, section 1(2) makes clear that intention or knowledge as to the facts or circumstances of the substantive offence is required even if such proof would not be required for the substantive offence itself.

---

[176] (1989) 90 Cr App Rep 340.
[177] *Ibid.*, 349.

Does the provision have any wider effect? No reference is made to any conduct or consequence elements of the substantive offence. No indication is given about the mens rea required for conspiracy when the substantive offence does require proof of knowledge of any particular fact or circumstance necessary for the commission of the offence. A basic principle of statutory interpretation is that, if express provision is made for a particular matter or issue and no provision is made for cognate matters or issues falling outside the situation expressly provided for, the inference to be drawn is that the same provision does not extend to those cognate matters or issues.[178] Prima facie, applying that rule of construction, we reach what has been aptly described as a "scandalous paradox":[179] on a conspiracy charge, knowledge or intent must be proved for any particular fact or circumstance necessary for the commission of the offence if such knowledge or intent would *not* be required in a trial for the substantive offence, but proof of such knowledge or intent may be dispensed with where such knowledge or intent *is* required for the substantive offence. Furthermore, on a conspiracy charge, no mens rea need be proved with respect to conduct and consequence elements of the substantive offence, regardless of whether such mens rea is required for the substantive offence.

This prima facie conclusion defies logic and cannot be defended in terms of policy. It is relevant to refer again to the legislative history of the Act. Recall that the original Bill put before Parliament contained a clause that provided for proof of intention as to any consequence elements necessary for commission of the substantive offence on a charge of conspiracy. Although the clause was deleted on the ground that it was excessively complex, the Lord Chancellor assured Parliament that what is now section 1(1) of the Criminal Law Act 1977 required proof of "full intention and knowledge before conspiracy can be established".[180] If these words are taken as an authoritative guide to the interpretation of section 1(1), intention or knowledge should be required as to all elements that make up the substantive offence. That is the position at common law;[181] one would have anticipated express provision in the Act were the well-established and long-standing common law position to be departed from. If we accept that section 1(1) requires intention or knowledge for all elements of the substantive offence, then section 1(2) may be regarded as a provision inserted to avoid any doubt that the same level of intention or knowledge is required on a conspiracy charge even when it is not required by the substantive offence. The word "nevertheless" adds force to this interpretation; it may be taken to stress that, even in cases where there is an element of strict liability within the substantive offence, mens rea as to those elements is required for conspiracy; *a fortiori* such intention or knowledge is required when proof of such intention or knowledge is required for the substantive offence. This reading, originally proposed by Sir John Smith,[182] has been endorsed by the House of Lords in *Saik*[183] and can be taken as established.

Accordingly, it seems clear that D will not be liable for conspiracy unless she intends or knows of any particular fact or circumstance necessary for the commission of the

---

[178] "*Expressio unius est exclusio alterius*"—"the mention of one thing is the exclusion of another".

[179] Elliot, "Mens Rea in Statutory Conspiracy" [1978] *Crim LR* 202, 204.

[180] See above, § 9.3(iv)(a).

[181] See below, § 15.9(iv), regarding the mens rea for conspiracy to defraud.

[182] "Mens Rea in Statutory Conspiracy: (3) Some Answers" [1978] *Crim LR* 210.

[183] [2006] UKHL 18, [2007] 1 AC 18, paras. 16–21 (Lord Nicholls).

substantive offence. Recklessness, even of the *Cunningham* variety,[184] as regards the actus reus of the substantive offence will not suffice for conspiracy. Suppose D and E agree to cut down a tree that they think may belong either to E or to V. Should it be the case that the ownership of the tree is V's, destruction of the tree by D and E would constitute criminal damage on their part, recklessness being sufficient culpability for the offence.[185] Yet there would not be a conspiracy to commit criminal damage: they would neither know[186] nor intend that the tree belongs to V.

The rule is different concerning any mens rea ingredients of the substantive offence that are ulterior where those ingredients are unrelated to the actus reus.[187] To be guilty of a conspiracy in respect of such an offence, D and E must themselves also satisfy those ulterior mental elements, even if they involve recklessness. So, for example, if D and E are charged with conspiracy to commit criminal damage being reckless as to whether life is endangered, since it need not be proved that life is actually endangered, this need not be intended or known, and recklessness as to endangerment suffices.

(e) Future facts

Under the terms of section 1(2), D must intend or know that "facts or circumstances necessary for the commission of [the substantive offence] shall or will exist at the time when the conduct constituting the offence is to take place". Clearly, it is possible to intend a future fact or circumstance. If D invites V for dinner on 1 November, he intends to have dinner with V on that day. Suppose that D and E agree to invite V to dinner on the 1st and to kill him when he comes on that day. D and E are guilty of conspiracy to murder as they intend a fact necessary for the commission of the crime—the presence of V for dinner—to occur.

Ordinarily, however, one would not say that D knows V will come to dinner on 1 November, at least until V responds affirmatively to the invitation. It is therefore possible to conceive of situations where D and E plan to kill V and it cannot be said that they intend or know of V's necessary presence. For example, suppose that D and E are aware that V always drives home by either route A or route B. They agree that, should V take route B on 1 November, they will intercept him and kill him. Strictly, they cannot *intend* the presence of V unless they have (or think they have) some means of influencing V to take route B. Moreover, they do not *know* which route V will take. Accordingly, on a literal interpretation of section 1(2), there is no conspiracy.

Such a literal interpretation would seriously undermine the law of conspiracy. As we saw earlier, when discussing conditional agreements (§ 9.3(ii)(c)), the successful implementation of agreements will often require the presence of facts or circumstances which can be neither known nor intended when the agreement is struck. Since it is generally not possible to "know" the future outcome of unresolved contingencies,[188] the interpretation of intend becomes crucial. It is submitted that, for the purpose of section 1(2), D's "intention"

---

[184] [1957] 2 QB 396.

[185] Criminal Damage Act 1971, s. 1(1).

[186] For general discussion of knowledge as a culpability term in criminal law, see Shute, "Knowledge and Belief in the Criminal Law" and Sullivan, "Knowledge, Belief and Culpability" in Shute and Simester (eds.), *Criminal Law Theory: Doctrines of the General Part* (2002) 184 and 207 respectively.

[187] *Saik* [2006] UKHL 18, [2007] 1 AC 18, para. 4 (Lord Nicholls).

[188] Above, § 5.4. Cf. *Sunair Holidays Ltd* [1973] 2 All ER 1233, where the Court of Appeal held that D could not be taken to "know" the existence of a future, contingent fact (the date of completion of a swimming-pool).

must embrace the preconditions of that intention, such that D should be taken to intend the existence of those facts or circumstances which he contemplates as necessary for the commission of the intended substantive offence.[189]

Subject to that qualification, whatever the mens rea requirements for the substantive offence, or the lack thereof, to be convicted of conspiracy D must know of or intend the presence of any material circumstances necessary for proof of the substantive offence. The decision in *Sakavicas*[190] is, however, in flat contradiction of this statement of the law. The money-laundering offences at issue in that case required proof of knowledge or suspicion of the illegal provenance of the funds: the Court of Appeal held that D and E were guilty of conspiracy to commit these offences on the basis of their suspicion that the funds they agreed to process were the proceeds of drug trafficking or other illegal activity. Happily, we need not consider the tortuous reasoning behind the decision.[191] In *Saik*,[192] the House of Lords ruled that, even where liability for an offence could be incurred without knowledge on the part of the person committing it of any particular fact or circumstance necessary for the commission of the offence, section 1(2) of the 1977 Act required proof that any conspirator knew or intended that the fact or circumstance "shall or will" exist when the conspiracy was put into effect. Baroness Hale, dissenting, considered that D would intend in a conditional sense the fact of the illegal provenance of the funds if he agreed to accept them for changing into another currency despite his suspicions.[193] But the concept of conditional intent is best reserved for where D resolves a course of action subject to a contingency as in, "I will steal that necklace if those are real diamonds". To adapt the concept in the manner of Baroness Hale is to render it a synonym for suspicion.

Special mention should be made of cases involving conspiracies to import or deal in controlled drugs. It seems that, if D takes himself to be agreeing to the importation of a Class A drug, he will be liable for conspiracy to import a Class B or C drug if that is what his co-conspirators take themselves to have agreed.[194] Even though importation of a Class A drug is a different offence from importation of a Class B or Class C drug, the mens rea for each different importation offence is the same. It suffices that there was awareness that the item in possession was some form of contraband.[195] Yet, strictly speaking, D neither knew nor intended the existence of the facts necessary for the commission of this lesser offence. The finding of conspiracy to commit the lesser offence can be defended if we are prepared to say in this context that the greater offence can comprehend the lesser offence, so that an intention to import a Class A drug can be taken to be an intent to import a Class B or Class C drug.

---

[189] Such an interpretation must underlie decisions such as *O'Hadhmaill* [1996] Crim LR 509 (CA), discussed above in § 9.3(ii)(c). In that case, D and others agreed to resume a bombing campaign if and when a ceasefire was revoked. Strictly, they could neither have known nor intended that hostilities would restart (the matter was not for them to decide). Their conviction for conspiracy indicates that it was enough for them to *contemplate* circumstances whereupon their agreement would take effect.

[190] [2004] EWCA Crim 2686 and see too *Ali* [2005] EWCA Crim 87.

[191] Expertly and critically dissected by Ormerod, "Making Sense of Mens Rea in Statutory Conspiracies" [2006] *Current Legal Problems* 185, an analysis endorsed by Lord Nicholls in *Saik* [2006] UKHL 18, [2007] 1 AC 18, para. 37.

[192] *Ibid.* See also *Suchedina* [2006] EWCA Crim 2543, [2007] 1 Cr App R 23; *K* [2007] EWCA Crim 1888, [2008] 1 Cr App R 1.

[193] *Ibid.*, paras. 97–100.

[194] *Patel*, unreported, 7 August 1991 (CA), transcript 89/4351/51; *Taylor* [2002] Crim LR 205.

[195] *Taafe* [1984] AC 539.

(f) Mens rea for statutory conspiracy—a summary

It may be helpful to summarise our conclusions on the mental element required for conspiracy:

(i)   D must intend that the agreement to which she is a party should be carried out.

(ii)   D must intend or know of the existence of any fact or circumstance necessary for the commission of the agreed offence.

(iii)   Where a fact or circumstance necessary for the commission of the agreed offence is not in existence at the time of the agreement, D must intend or know that any such fact or circumstance will exist at the time the offence takes place.

(iv)   If D is to be guilty of conspiracy, at least one other party to the agreement must satisfy conditions (i) through (iii) above.

(v)   It is not necessary for D to intend to play any active part in carrying out the agreement.

(g) Reform of the mens rea of conspiracy

The Law Commission[196] has reviewed the appropriate mens rea for conspiracy relating to the circumstance elements of the substantive offence and has recommended that it should be reformed so that: (i) where the substantive offence requires proof of no fault or only negligence as regards circumstance elements, it should be sufficient to prove recklessness as regards such elements for the conspiracy; and (ii) where the substantive offence requires proof of subjective fault as regards circumstance elements, that fault element should also apply as regards such elements for the conspiracy.

The adoption of such a reform to the law of conspiracy would be a significant change. It would result in an approach to mens rea which has sometimes been adopted for attempt[197] and would avoid the artificial restriction of a conspiracy to where D and E intended or knew that a relevant circumstance would or does exist, for there is culpability in agreeing to do something suspecting that the circumstance might exist and a need for social protection in such circumstances. Further, the line between conditional intent and recklessness is already narrow and increasingly difficult to draw, making the case for recognising recklessness for conspiracy even stronger.

The significance of this reform is illustrated by conspiracy to rape. As the law stands, for D and E to be guilty of conspiracy to rape they must intend one of them to have sex with V intending or knowing that V would not be consenting to intercourse. This would be particularly difficult to prove. However, since the mens rea of rape is absence of reasonable belief in consent—a form of negligence—if the law of conspiracy was reformed as the Law Commission recommends, D and E could be convicted of conspiracy to rape if they suspected that there was a possibility that V might not be consenting. An agreement to have sex even if V might not be consenting is properly characterised as a criminal conspiracy. Similarly, the effect of this reform would be that the defendant in *Saik* would be guilty of conspiring to launder money if he suspected that the money might be the proceeds of crime, since suspicion is the applicable mens rea for the substantive offence.

---

[196] Law Com. No. 318, *Conspiracy and Attempts* (2009) paras. 2.137 and 2.146.

[197] Below, § 9.4(iii)(b); although it is inconsistent with the approach to the mens rea for attempt recognised by the Court of Appeal in *Pace* [2014] EWCA Crim 186, [2014] 1 WLR 2867.

(v) D's co-conspirators: some limitations

Once it has been proved that D is a party to an agreement to commit a crime and is possessed of the necessary mens rea, and that at least one other party to the agreement has mens rea, liability for conspiracy will normally ensue against D and any other party with mens rea. However, liability will not arise if that other party is the only other party to the agreement and is either (a) D's spouse or civil partner; (b) a person under the age of criminal responsibility; (c) a victim of the intended substantive offence; or (d) a limited company. We must also consider the position (e) when the only other party to the agreement is acquitted.

(a) Spouses and civil partners

It was probably a rule at common law that an agreement between a husband and wife alone to commit a crime did not constitute a conspiracy. The common law was based upon the legal fiction that husband and wife constituted a single legal person.[198] In R,[199] the House of Lords decided that the same fiction no longer had any role to play in providing the husband with a defence to a charge of raping his wife. The view expressed in R, that this fiction was fundamentally at odds with the status of women in modern English life, is of general application and in principle would enable common law conspiracy charges to be brought on the basis of agreements confined to a husband and wife.[200] However, section 2(2) of the Criminal Law Act 1977 expressly provides that an agreement confined to a spouse or to a civil partner[201] will not constitute a statutory conspiracy.

This provision had been endorsed by the Law Commission as safeguarding "the stability of marriage".[202] One might think there are more serious threats to a marriage than conspiracy charges and, in any event, one spouse may be charged as a secondary party to the other spouse's crimes should the conspiracy be carried out. A spouse may also incur liability under section 4 of the Criminal Law Act 1967 if anything is done with intent to impede the apprehension or prosecution of the principal offender. Be that as it may, section 2(2) is unequivocal. Its terms are, however, confined to agreements where the parties are the spouse or civil partners alone. Should they be joined by any other party, such as a child of the marriage over the age of criminal responsibility, all parties will be liable for conspiracy.[203] The immunity in respect of conspiracy is anomalous and anachronistic but is undeniably part of the modern law of statutory conspiracy. The Law Commission has acknowledged that spousal immunity is out-dated and has recommended its removal.[204]

---

[198] *CLGP* 799–803.

[199] [1992] 1 AC 599.

[200] There is no English decision which rules that husband and wife cannot conspire at common law, although there is a statement to that effect in Hawkins 1 PC, ch. 27, § 8 and dicta in *Mawji* v. *R.* [1957] AC 126 (PC). In the civil law, a husband and wife can conspire: *Midland Bank Trust Co Ltd* v. *Green (No 3)* [1979] Ch 496.

[201] Civil Partnership Act 2004, sched. 27. The exception does not apply to agreements between "de facto" partners, who are living together as a couple but not in a formal marriage or civil partnership: *Suski* [2016] EWCA Crim 24.

[202] Law Com. No. 76, *Conspiracy and Criminal Law Reform* (1976) paras. 1.46–1.49.

[203] *Chrastny* [1991] 1 WLR 1381.

[204] Law Com. No. 318, *Conspiracy and Attempts* (2009) para. 5.16.

(b) Persons under the age of criminal responsibility

Section 2(2) further provides that D will not be guilty of conspiracy if the only other person with whom he agrees is a person under the age of criminal responsibility. If E is the only other party to the agreement and is under the age of 10, E has a complete defence to a charge of statutory conspiracy.[205] Section 2(2) makes it clear that, in such cases, D too is exempt from liability in conspiracy. It is not obvious why E's lack of criminal capacity should also provide immunity for D if E was capable of entering into an agreement with an intention that the agreement be carried out. However, arguably persons under 10 are generally incapable in any meaningful sense of making criminal agreements; if so, one way of justifying the subsection is to see it as a form of conclusive presumption against the existence of the actus reus of conspiracy. On that view, there would be no agreement to which D can be a party in any case where E, the only other party, is under 10. The Law Commission has recommended that this rule should not be changed,[206] but has recognised that the adult D could be guilty of encouraging or assisting a conspiracy, since the Law Commission considers that it is sufficient that D has done an act which is capable of encouraging or assisting the offence, it being irrelevant that this substantive offence has not been and cannot be committed because E is under 10.[207] It is not, however, clear that any of the assisting or encouraging offences will have been committed in such circumstances, because D will not have committed an act which is capable of assisting or encouraging an offence to be committed by E, since E lacks the capacity to commit any such offence.

(c) Where the only other party is a victim

At common law, where E would otherwise be party to a conspiracy with D, E will not be liable if she is to be regarded as the victim of the agreed crime. So, in *Tyrrell*,[208] E, a girl under the age of 14, was not a conspirator with D in the crime of unlawful sexual intercourse despite her readiness to participate. Section 2(2) confirms this immunity for statutory conspiracy. It also provides that D, too, is not liable for statutory conspiracy if the only other party to the agreement is an "intended victim" of the agreed offence.

It is difficult to appreciate why, in principle, this should be so. If E, notwithstanding her victim status, possesses the capacity to enter agreements with intent that they be carried out, there is a sufficient actus reus for D's liability to be assessed by reference to his own culpability. The rule in *Tyrrell* is protective of victims and, it is submitted, should confer no immunity on non-victim participants in the criminal activity. The effect of section 2(2) is to pass on the protection accorded to victims to persons who are fully accountable for the agreements they enter.

The range of persons who fall within the category of victim is not defined by the Act. At common law, in the context of immunity from charges of complicity and conspiracy, a "victim" has always been a member of a defined, vulnerable class, such as a young person below the age of consent or a statutorily protected tenant.[209] The absence of such

---

[205] The defence of infancy is discussed below, § 19.4.
[206] Law Com. No. 318, *Conspiracy and Attempts* (2009) para. 5.39.
[207] See above, § 9(2)(i)(e).
[208] [1894] 1 QB 710. See above, § 7.6(iv)(a).
[209] *Grace Rymer Investment* v. *Waite* [1958] Ch 831.

limiting characteristics specified in section 2(2)—there is simply an unqualified reference to "intended victim"—invites consideration whether the term is to be taken in a broader sense. This was considered by the Supreme Court in *Gnango*,[210] where Lords Phillips and Judge[211] recognised that the word "victim" might be interpreted broadly to mean any person who would be harmed by the offence. They went on, however, to emphasise that the word "victim" in section 2(2) had not previously received judicial consideration and the adoption of the broad interpretation could produce surprising results. For example, an agreement between D and E to commit a terrorist atrocity by E acting as a suicide bomber would not be a criminal conspiracy, because E would be characterised as a victim since he was intended to be killed. Similarly, a conspiracy between D and E to set fire to E's house fraudulently to obtain insurance money would not be a conspiracy, because E would suffer property damage and so would be characterised as a victim. In the light of such results, Lords Phillips and Judge suggested that "victim" for the purposes of section 2(2) should be interpreted narrowly so as to be confined to the person who was intended to be protected by the offence. This would be consistent with the interpretation of "victim" for the crimes of assisting and encouraging[212] and for complicity.[213] Further, as the policy of the provision is questionable, a narrow interpretation of "victim" should be adopted, and, preferably, and as the Law Commission has recommended, it should exempt the victim and not any other party to the conspiracy.[214]

The express provision in section 2(2) for the cases of infants (above, § 9.3(v)(b)) and for victims indicates that D will otherwise be liable for conspiracy in any situation where the only other party to the agreement is exempt from prosecution on some other ground (provided the ground of exemption is compatible with the capacity to enter an agreement with the intention that it be carried out). An illustration from the common law is provided by *Duguid*,[215] where D agreed with E, the mother of a child, to remove the child from the possession of the lawful guardian. Had the agreement been carried out, D would have been liable for an offence under section 56 of the Offences against the Person Act 1861, but not E, as it was provided that a mother could not be prosecuted for taking her own child. It was held that E's immunity from prosecution for the substantive offence did not preclude D from being convicted for conspiracy to commit the offence. The same should follow for statutory conspiracy.

(d) Limited companies

The position of limited companies as parties to conspiracies is not dealt with by the Act. It may be assumed that the common law rules will continue to apply in statutory conspiracy.

Companies, as legal persons with an identity, separate from that of shareholders and directors,[216] may commit crimes in their own right. It has been held that companies may

---

[210] [2011] UKSC 59, [2012] 1 AC 827.

[211] *Ibid.*, para. 49.

[212] Serious Crime Act 2007, s. 51; above, § 9.2(iii)(c). This is also the recommendation of the Law Commission: Law Com. No. 318, *Conspiracy and Attempts* (2009) para. 5.35.

[213] *Gnango* [2011] UKSC 59, [2012] 1 AC 827; above, § 7.6(iv)(a).

[214] Law Com. No. 318, *Conspiracy and Attempts* (2009) para. 5.35.

[215] (1906) 70 JP 294.

[216] *Salomon v. Salomon* [1897] AC 22 (HL).

become parties to conspiracies provided an agreement on behalf of the company is made by a person sufficiently senior to be identified with the company.[217] In *McDonnell*,[218] Nield J ruled there was no conspiracy where D, the managing director and sole shareholder in E Ltd, arranged the tax affairs of E Ltd so as to evade fraudulently the payment of corporation tax. For Nield J, conspiracy required the involvement of at least two human agents; he rejected the view that E Ltd could be regarded as possessing a mind separate from D's as "too artificial".

It may be noted that if, in *McDonnell*, D had enlisted the help of, say, F, an accountant, to create the fraudulent scheme of corporate tax evasion, a conviction of D, F, and E Ltd for conspiracy to evade corporation tax would have been possible. Yet a conviction of E Ltd for conspiracy in those circumstances would involve the same degree of artificiality which the learned judge found unacceptable on the facts of *McDonnell*. The conviction of E Ltd would be on the basis that D's agreement with F entailed the agreement of E Ltd. Whenever a company is convicted of conspiracy, an artificial duality is involved, since the state of mind of D (a person of requisite seniority) is not merely her own state of mind but, additionally, a state of mind attributable to the company. The same logic can be carried over to one-person companies, as the Privy Council decision in *Lee* v. *Lee's Air Farming*,[219] a civil case, demonstrates. In the civil law it is possible to identify a conspiracy where the company is alleged to have conspired with only one human agent, who is the very person identified with that company;[220] there is no reason of principle or logic why the position in criminal law should be any different. By virtue of the separate identity of the sole shareholder and the company, it would be appropriate for the criminal law to follow civil law so that a conspiracy between the sole shareholder and the company should result in liability under both regimes.[221]

(e) Acquittal of the only other party

Suppose that D and E are jointly tried for conspiracy and no other persons are alleged to have conspired with them. At one time the common law rule was that the acquittal of one of the alleged conspirators entailed the acquittal of the other. The reasoning behind this rule was that the acquittal of one conspirator and the conviction of the other in circumstances where only two persons had been charged with conspiracy would be incompatible with the requirement that two or more parties are necessary to constitute a conspiracy. The rule was criticised for confusing the requirements of formal legal proof with actual facts in the world. It may be the case, for example, that a confession or hearsay evidence is admissible against D but not against E,[222] resulting in proof beyond reasonable doubt against D but not against E. This criticism of the common law proved decisive for the House of Lords in

---

[217] *Kent and Sussex Contractors Ltd* [1944] KB 146.

[218] [1966] 1 QB 233. See also *AAH Pharmaceuticals* v. *Birdi* [2011] EWHC 1625 (QB), para. 31 (Coulson J).

[219] [1961] AC 12 (PC). It was held that Mr Lee could be identified with his company in his capacity as managing director and could be regarded as an employee, under the direction of the company, in his capacity as the company's one and only pilot. According to Lord Morris, "such is the logic of *Salomon*".

[220] *Barclay Pharmaceuticals Ltd* v. *Waypharm LP* [2012] EWHC 306 (Comm), paras. 227–9 (Gloster J); *Twentieth Century Fox Film Corp.* v. *Harris* [2014] EWHC 1568 (Ch), para. 151 (Barling J).

[221] Virgo, "'We Do This in the Criminal Law and That in the Law of Tort': A New Fusion Debate" in Pitel, Neyers and Chamberlain (eds.), *Tort Law: Challenging Orthodoxy* (2013) 95, 114.

[222] *CLGP* 678–9.

DPP v. *Shannon*.[223] Thereafter, the acquittal of one party to the conspiracy was no bar to the conviction of the other even for cases where only two parties were alleged to have formed a conspiracy. The Criminal Law Act 1977, in section 5(8) and (9), confirms the rule in *Shannon* for both statutory and common law conspiracies.

(vi) Conspiracies involving the commission of more than one offence

Section 1(1) of the Criminal Law Act 1977 refers to a course of conduct involving "the commission of any offence or *offences*", indicating that a course of conduct charged as a single conspiracy may have as its objective the commission of two or more offences. It is even permissible for a number of offences of differing degrees of seriousness to be charged in a single conspiracy; provided it can be proved against each conspirator that she agreed to the commission of the most serious offences referred to in the indictment. The effect of this proviso can be seen in *Roberts*,[224] where there was evidence that some of the defendants had agreed to acts of aggravated criminal damage whereas other defendants had agreed only to acts of simple criminal damage. The Court of Appeal ruled that the defendants in the latter group were not parties to the conspiracy as charged, namely to commit aggravated criminal damage. Presumably, they would have been parties if the indictment had charged only a conspiracy to commit acts of simple criminal damage.

When an agreement to commit two or more crimes is charged as a single conspiracy, particular care must be taken not to bring into association parties who are not truly partners in the same objectives. D and E may agree to rob V and W banks but decide that they will need the assistance of F with a further robbery of X bank. Accordingly, they enlist F for the X bank project. In a trial where only D and E are the defendants, the most appropriate course may be to charge D and E with a single conspiracy to rob V, W, and X banks. Such a course may be more economical of court-time and provide a jury with a better overall perspective of their wrongdoing. If F is joined too as a defendant, he may only properly be charged with conspiring to rob X bank, thus precluding the use against him of evidence that relates only to the robbery of V and W banks.

Although multi-offence conspiracies may be charged as a single conspiracy, there is nothing to preclude several, distinct conspiracy charges. In *Lavercombe*,[225] D and E agreed to buy cannabis in Thailand for importing into the United Kingdom. Although already convicted in Thailand for conspiracy to possess cannabis, the Court of Appeal confirmed their liability for conspiracy to import cannabis into the United Kingdom. Since there were two distinct offences there could be two distinct conspiracies and it was immaterial that both conspiracies were constituted by the one agreement on a course of conduct.

(vii) Conspiracy to commit murder—duress

Duress is not a defence to murder, either for a principal or for an accessory,[226] nor to attempted murder.[227] It has, however, been recognised that duress is a defence to conspiracy

---

[223] [1975] AC 717.
[224] [1998] 1 Cr App R 441.
[225] [1988] Crim LR 435.
[226] *Howe* [1987] AC 417. Below, § 22.3.
[227] *Gotts* [1992] 2 AC 412 (HL).

to commit murder,[228] apparently because conspiracy is considered to be more remote from the completed offence than attempt,[229] so there is greater opportunity for repentance and failure. Consequently, duress should also be a defence to assisting or encouraging murder. If focus is placed on the culpability of D, this distinction in the operation of the defence of duress is difficult to defend, because for each inchoate offence relating to murder there must be an intention that V be killed. It was because the mens rea for attempted murder is an intention to kill that duress was denied to that offence, and conspiracy to commit murder requires a similar intent. But, if the focus is placed on potential harm, that harm is more remote where there is a conspiracy to murder rather than an attempt, so it is possible to distinguish between the different inchoate offences, although this is artificial.[230] It would be preferable to allow the defence of duress in respect of all inchoate offences to commit murder, and even to murder itself.[231]

(viii) Conspiracy—an unnecessary offence?

If statutory conspiracy were to be abolished,[232] persons who agreed to commit a crime would be beyond the reach of the criminal law only until they encouraged or assisted others to commit crimes, committed some offence of a preliminary or possessory kind by way of preparation for the offence agreed, or engaged in conduct sufficiently proximate to the substantive offence to constitute an attempt. The ground covered by conspiracy and conspiracy alone is narrow and it may be non-existent following the enactment of the Serious Crime Act 2007. The only possible ground covered exclusively by conspiracy is limited to some non-consummated agreements where D's agreement with E that E should commit a crime does not constitute any form of encouragement or assistance in relation to the projected offence; usually the very act of making an agreement will constitute some form of encouragement in respect of the commission of the substantive offence and so be covered by the Serious Crime Act 2007. In practical terms, such conspiracies that have manifested themselves in nothing more than the fact of agreement are rarely prosecuted. Such bare agreements will seldom come to light, since criminals do not plan their crimes on the public record. Typically, evidence of a conspiracy is inferred from concerted criminal activity.[233] Moreover, when a crime has been committed, anyone who has agreed to its commission will, almost invariably, be an accomplice of the principal offenders. It may be doubted whether it is worth retaining such a complex body of law merely to proscribe non-consummated agreements.

Against that view, those who wish to retain conspiracy would argue that multi-party agreements to commit crimes are more dangerous and subversive than commitments to crime on the part of individuals.[234] There is a degree of plausibility in that claim, especially because, after a period when prosecutions were seldom brought in respect of conspiracies

---

[228] *Ness and Awan* [2011] Crim LR 645.

[229] *Gotts* [1991] 1 QB 660, 668 (Lord Lane CJ).

[230] *Ness and Awan* [2011] Crim LR 645, para. 29 (McCombe J).

[231] See Law Commission, *Murder, Manslaughter and Infanticide* No. 304 (2006), Part 6.

[232] Johnson, "The Unnecessary Crime of Conspiracy" (1973) 61 *Cal LR* 1137; Dennis, "The Rationale of Criminal Conspiracy" (1977) 93 *LQR* 39.

[233] *Mulcahy* (1868) LR 3 HL 306, 317; *Hammersley* (1958) 42 Cr App R 207.

[234] *Griffiths* [1966] 1 QB 589.

which did not result in the commission of substantive offences, non-consummated conspiracies are increasingly prosecuted as, for example, terrorist conspiracies to cause explosions which are intercepted by police at a preparatory stage. A joint trial of principals and accomplices in respect of the substantive offences actually committed or attempted enables the prosecution to lay appropriate stress on the dangers that may be posed by well-organised criminal activity.

At common law, conspiracy was employed for what has been described as its "useful elasticity". When conspiracy was entirely a common law crime, prosecutors were allowed to use conspiracy charges to evade time limits, sentencing restrictions, and procedural requirements imposed in respect of particular statutory offences. Happily such elasticity is no longer permitted; the Criminal Law Act 1977 ensures that the penalty for conspiracy cannot exceed that imposed for the substantive offence[235] and that any time or procedural requirements associated with the substantive offence equally apply to conspiracies to commit that offence.[236] As we noted at the outset of our discussion of conspiracy, one form of elasticity remains. It is still the case that some forms of conduct which would not be criminal if perpetrated by an individual may become criminal at common law if done in pursuance of an agreement by two or more persons, most notably in conspiracy to defraud.[237] It is very much a matter for regret that the Fraud Act 2006 did not abolish conspiracy to defraud despite the Law Commission's intention that it should.[238]

Supporters of conspiracy charges emphasise their procedural and evidential advantages. Following an allegation of conspiracy, each alleged conspirator may be treated as the agent of his co-defendants. Accordingly, evidence pertaining to one particular defendant becomes admissible against all other defendants for the purposes of the conspiracy charge that yokes them together.[239] Conspiracy counts, it is claimed, give proper emphasis to the group character of multi-party offending and allow the jury a clearer, more rounded, picture of what the defendants have done.[240] This is particularly useful, it is said, where the role played by one or more of the parties in the perpetration of the substantive offences is unclear. Yet, as Professor Glanville Williams pointed out many years ago, these benefits are equally accessible if defendants are charged with being each other's accomplices,[241] although that depends on establishing the commission of a substantive offence by the principal. It is habit of mind and long-standing practice that favours recourse to conspiracy rather than any unique advantage that the charge brings.

The Law Commission reviewed the law of conspiracy, particularly in the light of the creation of inchoate offences of encouragement and assistance, and concluded that there is still a role for the offence.[242] The Law Commission did, however, find the existing offence

---

[235] Criminal Law Act 1977, s. 3.

[236] *Ibid.*, s. 4.

[237] Below, § 15.9.

[238] Law Com. Consultation Paper No. 155, *Fraud and Deception* (1999).

[239] Cf. *Griffiths* [1966] 1 QB 589.

[240] *Cox and Mead, The Times*, 6 December 1984, discussed in Law Com. No. 104, *Conspiracy to Defraud* (1987) para. 6.6; *Simmonds* [1969] 1 QB 685, 690.

[241] *The Proof of Guilt* (2nd ed., 1958) chap. 9.

[242] Law Com. No. 318, *Conspiracy and Attempts* (2009). See further LCCP No. 183, *Conspiracy and Attempts* (2007) Part 2.

wanting in certain respects. As has already been observed, it has proposed amending the mens rea of the offence and certain aspects of the law concerning which parties can be exempt from liability. Further, from a desire to attain some measure of consistency between conspiracy and the offences of assistance and encouragement, it has recommended that the defence of acting reasonably should be available for conspiracy in the same form as it appears in section 50 of the Serious Crime Act 2007.[243] Whilst consistency between the inchoate offences is desirable, the case for consistency is less strong when the defence of acting reasonably is so far from satisfactory.[244]

§ 9.4 Attempt

The inchoate offence of attempt[245] penalises conduct which is sufficiently proximate to the commission of an indictable offence, when done with intent to commit that offence. At common law, attempt was a complex, vacillating body of law.[246] Considerable, albeit imperfect, simplification has been achieved by the Criminal Attempts Act 1981, which abolishes the common law offence and replaces it with the following statutory offence contained in section 1:[247]

> If, with intent to commit an offence to which this section applies, a person does an act which is more than merely preparatory to the commission of the offence, he is guilty of an attempt to commit the offence.

The most obvious justification for having a general law of attempts is to allow the timely prevention of future criminal harms. A concern with harms yet to be realised can be seen even in the early development of the common law. For instance, burglary, from its emergence in the twelfth century, penalised individuals who entered walled cities or inhabited premises at night with felonious intent. The threat to security from such entry called for intervention; it was not necessary to demonstrate that the felony D had in mind ultimately was committed.[248] Likewise, the offence of assault was devised to proscribe threats of immediate violence, supplementing the earlier offence of battery which penalised the actual use of force.[249] The crime of attempt itself, dealing in general terms with threatened harms, did not emerge until much later. We owe to the Star Chamber the notion that, if a crime exists, it is also an offence to attempt to commit that crime.[250] This idea was received into the common law and by the early nineteenth century it was possible to speak in terms of a general common law crime of attempt,[251] now replaced by the present statutory offence.

---

[243] *Ibid.*, para. 6.56.
[244] Above, § 9.2(iii)(b).
[245] Duff, *Criminal Attempts* (1996).
[246] See the definitive account in *CLGP*, chap. 14.
[247] The Act broadly gives effect to the recommendations in Law Com. No. 102, *Attempt and Impossibility in Relation to Attempt, Conspiracy and Incitement* (1980).
[248] Kenny, *Outlines of the Criminal Law* (1902) 170–1.
[249] Hawkins, *Pleas of the Crown*, chap. 62, § 1.
[250] Stephen, *History of the Criminal Law of England* (1883) vol. 2, 221–3.
[251] *Higgins* (1801) 2 East 5, 102 ER 269.

(i) Actus reus: the requirement of proximity

Resolving when conduct is sufficiently close to the commission of an offence to constitute an attempt has been a matter of intractable difficulty for English law.[252] It would be unfair to characterise this failure to devise a simple and clear test of proximity as a matter of judicial ineptitude. Ordinary language supplies little help in distinguishing conduct that is merely preparatory from conduct that is close enough to harm to constitute an attempt.[253] We would not say of D, a high jumper, that she was attempting to clear the bar until she had commenced her run-up to the jump. We can assume a general agreement that earlier conduct (warm-up, removal of track suit, etc.) is conduct preliminary to an attempt to clear the bar. Thereafter, dispute may arise. Some may argue that an attempt to clear the bar does not begin until D launches herself upwards, whereas others may insist that we are within the ambit of an attempt once the run-up commences. In terms of the rules of athletic competitions, the latter group would win the argument if the rule for competitions is that a run-up to the bar, however faltering and incomplete, constitutes an attempt at a jump. It will be readily appreciated that this rule would be a matter of stipulation and does not rest on any "correct" view of what, in any natural or philosophical sense, constitutes an attempt at jumping obstacles.

(a) The proximity requirement at common law

Unsurprisingly, the common law failed to identify a general test of sufficient proximity. Consensus on a test for proximity has been undermined by an unresolved tension between the claims of social protection, on the one hand, and an insistence that criminal liability should be confined to those who have perpetrated some wrongful deed, on the other. The latter approach was given its best expression in what was known as the "last act" test.[254] Under that test, D would not be liable for the attempted murder of V until, say, she had aimed the gun and squeezed the trigger (i.e. D had done the last act required of her to commit the crime). The test has its attractions. It allows certainty of application and confines liability to those who have perpetrated a wrong.[255] From the perspective of V, however, the test has grave limitations. Provided we can be sure that D has resolved to kill V, there is much to be said for intervening and stopping D well before V's life is imperilled by D's actually firing at him.

Such concerns were reflected in alternative formulations to the last act test such as the "substantial step"[256] test and the "unequivocal act" test.[257] Under the substantial step test, D could be convicted of attempted arson on the basis of, say, walking towards a haystack with matches in his pocket (should it be proved that he intended to set fire to the stack). Objections to D's conviction can be raised on the basis that, until he strikes a match in order to ignite the stack, he has done nothing wrong; there is nothing reprehensible about walking

---

[252] Duff, *Criminal Attempts* (1996) chap. 2; Smith, "Proximity in Attempt: Lord Lane's Midway Course" [1991] *Crim LR* 576; Stuart, "The Actus Reus in Attempts" [1970] *Crim LR* 505.

[253] For instructive discussion see Duff, *Criminal Attempts* (1996) 33–5.

[254] *Eagleton* (1855) 6 Cox CC 559.

[255] Assuming, as we do, that D can do wrong though she causes no material harm (even in the sense of alarm and apprehension). D does wrong if she fires at V, even if V remains unaware of D's actions.

[256] *Roberts* (1855) Dears 539, 169 ER 836.

[257] *Davey v. Lee* [1968] 1 QB 366.

in a field with matches in one's pocket.[258] An additional objection is that convictions in such circumstances may be unduly dependent on confession evidence. The "unequivocal act" test addressed these concerns. Under its terms, in our arson example, D would not commit attempted arson until his extrinsic conduct indicated in the clearest terms that his immediate project was arson. In application, however, this test was not consistently or strictly applied, and resort to D's state of mind was permitted to resolve the ambiguities of his conduct.[259]

(b) The proximity requirement under statute

No particular test achieved primacy at common law, although it is fair to say that the predominant trend in the thirty years or so prior to the Criminal Attempts Act 1981 was toward a restrictive rather than expansive approach to the test of sufficient proximity.[260] Following the recommendations of the Law Commission, the Criminal Attempts Act 1981 dispenses with any formal legal test of proximity. Instead, it addresses the proximity issue in terms of a question of fact to be placed before the jury: did D do an act which was "more than merely preparatory to the commission of the offence"?[261]

The Act provides explicitly that whether an act by D is more than merely preparatory "is a question of fact"[262] to be answered by the jury, provided that there is evidence sufficient in law to support such a finding. Accordingly, a judge must satisfy herself that the prosecution has adduced enough evidence to support a finding that D's act was more than merely preparatory to the commission of an offence. If the judge is satisfied, the question of sufficient proximity is put to the jury who must then make their own decision on the issue. However compellingly obvious it may seem that particular conduct is more than merely preparatory, it is a misdirection for a judge to instruct a jury that they *must* find the actus reus is proved.[263]

(c) The approach in the cases

The long title to the Criminal Attempts Act 1981 indicates that the Act is to reform the previous law.[264] Accordingly, it would be reasonable to suppose that the common law on the issue of sufficient proximity was superseded. Despite this, in the early cases decided under the Act, reference was made to pre-Act case law when addressing the question of sufficient proximity.[265] By contrast, subsequent cases, most notably *Jones*,[266] have stressed that the words "more than merely preparatory" must be allowed their natural meaning and

---

[258] On this view, punishing D might well be regarded as a form of preventative detention and a violation of D's rights.

[259] In *Davey* v. *Lee* [1968] 1 QB 366, the Court of Criminal Appeal adopted the unequivocal act test and, at the same time, permitted resort to confession evidence in order to clarify D's otherwise ambiguous conduct.

[260] E.g. *Kyprianou* v. *Reynolds* [1969] Crim LR 656; *Comer* v. *Bloomfield* (1971) 55 Cr App R 305.

[261] Criminal Attempts Act 1981, s. 1(1).

[262] *Ibid.*, s. 4(3).

[263] See *Stonehouse* [1978] AC 55 (HL), which resolved the position under the common law. The reasoning in *Stonehouse* is *a fortiori* applicable to the position under the Criminal Attempts Act 1981 which provides explicitly that the question of proximity is one of fact.

[264] "An Act to amend the Law of England and Wales as to attempt to commit offences …"

[265] *Widdowsen* (1985) 82 Cr App R 314; *Boyle* (1987) 84 Cr App R 270.

[266] [1990] 3 All ER 886.

not be expansively or restrictively glossed by reference to cases decided before the Act. This seems now to be the law. It follows that an appellate court, when reviewing a conviction for attempt, must satisfy itself simply that there was sufficient evidence to sustain the finding that D's conduct was more than merely preparatory. On the face of it, that is a question of evaluating the facts of each particular case. In *Geddes*, however, Lord Bingham LJ introduced a degree of rigour into the question by insisting that the necessary proximity would not occur until D reached the stage of trying to commit the offence:[267]

> "It is, we think, an accurate paraphrase of the statutory test and not an illegitimate gloss upon it to ask whether the available evidence, if accepted, could show that a defendant has done an act which shows that he has actually tried to commit the offence in question, or whether he has only got ready or put himself in a position or equipped himself to do so."

In *Geddes*, D was a trespasser who was apprehended in a school lavatory while in possession of a knife, rope, and binding tape. There was compelling reason to believe that D intended to abduct a pupil of the school. D was charged with attempted false imprisonment, but, applying Lord Bingham's test, he was not guilty because he had not tried before his arrest to detain any victim.

In light of *Geddes*, it seems that a person does not reach the stage of trying to commit the offence until he broaches commission of the actus reus of the substantive offence,[268] as occurred in *Jones*,[269] where D was convicted of attempted murder upon unlocking the safety-catch and pointing a loaded firearm at V, and in *A-G's Reference (No. 1 of 1992)*,[270] where a conviction for attempted rape was upheld after D had thrown V to the ground and exposed his penis. In *Mason v. DPP*,[271] D's conviction for attempting to drive a motor vehicle while under the influence of alcohol was quashed where D, being twice over the legal limit for alcohol, had opened his car door intending to drive the vehicle, which was then stolen from him. D was not considered to have embarked on the crime proper; he would have done had he managed to turn the engine on before the car was stolen. Similarly, in *Campbell*,[272] D, in possession of an imitation firearm, was arrested just before entering a Post Office which he intended to rob. The quashing of his conviction for attempted robbery followed from the fact that, however close he came to committing robbery, he had yet to commence those acts which would constitute theft by force—which is the actus reus of robbery.

Less easily explained in terms of Lord Bingham's test is *Tosti*.[273] D was observed concealing oxyacetylene equipment behind a hedge, approaching a barn door, and bending down to examine a padlock. His conviction for attempted burglary was sustained by the Court of Appeal, because, although his act was preparatory, it was not "merely" so. The

---

[267] [1996] Crim LR 894, 895. In *Gullefer* (1990) 91 Cr App R 356 the appropriate test had been described as being whether the defendant had "embarked on the crime proper".

[268] See Clarkson, "Attempt: The Conduct Requirement" (2009) 29 *OJLS* 25, 26, who concludes that in most cases there will have been an attempt where there has been a confrontation with the victim or property.

[269] (1990) 91 Cr App R 351 (CA). Contrast at common law, *Stevens v. R.* [1985] LRC (Crim) 17, noted (1986) 50 *J Crim L* 247.

[270] [1993] 2 All ER 190 (CA).

[271] [2009] EWHC 2198 (Admin).

[272] [1990] 93 Cr App R 350 (CA).

[273] [1997] Crim LR 746 (CA).

line dividing *Campbell* from *Tosti* may be considered so faint as to be invisible. It could, perhaps, be asserted that, by examining the padlock in *Tosti*, D was getting physically to grips with committing the crime itself, something that had yet to occur in *Campbell*. That at least was the view of Beldam LJ, who described the defendant in *Tosti* as taking "the first steps in the commission of the offence".[274]

Broadly, the approach to the question of sufficient proximity taken by Lord Bingham in *Geddes* is to be welcomed. In insisting that D must have commenced that series of acts which will constitute, if and when completed, the actus reus of the substantive offence, liability for attempt is confined to those who have demonstrated by their overt conduct that they are prepared to commit crimes. Moreover, a law of attempt cast in these restrictive terms is less dependent on confession evidence for convictions than would be the case under a more expansive test. To be sure, as in many areas of law, there will be decisions not easy to reconcile, as the contrasting decisions in *Campbell* and *Tosti* demonstrate. Yet, in general terms, the current law governing sufficient proximity in attempt is far more straightforward than it was under the common law, where incompatible legal tests competed for supremacy.

(ii) The scope of the actus reus of attempt

(a) Summary offences

To be guilty of an attempt, D must intend to commit an offence to which section 1 of the Criminal Attempts Act 1981 applies.[275] Section 1(4) of the Act provides that the offence must be an offence that would be triable in England and Wales as an indictable offence. In general terms, therefore, there is no offence of attempting to commit a summary offence. This must reflect the legislative view that attempts are systemically less serious than the perpetration of substantive offences and do not merit criminalisation where the substantive crime is of a minor nature. There are, however, a number of specific statutory offences of attempting to commit particular summary offences.[276] Despite this, the offence of attempted battery was recognised in *Nelson*,[277] even though the substantive offence is a summary offence.[278] This was because, exceptionally, battery (and common assault) can be tried on indictment where it is part of a series of offences of the same or similar character as an indictable offence.[279]

(b) Attempt, conspiracy, and complicity

Section 1(4) additionally provides that the offence of attempt does not apply to common law or statutory conspiracy, nor aiding, abetting, counselling, procuring, or suborning the commission of an offence. The reasoning lying behind these exceptions appears, in the case of conspiracy, to be its remoteness from any substantive offence and, in the case of secondary participation, because of the need to avoid unprincipled results arising from the

---

[274] *Ibid.*, 747.

[275] Section 1(1).

[276] Section 3 of the Criminal Attempts Act 1981 provides that, if any special statutory provision permits a charge of attempt in respect of a summary offence, liability for such an attempt will be governed by the same principles that apply to charges of attempt brought under the 1981 Act.

[277] [2013] EWCA Crim 30, [2013] 1 Cr App R 30.

[278] Criminal Justice Act 1988, s. 39.

[279] *Ibid.*, s. 40.

peculiar nature of secondary liability. Complicity is not an offence known to English law; rather, the accessory is convicted of the same offence as the principal. But where D has tried to assist or encourage P to commit a substantive offence, P may still have a number of acts still to do before that crime is committed, so that to say that D has attempted to commit that substantive offence, albeit as a secondary party, "stretches the language of attempts beyond acceptable limits".[280] If, for example, D had sent a gun to P to kill V but the police intercepted the gun before P could shoot V, it would be odd to convict D of attempting to assist P to commit murder as P could not even be convicted of attempted murder because she had not done a more than merely preparatory act towards the commission of that offence. If attempted complicity was confined instead to where the substantive offence had been committed but D failed to encourage or assist it, D's liability for attempt would be unprincipled. If, for example, P had committed murder as a principal but it could not be shown that D's act had assisted P to commit the crime (because, for example, the gun was sent to but not received by P), whether D had done a more than merely preparatory act towards being an accessory could not be determined at the point when D had sent the gun, but would depend on whether P had gone on to commit the substantive offence; adopting such a "wait and see" approach is not consistent with the principle which requires liability for attempt to be determined at the point of doing a more than merely preparatory act, and not in the light of subsequent events.[281] In both these cases it would now be possible to convict D, but by reference to the inchoate offence of assisting rather than complicity. In the example where D sent a gun to P but it was intercepted by the police, D had in fact committed the inchoate offence of assisting by doing an act which was capable of assisting the crime. If D had not supplied the gun to P but had done a more than merely preparatory act towards the supply of the gun (such as packing it in a parcel and taking it to the Post Office when he was stopped by the police), there is no objection to D being convicted of attempting to commit the inchoate offence of assistance, since this does not relate in any way to the commission of an offence by P, and this is not excluded by section 1(4) of the Criminal Attempts Act 1981.

Complicitous conduct may also be made the gravamen of a specific substantive offence, as in the statutory crimes of encouraging or assisting suicide and of procuring an act of gross indecency. These statutory offences can, in turn, be attempted.[282]

(c) Omissions

Section 1 of the Act makes reference to "a person who does an act which is more than merely preparatory". There is authority that statutory phrases which make reference to the "doing of acts" import a legislative intent to preclude liability for omission.[283] In the context of attempts, the practical effect of this limitation is likely to be limited. On occasion, however, it may leave unpunished conduct which should be censured. Suppose that D, a carer who is wholly responsible for the welfare of the bedridden V, intentionally omits to

---

[280] Child, "The Difference Between Attempted Complicity and Inchoate Assisting and Encouraging—A Reply to Professor Bohlander" [2010] *Crim LR* 924, 926.

[281] See Smith, "Secondary Participants and Inchoate Offences" in Tapper (ed.), *Crime, Proof and Punishment: Essays in Memory of Sir Rupert Cross* (1981) 38.

[282] *McShane* (1977) 66 Cr App R 97 (CA).

[283] *Ahmad* (1986) 84 Cr App R 64 (CA).

provide food or drink for him. All other things being equal, it would be appropriate to find D liable for the attempted murder if and when V's health becomes seriously impaired by a lack of sustenance.[284] Under the terms of the Criminal Attempts Act, however, D will not be liable for attempted murder, notwithstanding how parlous V's condition may become. The Law Commission has recommended that it should be possible to be liable for an attempt by omission, but only as regards attempted murder.[285] It would follow that the carer who omitted to provide food and drink to V would be guilty of attempt if she intended to kill, but not if she only intended to cause serious harm to V. This is a highly artificial distinction to draw and it would have been preferable had the Law Commission simply recommended that it should be possible to attempt by omission regardless of the offence attempted.

(d) Offences of negligence and strict liability

As will be discussed below in § 9.4(iii), liability for attempt requires proof of an intent to commit the substantive offence. It has been argued that this requirement places limits on the kind of offences that can be attempted:[286]

> "the requirement of an intent to commit the substantive offence whose attempt is charged means that a charge of attempt to commit involuntary manslaughter is inappropriate because the prosecution would have to prove an intent to kill and if they did this they would establish murder."

Not so. Admittedly, it would be odd to charge, say, attempted manslaughter by gross negligence. Negligence is a failure to attain reasonable standards and a person intentionally flouting such standards is acting culpably but not in a manner we would ordinarily call "negligent". To say that one is attempting to be negligent seems a contradiction in terms.

The oddity arises, however, not because manslaughter is an offence of negligence, but because, if the actus reus of manslaughter is intended, the appropriate offence is normally murder (since manslaughter and murder share the same actus reus and are differentiated by gradations of mens rea).[287] Even so, there is nothing that prevents an intentional killing from being charged as manslaughter—the greater offence includes the lesser.[288] The lesser forms of culpability provided for manslaughter are sufficient but not necessary conditions of liability. Accordingly, a charge of attempted manslaughter[289] is not a contradiction in terms, but must be proved by evidence which establishes an intent to kill. The fact that such evidence would satisfy the requirements of attempted murder does not preclude the lesser charge from being brought.

---

[284] The possibility of liability for attempts by omission may give rise to difficult questions of proximity. Suppose that V falls down a hole and D is under a duty to rescue V. D, however, walks away hoping that V will not be found and will perish of starvation. Does D's conduct amount to an attempt as soon as she walks away, or must V first come close to death?

[285] Law Com. No 318, *Conspiracy and Attempts* (2009) para. 8.151.

[286] Card, Cross, and Jones, *Criminal Law* (21st ed., 2014) 579.

[287] See below, Chapter 10.

[288] Not infrequently, prosecutors lay manslaughter charges where the evidence would support a charge of murder. They may do so for a variety of reasons, including evasion of time-consuming trial issues and avoidance of the mandatory sentence associated with murder. For discussion, see Farrier, "The Distinction between Murder and Manslaughter in its Procedure Context" (1976) 39 *MLR* 415, esp. at 430–1.

[289] Particularly of the constructive variety: below, § 10.6(i).

The point at issue here is simple but important. Most substantive offences do not require proof of an intent to commit them—many offences require no proof of culpability at all.[290] If they can be tried on indictment, these crimes can be attempted, provided that D intended to commit the crime. For example, if D takes a vehicle which is in a dangerous condition onto the highway, she will commit the offence of dangerous driving if the state of the vehicle should have been obvious to a careful and competent driver.[291] For the substantive offence, it is irrelevant that D herself was unaware of the danger her vehicle posed. Suppose she were to be stopped immediately prior to driving onto the highway and her vehicle examined. In principle, she would be guilty of attempted dangerous driving should she be aware of the dangerous condition of her vehicle, but not otherwise.

(iii) The mens rea of attempt

The mens rea requirement is simply stated: according to the Criminal Attempts Act 1981, D must act "with intent to commit [the substantive] offence".[292] Alas, judicial interpretation has rendered the explication of this requirement much less straightforward than it should be. It will assist our discussion if we look at the question of intent sequentially in respect of the separate elements that may make up the actus reus of a substantive offence. Almost invariably an offence will require some form of *conduct* on the part of D,[293] and usually conduct perpetrated in particular *circumstances*. For some offences, an additional *consequence* element is required; it must be proved that D's conduct caused a particular result, such as a wound or a death. The concept of intent is not univocal across these three elements. Hence, we need to discuss the intent required for attempt liability by reference to each of these elements separately.

(a) Conduct

By "conduct", we mean those movements on the part of D which are required of her as part of the actus reus of the substantive offence. In a case of murder by shooting, for example, the conduct element would include D's aiming of the gun and her squeezing of the trigger. Typically, such conduct will speak for itself in terms of its intentionality.[294] Were we to observe D picking up the gun and aiming it at V, we would thereby directly observe her intentionality. Generally, we would only be unsure whether or not her conduct was intentional were we to be told that, despite her appearance of consciousness, she was, say, sleepwalking or in a hypnotic trance. Outside such very special cases as these, and the more common cases of altered states of consciousness induced by drink or drugs, the intentionality of conduct will be straightforwardly established.

---

[290] See above, Chapter 6.
[291] Road Traffic Act 1988, s. 2, as substituted by s. 1 of the Road Traffic Act 1991.
[292] Section 1(1).
[293] For possible exceptions see above, § 4.1(ii).
[294] See Duff, *Intention, Agency and Criminal Liability* (1990) 116–20, where it is argued convincingly that intentions may take a form which can be directly observed and are inappropriately characterised as inner mental states severable from the conduct of the agent.

(b) Circumstances

Conduct is the most basic element of an offence and will rarely constitute the actus reus by itself. Attendant circumstances will need to be present. Frequently, the presence or absence of such circumstances will be matters beyond the control of D and, consequently, matters beyond the scope of his intention. Consider the case of D who finds a book on a seat in an airport lounge. Make two alternative assumptions: (i) the book was deliberately abandoned by its owner V, thereby divesting V of ownership; or (ii) V left the book inadvertently and would recover it if he could, so that ownership would remain with V. Suppose that D is about to deface the book but is prevented from doing so by the intervention of X. The substantive offence of criminal damage would have been possible only if the book were property belonging to another, e.g. on the facts of assumption (ii).[295] Whether or not the book belongs to V is a circumstance that, strictly, D cannot have intentions about—the facts are whatever they are. If the facts are those of assumption (ii) and D is aware of those facts, then clearly he intends to damage property belonging to another and is guilty of an attempt. His *knowledge* of the circumstances makes for an intention to damage someone else's property.[296] That intention would also subsist if D has a true *belief* that the facts were those of assumption (ii). His belief, though falling short of knowledge, still entails an intent to damage property belonging to another. The same applies if D has a *false* belief that the facts are as in (ii), where the truth is that V has indeed abandoned the book. Under the Criminal Attempts Act 1981, even in this last case D is guilty of an attempt—notwithstanding that the full offence is impossible to commit.[297] His false belief makes for an *intention* to damage property belonging to another.

But what if D lacks knowledge or any true or false belief? He observes V leaving for his flight and is unsure whether V has abandoned or inadvertently left the book. If he defaces the book, lacking any knowledge or belief about its ownership, it could not be said that he intends to damage property belonging to another—that would not be his purpose, neither would damage to another's property be something that he foresees as virtually certain. Here we should say that he is merely reckless about damaging *another's* property. He apparently lacks the intent that the Act requires. This conclusion is supported by section 1(3) of the Criminal Attempts Act 1981, which provides that, where D's intent would not be regarded as an intent to commit an offence, D shall be regarded as having the necessary intent to commit the offence, "if the facts of the case had been as he *believed* them to be" (emphasis added). These words demonstrate that, even where V has in fact abandoned the book, D may still be convicted of attempted criminal damage if, *and only if*, he has a *belief* that the property is owned by another. Unfortunately, there is no express provision covering the position where the facts are as D believes them to be; but as a matter of general principle it may be said that only a belief (here a true belief) that the property is owned property should

---

[295] On assumption (i), ownership in the book would not vest in the owners or tenants of the airport lounge but in the first person taking possession of the book intending to keep it: *Parker v. British Airways Board* [1982] QB 1004; below, § 13.4(v).

[296] Unless he made a mistake of civil law and believed that he was entitled to assume ownership of the book in such circumstances: cf. *Smith* [1974] QB 354.

[297] Criminal Attempts Act 1981, s. 1(2).

allow a conviction for attempted criminal damage. Recklessness or suspicion should not suffice. That was the position taken, at the time, by the Law Commission.[298]

The proper interpretation of the mens rea for attempt was considered by the Court of Appeal in the important decision of *Pace*,[299] which concerned a police operation to test whether scrap yards were prepared to buy stolen metal. The police offered scrap metal for sale to the defendants who purchased it. Had the metal been stolen, the defendants would have been guilty of converting criminal property[300] if they had suspected that the metal had been stolen.[301] In fact, the metal was the property of the police and so not stolen. Hence the defendants were charged with attempting to convert stolen property. The trial judge had held that it was sufficient for the attempt that the defendants had *suspected* that the metal was stolen. The Court of Appeal disagreed. It was held that the mental element for attempt according to section 1(1) required D to intend *all* the elements of the substantive offence; in the Court's view, there was no linguistic or purposive basis for any alternative interpretation.[302] Consequently, D had to intend the metal to be stolen. Since this had not been established, the convictions were quashed.

The decision in *Pace* has proved to be controversial, primarily for two reasons. The first reason is that the insistence on intention as to all elements of the substantive offence faces difficulties when engaging with circumstance elements of a crime, a problem highlighted by our example (above) of the book found in the airport lounge. As a matter both of statutory interpretation and of principle the intention to commit an offence should connote an intention with respect to the conduct or consequence elements of the offence, whereas it is knowledge or belief which should operate with respect to the circumstance elements of the offence.[303] The Court of Appeal in *Pace* did in fact acknowledge that knowledge or belief could be relevant to an attempt, despite its earlier insistence that intention is required for all elements of the offence, when it was recognised that the defendants could have been charged with attempting to handle stolen goods, for which the relevant mens rea relating to the goods' being stolen is knowledge or belief.[304] The inclusion of belief within the mens rea of an attempt is provided for by the Criminal Attempts Act 1981 through section 1(3), which is properly interpreted as allowing for belief as to circumstances, an appropriate interpretation of the word 'facts' which is used in the subsection.[305] It follows that it is possible to equate D's belief with intention for the purposes of section 1(1). In other words, it is legitimate to interpret the Court of Appeal's insistence on intention as to all the elements of the offence to include belief as to circumstances.

---

[298] Law Com. No. 102, *Attempt and Impossibility in Relation to Attempt, Conspiracy and Incitement* (1980) paras. 214–18. Note that the Law Commission later changed its mind on the underlying policy questions: Law. Com. No. 177, *A Criminal Code for England and Wales* (1989) cl. 49(2).

[299] [2014] EWCA Crim 186, [2014] 1 WLR 2867. See Virgo, "Criminal Attempts—The Law of Unintended Circumstances" [2014] *CLJ* 244; Simester, "The Mens Rea of Criminal Attempts" (2015) 131 *LQR* 169; Stark, "The Mens Rea of a Criminal Attempt" [2014] 3 *Arch Rev* 7; Dyson, "Scrapping Khan" [2014] *Crim LR* 445; Mirfield, "Intention and Criminal Attempts" [2015] *Crim LR* 142; Bruneau and Taylor, "In Defence of *Pace and Rogers*" [2015] 8 *Arch Rev* 6.

[300] Proceeds of Crime Act 2002, s. 327.

[301] *Ibid.*, s. 340(3)(b).

[302] This analysis is defended by Mirfield, "Intention and Criminal Attempts" [2015] *Crim LR* 142, 148.

[303] Simester, "The Mens Rea of Criminal Attempts" (2015) 131 *LQR* 169, 171.

[304] [2014] EWCA Crim 186, [2014] 1 WLR 2867, para. 81.

[305] Bruneau and Taylor, "In Defence of *Pace and Rogers*" [2015] 8 *Arch Rev* 6, 8.

The second controversial feature of the decision in *Pace* is that it is inconsistent with two earlier decisions of the Court of Appeal about the mens rea for attempt. The first of these was *Khan*,[306] where D had attempted to have sexual intercourse with V, aware that she might not consent to the act. On the interpretation of the mens rea for attempt adopted in *Pace*, D would be liable for attempted rape only if he intended to have sex with V intending that she did not consent. But in *Khan*, D was found to have been reckless about V's consent: that is, aware that she might not consent. In confirming D's conviction for attempted rape, the Court of Appeal in *Khan* ruled that, provided D possessed an intention with respect to the conduct element of the full offence (and D clearly intended to have sex), proof of recklessness as to any circumstance element would permit a finding that D intended to commit rape within the meaning of section 1 of the Criminal Attempts Act 1981. The Court emphasised that the mens rea for rape and attempted rape were the same,[307] since at the time recklessness as to absence of consent was the required mens rea for rape.[308]

Conceptually, the court's reasoning is unconvincing.[309] Where D lacks knowledge or belief regarding the absence of V's consent, D intends to rape only if it is his purpose "to have sexual intercourse without consent"—i.e. if it was *part* of his design that V should not consent.[310] Alternatively, if D's purpose was simply "to have sex", it being incidental to him whether V consents, then he would certainly intend "to have sex" but would intend "to have sex without consent" only if he knew or believed that V would not consent.

In confirming the conviction in *Khan*, the Court was heavily influenced by the fact that, had D succeeded in having intercourse, he would have been liable for the full offence of rape, an offence which could then be committed intentionally or recklessly. In the interests of public protection, the Court of Appeal considered that the mens rea for attempt should be aligned as closely as possible with the mens rea for the substantive offence. This is a powerful consideration. Undeniably, the conduct involved in *Khan* was gravely wrong and a considerable gap in social protection would have been allowed had his conviction been quashed. Nonetheless, the Court of Appeal seems in *Khan* to have departed from the statutory requirement of an intent to commit the full offence.[311]

---

[306] [1990] 1 WLR 813. The other decision is *A-G's Reference (No. 3 of 1992)* [1994] 1 WLR 409: below, § 9.4.(iii)(c).

[307] [1990] 1 WLR 813, 819.

[308] See now the Sexual Offences Act 2003, s. 1(1).

[309] See Sullivan, "Intent, Subjective Recklessness and Culpability" (1992) 12 *OJLS* 380, where the reasoning but not the outcome in *Khan* is criticised. For a defence and rigorous explication of the reasoning in *Khan*, see Duff, "The Circumstances of an Attempt" [1991] *CLJ* 100.

[310] Above, § 5.1(v).

[311] Furthermore, the Law Commission, reversing the position it took at the time the Criminal Attempts Act 1981 was framed (Law Com. No. 102, *Attempt and Impossibility in Relation to Attempt, Conspiracy and Incitement* (1980)), adopted the reasoning in *Khan* in its proposed Criminal Code: Law Com. No. 177, *A Criminal Code for England and Wales* (1989) cl. 49(2). The Law Commission has since recommended that, for substantive offences which have circumstance elements but no corresponding fault element or a fault element of negligence, D should only be convicted of attempting the offence if he is subjectively reckless as to the circumstance elements: Law Com. No. 318, *Conspiracy and Attempts* (2009) para. 8.133. Further, for those substantive offences which have fault elements not requiring negligence as regards facts or circumstances, D should only be convicted of attempting that offence if he possesses that fault element: *ibid.*, para. 8.137. These proposals are consistent with the Law Commission's recommendations for the reform of statutory conspiracy: above, § 9.3(iv)(g).

Khan was tentatively distinguished in *Pace* on the grounds that the mens rea for rape was recklessness and also because, had D succeeded in his act of penetration, he would have been guilty of rape, whereas the defendants in *Pace* could never have successfully converted stolen property because the property was not stolen. But neither ground is convincing. Although the relevant mens rea for the substantive offence in *Khan* was recklessness which is different from the relevant mens rea of suspicion in *Pace*, since recklessness requires D to foresee a risk which it is unreasonable to take, recklessness and suspicion are not in this context significantly different, and no indication was given as to why the existence of recklessness as a mens rea for the substantive offence should result in a different approach, especially where that approach is inconsistent with the mens rea requirement for attempt as interpreted by the Court in *Pace*. Further, whilst it is certainly the case that rape in *Khan* was possible, since V was not consenting to sex, and the conversion of stolen property in *Pace* was not possible, because the property was not stolen, it is unclear why this should make any difference to the mens rea requirement for attempt. It would have been preferable for the Court of Appeal in *Pace* to have held that *Khan* was incorrectly decided, being inconsistent with the mens rea requirement explicitly articulated in the Criminal Attempts Act 1981. It follows that the mens rea for attempted rape is preferably analysed as being that D must have intended to have intercourse with V, knowing or believing that V did not or would not consent, even though this is not what *Khan* decided and that decision was not overruled in *Pace*.

(c) Consequences

Prior to the Criminal Attempts Act 1981, in order to be liable for attempt D had to intend to cause any consequence specified in the actus reus of the full offence. A leading pre-Act case is *Whybrow*,[312] where D was charged with the attempted murder of his wife. Asserting that, in the case of attempt, "intent becomes the principal ingredient of the crime", Goddard LCJ ruled that for D to be guilty of attempted murder he must have intended to cause the death of V. He explicitly rejected the argument that, because an intent to cause grievous bodily harm would suffice for the full offence, it would also suffice for the attempt to commit it. The centrality of intent to attempt liability was confirmed in another pre-Act case, *Mohan*, where James LJ spoke of:[313]

> "a decision to bring about, in so far as it lies within the accused's power, the commission of the offence which it is alleged the accused attempted to commit, no matter whether the accused desired that consequence of his act or not."

In *Pearman*,[314] the Court of Appeal stated that this passage remained an authoritative guide to the interpretation of intent under the Criminal Attempt Act 1981, and the vital significance of intention to consequences was confirmed in *Pace*.[315] The words employed by James LJ in *Mohan* comprehend not only the primary meaning of the term intent (what

---

[312] (1951) 35 Cr App R 141 (CCA).
[313] [1976] QB 1, 3 (CA).
[314] (1984) 80 Cr App R 259.
[315] [2014] EWCA Crim 186, [2014] 1 WLR 2867, paras. 46–7.

is sometimes called direct intent), but also foresight that a consequence was a virtual certainty. This was confirmed in *Pearman*, where it was stated that:[316]

> "a man who is cornered by the police when he is in a car may have the primary purpose of simply escaping from that situation. If he drives straight at police officers at high speed, a jury is likely to conclude that he intended to injure a police officer and maybe cause him serious grievous bodily harm."

In the light of the House of Lords decision in *Woollin*,[317] where the consequence is not directly intended by D, a jury should be invited to make a finding of intent only where that consequence was a virtually certain result of D's conduct and where D was aware of this virtual certainty. Only then, in the words of James LJ, can we speak convincingly of a "decision to bring about, in so far as it lies within the accused's power, the commission of the offence which it is alleged the accused attempted to commit".

It has been argued that this constitutes too broad a view of what is required for a finding of intent as to consequences in the law of attempt. The argument runs that the term "attempt" is synonymous with "trying" and it can only be said that D is attempting to achieve a consequence if he is acting in order to bring that consequence about.[318] But ordinary English usage is not always clear cut in these matters, and need not foreclose discussion of issues of principle or policy in criminal law. Suppose, to use Glanville Williams's example,[319] that D places a bomb in the hold of a departing passenger plane. When asked why, he may truthfully reply that he was looking to make an insurance claim based on the loss of the plane and deny that his purpose was to take life. Yet he knows that success in his objective is inseparable from the sacrifice of people's lives. Arguably, it is not open to D to deny, even on ordinary language, that he was trying to kill—only to deny that this was his ultimate motive. Moreover, the grave wrongdoing involved and the requirements of social protection supply compelling reasons to treat such a case as one of attempted murder. The conclusion is supported by *Mohan*, by *Pearman*, and by the Court of Appeal decision in *Walker and Hayles*.[320]

Thus far, the mens rea required for consequence elements seems straightforward— direct intent or foresight of a virtual certainty, which is consistent with the language of the Criminal Attempts Act as interpreted in *Pace*. However, the decision of the Court of Appeal in *Pace* is inconsistent with an earlier decision of the Court of Appeal, *A-G's Reference (No. 3 of 1992)*,[321] which might be interpreted to support recklessness sometimes being sufficient in respect of the consequence element of a substantive offence. In that case D and others had thrown lighted petrol bombs at a car in which V and others were passengers. The bombs missed the car and smashed against a wall. D was charged with attempted arson being reckless whether life be endangered, contrary to section 1(2) of the Criminal Damage Act 1971. The trial judge directed that D would not be guilty of this aggravated form of attempted criminal damage unless it were proved that he *intended* that V's life

---

[316] (1984) 80 Cr App R 259, 263.
[317] [1999] 1 AC 82.
[318] Fletcher, *Rethinking Criminal Law* (1978) 161.
[319] Above, § 5.1(iv).
[320] (1989) 90 Cr App R 226 (CA).
[321] [1994] 1 WLR 409.

be endangered. The Court of Appeal, much influenced by its earlier decision in *Khan*,[322] disagreed. It adopted what has been called the "missing element"[323] analysis of the intent requirement in attempt:[324]

> "If the facts are that, although the defendant had one of the appropriate states of mind required for the complete offence, but the physical element required for the commission of the complete offence is missing, the defendant is not to be convicted unless it can be shown that he intended to supply the physical element."

The Court effectively divided the actus reus of an attempt into those elements of the substantive offence that D had satisfied, and those elements that were still "missing". For the former, whatever mens rea was required by the substantive offence would suffice also for the attempt. For the latter, intent would be required. Applying this analysis to the facts of *A-G's Reference* itself, the only element missing from commission of the full offence was damage to property, an element which, in the quaint language of the court, D was doing his best to supply. This was the only element that D was required to intend. So far as the remaining elements were required, for the full offence it sufficed at the time that D be *Caldwell*-reckless whether life would be endangered by his conduct. The Court ruled that *Caldwell* recklessness would equally suffice for the attempt.

A-G's Reference (No. 3 of 1992) could be read as deciding that, on a charge of attempt, recklessness may suffice for any "present" consequence element of the full offence provided that D intends to bring about any "missing" consequence or other element. The cases decided prior to *A-G's Reference* are reconcilable on the basis that, in the earlier decisions, the relevant consequence had always been a "missing element", i.e. something that had not materialised. An intention to bring about a non-realised consequence is still required, if this reading of *A-G's Reference* is accepted.

An alternative explanation of the result of the case, though not of the reasoning adopted, arises from dicta of Lord Nicholls in *Saik* in the context of conspiracy,[325] namely that it is not necessary for the substantive offence to show that life had actually been endangered, only that D was recklessly indifferent whether the criminal damage would endanger life. The consequence for conspiracy is that the mens rea for conspiring to commit criminal damage being reckless whether life is endangered is an intent to damage property and recklessness as to endangerment. *A-G's Reference (No. 3 of 1992)* could be analysed as reaching the same conclusion for an attempt to commit this offence, so recklessness as to endangerment is sufficient, not because it was a "present" consequence but simply because it was an ulterior mental ingredient of the substantive offence. In other words, the case should not be read as considering the mens rea in respect of the consequence element of the substantive offence. Rather, the requirement of endangering life should be treated as neither a conduct, consequence nor a circumstance of the substantive offence, but as an ulterior mens rea element.[326] If the recommendations of the Law Commission as to the mens rea

---

[322] [1990] 1 WLR 813: above, § 9.4.(iii)(b).

[323] Stannard, "Making up for the Missing Element: A Sideways Look at Attempts" (1987) 7 *LS* 194.

[324] [1994] 1 WLR 409, 417 (Schiemann J).

[325] [2006] UKHL 18, [2007] AC 18, para. 4 (Lord Nicholls); above, § 9.3(iv)(d).

[326] See Child, "The Structure, Coherence and Limits of Inchoate Liability: The New *Ulterior* Element" (2014) 34 *LS* 537. Child rationalises this, at 558, somewhat unconvincingly, on the basis that D's knowledge of her

for attempt are adopted,[327] the result in *A-G's Reference* would be confirmed, since the mens rea for the substantive offence relating to whether life was endangered should apply to the attempt. This reform would at least ensure consistency between the results in cases and the relevant legislation.

We are, however, left with dicta in *A-G's Reference* which adopts "the missing physical element test". These dicta were described in *Pace* as elliptical if not self-contradictory.[328] They are best forgotten and, indeed, in *Pace* the decision was mentioned but then ignored. That is appropriate: if intention were required only for those elements of the full offence which D has not brought about, the scope of attempt would be considerably enlarged. A noteworthy feature of *A-G's Reference* was that *Caldwell* recklessness (which was at that time sufficient mens rea for the substantive offence of arson) was found to constitute adequate culpability in the context of attempts liability. It is hardly any step further to allow negligence to suffice.[329] Suppose that D, who is driving a dangerous vehicle, is stopped immediately before joining the highway. It is established that he intended to drive onto the highway, but the evidence falls short of proof that he was aware of the condition of his car. If, however, a careful competent driver would have been aware, then D intended to bring about the missing element of driving on the highway and possessed the culpability for other elements required for the full offence, namely that the vehicle is dangerous.[330] On the authority of *A-G's Reference*, D would be guilty of a negligent attempt to drive dangerously. This is a bizarre result. Doubtless there is something to be said for this approach in terms of public safety, but it goes beyond anything Parliament intended when passing the Criminal Attempts Act 1981, it is clearly inconsistent with the decision in *Pace* and so, like *Khan*, *A-G's Reference (No. 3 of 1992)* is preferably treated as overruled.

(d) Conditional intent

Does a "conditional intent" satisfy the intent requirement for attempt? In *Husseyn*,[331] D was charged with attempting to steal sub-aqua equipment. He had been on the point of opening a holdall which contained the equipment. His conviction for attempted theft was quashed on the basis that he was searching for something that, for him, would be worth taking. A "present" intent to steal would not arise until D determined to take some particular item of property. By contrast, an intent to steal if and when some precondition should be satisfied was not sufficient for an attempt: it was not a "present" intent to steal.

The ramifications of *Husseyn* were considerable.[332] Many people enter property with intent to steal but propose only to steal things which are valuable, concealable, and portable,

---

own recklessness constitutes an intention that she should be reckless as to life being endangered; but he then acknowledges that this is best interpreted as a simple requirement of recklessness regarding the ulterior element.

[327] Law Com. No. 318, *Conspiracy and Attempts* (2009) para. 8.133.

[328] [2014] EWCA Crim 186, [2014] 1 WLR 2867, para. 53.

[329] See above, § 5.2(i). The abolition of *Caldwell* recklessness in *G* [2004] 1 AC 1034 and the endorsement by the House of Lords of a subjective approach to mens rea in serious offences may make such a prospect less likely; but in *Misra* [2004] EWCA Crim 2375, [2005] 1 Cr App R 21 it was held that the decision in *G* had no implications for gross negligence manslaughter. The Law Commission has recommended that negligence should not suffice for an attempt: Law Com. No. 318, *Conspiracy and Attempts* (2009) para. 8.133.

[330] Under s. 2 of the Road Traffic Act 1988, as substituted by s. 1 of the Road Traffic Act 1991, it suffices that the dangerous condition of the vehicle "would be obvious to a competent and careful driver".

[331] (1977) 67 Cr App R 131n. See also below, § 13.7(i)(f).

[332] See Williams, "Three Rogues' Charters" [1980] *Crim LR* 263.

such as money or jewellery. Prima facie, on the reasoning in *Husseyn*, such people would not be burglars until they encountered some property that they resolved to steal since, until then, there is no "present" intent to steal. However, a subsequent Court of Appeal decision, *A-G's Reference (Nos. 1 and 2 of 1979)*,[333] held that a conditional intent to steal is a "present" intent for the purposes of burglary.

How are the decisions in *Husseyn* and *A-G's Reference (Nos. 1 and 2 of 1979)* to be reconciled? In the latter case, the Court of Appeal put forward an explanation of *Husseyn* in procedural terms. In *Husseyn*, D had been charged with attempting to steal sub-aqua equipment. Such a charge could not succeed as D never formed an intent to steal sub-aqua equipment as such. Had he been charged with attempting to steal "some or all of the contents of the holdall", a conviction for attempted theft would have been sustainable. Yet, as observed in *Smith and Hogan*, unless it could be proved that D would have taken something from the receptacle, the issue found to be decisive in *Husseyn* is left intact.[334] In the circumstances that arose in that case, it is suggested that D should have been charged with "attempting to steal from a holdall".

Yet, even if that procedural solution is accepted, a further difficulty may remain. Liability for attempt still requires an act of sufficient proximity which, in the case of attempted theft, implies an act that is proximate to the appropriation of someone else's property.[335] If D has demonstrated that he does not want *that* property—he opens the door to a room and then closes it without taking its contents—how close has D come to appropriating *those* contents? Proving a sufficiently proximate act in these circumstances requires a fictional supposition that D did intend to acquire the items which, in reality, he went on to reject.[336]

The Law Commission has proposed that the Criminal Attempts Act 1981 should be amended to make clear that an intent to commit a crime includes a conditional intent to commit it.[337] This would be an appropriate clarification of the law.

(e) Mens rea for attempt—a summary

Regarding the mens rea for attempt, the Criminal Attempts Act 1981 merely refers to "an intent to commit the offence". We can now appreciate that this beguilingly simple statement requires considerable explication in the light of contradictory case law. It is not possible to reconcile the trilogy of Court of Appeal cases which have considered the mens rea for attempt. However, if it is assumed that *Pace* broadly reflects the appropriate mens rea, it is possible to summarise the preferred interpretation of the law as follows:

    (i)   D must intend to perpetrate any conduct element specified for the full offence.

---

[333] [1980] QB 180. And see too *Toothill* [1998] Crim LR 876.

[334] *Smith and Hogan* 468.

[335] The problem does not arise in burglary, the offence at issue in *A-G's Reference (No. 3 of 1992)*; there the intent to steal can be established in general terms; there is no need to prove that D came close to stealing something in particular.

[336] Fictional, or counterfactual, assumptions of this sort may properly to used to resolve the issue of proximity in cases where it is impossible to commit the substantive crime: Criminal Attempts Act 1981, s. 1(3), and see further below, § 9.5. This provision does not, however, apply to cases of property not wanted by D, since it is clearly possible to steal such property.

[337] Law Com. No. 318, *Conspiracy and Attempts* (2009) para. 8.106.

(ii)   For any circumstance elements of the full offence, it is sufficient if D intends, knows, or believes that those circumstances are or will be present at the time of her conduct, even if that circumstance will never exist in reality.

(iii)   For consequence elements it must be proved that D intended to realise that consequence.

(iv)   Finally, a conditional intent may be sufficient mens rea provided that D has resolved to commit the crime at issue should the condition be satisfied.[338]

In *Pace*, the Court of Appeal justified the restrictive interpretation of the mens rea of attempt on the ground that it was in accordance with the principle that a higher level of mens rea should be required for an attempt than for the substantive offence.[339] No attempt was made to identify what the relevant principle might be, although it can be assumed that it was that the criminality of inchoate offences turns on culpability rather than harm caused.

(iv) Voluntary withdrawal

In the case of substantive offences, full repentance and restoration after commission of the offence will be merely matters of mitigation. If D surreptitiously picks up an item in a department store, dishonestly intending to avoid paying for it, he commits theft notwithstanding a subsequent pang of conscience which leads him to put it back. What if that change of heart should strike D as he reaches for the item but before he makes contact with it?[340] The answer is the same. Analytically, if the actus reus and mens rea of attempted theft are present, he has reached the point of no return. In conceptual terms, liability for attempt should ensue if actus reus and mens rea are present, save where D can lay claim to any justification or excuse for his conduct.

In the case of attempts, however, there is something inapt about such an unyielding analysis. Although attempt is a crime in its own right, its principal rationales are to allow timely interventions by law enforcement personnel prior to the realisation of any harm and to allow lawful restraint of the socially dangerous. A genuine change of heart by D prior to bringing about harm indicates that intervention and restraint were not required for that occasion. Further, some voluntary withdrawals can considerably reduce D's culpability. As we shall argue in the next section, should D take aim at V and shoot with intent to kill, D's innate culpability remains the same whether or not she succeeds in killing V. Yet, if D should take aim and then voluntarily desist, the survival of V is to D's credit. Besides, from a purely instrumental perspective, there is something to be said for the law's giving D an incentive for voluntary withdrawal in such cases.

At the present time, such English case law as touches on voluntary withdrawal in attempt is inconclusive on whether, currently, a "change of heart" defence is allowed.[341] Ideally a

---

[338] Although, as noted above in § 9.4(iii)(d), there may be difficulties with the actus reus requirement of proximity in such cases.

[339] [2014] EWCA Crim 186, [2014] 1 WLR 2867, para. 74.

[340] See Wasik, "Abandoning Criminal Intent" [1980] *Crim LR* 785.

[341] For discussion of English and Commonwealth authority, see Stuart, "The *Actus Reus* in Attempts" [1970] *Crim LR* 505, 519–21.

defence should be created by legislation.[342] The main problem about providing such a defence concerns the difficulty of differentiating between voluntary and involuntary desistance. In *Page*,[343] for instance, D was observed climbing a ladder and inserting the point of a crowbar under a window frame. He then withdrew the implement and climbed down the ladder. He claimed that thoughts of his mother had brought him back to his good self. An alternative explanation was that he had become aware of police observation. To obviate these difficulties of establishing true motive, there is something to be said for placing the onus of proof, on a balance of probabilities, on the defendant. As a matter of general principle, the burden of proving constituent elements of the crime and of disproving any excuse or justification arising from the facts should lie with the prosecution.[344] Yet the defence proposed is highly exceptional. It would be raised where the formal elements of guilt were present and where there was nothing to suggest that the defendant lacked the capacity to choose to conform her conduct to law. Accordingly, a reverse burden of proof would not cause undue hardship and may encourage acceptance of such a defence.

(v) Liability for attempt and commission of the full offence

Failure is implicit in the ordinary notion of an attempt. When we watch a high jump competitor sail effortlessly over the bar, we do not describe her effort as a "commendable attempt" to clear the bar. For the purposes of legal analysis, it has been argued that the offence of attempt is subsumed and eclipsed by commission of the full offence.[345] If this idea of merger is taken literally then were D, say, to be charged with attempted murder, she would be able to answer the charge by demonstrating that she had, in fact, committed murder. Attempt liability would no longer subsist, as it would have been eclipsed by the commission of the full offence.

This argument has found favour in some jurisdictions,[346] but is manifestly unsatisfactory. As a matter of ordinary English usage, the term "attempt" may imply a failure to complete but there is no need here slavishly to follow the contours of ordinary language when addressing issues of principle and policy. For the purposes of the criminal law, "attempt" need not be construed as a description of D's conduct as a whole, but should be regarded as a description of the kind of liability his conduct will attract at a particular stage in his sequence of acts. That liability, once established, remains free-standing and is not subsumed within any subsequent liability for the full offence. This analysis is supported by section 6(4) of the Criminal Law Act 1967, which provides that D may be convicted for an attempt "notwithstanding that he is shown to be guilty of the completed offence". Indeed, attempt charges have been permitted in circumstances where the evidence supporting the charge was unequivocally evidence of the full offence. Such was the case in *Cox*,[347] a case of "mercy killing" by a doctor. The evidence of poisoning which secured a conviction for attempted

---

[342] However, the Law Commission made no such recommendation in its review of the law of attempt, and specifically rejected such a defence for conspiracy: Law Com. No. 318, *Conspiracy and Attempts* (2009).

[343] [1933] Argus LR 374 (Victoria). Cf. *Taylor* (1859) 1 F & F 511, 175 ER 831; *Lankford* [1959] Crim LR 209.

[344] See Roberts, "Taking the Burden of Proof Seriously" [1995] *Crim LR* 783.

[345] Hall, *General Principles of Criminal Law* (2nd ed., 1960) 577; Fletcher, *Rethinking Criminal Law* (1978) 131.

[346] E.g. *Commonwealth* v. *Crow* (1931) 303 Pa 91.

[347] (1992) 12 BMLR 38.

murder, the only charge preferred, was overwhelming evidence that V had met her death by poisoning.[348] A charge of attempted murder may have been preferred in order to avoid confronting the jury with a decision to convict for the full offence of murder—a decision that would result in the imposition of a mandatory life sentence—rather than leaving the sentence to the discretion of the judge, as is the case for attempted murder, in a case where the defendant had acted on the request of and from compassion for his patient. Whatever the merits of this prosecutorial decision, the conviction of Dr Cox suggests that liability for the attempt survives the commission of the full offence.

(vi) Attempt, luck, and punishment

Consider the following scenarios:

> D leaves a house heavily intoxicated. He makes for his car in the driveway but is so drunk that he stumbles before he reaches the driveway and falls asleep. Alternatively, he may succeed in getting to his car but be so befuddled by drink that he cannot fit his key into the ignition. Or, he may manage to drive his car onto the road and, despite his intoxicated condition, reach his destination without mishap. On the other hand, he may be involved in a collision with another vehicle and deaths or injuries may, or may not, ensue. Why was D drunk? He may be an alcoholic and that condition may have arisen because of a genetic disposition, the vagaries of life, weakness of will, or any combination thereof. Or he may be an overseas visitor, unfamiliar with alcohol, who is taken completely unawares by the effect it has on him.

The possible narratives sketched above reflect the all-pervasive influence of chance factors on the prospect of criminal liability, the kind of offence committed, and what punishment, if any, will be received. Certain forms of contingency are so intrinsic to the very substance of life that a system of criminal law must merely take them as read, and can seek no form of accommodation with them.[349] Social circumstances, the particularities of character, and the patterns of opportunity for criminal acts constitute the most powerful crimogenic factors in play—but only exceptionally will they generate matters to be taken into account when determining whether D has committed a crime. Critical theorists such as Kelman[350] and Norrie[351] rebuke the failure of the criminal law to take account of these background factors, particularly the question of social disadvantage. Mainstream theorists, such as Ashworth,[352] accept that the criminal law as currently theorised and practised must, save for exceptional circumstances, assume that persons subjected to the criminal

---

[348] On the facts of *Cox*, V was unquestionably alive when the poison was administered, and the dosage was sufficient to kill anyone instantly, whatever their state of health. See too *Burke* [2000] Crim LR 413, where there was a conviction for attempt despite evidence of commission of the full offence.

[349] See above, § 6.5(i). On the appropriate treatment of chance and contingency in the making of moral judgements see, especially, Williams, "Moral Luck" in *Moral Luck* (1981) 20; Nagel, "Moral Luck" in *Mortal Questions* (1979) 24.

[350] Kelman, "Interpretative Construction in the Substantive Criminal Law" (1981) 33 *Stanford LR* 591.

[351] *Crime, Reason and History* (2nd ed., 2001) chap. 3; also his "'Simulacra of Morality'? Beyond the Ideal/Actual Antinomies of Criminal Justice" in Duff (ed.), *Philosophy of Criminal Law* (1998) 101.

[352] "Criminal Attempts and the Role of Resulting Harm under the Code and in the Common Law" (1988) 19 *Rutgers LJ* 19; "Taking the Consequences" in Shute, Gardner, and Horder (eds.), *Action and Value in Criminal Law* (1993) 107.

law are capable of autonomy and choice. Nonetheless, indeed because of that assumption, Ashworth insists that a rational criminal law should seek to eradicate, so far as practicable, the influence of luck on a person's criminal liability and punishment. In our drunken driver scenario, what would matter for Ashworth is that D attempted to drive while in a condition that posed a serious threat to others: provided he committed an act sufficiently proximate to driving the car, his culpability would hold constant; irrespective of whether he succeeded in driving, whether he was involved in an accident, and whether fatalities or injuries ensued from the accident. In Ashworth's view, D should be punished in a manner commensurate with his culpability and his just punishment should not be affected by the vagaries of chance.

The impact of luck is particularly marked in the sphere of liability for attempt. A Chicago-based study revealed that over 45 per cent of gunshot victims struck in the head by a high-calibre bullet survive their ordeal.[353] If D shoots V in the head with intent to kill him and succeeds, in many US jurisdictions he will face the prospect of the death penalty and in England he will receive a mandatory life sentence. Should V survive, D will not be a murderer and, in general, he will receive a lesser sentence.[354] Here Ashworth's "culpability holds constant" argument has particular force: it is not obvious how contingencies, such as the availability of timely and skilled surgery, put D in a different moral case even if the deftness of a surgeon allows him to evade the status of murderer. Still, on one scenario D will have killed and brought into the world such harms as the loss of a life, feelings of loss and grief for those persons close to V, the elimination of a productive member of society, etc.; whereas if death does not ensue, the harm actually brought about by D will be less. Anthony Duff, in his exhaustive and richly layered treatise on criminal attempts, argues forcefully from a deontological perspective that results do matter morally; that the greater the harm we bring about, the deeper our culpability.[355] On this perspective, differential punishment for attempts and completed crimes is justified.

To minimise the influence of luck upon the imposition of blame and punishment is attractive, even if contrary to popular sentiment. Famously, Kant argued for the primacy of trying, in contradistinction to succeeding, in making moral judgements. Assuming the presence of autonomy and the capacity for choice, an agent is in control of her decisions but is not in control of outcomes. If moral judgement is to be based on the quality of our autonomous choices, outcomes matter for such judgements only in so far as they cast light on our choices and indicate our resolve. That said, outcomes matter enormously in terms of human welfare and our relations with others. We may invite a friend for dinner and laugh with relief when he catches reflexively a bottle he has carelessly elbowed from the table. Laughter may be absent for a while should a mop and bucket be needed. Clearly, if a bad outcome does not arise, the emotional drive to impose full severity of sanction loses force. That is no cause for concern—in fact the opposite. Merely because D has put himself in a position where he may be justly punished does not, *pace* Kant, entail that he must be

---

[353] Zimring, "The Medium is the Message: Firearm Caliber as a Determinant of Death from Assault" (1972) 1 *J Legal Studies* 97, 104.

[354] Attempts are consistently punished less severely than the equivalent full offence. For a defence of this practice, see Robinson and Darley, "Objectivist Versus Subjectivist View of Criminality: A Study in the Role of Social Science in Criminal Law Theory" (1998) 18 *OJLS* 409.

[355] *Criminal Attempts* (1996) chap. 12.

punished to the full measure of his culpability.[356] If all just punishment were fully exacted, the world would be even worse than it already is.[357] Indeed, a much greater cause for concern is excessive punishment. Frequently, outcome-specific sanctions, such as mandatory life sentences, inflict a punishment which exceeds D's innate culpability.[358] That is of more concern than any undue leniency offered to those guilty of attempts.

(vii) Reform of the law of attempt

Inherent in the very idea of an attempt is something done that is proximate to commission of a full criminal offence. This necessary proximity was found to be lacking in *Geddes*,[359] where D, a trespasser who apparently intended to abduct a pupil of the school, was apprehended in a school lavatory while in possession of a kitchen knife, rope, and binding tape. The Court of Appeal ruled that D's conduct did not constitute attempted false imprisonment because he had not tried to restrict anyone's movements. Similarly, in *Campbell*,[360] D was not convicted of attempted robbery when he was arrested just as he was entering a Post Office with an imitation firearm. Not unreasonably, both decisions could be castigated as failures to afford adequate social protection to victims of serious crimes. In *Geddes*, had D trespassed in the school with intent to steal or inflict grievous bodily harm, or cause damage to property, he could have been convicted of burglary;[361] and in *Campbell*, D could have been convicted of attempted robbery had he actually entered the Post Office. Prior to the Criminal Attempts Act 1981, Geddes could have been convicted of procuring an instrument to commit a crime,[362] were it the case that he obtained the knife, rope, or tape as aids to abduction.

The Law Commission reviewed this gap in social protection and, in a Consultation Paper, recommended that the law of attempt should be split into two separate inchoate offences.[363] The first would be committed where D had committed the last acts necessary to commit the intended offence, but this would not be limited to the commission of the very last act, so it would encompass D, who, wanting to kill V, aimed a gun at V but still had to remove the safety catch and pull the trigger. The second would be a newly created offence of criminal preparation where D had done acts of preparation which form part of the execution of the plan to commit the intended offence, such as gaining entry to a building, interfering with a lock, or lying in wait for V. This recommendation was not intended to extend the ambit of the law of attempt but simply to reflect society's understanding of attempt and the intention of Parliament when enacting the 1981 statute. The recommendation was

---

[356] Kant, *Philosophy of Law* (1796; transl. Clarke, 1887). Kant believed that mercy had no place in criminal justice and should be confined to dealings between individuals. In his view, the State is under a duty not to pardon or forgive crimes.

[357] For attempts to justify acts of mercy under specified circumstances in criminal justice settings, see Smart, "Mercy" (1968) 43 *Philosophy* 345; Card, "Mercy" (1972) 81 *Philosophical Review* 182.

[358] See the discussion below, § 10.3(ii).

[359] [1996] Crim LR 894 (CA).

[360] [1990] 93 Cr App R 350.

[361] Theft Act 1968, s. 9.

[362] As in *Gurmit Singh* [1986] 2 QB 53; but see now s. 6 of the Criminal Attempts Act 1981.

[363] LCCP No. 183, *Conspiracy and Attempts* (2007).

subject to much criticism,[364] primarily that the two offences do not involve sufficiently distinct wrongdoing,[365] and consequently the Law Commission concluded in its report[366] that there is no need for any subdivision of attempt and that the existing definition of the actus reus is workable and satisfactory.

Nonetheless, it remains a matter of concern that there is a gap in social protection where D clearly intends to commit a crime and has started to prepare for the commission of that crime but has not done more than a merely preparatory act for its commission. The appropriate response to this gap is not to reintroduce a general offence of procuring materials to commit a crime nor to relax the interpretation of the proximity requirement in attempt. If we were to take the former path, any convicted paedophile would obtain items like a rope or a kitchen knife at his peril. Likewise, if we were to extend the actus reus of attempted false imprisonment to encompass any step, however preliminary, towards the commission of the offence, his freedom from arrest would be threatened whenever he was in the vicinity of children. Such steps, if taken to fill the gap exposed by *Geddes* and *Campbell*, carry an undue risk of oppressive policing and unsafe convictions based on dubious confessions. This said, intervention at a stage earlier than currently allowed by the law of attempt is warranted, despite the conclusions of the Law Commission, in respect of situations notoriously associated with particular kinds of harm. We are aware that we acquire such things as guns or explosives at our peril should we lack a licence or justification to do so. If we drive a car, we should know that we will be in trouble if we drive dangerously or allow our vehicle to become unsafe, even if no accident results. Convictions for offences of this kind do not violate legitimate expectations of fair warning nor require undue reliance on confession evidence. The way forward is to craft specific offences for particular situations which presage the occurrence of serious harm. In circumstances such as *Geddes* it might be possible to convict D of being in possession of a blade in a public place,[367] or carrying an offensive weapon in a public place, if the weapon was made, adapted, or intended to be used to cause injury to the person.[368] In *Campbell*, D was in fact convicted for possession of an imitation firearm.[369] Following *Geddes*, there has been specific legislative reform in the form of section 63 of the Sexual Offences Act 2003, which creates an offence of trespass with intent to commit a sexual offence;[370] and it would be appropriate to create a new offence of trespass with intent to imprison falsely or kidnap, where a sexual offence cannot be proved to have been intended.[371] It is better to proceed in this piecemeal way than to resort to a broad and vague law of attempt susceptible to uncertainties of interpretation and oppressive modes of enforcement.

Unquestionably, resolving when the criminal law should intervene to restrain and punish D at a point before she has committed any material harm is a sensitive and difficult

---

[364] See Clarkson, "Attempt: The Conduct Element" (2009) 29 *OJLS* 25; Rogers, "The Codification of Attempts and the Case for 'Preparation'" [2008] *Crim LR* 937.

[365] Clarkson, *ibid.*, 32.

[366] Law Com. No. 318, *Conspiracy and Attempts* (2009).

[367] Criminal Justice Act 1988, s. 139.

[368] Prevention of Crime Act 1953.

[369] Firearms Act 1968, s. 16A.

[370] Note also the offence contrary to s. 62 of the Sexual Offences Act 2003 of committing an offence (e.g. battery) with intent to commit a relevant sexual offence (e.g. rape).

[371] Note also the crime of preparing to commit an act of terrorism: Terrorism Act 2006, s. 5(1)(a).

matter. Serious crimes should require proof of culpability. It has been forcefully argued that culpability does not arise until D's conduct releases a risk of harm to a legally protected interest of V, in circumstances where D cannot control the realisation of the risk. On that view, D is not culpable when he strikes the match to light the fuse but he is culpable when he lights the fuse.[372] Whatever the merits of that view, its implementation would not be politically feasible for societies understandably concerned with risk and security.

§ 9.5 Impossibility and inchoate offences

(i) The principle of an impossibility defence

In principle, if the substantive offence is impossible to commit, this need not preclude liability for encouragement, assistance, conspiracy, or attempt. V may already be dead, but that does not rule out the possibility that D and E, unaware of his recent death, could make an agreement to kill V. The question then arises whether this agreement constitutes a criminal conspiracy. Prior to 1981, the common law position was that, if the full offence was impossible to commit, there could be no liability for any incitement, conspiracy, or attempt to commit it. Since 1981, the position has changed for attempts[373] and statutory conspiracy,[374] but impossibility remains a defence to common law conspiracy. The Serious Crime Act 2007 makes no reference to a defence of impossibility to the crimes of assistance and encouragement. However, for reasons of consistency with the statutory inchoate offences of attempt and conspiracy, and because assistance and encouragement can be committed if D does an act which is capable of assisting or encouraging a crime without any requirement that there be actual encouragement or assistance of any offence, the better view is that impossibility is not a defence to assistance or encouragement either.[375] It is unfortunate, however, that a statute which contains so much detail about the assistance and encouragement offences fails to make any reference to whether or not they are subject to a defence of impossibility.

It seems therefore that, apart from common law conspiracy, impossibility is not a defence to the inchoate offences. Nonetheless it remains important to consider whether impossibility should preclude liability for all inchoate offences.

In the case law and voluminous literature that the impossibility issue has generated, no predominant rationale for the existence of a defence of impossibility has emerged. It has been argued that impossibility necessarily provides a defence to a charge of attempt on grounds of lack of proximity, yet this explanation does not carry over to encouragement, assistance, and conspiracy. Besides, the proximity objection is circular. It implicitly assumes the conclusion that impossibility should provide a defence: if we allow liability to be proved on the basis of facts that D assumes, then his act may have been sufficiently proximate on the facts mistakenly assumed. More persuasive is the view that, since no harm was in fact threatened, the matter is insufficiently serious to warrant criminal liability; a conclusion attractive for those theorists who assert that criminal liability should be for conduct which

---

[372] Alexander and Ferzan, *Crime and Culpability: A Theory of Criminal Law* (2009) chap. 6.
[373] Criminal Attempts Act 1981, s. 1(2).
[374] Criminal Law Act 1977, s. 1(1)(b) as amended by the Criminal Attempts Act 1981.
[375] This is the view of the Law Commission: Law Com. No. 318, *Conspiracy and Attempts* (2009) para. 5.42. See also LCCP No. 300, *Inchoate Liability for Assisting and Encouraging Crime* (2006) para. 6.61.

causes harm or threatens harm and should not be imposed just because of one's character, however bad that may be.[376] On this view, when D and E agree to kill V, a person already dead, the agreement does not give rise to any social danger. Yet impossibility defences have been allowed even when danger beckoned. Picking an empty pocket has been regarded as a case of impossibility,[377] yet such conduct is menacing. Moreover, conduct may deserve censure irrespective of its propensity for harm: trying to kill someone without justification or excuse, for instance, is a very bad thing to do and merits punishment for its badness alone, whatever danger, if any, was threatened. The lack of a consistent rationale has given rise to unstable and shifting case law in jurisdictions which recognise an impossibility defence.[378]

This lack of focus has entailed difficulties in the legal application of impossibility defences. Insufficiency of means to attain an achievable end will generally not constitute an impossibility defence, yet radical insufficiency of means may do so. Further distinctions have been drawn concerning the relevance of the success or failure of D's project. Where D's project was to obtain a video recorder as cheaply as possible, it has at one time been ruled by the House of Lords that D did not attempt to handle stolen goods when she acquired a second-hand recorder which, erroneously, she thought was stolen.[379] On the other hand, D has subsequently been held to be guilty of attempting to traffic in heroin when he acquired a substance which he took to be heroin but which in fact was snuff, thereby frustrating his scheme to acquire the drug.[380] One way to defend these different outcomes is to maintain that a project brought to fruition without committing a crime cannot be regarded as an attempt to commit a crime, rendering irrelevant the question of impossibility as a defence.[381] Alternatively, some theorists acknowledge that in both situations an issue of impossibility arises but that only in the case of the failure to obtain drugs can there be said to be an intent to commit an offence.[382] These matters will require more discussion below. Enough has been said for now to indicate the vagaries and complexity of the topic of impossibility; a topic which, thankfully, has diminished in importance since the 1981 and subsequent statutory reforms.

The impossibility at issue here concerns matters of fact and law, but not impossibility relating to the very existence of an offence. There is a broad consensus that this latter form of impossibility should not lead to criminal liability. It is impossible in England to attempt to commit, say, the crime of adultery, because adultery is not a crime and in *Taaffe*[383] it was held that D could not be guilty of attempting to import foreign currency, since the importation of foreign currency was not a crime, even though D thought that it was. The consensus is not, perhaps, uniform: it has been claimed that it is inconsistent to deny a defence of impossibility and yet acquit someone who commits adultery in the belief that

---

[376] For a robust statement of this view see Hogan, "The Criminal Attempts Act and Attempting the Impossible" [1984] *Crim LR* 584.

[377] *Collins* (1864) Le & Ca 471, 169 ER 1477; but contrast *Ring* (1892) 61 LJMC 116.

[378] For a discussion of cases from a variety of US jurisdictions see Perkins and Boyle, *Criminal Law* (3rd ed., 1982) 627–35.

[379] *Anderton v. Ryan* [1985] 1 AC 560; below, § 9.5(iii).

[380] *Shivpuri* [1987] AC 1; below, § 9.5(iii).

[381] Hogan, "The Criminal Attempts Act and Attempting the Impossible" [1984] *Crim LR* 584; *Anderton v. Ryan* [1985] 1 AC 560.

[382] Duff, *Criminal Attempts* (1996) 112–13.

[383] [1984] AC 539.

he is committing a crime.[384] Yet the principle of legality requires that attempt liability take its bounds from the norms of the substantive criminal law.[385] Non-existent crimes are an entirely different case from a crime which, in particular circumstances, it may be impossible to commit.

Less straightforward is the situation where D considers his conduct to fall within the boundaries of an extant offence because he is mistaken about the ambit of the offence. Suppose that D "borrows" V's lawnmower for the weekend when V is away, aware that V would not have given D permission to use it. On the basis of a conversation with E (a confused law student), D believes that dishonestly borrowing the mower constitutes theft despite his lack of intention to deprive V permanently of the mower. D has demonstrated that he is prepared to do something which he assumes is theft, a crime that assuredly exists. Yet, legally, he is in the same case as our adulterer. He believes that dishonestly borrowing a lawnmower is a crime: it is not. Even more complex is the case where the mistake as to the ambit of a crime is the product of a mistake of civil law. For exculpatory purposes, a mistake of civil law is put on the same footing as a mistake of fact[386] and, arguably, this should cut both ways. Suppose that D cuts down a particular tree that he mistakenly thinks belongs to V. The fence separating D's land from V's had been moved by V without D noticing this change for six years, and D assumes that ownership in the tree is vested in V because he believes that ownership to land is acquired by adverse possession after six years; whereas the legally effective period is twelve years. If D's belief were true he would be intentionally destroying property belonging to another, a clear case of criminal damage. There seems little difference here from the situation where D makes a valid contract for the acquisition of a video recorder in the mistaken belief that the item was stolen. Both cases should come out the same way on the question whether an inchoate offence has been committed. But which way remains a matter of controversy, as we shall see.

(ii) Impossibility at common law

The House of Lords decisions in *Haughton* v. *Smith* [387] and *DPP* v. *Nock* [388] established a defence of impossibility for inchoate offences at common law. As we have noted, these decisions still govern for common law conspiracy. Three distinctive situations were identified in *Haughton* and confirmed in *Nock*. They will be discussed in turn.

(a) Inefficient and insufficient means

Seeking an attainable end in a manner which will not attain success is not to be regarded as a case of impossibility. That D and E dishonestly agree to relieve V of money through a scheme never likely to fool V will not preclude a conviction for conspiracy to defraud. In practice this category is straightforward and uncontroversial. At the theoretical level, however, it might be considered that in those rare cases where D commits himself to a criminal

---

[384] Gross, *A Theory of Criminal Justice* (1979) 209.
[385] See *CLGP* 633–5.
[386] *Smith* [1974] QB 354.
[387] [1975] AC 476.
[388] [1978] AC 979.

endeavour by means which are radically deficient and which threaten no one's interests, this degree of deficiency of means should be classified as intrinsically impossible. So if D wished to kill V by sticking pins into an effigy of V, one may be inclined not to take the matter seriously—however convinced D may be of her diabolical powers. As a matter of principle, it might appear natural to dismiss any charge of attempted murder in such a case on the ground of impossibility. On the other hand, since the particular result *is* achievable, by some means or other, and is genuinely, if ineffectually, striven for, the situation does seem to be one of ineffective means and so the issue of impossibility would not even arise. Duff suggests that this sort of case should be dealt with by providing for an acquittal if the conduct alleged "failed to engage with the world as an attempt to commit [the] offence".[389] As matters stand, since impossibility is not a defence to attempt, one would have to rely on prosecutorial discretion. Given the absence of reported cases, the employment of radically deficient means does not appear to attract prosecution, perhaps because it does not normally come to light or is not taken seriously when it does.[390]

(b) Physical impossibility

Perhaps the voodoo doll case should be treated as a case involving physical impossibility, so the availability of the defence of impossibility would matter. In *Nock*,[391] D and others were in possession of an admixture of substances from which they attempted to obtain cocaine. The mixture was incapable of yielding cocaine whatever processes it was subjected to. The House ruled that should a particular objective be physically impossible, whatever the means employed, the defence of impossibility applied. Suppose that V falsely informs D and E that he has a large credit balance at X bank. In fact V has no funds at all at the bank. If D and E contrive a dishonest scheme in an attempt to access V's supposed account, they have a defence of impossibility to conspiracy to defraud.

This head of impossibility has given rise to great dissatisfaction. In the example above, V may have suspected the dishonest designs of D and E and led them a false trail in order to entrap them. Should this be regarded as a case of physical impossibility if V had the large balance he claimed, but at the Y bank? In the past, it has been ruled to be a case of impossibility when D shot at a tree stump thinking it was a human being,[392] but not a case of impossibility when D shoots into an empty room while V is located elsewhere in the house.[393] The "empty pocket" cases, too, have divided courts,[394] with exceptional variables (such as property situated elsewhere on the victim or the proximity of other victims) generating convictions for attempted theft against the general trend of acquittals. There are few academic defenders of acquittals in cases of physical impossibility (subject to Duff's "engagement with the world" reservation referred to earlier) and the matter is much less important than it was following the intervention of statute for most inchoate offences.

---

[389] *Criminal Attempts* (1996) 398.

[390] In a study conducted by Finkel *et al.*, subjects almost unanimously considered that a case involving radically deficient means (pins in a wax effigy) did not merit prosecution: "Lay Perspectives on Legal Conundrums: Impossible and Mistaken Act Cases" (1995) 19 *Law and Human Behaviour* 593.

[391] [1978] AC 979.

[392] *McPherson* (1857) 7 Cox CC 281, 169 ER 975 (CCR).

[393] *State* v. *Mitchell* (1902) 170 Mo 633.

[394] Contrast *Collins* (1864) Le & Ca 471, 169 ER 1477 with *Ring* (1892) 61 LJMC 116.

Nonetheless, the continuing presence of this defence for common law conspiracies under-scores the desirability of statutory intervention in respect of this offence.

(c) Completion of intended conduct without the commission of a substantive offence

This category is exemplified by *Haughton*,[395] where D arranged to take possession of corned beef that he assumed would be stolen. When he did take possession, the beef was no longer stolen as it had been taken into police custody[396] and then released under police supervi-sion in order to entrap D. The House of Lords ruled that D was not guilty of attempting to handle stolen goods. His (physical) conduct was "objectively innocent" and his belief that the goods were stolen did not alter that fact.

This notion of "objective innocence" has proved tenacious. Indeed, for some time it even withstood the statutory abolition of an impossibility defence in attempt and statutory con-spiracy (discussed in the following section). Two arguments support acquittals in these cases. First, it is claimed that situations which consist of D achieving everything he set out to do are ineptly described as attempts, which imply some form of miscarriage or failure. Secondly, where the conduct is "objectively innocent", convictions in these cases may argu-ably be castigated as involving punishment for thought alone. It is submitted that neither claim is defensible. As we noted earlier (§ 9.4(v)), "attempt" as a legal term of art need not imply any form of failure. Moreover, "impossible" attempts are no more thought crimes than are other attempts. D must do something which is more than merely preparatory on the facts that he assumed.

(iii) *Impossibility in attempt, statutory conspiracy, encouragement, and assistance*

Decisions such as *Haughton* and *Nock* were subjected to considerable criticism, princi-pally on the ground that people who unequivocally embarked on criminal projects, such as receiving stolen goods on a large scale or producing cocaine for trafficking purposes, were evading justified censure and restraint because of flukes which, although precluding concrete harm on particular occasions, allowed dangerous actors to remain at large.[397] This sentiment ultimately proved decisive and the Criminal Attempts Act 1981 abolished the impossibility defence for statutory conspiracy and attempt. For both offences it is provided that D may conspire or attempt to commit an offence, "even though the facts are such that the commission of the offence is impossible".[398] Those words seem apt to eradicate the defence of impossibility in all its forms and, although no explicit provision is made in the Serious Crime Act 2007, it is consistent with that statute to assume that the defence is not available either for assistance or encouragement. D will encourage P to traffic in a Class A drug even if the suitcase which D instructs P to collect contains snuff and not, as D believes, heroin. Similarly, D and E will be guilty of conspiracy to traffic in the drugs if they both believe the suitcase to contain heroin, even though it does not. D will attempt to

---

[395] [1975] AC 476.

[396] Theft Act 1968, s. 24(3).

[397] See the discussion in Law Com. No. 102, *Attempt and Impossibility in Relation to Attempt, Conspiracy and Incitement* (1980) paras. 2.85–2.100.

[398] Criminal Attempts Act 1981, s. 1(2); Criminal Law Act 1977, s. 1(1)(b).

handle stolen corned beef, notwithstanding that the beef has ceased to be stolen property, if D thinks it is stolen. In the case of attempt, for the avoidance of any conceivable doubt, it is provided that D's intention is to be judged as if "the facts of the case had been as he believed them to be".[399] This renders completely untenable the always fallacious argument which took the form, on facts such as *Haughton*, that "D intended to handle that particular consignment of beef: that particular consignment of beef was not stolen beef; accordingly, D did not intend to handle stolen beef".

Yet even the most clearly drafted legislation, emerging from a transparent and easily verifiable legislative history,[400] may not be proof against firmly entrenched judicial views, particularly where the facts of the instant case put these views in the best light. In *Anderton v. Ryan*,[401] D was questioned by police about her acquisition of a video recorder at a low price. She admitted that she believed the item was stolen, although it was never proved that it had been. She was charged with attempted handling. Clearly what D did was not intrinsically a criminal project. The project was the acquisition of a video recorder and D was not so perverse as to prefer a recorder that was actually stolen. Moreover, there was no evidence that she was a trader in stolen goods, rendering her prosecution heavy-handed, if not oppressive. Yet, according to the Criminal Attempts Act 1981, her conviction would seem assured. If the facts had been as she believed them to be, she would have acquired a stolen item. Judging her intent against the facts she supposed, she intended to handle stolen goods.

A unanimous House of Lords quashed D's conviction. The language of the 1981 Act was not so much interpreted as swept aside by the idea of "objective innocence". She had done everything she had wanted to do, it was said, and she had not been proved to have committed a crime. How could everyday, lawful acts such as acquiring goods for payment be turned into crimes by mere beliefs which could not be shown to correspond with the facts? The conduct was not of the sort intended to be regulated by the Criminal Attempts Act 1981 and, accordingly, application of the impossibility provisions to D's conduct simply, seemingly, did not arise.

Within a matter of months, in *Shivpuri*,[402] the House of Lords was confronted with facts from a very different milieu from *Anderton*. D was a suspected drug trafficker. In the context of an undercover police operation, he was induced to take possession of a suitcase full of snuff which he had been assured contained heroin, and was subsequently charged with attempting to commit the offence of being knowingly concerned with dealing in controlled drugs. Here D's project was intrinsically criminal. The absence of heroin entailed the failure of his project. Moreover, it is clearly in the public interest that "sting" operations should be carried out, where possible, with the aid of such props as powder masquerading as a drug, fake firearms, or explosives, etc., without risking circulation of the real things. It

---

[399] Criminal Attempts Act 1981, s. 1(3)(b).

[400] In the discussion in Law Com. No. 102, *Attempt and Impossibility in Relation to Attempt, Conspiracy and Incitement* (1980) paras. 2.85–2.100, no distinction was drawn between the fact patterns of cases such as *Anderton* and cases such as *Shivpuri*. The provisions in the Law Commission's draft Bill, reflecting this analysis, were adopted unchanged by Parliament.

[401] [1985] 1 AC 560.

[402] [1987] AC 1.

is not surprising then, that D's conviction for attempted drug trafficking was upheld by a unanimous House. More surprising, perhaps, was that *Anderton v. Ryan* was overturned. A majority of the House considered that differing outcomes in these cases could not be reconciled. Interestingly, two Law Lords considered that the two cases could be reconciled,[403] but they were not prepared to take this opinion to the point of dissent. Accordingly, *Anderton v. Ryan* was unequivocally overruled.

That there are differences between *Shivpuri* and *Anderton* is undeniable. But, as the majority in *Shivpuri* recognised, these differences can gain no purchase on the language of the 1981 Act.[404] If we judge Mrs Ryan on the facts that she supposed, she would have obtained a stolen item and would have intended to obtain a stolen item. The fact that this criminal act (on the supposed facts) was not done for its own sake but to gain some ulterior advantage is true of a great many acts which are indubitably criminal. That Mrs Ryan did not in fact obtain a stolen item (or could not be proved to have done so) prompts reactions of indulgence for her case. Yet it has not proved feasible to draft legislation on impossibility which leaves out a Ryan but includes a Shivpuri.

Duff, in his exhaustive treatise on attempts, maintains that the two cases can and should have different outcomes and, moreover, that different outcomes are compatible with the language of the Criminal Attempts Act 1981.[405] His position is that while Shivpuri intended to traffick in drugs, Ryan did not intend to handle stolen goods. According to Duff, Ryan lacked the requisite intent as obtaining a stolen recorder played no motivational part in her conduct. She wanted a cheap recorder, nothing else, and therefore the stolen quality which she mistakenly attributed to the item she acquired was not part, as Duff terms it, of the "content" of her intent. He does acknowledge, however, that had her belief been congruent with the facts, she would have intended to obtain a stolen item.

Duff's explication of this perceived difference is complex and subtle. Suffice it here to say that he would draw distinctions which, however fine-grained, do not necessarily carry moral weight. He says of D who intends to kill V, a person he takes to be the prime minister but whose identity is immaterial to D (a contract killer, say), that D intends to kill the prime minister if V is the prime minister but not if D mistakenly takes V to be the prime minister. Either way, of course, D is guilty of murder. But surely, in either case, he intends to kill the prime minister? Duff ties "intent" too tightly to "motive". Intention is a cognitive as well as a motivational state: the "content" of one's intent includes circumstances that are known about or believed even when not desired. Moreover, the claim that the content of one's intentions depends upon what actually happens is profoundly implausible. Intention is a mental state, a subjective phenomenon. We intend those acts and results which provide us with a reason for which we act—it is hard to see how those reasons could be constituted by unknown truths.

---

[403] Lords Hailsham and Mackay took the view that in *Shivpuri* D intended to deal in drugs whereas in *Anderton* D merely believed the recorder was stolen and did not intend to acquire a stolen recorder. It is submitted that, although there certainly is a distinction between the cases, the difference is one of motive rather than a lack of intention.

[404] Lord Bridge, in giving judgment for the House, acknowledged his indebtedness to an article by Glanville Williams, "The Lords and Impossible Attempts" [1986] *CLJ* 33.

[405] Duff, *Criminal Attempts* (1996) 378–84.

§ 9.6 Jurisdiction and inchoate offences

At common law, the dependence of jurisdiction upon territory ensured that "all crime is local".[406] For statutory crimes, there is a very strong presumption that criminal statutes are concerned only with the regulation of acts or omissions perpetrated in the United Kingdom.[407] There are, however, some long-standing statutory exceptions to the territoriality principle[408] and, in recent times, significant further exceptions have been enacted in response to the transnational character of some forms of criminality.[409]

In principle, inchoate offences need not be constrained by the territoriality principle, provided the inchoate offence in question relates to an offence to be perpetrated in England or Wales. As Lord Salmon observed, what difference does it make if a plan to rob a bank in London is hatched in Birmingham or Brussels?[410] In that spirit, the Privy Council in *Somchai Liangsiriprasent* v. *United States*[411] considered that parties to agreements made abroad to perpetrate offences in England are subject to English criminal jurisdiction, notwithstanding the absence of any steps taken in England to put the agreements into effect. The Court of Appeal has made similar rulings in *Sansom*[412] and *Naini*.[413] The position established for conspiracy may well apply also to attempt. In *DPP* v. *Stonehouse*,[414] D faked his death by drowning in Miami so that his wife, who was not involved in the fraud, could claim on life assurance policies. The House of Lords asserted jurisdiction over this attempted criminal deception. The majority of the House justified the assumption of jurisdiction on the basis that "effects" (reports in the press) of D's conduct in Miami were felt in England.[415] Lord Diplock, however, asserted jurisdiction on a different basis: that D's conduct abroad was sufficiently proximate to the commission of an offence of criminal deception in England. His Lordship's more straightforward approach gains strength from the subsequent adoption, in cases such as *Sansom*,[416] of the same approach to cases of conspiracy. If attempts or conspiracies are focused on substantive crimes which are themselves triable in England or Wales, there is no reason in principle why the attempt or conspiracy should take place in England or Wales. This has now been recognised explicitly for encouragement and assistance, so that if D knows or believes that the act amounting to the commission of the substantive offence might take place wholly or partly in England or Wales then he can be guilty of encouragement or assistance regardless of where he was at the relevant time.[417]

For most offences of fraud and dishonesty, it is now clearly the case, following the implementation of Part I of the Criminal Justice Act 1993,[418] that conspiracies, attempts,

---

[406] Williams, "Venue and Ambit of the Criminal Law" (1965) 81 *LQR* 276, 395, 518.
[407] *Cox* v. *Army Council* [1963] AC 48; *Air India* v. *Wiggins* [1980] 1 WLR 815.
[408] Notably murder, manslaughter, and bigamy: OAPA 1861, ss. 9, 57.
[409] E.g. Criminal Justice Act 1993, part 1; Suppression of Terrorism Act 1978, s. 4; Taking of Hostages Act 1982, s. 1(1).
[410] *DPP* v. *Doot* [1973] AC 602.
[411] [1991] AC 225.
[412] [1991] 2 QB 130.
[413] [1999] 2 Cr App R 398 (common law conspiracy to defraud).
[414] [1978] AC 55. See now Part I of the Criminal Justice Act 1993.
[415] For criticism of that approach see Sullivan, "Crossing the Rubicon in Miami" (1978) 41 *MLR* 215.
[416] [1991] 2 QB 130.
[417] Serious Crime Act 2007, s. 52(1).
[418] SI 1999 No. 1189 (32); SI 1999 No. 1499 (42). For discussion of Part 1 of the Criminal Justice Act 1993 in relation to substantive offences of fraud and dishonesty, see below, § 13.9.

encouragement, and assistance directed at those offences need not take place in England and Wales provided that English courts would have jurisdiction over the substantive offence.[419] As we have seen, that position has been established judicially for conspiracy in general, applies generally by statute for encouragement and assistance, and probably extends generally for attempts too.

We now turn to the converse case of inchoate offences in England and Wales to commit crimes within foreign jurisdictions. Classically, inchoate activity directed at breaching foreign laws did not constitute an offence under English law.[420] An exception has been recognised for the crime of soliciting murder contrary to section 4 of the Offences Against the Person Act 1861,[421] such that it is possible to solicit murder to be committed abroad from within England and Wales, even if the potential victim is not a British citizen. It is also a statutory offence to incite in England and Wales the commission of an act of terrorism outside the United Kingdom.[422] For conspiracy, too, the classical position is radically changed by section 1A of the Criminal Law Act 1977,[423] which provides jurisdiction over conspiracies notwithstanding that implementation of the agreement will involve an act or event by one or more of the parties taking place outside England or Wales. The act or event must constitute an offence in the country where it is to take place and must also constitute an offence under English law were the act or event to take place in England or Wales. Jurisdiction is triggered if "anything" relating to the conspiracy—e.g. the posting of a letter—is done in England by a party to the conspiracy or by the "agent" of a party, either before or after the agreement was made. The breadth of coverage is enormous. For instance, D and E, Australian tourists passing through London, could be tried for conspiracy were they to agree in a London pub to cheat on the Paris Metro. The Attorney General must give consent to any prosecution under section 1A. It will be interesting to see how he or she approaches that task in practice.[424]

The Serious Crime Act 2007 also gives the English courts jurisdiction over assistance or encouragement if the act of assistance or encouragement was committed wholly or partly in England or Wales and D knew or believed that the conduct element of the substantive offence might occur abroad, and the offence would be triable in England and Wales were it committed there,[425] or would be an offence in the place where it was committed.[426] So, for example, if D writes a letter in England which is posted to P in France encouraging P to

---

[419] Criminal Justice Act 1993, ss. 3, 4.

[420] *Board of Trade* v. *Owen* [1957] AC 602; *Abu Hamza* [2006] EWCA Crim 2918, [2007] QB 659.

[421] *Abu Hamza, ibid.*

[422] Terrorism Act 2006, s59.

[423] Interpolated by s. 5 of the Criminal Justice (Terrorism and Conspiracy) Act 1998, as amended by the Coroners and Justice Act 2009, s. 72(1). No provision is made for attempt. Note, also, s. 5 of the Criminal Justice Act 1993, which extends conspiracy to defraud to commit specified offences of fraud and dishonesty to situations where the fraudulent or dishonest conduct will take place outside England and Wales.

[424] The Criminal Justice (Terrorism and Conspiracy) Act 1998 was hurriedly passed during an emergency session of Parliament. There is no reference in the debates to the provision extending jurisdiction for conspiracy. Political groups active in London suspected of organising violent acts to take place overseas are generally considered to be the target group.

[425] Serious Crime Act 2007, sched. 4, para. 1. For the purposes of this provision it is to be assumed that the person assisted or encouraged satisfies any conditions of citizenship, nationality, or residence which must be met in order for the English court to have jurisdiction.

[426] *Ibid.*, para. 2.

kill V, who might be in England or France, the English court would have jurisdiction over D. This is because the English court has jurisdiction over murder if P is a British citizen.[427] Alternatively, the English court would have jurisdiction over D even if her act of assistance or encouragement occurred wholly outside England and Wales, if she believed that the conduct element of the substantive offence might occur abroad and D would be guilty of the offence were she to commit it in that country.[428] So, if D, a British citizen, was on holiday in Japan and encouraged P to commit rape there, the English courts would have jurisdiction over D's encouragement because, if he had committed rape in Japan, the English court would have jurisdiction to try him.[429] The only limitation on jurisdiction over assistance and encouragement offences would be where the act of assistance and encouragement was committed wholly abroad and the English court would have no jurisdiction over D were she to commit the offence there. So, if D encouraged P in Brazil to assault V there, the English court would not have jurisdiction.

The Law Commission has recommended that the jurisdictional code relating to conspiracy should be clarified, so that:

(i)   Statute should recognise that the English court has jurisdiction over a conspiracy made abroad where D knew or believed that the conduct or circumstance element of the substantive offence might occur in England and Wales.[430] This accords with the position at common law.

(ii)   The English court should have jurisdiction where a conspiracy is intended to be carried out abroad in circumstances broadly consistent with the regime under the Serious Crime Act 2007. So, for example, there would be jurisdiction in England and Wales if D made a communication in England and Wales leading to the formation of a conspiracy abroad, D knew or believed that the conduct or circumstances of the offence might be committed abroad, and to do so would be a crime in that country.[431]

There is no recommendation that these jurisdictional reforms should encompass attempt as well, since there is very little scope for a more than merely preparatory act to be committed in England and Wales in respect of an offence committed abroad.[432] Nevertheless, D, who posts a fraudulent letter in England with a view to making a false insurance claim in France, will have committed a more than merely preparatory act in respect of fraud by false representation, but the English court would not have jurisdiction in such circumstances.

---

[427] Offences Against the Person Act 1861, s. 9.
[428] Serious Crime Act 2007, sched. 4, para. 3.
[429] Sexual Offences Act 2003, s. 72 and sched. 2.
[430] Law Com No. 318, *Conspiracy and Attempts* (2009) para. 7.49.
[431] *Ibid.*, para. 7.56. See also paras. 7.60 and 7.65.
[432] However, it would be appropriate to confirm by statute that there is jurisdiction in England and Wales where an attempt is committed abroad in respect of a substantive offence which is intended to be committed in England and Wales.

10

HOMICIDE

§ 10.1 Death and liability

Homicide is the death of a human being in circumstances where the death can be attributed to the conduct of one or more other human beings, or exceptionally to a corporation or other organisation.[1] A homicide may be lawful or unlawful. An example of lawful homicide is where D kills V in justifiable self-defence.[2] If the homicide is unlawful it may constitute one of a variety of offences (including diverse forms of vehicular homicide): in this chapter we will consider murder, manslaughter, and some related offences.

If D is found to be causally responsible for V's death, important penal consequences may follow that are unparalleled elsewhere in the criminal law. For instance, in *Mallet*,[3] D quarrelled with his neighbour V and punched V in the face. Ordinarily, this would have been a case of battery, as the punch itself inflicted no injury upon V. Unfortunately, V fell awkwardly and died as a result of striking his head on a paving stone. The events therefore constituted, as will be explained later, a case of manslaughter,[4] and the Court of Appeal confirmed D's custodial sentence[5] even though it found that D was not at fault with regard to causing V's death. If a motorist, by his dangerous driving, were to cause dreadful but non-fatal injuries, he would receive, at most, a five-year prison sentence.[6] If his driving were to cause death, the maximum sentence would extend to 14 years.[7] A person may cause another individual serious injury by grossly negligent conduct. Outside special contexts, such conduct will not result in criminal liability. Should death ensue, however, liability may be incurred for manslaughter.[8] Formerly, all persons found guilty of murder would receive a mandatory death sentence.[9] Nowadays, the mandatory sentence is life imprisonment,[10]

---

[1] See below, § 10.6(iii).

[2] At one time the common law formally distinguished between justifiable homicides and merely excusable homicides. While an acquittal followed upon verdicts either of justifiable or excusable homicide, in the case of the latter D's goods were forfeited. In 1828 forfeiture was abolished and, so far as D is concerned, there is no difference between the various defences to homicide (or to any other crime).

[3] [1972] Crim LR 260.

[4] Below, § 10.6ff.

[5] Imprisonment for one year.

[6] Road Traffic Offenders Act 1988, sched. 2, as amended by Legal Aid, Sentencing and Punishment of Offenders Act 1988, s. 143.

[7] Criminal Justice Act 2003, s. 285(3).

[8] *Adomako* [1995] 1 AC 171.

[9] That is, until s. 5 of the Homicide Act 1957 (now repealed) created a distinction between capital and non-capital murder. Non-capital murder attracted a mandatory life sentence.

[10] Murder (Abolition of Death Penalty) Act 1965.

a unique case of penal inflexibility for a crime which, like many other offences, can encompass substantial variations of culpability in its range of applications.

Of course, the criminal law must take killings seriously. By its very finality, death is an irremediable harm and even if V is killed instantly and painlessly in circumstances which did not cause her any prior anxiety, she will normally have been done a very great wrong. Yet it is a mistake to hold that death as a harm will invariably transcend all other harms. True, death is the negation of life and life is a precondition for all other forms of value and disvalue. Yet it does not follow that death is always the worst alternative. There may be circumstances where death is the preferred outcome for a particular person for reasons that strike us as rational, whereas only in the most bizarre circumstances would a person welcome the infliction upon herself of significant disablement or other forms of serious harm. Death is special in terms of the impact it has on those with strong emotional[11] and material bonds with the person deceased. The anger and resentment of these "secondary" victims,[12] amplified in the media, is perhaps the most potent factor inhibiting a more equable penal response to causing death. As this chapter will show, causing death may involve morally debatable forms of liability and risk exposure to excessive punishment.

§ 10.2 Homicide defined

A homicide must contain the following elements:

(a) The victim must be a human being.
(b) Death must be caused through the act or omission of one or more human beings, or exceptionally by a corporation or other organisation.
(c) Death must occur within the Queen's peace.

We will now examine these elements.

(i) Human beings

Homicide is defined in terms of the taking of human life. In certain rare situations, dispute may arise about the human status of a victim of an alleged homicide. First, a foetus, even to the point of delivery at birth, is not accorded full human status, and until birth the interests of the foetus are protected by laws falling outwith the law of homicide.[13] Secondly, at one time, the advent of death—identified in terms of the absence of pulse and respiration—was a clearly defined terminus of homicide law. Advances in medical techniques have undermined the certainty with which we can apply or disapply the concept of death to persons with profound and permanent disabilities whose existence is sustained by artificial means.[14] Accordingly, homicide law requires criteria by which to establish the presence of

---

[11] For a searching study of impact on family and significant others see Rock, *After Homicide: Practical and Political Responses to Bereavement* (1998).

[12] It may be noted that close relatives of persons deceased have been treated as "victims" for the purposes of bringing actions before the European Court of Human Rights (*McCann and Others* v. *UK* (1996) 21 EHRR 97) in order to contest the legality of State action resulting in fatalities.

[13] Infant Life (Preservation) Act 1929; OAPA 1861, s. 58.

[14] See Skegg, *Law, Ethics and Medicine* (1984) chap. 9.

independent human life at the time of birth and to determine the life/death status of persons who may exhibit one or more of the traditional indicia of life, but only by virtue of technological intervention.

(a) Life at birth

In *A-G's Reference (No. 3 of 1994)*,[15] the House of Lords confirmed, *obiter*, the previous understanding that to destroy a viable foetus, however late in term, would not constitute any form of homicide. This is so whether the act of destruction terminates the life of the foetus in the womb or causes the foetus to be stillborn. For a live foetus to attain full personhood, the whole body of the child must emerge into the world and must sustain an existence independently of the mother for however brief a period of time. There is no modern case law on what constitutes an existence independently of the mother.[16] The preponderance of nineteenth-century authority on the topic favours a test of independent respiration,[17] which provides a serviceable criterion for the existence of life.[18]

The failure to accord full human status to a late-term viable foetus has been rationalised on the basis that, until the foetus is expelled from the mother, it is to be regarded as belonging to the mother and not constituting any kind of entity in its own right.[19] This rationalisation was forcefully rejected by Lord Mustill in *A-G's Reference (No. 3 of 1994)*[20] on the ground that it contradicted incontrovertible biological fact. From an early stage in pregnancy, a foetus becomes an entity unto itself, whose habitat is in the womb. Indeed, after eight months of pregnancy, no further metamorphic development of the foetus occurs, and from then on the difference between a foetus and a neonate is purely a matter of location.[21] The legal conferment of personhood reflects societal perceptions which are not underpinned by biological data. This results in some uncomfortable anomalies. If a late-term viable foetus is destroyed in the womb without justification or excuse, the applicable offences are child destruction or unlawfully procuring a miscarriage.[22] If, however, the pre-term attempt to destroy the foetus (when *en ventre sa mere*) is unsuccessful and a birth ensues, yet the neonate dies as a consequence of injuries sustained in the earlier attempt to destroy it, a verdict of murder or manslaughter may ensue.[23] Similarly, a lawful abortion may be performed outside the normally permitted period of 24 weeks if it seems likely that a child, if born, would be seriously handicapped.[24] By contrast, if a pre-term child

---

[15] [1998] AC 245 (HL).

[16] For general discussion see Temkin, "Pre-Natal Injury, Homicide and the Draft Criminal Code" [1986] *CLJ* 414.

[17] *Poulton* (1832) 5 C & P 329, 172 ER 997; *Brain* (1834) 6 C & P 349, 172 ER 1272; *West* (1848) 2 Cox CC 500; *Crutchley* (1857) 7 C & P 814, 173 ER 355.

[18] The Criminal Law Revision Committee, in its Fourteenth Report, *Offences Against the Person* Cmnd. 7844 (1980), did not recommend any statutory change in the law.

[19] A view adopted by the Court of Appeal in *A-G's Reference (No. 3 of 1994)* [1996] 2 All ER 10, 18.

[20] [1998] AC 245, 256.

[21] Although the location of a foetus does have implications when the interests of the foetus are irreconcilable with respect for the autonomous choices of the pregnant woman: *St George's Health Care NHS Trust v. S* [1998] 3 All ER 673.

[22] Infant Life (Preservation) Act 1929; OAPA 1861, s. 58.

[23] Confirmed by the House of Lords in *A-G's Reference (No. 3 of 1994)* [1998] AC 245.

[24] Abortion Act 1967, s. 1(1)(d).

is sustained alive outside the womb, the destruction of the child would be regarded as the destruction of a person, however handicapped the child.[25]

Debate about the appropriate legal status of the late-term foetus has arisen in other jurisdictions, most notably in the United States.[26] South Carolina has legislated that a late-term foetus is legally to be regarded as a full human subject.[27] A considerable number of states have enacted "feticide" statutes, which fall short of attributing personhood to foetuses but which stipulate that the non-therapeutic destruction of a foetus is to be regarded as equivalent to the taking of human life.[28] In England, however, there is high authority that a late-term foetus is *not* to be regarded as a person. The House of Lords in *A-G's Reference (No. 3 of 1994)*[29] regarded the matter as beyond argument and would have refused to convict D of murder had D stabbed E when she was pregnant, with the intent only to injure E. This induced premature labour and the child V survived for four months before dying, it was assumed, from the effects of the stabbing when V was a foetus in the womb of E. The House of Lords considered that it would be extending the concept of transferred malice too far to transfer the intention to injure from the mother to the foetus and then to the child V that the foetus subsequently became at birth. Although the ruling was expressed in terms of discountenancing a "double" transfer of malice, that objection could not have been sustained had there not been a perceived discontinuity and a lesser status as between the foetus and the child. Furthermore, in a civil case, it has been ruled unlawful to make a woman submit to surgery in order to save the life of the foetus (and her own life) at the time of confinement.[30] Such an assertion of autonomy would be difficult to sustain in legal terms had the claimant been regarded as the mother of a child rather than of a foetus.

Moreover, the passing of the Infant Life Preservation Act 1929 can be said to reinforce the non-person status of a late-term foetus. The Act was passed on the assumption that to destroy a foetus in the process of birth would not constitute an offence unless it could be proved that the child had taken breath after complete expulsion from the mother. Therefore, it may be asserted with some confidence that the recognition of a late-term foetus as a full person would require legislative intervention.[31] Any such initiative should proceed cautiously. As we have discussed, the present law gives rise to some anomalous distinctions when tested against the biological facts. Yet the reception of a child into the world after the

---

[25] There are civil cases, such as *Re C* [1990] Fam 26 and *Re J* [1990] 3 All ER 930, and the criminal trial case of *Arthur* (1981) 12 B Med LR 1, which indicate that lesser degrees of medical care may be owed to profoundly disabled neonates, but the deliberate killing of any person is murder regardless of the state of disability: *Airedale National Health Trust v. Bland* [1993] AC 789. In the very special circumstances of *Re A (Children) (Conjoined Twins: Surgical Separation)* [2001] 1 Fam 147, the separation of conjoined twins was held to be a lawful procedure even though it was known that it would entail the death of the weaker twin. The difficulty and significance of the case arise from the fact that the weaker, profoundly handicapped twin was, properly, accorded full human status: see further § 21.3(ii)(e). In the case of late-term abortions, a foetus may be delivered capable of survival outside the womb but, particularly in a case of handicap, be allowed to die.

[26] There are decisions to the effect that the common law recognises the personhood of a late-term viable foetus: *Commonwealth v. Lawrence* (1998) 404 Mass 378 (Mass SC).

[27] Code of Laws of South Carolina, Offenses Against the Person, s. 16-3-90.

[28] Schott, "Fetal Protection—An Overview of Recent State Legislative Responses" (1991) 22 *Memphis State University LR* 119; Kaufman, "Legal Recognition of Independent Fetal Rights" (1997) 17 *Children's Legal Rights J* 20.

[29] [1998] AC 245.

[30] *St George's Healthcare NHS Trust v. S* [1998] 3 All ER 673.

[31] Currently, the jurisprudence on Art. 2 of the ECHR seems unlikely to require any judge-made change to the law: *Vo v. France* (2005) 40 EHRR 259.

point of birth is an event of enormous cultural significance, laden with symbolism. These social facts may weigh more heavily than biological facts when resolving the parameters of the law of homicide.[32]

Post-natal deaths from pre-natal injuries.
Once a child has an existence independently of the mother, the death of the child by the agency of another will constitute homicide. This applies where a pre-birth injury causes a post-birth death. The early case of *Senior*[33] indicates the potential scope of the liability that may arise in such circumstances. D, a midwife, ineptly supervised a birth. As a consequence, the child died shortly after the birth and D was successfully prosecuted for manslaughter by gross negligence. A wide range of pre-birth conduct on the part of pregnant women may be associated with the deaths of infants, including substance abuse and sexual risk-taking. In English case law, at the present time, there is no reported case of a prosecution arising from such circumstances. There may be a very understandable ambivalence on the part of prosecuting authorities in seeking penal sanctions against persons who are in thrall to addictions of various kinds or burdened by other forms of social dysfunction, but in principle such prosecutions are possible.[34]

A-G's Reference (No. 3 of 1994) confirms that post-natal deaths resulting from pre-natal injury fall within the domain of homicide. In actus reus terms this is quite straightforward: a neonate is a person even when born in a condition inimical to ultimate survival. Yet the fact that the fatal injury was inflicted prior to birth may well have a bearing upon questions of mens rea. If D intends to destroy a foetus in the womb, he will lack an intent to kill *a person* and therefore will lack the mens rea for murder. Consequently, should the foetus survive D's destructive efforts but die some time after the birth as a consequence of them, a murder charge would seem to be ruled out.[35] D will be liable for murder only if he inflicts a pre-birth injury intending to cause the child to die after the birth[36] or to be born with a serious injury.[37]

Recall that on the facts of *A-G's Reference (No. 3 of 1994)*, D did not direct his violence at the foetus. His target was the pregnant woman, whom he stabbed in the small of the back. The mother gave birth but the child died four months later as a consequence of premature birth induced by the attack. The House of Lords considered D guilty of manslaughter of the kind known as constructive manslaughter, which merely requires a dangerous criminal act causally associated with the death. It is not necessary that the dangerous act be targeted at the deceased.[38]

---

[32] Becker, "Human Being: The Boundaries of the Concept" (1974) 4 *Phil & Public Aff* 334; Engelhardt, "The Ontology of Abortion" (1973) 84 *Ethics* 217.

[33] (1832) 1 Mood CC 346, 168 ER 1298.

[34] Prosecutions and civil law injunctions have been sought against substance-abusing pregnant women in the United States: Jos, Marshall and Perlmutter, "The Charleston Policy on Cocaine Use during Pregnancy: A Cautionary Tale" (1995) 23 *J Law, Med and Ethics* 120; Glaze, "Combatting Prenatal Substance Abuse: Court Ordered Protective Custody of the Fetus" (1997) 80 *Marquette LR* 793.

[35] D would, however, be guilty of constructive manslaughter, on the basis that he has caused death by an unlawful and dangerous act. See further below, § 10.6(i).

[36] According to Lord Mustill, in these circumstances D's mens rea may be regarded as not directed to the foetus but to the human being if and when it comes into existence: [1998] AC 245, 261.

[37] This should follow from the rule that an intent to cause grievous bodily harm is sufficient mens rea for murder.

[38] *Mitchell* [1983] QB 741, confirmed in *A-G's Reference (No. 3 of 1994)* [1998] AC 245, 270.

In ruling that D would be guilty of manslaughter, the House of Lords differed from the Court of Appeal,[39] which had thought that a murder verdict was possible on the basis of the transferred intent principle.[40] D had intended to cause grievous bodily harm to his pregnant girlfriend, and with that intention he had done an act causing the subsequent death of the child. Lord Mustill, in rejecting this view, expressed his dislike both of the rule that intent to cause grievous bodily harm sufficed as mens rea for murder and of the transferred intent principle generally. He accepted that these grounds of inculpation were too well entrenched to remove. Yet he declined, as we noted above, to "extend" the transferred intent principle to "double" transfers (first from the mother to the foetus, then from the foetus to the child it became).[41]

Clearly, *A-G's Reference (No. 3 of 1994)* decides that if D intends to cause serious harm to a pregnant V (which is sufficient mens rea for murder should V herself die) but does not intend to harm the foetus, he will be guilty of manslaughter but not murder should the foetus become a child who dies as a consequence of D's attack on the mother. The basis of this decision is elusive, giving rise to speculation about its ambit. Lord Mustill disliked the principle of transferred intent because he regarded it as based on a fiction. This fictional character of the principle may, however, be queried. The principle may, instead, be taken to prescribe that the mere occurrence of unforeseen consequences does not preclude liability if the presence of those consequences is compatible with proof of the elements of the offence, in this case intending serious bodily harm and causing death thereby. Moreover, the House of Lords clearly accepted the substance of the transferred intent principle when it ruled that, in the case of manslaughter, it sufficed that D's conduct was dangerous and that the dangerousness of the act need not be associated with any threat to the actual victim. Furthermore, recall that Lord Mustill refused to confirm the murder conviction on the basis of a compound dislike of the transferred intent principle and the rule that intent to cause serious harm sufficed as culpability for murder. Accordingly, we cannot be sure what the outcome would have been had D acted with intent to kill his girlfriend. Would Lord Mustill have countenanced a "double" transfer of intent then?

(b) Death[42]

At one time an entirely satisfactory legal account of death could be given in terms of the irreversible cessation of respiration and heartbeat. In most circumstances such an account will still suffice, but not in every case. Take a person who has been recovered unconscious from the sea. No heartbeat or respiration may be detectable, yet we would not pronounce that person dead if those faculties could be recovered by manual or technological means. If the point of no return has been reached, ruling out recourse to such means, then the person is assuredly dead. But suppose it is possible to re-establish respiration and heartbeat by artificial means. Can we assume that life has been restored?

The answer to that question will depend on the condition of the patient. It may be that, because of the length of time that the patient's brain was deprived of oxygen, the condition

---

[39] [1996] 2 All ER 10.
[40] Above, § 5.7.
[41] [1998] AC 245, 261.
[42] "Death" in Grubb, Laing, McHale (eds.), *Principles of Medical Law* (3rd ed., 2010) chap. 22.

known as "brain-death" has arisen. This is an irreversible condition involving the complete non-functioning of the brain stem.[43] Identification of this condition is straightforward— a confirmed flat printout from an electroencephalography (EEG) machine.[44] There is an international medical consensus that brain-death is death *ipso facto* and many jurisdictions have passed legislation stipulating brain-death as a criterion of death.[45] There has been no legislative response for England and Wales. However, in *Bland*,[46] three Law Lords assumed that destruction of the brain stem entailed death.[47] In *Re A (a minor)*,[48] a civil case, there was a first instance ruling that brain stem death was, for legal purposes, death. It would be surprising if a contrary view were to be taken in the criminal law.

Nonetheless, it is not universally agreed that brain-dead persons sustained mechanically are to be regarded as dead. Peter Singer, for instance, maintains that the locution "pink, supple and dead" is contradictory.[49] Certainly the body of a continuously respirated brain-dead person is a living organism. Should terminating the vitality of such an organism be regarded as causing the death of a human being? Current medical practice assumes that such organisms are no longer persons.[50] Considerable expense would be incurred and beneficent transplant and grafting surgery precluded were an appellate court to rule that brain-dead persons are live persons. It is not easy to see what value such a judgment would advance and, accordingly, we will assume here that brain-death is death in every case.

Any condition affecting the brain which is less radical than brain-death is unlikely to be legally designated a form of death. The House of Lords in *Bland*[51] decided that a person in a persistent vegetative state (PVS) was alive and made the same assumption for persons in profound and permanent coma. One may ponder whether persons permanently lacking any form of sentient life, wholly cut off from any form of interaction with other people, are a morally different case from persons who are brain dead. Yet there are strong pragmatic reasons for drawing a distinction between brain-death and other forms of non-sentience. There are reliable and easily applied criteria for determining the presence of brain-death.[52] The condition is completely irreversible and there is no prospect of any effective medical intervention. By contrast, diagnosis of the profundity and duration of states which fall short of brain-death is a far less certain procedure. Questions about the appropriate treatment of PVS and comatose patients can and should be debated in terms of the quality and meaning of life, a debate which should not be foreclosed by any stipulative definition of death.[53] Accordingly, it is submitted that any mental condition which does not amount to brain-death should be regarded as compatible with the presence of life.

---

[43] The brain stem controls reflexive functions of the body including breathing and heartbeat.
[44] "Criteria for the Diagnosis of Brain Stem Death" (1995) 29 *J Royal College of Physicians* 381.
[45] For references to international legislation, see Giesen, *International Medical Malpractice Law* (1988) 612, n. 73.
[46] [1993] 1 AC 789 (HL).
[47] *Ibid.*, 856 (Lord Keith), 863 (Lord Goff), 878 (Lord Browne-Wilkinson).
[48] [1992] 3 Med L Rev 303 (Fam D).
[49] *Rethinking Life and Death* (1995) 24.
[50] "Death" in Grubb, Laing, McHale (eds), *Principles of Medical Law* (3rd ed., 2010) 1135-9.
[51] [1993] 1 AC 789.
[52] "Criteria for the Diagnosis of Brain Stem Death" (1995) 29 *J Royal College of Physicians* 381.
[53] Dworkin, *Life's Dominion* (1993) chap. 7.

(ii) Causation in homicide

We have already discussed principles of causation in criminal law.[54] As there are no principles of causation distinctive to homicide, we need not discuss causation in any detail here. Nonetheless, some reference to causation is in order as homicide cases provide some striking examples of cases where causal principles are taken to their limits—and even beyond. When a person who is at fault is somehow connected to a result so grave as death, there is a disposition to attribute causal responsibility to the blameworthy agent. This sometimes results in strained causal attributions, particularly in cases where some other person, not morally at fault, seems more directly responsible for causing the death.

Pagett[55] is a case in point. D took V hostage before emerging from a flat, which was circled by armed police, with V clasped to him as a human shield. D fired at the police, who returned his fire. V died after being struck by a police bullet. The police response was found to be lawful conduct by way of self-defence. D was found guilty of manslaughter on the basis that his conduct was a cause of V's death.

Before we scrutinise the reasoning in the case, it should be stated at the outset that there would have been a failure of justice had not D been found guilty of the manslaughter of V as a principal offender. The police reaction was a reasonable one to an emergency not of their making. Goff LJ, however, eased the way for a finding of causal agency against D by describing the police reaction as "involuntary". Under that description, the police involved need not be regarded as voluntary informed actors and were allowed to drop out of the causal picture.

Yet it is possible to envisage circumstances where it would be inapt to describe interventions such as the police action in *Pagett* as involuntary conduct but where the moral pressure to attribute causal agency to someone not obviously the causal agent of the death would be as strong. Suppose that T, an armed duty policeman, is observing D, a terrorist. He sees that D is about to activate a remote controlled device which will detonate a bomb planted further down the crowded street. There are only seconds left, with no way to stop D except by shooting her. T takes the decision to shoot, aware of the risk that the bullet may strike someone else. The bullet kills V, an innocent person. There is a powerful case for holding D responsible for V's death. But it would be implausible to describe T's conduct as involuntary.

This example reveals that, in the context of intervening agents, something deeper than mechanical causal principles is at work when we designate a blameworthy person a causal agent. The sentiment lying behind the causal findings in such cases depends in part on a recognition of who bears primary moral responsibility for the untoward outcome. Such a finding may be made against a person who, under mechanical accounts of cause and effect, is not a causal agent. Risking a generalisation, we may say that if D, by her wrongful act or omission, places V in a situation where he is killed by the justified conduct of T, responsibility for the fact of V's death will be attributed to D as a principal offender.[56] Moreover, the same conclusion will follow even if T's conduct is merely excused, provided T's conduct is a reasonably foreseeable response to the situation D has created. In these situations, T's

---

[54] Above, § 4.2.
[55] (1983) 76 Cr App R 279 (CA).
[56] For discussion of the nature of justification and of excuse see further below, § 17.2.

conduct may even be fully informed and voluntary. As we saw in Chapter 4, what counts is not whether her conduct is "involuntary" but whether—to borrow a different phrase from *Pagett*—T's conduct is "free, deliberate and informed".[57] If, because of D's conduct, T does not intervene freely, D remains causally responsible for V's death.

This can be compared with *Kennedy (No. 2)*,[58] where D handed V a syringe containing heroin which V used to inject herself. V died from the effect of the drug. This was held to be a *novus actus interveniens* because V's conduct was considered to be voluntary and informed. The decision would have been different had V been unaware of what the syringe contained or was mistaken as to its contents, or if V could be considered to have acted involuntarily due to youth or particular vulnerability. The House of Lords did not examine whether a victim who was addicted to drugs should be considered to be vulnerable, wherefore the injection of the drug by V could be described as being involuntary.[59]

Less straightforward is a situation, as in *Dhaliwal*,[60] where V committed suicide after enduring considerable physical abuse over an extended period of time. The Court of Appeal was open to the argument that a suicide that was influenced by D's abuse could be considered an event caused by D.[61] That would seem a reasonable conclusion if V's suicide was an act of desperation induced by the abusive (and criminal) conduct of D.

Clearly moral questions of justification and excuse, as well as questions of foreseeability, can affect the attribution of an actus reus to D. The entanglement of moral issues with causal questions is evident in Devlin J's widely discussed judgment in *Adams*,[62] where he considered the position of a doctor dispensing analgesic drugs to a terminal patient. On the assumption that the drugs were administered to relieve pain, the underlying pathology responsible for the patient's terminal condition should, according to the learned judge, be regarded as the sole cause of death even if the drugs had brought forward the time of death by "minutes, hours or even, perhaps, days". This analysis should be doubted. It confuses motive with cause. If the same acceleration of death were brought about with a malevolent motive—say, to enjoy an inheritance sooner—then death would surely have been attributable to the drugs.[63] Similarly, subject to the *de minimis*

---

[57] (1983) 76 Cr App R 279, 288–9. See above, § 4.2(iii)(b) (Principle 1) and § 4.2(iii)(b) (Case 1).

[58] [2007] UKHL 38, [2008] 1 AC 269. See above § 4.2(iii)(b) (Principle 1).

[59] There might be circumstances where D, a supplier of drugs to V who injected himself, might be guilty of gross negligent manslaughter by failing to help V. See *Evans* [2009] EWCA Crim 650, [2009] 1 WLR 1999 (CA); below, § 10.2 (iii).

[60] [2006] EWCA Crim 1139, [2006] 2 Cr App R 24.

[61] In the event, the conviction for manslaughter was quashed as the prosecution based its case on the allegation that the last assault made by D on V was the cause of V's decision to commit suicide, declining to argue that D's abusive conduct overall was the cause of her suicide. The Court of Appeal considered that D's last assault in isolation was an insufficient cause of V's suicide but that the manslaughter charge might have succeeded had the prosecution's case proceeded on a wider basis: see further Horder and McGowan, "Manslaughter by Causing Another's Suicide" [2006] *Crim LR* 1035.

[62] [1957] Crim LR 365.

[63] See too *Le Brun* [1992] 1 QB 61 where, in the context of a manslaughter charge, different motivations made for different conclusions concerning the causal status of an act. D knocked V unconscious with a non-life-threatening blow and subsequently caused her death by picking her up and accidentally dropping her. The Court of Appeal held that the assault was to be regarded as a cause of death because D picked up V for a bad reason (to take her to a place where she did not want to go). If, however, he had picked her up with a good motive (seeking medical help) the assault would not have been, legally, a cause of death. The result reached in the case seems the right one, but it is unnecessary to resolve the issue in these confused causal terms: see further Sullivan, "Contemporaneity of Actus Reus and Mens Rea" [1993] *CLJ* 487, 495–500. The case is properly dealt with on the *Thabo Meli* principle: above, § 5.8(i)(b).

proviso,[64] medical treatment that hastens death is a cause of death; it is mens rea that may be missing, not the actus reus. Particularly in a homicide context, we must be alert to the drawing of causal distinctions, like Devlin J's, which are unwarranted by causal doctrine.[65]

(iii) Acts, omissions, and homicide

Well-known definitions of murder and manslaughter given by institutional authors such as Coke employ the terms "kill" and "killing" in their formulations of the conduct to be proved against D.[66] Accordingly, at one time, there was scope for an argument that "merely" allowing V to die could not constitute the actus reus of either murder or manslaughter, even if it could be established that D owed V a duty to act. This argument was put forward in *Gibbins and Proctor*,[67] where D was charged with murder on the basis of a deliberate failure to feed her infant stepdaughter. Unsurprisingly, on the facts of the case, the argument failed. A deliberate strategy to starve someone to death can legitimately be described as a killing—"I killed him by starving him to death" is a perfectly sensible statement. By contrast, failures to provide essential sustenance by mismanagement and incompetence, as in *Instan*,[68] or failures of supervision, such as the negligent failure of the railway crossing keeper in *Pittwood*[69] to close the gates before the arrival of the train, are less obviously designated "killings". The conviction for manslaughter in each of these cases indicates that the expressions "kill" and "killing" are not to be taken too literally. They should be regarded as synonymous with "cause death" and "causing death".[70] The notion of cause will accommodate failures by D to prevent the avoidable death of V where it can be maintained that it was D's duty to prevent V's death and that she possessed the capacity to do so.[71]

Accordingly, the distinction between acts and omissions presents no difficulties that are peculiar to homicide. That said, *ad hoc* use of the act/omissions distinction has sometimes been judicially employed in order to contain the scope of certain forms of homicide. The form of manslaughter known as constructive manslaughter is, as we shall see below, of very wide ambit. It would be broader still had not unlawful omissions been excluded from its scope by the definitional fiat of the Court of Appeal in *Lowe*.[72] In the same vein, it appears

---

[64] Above, § 4.2(ii)(a). This seems to be the best explanation of *Adams* itself.

[65] For an effective critique of causal doctrine featuring some well-known homicide decisions, see Norrie, "A Critique of Criminal Causation" (1991) 54 *MLR* 685.

[66] "Murder is when a man of sound memory, and of the age of discretion, unlawfully killeth within any county of the realm any reasonable creature in *rerum natura* under the king's peace, with malice aforethought, either expressed by the party or implied by law": Coke, 3 Inst 47.

[67] (1918) 13 Cr App R 134.

[68] [1893] 1 QB 450.

[69] (1902) 19 TLR 37.

[70] Stephen, *Digest of Criminal Law* (4th ed., 1887) 138, cited with approval in *A-G's Reference (No. 3 of 1994)* [1998] AC 245 (HL).

[71] Moore, amongst others, has argued against the view that omissions can be causes of events: *Act and Crime* (1993) 30–1. His position seems well founded in terms of mechanical causation. As is argued above, § 4.2(iv)(a), causative effect may only be attributed to omissions on the basis of a counterfactual narrative—the daughter would have lived had she been fed; the driver of the cart would not have been killed had the gate been shut etc. Bearing in mind the burden of proof, one should have great confidence that death would have been averted if D had performed the relevant duty. Unfortunately, this requirement is sometimes overlooked: see *Stone* [1977] QB 354.

[72] [1973] QB 702 (CA).

that V does not commit suicide should he refuse food or essential medical treatment while aware that refusal entails his certain death;[73] a matter of great moment for those caring for V, who might otherwise find themselves assisters in his suicide.[74] Likewise, V does not commit suicide should she ask to be removed from a life-support system;[75] but V will be asking for help in an act of suicide should she request assistance to take a substance that will end her life.[76] In both cases, the exercise of V's autonomy requires the assistance of others. However, the former situation is characterised as the refusal of treatment: her physical removal from life support is said, legally, to be an omission to provide further treatment, whereas active assistance in the taking of a fatal substance remains an illegal act.[77]

Liability for omissions will arise only if D can be said to be under a duty to prevent V's death. The identification of this duty proved controversial in *Evans*,[78] where D had supplied heroin to her half-sister, who self-injected and died from an overdose. D could not be considered to have caused V's death through the supply since the voluntary act of self-injection broke the chain of causation. However, D was liable for her failure to summon medical assistance because she had contributed to the creation of a state of affairs which she should have known had become life threatening. The recognition of a duty to act in such a case expands liability for omissions, since previously D would only owe a duty to act where she had created the state of affairs.[79] This could not have been established in *Evans* because the creator of the life-threatening state of affairs was V herself.

Particularly in medical contexts, D may find herself under a duty to sustain V's life in the first instance but then be relieved from that duty should it be determined by the court that V's best interests do not require the sustaining of his life.[80] The cessation of the duty to keep V alive is without prejudice to the overarching duty imposed on us all not to cause the death of others by a positive act.[81] That latter duty sits awkwardly with the well-established practice of closing down systems of life support in the light of a patient's wishes or a decision that the patient's best interests no longer require the sustaining of his life. On the face of it, the step-by-step procedure involved in shutting down a life-support system seems, indubitably, an act of commission comparable, say, to the simpler task of switching off a television. Be that as it may, Lord Goff in *Bland* considered that the removal of life support was to be regarded as an omission: in such cases the cause of death is attributed to the underlying pathology which necessitated life support, and the removal of life support is merely a failure to suppress this underlying cause.[82] In *Nicklinson* v. *Ministry of Justice*,[83]

---

[73] *Secretary of State* v. *Robb* [1995] 1 All ER 677 (CA).

[74] Suicide Act 1961, s. 2.

[75] *Re B (adult: refusal of Medical Treatment)* [2002] 2 All ER 449.

[76] *R (on the application of Pretty)* v. *DPP* [2002] 1 All ER 1.

[77] For critical discussion see Tur, "Legislative Technique and Human Rights: The Sad Case of Assisted Suicide" [2003] *Crim LR* 3.

[78] [2009] 1 WLR 1999.

[79] *Miller* [1983] 2 AC 161. For discussion, see above, § 4.1(i)(b) (Case 5).

[80] *Airedale NHS Trust* v. *Bland* [1993] AC 789; *Aintree University Hospitals NHS Foundation Trust v James* [2013] UKSC 67, [2014] AC 591, paras 18–22 (Baroness Hale).

[81] All the judgments in *Bland* emphasise that, although it may be in a patient's best interests not to be kept alive, no patient, whatever her condition and whatever her wishes, may be actively killed. See too *Cox* (1992) 12 BMLR 38.

[82] [1993] AC 789, 866.

[83] [2014] UKSC 38, [2015] AC 657, para. 22.

Lord Neuberger confirmed the distinction between a doctor who switches a life support machine off, which he characterised as an omission, and an interloper who maliciously switches the machine off, which he characterised as an act. Hence the interloper would be liable for a homicide offence, depending on his mens rea. The distinction is highly artificial and analytically unconvincing, but it does have the instrumental value of protecting medical personnel from liability for murder or manslaughter when carrying out what are now routine procedures of terminating life support.

(iv) Abolition of the year and a day rule

At common law, in order for D to be held responsible for V's death, the death had to occur within one year and a day of the act or omission by D that caused it.[84] The rule was of great antiquity and obscure in origin and rationale.[85] By early modern times, the rule was justified in terms of the difficulty of proving that D's conduct was a cause of V's death after the lapse of such a period of time. The current wide availability of life-support technology for the seriously injured renders such a rationalisation untenable, and the rule was abolished by the Law Reform (Year and a Day Rule) Act 1996[86] in respect of offences concerned with the causing of death and of suicide.

The Act brings homicide cases into line with other indictable offences. However, there are potentially oppressive situations for an accused person which may arise in homicide contexts. There may be a considerable lapse of time occurring between the injury caused by D and the ultimate death of V. During that time D will face the prospect of prosecution for some form of homicide in circumstances where he may already have been tried and convicted for an offence arising from the initial injury. Accordingly, the Act provides that proceedings in respect of a "fatal offence" may be instituted only if the Attorney General gives consent whenever the injury that causes death is sustained more than three years before death occurs or if the accused has previously been convicted of an offence in circumstances alleged to be connected with the death.[87]

(v) The Queen's Peace

Any human being can be the victim of homicide with the exception of persons who are not "under the Queen's Peace". Accordingly, causing the deaths of alien enemies in the course of war supplies no ground for a homicide prosecution.[88] The same probably applies to rebels who, at the time they were killed, were engaged in hostile operations against the Crown.[89]

---

[84] In the classic definition of murder given by Coke, V must die "of the wound or hurt, etc., within a year or a day of the same": 3 Inst 47.

[85] Yale, "A Year and a Day in Homicide" [1989] *CLJ* 202.

[86] Section 1.

[87] Section 2.

[88] See Rowe, "The Criminal Liability of a British Soldier Merely for Participating in the Iraq War 2003: a Response to Chilcot Evidence" [2010] *Crim LR* 752, 753–4. It is homicide if an enemy alien is killed other than in the course of war: *Maria v. Hall* (1807) 1 Taunt 33, 36, 127 ER 741.

[89] 1 Hale PC 433; *Page* [1954] 1 QB 170, 175 (Lord Goddard CJ).

As a matter of history, operations of war involving subjects of the Crown have been predominantly carried out overseas. On normal rules of criminal jurisdiction, which apply a territoriality principle, killings perpetrated overseas would in any event not be justiciable here. However, section 9 of the OAPA 1861 provides that any murder or manslaughter committed by any subject of the Crown on land out of the United Kingdom may be tried and punished in England.[90] The specific exception for those not under the Queen's Peace is therefore essential.

§ 10.3 Murder

(i) The mental element in murder[91]

The traditional definition of murder is that it is a homicide committed with "malice afore-thought". This definition is no longer useful; neither malice[92] nor forethought[93] is neces-sary, or sufficient, for a finding of murder. For many years past, malice aforethought has been a purely technical expression meaning nothing more than those mental states recog-nised by the common law as sufficiently culpable to make a homicide murder. Before the Homicide Act 1957, there were three kinds of malice aforethought—"express", "implied", and "constructive". Express malice required an intent to cause death. Implied malice was established by proof of an intention to cause grievous bodily harm. Constructive malice was present if D caused death while committing or attempting to commit a felony or when resisting lawful arrest. If a causal connection between the causing of death and commission of the felony or resistance to the arrest was established, it was immaterial that D intended neither to kill nor to cause grievous bodily harm.

Constructive malice was taken to be too indiscriminate in its operation[94] and was abol-ished by section 1 of the Homicide Act 1957. The Act makes clear that implied as well as express malice survives the abolition of constructive malice.[95] We will not further employ these anachronistic terms; it is better simply to refer to *an intent to cause death* and *an intent to cause grievous bodily harm* as the two forms of mental element currently sufficient under English law to constitute the mens rea of murder.

---

[90] Section 4 of the Suppression of Terrorism Act 1978 gives the English court jurisdiction if a murder is com-mitted in a country which is a party to the European Convention on Human Rights, regardless of whether D or the victim is a British citizen. So, in *Venclovas* [2013] EWCA Crim 2182, it was possible to convict D, a Lithuanian, of murder even though it was unclear whether the victim was killed in England or in Poland (where her body was found). This expands the jurisdiction of the English court significantly, although the assertion of jurisdiction under the 1978 Act requires the consent of the Attorney-General.

[91] Goff, "The Mental Element in the Crime of Murder" (1988) 104 *LQR* 30; Williams, "The Mens Rea for Murder: Leave it Alone" (1989) 105 *LQR* 387; Wilson, "A Plea for Rationality in the Law of Murder" (1990) 10 *LS* 307; House of Lords, Report of the Select Committee on Murder and Life Imprisonment (Session 1988–89) HL Paper 78, paras. 30–8.

[92] It is murder, for example, if D's intentional killing of V is done from motives of compassion, say because V has a painful, terminal illness.

[93] A spontaneous intentional killing is murder in the absence of any justification, excuse, or extenuation.

[94] *Royal Commission on Capital Punishment* Cmnd. 8932 (1953) 24–8.

[95] Homicide Act 1957, s. 1: "where a person kills another in the course or furtherance of some other offence, the killing shall not amount to murder unless done with the same malice aforethought (*express or implied*) as is required for a killing or to amount to murder when not done in the course or furtherance of some other offence" (emphasis added).

(a) Intent to cause grievous bodily harm

As indicated, an intent to cause grievous bodily harm remains sufficient mens rea for murder. It has survived several attempts to unseat it. In *Vickers*,[96] D had been convicted of murder on the basis that he intended to cause grievous bodily harm. The argument was put on behalf of D that, since causing grievous bodily harm with intent was, at that time, a felony in its own right, to convict someone of murder on the ground of proof of such an intent was effectively to resurrect the principle of constructive malice. The Court of Criminal Appeal rejected this argument. To kill by causing grievous bodily harm was not to cause death by an offence separate from the killing. The infliction of bodily harm was the direct cause of death.

In the subsequent case of *Hyam*,[97] where the House of Lords sought to resolve the definition of the mens rea for murder, Lord Diplock, with the assent of Lord Kilbrandon, rejected as a sufficient mental element the mere intent to cause grievous bodily harm. He considered that, historically, the erstwhile constructive malice doctrine had unduly inhibited the development and refinement of the mental element for the crime. Without that restraint, he considered that judges would have confined murder to circumstances where D either intended to kill or intentionally caused grievous bodily harm knowing that his conduct threatened the life of the victim.[98] With constructive malice abolished, Lord Diplock concluded that the House was free to express the mens rea for murder in the form it would have attained without the constraint of the felony/murder rule.

Of the three remaining Law Lords in *Hyam*, Lords Hailsham and Dilhorne refused to go along with Lord Diplock's striking version of counterfactual history. Remarkably, the fifth judge, Lord Cross, refused to make a decision on the matter, acknowledging force in both positions. Instead, he confirmed the verdict of murder on the "assumption" that an intent to cause grievous bodily harm constituted sufficient mens rea.[99] This lack of resolution entailed a subsequent appeal on the matter in *Cunningham*.[100] Here, a differently constituted House of Lords ruled by a majority that an intent to cause grievous bodily harm was sufficient mens rea for murder. Criticism continues at the highest judicial level of a law of murder which allows convictions for this grave offence without proof of any culpability element that refers to the element of death—a "fiction" according to Lord Mustill.[101] The criticism has particular force in circumstances where the harm in question, although "really serious", is not harm which constitutes, of itself, a threat to life. As Lord Edmund-Davies observed in his dissenting speech in *Cunningham*, a broken arm is "really serious"[102] but an intent to inflict such an injury should be regarded as insufficient for the most serious of crimes.[103] Yet, despite the continuing vein of judicial

---

[96] [1957] 2 QB 664.

[97] [1975] AC 55.

[98] *Ibid.*, 89–93.

[99] *Ibid.*, 97–8.

[100] [1982] AC 566.

[101] *A-G's Reference (No. 3 of 1994)* [1998] AC 245, 262.

[102] The interpretation of grievous bodily harm given in *DPP* v. *Smith* [1961] AC 290, 334. See too *Bollom* [2003] EWCA Crim 2846, where the Court of Appeal confirmed that harm which raised no risk to the life of V could constitute serious bodily harm.

[103] [1982] AC 566, 582–3. In terms of the discussion of moral luck above, § 6.5(i), this would be an injury where consequent death was a matter of extrinsic rather than intrinsic luck.

criticism,[104] the law is settled by *Cunningham* and was approved by the House of Lords in *Rahman*.[105] Any future change to the mens rea for murder will require legislation. Such a change had been recommended by the Law Commission,[106] so that a person who caused death but only intended to cause serious injury would be guilty of second degree murder—which would not attract the mandatory life sentence. Although Parliament subsequently reformed aspects of the law of murder, this recommendation was not adopted.

(b) Intent is subjective

The intent to be proved in a case of murder is the intent possessed by D herself at the time of the acts or omissions alleged to be the cause of death. This may appear so obvious a requirement as not to be worth stating. Such a statement of the obvious needs to be made, however, because of the notorious decision of the House of Lords in *DPP* v. *Smith*.[107] The House of Lords startled professional and academic opinion by ruling that D could be presumed to have intended to cause death or grievous bodily harm to V if a reasonable person, placed in the same situation as D and with D's knowledge of the surrounding circumstances, would have foreseen the causing of death or grievous bodily harm to V as a natural and probable consequence of her conduct. What precisely this formulation conveyed was a matter of intense debate.[108] An entirely tenable view of the decision was that it allowed a conviction for murder on the basis of negligence, on the foresight of the reasonable person rather than the accused. The controversy the decision aroused led to the preparation of a two-clause Bill by the Law Commission which, had it been enacted as it stood, would clearly have overturned *Smith*.[109] However, only one clause was enacted, being the clause that subsequently became section 8 of the Criminal Justice Act 1967. The clause that focused directly on the decision in *Smith* was dropped.

It will be recalled that section 8 deals with *proof* of intent and foresight;[110] it has nothing to say on the definition of these terms, or about when intent or foresight need be proved. On one reading of this legislative history, the decision in *Smith* remained intact, Parliament having explicitly rejected a provision that would have reversed it. If *Smith* still stood, it followed that murder was defined in a manner that did not require proof of intent or foresight on the part of D. Accordingly, section 8 would be irrelevant to the issue of the culpability required for murder; the section applies only when the definition of an offence requires proof of intent or foresight on the part of D.

Whatever the force of this reasoning, from the moment section 8 came into force, appellate courts regarded *Smith* as overturned[111] and this has been uncritically reiterated many times, most recently by the House of Lords in *Woollin*.[112] Furthermore, the Privy Council

---

[104] *Powell, Daniels and English* [1999] 1 AC 1, 11 (Lord Mustill), 14–15 (Lord Steyn); *Woollin* [1999] AC 82, 90 (Lord Steyn).

[105] [2008] UKHL 45, [2009] 1 AC 129, para. 51 (Lord Brown).

[106] Law Com. No. 304, *Murder, Manslaughter and Infanticide* (2006) para. 1.69.

[107] [1961] AC 290.

[108] Contrast Denning, *Responsibility Before the Law* (1961) with Williams, *The Mental Element in Crime* (1965) chap. 1.

[109] Law Com. No. 10, *Imported Criminal Intent (Director of Public Prosecutions v. Smith)* (1967) 17.

[110] See above, § 5.1(ix), where s. 8 is quoted in the text.

[111] *Wallett* [1968] 2 QB 367.

[112] [1999] AC 82.

in *Frankland*[113] advised that *Smith* had been based on a misunderstanding of the common law and should no longer be followed in a common law jurisdiction which did not possess the equivalent of section 8. *Smith*, it seems, has been remaindered safely to legal history: the intent required for murder is an intent that the accused herself must be proved to have possessed.

(c) The meaning of intent in murder

In our discussion in Chapter 5 of intent, a "core" meaning of the term was identified as well as an alternative, non-core meaning. D intends to cause V's death (or grievous bodily harm), in the core or primary sense, if he acts in order to cause death (or grievous bodily harm) to V or if he causes death (or grievous bodily harm) as a necessary means to some other end. When D acts in one of these states of mind, his conduct will normally take the form of a direct attack on V. In such cases Lord Bridge's "Golden Rule" applies:[114]

> "When directing a jury on the mental element necessary in a crime of specific intent, the judge should avoid any elaboration or paraphrase of what is meant by intent and leave it to the jury's good sense to decide whether the accused acted with the necessary intent."

This approach is commendably straightforward. Where V has died following an attack by D with a gun, knife, or heavy implement, a very strong inference arises that D attacked in order to kill or seriously hurt V. The jury may be safely left to draw that inference in the absence of any reason why they should not do so.

Such an uncomplicated approach is impossible where there is no compelling evidence that D intended to kill or cause grievous bodily harm in this core sense. Take a case where D sets fire to a house in order to make a fraudulent insurance claim in respect of the damage he will cause. He is aware that the house is occupied by V and that it is virtually certain that V will perish in the fire. Here there may be no evidence that D intends the death of V in the core sense of that term. He may be wholly indifferent whether V lives or dies. The existence or non-existence of V may have no bearing whatever on the success of his fraudulent claim. Consequently, were D to be charged with the murder of V, this would be one of those "rare cases" where a direction on intention of the kind laid down by the House of Lords in *Woollin* would be required:[115]

> "the jury should be directed that they are not entitled to find the necessary intention, unless they feel sure that death or serious injury was a virtual certainty (barring some unforeseen intervention) as a result of the defendant's actions and that the defendant appreciated that such was the case."

As we saw above in § 5.1(iv), *Woollin* establishes that foresight of virtual certainty is the basis of finding intention in the secondary, non-core sense. Ideally, *Woollin* should be read as establishing that proof of foresight on the part of D that it is virtually certain he will cause death or grievous bodily harm to V constitutes an intent, in the secondary non-core sense, to cause death or grievous bodily harm.[116] But, as previously discussed, because of

---

[113] [1987] AC 576.
[114] *Moloney* [1985] AC 905, 926.
[115] [1999] AC 82, 90.
[116] Simester, "Murder, Mens Rea and the House of Lords—Again" (1999) 115 *LQR* 17.

the way the *Woollin* direction is expressed and because of pre-*Woollin* case law, there is space for an interpretation to the effect that proof of the state of mind the direction identifies is merely evidence from which intent may be inferred and does not constitute intent *per se*.[117] Such a reading was endorsed by the Court of Appeal in *Matthews and Alleyne*.[118] To read the decision in this manner is unfortunate. It is when we lack evidence of intent in the core sense that a *Woollin* direction is required. It would be puzzling to insist that foresight that an outcome is virtually certain is mere evidence on which a finding of intent (in the secondary sense) to cause that outcome may be based. Far better to hold that appreciation on the part of D that his conduct is virtually certain to cause a particular result constitutes an intent (in a secondary, non-core sense) to cause that result, otherwise we are in the dark as to what constitutes this alternative form of intent. This is exemplified by *Matthews and Alleyne* itself. D and others threw V into a river when it was in mid-winter flood, despite their awareness that V could not swim. The trial judge directed the jury that they should convict D of murder if D appreciated that V's death by drowning was a virtual certainty. That was held to be a misdirection. The jury should have been told that they were entitled to find D guilty of murder should they choose to do so. Yet the conviction for murder was confirmed on the basis that any reasonable jury properly directed would have convicted on such evidence. Why such certainty? Because the jury could have had no doubt that D knew V was virtually certain to drown. So it seems that for non-core intent there is in reality nothing beyond the perception of practical certainty; it is unfortunate that obfuscation was not put to one side.

To conclude, we can say that D will have the mens rea for murder if:

(i)   he acts in order to kill or cause grievous bodily harm; or
(ii)   he kills or causes grievous bodily harm as a means to some other end he is seeking to achieve.

Additionally, members of the jury can be told that they are entitled to make a finding of intent against D if:

(iii) his conduct is virtually certain to cause death or grievous bodily harm and he appreciates that his conduct is virtually certain to cause death or grievous bodily harm.

There may be one situation, however, where the state of mind identified in (iii) may not suffice for murder. In *Bland*, Lord Goff considered that a doctor administering pain-relieving drugs to a terminal patient would not be guilty of murder, or any other offence, if the patient's death were accelerated as a known side-effect of this palliative care.[119] *Dicta* from other appellate cases[120] indicate that a doctor will not be criminally responsible for any consequences brought about as a side-effect of treatment given in what a responsible body of medical opinion would consider the best interests of the patient. Indeed, in *Gillick* Lord Scarman went so far as to state that "the bona fide exercise by a doctor of his clinical

---

[117] Above, § 5.1(iv). See also Norrie, "After *Woollin*" [1999] *Crim LR* 532.
[118] [2003] 2 Cr App R 30.
[119] [1993] AC 789.
[120] *Re J* [1990] 3 All ER 930, 938.

judgment must be a complete negation of the guilty mind".[121] Whatever scope is given to that statement, in the context of murder it is clear that any exemption for medical personnel from the scope of the offence is confined to the side-effects of treatment and does not embrace fatal means to a desired objective. If, as in *Cox*,[122] the acceleration of death is used as a means of terminating pain, liability will be incurred irrespective of the gravity of the pain, the lack of any other means of palliation, and the considered wishes of the patient. Whether a distinction between means and side-effects should be accorded such decisive effect in these distressing cases is, of course, a matter of intense ethical debate.

The Law Commission has in substance recommended codifying the law relating to intent in murder.[123] Under its proposals, D will be taken to intend a result if she acts in order to bring it about and, additionally, a jury "may" make a finding of intent if it is shown that D "thought the result was a virtually certain consequence of his or her action". A welcome advance on the current position is that D need only think a result to have been virtually certain: the prosecution would not have to prove that the result was in fact virtually certain, so ensuring an exclusive focus on the culpability of D. But, as under the current law, the jury in this case of non-core intent may choose whether or not to make the ultimate finding of intent. The basis of such a finding is left a deliberate blank by the Law Commission, which favours unstructured moral evaluations as a basis for findings of intent. Although Parliament subsequently reformed aspects of the law of homicide, it did not use the opportunity to adopt the Law Commission's proposed codification of the law relating to intent in murder.

(ii) The ambit of murder—an evaluation

Any evaluation of the defining elements of murder cannot leave out of account the mandatory sentence of life imprisonment that the offence attracts.[124] Many offences are defined in very general terms and encompass conduct that varies enormously in terms of its content and its culpability. Theft, for instance, ranges from taking the apple from the orchard to sophisticated frauds involving the electronic manipulation of huge sums of money. Of course, the apple thief and the large-scale fraudster will receive very different treatment at the hands of the court, a latitude facilitated by the discretionary sentencing scheme provided in the event of a conviction for theft.[125] By contrast, because each murder receives the same draconian penalty, in principle there ought to be a large degree of similarity in the culpability evinced by each particular murder. A moment's reflection, however, reveals that murder, like other offences, spans a range of differing culpabilities:[126]

> "Murder, as every practitioner of the law knows, though often described as one of the utmost heinousness, is not in fact necessarily so, but consists in a whole bundle of offences of vastly differing degrees of culpability, ranging from brutal, cynical and repeated offences like the

---

[121] [1986] 1 AC 112, 190.
[122] (1992) 12 BMLR 38.
[123] *Murder, Manslaughter and Infanticide*, Law Com. No. 304 (2006). For discussion, see Norrie, "Between Orthodox and Moral Contextualism" [2006] *Crim LR* 486.
[124] Murder (Abolition of the Death Penalty) Act 1965.
[125] From an absolute discharge to 7 years' imprisonment: Criminal Justice Act 1991, s. 26.
[126] *Howe* [1987] 1 All ER 771, 781.

so-called Moors murders (*R* v. *Brady and Hindley* (6 May 1966, unreported)) to the almost venial, if objectively immoral, 'mercy killing' of a beloved partner."

Why, then, the unyielding fixed penalty? The origin of the mandatory life sentence is to be found in the political process that lead to the passing of the Murder (Abolition of Death Penalty) Act 1965. There would not have been a Parliamentary majority for the abolition of the death penalty in murder had not the supporters of abolition undertaken that each and every conviction for murder should attract a mandatory life sentence.[127] There was then, and remains now, a strong public sentiment that murder is a special offence which should be marked on each occasion by a special penalty. Those who argue for retention of the mandatory life sentence (or for reintroduction of the death penalty) assert that the intentional taking of any life merits a life sentence and/or that an unyielding and draconian response is an effective deterrent for those who would otherwise kill. *Contra*, two authoritative committees which have investigated the issue found neither argument persuasive and recommended a discretionary sentencing regime for the offence.[128] Nonetheless, the Government has indicated its intention to retain the mandatory sentence.[129]

There have been other proposals to limit the effects of the mandatory life sentence for murder. One, proposed by Spencer,[130] was that the jury should be given the power to add to a verdict of guilty of murder that they found "extenuating circumstances" so that the judge would not be obliged to impose a mandatory life sentence. The proposal has not, however, been adopted.

The continuation of the mandatory life sentence for the indefinite future makes it all the more important that the definition of murder should be focused on the most culpable forms of killing. Beyond argument, the current definition of murder includes many persons convicted of the offence who do not merit a life term. Even though legal forms of extenuation, such as the defences of loss of control and diminished responsibility, take outside the ambit of murder some defendants who would otherwise be convicted for the offence, murder remains too inclusive an offence. It may be argued that the situation is not as draconian as it might seem because, as is well known, a prisoner serving a mandatory life term will rarely spend the rest of his life in prison. Nonetheless, the position of a person serving a mandatory life sentence is unenviable. A life sentence contains a literal truth in that any release is a release on licence that may be revoked by administrative rather than judicial decision. The release decision for a mandatory lifer is now entrusted to the Parole Board rather than the Home Secretary, following reform of the mandatory life-sentencing process instituted by the Criminal Justice Act 2003.[131] Under the scheme of the Act, the trial judge must recommend a minimum term of years which D should serve by way of retribution for his offence. Although what period of time should be served on this retributive basis is ultimately a matter for the judge,[132] there is a strong statutory presumption that the term

---

[127] The Bill that became the Murder (Abolition of Death Penalty) Act 1965 was a private member's Bill passed on a free vote.

[128] Report of the Advisory Council on the Penal System: *Sentences of Imprisonment* (1978) paras. 235–44; House of Lords, Select Committee on Murder and Life Imprisonment (Session 1988–89) HL Paper 78, paras. 108–18.

[129] *Hansard*, HL, 11 June 1997, WA 83.

[130] (2009) 173 *Criminal Law and Justice Weekly* 165.

[131] Section 269 and sched. 21.

[132] *Sullivan* [2004] EWCA Crim 1762, [2005] 1 Cr App R 3.

should be at least 15 years[133] or, according to the circumstances of the offence, 25 years, 30 years, or whole life. The last will be appropriate, for example, if the murder was the result of premeditated planning of at least two people or sought to advance a political, religious, racial, or ideological cause.[134] If D was over 18 at the time of the offence and he had taken a knife or other weapon with him which he used to commit murder, the starting point for the assessment of sentence is 25 years' imprisonment.[135] When the retributive part of the sentence is served, the Parole Board may delay release on licence if the prisoner's release is considered a risk for particular persons or the public generally. This regime is severe. Unlike prisoners serving a fixed term of years who are normally released after serving one-half of the term, persons subject to a mandatory life sentence must serve the retributive period of the sentence in full. It is imperative, therefore, that the scope of the offence of murder ensures as far as is possible that only those who warrant such treatment are convicted of the offence.

Criticism of the current scope of murder predominantly fixes on the fact that, in addition to an intention to kill, an intention to cause grievous bodily harm will suffice as mens rea. Those who support the current position argue that a person who acts with an intention to cause serious harm is sufficiently heinous to warrant full responsibility for the fact of death, should that occur. Yet, even if this is sometimes true, as a general proposition it is too broad; it may, for example, be murder if V dies as an untoward consequence of D's act of deliberately breaking V's arm, arising for example from poor treatment of the injury. In the light of judicial criticism of this form of culpability,[136] it is surprising that grievous bodily harm has not been reinterpreted in the context of murder to require the causing of harm that is intrinsically dangerous to life. Yet, even if that were done, there remains force in the argument that an offence designed to pick out the worst kinds of killings should require some advertence to the chance of causing death.

The Law Commission proposed an offence of first-degree murder along these lines.[137] As recommended, it would be first-degree murder to kill with intent to kill, or to kill with intent to cause serious injury when aware of a serious risk of causing death.[138] Only first-degree murder with this welcome narrowing of culpability would attract a mandatory life sentence.[139]

Suppose the mens rea for the form of murder attracting a mandatory sentence were to be reformulated along these lines. The range of culpability falling within the compass of the offence, though significantly narrower than the current offence, nonetheless would remain extensive, as the range of circumstances where the mens rea for the offence may arise would still be considerable. At one time, English law looked to features beyond mens

---

[133] Or 12 years if D was under 18 at the time of the offence.

[134] Criminal Justice Act 2003, sched. 21, s. 4(2).

[135] Criminal Justice Act 2003 (Mandatory Life Sentence: Determination of Minimum Term) Order 2010.

[136] *Cunningham* [1982] AC 566, 582–3 (Lord Edmund-Davies); *Powell and Daniels and English* [1999] 1 AC 1, 11 (Lord Mustill), 14–15 (Lord Steyn); *Woollin* [1999] AC 82, 90 (Lord Steyn).

[137] *Murder, Manslaughter and Infanticide*, Law Com. No. 304. (2006).

[138] For discussion, see Wilson, "The Structure of Criminal Homicide" [2006] *Crim LR* 471.

[139] The Law Commission proposed an offence of second-degree murder defined in terms of killings done with intent to cause serious injury or intended to cause injury or fear or risk of injury if D was aware of a serious risk of causing death. Additionally, it would be second-degree murder if D successfully raised diminished responsibility or loss of control to a charge of first-degree murder. This second-degree form of murder would not attract the mandatory penalty but could be punished with a life term if appropriate.

rea in an attempt to identify what forms of murder should attract a capital sentence. The same technique might be employed to determine which kinds of murder should attract a mandatory life sentence. Under now-repealed provisions of the Homicide Act 1957, factors such as killing a policeman or use of a firearm would make the offence a capital one.[140] Other jurisdictions make reference to such matters as the use of torture,[141] the use of poison,[142] a sexual motive, or the age of the victim.[143] However, in England, such an approach proved unsatisfactory. The grounds of aggravation were controversial and it was generally agreed that these subdivisions of the offence entailed fine distinctions which did not reliably track gradations of culpability.[144] Because, for political reasons, the mandatory penalty seems set to remain for the indefinite future,[145] there is much to be said for a definition of first-degree murder confined to killings done with intent to kill and it is to be regretted that the Law Commission did not remain faithful to its original proposal to this effect.[146] However, when Parliament subsequently took the opportunity to reform the law of murder, it did not adopt the Law Commission's recommendations concerning first- and second-degree murder. Consequently, the partial defences to murder of loss of control and diminished responsibility, which Parliament did revise, will be important palliatives for an offence punished in such a rigid fashion.

§ 10.4 Manslaughter

(i) Introduction

At one time, under the common law, any killing which was unlawful but insufficiently grave to amount to murder would be designated manslaughter.[147] Nowadays, the element of unlawfulness attendant on the killing of V by D no longer suffices *per se*. The unlawfulness must take particular forms if a verdict of manslaughter is to follow. Yet, even in its modern form, manslaughter is a crime of enormous scope. It is an offence that can be committed with several differing forms of culpability. Between these various ways of committing what is but a single offence, there is a major divide: the division between voluntary and involuntary manslaughter. Voluntary manslaughter refers to those killings perpetrated with an intent to kill or to cause grievous bodily harm, in circumstances which do

---

[140] Section 5(1) provided that murders done in furtherance of theft, by shooting or explosion, when avoiding arrest or escaping from custody, or of police officers and prison officers (and those assisting them) would constitute capital murder.

[141] Selaho Code, s. 18-4003(a).

[142] California Penal Code, s. 189.

[143] Ariz. Rev. Stat. Ann; s. 13-604.01(A).

[144] The class of capital murder in England and Wales was designed to capture not so much the worst killings in terms of innate culpability but those killings which most threatened order and stability, thereby warranting maximum deterrence. But this approach became discredited precisely because the line between capital and non-capital murder did not reliably track differing degrees of heinousness.

[145] The terms of reference given to the Law Commission by the Home Office for a review of the law of murder instructed that the mandatory penalty was to remain.

[146] LCCP No. 177.

[147] Up to the nineteenth century manslaughter was regarded as the residual category of homicide, into which fell all killings that were not justified, excusable, or murder: see Turner, *Kenny's Outlines of Criminal Law* (16th ed., 1952) 139–40.

not disclose any justification or excuse but where there is some form of legally recognised extenuation, established at the trial stage, which reduces what would otherwise be murder to manslaughter. Involuntary manslaughter does not require proof of an intent to kill or cause grievous bodily harm. In the sphere of involuntary manslaughter, recklessness, or gross negligence, or the commission of certain "dangerous" criminal acts, each provides a sufficient culpability for a manslaughter conviction.

(ii) Voluntary manslaughter

There are three forms of voluntary manslaughter: committing a prima facie murder in response to some incident or event which constitutes loss of control; committing a prima facie murder when afflicted by one or more of the conditions specified in section 2 of the Homicide Act 1957 (diminished responsibility); and committing prima facie murder in pursuance of a suicide pact. In each case, these grounds of mitigation will be relevant as legal extenuation only if it can be proved that D acted with intent to cause death or to cause grievous bodily harm. In the absence of proof of the culpability for murder, D may, in any event, be guilty of involuntary manslaughter or one of the statutory forms of homicide. Evidence of loss of control or of diminished responsibility may also be used to throw reasonable doubt on whether D did intend to kill or cause grievous bodily harm.[148] If proof of the mens rea for murder is not established, evidence of loss of control or mental disorder may still be relevant, but only at the sentencing stage following a verdict of manslaughter. But that is not our present concern, which is with legal extenuation; that is, situations where all the elements of murder are made out and loss of control, diminished responsibility, or membership of a suicide pact is adduced to reduce the conviction to manslaughter.

At this juncture, only loss of control will be discussed. The defence of diminished responsibility was introduced to remedy some of the deficiencies of the defence of insanity; diminished responsibility and insanity will be considered when we discuss the mental condition defences.[149] Membership of suicide pacts will be discussed when we consider the legal response to suicide and to those who assist it.[150]

§ 10.5 Loss of control

For many centuries, English law has partially condoned killings when done in a state of anger aroused by some form of provocation. The origins of this form of extenuation have been traced back to verdicts of medieval juries whereby certain spontaneous angry killings were treated, indulgently, as killing *se defendendo*, thereby avoiding a verdict of murder and all its consequences.[151] From these beginnings, provocation ultimately emerged as a distinct partial defence to murder at common law and generated its own body of principles

---

[148] As was pointed out in the context of the previous common law defence of provocation in *Richens* [1993] 4 All ER 877, the loss of self-control has to be compatible with proof of an intent to kill or to cause grievous bodily harm.

[149] Below, Chapter 19.

[150] Below, § 10.9.

[151] Horder, *Provocation and Responsibility* (1992) chap. 1.

and rules.[152] This defence proved controversial and, following recommendations of the Law Commission,[153] was abolished by section 56 of the Coroners and Justice Act 2009, being replaced with a new, narrower, defence of loss of control, which came into force on 4 October 2010.[154] The new statutory defence has been described as "self-contained",[155] in the sense that the ambit of the defence is encompassed within the statutory provisions, unaffected by its common law heritage. Nevertheless, to understand the operation of the defence, it is important to be aware of the operation of the common law defence of provocation and why the Law Commission and Parliament considered that it needed to be replaced. Further, although the authorities on the old common law defence have no influence on the interpretation of the new defence, it remains useful to apply the new defence to the facts of the old cases in order to determine how the new defence will operate. In doing so, it will be seen, as the Court of Appeal has observed, that there are aspects of the legislation which are "likely to produce surprising results".[156]

(i) The defence of provocation

The old defence of provocation existed at common law.[157] As with the new defence of loss of control, it was only available as a defence to murder.[158] When the defence was raised the relevant issues fell within two tests, commonly referred to as the subjective and objective tests. The subjective test concerned whether D had lost self-control suddenly and temporarily because of something said or done. The objective test concerned whether a reasonable person would have lost control on account of the provocation and would have acted as D did. The interpretation of both tests proved to be controversial. As regards the subjective test, the need for a "sudden and temporary loss of self-control" indicated that there had to be something in the nature of a spontaneous response to the provocation if it was to be claimed that D lost self-control.[159] Any indication of a plan or design to kill V would sit uncomfortably with a plea that the killing was something beyond D's control. Similarly, any lapse of time between the last provocative incident and D's reaction would undermine D's claim to have lost control. There were, however, a series of cases in which trial judges allowed the defence to go to the jury despite significant passages of time between the killing and the last provocative incident. In none of these cases did the Court of Appeal deprecate

---

[152] Ashworth, "The Doctrine of Provocation" [1976] *CLJ* 292; Horder, *Provocation and Responsibility* (1992); Sullivan, "Anger and Excuse: Reassessing Provocation" (1992) 12 *OJLS* 380.

[153] Law Com. No. 304, *Murder, Manslaughter and Infanticide* (2006).

[154] Although the details of the new statutory defence are not closely linked to the recommendations of the Law Commission.

[155] *Clinton* [2012] EWCA Crim 2, [2013] QB 1, para. 2; *Gurpinar* [2015] EWCA Crim 178, [2015] 1 WLR 3442, para. 4.

[156] *Ibid.*

[157] Although it was supplemented by s. 3 of the Homicide Act 1957.

[158] In *Cunningham* [1958] 3 All ER 711, where a charge of wounding with intent to cause grievous bodily harm was brought, and in *Bruzas* [1972] Crim LR 367, which concerned a charge of attempted murder, it was confirmed that provocation could not be argued at trial in order to avoid conviction for the offence charged: outwith murder, provocation was relevant only at the sentencing stage as a possible ground of mitigation. Contrast, for example, the Indian Penal Code, ss. 334–5 (a partial defence to voluntarily causing hurt and grievous hurt).

[159] *Ibrams* (1982) 74 Cr App R 154 (CA).

this more accommodating approach.[160] These decisions changed the significance of lapse of time from being a formal legal barrier into an item of evidence relevant to the subjective issue of whether D did, in fact, lose self-control.

The chief controversy relating to the objective test concerned the identification of any characteristics of D which could be taken into account when assessing the impact that the provocation would have had on a reasonable person. This reasonable person standard was a judicial controlling device to prevent what were seen as undeserving pleas from being placed before a jury. The reasonable person was an ordinary person from whom a normal capacity to exercise self-control should be expected.[161] In evaluating D's response by reference to the standard of the ordinary person, there may be particular facets of D herself which explain the loss of self-control and its fatal consequences. D might be unusually pugnacious, abnormally sensitive, mocked about a particular form of affliction, and so on. The question thus arose as to what characteristics associated with D could be attributed to the reasonable person when assessing whether the reasonable person would have acted as D did. Two distinct lines of authority developed. First, the defence was premised on the reactions of persons capable of an ordinary level of self-restraint, so an objective standard of expectation applied, mediated only by the age or gender of the particular defendant.[162] However, when considering the weight or sting of the provocation, particular facets of D's person or character could be attributed to the reasonable person if germane to the weight of the provocation at issue in the case. So, a taunt about D's height might be more provocative to D if she was extremely short, or an adolescent may have less capacity for self-control than a mature adult.[163] A state of addiction would also count.[164] The second line of authority allowed conditions which were relevant on account of the effect they had on D's capacity for self-control in general, such as a personality disorder[165] or a mental impairment such as "battered woman syndrome",[166] even if the provocation was not directed at those characteristics. This second approach was criticised by the Privy Council,[167] but was endorsed by the House of Lords.[168] This was eventually rejected by the Privy Council in *A-G for Jersey* v. *Holley*,[169] where it was considered that D's alcoholism might have been a relevant consideration in evaluating the provocative sting of V's conduct had his quarrel with V related to his state of addiction, but his addiction had no relevance to the level of self-control to be expected of him. On that matter the only variables that the jury should take into account were age and gender. A consequence of this appeared to be that if D was, for example, a woman who was suffering from battered woman syndrome as a result of years of abuse from her partner, whom she had killed, the syndrome would not usually be relevant when

---

[160] In particular cases involving "battered woman syndrome", such as *Thornton (No. 2)* [1992] 1 All ER 306 and *Ahluwalia* [1992] 4 All ER 889.

[161] *Morhall* [1996] AC 90, 97–8 (Lord Goff).

[162] *Camplin* [1978] AC 705, 718 (Lord Diplock).

[163] *Ibid.*

[164] *Morhall* [1996] AC 90.

[165] *Dryden* [1995] 4 All ER 987.

[166] *Ahluwalia* [1992] 4 All ER 889; *Thornton (No. 2)* [1996] 2 All ER 1023; *Humphreys* [1995] 4 All ER 1008.

[167] *Luc Thiet Thuan* v. *R.* [1997] AC 131.

[168] *Smith* [2001] 1 AC 146. For critical commentary see Gardner and Macklem, "Compassion without Respect? Nine Fallacies in *R.* v. *Smith*" [2001] *Crim LR* 623; Macklem and Gardner, "Provocation and Pluralism" (2001) 64 *MLR* 815.

[169] [2005] UKPC 23, [2005] 2 AC 580.

evaluating whether the reasonable person would have killed, since the syndrome would relate to the ability to exercise self-control rather than to the gravity of the provocation.[170] This implication of the decision in *Holley* was a matter of particular concern and proved ultimately significant in the decision of Parliament that the law needed to be reformed; although, as will be seen, the decision in *Holley* has effectively been replicated in the new defence of loss of control.

(ii) A critique of provocation

The defence of provocation was subject to widespread criticism, most notably from Horder, who, in a monograph, recommended the abolition of the defence.[171] Subsequently, as a Law Commissioner, he was responsible for the report which made a similar recommendation.[172] There were many aspects of the defence which proved to be a cause for concern, but ultimately its key failing was that no acceptable rationale for it could be readily identified.

A condition of angry loss of self-control was at the core of provocation. Yet anger is a criminogenic emotion and one of the key deterrent tasks of the criminal law is to provide incentives for citizens to curb violent responses induced by their angry states. A person disposed to respond to frustrations and setbacks with an angry loss of control culminating in serious violence would thereby demonstrate a dangerous and deficient character and should not be accorded any form of condonation. Moreover, the partial condonation of angry violence through a provocation defence comes with an inbuilt gender bias because it clearly privileges persons with an effective capacity and disposition spontaneously to kill others. Such killings occur frequently in domestic contexts against physically vulnerable members of the household.[173] The historical origins of provocation lay in a perception, long discarded as part of our law, that killings emerging from sudden falling-outs ("chance-medleys") were less heinous than killings which were the product of premeditation. From the early modern period the continuation of the defence was reinforced by an acceptance that male honour can (even should) be vindicated by acts of retaliatory violence.[174] These paradigms are unsuited to a modern liberal democracy. They merely strengthen the view that the survival of the defence is an historical anomaly that is acceptable, if at all, only because of the mandatory penalty for murder.

Attempts were made to offer a modern rationale for the defence. McAuley[175] defended the extenuating force of provocation on the basis of what he termed "partial justification". For him, there needed to be some element of the victim's "asking for it", so that blame for the killing is in some sense shared between defendant and victim. As Macauley observed himself, such a rationale could not underpin the English version of the provocation defence

---

[170] Although it might still be possible for the jury to conclude that a person of normal self-control in the circumstances of D might reasonably have developed battered woman syndrome.

[171] *Provocation and Responsibility* (1992) chap. 9.

[172] Law Com. No. 304, *Murder, Manslaughter and Infanticide* (2006) part 5.

[173] In 2010/11 47% of female homicide victims who were acquainted with the suspect were killed by a partner or ex-partner, whereas 5% of male homicide victims who were acquainted with the suspect were killed by a partner or ex-partner: Smith, Osborne, Lau and Britten, *Homicide, Firearm Offences and Intimate Violence 2010/11* (2012). According to Edwards, "The Strangulation of Female Partners" [2015] *Crim LR* 949, strangulation is one of the principal methods used by men to kill women in intimate relationships.

[174] Horder, *Provocation and Responsibility* (1992) chaps. 1–3.

[175] "Anticipating the Past: The Defence of Provocation in Irish Law" (1987) 50 *MLR* 133.

because provocation could apply where the victim was someone other than the provocateur and, more importantly, the issue was raised if D was provoked by anything, such as the crying of a baby or a predictable reaction to his own unlawful or offensive behaviour. These are not cases where the victim "asks for it". In any event, the notion of partial justification is incoherent. Conduct is either justified, all things considered, or it is not (although in the latter case it may be condonable). Even in the case of the gravest provocation—say D has just witnessed the murder of his wife by V—D's killing V cannot be justified. Understandable, yes. Excusable, perhaps. But not justified. Viewed from the perspective of a general rule of conduct, his action is clearly wrong and impermissible.

Dressler[176] located the rationale of the provocation defence in the realm of excuse, the excuse consisting of D's reduced capacity to conform his conduct to law when induced to lose self-control in angry reaction to provocation. But, as he recognised, our judgmental reaction to loss of control greatly depends on the nature of the conduct which caused the reaction. In the example where V kills D's wife, we readily condone, at least in part, D's response. By contrast, where the precipitating incident is trivial, we may, quite reasonably, see E's loss of self-control as a ground of censure. Yet the emotions gripping E may be just as strong, just as choice-constraining, as the emotions aroused in a person who has endured grave provocation. The loss of self-control does not in itself explain why we feel blame is extenuated in some cases. Indeed, in some cases where murder verdicts have been sustained because of insufficient evidence of loss of self-control, there may be a strong case for extenuation, even in a case of considered, deliberate killing.

The rigidity of the mandatory sentence in murder calls for flexible, fact-sensitive grounds of extenuation. Some members of the judiciary sought to make provocation more flexible and fact-sensitive, particularly through reception of syndrome evidence. In so doing, they created an awkward overlap with the grounds of extenuation afforded by diminished responsibility, undermining the coherence of provocation as a defence for ordinary people. That tendency was halted by the decision in *Holley*; but this swapped one set of concerns for another. Take, for instance, the post-*Holley* decision in *Mohammed*.[177] D had killed his daughter V, enraged that she was continuing a relationship with a man after he had ordered her to end the connection. Not merely was this defiance but, according to the version of the Muslim faith to which D subscribed, it was in breach of V's religious obligation to obey her father, placing her beyond the bounds of her community. In an accurate rendering of the post-*Holley* law, the trial judge, in a direction approved by the Court of Appeal, instructed the jury that they should consider D's religion and culture in determining how a reasonable person so situated would have regarded V's defiance of her father. When it came to evaluating how a reasonable person would have reacted to the defiance (on discovering the couple in his house), the test to be employed was the likely reaction of a person of ordinary stability and temperament. This awkward amalgam of cultural relativism and mainstream expectations concerning self-control was not easy material with which a jury could achieve justice.

Cases such as *Mohammed* raised the question whether a soundly based defence of provocation could be worked out or whether the defence should be abolished. After careful consideration of the law and searching for a rationale for the defence, the Law Commission

---

[176] "Rethinking Heat of Passion: A Defence in Search of a Rationale" (1982) 73 *J Crim L and Crim* 421.
[177] [2005] EWCA Crim 1880.

recommended its abolition and replacement with a new defence of loss of control.[178] These recommendations were incorporated, subject to certain key amendments, in the Coroners and Justice Act 2009.

(iii) Loss of control

The defence of loss of control is defined by sections 54 and 55 of the Coroners and Justice Act 2009.[179] The heading to these provisions describes the defence as a "partial defence to murder". As with the old common law defence of provocation, loss of control is only available for the crime of murder, which first needs to be established, and results in D's being liable to conviction for manslaughter,[180] thus avoiding the mandatory life sentence. The defence is available whether D is the principal offender who killed V or an accessory who was party to the killing.[181]

To establish the defence, three components need to be established. Loosely summarised, these are:

(a)   D must actually lose self-control because of a triggering event;
(b)   the triggering event must be a qualifying one;
(c)   the loss of self-control must be objectively understandable, in that a "normal" person might also have lost self-control in the circumstances.

All three components need to be identified; if one is absent, the defence fails. Although the components should be analysed sequentially and separately, typically they will arise simultaneously at the point when the fatal violence is used.[182]

The trial judge must leave the defence to the jury, even if D has not raised the defence or given any evidence of loss of self-control, but only if sufficient evidence is adduced to raise an issue with respect to each[183] of the components of the defence on which, in the opinion of the judge, a properly directed jury could reasonably conclude that the defence might apply.[184] If the defence is left to the jury its members must assume that the defence is satisfied unless the prosecution proves beyond reasonable doubt that it is not.[185] We discuss the three components of the defence in the following subsections.

---

[178] Law Com. No. 304, part 5. The proposals are in substance the same as recommended in LCCP No. 177, part 6, on which see Mackay and Mitchell, "But Is this Provocation? Some Thoughts on the Law Commission's Report on Partial Defences to Murder" [2005] *Crim LR* 44; Quick and Wells "Getting Tough with Defences" [2006] *Crim LR* 514.

[179] See Norrie, "The Coroners and Justice Act 2009—Partial Defences to Murder (1) Loss of Control" [2010] *Crim LR* 275; Withey, "Loss of Control: Loss of Opportunity?" [2011] *Crim LR* 263.

[180] Coroners and Justice Act 2009, s. 54(7).

[181] *Ibid.*, s. 54(1). If the defence is successful for one party to the killing this does not affect the liability of any other party to the murder: s. 54(8).

[182] *Clinton* [2012] EWCA Crim 2, [2013] QB 1, para. 9.

[183] *Gurpinar* [2015] EWCA Crim 178, [2015] 1 WLR 3442, para. 22.

[184] Coroners and Justice Act 2009, s. 54(6). See *Gurpinar* [2015] EWCA Crim 178, [2015] 1 WLR 3442, where it was recognised that this requires more rigorous evaluation of the evidence by the trial judge than was required under the old defence of provocation.

[185] Coroners and Justice Act 2009, s. 54(5).

(a) D's loss of self-control

It must first be established that D's acts and omissions, in killing V or being a party to V's killing, resulted from D's loss of self-control.[186] Loss of self-control is not defined in the legislation but it has been interpreted by the courts as involving "D's loss of ability to maintain his actions in accordance with considered judgment or [where] he had lost normal powers of reasoning".[187] This is a subjective test which focuses on D's reaction, and it is necessary to establish a causative link between the loss of self-control and the relevant act or omission. Exactly what psychological state represents a loss of self-control cannot precisely be pinned down. In *Gurpinar*[188] the Court of Appeal was asked to consider whether loss of self-control encompassed a loss of temper and whether the loss of self-control had to be total, but declined to do so because the issues did not arise on the facts of the appeals and because the issue of what constituted a loss of self-control was considered to be generally fact-sensitive.

Loss of self-control was also a key requirement of the defence of provocation. So, in *Cocker*,[189] where D killed his terminally ill wife in response to her incessant requests for him to do so, no issue of provocation arose. The circumstances of the killing indicated calm and deliberation. The "classic" direction on the matter given by Devlin J in *Duffy*,[190] in respect of the defence of provocation, referred to "a loss of self-control, rendering the accused so subject to passion as to make him or her not master of his [*sic*] mind". Obviously, then, D had to be in some extremity of anger, but the anger need not be so overwhelming as to render D incapable of knowing what she was doing. In principle, if S's anger was as radically destabilising as that, she could claim that she lacked the mens rea for murder. In *Richens*,[191] it was stressed that awareness of the nature and quality of one's actions and of the consequences that will ensue from them was quite compatible with a successful plea of the old defence of provocation. All that was required was that D must be so angry that he was unable to restrain himself. Presumably this remains the case in respect of the defence of loss of control.

The old defence of provocation required the defendant's loss of self-control to arise from something said or done. There is no such requirement for the new defence; it is sufficient that D lost self-control and this need not arise from human agency. For example, D, a farmer, might look out upon his flood-devastated land and feel a great surge of anger towards V, his prosperous neighbour, who farms on higher ground. Should D's resentment lead him to kill V, the subsequent trial of D for murder might require consideration of whether D had lost self-control.[192] Further, loss of self-control will be established where it arises from a mistake made by D. For the common law defence of provocation it was recognised that, where D had mistakenly assumed that V had done something to him amounting to provocation, he was entitled to be tried on the basis that his mistaken assumptions were true.[193] The same should be true under the statutory defence of loss of self-control,

---

[186] *Ibid.*, s. 54(1)(a).
[187] See *Jewell* [2014] EWCA Crim 414, para. 24, relying on *Smith and Hogan*, § 15.1.2.5.
[188] [2015] EWCA Crim 178, [2015] 1 WLR 3442, para. 20.
[189] [1989] Crim LR 740 (CA).
[190] [1949] 1 All ER 932n (CCA).
[191] [1993] 4 All ER 877 (CA).
[192] Although there would be grave difficulty in establishing the other elements of the defence in such a case.
[193] *Brown* (1776) 1 Leach 148, 168 ER 177.

and even if the mistake was induced by alcohol, as was also the case at common law.[194] Consequently even loss of self-control arising from an honest but unreasonable mistake should suffice. This can be justified because a successful plea of loss of control merely extenuates and does not completely excuse.

Whereas the old defence of provocation required the loss of self-control to be sudden and temporary, for the new statutory defence the loss of control need not be sudden.[195] Although it might appear that this reform dramatically widens the ambit of the defence, since it is no longer necessary to show in effect an instinctive loss of control, and a killing which occurs days or even weeks after a particular triggering event might still be one which resulted from loss of self-control, the reform is not as radical as it might first appear, for four reasons. First, the interpretation of the defence of provocation had developed significantly so that, although there remained a formal requirement of sudden and temporary loss of self control, whether this was satisfied was a question of fact for the jury, meaning that longer gaps between a provocative event and killing would not necessarily mean that the defence failed. Secondly, the loss of control defence will only operate where a person with "a normal degree of tolerance and self-restraint" would have acted in a similar way. Consequently, the fact that the loss of self-control is not sudden may be relevant to a jury's concluding that a normal person would not have acted as D did. Thirdly, the defence will not be available where D has "acted in a considered desire for revenge".[196] The longer the gap between a triggering event and the killing, the more likely it will be that the jury concludes that the killing was motivated by revenge. The Court of Appeal has recognised that a jury was properly directed about the relevance of a considered desire for revenge when the trial judge referred to a "deliberate and considered decision ... one that has been thought about" by D.[197]

Finally, although the key implication of the absence of any requirement that the loss of self-control was "sudden" is that the judge should not exclude the defence from the jury merely because of the delay between a relevant triggering event and the loss of control, the jury may still legitimately conclude that the lapse of time means that there was no operative loss of control at the time of the killing. For example, in *Ibrams*,[198] which concerned the defence of provocation, the last provocative act perpetrated by V occurred on 7 October. On 10 October, D planned with others the killing of V. The attack was successfully carried out on 12 October. On such facts, the trial judge ruled that there was no evidence of any loss of self-control. It is submitted that the important feature in *Ibrams* was the planning and deliberation, with the lapse of time underscoring the organised nature of the killing. This would presumably be decided the same way under the new defence of loss of control. But evidence of premeditation and planning may not necessarily be incompatible with a finding of loss of self-control. In *Thornton (No. 2)*,[199] for instance, D declared her intention

---

[194] *Letenock* (1917) 12 Cr App R 221 (CCA); *Wardrope* [1960] Crim LR 770. Intoxication is not generally relevant to the third component of the defence if it relates to D's capacity for tolerance and self-restraint (*Asmelash* [2013] EWCA Crim 157, [2014] QB 103), but that should not exclude it from being relevant to the first component, i.e. whether D had lost self-control.

[195] Coroners and Justice Act 2009, s. 54(2).

[196] *Ibid.*, s. 54(4).

[197] *Clinton* [2012] EWCA Crim 2, [2013] QB 1, para. 131.

[198] (1982) 74 Cr App R 154 (CA).

[199] [1992] 1 All ER 306.

of killing V, her brutal husband, and went into another room to obtain and sharpen a knife, before returning and stabbing him. Similarly, in *Ahluwalia*,[200] D waited until her abusive husband V was asleep, fetched a can of petrol, doused his bed with fuel, and then set it alight. Most strikingly, in *Pearson*,[201] D and E had armed themselves with weapons and killed V, their abusive father, in the course of a planned joint enterprise. In each of these cases, the jury was asked to consider whether D had acted in a state of loss of control. This insistence upon a finding of loss of self-control has been criticised—a criticism founded on a very understandable concern with the provocation endured by the defendants in these cases.[202] But the old defence of provocation had a requirement that there must be a loss of self-control, and this has not changed under the new defence. Similarly, for the old defence it was possible to have regard to the cumulative impact of earlier events to assess whether D had lost self-control. Such cumulative impact remains relevant to the statutory defence of loss of control.[203]

(b) Qualifying trigger

D's loss of self-control must have a qualifying trigger.[204] There are two alternative qualifying triggers, either of which must be satisfied in their own right or in combination.[205] As the Court of Appeal correctly observed in *Clinton*:[206]

> "There is no point in pretending that the practical application of [section 55] will not create considerable difficulties."

The effect of the qualifying triggers is to limit the circumstances where the defence of loss of control will operate when compared with the old defence of provocation.[207]

Fear of serious violence.

The loss of self-control will have a qualifying trigger if it was "attributable to D's fear of serious violence from V against D or another identified person".[208]

This can be welcomed without reservation. It seems entirely suitable to cover without strain domestic violence cases such as *Thornton (No. 2)*[209] and *Ahluwalia*.[210] Furthermore, it repairs the failure of English law to provide some extenuation for cases where there is a right to use some force in self-defence but where the right was abused by D's recourse to excessive force, so that the complete defence of self-defence will not be available.[211]

---

[200] [1992] 4 All ER 889.

[201] [1992] Crim LR 193 (CA).

[202] O'Donovan, "Defences for Battered Women Who Kill" (1991) 18 *J Law and Soc* 219; Nicholson, "Telling Tales: Gender Discrimination Gender Construction and Battered Women Who Kill" (1995) 3 *Feminist Leg Stud* 185; McColgan, "In Defence of Battered Women Who Kill" (1993) 130 *J Law and Soc* 508; Wells, "Battered Women Syndrome and Defences to Homicide: Where Now?" (1994) 14 *LS* 266; Dressler, "Battered Women Who Kill Their Sleeping Tormenters: Reflections on Maintaining Respect for Human Life while Killing Moral Monsters" in Shute and Simester (eds.), *Criminal Law Theory: Doctrines of the General Part* (2002) 259.

[203] *Dawes* [2013] EWCA Crim 322, [2014] 1 WLR 947, para. 54.

[204] Coroners and Justice Act 2009, s. 54(1)(b).

[205] *Ibid.*, s. 55(5).

[206] [2012] EWCA Crim 2, [2013] QB 1, para. 11.

[207] *Dawes* [2013] EWCA Crim 322, [2014] 1 WLR 947, para. 60.

[208] Coroners and Justice Act 2009, s. 55(3).

[209] [1992] 1 All ER 306.

[210] [1992] 4 All ER 889.

[211] *Clegg* [1995] 1 AC 482.

But, whereas the defence of self-defence applies where there is a threat of any violence, the qualifying trigger will only be engaged where D fears serious violence. D's fear of serious violence is to be disregarded to the extent that the fear itself was caused by a thing which D incited to be done or said for the purpose of providing an excuse to use violence.[212] This restriction on the trigger embodies the notion that D cannot rely on a self-induced loss of control, at least when D's purpose was to create a situation where he could resort to violence. Further, the defence is not available where, even though D feared serious violence, she "acted in a considered desire for revenge".[213] But this qualifying trigger would appear to be satisfied if the facts of *Johnson*[214] arose again, where D was allowed to raise the defence of provocation in respect of V's extreme but predictable reaction to D's own objectionable and aggressive behaviour. This has been confirmed by the Court of Appeal in *Dawes*,[215] where it was held that the mere fact that D was behaving badly and was looking for and provoking trouble does not necessarily lead to the disapplication of the qualifying trigger. It is only where D intended that his actions would provide him with the excuse or opportunity to use violence that the qualifying trigger will not operate.

Sense of being seriously wronged by things done or said.
The loss of self-control will also have a qualifying trigger if it was attributable to something done or said or both which:[216]

(a)   constituted circumstances of an extremely grave character, and
(b)   caused D to have a justifiable sense of being seriously wronged.

A sense of being seriously wronged by something done or said will not be justifiable, however, where D has incited what was done or said in order to provide an excuse to use violence.[217]

Both the scope and the interpretation of this second qualifying trigger are troubling, with much of the concern being focused on the meaning of the phrases "extremely grave character" and "justifiable sense of being seriously wronged". Whether D has a sense of having been seriously wronged is a subjective test to be assessed with reference to D's own perception.[218] But, whether the circumstances were extremely grave and D was seriously wronged and whether D's sense of grievance was justifiable, are to be evaluated objectively.[219] It remains unclear, however, when D's sense of being seriously wronged can be considered to be justifiable rather than being merely excusable or understandable. In particular, when determining whether the sense of being seriously wronged is justifiable, it is not clear whether D's own circumstances can be taken into account or whether this is simply a matter for the jury to determine without regard to D's individual circumstances.

---

[212] Coroners and Justice Act 2009, s. 55(6)(a).
[213] *Ibid.*, s. 54(4).
[214] [1989] 1 WLR 740 (CA).
[215] [2013] EWCA Crim 322, [2014] 1 WLR 947, para. 58.
[216] Coroners and Justice Act 2009, s. 55(4)
[217] *Ibid.*, s 55(6)(b). This has been called "self-induced loss of control": *Clinton* [2012] EWCA Crim 2, [2013] QB 1, para. 13.
[218] *Ibid.*, para. 12.
[219] *Ibid.*; *Dawes* [2013] EWCA Crim 322, [2014] 1 WLR 681, para. 61.

It is undeniably the case that the effect of this trigger is that certain cases where the old defence of provocation applied will no longer fall within the loss of control defence. So, for example, the defence of provocation was available in *Doughty*,[220] where D killed his crying baby. Such a defendant would not have a defence of loss of control, since he would have no fear of serious injury and, even if the circumstances are extremely grave (which is unlikely), he has no justifiable sense of being seriously wronged by the crying. However, the defendant in *Mohammed*[221] might establish such a qualifying trigger by virtue of his daughter's continuance of a relationship which he had forbidden, arguably an "extremely grave" matter, and, having regard to the norms of his religion and culture, he might be characterised as having a justifiable sense of being seriously wronged. The prospect of the defence of loss of control being available in such cases of so-called "honour killings" is at least curtailed if D "acted in a considered desire for revenge",[222] although much will turn on whether D's motive can really be characterised as one of revenge. Alternatively, the defence would not succeed in such a case if the daughter's continuance of the relationship is not considered to be of "an extremely grave character", which is an objective test and not what D himself considered to be extremely grave. Further, the defence would only succeed if a person of a normal degree of tolerance and self-restraint would have reacted in a similar way. As we will see below, when determining how such a person would have reacted, the circumstances of D should be taken into account. If those circumstances include D's religious and cultural norms, however, as they did in *Mohammed* itself, the objective standard might potentially be regarded as satisfied by a particular jury.

At first glance, the operation of this second qualifying trigger might be thought applicable in one of the areas traditionally covered by the old defence of provocation, namely where D lost his self-control by virtue of his partner's infidelity and killed either the partner or her lover, or both of them. The infidelity could be characterised as being "of an extremely grave character" and D could be considered to have a justifiable sense of being seriously wronged by the betrayal. Under the statute, however, the fact that what was done or said "constituted sexual infidelity" must be disregarded when considering this qualifying trigger.[223] The interpretation of this exclusion was examined by the Court of Appeal in *Clinton*.[224] The Court emphasised that there was no definition of "sexual infidelity". It was acknowledged that the concept could be interpreted restrictively to confine it to conduct which relates directly and exclusively to sexual activity, so that words and acts constituting sexual activity would count but the effect of infidelity would not, such as envy, jealousy or possessiveness. The inclusion of the word "infidelity" would suggest that there needs to be a relationship of some kind to which one party could be unfaithful,[225] although the relationship need not be a legally recognised one through marriage or a civil partnership. Consequently, on the facts of the Australian case *Stingel*,[226] the exclusion would not apply

---

[220] (1986) 83 Cr App R 319.

[221] [2005] EWCA Crim 1880.

[222] Coroners and Justice Act 2009, s. 54(4).

[223] *Ibid.*, s. 55(6)(c). *Ibid.*, s. 55(6)(c). See Reed and Wake, "Sexual Infidelity Killings" in Reed and Bohlander (eds.), *Loss of Control and Diminished Responsibility: Domestic, Comparative and International Perspectives* (2011) 117.

[224] [2012] EWCA Crim 2, [2013] QB 1.

[225] *Ibid.*, para. 17.

[226] [1990] 171 CLR 313.

where a stalker found his victim having sexual intercourse. There was no infidelity by the victim, so the exclusion would not be engaged. Further, the infidelity must be sexual. So, for example, if one partner told the other that she considered their relationship to be at an end and that she considered herself free to have sexual intercourse with anyone she wished, this would not be considered to be "sexual infidelity", because the sex would take place after the relationship had ended. It would, presumably, be different if she had sex with others whilst she continued in a relationship with her partner.

A further difficulty of interpretation relates to the treatment of things "said" constituting sexual infidelity. Whilst this might encompass a D who overhears her partner tell his lover, "I love you", it is not clear that this necessarily constitutes infidelity which is "sexual", but equally it is not clear that it necessarily "constitutes" sexual infidelity; that would depend on the context and the circumstances in which it was said.[227] A further difficulty arises where the words said are untrue. This would apparently not constitute sexual infidelity, so could not be excluded when considering the qualifying trigger, but a truthful statement would be excluded. As the Court of Appeal recognised, such a distinction would be "illogical".[228] For this reason, the Court sensibly held that "things said" include admissions of sexual infidelity, true or untrue, and reports by others of sexual infidelity.

Whilst the provision appears to prevent sexual infidelity constituting a qualifying trigger, the Court of Appeal recognised that, to avoid injustice and absurdity of result, a more subtle interpretation must be adopted. The provision was interpreted as excluding sexual infidelity when it is the only qualifying trigger. But this is not a blanket exclusion, since events cannot be isolated from their context. Where sexual infidelity is integral to and forms an essential part of the context, sexual infidelity cannot be excluded and must be taken into account in order to evaluate whether other circumstances are grave and establish a justifiable sense of being wronged.[229] This is illustrated by the facts of *Clinton* itself. In that case, D had an argument with his wife following realisation that their marriage was at an end. During the argument, D's wife informed him that she was having an affair and had sexual intercourse with a number of other men, which she described in graphic detail, and taunted him about his previous failed attempts to commit suicide. The trial judge had withdrawn the defence of loss of control from the jury, on the ground that the defence was founded on sexual infidelity. The Court of Appeal considered this to be a misdirection because the wife's confession of sexual infidelity was relevant to the evaluation of the totality of the matters relied on as a qualifying trigger. A retrial was ordered, but D subsequently pleaded guilty to murder, so the jury did not have the opportunity to consider whether the totality of the evidence, including sexual infidelity, was sufficient to establish the qualifying trigger.

Whilst the exclusion of sexual infidelity as a circumstance to establish a qualifying trigger was motivated by a concern that evidence of sexual infidelity had been abused when establishing the old defence of provocation, it is unclear why it was felt that express provision was required for the exclusion of sexual infidelity when the defence of loss of control will anyway only be available where a person of a normal degree of tolerance and self-restraint would have acted as D did. Surely this objective standard provides a sufficient safeguard

---

[227] *Clinton* [2012] EWCA Crim 2, [2013] QB 1, para. 25.
[228] *Ibid.*, para. 26.
[229] *Ibid.*, para. 39.

against potential abuse of the defence of loss of control, for if the "normal person" would have acted as D did had she found her partner having an extramarital affair the defence ought to be available.

(c) Objective standard

Finally, D's loss of control must be judged by reference to an objective standard, namely whether "a person of D's sex and age, with a normal degree of tolerance and self-restraint and in the circumstances of D, might have reacted in the same or in a similar way to D".[230] The reference to D's circumstances is a "reference to all D's circumstances other than those whose only relevance to D's conduct is that they bear on D's general capacity for tolerance or self-restraint".[231]

This test broadly replicates the objective test at common law after the decision in *Holley*,[232] although without reference to "the reasonable person" and replacing the language of characteristics with that of circumstances. This is because circumstances of D relating to her general capacity for tolerance or self-restraint are to be excluded, as was recognised in *Holley*.[233] Consequently the effect of the line of authority ultimately endorsed in *Smith*, that mental disorder was relevant when evaluating D's conduct on the ground that it affected the capacity to exercise self-control, has not been adopted for the new defence. All other circumstances of D are relevant, including D's social, religious and cultural context, and any circumstance which relates to the effect of the triggering event on D. So, in *Holley*, the fact that D was an alcoholic would not be a relevant circumstance for the new defence since it related only to D's general capacity for tolerance and self-restraint; things would be different had D been taunted about his alcoholism, which would then be relevant when assessing the impact of the qualifying trigger on the normal person. So, if D was addicted to solvents and on that account was taunted by V,[234] this would be a relevant circumstance for the defence of loss of control, as would D's ethnicity, sexual orientation, impotence,[235] or eczema[236] if he was taunted about that, and even though the latter condition might be temporary. The age of D continues to be relevant as well. Consequently, *Camplin*[237] would be decided in the same way in respect of the defence of loss of control. In that case D, a 15-year-old boy, struck and killed V after V had sodomised and subsequently mocked him. The House of Lords recognised that the jury should be allowed to take into account D's age when determining the degree of self-control to be expected, since an adolescent would typically be more sensitive and volatile, when mocked, than would be a person of mature years. Further, presumably a qualifying trigger could be identified on the basis of a justifiable sense of being seriously wronged.

---

[230] Coroners and Justice Act 2009, s. 54(1)(c).
[231] *Ibid.*, s. 54(3).
[232] [2005] 2 AC 580.
[233] Although *Holley* might be considered to have left open the possibility that, although characteristics affecting self-control were excluded, the jury might conclude that a person of normal self-control in the circumstances of the defendant might reasonably have developed battered woman syndrome. Such a conclusion is not open to the jury under s. 54(3).
[234] *Morhall* [1996] AC 90. See also *Asmelash* [2013] EWCA Crim 157, [2014] QB 103, para. 25.
[235] Cf. *Bedder* [1954] 2 All ER 80.
[236] *Morhall* [1996] AC 90, 99 (Lord Goff).
[237] [1978] AC 705.

All circumstances other than those bearing on D's general capacity for tolerance or self-restraint can be taken into account. This is illustrated by cases relating to the old defence of provocation. So, for example, in *McArthy*,[238] D lost control after receiving an unwelcome sexual request from V. The jury was entitled to consider the fact that, some 20 minutes earlier, V had indecently assaulted D. Similarly, in both *Thornton*[239] and *Ahluwalia*,[240] the whole course of marital discord endured by the respective defendants was admitted as evidence relevant to the weight of the provocation and the impact it would have had. But the recognition in those cases that "battered woman syndrome" was a relevant characteristic for the defence of provocation would appear not to be relevant for the defence of loss of control, because the syndrome relates to the ability to exercise self-control.[241] The same applies to *Humphreys*,[242] which concerned immaturity and attention seeking by wrist slashing, and *Dryden*,[243] involving "obsessive and eccentric" personality. Common to all these cases was the presence of expert testimony indicating that these conditions were beyond the normal range of personality variation and constituted discrete syndromes. But they were considered to be relevant simply because they affected D's ability to exercise self-control. In other words, they "bear on D's general capacity for tolerance or self-restraint" and so must now be ignored. Such a conclusion is consistent with the approach adopted in *Roberts*,[244] where, although expert witnesses were prepared to testify that pre-lingual deaf-mutes typically experienced raised anger levels because of the frustrations inherent in coping with their disability, such evidence was not considered to be relevant to the provocation defence. The degree of self-control to be required of a deaf-mute was the same degree of self-control to be expected of any normal person of D's age and gender. Similarly, the decision of the Privy Council in *Luc Thiet-Thuan* v. *R.*[245] that D's brain damage (which induced impulsive behaviour in D) should not be taken into account remains relevant for the defence of loss of control. The decision of the House of Lords in *Smith*[246] would, however, be different. In that case, it was held that D's depression was relevant to the defence of provocation, even though the quarrel leading to V's death at the hands of D did not involve any pejorative reference by V to D's depressed condition. The depression simply affected D's capacity to exercise self-control and so would not be relevant under the statutory test. Further, self-induced intoxication is generally not a relevant circumstance, because it relates to D's capacity for tolerance and self-restraint;[247] similarly if D was suffering from withdrawal symptoms.

---

[238] [1954] 2 QB 105 (CCA).

[239] [1992] 1 All ER 306 (CA).

[240] [1992] 4 All ER 889.

[241] For criticism of the relevance of this syndrome and the related notion of learned helplessness to defences, including loss of control, on the ground that its recognition lacks sufficient scientific integrity, see Loveless, "R v GAC: Battered Woman 'Syndromization'" [2014] *Crim LR* 655.

[242] [1995] 4 All ER 1008.

[243] [1995] 4 All ER 987.

[244] [1990] *Crim LR* 122 (CA).

[245] [1997] AC 131.

[246] [2001] 1 AC 146 (HL). For critical commentary on *Smith* see Gardner and Macklem, "Compassion without Respect? Nine Fallacies in *R.* v. *Smith*" [2001] *Crim LR* 623.

[247] *Asmelash* [2013] EWCA Crim 157, [2014] QB 103. Intoxication might, however, be relevant where D has made a mistake because then it is not only relevant to D's capacity for tolerance and self-restraint: see Ashworth's commentary at [2013] *Crim LR* 599, 601.

Crucially, the fact that all circumstances other than those bearing on D's general capacity for tolerance or self-restraint can be taken into account when assessing the objective standard means that sexual infidelity is relevant at this stage of the analysis, even if it has been excluded when considering the second qualifying trigger. This was confirmed by the Court of Appeal in *Clinton*.[248] This emphasises the absurdity of the exclusion of "sexual infidelity" in the first place. If this can be taken into account at the third stage but may be excluded at the second stage, this makes the task of the judge in directing the jury very difficult, and the task of the jury almost impossible. As the Court said in *Clinton*:[249]

> "there will be occasions when the jury would be both disregarding and considering the same evidence. That is, to put it neutrally, counter intuitive."

It is simply not possible to compartmentalise evidence of sexual infidelity so that it is only considered at the third stage. If evidence of such infidelity is adduced, it will inevitably be taken into account at the second stage as well when evaluating the qualifying trigger.

(d) Critique of the loss of control defence

It is clear that the application of the defence of loss of control will be more limited than the defence of provocation, largely because of the need to establish a qualifying trigger. However, the reality is likely to be that in many cases the same result would be achieved whether at common law or under the statute, but some cases would be decided differently under the new defence. This can be assessed with reference to the case of a woman who, having been abused for many years by her partner, suffers from a recognised psychological syndrome and then murders her abusive partner. In determining whether she will have a defence of loss of control, it is necessary to consider the three requirements in turn. First, she must have killed as the result of a loss of self-control, even though this need not happen as a sudden response to a particular event. Secondly, the relevant trigger is most likely to be that her loss of self-control was attributable to her fear of serious violence from V. Finally, it must be considered whether a woman of her age and in her circumstances with normal tolerance and self-restraint would have reacted in a similar way. The key question is whether it is relevant that she has been abused for a long time and suffers from a syndrome as a consequence. Since the syndrome relates to D's general capacity for tolerance or self-restraint, it could not be taken into account under the Act. However, it is likely that the history of abuse will be relevant since it supports the existence and impact of the relevant qualifying trigger and would make it more likely that the normal person would have reacted as D did. Crucially, it is not obvious that a battered woman who kills her abusive partner is any more likely to have a successful partial defence of loss of control than she would a defence of provocation at common law.

The structure of the defence of loss of control is complicated: the meaning of the qualifying triggers is opaque, especially as regards a justifiable sense of being seriously wronged; moreover, the objective test, while avoiding the language of the reasonable person and D's characteristics, will still be difficult for the jury to apply, especially as the jury must disregard those circumstances of D which relate to a general capacity for tolerance and

---

[248] [2012] EWCA Crim 2, [2013] QB 1.
[249] *Ibid.*, para. 32.

self-restraint. Judicial directions to the jury relating to this defence are likely to be excessively complicated.

(iv) Relationship with diminished responsibility

There may be circumstances where the defences of loss of control and of diminished responsibility[250] will be raised in the same proceedings. Any diagnosable personality disorder or mental impairment presumptively falls within section 2 of the Homicide Act 1957[251] provided it is a "recognised medical condition". This may well lead a jury to conclude that D's responsibility for his acts was substantially impaired within the terms of that section where she had a personality disorder or mental impairment which was medically recognised. Equally, such evidence might be relevant to a plea of loss of control,[252] at least to the extent that it has a relevance to D's conduct other than as regards D's general capacity for tolerance or self-restraint. In an appropriate case, therefore, D may raise both defences of her own motion. This points up a major anomaly: for diminished responsibility, the burden of proof, on a balance of probabilities, lies with the defendant;[253] for loss of control, the burden of disproof is on the prosecution once sufficient evidence has been adduced to raise an issue in respect of it.[254] This burden is discharged by proof beyond any reasonable doubt.[255] It cannot be easy, even for the most conscientious and capable jury, to deal with the same evidence under different heads, applying differential burdens and quantums of proof. A further difficulty for the jury, as recognised in *Clinton*,[256] is that evidence of sexual infidelity may be relevant to the defence of diminished responsibility, since the discovery of sexual infidelity may lead to a recognised medical condition such as severe depression and impair D's ability to form a rational judgement, but it may be excluded for the defence of loss of control. One of the reasons why it has been held that self-induced intoxication is not a relevant circumstance when assessing the objective condition for the defence of loss of control[257] was because self-induced intoxication is not relevant to the assessment of diminished responsibility,[258] and "the potential for uncertainty and confusion which would follow the necessarily very different directions on the issue of intoxication, depending on which partial defence was under consideration, does not bear contemplation".[259] But

---

[250] Diminished responsibility is discussed in detail below, § 19.2.

[251] Section 2, as amended by section 52 of the Coroners and Justice Act 2009, provides that: "A person ("D") who kills or is a party to the killing of another is not to be convicted of murder if D was suffering from an abnormality of mental functioning which (a) arose from a recognised medical condition, (b) substantially impaired D's ability to do one or more of the things mentioned in subsection (1A) and (c) provides an explanation for D's acts and omissions in doing or being a party to the killing". The things mentioned in subsection 1A are: "to understand the nature of D's conduct; to form a rational judgment; to exercise self-control".

[252] In *Ahluwalia* [1992] 4 All ER 889 and *Thornton (No. 2)* [1996] 2 All ER 1023, evidence of battered woman syndrome was taken to be relevant to provocation and diminished responsibility. Both grounds of extenuation may be raised in the same trial.

[253] Homicide Act 1957 s. 2(2).

[254] Coroners and Justice Act 2009, s. 54(6).

[255] *Ibid.*, s. 54(5).

[256] [2012] EWCA Crim 2, [2013] QB 1, para. 33.

[257] *Asmelash* [2013] EWCA Crim 157, [2014] QB 103.

[258] *Dowds* [2012] EWCA Crim 281, [2012] 1 WLR 2576.

[259] *Asmelash* [2013] EWCA Crim 15, [2014] QB 103, para. 24.

such uncertainty and confusion does need to be contemplated for other aspects of the two defences.

§ 10.6 Involuntary manslaughter

The term "involuntary manslaughter" refers to those killings made criminal at common law notwithstanding a lack of intention to kill or cause grievous bodily harm.[260] The ambit of involuntary manslaughter is wide, ranging from killings which have a strong affinity with murder to situations where D would lack the culpability for any serious criminal offence had he not caused death. Nowhere is the role of chance factors more prevalent. Beyond the sphere of regulatory offences, negligence does not attract criminal liability unless the negligence is gross and results in death.[261] Assault is now a summary offence;[262] should a death be causally linked to an assault a manslaughter verdict will likely ensue, however unexpected and unforeseeable that eventuality may have been.[263] Certain forms of eccentric sexuality, not in themselves criminal, may attract a manslaughter verdict should death inadvertently occur.[264] The various ways in which liability for involuntary manslaughter may arise are not explicable by reference to any conceptual scheme or overarching principle. They merely reflect the assessments of judges down the years of which killings merit a punitive response. To an extent, the wide scope of involuntary manslaughter is a function of the complete sentencing discretion that judges are permitted at common law; D may receive anything from an absolute discharge to life imprisonment. If judges had accepted as a restraining principle that the minimum culpability requirement for manslaughter should, at least normally, be such as to merit a substantial custodial sentence, we would have a narrower and more defensible law of manslaughter.

It is impossible to state the ambit of involuntary manslaughter with precision. Four broad areas of liability can be identified and will now be discussed.

(i) Constructive manslaughter

What is now known as constructive manslaughter, or "unlawful act" manslaughter,[265] used to be the manslaughter counterpart of the felony/murder rule. If the unlawful act responsible for the death was not a felony but involved any other form of illegality, criminal or civil, then the perpetrator of the unlawful act was automatically guilty of manslaughter.[266] The extraordinary breadth of this form of liability needs no emphasis. Unfortunately, unlike the felony/murder rule itself, constructive manslaughter has not been abolished. The kinds of unlawful act on which a manslaughter verdict may be based have been significantly

---

[260] 1 Russ 611–33 (views about the scope of manslaughter from Coke, Hale, Hawkins, Forster, Black, and East). See generally on manslaughter Ashworth, "Manslaughter: Generic or Nominate Offences?" in Clarkson and Cunningham (eds.), *Criminal Liability for Non-Aggressive Deaths* (2008) chap. 11.

[261] *Adomako* [1995] 1 AC 171 (HL).

[262] Criminal Justice Act 1988, s. 39.

[263] See the facts of *Mallett* [1972] Crim LR 260 (CA).

[264] *Pike* [1961] Crim LR 547.

[265] Kenny, *Outlines of Criminal Law* (1902) 119–20.

[266] Buxton, "By Any Unlawful Act" (1966) 82 *LQR* 174.

narrowed since the eighteenth century, yet it remains a broad and frequently unpredictable ground of liability. Constructive manslaughter requires:

(i)   a criminal act which causes death;
(ii)   an act which is criminal *per se*; and
(iii) an act which is dangerous.

(a) A criminal act

In *Franklin*,[267] D was strolling along Brighton Pier on a bank holiday Monday and, we know not why, threw an empty wooden beer crate into the sea. The crate struck and killed V, who had been swimming in the sea below. The prosecution argued that liability for constructive manslaughter followed from the trespass to goods perpetrated by D on taking and disposing of the stallholder's crate. Field J rejected this argument by insisting that the unlawful act that causes V's death must be a crime. While merely a trial direction, it has been widely cited as authoritative, and despite the breadth of *dicta* employed by the House of Lords in *Newbury*[268] (where there was, *obiter*, undiscriminating reference to an "unlawful act" *tout court*)[269], since *Franklin* there has been no imposition of liability for constructive manslaughter on the basis of mere civil law wrongdoing.[270] That this absence reflects doctrinal limitations rather than mere prosecutorial practice is implied by the Court of Appeal decision in *Scarlett*.[271] D had been convicted of constructive manslaughter on the basis that he had assaulted V. His conviction was quashed on appeal because the trial court, improperly according to the Court of Appeal, had not permitted D to defend himself on the basis that he had thought that the force he had employed to eject a trespasser was reasonable even though, in objective terms, it was found by the jury to have been excessive.[272] There is little doubt that, under civil law, by employing excessive force D had committed the tort of battery,[273] and it is notable that no attempt was made to argue that this civil liability was a sufficient underpinning to sustain the conviction for manslaughter.

(b) An act of commission

Since the Court of Appeal decision in *Lowe*,[274] it appears that the criminal act must take the form of an act rather than an omission. D was found to have wilfully neglected her child

---

[267] (1883) 15 Cox CC 163.

[268] [1977] AC 500.

[269] In *Newbury*, D threw a piece of paving stone from a bridge as a train approached: it smashed through the cab window, killing V. We cannot assume the commission of any underlying offence against the person because, as will be discussed below, the House of Lords rejected, as a requirement for constructive manslaughter, any need for D to foresee that his act would cause physical harm to someone. Nonetheless, D seems to have committed the offences of criminal damage contrary to the Criminal Damage Act 1971 and of endangering passengers contrary to s. 32 of the OAPA 1861. Accordingly, there is no need to resort to the tort of trespass to sustain D's conviction for constructive manslaughter.

[270] In *Lamb* [1967] 2 QB 981, a case of horseplay involving a gun but not involving any assault, Sachs LJ held that it was a misdirection to speak in general terms of "an unlawful and dangerous act" and "not in point to consider whether an act is unlawful merely from the angle of civil liabilities". What was required was an act "unlawful in the criminal sense of the word".

[271] [1993] 4 All ER 629.

[272] But see now *Owino* [1996] 2 Cr App R 128 and *Armstrong-Braun* [1999] Crim LR 416.

[273] See now *Ashley v. Chief Constable of Sussex Police* [2008] UKHL 25, [2008] AC 962.

[274] [1973] QB 702; disapproving *Senior* [1899] 1 QB 283. Although *Lowe* has been superseded in other respects by *Sheppard* [1981] AC 394, it remains authoritative on the present point.

contrary to section 1 of the Children and Young Persons Act 1933 by her failure to arrange for medical treatment despite the obvious need of her child for medical attention. Phillimore LJ drew a sharp distinction between a child's dying as the result of a parent's blow and death resulting from parental neglect of the child. The former incident but not the latter will attract liability for constructive manslaughter. His Lordship did not offer any defence of this distinction and it is not obvious why indifference and neglect of one's parental duties to catastrophic effect is systemically less culpable than parental violence. Yet it is well to remember that we are dealing here with *constructive* liability, in the sense that there need be no mens rea regarding death or serious injury: if the ruling had been the other way, *all* child deaths associated with wilful neglect would constitute manslaughter without any necessity to demonstrate parental culpability in respect of the risk of death. Cases of egregious parental neglect resulting in the death of children can be charged as manslaughter on the basis of the gross negligence of the parents.[275] For that form of manslaughter, the better view is that the negligence must relate to the risk of death.[276] With this in mind, the decision in *Lowe* may be welcomed. It is regrettable enough that the causing of inadvertent death by a positive criminal act may frequently sustain a charge of manslaughter; there is no virtue in imposing this harsh doctrine on omissions, even on the assumption that, other things being equal, acts and omissions are morally equivalent.[277]

(c) An act criminal per se

The sheer number of criminal offences, particularly regulatory offences, leaves enormous scope for constructive manslaughter. A random example is the selling of food non-compliant with food safety standards, an offence of strict liability.[278] Each year, deaths ensue from food-poisoning. The lack of manslaughter verdicts associated with such deaths is, in part, attributable to the decision of the House of Lords in *Andrews*.[279] D had committed the offence of dangerous driving, and in so doing had caused the death of V. According to Lord Atkin, a verdict of manslaughter did not necessarily flow from such facts. For constructive manslaughter there had to be an underlying crime which was intrinsically criminal and not merely "a lawful act [done] with a degree of carelessness which the legislature makes criminal".[280] The distinction is not an easy one but in practical terms the effect of *Andrews* has been to take driving offences and regulatory offences concerned with public and workplace safety outside the ambit of constructive manslaughter.[281] Serious transgressions in those areas which result in death may, instead, constitute manslaughter by gross negligence.

---

[275] See also the offence contrary to s. 5 of the Domestic Violence, Crime and Victims Act 2004; below, § 10.8.

[276] See below, § 10.6(ii).

[277] On the question of equivalence, see the penetrating discussion in Bennett, *The Act Itself* (1995) 139–42.

[278] Food Safety Act 1990, s. 8. A defence of due diligence, with an onus of proof on D, is provided by s. 21.

[279] [1937] AC 576.

[280] *Ibid.*, 585.

[281] According to the *Mortality Statistics—Deaths Registered in England and Wales 2014* (2015), there were 13,111 deaths by accident in that year, of which 1,849 were transport accidents. Many of these deaths in workplace and road-traffic situations will involve criminal offences, yet the number of prosecutions for manslaughter form a tiny percentage of prosecutions compared with the prosecutions for health and safety offences and road traffic offences that may be brought following death from unnatural causes.

Otherwise there is increasing statutory regulation concerning deaths by driving[282] and in the workplace.[283]

Although the practical effect of *Andrews* is easily grasped, its conceptual underpinning is problematic. Lord Atkin's informing idea is straightforward: driving is not of itself illegal; it becomes illegal if done carelessly or dangerously. Therefore, dangerous or careless driving does not, of itself, provide a basis for manslaughter. But this distinction soon runs into difficulties. What if D takes his car on to the public roads with a blood alcohol level above the permitted limit or uses a mobile phone while driving a vehicle in contravention of section 41D of the Road Traffic Act 1988? And why is it the case that driving in a manner which is dangerous or, indeed, which exceeds the speed limit is not something intrinsically illegal? There is a host of things which are otherwise legal but which become illegal if done the wrong way or with the wrong motivation, and it is odd to base any classificatory scheme on this otherwise unremarkable fact. Here, we may discern judicial policy masquerading as a conceptually driven distinction. As we will see, constructive manslaughter is allowed free rein over such conduct as fighting, vandalism, drug-taking, and exotic sexual practices. It does not spill over to the quotidian criminalities of the majority population. This, it must be stressed, is not an argument for employing constructive manslaughter to its full extent.[284] It is an argument for abolition of this form of liability.[285]

Some writers have interpreted *Andrews* as authority for a much simpler proposition: that the unlawful act must be not merely a crime, but a crime of more than negligence or strict liability.[286] Strictly speaking, this is a misreading of the distinction drawn by Lord Atkin. But it is perhaps defensible to reread the decision in this way, since doing so provides a better underpinning to the practical distinction Lord Atkin sought to make. Nevertheless, in a later case also called *Andrews*,[287] D was convicted of unlawful act manslaughter where he injected V with insulin contrary to the Medicines Act 1968, even though this was a strict liability offence, and in *Meeking*[288] D was convicted of unlawful act manslaughter where she had interfered with a motor vehicle by pulling on the handbrake, thereby endangering road users contrary to the Road Traffic Act 1988, even though this is an offence of negligence, since it had to be obvious to a reasonable person that the conduct was dangerous. In this

---

[282] Notably, causing death by dangerous (Road Traffic Act 1991, s. 1), but also causing death by careless or inconsiderate driving (Road Traffic Act 1988, s. 2B), causing death by careless driving whilst under the influence of drink or drugs ((Road Traffic Act 1988, s. 3A) and causing death by unlawful driving where D was an unlicensed, disqualified or uninsured driver (Road Traffic Act 1988, s. 3ZB). See generally Cunningham, "Has Law Reform Policy Been Driven in the Right Direction? How the New Causing Death by Driving Offences Are Operating in Practice" [2013] *Crim LR* 711.

[283] Notably, the Health and Safety at Work Act 1974. See *Chargot Ltd* [2008] UKHL 73, [2009] 1 WLR 1(HL), where it was held that liability for failure to ensure health and safety at work is strict, with the burden placed on D to prove that it was not reasonably practicable for her to prevent the accident. The Health and Safety (Offences) Act 2008 enables the court to impose custodial sentences of us to two years' imprisonment for committing an offence under the 1974 Act.

[284] But see Wells, *Corporations and Criminal Responsibility* (2nd ed., 2001) 75–8, who argues for more frequent resort to this category of manslaughter in the interests of industrial and transportation safety.

[285] As recommended by the Law Commission in *Involuntary Manslaughter*, Law Com. No. 237 (1996) 127. Unfortunately, as will be discussed below, the Commission then substantially reversed its earlier position in Law Com. No. 304 (2006).

[286] See, e.g., *Smith and Hogan* 628; Ashworth and Horder, *Principles* 287.

[287] [2002] EWCA Crim 3021.

[288] [2012] EWCA Crim 1641, [2012] 1 WLR 3349.

latter case at least, as the unlawful act was one of negligence it would have been preferable to base the prosecution on gross negligent manslaughter,[289] since liability would then depend on the negligence being characterised as gross, which would have been established on the facts.[290]

(d) A dangerous criminal act

The House of Lords in *Newbury*[291] confirmed earlier authority to the effect that the criminal act in question must also be "dangerous". Because dangerousness may be so readily inferred from the fact that death has arisen, it should be stressed that the requirement for a dangerous act is a principle of limitation. The House adopted an earlier statement of the law made by the Court of Appeal in *Church*:[292]

> "the unlawful act must be such that all sober and reasonable people would inevitably recognise
> it as an act which must subject the other person to at least the risk of some harm resulting
> therefrom albeit not serious harm."

Two points may be made about this passage. First, the property of dangerousness need not be perceived by D; it is a matter of objective appraisal from the perspective of an ordinary, prudent person. Secondly, the danger in question need not relate to a risk of death or even serious bodily harm; the risk of minor physical harm is quite sufficient. Thus the constructive nature of unlawful act manslaughter is mitigated only to a slight degree. Nonetheless, the requirement for a dangerous act is not without limiting effect. In *Dawson*,[293] D pointed an imitation firearm at V in the course of a robbery. V, a middle-aged man with coronary illness, suffered a fatal heart attack induced by the fright engendered by his confrontation with D. This was held not to be a case of constructive manslaughter. The ordinary person would have foreseen that V would be frightened, even extremely frightened, but fright *per se* (falling short of psychiatric injury) was not a form of harm within the *Church* formulation. According to the Court of Appeal, it was clear that some form of bodily harm is required. A coronary was to be regarded as a form of bodily harm, but the ordinary person would not inevitably have recognised the risk of that eventuality arising from these circumstances. The ordinary person was to be invested with the knowledge available to D at the time of his act, no less, no more.[294] Middle-aged men did not comprise a class of individuals susceptible to heart attacks induced by fright. By contrast, in *Watson*,[295] *Dawson* was distinguished on facts where an 87-year-old man died as a result of a coronary induced by the stress of D's burglarious entry into his home. Elderly men did comprise a class of individuals susceptible to stress-induced heart attacks. D knew his victim to be an elderly man so it followed that the ordinary person test should be applied with that in mind. *Dawson* was also distinguished in *JM and SM*,[296] where the defendants fought with a doorman who died from an undiagnosed heart defect as a result of shock and a surge in blood pressure during the fight.

---

[289] Below, § 10.6(ii).
[290] [2012] EWCA Crim 1641, [2012] 1 WLR 3349, para. 14.
[291] [1977] AC 500.
[292] [1966] 1 QB 59, 70.
[293] (1985) 81 Cr App R 150 (CA).
[294] *Ibid.*, 157.
[295] (1989) 89 Cr App R 211 (CA).
[296] [2012] EWCA Crim 2293, [2013] 1 WLR 1083.

It was accepted that the fight was a cause of V's death. The trial judge had directed the jury that the prosecution had to prove both that the reasonable person would have foreseen the risk of some harm and that the victim died as a result of the sort of harm that a reasonable person would realise that the unlawful act risked causing. This would have constituted a significant (and defensible) restriction on the operation of unlawful act manslaughter. This direction was, however, rejected by the Court of Appeal, which held that it was not necessary to establish that the reasonable person would have foreseen the risk of the type of harm suffered by V; it was simply sufficient that some harm would have been foreseen, namely the physical harm to V arising from his restraining the defendants during the fight, even though the effect of the heart defect would not have been foreseen. *Dawson* was different because, on the facts of that case, no physical harm would have been foreseen arising from threatening with an imitation firearm. *Dawson* was also distinguished, questionably, in *Ball*.[297] D was quarrelling with V and reached into his pocket to take a cartridge which he placed in his shotgun. He fired the gun, killing V. The pocket contained live and blank cartridges. D claimed that he had intended to load his gun with a blank cartridge. His counsel argued that the reasoning in *Dawson* obliged the judge to direct the jury that, in applying the ordinary person test, the ordinary person must be taken to assume the presence of a blank cartridge in the gun because that was the assumption made by D. The Court of Appeal dismissed this argument on the ground that *Dawson* was a case concerned with the vulnerability of the victim, whereas the facts of *Ball* involved a question about the inherent danger of D's act. In the latter kind of case the jury was entitled to appraise the dangerousness of the act in the light of all the circumstances actually present at the time of D's act, not merely those circumstances known to D himself. Yet this distinction would lead to absurd consequences. Suppose that, on facts otherwise similar to *Ball*, D had bought a carton of blank cartridges which, due to a packaging mishap of which he was unaware, contained some live cartridges. In those circumstances, surely, the ordinary person should be invested with the same assumption as D; the assumption that the gun was loaded with a blank cartridge. Moreover, distinguishing *Dawson* was unnecessary. On the actual facts of *Ball*, D was aware that his pocket contained live cartridges as well as blanks. His manslaughter conviction is entirely in keeping with the reasoning of *Dawson*: D's act was dangerous given the facts that D knew. The argument of defence counsel in *Ball*, as sketched here, was a fallacious reading of *Dawson*. It should have been dismissed on that ground.

(e) No "aimed at" requirement

In the now discredited case of *DPP* v. *Smith*,[298] the House of Lords spoke in terms of an act "aimed at the victim" as a defining element of the crime of murder. That requirement, if such it ever was, did not survive the later decision of the House in *Hyam*.[299] Yet in *Dalby*,[300] Waller LJ, giving the judgment of the Court of Appeal, incorporated this limitation into the definition of constructive manslaughter. D unlawfully supplied V with drugs contrary

---

[297] [1989] Crim LR 730.
[298] [1961] AC 290. In *Frankland* [1987] AC 576, the Privy Council ruled that *Smith* had been based on a misunderstanding of the law of murder.
[299] [1975] AC 55.
[300] [1982] 1 All ER 916 (CA).

to section 4 of the Misuse of Drugs Act 1971. V injected the drugs intravenously and subsequently died from their effects. The illegal supply of drugs was not a sufficient predicate for a verdict of manslaughter because, according to Waller LJ, it lacked the quality of being "directed at the victim".[301] The validity of this requirement was soon tested against the facts of *Mitchell*,[302] where D began a fight with E in a crowded Post Office. In the ensuing fracas, V, a frail old lady, was crushed to death. D's manslaughter conviction was confirmed by the Court of Appeal notwithstanding that D's violence was directed at E and not V. All that was required was a criminal and dangerous act which was a legal cause of V's death, an approach followed by the Court of Appeal in *Goodfellow*[303] and vindicated by the House of Lords in *A-G's Reference (No. 3 of 1994)*.[304]

Despite the rejection of the "aimed at" requirement, the result in *Dalby* can now be defended on the basis of the absence of a causal nexus between D's act of supply and V's subsequent death. Following the decision of the House of Lords in *Kennedy (No. 2)*,[305] the fully informed and voluntary decision of V in injecting drugs into his bloodstream will break the chain of causation.

(f) Constructive manslaughter—a critique

In the late Victorian case of *Franklin*,[306] Field J expressed a "horror" of constructive crime. Such a reaction is by no means universal. In *Cato*,[307] two drug addicts, D and V, obtained heroin of a high degree of purity. As was their practice, they consensually injected heroin for each other. Each of them became comatose. Because of contingencies with no bearing on the respective culpability of each actor, D received medical treatment and survived, whereas V died. D was successfully prosecuted for manslaughter, receiving five years' imprisonment. At trial, the unlawful act was found to be the malicious administration of a noxious substance.[308] On appeal, Lord Widgery CJ suppressed his doubts about the propriety of that finding[309] by ruling that, alternatively, the unlawful act was "injecting [V] with a mixture of heroin and water which at the time of the injection and for the purposes of the injection [D] had unlawfully taken into his possession".[310] The difficulty about the latter "offence", a difficulty which should have daunted even a judge so robust as Lord Widgery CJ, is that no such crime is known to English law.[311]

What drives Lord Widgery CJ's judgment is an abhorrence of drug-taking and a determination to impose penal consequences on those involved in it. It is hard to discern any

---

[301] *Ibid.*, 919.

[302] [1983] QB 741.

[303] (1986) 83 Cr App R 23.

[304] [1998] AC 245.

[305] [2007] UKHL 38, [2008] 2 AC 269; above, § 4.2(iii)(b) (Principle 1).

[306] (1883) 15 Cox CC 163.

[307] [1976] 1 All ER 260 (CA). See the valuable note by Wells (1976) 39 *MLR* 474.

[308] OAPA 1861, s. 23.

[309] The effect of V's consent to the injection was insufficiently considered at trial in relation to a conviction under s. 23. Difficult questions would require resolution—particularly, at the present time, concerning the impact of the House of Lords decision in *Brown* [1994] 1 AC 212 about whether, as a question of public policy, V could legitimately consent to the injection.

[310] [1976] 1 All ER 260, 267.

[311] While *possession* and *supply* of controlled drugs are criminalised, it is not an offence to *administer* a controlled drug.

moral or social difference between drugs taken by an individual and those taken with the assistance of a mutual addict. Yet it was only the latter feature that created scope for a conviction for constructive manslaughter in *Cato* (and even then the decision is hard to justify in legal terms). A striking feature is the fortuity surrounding the verdict. Both V and D may easily have died; equally likely was joint survival or the sole death of D.

In our discussion of the law of attempt, we conceded both the impossibility of eradicating "outcome luck" from the criminal law, and that outcome luck could have legitimate implications for the grading of offences and the quantum of punishment.[312] But luck is too potent a factor in the imposition of liability for constructive manslaughter. It can turn a "trivial" assault between quarrelling neighbours into a serious crime involving a custodial sentence where, as in *Mallett*,[313] V falls awkwardly and fatally bumps his head on concrete. Such a verdict can be defended only on the basis that, if D engages in criminal conduct, he must take responsibility for the consequences of his criminality, whatever those consequences may be. No doubt such reasoning may have its place where D's conduct gives rise to a clear and vivid danger that serious consequences may occur. Yet, in constructive manslaughter, the connection between the unlawfulness of D's act and its dangerousness may be extremely tenuous. In *Arobieke*,[314] D terrified V by following him closely to the railway station and then searching for him on the train V had boarded. V had good reason to fear serious violence at the hands of D and, in his fear, sought to escape across the live tracks, thereby electrocuting himself. A conviction of constructive manslaughter against D was properly ruled out because, *inter alia*, the facts disclosed no unlawful act on his part. Contrast *Mallett*, where there was no threat of serious violence but D was nonetheless convicted of manslaughter.

Unfortunately, there is no likelihood that the legislature will abolish constructive manslaughter. Rather, the Government does not hesitate to impose heavy penalties based substantially on the fact of causing death, as witness the increase in the maximum penalty for causing death by dangerous driving from five years' to 10 years' imprisonment and thence to 14 years'.[315] The (in many ways admirable) heightened concern with the wrongs suffered by the victims of crime and the relatives of those victims appears for now to militate against rational appraisals of culpability in the face of death.[316] The most recent Law Commission proposals[317] recommend the creation of an offence of criminal act manslaughter, to cover cases where D kills V intending to cause injury or foreseeing a serious risk of causing injury. Although the trigger for liability is a subjective state of mind, a conviction for an offence which carries a possible penalty of life imprisonment is possible without proof of any culpability relating to death or even substantial harm. Even if this reform was enacted, therefore, it would maintain the unprincipled nature of this form of manslaughter.

---

[312] Above, § 9.4(vi). See also above, § 6.5.

[313] [1972] Crim LR 260.

[314] [1988] Crim LR 314 (CA).

[315] Criminal Justice Act 2003, s. 285, and the sentence for causing death by careless driving is now five years: Road Safety Act 2006, s. 20. Contrast the maximum penalty for dangerous driving *simpliciter* (contrary to s. 2 of the Road Traffic Act 1988), which remains pegged for now at two years' imprisonment.

[316] See also *Attorney-General's Reference (No. 60 of 2009)* [2009] EWCA Crim 2693, [2010] 2 Cr App R (S) 311, para. 22 (Lord Judge).

[317] Law Com. No. 304, para. 9.9

(ii) Manslaughter by gross negligence

Carelessness may be thought to be a problematic form of culpability for a serious criminal offence. The breadth of constructive manslaughter has been criticised. Nonetheless, liability for that form of manslaughter will be triggered by some form of chosen, criminal conduct. By contrast, gross negligence manslaughter requires no advertent wrongdoing and may penalise "the ethically well-disposed agent",[318] a person who lacks any violent or predatory designs on the persons or property of others. To be convicted of manslaughter by gross negligence, it is enough for D to cause the death of V by doing something or omitting to do something in circumstances which reveal a clear failure to exhibit minimum standards of competence or concern. Such standards are largely objective.[319] It was no answer for D to claim, in *Stone and Dobinson*,[320] that his intelligence and skills were so deficient as to preclude performance of the most basic of social tasks. Yet if we do not pay heed to such deficiencies, what is the basis of our censure?[321] If a person is capable of attaining basic skills and competence, then it is conventional and acceptable to criticise her for failure to exercise that competence. If the consequences of such failure are minor, criticism should normally be restrained. She would rightly be aggrieved to receive the same degree of censure for carelessly losing another person's £10 as for dishonestly taking that £10. Yet what if D, a child-minder, allows V, an infant in her care, to wander with fatal consequences onto a busy road because she was preoccupied by a conversation with E? The urge to punish would arise. Would it be in point that D was distraught at what she had allowed to happen? If the child had survived, however badly injured, no criminal offence would have been committed by D. Does the impact of death override the lack of recklessness or intent, levels of culpability that otherwise are required for a stigmatic offence? Or should gross negligence receive criminal censure on a broader and more consistent basis than it now does?[322] The answer to such questions depends ultimately on value judgements which are psychologically grounded, lying beyond proof and refutation.[323]

(a) The meaning of gross negligence

To cause or allow the death of another negligently will not, of itself, incur liability in manslaughter. The failure of care or concern must be rather more egregious than is required for civil liability. According to Lord Hewart CJ in *Bateman*, it must be the case that:[324]

> "in the opinion of the jury, the negligence of the accused went beyond a mere matter of compensation between subjects and showed such disregard for the life and safety of others, as to amount to a crime against the state and conduct deserving of punishment."

---

[318] An expression attributable to Bernard Williams.

[319] There is, however, uncertainty whether the standards are *entirely* objective: above, § 5.5(ii).

[320] [1977] QB 354 (CA).

[321] See too the facts of *Elliot v. C* [1983] 2 All ER 1005.

[322] As is argued in Schulhofer, "Harm and Punishment: A Critique of the Emphasis on the Results of Conduct in the Criminal Law" (1974) 122 *U Pa L Rev* 1497, 1605.

[323] Acceptance of the salience of psychological reactions as precipitates for moral judgments entails the rejection of moral realism but not an acceptance of moral relativism. On psychological reactions and moral judgments see Bennett, *The Act Itself* (1995) 12–16.

[324] (1925) 19 Cr App R 8, 11.

The dictum has been criticised for vacuity, yet it usefully stresses that juries should be cautious when attributing criminality to a defendant who has neither intended nor foreseen that she would cause or allow harm to another. The dictum was approved by the House of Lords in *Andrews*[325] and reflects a consistent pattern of jury directions. Exemplifying this approach is the decision in *Finney*,[326] where D, a lunatic asylum attendant, was not found guilty of manslaughter even though he made no visual check to see if his patient, V, had left the bath following D's direction to do so. V had remained in the bath and had been killed when, for cleaning purposes, D released scalding water into it. The evidence fell short of establishing the abject failure of care necessary to justify a finding of gross negligence with penal consequences.

Sometimes, the courts equate gross negligence with a form of recklessness. For instance, Lord Atkin opined in *Andrews* that a useful synonym for gross negligence was the term recklessness. It is clear from the context (the approval of the decision in *Bateman*) that Lord Atkin was not in any sense seeking to dilute the degree of egregiousness required for a finding of gross negligence.[327] However, the House of Lords went further in *Seymour*.[328] Lord Roskill, in giving judgment for the House, took recklessness to be the most suitable term to express the kind of culpability required for this head of manslaughter. Moreover, he ruled that the recklessness required should be of the kind expounded in *Caldwell*[329] and *Lawrence*.[330] Furthermore, whereas the better view had been that gross negligence should relate to the risk of death or, at least, grievous bodily harm, for Lord Roskill recklessness as to the risk of any degree of harm would suffice.[331] The upshot was an enormously wide form of manslaughter. Liability would ensue if D's conduct had given rise to an obvious and serious risk of physical harm, a risk which D had either foreseen or failed to give any thought to. The breadth of this new approach is readily appreciated if we return to the facts of *Finney*; a manslaughter verdict would seem assured were a jury to be directed along the lines indicated by Lord Roskill.

In *Adomako*,[332] the House of Lords reviewed the fundamentals of this form of manslaughter. *Seymour* was not overruled but was seen as no longer relevant. Lord Mackay noted that the House in *Seymour* was concerned with liability for the offence of causing death by reckless driving alongside liability for manslaughter. Indeed it was, and one of the most telling criticisms of *Seymour* was that Lord Roskill took the constituents of each offence exactly to correspond. According to Lord Mackay, the statutory abolition of causing death by reckless driving therefore remaindered *Seymour* to legal history. Unfortunately, he did not explain the mystery of how the abolition of the offence of reckless driving had also undone what *Seymour* had decided about manslaughter. It would have been far better to have overruled the decision by using the 1966 Practice Direction. Judicial comity restrains judicial candour.

---

[325] [1937] AC 576, 582–3.
[326] (1874) 12 Cox CC 625.
[327] [1937] AC 576, 583.
[328] [1983] 2 AC 493.
[329] [1982] AC 341.
[330] [1982] AC 510.
[331] [1983] 2 AC 493, 505 where the elements of reckless manslaughter are assimilated to the elements of reckless driving.
[332] [1995] 1 AC 171. For valuable notes discussing the decision see Smith [1994] *Crim LR* 758; Virgo [1995] *CLJ* 14; and Gardner (1995) 111 *LQR* 22.

Be that as it may, *Caldwell* recklessness has been removed from the ambit of manslaughter. *Adomako* asserts the continuing relevance of the approach taken in *Andrews* and *Bateman* and reinstates gross negligence as the required form of culpability. To incur liability for this form of manslaughter, D must have been in breach of a duty of care under the ordinary principles of the tort of negligence and her negligence must have caused the death of V. Whether D owed a duty of care to V is a question of law for the judge, who should direct the jury that a duty of care is owed if certain facts are established, the determination of those facts being for the jury.[333] Although the civil law of negligence is to be applied to determine whether a duty of care was owed, some of the implications of tortious liability will not be relevant. So, for example, if D and V are engaged on a joint criminal enterprise—such as illegal immigration[334] or arson of a building[335]—D may be liable for the manslaughter of V on the basis of his gross negligence irrespective of the fact that public policy would preclude a successful civil action in negligence against V.

While there is a general duty imposed on us all not to cause death by a positive act, the duty requirement requires closer attention where the allegation of gross negligence relates to D's omission rather than actions.[336] In such cases it is necessary to identify a legal duty to act as distinct from a duty of care,[337] but, once a duty *to act* has been identified, it will be necessary to identify that a duty *of care* was owed to V, although this will usually follow inexorably from the duty to act. So, in *Pittwood*,[338] where D had failed to close a railway-crossing gate, D's liability for manslaughter rested on a finding that he had a contractual duty owed to his employer to close the gate and a general duty of care which was owed to the users of the crossing. Similarly, in *Evans*,[339] D, who had supplied heroin to her half-sister, who had then self-injected and died from an overdose, owed a duty to obtain medical assistance because D had contributed to the creation of a state of affairs by the supply of drugs which she ought to have known was life threatening. The duty to act meant that she also owed a duty of care towards her sister. Her failure to take the reasonable step of obtaining medical assistance constituted a breach of this duty that was considered to be grossly negligent and so she was guilty of manslaughter. As was seen in Chapter 4,[340] the identification of a duty to act in *Evans* is controversial. Although the recognition of the duty was founded on *Miller*,[341] in that case D had created the dangerous situation, whereas in *Evans* it was sufficient that D had contributed to the creation of the risk of the danger occurring. D could not be considered to have created the dangerous situation because, following the decision of the House of Lords in *Kennedy (No. 2)*,[342] V's self-injection broke the chain of causation; it was V's own act of injection that created the danger.

---

[333] *Evans* [2009] EWCA Crim 650, [2009] 1 WLR 1999. See also *Moore* [2015] NSWCCA 316, where it was recognised that a director of a bricklaying company might have owed a duty of care to an employee bricklayer who was killed by a falling wall. Various factors indicated a duty of care, including that D had control of the building site and the ability to direct that steps be taken to secure the wall.

[334] *Wacker* [2003] 1 Cr App R 22.

[335] *Willoughby* [2004] EWCA Crim 3365.

[336] See generally Ashworth, "Manslaughter by Omission and the Rule of Law" [2015] *Crim LR* 563.

[337] *Evans* [2009] EWCA Crim 650, [2009] 1 WLR 1999, para. 21.

[338] (1902) 19 TLR 37; above, § 4.1(i)(b) (Case 3).

[339] [2009] EWCA Crim 650, [2009] 1 WLR 1999.

[340] § 4.1(i)(b) (Case 5).

[341] [1983] 2 AC 161.

[342] [2007] UKHL 38, [2008] 2 AC 269.

Once the duty of care (in the qualified sense identified above), its breach and causation arising from the breach are established, the jury must next ask themselves (for Lord Mackay, it is "supremely a jury question"):[343]

"having regard to the risk of death involved, [was] the conduct of the defendant ... so bad in all the circumstances as to amount to a criminal act or omission?"

The harshness introduced by *Seymour* is, for the moment at least, a thing of the past; witness the quashing of several of the convictions in the consolidated appeals heard by the House in *Adomako*, convictions which were entirely well-founded under a *Caldwell* recklessness standard. The phrase of Lord Mackay's, "having regard to the risk of death involved", suggests that the gross negligence of D must be as to death and not as to any lesser harm, albeit the test is whether a reasonably prudent person would have foreseen a serious and obvious risk of death.[344] As Glanville Williams observed, if gross negligence as to any physical harm were to suffice, constructive manslaughter would effectively be made redundant.[345] Note, too, that "badness" in this context is not a matter of evil disposition or even indifference to the victim's welfare. It is a matter of D's conduct. In one of the cases disposed of in *Adomako* where a conviction for gross negligence manslaughter was confirmed, an anaesthetist had failed for 11 minutes or so to identify the cause of the patient's respiratory difficulty as a dislodged endotracheal tube. Other means of restoring the supply of oxygen were frantically tried but the simple and obvious procedure of reattaching the tube was not performed, something that, according to expert evidence, would have been done by a competent anaesthetist within 30 seconds of observing the patient's difficulties. As a qualified professional person, he was required to demonstrate competence. His incompetence was so bad as to allow his conviction for manslaughter to be confirmed.

(b) A critique of gross negligence manslaughter

Whether negligence, however gross, is a sufficient form of culpability for a serious offence is a matter that has divided theorists.[346] In the light of the House of Lords decision in *G*,[347] which rejected objective recklessness as a suitable form of culpability for serious offences, the optimistic argument was put in *Misra*[348] that abolition of objective recklessness implied the abolition of gross negligence as a form of culpability for an offence as serious as manslaughter. The argument predictably failed,[349] since gross negligence manslaughter has been well established for many years and was recently endorsed and refurbished by the House of Lords in *Adomako*. Moreover, there is clearly ground for serious criticism of D if she has failed to conduct herself to the standard that she is reasonably capable of achieving; equally so were she to attempt a task that she knows she is incapable of achieving. It has been argued that penal consequences in respect of negligence are pointless because the thoughtless and the careless cannot be deterred, whereas reckless or intentional criminality

---

[343] [1995] 1 AC 171, 187.
[344] Confirmed in *Singh (Gurphal)* [1999] Crim LR 582; *Misra* [2004] EWCA Crim 2375, [2005] 1 Cr App R 21; *Yaqoob* [2005] EWCA Crim 2169.
[345] *CLGP*, 111.
[346] See above, § 5.5(iv).
[347] [2004] 1 AC 1034; above, § 5.2(i)(b).
[348] [2005] 1 Cr App R 21.
[349] As was also the case in *Mark* [2004] EWCA Crim 2490.

can be influenced by the prospect of hard treatment. The point has been put as a matter of logic, but it is a question of fact. We all have prudential reasons to drive carefully because, if we do, our chances of being killed or injured on the road are diminished. Another reason for driving carefully is to avoid liability for the crime of driving without due care and attention.[350] Whether that offence and other motoring offences improve driving standards on a significant scale is something to be investigated and not dismissed out of hand.[351] The argument from deterrence has gained force recently, particularly by way of reaction to several large transportation disasters.[352] The Law Commission is now of the view, reversing an earlier stance, that there is a valid role for the offence of gross negligence manslaughter in English law.[353] Further, gross negligence—"conduct falling far below what can reasonably be expected"—is the informing idea behind the new offence of corporate manslaughter.[354] Yet legitimate concern with effective deterrence should not override an insistence that convictions for serious, stigmatic, offences should be based on a sufficient degree of culpability. Should an anaesthetist, doing his hapless and inadequate best, receive a custodial sentence for the disastrous consequences of his ineptitude? Yes, it might be answered, if he was capable of doing better or had reason to know that he was not up to the demands of his job. A negative response would be made by those who would restrict imprisonment to persons who *choose* to harm the interests of others. We can introduce but not resolve this issue here. As was said earlier, disagreement arises from different psychological responses to the occurrence of harm and cannot be resolved by any resort to principle. Even if we allow findings of negligence to be a basis of criminal liability, liability for manslaughter is based not on mere negligence but *gross* negligence which is "so bad ... as to amount to a criminal act or omission". This judgment is to be made by the jury and allows considerable scope for different verdicts on similar facts. Such is the latitude for the fact-finder, the argument was put in *Misra*[355] that this variant of manslaughter failed to give the fair notice required by Article 7 of the ECHR. The argument failed. As we have seen, the fair notice requirements of Article 7 have not been rigorously applied.[356] Furthermore the criminalisation of negligence entails fact-specific judgments made on the basis of general criteria. It is simply impossible to lay down specific rules about the standard of care for the myriad of circumstances where a claim can be made that D has acted negligently.

(iii) Corporate manslaughter

There is no reason in principle why a company cannot be convicted of manslaughter, since a company has legal personality in its own right.[357] But securing convictions of companies proved difficult at common law by virtue of the attribution theory of corporate criminal

---

[350] Road Traffic Act 1988, s. 3, as substituted by s. 2 of the Road Traffic Act 1991.

[351] Although the difficulties of measuring the deterrent effects of criminal laws are very considerable: see Walker and Padfield, *Sentencing: Theory, Law and Practice* (2nd ed., 1996) 79–95.

[352] Which proved influential regarding the creation of the new crime of corporate manslaughter: below, § 10.6(iii).

[353] Law Com. No. 304, para. 9.9.

[354] Below, § 10.6 (iii).

[355] [2005] 1 Cr App R 21.

[356] See above, § 2.3.

[357] See above, § 8.2.

liability,[358] whereby a single senior manager[359] in the corporate hierarchy had to be identified whose fault could be attributed to the company.[360] That it could be established that
there was widespread negligence in the management of the company was not sufficient to
impose corporate liability for manslaughter. It was only in very rare cases that it could be
shown that a senior manager was personally grossly negligent for the purposes of establishing corporate liability.

The Corporate Manslaughter and Corporate Homicide Act 2007[361] was enacted as a
result. This statute creates corporate liability for what is in effect gross negligent manslaughter but without the need to rely on the attribution theory. Consequently, instead of needing
to show that a manager possessed sufficient culpability for the crime, it is sufficient to show
that there was general culpability in the management or organization of the company.

Although the statute creates a new offence of corporate manslaughter and abolishes corporate manslaughter by gross negligence at common law,[362] the reach of liability encompasses a variety of organisations other than companies, including most corporations,
partnerships, trade unions, police forces, and various government departments.[363]

An organisation will be guilty of corporate manslaughter if the way its activities are
managed or organised causes a person's death and amounts to a gross breach of a relevant
duty owed by that organisation to the deceased.[364] The organisation will only be liable if
the way its activities are managed or organised by its senior management[365] is a substantial
element in the breach of duty.[366] Key to this offence is the need to identify a relevant duty
of care and whether the breach was "gross". A variety of relevant duties of care in the tort of
negligence are specifically identified, including duties owed by virtue of being an employer,
the occupier of premises, the supplier of goods or services, construction or maintenance,
use of plant or vehicle, or the carrying on of any activity on a commercial basis.[367] Whether
a duty of care is owed is a question of law for the judge,[368] as is now the case for the common law offence of gross negligent manslaughter. The range of the relevant duties is extensive and encompasses, for example, duties relating to building, transport, and even leisure
activities; it does not, however, include duties of care owed by a public authority relating to
matters of public policy, such as the allocation of resources or the weighing of competing
public interests.[369] So, a government department which implements a policy of extensive
reductions in public spending will not be guilty of the offence if deaths result from that
policy.[370]

---

[358] See above, § 8.2(iii)(b).

[359] *P & O Ferries (Dover) Ltd* (1990) 93 Cr App R 72.

[360] *Tesco Supermarkets Ltd v Nattrass* [1972] AC 153; *A-G's Reference (No. 2 of 1999)* [2000] 1 QB 796.

[361] Ormerod and Taylor, "The Corporate Manslaughter and Corporate Homicide Act 2007" [2008] *Crim LR*
589.

[362] Corporate Manslaughter and Corporate Homicide Act 2007, s. 20.

[363] *Ibid.*, s. 1(2) and sched. 1.

[364] *Ibid.*, s. 1(1).

[365] People are "senior management" if they play significant roles in making decisions about how the organisation's activities are managed or organised or actually manage or organise those activities: *ibid.*, s. 1(4)(c).

[366] *Ibid.*, s. 1(3).

[367] *Ibid.*, s. 2(1). The Act extends to duties owed to people in custody (s. 2(2)).

[368] *Ibid.*, s. 2(5).

[369] *Ibid.*, s. 3(1).

[370] There are further statutory exclusions for statutory inspections (s. 3(3)), certain military activities (s. 4),
certain policing activities (s. 5), and certain organisations which respond to emergency circumstances (s. 6).

Once a duty of care has been established, it is then necessary to show that its breach is gross—something defined as conduct which "falls far below what can reasonably be expected of the organisation in the circumstances".[371] This mirrors the standard of gross negligence for the common law offence. However, the statute identifies certain factors which the jury should take into account when deciding whether there was a gross breach of duty.[372] These factors include whether there was a serious failure to comply with health and safety legislation and the consequent risk of death, and the existence of attitudes, policies, systems, or accepted practices within the organisation which are likely to have encouraged failure to comply with health and safety legislation or tolerance of it.

The liability created by this offence is fixed only on the corporation itself. Consequently, it is not possible for an individual, such as a director of the company, to be an accessory to corporate manslaughter,[373] although directors continue to be prosecuted for manslaughter or breach of health and safety legislation in their own right.[374]

The 2007 Act is a significant piece of legislation for corporate liability, although it appears that prosecutions under it are not common, being confined to the clearer cases of gross negligence since proceedings cannot be commenced without the consent of the Director of Public Prosecutions.[375] The first company to be convicted of this offence was Cotswold Geotechnical Holdings Ltd,[376] a small family-run business, with the prosecution arising from the death of an employee who was working in a deep and unsupported pit which collapsed.

(iv) Reckless manslaughter

In *Hyam*,[377] the House of Lords ruled by a majority that a high degree of *Cunningham* recklessness—foresight of the probability of death or grievous bodily harm—sufficed for malice aforethought in murder. *Hyam* was, in substance, reversed by *Moloney*,[378] where the House decided that nothing less than an intent to kill or cause grievous bodily harm would suffice as the culpability required for murder. The dissenting judges in *Hyam* assumed that the high form of recklessness that the majority found sufficient for murder would suffice to support a verdict of manslaughter. This must surely be the case, at least where D foresees he may kill or seriously injure V; yet there is a dearth of authority on subjective reckless-ness as a form of culpability for manslaughter.[379] In the vast majority of cases when there is foresight on the part of D that his conduct may unjustifiably or inexcusably kill or seri-ously injure V, his conduct will involve the commission of some offence, irrespective of the causing of any injury or death to V. In *Hyam* itself, D had perpetrated arson. Consequently, a conviction for constructive manslaughter would straightforwardly be obtained on facts

---

[371] *Ibid.*, s. 1(4)(b).

[372] *Ibid.*, s. 8.

[373] *Ibid.*, s. 18(1).

[374] See Antrobus, "The Criminal Liability of Directors for Health and Safety Breaches and Manslaughter" [2013] *Crim LR* 309.

[375] Corporate Manslaughter and Corporate Homicide Act 2007, s. 17(a).

[376] [2011] EWCA Crim 1337. See Dobson, "Shifting Sands: Multiple Counts in Prosecutions for Corporate Manslaughter" [2012] *Crim LR* 200.

[377] [1975] AC 55.

[378] [1985] AC 905.

[379] The existence of this form of manslaughter was, however, confirmed in *Lidar* [2000] 4 Archbold News 3.

such as those without regard to the question whether D foresaw death or serious injury to another.

There may, nonetheless, occasionally be circumstances where D is subjectively reckless as to the causing of death or serious injury but where his conduct would not involve any offence for constructive manslaughter. For instance, D, an archer, might continue with his target practice even though V is present within the vicinity. When aiming at the target, D would not necessarily commit any offence against V.[380] Accordingly, if V were killed by D's overshooting arrow, it might not be a case of constructive manslaughter but it would be reckless manslaughter if D foresaw a risk of causing death or serious bodily harm.

Does foresight of harm of a lesser magnitude than death or serious harm suffice? In *Adomako*, Lord Mackay gave his approval to earlier *dicta* which suggest that the mens rea for manslaughter will be present in circumstances where D foresees that his acts or omissions may cause physical harm to V or where D is indifferent to the effects of his conduct upon V's health or welfare.[381] It is unfortunate that Lord Mackay approved these *dicta*, which are vaguely expressed and of uncertain ambit. In any event, they are no more than *obiter dicta*: the cases wherein they occur involved questions of gross negligence regarding V's death.[382] There is nothing to preclude the adoption of a rule that the mens rea for reckless manslaughter is foresight of an unwarranted risk of death or grievous bodily harm. In *Lidar*,[383] the Court of Appeal assumed that foresight of death or serious harm was required.

This form of manslaughter is rarely prosecuted, because any qualifying cases are likely also to fall within the ambit of either constructive manslaughter, as noted above, or gross negligence manslaughter. In *A-G's Reference (No. 2 of 1999)*,[384] Rose LJ considered that recklessness in the form of advertence to risk or indifference to risk, might lead to a finding of gross negligence in the criminal law; confirming the view that there is very little scope for a species of manslaughter based exclusively on recklessness. It is true that a finding of gross negligence must rest on a finding that D's conduct was "so bad in all the circumstances as to amount to a criminal act or omission", but that quality is surely present where D takes or is indifferent to an unwarranted risk of causing death or serious bodily harm. It seems negligent as well as reckless to take a known risk—and frequently grossly negligent. The only discrete ground covered by this variant of manslaughter would be situations where D knowingly takes an unwarranted risk of causing serious bodily harm but is not grossly negligent as to causing V's death, essentially a theoretical rather than practical possibility. It is noteworthy that in the Law Commission's final report on the reform of homicide, no provision is made for a statutory version of reckless manslaughter.

§ 10.7 Reform of the law of homicide

A decade ago the Law Commission conducted a major review of the English law of homicide, with consultation papers and a final report on the partial defences to murder,[385] and

---

[380] There might be an assault if V were made apprehensive by D's continuing to shoot his arrows and D was aware that this was the case, but not otherwise.

[381] [1995] 1 AC 171, 187.

[382] *Stone and Dobinson* [1977] QB 354; *West London Coroner, Ex parte Gray* [1988] QB 467.

[383] [2000] 4 Archbold News.

[384] [2000] 3 All ER 182.

[385] LCCP No. 173 (2003); Law Com. No. 290 (2004).

a consultation paper and final report on the structure and content of homicide.[386] Looking in the round at this body of work,[387] and without repeating our earlier remarks on specific aspects of the proposals, the principal impression is how much the future envisaged by the Commission is so similar to the present. There will be a crime of murder—first-degree murder—with a mandatory penalty of life imprisonment. There will be partial defences of loss of control and diminished responsibility, reducing first-degree murder to second-degree murder and so displacing the mandatory penalty. Gross negligence manslaughter will be retained and the proposal for an offence of criminal act manslaughter has a large affinity with the current constructive manslaughter. To be sure, there are some significant changes. First-degree murder will require some degree of culpability as to causing death, and duress will be a defence to first-degree and second-degree murder, albeit with a reverse burden of proof. The subsequent statutory reform of the partial defences is essentially a refurbishment rather than a new blueprint. The defence of diminished responsibility is essentially unchanged and the new defence of loss of control is not as radical as might first be thought, with a large degree of codification of aspects of the common law, especially regarding the objective test.

The crucial decision was the retention of one form of murder attracting a mandatory penalty. Much of the design and content of the new dispensation follows from that. A radical, simplifying reform, suggested by Lord Kilbrandon in *Hyam*,[388] would be to reduce all the categories of homicide to one: a general, all-embracing offence of unlawful homicide. This proposal has been defended and elaborated by Blom-Cooper and Morris.[389] Certainly, many of the post-*Hyam* appeals on the demarcation of the murder/manslaughter boundary, the limits of what has become the loss of self-control defence, and the applicability of duress to murder would have been unnecessary had this bold proposal been taken up by the legislature. The principal casualty of such a change would be a distinct crime of murder. The pay-off would be radical simplification of a complex body of law and a sentencing discretion for every case of homicide.

These are powerful attractions, yet it may cogently be objected that to scrap all the current gradations of homicide would bring under one label an enormous range of differing conduct with very different forms of culpability. Besides, there is a strong sentiment to retain the evocative term murder; a feeling that an important cultural value would be lost if the worst killings did not attract that label. That sentiment proved decisive for the Law Commission.[390] It remains to be seen what price must be paid in terms of appeals and complexity should these wider reforms ever be implemented. Enlightenment seems unlikely since, when Parliament had the opportunity to reform the law of homicide, it chose to concentrate on reforming the partial defences to murder; leaving the recommendations of the Law Commission for structural changes to the law to gather dust, as has so often been the case.

---

[386] LCCP No. 177; Law Com. No. 304 (2006).

[387] For reviews, see Wilson, "The Structure of Criminal Homicide" [2006] *Crim LR* 471; Ashworth, "Principles, Pragmatism and the Law Commission's Recommendations on Homicide Law Reform" [2007] *Crim LR* 345.

[388] [1975] AC 55, 98.

[389] *With Malice Aforethought* (2004) and *Fine Lines and Distinctions: Murder, Manslaughter and the Unlawful Taking of Human Life* (2011).

[390] Law Com. No. 304, part 2.

§ 10.8 Causing the death of a child or vulnerable adult

There have been difficult cases where a child has been killed by a parent but it cannot be proved whether it was the mother or the father who killed the child, so neither is convicted. To ensure a conviction in such circumstances, a new offence was created by section 5(1) of the Domestic Violence, Crime and Victims Act 2004 where D failed to take reasonable steps to protect V. To establish this offence, it must be shown that V, who is a child or a vulnerable adult,[391] was killed[392] as the result of an unlawful act by somebody who was a member of the same household and who had frequent contact with V, and that there was a significant risk of serious physical harm being caused to V by such a person. D will be guilty of the offence if, as well as being a member of the same household as V and having frequent contact with him, she either

(i) caused V's death; or
(ii) was aware, or ought to have been aware, of the risk of serious harm to V; she failed to take reasonable steps to protect V from the risk;[393] and the unlawful act occurred in circumstances of the kind which D foresaw or ought to have foreseen.

The Act imposes a penalty of up to 14 years' imprisonment.

Although the offence appears complex, its application is clear. Suppose, for example, that D is the mother of V, a baby. She lives with her partner P, who has physically abused V on a number of occasions. P murders V. D would be guilty of the section 5 offence if: she was aware, or should have been aware, of the significant risk of physical harm being caused to V by P; she failed to take reasonable steps to protect V from the risk, such as contacting the social services; and the murder occurred in circumstances which she did or should have foreseen. It is notable that her liability could depend on objective recklessness and takes the form of liability for an omission, the statute creating a duty to act if there is no pre-existing legal duty to do so. There would be such a pre-existing duty in the case of a mother and her child.

It has been suggested that there is a danger that this offence will criminalise mothers of abused children who are themselves victims of domestic abuse.[394] This was discounted in *Khan*[395] on the ground that D would only be liable if she had failed to take reasonable steps to protect her child; what is reasonable being assessed with reference to D's own circumstances, having regard to her own suffering of domestic abuse.[396]

---

[391] The state of vulnerability need not be long-standing and may arise from injury, illness, or circumstance, such as being a recent immigrant who does not speak any English and who is utterly dependent on others in the household: *Stephens and Mujuru* [2007] EWCA Crim 1249; *Khan (Uzuma)* [2009] EWCA Crim 2, [2009] 1 WLR 2036.

[392] The offence was extended to cases where V suffers serious physical harm by the Domestic Violence, Crime and Victims (Amendment) Act 2012, s. 1.

[393] Morrison, "Should there be a Domestic Violence Defence to the Offence of Familial Homicide?" [2013] *Crim LR* 826, 830 considers this reasonable steps test to constitute both actus reus and mens rea, sine it determines both breach of duty and fault.

[394] Herring, "Familial Homicide, Failure to Protect and Domestic Violence—Who's the Victim?" [2007] *Crim LR* 923.

[395] *Khan (Uzuma)* [2009] EWCA Crim 2, [2009] 1 WLR 2036, para. 33.

[396] See further Morrison, "Should There Be a Domestic Violence Defence to the Offence of Familial Homicide?" [2013] *Crim LR* 826.

§ 10.9 Suicide, encouraging or assisting suicide, and suicide pacts

(i) Suicide

For centuries, death by suicide entailed for the deceased a form of post-mortem disgrace. Burial rites were prohibited and real and personal property were forfeit to the Crown.[397] That stigma was reflected in law. Until the passing of the Suicide Act 1961, it was an offence at common law to attempt suicide. Because of the Act, however, a survivor of a suicide attempt will no longer attract criminal liability for her self-directed conduct.[398] In *Nicklinson v Ministry of Justice*[399] Lord Sumption noted that the move to decriminalise was not taken because suicide had become morally acceptable but because the imposition of criminal sanctions on those who had attempted suicide was perceived as inhumane and ineffective. As will be seen, it remains criminal to assist or encourage the suicide of others, whether by helping others to kill themselves or simply by doing an act which is capable of assisting or encouraging another to commit suicide (even if no suicide is ultimately attempted).[400]

The residual criminality still associated with suicide requires some attempt at determining what acts are to be regarded as suicides.[401] In *Bland*,[402] Lord Goff took the view that a person was legitimately entitled to insist on the cessation of forms of life support such as mechanical respiration. Such an exercise of autonomy was not to be regarded as a form of suicide, merely a refusal of medical treatment. Lord Goff did not explain why, in particular circumstances, to decline further treatment is not to opt for suicide. It is not obvious why a request to be taken off life support is not a form of suicide in circumstances where the removal of support entails a rapid and certain death. Prima facie, it seems to be a case of opting for non-existence by rejecting an unacceptable form of life. Be that as it may, Lord Goff's denial that such a choice was equivalent to suicide both ensures patient autonomy and shields doctors and other medical personnel from the possibility of criminal liability in respect of assisting suicide. It remains the case that the taking of any drug or poison to end life will be suicide whatever the degree of pain and disability the patient must otherwise endure. That position has not changed following the incorporation of the ECHR into English law.[403]

In *Bland*, Hoffmann LJ took the decriminalisation of suicide to be a recognition of the principle of self-determination.[404] If this is indicative of a right in the strict sense, it should follow that if a person of sufficient maturity and competent decision-making capacity has resolved to take her life, any physical intervention to prevent her from doing so will constitute an assault. This analysis throws into question the legality of such interventions as

---

[397] Kenny, *Outlines of Criminal Law* (1902) 112–14.

[398] Suicide Act 1961, s. 1.

[399] [2014] UKSC 38, [2015] AC 657, para. 212.

[400] Suicide Act 1961, s. 2.

[401] See also Wheat, "The Law's Treatment of the Suicidal" [2000] *Med LR* 182.

[402] [1993] AC 789, 864.

[403] In *Re B (Adult: refusal of medical treatment)* [2002] 2 All ER 449, the Court of Appeal ruled that the continuation of life support should cease on notification by a competent patient that such treatment was no longer wanted. However, assisting a person wishing to die by providing a substance that will terminate life is unlawfully to assist that person's suicide: *R (on the application of Pretty)* [2002] 1 All ER 1. For critical discussion, see Tur, "Legislative Technique and Human Rights: The Sad Case of Assisted Suicide" [2003] *Crim LR* 3.

[404] [1993] AC 789, 827.

non-consensual medical treatment to prevent loss of life following a suicide attempt. It may be doubted, however, whether there is a right to commit suicide, at least in the full sense. If there were such a right, the right-holder should be entitled to call upon others to help her in the vindication of the right. But it is quite clear that if others were to help her they would become liable for assisting suicide, contrary to section 2 of the Suicide Act 1961. The existence of section 2 rather suggests that the abolition of the offence of attempted suicide does not make the choice to commit suicide a legally protected sphere of autonomy, merely that such a choice will not incur a criminal sanction. On the other hand, the mere fact that life-preserving intervention *may* be lawful does not mean that it *should* be employed in every possible case.

(ii) Encouraging or assisting suicide

Following the decision of the House of Lords in *Kennedy (No. 2)*,[405] V's voluntary act of committing suicide will break the chain of causation so that persons who assist or encourage V are not liable as a principal for a homicide offence in respect of V's death.[406] Rather, liability is under section 2 of the Suicide Act 1961.[407] When first enacted, section 2 created an offence of aiding, abetting, counselling, or procuring suicide or attempted suicide. This involved the standard complicity formula and it required proof that V had committed suicide and that D had done an act which helped, encouraged, or procured this offence with the necessary mens rea for accessorial liability. However, the section created a free-standing crime, not a way of participating in the crime of another, since V's act of committing suicide or attempting suicide is not an offence in its own right.

This original offence of complicity in suicide has now been replaced by what is, in effect, a new offence of doing an act which is capable of encouraging or assisting suicide, contrary to section 2(1) of the Suicide Act 1961.[408] Whereas the old offence required proof of suicide or a suicide attempt, under the new version of the offence it is not necessary to prove that any suicide or attempted suicide has occurred.[409] This version uses the language of the new inchoate offences of assisting and encouraging a crime,[410] and it is an inchoate offence too. The maximum sentence for this offence is imprisonment for 14 years.[411] The old complicity offence could be attempted, whereas it is not possible to attempt the new offence,[412] so it is unlikely that the scope of liability will be expanded by this reform, since an act which is capable of encouraging or assisting suicide is likely to have been a more than merely preparatory act in respect of the aiding, abetting, counselling, or procuring a suicide or a suicide attempt.

---

[405] [2007] UKHL 38, [2008] 2 AC 269.
[406] But see *Dhaliwal* [2006] EWCA Crim 1139, [2006] 2 Cr App R 24; above, § 10.2(ii).
[407] There is no such liability in Scotland, as confirmed in *Ross v. Lord Advocate* [2016] CSIH 12 (Inner House, Court of Session).
[408] Inserted by s. 59 of the Coroners and Justice Act 2009.
[409] Suicide Act 1961, s. 2(1B).
[410] Serious Crime Act 2007, Part 2. See above, § 9.2.
[411] Suicide Act 1961, s. 2(1C).
[412] Criminal Attempts Act 1981, s. 1(4)(ba). Neither is it possible to commit the offence of encouraging or assisting contrary to section 44 of the Serious Crime Act 2007 in respect of the offence of encouraging or assisting suicide: Serious Crime Act 2007, s. 51A.

The actus reus of this offence requires D to do an act which is capable of assisting or encouraging suicide or attempted suicide of another person. The encouragement and assistance need not relate to a specific person or class of person known to D or even identified by her. So a person who writes an article in a blog which advocates those readers who are terminally ill to commit suicide would in principle be guilty of the offence. Encouragement is defined as including the making of threats or putting pressure on a person to commit suicide.[413] It is possible to assist or encourage indirectly by arranging for D2 to do the act of assisting or encouraging.[414] As, with the Serious Crime Act offences of encouraging and assisting crime, it is not necessary to show that D's act had any effect on V; D may be guilty of the offence even if V is unaware of D's act.

The mens rea of the offence is an intent by D's act to encourage or assist suicide or attempted suicide.[415] For assisting or encouraging crime under section 44 of the Serious Crime Act 2007, foresight does not constitute intent, so oblique intent appears not to be sufficient; but no similar provision is made for assisting or encouraging suicide, so presumably foresight of a virtually certain consequence will suffice.

If D's act is not actually capable of assisting or encouraging suicide, the facts should be judged as D believed that they were or would be, and, in the light of D's belief, it should be determined whether the act was capable of encouraging or assisting suicide.[416] The effect of this qualification is that impossibility should not defeat liability for this offence. So, for example, if D writes a letter to encourage V to commit suicide but, unknown to D, V had already killed himself, D's act of sending the letter should be treated as capable of encouraging suicide on the facts as she believed them to be.

Under the previous law, where D aided or abetted V to commit suicide in a country abroad where suicide is lawful, there was some doubt as to whether England would have jurisdiction over D.[417] There can be no doubts about this under the newly reformed section 2. This is because, as long as D does the act which is capable of assisting or encouraging suicide in England, it is irrelevant that it has no effect on V and equally irrelevant that any possible suicide might be committed abroad.

Although in medical contexts life-sustaining treatment can be withdrawn or refused without embroiling medical or caring personnel in assisting suicide charges, outside these contexts encouraging self-determination by way of omission will result in potential liability. So, if V determines to die by way of starvation, D may incur liability under section 2 were he to encourage and strengthen her resolve not to take food during the critical period. However, if V were to go on a hunger strike to make a political point, it is by no means obvious that persons strengthening her resolve up to the point of death will incur liability under section 2. It may well be that the doctrine of double effect will operate in this context,[418] so that D's liability will depend on whether he intended V to die or merely foresaw death as a side-effect. However, if he foresaw suicide as a virtually certain consequence, this may well

---

[413] Suicide Act 1961, s. 2A(3).

[414] *Ibid.*, s. 2A(1).

[415] *Ibid.*, s. 2(1)(b).

[416] *Ibid.*, s. 2A(2).

[417] This was considered by some of the judges in *R (On the application of Purdy)* v. *DPP* [2009] UKHL 45, [2010] 1 AC 345, but was left open.

[418] *Secretary of State for the Home Department* v. *Robb* [1995] 1 All ER 677; *Nicklinson v Ministry of Justice* [2014] UKSC 38, [2015] AC 657, para. 18 (Lord Neuberger).

be sufficient for liability under section 2. In *Nicklinson v Ministry of Justice*,[419] Lord Sumption recognised that, whilst a doctor cannot advise a patient on how to kill herself, there is no danger of criminal liability if the doctor provides advice about the clinical options, such as sedation and other palliative care, available to a patient who wishes to kill herself. This constitutes an impossibly fine line between the doctor's legitimate duty of care of the patient and the illegitimate assistance or encouragement of suicide.

The offence can only be prosecuted with the consent of the Director of Public Prosecutions (DPP).[420] The exercise of the DPP's discretion to prosecute has proved controversial. In *Pretty* v. *DPP*,[421] the claimant sought a declaration of immunity from prosecution if her husband subsequently aided her suicide. The House of Lords refused to grant such an exemption. Subsequently, in *R (On the application of Purdy)* v. *DPP*[422] the claimant sought and obtained an order requiring the DPP to specify the facts and circumstances which he would take into account when considering whether to prosecute for assisting suicide.

Consequently, the DPP issued a policy document identifying the factors he will take into account when determining whether to prosecute.[423] Relevant factors in favour of prosecution include that V was under 18; V had not reached a voluntary, clear, settled, and informed decision to commit suicide; D was not wholly motivated by compassion; D was acting as a healthcare professional, a professional carer, or as a person in authority, such as a prison officer, and the victim was in his or her care; or D pressured V to commit suicide. The purpose of such a policy document, as identified by the House of Lords, is that it will enable V to make an informed decision when, at some future date, she wishes to die but needs assistance to do so.[424] The essence of the DPP's policy, consistent with the attitude of the House of Lords in *Purdy*, is that the autonomy of V should prevail, and D should not be prosecuted for assisting V's suicide, where V had a settled and clear intent to die for reasons of debilitating illness and had the clear capacity to make such a decision. The uncertainty of this policy was subsequently challenged in *Nicklinson v Ministry of Justice*,[425] but the Supreme Court held that the policy did not require clarification and it would be inappropriate for the court to dictate to the DPP what the policy on prosecution should be; the court could review that policy, but could not dictate its terms.

In *Nicklinson v Ministry of Justice*,[426] the Supreme Court acknowledged for the moment that the criminalisation of assisted suicide is not necessarily incompatible with the right to private life under Article 8 of the European Convention on Human Rights, because interference with that right has to be balanced against the interests of society in protecting vulnerable people from being pressured into suicide; at least, the Court concluded that it was not able to declare such compatibility on the evidence before it, although some of their Lordships did not rule out such a declaration in the future. Others of their Lordships considered that reform of the crime of assisted suicide was a matter for Parliament and not the courts.

---

[419] *Ibid.*, para. 255(3).
[420] Suicide Act 1961, s. 2(4).
[421] [2002] 1 All ER 1.
[422] [2009] UKHL 45, [2010] 1 AC 345. Heywood, "Clarification on Assisted Suicide" (2010) *LQR* 5.
[423] *Policy for Prosecutors in Respect of Cases of Encouraging or Assisting Suicide* (2010), updated October 2014. See Daw and Solomon, "Assisted Suicide and Identifying the Public Interest in the Decision to Prosecute" [2010] *Crim LR* 737; Rogers, "Prosecutorial Policies, Prosecutorial Systems, and the Purdy Litigation" [2010] *Crim LR* 543.
[424] [2009] UKHL 45, [2010] 1 AC 345, para. 30 (Lord Hope).
[425] [2014] UKSC 38, [2015] AC 657.
[426] *Ibid.*

(iii) Suicide pacts

If D kills V with the "settled intention" of dying too in pursuance of a suicide pact between herself and V, D will be guilty of manslaughter rather than murder by virtue of section 4 of the Homicide Act 1957. To be a member of such a pact, one must intend to die in pursuance of the pact. If that is not the case, D will be guilty of murder. It is not a defining element of a suicide pact that each member of it must intend to die on the same occasion. Accordingly, D should be entitled to a verdict of manslaughter even if a time comes when she no longer intends to fulfil the pact, provided she intended to observe the pact at the time she killed V. One aspect of the extenuation that underlines section 4 is that D's mental state must be so desperate as to induce a decision to commit suicide *at the time of the killing*. It is irrelevant that the condition may pass.

For obvious reasons, it may be difficult to resolve what part the survivor of a suicide pact played in enacting the pact. The Suicide Act 1961 provides that, on a charge of murder or manslaughter in pursuance of the pact, a verdict of encouraging or assisting suicide may be given.[427]

---

[427] Suicide Act 1961, s. 2(2).

11

NON-FATAL OFFENCES AGAINST
THE PERSON

Offences of violence cover an enormous spectrum of human conduct. D commits battery if he takes hold of V's arm, should V have made it clear that she objects to such contact by D.[1] Or D may shoot and seriously injure V and thereby commit serious offences such as attempted murder or wounding with intent. What links the arm-holding with the shooting is the right of all persons not to be subjected to any unwarranted intrusion upon the body.[2] This most basic of rights is jealously guarded by the criminal law and, because of this, the concept of violence employed in the foundation offences of assault and battery extends to the mere touching of the clothes of the victim and even to the threat of such touching.[3] This is not overreaction: the right not to be physically touched, outside the sphere of consensual touchings and the exigencies of normal life, is fundamental to ordered liberty. Even where no harm occurs, the raw battery or assault in itself violates D's right to be left alone and not be interfered with by others. This shows that there is a further dimension to the offences against the person, additional to the concern for personal integrity and our right not to be hurt. This further dimension is a matter of privacy. The very act of interfering with another's person is a wrong; not because of any harmful consequences, but because it violates one of the core interests implicated in the right to privacy, guaranteed by Article 8 of the ECHR.

There are a considerable number of offences which deal with the infliction or the threat of violence. Many of them are to be found in the Offences against the Person Act 1861, a statute which remains of central importance today. The Act was in no sense a codification of non-fatal violent offences; it merely brought together a disparate collection of existing statutory offences. There is much overlap and inconsistent terminology. Even at the time of its enactment it was castigated as "singularly fragmentary and unsystematic".[4] Yet it remains, today, at the centre of the law's response to violence against the person[5] and continues to generate a stream of appellate, interpretative case law.

---

[1] *Collins* v. *Wilcock* [1984] 3 All ER 374 (CA).

[2] The right inheres in all persons capable of autonomous choices, however irrational the choice made by the particular agent: *St George's Healthcare NHS Trust* v. *S* [1998] 3 All ER 673. By contrast, if a person is considered unable to choose, quite drastic physical interventions may become lawful, such as the sterilisation of a learning-disabled woman: *F* v. *West Berkshire Health Authority* [1990] 2 AC 1 (HL).

[3] *Day* (1845) 1 Cox CC 207; *Thomas* (1985) 81 Cr App R 331 (CA).

[4] Greaves, *The Criminal Law Consolidation and Amendment Acts* (2nd ed., 1862) 3–4.

[5] It is assumed that "person" is a reference to a human being and that pre-natal injury does not fall within provisions relating to the inflicting, occasioning, or causing of injury. There is no authority or dictum to the contrary and no reason of principle why the law relating to non-fatal offences against the person should differ on this point from the law of homicide (see above, § 10.2(i)(a)). If V should be born in an injured condition because of something done by D prior to V's birth, then, applying the reasoning in *A-G's Reference* (*No. 3 of 1994*) [1998] AC 245, in principle a charge against D under a suitable provision of the OAPA 1861 should be possible.

In this chapter, no attempt will be made at a comprehensive coverage of offences of violence. We will look first at the two basic offences, assault and battery, which police the frontier between lawful conduct and violent acts. Then we will turn to offences involving some form of bodily (which now includes psychiatric) harm, namely assault occasioning actual bodily harm, malicious wounding or infliction of grievous bodily harm, and wounding or causing of grievous bodily harm with intent to do grievous bodily harm. As we shall see, these offences have been extended to include the intentional and reckless transmission of diseases and infection. Following that, we will briefly consider offences concerned with poisons and noxious substances and then go on to discuss harassment offences—what might be termed psychic violence. Finally, we will examine versions of these offences aggravated by racial or religious hostility.

§ 11.1 Assault and battery

Assault and battery are two distinct offences. V is assaulted if she *apprehends* the possibility of imminent unlawful violence: if D has "done something of a physical kind which causes someone else to apprehend that they are about to be struck".[6] A battery is inflicted upon V if unlawful violence is *inflicted* upon her.[7] The former tends to be called "common assault" and the latter "assault by beating".[8] The distinction may seem odd. Ordinary people, and lawyers too, would naturally describe D's punching V simply as an assault. It would seem pedantry of the most tiresome kind to insist that, if V saw the punch coming, she was first assaulted as she apprehended its impact and subsequently battered when the punch landed. The pedant might add for good measure that if V was struck without warning from behind by D, D would be guilty of battery but not of assault. It would be far better to do away with such nit-picking and use the single word "assault" to cover situations where V *either* apprehends *or* suffers violence (in the latter case, whether she apprehended it or not). The term battery (or even "assault" with the addition of "by beating") could be allowed to wither away as an archaism. Indeed it looked as if that was the way that things were going. In 1980, the Criminal Law Revision Committee took the view that the term "assault" could be safely used in legal discourse to cover assaults in the narrow sense (i.e. causing an apprehension of violence) and in the sense of inflicting violence, rendering the term battery otiose.[9] A similar position has been taken by the Law Commission, although it recommends distinguishing between threatened and physical assault.[10]

Pedantry returned with a vengeance in *DPP* v. *Little*.[11] The information laid against D charged that he "did unlawfully assault and batter [V] contrary to [section 39 of the Criminal Justice Act 1988]". The Divisional Court ruled that the information was bad for duplicity because it charged two separate offences instead of the permissible single offence.

---

[6] *Nelson* [2013] EWCA Crim 30, [2013] 1 WLR 2861, para. 3. See *Logdon* [1976] Crim LR 121 (DC) for an example of a "pure" assault, i.e. a situation where D intended V to apprehend violence by showing him a gun in a desk drawer but lacked any present intention to inflict violence.

[7] *Nelson* [2013] EWCA Crim 30, [2013] 1 WLR 2861, para. 3.

[8] *Ibid.*

[9] Criminal Law Revision Committee, Fourteenth Report, *Offences Against the Person* Cmnd. 7844 (1980).

[10] *Reform of Offences Against the Person* Law Com. No. 361 (2015); discussed below, § 11.10.

[11] [1992] QB 645 (DC).

Assault, said the Court, was to cause an apprehension of violence and battery was to inflict violence, which does not require proof of any apprehension by V.[12] If assault and battery were to be charged, they would have to be laid by separate informations. It is not, as might have formerly been thought, mere verbiage to charge D's physical attack on V as an assault and battery: it is to charge D with two separate offences with different definitions.

In historical terms, the decision in *Little* is correct. Battery emerged as a crime from the tort of trespass to the person.[13] The etymology of assault—*adsaltare*, to jump at—indicates the focus on frightening rather than hitting people. Yet it is remarkably inconvenient to revert to the medieval origins of these offences. For example, section 47 of the OAPA 1861 penalises "any *assault* occasioning actual bodily harm". There is no reference whatever to battery. By far and away the most common incident giving rise to a charge under section 47 is a direct attack by D on V. The standard form of indictment for such an occurrence is "D assaulted V, thereby occasioning him actual bodily harm". If V apprehended the attack, the reference to assault is sustainable in terms of the presence of the elements of that offence. Yet it is the battery rather than the assault that occasions the actual bodily harm. What if D succeeds in striking V without first causing him apprehension? (Suppose V is looking the other way or is asleep.) This would constitute a section 47 offence.

In *Little*, the Divisional Court accepted that the legislature, in section 47 and in other provisions, used the term "assault" to embrace both assault in the pure sense of the term and the offence of battery. That points up the fact that the standard form of indictment referred to above, used in respect of section 47, is duplicitous, in that the term "assault" when used in that section is a reference to the two distinct offences of assault or battery. To avoid this problem it would be appropriate for prosecutors to make it clear that the section 47 charge involves an assault or battery but not both.

Until the long-overdue reform of offences against the person is in place,[14] we must take seriously the separateness of assault and battery.

§ 11.2 Assault

(i) The actus reus

According to the decision in *Little*,[15] assault is a statutory offence. Therefore, one should consult the statutory definition to determine the actus reus of the offence. But there is no statutory definition. *Little* states that assault became a statutory offence upon the passing into law of section 47 of the OAPA 1861. This is a puzzling conclusion, since section 47 merely states that the maximum penalty for assault occasioning actual bodily harm is five years' imprisonment and that it may be tried on indictment. *Little* goes on to rule that the relevant constitutive statutory provision is now section 39 of the Criminal Justice Act 1988, which provides that common assault (and battery) are summary offences punishable by a fine not exceeding level 5 or a term of imprisonment not exceeding six months. Again,

---

[12] *Nelson* [2013] EWCA Crim 30, [2013] 1 WLR 2861, para. 7.
[13] Milsom, *Historical Foundations of the Common Law* (2nd ed., 1981) chap. 11.
[14] See below, § 11.10.
[15] [1992] QB 645 (DC).

no definition of assault is to be found there. We must still turn to the common law in order to delineate the nature and ambit of the offence, notwithstanding that the practice after *Little* is for informations to refer to assault as an offence charged under section 39.[16]

The actus reus of assault is any act by D that causes V to apprehend immediate and unlawful personal violence. There is high authority endorsing this statement of the actus reus in assault and a degree of stability of definition has been achieved.[17] However, as we shall see, key elements of this judicially derived formula have been expansively interpreted. Before turning to those elements, some general remarks concerning the actus reus need to be made.

(a) Unlawfulness and consent

V must apprehend *unlawful* violence. Sometimes, the application of force may be quite lawful, as in the application of defensive or preventive force.[18] Consent of the victim, too, may legitimate what would otherwise count as unlawful violence. Although consent is further discussed below,[19] given the crucial role that it may play in constituting an assault, some additional discussion of that element is appropriate here.

There is some uncertainty whether lack of consent is an element of the actus reus of assault or a defence to assault.[20] The former is the better view. The threshold of violence in assault is, properly, set at a very low level. V suffers the actus reus of an assault if she apprehends an imminent touching by D to which she has not consented and which is not an inevitable concomitant of ordinary life (like being jostled on a crowded underground train). Because an assault may include the threat of things that (should they happen) will not even hurt, we can see that lack of consent, and D's corresponding disrespect for V's autonomy and privacy, are at the heart of the wrong that constitutes an assault.[21] Certain forceful interventions may be well intentioned and, from a paternalist standpoint, be in the interests of V. But it is for V to decide what is in her interest. In *St George's Trust*,[22] a tort

---

[16] It is obscure why providing statutory penalties for a common law offence changes the offence into a statutory offence. If it does, murder, for instance, becomes a statutory offence because the penalty for murder is prescribed by the Murder (Abolition of Death Penalty) Act 1965. That conclusion has never been suggested. Subsequently, the Court of Appeal has left open the question whether assault and battery should be regarded as separate statutory offences: *Lynsey* [1995] 3 All ER 654. Further, in *Haystead* v. *Chief Constable of Derbyshire* [2000] 3 All ER 890, Laws LJ observed that assault and battery were "in truth" common law offences. However, unless and until *Little* is overruled, charges of assault and battery should be brought under s. 39 of the Criminal Justice Act 1988.

[17] *Ireland* [1998] AC 147.

[18] Below, § 21.2. This includes reasonable force as self-help to recover property from a trespasser: *Burns* [2010] EWCA Crim 1023, [2010] 1 WLR 2694.

[19] § 21.1.

[20] In *Brown* [1994] 1 AC 212 (HL), Lords Jauncey, Lowry, and Templeman considered consent to be a defence to assault, whereas Lords Mustill and Slynn considered the absence of consent to be part of the harm that constituted the offence. However, the views expressed on this point were *obiter* in respect of simple assault, since the case involved the causing of actual bodily harm—which in the circumstances was taken by the majority to negative the relevance of consent altogether (below, § 21.1(iv)). In *Kimber* [1983] 3 All ER 316, the Court of Appeal considered absence of consent to be an integral element of the actus reus in assault.

[21] Consequently, in principle there should be no finding of *assault*, even where D has caused significant physical harm to V, if D acts with V's consent. (There may well be liability for other offences which do not require an assault upon V, such as ss. 18 and 20 of the OAPA 1861.) However, this may not be the position under English law at present; on the majority view in *Brown* (see previous note), the most minor of apprehended contacts will constitute the actus reus of assault and consent is simply a qualified defence.

[22] [1998] 3 All ER 673 (CA).

case, D performed an operation to save V's life and the late-term foetus she was carrying. However, he did so despite V's lack of consent. This was held to be trespass to the person and, undoubtedly, was also an assault.

Consequently, it is not necessary for V in any sense to be *frightened* by what D intends to do. It is enough that she does not want D to do it. If D threatens any form of immediate touching which V has not consented to, or which need not be tolerated as an incident of everyday life, D commits the actus reus of assault.

(b) The conduct element in assault

In *Fagan* v. *MPC*,[23] the Divisional Court reiterated the traditional view that assault requires a positive act and that a mere omission will not suffice. In *Fagan*, D's conviction for assault[24] was confirmed on the basis of intentional failure to remove the wheel of a car which he had inadvertently parked on V's foot. The decision demonstrates that the act requirement will be fulfilled if D persists with a threatening posture that he may have adopted without any intent to cause apprehension of harm. Suppose that D, believing himself to be alone in a railway carriage, puts on a "horror" mask to amuse himself. In fact there is another passenger, V, in the carriage, and donning the mask causes V to fear an imminent attack from D. The actus reus of assault has occurred: and it continues while D does not remove the mask. Thus it will be possible for D to commit the offence later, once he becomes aware of V's presence (and of V's fear).

The act requirement will not be satisfied, however, if D's *lawful* presence, without more, is perceived as a threat by V. Suppose that D enters an enclosed railway carriage on a train. The only other occupant is V, a lone woman. D notes that V seems agitated: moments later she says, "Please do not touch me". It would be appropriate socially for D to remove himself from the carriage at the first safe opportunity, but his failure to do so should not constitute the actus reus of assault. Arguably, that conclusion would not hold if D had knowingly entered a "women-only" carriage, i.e. if D were a trespasser. In *Smith* v. *Superintendent of Woking Police Station*,[25] D had trespassed onto enclosed grounds and looked through the window of a ground-floor bedroom. V, undressing for sleep, was terrified when she saw him standing there; conduct which constituted an act of assault.

To speak is clearly an act. However, there are dicta to the effect that "mere words" would not constitute an assault.[26] Applying such *dicta*, the Court of Appeal of British Columbia ruled in *Byrne*[27] that to say, threateningly, "I've got a gun, give me all your money or I will shoot" did not constitute an assault. The court insisted on some form of physical act. This remarkable indulgence is no longer on offer in England and Wales. The decision in *Smith*, above, holds that mere presence in unlawful threatening circumstances may constitute an assault. Those features were present in *Byrne* and, in addition, there were threatening words,

---

[23] [1969] 1 QB 439 (DC); above, § 4.1(i)(b) (Case 4). This point was not taken, however, in *Santana-Bermudez* [2003] EWHC 2908 (Admin), [2004] Crim LR 471.

[24] Strictly, the case involved battery rather than assault, as it was concerned with the application of force and not the threat of force. The Divisional Court spoke in terms of assault and there is no reason to suppose that its reasoning does not extend to assault in the pure sense of that term.

[25] (1983) 76 Cr App R 234 (DC).

[26] *Meade and Belt* (1823) 1 Lew CC 184.

[27] [1968] 3 CCC 179.

making *Byrne* an *a fortiori* case from the standpoint of *Smith*. Any remaining doubt on the matter is resolved by the decision of the House of Lords in *Ireland*.[28] One of the matters requiring resolution in this important case was whether silent telephone calls could, *in principle*, constitute an assault. (The ruling was in principle because D had pleaded guilty to a charge of assault occasioning actual bodily harm, in the sense of psychiatric harm by silent telephone calls; accordingly the facts of the case were not under review.) The court ruled unanimously that a silent telephone call would constitute an assault if, *inter alia*, it caused V to apprehend the possibility of immediate violence. Although it would be possible to draw a distinction between telephone calls *per se* and "mere words", the two full judgments given in *Ireland* take their decision to have abolished the rule that mere words cannot constitute an assault if it ever truly existed in English law.[29] Similarly, in *Constanza*[30] (discussed below), the Court of Appeal held that written threats by letter could found an assault. Presumably this would extend to threats by text message or the use of social media.

(c) A threat of immediate violence

Assault in its pure form is a *threat* offence, whereas battery is a *contact* offence. Although they have differing histories, the two offences are closely linked. The actus reus of assault is the threat of an immediate battery. But it would be a mistake to describe assault as an attempted battery. To be guilty of assault, D need not possess any intention to inflict violence on V; it is enough that he intentionally or recklessly causes V *to apprehend* immediate violence.[31] On the other hand a threat to inflict violence later is not enough. So, if D were to say, "I will come round next Monday and cut your right leg off", he would not have assaulted V, notwithstanding V's state of terror, because the violence which was threatened was not intended to occur immediately. Presumably this is to encourage V to escape the threat, for example by going to the police.

An understandable judicial concern with the life-wrecking consequences of the abusive conduct familiarly called "harassment" has led to a significant attenuation of the immediacy requirement in assault, making for considerable doubt about the current scope of the offence. In *Constanza*, the Court of Appeal reviewed D's conviction for assault occasioning actual bodily harm arising from circumstances where D, among other things, sent threatening letters to V. Confirming D's conviction, the Court noted that D lived in the same neighbourhood as V and that it was enough to prove "fear of violence at some time not excluding the immediate future".[32] These words are not conspicuously clear but, in the context of the case, they appear to mean that it sufficed that among the fears that V entertained was the fear of a possible imminent attack. That this is enough is confirmed by the House of Lords in *Ireland* where Lord Steyn, speaking for the judicial committee, concluded that the immediacy requirement was made out if D's conduct caused V to apprehend the "possibility" of an immediate attack.[33]

---

[28] [1998] AC 147 (HL).

[29] *Ibid.*, 161–2 (Lord Steyn), 166 (Lord Hope).

[30] [1997] 2 Cr App R 492 (CA).

[31] *Logdon* [1976] Crim LR 121 (DC). For a discussion of assaults not culminating in bodily contact, see Horder, "Reconsidering Psychic Assault" [1998] *Crim LR* 392.

[32] [1997] 2 Cr App R 492, 494.

[33] [1998] AC 147, 162.

In *Ireland*, D's conduct took the form of silent telephone calls which were made miles from the homes of his victims. As mentioned already, their Lordships did not decide whether the actual calls placed by D constituted assaults; in the light of D's guilty plea it merely had to be decided whether silent calls could in principle constitute assaults. Of course, on particular facts, a silent call might cause a fear of an immediate attack (e.g. where V believes the caller is in the flat below). Yet, even though V may know that the caller is many miles away, she may still be reduced to a state of great fear. It seems from *Ireland* that in such cases the issue of assault may now be put to the jury. As Lord Steyn acknowledged, whether V is put in fear of the possibility of an immediate attack is a question of fact. Nonetheless, he recommended that trial judges might advise juries that, if they found that V was put in fear, they should consider "what, if not the possibility of imminent personal violence, was the victim terrified about?"[34]

This, with respect, relaxes the imminence requirement in assault beyond any point previously contemplated. It is simply not the case that a state of fear is, necessarily, a fear of the possibility of imminent attack. It is perfectly possible to experience fear and, at one and the same time, be aware that one is perfectly safe, as anyone who has watched a well-crafted horror film well knows. Many recipients of such hateful things as threatening letters or calls may be traumatised by the experience, particularly if it is an extended one, yet at no time fear an *immediate* attack. Certainly, there should be legal protection from such conduct.[35] But the law of assault is the wrong medium (as Lord Steyn seemingly concedes at one point in his judgment).[36] In cases involving threatening calls or letters, it is submitted that judges should refrain from leaving assault-based offences to juries unless there is some evidence from the facts of the instant case that V was actually put in fear of the possibility of an immediate attack. *Pace* Lord Steyn, evidence of fear of something inchoate or non-immediate should not be placed before juries with an invitation to find that the only plausible basis for the fear was the threat of immediate attack.

(d) Conditional threats

There is some authority that a "conditional" threat cannot constitute an assault. In *Blake v. Barnard*,[37] there was held to be no assault where D pointed a pistol at V's head with the words, "Shut up or I will blow your brains out". The reasoning behind this remarkable decision was that there was no threat of immediate violence because V could negate the threat by doing what he was told.

Several criticisms may be made. In *Blake*, the famous civil case of *Tuberville v. Savage*[38] was perceived to be in point. This was an error. In *Tuberville* D touched his sword and informed V that "If it were not assize time, I would not take such language". We can see that D was informing V that, despite V's impertinence, D was not going to use his sword for

---

[34] *Ibid.*, 162. See also *DPP* v. *Ramos* [2000] Crim LR 768.

[35] Protection from Harassment Act 1997; Communications Act 2003. On the latter see *Collins* [2005] Crim LR 794.

[36] [1998] AC 147, 162

[37] (1840) 9 C & P 626, 173 ER 985.

[38] (1669) 1 Mod Rep 3, 86 ER 684.

fear of being tried, by the judges who were in the neighbourhood, and hanged:[39] a case of a non-threat rather than a conditional threat. Moreover, as already discussed, assault is as much about the protection of autonomy as protection from hurt. In *Blake*, D had no right to put such a coercive condition to V. Accordingly, V was under no duty to comply with the threat and was being confronted with a risk of violence should he assert his right to speak. In principle, such threats should normally constitute assaults. Indeed, there are *dicta* in the later case of *Read* v. *Coker*[40] to that effect.

(ii) The mens rea for assault

The mental element for the crime of assault can be stated briefly and with some assurance. D must intend that V should fear the possibility of immediate violence, or recklessly cause V to fear the possibility of immediate violence.[41] There is no authority or any reason of principle why intent should bear any special or restricted meaning in this context. The reck-lessness in question is *Cunningham* recklessness:[42] accordingly, D must intend or foresee that V will fear the possibility of immediate violence.

Because assault is a crime which may be committed recklessly, it is, in the confusing terminology employed by the courts, a crime of "basic" intent and therefore a crime where the liability of voluntarily intoxicated persons is resolved under the principles of *Majewski*.[43]

§ 11.3 Battery

(i) Actus reus

The actus reus of battery is the infliction of violence on V by D. It has emerged from our discussion of assault that violence is used in a very extended sense, reflecting the values of autonomy and privacy as well as protection from physical harm. Accordingly, D commits battery if he makes contact with V in any fashion to which she has not consented or which is not a contact in keeping with the normal expectations of the relevant time and place.[44] To kiss someone without consent has been considered a battery,[45] as has the act of spitting upon someone,[46] and the unauthorised cutting of hair.[47] If D makes contact with clothes that V is wearing, that will also suffice for battery.[48]

---

[39] Assuming, as the Court seemingly did, that D's words were a reliable indication that V was in no immediate danger. It is easy to imagine circumstances where reaching for a weapon is construed as a threat of immediate violence despite placatory words.

[40] (1853) 13 CB 850, 138 ER 1437.

[41] *Savage* [1992] 1 AC 699.

[42] *Spratt* [1991] 2 All ER 210 (CA); *Parmenter* [1992] 1 AC 699 (CA). *Dicta* in the House of Lords in *Savage* (which overruled *Spratt* and *Parmenter* on other grounds) assume that advertence is required for assault: [1992] 1 AC 699, 736 (Lord Ackner).

[43] [1977] AC 443 (HL); discussed below, § 18.3(ii).

[44] "An assault [*sc.* meaning "battery"] is an intentional touching of another person without the consent of that person and without lawful excuse": *Faulkner* v. *Talbot* [1981] 3 All ER 468, 471; applied in *Thomas* (1985) 81 Cr App R 331 (CA).

[45] *Dungey* (1864) 4 F & F 99, 102, 176 ER 487.

[46] *Smith* (1866) F & F 1066, 176 ER 910.

[47] *Smith* [2006] EWHC 94 (Admin), [2006] 1 WLR 1571.

[48] *Day* (1845) 1 Cox CC 207.

If one wishes to have the benefits of moving about in a modern urban society, one must accept the inevitable bodily contacts arising therefrom. Suppose that V has a horror of bodily contact with strangers but must take an underground train in order to get to work. She cannot complain of battery when she is crushed together with others in the rush hour. However, she is entitled to resist what would otherwise be normal lawful contact provided she has made it clear to D that she does not want such contact with him and it is practicable for him to desist from such contact.[49]

There is dispute about how direct the contact with V must be to constitute battery. Person-to-person contact is obviously sufficient but not necessary. Using any form of weapon will suffice. Just as a knife wielded in the hand is within the offence, so too a knife that is thrown. As *Scott* v. *Shepherd*[50] illustrates, it does not matter if a dangerous weapon, such as a grenade, passes through several panic-stricken hands after being thrown by D prior to the impact on V. Such a response would not constitute a *novus actus interveniens*. Extending the offence further, there are *dicta* to the effect that to set a booby trap[51] or to cause crushing by inducing panic[52] may constitute battery. There seems a clear public interest in including such events within the scope of the offence; it should not matter in principle whether D causes violence to the person of V by direct or indirect means, provided the causing of violence is attributable to some act by D.

As with assault, battery requires an act. However, it seems that the normal rules about omissions apply.[53] Thus a qualifying "act" was found to be present in *Santana-Bermudez*,[54] where V's finger was pierced by a syringe-needle lying in D's pocket. Prior to searching D, V (a police officer) asked if he had any needles on his person, and D replied "No". The danger that D had created was found to come within the decision in *Miller*[55] and, on the Divisional Court's reading of that decision, his failure to inform V was tantamount to an act of battery.

Accordingly, acts indirectly causing violence seem to fall within the crime of battery. However, in *Ireland*, Lord Steyn strongly discountenanced any assumption that a battery had occurred on the facts of that case. The silent telephone calls had caused psychiatric injury to V, injury which was taken to constitute bodily harm. The prosecution had argued that causing such bodily harm through the medium of the telephone was a form of battery. This was decisively rejected, on the ground that the concept of battery could not accommodate the causing of psychiatric injury by telephone.[56] Moreover, in *Wilson*,[57] the House of Lords had earlier ruled that the statutory offence of maliciously inflicting a wound or grievous bodily harm would encompass percussive and impact injuries whether directly or indirectly caused. In so ruling, their Lordships had considered that, so construed, the offence of malicious wounding[58] would take in a broader swathe of conduct than battery.

---

[49] *Collins* v. *Wilcock* [1984] 3 All ER 374 (CA).
[50] (1773) 3 Wils 403, 96 ER 525; above, § 4.2(iii)(b) (Case 1). *Scott* v. *Shepherd* is a civil case but there is no reason why a narrower conception should be adopted in the criminal law.
[51] *Clarence* (1888) 22 QBD 23, 36 (Wills J), 45 (Stephen J) (CCR).
[52] *Martin* (1881) 8 QBD 54 (CCR); see also *Lewis* [1970] Crim LR 647 (CA).
[53] Above, § 4.1(i).
[54] [2004] Crim LR 471.
[55] [1983] 2 AC 161. See above, § 4.1(i)(b) (Case 5).
[56] [1998] AC 147, 161. The conduct was held to constitute an assault.
[57] [1984] AC 242; followed in *Mandair* [1995] 1 AC 208 (HL).
[58] OAPA 1861, s. 20.

The cases which take a broader view of battery are not binding on the House of Lords.[59] In the one decision directly in point (and uncomplicated by any creative use of the *Miller* principle), *DPP* v. *K*,[60] the Divisional Court held that a battery had occurred where D had secreted acid in a hand-dryer, causing V to be burnt with acid upon using the machine. It is submitted that the Divisional Court was correct. Particularly in cases where such means are intentionally employed to cause harm, it would be absurd to draw any distinction between indirect methods and more standard forms of weapon. The idea that battery requires a very direct form of violence gains force from the term "inflict", which features in standard formulations of the offence. Yet the same verb also features in the statutory offence of malicious wounding and, in that context, is no longer taken to require a directly caused injury.[61] Indeed in *Burstow*, an appeal heard jointly with *Ireland*, the House of Lords approved (in the context of maliciously inflicting grievous bodily harm) a reading of inflict as a near synonym for cause when the harm consisted of psychiatric injury.[62] The restrictive view of battery taken in *Ireland* was *obiter*.[63] It is submitted that, in cases of physical contact, the more relaxed reading of inflict in *Wilson*[64] should be extended to battery. It follows that the indirect infliction of violence should suffice.[65]

(ii) Hostility

In *Brown*,[66] the House of Lords confirmed that the contact required for battery was a "hostile" contact. This requirement is not straightforwardly classified as an element of either actus reus or mens rea. The presence of hostility is a function of the motivation and attitude of D (seemingly a matter of mens rea) but which serves to fix and identify the nature of the conduct itself (prima facie, a matter of actus reus). A hand placed on V's shoulder in friendship is different in kind from a hand that will pull V into the violent clutches of D, notwithstanding that the force applied in the initial placing of the hand may be the same.

The requirement for hostility has come under strong judicial and academic attack. Lord Goff, in particular, has criticised the requirement as too vague and restrictive. For him, the boundaries of "physical contact which is generally acceptable in the ordinary conduct of daily life" should inform decisions concerning the ambit of the offence.[67] But does this

---

[59] *Martin* (1881) 8 QBD 54 and *Lewis* [1970] Crim LR 647 did involve assumptions that a battery had occurred, as the view was taken in those cases that a conviction under s. 20 of the OAPA 1861 required proof of a battery; an assumption no longer tenable in the light of *Wilson* [1984] AC 242 and *Mandair* [1995] 1 AC 208.

[60] [1990] 1 All ER 331.

[61] See *Wilson* [1984] AC 242 and *Mandair* [1995] 1 AC 208.

[62] [1998] AC 147, 160 (Lord Steyn), 164 (Lord Hope).

[63] The convictions were sustained on a finding of assault.

[64] [1984] AC 242.

[65] For a view that this conclusion, while desirable in terms of policy, is untenable on the state of the authorities, see Hirst, "Assault, Battery and Indirect Violence" [1999] *Crim LR* 557. But see also *Haystead* v. *Chief Constable of Derbyshire* [2000] 3 All ER 890, where D caused V, a baby, to fall to the floor by hitting V's mother who was carrying V. Laws LJ took the view that battery did not require a directly inflicted injury. Although this opinion was strictly *obiter* (on the facts there was, on analysis, a directly inflicted injury), Laws LJ made it clear that he would have confirmed D's conviction even had he found V's injuries to be indirectly inflicted.

[66] [1994] 1 AC 212. A requirement for hostility was also endorsed by the Court of Appeal in the civil case of *Wilson* v. *Pringle* [1987] QB 237.

[67] *Collins* v. *Wilcock* [1984] 3 All ER 374, 378 (CA); see too *F* v. *West Berkshire Health Authority* [1990] 2 AC 1 (HL).

provide a clearer cutting edge? Suppose V is embraced by D, an exuberant stranger, in a crowded bar one minute after midnight on New Year's Day. He does not like it. Is this a battery or, in the context of the time and place, an "acceptable standard of conduct"? If one takes the view that a *faux pas* should not necessarily entail criminal liability, there may be something to be said for a requirement of hostility.

While the majority in *Brown* endorsed the need for hostility in battery, it has been remarked that, in the context of that case, the word was interpreted in such a way as to deprive it of any meaning.[68] In *Brown*, all the defendants had fully consented to participation in sadomasochistic activities. Nonetheless, the hostility requirement was found to be satisfied. The contacts between the defendants in *Brown* caused actual bodily harm or wounds and were intended to do so. They were more than mere batteries. From *Brown*, we may infer that conduct intentionally causing that degree of harm for a purpose not judicially recognised as acceptable will *ipso facto* be found to be hostile.[69] In such cases the requirement is meaningless. That still leaves a role for the hostility requirement in cases where the contact does not cause bodily harm or where bodily harm was unintended and unforeseen.

(iii) Mens rea

The mens rea for battery mirrors the mens rea for assault. D must intend to inflict unlawful violence or do so recklessly. The recklessness is *Cunningham* recklessness.[70] D must actually have foreseen the risk of inflicting violence upon V. This requirement is subject to the standard *Majewski* exception for voluntary intoxication.[71]

§ 11.4 Assault occasioning actual bodily harm

Section 47 of the OAPA 1861 provides:

> whosoever shall be convicted upon an indictment of any assault occasioning actual bodily harm shall be liable to be imprisoned for any term not exceeding five years.

(i) Actus reus

The term assault is used here as an umbrella term to cover the discrete offence of assault, in the pure sense of that term, and the offence of battery.[72] By far and away the most common form of this offence will be a battery which causes the requisite degree of bodily harm.

---

[68] *Smith and Hogan*, 708.

[69] But see *Wilson* [1997] QB 47 (CA); discussed below, § 21.1(v).

[70] *Savage* [1992] 1 AC 699; *Fagan v. Metropolitan Police Commissioner* [1969] 1 QB 439. The cases do not discriminate between the separate offences of assault and battery when discussing mens rea issues; it is safe to assume equivalence.

[71] Below, § 18.3(ii).

[72] In *Savage* [1992] 1 AC 699, 736, 740, Lord Ackner described the mens rea for s. 47 in terms of the mens rea for assault and in terms of the mens rea for battery: we can safely assume that in this context, the term "assault" covers "pure" assault and battery.

However, it is possible for a pure assault to occasion bodily harm; in *Lewis*,[73] a frightened V was injured when escaping the threatened violence of D.

In "fright" cases such as *Lewis*, where harm arises in the course of a reaction to a threat of violence, a causal link between D's threatening conduct and V's injury exists even though V's frightened reaction may be considered ill-advised. It is unrealistic to expect frightened people to take measured responses and it is quite foreseeable that they will not do so. In the leading case of *Roberts*,[74] where V jumped from a moving car in order to escape the sexual gropings of D, causal responsibility for V's injuries was attributed to D on the footing that V's reaction was not so "daft" as to be unforeseeable.[75] There seems, in this context, to be no difference between "occasioning" bodily harm and "causing" bodily harm.[76]

What constitutes actual bodily harm is set at a very low threshold: "any hurt or injury calculated to interfere with the health or comfort of [D]", provided it is more than "transient and trifling"[77] Bruisings, abrasions, blooded noses, etc., will be enough, as will even momentary unconsciousness.[78] Practically any sustained attack or fighting will involve occasioning actual bodily harm. Enormous scope is thus afforded to prosecutorial discretion. However, the Crown Prosecution Service's charging standard[79] adopts a much more restrictive interpretation of actual bodily harm, which is equated with serious injury. Various factors may be relevant in determining this, but in particular whether significant medical intervention is required (such as a need for a number of stitches or a hospital procedure under anaesthetic) and/or whether permanent effects have resulted. The vast majority of the common assaults that are tried summarily by virtue of section 39 of the Criminal Justice Act 1988 are also triable on indictment under section 47 of the OAPA 1861, with the maximum term of imprisonment inflated from six months to five years. The gravity of the injury is but one of the many variables determining whether a violent incident is tried summarily or indictably, or, indeed, tried at all.[80]

The expression *actual* bodily harm might be taken to signify that only physical harm will fall within the section. However, as interpreted in *Miller*, the expression includes "a hysterical and nervous condition".[81] In *Chan-Fook*,[82] the Court of Appeal asserted that non-physical harm falls within section 47 provided that it constitutes some form of psychiatric injury attested to by expert evidence. This ruling was confirmed by the House of Lords in *Burstow*.[83] Accordingly, mere fright will not constitute bodily harm, even where a nervous

---

[73] [1970] Crim LR 647 (CA); see also *Cartledge v. Allen* [1973] Crim LR 530.

[74] (1971) 56 Cr App R 95 (CA).

[75] *Ibid.*, 102. *Williams* [1992] 2 All ER 183 (CA) adopts the same approach to causation in homicide. For discussion of interventions by victims see above, § 4.2(iii)(e).

[76] John Gardner has claimed that "occasion" is a broader term than "cause" and includes liability for outcomes which would not be attributed on the basis of a causal analysis: "Rationality and the Rule of Law in Offences against the Person" [1994] *CLJ* 502, 509–10. Gardner cites no authority for his claim, merely stating that the distinction between "occasion" and "cause" was "neglected" in *Roberts*.

[77] *Donovan* [1934] 2 KB 498 (CCA).

[78] *T v. DPP* [2003] EWHC 266 (Admin).

[79] Crown Prosecution Service, *Offences Against the Person, Incorporating the Charging Standard.*

[80] For an illuminating study, in the context of assaults, of which factors determine a decision to prosecute and for what offence, see Clarkson, Cretney, Davis, and Shepherd, "Assaults: The Relationship between Seriousness, Criminalisation and Punishment" [1994] *Crim LR* 4.

[81] *Miller* [1954] 2 QB 282, 292.

[82] [1994] 2 All ER 552.

[83] [1998] AC 147.

or hysterical condition is induced, unless there is uncontroverted expert testimony that V's state constitutes a form of psychiatric injury.[84] The CPS charging standard recognises that psychiatric injury may suffice as actual bodily harm if it goes beyond fear, distress, or panic.[85]

The inclusion of psychiatric injury as a harm within the sphere of offences concerned with violence has considerable ramifications, discussed in more detail below.[86] In the context of section 47, the range of conduct penalised which caused psychiatric injury is limited by the need for an assault or battery: D must threaten or inflict unlawful violence on V. Only if psychiatric injury ensues from those circumstances is a charge under section 47 in order.

(ii) Mens rea

The mens rea for section 47 is the mens rea for assault or battery, discussed previously. There is no need to prove any mental element with respect to occasioning bodily harm.[87] Accordingly, this is an offence of constructive liability.[88] The element of the offence constituting the aggravating feature is an element of strict liability. In the context of aggravated offences of violence, constructive liability seems wrong in principle. This is disputed by Gardner, who argues that persons who threaten or use violence cross a moral threshold when they do so and occupy a position of responsibility for any consequences that ensue from such conduct.[89] Gardner's view finds great support in popular sentiments and from some judges. By contrast, in the context of offences against the person, the correspondence principle mandates that sufficient culpability is most reliably evidenced by proof that D intended or at least foresaw those consequences of her conduct which are elements of the offence with which she is charged.[90] There is room in the criminal law for liability based on negligence (even, perhaps, strict liability for minor regulatory offences)[91], but not when the crimes are concerned with violence (as opposed to its consequences). It is true that many cases of assault occasioning actual bodily harm will arise spontaneously in street and recreational settings, frequently where D has consumed significant quantities of drink or drugs.[92] Difficulties of proving mens rea in such circumstances are considerably eased by the special regime for the voluntarily intoxicated.[93] Since assault occasioning actual bodily

---

[84] In *Morris* [1998] 1 Cr App R 386, evidence from a general practitioner that V suffered anxiety, fear, and sleeplessness was held to be insufficient to establish actual bodily harm. Ashworth argues that the insistence on psychiatric injury is unduly limiting in the light of research which demonstrates that fright and lasting fear are produced by many attacks: *Principles*, 302. A more expansive approach to the question of harm, however, would entail considerable difficulties of definition and proof in cases of non-corporeal bodily harm.

[85] Crown Prosecution Service, *Offences Against the Person, Incorporating the Charging Standard*.

[86] § 11.5(i).

[87] *Savage* [1992] 1 AC 699 (HL), affirming *Roberts* (1971) 56 Cr App R 95 (CA), overruling *Spratt* [1991] 2 All ER 210 (CA) and *Parmenter* [1992] 1 AC 699 (CA).

[88] Above, § 6.5.

[89] "Rationality and the Rule of Law in Offences Against the Person" [1994] *CLJ* 502. For different views on the merits of the correspondence principle, see Horder, "A Critique of the Correspondence Principle" [1995] *Crim LR* 759 and Mitchell, "In Defence of the Correspondence Principle" [1999] *Crim LR* 195.

[90] Above, § 6.5.

[91] Though see above, § 6.3, for a full discussion of this issue.

[92] *Focus on Violent Crime and Sexual Offences* 2014, chap. 5.6 (Office for National Statistics).

[93] See below, § 18.3.

harm is the least serious of the aggravated offence of violence, it may be that on proof of mens rea for the *assault* element, negligence as to the consequence—the infliction of actual bodily harm—would be an acceptable form of culpability. But there should be some form of culpability for the aggravating element of the offence.

§ 11.5 Maliciously wounds or inflicts grievous bodily harm

Section 20 of the OAPA 1861 provides:

> whosoever shall unlawfully and maliciously wound or inflict any grievous bodily harm upon any other person, either with or without any weapon or instrument, shall be guilty of an offence, and being convicted thereof shall be liable ... to imprisonment for a term not exceeding five years.

It is noteworthy that the maximum penalty, five years, is the same penalty provided under section 47. In practice, section 20 is regarded as the more serious offence, and the legal guidance of the Crown Prosecution Service reflects this, with the offence considered to be relevant only when really serious injury has been suffered.[94] Further, in terms of punishment, the sentences handed down in respect of section 20 convictions are typically in a higher range than are the sentences imposed in respect of section 47.[95]

(i) Actus reus

(a) Wounds or inflicts grievous bodily harm

The harm element of the offence is present if D wounds or inflicts grievous bodily harm on V. A wound, as defined, requires all the layers of the skin to be pierced.[96] There must be an external aspect to an injury for it to be regarded as a wound. Internal ruptures, even if they cause significant internal bleeding, are not wounds.[97] Even so, the range of what counts as a wound is considerable. If sufficiently serious, a wound may also constitute grievous bodily harm while, at the other end of the spectrum, even a very minor injury may satisfy the definitional requirement of a wound, such as a pin prick.

In *Metheram*,[98] the phrase "really serious harm" was thought best to express the meaning of grievous bodily harm. As explained in *Grundy*,[99] the totality of the injuries suffered by V should be taken into account; it may be that no one particular injury is really serious yet, taken as a whole, V's injuries may amount to grievous bodily harm. This approach was confirmed in *Bollom*,[100] where it was applied with the sensible observation that far less by way of bodily harm would constitute serious harm if V were a young child. According to the

---

[94] Crown Prosecution Service, *Offences Against the Person, Incorporating the Charging Standard*.

[95] Sentencing Guidelines Council, *Assault and Other Offences Against the Person* (2008) 14.

[96] Both the dermis and the epidermis must be broken: *Moriarty v. Brooks* (1834) 6 C & P 684, 172 ER 1419; a break in the outer skin is insufficient: *M'Loughlin* (1838) 8 C & P 635, 173 ER 651.

[97] *JCC (a minor) v. Eisenhower* (1984) 78 Cr App R 48 (DC).

[98] [1961] 3 All ER 200 (CCA).

[99] [1977] Crim LR 543 (CA).

[100] [2004] 2 Cr App R 50.

Crown Prosecution Service's charging standard,[101] grievous bodily harm includes injury which results in permanent disability, loss of sensory function, or visible disfigurement; broken or displaced limbs or bones, including fractured skull, compound fractures, broken cheek bone, jaw, or ribs; injuries which cause substantial loss of blood, usually necessitating a transfusion or resulting in lengthy treatment or incapacity; and serious psychiatric injury.

It has been recognised that infection by the HIV virus can constitute grievous bodily harm.[102] In *Burstow*,[103] the House of Lords confirmed that psychiatric injury, attested to by expert evidence, could constitute *bodily* harm. Further, if the adverse psychiatric condition inflicted on V by D were sufficiently serious, it would constitute grievous bodily harm falling within section 20 (and section 18) of the OAPA 1861. In the context of psychiatric injury, it was ruled in *Burstow* that D would "inflict" such harm if his conduct was a cause of V's psychiatric condition, a matter to be determined on normal causal principles.[104]

The effect of *Burstow* is to enlarge significantly the kinds of setback to personal wellbeing that fall within the section and, consequentially, the kinds of conduct coming within the scope of the offence. On the facts of *Burstow*, there was no physical contact that impacted upon V, directly or indirectly. V had endured a long process of harassment by D, which included such abuses as threatening letters and telephone calls, following, photographing, etc. A reading of the case leaves no doubt about the extent of V's suffering and the wrongfulness of D's conduct. There can be no qualms about the actual decision in the case. However, the limits of the decision are difficult to identify.[105]

In *Burstow*, psychiatric injury was held to be a form of *bodily* injury. How literally are we to take this? If no distinction is to be taken between psychiatric and physical injury *in general*, the effects of the decision could be profound. For example, suppose that D, an employer, wishes to terminate the contract of V, her employee. D has good reason to consider V's job performance unacceptable. Of course, in no circumstances whatsoever may D inflict physical harm on V to force his resignation. Instead of that, however, she calls V to her office, gives him three months' salary in lieu of notice, and explains how he has fallen down on his job. She is aware of V's previous psychiatric history and foresees that his mental health will once again break down if sacked. That proves to be the case. On these facts, D has caused psychiatric injury and foresaw that she would do so. A section 20 offence? One's initial response is to stress that section 20 requires *unlawful* conduct on the part of D. How can a legitimate termination of employment be unlawful? The answer, if one takes literally the finding in *Burstow*, is that any course of conduct whereby D foresees that she will cause V grievous *bodily* harm cannot be legitimate conduct unless she is acting in self-defence or under duress.

It is unlikely that the limits of *Burstow* will be tested in this way. The Crown Prosecution Service will probably not prosecute in those cases where such commonplaces as adultery, verbal cruelty, termination of employment, promises made for the purposes of seduction,

---

[101] *Offences Against the Person, Incorporating the Charging Standard.*

[102] *Dica* [2004] EWCA Crim 1103, [2004] QB 1257 (CA); *Konzani* [2005] EWCA Crim 706, [2005] 2 Cr App R 14; *B* [2006] EWCA Crim 2945, [2007] 1 WLR 1567. As can the transmission of genital herpes: *Golding* [2014] EWCA Crim 889.

[103] [1998] AC 147.

[104] *Ibid.*, 160, 164.

[105] For an incisive discussion see Gardner, "Stalking" (1998) 114 *LQR* 33.

and the like cause serious mental distress amounting to psychiatric injury. These things will be tolerated as part of "normal" life, as they should be. Any attempt rigorously to police such matters would make for an intolerable society. There would need to be something extreme and visible—the kind of conduct that occurred in *Burstow* or, perhaps, sustained classroom or workplace bullying, to trigger a police investigation and a file of evidence for the Crown Prosecution Service. Psychiatric injury may have devastating consequences, but it is *different* from physical injury. Policing the causing of psychiatric injury by way of nineteenth-century laws focused on matters physical is not the way forward. New legislation is required which should pay particular attention to the kind of conduct which is to be penalised.[106]

(b) Inflict

The verb "inflict", which features in section 20, was for a very long time thought to include a narrower range of conduct than would be captured by employing the term "cause". In the context of psychiatric injury, *Burstow* decided that inflict is to be interpreted as a synonym for cause.[107] We will consider first the meaning of inflict derived in cases of physical injury, and then consider whether the extensive interpretation adopted in *Burstow* has implications for cases which involve physical injury.

For many years, *Clarence*[108] was regarded as the leading case on the meaning of "inflict". D had been charged with the malicious infliction of grievous bodily harm upon V, on account of his infecting her with gonorrhoea. Despite V's ignorance of D's infected state, her consent to intercourse was taken to be valid; accordingly, the bodily contact involved in intercourse did not constitute a battery by D. For the majority, this ruled out a conviction under section 20 because of the need for a:[109]

> "direct causing of some grievous injury to the body itself with a weapon, as by a cut with a knife, or without a weapon, as by a blow with the fist, or by pushing a person down. Indeed, ['inflict' implies] an assault and battery of which a wound or grievous bodily harm is the manifest immediate and obvious result."

The restrictive definition in *Clarence* was relaxed to a degree in cases such as *Martin*[110] and *Halliday*.[111] These and other cases were considered by the House of Lords in *Wilson*, where the House of Lords ruled, *contra Clarence*, that section 20 did not require the commission of an assault or battery:[112]

> "grievous bodily harm may be inflicted where the accused has directly or violently inflicted it by assaulting the victim or where the accused has 'inflicted' it by doing something intentionally which though it is not in itself a direct application of force to the body of the victim does

---

[106] To some extent, the Protection from Harassment Act 1997 provides appropriate protection from conduct of this kind: see below, § 11.8.

[107] [1998] AC 147.

[108] (1888) 22 QBD 23 (CCR).

[109] *Ibid.*, 41 (Stephen J).

[110] (1881) 8 QBD 54 (CCR) (D held to have inflicted grievous bodily harm by causing victims to rush to locked exits).

[111] [1886–90] All ER 1028 (CCR) (D held to have inflicted grievous bodily harm when V was injured in the course of escaping the threatened violence of D).

[112] [1984] AC 242.

directly result in some force being applied violently to the body of the victim so that he suffers grievous bodily harm."

This passage was subsequently endorsed by the House of Lords in *Mandair*.[113] An injury caused by way of an "infliction" is an injury caused by an impact or percussion set in motion by D. The injury must arise directly from the impact but the impact itself need not be something that D has directly caused; any direct or indirectly caused impact or percussive connection will suffice. Returning to the facts of *Clarence*, we can now appreciate that if an assault or battery is no longer required, the fact of consensual intercourse will not, of itself, be a barrier to a conviction. Yet to convict on the facts of *Clarence*, we must still find that "force [was] applied violently" and that, because of the violent application of force, injury (infection) was sustained. Even if we regard consensual intercourse as involving the violent application of force (which is doubtful), the injury is not caused by the application of force but by the process of infection.

To allow diseases and infections within the scope of section 20, "inflict" must be interpreted as a near synonym for cause. That, as we know, was the course taken in the context of psychiatric injury in *Burstow*, where there had been no physical contact between D and V. Lord Hope considered that inflict bore the same meaning as cause, save that for the former term there was an implication that the consequences of the act were likely to be unpleasant or harmful.[114] In the context of crimes, his approach effectively assimilates "inflict" to "cause", and would ensure a conviction on facts such as *Clarence*. Lord Steyn, whose judgment was that of the majority, was more circumspect. He did not consider the two terms to be synonymous but took it to be natural to speak of inflicting psychiatric injury without implying, in that context, any direct or indirect violent contact.[115] In the important decisions of *Dica*[116] and *Konzani*,[117] the Court of Appeal took the analysis of Lord Hope to be of general application. Departing from the ruling in *Clarence*, it was held in both cases that for D to pass on a sexually transmitted disease to his sexual partner V, where V was unaware and had not consented to the risk of infection, was conduct falling within section 20. These cases have considerable ramifications for questions relating to what constitutes a valid consent to harm, for the scope of some key sexual offences, and for the appropriateness of using laws designed to curb violence to penalise sexual risk-taking. The first two issues will be treated in later chapters,[118] and the third matter later in this chapter (§ 11.7); for now, we need merely note that, unless and until they are overruled by the House of Lords, *Dica* and *Konzani* resolve that "inflict" is a synonym for "cause" for the purposes of section 20.

(ii) Mens rea

The key term is malice: in modern English criminal law this is interpreted as intention or recklessness. The recklessness is *Cunningham* recklessness.[119] However, the foresight

---

[113] [1995] 1 AC 208.
[114] [1998] AC 147.
[115] *Ibid.*, 160–1.
[116] [2004] EWCA Crim 1103, [2004] QB 1257.
[117] [2005] EWCA Crim 706, [2005] 2 Cr App R 14.
[118] See Chapters 21 and 12 respectively.
[119] *Savage* [1992] 1 AC 699.

required for this offence is not foresight on the part of D that he will wound or inflict grievous bodily harm on V. It is enough, according to a line of authority originating in *Mowatt*[120] and endorsed by the House of Lords in *Savage and Parmenter*,[121] that D foresees that he may[122] inflict some, even minor, bodily harm on V. This is unfortunate. More than that: this violation of the correspondence principle is unacceptable in the context of a serious offence of violence.

Most section 20 cases will involve physical attacks. The Court of Appeal sensibly ruled in *Beeson*[123] that, if a wound or grievous bodily harm is caused by a direct attack inherently likely to cause physical harm, no guidance to the jury on the meaning of malice is necessary. Guidance should be given only if D raises an argument that his conduct was in some sense mistaken or accidental or that, for some other reason, he failed to recognise that he might cause harm.

§ 11.6 Wounding with intent

Section 18 of the OAPA 1861 provides:

> Whosoever shall unlawfully and maliciously by any means whatsoever wound or cause grievous bodily harm to any person ... with intent ... to do some ... grievous bodily harm to any person, or with intent to resist or prevent the lawful apprehension or detainer of any person, shall be guilty of an offence, and being convicted thereof shall be liable ... to imprisonment for life.

Section 18 creates one offence with several modes of commission. It may be helpful to set out these various modes of commission:

(a) unlawfully and maliciously wounding, with intent to do grievous bodily harm;
(b) unlawfully and maliciously wounding, with intent to resist or prevent the lawful apprehension or detainer of any person;
(c) unlawfully and maliciously causing grievous bodily harm, with intent to do grievous bodily harm;
(d) unlawfully and maliciously causing grievous bodily harm, with intent to resist or prevent the lawful apprehension or detainer of any person.

(i) Actus reus

We are already familiar with the meanings of "wounding" and "grievous bodily harm".[124] As we have discussed, the term "grievous bodily harm" includes serious psychiatric injury and now will include serious infection or disease. In the context of section 18, where the culpability requirement is intention, there may be less concern about the extension of liability

---

[120] [1968] 1 QB 421 (CA).
[121] [1992] 1 AC 699.
[122] *Rushworth* (1992) 95 Cr App R 252, 255 (CA), dismissing an argument that D must foresee that some harm to V will result from his conduct.
[123] [1994] Crim LR 190 (CA).
[124] Above, § 11.5(i)(a).

into these areas. The requirement of intention will narrow and focus the potential range of conduct that may be penalised and ensure a culpability that warrants a criminal sanction. What constitutes "lawful apprehension or detention" will depend on the validity of the arrest and detention, a matter dependent on the particular facts of each case.

With the omission of the verb "inflict", the former uncertainties associated with that term in section 20[125] are avoided. It is necessary only that D wounds or causes serious injury. Normal principles of causation apply.[126]

(ii) Mens rea

The core of the offence is intention. In variants (a), (b), and (d) (set out above), this is an ulterior intent,[127] while in variant (c) the required intent coincides with the actus reus. The most common variants of the offence are (a) where D wounds V with intent to cause grievous bodily harm or (c) where D causes V grievous bodily harm with intent to cause grievous bodily harm.

In variant (c), where mens rea coincides with actus reus, if the grievous bodily harm is caused by way of a direct attack, the jury should simply be invited to consider whether D intended that result: there is no need for any direction on the meaning of intent.[128] By contrast, where D has caused V grievous bodily harm by some dangerous act not in the nature of a direct attack and asserts that she did not act in order to cause such harm, it will be sufficient for the matter to go to the jury if she foresaw that harm is virtually certain to occur.[129] In both of the cases under discussion—direct attack causing grievous bodily harm; dangerous act causing grievous bodily harm—the term "maliciously", which appears in section 18, is redundant. The mens rea issue is whether D intended grievous bodily harm: if she did, a fortiori it was done maliciously in the sense that term carries in modern English criminal law.

Under variant (b), where the section 18 offence takes the form of a wound falling short of grievous bodily harm, an ulterior intent to cause grievous bodily must be proved. In practice, there is no room in this kind of case for intent proved on the basis of foresight that the grievous bodily harm was a virtual certainty: if grievous bodily harm did not arise, then it could not have been a virtually certain result of D's actual conduct. Accordingly it must be proved that D acted with intent in the core sense[130] to cause V grievous bodily harm. Again, the term maliciously is redundant; if D acted in order to cause serious harm, a fortiori he acted maliciously with respect to that consequence.

The requirement of malice may have a role to play in variants (b) and (d), where D's intent is to prevent or resist the lawful apprehension or detention of any person. In principle, the requirement of malice in section 18 entails that D must at least foresee the

---

[125] For the moment resolved: above, § 11.5(i)(b).
[126] See above, § 4.2.
[127] Above, § 5.1(vii).
[128] Moloney [1985] AC 905, 926 (HL).
[129] Woollin [1999] AC 82 (HL); above, § 5.1(iv).
[130] Above, § 5.1.

possibility that she might cause a wound or grievous bodily harm in cases where her intent is to resist arrest or detention.[131]

In variants (b) and (d), it is clear from the terms of section 18 that D must *intend* to resist an apprehension or detention. Recklessness does not suffice. However, section 18 further requires that D must intend to resist a *lawful* apprehension or detention. What mens rea is required for the element of lawfulness? In principle, what is needed is that, in the circumstances that D believes to exist, the arrest is lawful. Thus if D wrongly believes in facts which, if true, would have made the arrest unlawful, he lacks mens rea. On the other hand, if D has made no mistake about the circumstances, it suffices that the apprehension or detention is, in fact, lawful. It would not go to liability, merely mitigation, that D believed the apprehension or detention was illegal.[132]

§ 11.7 Transmitting diseases and infection

Concern about the spread of Acquired Immune Deficiency Syndrome (AIDS) has led to consideration whether current offences against the person may apply to conduct associated with transmission of that condition.[133] More generally, as we will see, there are justified concerns over the appropriateness of the existing range of offences that protect the person in the context of harms inflicted by the transmission of diseases and infection. Our discussion will focus on AIDS; there are, of course, implications for other forms of transmission of disease and infection whether sexually transmitted or otherwise.

(i) Cases where harm was intended

The most straightforward situation will be where V dies as a consequence of AIDS and it can be proved that D infected V with Human Immunodeficiency Virus (HIV) in order that she should die. With the abolition of the year-and-a-day rule,[134] there is no impediment to a charge of murder. Such cases are likely to be very rare (although they are not unknown).

What offences, if any, are committed if D intentionally causes V to become HIV-positive? From the decisions in *Dica*[135] and *Konzani*,[136] we know that to be made HIV-positive is to be seriously harmed in a bodily sense. If the infection is intentionally transmitted there seems no impediment to a conviction under section 18 of the OAPA 1861, a conclusion consistent with the judgment of Stephen J in *Clarence*.[137] Although the condition of being HIV-positive is compatible with years of normal healthy existence, given access to suitable drugs, the condition is a significant setback to the interests of the person so afflicted and

---

[131] *Morrison* (1989) 89 Cr App R 17. The case confirms that the test is actual foresight of injury on the part of D but it did not rehearse the question whether the foresight must be of a wound or grievous bodily harm. In principle it should; but see *Mowatt* [1968] 1 QB 421.

[132] Cf. *Bentley* (1850) 4 Cox CC 406. Such a mistake should be characterised as a mistake of law, discussed below, § 18.2.

[133] Bronitt, "Spreading Disease and the Criminal Law" [1994] *Crim LR* 21.

[134] Law Reform (Year and a Day Rule) Act 1996; discussed above, § 10.2(iv).

[135] [2004] EWCA Crim 1103, [2004] QB 1257.

[136] [2005] EWCA Crim 706, [2005] 2 Cr App R 14.

[137] (1888) 22 QBD 23.

the setback is, in a broad sense, to bodily integrity. Whatever reservations there may be concerning the extension of bodily harm to psychiatric injury,[138] it would, in the light of that extension, have been perverse to hold that the condition of being HIV-positive did not amount to grievous bodily harm. That said, the expression is not a natural one to employ in this context, pointing up the need for specific legislation. The Law Commission has, however, recommended that specific offences concerning the transmission of disease should not simply be enacted; rather, there should be a wider review of the law, in consultation with health professionals, to determine whether specific offences should be created.[139]

(ii) Cases where the harm was knowingly risked

Far more common than intentionally transmitting infection will be taking risks relating to infection, notably through forms of unprotected sexual activity engaged in by persons who are aware that they have a condition that can be passed on by sexual contact. By reading "inflict" as synonymous with cause, the Court of Appeal in *Dica* and *Konzani* has laid the ground for straightforward convictions of maliciously inflicting grievous bodily harm, within the terms of section 20, in cases where D infects his sexual partner having foreseen the risk of doing so, and where V has not given an informed consent to that risk.

In *Dica*, on the facts assumed for the purposes of the appeal, and on the facts themselves in *Konzani*, V had not consented to the risk of infection. In light of the decision of the House of Lords in *Brown*,[140] however, it might be considered that whether V had actually consented was irrelevant, since it was held in that case that, save for special circumstances,[141] valid consent is restricted to the infliction of harms falling short of actual bodily harm and the harm in *Dica* and *Konzani* was much more serious than that. Since, however, the victims in *Dica* and *Konzani* clearly had not consented to the *deliberate* infliction of actual bodily harm or worse, it followed that Brown was not engaged. Consequently, if they had consented to the *risk* of the disease being transmitted, this might have negated D's liability. In *Dica*, reference was made to a couple trying to start a family and to another couple organising their sex life according to the strictures of the Roman Catholic church. The assumption was made that in those circumstances it would be legitimate to take the risk of becoming HIV-positive. More significantly, however, following *Konzani*, if D was aware that he might be HIV-positive and did not disclose this to V, V's consent to unprotected sexual intercourse would be assumed not to be an informed consent, so liability would be possible. In such circumstances, should V subsequently die, D could face a charge of manslaughter of the constructive or gross negligence varieties.[142]

If V has not given a valid consent to the risk of HIV, will each incident of risky sexual intercourse constitute rape of the penetrated V? Is V's consent to the sex act vitiated? According to *Clarence*,[143] the answer is no: V, even in her state of ignorance, understood

---

[138] *Burstow* [1998] AC 147 (HL); *Chan-Fook* [1994] 2 All ER 552 (CA).

[139] *Reform of Offences Against the Person*, Law Com. No. 361 (2015).

[140] [1994] 1 AC 212.

[141] Such as organised sport; one may safely assume that sexual activity would not in itself qualify as a special circumstance. See below, § 21.1(iv).

[142] See the discussion of these ways of committing manslaughter in Chapter 10.

[143] (1888) 22 QBD 23; confirmed in *EB* [2006] EWCA 2945. See below § 21.1(ii)(d).

the essential nature of the act to which she was consenting. The matter is controversial, yet on balance it is submitted that *Clarence* is correct on this point and is supported by dicta in *Dica* and *Konzani* and by the decision in *B*.[144] However, the situation is different if V's "consent" to sexual intercourse was procured through active deception by D regarding D's use of a condom or, it seems, D's HIV status.[145] We return to this matter in the next chapter and, later, in § 21.1(iii)(d).

(iii) *Administering noxious things*

Finally, mention should be made of section 23 of the OAPA 1861, which concerns the malicious administration (or causing to be administered or taken) of noxious things which endanger life or inflict grievous bodily harm. It has been suggested that bodily fluids containing HIV are "noxious" things and that sexual transmission of fluids can be regarded as an "administration" or a "taking" within the meaning of this section.[146] These are by no means untenable claims and, if this interpretation is accepted, a defendant could be convicted on the basis of having unprotected sex knowing or suspecting himself to be HIV-positive since that fact, of itself, would be life-endangering to an HIV-negative person. Under the section, the element of malice (recklessness) merely relates to the administration of the noxious substance; it need not be proved that D foresaw life endangerment or the infliction of grievous bodily harm.[147]

Save for cases involving the intentional transmission of disease, it is submitted that the vigorous application of the laws regulating physical and sexual violence to cases involving transmission of diseases would be a far from ideal response to a difficult area of social and health policy, where confident and confidential reporting of an HIV status is at least as important as deterring sexual irresponsibility.[148]

---

[144] [2006] EWCA Crim 2945, [2007] 1 WLR 1567.

[145] See *Assange* v. *Swedish Judicial Authority* [2011] EWHC 2849 (Admin), paras. 82–90. The view taken in *Assange* would bring English law on consent closer to the position in Canada, where the fraudulent concealment of HIV-positive status vitiates consent if there was a "realistic possibility of transmission"—thereby constituting an aggravated sexual assault through endangerment of life (rather than an offence of violence) even if the disease was not transmitted: *Mabior* 2012 SCC 47.

[146] Bronnitt, "Spreading Disease and the Criminal Law" [1994] *Crim LR* 21.

[147] *Cato* [1976] 1 All ER 260. The Law Commission recommends that the poisoning offences in the OAPA 1861 should be replaced with a single offence of knowingly or recklessly administering a substance which is capable of causing injury: Law Com. No. 316, *Reform of Offences Against the Person* (2015). It would not be necessary to prove that injury was caused.

[148] A position acknowledged by the Law Commission in *Reform of Offences Against the Person*, Law Com. No. 361 (2015). See the critiques in Weait, "Taking the Blame: Criminal Law, Social Responsibility and the Sexual Transmission of HIV" (2001) 23 *Journal of Social Welfare and Family Law* 441 and Weait, "Knowledge, Autonomy and Consent: *R v Konzani*" [2005] *Crim LR* 763. The sensitivities of prosecution of such cases is also acknowledged by the Crown Prosecution Service in *Intentional or Reckless Sexual Transmission of Infection*.

§ 11.8 Harassment

The Protection from Harassment Act 1997[149] provides, *inter alia*:[150]

1(1) A person must not pursue a course of conduct—
(a)   which amounts to the harassment of another, and
(b)   which he knows or ought to know amounts to harassment of the other.
(1A) A person must not pursue a course of conduct—
(a)   which involves harassment of two or more persons, and
(b)   which he knows or ought to know involves harassment of those persons, and
(c)   by which he intends to persuade any person (whether or not one of those persons mentioned above)—
    (i)   not to do something that he is entitled or required to do, or
    (ii)   to do something that he is not under any obligation to do.
(2) For the purposes of this section ..., the person whose course of conduct is in question ought to know that it amounts to or involves harassment of another if a reasonable person in possession of the same information would think the course of conduct amounted to or involved harassment of the other.
(3) Subsection (1) or (1A) does not apply to a course of conduct if the person who pursued it shows—
(a)   that it was pursued for the purpose of preventing or detecting crime,
(b)   that it was pursued under any enactment or rule of law or to comply with any condition or requirement imposed by any person under any enactment, or
(c)   that in the particular circumstances the pursuit of the course of conduct was reasonable.
2(1) A person who pursues a course of conduct in breach of section 1(1) or (1A) is guilty of an offence.
...
4(1) A person whose course of conduct causes another to fear, on at least two occasions, that violence will be used against him is guilty of an offence if he knows or ought to know that his course of conduct will cause the other so to fear on each of these occasions.
(2) For the purposes of this section, the person whose course of conduct is in question ought to know that it will cause another to fear that violence will be used against him on any occasion if a reasonable person in possession of the same information would think the course of conduct would cause the other so to fear on the occasion.

The expression "violence" in section 4 evokes some kind of physical attack. As we have seen in this chapter, in *Ireland and Burstow*[151] the House of Lords brought non-contact acts that cause psychiatric injury into the mainstream of the criminal law in terms of offences and punishment. While the reasoning and ultimate implications of these decisions have been questioned, no one would deny that courses of conduct aimed at destabilising and diminishing the quality of the victim's life are properly regarded as species of violence, notwithstanding the lack of any blow or physical attack. The activities known as stalking

---

[149] Wells, "Stalking: The Criminal Law Response" [1997] *Crim LR* 463; Finch, *The Criminalisation of Stalking* (2001); Finch "The Perfect Stalking Law: An Evaluation of the Efficacy of the Protection from Harassment Act 1997" [2002] *Crim LR* 702.

[150] Subsection (1A) was inserted by s. 125 of the Serious Organised Crime and Police Act 2005. See also the new stalking offences inserted by the Protection of Freedoms Act 2012: below, § 11.8(iv).

[151] [1998] AC 147 (HL).

and harassment are now widely regarded as serious wrongs in our culture and cause considerable suffering.[152]

The Protection from Harassment Act 1997 is a legislative attempt directly to confront these wrongs, although it impinges on other conduct too, such as protests, demonstrations, and intrusive press activity. In its criminal law part, the Act creates the three offences set out above: two harassment offences in section 1 and a fear of violence offence in section 4. Offences have also been created within the Act relating specifically to stalking. We consider these offences in turn.

(i) Harassment of another

Turning to the first, and primary, harassment offence set out in section 1 of the Act, the most striking feature is the absence of any definition of "harassment", the very activity to be proscribed, save that harassment includes alarming a person or causing them distress.[153] In *Hayes* v. *Willoughby*,[154] Lord Sumption described "harassment" as being "an ordinary English word with a well understood meaning". In *Thomas* v. *News Group Newspapers Ltd*,[155] Lord Phillips MR defined harassment as "a persistent and deliberate course of unreasonable and oppressive conduct, targeted at another person, which is calculated to and does cause that person alarm, fear or distress". For the purposes of the criminal law, in *Curtis*[156] "harassment" was unhelpfully defined as conduct which "must be unacceptable to a degree which would sustain criminal liability and also must be oppressive".

Section 1(2), in effect, provides that if a reasonable person would interpret D's course of conduct as amounting to harassment, then that course of conduct is harassment. Since the offence may be tried only summarily, the "reasonable person" in effect will be the stipendiary magistrate or the lay justices trying the case.

The scope of the primary offence is quite enormous. An admissions tutor may understandably consider herself harassed after the fifth telephone call from an importunate applicant. But, even in her blackest mood, the tutor is unlikely to regard herself as the victim of an offence. In *James*,[157] for example, D was abusive in a number of phone calls whilst making a complaint. He was convicted of the offence, notwithstanding that some of the calls were return calls initiated by V.

The scope of the offence is curbed to a degree by section 1(3), which provides a defence, with the burden of proof on D, of acting for the purpose of preventing or detecting crime, complying with a statutory enactment, or acting reasonably. The interpretation of the first limb of this defence was considered by the Supreme Court in *Hayes* v. *Willoughby*,[158] a case concerning civil liability for harassment. Since this limb of the defence is not curtailed by the word "reasonableness" and the focus is on D's purpose of preventing or detecting a

---

[152] *Focus on Violent* Crime and *Sexual Offences 2013/14: Chapter 4: Intimate Personal Violence and Serious Sexual Assault* (Office for National Statistics) reports that, after the age of 16, stalking affects over 1 in 5 women (21.5%) and nearly 1 in 10 men (9.8%).

[153] Protection from Harassment Act 1997, s. 7(2).

[154] [2013] UKSC 17, [2013] 1 WLR 935, para. 1.

[155] [2001] EWCA Civ 1233, [2002] EMLR 78, para. 30.

[156] [2010] EWCA Crim 123, [2010] 1 WLR 2770, para. 29.

[157] [2009] EWHC 2925.

[158] [2013] UKSC 17, [2013] 1 WLR 935.

crime, this appears to embody a subjective test; but that was not considered to be appropriate without some control mechanism, because, to use the words of Lord Sumption, a large proportion of those participating in conduct involving harassment will be "obsessives and cranks, who will commonly believe themselves to be entitled to act as they do".[159] Consequently, a hybrid interpretation was adopted. First, D's state of mind needed to be considered, to determine whether he did have the purpose to prevent or detect crime. Secondly, however, this needed to be a rational purpose: which imports a requirement of good faith, so that "there should be some logical connection between the evidence and ostensible reasons for the decision ... an absence of arbitrariness, of capriciousness or of reasoning so outrageous in its defiance of logic as to be perverse".[160] This is a radical interpretation of the defence, which limits its ambit. It means that D will not be able to rely on the defence unless he can prove that he had applied his mind to the matter and concluded that his conduct was an appropriate method of preventing or detecting crime. This is not a test of whether the reasonable person would have reached the same decision; it is simply a matter of whether D's decision can be characterised as rational in the light of the evidence available to him. Significantly, Lord Reed dissented, preferring to interpret the first limb of the defence in purely subjective terms, both because Parliament did not qualify the defence by reference to rationality and because the defence operates in both the civil and the criminal context, and in the latter it is not appropriate to restrict the defence artificially. With respect, Lord Reed is correct. Whilst the interpretation of the defence by the majority may be appropriate in the context of civil law claims, it is inappropriate artificially to restrict the defence for the criminal law by reference to vague notions of rationality.

There must, at least, be a "course of conduct". This requires the harassment of V on at least two occasions[161] and must involve some degree of connection between the two occasions.[162] The Act provides that if D aids, abets, counsels, or procures E's conduct on one occasion and, should E's conduct on a subsequent occasion taken with the first occasion make for a course of conduct by E, there is also a course of conduct on D's part whether or not D was present on the second occasion.[163] However, two self-contained incidents involving interactions between the same persons will not constitute a course of conduct, as where D is unpleasant to V after some disagreement, is then reconciled to V, but on some future occasion is unpleasant again. But, provided there is the necessary degree of connection between the two episodes of harassment, it will not matter if there is a considerable time elapsing between them—annual demonstrations outside, say, a synagogue on a particular anniversary might well constitute an offence of harassment.

Although the offence requires the harassment of another by way of at least two episodes of conduct (to make for a course of conduct), it is not necessary that V be present to experience the harassment. In *Dunn*,[164] the Court of Appeal ruled that V had been harassed by D's conduct at V's home. D had intended to frighten all members of the household (including V) and it was immaterial that she was not present at the time.

---

[159] *Ibid.*, para. 12.

[160] *Ibid.*, para. 14 (Lord Sumption).

[161] Protection from Harassment Act 1997, s. 7(3), as inserted by the Serious Organised Crime and Police Act 2005, s. 125(7).

[162] *Lau v. DPP* [2000] Crim LR 580; *Hills* [2001] Crim LR 318.

[163] Section 7(3A), as inserted by the Criminal Justice and Police Act 2001, s. 44.

[164] [2001] Crim LR 130.

To be guilty of the primary harassment offence, contrary to section 1(1), D must know or ought to know that his conduct is harassment. One might think that a negligence requirement is rather low for a serious offence, but in fact the requirement here falls short even of true negligence, especially in the context of group activity. If D aids, abets, counsels, or procures E's conduct on one occasion, D will be taken to know any matter that E knew or ought to have known on a subsequent occasion—whether or not D was present on that subsequent occasion.[165] Moreover, in determining what D ought to have known (even when acting alone), no account is to be taken of a cognitive disability such as schizophrenia.[166] In *Thomas* v. *News Group Newspapers*,[167] in a preliminary ruling in civil proceedings,[168] the Court of Appeal held that there was no reason in principle why articles in a newspaper showing V in an unfavourable light should not constitute harassment of V. The decision in *Thomas* confirms that the parameters of this offence are very broad indeed, and it may well be that prosecutions on particular facts will be open to objections under Articles 7 (non-retroactivity), 10 (freedom of expression), and 11 (freedom of peaceful assembly and association) of the ECHR.

(ii) "Persuasive" harassment of others

The second, subsidiary, harassment offence, contrary to section 1(1A), has many features in common with the primary offence, contrary to section 1(1), but also points of difference. First, at least two persons must be subjected to conduct which *involved* harassment. For the primary offence, one or more persons must be subjected to conduct which *amounted* to harassment. The difference between involving and amounting is far from obvious: if conduct does not amount to harassment it can hardly involve harassment. Perhaps different terms are used because for the primary offence D need not have any particular objective, it being enough that his conduct amounts to harassment. By contrast, for the subsidiary offence, D must intend to persuade at least two persons not to engage in some form of lawful conduct. The different phraseology is perhaps to emphasise that conduct which is part of a bigger scheme than harassment for harassment's sake is within the subsidiary offence. (And yet the same is true of the primary offence!) Be that as it may, this form of the harassment offence seems designed to cover a situation where, say, D, an animal rights activist, seeks to persuade employees not to continue working for a company that tests its products on animals. If her persuasive efforts constitute harassment in the opinion of a reasonable person, and if a judgment is made that she should have known this, she will be guilty of the subsidiary offence.

(iii) Causing fear of violence

The offence created by section 4 has been interpreted as an alternative version of the section 2 offence. Consequently, it must be established that D has put V in fear

---

[165] Protection from Harassment Act 1997, s. 7(3A)(b), as inserted by the Criminal Justice and Police Act 2001, s. 44.

[166] *Colohan* [2001] EWCA Crim 1251.

[167] [2001] EWCA Civ 1233, [2002] EMLR 78.

[168] The 1997 Act also provides civil remedies for harassment.

of violence on at least two occasions by a course of conduct which amounts to harassment.[169] It should be noted that, unlike assault, the fear of violence need not be fear of immediate violence. Yet a blatant threat, say, to kneecap V next Wednesday will not of itself fall within section 4 because V's fear of violence must be caused by D on at least two occasions. Moreover, V must fear that violence *will* be used against her.[170] A well-founded apprehension even of the probability of violence will not suffice.[171] In the light of these factors, Lord Steyn in *Ireland and Burstow* considered that the Act offered deficient protection to recipients of telephone calls or messages redolent with threatened violence but short on the specifics of intended action.[172] Lord Steyn was right.

Moreover, it is necessary to show that there was a course of conduct which amounted to harassment and that there must be some nexus between the two or more occasions when V was caused to fear violence. In *Curtis*,[173] the Court of Appeal held that six incidents involving the use or threats of violence by one partner against the other did not constitute a "course of conduct" when this occurred over a nine-month period, particularly when the aggressive behaviour was interspersed with affection.

The offence under section 4 does not require any intent or recklessness on the part of D in causing V to fear violence. It is enough that a reasonable person would have foreseen that result. It might be thought that an offence which can be committed negligently should not have a maximum sentence of imprisonment for five years. Lord Steyn, on the other hand, considered five years too low a sentence for the worst kind of offending within section 4. That may well be true for cases where D has intentionally subjected V to a reign of terror with devastating effect. It would have been far better had there been gradations of offence in terms of a hierarchy of intention, recklessness and, if need be, negligence, with differential penalties attached.

(iv) Stalking

The Protection of Freedoms Act 2012 created two new offences specifically relating to stalking.[174] The first of these is a summary offence of stalking, contrary to section 2A of the Protection from Harassment Act 1997. This involves a course of conduct which is in breach of section 1(1) of the Act and which amounts to stalking of another person; namely, that the conduct amounts to harassment of another person, the acts or omission are associated

---

[169] *Curtis* [2010] EWCA Crim 123, [2010] 1 WLR 2770, para. 20; *Widdows* [2011] EWCA Crim 1500. Concern about the interpretation of the offence requiring proof of harassment was expressed by the same court in *Haque* [2011] EWCA Crim 1871, [2012] 1 Cr App R 5, para. 69. The court recognised that the need to establish harassment meant that the prosecution had to establish that the conduct was targeted at an individual; that it was calculated to alarm, or cause distress to, that person; and that it was oppressive. The emphasis on "calculation" can be considered to contradict the objective test of fault, namely that a reasonable person would have foreseen that V would fear violence.

[170] Fear that D will be violent to someone other than V does not suffice: *Caurti v. DPP* [2002] Crim LR 131.

[171] In *Henley* [2002] Crim LR 582, it was held to be an error to rule that it sufficed that V was "seriously frightened as to what *might* happen".

[172] [1998] AC 147, 153. This might now be covered by the new offence of stalking which causes serious alarm or distress. See below § 11.8(iv).

[173] [2010] EWCA Crim 123, [2010] 1 WLR 2770. See also *Widdows* [2011] EWCA Crim 1500.

[174] See MacEwan, "The New Stalking Offences in English Law: Will They Provide Effective Protection from Cyberstalking?" [2012] *Crim LR* 767.

with stalking, and D knows or ought to know that conduct amounts to harassment.[175] Particular examples are given of acts or omissions which are associated with stalking,[176] such as following a person, contacting them, monitoring their use of electronic communication, watching or spying on them, or interfering with their property.

In addition, a new offence is created of perpetrating acts or omissions associated with stalking which either (i) cause another to fear violence on at least two occasions[177] or (ii) cause serious alarm or distress which has a substantial effect on another's usual day-to-day activities.[178]

For the most part, these new offences add nothing to the existing offences of harassment, save to label criminal conduct specifically as stalking, although liability is expanded to cover causing serious alarm or distress. The maximum sentence for both stalking offences is the same as for the equivalent harassment offences. The intention behind the creation of the new offences is to label criminal conduct specifically as stalking; even though a stalker may still be charged with one of the original harassment offences, if their course of conduct can be described as stalking then it is more likely and more appropriate that they will be prosecuted under the new offences.

The Protection from Harassment Act 1997 is an unimpressive measure; a hasty product driven by political exigencies with legislative revisions and extensions made in the same vein, the most recent largely being of cosmetic effect to ensure that the language of stalking is now used. The legislation uses undefined terms and takes objective liability to the extent of deeming D to know of matters which were the thoughts and motivations of others at occasions where he was not present. A better solution to the genuine problem of threats, harassment, and stalking is required.

§ 11.9 Racial and religious aggravation

There is considerable evidence that a significant number of violent attacks which take place in public are racially motivated and that the number of such attacks is on the increase.[179] Part II of the Crime and Disorder Act 1998 sought to strengthen the law's response to such attacks by providing that a racist motivation for violent and some cognate offences will constitute a racially aggravated form of the offence (a separate offence) subject to higher penalties.[180] Pursuant to section 39 of the Anti-Terrorism Crime and Security Act 2001, religious aggravation is folded into this legislation on the same terms. Of the offences we have examined in this chapter, the maximum term of imprisonment for a racially or religiously aggravated assault is two years' imprisonment; for racially or religiously aggravated

---

[175] Protection of Harassment Act 1997, s. 2A(2).

[176] *Ibid.*, s. 2A(3).

[177] *Ibid.*, s. 4A(b)(i).

[178] *Ibid.*, s. 4A(b)(ii).

[179] In 1988 there were 4,383 race hate crimes reported to the police, rising to 12,222 reports in 1995–6: Home Office, *Racial Violence and Harassment: A Consultation Document* (1997). In 2014/15 there were 42,930 race hate crimes reported to the police: *Hate Crime England and Wales 2014/15* (Home Office). This was 82% of the 52,238 hate crimes recorded. 11% were sexual orientation hate crimes; 6% were religion hate crimes; 5% were disability hate crimes; and 1% were transgender hate crimes.

[180] Crime and Disorder Act 1998, s. 28. Note also the Public Order Act 1986, ss. 18–23 of which create offences of stirring up hatred by reference to race, religion, or sexual orientation.

assault occasioning actual bodily harm, seven years; for racially or religiously aggravated malicious wounding or grievous bodily harm, seven years; for racially or religiously aggravated harassment, two years; and for racially or religiously aggravated putting people in fear of violence, seven years.[181] As the aggravated version of these offences are separate offences in their own right, the element of D's hostility to V based on V's race or religion is something that has to be proved at trial or conceded by the defence. There is no provision for a racially or religiously aggravated version of wounding or causing grievous bodily harm with intent. As the maximum penalty for that offence is life imprisonment there is, of course, no scope for further aggravation. However, section 145 of the Criminal Justice Act 2003 provides that racial or religious motivation is an aggravating factor in sentencing for all offences, save for those covered by the Crime and Disorder Act 1998, and if either form of hostility is proved there must be an announcement to that effect in open court.[182] This provision does not, however, increase the maximum sentence for the crime, unlike the Crime and Disorder Act. The trial judge can have regard to racial or religious motivation as an aggravating factor in sentencing even though D could have been but was not charged with the aggravated offence contrary to the Crime and Disorder Act 1998.[183]

Racial or religious aggravation is defined in section 28 of the Crime and Disorder 1998. The section provides:

(1) An offence is racially or religiously aggravated … if—

(a) at the time of committing the offence, or immediately before or after doing so, the offender demonstrates towards the victim of the offence hostility based on the victim's membership (or presumed membership) of a racial or religious group; or

(b) the offence is racially motivated (wholly or partly) by hostility towards members of a racial or religious group based on their membership of that group.

(2) In subsection (1) (a) above—

"membership" in relation to a racial or religious group includes association with members of that group;

"presumed" means presumed by the offender.

(3) It is immaterial for the purposes of paragraph (a) or (b) of subsection (1) above whether or not the offender's hostility is also based, to any extent, on a factor not mentioned in that paragraph.

(4) In this section "racial group" means a group of persons defined by reference to race, colour, nationality (including citizenship) or ethnic or national origins.

(5) In this section "religious group" means a group of persons defined by reference to religious belief or lack of religious belief.

If D assaults V, a member of a different racial or religious group, the fact that his victim belongs to a different group will not of itself establish the element of racial aggravation. The possibility of proving racial aggravation will arise only if D is aware that V is a member of a particular racial group or presumes, rightly or wrongly, that V is a member of the group.

---

[181] See ss. 29 and 32 of the Crime and Disorder Act 1998.

[182] Section 146 of the Criminal Justice Act 2003 provides that sentences can be increased by aggravation relating to disability, sexual orientation, or transgender identity.

[183] *O'Leary* [2015] EWCA Crim 1306. See Owusu-Bempah and Walters, "Racially Aggravated Offences: When Does Section 145 of the Criminal Justice Act 2003 Apply?" [2016] *Crim LR* 116.

Ultimate proof of racial or religious aggravation may take two forms. First, under section 28(1)(a) of the Crime and Disorder Act 1998 the prosecution may be able to prove that at the time of the offence, or immediately before or after it, D "demonstrated" racial or religious hostility towards V based on V's membership or presumed membership of a racial or religious group. Here, the racial hostility is something extraneous to the offence itself. It is something that accompanies offences, not something to be inferred from an offence *per se*, even if D is aware of V's membership of a particular racial or religious group. So, something like a racial or religious insult aimed at V immediately before, during, or after the attack is required.[184] It is not necessary to show that racial or religious hostility is at least part of the explanation for the attack: it suffices that hostility is manifested in some way.

By contrast, under section 28(1)(b) it must be proved that in the absence of any demonstration of racial or religious hostility, D's offence was motivated by hostility towards V, a hostility explained by V's membership or presumed membership of a racial or religious group.

What constitutes membership of a racial group has been widely construed. In *White*,[185] D referred to V as an "African". This was held sufficiently specific to indicate hostility to V because of her membership of a racial group. Similarly in *M (A minor)*[186] "bloody foreigner" sufficed, as did "immigrant doctor" in *A-G's Reference (No. 4 of 2004)*.[187] These are undeniably broad interpretations of what constitutes membership of a racial group; but any other approach would lead to some unedifying distinctions and benefit those who express their racial hostility in a coarse-grained way. A similar approach to "religious group" is more problematic. Understandably, there is no legislative list of approved religions. So a cult where V claims some special relationship with the supernatural, and persuades D and other followers that the best guarantee of the afterlife is to follow his precepts, may well constitute a religious group. Should D lose his faith in V and physically attack him on the ground that he is a false prophet, his attack may be considered aggravated by religious hostility. That hardly seems in the public interest.

Sensibly, what makes for hostility is undefined.[188] Where abusive language is used immediately before, during, or immediately after the offence, making pejorative references to race or religion hostility of the relevant kind will typically be present. But not invariably. In *DPP v. Pal*,[189] D referred to V as a "brown Englishman" and a "white man's arse-licker". Racial aggravation was held not to be present: D had taken exception to V's conduct, not to his race. D's hostility to V was based on his conception of how members of their racial group should interact with members of another racial group. The decision is understandable as an interpretation of the provisions but is uncomfortable in terms of social policy.[190]

---

[184] In *Parry* [2004] EWHC 3112, an admission to the police 20 minutes after D's attack that his attack on V was racially motivated was held to be a demonstration of racial hostility immediately after the attack.

[185] [2001] 1 WLR 1352.

[186] [2004] EWHC 1453; similarly *Rogers* [2005] EWCA Crim 2863.

[187] [2005] EWCA Crim 889.

[188] Walters, "Conceptualizing Hostility for Hate Crime Law: Minding 'the Minutiae' when Interpreting Section 28(1)(a) of the Crime and Disorder Act 1998" (2014) 34 *OJLS* 47 argues that D should be considered to have demonstrated hostility where she is aware that her behaviour is likely to be received as indicating hostility towards V's identity.

[189] [2000] Crim LR 756.

[190] In *Mcfarlane* [2002] EWHC Admin 485, *Pal* was said to be heavily dependent on its facts and that normally, where a racialist epithet was used during an attack, racial hostility would be made out.

Suppose that V marries outside her religious group, an act of apostasy according to the group's religious norms, for which the sanction is a severe beating. The beating would not be religiously aggravated on the logic of *Pal*.[191] Perhaps the most disturbing feature of *Pal* is that it comports with the grain of the provisions. But protection can also be needed from the strictures of religion and claims of dominion or containment based on ethnic loyalties.[192]

Proof of an attack by D on a member of a different racial or religious group will not, of itself, establish racial or religious hostility. That fact will not even be prima facie proof of hostility if there is evidence of some non-racial or religious explanation for the attack. On the other hand, as a matter of evidence, if the prosecution can prove that D knew or presumed that V was a member of a different racial or religious group and there is no overt explanation for D's aggression (such as a non-religious or non-racial quarrel), D may legitimately be expected to raise some credible evidence of non-racial or non-religious motivation. If he does not do so, the prosecution's allegation of racial or religious hostility is likely to be sustained. In the absence of a credible explanation, actions may be allowed to speak loudly and clearly.[193]

The Law Commission was asked by the Ministry of Justice to review aspects of the current law on hate crime, particularly whether the aggravated offences should be extended to include other protected characteristics of disability, sexual orientation, or transgender identity. In its report,[194] the Law Commission decided that, before it could make any such recommendation, there needed to be wider review of the operation of the existing aggravated offences, in part to identify a theoretical framework for determining which protected characteristics should be included in hate crime legislation. Pragmatically, however, the Law Commission acknowledged that, if such a review was not possible, the aggravated offences should be extended to include these additional characteristics, which are already relevant to the enhanced sentencing regime under the Criminal Justice Act 2003.

§ 11.10 Reforming the law of violence

Judges and commentators have expressed a great deal of dissatisfaction with the law relating to non-fatal offences. The main focus of discontent has been with sections 47, 20, and 18 of the OAPA 1861, by far the most important sections of that Act in terms of the number of

---

[191] In *Pal*, the court claimed that its reasoning would not extend, in the Court's own example, to a white man attacking another white man because of the latter's association with a black woman; but it is hard to see the difference in principle between this example and the facts of the case.

[192] Section 28(5) of the Crime and Disorder Act 1998 makes some movement in this direction by defining religious group to mean a group defined either by religion or the absence of religion. Hence an attack on atheists, where hostility to atheism is demonstrated as part of the motivation for the attack, will constitute religious aggravation.

[193] Inferences against D may be drawn from a failure to give evidence: Criminal Justice and Public Order Act 1994, s. 35.

[194] Law Commission, *Hate Crime: Should the Current Offences be Extended?*, Law Com. No. 348 (2014). See Bakalsi, "Legislating Against Hatred: The Law Commission's Report on Hate Crime" [2015] *Crim LR* 192. See also Owusu-Bempah, "Prosecuting Hate Crime: Procedural Issues and the Future of the Aggravated Offences" (2015) 35 *LS* 443, who argues that the aggravated offences should be repealed, with reliance on the enhanced sentencing regime alone.

prosecutions. On one view, these offences may be viewed as an escalating ladder of gravity, in terms of the harm caused to the victim. From that perspective, the coverage provided is quirky and not easily rationalised. Section 47 requires an assault or battery which must occasion actual bodily harm. No mental element is required in respect of the bodily harm. What degree of directness is required for a battery is unclear. The maximum penalty for section 47 is five years' imprisonment, the same as for malicious wounding or infliction of grievous bodily harm under section 20, which does not reflect the fact that section 20 is regarded as a more serious offence.

In turn, section 20 concerns two different forms of harm—wounds and grievous bodily harm—which may well involve very different orders of magnitude. Whereas grievous bodily harm is by definition serious, a wound may be very minor. There seems no obvious reason to bracket wounds and serious bodily harm within the actus reus of one offence. Further, under section 20 a minimum mens rea of recklessness is required, but not as to a wound or grievous bodily harm; foresight of some, minor, bodily harm suffices.

Section 18 has given less ground for criticism. Although wounds and grievous bodily harm are again bracketed together, there must always be proof of an intent to cause grievous bodily harm or to resist lawful arrest or detention. This ensures that some measure of serious wrongdoing is involved for this very serious offence with its maximum term of life imprisonment. Nonetheless, it remains an offence that draws together things not obviously connected. Questions relating to arrest and detention are best dealt with in the family of offences relating to assaults on the police and other criminal justice officials. The term grievous bodily harm covers a wide range of injury, from, say, a broken arm to horrendous life-threatening injuries. Moreover, the offence takes two very different forms: as either an offence where a serious harm was intentionally caused or an offence where a serious harm was intended but not brought about.

In 1998, the Home Office proposed replacement offences that would constitute a simpler and more coherent pattern of offences,[195] largely reflecting recommendations made in 1993 by the Law Commission.[196] More recently, the Law Commission[197] has reconsidered these proposals and, whilst broadly endorsing them, has made some significant modifications. The Law Commission has identified various criticisms of the existing offences: these include the thought that there are too many offences in the OAPA 1861 which are narrowly defined and differentiated by highly particularised factual scenarios; conversely, other offences, such as section 18, tend to assimilate morally different albeit related situations; the order and grading of the offences is unclear; and the language used is archaic and words are used without a clear meaning. At the heart of the Law Commission's recommendations is the need for a logical hierarchy of offences and recognition of the principle of correspondence between mens rea and actus reus, such that the harm which needs to be intended or foreseen matches the harm done.

The Law Commission proposes the replacement of sections 18, 20, and 47 with three new offences:

(i)   Intentionally causing serious injury to another, for which the maximum sentence would be life imprisonment.

---

[195] Home Office, *Violence: Reforming the Offences Against the Person Act 1861* (1998).
[196] Law Com. No. 218, *Legislating the Criminal Code: Offences Against the Person and General Principles* (1993).
[197] Law Com. No, 361, *Reform of Offences Against the Person* (2015).

(ii) Recklessly causing serious injury to another, for which the maximum sentence would be seven years.
(iii) Intentionally or recklessly causing injury to another, for which the maximum sentence would be five years.

Although the Home Office had recommended that intention (including oblique intention) and recklessness should be defined, the Law Commission considers that this is not necessary, since such terms should be understood in accordance with the general law. It is noteworthy that the language of injury is used, without distinguishing between bodily harm and wounding. It would follow that, for the most serious offences, wounding as presently defined will only constitute relevant harm if it can be characterised as serious. Further, injury would be defined to include both the transmission of disease, pending a wider review of the law on transmission of disease to determine whether specialised offences are required, and recognised psychiatric conditions—but not, as the Home Office Bill originally stated, all mental harm, which would have gone far beyond the existing law and beyond the domain of offences of violence.

For many criminal lawyers, the enactment of these proposals in place of sections 47, 20, and 18 would constitute a significant advance. The most obvious feature of the proposed offences is the absence of clutter; the expression is simple and direct, with actus reus linked to mens rea through nothing more than a causal connection. The mens rea terms are unexceptionable from the perspective of subjectivism and the correspondence principle. It is difficult to imagine that this scheme of offences would give rise to the same number of appeals, confusions, and complexities as does the current order.

If simplicity and economy of means are taken to be virtues (and this has been contested), there are nonetheless some criticisms that may be offered. The proposals draw a distinction between injuries and serious injuries, yet provide no guidance on seriousness. As under the current law, what constitutes a serious injury will be a question of fact. Potentially, this brings an unduly large swathe of injury into the most grave offence—intentionally causing serious injury—which, like the present section 18, carries a maximum term of life imprisonment. There is something to be said in favour of a greater particularity here, with a tripartite division of physical harm offences into cases of (i) injury, (ii) serious injury, and (iii) grievous injury. These terms should have some degree of definition, with grievous injury confined to physical or mental harm that causes extreme pain and suffering, significant disfigurement, or significant disability.

In the sphere of serious injury, the proposals sharply demarcate causing serious injury with intent (maximum penalty life imprisonment) from recklessly causing serious injury (seven years maximum). For cases of causing injury, however, there is but one offence which can be committed either intentionally or recklessly. It is difficult to appreciate why the distinction between intent and recklessness loses its moral significance for cases involving lesser injury.[198]

---

[198] If, as we believe, the distinction between intention and recklessness retains moral purchase at this lower level of offending, the provision of separate offences of intentionally causing injury and recklessly causing injury would provide the further advantage that the former offence, being a crime where the culpability is confined to intent, would not come within the *Majewski* principle: see further below, § 18.3.

The conditional welcome given here for these proposals was by no means universally shared among reactions to the Law Commission's original proposals in 1993, and much of the criticism expressed then remains applicable to the Law Commission's new recommendations. Horder complained that such reforms would strip the law of too much moral substance.[199] He emphasised the importance of "representative" or "fair" labelling,[200] which is achieved only if the definition of an offence conveys an accurate moral picture of what the defendant has done. To that end, he favoured the use of such graphic terms as "castrates, disables, disfigures, or dismembers … or removes an internal body part" in the definition of offences.[201] One may question, however, whether the awful details of the worst forms of violence need to feature in the *definition* of offences. Such cases receive close attention from the media and the factual details are widely disseminated in the press. The moral resonance of an offence need not require details of the *modus operandi*. For example, the term "murder" has great evocative power. Murder may extend over a vast range of particulars from, say, a painless lethal injection to agonising and protracted forms of death; but there is no need to identify gruesome ways of killing in order to convey the gravity of murder. Besides, if charges were to contain the amount of particularity recommended by Horder, there arises the risk of unmeritorious arguments on the applicability of the charge brought. Arguments concerning whether D's act was a disablement or disfigurement would be thoroughly unattractive. That said, we have commented already on the fact that the term "serious injury" is too broad and that a greater degree of subdivision and definition is required. To this extent Horder is clearly right.

Another critical voice was that of Gardner.[202] For him, sections 47, 20, and 18 of the OAPA 1861 each has a distinctive value and ambit, which would be swept away by the proposals. Gardner argues that the central point about section 47 is that liability is triggered by an assault or battery: "By committing an assault one changes one's own normative position, so that certain adverse consequences and circumstances which would not have counted against one but for one's original assault now count against one automatically, and add to one's crime".[203] On this view, it is no surprise that section 47 has the same maximum penalty as section 20, that no mental element is required for the occasioning of actual bodily harm, and that (according to Gardner) "occasion" is a broader term than cause.

In Gardner's scheme, section 20 concerns the *infliction* of violence, which can take in a broader field of conduct than assault but keeps the offence away from such things as transmitting diseases. Here some degree of foresight should be required about the possible infliction of physical harm. Section 18, in dealing with *intended* consequences, appropriately moves to a broader *causal* standard when determining the presence of actus reus. We cannot discuss here whether this schema is persuasive in normative terms. What can be said is that Gardner's schema has never been firmly established as part of English law. In actus reus terms, there was for many years a close association between sections 47 and 20, as it was considered that "inflict" required proof of an assault or battery. Although that

---

[199] "Rethinking Non-fatal Offences Against the Person" (1994) 14 *OJLS* 335.
[200] See above, § 2.4.
[201] Horder, "Rethinking Non-fatal Offences Against the Person" (1994) 14 *OJLS* 335, 345.
[202] "Rationality and the Rule of Law in Offences Against the Person" [1994] *CLJ* 502.
[203] *Ibid.*, 509.

connection was relaxed in *Wilson*,[204] there remains considerable doubt about the extent to which battery itself can accommodate forms of indirectly caused injury, rendering problematic the degree of disassociation between sections 47 and 20 when physical injury is in issue. Moreover, there is no authority that "occasion" in section 47 is a broader term than cause, although there is authority that it is synonymous with cause.[205] Indeed when psychiatric injury is an issue, "inflict" itself has been interpreted as "cause",[206] making for points of contact between sections 20 and 18 as well as section 47. Gardner seems to be seeking a preservation order on a house never built. The degrees of difference and similarity between the three offences follow no overarching pattern, a fact which by itself makes a case for reform.

Finally, something should be said about the proposals to reform assault and battery. The Law Commission envisages that the existing offences of assault and battery should be replicated in legislation by two renamed offences, with "battery" being called "physical assault" and what is presently called "assault" being called "threatened assault". This would have the virtue of fairly labelling the offences by reference to the distinction between contact and threat. The language of "physical assault" might be criticised, however, because it suggests direct physical contact between D and V; whereas under the existing law of battery, force can be applied indirectly to establish the offence.[207] This would be reflected in the definition of "physical assault" which would be committed if D intentionally or recklessly applies force to, or causes an impact on, the body of another. "Threatened assault" would be committed where D intentionally or recklessly causes the other to believe that any such force or impact is imminent.

The Law Commission also recommends the creation of a new offence of aggravated assault, which would be a summary offence with a maximum sentence of 12 months. This offence would be committed where D committed a physical or threatened assault that causes injury, regardless of whether D intended or was reckless about causing the injury. The Law Commission's reasons for recommending this offence are unconvincing: namely, to bridge the gap between the lowest level offence of assault, for which the maximum sentence is six months, and of causing injury, for which the maximum sentence is five years, by creating an offence to provide for cases where relatively low levels of injury are caused. The Law Commission considers that such an offence would provide an appropriate label for the person who causes injury but who does not deserve a sentence of more than 12 months, and would also allow for considerable cost-saving by confining this offence to Magistrates' Courts. But liability for this aggravated assault would be constructive, since no mens rea is required regarding the injury caused; undermining one of the Law Commission's core principles for reform of the offences against the person, namely the correspondence principle. Further, injury is undefined, so it will be unclear where the lines should be drawn between "physical assault" and "aggravated assault", and between that offence and the offence of causing injury. It would have been preferable for the Law Commission to recommend that

---

[204] [1984] AC 242 (HL).
[205] *Roberts* (1971) 56 Cr App R 95 (CA).
[206] *Burstow* [1998] AC 147 (HL).
[207] *K* (1990) 91 Cr App R 23 (CA). See above, § 11.3(i).

the maximum sentence for both physical and threatened assault be increased from 6 to 12 months, in order to enable the judge to reflect the aggravating effect of injury in the sentence imposed.

Although the Law Commission's proposals for reform are not perfect, they are workable and generally build sensibly on the current law with useful simplification and clarification: a striking contrast to more recent legislation. It is vital that Parliament enacts these proposals without delay.

12

THE PRINCIPAL SEXUAL OFFENCES

The regulation of sexual activity by the criminal law is not easy. The law must respond to wrongful and harmful sexual behaviour, and ensure that sexual autonomy—a core part of personal identity—is respected. These demands will not push unilaterally in the direction of expansive criminalisation. Sometimes the idea of sexual autonomy will tell against criminalisation. Although the majority of citizens might view a certain sexual activity as distasteful, this is not necessarily reason enough for the criminal law to become involved. There are some aspects of sexual behaviour that are simply "not the criminal law's [and thus the public's] business", and which must remain part of the private sphere of sexual morality.[1] Even if this tension between reacting to public wrongdoing and respecting personal choice is recognised, resolving it is difficult. Compounding the problem is the need for certainty and clarity in the criminal law.[2] Drawing such lines in a complex and sensitive area such as sexual relations is fraught with challenges.

English law's main attempt to mediate these competing concerns is contained in the Sexual Offences Act 2003 (SOA 2003), which came into force on 1 May 2004.[3] The Act was intended to "to provide a clear, coherent and effective set of laws that increase protection, enable the appropriate punishment of abusers and ensure that the law is fair and non-discriminatory".[4] It also aimed to address the low conviction rate in sexual offences.[5] These aims are laudable and, to the extent that it achieves them, the SOA 2003 is an improvement on the previous law. As will be seen in this chapter, however, many aspects of the SOA 2003 are unsatisfactory. Some parts of the legislation are vague or insufficiently nuanced, leaving the courts to ensure the effective working of its provisions. There is also a tendency towards

---

[1] *Committee on Homosexual Offences and Prostitution: Report* (CM 247, 1957) 62.

[2] Above, § 2.3.

[3] Some sexual offences are dealt with in other legislation. See, for instance, the offence of "disclosing private sexual photographs and films with intent to distress"—a response to "revenge pornography"—in s. 33 of the Criminal Justice and Courts Act 2015.

[4] From a Home Office press release, quoted by Arabella Thorp in Parliamentary Research Paper 03/62 (10 July 2003). On the genesis of the 2003 Act, see: Home Office, *Setting the Boundaries: Reforming the Law on Sex Offences* (2000); Lacey, "Beset by Boundaries: The Home Office Review of Sex Offences" [2001] *Crim LR* 3; Rumney, "The Review of Sex Offences and Rape Law Reform: Another False Dawn?" (2001) 64 *MLR* 890; *Protecting the Public: Strengthening Protection against Sex Offenders and Reforming the Law on Sexual Offences* (CM 5668, 2002); Home Affairs Committee, *Sexual Offences Bill* (Fifth Report of Session 2002–03, HC 639, 2003); *The Government Reply to the Fifth Report from the Home Affairs Committee Session 2002–2003* (HC 639); *Sexual Offences Bill* (CM 5986, 2003).

[5] See *An Overview of Sexual Offending in England and Wales* (2013), available at www.gov.uk/government/uploads/system/uploads/attachment_data/file/214970/sexual-offending-overview-jan-2013.pdf.

verbosity and overlapping offence definitions within the statute,[6] which leaves much in the hands of prosecutorial discretion.

This chapter begins by outlining the law regarding the main non-consensual sexual offences. It then considers offences relating to children, which do not require proof that the complainant was not consenting, before considering certain familial sexual offences.

§ 12.1 Non-consensual sexual offences: common elements

The SOA 2003 contains four major offences that penalise D in respect of non-consensual sexual acts: rape (section 1); assault by penetration (section 2); sexual assault (section 3); and causing a person to engage in sexual activity without consent (section 4).[7] These offences replace the former version of rape and the offence of indecent assault.[8] They also extend the law's reach, and alter the labelling and punishment of certain conduct that was already criminal. For instance, non-consensual digital penetration of the vagina or anus would previously have been an indecent assault (maximum penalty: 10 years' imprisonment), but is now assault by penetration (maximum penalty: life imprisonment). Much conduct that would previously have fallen under (now abolished) offences relating to obtaining sexual activity by threat or deception now falls under the main non-consensual offences, such as rape.

Before getting further into the specific elements of the SOA 2003's non-consensual offences, it is useful to consider the general elements that they have (by and large) in common. First, each of the non-consensual offences involves "sexual" conduct (this requirement is implicitly satisfied in every case of rape; it is an explicit requirement in sections 2–4). The Act makes provision for determining when conduct is sexual,[9] and we consider this provision in § 12.2. Secondly, all four offences involve the absence of the complainant's consent.[10] The absence of consent is centrally important to identifying the wrong that D has perpetrated against V.[11] Consent is defined in the Act, but in such a vague manner that a significant, and at times problematic, body of case law has built up around the statutory definition. Moreover, the Act creates various evidential[12] and

---

[6] By way of contrast, to modernise the "core" areas of non-consensual sex, plus the sexual abuse of minors, in 1996 the Italian legislature inserted new provisions into the Italian Penal Code that consisted of nine articles, creating four criminal offences. To cover the same ground, the English legislature has found it necessary to enact 29 sections creating no less than 21 separate offences, many of which overlap with one another. One of the proclaimed aims of the SOA 2003 was to make the law "clear and coherent". "Convoluted and prolix" was what we got.

[7] For exposition and critique of these four offences, see Temkin and Ashworth, "The Sexual Offences Act 2003: Rape, Sexual Assaults and the Problems of Consent" [2004] *Crim LR* 328.

[8] Formerly found in the Sexual Offences Act 1956, ss. 1 (rape), 14–15 (indecent assault).

[9] SOA 2003, s. 78.

[10] Following the approach adopted in the other chapters, the text will refer to the defendant as D and the complainant as V. Note, however, that the SOA 2003 refers to "A" (the person performing/causing the activity) and "B" (another person engaging in, or being subjected to, the activity). Note, further, that efforts have been taken, where possible, to avoid language that suggests D is necessarily male and V is necessarily female.

[11] Some view at least some instances of penile penetration as being *prima facie* wrongful, with consent providing a defence: Dempsey and Herring, "Why Sexual Penetration Requires Justification" (2007) 27 *OJLS* 467; Wall, "Sexual Offences and General Reasons Not to Have Sex" (2015) 35 *OJLS* 777. The orthodox view is that penile penetration is wrongful (even on a *prima facie* level) only if there is an absence of consent. For discussion, see Dsouza, "Undermining Prima Facie Consent in the Criminal Law" (2014) 33 *Law and Philosophy* 489, 494–6.

[12] SOA 2003, s. 75.

conclusive[13] presumptions about V's non-consent (an aspect of the actus reus) and about the lack of D's reasonable belief in consent (an aspect of mens rea). These matters are covered in § 12.3. Thirdly, D's conduct, or the activity caused by D, must be intended. This element is discussed in § 12.4. Finally, in relation to that part of the mens rea concerning V's lack of consent, the prosecution need only prove that D had no *reasonable belief* that V consented.[14] This form of mens rea is explored in § 12.5.

After these general matters have been covered, we will consider the specific definitions of each of the non-consensual offences.

§ 12.2 Common element 1: Sexual conduct or activity

The offences of assault by penetration, sexual assault, and causing a person to engage in sexual activity without consent explicitly require proof of *sexual* conduct or activity. The same requirement is not included explicitly in the definition of rape. The reason for this, presumably, is that the sexuality of penile penetration is self-evident. If so, then every case of penile penetration is, inherently, a case of *sexual* conduct under the SOA 2003. Were this not so, it could be argued that the definition of rape excludes "non-sexual" penile penetrations, as where D penetrates V not for sexual gratification but to cause distress and humiliation.[15] We think, however, that any argument that penetrations so motivated are not sexual should be rejected. The humiliation and distress arises from non-consensual connection of this particularly intimate, *sexual* sort, regardless of whether D seeks sexual gratification from his conduct.[16]

Moving beyond the context of penile penetration, section 78 of the Sexual Offences Act 2003 provides that activity is sexual if:

(a) whatever its circumstances or any person's purpose in relation to it, it is because of its nature sexual, or

(b) because of its nature it may be sexual and because of its circumstances or the purpose of any person in relation to it (or both) it is sexual.

In terms of providing a definition of the word "sexual", section 78 is deficient, because it is circular—i.e. it includes within its terms the very word that it sets out to define.[17] In effect, section 78 leaves open the basic question: what, exactly, is meant by the word "sexual"? Much interpretational work is left for the courts and juries. It is clear from its bifurcated structure that section 78 was intended to preserve the type of approach the courts had taken under the old law to the meaning of the word "indecent", in the (now abolished) offence of indecent assault.[18] Thus, although there is an obvious distinction between the words

---

[13] SOA 2003, s. 76.

[14] This is a fundamental shift from the subjective mens rea requirements contained in the former offences of indecent assault and rape. For an account of the previous law, see Chapter 12 of the first edition of this work.

[15] Under the old law of indecent assault, acts intended to humiliate could still be, by their nature, inherently indecent. See *Lemmon* [2005] EWCA Crim 994.

[16] It is noteworthy that Lord Ackner, in giving judgment for the House of Lords in *Court* [1989] AC 28, considered that intimate touching not motivated by sexual gratification would fall within the (former) offence of indecent assault. The relationship between indecency and sexual activity is considered later in this section.

[17] Bennion, "The Meaning of 'Sexual' in the Sexual Offences Bill" (2003) 167 *Justice of the Peace* 784.

[18] On which, see *Court* [1989] AC 28.

"indecent" (which implies wrongfulness) and "sexual" (which does not), some instructive illustrations can be drawn from the previous law on indecency.

(i) Activity "by its nature" sexual

Obvious examples of activities that would be *of their nature* sexual are penile penetration of the vagina, anus, or mouth; and oral sex. Beyond that, matters quickly become more complicated. In *Court*,[19] a decision concerning the old offence of indecent assault, it was said that the touching of a vagina was *inherently* indecent even if done for a non-sexual reason. Lord Ackner proposed a case where D, a doctor, takes a vaginal sample from V ostensibly for diagnosis but, in reality, for the purposes of some general research he is undertaking. Assuming no valid consent to the touching has been given in such circumstances, and that D had no belief in such consent, the offence of indecent assault would have been committed because D's act is (according to Lord Ackner) inherently indecent. A similar view was applied in *Tabassum*,[20] again to convict D of indecent assault, where D examined V's breasts for a non-sexual reason (namely, to build up a data set for a computer program he was developing for sale to doctors).[21] Should the same approach be taken under the SOA 2003?

On one view, a conviction for battery in Lord Ackner's example and in *Tabassum* might be said to underplay the gravity of the situation. Touching another person's private parts involves an affront to their modesty which makes the matter significantly more shocking than the sort of behaviour—pushes, kicks, and blows—constituting the usual type of common assault. Yet there are convincing reasons why such activities should not be considered to be *in their nature* sexual. Deeming all such touchings as sexual pushes the boundaries of the criminal law too far.[22] It seems wrong to conceive the taking of a vaginal swab, legitimately performed in order to screen for cervical cancer, as an inherently "sexual" activity, even though it involves an intimate touching. The medical professional taking the swab is not engaged in prima facie "sexual" conduct, which she must *justify* as preventive medicine. She is simply performing preventive medicine. Secondly, consider the case of a medically appropriate vaginal examination of a patient in circumstances where the patient cannot validly consent to sexual activity. (Baby girls, still in nappies, often get thrush. The practice nurse will take a vaginal swab to confirm the diagnosis.) Where the patient is a child, consent by a parent or someone *in loco parentis* may suffice.[23] If such consent is unavailable, however, resort to the defence of best-interests medical necessity will presumably be required in order to legitimate any such examination.[24] Again, however, necessity is a

---

[19] [1989] AC 28, 44 (Lord Ackner).

[20] [2000] 2 Cr App R 328.

[21] D carried out what may have been genuine research into breast cancer, aware that women whom he examined mistakenly assumed he was a medical doctor. The Court of Appeal held that their mistake vitiated the women's consent (as to which see below, § 12.3) and that, even if the research was genuine, the examinations were inherently indecent and therefore indecent assaults rather than mere assaults.

[22] Cf. Sullivan, "The Need for a Crime of Sexual Assault" [1989] *Crim LR* 331, where it was argued that the term "indecent assault", now superseded by "sexual assault", was both over-inclusive (in that the touching of intimate bodily parts was taken to be inherently indecent whatever D's reasons for touching V's body) and under-inclusive (in that certain acts, even if done in pursuit of sexual arousal, would remain inherently decent).

[23] But can even a parent consent to something deemed to be sexual activity, on behalf of his or her child?

[24] See below, § 21.3(ii)(b).

defence against prima facie wrongdoing, and it is tenuous at best to suggest that the medical professional has done anything wrong in the circumstances.

There is nothing remotely sexual about a typical colonoscopy. If the foregoing arguments are persuasive, then touching a person's vagina, anus, or breasts cannot be an activity that is automatically and always—by its nature—sexual. In turn, this means that the category of activities falling within paragraph (a) is very small indeed, since that category is blind to the context. Perhaps it only includes penile penetration and oral sex. Most activities will fall within category (b) below. Indeed, it might justifiably be asked whether paragraph (a) is worth keeping, if all it covers is activities such as penile penetration and oral sex.

(ii) Activity ambiguous by nature

Where conduct is not inherently sexual, but "because of its nature it *may* be sexual", paragraph (b) of section 78 requires us to consider whether it *is* sexual "because of its circumstances or the purpose of any person in relation to it (or both)". The facts of *Court* provide an illustration of this type of case. D put V, a 12-year-old girl, over his knee and smacked her fully clothed bottom. If this was an act of unauthorised discipline for misbehaviour by V, it was a case of simple assault. D revealed that he had smacked V's bottom because of his "buttock fetish". Accordingly, D was guilty of indecent assault. He would nowadays be guilty of sexual assault.

The structure of s. 78, distinguishing acts that (a) simply *are* sexual from those that merely (b) *may* be sexual, might be taken to imply that certain acts, because of their nature, *cannot* be regarded as sexual under section 78 at all, even if they are done for sexual gratification. That was certainly the position under the old law of indecent assault. For example, it was held in *George*[25] that when, for fetishistic reasons, D touched the shoes that V was wearing, D's sexual motive could not turn an inherently decent act into an indecent one. The law of indecency was, as a matter of authority, swept away by the reforms introduced by section 78. The approach in *George* seems, however, to have survived, thanks to the decision in *H*.

In *H*, the Court of Appeal distinguished between two questions in the context of section 78(b): first, whether the touching because of its nature *could* be sexual; and secondly, whether the touching because of its circumstances or any person's purpose *was* sexual. The adoption of this distinction, which admittedly follows the wording of section 78(b), means that the Court of Appeal envisaged a category of conduct that can *never* be sexual (perhaps tellingly, no concrete examples of absolutely non-sexual conduct were provided). It was considered doubtful whether a sexual assault would occur on facts such as *George*, although the Court of Appeal acknowledged that the ultimate decision might be for the jury within the terms of section 78(b).[26] In other words, *George* might or might not involve a sexual assault. This uncertainty over whether the jury *should* be asked to decide whether D's conduct *was* sexual is problematic. Indeed, the first question posed in *H* is an unnecessary distraction. In our view, the practical answer is *always* going to be yes: the nature of *any* act can be changed into a sexual act if done in pursuit of sexual gratification. If D touches V in any manner to attain a state of arousal, it is submitted that a sexual assault has occurred

---

[25] [1956] Crim LR 52.
[26] *H* [2005] EWCA Crim 732, [2005] 1 WLR 2005, para. 11.

(assuming the touching is non-consensual, and D has the relevant mens rea). Such a touching is qualitatively different from, not to mention more threatening than, a touching where D, say, takes hold of V's shod foot in order to ascertain V's shoe size.[27]

Could section 78(b) be interpreted consistently with our position? We think it could be. Section 78(a) explains that some conduct is by its nature *always* sexual. Section 78(b) explains that there is a category of conduct that is not by its nature *always* sexual, but is *capable* of being so. This does not imply, in terms of logic, a category of conduct that can *never* be sexual, although it does imply a category of conduct (on our view, *all* conduct) that *can* be rendered sexual in the light of the circumstances and/or any person's purpose. On the view taken here, then, where D's conduct was not by its nature sexual, the sole relevant question for the jury should be whether the circumstances and/or any person's purpose rendered D's conduct sexual. In our view, there is neither practical nor statutory imperative for a category of inherently non-sexual activity.

(iii) Mens rea and section 78

A question left unanswered by section 78 is whether the defendant must have a form of mens rea with regard to the sexual nature of the activity, especially in cases where the activity has been classed as "sexual" on an objective basis, without reference to D's purpose: must D, for instance, intend it to be sexual, or know it to be sexual, or lack a reasonable belief that it is not sexual? Under the old law of indecency, it appeared that the defendant simply had to know or be reckless as to the circumstances that were unambiguously indecent, which suggests that no fault was actually required with regard to the indecent nature of the circumstances *itself*.[28] As the indecent nature of D's conduct was an evaluative concept, this approach is defensible and consistent with other areas of the criminal law—for instance, D's driving can be "dangerous", even if D himself thinks his driving is perfectly acceptable.

The same approach should be followed in relation to the SOA 2003's concept of sexual conduct: if D's conduct is of its nature sexual, D need only be aware of engaging in the relevant conduct.[29] If it is the circumstances that render D's conduct sexual, D need only be aware that those circumstances exist or might exist. In cases where it is D's purpose that *makes* the conduct sexual, there is presumably no additional requirement that D *recognises* this to be the case.

What if D digitally penetrates V's anus (without, of course, V's consent) in order to hurt V, rather than for any purpose of gaining sexual gratification? It is submitted that D's failure to advert to the inherently sexual nature of this conduct does not render D's act any less "sexual".[30] D has committed the section 2 offence of assault by penetration. D's motivation to hurt V does not change this.

---

[27] See, further, Sullivan, "The Need for a Crime of Sexual Assault" [1989] *Crim LR* 331.

[28] *Parsons* [1993] Crim LR 792.

[29] Admittedly, this subjective requirement of awareness runs counter to the more general objective approach to fault adopted in the SOA 2003. It could be that, consistent with that objective focus, the courts could impose liability where D *ought* to have been aware of engaging in the relevant conduct.

[30] Cf. *Hill* [2006] EWCA Crim 2575.

§12.3 Common element 2: the absence of consent

For each of the non-consensual offences, it must be proved that V did not consent. Consent has a specific meaning within the SOA 2003, which differs from the understanding of consent in other areas of the law (such as in non-sexual offences against the person).[31] Section 74 of the SOA 2003 provides that a person consents "if he agrees by choice, and has the freedom and capacity to make that choice". This definition is meant to offer more clarity than the previous law's rudimentary distinction between consent, however reluctant, and mere "submission" falling short of consent.[32]

Even if section 74 says more than the previous understanding of consent, it raises difficult questions. The matters of when a person has the "capacity" and "freedom" to consent are difficult to resolve. This has meant that a substantial body of case law on the statutory definition of consent has built up. It is thus useful to consider the factors that have been identified by the courts as going to the question of capacity and freedom to choose under section 74. The discussion here will be limited to the context of sections 1–4 of the SOA 2003. We shall consider general difficulties regarding consent's role in the criminal law in § 21.1.

To understand the type of situation that will fall under section 74, it is necessary first to explore sections 75 and 76 of the SOA 2003. These contain presumptions regarding the questions of consent and reasonable beliefs about consent. One objective of the SOA 2003 was to make it easier to convict sex offenders. Amongst the reasons why it was said to be difficult to secure their conviction under the old law were the problems of proving that the victim did not consent (especially when the only evidence of this was the complainant's word), and of proving that the defendant knew or was reckless about the complainant's non-consent. As will be seen below, it is no longer necessary to prove that the defendant had such knowledge or was reckless about the matter of consent: the absence of a reasonable belief in consent is the relevant mens rea element employed in relation to the absence of consent under the SOA 2003. Proving the absence of such a belief might still, however, be difficult. In the hope of alleviating these remaining evidential difficulties, the SOA 2003 sets out a range of situations where it will be presumed both that V did not consent *and* that D did not reasonably believe that V consented.

(i) *"Conclusive presumptions" about non-consent: section 76*

Section 76 of the SOA 2003 provides that it is to be *conclusively* presumed that V did not consent, and—equally importantly—that D did not reasonably believe V consented, where it is proved that D did the "relevant act" (e.g. in rape, that D penetrated V's vagina, anus or mouth with D's penis) and either:

(a) [D]intentionally deceived [V] as to the nature or purpose of the relevant act; [or]

(b) [D]intentionally induced [V] to consent to the relevant act by impersonating a person known personally to [V]

---

[31] See below, § 21.1.

[32] *Olugboja* [1982] QB 320 (CA). On *Olugboja*, see Gardner, "Appreciating *Olugboja*" (1996) 16 *LS* 275. As will be seen below, the distinction in *Olugboja* has been treated inconsistently under the SOA 2003.

Althhough expressed in terms of a rule of *evidence*, a "conclusive presumption" of this sort is in truth a rule of substantive law. The same notion could have been expressed more simply by saying "a person does not in law consent to a sexual act in the following circumstances";[33] and if the presence of these circumstances meant that V in law did not consent, and D was aware—or should have been aware—of those circumstances, D would then be deemed to have mens rea.

Section 76(a) envisages intentional deceptions as to two elements of a sexual activity: nature and purpose. It is useful to consider these matters separately.

(a) Deceptions regarding the nature of the activity

Implicit in the concept of the *nature* of an act is a distinction between the essence of the act and its non-essential attributes. Provided V understands the essence of the act, V's consent to that act will not be undermined even if V is mistaken or ignorant as to one or more non-essential attributes. An example of a deception as to an *essential* attribute is the old case of *Williams*,[34] where D—astonishingly—passed off his act of intercourse as *only* a medically approved method of improving V's singing voice.[35] Such a case would now be dealt with under section 76: if D was proved to have intentionally penetrated V's vagina with his penis, having *intentionally* deceived V by representing the activity as a medical procedure rather than a sexual activity, V would be presumed conclusively not to have consented, and D would be presumed conclusively not to have reasonably believed that V consented.

This leaves open the question what will be regarded merely as a *non-essential* attribute of conduct, a deception as to which will not trigger the conclusive presumptions in section 76. Some guidance can now be derived from cases decided under the SOA 2003. In *B* it was held that, where D does not disclose that he may pass on a sexually transmitted infection to V, this does not vitiate V's consent to the *sexual* act.[36] (At the same time, because V does not consent to the risk of infection, D may commit a non-sexual offence against the person if V is infected.)[37] Similarly, V's consent was not vitiated by applying section 76 in *Jheeta* when she agreed to have sex with D in the mistaken belief, induced by D, that he was suicidal and likely to kill himself unless she agreed.[38] (D was nevertheless convicted using the general

---

[33] See Tadros, "Rape without consent" (2006) 26 *OJLS* 515. Cf. Sexual Offences (Scotland) Act 2009, ss. 12, 14.

[34] [1923] 1 KB 340 (CA); see too *Flattery* (1877) 2 QBD 410.

[35] Importantly, the complainant in *Williams* did not know that the defendant was going to penetrate her with his penis. If she had known that, a difficult question would then have arisen over whether she was, in fact, deceived as to the "nature" of the activity—see below.

[36] [2006] EWCA Crim 2945, [2007] 1 WLR 1567; confirming *dicta* in *Dica* [2004] EWCA Crim 1103, [2004] QB 1257 and *Konzani* [2005] EWCA Crim 706, [2005] 2 Cr App R 14.

[37] In *Dica*, the Court of Appeal considered *Clarence* to be overruled by *Wilson* [1984] AC 242, *Ireland and Burstow* [1998] AC 147, and *Chan-Fook* (1994) 99 Cr App R 147, in so far as *Clarence* was authority to the effect that s. 20 of the OAPA 1861 required proof of assault or battery. It was held in *Dica* that to cause V to become HIV-positive was to cause her grievous bodily harm, and that a s. 20 offence would be committed if D was aware of the risk of infecting V and had not informed her of that risk, an analysis upheld in *Konzani*. A similar analysis was adopted in *Golding* [2014] EWCA Crim 889, where the infection was genital herpes. Interestingly, in *Dica* the Court considered that, notwithstanding the decision in *Brown* [1994] 1 AC 212, V could consent to certain risks in the context of sexual activity if informed of the risk. An example was given of a Roman Catholic married couple who could not practice protection despite the infection of one of the partners. As it had not been ascertained at trial in *Dica* whether the victim had known of the risk, the appeal resulted in an order for a retrial—at which he was again convicted.

[38] *Jheeta* [2007] EWCA Crim 1699, [2008] 1 WLR 2582.

definition of consent in section 74, as explained below.) In the same spirit, it was held in *Assange*[39] that the wearing or not wearing of a condom does not alter the "nature" of the sexual activity under section 76.[40] V's consent is thus not vitiated under section 76 where D tells V that he will use a condom but in fact does not. (The Divisional Court then went on to say that, if V had made it clear that she would only consent if D used a condom, D's intentional and deceptive failure to respect the condition would vitiate her consent in the light of section 74, a matter to which we return below.) Finally, D's deception regarding his or her gender might not alter the "nature" of the act, for the purposes of section 76 (though, again, it may be relevant under section 74).[41] The lesson to take from these cases is that the courts have been restrained when considering what will alter the "nature" of the act under section 76.

(b) Deceptions regarding the purpose of the activity

Similar conservatism has been visible in cases under section 76 concerning deceptions concerning the *purpose* of the act. Frequently, deception about the purpose of the act will be indistinguishable from a deception about its nature, but this is not inevitable. Consider a situation where V has been led by D to expect to be paid for providing sex.[42] On one view, V understands both that it is a sexual act (hence is not deceived about its nature) and that D's purpose is to have sex with V in order to achieve sexual gratification. V's position is the same as anyone who has offered a service as a consequence of a deception about payment. The gravamen of D's wrongdoing is dishonesty rather than sexual violation. On another view, V lacks any true understanding of the nature or purpose of D's conduct if, but for some ignorance of fact or false belief on V's part, consent would not have been given.[43] The first view is to be preferred, because the second is based on an unduly stringent view of consent in the context of very serious offences.[44] Suppose, for instance, that V, a prostitute, were to ask D if he is a supporter of Aberdeen Football Club. She informs him, truthfully,

---

[39] *Assange v. Swedish Prosecution Authority* [2011] EWHC 2849 (Admin). The issue arose in context of a European Arrest Warrant, for which Assange's liability to surrender depended on whether the acts in question would have amounted to criminal offences in England. The Divisional Court concluded that they would. Assange appealed unsuccessfully to the Supreme Court, but on grounds unrelated to this aspect of the Divisional Court's decision.

[40] Cf. the opinion of Abella, Moldaver and Karakatsanis JJ in *Hutchinson* 2014 SCC 19, [2014] 1 SCR 346.

[41] In *McNally* [2013] EWCA Crim 1051, [2014] QB 593, the Court of Appeal held that, as a matter of "common sense", the "nature" of D's act had been altered by D's deception regarding her gender: para. 26. The case was, however, decided under section 74's general definition of consent, the view being taken that section 76 was beside the point (para. 18). This treatment of the issue suggests that gender is not relevant to section 76, but *McNally* is by no means determinative. See, further, Rogers, "Further Developments under the Sexual Offences Act" [2013] 7 *Arch Rev* 7, 7–8. Rogers notes correctly that deciding the case under s. 74 means that the prosecution is relieved of having to prove *intentional* deception regarding gender, though the defendant's intentional deception appears to have been a factor employed by the court to find that no consent had been given in *McNally*.

[42] Cf. the pre-SOA 2003 case of *Linekar* [1995] QB 250 (CA).

[43] Herring, "Mistaken Sex" [2005] *Crim LR* 511.

[44] See further Gross, "Rape, Moralism and Human Rights" [2007] *Crim LR* 220; Herring, "Human Rights and Rape: A Reply to Hyman Gross" [2007] *Crim LR* 228; Bohlander, "Mistaken Sex, Political Correctness and Correct Policy" (2007) 71 *J Crim L* 412. For Herring's most recent thoughts, see Herring, "Rape and the Definition of Consent" (2014) 26 *NLSI Rev* 62.

that she would not have sex with him if he were in that category because of her strong allegiance to Dundee United. D untruthfully replies that he does not support Aberdeen and pays V for sexual intercourse. It would be inappropriate to conclusively presume, in such circumstances, that V did not consent and that D did not reasonably believe that V consented. That would, of course, make it a straightforward case of rape. Yet to characterise the unpleasantness of this episode as rape seems, in some important respects, to misrepresent what is wrong about it.[45] In turn, reliance on conclusive presumptions which turn it into a clear case of rape is troubling.

The purpose limb of section 76 has given rise to some difficult case law. In *Devonald*,[46] D, a man of 37, wishing to humiliate V, a boy of 16 who had jilted D's daughter, assumed the identity of a non-existent girl of 20 ("Cassey"). Having engaged V in a salacious email correspondence, D persuaded V to masturbate in front of a webcam. In a brief unreserved judgment, the Court of Appeal upheld D's conviction for causing a sexual activity without consent on the ground that D had deceived V as to the "nature or purpose of the act".

Devonald was trenchantly criticised,[47] and its scope appears now to be severely limited, seemingly applying only to cases where V fails *entirely* to appreciate D's purposes (in engaging, or having V engage, in the relevant activity). Contrast *Bingham*,[48] in which D (V's boyfriend) created a fake online persona ("Grant"). "Grant" persuaded V to take intimate photographs of herself and send them to him. "Grant" then threatened to send the photos to V's employer unless she continued to take intimate photographs for him. V complained to D, who in turn purported (valiantly) to kill "Grant". Next, however, D created a second persona ("Chad"). "Chad" claimed to know both about the photos and the murder of "Grant". When V eventually contacted the police, D was found to be behind all of this, and was charged with the section 4 offence (causing a person to engage in sexual activity without consent). D explained initially that he was trying to make V stand up for herself. He eventually admitted that he had the purpose of achieving sexual gratification. The Court of Appeal distinguished *Devonald* on the basis that, in that case, V had not appreciated D's purpose (humiliation) at all. V would, if asked, presumably have said that Devonald's purpose was to obtain sexual gratification, which it was not. In *Bingham*, V had presumably appreciated at least *part of* D's purpose (to obtain sexual gratification), even if another potential aspect of D's purpose (making V stand up for herself) was hidden. V would, if asked, then have said that D's purpose was to obtain sexual gratification, and at least in part it was.[49] This was enough to take the case out of section 76's conclusive presumptions. Indeed, the conclusive nature of the presumptions under section 76 evidently weighed heavily with the Court in *Bingham*.[50]

Bingham is correctly decided. None the less, while the reasoning in *Devonald* is unconvincing, and not easy to reconcile with that in *Bingham*, it is quite clearly the view of

---

[45] This might be disputed by Gardner and Shute, who place the use of V as a mere sex object by D at the core of the wrong of rape: "The Wrongness of Rape" in Horder (ed.), *Oxford Essays in Jurisprudence* (4th series, 2000) 193. It is all too likely in our example that D's interest in V is purely confined to sex. But the commodification of sex is neither a necessary nor a sufficient condition of rape, the essence of which is penetration without consent.

[46] [2008] EWCA Crim 527.

[47] See Rogers, "Sexual Offences: Consent; 'Purpose' of Defendant" (2008) 72 *J Crim L* 280; also the commentary by Richardson at [2008] 32 *Criminal Law Week* 3–4.

[48] [2013] EWCA Crim 823, [2013] 2 Cr App R 29.

[49] See, too, *Jheeta* [2007] EWCA Crim 1699, [2008] 1 WLR 2582.

[50] At para. 20.

the Court in the latter case that *Devonald* was to be distinguished rather than overruled. Accordingly, section 76 remains in play where the deception about D's purpose is comprehensive.

(c) Impersonation of a person known personally to V

Conclusive presumptions of non-consent, and of no reasonable belief in consent, will arise under section 76 if D intentionally impersonates someone known to V, and V is induced by the impersonation to consent to the sexual act. The requirement for *personal* acquaintance will exculpate someone who exploits a strong resemblance to, say, Cristiano Ronaldo (assuming Ronaldo is not a personal acquaintance of V's). It would also create a potential obstacle to using this limb of section 76 in a case like *Devonald*—"Cassey" was fictitious, and V had never "met" her. That said, it is not unimaginable that the idea of personal acquaintance might well be stretched beyond persons who have been met *physically* by V. Long-term pen friends may be said to have a *personal* relationship even if they have not met: it would be natural, for example, to say that of the friendship between Helene Hanff and Frank Doel, notwithstanding that it bloomed from a transatlantic correspondence and they never met in person.[51] Updating the scenario, suppose that A (a real person) creates a genuine online profile and interacts with V.[52] D logs on to A's online account and arranges to meet with V. V thinks D to be A, and willingly has sex with D under that misapprehension. Has D intentionally induced V's consent by impersonating someone "known personally" to V? No case raising this point has come before the courts, but there is no good reason to restrict impersonation to *physical* acquaintances, particularly given the prevalence of online relationships in contemporary society. There is no stretch of language here. D may not have met V "in person", but the range of meanings covered by "personally" includes reference to D "as an individual person (as distinct from others)",[53] and that is the sense in play here.

   An important limitation on the impersonation limb of section 76 is that the impersonation must *induce* consent. Suppose that D's impersonation—of, say, a second cousin who V has not seen in 15 years—did not play any part in V's decision to engage in sexual activity with D. No conclusive presumption applies.

(ii) Section 75 and the "evidential presumptions"

Section 75 of the SOA 2003 lists a set of circumstances in which an "evidential presumption" arises against D that V did not consent and—again, equally importantly—that D had no reasonable belief in consent.[54] V's lack of consent, and D's lack of a reasonable belief in V's consent, can be presumed if the prosecution proves that:

   (i)   D did the "relevant act" (e.g. in rape, penetrated V's vagina, anus or mouth with D's penis);

---

[51] Hanff, *84, Charing Cross Road* (1970).
[52] Or A and V begin corresponding by letter, having responded to an advert in the newspaper.
[53] *Oxford English Dictionary* (3rd ed., 2008).
[54] The government's original idea was to go further and place a reverse legal burden on D. This would have meant that, if the prosecution could prove the existence of one of the set of circumstances, D would then have the burden of proving on the balance of probabilities that V consented, and/or that D reasonably believed V did. If the defendant failed to offer such proof, the court would be obliged to presume that V had not consented, and

(ii)   one of the circumstances listed in section 75(2) existed; and

(iii) D *knew* that the relevant circumstance(s) existed.

In contrast to the *conclusive* presumptions in section 76 (discussed above), the evidential presumptions in section 75 are *rebuttable*. D can overcome the presumptions under section 75 by leading evidence that suggests that V did in fact consent, or that D reasonably believed V consented, or both. In terms of the law of evidence, D has an "evidential burden" to satisfy if wishing to combat the section 75 presumption. To satisfy this evidential burden and rebut the relevant presumptions, D must point to evidence that raises a reasonable doubt regarding V's lack of consent and/or the absence of a reasonable belief in consent on D's part. Once such evidence is before the court, both sides are, in legal terms, "back to square one"—the prosecution has the full burden of persuading the court that V did not consent, and that D had no reasonable belief in consent; and D has the benefit of any reasonable doubt concerning those matters.[55]

The evidence suggesting that V consented (or that D reasonably believed V did) may, in theory, consist of nothing more than D's oral evidence. At first sight, this could mean that, in order to nullify the effect of section 75, all D needs to do is to go into the witness box and aver that V consented and/or that D reasonably believed V consented.[56] Section 75 would then have added a new complication to the law of sexual offences but to little effect. In *Ciccarelli*, however, the Court of Appeal held that D did not discharge the evidential burden by *merely* asserting in the witness box that he reasonably believed V was consenting. In order to discharge the evidential burden, "some evidence *beyond the fanciful or speculative* had to be adduced to support the reasonableness of his belief".[57] In other words, the evidence called by D must be such that it could raise, in the mind of a reasonable jury, a *reasonable* doubt about the prosecution's claim that D lacked a reasonable belief in V's consent. Although it sets a relatively low bar, the decision in *Ciccarelli* helps to avoid completely neutering section 75.

The circumstances that give rise to the evidential presumption are set out in section 75(2). The first three circumstances are as follows:

(a)   any person was, at the time of the relevant act or immediately before it began, using violence against the complainant or causing the complainant to fear that immediate violence would be used against him;

(b)   any person was, at the time of the relevant act or immediately before it began, causing the complainant to fear that violence was being used, or that immediate violence would be used, against another person;

(c)   the complainant was, and the defendant was not, unlawfully detained at the time of the relevant act;

---

that D had not reasonably believed V was consenting: *Protecting the Public—Strengthening Protection against Sex Offenders and Reforming the Law on Sexual Offences* (CM 5668, 2002) 16. This proposal was retracted because of concerns about the compatibility of a reverse legal burden with Art. 6(2) of the ECHR, which guarantees the presumption of innocence: see above, §§ 2.5 and 3.2.

[55] Above, § 3.2.

[56] Cf. McEwan, "'I Thought She Consented': Defeat of the Rape Shield or the Defence that Will Not Run?" [2006] *Crim LR* 969.

[57] *Ciccarelli* [2011] EWCA Crim 2665, [2012] 1 Cr App R 15, para. 18 (emphasis added). A similar approach has been taken in respect of weak defence evidence in sex cases in Canada: see, e.g., *Pappajohn* [1980] 2 SCR 120.

One may wonder why conditions (a)–(c) required specific provisions. Under the general test set down in section 74, one would have thought that, in such circumstances, a lack of freedom and capacity to consent would readily be found. D would have to produce some exceptional evidence to avoid a finding of non-consent.[58] That is, effectively, the position under section 75(2)(a)–(c); the use or threat of immediate violence or unlawful detention must surely, ordinarily, be incompatible with the free consent of V. The inclusion of circumstances (a)–(c) is no easier to understand when regard is had to the presumption that D had no reasonable belief in V's consent. It will be remembered that D must *know* about the relevant circumstance, for instance that someone had threatened V with violence. In such circumstances, the absence of D's reasonable belief in consent is (again absent exceptional circumstances) readily found.

The next circumstance in which an evidential presumption will arise is where:

(d)   the complainant was asleep or otherwise unconscious at the time of the relevant act;

Again, it might be wondered why this provision is necessary. Under the previous law, the fact that V was asleep or otherwise unconscious would normally constitute incapacity to consent.[59] It seems that the effect of condition (d) is to allow for a possibility that, between persons in an intimate relationship, one of them may sometimes, legitimately, sexually fondle a sleeping partner. In such a case, while V's non-consent (and D's lack of reasonable belief in consent) is to be presumed, D still has an opportunity to raise a reasonable doubt about these matters, making them a contested issue in the proceedings, and overcoming the evidential presumptions under section 75.

Similar issues in the context of existing sexual relationships might arise in relation to the next circumstance:

(e)   because of the complainant's physical disability, the complainant would not have been able at the time of the relevant act to communicate to the defendant whether the complainant consented;

In general, where a person performs a sexual act on a person who cannot at the time communicate consent because of disability, a very serious wrong is perpetrated.[60]

The final circumstance in which a presumption of no consent, and no reasonable belief in consent, can arise requires more explanation:

(f)   any person had administered to or caused to be taken by the complainant, without the complainant's consent, a substance which, having regard to when it was administered or taken, was capable of causing or enabling the complainant to be stupefied or overpowered at the time of the relevant act.

Where, in fact, V *is* overpowered or stupefied by the relevant substance, the finding of non-consent within the terms of section 74 would normally be straightforward, even without the benefit of condition (f).[61] Condition (f) is, however, necessary for cases where the

---

[58]   It is conceivable that some sadomasochistic practices could fall under condition (a). D might then be able to raise the issue of consent. Similarly, subject to questions about V's freedom and capacity, it may be that V could consent to sexual intercourse with a kidnapper or guard.

[59]   *Mayers* (1872) 12 Cox CC 311; *Larter* [1995] Crim LR 75 (CA).

[60]   The exception comprises a case where V *is* consenting, but cannot communicate that at the time. Difficulties of proof abound.

[61]   To raise an issue of consent in such circumstances, D would presumably have to adduce evidence that V agreed in advance that D could make covert attempts to stupify or overpower V and could be allowed

substance, although *capable* of causing (or enabling) V to be overpowered or stupefied at the time of the relevant act, fails to do so. In such circumstances, section 75 requires D to raise evidence suggesting that V had not succumbed to (or even been affected by) the substance and was in fact consenting to the relevant sexual activity.[62]

(iii) *Beyond the evidential and conclusive presumptions*

If a prosecution is brought on facts not covered by any evidential or conclusive presumption (or, indeed, if an evidential presumption is rebutted by D), the normal rules of proof will apply: the prosecution must establish that V did not consent (and that D lacked any reasonable belief that V consented). The definition of consent will be that given in section 74: that V "agrees by choice, and has the freedom and capacity to make that choice".

The Court of Appeal has identified various situations in which there will be an absence of freedom and capacity to make a choice.

(a) *Capacity*

With regard to capacity, the focus of attention is on V's ability to understand the meaning and implications of his decisions.[63] Those questions, at least, involve consideration of matters of objective fact, albeit of a psychological rather than physical kind. The prosecution must prove the absence of V's ability beyond reasonable doubt.[64]

Of particular difficulty are cases where V's incapacity arises from a state of voluntary intoxication. In what circumstances is the consent of a voluntarily intoxicated person valid?[65] If V was so drunk or drugged as to be unconscious, then, except in the unlikely but possible situation where V had intimated consent in advance,[66] there would be no question of V's having consented. At the other end of the scale, there is equally no doubt that where V

---

intercourse (or whatever sexual touching is at issue) if V were reduced to that condition. In *R (T)* v. *DPP* [2003] EWHC 226 (Admin), it was held that even a momentary loss of consciousness constituted actual bodily harm for the purposes of s. 47 of the OAPA 1861. In the light of the decision in *Brown* [1994] 1 AC 212, which precludes the validity of any consent to the infliction of actual bodily harm save in limited circumstances (below, §§ 21.1, 21.1(iv)), D may well commit an offence against s. 47 or s. 23 of the OAPA 1861.

[62] Even then, D might be convicted of the offence under s. 61 of the SOA 2003: "administering a substance with intent".

[63] In *D Borough Council* v. *B* [2011] EWHC 101 (Fam), [2012] Fam 36, a civil case, Mostyn J held that capacity for these purposes requires an understanding and awareness of "the mechanics of the act; that there are health risks involved, particularly the acquisition of sexually transmitted and sexually transmissible infection; [and] that sex between a man and a woman may result in the woman becoming pregnant". See further *A* [2014] EWCA Crim 299, [2014] 1 WLR 2469, where the guidance on mental capacity found in the Mental Capacity Act 2005, ss. 2–3 was relied upon in the context of establishing capacity to consent under the SOA 2003. In practice, a person who has sex with an adult whose mental capacity to consent is doubtful will probably be prosecuted for one of the specific offences relating to mentally disordered persons created by SOA 2003, ss. 30–42. On the issue of capacity in relation to those offences, see *Cooper* [2009] UKHL 42, [2009] 1 WLR 1786.

[64] *A* [2014] EWCA Crim 299, [2014] 1 WLR 2469.

[65] For an account of the difficult issues that arise in estimating the effect on consent of drink, drugs, and mind-altering substances, see Finch and Munro, "Intoxicated Consent and the Boundaries of Drug Assisted Rape" [2003] *Crim LR* 773. See, further: Finch and Munro, "The Demon Drink and the Demonized Woman: Socio-sexual Stereotypes and Responsibility Attribution in Rape Trials Involving Intoxicants" (2007) 16 *Social & Legal Studies* 591; Gunby et al., "Alcohol-related Rape Cases: Barristers' Perspectives on the Sexual Offences Act 2003 and its Impact on Practice" (2010) 74 *J Crim L* 579.

[66] For example, if V (a prostitute) agrees to be rendered unconscious to gratify the desire of D, who enjoys intercourse with unconscious people: cf. the facts of *Pike* [1961] Crim LR 114 and 547 (CA).

is disinhibited by alcohol or drugs to the point of engaging willingly in sexual activity that would have been refused had V been sober, V's consent is valid: just as a drunken intent is still an intent,[67] so for present purposes a "drunken consent is still consent".[68] Between those two extremes there is a point where the "freedom and capacity" to choose that section 74 requires is lost.[69] The difficulty is identifying this point.[70] In *Bree*,[71] the Court of Appeal remarked that:

> "We should perhaps underline that, as a matter of practical reality, capacity to consent may evaporate well before a complainant becomes unconscious. Whether this is so or not, however, is fact-specific, or more accurately, depends on the actual state of mind of the individuals involved on the particular occasion."

These remarks, it should be stressed, were made in the context of complainants who were voluntarily intoxicated, and the courts can be expected to take a sterner line with defendants in cases where the complainant's intoxication is involuntary. Judgments about consent, or the lack of consent, can be affected by the disapproval of D's conduct quite as much as estimates of V's state of mind.[72] Thus, where D has administered or caused V to take a substance without V's consent, it may be said that V's consent was not valid where V does something *only because of* the substance's disinhibiting effects.[73]

Questions about *freedom* to consent have generated far more appellate decisions than questions about capacity. The next sections present overviews of the case law on freedom to make a choice as it stands.

(b) Pressure on V

The first factor that can remove V's freedom to choose is circumstantial pressure. Suppose that D offers V work in D's brothel, fully aware that V, an asylum seeker who has not applied for asylum at the port of entry, is without means of support? Did V make a choice whilst possessing "the freedom ... to make that choice"? If D does no more than offer V work in the brothel, D may seek to argue that V's choice was a free one. D may firmly believe this, but that of itself will not determine the question. Whether, on the facts, V's consent is vitiated is not for D to decide; it is a question for the jury.[74]

---

[67] Below, § 18.3. However, if D spikes V's drink in order to get V into this condition D will commit an offence under s. 61 of the SOA 2003 of "administering a substance with intent", an offence that the courts view particularly seriously—see *Attorney General's Reference (No. 31 of 2006)* [2007] EWCA Crim 1623, [2008] 1 Cr App R (S) 46, where the Court of Appeal increased a sentence of two years' imprisonment to three and a half.

[68] *Bree* [2007] EWCA Crim 804, [2008] QB 131, para. 34.

[69] Importantly, the issue is not whether V can remember the incident clearly, but rather whether V had the capacity to consent: *Seedy Tambedou* [2014] EWCA Crim 954.

[70] See Wallerstein, "'A Drunken Consent Is Still Consent'—Or Is It? A Critical Analysis of a Drunken Consent Following *Bree*" (2009) 73 *J Crim L* 318.

[71] [2007] EWCA Crim 804, [2008] QB 131, para. 34. The matter of directing the jury on matters of voluntary intoxication and consent was considered in *Kamki* [2013] EWCA Crim 2335.

[72] See, for instance, *Kirk* [2008] EWCA Crim 434, discussed in the next section. For proposals to define rape more in terms of the conduct of D rather than the state of mind of V, see Dripps, "For a Negative, Normative Model of Consent, with a Comment on Preference-skepticism" (1996) 2 *Legal Theory* 113 and West, "A Comment on Consent, Sex and Rape" (1996) 2 *Legal Theory* 233. Contrast Bogart, "Commodification and Phenomenology: Evading Consent in Theory Regarding Rape" (1996) 2 *Legal Theory* 253.

[73] This supports the case for having the evidential presumption in s. 75(2)(f).

[74] An analogy may be drawn with a situation where D uses what he himself believes to be reasonable force in self-defence but where a jury finds that the force used was excessive. Notwithstanding the decision in *Scarlett*

It is far from easy to determine whether the brothel keeper would be found guilty of the offence of causing V to engage in sexual activity.[75] Many other difficult examples could be given, particularly outside the circumstances covered by presumptions. For instance, as we saw in § 12.3(ii), an evidential presumption that V did not consent arises if D makes a threat of *immediate* violence to V or another.[76] What if D threatens to disfigure V in a few days' time unless V has sex with D now? As such a threat does not give rise to an evidential presumption, are we to infer that such threats are of a lesser order of magnitude? Such an inference should be resisted: the issue is, simply, whether V had the freedom and capacity to choose. Given the nature of this particular threat, the jury may readily find a lack of consent under the general definition in section 74. But make the threat less horrific, expand the timeline, and uncertainties may arise. If working as a prostitute is something she detests, has V been "caused to engage in sexual activity without consent" or has she taken, however reluctantly, an opportunity to earn money provided by D?[77] What if D had forcibly taken what money V had before offering work in the brothel? In *Kirk*,[78] a 13-year-old girl had run away from home. She went to the workplace of a man who had previously abused her and, after waiting until everyone else had left, had sex with him for money. Her evidence, as summarised by the trial judge in his direction to the jury, was: "I was very hungry and needed to eat so I went to [D's place of work] … All I can say is that I ended up having sex with [D] for £3.25. I used the money to buy food." The Court of Appeal upheld D's conviction for rape.

A similar problem can arise when an adult, with apparent willingness but inward revulsion, complies with a request for sex made by a person in a dominant position—a step-parent, for example—who has been sexually abusing V since childhood. In *C*,[79] the Court of Appeal held that it was open to the jury in such a case "to conclude that the evidence of … consent when the complainant was no longer a child was indeed apparent, not real, and that the appellant was well aware that in reality she was not consenting".

It is even possible that victims of alleged sexual offences might think they *were* consenting, when, due to the circumstances in which that choice was made, they lacked the freedom to consent in legal terms. In *Ali*,[80] the Court of Appeal noted that:

> "One of the consequences of grooming is that it has a tendency to limit or subvert the alleged victim's capacity to make free decisions, and it creates the risk that he or she simply submitted

---

[1993] 4 All ER 629 (CA), D cannot rely on a mistake of fact based on his own normative standards: *Owino* (1996) 2 Cr App R 128; *Martin (David)* [2000] 2 Cr App R 42; Criminal Justice and Immigration Act 2008, s. 76(6); below § 18.1(v). *A fortiori*, this will be the case where a *reasonable* belief on D's part is required.

[75] For general discussion of the circumstances that vitiate consent at common law, see below, § 21.1(iii). In practice, the Crown would probably avoid this area of difficulty (and difficult questions of causation) by prosecuting the brothel keeper for causing or inciting prostitution for gain (SOA 2003, s. 52) or for controlling prostitution for gain (SOA 2003, s. 53), both of which carry a maximum sentence of seven years' imprisonment.

[76] SOA 2003, s. 75(2)(a)–(b).

[77] Note, too, the question whether her conduct is "caused": below, § 12.9.

[78] [2008] EWCA Crim 434. The decision is criticised by Richardson [2008] 46 *Criminal Law Week* 2–3. It has further been suggested that *Kirk* and *Jheeta* (discussed below) are cases of undue influence by D, rather than pressure on V: Dsouza, "Undermining Prima Facie Consent in the Criminal Law" (2014) 33 *Law and Philosophy* 489, 516. Although this argument is interesting in theory, it is clear that the courts understood these cases to be ones of pressure, rather than influence.

[79] [2012] EWCA Crim 2034, para. 16.

[80] [2015] EWCA Crim 1279, [2015] 2 Cr App R 33.

because of the environment of dependency created by those responsible for treating the alleged victim in this way. Indeed the individual may have been manipulated to the extent that he or she is unaware of, or confused about, the distinction between acquiescence and genuine agreement at the time the incident occurred."[81]

The comment in *Ali* about the distinction between "acquiescence and genuine agreement" harks back to the pre-2003 distinction between consent and submission.[82] Indeed, it had been thought that the traditional line between consent and submission remained relevant to the definition of consent in section 74.[83] However, room for doubt on this point has been introduced by the following *obiter* comment in *W*:[84]

"the dichotomy set up by the judge (free consent/submitting to a demand that [V] felt unable to resist) … does not reflect the law. It is possible for a person to submit to a demand which he or she feels unable to resist, but without lacking the capacity or freedom to make a choice. This is an example of reluctant consent."

Consider two examples. In the first, D pesters V for sex, until V eventually agrees. This is perhaps "reluctant consent" (as the Court of Appeal puts it); one might argue that it is a form of "submission", but the Court of Appeal would then say that it is not the type of submission that denies consent. In the second example, V agrees because of fears that, if V refuses D sex, D will attack V. This is pure submission, and no consent at all. In our view, it is this kind of distinction (admittedly a vague one) that the Court of Appeal was attempting to articulate in *W*.

A final, difficult, case is *Jheeta*.[85] D persuaded his over-trusting girlfriend, V, to continue a sexual relationship with him by sending her messages, purporting to come from the police, warning her that if she ended the relationship D was likely to commit suicide. His deceptive conduct began before, and continued after, the SOA 2003 came into force. On counts in the indictment charging the former offence of procuring sex by false representations (relating to the earlier period), he was unquestionably guilty.[86] In relation to the post-2003 Act counts, the Court of Appeal held that V's consent had been vitiated, but the basis for the court's decision is not clear. *Jheeta* should be recognised principally as a case of pressure that vitiated consent: the nature of the defendant's deception meant that V lacked the freedom and capacity to choose to engage in the relevant sexual activities.

Jheeta demonstrates that deceptions can give rise to pressure on V and, thereby, potentially vitiate consent. It is also possible for deceptions, even if they do not generate such levels of pressure, to vitiate consent more directly: a possibility to which we now turn.

(c) Deceptions and mistakes

Difficulties concerning freedom to choose under section 74 also arise when D obtains V's agreement to a sexual activity by deception.[87] One example of such a case is where D

---

[81] *Ibid.*, para. 58.
[82] *Olugboja* [1982] QB 320 (CA).
[83] See, e.g., *Robinson* [2011] EWCA Crim 916.
[84] [2015] EWCA Crim 559, para. 34.
[85] [2007] EWCA Crim 1699, [2008] 1 WLR 2582.
[86] Sexual Offences Act 1956, s. 3.
[87] Laird, "Rapist or Rogue? Deception, Consent and the Sexual Offences Act 2003" [2014] *Crim LR* 492.

intentionally breaches an express condition for consent laid out by V. The deception in such cases is that D intends to abide by V's request. In *Assange* (an extradition case),[88] it was suggested that if V agrees to have sex with D on the condition that he wears a condom, and D intentionally breaches this condition, there is no consent under section 74. *Assange* was applied in *R(F)* v. *DPP*,[89] where the High Court ruled that, where V had made it clear to D that she consented on condition that D would not ejaculate inside her vagina, her consent was vitiated if he then deliberately did so, or if he penetrated her with that intent. Following these decisions, a man's consent might be vitiated if he made it clear that he would not have sexual intercourse with a woman unless she was using contraception, and the woman, wishing to get pregnant, told him that she was when she was not. She could be convicted, on that basis, of sexual assault, or of causing a person to engage in sexual activity without consent (but not, as we will see, of rape or assault by penetration).[90]

What cases such as *Assange* and *R(F)* show is that, contrary to previous understandings,[91] section 76 does not contain an exhaustive list of deceptions that will vitiate consent. Other deceptions can engage section 74.

Recognising this, the courts have begun to acknowledge cases where D's active deception can vitiate consent even *without* an express precondition such as that found in *Assange* or *R(F)*. In *McNally*,[92] D, who was born with female genitalia but identified as male,[93] claimed to be a young man and entered into a relationship with V, a young woman. D and V engaged in a number of sexual activities, V thinking throughout that D was male. Importantly, V indicated that she would not have engaged in those activities had she known the truth about D. The Court of Appeal held that, *in the circumstances*, D's *active* deception had vitiated V's consent—she did not have the freedom to make the relevant choice (to engage in sexual activity with a man or a woman).[94]

It is important to register the circumstances of *McNally*: D was actively deceiving V about D's gender—a feature of the case that was emphasised by the Court of Appeal[95]—and V would not have engaged in sexual activities with D had she known the truth. Had V simply made a mistake in this regard (with no encouragement from D), it is possible that the Court of Appeal would not have upheld a conviction for a non-consensual offence. It is also not clear what the position is where D is aware that V has made a mistake and does nothing to correct it. It might be argued that what matters is the *attribute* of the activity (such as D's gender), rather than what D says about it, when determining whether V consented.[96] This is not, however, the approach that the cases to date have taken. So it seems that if V thinks D is male, when in fact D is female, V's consent is not—without

---

[88] [2011] EWHC 2849 (Admin).

[89] [2013] EWHC 945 (Admin), [2014] QB 581.

[90] Rape requires penile penetration of V's vagina, anus, or mouth; assault by penetration requires the penetration of V's vagina or anus.

[91] Miles, "Sexual Offences: Consent, Capacity and Children" [2008] 10 *Arch News* 6, 6. See, too, Rogers, "The Effect of 'Deception' in the Sexual Offences Act 2003" [2013] 4 *Arch Rev* 7, 9.

[92] *McNally* [2013] EWCA Crim 1051, [2014] QB 593, esp. paras. 23–7.

[93] For discussion of this aspect of the case, see Sharp, "Criminalising Sexual Intimacy: Transgender Defendants and the Legal Construction of Non-consent" [2014] *Crim LR* 207.

[94] Whether the Court of Appeal decided *McNally* under s. 74 or s. 76 is disputed—but see above, n. 41.

[95] *McNally* [2013] EWCA Crim 1051, [2014] QB 593, para. 27.

[96] Cf. Miles, "Sexual Offences: Consent, Capacity and Children" [2008] 10 *Arch News* 6, 6.

more—necessarily vitiated, even if V would not have engaged in the relevant activity had V known the truth.

Beyond cases of active deceptions about gender, what other factors might be relevant to the definition of consent in section 74? There are hints in *McNally* that active deception regarding HIV status could well vitiate consent.[97] This view restricts the decision in *B* (above, § 12.3(i)(a)) to non-deceptive *omissions* to inform a partner of HIV status, or cases where V simply makes a mistake about D's HIV status. If D lies to V that he is not HIV-positive, V's consent could be vitiated (assuming that V would not have had sex with D without the assurance). For other cases, the Court of Appeal has urged that a "common sense" approach be taken towards deceptions and the vitiation of consent.[98] Perhaps this is the only response that can be given: once it is accepted that deceptions beyond those covered in section 76 can vitiate consent, it is difficult to draw bright lines regarding *which* deceptions will have that effect.[99] The courts have thus been short of examples of deceptions that will not vitiate consent. One example that has been given is a deception as to D's wealth—e.g. D tells V that D is a millionaire when D is, in fact, of modest means.[100] If V would not have had sex with D had V known this, then there has been a deception that induced consent, but the "common sense" approach adopted by the Court of Appeal would protect D from liability for a sexual offence. It must be assumed that the same would true even if V had specifically ascertained from D that D was a millionaire prior to sex. Beyond this example, there is only possibility and, alas, conjecture. The courts will be thrust into case-by-case decisions whether a deception or mistake has vitiated consent. This is a highly unsatisfactory position for the law of sexual offences to have reached.

What ways forward might there be? Two extremes might be envisaged. Herring has, for instance, proposed that all deceptions that induce V to engage in a sexual activity when otherwise V would not have done so should vitiate consent under section 74. As noted already, such an approach risks making the concept of consent in sexual offences unduly stringent. At the other extreme, criminal liability could be excluded altogether if D's deception does not fall within section 76. The latter option seems implausible, in as much as it would arbitrarily downgrade deceptions falling outside section 76, and underplay D's wrongdoing in other cases where, but for the deception, the activity would not have occurred.

Another option that would still engage with deceptions beyond the scope of section 76 would be to turn back the clock: to restrict the type of deceptions that can vitiate consent to those listed in section 76, and reinstate (and expand, to cover men) a distinct offence such as procuring a woman to have sexual intercourse by "false pretences or false representations".[101] A similar offence was abolished when the SOA 2003 came into

---

[97] *McNally* [2013] EWCA Crim 1051, [2014] QB 593, para. 24.

[98] *R(F)* v. *DPP* [2013] EWHC 945 (Admin), [2014] QB 581, para. 26; *McNally* [2013] EWCA Crim 1051, [2014] QB 593, para. 25.

[99] For an attempt to bring more rigour to this area, see Williams, "Deception, Mistake and Vitiation of the Victim's Consent" (2008) 124 *LQR* 132.

[100] See *McNally* [2013] EWCA Crim 1051, [2014] QB 593, para. 25.

[101] Sexual Offences Act 1956, s. 3. The offence was originally devised as part of the legislative response to the "white slave traffic", but case law interpreted it as applying to men who told lies to persuade women to have sexual intercourse with themselves, as well as those who did so in order to procure women to gratify the lust of third parties.

force—possibly because the view was taken that the section 4 offence of causing a person to engage in sexual activity without consent would cover such situations.[102]

Obviously, any proposal to resurrect the old procurement offence itself raises difficulties.[103] Although, in terms of the labelling of offenders, a conviction for a procurement offence might be an improvement over the present law, more thought needs to be given to exactly *which* deceptions should trigger liability for a sexual offence—and for *which* offence. To an extent, this concern can be met by insisting that D must be aware (or, if that is too narrow an approach, that D ought to have been aware) that the deception is material to V's consent, and not something to which V is indifferent. Even so, the core issue remains. Is it really the case that *any* deception impacting on V's consent should be the stuff of criminal liability? Or should there be a requirement that the concern would be considered material by a reasonable person?[104]

An additional concern relates to the viewing of any reinstated procurement offence as a less serious form of rape. There is tremendous pressure to secure convictions in sexual offences cases, and concern has been expressed at the risk that borderline cases would be charged as the new offence, rather than as—say—rape, simply to encourage a jury to convict more readily, or the defendant to plead guilty.[105] These difficulties are not insurmountable, but they are real. If they could be addressed satisfactorily, reinstating an offence of procuring sexual activity by deception, and reducing the scope for the vitiation of consent under section 74, could offer an improvement upon the present situation.[106]

§ 12.4 Common element 3: intentional performance or causing of conduct

The discussion thus far has focused primarily on the actus reus aspects of the main non-consensual offences. We now turn to the mens rea. The first three non-consensual offences considered in this chapter include a requirement that D intended the behavioural element of the actus reus: an intentional penetration with the penis in section 1 (rape);[107] an intentional penetration in section 2 (assault by penetration); an intentional touching of another person in section 3 (sexual assault). The fourth non-consensual offence considered in this chapter requires the intentional causing of a consequence (that another person engages in an activity) in section 4.

In practice, if an act of penetration is proved, almost invariably the inference will be that it was intended. Other acts might be more difficult to interpret. It is easy to envisage

---

[102] Spencer, "Sex by Deception" [2013] 9 *Arch Rev* 6, 7.

[103] One misplaced concern would be that the old offence was too caught up in the paradigm of "an 'evil' man deceiving a 'gullible' woman" into sex, and that more specific offences (such as those targeting people-trafficking) capture the relevant wrong. See Sjolin, "Ten Years On: Consent under the Sexual Offences Act 2003" (2015) 79 *J Crim L* 20, 31. This is to take too narrow a view of the decided cases under s. 74, some of which (e.g. *Jheeta*) do live up to a gender-neutral and more modern paradigm: D takes advantage of C's vulnerability by lying in order to secure assent to sexual activity.

[104] There was uncertainty on this point under the old offence: Smith, *Smith and Hogan: Criminal Law* (10th ed., 2002) 475.

[105] Sjolin, "Ten Years On: Consent under the Sexual Offences Act 2003" (2015) 79 *J Crim L* 20, 32.

[106] See, further, Spencer, "Sex by Deception" [2013] 9 *Arch Rev* 6.

[107] Contrast the Sexual Offences (Scotland) Act 2009, s. 1(1) (rape), which covers intentional *and* reckless penetration.

circumstances where the touching of a fully clothed person in a "sexual" manner may be completely accidental or inadvertent. For instance, the sudden stopping of a tube carriage might jolt D, with the consequence that D's hand touches V's breast. D should not be convicted of sexual assault (or any other form of assault), as the touching was not intended.

Can D deny that her behaviour was intentional by pointing at her extreme state of voluntary intoxication? The criminal law doctrines governing voluntary intoxication are set out below, in § 18.3. In general, where D lacks the requisite mens rea in respect of one or more elements of the actus reus, the doctrines allow a legal inference to be made that D actually has mens rea (in effect, deeming D to have mens rea), for any "basic intent" offence—but not where the offence requires proof of a "specific intent". In turn, this raises the question whether the offences in sections 1–4 are crimes of basic or specific intent.[108]

The question was considered in *Heard*.[109] D, who was waiting to be seen at a hospital, became angry and punched one of the police officers accompanying him. He then undid his trousers, took his penis in his hand, and rubbed it up and down the thigh of the officer. D was arrested and charged with sexual assault. D was at the time extremely drunk.

On the facts, the Court of Appeal concluded that D was not intoxicated *enough* to raise the issue. None the less, the Court went on to rule that the intention at issue in section 3 was a basic intention, on the ground that no purposive element was involved in the section: a deliberate touching that was in fact sexual sufficed, and it was not necessary to show that the touching was done for any purpose. The Court explained that, had D been sufficiently intoxicated to raise a reasonable doubt over his intention, evidence of his intoxication would have been inadmissible to deflect a finding that D's act of rubbing his penis against V's trousered leg was intentional. Presumably, a similar analysis will apply to a charge of rape and assault by penetration where D achieves penetration despite his extreme intoxication. The situation with regard to the section 4 offence (causing a person to engage in sexual activity without consent) is less clear, because D must intend a *consequence*, rather than his own bare behaviour. The point of whether the section 4 offence is one of basic or specific intent awaits decision.

The court's decision in *Heard* also recognised an important further distinction. According to *Heard*, the voluntary intoxication rules apply if D's *touching* of V is deliberate. But where D bumps into V while in a drugged or drunken state, the crucial requirement of intentional touching (or penetration, as the case may be) is not supplied by the standard intoxication doctrines. As recognised in *Heard* itself, even in a case of basic intent, a finding of such intent will not be made if "the mind did not go with the physical act".[110] It seems that "a drunken accident is still an accident":[111] where, viewed objectively, the physical conduct that caused the actus reus was patently non-intentional, the law of voluntary intoxication will not convert accidents into intentional sexual conduct.

---

[108] Under its previous definition, rape was construed as a crime of basic intent. See *Woods* (1982) 74 Cr App R 312 (on recklessness as to consent) and *Fotheringham* (1989) 88 Cr App R 206 (on recklessness as to mistaken identity).

[109] [2007] EWCA Crim 125, [2008] QB 43; below, § 18.3(i).

[110] *Ibid.*, paras. 19–23. See, also, the decision in *Brady* [2006] EWCA Crim 2413 (discussion below, § 18.3(iii)).

[111] *Heard* [2007] EWCA Crim 125, [2008] QB 43, para. 23.

§ 12.5 Common element 4: the absence of a reasonable belief in consent

In addition to an intention to carry out the relevant conduct, the non-consensual offences include a mens rea element in relation to the absence of V's consent: the defendant must lack a reasonable belief that V is consenting. Importantly, this formulation means that the following situations will satisfy the fault requirement with regard to the absence of consent: D intends that V not consent; D knows that V is not consenting; D believes that V is not consenting; D is (subjectively) reckless whether V is consenting; D does not think about whether V is consenting; and D believes that V is consenting, but that belief is not based on reasonable grounds (in essence, a form of negligence with regard to belief-formation).

This approach to fault marks a notable change from the old law, by introducing an objective test in cases where D claims to have believed that V was consenting. For the purposes of the old law, in *Morgan*[112] (discussed in Chapter 18) the House of Lords had ruled that, in principle, a man who had sexual intercourse with a woman without her consent was not guilty of rape if he had honestly believed that she was consenting, however unreasonable his belief might have been. Although there was little evidence that in practice juries acquitted defendants who claimed that they honestly, but unreasonably, believed the complainant had consented, the decision in *Morgan* was widely thought to send an undesirable message about what was permissible in sexual relations.[113] Unsurprisingly, the government that promoted the reforms in the 2003 Act made the reversal of *Morgan* one of the key elements in its revision of the law sexual offences.

Whether the absence of a reasonable belief formula has the desired effect is questionable, and depends on how the courts eventually decide to interpret it. Regrettably, there are at least two ways in which the legislation might have missed its mark. The first concerns the nature of "reasonableness" itself—the 2003 Act does not make clear *to whom* the defendant's belief must be reasonable, and this opens up the possibility that harmful stereotypes about the nature of sexual offending and victimhood will influence judgements about the defendant's mens rea.[114]

Secondly, the legislation provides that:

> Whether a belief is reasonable is to be determined having regard to all the circumstances, including any steps [D] has taken to ascertain whether [V] consents.[115]

An obvious question is what "all the circumstances" include. In other situations where the courts are called upon to decide whether behaviour was reasonable—for example, in the

---

[112] [1976] AC 182.

[113] The Sexual Offences (Amendment) Act 1976 was passed after *Morgan*. Section 1(2) provided that the jury was to consider the grounds for D's belief in ascertaining whether it thought he might have actually held it. The substantive law remained unchanged, however. If the the jury concluded it was reasonably possible that D honestly believed that V had consented, D was still to be acquitted.

[114] Cowan, "'Freedom and the Capacity to Make a Choice': A Feminist Analysis of Consent in the Criminal Law of Rape" in Munro and Stychin (eds.), *Sexuality and the Law: Feminist Engagements* (2007) 51, 60.

[115] This formula is repeated four times in the Act, once in relation to each of the offences: see SOA 2003, ss. 1(2), 2(2), 3(2), and 4(2). If D has a reasonable belief that X is consenting, and then (reasonably) mistakes V for X, D

tort of negligence—it goes without saying that they make the decision taking account of "all the circumstances"; but by "all the circumstances" they normally mean those that are *external* to the defendant. If a driver is sued for negligence it helps her not at all to argue that, though her driving fell short of the objective standard of the reasonable person, by the standards of a person with her mental disabilities she was doing rather well.[116] The courts tend to take an equally hard-nosed line when dealing with prosecutions for offences of negligence.[117] Thus, in the context of the offence of dangerous driving, they have said that the question is whether his driving was objectively dangerous, and it is irrelevant that he was "doing his incompetent best".[118] This might suggest that, in the context of sections 1–4 of the SOA 2003,[119] no allowance would be made for the defendant who, as a result of learning disabilities, believed V had consented when a person of normal intellect would have realised V did not.

In its original form, the Sexual Offences Bill provided a test that was purely objective: the defendant would have been guilty if "a reasonable person would in all the circumstances doubt whether [the complainant] consents". But in Parliament this evoked opposition on the ground that it potentially bore too heavily on those with learning disabilities, who might in consequence be judged by standards they could not attain.[120] This is why the "all the circumstances" provision was added. The general idea behind this formulation is that, in the case of a defendant with learning disabilities, these would form part of the "circumstances", and hence be taken into account in whether the belief was reasonable.[121]

If "all the circumstances" were taken to include *all* those that are internal to the defendant, this could have the effect of defeating the intended reform. Taken to the limit, it would mean making allowance not only for the fact that D had learning disabilities, but also that D's judgement was clouded by mental illness—and indeed that D was by nature arrogant, impetuous, or stupid. The practical effect of this might be to make the test of mens rea essentially subjective, effectively restoring the position as it was under *Morgan*.

Moved by considerations of this sort, in *B*—a case involving a schizophrenic defendant—the Court of Appeal said:[122]

> "We conclude that unless and until the state of mind amounts to insanity in law, then under the rule enacted in the Sexual Offences Act beliefs in consent arising from conditions such as delusional psychotic illness or personality disorders must be judged by objective standards of reasonableness and not by taking into account a mental disorder which induced a belief which could not reasonably arise without it."

---

still has a reasonable belief in consent and should not be guilty. Cf. the bizarre facts at issue in *Attorney-General's Reference (No 79 of 2006)* [2006] EWCA Crim 2626, [2007] 1 Cr App R (S) 122.

[116] *Nettleship* v. *Weston* [1971] 2 QB 691 (CA).

[117] See the discussion of abnormal characteristics in negligence, above, § 5.5(ii).

[118] *Evans* [1963] 1 QB 412 (CA).

[119] There is a possible distinction: it could be said that in driving offences this is a "behavioural" element of the actus reus rather than, as here, a "circumstances or consequences issue". See above, § 5.5(iii).

[120] See Temkin and Ashworth, "The Sexual Offences Act 2003: Rape, Sexual Assaults and the Problems of Consent" [2004] *Crim LR* 328, 340–41.

[121] *Ibid.*, 341.

[122] [2013] EWCA Crim 3, [2013] 1 Cr App R 36, para. 40.

In so ruling, however, they were prepared to accept that, despite this, "cases could arise in which the reasonableness [of D's belief] depends on the reading by the defendant of subtle social signals, and in which his impaired ability to do so is relevant to the reasonableness of his belief".[123] Further litigation on this point seems inevitable. The approach outlined in *B* fails to separate the truly culpable from those in need of treatment. Such conditions should, therefore, be taken into account when assessing the reasonableness of the defendant's beliefs about consent.

§12.6 Rape

We turn now to consider the more specific components of the offences contained in sections 1–4 of the SOA 2003. We start with rape. Section 1 of the Act provides:

(1) [D]commits an offence if—
  (a) he intentionally penetrates the vagina, anus or mouth of [V] with his penis,
  (b) [V]does not consent to the penetration, and
  (c) [D]does not reasonably believe that [V] consents.

The maximum sentence is life imprisonment.[124]

Rape is the only one of the offences to be considered here that (subject to certain exceptions)[125] requires a male perpetrator, someone who intentionally penetrates the vagina, anus, or mouth of another non-consenting person with *his* penis. There was some controversial authority that the former offence of rape could be committed by a woman through an innocent agent.[126] Such a verdict now seems precluded by the new wording of the offence.[127]

D must penetrate V's vagina, anus or mouth, and penetration continues from entry to withdrawal.[128] Accordingly, D may rape V if he continues to penetrate V when an initial consent is revoked prior to withdrawal.[129] Vaginal penetration occurs as soon as there is entry of the vulva.[130] It is immaterial if the vagina penetrated is surgically constructed, for example through gender reassignment surgery.[131] Anal and oral penetrations also

---

[123] *Ibid.*, para. 41; above, § 5.5(ii). Cf. *TS* [2008] EWCA Crim 6.

[124] SOA 2003, s. 1(4).

[125] First, as explained in SOA 2003, s. 79(3): "References to a part of the body include references to a part surgically constructed (in particular, through gender reassignment surgery." This leaves open the possibility that a person who is legally a woman, but has a surgically constructed penis, could commit rape. Secondly, legally female persons can have a penis if they: (a) are intersex and have been registered as female, yet have a functioning penis; or (b) were registered as male upon birth but later legally transitioned to female—which does not, under English law, require any kind of surgical intervention.

[126] *Cogan and Leak* [1976] QB 217 (CA); above, § 7.3(i).

[127] Secondary liability remains possible. If D1 assists or encourages D2 to penetrate V's vagina, mouth, or anus with D2's penis, D1 will (assuming she possesses the relevant mens rea) be an accomplice to any rape that D2 perpetrates. Further, should D1 procure D2 so to act while D2 reasonably believes that V consents, D2 would nonetheless have committed the actus reus of rape, a sufficient basis with which to find complicity by D1: *DPP* v. *K and B* [1997] 1 Cr App R 36; above, § 7.6(ii)(b). Furthermore, a defendant who caused a person to engage in sexual activity without consent might be liable for the offence under s. 4 of the SOA 2003.

[128] SOA 2003, s. 79(2).

[129] As was the position under the previous law: *Kaitamaki* [1985] AC 147; *Cooper* [1994] Crim LR 531 (CA).

[130] SOA 2003, s. 79(9).

[131] *Ibid.*, s. 79(3).

constitute rape, entailing male as well as female victims. Non-consensual penile penetration of V's anus has been rape since 1994.[132] Prior to the 2003 Act, non-consensual penile penetration of V's mouth would not have been rape.

§ 12.7 Assault by penetration

Section 2 of the SOA 2003 provides:

(1) [D] commits an offence if—
(a) he intentionally penetrates the vagina or anus of another person [V] with a part of his body or anything else,
(b) the penetration is sexual,
(c) [V] does not consent to the penetration, and
(d) [D] does not reasonably believe that [V] consents.

A striking feature of this offence is its potential breadth, particularly considering the maximum penalty of life imprisonment.[133] Although the intentional, non-consensual, penetration must be of the anus or vagina, it may be done with any part of the body or with anything else.[134]

It will be noted that there is an overlap with the offence of rape whenever the vagina or anus of V is penetrated by D's penis. This was a deliberate act by the legislature, to allow for cases where it can be proved that D was responsible for an act of penetration by some bodily part or object but it cannot be proved with certainty that D used his penis.[135]

Conversely, one may question whether rape should be limited to penile penetration. Why not expand the boundaries of rape to include what is covered by the section 2 offence? The answer is that the legislature has taken the view that there is something *special* about penile penetration. Such penetration may be thought to be the ultimate kind of forced intimacy, as well as being the form most redolent of risk of disease and unwanted pregnancy.[136] This point is of limited practical import. Both rape and assault by penetration attract maximum sentences of life imprisonment. There is nevertheless an important point of principle (and symbolism) about whether D, who penetrates V's anus with a sex toy, without V's consent, should be labelled as a "rapist". Perhaps not, but the point is debatable.

---

[132] As a result of Criminal Justice and Public Order Act 1994, s. 142.

[133] SOA 2003, s. 2(4).

[134] Herein lies another reason why routine medical procedures involving a speculum, swabs, and the like should not be considered *by their nature* to be sexual (above, § 12.2). If they were, D, a doctor, who takes a vaginal swab from a patient, ostensibly for the sake of a treatment required by V but, covertly, to collect data for a study unconnected with V's medical needs, could be liable for the s. 2 offence (if D's deception is significant enough to vitiate consent and assuming that D has no reasonable belief in V's consent).

[135] Cf. the Scottish case of *Garvock* v. *HM Advocate* 1991 SCCR 593.

[136] It has been argued that the core of the wrong of rape is disrespect for V's autonomy, the use of her body in a purely instrumental manner which disregards her personhood. As such, rape in its "pure" form would take place where D, using a condom, penetrates an insensate V who never becomes aware of what D has done and suffers no adverse physical or psychological effects: Gardner and Shute, "The Wrongness of Rape" in Horder (ed.), *Oxford Essays in Jurisprudence* (4th series, 2000) 193. On this view, the "core" wrong would have occurred whenever D uses the body of an insensate V for sexual gratification and whatever form his conduct takes, implying no difference in the basic wrong of the offences of rape, assault by penetration, and sexual assault. But, of course, a typical instance of rape will be fully experienced by the victim and will inflict serious psychological trauma, as well as risking

§ 12.8 Sexual assault

Section 3 of the SOA 2003 provides:

(1) [D] commits an offence if—
(a) he intentionally touches another person [V],
(b) the touching is sexual,
(c) [V] does not consent to the touching, and
(d) [D] does not reasonably believe that [V] consents.

The maximum penalty is 10 years' imprisonment if tried on indictment, or 6 months' imprisonment if tried summarily.[137]

Sexual assault covers non-consensual, non-penetrative, sexual acts, requiring proof that D touched V. V's person includes reference to a body part surgically constructed, in particular through gender reassignment surgery.[138] A "touching" includes a touching amounting to penetration,[139] another aspect of overlap within the major non-consensual offences. The term "touching" covers much else besides, including touching made with any part of the body, or using anything else, and *through* anything.[140] It was confirmed in *H*[141] that V's body includes V's clothes and it seems that V need feel no pressure on V's body. For example, should D intentionally brush V's fully clothed crotch without V's consent, D may well commit sexual assault.

One point of restriction, however, is that the offence is confined to *touching*; which, in the pedantic terms of English law, is strictly speaking a battery. Accordingly, to continue our example, if D attempts but fails to touch V's crotch, yet puts V in fear of an imminent touching, D may well perpetrate a simple assault but not a sexual assault.[142]

§ 12.9 Causing a person to engage in sexual activity without consent

Section 4 of the SOA 2003 provides:

(1) [D] commits an offence if—
(a) he intentionally causes [V] to engage in an activity,
(b) the activity is sexual,
(c) [V] does not consent to engaging in the activity, and
(d) [D] does not reasonably believe that [V] consents.

---

physical injury, infection, and—in the case of vaginal penetration—unwanted pregnancy. Although such effects are not within the formal definition of rape (and will often accompany other non-consensual sexual offences), they are very much part of our conception of rape and explain why rape is appropriately characterised as a form of violence (although it need not involve *physical* violence) against V as well as a wrong of disregard for V's autonomy.

[137] SOA 2003, s. 3(4).
[138] *Ibid.*, s. 79(3).
[139] SOA 2003, s. 79(8).
[140] SOA 2003, s. 79(8).
[141] [2005] EWCA Crim 732, [2005] 1 WLR 2005.
[142] There may, of course, be an attempted sexual assault on such facts. Concerning the mens rea of criminal attempts in this area, see below, § 9.4(iii).

The maximum penalty is life imprisonment in certain circumstances.[143] Otherwise, it is 10 years' imprisonment if tried on indictment, or 6 months' imprisonment if tried summarily.[144]

A perusal of this offence immediately informs the reader that where the interchange is between D and V, and no one else, much of the conduct covered in sections 1–3 will fall also within this offence. With the exception of sexual violations of overwhelmed or passive victims (who could not be said to be "engaged in an activity"), the overlap of section 4 with the other three offences is considerable.

What, then, is the distinctive coverage of this offence? For the moment, confining ourselves to interactions between D and V, situations where D causes V to touch D (or indeed V) sexually seem to be included.[145] Consider also a case where D compels V to have intercourse with her. This means that what might loosely be described as "female rape" is still an offence, potentially carrying with it a maximum penalty of life imprisonment.[146] Moving beyond two-party interactions, D commits this offence if D causes V to engage in non-consensual sexual activity with T: T may be innocent of D's machinations, an accomplice of D, or even a co-complainant with V.

D must cause V to engage in an activity to which V does not consent. If V acts because of something violent or coercive that D does, or threatens to do, it is inevitable that D will be found to have caused V to do it. Significant deceptions by D could also lead to a finding that D caused V to engage in a sexual activity without consent. As we saw in § 12.3, these very facts can establish V's lack of consent. But the two elements may not coincide. On a very loose view of causation, for example, D might be said to have "caused" V to have sex with D by overcoming V's reluctance with a very large sum of money.[147] It does not follow that the ensuing sexual act was non-consensual, even in cases where D has exploited the economic circumstances of V.

It is worth dwelling briefly on the last point. A real difficulty in this area is that extreme economic hardship can be highly coercive. In the example of the brothel keeper (§ 12.3(ii)(b) above), it is no great stretch of the English language to say that—through offering V work in his brothel—D has caused V (a desperate asylum seeker) to engage in sexual activity. Such a conclusion would have significant implications not merely for the scope of section 4 but also for the other non-consensual offences in the Act. No doubt those responsible for formulating and implementing a draconian asylum policy are effectively beyond the purview of this offence and, if they are exempt, D should be too. Yet it is remarkable that modern drafting of serious offences can give rise to such conjectures about their scope.

---

[143] These circumstances are where the activity involves "penetration of [V]'s anus or vagina ... penetration of [V]'s mouth with a person's penis ... penetration of a person's anus or vagina with a part of [V]'s body or by [V] with anything else, or ... penetration of a person's mouth with [V]'s penis": SOA 2003, s. 4(4).

[144] SOA 2003, s. 4(5).

[145] See, e.g., *Devonald* [2008] EWCA Crim 527.

[146] Assuming penile penetration of D's vagina is involved: SOA 2003, s. 4(4).

[147] A broad view of causation, one that would plot a causal pathway connecting the conduct of D and the voluntary actions of V, has occasionally been taken by the courts. But see the critical analysis at § 4.2(iii)(d).

§ 12.10 Consensual sexual offences

The SOA 2003 creates five groups of what might be called "consensual sex offences"—that is, cases where a form of sexual behaviour constitutes a criminal offence, even if the other person involved consents to it. (The presence of consent is not, of course, a legal ingredient in these offences, and defendants can be prosecuted for them in cases where consent was absent and their behaviour therefore constituted one of the non-consensual offences discussed earlier.)

The first two groups involve sexual acts with persons who are under the age of consent (16). The third penalises sexual acts with persons under the age of 18 when done by those whom the law regards as being in a "position of trust". The fourth penalises sexual acts with persons under 18 when done by any of a wide range of "family members". The fifth penalises "sex with an adult relative": sexual acts when performed by persons over the age of consent who are closely related to one another.

§ 12.11 Child sex offences[148]

(i) Offences involving children under 13

Sections 5–8 of the SOA 2003 create four criminal offences of sexual behaviour with children who are under 13. The first is called "rape of a child under 13",[149] the second is "assault of a child under 13 by penetration",[150] and the third is "sexual assault of a child under 13".[151] In each case, the actus reus is the same as for the similarly named non-consensual offence set out earlier in the Act, except that the words "[V] does not consent" are replaced by the words "the other person is under 13". The fourth offence is "causing or inciting a child under 13 to engage in sexual activity".[152] This offence is similar to the offence in section 4 of "causing a person to engage in sexual activity without consent", except that presence of consent is irrelevant and the offence extends beyond "causing" sexual activity to include "inciting" it.[153]

These four offences are constructed on the basis that, because a child under 13 is unable to consent, to engage them in consensual sexual activity is morally equivalent to forcing it upon an older person who does not consent. In many situations—for example, where D is 50 and performs a sexual act with a child of 5—this will obviously be so. However, where

---

[148] For a detailed examination and criticism of the law on this area, see Spencer, "Child and Family Offences" [2004] *Crim LR* 347.

[149] SOA 2003, s. 5. The maximum penalty for this offence is life imprisonment: s. 5(2).

[150] *Ibid.*, s. 6. The maximum penalty for this offence is life imprisonment: s. 6(2).

[151] *Ibid.*, s. 7. The maximum penalty for this offence is 14 years' imprisonment on indictment and 6 months' imprisonment if tried summarily: s. 7(2).

[152] *Ibid.*, s. 8. The maximum sentence is dependent on the activity engaged in. If it involves "penetration of [V]'s anus or vagina … penetration of [V]'s mouth with a person's penis … penetration of a person's anus or vagina with a part of [V]'s body or by [V] with anything else, or … penetration of a person's mouth with [V]'s penis", the maximum penalty is life imprisonment: s. 8(2). In other cases, the maximum penalty is 14 years' imprisonment on indictment, and 6 months' imprisonment when tried summarily: s. 8(3).

[153] Indeed, it has been held that s. 8 creates two offences, one involving causation and the other involving incitement: *Walker* [2006] EWCA Crim 1907. This drafting avoids issues of causation arising in cases where V (factually, if not legally) consents to the relevant activity.

the participants are of a similar age, or where (as is possible) the defendant is even younger than the other participant, an issue of fair labelling arises.[154] If, at her suggestion, a boy of 12 has sexual intercourse with a girl of the same age, or allows her to fellate him, it is surely questionable whether it is appropriate to label him a "rapist". Furthermore, these offences, unlike their equivalents under the old law,[155] carry strict liability as to the age of the other participant. Although the drafting of the provisions does not make this explicit, Parliament plainly intended strict liability to apply.[156] So it follows that, in the previous example, the boy of 12 would be in law a "rapist", even if the girl told him she was 13—or 16—and he honestly and reasonably believed it.

(ii) Offences involving children under 16

Sections 9–15 of the Act create a further six offences penalising various forms of sexual behaviour with a person under the age of 16. Although mainly directed against sexual acts with older children, they apply no less to sexual acts with younger ones, and where the child is under 13 they overlap with the offences discussed in the previous section.[157] Although less severely punishable than those created by sections 5–8, all of these offences are potentially triable on indictment and punishable with imprisonment.[158]

Section 9 creates an offence of "sexual activity with a child", which is committed by any intentional touching of a person under 16 that is "sexual" in the sense given to that word by section 78, which was discussed earlier.[159] The defendant must be aged over 18 to commit the offence. The maximum penalty (depending on the activity engaged in) is either life imprisonment, or 14 years' imprisonment when tried on indictment (6 months' imprisonment when tried summarily).[160]

Section 10 creates the offence of "causing or inciting a child to engage in sexual activity". The defendant must be over 18, and the maximum penalties are the same as for the section 9 offence.[161] Section 11 creates a third offence of "engaging in sexual activity in the presence of a child", and section 12 a fourth offence of causing a child to watch a sexual act, or showing a child a pornographic picture. Again, the defendant must be over 18. The maximum sentences for both offences are 10 years' imprisonment if tried on indictment, or six months' imprisonment if tried summarily.[162] These (and the "under 13" offences)

---

[154] Above, § 2.4.

[155] See: B (a minor) v. DPP [2000] 2 AC 428; K [2002] 1 AC 462; Kumar [2004] EWCA Crim 3207, [2004] 1 WLR 1352.

[156] Confirmed in G [2006] EWCA Crim 821, [2006] 1 WLR 2052; G [2008] UKHL 37, [2008] 1 WLR 1379.

[157] This is a deviation from the original plan, which was that the second group of offences should be entirely separate from the first. For the history of the matter, see Spencer, "Child and Family Offences" [2004] Crim LR 347, 353.

[158] Maximum penalties range from 6 months to 14 years, depending on the nature of the sexual act and the court before which the offence is tried.

[159] See above, § 12.6.

[160] Life imprisonment applies if the activity involves "penetration of [V]'s anus or vagina ... penetration of [V]'s mouth with a person's penis ... penetration of a person's anus or vagina with a part of [V]'s body or by [V] with anything else, or ... penetration of a person's mouth with [V]'s penis": SOA 2003, s. 9(2). For other activities, see s. 9(3).

[161] SOA 2003, ss. 10(2)–(3).

[162] Ibid., ss. 11(2), 12(2).

are supplemented by two specific preliminary offences: "arranging or facilitating the commission of a child sex offence"[163] and the offence usually called "grooming"—having communicated with a child on at least two earlier occasions, meeting them, or travelling to meet them, with the intention of committing a sexual offence.[164]

Unlike the "under 13" offences, the "under 16" offences are drafted so as to provide some protection for defendants who engage in sexual acts with a child or young person whom they believe to be over the age of consent. D does not commit any of the offences in sections 9–12 unless D had no reasonable belief that the child was aged 16 or over. If the child was under 13, however, strict liability is imposed with regard to the age of the child.[165]

Although both groups of child sex offences were aimed at adult paedophiles who prey upon the young and vulnerable, they are not so limited, and also punish all forms of sexual behaviour between consenting children. By section 13, persons under 18 who commit what would otherwise be one of the "under 16" offences set out in sections 9–12 incur a lower range of penalties: 5 years' imprisonment if tried on indictment, and 6 months' imprisonment if tried summarily. But even this limited concession does not apply to the "under 13" offences, however young the defendant who commits them. The result is to bring within the criminal law a range of sexual acts, some of which are usually thought to be normal and not improper, and others at least not seriously wrong. They include, for example, mouth-to-mouth kissing[166] or minor acts of sexual exploration between consenting 14- or 15-year-olds, and erotic play between children of the age of 10. In 1994 a study reported that the average age of young people's first sexual experiences (kissing, cuddling, petting, etc.) then stood at 14 for women and 13 for men,[167] and a 2013 study suggested that around 30% of 16–24 year olds had had full sexual intercourse before they were 16.[168] So far are these relevant provisions out of line with the normal sexual behaviour of young people that their practical effect must be to make indictable offenders out of all but a minority of the population. This was a feature of the old law as well, and one for which it was forcefully criticised.[169] It seems paradoxical that in a law intended to "modernise Victorian laws on sex offences" this blemish should have been not cured, but reinforced and, through the use of strict liability in some offences, exacerbated.

This point concerning overcriminalisation was made when the Sexual Offences Bill was before Parliament, but all moves to restrict the scope of the child sex offences were resisted by the government on the ground that they might provide unwanted loopholes for paedophiles. The resulting "legislative overkill" did not matter, it was said, because the police and

---

[163] *Ibid.*, s. 14. The maximum penalty for this offence is 14 years' imprisonment on indictment, and 6 months' imprisonment if tried summarily: s. 14(4).

[164] *Ibid.*, s. 15. The maximum penalty for this offence is 10 years' imprisonment on indictment, and 6 months' imprisonment if tried summarily: s. 15(4).

[165] *Ibid.*, ss. 9(1)(c), 10(1)(c), 11(1)(d), 12(1)(c).

[166] Mouth-to-mouth kissing, if done for erotic pleasure, is unquestionably "sexual behaviour", and prosecutions are sometimes brought where matters go no further than this. For an example, see *Lamb* [2007] EWCA Crim 1766, (discussed below, § 12.13).

[167] Wellings et al., *Sexual Behaviour in Britain: the National Survey of Sexual Attitudes and Lifestyles* (1994) 40; Erens, McManus, Prescott, Field et al., *National Survey of Sexual Attitudes and Lifestyles II* (2003) 5.

[168] Mercer et al, "Changes in Sexual Attitudes and Lifestyles in Britain Through the Life Course and Over Time" (2013) 382 *The Lancet* 1781, 1786.

[169] Hogan, "Modernising the Law of Sexual Offences" in Glazebrook (ed.), *Reshaping the Criminal Law* (1978) 174.

the Crown Prosecution Service have a discretion to prosecute which they can be expected to exercise intelligently.[170] They were wrong about that, and in this connection two things should be noted. One is that English law contrives to make this problem particularly acute, first by setting an age of consent that it is among the highest in Western Europe, and secondly by setting an age of criminal responsibility which, at 10, is among the lowest—and by extending the bite of it by abolishing the "doli incapax" rule, which until 1998 prevented children between the age of 10 and 14 incurring criminal liability except where they realised that their conduct was morally wrong.[171] The second is that, in a number of other countries, the problem has been avoided by drafting criminal offences of sex with minors so as to exclude consensual acts between minors who are close in age.[172]

This part of English law is inconsistent, in that it permits persons under 16 who understand their implications to consent to medical procedures, however serious—and indeed to the prescription of contraceptive medication[173]—whilst at the same time forbidding them to consent to sexual acts, however trivial. It is also oppressive because, despite the government's assurances at the time the Sexual Offences Act was passed and the formal guidance issued by the Crown Prosecution Service stressing that "the overriding purpose of the legislation is to protect children and it was not Parliament's intention to punish children unnecessarily or for the criminal law to intervene where it was wholly inappropriate", and adding that "[c]onsensual sexual activity between, for example, a 14 or 15 year-old and a teenage partner would not normally require criminal proceedings in the absence of aggravating features",[174] heavy-handed prosecutions do indeed take place.[175] (In theory, a prosecution brought in breach of the prosecutor's publicly stated policy can be attacked

---

[170] "We should create the offence and leave it to the prosecutor to decide": Paul Goggins, Under-Secretary of State, Standing Committee B, 11 September 2003, 135. At the second reading of the Bill, the Home Secretary, David Blunkett, had famously offered "to buy a flagon of champagne for anyone who comes up with a satisfactory answer" as to how the law could be framed without leaving undesirable loopholes: Hansard (HC), vol. 429, no. 129, col. 195 (15 July 2003).

[171] See below, § 19.4 and, in particular, *JTB* [2009] UKHL 20, [2009] 1 AC 1310.

[172] In France, for example, the criminal offence of consensual sex with minors is defined so as to exclude defendants who are themselves under the age of 18 (Code pénal Art. 227–25); and in Italy the equivalent offence does not apply to sexual acts with minors provided (i) the minor is over 13 and (ii) there is no more than three years' difference in age between them (Codice penale Art. 609 quater, para. 5). Under Scots law, the fact that the difference in age between the parties does not exceed two years can constitute a defence to some consensual sexual offences: Sexual Offences (Scotland) Act 2009, s. 39(3).

[173] See, further, SOA 2003, s. 73, which provides a limited defence for those who would otherwise be aiding, abetting, or counselling an offence under certain sections of the Act. This defence would be available to a doctor prescribing contraception to V, a 13-year-old girl, to limit the risk of V becoming pregnant, well aware that this might encourage V to engage in sexual activity.

[174] Crown Prosecution Service, *Rape and Sexual Offences: Chapter 11: Youths* www.cps.gov.uk/legal/p_to_r/rape_and_sexual_offences/youths/.

[175] For one example out of many, see *C* (2009) 173 CL & JW 303 (CA). D, a boy of 14, had consensual sex with his girlfriend, A, aged 14. After they broke up, D started going out with A's friend B, aged 13, and these two also had consensual sex. B's mother found out and told the police, when by chance she read on B's mobile phone a text conversation between A and B comparing notes. For this, D, a "good student" from a "respectable family", was prosecuted for "sexual activity with a child" contrary to s. 13, pleaded guilty, and initially received an eight-month custodial sentence—reduced to a supervision order on appeal. The girls were equally guilty, yet were not prosecuted. For other examples of proceedings that seem heavy-handed, see: *R(S)* v. *DPP* [2006] EWHC 2231 (Admin); *D* [2006] Cr App R (S) 330 (53); *C* [2006] All ER (D) 293. Cf. *BH* v. *Llandundo Youth Court* [2014] EWHC 1833 (Admin), where the decision to commit two boys (who were 11 at the time of the alleged offence) to trial in the Crown Court for causing or inciting a child under 13 to engage in sexual activity was quashed, and the case was referred to the Youth Court. In that case, V was *not* consenting.

either by inviting the court of trial to stay the proceedings as an abuse of process or by seeking judicial review of the decision to institute it. In practice, however, such attacks are usually unsuccessful.)[176]

As we have seen, Article 8 of the ECHR obliges contracting states to respect, within limits, the right of its citizens to respect for private and family life. In the case of a prosecution for under-age sex that was particularly oppressive, could this guarantee be invoked? The attempt was made, unsuccessfully, in G.[177] A boy aged 15 had sexual intercourse with a girl of 12 and later pleaded guilty to the offence of "rape of a child under 13" contrary to section 5 of the SOA 2003, on the basis that she had consented but that she had told him that she too was 15. G later sought to argue that a conviction on these facts for such a grave and stigmatic offence was disproportionate and infringed his rights under Article 8. If criminal proceedings were appropriate, he contended, he should have been prosecuted for the less serious offence under section 13 ("child sexual offences committed by children or young persons"). This argument was accepted by two members of the House of Lords, but the majority gave it short shrift. Lord Hoffmann contemptuously dismissed the proceedings as "another example of the regrettable tendency to try to convert the whole system of justice into questions of human rights".[178] Using more moderate language, Baroness Hale said "the prosecution, conviction and sentence were both rational and proportionate in the pursuit of the legitimate aims of the protection of the health and morals and rights and freedoms of others",[179] while Lord Mance said that the statutory scheme was justified by "the strong protective needs of children under 13"—protective needs which, it seems, are sufficiently strong to justify making criminals out of both parties where two children engage in consensual sex.[180]

§ 12.12 "Abuse of trust"

Sections 16–24 of the Act create four offences of sexual behaviour with children by persons who are in a position of trust. For the purposes of these provisions, "children" are those aged under 18; hence some persons over the age of consent are included. The sexual acts that are so prohibited are the same as those set out in the "under 16" offences: "sexual activity" (meaning any sexual touching), causing or inciting a "child" to engage in sexual activity", engaging in sexual activity when a "child" is present, and causing a "child" to watch a sexual act or see a pornographic image. What amounts to a "position of trust" is set out, in minute detail, in sections 21 and 22; the persons listed include schoolteachers, staff in hospitals and care homes, and, for good measure, any other categories of person designated by the Secretary of State.

---

[176] As in S v. DPP [2006] EWHC 2231 (Admin). Unusually, a judicial review did succeed in R (E, S and R) v. DPP [2011] EWHC 1465, [2012] 1 Cr App R 68, noted in Spencer, "Controlling the Discretion to Prosecute" (2012) 71 CLJ 27. Cf. R (CM) v. CPS [2014] EWHC 4457 (Admin).

[177] [2008] UKHL 37, [2009] 1 AC 92. See, further, Brown [2013] UKSC 43, [2013] 4 All ER 860.

[178] G [2008] UKHL 37, [2009] 1 AC 92, para. 10.

[179] Ibid., para. 55.

[180] Ibid., para. 72. The defendant later raised the Art. 8 issue again an application to Strasbourg, but his application was ruled inadmissible: G v. United Kingdom (2011) 53 EHR SE 25.

Whether there is really any need for these offences is questionable. Where the "child" is under 16 they overlap, of course, with the "under 16" offences. No such offence was known to English law until 2000, when the precursor to these provisions was hastily created,[181] not in response to any public pressure but as a gesture needed to persuade Parliament to agree to lower the age of consent for homosexual acts from 18 to 16: opposition focused on the risk that a change in the law would leave homosexual teachers free to form sexual relationships with their older pupils. In practice, the main impact of these offences is to criminalise all forms of sexual contact—however minor—between teachers and sixth-form pupils aged 16 and 17. For teachers to form consensual sexual relationships with their older pupils may be misbehaviour that fully justifies dismissal, but does it follow that it ought to be a criminal offence?[182] Not least of the incongruities that result is that it renders criminal any sexual contact between persons who, according to the civil law, are legally competent to marry (and, since 2005, to form civil partnerships): a point that is recognised by section 23, which solemnly provides a defence for sexual acts performed in the context of a marriage or a civil partnership.

§ 12.13 "Familial child sex offences"

In similar vein, sections 25–9 create four offences of sexual acts when performed with persons under the age of 18 by those whom the Act defines as "family members". The range of sexual acts prohibited is slightly narrower than is covered by the "under 16" and "abuse of trust" offences, being limited to "sexual activity" in the sense of any form of sexual touching,[183] and inciting the other family member to touch him.[184] The "family relationships" to which these offences apply are set out in some detail in section 27. In essence, there are three groups. The first consists of parents, grandparents, brothers, sisters, half-brothers, half-sisters, aunts, uncles, and foster-parents; these count as "family members" whether or not the "victim" of the offence has ever lived with them. The second comprises step-parents, cousins, step-brothers, step-sisters, and people who have shared a common foster-parent. These count as family members if they have ever lived in the same household as the "victim", or at some point have been involved in caring for him or her. The third group includes all persons whatsoever who are currently living with the victim and are currently involved in providing care.

---

[181] Sexual Offences (Amendment) Act 2000, s. 3.

[182] In *Lamb* [2007] EWCA Crim 1766, a 31-year-old teacher was prosecuted for allegedly kissing, on two occasions, 17-year-old sixth-form girls, with their consent, at balls celebrating the end of the school year. The proceedings involved a six-day trial in the Crown Court, at the end of which he was convicted and given a suspended sentence, and then a further hearing in the Court of Appeal, which ultimately quashed his conviction because of a misdirection on the evidence. Was this, one wonders, an appropriate use of scarce resources?

[183] SOA 2003, s. 25. The maximum sentence varies with the age of the defendant and the activity engaged in. If the defendant is over 18 years of age, and the activity involved "penetration of [V]'s anus or vagina … penetration of [V]'s mouth with a person's penis … penetration of a person's anus or vagina with a part of [V]'s body or by [V] with anything else, or … penetration of a person's mouth with [V]'s penis", the maximum penalty is 14 years' imprisonment and summary trial is unavailable: s. 25(4)(a). In other cases where the defendant is over 18, the maximum penalty is 14 years' imprisonment on indictment, or 6 months' imprisonment if tried summarily: s. 25(4)(b). If the defendant is under 18, the maximum penalty is 5 years' imprisonment on indictment, or 6 months' imprisonment if tried summarily: s. 25(5).

[184] *Ibid.*, s. 26. The maximum penalties are the same as under s. 25.

These offences were completely new: the previous law contained an offence of incest, but this was limited to vaginal intercourse between a small number of close relatives; the new law, by contrast, penalises a much wider range of sexual activity.[185] As with the "abuse of trust" offences, these offences overlap with the "under 16" offences, and their practical impact is limited to sexual acts with persons aged 16 and 17. Although the offences created by these sections of the Act include a considerable amount of supposedly consensual behaviour that is likely to be unpleasantly abusive, it also criminalises much that seems completely innocent: for example, mouth-to-mouth kissing between first cousins aged 17 who at some point in their life lived under the same roof—punishable with (theoretically) five years' imprisonment. As with the "abuse of trust" offences, this group of offences also potentially incriminates sexual conduct between persons whom the civil law permits to marry or form a civil partnership; and with this in mind, section 28, like section 25, creates a defence for those who have done so.

§ 12.14 Sex with an adult relative

The offences discussed in the previous section are complemented by two further new offences entitled "sex with an adult relative". Section 64 makes it an offence for a person over 16 to perform an act of penetrative sex with another person who is a parent, grandparent, child, grandchild, brother, sister, half-brother, uncle, aunt, nephew, or niece, and who is over the age of 18,[186] while section 65 creates a "passive" version of the same behaviour. The previous law contained a precursor to these offences in the crime of incest, which criminalised consensual sex between close relatives irrespective of their age, but these replacement offences go much further. First, whereas incest was limited to acts of "ordinary" vaginal intercourse, the new offences cover any form of penetrative sex (including oral sex). And secondly, whereas incest was limited to sexual intercourse between a narrow range of close relatives, the new offences extend to a wider list, including uncles and aunts and nephews and nieces, and—true to the policy of making the new law on sexual offences gender neutral—to sex between consenting males as well as to sex between consenting men and women.

Since homosexual acts between consenting males were legalised in 1967, it has been widely accepted that criminal liability should not attach to sexual acts done between consenting adults in private. So what possible justification could there be for retaining, as between consenting adults, the offence of incest—the existence of which was defended on eugenic grounds[187]—and extending it to cover acts that are incapable of causing pregnancy? The utilitarian reasons given at the time[188] were spectacularly weak and the real

---

[185] For example, the behaviour in *R* [2009] 2 Cr App R (S) 184 (24), where a boy of 19 received a three-year custodial sentence for putting his finger into the vagina of his 17-year-old sister, with her consent. Prior to the Sexual Offences Act, no criminal offence would have been committed.

[186] A bizarre consequence of the offences being limited in this way appears to be that D could mount a defence along the lines that the Crown cannot prove the other person was under the age of 18 at the time.

[187] Bailey and Blackburn, "The Punishment of Incest Act 1980: A Case Study in Law Creation" [1979] *Crim LR* 708; Wolfram, "Eugenics and the Punishment of Incest Act 1908" [1983] *Crim LR* 308.

[188] In *Setting the Boundaries—Reforming the Law on Sex Offences* (2000), paras. 5.8ff, the Home Office argued that the offence was necessary to provide "redress" for those who in later life realise that "the relationship they have been involved in has not been appropriate": which overlooks the fact that if the course of conduct began

reason appears to be that incest, like homosexual acts between males before 1967, is viewed by many or most people with horror and disgust. But where such acts are done in private, is the fact that other people would be disgusted if they knew about them a sufficient reason for making such behaviour a criminal offence?

In *Stübing* v. *Germany*,[189] a German law criminalising incest between consenting adults was challenged by a man who had had consensual sexual intercourse with his adult sister. Though accepting that Article 8 of the Convention was engaged, the Strasbourg Court held that the German offence could be justified under Article 8(2), which permits the state to interfere with private lives where this is "necessary in a democratic society ... for the protection of health or morals, or for the protection of the rights and freedoms of others". In so holding, the Court took into account, among other things, the risk of genetic abnormalities when children are born as a result of incestuous relationships. As the English offence, unlike the German one, extends to cover sexual acts from which the birth of children could not possibly result, its justification under Article 8(2) would be less easily established.

§ 12.15 Jurisdiction

Traditionally, the basic rule of English criminal law was *territoriality*.[190] To be punishable as a criminal offence in England and Wales, the act in question must take place there. As Viscount Simonds put it in one case, "apart from those exceptional cases in which specific provision is made in regard to acts committed abroad, the whole body of the criminal law of England deals only with acts committed in England".[191] The increasing ease of foreign travel, particularly within Europe but also beyond, has led to a growing number of statutory exceptions. One important exception concerns sexual offences. Section 72 of the Sexual Offences Act 2003[192] gives the courts in England and Wales jurisdiction over a range of sexual offences involving children or young persons where these are committed outside the United Kingdom by a "United Kingdom national"[193] or by a person who is resident within the UK, provided that the behaviour also constitutes a criminal offence in country where it occurred.

---

during the complainant's early life the defendant would be guilty of a range other offences. It was also argued that the offence is necessary to "protect the family unit" from behaviour that is likely to endanger it: an argument that would equally justify the criminalisation of adultery, refusal to have sexual intercourse, persistent drunkenness, and a range of other matrimonial misdeeds. See further Spencer, "Child and Family Offences" [2004] *Crim LR* 347, 358.

[189] (2012) 55 EHRR 24. See Spencer, "Incest and Article 8 of the European Convention on Human Rights" (2013) 72 *CLJ* 5.

[190] The classic study is Glanville Williams, "Venue and Ambit of the Criminal Law" (1965) 81 *LQR* 276, 395, 518.

[191] *Cox* v. *Army Council* [1963] AC 48, 67.

[192] Re-enacting a rule first introduced by the Sex Offenders Act 1997.

[193] A term which s. 72(9) defines as British citizens, plus certain other stated groups.

13

THEFT

§ 13.1 Property, rights, and justice

"A man's property is something related to him: This relation is not natural, but moral and founded upon justice. 'Tis very preposterous, therefore, to imagine, that we can have any idea of property, without fully comprehending the nature of justice…. The origin of justice explains that of property."[1]

The recognition and protection of property rights in our society raise deep questions of political philosophy. In part, this is because the concept of "property" is itself amorphous. There is a tendency to associate property with "things"—to think of property in terms of objects endowed with spatial dimensions, that can be touched and seen. The association is often appropriate, but can be misleading. Property, understood in the context of a legal system, is a legal phenomenon—and rights of property are not physical things but legal constructs. Indeed, in an important sense proprietary rights are a species of personal right. They are rights between persons, which are held by one person against another person or persons.[2] That I own something means, in law, that I have certain rights to deal with that thing which others do not have and that others owe me certain duties not to deal with it.

These rights and duties are not absolute. D is not free to torture her cat. Ownership of land does not mean the police have no right, under any circumstances, to enter; neither does it make one free to build upon the land without permission. Property may be subject to taxation and even expropriation by the State.

Moreover, the rights associated with ownership of property vary across different types of property. As we shall see, the human body is not susceptible of ownership in the same way as is a kettle. Similarly, the legal nature of property has varied across different periods of social and legal development. In the early common law, ownership was conceived of in terms of the right to possession,[3] which explains the emphasis on possession in the Larceny Act 1916, the statutory predecessor to our modern law of theft; and also why the tort of

---

[1] Hume, *A Treatise of Human Nature* (Selby-Bigge and Nidditch, eds., 2nd ed., 1978) 491.

[2] Cf. Hohfeld, *Fundamental Legal Conceptions as Applied in Judicial Reasoning* (1919) 71ff; Harris, *Property and Justice* (1996) 120ff. According to Grey, "The Disintegration of Property" in *NOMOS xxii: Property* (1980) 69, 81, "the substitution of a bundle-of-rights for a thing-ownership conception of property has the ultimate consequence that property ceases to be an important category in legal and political theory".

[3] Pollock and Maitland, *The History of English Law* (2nd ed., 1911) vol. I, 57, vol. II, 153ff; Tigar, "The Right of Property and the Law of Theft" (1984) 62 *Texas LR* 1443.

conversion could only be committed against a plaintiff in possession or with an immediate proprietary right to possession.[4]

The extent to which property is a pre-legal concept (rather than a creation of law) is a matter of controversy. Property rights are distinguished from other interpersonal rights by the fact that they exist in respect of some *thing*; yet that thing may be tangible or intangible and, independent of the law, property seems to lack any clear-cut definition.[5] Despite this, much of our law and society takes property to be a foundational concept. In both civil and criminal law, sanctions for wrongs such as conversion, theft, and the like, normally require proof of a harm. Implicitly, these sanctions take it for granted that there is some right of property that can be harmed, such that corrective justice is called for; or even, in Locke's work, so that the government of a society is warranted.[6] This sort of proposition—that property may be prior to tort and criminal law, and even prior to law—informs much political theory, especially by libertarian philosophers.[7] Property rights are defended by liberal political philosophers, too, on the ground that autonomy is augmented when individuals are able to choose for themselves how they deal with their property, spend their money, etc.[8] If my well-being is increased by breaking crockery from time to time, without risking harm to others, that should be my affair—provided the crockery is mine.

At the same time, the reasons for law to recognise property are not only individualistic. Donne's admonition that no man is an island also has communitarian implications for the law of property. In a social context, property rights help to co-ordinate the activities of society members, by limiting the freedom of citizens to conduct themselves without trespassing unduly upon the private lives of others. Property rights can enhance liberty, yet their free use by one may restrict the capacity for well-being of another. Even in societies which endorse free-market economic activity, the law typically contains a panoply of constraints on monopolistic, exploitative, or otherwise unfair action. Similarly, taxation derogates from absolute notions of dominion over property, but may be justified by redistributive arguments—including the need to foster minimum standards of living in others. In economic terms, a selective recognition of property rights offers chances both to foster economic prosperity and to provide for values that markets may not deliver, including values related to basic needs and human rights.

Legal institutions of property, therefore, must accommodate both the principles and privileges of ownership, with its implications for corrective justice, and the need to allocate social wealth, driven by concerns of distributive justice. However, by contrast with corrective justice, which presupposes a notion of property, distributive justice may operate prior to the law's conception of property.[9] An absolutist legal conception of property

---

[4] Who may be the bailee rather than the owner: *Gordon* v. *Harper* (1796) 7 TR 9; *Wertheim* v. *Cheel* (1885) 11 VLR 107; *Nyberg* v. *Handelaar* [1892] 2 QB 202; Warren, "Qualifying as Plaintiff in an Action for Conversion" (1936) 49 *Harv LR* 1084. Indeed, even the owner is capable of converting her own goods, if someone else has an indefeasible possessory right to them: *Roberts* v. *Wyatt* (1810) 2 Taunt 268, 127 ER 1080; *City Motors* v. *S. Aerial Service* (1961) 106 CLR 477.

[5] Gray, "Property in Thin Air" [1991] *CLJ* 252.

[6] Locke, *Two Treatises of Government*, Book II § 123. Cf. *Entick* v. *Carrington* (1765) 19 St Tr 1029, 1060: "The great end for which men entered into society was to secure their property".

[7] See, e.g., Nozick, *Anarchy, State and Utopia* (1974).

[8] See Waldron, *The Right to Private Property* (1988); Simmonds, "The Possibility of Private Law" in Tasioulas (ed.), *Law, Values and Social Practices* (1997) 129.

[9] Cf. Simester and Sullivan, "On the Nature and Rationale of Property Offences" in Duff and Green (eds.), *Defining Crimes: Essays on the Criminal Law's Special Part* (2005) 168, §§ 1–2.

would generate a system in which autonomy, consent, and individual fault are determinative. These concepts are certainly important to the common law. But they are not the only considerations. For example, in many jurisdictions constructive trusts are now recognised for reasons of fairness, say upon the break-up of a domestic relationship where no formal arrangements existed regarding distribution of property. Land owners may now owe involuntary duties to trespassers.[10] The recognition of property in commercial contexts may be determined by the need to allocate risk in unforeseen circumstances, or by considerations of priority in insolvency. Indeed, the Canadian Supreme Court has even suggested that proprietary remedies can be created, or even refused, on a discretionary basis according to whether "there is reason to grant to the plaintiff the additional rights that flow from a recognition of a right of property".[11]

By and large, these distributive factors are not the concern of the criminal law, since it is not for the criminal law to decide when property rights exist. Rather, property offences exist primarily to reinforce and protect those rights once recognised by the civil law. Indirectly, therefore, property offences are not merely a means to protect individuals' autonomous rights over property, but also a tool for reinforcing political decisions about the distribution of scarce resources in society. Prima facie rules of property arise in the civil law for a variety of underlying reasons. Yet the criminal law does not look behind the prima facie rules. It takes ownership, and its facets, as an axiom.

Inevitably so. Both civil and criminal law share a conception of ownership. Notwithstanding what has been said here about *when* ownership should be recognised, its recognition necessarily involves certain legal consequences, at least in a liberal society.[12] Ownership of property confers upon the owner a set of powers, in particular to use and to alienate (transfer) the property, and to exclude others from doing the same.[13] Without these powers there is no ownership. In the context of property offences, the function of the criminal law is to protect those rights of ownership. This means that the criminal law must take its lead from the civil law: the creature it protects is a creation of the civil law.

In the criminal law, that protection is achieved by a variety of offences which impose obligations on non-owners not to usurp the powers of an owner. First among them, and the subject of this chapter, is the prohibition of theft.

§ 13.2 The definition of theft

Theft is defined in section 1(1) of the Theft Act 1968, which radically recast this area of law along lines proposed by the Criminal Law Revision Committee.[14] Section 1(1) provides:

> A person is guilty of theft if he dishonestly appropriates property belonging to another with the intention of permanently depriving the other of it; and "thief" and "steal" shall be construed accordingly.

---

[10] Occupiers' Liability Act 1984.

[11] *Lac Minerals v. Corona Ltd* (1989) 61 DLR 14, 51.

[12] Cf. Honoré, "Ownership" in Guest (ed.), *Oxford Essays in Jurisprudence* (1961) 107.

[13] In Roman law it was traditionally said that the owner had the right *ius utendi fruendi abutendi*: to use, enjoy or destroy. See Buckland, *A text-book of Roman Law from Augustus to Justinian* (3d ed., 1963) § LXVIII.

[14] Criminal Law Revision Committee, Eighth Report, *Theft and Related Offences*, Cmnd. 2977 (1966). A prominent part in the preparation of this report was played by the two of the most respected legal writers of the day: Professors Glanville Williams, and J.C. Smith (the original author of *Smith's Law of Theft*, now in its ninth edition

The offence contains five elements, each of which must be proved by the prosecution. The first three elements comprise the actus reus:

(i)   there must be *property* (i.e. something capable of being stolen);
(ii)   that property must *belong* to another; and
(iii) D must *appropriate* the property.

The final two elements constitute the mens rea:

(iv) D must intend permanently to deprive another person of the property; and
(v)   D must act dishonestly.

Each of these elements will be considered below.[15]

§ 13.3 Property

Most things can be stolen. At common law and under the Larceny Act 1916, land and intangible property were excluded from the ambit of a larceny.[16] This limitation is undone by section 4(1) of the 1968 Act, which enacts a general rule that:

> "Property" includes any money and all other property, real or personal, including things in action and other intangible property.

The current position is therefore that, subject to certain exceptions in section 4(2)–(4), any type of property can be stolen. But it remains necessary to show (a) that the thing stolen is, in law, an item of property; and (b) that none of the exceptions apply.

(i) What counts as property?

To fall within section 4(1), the thing stolen must first be some type of property (real or personal, tangible or intangible). Most instances of theft are straightforward: D absconds with a television set or some other chattel—a piece of tangible personal property. Other cases, however, may be less obvious. Suppose D usurps V's right of way, or takes a train ride without first buying a ticket. Are these cases of theft? In order to answer that question, we need first to know whether the thing taken is, in law, "property". That term is not defined by the Theft Act, and its definition is a matter for the civil law. Although most things are capable of being owned, even in the civil law it is sometimes unclear whether particular rights constitute a form of legal or equitable property (i.e. rights *in rem*) or merely give rise to entitlements to sue others in contract, tort, or equity (rights *in personam*). In what follows we will survey the main areas of difficulty.

---

by Ormerod and Williams, 2007). For an account of the earlier law in its final stages, see the first edition of Smith and Hogan, *Criminal Law* (1965).

[15] For more detailed treatment, see also *Smith's Law of Theft, ibid.*

[16] The central element of the actus reus of larceny was "taking and carrying away", alias "asportation": something it is impossible to do to intangible property, and very difficult to do with land.

(a) Things in action and other intangible property

A thing in action, also called a chose in action, is something in which the law acknowledges property rights but which has no physical existence. The rights cannot be asserted physically and can be vindicated only by legal action (hence a thing "in action"). Examples of choses in action are a debt, shares in a company,[17] and a trade mark or copyright. Under section 4(1), all these things are capable of being stolen.

However, mere information, even a trade secret, does not qualify for protection as intangible property.[18] In *Oxford* v. *Moss*,[19] a university student took an examination paper before the examination and copied it before returning the paper to its original location. He was held not to have committed theft. Even though the information on the examination paper was no longer confidential, in the eyes of the law the university had not been deprived of any property. It would have been different if the student had not returned the examination paper itself, since he could then have been convicted of stealing the paper on which the examination was typed.[20]

Even where the right being interfered with is property for the purposes of the Act, the interference may not always count as theft. Breach of copyright, for instance, violates a chose in action. But photocopying a textbook does not deprive the copyright owner of the book. Neither does it deprive her of copyright in that book.[21]

There are hard questions of policy at issue here. Industrial espionage is a serious matter. Information can be worth an enormous amount of money. It may be the subject of contract, and its acquisition often involves the expenditure of considerable human and financial resources. We take it for granted that the recipe for Coca Cola is secret, both from us and from the manufacturer's competitors. Certainly it receives protection under the civil law, albeit not from the law of property.[22] Why not from the law of theft? In modern times, a nation's economic activity depends upon owners being able to protect the intangible rewards of their labours just as much as the tangible chattels they produce. The knowledge generated by research and development activities is vital to economic growth, and the case for criminalising theft of that knowledge is at least arguable.[23]

On the other hand, this is not to say that the decision in *Oxford* v. *Moss* was wrong. Extending the law of theft to include the appropriation of information raises difficult questions concerning the proper scope of protection. Should all confidential information be protected, or just trade secrets? When is information sufficiently confidential? What if the

---

[17] Cf. *Grubb* [1915] 2 KB 683.

[18] Cf. *The Federal Commissioner of Taxation* v. *United Aircraft Corp* (1943) 68 CLR 525, 534–5 (Latham CJ); *Boardman* v. *Phipps* [1967] 2 AC 46, 102–3 (Lord Cohen), 127–8 (Lord Upjohn), though for more equivocal views see at 89–91 (Viscount Dilhorne), 107 (Lord Hodson), 115 (Lord Guest).

[19] (1978) 68 Cr App R 183. See [1979] Crim LR 119.

[20] As happened to a schoolteacher who intercepted GCE papers in advance of the exam, read them, and then destroyed them: see Coleman, *Daily Telegraph*, 15 September 1981. (D was fined £1,000 and given a 12-month suspended prison sentence.)

[21] Cf. *Lloyd* [1985] QB 829; *Rank Film Distributors Ltd* v. *Video Information Centre* [1982] AC 380, 445; *Storrow and Poole* [1983] Crim LR 332.

[22] *Fraser* v. *Thames Television* [1984] QB 44; *A-G* v. *Observer Ltd* [1990] 1 AC 107, Stuckey, "The Equitable Action for Breach of Confidence: Is Information Ever Property?" (1981) 9 *Sydney LR* 402.

[23] See Cross, "Protecting Confidential Information under the Criminal Law of Theft and Fraud" (1991) 11 *OJLS* 264; Davies, "Protection of Intellectual Property—A Myth?" [2004] *J Crim Law* 398. Compare the Model Penal Code, § 223.0(6): "'Property' means anything of value".

information is a matter of public interest?[24] An ingredient in theft is "intention permanently to deprive" (§ 13.7 below); how would that concept apply to theft of information? The area, while ripe for reform, calls for legislative rather than judicial innovation.

(b) Services

A service is not by itself property.[25] So, for example, a ride on a train cannot be stolen,[26] though D's activity may comprise some other offence such as obtaining services dishonestly;[27] and one may steal the piece of paper on which the ticket is printed.

(c) Bank accounts

The relationship between banker and customer is one of debtor and creditor[28] or, if the account is in overdraft, vice versa. Since debts are a type of chose in action, it follows that the customer's right to draw on a credit balance is property within the scope of section 4(1), and can be stolen. Additionally, an agreed overdraft facility, which has not been fully drawn down, gives the customer a legal right against the bank and so also constitutes a chose in action.[29]

The case of *Kohn*[30] provides a useful example. D was a director of company C, which had an account with bank B. D had signing authority on the company's account. He dishonestly drew cheques on that account for personal purposes, thereby causing C's account with B to be debited. D was convicted of theft: he had stolen C's right of action, against B, for the amount by which C's account was debited.

D was not, however, convicted of theft in respect of every cheque. Most of the cheques had been drawn when C's account was in credit or within the authorised overdraft limit. In these cases D appropriated C's chose in action. One cheque, however, was drawn when the account was in overdraft beyond the authorised limit. The Court of Appeal held that in the last situation there was no theft. If an account is overdrawn beyond its agreed limit, the bank has no legal obligation to meet the cheque. Hence, C had no chose in action against B, and there was nothing for D to steal.[31]

In addition to the question of identifying what property is stolen, theft from a bank account also presents problems concerning the act of appropriation and the intention to deprive permanently. We consider these issues below, in § 13.6(vi) and § 13.7.

---

[24] Cf. Cripps, "The Public Interest Defence to the Action for Breach of Confidence and the Law Commission's Proposals on Disclosure in the Public Interest" (1984) 4 *OJLS* 361.

[25] *Bagley* (1923) 17 Cr App R 162.

[26] Cf. *Boulton* (1849) 1 Den 508, 169 ER 349; *Beecham* (1851) 5 Cox 181.

[27] Contrary to s. 11 of the Fraud Act 2006. Under s. 5(3) of the Railway Regulation Act 1889 it is a criminal offence to travel or attempt to travel without a ticket, or to intentionally travel beyond the point covered by a valid ticket, with intent to avoid payment of the fare; an offence now ferociously reinforced by ss. 17 and 18 of the Railway Byelaws 2005, which make it a criminal offence to travel without a valid ticket, even without fraudulent intent. Under Art. 143 of the Air Navigation Order 2009/3015 it is a criminal offence to be a stowaway upon an aircraft.

[28] *Foley* v. *Hill* (1848) 2 HLC 28, 9 ER 1002.

[29] *Kohn* (1979) 69 Cr App R 395.

[30] *Ibid.* Cf. *Williams (Roy)* [2001] 1 Cr App R 362, in which D, a builder, dishonestly overcharged customers for work done. D's conviction for theft was upheld on the basis that, by presenting a customer's cheque for payment, he appropriated that customer's bank account (i.e. the chose in action held by that customer against the bank).

[31] Cf. *Navvabi* [1986] 3 All ER 102. D might, however, have been guilty of stealing the proceeds of the cheque, following the decision in *Gomez* (below, § 13.6(ii)).

(d) Body parts

Some things, though corporeal, cannot be owned at all. At common law this included wild animals (*ferae naturae*) when at large,[32] and the human body, even when deceased;[33] so a human corpse cannot be stolen, by contrast with the corpse of a farm animal.[34] The position with regard to animals is now covered by section 4(4) (see below, § 13.3(ii)(c)). However, the question of the human body or body parts is not covered in the Theft Act, and remains somewhat uncertain. There is an interim right to possession (not ownership) of a corpse which vests in those charged with its burial.[35] Apart from this, the courts have recognised a limited possessory right in a corpse or body part if being used as a medical specimen or as an exhibit in a museum, at least where the item has acquired different attributes by undergoing a lawful application of skill (e.g. dissection or embalming),[36] and the Human Tissue Act 2004 allows certain persons a right to possess body parts in particular circumstances (while making it a criminal offence for them to do so when the procedures laid down by the Act have not been followed).

At the level of principle, there are difficult legal issues here. The fact that there may be certain limited rights to a corpse or parts thereof does not resolve the question whether that corpse or its parts can be stolen. The problem can be summarised as follows. First, although there may be possessory rights in some circumstances, it appears those rights do not amount to full ownership. And if parts of dead bodies are incapable of being owned, then it is arguable that they are not *property* within section 4(1), and therefore cannot be stolen.[37]

The contrary position is that since possession is one of the rights of ownership, such limited rights as may be had in body parts or a corpse nonetheless amount to *property* rights, enforceable by proprietary remedies, which fall short of ownership.[38] They are rights *in rem*,[39] enforceable against third parties. And since limited property rights are available, this suggests that, arguably, a corpse *is* property, albeit property that is incapable of being owned. This second analysis has now been accepted by the Court of Appeal in *Kelly*.[40] In our view, it is to be preferred: a taking in contravention of any property right suffices.

---

[32] Even a landowner does not own or possess the wild animals on his land. Cf. *Howlett and Howlett* [1968] Crim LR 222.

[33] *Williams* v. *Williams* (1880) 20 Ch D 659, 662f (extending to a corpse the logic of the proposition that a live human body cannot be subject to ownership).

[34] *Edwards* (1877) 13 Cox CC 384.

[35] *Calma* v. *Sesar* (1992) 106 FLR 446; *Dobson* v. *North Tyneside HA* [1996] 4 All ER 474, 478.

[36] *Kelly* [1998] 3 All ER 741; applying *Doodeward* v. *Spence* (1908) 6 CLR 406. In the latter case, Griffith CJ was careful not to say that a corpse could be owned, but rather that it could be in the lawful possession of someone, and that the law would protect that lawful possession. Note that preserving a brain in paraffin prior to a post-mortem examination does not turn it into an item in which others could have a right of possession or property: *Dobson* v. *North Tyneside HA* [1996] 4 All ER 474. See Maclean, "Resurrection of the Body Snatchers" (2000) 150 *NLJ* 174.

[37] Even though s. 5(1) of the Theft Act 1968 provides that for the purposes of theft, "property shall be regarded as belonging to any person having possession or control of it, or having in it any proprietary right or interest", this does not dispense with the separate requirement in ss. 1 and 4 that the thing stolen be property.

[38] Cf. de Stoop, "The Law in Australia Relating to the Transplantation of Organs from Cadavers" (1974) 48 *ALJ* 21, 22.

[39] I.e. a right that held *in respect of* a particular thing and which is enforceable against others generally (e.g. ownership of a car); by contrast with a right *in personam*, which is enforceable only against particular persons (e.g. a debt).

[40] [1998] 3 All ER 741.

Adopting such analysis has the practical advantage of allowing a conviction for theft when, say, a corpse is stolen from the executors. Even after *Kelly*, however, a second problem for the law is to identify *when* such rights can arise. For example, it remains unclear under present law whether anyone has a property right to a human embryo or to a body part designated for transplant surgery;[41] and thus whether such items can be stolen. It is certainly arguable that such items deserve the protection of the criminal law.[42]

In *Yearworth* v. *North Bristol NHS Trust*,[43] the Court of Appeal were faced, in the context of a civil action for negligence, with the related but distinct question whether property rights exist in products of a living body: in this case, frozen sperm stored in sperm bank, which negligent storage by the defendant's employees had allowed to perish. A powerful court consisting of the Lord Chief Justice, the Master of the Rolls, and a Lord Justice of Appeal decided the question in the affirmative, and ruled that the men's claim was therefore entitled to succeed. In this case they might have reached their decision by applying the reasoning in *Kelly* and related cases—namely that in principle there is no property in sperm, but an exception applies where it has undergone treatment (in this case, freezing)—but they declined to do so. Instead, they decided the case on the broader basis that "for the purposes of their claims in negligence, the men had ownership of the sperm which they ejaculated". As well as deciding the point in relation to products of the living body, and presumably amputated parts of living bodies too,[44] this case impliedly casts doubt on the correctness of the traditional reasoning in respect of ownership of dead bodies and their parts, suggesting the possibility that the courts in future might discard it and decide that there are property rights in these as well.

More straightforwardly (and more generally), there is a case for statutory reform, which need not be achieved through the law of property offences. Arguably, interference with such things as body parts is not the sort of wrongdoing for which property offences are the suitable means of control, and warrants criminalisation by means of separate, more specific legislation.[45]

(e) Electricity, gas, and water

Section 13 of the 1968 Act enacts a separate offence of dishonestly abstracting electricity. The separate offence is needed because electricity, like other forms of energy such as heat,[46] is not property. In *Low* v. *Blease*,[47] D broke into a house and sought to warm himself by switching on the electric fire. He was held not guilty of burglary; he had not entered with intent to steal because the electricity consumed by the fire could not be stolen.

---

[41] See, e.g., Andrews, "The Legal Status of the Embryo" (1986) 32 *Loyola LR* 257.

[42] Lavoie, "Ownership of Human Tissue: Life after *Moore* v. *Regents of the University of California*" [1989] 75 *Virginia LR* 1363. See also Wall, "The Legal Status of Body Parts: a Framework" (2011) 31 *OJLS* 783.

[43] [2009] EWCA Civ 37, [2010] 2 QB 1; Quigley, "Property: The Future of Human Tissue?" (2009) 17 *Medical LR* 457.

[44] At para. 45(d) the Court of Appeal suggested that a surgeon presented with a finger amputated in a factory accident who then negligently damaged it before starting the medical procedure to reattach it would be liable, whether or not the finger had been the subject of any preliminary work that had "changed its attributes".

[45] As has already happened, to a limited extent. For specific offences, see the Human Tissue Act 2004, s. 5, and the Sexual Offences Act 2003, s. 70 (creating a specific offence of necrophilia); and see Spencer, "Criminal Liability for the Desecration of a Corpse" [2004] *Archbold News*, Issue 6, 7.

[46] *Clinton* v. *Cahill* [1998] NI 200.

[47] [1975] Crim LR 513.

Gas, on the other hand, is property and can be stolen.[48] The same is true for water that has been placed in a container such as a pipe.[49] Water in a lake or pond is a severable part of the land on which it stands,[50] and is therefore subject to the rules governing theft of land (below).

(f) Identity

Although "identity theft" is phrase in common usage, a person's identity is not considered to be their property for the purpose of the law of theft. Neither need it be, because "identity thieves" usually impersonate others with a view to gain, which makes them guilty of the crime of fraud (discussed in Chapter 15 below). In addition, by statute there exists a range of specific offences of "personation", of which the impersonator is guilty even if his motive is not financial.[51]

(ii) The exceptions in section 4(2)–(4)

Notwithstanding the general rule in section 4(1) that any type of property can be stolen, section 4 itself contains special provisions applicable where the subject matter of the theft is real property, a plant growing wild, or a wild animal.

(a) Land

The ruling in section 4(1) that real property can be stolen is significantly qualified by section 4(2), which provides:

> A person cannot steal land, or things forming part of land and severed from it by him or by his directions, except in the following cases, that is to say—
>
> (a)   when he is a trustee or personal representative, or is authorised by power of attorney, or as a liquidator of a company, or otherwise, to sell or dispose of land belonging to another, and he appropriates the land or anything forming part of it by dealing with it in breach of the confidence reposed in him; or
>
> (b)   when he is not in possession of the land and appropriates anything forming part of the land by severing it or causing it to be severed, or after it has been severed; or
>
> (c)   when, being in possession of the land under a tenancy, he appropriates the whole or part of any fixture or structure let to be used with the land.

Section 4(2)(a) covers trustees and the like[52] who fraudulently convert land in breach of the terms under which the land is entrusted to them. Section 4(2)(b) makes it possible for anyone to steal part of the land—including fixtures, plants, trees, and soil—by severing the item from the land, or by appropriating it after severance.[53] Under section 4(2)

---

[48] *White* (1853) Dears 203, 169 ER 696; *Firth* (1869) LR 1 CCR 172.

[49] *Ferens* v. *O'Brien* (1883) 11 QBD 21.

[50] Burn, *Cheshire and Burn's Modern Law of Real Property* (18th ed., 2011) 163.

[51] For a list, see *Archbold* (2016 edition) § 22.72–22.76.

[52] Cf. *Daniels* v. *Daniels* [1978] Ch 406 (company directors).

[53] Cf. *Foley* (1889) 17 Cox CC 142 (grass); *Skujins* [1956] Crim LR 266 (farm gate); *Carver* v. *Pierce* (1648) Style 66, 82 ER 534 (dung).

(c), a tenant is capable of stealing fixtures and structures which he removes from the property.[54]

The exceptions leave intact the general rule, which is that a person, however dishonest, does not commit theft by entering upon another person's land with a view to making it his own. At the date when the Theft Act was passed it was widely felt that such behaviour should not fall within the ambit of the criminal law. This was largely because a squatter who succeeds in staying put for 12 years can thereby acquire legal title and it was thought that, if the conduct was capable of transferring ownership it could not properly be treated as a theft: a once scrupulous attitude towards the need for compatibility between the civil and the criminal law which, as we shall see later in this chapter, is nowadays very much dissipated.[55] Meanwhile, although the general rule is still that land cannot be stolen, in the years since 1968 Parliament has repeatedly intervened to render criminal various different forms of civil trespass: most recently in 2012, with a new offence of squatting in a residential building.[56]

(b) Things growing wild

At common law, things growing wild are part of the land on which they grow. Prima facie, therefore, under section 4(2)(b) anything growing wild on land can be stolen through being severed from the land or, once severed, through being then appropriated by D. However, section 4(3) creates a further restriction:

> A person who picks mushrooms growing wild on any land, or who picks flowers, fruit or foliage from a plant growing wild on any land, does not (although not in possession of the land) steal what he picks, unless he does it for reward or for sale or other commercial purpose.
>
> For purposes of this subsection "mushroom" includes any fungus, and "plant" includes any shrub or tree.

In essence, this means that D is exempt from liability provided:

(i)   he removes *part* of the plant (not the whole, unless it is a mushroom);
(ii)   the plant is growing *wild* (not cultivated);
(iii)   he *picks* it (rather than, say, chops it down); and
(iv)   he does so for a non-commercial purpose.

(c) Wild creatures

At common law a wild creature is owned by no one, and so cannot be stolen.[57] However, if such an animal is captured or killed, the person on whose land the capture or killing occurs thereupon acquires ownership of the creature.[58] Consequently, any subsequent

---

[54] For discussion of some of the difficulties and anomalies associated with s. 4(2) see A.T.H. Smith, *Property Offences* (1994) § 3.34ff.

[55] Below, § 13.6.

[56] Legal Aid, Sentencing and Punishment of Offenders Act 2012, s. 144. See Cobb, "Property's Outlaws: Squatting, Land Use and Criminal Trespass" [2012] *Crim LR* 114.

[57] Cf. *Cresswell v. DPP* [2006] EWHC 3379, [2007] Env LR D8: badgers not reduced into possession are not property (either at common law or in the context of s. 10 of the Criminal Damage Act 1971). There are, however, a number of specific offences of poaching: see *Blackstone's Criminal Practice* (2016), § B.13.91.

[58] *Blades v. Higgs* (1865) 11 HL Cas 621, 11 ER 1474.

appropriation of the animal or its carcass would prima facie be a theft. Section 4(4) abrogates this result. For the purposes of the 1968 Act:

> Wild creatures, tamed or untamed, shall be regarded as property; but a person cannot steal a wild creature not tamed nor ordinarily kept in captivity, or the carcase or any such wild creature, unless either it has been reduced into possession by or on behalf of another person and possession of it has not since been lost or abandoned, or another person is in course of reducing it into possession.

It follows that a wild creature may be stolen only if (i) it is tamed or ordinarily kept in captivity, or (ii) it has been reduced into and remains in another person's possession, or (iii) it is in the process of being reduced into possession by another person. By way of example, domestic pets or the animals in a zoo are capable of being stolen, since they are (i) tamed or ordinarily kept in captivity. Bees that return to a hive can also be stolen, not because they are tamed or kept but because (ii) they have been reduced into possession (and possession has not since been lost). A poacher, on the other hand, does not steal the rabbit he captures. But if a second person, D, takes the rabbit from the poacher when the latter is (iii) in the process of capturing it, D then steals the rabbit.[59]

To count as property, the thing in question must be something capable of being owned. The fact that the victim of the alleged theft herself committed a criminal offence by owning or possessing it is, of course, irrelevant. So where three equal villains attacked a drug dealer and forcibly took his heroin, they committed robbery[60] (that is, theft accompanied by violence).[61]

§ 13.4 Belonging to another (I)—the basics

It is impossible to steal property from oneself.[62] Some other person must have an interest in the subject matter of the theft before that item can be stolen. This is not to deny that D can steal something she owns. While D may be the owner, other persons may have an immediate right to possession or control, or some proprietary interest that can be asserted against the owner: V, say, may have a lien,[63] or some other interest in the property. In such a case the property can be stolen by D (or by anyone else). But if D is the absolute owner of the property, so that no one else is joint owner or has any lesser proprietary right or a right to possession or control, she cannot steal it. It does not "belong to another" for the purposes of section 1 of the Act.

The meaning of "belonging to another" is elaborated in section 5. The key provision is section 5(1):

> Property is to be regarded as belonging to any person having possession or control of it, or having in it any proprietary right or interest (not being an equitable interest arising only from an agreement to transfer or grant an interest).

---

[59] This extends the common law, which formerly required that the reduction into possession be completed before the animal or carcass could be stolen. See *Roe* (1870) 11 Cox 554.

[60] *Smith* [2011] EWCA Crim 66, [2011] 1 Cr App R 30; noted by Smith, [2011] CLJ 289.

[61] As is explained in § 14.3.

[62] Although, remarkably, one can steal property by the very act of acquiring absolute ownership of it: *Hinks* [2000] UKHL 53, [2001] 2 AC 241. See further below, § 13.6(ii)(c).

[63] See below, § 13.4(ii).

In general, this means that for the purposes of theft an item "belongs" to everyone with any form of proprietary interest in the item, whatever the nature of that interest—i.e. whether it be a right of ownership or possession, or a proprietary interest existing only at equity. Generally speaking, therefore, D commits the actus reus of a theft whenever he appropriates property in which someone else has a proprietary interest.

The rule stated here gives rise to a number of special cases, which benefit by further discussion here and in § 13.5.

(i) What interests are protected by section 5?

We have noted that section 5(1) protects virtually any form of proprietary interest, whether of ownership or possession, and whether at common law or equity. Although the section mentions "possession *or* control", it is not clear that the latter term adds anything much. Physical control would in any event also constitute a possessory interest, and any other right of control would presumably only qualify if it were enforceable *in rem*, i.e. if it were a proprietary interest.

On the other hand, equitable proprietary interests should be distinguished from interests that may arise when D enters into an agreement to sell goods to V on some future date. The provision in section 5(1) makes it clear that the latter sort of interest is not protected, by contrast with contracts of sale that transfer ownership immediately. Hence if, before the agreed date of the future transfer, D were to resell the goods to T, D would not commit theft from V.

The inclusion of equitable proprietary interests has opened the way for a significant expansion of the scope of theft in recent years, given the important role of the constructive trust in modern civil law. Because of the complexity of the law of constructive trusts, we will deal with this topic separately, in § 13.5(i).

The scope of theft in section 5(1) is also extended by supplementary provisions in section 5(2)–(4), which is designed to capture certain specific types of theft. These provisions are dealt with below, in § 13.5(ii)–(iv).

(ii) Theft by an owner under section 5(1)

As we have mentioned, one implication of section 5(1) is that even an owner may commit theft, provided the victim of the theft is deprived of an interest recognised under section 5. This might occur in a case where someone else has a lien[64] over the goods. In the New Zealand case of *Cox*,[65] a garage repairing a car had a lien over it. D dishonestly retrieved the car and was convicted of theft, as the lien had conferred a possessory interest. Similarly, in *Slowly*[66] V sold onions to D, for which he had not yet been paid. Until paid, V (being a seller in possession) was entitled to assert a lien over the goods.[67] Accordingly, D's

---

[64] That is, a right to retain possession that is enforceable even against the owner until some condition is met: *Hammonds* v. *Barclay* (1802) 2 East 227, 235, 102 ER 356, 359.

[65] [1923] NZLR 596.

[66] (1873) 12 Cox 269.

[67] Sale of Goods Act 1979, s. 39; *Dennant* v. *Skinner* [1948] 2 KB 164.

dishonest taking of the goods was theft, and similarly in *Rose v Matt*,[68] where the owner of a travelling clock deposited it as security for the price of unpaid goods then later removed it from the shop when nobody was looking.

Another standard case in which an owner may commit theft is if there is more than one owner. If D and V are co-owners of a chattel and D dishonestly sells the chattel, D is guilty of theft. Similarly, it has been ruled that a partner may be convicted of theft of property belonging to the partnership.[69]

(iii) Theft by an absolute owner? When D's interest is better than V's

In principle, there should be one important exception to the general proposition that property may be stolen from anyone having a proprietary interest therein. Consider the following, fairly straightforward, case:

> Suppose that V is a thief who has stolen a television set from D. D remains absolute owner of the television, but while in possession V has a lesser proprietary (possessory) interest in the television, which he may maintain against anyone save D. V's interest is sufficient for section 5(1). Consequently, if T dishonestly removes the television from V's house, T is himself guilty of stealing from V.[70]

Now the exception. In a case of this sort, D—the owner—surely cannot steal the television by retaking it from V. This is because V has no property right in the television maintainable against D. *Vis-à-vis* D, the television belongs to no one else. By contrast, *vis-à-vis* T, the television belongs to both D and V; hence T can steal it from V and from D.[71]

One illustration of this exception is the Crown Court decision in *Meredith*.[72] D's car had been impounded by the police and removed to a police station. Without consent, D then recovered his car from the police station. D was acquitted of theft, after the trial judge ruled that the police had no right to retain possession of the car against the owner.

Obvious as all this may seem, there is appellate authority to the contrary. In *Turner (No. 2)*,[73] D had taken his car to a garage for repair. Subsequently and dishonestly, he recovered the car without paying for the repairs. D was convicted of theft. Prima facie, this looks right: the car surely "belonged to" the garage for the purpose of section 5(1), since the garage would have been entitled to assert a lien over the car until the repairs were paid for.[74] Unfortunately, the trial judge directed the jury to disregard the issue of liens. Consequently, the Court of Appeal was obliged to consider D's appeal on the footing that there was no lien. The Court nonetheless upheld the conviction, reasoning that even as a mere bailee at will,

---

[68] [1951] 1 KB 810.

[69] *Bonner* [1970] 2 All ER 97n.

[70] *Buckley* v. *Gross* (1863) 3 B & S 566, 122 ER 213; *Daniel* v. *Rogers* [1918] 2 KB 228, 234; *Parker* v. *British Airways Board* [1982] QB 1004, 1009 (Donaldson LJ).

[71] A helpful illustration of the priority of interests is *Costello* v. *Chief Constable of Derbyshire* [2001] All ER 150 (CA). D was in possession of a stolen car that was seized by the police. The owner, however, could not be traced. In those circumstances, the Court held that D was entitled to recover the car from the police, because he had better title to the car than anyone apart from the original owner.

[72] [1973] Crim LR 253. Cf. Model Penal Code, § 223.0(7): "'property of another' includes property in which any person other than the actor has an interest *which the actor is not privileged to infringe*" (emphasis added).

[73] [1971] 2 All ER 441.

[74] Cf. *Cox* [1923] NZLR 596; above, § 13.4(ii).

the garage had a possessory interest in the car (maintainable against anyone except D) sufficient to qualify for section 5(1). According to the Court of Appeal, "there is no ground for qualifying the words 'possession or control' in any way", i.e. by excluding from section 5(1) any proprietary interests inferior to those of the defendant.

The decision is absurd.[75] If no lien existed, the car belonged to D and D alone. The gist of theft is interference with someone else's property rights. D did no such thing. He merely exercised proprietary rights to which he was entitled (albeit in order to evade a debt).

(iv) Has D become an absolute owner?

Assuming that an absolute owner cannot steal her own goods, and subject to section 5(2)–(4),[76] cases will often arise when D acquires possession or control of property innocently enough but subsequently, and dishonestly, decides to keep it from the person from whom the property was acquired. For example:

> D enters into a hire-purchase contract with V Ltd. to acquire a television set. She takes the television set home, intending to honour the agreement. However, a few months later, she finds herself in financial difficulties. She stops paying V Ltd., sells the television, and pockets the proceeds.

In this case, D steals the television set when she offers it for sale.[77] In a hire-purchase agreement, possession passes but the property in the goods remains with the seller until all instalments have been paid. Thus an on-sale by the possessor is theft. Likewise, borrowing something, and then keeping it having decided not to return it, may amount to theft—on the basis of the keeping rather than the borrowing—since the borrower legitimately acquires possession but does not acquire ownership.

However, other cases may be more difficult:

> D purchases a table from V on one month's credit. When he takes delivery of the table, D intends to honour his obligation to V. Later, however, D decides not to pay. He sells the table to T, an innocent third party, and absconds with the cash.

Does D steal the table? The general rule is that if V—the person from whom the property is acquired—retains ownership or some other interest in the property, D will be guilty of theft by his later dishonest appropriation of the goods. Otherwise, if V delivers the goods and transfers property in them to D, who subsequently forms the intent not to pay for them, D does not commit theft. It is therefore crucial to determine whether, and at what point in time, D has become the owner of property that formerly belonged to V. Apart from some specific provisions in section 5(2)–(4) of the Theft Act 1968, to be considered in due course, the criminal law provides no answer to this question, which must be decided by reference to civil law rules.

---

[75] The same adjective is used by A.T.H. Smith, *Property Offences* (1994) § 4–43. A factor underlying the decision may have been that, as the rules of criminal procedure then stood, the result of quashing the defendant's conviction would have been that a man who was almost certainly guilty was acquitted; since 1988, however, the Court of Appeal has had a general power when quashing a conviction to order a retrial.

[76] Below, § 13.5(ii)–(iv).

[77] Below, § 13.6(i).

This point is of central importance. In principle, consistency of criminal law and civil law concepts is essential in theft, which after all is concerned with the protection of property rights.[78] It would be more than odd if D could be convicted of theft when she had not in fact interfered with V's property rights. As Williams writes, "the object of the law of theft is to attach a penal sanction to certain violations of property rights; so (it may be urged) if there is no violation of property rights under the general (civil) law, there should be no theft".[79] It was said in this text, as far back as Chapter 1, that there ought to be no criminalisation without harm.[80] In theft, the relevant harm is infringement of another's property rights. Protection against that harm *is the very purpose* of criminalising theft. The rights (specifically, ownership and possession) which are protected are creatures of civil law. Therefore, unless those civil law rights are in fact infringed, the harm does not occur and theft should not lie.

In deciding whether ownership has passed already to D for the purposes of section 5(1), there are two principal issues. One is to ascertain whether title has prima facie passed, or whether D merely has possession. Here one needs to look at the terms of the agreement between V and D, in particular whether V has reserved some property right in the goods.

The second issue is that, even where a prima facie transfer of title has been identified, the transfer may be vitiated. In general, there are three ways in which this may occur. First, the transaction may be induced by D's wrongful duress, fraud, false pretences, etc. In such cases, any title acquired by D will be at least voidable, if not void, and the transaction can constitute theft.[81] Secondly, even though D has not induced the transaction by any wrongdoing, V may have made a fundamental mistake. In that case, the transaction is void.[82] V retains title to the goods and they can be stolen by D. Finally, V, acting on behalf of the true owner, may not have authority to pass title. In that case, again, the transaction is void and D cannot become owner of the property.

In the following sections, we discuss aspects of these problems in more detail. (A third issue, to be discussed later, arises where D does become the legal owner of the property but is subject either to a constructive trust or to one of the extensional provisions in section 5(2)–(4), in which case theft may still be possible. These cases will be explored in § 13.5.)

(a) Has ownership passed, prima facie?

The general rule, which is subject to a number of statutory and common law provisos, is that title passes if and when the transferor so intends it to pass. It is not possible here to give

---

[78] Cf. J.C. Smith, "Civil Law Concepts in the Criminal Law" [1972B] *CLJ* 197. Although see *Morris* [1984] AC 320, 334, for the dubious (and unnecessary) claim that the criminal law should not be concerned with the niceties of the civil law. The approach taken in *Walker* [1984] Crim LR 112 and in *Tillings v. Tillings* [1985] Crim LR 393 is to be preferred; cf. *Nabina* [2000] Crim LR 481. Compare too *Dobson v. General Accident Fire and Life Assurance Corp* [1989] 3 All ER 927, 937: whether property belongs to another "is a question to which the criminal law offers no answer and which can only be answered by reference to civil law principles".

[79] Glanville Williams, "Theft, Consent and Illegality" [1977] *Crim LR* 127, 138. *Per* A.T.H. Smith, *Property Offences* (1994) § 5–49, "if the civil law sees no reason to permit the owner to complain of an interference with his property why should the criminal law do so?"

[80] Above, § 1.2.

[81] The leading case is *Gomez*: below, § 13.6(ii)(a)–(b).

[82] Voidability is not an option in the case of a unilateral mistake. A transaction can be voidable, as opposed to void, only when D has acted in some way wrongfully. If P's mistake is fundamental, the transaction is void; if not, the transaction is entirely valid and unimpeachable.

a comprehensive account of the civil law regarding transfer of property. Rather, we propose briefly to mention some well-known situations, and to illustrate the relationship between the relevant civil law rules and the criminal law of theft.

Case 1: Contracts for sale of goods.
Where ascertained goods are sold, the rules on passing of title are to be found in the Sale of Goods Act 1979. The basic rule, stated in section 17, is that where there is a contract for the sale of specific or ascertained goods, property in them passes when the buyer and seller so intend. In the case of sale of unascertained goods, section 16 provides that no property in them can be transferred to the buyer unless and until the goods are ascertained.[83] Section 18 provides that if there is no agreement regarding the passing of title, then property passes at the time the contract is made.[84]

One consequence of section 17 is that a seller may pass possession but reserve ownership. This is standard, for example, in hire-purchase contracts, where property remains in the seller until the buyer has paid for the goods. Although the buyer has lawful possession, a charge of theft would lie where the buyer then usurps the seller's rights of ownership over those goods, e.g. by dishonestly selling them.

Case 2: Rescission.
In *Walker*,[85] D sold V a defective video recorder which V returned for repair. After some time, V then issued a summons claiming the price of the video as the "return of money paid for defective goods". D thereafter sold the video. His conviction for theft was quashed. Arguably, the summons had the effect of rescinding the original contract of sale; revesting ownership of the machine once again in D.

Case 3: Receptacles.
The owner of a vending or similar machine, such as a coin-operated telephone, becomes the owner of any money as soon as it is inserted.[86] This is explicable on the general rule: the depositor intends to pass ownership when he inserts a coin in prepayment. Even if the machine malfunctions and he does not get what he pays for, his remedy is a refund, not a retrieval of the particular coin inserted. It is thus the actus reus of theft to retake money from such a machine, except by authorised means (e.g. pressing the refund button).

Similarly, when petrol is sold at a service station, ownership passes when the petrol is pumped into the tank of the vehicle. Thus a motorist who fills his tank intending to pay for the petrol, but then decides not to pay for it and drives off, commits no theft.[87] He already owns and has possession of the petrol before he forms the mens rea of theft, and instead commits the offence of making off without payment.[88]

---

[83] See, e.g., *Re Goldcorp Exchange* [1995] 1 AC 74 (PC): buyers had no legal or equitable interest in an undifferentiated bulk of gold bullion. This rule is subject to certain exceptions for sales of undivided shares in an ascertained bulk (see, in particular, the Sale of Goods Amendment Act 1979).

[84] Provided the goods are specific and deliverable, and the contract is unconditional. Other rules in s. 18 apply where these criteria are not met.

[85] [1984] Crim LR 112.

[86] *Martin* v. *Marsh* [1955] Crim LR 781; *Hollings* (1940) 4 J Cr L 370; cf. *Jean* [1968] 2 CCC 204.

[87] *Greenberg* [1972] Crim LR 331; *Edwards* v. *Ddin* [1976] 3 All ER 705. This assumes that the controversial decision in *Hinks* [2000] UKHL 53, [2001] 2 AC 241 (below, § 13.6(ii)(c)) applies only to circumstances where the act of appropriation is coincident with, and not subsequent to, the obtaining of ownership.

[88] Theft Act 1978, s. 3.

Case 4: Contents.

If a person puts a valuable ring in a desk drawer, and after death her executor sells the desk, the buyer may not keep the ring on finding it since it was not included in the sale,[89] and a dishonest failure to return it would constitute theft. Ownership of the ring remains in the executor since he does not intend to pass title thereto when he sells the desk.

(b) Is the passing of title voidable for duress, misrepresentation, etc?

It is clear that transfers, even those pursuant to a contract, are voidable at common law if they are induced by the recipient's wrongdoing, e.g. by duress or misrepresentation.[90] Similarly, transfers affected by undue influence are voidable in equity.[91] In light of the House of Lords decision in *Gomez*,[92] the dishonest receipt of goods pursuant to such a voidable transfer can now be theft. (This, strictly, puts the criminal law at odds with the civil law, as a voidable title is a "perfect title"[93] until the transaction conferring ownership on D is set aside.)

(c) Is the passing of title void for mistake?

O's consent to the transfer of title may be negated by a "fundamental" mistake, whether or not induced by fraud or misrepresentation. A mistake is fundamental if and only if its existence makes it reasonable to say that there is no intention on O's part to transfer *this* property to *this* person.[94] As the High Court of Australia put it, what this means is that a mistake is sufficiently fundamental if it is "as to the identity of the transferee or as to the identity of the thing delivered, or as to the quantity of the thing delivered".[95] However, applying this test is not always clear cut. Moreover, even where O's mistake is not sufficiently fundamental, it may well generate liability under section 5(4), which we will consider below (§ 13.5(iv)).

Case 1: Mistake regarding property.

Mistake as to the identity of the property will always defeat consent. In *Davies*[96] the proprietor of a nursing home induced two old ladies to endorse cheques made out to them by signing on the back, and then paid the cheques into his own account. The victims had not known that they were endorsing cheques, but merely thought that they were signing pieces of paper. For this reason property in the cheques never passed to D, who was thus rightly convicted of theft. Here the mistake was obviously fundamental: in each case V believed

---

[89] *Thomas* v. *Greenslade* [1954] CLY 3421; *Moffatt* v. *Kazana* [1969] 2 QB 152; *Merry* v. *Green* (1841) 7 M & W 623, 151 ER 916.

[90] See, e.g., Furmston, *Cheshire, Fifoot and Furmston's Law of Contract* (16th ed., 2012) ch. 9; Winfield, "Quasi- Contract Arising from Compulsion" (1944) 60 *LQR* 341; *Cooper* v. *Joel* (1859) 1 De GF & J 240, 45 ER 350; *Wauton* v. *Coppard* [1899] 1 Ch 92. Indeed, in cases of grave physical duress or fundamental misrepresentation the transfer may even be void: Lanham, "Duress and Void Contracts" (1966) 29 *MLR* 615.

[91] [1993] AC 442. This should have been the approach taken by the Court of Appeal in *Hinks* [2000] UKHL 53, [2001] 2 AC 241; below, § 13.6(ii)(c).

[92] Below, § 13.6(ii)(a).

[93] A legal term of art, meaning that the person with such title is able to pass valid title to another; it is not, of course, a "perfect title" in the literal sense of the word because it is liable to be set aside.

[94] Williams, "Mistake in the Law of Theft" [1977] *CLJ* 62, 64.

[95] *Ilich* (1986) 162 CLR 110, 126.

[96] [1982] 1 All ER 513.

the property to be a valueless piece of paper, whereas in reality it was a bill of exchange—a different type of thing altogether.

Case 2: Mistake regarding quantity.

If the owner intends to deal only with a specific number of goods handed over, then there is no consent as to the excess. But if O's intention is to hand over a group of things, a mistake as to the number of items in the group does *not* negate the intention to hand them all over.

An example of the former variety is *Russell v. Smith:*[97]

> D was a driver for a haulage company. He was instructed to collect a one-ton load of pig meal from P. P, when loading the meal, inadvertently loaded an additional eight sacks. When D discovered the error, he appropriated the eight sacks and sold them.

P intended to give D the number of sacks corresponding to one ton of meal; there was no intention to put the additional sacks on the lorry. Thus P remained owner of the eight extra sacks, which D stole when he appropriated them. Contrast this decision with an example where P offers to sell D all the pig meal then stored at his warehouse; which P mistakenly think amounts to one ton's worth, when in fact it is eight sacks more than that weight. In the latter case, D acquires ownership of the entirety.

The distinction at work here is between a mistake which simply motivates or underlies P's intention to pass title to certain goods, and one which negates P's intention to pass title in those very goods which were in fact delivered. It is, in short, the difference between a mistake as to *what* P is passing to D, and a mistake as to *why* he is doing so.[98]

Case 3: Mistake regarding transferee.

Mistake as to the identity of the other party may vitiate consent, but only if the identity was crucial to O's decision to give consent.[99] In *Hudson*, D received and paid into his bank account a cheque which was inadvertently made out to him, but obviously intended for someone else with the same surname. He was convicted of stealing the cheque.[100]

It seems that a mistake about the transferee's identity supplies the best explanation of another well-known case, *Middleton*.[101] In that case, D went to withdraw 10 shillings from his Post Office savings account, which had at that time a balance of 11 shillings. The Post Office practice was to pay out withdrawals pursuant to a warrant obtained by D and a letter of advice from the Postmaster General sent direct to the relevant branch. Unfortunately the clerk consulted the wrong letter of advice, which related to a different account holder, and paid out £8 16s 10d. The Court of Criminal Appeal held that D was properly convicted of larceny, as the clerk's intention to pass title to the money was vitiated by his mistake. Since

---

[97] [1958] 1 QB 27.

[98] Analogous to the distinction in contract law between a mistake "in the motive or reason for making the offer", and a mistake in the terms of the offer itself: *Imperial Glass* v. *Consolidated Supplies* (1960) 22 DLR (2d) 759.

[99] Thus *Cundy* v. *Lindsay* (1878) 3 App Cas 459 may be distinguished from *King's Norton Metal Co* v. *Edridge* (1897) 14 TLR 98, where the rogue's assumed name was of no particular significance.

[100] [1943] KB 458. But this is not an absolute rule, at least where the parties deal face to face. In *Ingram* v. *Little* [1961] 1 QB 31 a contract for sale of a car to a rogue under a false name (whose cheque bounced) was held void, but in *Lewis* v. *Averay* [1972] 1 QB 198 a similar sale to a rogue believing him to be a certain TV actor was held valid. Possibly the only explanation for this anomaly is that in the latter case there was no actual misrepresentation by the buyer. Even before these cases, the considerable difficulties in this area of law had been pointed out by Williams, "Mistake as to Party in the Law of Contract" (1945) 23 *Can Bar Rev* 271.

[101] (1873) 12 Cox CC 417.

the clerk clearly did intend to give D £8 16s 10d, and not 10 shillings, he made no mistake about the nature or quantity of the property transferred.[102] Rather, his mistake is best seen as being about D's identity, which he had mistaken for that of the person named in the letter of advice.[103]

In 1972, the Court of Appeal purported to follow *Middleton* in *Gilks*.[104] G placed various bets at a betting shop, including one on "Fighting Taffy", which was unplaced in a race won by "Fighting Scot". When he went to collect his winnings on the various bets he had placed, the bookmaker mistakenly thought G had backed the winner, and calculated and paid out an amount well in excess of G's true winnings. G, realising the mistake, decided to pocket the entirety. His conviction for theft was upheld on the footing that *Middleton*[105] had established, in such cases, that property in money paid by mistake does not pass. It is submitted, however, that the Court of Appeal's reasoning was flawed. The bookmaker's error was an antecedent one of calculation[106] and not of the sort found in *Middleton*, where the clerk had paid the right amount to the wrong person. The bookmaker paid G (the right person) exactly the amount he intended. Therefore ownership of the money had passed to G.[107]

However, even assuming that ownership did pass to G, as the law now stands this may not matter; because, as we shall explain in § 13.6 when discussing appropriation, a line of cases decided after *Gilks* suggests—surprisingly—that it is now possible to commit theft by a dishonest act notwithstanding that the act has the legal effect of passing ownership.[108]

(d) Other mistakes—and the possibilities of constructive trusts or section 5(4)

The general rule is that, failing a "fundamental" mistake of the kinds identified in the foregoing paragraphs, the transaction is effective to pass title in the relevant property from O to D; thereafter, prima facie, that property cannot be stolen by D. In such cases, a charge of theft may still be available if the property still belongs to O in equity or by virtue of section 5(1)–(4). These extensions to section 5(1) are discussed in detail below (§ 13.5); but, in the context of mistakes, it is worth drawing particular attention to the role of section 5(4) and to developments in equity. Suppose that O mistakenly imagines she owes D £100 when, in fact, she owes £70. If she then pays him £100, D normally acquires absolute title to all of the money (O makes no fundamental mistake about what she is paying him),

---

[102] *Per* Bramwell B (dissenting): "No doubt the clerk did not intend to do an act of the sort described, and give to Middleton what did not belong to him. Yet he intended to do the act he did. What he did he did not do involuntarily, nor accidentally, but on purpose": (1873) 12 Cox CC 417, 428.

[103] (1873) 12 Cox CC 417, 419: the clerk "certainly meant that the prisoner should take up that money, though he only meant this because of a mistake as to the identity of the prisoner with the person really entitled to that money." Cf. Smith and Hogan, *Criminal Law* (1965) 354. On whether the facts really support such a finding, *contra* the dissent by Cleasby B (1873) 12 Cox CC 417, 441–2. Cf. Turner, "Two Cases of Larceny" in Turner and Radzinowicz (eds.), *The Modern Approach to Criminal Law* (1948) 356, 359.

[104] [1972] 3 All ER 280 (CA). See the criticism by J.C. Smith in [1972] Crim LR 586. Compare *Prince* (1868) LR 1 CCR 150.

[105] (1873) 12 Cox CC 417.

[106] Of the sort found in *Moynes* v. *Coopper* [1956] 1 QB 439; below, § 13.5(iv).

[107] There is some authority (*Chase Manhatten Bank* v. *Israel British Bank* [1981] 1 Ch 105 and *Shadrokh-Cigari* [1988] Crim LR 465) to the effect that, when making a mistake of this sort, V may retain equitable title in the money. These cases, which are controversial, are discussed in § 13.5(i)(a).

[108] Note also that, quite apart from subsequent legal developments, s. 5(4) would ordinarily apply to such overpayments, but did not do so in this case because it arose out of a wager: below, § 13.4(iv)(d), 13.5(iv).

but he becomes liable under civil law to repay the excess £30. In those circumstances, section 5(4) operates to deem that excess as belonging to O for the purposes of theft. If D dishonestly keeps the £30, he then commits theft. Section 5(4) is the subject of § 13.5(iv) below. Additionally, there is authority that, under certain conditions, O retains equitable title to the excess and D holds the excess as a constructive trustee; in which case the property still belongs to O within the core terms of section 5(1). This possibility is considered in § 13.5(i)(a).

(e) Was the transferor authorised to pass title?

Property will not pass if the transferor does not have the owner's authority to pass title. In *Bhachu*, a dishonest cashier acted in collusion with D by "selling" the goods to her at a price below the authorised price.[109] In such a case, the cashier does not have the authority to pass title on O's behalf, and the goods are converted by D when she takes them out of the shop.[110] By contrast, an unintentional error on the part of an agent does not mean that the agent's conduct is unauthorised, even if the recipient is dishonest.[111]

(v) Abandonment and loss: is finding theft?

It is possible for ownership to be relinquished through abandonment. If an owner intentionally abandons goods, they become ownerless, and therefore cannot be stolen.[112] However, an item may be lost rather than abandoned. Consider the following example:

> David finds a wallet in a busy street, and picks it up. He looks in the wallet for evidence of the owner's identity and finds none, but does find some money. He puts the wallet in his pocket. Does David commit the actus reus of a theft?

Typically, in "finding" cases, it is important to resolve whether the thing found belongs to another: whether, in this scenario, there is another person with a right of property in the wallet and its contents. In turn, this is likely to depend on whether the wallet is abandoned or merely lost. If lost, then the person who originally lost the wallet remains its owner. By contrast, if abandoned, the wallet is unowned until David picks it up and puts it in his pocket.

Generally speaking, the courts are reluctant to find that goods have been "abandoned" rather than merely lost.[113] It will not suffice, for example, merely to put rubbish out for collection,[114] or to bury a dead animal.[115] Normally, as in these examples, some right in

---

[109] (1976) 65 Cr App R 261. Cf. *Tideswell* [1905] 2 KB 273.

[110] In such circumstances, it seems that the cashier herself steals the goods when she offers to sell them at an undervalue: see *Pitham and Hehl* (1976) 65 Cr App R 45, below, § 13.6(i).

[111] *Jackson* (1826) 1 Mod 119, 168 ER 1208; *Prince* (1868) LR 1 CCR 150.

[112] Cf. *Ellerman Wilson Line* v. *Webster* [1952] 1 Lloyd's Rep 179, 180.

[113] Cf. Hudson, "Is Divesting Abandonment Possible at Common Law?" (1984) 100 *LQR* 110.

[114] *Williams* v. *Phillips* (1957) 41 Cr App R 5. As long as the rubbish remained on the owner's premises it was not abandoned; property in it passed when collected by the local authority. In *Ricketts* v. *Basildon Magistrates* [2010] EWHC 2358 (Admin) the defendant had helped himself to items left outside a charity shop when it was closed. It was held that the would-be donors, by attempting in this way to give them to the charity shop, had not abandoned them.

[115] *Edwards* (1877) 13 Cox CC 384.

the subject matter (such as the right of exclusion of others from the subject matter) will be preserved. Abandonment of ownership requires a giving up of the owner's physical control of an item, accompanied by the cessation of any intention to possess that item and of any intention to exclude other persons from its possession—i.e. a deliberate relinquishing of all rights over the item.[116]

Let us assume, since it contains money, that in David's case the wallet was not abandoned. It is worth noting that if David had formed an honest belief that the goods were abandoned rather than lost, he would not commit theft.[117] However, this is because of the lack of mens rea (dishonesty), rather than the absence of an actus reus.

(a) When does a finder acquire ownership?

Once abandoned, ownership of items vests in the first person to take possession of them. Possession, in turn, is normally taken by intentionally exercising control over the items. This may be done physically (as David does with the wallet, in the example above). Where chattels are abandoned on occupied land, however, the occupier will often acquire possession even before the chattel is found. In general, there are three types of cases in which the occupier acquires a better title than the finder.[118]

First, if the thing found is embedded in,[119] under,[120] or otherwise attached[121] to the land, it belongs to the occupier or owner (as the case may be)[122] of the land regardless of who finds it.[123]

Secondly, if something is found loose by an employee on the employer's property, the employer has a superior right to possession of that thing, in priority to the employee—finder.[124]

Finally, where the item is found lying loose on the land, the occupier can acquire a prior title either by (a) restricting public access to the land upon which the items lie,[125] or (where the land is open to public access) by (b) manifesting an intention to exercise control over the land and the things thereon.[126] Obviously if the item is found by a visitor inside D's private home, D has a superior title since the public does not have general

---

[116] Cf. Hudson, "Abandonment" in Palmer and McKendrick, *Interests in Goods* (1993); *The Crystal* [1894] AC 508.

[117] *Small* [1987] Crim LR 777; *White* (1912) 7 Cr App R 266.

[118] See Reisman, "Possession and the Law of Finders" (1939) 52 *Harv LR* 1105; Tay, "Problems in the Law of Finding" (1964) 37 *ALJ* 350; Harris, "The Concept of Possession in English Law" in Guest (ed.), *Oxford Essays in Jurisprudence* (1961) 69, 80ff.

[119] *Elwes* v. *Brigg Gas Company* (1886) 33 Ch D 562.

[120] *Rowe* (1859) Bell 93, 169 ER 1180; *South Staffordshire Water Co* v. *Sharman* [1896] 2 QB 44 (items lying under water; though in the latter case the defendant was also an employee).

[121] E.g., sealed inside a fixture: *City of London Corporation* v. *Appleyard* [1963] 2 All ER 834; *Moffatt* v. *Kazana* [1969] 2 QB 152.

[122] Itself a matter of potential controversy: see, e.g., *Elwes* v. *Brigg Gas Company* (1886) 33 Ch D 562.

[123] *Waverley* [1995] 4 All ER 756.

[124] *The Title of the Finder* (1899) 33 ILT 225; *Willey* v. *Synan* (1937) 57 CLR 200; *Grafstein* v. *Holme* [1958] 12 DLR (2d) 727.

[125] *Parker* v. *British Airways Board* [1982] QB 1004, 1013, 1019 (Donaldson LJ), 1020 (Eveleigh LJ), 1021 (Sir David Cairns).

[126] *Waverley* [1995] 4 All ER 756; cf. *Parker* v. *British Airways Board* [1982] QB 1004, 1018.

access to the home. Less straightforward illustrations of possibility (a) are the following two cases:

> In *Woodman*,[127] D took scrap metal from a factory site. E, the occupier of the site, had no knowledge of the existence of the scrap, as it had sold all the scrap on the site to B for removal. In fact, B had removed the bulk of the scrap but left some pieces behind, which B deemed too inaccessible to be worth the cost of removing. The site had been wound down and was now disused, although a barbed-wire fence had been erected around the site to exclude trespassers.

D's conviction was upheld by the Court of Appeal. Even if ownership of the remaining scrap had been abandoned by B, ownership would have reverted to D as the occupier of the land, since D had manifested an intention to exclude trespassers by fencing off the site.

> In *Hibbert* v. *McKiernan*,[128] D trespassed on a private golf course and dishonestly took eight golf balls which had been lost—and, it was found, subsequently abandoned— by their former owners.

The Divisional Court held that D was rightly convicted of theft from the golf club. Even if the balls had truly been abandoned (a doubtful conclusion, since clearly they had been lost unintentionally),[129] the golf club, as occupier of the land, had a better possessory title than D. D was a trespasser whose presence on the course was excluded.

On the other hand, where the premises are open to the public, the occupier's position is weaker, and she gains prior title only if she has manifested an intention to exercise control over the things that are or might be on the premises. In *Parker* v. *British Airways Board*,[130] Parker found a gold bracelet in an executive lounge at Heathrow airport. He handed the bracelet in to British Airways (who, as lessees, occupied the lounge), asking that the bracelet be returned to him if unclaimed. British Airways sold the bracelet. Parker succeeded in an action for conversion of the bracelet. The Court of Appeal held that Parker's rights as finder could be displaced only if British Airways could show as occupiers an obvious intention to exercise such control over the lounge and things in it that the bracelet was in their possession before the plaintiff found it.[131] On the evidence, there was no manifestation of such an intention as would give the defendants a right superior to that of the plaintiff; the airline's instructions to staff for dealing with lost articles were not published to users of the lounge, and it did not carry out searches for lost articles.

---

[127] [1974] QB 754.

[128] [1948] 2 KB 142.

[129] A finding made by the justices at first instance (who seem to have confused abandonment of the search with abandonment of the balls themselves) and accepted, without being approved (cf. *ibid.*, 151), by the Divisional Court for purposes of the appeal. If lost rather than abandoned, a charge of theft from the original owners of the balls would have been straightforward. A slightly different case with identical result is *Rostron* [2003] EWCA Crim 2206 where, under the rules of the club by which players were bound, lost balls were deemed to be "surrendered" to the club. Thus title passed to the club by contractual assignment rather than by the law governing possession of abandoned property; and the defendants were rightly convicted of stealing from the club.

[130] [1982] 1 All ER 834; discussed by Roberts, "More Lost Than Found" (1982) 45 *MLR* 683.

[131] It was also suggested that D's rights might be displaced had he acted dishonestly. However, unless D's dishonesty were such as to make him a trespasser *ab initio*, it is hard to see how this qualification can be justified. See A.T.H. Smith, *Property Offences* (1994) § 4–20, 4–21.

A special exception is "treasure", as defined in section 1 of the Treasure Act 1996. Any items falling within that definition (such as articles over 300 years old when found that are composed of at least 10 per cent gold or silver) are, by virtue of the Act, the property of the Crown.

§ 13.5 Belonging to another (II): extensions in the Act and in equity

There is a variety of ways in which the reach of the criminal law has been extended to protect interests in property rights beyond those falling within section 5(1). Much of the variety is added by sections 5(2),[132] 5(3),[133] and 5(4).[134] These subsections are intended to cover specific *lacunae* in the scope of section 5(1). In at least one other area, however, liability under section 5(1) itself has been enlarged as a result of changes in the civil law, notably the expansion of the constructive trust since the passing of the 1968 Act.

(i) *The growth of the constructive trust*[135]

In § 13.4, we saw that section 5(1) includes almost any form of proprietary right or interest within the range of what may be stolen, including, in particular, equitable proprietary interests. This obviously covers, first and foremost, the case where property is held on an express trust. However, a consequence of embracing any proprietary interest within the terms of section 5(1) is that, in recent years, developments in the law governing constructive trusts have brought a variety of new situations potentially within the net of criminal liability.

A constructive trust is a type of trust that arises by operation of law, rather than pursuant to the intention of the parties.[136] If D holds property in circumstances where, in equity and good conscience, the property ought to be owned or enjoyed by V, a constructive trust may be imposed upon D; with the consequence that, although D is the legal owner of the property, he holds that property for the benefit of V—the equitable owner. Such equitable ownership is sufficient for the purposes of section 5(1).

The law of constructive trusts is too complex to be treated in any depth here. We will simply introduce and briefly discuss some of the paradigm cases. What will be said in the following paragraphs assumes—unavoidably—some familiarity with the relevant civil law concepts.

(a) *Property obtained by mistake*

In § 13.4(iv)(c) and (d), we considered the situation where D obtains property pursuant to another's mistake. Where D has induced the mistake we saw that title to the property

---

[132] Below, § 13.5(ii).

[133] Below, § 13.5(iii).

[134] Below, § 13.5(iv).

[135] See generally Virgo, *Principles of Equity and Trusts* (2nd ed., 2016) ch. 9.

[136] Trust lawyers are divided as to whether constructive trusts are "institutional", meaning that they arise automatically, or "remedial", meaning that they are (in effect) a fiction employed by the courts, in their discretion, to secure a just result. In *FHR European Ventures LLP v. Cedar Capital Partners LLC* [2014] UKSC 45, [2015] AC 250 the Supreme Court opted for the first of these two views. For a discussion, see Virgo, *ibid*.

normally passes but is voidable, so that D may still be convicted of theft.[137] Otherwise, if the mistake is not fundamental, title passes; therefore, since D becomes absolute owner, section 5(1) does not apply and he cannot be convicted of theft unless (as will be discussed in § 13.5(iv)) the case falls exceptionally within section 5(4).

Such was the backdrop of settled law against which the Theft Act 1968 was enacted. But there is now authority that, while title passes at law, the law may recognise an equitable interest in the property—which would be a sufficient property interest to qualify within section 5(1). In *Chase Manhattan Bank* v. *Israel British Bank*,[138] the plaintiff bank paid $2 million by mistake into another bank for the account of the defendant, which then went bankrupt. The plaintiff sought to recover the overpayment. Goulding J ruled in favour of the plaintiff, holding that a person who pays money to another under a mistake of fact retains an equitable proprietary right or interest in the money, as opposed to a purely personal right. This reasoning was later doubted by Lord Browne-Wilkinson in his speech in *Westdeutsche Landesbank Girozentrale* v. *Islington LBC*.[139] The basis for a constructive trust, he said, was "unconscionabilty"; and it was not unconscionable conduct, as such, to receive a mistaken payment. However, if a person who had received such a payment, having discovered the mistake, then used the money, or failed to pay it back, his conduct would be unconscionable, and a constructive trust could then arise. "Although the mere receipt of the moneys, in ignorance of the mistake, gives rise to no trust, the retention of the moneys after the recipient bank learned of the mistake may well have given rise to a constructive trust."

In *Shadrokh-Cigari*,[140] a child's bank account was mistakenly credited with £286,000. D, the child's guardian, procured the child to authorise the issue of four banker's drafts in D's favour. Applying *Chase Manhattan*, the Court of Appeal held that D stole the drafts from the bank. Since the drafts had been drawn by the bank in error, the bank retained an equitable interest in them. Hence, for the purposes of section 5(1), they belonged to the bank. This was before the reasoning in *Chase Manhatten* had been disapproved in the *Westdeutsche* case. But as D was aware of the mistake and consciously took advantage of it, even under Lord Browne-Wilkinson's narrower formulation of the law a constructive trust presumably arose at the point when D handled the property, even if it did not arise before. In the light of this, it seems that the right result was reached in *Shadrokh-Cigari*, if not for exactly the right reason.[141] In *Shadrokh-Cigari* the Court of Appeal also upheld the conviction on a second basis: namely that, because the property was received under a mistake, the situation was covered by section 5(4) (which is discussed in § 13.5(iv) below). D's conviction can be justified on this basis too, surely, irrespective of the existence (or non-existence) of a constructive trust.[142]

Shadrokh-Cigari was later applied by the Court of Appeal in *Webster*.[143] Here an army officer who had won a medal was later sent a second duplicate medal by mistake. He passed

---

[137] Above, § 13.4(iv)(b).
[138] [1981] Ch 105, 119.
[139] [1996] AC 669, 714.
[140] [1988] Crim LR 465.
[141] See Ormerod and Williams, *Smith's Law of Theft* (9th ed., 2007) §§ 2.257–2.258.
[142] Though this basis was also doubted by Professor J.C. Smith in his comment on the decision in [1988] Crim LR 465, 467.
[143] [2006] EWCA Crim 2894.

it over to D, his administrative officer, to deal with, intending him to return it, but instead of doing so he sold it on eBay. His theft conviction was affirmed on the basis, inter alia, that the Secretary of State retained an equitable interest in the duplicate medal that had been given to the officer in error.

(b) Property obtained by fraud

In *Re Holmes*,[144] an extradition case, D was alleged to be a dishonest employee of the X bank in Germany who had abused his position to cause the X bank to make a direct transfer of 15.5 million US dollars from its own funds, using the SWIFT[145] system of inter-bank transfers, to the Y bank in Holland, where it was credited to an account which D controlled, and whence D had then spirited it away to the Bahamas, Switzerland, Australia, Austria, and Indonesia. Under the law of extradition as it then stood,[146] D was liable to be extradited to Germany only if his behaviour constituted an offence under English law as well, which—remarkably—he claimed it was not. The Divisional Court held that in England D would have committed an offence of fraud.[147] For good measure it added, obiter, that he would also be guilty of theft in relation to the funds received by the Y bank, in respect of which there existed a constructive trust in favour of the X bank. In so holding, the Court quoted the following passage from Lord Browne-Wilkinson's speech in the *Westdeutsche* case:

> "Although it is difficult to find clear authority for the proposition, when property is obtained by fraud equity imposes a constructive trust on the fraudulent recipient: the property is recoverable and traceable in equity."[148]

(It also added that, if the money had been transferred by the X bank from an account at that bank that could be identified, D would also have been guilty of theft of the chose in action represented by that bank account.)[149]

(c) Making a profit from abuse of fiduciary position

If D "occupies a position in which he is expected to safeguard, or not to act against, the financial interests of another person" and dishonestly abuses that position with a view to financial gain, he will be guilty of the offence of fraud by abuse of position, as will be explained later (§ 15.5 below). If such a person does make a financial gain, the civil law will make him personally liable to account for it to the person, V, whose interests he was expected to protect. And in some situations the civil law goes even further in protecting the victim of his misbehaviour by treating D as holding the profit he has made on a constructive trust in favour of V. In this situation, V has, once again, a proprietary right over the

---

[144] [2004] EWHC 2020 (Admin), [2005] 1 WLR 1857; noted [2005] Crim LR 229.

[145] SWIFT stands for Society for Worldwide Interbank Financial Telecommunication.

[146] Under Part I of the Extradition Act 2003, which was not yet in force, this "double criminality" requirement has been curtailed in the context of extradition between the UK and other EU Member States. See Spencer, "The European Arrest Warrant" (2003–4) 6 *Cambridge Yearbook of European Legal Studies* 201.

[147] The offence, now abolished, of obtaining a money transfer by deception, contrary to the Theft Act 1968, s. 15A; today he would be guilty of fraud, under ss. 1 and 4 of the Fraud Act 2006 (fraud by abuse of position). See Chapter 15 below.

[148] Followed and applied in *Armstrong DLW GmbH v. Winnington Networks Ltd* [2012] EWHC 10 (Ch), [2013] Ch. 156; and see further Virgo, *Principles of Equity and Trusts* (2nd ed., 2016) 310–11.

[149] *Williams* [2001] 1 Cr App R 362, §13.3(c) above; and see *Chan Man-sin*, § 13.6(vi) below.

property; and in consequence, section 5(1) of the Theft Act potentially applies to make D guilty of the offence of theft, as well as fraud by abuse of position.

Whether a constructive trust arises in this situation depends on whether D occupied, in law, the position of "fiduciary". Of this term there is no precise legal definition, but

> [a] "fiduciary" is essentially somebody, person A, who is in a relationship with another person, B, in which B is entitled to expect that A will act either in B's best interests or in their joint interests, to the exclusion of A's own interest. In determining whether a person is a fiduciary, it is first necessary to consider whether that person is in a relationship with another that falls within one of the recognized categories of fiduciary relationships. If it does not, it is then necessary to examine the factual circumstances of the relationship to determine whether there are sufficient hallmarks of a fiduciary relationship to enable the court to conclude that the relationship is indeed fiduciary.[150]

Recognised categories of fiduciary relationship include those involving agents, solicitors, company directors, and partners.[151] Beyond that, whether a given person counts as one will depend on the facts of the case, and this is a question that it is sometimes difficult to answer.

Until recently, there was a further difficulty, this time in relation to the types of gain to which a constructive trust might possibly attach. It would certainly attach to profits made from interference with the principal's property, or improperly exploiting an opportunity that should have been available to him; but according to some of the authorities it would not attach to profits derived from a third party, such as bribes or unauthorised commissions.[152] Thirty years ago, these decisions were relied on by the Court of Appeal to endorse an acquittal in *A-G's Reference (No. 1 of 1985)*.[153] D was the manager of a public house and an employee of the brewers to whom the house was tied. In contravention of the terms of his employment, he sought to sell beer purchased privately from a wholesaler to supplement his profits. The Court thought that such circumstances would not give rise to a trust and, even if it did, that it would not be such a trust as falls within the ambit of section 5(1). (We will consider the policy merits of this view below, in § 13.5(i)(d).) But in 2014 the Supreme Court in *FHR European Ventures LLP v. Cedar Capital Partners LLC*[154] disapproved of this line of cases and declared them overruled, together with *A-G's Reference (No. 1 of 1985)* insofar as it depended on them. It now follows that a constructive trust can indeed attach to bribes and other improper benefits deriving from third parties.

The other difficulty remains. A widely accepted view is that a person who falls outside the recognised categories may be a fiduciary if (i) he or she has expressly or implied undertaken to act in the best interests of the other and (ii) he or she has a discretionary power to affect the principal's legal or practical interests.[155] On this basis, an ordinary employee is unlikely to be a constructive trustee, and hence unlikely to be guilty of theft by virtue of section 5(1) if he accepts a bribe or makes an unauthorised profit on the side. So for example where, as

---

[150] Virgo, *Principles of Equity and Trusts* (2nd ed., 2016) 498.
[151] *Ibid.*, 499.
[152] In particular, *Lister v Stubbs* (1890) 45 Ch D 1.
[153] [[1986] QB 491. An earlier decision to similar effect is *Powell v. MacRae* [1977] Crim LR 571.
[154] [2014] UKSC 45, [2015] AC 250.
[155] Virgo, *Principles of Equity and Trusts* (2nd ed., 2016) 501; quoting the Canadian case of *Galambos v. Perez* 2009 SCR 48, [2009] 3 SCR 247.

in the old case of *Cullum*,[156] the captain of a barge carries cargo contrary to his instructions and appropriates the resulting profits he is probably not guilty of stealing the profits; nor, likewise, the manager of the public house in *A-G's Reference (No. 1 of 1985)*. (However, as previously mentioned, they would now commit the offence of fraud by abuse of position.)

(d) The merits of criminalising theft as a constructive trustee

We noted above that the Court of Appeal in *A-G's Reference (No. 1 of 1985)*[157] refused to accept that constructive trusts fall within the scope of section 5(1). If now shown to be incorrect in law, as matter of policy its position was understandable. Constructive trusts were developed by the civil law with aims in mind that are characteristically irrelevant to the criminal law,[158] and often in the context of litigation to determine whether V should have a prior claim in insolvency over a third party, T. It is not obvious that the question whether D steals from V should be determined by the unrelated issue of priority between V and T.

Moreover, in this area the label "theft" does not always accurately capture the nature of D's wrongdoing. Consider the example where D, a fiduciary, accepts a bribe. In such a case the obvious charge to bring is one for the offence of bribery,[159] in respect of his initial acceptance of the bribe, or fraud by abuse of position, and not for subsequent theft of the proceeds. And issues of fair labelling aside,[160] extending theft liability to constructive trusts has the further disadvantage of decreasing certainty in the law, and reducing the level of fair warning available to prospective thieves.[161] As Lord Lane pointed out in *A-G's Reference* itself, "if something is so abstruse and so far from the understanding of ordinary people as to what constitutes stealing, it should not amount to stealing".[162] If conduct of this sort should fall within criminal law, the proper place for it is surely in the law of fraud. In 2006, as we shall see in Chapter 15, Parliament enacted a new Fraud Act, which creates a new tripartite offence of fraud, one form of which is "fraud by abuse of position". This offence unquestionably covers dishonest employees who abuse their position to make money on the side. For this offence, as we shall later see, it is not a legal requirement that D should be a "fiduciary". It is for this offence, and not some inflated form of theft, that dishonest employees and should now be prosecuted.[163]

(ii) Theft of an interest protected by section 5(2): trust property

As we have seen, a trustee can typically be convicted of theft of trust property under section 5(1), since any beneficiary of the trust would normally have an equitable interest

---

[156] (1873) LR 2 CCR 28.

[157] [1986] QB 491; above, § 13.5(i)(c).

[158] *Per* A.T.H. Smith, "Constructive Trusts in the Law of Theft" [1977] *Crim LR* 395, 400: "the civil law imposes constructive trusts in situations, and for multifarious reasons, which may have nothing to do with the purposes of the criminal law."

[159] Contrary to the Bribery Act 2010.

[160] Cf. the discussion of fair labelling in § 2.4.

[161] Above, § 2.3.

[162] [1986] QB 491, 507; adding the telling comment that "There are topics of conversation more popular in public houses than the finer points of the equitable doctrine of the constructive trust."

[163] Making secret profits had previously been held indictable as conspiracy to defraud: *Button* (1848) 3 Cox CC 229; *Rashid* [1977] 2 All ER 237; *Doukas* [1978] 1 All ER 1061.

in the trust property, which would qualify for protection as a proprietary interest under section 5(1). However, particularly in the case of charitable trusts, or discretionary trusts for a very large class,[164] sometimes there may be no individual beneficiary with an equitable interest in the trust. Such cases are covered by section 5(2):

> Where property is subject to a trust, the persons to whom it belongs shall be regarded as including any person having a right to enforce the trust, and an intention to defeat the trust shall be regarded accordingly as an intention to deprive of the property any person having that right.

A charitable trust is enforceable by the Attorney General. For the purposes of theft, therefore, its property belongs to the Attorney General, and may be stolen by the trustee.[165]

(iii) Theft of an interest protected by section 5(3): property received on account

What if a person such as stockbroker, solicitor, or estate agent, having received property from a client, fraudulently misuses it for his own benefit? One way of dealing with such persons is under section 5(3):

> Where a person receives property from or on account of another, and is under an obligation to the other to retain and deal with that property or its proceeds in a particular way, the property or proceeds shall be regarded (as against him) as belonging to the other.

The section overlaps to a considerable extent with section 5(1), since persons receiving property on account will generally be fiduciaries who have legal but not equitable title to that property. In such cases, for purposes of theft the property can be stolen from the equitable owner (*per* section 5(1)) and from the person on whose account it is received (*per* section 5(3)). Section 5(3) comes into its own, however, when no one apart from D has any legal or equitable interest in the property stolen.[166] Suppose T gives D money for a specific purpose, e.g. to pay the gas bill. There would normally be no expectation that D will pay the bill using the exact banknotes, cheque, etc., that T gives him. T intends, rather, that D should pay out either the money T gives him, its proceeds, or (if D has it) an equivalent sum; in effect, that D should maintain a sufficient fund to make the payment. In this situation D is the owner of the money, but may have a duty to account falling within section 5(3).[167]

Section 5(3) would also capture situations in which we would hold D to be under a fiduciary obligation notwithstanding that he has legal and equitable ownership of a thing. There is authority for the proposition that the residuary legatees of an estate have no proprietary interest before the estate is administered,[168] but we would think the executor guilty of theft were he dishonestly to appropriate the estate property to his own use. Another example is provided by the *Quistclose*[169] line of cases, where the transferees of money were

---

[164] Cf. *Vestey* v. *IRC* [1980] AC 1148.

[165] The analysis was missed by the Court of Appeal in *Dyke and Munro* [2002] 1 Cr App R 404.

[166] Cf. *Klineberg* [1999] 1 Cr App R 427, 432: s. 5(3) "is essentially a deeming provision by which property or its proceeds 'shall be regarded' as belonging to another, even though, on a strict civil law analysis, it does not".

[167] As the court held in *Davidge* v. *Bunnett* [1984] Crim LR 297.

[168] *Commr of Stamp Duties (Queensland)* v. *Livingstone* [1965] AC 674.

[169] *Quistclose Investments Ltd* v. *Rolls Razor Ltd* [1968] 1 All ER 613.

obliged to keep it separate and to use it for specific purposes, even though there was no beneficial interest vesting in the intended recipients, nor, initially, in the transferors.

On the other hand, it is not always easy to determine when a person receives money on account. The obligation must be a *legal* obligation. A moral or social obligation is not sufficient.[170] When does this legal obligation arise?

(a) The receipt on account distinguished from mere personal liability

A duty to account does *not* exist where the relationship between D and the transferor of the property is that of debtor and creditor, such that the transferor's remedy against D is merely *in personam*. In theory, the difference between a duty to account and a liability *in personam* is clear enough. There is no duty to account when the recipient is entitled to the property both legally and beneficially, without any particular obligations attaching to her use of that property or its proceeds, so that she may deal with it as her own. In that case, the recipient's obligations operate as collateral, independent liabilities (e.g. a contractual debt). By contrast, where there is a receipt on account, D does not have untrammelled ownership of the property, and is entitled to dispose of and deal with the property or its proceeds only subject to the terms on which it was received.

However, it is not always a simple matter to distinguish them in practice. J.C. Smith, discussing the (former) offence of fraudulent conversion, has suggested the following test where money is transferred:[171]

> "Was the transferee permitted, under the terms of the contract, to use the money as he thought fit; or was he obliged to apply it in a particular way or to retain an equivalent sum, either in his possession or in a bank? Only in the latter event can the transferee commit fraudulent conversion."

The distinction is often relevant in a civil law context, especially in an insolvency, where it may be important to decide whether the money forms part of a debtor's general assets to be distributed among creditors, or whether it may be recovered intact by the transferor.[172] In the criminal context, a simple example may be found in the travel agency business. A travel agent generally receives money from customers in return for an obligation to provide the ticket, and may use the money received from customers as he chooses. It was held in *Hall*[173] that this creates a debtor–creditor relationship. In that case, D had received deposits for air tickets and paid the money into a general trading account; he then failed to supply tickets to the clients. Although his conduct was "condemned as scandalous",[174] in the absence of special arrangements imposing on him an obligation to deal with clients' money in a particular way, he had no duty to account and therefore did not commit theft. By contrast, in

---

[170] Cf. *Huskinson* [1988] Crim LR 620; *Meech* [1974] QB 549, 554; *Hall* [1973] QB 126; J.C. Smith, "The Scope of Fraudulent Conversion" [1961] *Crim LR* 741 and 797, 799ff.

[171] J.C. Smith, "The Scope of Fraudulent Conversion" [1961] *Crim LR* 741 and 797, 800. This test was adopted in *Stephens* v. *R.* (1978) 52 ALJR 662, 669. For a useful illustration, compare *Hotine* (1904) 68 JP 143 with *Donald Smith* [1924] 2 KB 194.

[172] For example in the *Quistclose* line of cases: *Quistclose Investments Ltd* v. *Rolls Razor Ltd* [1968] 1 All ER 613.

[173] [1973] QB 126. Cf. *Robertson* [1977] Crim LR 629—but contrast *Brewster* (1979) 69 Cr App R 375 (insurance brokers).

[174] [1973] QB 126, 131.

Re Kumar,[175] D, also a travel agent, had specifically agreed a trustee relationship in respect of moneys received from airline ticket sales. After deducting commission, D was required each month to remit the proceeds to IATA; which he failed to do. In these circumstances D had a duty to account and was ruled to have committed a theft.

One standard application of section 5(3) is to charity collectors.[176] In *Wain*,[177] D raised money from the public by conducting charitable discotheques and other events. Subsequently, he failed to hand the money over and instead spent it. D's conviction was upheld by the Court of Appeal on the basis that he was obliged to retain the proceeds of his fundraising for the benefit of the charity; hence, under section 5(3), the money belonged to the charity for the purposes of theft.

(iv) Theft of an interest protected by section 5(4): where there is an obligation to make restitution

Suppose that C is a wages clerk. When making up the pay packets one week, he accidentally puts a £50 note, which has stuck to another note, into D's packet, so that it now contains £200 instead of £150. Upon discovering the error, D resolves to say nothing and spends the money. He is guilty of stealing the £50 note. C's mistake was a fundamental one of quantity (above, § 13.4(iv)(c)), and the £50 note still belongs to the employer. Section 5(1) applies straightforwardly.

Compare, on the other hand, *Moynes* v. *Coopper*,[178] where a wages clerk miscalculated the amount due to D. Although the employee was thus overpaid, the clerk intended to pay the amount of money actually paid. Hence title in the whole amount paid passed to D, and D could not be convicted of larceny. The employer had no proprietary claim to the money in D's hands, merely a personal claim in restitution against D for money had and received.[179]

However, since the passing of the Theft Act 1968 mistakes of the latter variety are now covered by the special provisions of section 5(4):

> Where a person gets property by another's mistake, and is under an obligation to make restoration (in whole or in part) of the property or its proceeds or the value thereof, then to the extent of that obligation the property shall be regarded (as against him) as belonging to the person entitled to restoration, and an intention not to make restoration shall be regarded accordingly as an intention to deprive that person of the property or its proceeds.

---

[175] [2000] Crim LR 504.

[176] *Quaere* whether such cases in any event give rise to a constructive trust, falling within the scope of s. 5(1)–(2).

[177] [1995] 2 Cr App R 660; rightly disapproving *Lewis* v. *Lethbridge* [1987] Crim LR 59 (DC). In the latter case, D had obtained sponsorships for the benefit of a charity, but then kept the money. D's conviction was quashed because the magistrates had made no finding of fact that the charity expected D to maintain a separate fund with the money; but, as the Court in *Wain* pointed out, an obligation to account for the moneys or their proceeds need not come from the beneficiary. It can originate from the donors.

[178] [1956] 1 QB 439. Cf. *Davis* (1988) 88 Cr App R 347 (CA).

[179] There is, however, controversial authority to the effect that even though title passes at law, the unilaterally mistaken payer may sometimes retain an equitable interest in the goods—which would be a sufficient property interest to qualify within s. 5(1). Because of its complexity, we consider this possibility separately, in § 13.5(i)(a).

Moynes would now be guilty of theft, notwithstanding that he in no way infringed his employer's property rights. The effect of section 5(4) can be seen in *A-G's Reference (No. 1 of 1983)*.[180] D, a police constable, had her salary paid by direct debit. By mistake, she was overpaid on one occasion by £74.74. On the assumption that she subsequently decided, dishonestly, not to repay the sum, the Court of Appeal ruled that she would be guilty of theft. Notwithstanding that she owned outright the content of her bank account, and was entitled to draw upon it as she wished, there was a legal obligation upon D to repay to her employer a sum equivalent to the overpayment once she discovered the mistake. By virtue of section 5(4), that sum (of £74.74) was *deemed* for the purposes of theft to belong to the employer, and so could be stolen.

The obligation must be a legal and not a moral obligation to make repayment.[181] Recall the betting case of *Gilks*,[182] discussed in § 13.4(iv)(c). While the mistake in that case was of the same type as that in *Moynes* v. *Coopper*, as the law then stood no legal obligation to make repayment arose in *Gilks* because the overpayment was in virtue of a wager.[183] Thus *Gilks* did not fall within the ambit of section 5(4).

Although the decision in *Moynes* was much criticised at the time,[184] its undoing by section 5(4) seems something of an overreaction. The defendant in *Moynes* is a mere debtor; section 5(4) effectively makes personal liability the stuff of theft. This, surely, is a misuse of the concept of theft.

Moreover, it is debatable whether the defendant's behaviour should be criminalised under any other description either. If, through V's own error, V mistakenly gives D an unjustified windfall, prima facie his proper remedy is a civil law claim in money had and received. It is not obvious that the criminal law should wade to his rescue. This is not a case where D has done anything wrong to induce V's blunder. Like the difference between silence and active misrepresentation in contract law, taking studious advantage of another's unilateral mistake is not normally the stuff of legal intervention. Sometimes such circumstances warrant a civil law remedy; but it does not necessarily follow that the criminal law should be available here as a creditors' device.

§ 13.6 Appropriation

So far, we have considered what can be stolen: what sort of *property*, and what sort of *interest* in that property, is susceptible of theft. The third issue for the actus reus of theft is what sort of *action*, in connection with that property, is prohibited? Under section 1, D must "appropriate" the stolen property, a term elaborated upon by section 3(1):

> Any assumption by a person of the rights of an owner amounts to an appropriation, and this includes, where he has come by the property (innocently or not) without stealing it, any later assumption of a right to it by keeping or dealing with it as owner.

---

[180] [1985] QB 182 (CA).

[181] *Gilks* [1972] 3 All ER 280, 283. Cf. the discussion of s. 5(3) above, § 13.5(iii).

[182] [1972] 3 All ER 280; above, § 13.4(iv)(c) (Case 3).

[183] Gaming Act 1845, s. 18; Gaming Act 1892, s. 1. Since then, the Gambling Act 2005 has repealed the legislation which formerly rendered all gaming debts legally unenforceable.

[184] See, e.g., [1956] Crim LR 516.

Although this definition is not intended to be exhaustive,[185] it appears to be at least as wide as any ordinary language concept of appropriation, and for practical purposes it is comprehensive. The history of the interpretation of section 3(1) is the sorry story of a statutory provision being construed so loosely as to deprive it of any solid content. We shall try to avoid its retelling here, save in so far as necessary. As things stand, the gist of appropriation is as follows:

> D appropriates an item when he does anything in connection with it that only an owner (or someone having rights derived from ownership) has the right to do, or that an owner has the right to exclude others from doing.

For instance, D appropriates something when he touches it, destroys it, gives it to another person, sells it, or even offers it for sale. The right to do each of these things is a right of ownership, and D assumes one of those rights when he does any of these actions. Note that D need only assume any one of the rights of ownership, not all of them, by his action.[186] Thus touching something is an appropriation even though one may do so without presuming all the facets of ownership.

Any act of appropriation is sufficient. There is no need for it to be the very act by which D intends to deprive V of the item stolen. It is sufficient that D appropriates the item while intending that the owner should be deprived, even if that deprivation will be accomplished only by some later act of D's.[187] Suppose, for example, that D changes the labels on two products (say, product A and product B) in a supermarket, intending to buy the more expensive item, product A, at an undervalue. He steals product A as soon as he touches it, even though this act is only preliminary to the act of appropriation by which the owner will be deprived.[188]

Before we elaborate upon this analysis in the following pages, it is worth commenting that, although this interpretation of section 3(1) must now be accepted, it seems at variance with the plain words of the statute: any assumption of "the rights of an owner" seemingly indicates an assumption of the *entirety* of the owner's rights. As we shall see, because of questionable interpretations, acts which previously would have been merely preparatory to theft—and which are not part of the gravamen of theft—are now treated as the theft itself.[189]

---

[185] Cf. Report of the Criminal Law Revision Committee, *Theft and Related Offences* Cmnd. 2977 (1966) para. 34.

[186] *Morris* [1984] AC 320, where the House of Lords rejected the appellant's argument to the contrary.

[187] *Ibid.*

[188] That said, it is arguably the case that in order to amount to an appropriation the act must be done with the intention of assuming the rights of an owner. If that is right, a person who picks up a purse in the street intending to hand it in to the police does not "appropriate" it, and would not be guilty of theft for that reason, quite apart from that he acts without dishonesty or the intent permanently to deprive. See Melissaris, "The Concept of Appropriation and the Offence of Theft" (2007) 70 *MLR* 581.

[189] In *Morris, ibid.*, Lord Roskill conceded that there was force in the view that the expression, "the rights of an owner", means all rights, not one or some. For his Lordship, however, it was decisive that s. 3(1) goes on to speak of "any later assumption of *a* right." Remarkably, he omitted the subsequent words, "by keeping or dealing with it as an owner", which make it clear that D must keep or deal with the property by assuming the entirety of the rights to it.

(i) Some examples of appropriation

It may be helpful to illustrate the variety of forms of conduct that can constitute theft. In *Pitham and Hehl*,[190] M offered to sell P and H some furniture, which all concerned knew did not belong to M. Convictions for handling by P and H were upheld on appeal, on the footing that M committed theft when he offered to sell the goods; hence P and H were guilty of handling goods that were stolen when they received them. The decision may be doubted on the facts,[191] but is clear authority that offering to sell goods assumes a right of the owner and is therefore an appropriation.

In *Chan Nai-Keung*,[192] D, a director of a company which exported textiles, dishonestly sold a large quantity of the company's export quotas (a form of intangible property). D's conviction for theft was upheld by the Privy Council.

The framers of the Theft Act 1968 envisaged that the term "appropriation" would cover the same ground as the civil law concept of conversion,[193] and it seems clear that any form of conversion will also be an appropriation. This includes conversion by a person who legitimately has possession of the goods: for example, it is a theftuous conversion for a bailee to grant a chattel security over the property lent to her,[194] or to obliterate the identifying marks by painting it.[195]

(ii) Restrictions on the scope of appropriation?

Prima facie, the scope of appropriation is astoundingly wide, with the consequence that the actus reus of theft is usually a simple matter for the prosecution to establish. Provided D does anything whatsoever in connection with property belonging to another person, the actus reus is made out; if he is dishonest and has an intention permanently to deprive, he steals it. Consider the following situation:

> Walter decides to steal a car. He walks down the street until he finds a Ford Mondeo with its doors unlocked. He opens the door and gets into the car. Unfortunately for him, he finds that his skeleton ignition key does not work. He gives up and goes home.

This looks like an attempted theft, subject to the question whether Walter had passed the stage of mere preparation and had in fact commenced the attempt. But it is not. It is a consummated theft, complete as soon as Walter opened the door. That was an appropriation: since all the other elements of theft were present, the offence was committed at that point.

The result is worrying as well as surprising. In Chapter 1 of this book, we discussed the proposition that criminal offences should require both harm and culpability before

---

[190] (1976) 65 Cr App R 45. Cf. *Rogers v. Arnott* [1960] 2 QB 244.

[191] Since all three knew that M had no authority to sell the furniture, M's "offer" seems to have been a mere sham rather than an appropriation. As Smith wrote, "D did not purport to be the owner or to be acting with his authority. It was not really an offer to sell at all but a proposal for a joint theft of the goods": Ormerod and Williams, *Smith's Law of Theft*, 9th ed. (2007) §2.79.

[192] *A-G of Hong Kong v. Chan Nai-Keung* (1987) 86 Cr App R 174.

[193] See below, § 13.6(ii)(b).

[194] Cf. *Dunbar* [1963] NZLR 253. (D had the loan of a boat, which he pledged as security for a financial transaction.)

[195] As in *Russell* [1977] 2 NZLR 20.

imposing the sanctions of conviction and punishment. Unfortunately, the modern law of theft appears virtually to have dispensed with harm. Conceptually, and at the level of ordinary language, the gist of theft is depriving another person of his property rights. Legally, theft is no such thing. Looked at objectively, D's behaviour may be ordinary and harmless, yet be the actus reus of theft. Consider the case of *Dip Kaur* v. *Chief Constable for Hampshire*:[196]

> D was in a shop where she found a pair of shoes, one of which was marked for sale at £6.99, the other at £4.99. She took the shoes to the cashier, hoping that the cashier would see the lower (incorrect) price. She was charged £4.99. Her conviction for theft was quashed, for the reason that the cashier's mistake (in thinking £4.99 was the correct price) did not negate her intention to sell the goods to D for £4.99; thus, when D left the shop, she owned the shoes and could not steal them.

As things stand, the case would now be decided differently. D, if dishonest, stole the shoes as soon as she picked them off the sale rack—notwithstanding that the subsequent transaction was valid and she became their owner.

(a) Possible qualification 1: unauthorised or wrongful appropriations?

It might be thought that one way out of this difficulty is to read an implicit qualification into section 3(1): rather than simply "any assumption" of the rights of the owner, section 3(1) may be interpreted as requiring "any unauthorised assumption", or perhaps any "usurpation" of the owner's rights. This approach would better reflect the core idea that theft involves some form of harmful interference with another person's property rights, and that appropriation lacks a theftuous character unless it conflicts with the victim's rights.[197]

At one point, the House of Lords appeared to favour such a qualification. In *Morris*,[198] D took goods from the shelves of a supermarket. He replaced the price labels attached to them with labels showing a lesser price than the originals. He was arrested after buying the goods at the lesser price and was subsequently convicted of theft. The House upheld the conviction, on the basis that D appropriated the goods and committed theft when he switched the price labels. The decision is clearly right, since D's act was an unauthorised appropriation of the goods. However, in the course of his judgment Lord Roskill dealt specifically with a point raised by counsel for the Crown:[199]

> "My Lords, Mr. Jeffreys sought to argue that any removal from the shelves of the supermarket, even if unaccompanied by label switching, was without more an appropriation. In one passage in his judgment in Morris's case, the learned Lord Chief Justice appears to have accepted the submission, for he said [1983] QB 587, 596 [CA]: 'it seems to us that in taking the article from the shelf the customer is indeed assuming one of the rights of the owner—the right to move the article from its position on the shelf to carry it to the check-out.' With the utmost respect, I cannot accept this statement as correct. If one postulates an honest customer taking goods

---

[196] [1981] 2 All ER 430.
[197] Cf. Model Penal Code, § 223.2 (the interference must be "unlawful").
[198] [1984] AC 320; discussed by Leigh, "Some Remarks on Appropriation in the Law of Theft after *Morris*" (1985) 48 *MLR* 167. Cases exhibiting similar reasoning include *Meech* [1974] QB 549; *Hircock* (1978) 67 Cr App R 278; *Morgan* [1991] RTR 365; *Fritschy* [1985] Crim LR 745.
[199] [1984] AC 320, 332.

from a shelf to put in his or her trolley to take to the checkpoint there to pay the proper price, I am unable to see that any of these actions involves any assumption by the shopper of the rights of the supermarket. *In the context of section 3(1), the concept of appropriation in my view involves not an act expressly or impliedly authorised by the owner but an act by way of adverse interference with or usurpation of those rights.* When the honest shopper acts as I have just described, he or she is acting with the implied authority of the owner of the supermarket to take the goods from the shelf, put them in the trolley, take them to the checkpoint and there pay the correct price, at which moment the property in the goods will pass to the shopper for the first time.... I do not think that section 3(1) envisages any such act as an 'appropriation', whatever may be the meaning of that word in other fields such as contract or sale of goods law."

We have italicised the key proposition asserted by Lord Roskill, but the example he discusses is also helpful. It is this reasoning that justifies the quashing of D's conviction in *Dip Kaur* (above) where, by contrast with the defendant in *Morris*, D's handling of the shoes involved no unauthorised action. She simply picked them up and took them to the counter, something any shopper has an implied licence to do.[200]

Unfortunately, Lord Roskill's analysis was inconsistent with the earlier House of Lords decision in *Lawrence v. Metropolitan Police Commissioner*.[201] In that case D, a taxi-driver, drove a newly arrived foreign student with little English from Victoria Station to an address in London. The student had offered a £1 note for the fare, which D said was not enough before extracting a further £6 from the student's open wallet. In truth, the legally authorised fare for the journey was approximately 50 pence. Although the student had permitted D to take the excess money, the House upheld D's conviction for theft. The student's consent was irrelevant:[202]

"I see no ground for concluding that the omission [from section 1(1) of the Theft Act 1968] of the words 'without the consent of the owner' was inadvertent and not deliberate, and to read the subsection as if they were included is, in my opinion, wholly unwarranted. Parliament by the omission of these words has relieved the prosecution of the burden of establishing that the taking was without the owner's consent. That is no longer an ingredient of the offence.

... That there was appropriation in this case is clear. Section 3 (1) states that any assumption by a person of the rights of an owner amounts to an appropriation. Here there was clearly such an assumption.... [An appropriation] may occur even though the owner has permitted or consented to the property being taken."

The conflict in approach between *Lawrence* and *Morris* was resolved in *Gomez*,[203] in which their Lordships affirmed *Lawrence*. D, the assistant manager of a shop, had formed a plan with R, a customer, to acquire goods in exchange for two stolen cheques. Knowing that the cheques were stolen, D deceived the shop manager into authorising the sale of the goods to R in exchange for the cheques. Instead of charging him with obtaining property by

---

[200] Admittedly, it could be argued that such a licence (to carry goods within the shop) extends only to honest shoppers; a similar restriction has been allowed in the context of burglarious trespass (criticised below, § 14.3(ii)(a)). Besides being an artificial construction, however, such a move could be said to make proof of the actus reus dependent on proving an element of mens rea, which would be to put the cart before the horse; though see note 188 above.

[201] [1972] AC 626.

[202] *Ibid.*, 632. Cf. *Dobson v. General Accident Fire and Life Assurance Corporation plc* [1990] 1 QB 274 (CA).

[203] [1993] AC 442.

deception[204] (as should have occurred), the prosecution charged D with theft. The Court of Appeal quashed his conviction, on the ground that ownership of the goods had passed; since the manager had consented to the transaction, possession of the goods was authorised and therefore there was no appropriation. The House of Lords, by a majority, restored the conviction:

> "The decision in *Lawrence* was a clear decision of this House upon the construction of the word 'appropriate' in section 1(1) of the Act, which had stood for 12 years when doubt was thrown upon it by obiter dicta in *Morris*. *Lawrence* must be regarded as authoritative and correct, and there is no question of it now being right to depart from it."[205]

The upshot of *Gomez* is that the scope of "appropriation" in theft is not limited to unauthorised or wrongful appropriations but includes even appropriations made with consent of the owner.[206]

(b) What was wrong with Gomez?

Quite apart from the fact that it virtually demolished any distinction between theft and the (then) offence of obtaining by deception,[207] the decision was questionable for other reasons. The majority judgments by Lord Keith and Lord Browne-Wilkinson treated the matter largely as an issue of precedent: the analysis of appropriation in *Lawrence* was part of the *ratio decidendi* of that case, whereas it was merely *obiter dicta* in *Morris*. They barely mentioned the issues of principle at stake, and were unswayed by the evidence that the legislature could not have intended such a broad interpretation of appropriation. The majority judgments are also profoundly disappointing because they contain no recognition, anywhere, that the interpretation of criminal statutes is a matter that should be governed by general principles, which include the principle that, in the absence of any compelling policy reason suggesting Parliament really intended the wider meaning, statutes creating criminal liability should not be extensively construed.[208]

The better view is surely that if V transfers ownership of the goods to D, D as owner should be incapable of stealing those goods. As Lord Lowry pointed out in his minority judgment,[209] this was certainly the view of the Criminal Law Revision Committee (CLRC),

---

[204] Contrary to s. 15 of the Theft Act 1968; an offence later abolished and replaced by a new and broader offence of fraud: below, § 15.1.

[205] *Ibid.*, 464.

[206] See, e.g., *Williams (Roy)* [2001] 1 Cr App R 362. D dishonestly overcharged a number of clients for building work. He was convicted of stealing from his clients' bank accounts, notwithstanding that each appropriation from those accounts was with the consent of the customer who wrote the cheque.

[207] See Shute and Horder, "Thieving and Deceiving—What Is the Difference?" (1993) 56 *MLR* 548; Clarkson, "Theft and Fair Labelling" (1993) 56 *MLR* 554. A few instances of non-overlap are identified in Heaton, "Deceiving without Thieving" [2001] *Crim LR* 712. Earlier writing prior to *Gomez* includes Koffman, "The Nature of Appropriation" [1982] *Crim LR* 331; Leigh, "Some Remarks on Appropriation" (1985) 48 *MLR* 167; Gardner, "Is Theft a Rip-off?" (1990) 10 *OJLS* 441; Halpin, "The Appropriate Appropriation" [1991] *Crim LR* 426. Glazebrook, however, approves of *Lawrence* for pragmatic reasons: "Thief or Swindler: Who Cares?" [1991] *CLJ* 389. For discussion of the former offence of obtaining by deception and its successor under the Fraud Act 2006, see Chapter 15 below.

[208] As explained in § 3.1 above. In some Continental criminal codes, the rule against the extensive construction of criminal statutes is laid down explicitly. Article 111-4 of the French *Code pénal* provides, "*La loi pénale est d'interprétation stricte*"—"criminal statutes are to be strictly construed".

[209] *Gomez* [1993] AC 442, 470ff.

upon whose report the Theft Act 1968 was based.[210] When framing the Act, the CLRC equated appropriation with conversion[211]—a term that certainly requires unauthorised usurpation of another's property rights—and preferred the former word only because the latter was regarded as unduly technical terminology.

At the level of principle, the reasons a defendant who acquires ownership should not be convicted of theft are also compelling. The difficulty with *Gomez* is not the particular outcome, but the wider implications. The actus reus of theft was so broadened that in practice it has no boundaries. Every transaction between two parties that pertains to property, whether corporate or private, whether consensual or involuntary, is now, apparently, the actus reus of a theft. This result has two effects. The first is to make a nonsense of the relationship between theft and the civil law of property. On the face of it, *Gomez* means that a defendant who acquires ownership by a transaction can also, by that very transaction, commit a crime. These two results cannot stand together. It is a long-standing rule of equity "that the Courts will not recognize a benefit accruing to a criminal from his crime":[212] no one may benefit by his wrong.[213] If so, either there should be no crime, or the civil law must change (so that D does not get title). Given that the purpose of an offence such as theft is to protect property rights, and that the existence of property rights is a matter for the civil law, it is not for the criminal law to change the civil law of property. Unlike crimes such as assault, the rights being protected are necessarily rooted in the civil law. Remove dependence on the law of property, and property offences have no rationale. The decision in *Gomez* ignores that constraint.

The other effect of *Gomez* is to extend the offence of theft backwards in time, violating the harm principle in a second way. Earlier, we discussed the case of *Dip Kaur* v. *Chief Constable for Hampshire*,[214] and noted that this case could now be theft as soon as D picked the shoes off the sale rack—well before she approached the cashier. Previously, picking the shoes up would have been mere preparation, and not even an attempt to steal. Now (if accompanied by mens rea) it is not merely an attempt, but a full-blown theft. This result contravenes all the principles guiding the parsimonious criminalisation of harmless, preparatory activity.[215] Touching a pair of shoes inside a shop is hardly theftuous behaviour. It is in no way wrongful. There is no harm. Sometimes, where there is no harm and the behaviour is by itself innocent, liability for an attempt may be appropriate. But merely touching the shoes, a precursor to approaching the cashier with them, should be regarded as mere preparation for theft. Yet on the authority of *Gomez*, it could be the full-blown offence.

(c) Possible qualification 2: void versus voidable appropriations?

At first it was thought that *Gomez* was subject to an important limitation. In that case, D had induced the manager to part with the goods by deception. Thus, although title passed to D and his accomplice, at common law that title was voidable—like any transaction induced

---

[210] Cmnd. 2977, *Theft and Related Offences* (1966).
[211] *Ibid.*, para. 34.
[212] *Beresford* v. *Royal Insurance Co Ltd* [1938] AC 586, 599 (Lord Atkin).
[213] See, e.g., *Cleaver* v. *Mutual Reserve Fund Ass.* [1892] 1 QB 147; *Re Giles, decd.* [1972] 1 Ch 546.
[214] [1981] 2 All ER 430. Above, § 13.6(ii).
[215] Above, § 1.2(i). Cf. Giles and Uglow, "Appropriation and Manifest Criminality in Theft" (1992) 56 *J Crim L* 179.

by deception, fraud, undue influence, or misrepresentation.[216] Arguably, therefore, *Gomez* could be distinguished from cases where D acquires full, unimpeachable ownership of the goods. *Gomez* rules that the acquisition of a voidable title is the actus reus of theft. But it does not decide that D appropriates goods when she acquires a fully valid title to them.

For good or ill, the House of Lords then rejected this distinction in the subsequent case of *Hinks*.[217] The facts were as follows:

> D had become friendly with V, a 53-year-old man described as naïve, gullible and of limited intelligence but with a considerable sum in his building society account. She successfully encouraged him to make a series of gifts totaling £60,000 and a TV set. The transfers were, it seems, valid gifts; though unintelligent, V clearly had the necessary capacity to dispose of his property if chose. Gifts made by vulnerable persons to those who make abusive use of their moral hold over them, like transactions brought about by fraud, are potentially voidable, and V's gifts to D might well have been voidable on this ground.[218] However, this point was not explored at trial, and the judge did not direct the jury's attention to it, treating D's improper use of her influence over V merely as a matter relating to the issue of dishonesty.

Notwithstanding this omission, the House of Lords (by a majority of three to two) upheld D's conviction. Concurring in a speech delivered by Lord Steyn, the majority rejected D's argument that a finding of theft under the Act is subject to an exception where the relevant appropriation was an acquisition of fully valid title, holding that the language of the 1968 Act stipulates no such exception. Any appropriation, with or without the consent of the owner, falls within the Act. Even the *very acquisition* of indefeasible ownership, in accordance with the transferor's intentions, is an appropriation from V and the actus reus of theft. Provided D is dishonest, and intends not to return the property, she steals it. In so holding, the majority accepted that this created a potential conflict between the criminal and the civil law, but were undeterred by this. "In a practical world," said Lord Steyn, "there will sometimes be some disharmony between the two systems. In any event, it would be wrong to assume on a priori grounds that the criminal law rather than the civil law is defective."[219]

Although, in many respects, it takes only one small step beyond *Gomez*, this is an extraordinary decision.[220] No doubt exploitation of the vulnerable warrants redress. The exploitation of those who are weak minded, especially the old, by unscrupulous and grasping persons is a real and recurrent problem, one that is likely to get worse as the number of old people in the population increases. What was done by the defendant in *Hinks* was not the worst of the cases that arise, but it is right in principle that such conduct should be a criminal offence. All this is no doubt what the majority had in mind when they upheld the defendant's conviction for theft in this case. However, the law of theft is fundamentally unsuited to that task. Such behaviour is surely a form of fraud, not a form of theft. (Indeed,

---

[216] Cf. *Wheatley and Penn v. The Commissioner of Police of the British Virgin Islands* [2006] UKPC 24, noted below in this section.

[217] [2000] UKHL 53, [2001] 2 AC 241. Cf. *Hopkins and Kendrick* [1997] Crim LR 359; *contra Mazo* [1997] 2 Cr App R 518. The earlier cases are usefully discussed by Smith, *The Law of Theft* (8th ed., 1997) §§ 2–21, 2–22.

[218] For a discussion of the authorities, see *Cresswell v. Potter* [1978] 1 WLR 255.

[219] [2001] 2 AC 241, 252.

[220] A decision not, however, without defenders: see Shute, "Appropriation and the Law of Theft" [2002] *Crim LR* 445; Bogg and Stanton-Ife, "Protecting the Vulnerable: Legality, Harm and Theft" (2003) 23 *Legal Studies* 402. The law established in *Hinks* had also been advocated by Gardner, "Property and Theft" [1998] *Crim LR* 35.

as we see in Chapter 15, some such cases can now be prosecuted under the Fraud Act 2006 as "fraud by abuse of position".)

The main problem with *Hinks*, surely, is that it turns the very rationale of property offences on its head. Theft is not a crime in thin air. It is designed to protect and reinforce property rights. That is the whole point of theft.[221] Since the offence has no other *raison d'être*, it is inherently dependent upon the civil law of property. The law of theft cannot dispense with the requirement for violation of a property right because its whole purpose is dependent upon and secondary to the allocation of rights through property law. The effect of *Hinks* is to cut property offences adrift from the law of property rights: the cart is now before the horse.[222] Consider the law of contract. It is standard law that if D stays silent in the face of a mistake by P which is not reflected in the terms of the transaction, P is bound to that transaction and has no remedy.[223] Adapting the facts of *Leaf* v. *International Galleries*,[224] the purchase of a painting in the mistaken belief that it was a Constable from a gallery owner, D, who knows of the mistake but says nothing is, in the law of contract, valid; and D could sue for the unpaid purchase price. Yet if *Hinks* is right, the price paid by the buyer is stolen by D should a jury be persuaded that D is dishonest. But this would surely be absurd.[225]

In the later case of *Wheatley and Penn* v. *The Commissioner of Police of the British Virgin Islands*,[226] the defendants were convicted of theft after D1 corruptly allocated government construction contracts to D2, notwithstanding that the contracts were at an appropriate price. The Privy Council, after noting that considerations of gain or loss were now irrelevant to the question of appropriation,[227] went on to emphasise that, in the present instance, "there is no dissonance between the criminal and the civil law, since the contracts made by the first appellant, contrary to his authority and with the connivance of the second appellant, were plainly voidable at the suit of the Government".[228] If *Hinks* is right, voidability is now irrelevant: that is the very point at which *Hinks* expands upon *Gomez*. Yet it is no surprise that the courts still find the point significant. *Hinks* is a troubling decision.

Given the potential expansiveness of the decision, a point of limitation should be stressed. *Hinks* deals with the scenario where the act of acquiring title is charged as

---

[221] Cf. Simester and Sullivan, "On the Nature and Rationale of Property Offences" in Duff and Green (eds.), *Defining Crimes: Essays on the Criminal Law's Special Part* (2005) 168, § 2.

[222] Lord Hobhouse (dissenting) sees this when he observes that "[t]here is no law against appropriating your own property" (at 856c; see generally 854–6; also 865b).

[223] *Smith* v. *Hughes* (1871) LR 6 QB 597; *Bell* v. *Lever Brothers Ltd* [1932] AC 161.

[224] [1950] 2 KB 86.

[225] That the problems of the conflict between the civil and the criminal law that result from *Hinks* are not imaginary is illustrated by a first instance case in which a couple, who had become the care-givers of a vulnerable man, persuaded him to give to them most of his property inter vivos and to leave the rest of it to them in his will. For this, they were prosecuted and convicted of conspiracy to steal; and two-and-a-half years after their victim's death his body remained unburied because the defendants—whom his will made his executors—were in prison, and in no position to organise a funeral. "Anger as Swindled Farmer Lies Unburied", *Western Gazette*, 23 April 2009. The facts of the case were truly shocking because the couple also physically neglected the man—to the point where they were seemingly fortunate to avoid a prosecution for manslaughter.

[226] [2006] UKPC 24.

[227] *Ibid.*, paras. 9–10.

[228] *Ibid.*, para. 11.

theft; where the acquisition of title by D is coincident with the transfer from V. From that perspective D, in the extended sense that the law allows, has appropriated property belonging to V if the deprivation and acquisition of the property are regarded as two aspects of the one transaction. The case does not decide that once D has acquired valid title to property, any *subsequent* dishonest appropriation of that property by D, *after* absolute ownership is transferred, will amount to theft. (Such cases can only be theft if section 5(3)–(4) applies.)

One other point of qualification is made by Lord Hutton in his dissent in *Hinks*. His Lordship observes that section 2(1)(a) of the Theft Act 1968 provides that a person's appropriation is not to be regarded as dishonest if he appropriates property in the belief that he has, in law, the right to deprive the other of it.[229] Typically, a person who acquires ownership of goods will also *believe* that she has a right to them. Where this is so, a charge of theft will fail for lack of dishonesty.[230] Hence, in the example based on *Leaf v. International Galleries* above, the gallery owner may say: "I know it was sharp practice, but I also knew it was permissible within the (civil) law, otherwise I would not have done it. I sought throughout to abide by the law and made all the disclosures that the law required of me in order for the transaction to be valid." In such a scenario it is arguable that, by virtue of section 2(1)(a), D may not in law be considered dishonest. Furthermore, even if D does not reason with himself in that fashion and is merely keen to make the contract at that price, he will be aware of the facts which in law make the contract valid. From the perspective of the civil law, he does not have to believe in a claim of right to the money that V pays; he simply *has* the right to the money at civil law. It is quite remarkable that persons who unreflectingly enter valid contracts may find themselves facing a charge of theft, a matter with clear implications for the fair notice protection guaranteed by Article 7 of the ECHR.[231]

(iii) Theft by keeping or omission

The mere decision to steal is not sufficient for theft.[232] There must be conduct as well, amounting to an appropriation. We have noted, however, that this is not a very stringent restriction: picking a tin of beans off the shelves of a supermarket is theft if D does so with intent to steal. Thus, although a decision to thieve is not enough, some very preliminary conduct is.

Moreover, the conduct may be an omission, as distinct from a fresh positive act, and it is sufficient for theft that D keeps property lawfully obtained: indeed, section 3(1) expressly states that a person may steal something by "keeping … it as owner". In the New Zealand

---

[229] Below, § 13.8(i).

[230] As it happens, Lord Hutton's dissent goes further: it advocates a general rule that there can never be a finding of dishonesty where the transfer of ownership is fully valid. But such a rule was implicitly rejected by the majority decision. The exploitative conduct by Karen Hinks was dishonest: everyone, and most importantly the jury, agreed on this. Nonetheless, on the particular facts of a different case, there may be room to invoke s. 2(1)(a).

[231] Whilst accepting the need for the civil law of property and the law of theft to sing in unison, Green argues that it is the civil law, not the criminal law, that is out of tune with the needs of modern society—and that the civil law which should therefore be reformed: "Theft and Conversion" (2012) 128 *LQR* 564.

[232] Cf. *Eddy v. Niman* (1981) 73 Cr App R 237; though the decision must now be read in light of *Gomez* [1993] AC 442 (above, § 13.6(ii)(a)).

case of *Subritzky*,[233] failing to return a toy taken innocently by D's child was held to be theft by conversion and, it is submitted, would be theft by appropriation also. Likewise borrowing a thing, and then keeping it having decided not to return it, may amount to theft—on the basis of the keeping rather than the borrowing.

The possibility of theft by keeping must, however, be approached with some caution. Generally, there is no liability for omissions in the criminal law and it seems that theft by keeping may be subject to special restrictions. In *Broom* v. *Crowther*,[234] D purchased a stolen theodolite. Subsequently, he discovered that the device was stolen. D kept the theodolite for a further week until it was seized by the police. On appeal, D claimed that, after learning the truth of the matter, he had merely left the theodolite sitting in his bedroom while he pondered what to do; and that this was not an appropriation within the terms of the Theft Act 1968. The Divisional Court quashed his conviction for theft.

Usually, such a defendant may escape conviction by denying mens rea, since it will be difficult to prove dishonesty is these circumstances. It seems, however, that not all omissions to return something ("keepings") will count as appropriations. The qualifications are twofold. First, section 3(1) states that a person may steal something by "keeping … it *as owner*". This suggests, as *Broom* v. *Crowther* seems to emphasise, that a mere "keeping" which does not manifest any decision to treat the property as D's own will not count as an appropriation. The keeping must amount, in effect, to a conversion: D's conduct must amount to a *usurpation* or denial of O's rights. This may depend upon the intention with which D acts: thus merely leaving the item in a drawer for safekeeping, as opposed to keeping the thing for oneself, is not a conversion[235] and, if *Broom* v. *Crowther* is right, neither is it an appropriation for the purposes of theft.

Secondly, the essence of keepings is that they are omissions. As we saw in Chapter 4, the law is rightly reluctant to impose criminal liability for mere omissions, unless the circumstances give rise to a specific duty obligating D to act. It is submitted that this general principle of the common law applies also to theft. In other words, an omission cannot be an appropriation unless it is in contravention of D's duty to return the goods to V. Suppose the following three cases:

(1)   D1 has hired a car from V. The period of hire has not expired. D1 decides to keep the car, which he leaves sitting on the driveway.

(2)   D2 has hired a car from V. The period of hire has not expired. D1 decides to sell the car, which he then drives to Ireland, intending to trade it in there for a new vehicle.[236]

(3)   D3 has hired a car from V. The period of hire has since expired. D1 decides to keep the car, which he leaves parked on his driveway.

Case (2) is straightforwardly one of theft: D appropriates the car by his positive act of driving it to Ireland. Equally, however, it is submitted that case (1) is not theft. Since the bailment has not expired, D is under no duty to do return the car, and his omission to do so should not be regarded as an actus reus of theft.

[233] [1990] 2 NZLR 717. Similar facts occurred in the English case of *Walters* v. *Lunt* [1951] 2 All ER 645, a decision based on the old law of larceny. See also *Thomas* (1953) 37 Cr App R 169.

[234] (1984) 148 JP 592. The case is also notable on a point concerning bona fide purchasers: below, § 13.6(v).

[235] Cf. *Police* v. *Moodley* [1974] 1 NZLR 644.

[236] *Morgan* [1991] RTR 365.

Case (3) is more complex. D's omission to return the car is in breach of the duty he owes to V, so prima facie is a "keeping" for the purposes of section 3(1). It is necessary, therefore, also to determine whether he has kept the car "as owner", or whether the *Broom v. Crowther* exception is available. In our view, this is a case of theft.

(iv) Multiple and continuing appropriations

Consider the following scenario, which is based on an example discussed in § 13.4(v):

> David finds a wallet in a busy street, and picks it up. He looks in the wallet for evidence of the owner's identity and finds none. The wallet contains no money. David puts the wallet in his pocket, concluding that it is lost rather than abandoned but that the true owner cannot be found. He then takes the wallet home and, on looking more carefully inside, finds the owner's name and address. Deciding to keep the wallet anyway because of its attractive appearance, he puts the wallet in a drawer. A month later, he takes the wallet out of the drawer and starts to use it.

How many times does David appropriate the wallet? When does he steal it? The key to the answer is section 3(1), which states that *any* assumption of the rights of an owner is an appropriation, "and this includes, where he has come by the property (innocently or not) *without stealing it*, any later assumption of a right to it by keeping or dealing with it as owner". The specific inclusion of later appropriations, subject to the qualification "without stealing it", means that David appropriates the wallet *every* time he does anything with it, *until* he steals it. Once there is a moment in time when all the elements of theft are present, the wallet is stolen and he does not keep restealing it thereafter.[237] Let us conclude, in the above example, that David is not dishonest and lacks the mens rea for theft until he gets home and discovers the owner's name.[238] It follows that David appropriates the wallet (*inter alia*) when he picks it up, when he looks through it, when he puts it in his pocket, when he carries it with him, and when he puts it in the drawer. But not when he starts to use it a month later: by then, it is already stolen.

Sometimes the location or timing of a theft matters. In *Atakpu and Abrahams*,[239] the defendants used false documents to hire cars in Germany and Belgium. They drove the cars to England, intending to sell them, but were arrested by customs officials on arrival at Dover. The convictions for conspiracy to steal the vehicles were quashed, on the ground that the thefts were not committed in England and therefore English courts lacked jurisdiction. On the authority of *Gomez*,[240] the cars were first appropriated in Germany and Belgium. Given that the defendants had the mens rea for theft at that time, the cars were

---

[237] Williams, "Appropriation: A Single or Continuous Act?" [1978] *Crim LR* 69, 69: "A man steals a watch, and two weeks later sells it. In common sense and ordinary language he is not guilty of a second theft when he sells it. Otherwise it would be possible, in theory, to convict a thief of theft of a silver teapot every time he uses it to make the tea."

[238] *Per* s. 2(1)(c): below, § 13.8(iii).

[239] [1994] QB 69. See also *Morgan* [1991] RTR 365, where D took a leased car to Ireland and traded it in for a new car; he was convicted of theft in England.

[240] Above, § 13.6(ii)(a). If *Gomez* had adopted the analysis in *Morris*, the problem would not have arisen since the first theftuous (in the sense of unauthorised) appropriation would have been when the cars were offered for sale in England.

therefore already stolen before being brought into this country.[241] Hence, there could be no conspiracy to steal them in England.[242] As Ward J put it:[243]

> "Endeavouring to summarise it would seem that (1) theft can occur in an instant by a single appropriation but it can also involve a course of dealing with property lasting longer and involving several appropriations before the transaction is complete; (2) theft is a finite act—it has a beginning and it has an end; (3) at what point the transaction is complete is a matter for the jury to decide upon the facts of each case; (4) though there may be several appropriations in the course of a single theft or several appropriations of different goods each constituting a separate theft as in *Reg. v. Skipp* [1975] Crim LR 114, no case suggests that there can be successive thefts of the same property…."

Similarly, D can be convicted of robbery only if the use or threat of force occurs immediately before or at the time of the theft.[244] Thus if D steals goods from a supermarket, and after leaving the shop threatens the driver of the taxi carrying him, D commits no robbery since the theft is already complete.

It seems that an appropriation can also be a *continuing* act,[245] as opposed to one which is always completed instantaneously. Suppose the following variation:

> D picks goods off the shelf at a supermarket and puts them inside her jacket, intending to leave without paying for them. On the authority of *Gomez*, she has already stolen the goods. While approaching the cashier, however, she is accosted by the store's security guard. D strikes the guard violently, and runs from the store with the goods.

Does D commit robbery? The common-sense answer must be yes—even though, if the goods are already stolen, it is hard to see how that answer can be justified in law. The answer is justified by holding that D's appropriation of the goods was a single continuing act, lasting (say) for the period during which she puts the goods in his jacket and carries them out of the supermarket. While such an analysis sits somewhat uneasily with *Gomez*,[246] a number of decisions appear to recognise the possibility.[247] (An alternative approach, in the specific context of robbery, might be to construe liberally the requirement in section 8(1) that the force be used "at the time of" the stealing; thereby embracing force used in the proximate aftermath of D's theftuous act.)[248]

---

[241] Contrast *Ashcroft* [2003] EWCA Crim 2365, where D, a haulier, was convicted of conspiring to steal goods in England which were first loaded onto his lorries in Scotland before being diverted in England. The Court of Appeal—it is submitted wrongly—dismissed D's claim that the theft occurred in Scotland, describing that analysis (paras. 43, 45) as "some way removed from reality and we do not believe that *Gomez* was ever intended to apply to the sort of situation that obtains in this case…. In our judgment there never was in any ordinary sense of the word an 'appropriation' of the stolen goods until the conspirators removed them from the containers." But it is an ineluctable implication of *Gomez* that the goods were first appropriated in Scotland.

[242] For criticism of the jurisdictional aspects of *Atakpu* see Sullivan and Warbrick, "Territoriality, Theft and *Atakpu*" [1994] *Crim LR* 650, who argue that since the Theft Act 1968 does not have extra-territorial effect, the defendants' actions in Germany and Belgium were not appropriations within the Act. See also below, § 13.9.

[243] [1994] QB 69, 79.

[244] Theft Act 1968, s. 8(1). See below, § 14.3; and *Vinall*, n. 306 below.

[245] Cf. *Fagan v. Metropolitan Police Commissioner* [1969] 1 QB 439; above, § 4.1(i)(b) (Case 4).

[246] Cf. *Atakpu and Abraham* [1994] QB 69, 80; but contrast *Lockley* [1995] Crim LR 656.

[247] e.g. *Bowden* [2002] EWCA Crim 1279; *Donaghy v. Marshall* [1981] Crim LR 644; *Hale* (1978) 68 Cr App R 415; *Pitham and Hehl* (1976) 65 Cr App R 45, 49 (while denying it in the instant case). See Williams, "Appropriation: A Single or Continuous Act?" [1973] *Crim LR* 69.

[248] Cf. *Hale* (1978) 68 Cr App R 415; below, 14.2(iii).

(v) Bona fide purchasers

The *nemo dat* rule means that if R steals a book from O, O retains ownership of the book even when R then sells the book to D, a purchaser who acts in good faith. Prima facie, if D were then to discover that the book was stolen, she would herself become liable to be convicted for theft. This possibility is avoided by section 3(2), which provides:

> Where property or a right or interest in property is or purports to be transferred for value to a person acting in good faith, no later assumption by him of rights which he believed himself to be acquiring shall, by reason of any defect in the transferor's title, amount to theft of the property.

In *Wheeler*,[249] a dealer purchased a variety of military antiques. He then sold one of the items, a medal. Subsequently, before delivering the medal and receiving payment, he discovered that the medal was stolen. His conviction was quashed: the application of section 3(2) meant that D committed no theft by completing the transaction. Neither was D guilty of handling.[250] (He might, however, be guilty of the offence of fraud if the purchaser had been induced to make payment by D's representation, implied or express, that D was their owner.)[251]

It appears that a purchaser will not be regarded as "in good faith" for the purposes of section 3(2) if she suspects that the goods are stolen. It is not necessary for her to be convinced of the matter. In *Broom* v. *Crowther*,[252] D purchased a theodolite from R for £5. The instrument was worth about £200. After later discovering that it was in fact stolen, D kept the theodolite for a further week until it was seized by the police. In convicting him for theft, the magistrates ruled that the defence in section 3(2) was unavailable, since D had not acted in good faith: at the time when he made the purchase, D had suspected the device was stolen and had accepted R's denial without pursuing the matter because the bargain was so advantageous. (The conviction was quashed on other grounds: see § 13.6(iii) above.)

(vi) Bank accounts

Suppose D, a company director of V Ltd., forges a cheque on V's account with bank B. Does D commit theft? The answer, it appears, is yes. V's account with B is a chose in action that can be stolen[253] and, according to the Privy Council in *Chan Man-sin*,[254] V appropriates that account when he assumes V's right, as owner, to draw cheques on the account.

---

[249] (1991) 92 Cr App R 279.

[250] *Bloxham* [1983] 1 AC 109.

[251] Surprisingly, the Court also quashed D's conviction for obtaining by deception (as the offence then was), apparently reasoning that there was no deception: because the sale was in market overt, D's implied representation that the buyer would get good title to the medal was true. But D had *expressly* stated that the medal was not stolen, which was a deception.

[252] (1984) 148 JP 592. See Spencer, "Handling, Theft and the *Mala Fide* Purchaser" [1985] *Crim LR* 92; Williams, "Handling, Theft and the Purchaser who takes a Chance" [1985] *Crim LR* 432; Spencer, "Handling and Taking Risks—A Reply to Professor Williams" [1985] *Crim LR* 440. The case is discussed earlier, in § 13.6(iii), in respect of a different point taken by D in his successful appeal.

[253] Above, § 13.3(i)(c).

[254] *Chan Man-sin* v. *A-G of Hong Kong* [1988] 1 All ER 1. The same analysis appears in *Burke* [2000] Crim LR 413 (CA). See also below, § 13.7(ii).

It must be said that this reasoning is debatable. Prima facie, D obtained by deception; he stole nothing—at least, nothing from V.[255] In particular, although the bank account was clearly property belonging to V, it is arguable that nothing done by D affected or was even relevant to that account. The forged cheque was a nullity, nothing more.[256] Although D *pretended* to deal with V's bank account, in law he no more dealt with V's chose in action against B than he dealt with any of the accounts held by anyone else at the bank. The real wrong was obtaining by deception the *proceeds* of the cheque[257]—but the victim of that crime was bank B, not V. No property right of V's was harmed by D. If that is right, why should V be treated as the victim of a theft?

On the other hand, and in defence of the current law, it may be argued that by pretending to deal with V's bank account, D "assumed" the right of an owner over the account and therefore appropriated it within the meaning of section 3(1).[258] Moreover, V *will* normally suffer the disadvantage of a wrongful debit against its account, which will remain in place, and cause an effective loss to V, until the forgery is discovered (if ever). So, although the law on this point is problematic, it is not without justification.

The analysis is different where the cheque is not a nullity. *Chan Man-sin* may be contrasted with the case of *Kohn*,[259] where D had authority to draw cheques.[260] He abused that authority by withdrawing money for personal gain. In that case, the cheques were valid and not mere forgeries, so that the company's bank account was rightfully debited. Thus D was properly convicted of theft, from the company, by appropriating its bank account.

Another difficult case is where D, by dishonest conduct, induces V to debit her bank account in D's favour. In *Williams*,[261] as we saw earlier, the Court of Appeal decided this could be an appropriation, and so upheld the conviction of D, a dishonest builder, who had presented V with a dishonestly inflated bill, which V had paid by writing a cheque that D presented to V's bank, which duly debited V's account in D's favour. However, in the later case of *Briggs*[262] the Court of Appeal thought otherwise.

> D, a predatory great-niece of V1 and V2, "helped" the Vs to sell their big house and buy a little one more suited to their current needs. The big house was sold, and the proceeds of sale held by a firm of conveyancers, Bentons. D then arranged for the Vs to get Bentons to transfer the necessary slice of the proceeds to the vendors of the little house and, against the wishes of the Vs, induced the vendors of the little house to convey it to D instead of to the Vs. The Court of

---

[255] Unless, perhaps, he stole the paper on which the cheque was written. Given that D obtained by deception—pursuant, therefore, to a voidable transfer—the decision in *Gomez* (above, § 13.6(ii)(a)) means that he may also have stolen whatever he obtained in return for the forged cheque.

[256] *Tai Hing Cotton Mill Ltd* v. *Liu Chong Hing Bank Ltd* [1986] AC 80 (PC).

[257] This proposition is subject to further complication where the "proceeds" take the form of a money transfer (cf. *Preddy* [1996] AC 815, swiftly remedied by s. 15A of the Theft Act 1968). See below, § 15.1.

[258] That was also the conclusion of the Court of Appeal in *Re Osman* [1990] 1 WLR 277, 294–5, where D, a company chairman, sent a telex instructing the company's bank to transfer money from the company's account. The Court ruled that purporting to deal with the bank account qua owner was, in itself, an appropriation regardless of the effect on the account itself and even if the account was never debited. For approving comment, see [1988] Crim LR 611.

[259] (1979) 69 Cr App R 395; discussed above, § 13.3(i)(c).

[260] To similar effect is *Hilton* [1997] 2 Cr App R 445, where D controlled a charity's bank account and had authority to instruct the bank to make transfers.

[261] [2001] 1 Cr App R 362.

[262] [2004] EWCA Crim 3662, [2004] 1 Cr App R 34 (451).

Appeal quashed D's conviction for theft on the ground that D's conduct did not amount to an appropriation of the fund, belonging to the Vs, and currently in the hands of Bentons.

With ingenuity it is possible to distinguish the facts of this case from those of *Williams*, but as the judgment in *Briggs* was given unreserved, and without reference to *Williams* (or indeed to *Gomez* or to *Hinks*), it is probably better seen as an aberration.[263] If such a case were to arise today, D would undoubtedly be guilty of fraud under the Fraud Act 2006.[264]

§ 13.7 Intention permanently to deprive

(i) The core definition

Dishonest borrowing is not theft, no matter how much inconvenience it causes the owner. If D, a law student, dishonestly takes a book from the law library by concealing it in his bag, he commits theft if he intends not to return the book, but not if he means to keep the book only until the end of term.[265] It is not theft even if D realises there is a chance he will be unable to return the book (e.g. because he has a habit of losing books in his possession).[266] To fulfil the requirements of theft, D must have the *intention* permanently to deprive V of her property. This requirement, stated in section 1(1), is not defined in the Theft Act 1968, although there are some complex supplementary provisions in section 6 (see § 13.7(ii)). For the most part, however, the core meaning of "intention permanently to deprive" has presented few problems. Generally, it is sufficient that D has an intention indefinitely to exclude V from exercising her right to the property.

(a) Dishonest borrowing

Some writers have questioned the rule that borrowing is not theft,[267] and its wisdom is certainly arguable. The owner may well have a civil action against D for use and enjoyment, and in many cases the very point of her ownership is to monopolise the use and enjoyment of which she is deprived by D. Suppose that O, a law student, owns a textbook on criminal law. D dishonestly takes the book, intending to keep it until the criminal law exam has been sat by both D and O. As things stand, D has not stolen the book.[268] Yet O has been frustrated in the very reason she bought the book. She is likely to have to buy another copy in the meantime. Provided D is dishonest, there is a good case for treating such behaviour as criminal.

---

[263] The case is criticised by Heaton, "Cheques and Balances" [2005] *Crim LR* 747, and by Ormerod in a note at [2004] *Crim LR* 409.

[264] D would be guilty of fraud by abuse of position contrary to s. 4 of the Fraud Act, and probably fraud by false representation contrary to s. 3; see Chapter 15 below. (No substantive injustice was done in *Briggs* because although her conviction for theft was quashed, she remained convicted of forgery, obtaining services by deception, and—for good measure—social security fraud too.)

[265] Cf. *Neal* v. *Gribble* [1978] RTR 409.

[266] Cf. *Crump* (1825) 1 C & P 658, 171 ER 1357. This would be a case of recklessness whether the owner is deprived, rather than of intention: above, §§ 5.1(iii), 5.2.

[267] Williams, "Temporary Appropriation should be Theft" [1981] *Crim LR* 129; Bein, "The Theft of Use and the Element of 'Intent to Deprive Permanently' in Larceny" (1968) 3 *Israel LR* 368.

[268] Neither does s. 6(1) apply: below, § 13.7(ii)(b).

Additionally, criminalisation of dishonest borrowing may assist in resolving an evidential difficulty. Sometimes where D claims that he intended to return the thing "borrowed"
(e.g. where D takes a book from the library), it may be hard to prove that he intended to
keep the thing permanently.

Against these arguments, it may be thought harsh to equate a mere borrowing with theft.
Although the inconvenience to O may sometimes be comparable, as a *general* proposition
the wrong of permanently taking O's property is far more substantial than the wrong of
temporarily interfering with her use and enjoyment. In practice, evidential difficulties with
the present law have not been overwhelming, and are surely insufficient to justify a radical change in the substantive law. Moreover, enacting an offence of dishonest borrowing
would place even greater pressure on the issue of dishonesty, itself (as we shall see) a judgement call by the jury. To do so would leave the law of theft both extraordinarily wide and
extremely vague, thereby undermining the principle of fair warning and the rule of law.

While not enacting a general offence, the 1968 Act does criminalise specific forms of
borrowing. Certain cases are treated as theft by virtue of section 6, which is considered
in § 13.7(ii) below. There are also some specific offences. Section 12 creates an offence of
taking a motor vehicle or other conveyance without authority; section 12A enacts a related
offence of aggravated vehicle-taking; while section 11 criminalises the removal (with or
without an intention permanently to deprive) of items from public buildings.[269]

(b) Deprivation

The essence of theft is deprivation, not gain. Thus, what must be intended is that the owner
be deprived (permanently), not that any benefit endure to D or anyone else. Thus it is theft
for D to appropriate O's goods intending to destroy them,[270] to hide them so that they are
never found,[271] or to give them away. The point, which was also true under the pre-Act law
of larceny,[272] is now made explicit in section 1(2) of the 1968 Act:

> It is immaterial whether the appropriation is made with a view to gain, or is made for the thief's
> own benefit.

(c) Change of mind

If D steals something, intending to keep it, then later changes his mind and decides to
return the thing, this is theft.[273] It is too late. At the time the actus reus occurs, D has the
mens rea for theft.

---

[269] And students should note the Highways Act 1980, s. 174(4), under which a person commits an offence
if he "takes down, alters or removes any barrier, traffic sign, support or light erected or placed in pursuance of
subsection (1) above or any fence, barrier, traffic sign or light erected or placed on or near a street in pursuance
of any other enactment for the purpose of warning users of the street of any obstruction, whether caused by the
execution of works in or near the street or otherwise, or of protecting them from danger arising out of such an
obstruction".

[270] *Welsh* [1974] RTR 478 (D, a motorist stopped on suspicion of drink-driving, destroyed a urine sample that
he had given for analysis); cf. *Cabbage* (1815) R & R 292, 168 ER 809 (D backed a horse down a mineshaft in order
to destroy evidence of the horse's theft).

[271] Cf. *Wynn* (1848) 1 Den 365, 169 ER 283 (D, a postal worker, flushed letters down a lavatory in order to
conceal the fact that he had sorted them incorrectly).

[272] Turner, "Larceny and Lucrum" (1941) 4 *Toronto LJ* 296.

[273] Cf. *Easom* [1971] 2 QB 315, 320.

(d) An ulterior intention

The intent to deprive is an ulterior intention,[274] accompanying the actus reus rather than directed toward the actus reus itself. Thus the requirement is not merely that D intend the appropriation *per se*, but that the act of appropriation be done with the *further* intent that the owner be deprived permanently, either by that act or by some other act.

The importance of this point is that there is no requirement that D should intend to deprive V by *that very* act of appropriation. As was noted in § 13.6, it is sufficient that D appropriates the goods while intending that the owner should be deprived, even if the deprivation will be accomplished only by some later act of D's.[275] Suppose, for example, that D changes the labels on two products (say, product A and product B) in a supermarket, intending to buy the more expensive item, product A, at the lower price of product B. He steals product A as soon as he touches it, even though this is not the act of appropriation by which the owner will be deprived.

(e) Paying for or returning similar goods

In *Velumyl*,[276] D dishonestly borrowed £1,050 from his employer's safe, without authority and in breach of company rules. D apparently intended to repay the amount borrowed. He was nonetheless convicted of theft. Although D intended to return an equivalent sum of moneys, these would not be the identical notes and coins that he had taken, merely substitute moneys to the same value. Hence, the Court concluded, D intended to deprive V permanently of the particular notes and coins that he appropriated.

Similarly, if D were to take a bag of sugar from V's kitchen, intending to buy another bag and replace it, D would still intend to deprive V permanently of the particular bag taken. *A fortiori*, a case where D intends to give V some money to pay for the sugar.[277] (Of course, an issue may arise in such cases whether D has acted dishonestly.)

(f) Conditional intention

In *Easom*,[278] D picked up a handbag in a cinema. He searched through the handbag in order to ascertain its contents, then put the handbag back having decided that none of the contents were worth stealing. D was charged with theft of "one handbag, one purse, one notebook, a quantity of tissues, a quantity of cosmetics and one pen", and at first instance was convicted. However, the Court of Appeal quashed his conviction, ruling that:[279]

> "In every case of theft the appropriation must be accompanied by the intention of permanently depriving the owner of his property. What may be loosely described as a 'conditional' appropriation will not do. If the appropriator has it in mind merely to deprive the owner of such of his property as, on examination, proves worth taking and then, finding that the booty is valueless to the appropriator, leaves it ready to hand to be repossessed by the owner, the

---

[274] Above, § 5.1(vii).

[275] *Morris* [1984] AC 320.

[276] [1989] Crim LR 299. Cf. *McCall* (1971) 55 Cr App R 175; *Duru* [1973] 3 All ER 715; *Williams* [1953] 1 All ER 1068, 1070.

[277] Cf. Theft Act 1968, s. 2(2).

[278] [1971] 2 QB 315.

[279] *Ibid.*, 319.

appropriator has not stolen. If a dishonest postal sorter picks up a pile of letters, intending to steal any which are registered, but, on finding that none of them are, replaces them, he has stolen nothing."

The decision is probably right, but only in terms of the precise charge that was brought. D certainly appropriated the purse, notebook, tissues, etc., inside the handbag. However, at no time did D intend to deprive the owner of such things. He was looking for something else.

Suppose, however, that D had been charged with stealing "the contents" of the handbag. In that case, D should have been convicted.[280] Again, he certainly appropriated the contents.[281] Thus the actus reus element of theft is satisfied. This time, however, the mens rea requirement is also satisfied—by a conditional intention.[282] Not yet knowing what they were, D intended to steal any of "the contents" of the handbag should they prove desirable. Thus, it is submitted, he appropriated the contents with intent (conditionally) to deprive the owner of them. Since conditional intention is treated in law as intention,[283] that looks like theft. The fact that he subsequently returned the bag and its contents is irrelevant. They were already stolen.[284]

At the level of policy, there seems little merit in acquitting the defendant. Pre-*Gomez*, it may have been appropriate to treat such cases either as mere preparatory action or as an attempted theft, but that possibility is now gone. D plans to steal the contents, subject only to a condition outside his control (i.e. that they are valuable); he executes the plan; he appropriates the contents. The actus reus of theft has already occurred. Certainly, D's conduct can no longer be regarded as merely preparatory. Given his moral culpability, D ought to be convicted of theft.

A different type of case is where D intends to steal valuable contents, if any, from a handbag which he has no intent to take but puts the handbag back because it is empty. That is a case of attempted theft;[285] because there is no actus reus. Although, in such a case, D has a (conditional) intent to steal the contents, he does not appropriate them since they do not exist.

There is a third type of case. Consider the following variation:

> D takes V's handbag, intending to keep the diamond ring that (he thinks) is in the bag. Later, he discovers that the handbag contains no ring, merely some credit cards (for which D has no use). He returns the bag with the credit cards inside.

---

[280] *Re A-G's References (Nos. 1 and 2 of 1979)* [1980] QB 180.

[281] Note that the terminology of a "conditional appropriation", coined in the quotation from *Easom* in the text, must be regarded as outmoded in the wake of *Gomez* (above, § 13.6(ii)(a)). If even an authorised touching of goods is now regarded as an appropriation, D's conduct in *Easom* is surely also an appropriation.

[282] A fine distinction exists between the case of a defendant who investigates the contents with a view to later deciding whether to steal (i.e. one who has not yet made any decision to steal) and that of one who has decided to steal the contents should they prove upon investigation to be valuable. Arguably, the close psychological relationship between decisions and intentions suggests that in the former case (and perhaps in *Easom* itself) the defendant has not yet formed an intention to steal, provided D's conduct is more than preparatory. However, such a fine distinction arguably is out of place here, since the condition upon which the decision depends is merely a matter of circumstances external to the defendant. It certainly would not operate to exculpate the postal sorter in the example cited by the court.

[283] Above, § 5.1(viii). See Campbell, 'Conditional Intention' (1982) 2 *LS* 77.

[284] Cf. above, § 13.6(ii)(b).

[285] Cf. *Smith and Smith* [1986] Crim LR 166.

D does not steal the handbag, since he has no intention to keep the bag itself. He does not steal a ring, since there is none; though he could now be charged with attempted theft of the ring.[286] Neither does he steal the credit cards *per se*, since he has no intention to deprive the owner of them. Moreover, this is not a case of conditional intention to steal anything valuable. Rather, it involves a specific, frustrated, intention to steal a diamond ring. Should D be convicted of theft of "the contents" of the handbag, or only of attempted theft of the ring?

As the law stands, it appears that D can be convicted of theft of the contents.[287] This description may seem rather vague, but it should be recalled that the Theft Act criminalises theft of any "property belonging to another". Even though it matters to D, from the point of view of the law the difference between a ring and credit cards is an immaterial variation.[288] D had the actus reus for theft of the cards and the mens rea for theft of a ring. Both are forms of property, which is all the Act requires.

If doubts exist as to how far a conditional intent will do for the completed offence of theft, there is no doubt that such an intent will usually satisfy the mens rea requirement for a number of other related offences: in particular, conspiracy,[289] attempted theft,[290] and burglary.[291]

(ii) Section 6: extensions and special cases

Often, a thief has no particular agenda regarding the fate of the property he steals. If D means to pawn stolen goods, or to use them before discarding them, he may not intend that the original owner be permanently deprived. He may be indifferent to their ultimate destiny. While many of these cases can be treated as intention on the basis that it is virtually certain the owner will be deprived permanently,[292] sometimes it may be quite likely that the owner will recover the property. In order to make it explicit that the Act extends to such cases, Parliament supplemented the work of the Criminal Law Revision Committee by enacting section 6:

> (1) A person appropriating property belonging to another without meaning the other permanently to lose the thing itself is nevertheless to be regarded as having the intention of permanently depriving the other of it if his intention is to treat the thing as his own to dispose of regardless of the other's rights; and a borrowing or lending of it may amount to so treating it if, but only if, the borrowing or lending is for a period and in circumstances making it equivalent to an outright taking or disposal.
>
> (2) Without prejudice to the generality of subsection (1) above, where a person, having possession or control (lawfully or not) of property belonging to another, parts with the property under a condition as to its return which he may not be able to perform, this (if done for purposes of his own and without the other's authority) amounts to treating the property as his own to dispose of regardless of the other's rights.

---

[286] Contrast *Husseyn* (1977) 67 Cr App R 131n, a case decided before the law on impossible attempts was altered by the Criminal Attempts Act 1981 (see above, § 9.4(iii)(d), 9.5(iii)).

[287] Cf. *Re A-G's References (Nos. 1 and 2 of 1979)* [1980] QB 180.

[288] See above, § 5.7.

[289] § 9.3(ii) above.

[290] § 9.4(iii) above.

[291] § 14.3(iv) below; this was the point at issue in *Re A-G's References (Nos. 1 and 2 of 1979)* [1980] QB 180.

[292] Above, § 5.1(iv).

Unlike most of the other sections of the Theft Act, which were drafted by the Criminal Law Revision Committee, section 6 is not clearly worded and the drafting makes a straightforward interpretation of this section impossible. The history of the provision suggests that the idea was simply to codify the case law that had interpreted the phrase "intention permanently to deprive" when it appeared in the definition of larceny, the precursor offence to theft (which replaced larceny in the reform in 1968). According to this earlier case law, an intention to deprive (as against mere recklessness) was normally required, but there were three cases in which recklessness, or something akin to it, was sufficient. The first was the "ransom principle", whereby it counted as an intention to deprive if the defendant's idea was to return the property only if the owner was prepared to pay for it.[293] The second was the "essential quality" principle, whereby it counted as an intention permanently to deprive if the defendant meant the owner to get his property back only after it had undergone a fundamental change; for example, a live horse taken and a dead horse returned.[294] The third was the "pawning principle", whereby it counted as an intention permanently to deprive if the defendant pawned another person's property without his consent, hoping to be able to redeem the pledge but realising he might be unable to do so.[295] However, the wording of the section does not make it clear that this was the intended aim, and the purpose can only be detected by reading the parliamentary debates.[296] As the language of section 6(1) is singularly opaque, it is possible to give it a wide meaning, or a narrow one—so some cases interpret it in the narrow sense, others in the wider one.

One of the earlier decisions on section 6 is *Lloyd*.[297] D, a film projectionist, borrowed films and passed them to E, who made and sold pirate copies of the films. The Court of Appeal ruled this was not theft.[298] In reaching this decision the court referred to pre-1968 case law, and (in essence) took the position that section 6 merely confirmed it. Although section 6 makes it clear that some "borrowings" do involve an intention permanently to deprive, the court said:

> "Borrowing is *ex hypothesi* not something which is done with intention permanently to deprive. This half of the subsection, we believe, is intended to make it clear that a mere borrowing is never enough to constitute the necessary guilty mind unless the intention is to return the 'thing' in such a changed state that it can truly be said that all its goodness or virtue is gone."

More recently, a similar approach was taken in *Mitchell*.[299] Here D was one of a gang of thieves who, having crashed their getaway car, violently hijacked V's BMW, eventually abandoning it a few miles away on the road with its hazard lights flashing. For this D was convicted of robbery—a crime which, as we explain in Chapter 14, is theft aggravated by violence. Having referred to *Lloyd*, the Court of Appeal quashed D's robbery conviction on the ground that there was no underlying theft. In this case, D did not intend V to lose her car permanently, and his intention to take it temporarily could not be converted into an intention permanently to deprive by invoking section 6(1).

---

[293] *Hall* (1849) 3 Cox 245; *Peters* (1843) 1 Car and Kir 246, 174 ER 795.
[294] Cf. *Cabbage* (1815) Russ & Ry 292, 168 ER 809; *Richards* (1844) 1 Car & Kir 532, 174 ER.925.
[295] *Beecham* (1851) 5 Cox 181.
[296] See Spencer, "The Metamorphosis of Section 6 of the Theft Act" [1977] *Crim LR* 653.
[297] [1985] QB 829.
[298] *Ibid.*, 836 (Lord Lane CJ). Cf. *Bagshaw* [1988] Crim LR 321.
[299] [2008] EWCA Crim 850.

However, section 6(1) does say, *inter alia*, that a defendant is "to be regarded as having the intention of permanently depriving the other of it if his intention is to treat the thing as his own to dispose of regardless of the other's rights". Although the phrase "dispose of" can be read in a narrow sense, as meaning "to get rid of once and for all", it can also be read in a wide sense, to mean "to deal with". And there are cases in which the courts have taken it in the wider sense, thereby converting into theft acts by defendants who did not really mean the owner to lose his property at all. One such case is *DPP* v. *Lavender*,[300] where D dishonestly removed two doors from a house and hung them in another house. Both houses were owned by the council. The Divisional Court ruled that D had committed theft. Although the council had not in fact been deprived of the doors, D had nonetheless "disposed" of them within the meaning of section 6(1). With respect, this result seems odd. There was no disposal of the doors in the narrow sense—they were not thrown out, destroyed, or sold.[301] They were merely moved, and there was no suggestion by his conduct that D intended to treat them as his own, since they continued to be affixed to council property. Another case to take this line is *Marshall*.[302] In this case, D had been making money in the London underground by begging unexpired day tickets from passengers who had completed their last journeys of the day and reselling them to other passengers. For this D was convicted of theft of the tickets from London Transport, which had issued them. On appeal, he sought to argue that, as he knew the tickets would eventually find their way back to London Transport at the end of the day, he had no intention permanently to deprive. Rejecting the narrow construction that was put on section 6 in *Lloyd*, the Court of Appeal upheld the conviction.

The courts have also taken a broad view of section 6 when dealing with those who have improperly interfered with other people's bank accounts. In *Chan Man-sin*,[303] discussed earlier, D dishonestly drew cheques on his employer's bank account. The Privy Council ruled that D had dealt with the company's property (i.e. its chose in action against the bank) as if it were his to dispose of without regard to the company's rights. But if, as we saw in § 13.6(vi), unauthorised drawings of this sort are a nullity, then arguably D did not dispose of the account at all. At law, nothing done by D in any way affected the relationship between the company and the bank. D merely tricked the bank into crediting D's own account (and purporting to debit V's account). The Privy Council appears to have equated "purporting or pretending to dispose of the thing as one's own" with "disposing of the thing as one's own". The decision is debatable. Nonetheless, as things stand, this is the law: the intent to make an apparent or pretended disposal is sufficient for section 6(1).

What can be said with some degree of certainty is that section 6(1) covers both the "ransom principle" and the "essential quality principle", by which the courts extended the concept of intention permanently to deprive before 1968. An example of the first is *Raphael*,[304] where D's conviction for theft was affirmed where he had taken V's car away from him by force, and then attempted to sell it back to him. And an example of the second is *DPP* v. *J*,[305]

---

[300] [1994] Crim LR 297. Cf. *Cahill* [1993] Crim LR 141.
[301] For discussion, see A.T.H. Smith, *Property Offences* (1994) §§ 6-33, 6-34.
[302] [1998] 2 Cr App R 282.
[303] [1988] 1 All ER 1; also *Burke* [2000] Crim LR 413; *Re Osman* [1990] 1 WLR 277, 294–5. See above, §§ 13.3(i)(c), 13.6(vi).
[304] [2008] EWCA Crim 1014.
[305] [2002] EWHC (Admin) 291.

in which the defendants forcibly took V's headphones, snapped them, and returned them to V. On appeal, it was held that the magistrates had been wrong to accept a submission of no case to answer: a person who took something and dealt with it for the purpose of rendering it useless demonstrated the intention of treating that article as his own to dispose of. But a definitive answer to the question of how much other ground (if any) the section covers is obscure, and destined to remain so until the day—if it comes—that the matter is finally resolved by the Supreme Court.[306]

(a) Parting with property under a condition as to its return

If D dishonestly takes goods and pawns or pledges them, intending to redeem and return the goods but aware there is a risk he may be unable to do so, the operation of section 6(2) means that he commits theft. It is difficult to see why pledging goods should not count as a disposition within the scope of section 6(1), in which case section 6(2) is unnecessary.

§ 13.8 Dishonesty

In addition to the other elements required for theft, D must appropriate the property dishonestly. Unfortunately, the 1968 Act gives no definition of dishonesty. This is not to say that the Act is silent on the matter. According to section 2:

> (1) A person's appropriation of property belonging to another is not to be regarded as dishonest—
> (a) if he appropriates the property in the belief that he has in law the right to deprive the other of it, on behalf of himself or of a third person; or
> (b) if he appropriates the property in the belief that he would have the other's consent if the other knew of the appropriation and the circumstances of it; or
> (c) (except where the property came to him as trustee or personal representative) if he appropriates the property in the belief that the person to whom the property belongs cannot be discovered by taking reasonable steps.
> (2) A person's appropriation of property belonging to another may be dishonest notwithstanding that he is willing to pay for the property.

The operation of these provisions is, however, purely negative. If D falls within section 2(1), he is not dishonest. But if he falls outside the section, it does not follow that he *is* dishonest. The question whether he is dishonest must then be asked and answered independently. Similarly, section 2(2) merely excludes one defence from operating as a matter of law. If D was willing to pay for the property, he may or may not be dishonest—that question must be asked, and answered, separately—when account may be taken of the fact that she was willing to pay.

In deciding the issue of dishonesty, therefore, it is necessary to begin with section 2(1). It is only if those provisions do not apply that we must investigate the issue more generally.

---

[306] The Court of Appeal reviewed a long list of authorities on s. 6 in *Vinall* [2011] EWCA Crim 2652, [2012] 1 Cr App R 29, concluding that, uncertain as its outer limits may be, the section does extend the concept of intention permanently to deprive beyond the limits of the pre-existing common law. The case is further discussed in relation to robbery: below, § 14.3.

(i) Belief that he has the right to deprive: section 2(1)(a)

Section 2(1)(a) codifies the old common law defence of colour of right: D's belief that he is legally entitled to act as he does forecloses any finding of dishonesty. The defence means that D does not commit theft if she honestly believes her appropriation of the thing is *legally* entitled, even where her belief is based on ignorance, mistake of fact, or even mistake of law.[307] Examples of colour of right defences abound in the common law. In *Bernhard*,[308] for example, a woman who blackmailed her former lover thought she had a right to the money claimed; she was acquitted of demanding money with menaces. Similarly, in *Skivington*,[309] D held up a wages clerk and demanded his wife's wages: though this was an assault, it was held there was no theft and therefore no robbery, since he believed he had a lawful claim.

Skivington demonstrates that since colour of right is a defence to theft, it is also a defence to other crimes in which theft or an intent to steal is an ingredient, such as robbery and burglary. In such cases, if D believes he is entitled to the money, the charge fails for lack of the theftuous element; it is irrelevant whether D believes he had a right to use force.

It may seem odd that the defence can be based on a mistake of law. But, as we have said, the moral wrong of theft is the deliberate assumption of, or interference with, another's property rights. It is D's mental state that marks out that interference as deserving the attention of the criminal law, and more than a mere tortious conversion. It follows that someone who thinks she is not violating another person's property rights lacks the guilty mind that makes her actions worth criminalising. For similar reasons, it is clear that an honest mistake is sufficient even if it be unreasonable. In *Holden*,[310] D, who worked for a tyre company, was charged with theft of scrap tyres from his employer. He claimed that he had seen others take tyres and had been permitted to do so by a supervisor. It was company policy that taking tyres, or permitting others to do so, was sackable conduct. D was convicted of theft after the judge directed the jury that the test of dishonesty was whether D reasonably believed he had a right to take the tyres. The Court of Appeal quashed the conviction. D's conduct was certainly a civil wrong. But, if the defendant was to be believed, he did not mean to act wrongfully. A mistake may be honest even when unreasonable, and negligent violation of another's property rights is not, and should not be, the stuff of theft.

A distinction should be drawn between the defence that D believes she has a *legal* right to the thing allegedly stolen, which operates through section 2(1)(a), and a belief that she has a *moral* justification for her act. Belief in moral justification may, but will not necessarily, include a belief that D is legally entitled to the thing taken. Where D knows she has no legal right to the thing, her belief in a moral right alone is not sufficient for the colour of right defence in section 2(1)(a).[311] It may, however, lead to her being found not dishonest on the general test (below, § 13.8(iv)).

---

[307] *Bernhard* [1938] 2 KB 264.
[308] *Ibid*. V agreed to pay his mistress (D) a sum of money, which he did not; she then threatened to expose him to his wife and the public unless he paid up. D was acquitted of demanding money with intent to steal, as she—mistakenly—thought she had a valid claim to the money.
[309] [1968] 1 QB 166; cf. *Robinson* [1977] Crim LR 173.
[310] [1991] Crim LR 478.
[311] Cf. *Harris v. Harrison* [1963] Crim LR 497 (at common law). In *Hemmerly* (1976) 30 CCC (2d) 141, D, a drug dealer, was convicted of robbery. In his defence he argued that he was entitled to the money taken, as the victim owed it to him. However, it was clear that D did not believe he had a legal claim to the money; although belief in a moral right might negative dishonesty, it was held not to do so in this case.

(ii) Belief that the other would consent: section 2(1)(b)

Social life is unavoidably a co-operative enterprise. Frequently, we anticipate the generosity of our family and friends by taking and using property in their absence. When we do so, we assume that the owner will not object. For example, in a prosecution for larceny prior to the Theft Act 1968, a farmer borrowed a bale of his neighbour's hay expecting to replace it with a bale of his own.[312] Although he had an intention permanently to deprive his neighbour of the particular bale he "borrowed",[313] his behaviour was accounted not dishonest and he was acquitted of larceny. This type of case is now covered by section 2(1)(b).

(iii) Belief that the owner cannot be found: section 2(1)(c)

Section 2(1)(c) encapsulates the finder's defence.[314] Recall the example stated earlier in this chapter:[315]

> David finds a wallet in a busy street, and picks it up. He looks in the wallet for evidence of the owner's identity and finds none, but does find some money. He puts the wallet in his pocket.

Does David commit theft? Assuming the wallet is indeed lost rather than abandoned, the question turns on whether David is dishonest. If he believes the owner cannot be found by taking reasonable steps, section 2(1)(c) will operate to absolve him.

The three points about this defence should be emphasised. First, David need not consider whether the owner can be found if *all possible* steps are taken. Only reasonable steps need be considered. What is reasonable will depend on the circumstances. If the wallet is inexpensive and contains very little money, David will probably not be required to make any great effort (even so, were a police station close by, it may be adjudged unreasonable not to hand in the wallet). If the wallet contains hundreds of pounds, rather more may be expected.

The second point is that the question of what D *believes* is subjective. Consider the following variation:

> Joan finds a wallet in a busy street, and picks it up. She looks in the wallet for evidence of the owner's identity and finds none, but does find a few pound coins. (In fact, there is a name and address label in the wallet, but Joan's examination of the wallet is a careless one and she does not see it.) Joan puts the wallet in her pocket, concluding that it is lost rather than abandoned but that the true owner cannot be found. She then spends the money and takes the wallet home. On reaching home and looking more carefully inside the wallet, she finds the owner's name and address. Deciding to keep the wallet anyway, she puts it in a drawer.

Joan's initial mistake about the impossibility of tracing the owner need not be a reasonable one. Since she genuinely believes that the owner cannot be found, she is entitled to be

---

[312] Case noted [1956] Crim LR 360.

[313] Above, § 13.7(i)(e).

[314] Though its application is not restricted to finders, and would exculpate bailees where the bailor was now untraceable. See A.T.H. Smith, *Property Offences* (1994) § 7-42.

[315] Above, § 13.4(v).

regarded as honest by virtue of section 2(1)(c). Hence, when she spends the money, she commits no theft. However, facts may change, and the defence may cease to be available—as in the example here. Joan is guilty of stealing the *wallet* when she puts it in the drawer.[316]

The foregoing points intersect at the requirement of "reasonable steps". In principle, while it is a subjective enquiry into what D's beliefs are about the circumstances, the assessment whether the steps (she believes to be) required to locate the owner are *reasonable* is an objective matter, which it is for the court to determine rather than D.[317] Suppose that D finds a wallet containing £1,000 in notes, but has little sense of obligation and genuinely believes it is unreasonable to expect her to be inconvenienced by walking some 600 yards to the nearby police station in order to notify them of her discovery (which, she recognizes, may help to locate the owner). Section 2(1)(c) would not be available.

(iv) The general test for dishonesty

Assuming the defendant cannot avail herself of the defences contained in section 2(1), dishonesty falls to be resolved under the general test. Whether the defendant was dishonest is a question of fact—albeit secondary or evaluative fact—in much the same way as the evaluation whether force used was "reasonable" in the context of self-defence.[318] This is a departure from the position as it was before 1968. In the old crime of larceny (which theft has replaced), the defendant's guilt or innocence depended on whether he had acted "fraudulently". This, by contrast, was treated as a question of law, and narrowly interpreted by the judges. Their interpretation led some commentators to argue in favour of a general "safety valve" that would avoid convictions in hard cases:[319] a view that seems to have influenced the way in which the replacement concept of "dishonesty" was later treated by the courts.

Initially, there was uncertainty about exactly what it was that the tribunal of fact is called upon to decide here. Some of the earlier cases took the position that the test of dishonesty was purely objective ("Was D dishonest according to generally accepted standards of behaviour"),[320] while others took the view that it was subjective ("Did D believe that his behaviour was dishonest?").[321] In 1982 the confusion was resolved in *Ghosh*,[322] in which the Court of Appeal set out a two-part test for the jury or magistrates to apply, incorporating elements of both approach:[323]

    (i)   Was what was done dishonest according to the ordinary standards of reasonable and honest people?

---

[316] Cf. *Minigall* v. *McCammon* [1970] SASR 82.

[317] This is generally true of reasonableness requirements: cf. the justificatory defences, discussed below, § 21.2(ii), (iv). Contrast, unusually, the defence of lawful excuse under s. 5 of the Criminal Damage Act 1971: below, § 14.5(vi)(b) (a reasonable means of protection). The emphatic role of s. 5(3) in that Act finds no correspondent here.

[318] Below, § 21.2.

[319] Smith and Hogan, *Criminal Law* (1965) 381.

[320] *Feely* [1973] QB 530, 537–8 (CA).

[321] *Boggeln* v. *Williams* [1978] 2 All ER 1061. Cf. *Gilks* [1972] 3 All ER 280, 283, where the Court of Appeal approved the trial judge's direction that the jury should "try and place yourselves in [the appellant's] position at that time and answer the question whether in your view he thought he was acting honestly or dishonestly". See also *Landy* [1981] 1 All ER 1172 (conspiracy to defraud); contrast *Greenstein* [1976] 1 All ER 1 (obtaining by deception).

[322] [1982] QB 1053.

[323] *Ibid.*, 1064.

    (ii)   Did the defendant realise that reasonable and honest people would regard what he did as dishonest?

If the answer to both questions is yes, the jury should conclude that the defendant was dishonest.

    An important point of principle arises where D belongs to a particular group. In such a case, who are the "reasonable and honest people" by whose standards the issue of honesty is determined? Is it "reasonable and honest" members of D's specialist group, or "reasonable and honest" members of society in general? The point arose in *Hayes*.[324] D, a banker, had been accused of conspiring with others to rig the LIBOR rate[325] in favour of the bank for which he worked and thereby, indirectly, in favour of himself. For this he was prosecuted for conspiracy to defraud (another crime in which dishonesty is an ingredient)[326] and convicted at a trial conducted on the basis that the appropriate standard was that of reasonable and honest members of society in general, rather than reasonable and honest bankers. Affirming his conviction, the Court of Appeal held that the trial judge's approach had been correct.[327] In *Hayes*, the defendant's argument centred around the first, objective limb of the *Ghosh* test and in rejecting it, the Court of Appeal seems to have accepted—albeit without argument—that the standards of the specialist group to which D belongs might be relevant to the second, subjective limb of the test. This is surprising because, as we explain below, the issue in the second limb of the test is whether D believed that "reasonable and honest" members of society would approve of what he did—a reference seemingly to the same group as for the first limb of the test.[328]

    The *Ghosh* direction on dishonesty need not be given in every case, only when there is evidence of a divergence between the defendant's standards of honesty and those of "reasonable and honest people".[329] By contrast with the purely subjective approach, the defendant is not entitled to rely simply on her own views whether her conduct is honest. This point was made explicitly by the Court of Appeal in *Ghosh*:[330]

> "For example, Robin Hood or those ardent anti-vivisectionists who remove animals from vivisection laboratories are acting dishonestly, even though they may consider themselves to be morally justified in doing what they do, because they know that ordinary people would consider those actions to be dishonest."

On the other hand, according to Lord Lane, neither is the test exclusively objective:[331]

> "Take the man who comes from a country where public transport is free. On his first day here he travels on a bus. He gets off without paying. He never has any intention of paying. His mind is clearly honest; but his conduct, judged objectively by what he has done, is dishonest."

---

[324] [2015] EWCA Crim 1944.

[325] LIBOR is an acronym for the London Interbank Offered Rate. This is the interest rate which banks can charge each other on commercial loans in the London market.

[326] See § 15.9 below.

[327] An earlier decision to similar effect was *Lockwood* [1986] Crim LR 244. So it seems that even in corporate frauds we apply the standards of ordinary decent people, not "current notions of fair trading among commercial men", as was suggested in *re Patrick Lyon* [1933] Ch 786, 790 and *Landy* [1981] 1 All ER 1172, 1181 ("a man of his intelligence and experience"). For discussion, see Levi, "Fraud Trials in Perspective" [1984] *Crim LR* 384; Elliott, "Directors' Thefts and Dishonesty" [1991] *Crim LR* 732.

[328] See the comment by Rogers, [2016] 3 *Archbold Review* 7.

[329] Cf. *Roberts* (1987) 84 Cr App R 117; *Price* (1990) 90 Cr App R 409; *Brennan* [1990] Crim LR 118; *Wood* [2002] EWCA Crim 832.

[330] [1982] QB 1053.

[331] *Ibid.*, 1063.

Even if the foreigner satisfies the first limb,[332] such a case is now exculpated by the second limb of the *Ghosh* test.

(a) Problems with the Ghosh test

Both *Feely* and *Ghosh* have attracted an extensive critical literature.[333] For one thing, it may be thought rather open-ended to ask the jury to apply a standard of "reasonable and honest people" (in *Ghosh*) or of "ordinary decent people" (in *Feely*). Even though, in *Ghosh*, this is done with the intention of imposing an objective standard for dishonesty, it assumes juries and magistrates are heterogeneous and have consistent values. That is surely not the case. Values in this country vary widely, both across and within socio-economic and cultural divides. There is no reason to suppose such variation does not extend to judgements of dishonesty. When a batsman at cricket refuses to walk, is that dishonest? It depends who you ask. Perhaps we can agree that shoplifting is dishonest; what about making an otherwise lawful profit from information about a company that is not widely known?[334] Do we really all concur, *pace* Lord Lane, that Robin Hood was dishonest—or that openly using force to release battery hens or destroy genetically modified crops is dishonest? Obviously, if different persons can reasonably hold different views about these questions, there is a real danger of different verdicts, on the same set of facts, from different juries. In turn, this undermines the rule of law. Even an informed defendant may be unable to predict whether his behaviour will contravene the law. Arguably, such uncertainty contravenes Article 7 of the ECHR.[335]

On the other hand, the subjective element in the *Ghosh* test produces its own problems. To some extent, dishonesty is a matter of personal morality, but defendants cannot be permitted entirely to supplant their own values (or even their own views of what society's values are) for those of the law. It is vital to the authority of a legal system that its laws set an objective touchstone. Law works by preventing people from doing what they want, through imposing a standard of acceptable behaviour and demanding that they conform to that standard. If the values that the law would have us act upon were displaced, in each case, by those of the particular defendant, then the law would have no standard to impose.[336] Where defendants are prosecuted for groping their secretarial staff, for possession of cocaine, or for persuading family members to "take" the penalty points they have incurred for speeding, we do not expect them to be acquitted if they say, however truthfully, "But I thought everybody

---

[332] Arguably, the foreigner is not even within the first limb of the *Ghosh* test. This illustrates one of the difficulties about that test: even under limb one, D's subjective state of mind must be considered. Lord Lane's concept of "objective dishonesty" is therefore problematic.

[333] See, e.g., Elliott, "Dishonesty under the Theft Act" [1972] *Crim LR* 625; Wasik, "Mens Rea, Motive and the Problem of 'Dishonesty' in the Law of Theft" [1977] *Crim LR* 543; Campbell, "The Test of Dishonety in R v. Ghosh" [1984] *CLJ* 349; Griew, "Dishonesty: The Objections to Feely and Ghosh" [1985] *Crim LR* 341; Halpin, "The Test for Dishonesty" [1996] *Crim LR* 283; Halpin, *Definition in the Criminal Law* (2004) chap. 4.

[334] See n. 327 above.

[335] See, in particular, the discussion of this point in the Law Commission's Consultation Paper No. 155, *Fraud and Deception* (1999) § 5.33ff. A prescient early note is McKenna, 'The Undefined Adverb in Criminal Statutes' [1966] *Crim LR* 548, 552–3.

[336] "To permit one who knows but does not accede to the community valuation of interests to have an individual standard would at once destroy the law": Seavey, "Negligence—Subjective or Objective?" (1927) 41 *Harvard LR* 1, 11.

does it". One would have thought the law should equally refuse to listen to excuses of this sort when they are put forward by those accused of thieving by dipping into tills or of fraud by fiddling their expenses. These are weighty objections. They seem all the stronger now that, thanks to the elastic interpretation of "appropriation", the dishonesty requirement has ceased to be residual and plays a central role in the offence.

Despite that, however, it seems that, at least until recently, the *Ghosh* test has proved surprisingly popular with judges and with the legislature. The courts themselves decided that dishonesty, as interpreted in *Ghosh*, is an element of the common law offence of conspiracy to defraud,[337] and more recently in at least some cases of the common law offence of misconduct in public office.[338] And Parliament, presumably well aware of the way in which the term is interpreted, has repeatedly used the word "dishonestly" when enacting new legislation in relation to fraud;[339] indeed, as will be seen in Chapter 15, in 2006 it reformed the law of fraud in such a way as to make dishonesty the central element in a new general offence of fraud.

Nonetheless, there are now signs that opinion may be changing. In 2013, Parliament amended the "cartel" offence created by section 188 of the Enterprise Act 2002 so as to remove dishonesty as an ingredient in the offence, on the ground that it made the offence unworkable.[340] In 2011, the country was treated to the unedifying spectacle of Members of the House of Lords, on trial for frauds in relation to their official expenses, trying to persuade juries to acquit them because they believed fraudulent expenses claims to be part of the "office culture".[341] It has also been suggested that uncertainty resulting from the *Ghosh* test was one of the reasons why the police failed to bring theft charges against any of the large number of people who, in 2007, helped themselves to the cargo of a ship wrecked in Branscombe Bay.[342] It is possible that these developments will eventually cause the *Ghosh* test to be reconsidered.

§ 13.9 Jurisdiction over Theft Act offences

(i) National cases

For criminal procedure purposes, theft is an "either-way offence". This means that, in principle, a case of theft can be dealt with either by summary proceedings in a Magistrates' Court, or on indictment in a Crown Court (with a trial by jury if D elects to plead not guilty). The general idea is that petty thefts are dealt with summarily, and the Crown Court is reserved for cases of importance; but as defendants charged with either-way offences have

---

[337] Below, § 15.9.

[338] *W* [2010] EWCA Crim 372, [2010] QB 787.

[339] See, e.g., s. 111A of the Social Security Administration Act 1992.

[340] Some 10 years earlier, in 2003, the legislature in New Zealand reformed the law so as to avoid the *Ghosh* test. Section 217 of the Crimes Act 1961, as amended, provides that "dishonestly, in relation to an act or omission, means done or omitted without a belief that there was express or implied consent to, or authority for, the act or omission from a person entitled to give such consent or authority". For interpretation, see the New Zealand Supreme Court in *Hayes* [2008] 2 NZSC 3, 2 NZLR 321.

[341] Lord Taylor of Warwick (BBC News, 25 January 2011) and Lord Hanningfield (BBC News, 26 May 2011).

[342] Glover, "Can Dishonesty be Salvaged? Theft and the Grounding of the *MSC Napoli*" (2010) 74 *J Crim Law* 53.

a right to insist on jury trial, a number of trivial cases of theft have regularly found their way into the Crown Court. As Crown Court proceedings are much more expensive than summary proceedings, this has led to repeated moves to make petty theft a purely summary offence. To date, all such moves have failed. The most recent attempt was section 176 of the Antisocial Behaviour, Crime and Policing Act 2014,[343] which has now made low-value shoplifting[344] a purely summary offence; but as the new provision then goes on to preserve the defendant's right to jury trial, its practical impact is likely to be very small.[345]

(ii) International cases

Nowadays, theftuous and fraudulent conduct frequently has a transnational dimension. For example, D, from London, may obtain access by electronic means to V's New York bank account and dishonestly transfer funds from that account to an account he has opened for himself in a Swiss bank. Or D may send a deceptive telex from London to Hong Kong, causing V to transfer for D's benefit funds held in a Hong Kong bank. It may well be that the conduct just described merits trial and punishment before an English court, since there may be damage to interests which fall properly within the purview of English criminal law.[346]

At common law, any claim to jurisdiction now requires proof that either (i) the last constituent element, or (ii) a "substantial" component, of the actus reus of the offence took place in England or Wales; and that there is no reason of comity with foreign legal systems not to try the offence here.[347] Frequently, asserting jurisdiction will be possible notwithstanding a substantial transnational element on the facts.[348] In *Re Osman*,[349] acts were done in Hong Kong (where the law of theft was the same as in England) which took effect on property situated in other countries. It was held that the property had been appropriated in Hong Kong, without prejudice to the possibility that appropriation also occurred where the property was located. Similarly, a blackmailing demand is made when a letter is posted in England, even if the addressee will receive the letter in Germany.[350]

---

[343] By adding a new s. 22A to the Magistrates' Courts Act 1980.

[344] Meaning goods the value of which does not exceed £200.

[345] Redesignating low-value shoplifting as a summary offence does deprive the magistrates and the Crown Prosecution Service of their previous right to insist that the case should be dealt with in the Crown Court; but unlike the defendant's equivalent right, it was very rarely exercised.

[346] UK nationals, including companies, may suffer loss of property owned overseas. Moreover, the City of London and other financial centres may suffer loss of reputation and confidence if perceived as havens for international fraud: see further Law Com. No. 180, *Jurisdiction over Offences of Fraud and Dishonesty with a Foreign Element* (1989).

[347] *Smith (Wallace Duncan) (No. 4)* [2004] EWCA Crim 631, [2004] QB 1418; overruling *Manning* [1999] QB 980 (CA).

[348] Save for specific statutory exceptions, English courts do not accept jurisdiction over conduct perpetrated entirely outside England and Wales, even in respect of a British subject. For common law crimes, constraints of venue and ambit ensured that "all crime is local". For statutory crimes, there is a very strong presumption that criminal statutes are concerned and only concerned with prescribing acts or omissions perpetrated in the United Kingdom: *Cox v. Army Council* [1963] AC 48.

[349] [1990] 1 WLR 277.

[350] *Treacy* [1971] AC 537.

The modern common law has fallen broadly into line with Part I of the Criminal Justice Act 1993,[351] which attempts to achieve consistency between theft and offences of fraud and dishonesty regarding jurisdiction over offences with transnational elements. If an offence is listed in Part I of the Criminal Justice Act 1993,[352] under section 2 of that Act an assumption of jurisdiction will be permitted notwithstanding that elements of the offence have taken place overseas provided a "relevant event"—i.e. any definitional element of the offence— occurs in England and Wales.[353]

---

[351] Part I came into effect in August 1999: SI 1999, No. 1189 (32); SI 1999, No. 1499 (42).

[352] The listed offences in s. 1 of the Criminal Justice Act 1993 include: theft; false accounting; false statements by company directors; blackmail; handling stolen goods; fraud and related offences; forgery and allied offences; conspiracy to defraud; and the common law offence of cheating in relation to the public revenue.

[353] "For the purposes of this Part, 'relevant event' ... means ... any act or omission or other event (including any result of one or more acts or omissions) proof of which is required for the commission of the offence": Criminal Justice Act 1993, s. 2(1).

14

RELATED OFFENCES

It is impossible, in a work of this nature, to analyse all the offences besides theft which concern themselves with harms to property.[1] In Chapter 15, fraud offences will be considered. Those are offences which, unlike theft and the offences considered in this chapter, often involve the wrongful manipulation of other persons, so that invasion of a victim's property interests is, at least prima facie, consensual: "whereas the thief makes war on a social practice from the outside, the deceiver is the traitor within".[2] Besides theft, however, there are many other property offences which are external to, and attack rather than insidiously use, the law's established processes for allocating and transferring property rights. In this chapter, we consider five such offences.

§ 14.1 Handling stolen goods

"There would not be so many thieves if there were no receivers."[3] The crime of handling is in many ways a special case of being an accessory to theft,[4] one which deserves independent criminalisation because of the important role that "fences"—and indeed end-purchasers—of stolen goods play in the economics of the offence. Recognition of the importance of handling was relatively slow in coming. As its early legal status suggests, in some respects handling *is* a secondary offence. Logically and temporally, theft is prior to handling: the latter presupposes the former. (It should be noted, however, that although receiving is normally associated with theft, the modern offence can also be committed in respect of blackmail, fraud, and by withdrawing a wrongful credit. Thus one who launders the proceeds of blackmail may be guilty of handling under the Theft Act 1968.)[5] Historically, too, theft was originally a far more significant crime than handling. Prior to the

---

[1] For detailed treatments, see further Ormerod and Williams, *Smith's Law of Theft* (9th ed., 2007).

[2] Shute and Horder, "Thieving and Deceiving: What Is the Difference?" (1993) 56 *MLR* 548, 553.

[3] *Battams* (1979) 1 Cr App R(S) 15, 16. According to Klockars, *The Professional Fence* (1974) 165–6, "the observation itself is better understood as an hyperbolic plea for attention to the criminal receiver than as an accurate statement of his relationship to theft.... In brief, if there were no receivers, there would still be all sorts of thieves, and possibly more thieves of sorts we don't like than we have now."

[4] Indeed, this was how it was first criminalised, in 1692, 3 & 4 W. & M. c. 13 (receivers deemed to be accessories). Earlier law disclosed an offence only if D actually received or abetted the thief himself: *Dawson's Case* (1602) 2 Bracton 337, 339, 80 ER 4. For a brief history, see Hall, *Theft, Law and Society* (2nd ed., 1952) 52–8. The old position is now reversed, and receiving the thief does not constitute receiving the goods stolen: *Wiley* (1850) 4 Cox CC 412, 169 ER 408.

[5] It is unclear why handling should be restricted to these specific crimes and not apply to the proceeds of crime more generally, as it does in some other jurisdictions. (Cf. Howarth, "Handling Stolen Goods and Handling Salmon" [1987] *Crim LR* 460.) Contrast, e.g., s. 246 of the Crimes Act 1961 (NZ), which makes it an offence to receive anything "stolen or obtained by any other crime". However, as will be noted in § 14.2, the expanded scope

Industrial Revolution, chattels were relatively few and there was little mobility between population centres.[6] Hence, stolen property could be traced fairly easily and there were few commercial opportunities for redistribution of such property. Theft, in turn, tended to be committed to satisfy personal needs rather than for profit.

In modern society, the explosion of property offences is a simple matter of economics: in the market for stolen goods, supply has increased to meet demand. Professional fences are the brokers who make that market: handling is the channel through which commercial forces drive theft.[7] Reflecting this, the maximum penalty for handling is imprisonment for 14 years, by contrast with a maximum of seven years for theft.

In addition, those who deal in stolen goods also provide the means by which merchandise can be "laundered", so that the tangible evidence of theft effectively disappears.[8] Mass-produced items, once sold on, cannot normally be traced. By providing an outlet for the efficient disposal of such items, handlers reduce the risk that theft will be detected. Thus one, largely unrecognised, role that professional fences perform is the obstruction of justice.

Yet these considerations are somewhat abstract, and their victims are not harmed so immediately as they are by the theft itself. Consequently, the wrongness of handling—unlike that of another offence of profiting from others' crimes, the possession of child pornography—has never caught the popular imagination. Indeed, in practice those accused of theft or burglary are often prepared to plead guilty to handling if the charge of theft of burglary is dropped, even though the offence of handling carries a higher penalty.[9] This may be in part because the Theft Act draws no distinction between the lay receiver, who may once in his lifetime buy stolen goods for his own consumption, and the criminal businessman who maintains an organisation and thus supports the theft industry. With this in mind, in previous editions of this book we suggested that that the law was at fault in failing to deal strongly enough with professional handling. As we shall see later, in 2002, Parliament, mindful of this problem, created the new and broadly based offence of "laundering", which was designed to strike hard at professional money launderers. But, as we shall also see later, this new offence, like handling, is as apt to catch the little fish as it is the big one: to the point where, if exploited to the limit, it would make the offence of handling stolen goods redundant.[10]

Section 22(1) of the Theft Act 1968 defines handling as follows:

> A person handles stolen goods if (otherwise than in the course of the stealing) knowing or believing them to be stolen goods he dishonestly receives the goods, or dishonestly undertakes or assists in their retention, removal, disposal or realisation by or for the benefit of another person, or if he arranges to do so.

of modern laundering legislation compasses the proceeds of any criminal conduct—effectively swallowing the traditional offence of handling.

[6] Chappell and Walsh, "'No Questions Asked', A Consideration of the Crime of Criminal Receiving"(1974) 20 *Crime and Delinquency* 157, 160.

[7] Cf. Klockars, *The Professional Fence* (1974); Blakey and Goldsmith, "Criminal Redistribution of Stolen Property: The Need for Reform" (1976) 74 *Mich LR* 1512; Sutton, Schneider and Hetherington, *Tackling theft with the market reduction approach* (2001); *Shelton* (1986) 83 Cr App R 379, 385.

[8] Chappell and Walsh, "Receiving Stolen Property: The Need for a Systematic Inquiry into the Fencing Process" (1974) 11 *Criminology* 484, 494.

[9] An instructive example is *Sainthouse* [1980] Crim LR 506, where a casual (i.e. non-professional) receiver was prepared to plead guilty to handling but not to theft.

[10] See below, § 14.2.

The section stipulates four main elements. The actus reus is:

(i)   that D handles goods; and
(ii)   the goods were stolen.

The mens rea components are:

(iii)   D knows or believes the goods were stolen or dishonestly obtained; and
(iv)   dishonesty.

(i) Handling

Prior to the passing of the Theft Act 1968, the only mode of handling goods was receiving them, something that required the defendant to take possession or control over the goods. This limitation made it more difficult to convict those professional fences who facilitated dispositions of goods without themselves ever coming into physical contact with or acquiring the goods. Under section 22(1), the behavioural element of the offence can now be done in the following ways:[11]

(i)   through receiving, or arranging to receive, the goods;
(ii)   through assisting in their retention, removal, disposal, or realisation by another person, or through arranging to do so;
(iii)   through assisting in their retention, removal, disposal, or realisation for the benefit of another person, or through arranging to do so.

In each of these cases, the handling must occur otherwise than in the course of the original stealing. It must be observed, at the outset of this discussion, that the drafting of section 22(1) is rather inelegant and does not lend itself to clear elucidation. In particular, the actus reus of handling is specified in terms both wide and uncertain.[12]

(a) Receiving

The law on receiving pre-dates the Act.[13] The actus reus requirement in receiving is that H acquires (joint or sole) possession or control over the goods from another person.[14] The acquisition of possession or control is a single finite act: once possession or control is acquired, the receiving is complete and later dealing with the goods cannot be treated as a continuing or further act of receiving.

H need not take personal physical custody of the goods. Possession *or* control is sufficient. Regarding the first of these, "possession" is established by showing (i) that the goods

---

[11] *Bloxham* [1983] 1 AC 109, 113–14; below, § 14.1(i)(c).
[12] Spencer, "The Mishandling of Handling" [1981] *Crim LR* 682, 683–4; Blake, "The Innocent Purchaser and Section 22 of the Theft Act" [1972] *Crim LR* 494.
[13] Cf. *Smythe* (1980) 72 Cr App R 8, 11 ("receiving, or handling as it has now become").
[14] In *Seymour* [1954] 1 All ER 1006 the Court of Criminal Appeal sought to correct a tendency to find people guilty of receiving, rather than theft, whenever they were found in possession of stolen goods. Lord Goddard CJ emphasised that to find someone guilty of receiving, the jury must be satisfied that D received from *someone else*: "[i]f he is the thief, he cannot be guilty of receiving because a man cannot receive from himself, but must receive the property from somebody else". Thus, where the evidence is as consistent with theft as it is with handling, the indictment ought to contain a count for theft and a count for handling. See below, § 14.1(vi).

are either in H's immediate physical custody or located at a place over which H has control (e.g. in H's house); together with (ii) a mental element, the intent by H to possess the goods.

The mental element is essential. D cannot be in possession of property that he does not know exists.[15] Suppose, for instance, that T, having stolen a wallet, disposes of it by slipping the wallet into H's bag without H's knowledge. In such a case, for the purposes of receiving H does not take possession of the wallet, at least until she knows she has it. Similarly, if goods stolen by another are found in H's house, it must be shown either that H had arranged for them to be delivered there[16] or, alternatively, that H had realised the goods were present and intentionally exercised control over them. In *Cavendish*,[17] Lord Parker CJ put the test in the following way:

> "It is quite clear, without referring to authority, that for a man to be found to have possession, actual or constructive, of goods, something more must be proved than that the goods have been found on his premises. It must be shown either, if he was absent, that on his return he became aware of them and exercised some control over them or ... that the goods had come, albeit in his absence, at his invitation or by arrangement."

The importance of the mental ingredient involved in acquiring possession or control can be seen in *Healey*.[18] In that case, the defendant was hired to assist in melting down some tin. The tin was stolen. The defendant's conviction for receiving was quashed by the Court of Criminal Appeal, because the trial judge had not drawn the jury's attention to the difference between a person who was merely assisting, even if dishonestly, and a person who by his assistance had become a joint possessor with the principal whom he was assisting. The Court cited a passage from *Hobson v. Impett*:[19]

> "It is not the law that, if a man knows goods are stolen and puts his hands on them, that in itself makes him guilty of receiving, because it does not follow that he is taking them into his control. The control may still be in the thief or the man whom he is assisting, and the alleged receiver may be only picking the goods up without taking them into his possession, the goods all the time remaining in the possession of the person whom he is helping."

As this passage makes clear, physical possession, e.g. in the sense of touching something, is insufficient without the accompanying intent thereby to possess or control the thing. To similar effect is the decision in *Hawes v. Edwards*.[20] A parcel containing stolen goods was delivered to D's address. After the delivery, police officers entered the premises and found the defendant together with the opened parcel. One of the officers asked D whether he had signed for the parcel, to which he responded, "No, I am examining the contents before I sign for it". D's conviction for receiving was quashed. Although he had opened the parcel, he had not yet decided whether to acquire possession from the thieves. In effect, the thieves had offered to transfer the goods to him, and D had yet to accept their offer.

Conversely, physical possession is not always *required*. If the defendant lacks actual custody of the stolen goods, she may nonetheless be found to have "control" over them. This

---

[15] See also above, § 5.6 (ii).
[16] *Lloyd* [1992] Crim LR 361; *Cavendish* [1961] 2 All ER 856.
[17] [1961] 2 All ER 856, 858.
[18] [1965] 1 All ER 365.
[19] (1957) 41 Cr App R 138, 141 (Lord Goddard CJ). See *Healey* [1965] 1 All ER 365, 369.
[20] (1949) 113 JP 303; cf. *Freedman* (1930) 22 Cr App R 133.

occurs when custody is in the hands of an agent or servant acting under the defendant's direction; through whom the defendant exercises control over the goods.[21] Again, the exercise of control imports a mental element, and one cannot unknowingly exercise control over something. Hence, according to Lord Parker CJ, "a man cannot be convicted of receiving goods of which delivery has been taken by his servant unless there is evidence that he, the employer, had given the servant authority or instructions to take the goods".[22]

(b) Arranging to receive

Handling can also be committed in inchoate form. Under section 22(1) what, prior to 1968, would have been (at most) an attempt or a conspiracy to receive is now a full offence. If the prosecution can prove that H made an arrangement to receive the goods, she is guilty of handling them; there is no need to prove that she actually received the goods. However, the arrangement must be made after the goods are stolen, since it is necessary that H should know or believe the goods are stolen property at the time of making the arrangement.[23]

(c) Undertaking or assisting in the retention, removal, disposal, or realisation

Section 22(1) makes H guilty of handling if he undertakes or assists to retain, remove, dispose of, or realise the goods, by or for the benefit of another person. According to Lord Bridge:[24]

> "First, the offender may himself undertake the activity for the benefit of another person. Secondly, the activity may be undertaken by another person and the offender may assist him. Of course, if the thief or an original receiver and his friend act together in, say, removing the stolen goods, the friend may be committing the offence in both ways."

Typically, this encompasses cases where H organises the on-sale of stolen goods without herself ever taking possession of them,[25] or where H assists the thief to fence or realise the goods. The formula would also capture situations where H promises to destroy or assists in destroying (or otherwise "disposing" of) stolen property; as well as cases where H undertakes or assists to store ("retain") the stolen items.[26] Merely using the goods, however, is not sufficient. In *Sanders*,[27] D used a stolen heater in his father's garage, where D was employed. Although the father was guilty of handling, D was not.

Neither is passive acquiescence sufficient. In *Coleman*,[28] H's wife used money she had stolen to pay for legal fees which had been incurred jointly by H and his wife. H was charged with assisting his wife to dispose of the money. The Court of Appeal quashed his conviction after the trial judge misdirected the jury that it was sufficient for handling that H was

---

[21] *Smith* (1855) Dears 494, 169 ER 818; *Miller* (1854) 6 Cox 353.

[22] *Cavendish* [1961] 2 All ER 856, 858; a continuation of the remarks quoted earlier in this section.

[23] *Park* (1987) 87 Cr App R 164. If an agreement to handle stolen goods is made prior to the theft, the proper charge is conspiracy (*ibid.*, 173). It may also be appropriate to charge the would-be handler as an accessory to the contemplated theft, or with an inchoate offence of encouraging or assisting it.

[24] *Bloxham* [1983] AC 109, 113–14.

[25] Cf. the facts of *Watson* [1916] 2 KB 385.

[26] *Pitchley* (1972) 57 Cr App R 30, 37: retain means "keep possession of".

[27] (1982) 75 Cr App R 84. Cf. the law governing the taking of possession by employees who find goods: above, § 13.4(v)(a).

[28] (1985) 150 JP 175.

dishonest and was getting the benefit of the disposal. Knowingly standing by while a benefit is conferred is not in itself assistance, though it may be circumstantial evidence supporting a wider case that H encouraged or assisted his wife in the disposal. The decision seems right, on the principle that there is generally no criminal liability for omissions. Thus, in *Brown*,[29] H's failure to tell the police that stolen goods were in his flat when instructing them to "get lost" was held not to be assisting in their retention. In the absence of a duty to disclose, H's omission was an insufficient basis for criminal liability.[30]

By contrast, in *Kanwar*,[31] H actively lied by telling the police that she had purchased articles which her husband had stolen. The effect of these lies, had they been believed by the police, would have been to assist her husband to retain the stolen articles. H's appeal against conviction for handling stolen goods was therefore dismissed by the Court of Appeal.

In *Kanwar*, the finding that positive representations by H could be assistance seems right. Nonetheless, the decision itself is problematic for a different reason: H's "assistance" was ineffective because her lies were not believed. The Court met this difficulty with the bald assertion that "[t]he requisite assistance need not be successful in its object".[32] With respect, this proposition must be qualified. It is possible to assist in a project which, ultimately, is unsuccessful. If H's lies had been temporarily believed but, later, the police had discovered the truth, it might then be reasonable to say that H provided assistance towards the retention of the stolen articles. But on the facts of the case, her lies were wholly ineffectual. She merely attempted to assist.

(d) Arranging to undertake or assist in the retention, removal, disposal, or realisation

One might think that "arranging to assist" in disposing of stolen goods has the hallmarks of an inchoate offence. But under section 22(1), it constitutes the full offence of handling. Thus if, in *Kanwar*, H had promised the thief (i.e. "undertaken") to tell lies, or had made a plan ("arrangement") with someone else to conceal stolen the stolen goods, no difficulty would have arisen: she would be guilty of handling even before the undertaking or arrangement was implemented.

Potentially, this extends the substantive law of handling far into the realm of inchoate offences. Indeed, in extreme cases it would take handling through inchoate wrongs and out the other side, into the field of mere preparation. Given that an undertaking to retain is itself inchoate in nature, making arrangements in advance of giving such an undertaking must be preparatory even to the inchoate wrong. Yet, under section 22(1), both of these constitute the full offence of handling. To some extent, the apparent width of this provision is narrowed in practice by the requirement that there be in existence, at the time, stolen goods to which H's arrangement relates. Nonetheless, it may be questioned whether the mere making of an arrangement to undertake to dispose of those goods comprises a crystallised harm sufficient to warrant criminalisation.

---

[29] [1970] 1 QB 105.
[30] Above, § 4.1(i).
[31] [1982] 2 All ER 528.
[32] *Ibid.*, 529.

(e) By or for the benefit of another

The requirement that the arranging, assisting, or undertaking be "by or for the benefit of another person" is awkwardly expressed. What it seems to mean is that, apart from traditional receiving, there are two types of handling by dealing:

(i)   where H acts as a principal, by arranging or undertaking to deal with (i.e. retain, dispose of, etc.) the property *for the benefit of someone else*; and

(ii) where H has a secondary role, by arranging or assisting *someone else to* deal with the property (i.e. "by another person").

What this means is that if H deals with the property on his own, solely for his own benefit, he does not handle.[33] (That is, unless he receives the property.) In *Bloxham*,[34] H purchased a car in good faith. Later he realised the car was stolen, whereupon he sold it at an undervalue to T, an innocent party. H's conviction for handling was quashed by the House of Lords. Although he had disposed of the car, and T had benefited thereby, H had not dealt with the car *for the benefit* of T or anyone else. Rather, H had acted on his own behalf. Moreover, because H also acted by himself, neither could he be convicted on the alternative basis that he had arranged or assisted in the disposal *by another person*.[35]

(f) Otherwise than in the course of stealing

The original theft cannot also be a handling: the goods must be stolen before they can be handled. Section 22 re-enacts this rule, which was part of the common law of receiving,[36] by the proviso that the handling must occur "otherwise than in the course of the stealing". In so doing, it helps to preserve the functional distinctiveness of handling, which involves wrongdoing by receiving or dealing with goods *after* they are stolen.

The converse does not hold. Virtually every handling is also a theft, since both receiving and dealing with property will count as an "appropriation" for the purposes of theft.[37] This overlap is less problematic, however, since theft carries a lesser maximum penalty than handling.[38] We consider the issue of overlaps further in § 14.1(vi).

It is unclear how long a period is included within "the course of the stealing". Suppose the following example:

D picks goods off the shelf at a supermarket and puts them inside her jacket, intending to leave without paying for them. On the authority of *Gomez*, she has already stolen the goods. As part of the plan, however, D then meets H, her accomplice, in another aisle and passes over some of the goods. H conceals them and leaves separately.

[33] Cf. *Sloggett* [1972] 1 QB 430, 434; also the commentary on *Slater and Suddens* [1996] Crim LR 494.

[34] [1983] 1 AC 109 (HL); reversing [1981] 2 All ER 647 (CA). The decision by the Court of Appeal was strongly criticised by Spencer, "The Mishandling of Handling" [1981] *Crim LR* 682.

[35] As occurred in *Tokeley-Parry* [1999] Crim LR 578, where D arranged for T to smuggle (i.e. "remove", within the terms of s. 22(1)) stolen antiques from Egypt into England.

[36] *Seymour* [1954] 1 All ER 1006; *Thompson* [1965] Crim LR 553.

[37] Cf. *Stapylton* v. *O'Callaghan* [1973] 2 All ER 782; Smith, "Theft and/or Handling" [1977] *Crim LR* 517.

[38] Seven years' imprisonment, by contrast with 14 for handling. See ss. 7 (as amended by the Criminal Justice Act 1991, s. 26) and 22(2).

Does H handle the goods? Common sense suggests not (and that it is a joint theft), but the law has yet to answer this question unequivocally. In principle, once there is an appropriation by the thief, the offence of "theft" is complete and committed. This suggests that, in law, the theft is finished—which would make H guilty of handling.[39]

There are two possible ways round this conclusion. One is to rule that D's appropriation of the goods was a single continuing act, lasting (say) until she left the supermarket. While there is no case post-*Gomez* wholeheartedly adopting such an analysis—and it is not easy to reconcile with *Gomez*[40]—the balance of the decisions appears to favour this analysis.[41]

Alternatively, and perhaps equally plausibly, it is open to the courts to rule that the phrase "the course of the stealing" covers a period extending beyond the duration of the theftuous act of appropriation.[42] As a matter of ordinary language, the term "theft" legitimately describes the whole transaction by D and H in the supermarket; moreover, it seems an appropriate word to capture the moral significance of their course of activity, when viewed as a whole. For the purposes of section 22(1), there seems no reason to restrict interpretation of "the course of the stealing" to the technical instant of appropriation required to be proved under section 1.

Even granted the analysis suggested here, however, the boundaries of theft will be vague. In the example set out above, when is the course of the theft by D (and H) completed, so that the goods can thereafter be handled? Is it after D moves past the cashier's counter, when she is outside the premises, when she is some metres down the road, or at some other moment? To some extent, the answer will involve drawing lines intuitively, depending on such factors as whether the thief is still at the scene of the crime.[43]

(ii) Stolen goods

The things handled must be "stolen", and they must be "goods", within the meaning of the Act. Both these terms require discussion.

(a) Goods

The definition of "goods" is set out in section 34(2)(b):

> "goods", except in so far as the context otherwise requires, includes money and every other description of property except land, and includes things severed from the land by stealing.

This definition is almost coextensive with the definition of "property" for the purposes of theft (above, § 13.2), with the main exception that D cannot be guilty of handling land

---

[39] Cf. *Pitham and Hehl* (1976) 65 Cr App R 45, 49, where D's offer dishonestly to "sell" V's goods to H was held to constitute theft, such that H's purporting to buy the goods and carry them away was handling. For criticism of the decision, see § 13.6(i); also the text below, § 14.3(iii).

[40] Cf. *Atakpu and Abraham* [1994] QB 69, 80. Contrast, however, *Lockley* [1995] Crim LR 656.

[41] E.g. *Hale* (1978) 68 Cr App R 415; *Donaghy* v. *Marshall* [1981] Crim LR 644; *Lockley* [1995] Crim LR 656; *Bowden* [2002] EWCA Crim 1279. See Williams, "Appropriation: A Single or Continuous Act?" [1973] *Crim LR* 69.

[42] Cf. *Hale* (1978) 68 Cr App R 415, regarding the requirement in robbery, *per* s. 8(1), that force be used "at the time of" the stealing. See below, § 14.3(iii).

[43] Contrast *Pitham and Hehl* (1976) 65 Cr App R 45 (theft of furniture complete as soon as D offered to sell it to H) with *Gregory* (1981) 77 Cr App R 41 (during a burglary, theft might continue before property is removed from the building).

unless severed.[44] In *A-G's Reference (No. 4 of 1979)*,[45] the Court of Appeal confirmed that things in action can be handled. Although they cannot be "received" (which requires a physical taking of possession or control over the goods), following the enactment of the 1968 Act intangible property can now be handled by retention, removal, disposal, or realisation. Thus, if H assists D to negotiate a cheque obtained by fraud, she becomes guilty of handling.[46]

(b) Stolen

It is not sufficient that the goods have been obtained by crime. They must have been obtained pursuant to certain particular crimes. *Per* section 24(4), the three main offences are theft contrary to section 1, blackmail contrary to section 21, and fraud contrary to section 1 of the Fraud Act 2006.[47] In light of *Gomez*,[48] cases of obtaining by blackmail or fraud generally also constitute theft, and theft is the most important principal offence lying behind convictions for handling. Goods which are obtained by offences of which theft is an element—e.g. burglary and robbery—can also be handled.[49]

It is not necessary to prove the identity of either the person who actually committed the crime or the owner of the property.[50] Provided the evidence discloses that the property was obtained by theft or another crime, even the acquittal of the particular person charged with committing that theft is irrelevant to the charge of receiving.[51] However, it *is* essential to prove that the property was stolen,[52] or obtained by blackmail or fraud that constitutes a *crime*. So, for example, where the person charged with originally stealing a thing is acquitted (or cannot be charged at all) on the ground of legal incapacity such as minority or insanity,[53] the handler cannot be convicted in the absence of other evidence showing the property was obtained by theft. An illustration of this is the pre-Act case of *Walters* v. *Lunt*,[54] in which the defendants took possession of a tricycle that their child, aged seven years, had wrongfully brought home. The Court ruled they could not be convicted of receiving since the child, being under eight years old, could not be guilty of larceny.

---

[44] The possible theft of land is subject to different restrictions, set out in s. 4(2) of the Theft Act 1968. See above, § 13.3(ii).

[45] [1981] 1 All ER 1193. The decision must now be doubted on other grounds, in light of *Preddy* [1996] AC 815; below, § 15.1. However, there seems no reason to doubt its authority on this point.

[46] Cf. *Pitchley* (1972) 57 Cr App R 30 (money in a bank account).

[47] Section 24A(8) adds obtaining by withdrawal of a wrongful credit. Thus, whereas it is now a separate criminal offence merely to retain a wrongful credit (s. 24A(1)), it is handling to withdraw the proceeds.

[48] Above, § 13.6(ii)(a).

[49] *Pitham and Hehl* (1976) 65 Cr App R 45; *Smythe* (1980) 72 Cr App R 8; *Gregory* (1981) 77 Cr App R 41.

[50] *Carr & Wilson* (1882) 10 QBD 76 (bonds stolen from an English ship moored in Holland, thief and circumstances of the theft unknown). In *Fuschillo* [1940] 2 All ER 489, D was charged with receiving a vast quantity of sugar, although it was not proven who had stolen it or from whom it was stolen. The Court of Criminal Appeal applied *dicta* in *Sbarra* (1918) 13 Cr App R 118, 120 to the effect that "the circumstances in which a defendant receives goods may of themselves prove that the goods were stolen, and further may prove that he knew it at the time when he received them. It is not a rule of law that there must be other evidence of the theft."

[51] *Close* [1977] Crim LR 107. For criticism of that decision on its particular facts, see Smith, *Property Offences* (1994) §§ 30-08, 30-09.

[52] *Cording* [1983] Crim LR 175; cf. *Creamer* [1919] 1 KB 564.

[53] Cf. *Farrell* [1975] 2 NZLR 753, in which the person from whom H received a stolen cheque was acquitted of theft on the ground of insanity. Consequently, the Court held, the evidence against H lacked an essential ingredient of the receiving charge, namely that the cheque was "stolen" within the meaning of the criminal law.

[54] [1951] 2 All ER 645.

In cases of this sort, the defendants may still be convicted of an attempt to handle sto-len goods,[55] at least where they are unaware of the circumstances exculpating the original "thief". More straightforwardly, as the Court pointed out in *Walters* v. *Lunt*, their subse-quent dealing with the tricycle would itself have been larceny, and would now be theft under section 1.

(c) Proceeds

The handler need not handle the whole of the thing stolen. It is sufficient, for example, that D receives parts of a car which has been stolen (e.g. the wheels or radio), or parts of a stolen stereo system, such as the tape deck or amplifier. Furthermore, the property need not be in the same state or condition as it was when stolen. A stolen car can be received even though substantially damaged in an accident before it arrives in D's hands. Similarly, section 22 would apply to the handling of mutton from a sheep that was alive when stolen.[56]

These are examples where the identity of the stolen property is unchanged in the hands of the handler, even though its character may have partially altered. What about changes of identity? At common law, the thing received had to be the actual thing that was first stolen, not its proceeds or a substitute.[57] In this form, the law was rather too generous to those involved in laundering the proceeds of theft, since it conferred an immunity from prosecu-tion upon subsequent participants in the laundering "chain", once the original item was exchanged.[58] That immunity is now overridden by section 24(2), which extends the scope of stolen goods to include:

(a)   any other goods which directly or indirectly represent or have at any time represented the stolen goods in the hands of the thief as being the proceeds of any disposal or realisation of the whole or part of the goods stolen or of goods so representing the stolen goods; and

(b)   any other goods which directly or indirectly represent or have at any time represented the stolen goods in the hands of a handler of the stolen goods or any part of them as being the proceeds of any disposal or realisation of the whole or part of the stolen goods handled by him or of goods so representing them.

The upshot of this rather tortuous prose is that if a thief or handler exchanges stolen goods for other goods, the other goods are deemed also to be stolen.[59] But if an innocent person, into whose hands stolen goods fall, exchanges those stolen goods for other goods, the other goods she receives are not deemed stolen. For example:

> D steals a television set. She fences it to H in exchange for a video recorder. H knows the set is stolen. In turn, H sells it at a car boot sale to T for £30. T is an innocent buyer. Later, T swaps the television with his neighbour for a lawnmower.

The television is stolen property throughout this example. The video recorder becomes sto-len property when D receives it in exchange for the television. The £30 also becomes stolen

---

[55]   Cf. *Toye* [1984] Crim LR 555.

[56]   Cf. *Cowell and Green* (1796) 2 East PC 617.

[57]   *Walkley* (1829) 4 C & P 133, 172 ER 640.

[58]   It appears that the civil law is in the process of filling this lacuna. Common law tracing now allows P to claim the proceeds of an unauthorised exchange-transaction: see *Trustee of the Property of FC Jones and Sons* v. *Jones* [1997] Ch 159; *Foskett* v. *McKeown* [2001] AC 102. On this analysis, the victim of a theft may acquire title in the exchange proceeds, and subsequent handlers may be guilty of theft.

[59]   *Forsyth* [1997] 2 Cr App R 299. See especially the commentaries at [1997] Crim LR 589 and 755.

when H receives it from T. The lawnmower, however, never becomes stolen property, since it was received only by T, who was innocent and neither a thief nor a handler.

(d) Goods which are no longer stolen

Goods are no longer stolen, and cannot be handled, once they re-enter into the possession of the legal owner or a person authorised by the owner to possess them. By section 24(3), this may occur in two ways:

> But no goods shall be regarded as having continued to be stolen goods after they have been restored to the person from whom they were stolen or to other lawful possession or custody, or after that person and any other person claiming through him have otherwise ceased as regards those goods to have any right to restitution in respect of the theft.

The first way in which goods become not stolen, then, is if they are restored to the original owner or to an authorised possessor. Suppose, for example, that the police recover stolen goods but then, with the consent of the owner, return them to the location where they were discovered in order to trap a would-be receiver. In that case, the subsequent purchaser cannot be convicted of handling.[60] However, she would remain guilty of attempting to handle the goods,[61] and would normally also commit a fresh theft.[62]

Whether goods have been reduced into possession is a question of fact, and turns on the intention of the possessor. In *A-G's Reference (No. 1 of 1974),*[63] a policeman spotted a van containing packages of new clothing which he (rightly) suspected were stolen. He immobilised the vehicle by removing its rotor arm, and kept observation. The defendant later got into the van and attempted to start it, whereupon he was questioned by the policeman. After offering an implausible explanation for the packages, the defendant was arrested. At issue both during trial and on appeal was whether the policeman had taken possession of the clothing or whether he was merely watching it with a view to catching the handler. In the judgment of the Court of Appeal:[64]

> "it depended primarily on the intentions of the police officer. If the police officer seeing these goods in the back of the car had made up his mind that he would take them into custody, that he would reduce them into his possession or control, take charge of them so that they could not be removed and so that he would have the disposal of them, then it would be a perfectly proper conclusion to say that he had taken possession of the goods. On the other hand, if the truth of the matter is that he was of an entirely open mind at that stage as to whether the goods were to be seized or not and was of an entirely open mind as to whether he should take possession of them or not, but merely stood by so that when the driver of the car appeared he could ask certain questions of that driver as to the nature of the goods and why they were there, then there is no reason whatever to suggest that he had taken the goods into his possession or control."

---

[60] *A-G's Reference (No. 1 of 1974)* [1974] QB 744. Cf. *Dolan* (1855) Dears 436, 169 ER 794; *Schmidt* (1866) LR 1 CCR 15; *Hancock* (1878) 14 Cox CC 119. For discussion, see Blakey and Goldsmith, "Criminal Redistribution of Stolen Property: The Need for Reform" (1976) 74 *Mich LR* 1512, 1552ff.

[61] Cf. Criminal Attempts Act 1981, s. 1(2)(3); above, § 9.5(iii).

[62] *Greater Manchester Metropolitan Police Commissioner* v. *Streeter* (1980) 71 Cr App R 113, 119.

[63] [1974] QB 744.

[64] [1974] QB 744, 753.

The rule, then, is analogous to that governing the possession of abandoned goods:[65] a person takes possession if he intentionally exercises control over the goods. In principle, merely standing by is not sufficient. However, the decision is one for the jury on the facts of each case. Consequently, the Court concluded:[66]

> "that the trial judge was wrong in withdrawing the issue from the jury. As a matter of law he was not entitled to conclude from the facts … that these goods were reduced into the possession of the police officer. What he should have done in our opinion would have been to have left that issue to the jury for decision, directing the jury that they should find that the prosecution case was without substance if they thought that the police officer had assumed control of the goods as such and reduced them into his possession. Whereas on the other hand, they should have found the case proved, assuming that they were satisfied about its other elements, if they were of the opinion that the police officer in removing the rotor arm and standing by and watching was doing no more than ensure that the driver should not get away without interrogation and was not at that stage seeking to assume possession of the goods as such at all."

Secondly, goods may cease to be stolen if a third party acquires indefeasible legal ownership of them, usually by purchasing them in good faith. Normally in such cases the rule *nemo dat quod non habet* will prevent other persons from acquiring ownership, since at law a person cannot transfer to another any better title to goods than she has herself.[67] However, there are some exceptions to this, enacted by statutes such as the Sale of Goods Act 1979.[68] Alternatively, where the goods are obtained by blackmail or fraud, the transaction is likely to be voidable rather than void, in which case they will cease to be stolen should the original owner elect to affirm the transaction (e.g. through ratifying the contract by which the goods were obtained), even without the intervention of a *bona fide* purchaser for value.

(iii) Knowledge or belief

At the time the actus reus occurs (i.e. the goods are received or otherwise handled), the defendant must *know or believe that the goods are stolen*. It is not necessary that the defendant should know the particular way in which the goods were obtained,[69] or their owner,[70] or even the specific nature of the goods,[71] provided she knows they were obtained by theft, fraud, or blackmail.

The meaning of "knowledge" was considered in § 5.4, where it was said that knowing means "knowing, or correctly believing".[72] In essence, this requires that the defendant must accept, or assume, and have no serious doubt, that the goods he handles were obtained by crime. In particular, it is not enough that the defendant thinks the goods are "probably"

---

[65] Above, § 13.4(v)(a).
[66] [1974] QB 744, 754.
[67] Sale of Goods Act 1979, s. 21.
[68] E.g., if the rogue has obtained a voidable title to the goods that has not been avoided at time of on-sale (Sale of Goods Act 1979, s. 23), or is a mercantile agent with authorised possession (Factors Act 1889, s. 2).
[69] Cf. *DPP* v. *Nieser* [1959] 1 QB 254.
[70] *Fuschillo* [1940] 2 All ER 489.
[71] *McCullum* (1973) 57 Cr App R 645.
[72] See also Griew, "Consistency, Communication and Codification" in Glazebrook (ed.), *Reshaping the Criminal Law* (1978) 57.

stolen.[73] Neither is it sufficient that D *suspects* the goods are stolen: " 'Knowing' is not the equivalent of 'having a pretty good idea'".[74] In *Griffiths*,[75] the trial judge instructed the jury that it would be sufficient if the defendant "suspects that goods are stolen and then deliberately shuts his eyes to the circumstances". The Court of Appeal held that this was a misdirection. (However, as we shall note in § 14.2(ii)(b), suspicion may warrant a conviction for a laundering offence.)

For practical purposes, knowledge and belief are coextensive.[76] The case law has sometimes sought to draw minor distinctions between these two cognitive states. According to the 1859 case of *White*:[77]

> "The knowledge charged in this indictment need not be such *knowledge* as would be acquired if the prisoner had actually seen the lead stolen; it is sufficient if you think the circumstances were such, accompanying the transaction, as to make the prisoner *believe* that it had been stolen."

Similarly, in *Hall*,[78]

> "A man may be said to know that goods are stolen when he is told by someone with first-hand knowledge (someone such as the thief or the burglar) that such is the case. Belief, of course, is something short of knowledge. It may be said to be the state of mind of a person who says to himself: 'I cannot say I know for certain that these goods are stolen but there can be no other reasonable conclusion in the light of all the circumstances, in the light of all that I have heard and seen.'"

But these distinctions, which merely concern the *basis* of one's knowledge or belief, are without great value. It is generally impossible to know anything with utter certainty: even the evidence of one's own eyes may occasionally be doubted. What counts is whether the defendant has a settled belief, with no serious doubt, that the goods are stolen. Consistent with this view, the better guidance is that set out by the Court of Appeal in *Moys*:[79]

> "The question is a subjective one and it must be proved that the defendant was aware of the theft or that he believed the goods to be stolen. Suspicion that they were stolen, even coupled with the fact that he shut his eyes to the circumstances, is not enough, although those matters may be taken into account by a jury when deciding whether or not the necessary knowledge or belief existed."

(a) Wilful blindness

What, however, if H suspects the goods are stolen and deliberately refrains from enquiring any further into the question? In this situation H's mental state may be described as one of

---

[73] *Reader* (1977) 66 Cr App R 33, 36 (CA).

[74] *Woods* [1969] 1 QB 447, 452. Although a pre-Act decision, this still represents the law: *Grainge* [1974] 1 All ER 928; *Reader* (1977) 66 Cr App R 33. A helpful review of the law is found in *Forsyth* [1997] 2 Cr App R 299, 317–21. More recently, the distinction between suspicion and knowledge or belief has been affirmed by the House of Lords in the context of conspiracy: *Saik* [2007] 1 AC 18, at para 32 (Lord Nicholls), para 78 (Lord Hope), and para 120 (Lord Brown).

[75] (1974) 60 Cr App R 14, 16. Taken as a whole, however, the judge's direction was thought to be adequate, and the defendant's appeal was dismissed.

[76] Subject to the point that "knowledge" implies a *correct* belief: above, § 5.1(v).

[77] (1859) 1 F&F 665, 175 ER 898 (Bramwell B, emphasis added).

[78] (1985) 81 Cr App R 260, 264.

[79] (1984) 79 Cr App R 72, 76 (Lord Lane CJ); preferred in *Forsyth* (1997) 2 Cr App R 299, 321 as guidance that is "clear and more readily understandable by a jury and avoids the potential for confusion inherent in a *Hall* direction".

wilful blindness. Does H's failure to make that further enquiry itself establish the requisite knowledge or belief? As was stated in § 5.4(i), generally the answer is no. That wilful blindness is not automatically deemed to be knowledge[80] for the purposes of handling was made clear by the Court of Appeal in *Griffiths*:[81]

> "To direct the jury that the offence is committed if the defendant, suspecting that the goods were stolen, deliberately shut his eyes to the circumstances as an alternative to knowing or believing the goods were stolen is a misdirection. To direct the jury that, in common sense and in law, they may find that the defendant knew or believed the goods to be stolen because he deliberately closed his eyes to the circumstances is a perfectly proper direction."

Knowledge and belief are subjective phenomena. They cannot be established by showing that the defendant *ought* to have realised the goods were stolen.[82] However, as the closing sentence of the quotation makes clear, the obviousness of the truth may be an *evidential* factor, supporting the inference that in fact H knew he was handling stolen property. A failure by H to make some enquiry may, in certain circumstances, be taken into account in considering whether the prosecution has proved beyond reasonable doubt the existence of knowledge or belief. A jury may legitimately come to the conclusion that the defendant abstained from enquiry because he knew already what the answer was going to be, and thence infer that his omission to enquire stemmed not from mere suspicion, but from his positive belief that the goods had been stolen.[83]

Nonetheless, there is still room for the wilful blindness doctrine, as the basis for deeming in law a belief that goods were stolen. It operates where H believes the goods are almost certainly stolen, and where any slight doubt on the matter could easily be resolved by his further enquiry. If H deliberately refrains from making that enquiry, especially if he does so in order later to be able to deny knowledge, he is to be attributed with knowledge. However, the scope of the doctrine is very narrow.[84] Its ambit is discussed in more detail above, in § 5.4(i).

(b) Recklessness: a case for law reform?

Apparently, the approach of the courts to wilful blindness is contrary to the intention of those who drafted the Act. According to the Criminal Law Revision Committee, commenting on the law prior to the 1968 Act:[85]

> "The man who buys the goods at a ridiculously low price from an unknown seller whom he meets in a public house may not *know* that the goods were stolen, and he may take the precaution of asking no questions. Yet it may be clear on the evidence that he *believes* that the goods were stolen. In such cases the prosecution may fail (rightly, as the [pre-Act] law now stands) for want ... of guilty knowledge."

---

[80] As might be suggested by somewhat ambiguous *dicta* in *Atwal* v. *Massey* [1971] 3 All ER 881 (DC).

[81] (1974) 60 Cr App R 14, 18; cf. *Saik* [2007] 1 AC 18, at [62] (Lord Hope). Similarly, in *Smith* (1976) 64 Cr App R 217, 220, Lawton LJ stated: "We are satisfied that except in most unusual cases juries are capable of understanding what is meant by the word 'believing'.... Phrases such as 'suspecting that the goods were stolen and then wilfully shutting one's eyes to the obvious' should not be used as a definition of 'believing.'"

[82] *Atwal* v. *Massey* [1971] 3 All ER 881, 882; *Bellenie* [1980] Crim LR 437; *Havard* (1914) 11 Cr App R 2.

[83] Cf. *Crooks* [1981] 2 NZLR 53, 59 (NZCA), which contains a useful discussion of knowledge and belief.

[84] Wilful blindness is discussed further in § 5.4(i).

[85] *Theft and Related Offences* Cmnd. 2977 (1966) para. 134. But see the important gloss by Williams, "Handling, Theft and the Purchaser Who Takes a Chance" [1985] *Crim LR* 432, 433–4.

By inserting "or believing" into the mens rea requirement for handling, the Committee seemingly sought to extend the law to capture such cases. As it turns out, they have not done so. That should not surprise, because the meaning of "believe" is too close to that of "know" to mark a meaningful extension. It certainly does *not* mean "suspect". What the Committee might have been better to do was to signal its intention more clearly by expressly widening the mens rea requirement into the realm of recklessness: e.g. by stipulating "believing the goods are probably stolen" or "believing the goods may be stolen" to be sufficient mens rea.

It is a difficult question whether the law ought to have been extended into recklessness, or whether it is right to insist on knowledge or belief. On the one hand, it is difficult to prove the mens rea of handling, hence the perceived need for a recent possession doctrine and statutory evidential aids;[86] fewer dishonest handlers would escape conviction if recklessness were sufficient. The concern about convicting for mere suspicion could be allayed by requiring that H believe the goods are *probably* stolen (i.e. more probably stolen than not).[87] Moreover, dishonestly buying goods which are (correctly) thought by H to be probably stolen satisfies the twin criteria of harm and culpability. It is harmful to the original owner and helpful to the thief, and it is culpable. Hence, it may be thought, there are strong reasons in favour of criminalisation.

Against this argument, it is improbable that the change would much affect the position of professional fences, who are likely to know rather than suspect the provenance of the goods. Thus its greatest value would be against the casual or occasional receiver—the purchaser at a car boot sale, or the pawnbroker, who suspects but is uncertain whether the goods are stolen, and would not buy or accept the goods if she knew the truth. These forms of legitimate commercial activity might be stifled if the purchaser or broker were required consciously to risk criminal conviction by her activity.[88]

On balance, we incline toward the former argument. The risk of over-extending the criminal law is safeguarded against by the further mens rea requirement that the defendant must not only be reckless but also *dishonest*.[89] The pawnbroker who suspects goods are stolen but has no way of knowing the truth should not (and probably would not, by a jury) be accounted dishonest, especially if his acceptance of the goods is consistent with standard practice in the industry.[90] By insisting on knowledge or a firm belief, the law condones rather than stigmatises the "fallen off the back of a lorry" culture in our society—a culture, it must be said, that is overdue for eradication. (But as we shall explain below in § 14.2, some of those who escape criminal liability for handling because they merely suspect the goods are stolen will now commit one of the offences of money-laundering.)

---

[86] Below, § 14.1(iii)(c), (d).

[87] Spencer, "Handling, Theft and the *Mala Fide* Purchaser" [1985] *Crim LR* 92, 95–6. Blakey and Goldsmith, "Criminal Redistribution of Stolen Property: The Need for Reform" (1976) 74 *Mich LR* 1512, 1560 advocate a standard of awareness of "a substantial risk" that the property was stolen.

[88] See Williams, "Handling, Theft and the Purchaser Who Takes a Chance" [1985] *Crim LR* 432, 435–6.

[89] Spencer, "Handling and Taking Risks—A Reply to Professor Williams" [1985] *Crim LR* 440. See below, § 14.1(iv).

[90] On the relevance of standard practices, see Smith, *Property Offences* (1994) § 7-84.

(c) Evidence of mens rea: the doctrine of recent possession

Proof of mens rea in handling can be difficult. The prosecution may be able to establish that H had possession of stolen goods, but unless it can give some account of how those goods were acquired, or of what H intended to do with the goods, it may be very difficult to prove that H knew or believed the goods were stolen. To meet this challenge, judges have evolved a device of prima facie inference, from which proof of possession can, under certain circumstances, support an inference of criminality. This is known as the doctrine of recent possession.

The "doctrine" of recent possession, which originates in the common law, is a common-sense rule that the proof of possession by D of property recently stolen is sufficient evidence to justify a finding that D is either the thief or a dishonest receiver, in the absence of a credible explanation of how D came by the property.[91] It has been described as

> "a convenient way of referring compendiously to the inferences of fact which, in the absence of any satisfactory explanation by the accused, may be drawn as a matter of common sense from other facts, including, in particular, the fact that the accused has in his possession property which it is proved had been unlawfully obtained shortly before he was found to be in possession of it."[92]

Although in some jurisdictions it has been held that the rule is limited to theft, its application to receiving may be justified on the pragmatic ground that criminal receivers can rarely be detected in the act of receiving, so that direct evidence is rarely available.[93]

Before the inference from recent possession can be invoked, the prosecution must prove the relevant property was stolen, and that it was stolen recently. How recent is "recent"? It depends on the facts, and in particular on the nature of the property. Possession of a stolen £20 pound note would ordinarily be unlikely to support an inference of theft or handling after more than a few days; 11 months was too long for stereo equipment in *Simmons*;[94] but the doctrine was applicable after four months in the case of a corporate bond.[95]

The classic direction is found in *Aves*:[96]

> "Where the only evidence is that an accused person is in possession of property recently stolen, a jury may infer guilty knowledge (a) if he offers no explanation to account for his possession, or (b) if the jury are satisfied that the explanation he does offer is untrue. If, however, the explanation offered is one which leaves the jury in doubt whether he knew the property was stolen, they should be told that the case has not been proved, and, therefore, the verdict should be Not Guilty."

Thus stated, it is clear that recent possession is simply a matter of ordinary evidential inference from circumstances. The onus of proving both actus reus and mens rea remains on the prosecution. Its dependence upon the fact of possession makes the evidential inference of limited value against sophisticated professional fences, who are unlikely to take actual

---

[91] Cf. *Smythe* (1980) 72 Cr App R 8, 11.

[92] *DPP v. Nieser* [1959] 1 QB 254, 266. See also *Raviraj* (1986) 85 Cr App R 93 (CA): the doctrine is only an extension of a general proposition that guilt may be inferred from unreasonable behaviour by the accused in response to his being confronted with facts which prima facie suggest his guilt.

[93] Cf. Hall, *Theft, Law and Society* (2nd ed., 1952) 175.

[94] [1986] Crim LR 397.

[95] *Livock* (1914) 10 Cr App R 264.

[96] [1950] 2 All ER 330. See also *Ketteringham* (1926) 19 Cr App R 159; *Hepworth* [1955] 2 QB 600; *Cash* [1985] QB 801, 804 (CA).

possession of the goods for themselves; or who, if they do take possession, are likely to take the precaution of ensuring they can offer a plausible explanation, e.g. by integrating possession of stolen goods with their other, legitimate, business activities.[97]

(d) Proof of guilty knowledge under section 27(3)

In addition to the doctrine of recent possession, the prosecutor has long-standing statutory aid. Section 27(3) provides that, in proving knowledge or belief on a charge of handling, the prosecution may give as evidence (a) the fact that other stolen property was handled by D or in D's possession at some time during the 12 months preceding the current offence charged (i.e. prior possession), or (b) the fact that D was convicted of theft or handling within the period of five years before being charged with the current offence (i.e. previous convictions).[98]

Formerly these provisions stood out as an uncomfortable exception to the general rule that rendered inadmissible a defendant's previous misdeeds as evidence of his present guilt, and the provisions were criticised on that account. The general rule was radically amended by the Criminal Justice Act 2003, which now makes such evidence admissible in any case where it is logically relevant to a matter in dispute between the prosecution and the defence.[99] In the light of this, section 27(3) is now redundant.[100]

(iv) Dishonesty

It is an essential element of the offence that the goods have been handled dishonestly. Suppose, for instance, that H knowingly takes possession of stolen goods and passes them to someone else. H may well have done the actus reus of handling (a disposal for the benefit of another person). But if H is a police officer, recovering the goods on behalf of the owner, he is not guilty of an offence—because his actions are most unlikely to be regarded by the jury as dishonest. This analysis is illustrated by the pre-Act case of *Matthews*,[101] in which the Court of Criminal Appeal held that a person who has received stolen property intending to hand it over at once to the police or the true owner could not be guilty of receiving stolen property.

The test of dishonesty in handling is the same as that in theft, and the leading case in both contexts is *Ghosh*.[102] Note, however, that the specific defences provided by section 2 of the Theft Act 1968 apply only in the context of theft and not to handling. Where such exculpatory circumstances exist on a handling charge, they operate simply as factors to be considered when determining dishonesty on general principles.[103] The issue is one of fact, and is for the jury to decide.

---

[97] See Klockars, *The Professional Fence* (1974) 80–93; Hall, *Theft, Law and Society* (2nd ed., 1952) 189–90.

[98] These rules date from the Prevention of Crime Act 1871, which replaced even more stringent provisions enacted two years earlier by s. 11 of the Habitual Criminals Act 1869.

[99] Criminal Justice Act 2003, s. 101(1)(d). On the 2003 reform, see Spencer, *Evidence of Bad Character* (3rd ed., 2016).

[100] Indeed, in the Report from which the 2003 reform derives, the Law Commission recommended their repeal: Law Com. No. 273, *Evidence of Bad Character in Criminal Proceedings* Cm. 5257 (2001) para. 11.55.

[101] [1950] 1 All ER 137, 138.

[102] [1982] QB 1053; cf. *Brennen* [1990] Crim LR 118.

[103] See above, § 13.8.

(v) Concurrence of actus reus and mens rea

As we saw in § 5.8, it is a fundamental principle of criminal law that the actus reus and mens rea must coincide: there must be a moment in time at which all the elements of the offence are simultaneously made out. In the context of handling, this means that knowledge acquired, or dishonesty formed, after the actus reus is insufficient.

Suppose D takes possession of goods innocently and then learns they are stolen, or receives them intending to hand the goods over to the police (so without dishonesty) and later changes her mind. At this point she cannot commit handling by receiving. Once possession is taken, it cannot be retaken; the actus reus of receiving is completed and is not a continuing act.[104] Other forms of handling, however, can be repeated or continuing.[105] Thus D would become guilty of handling if, having become dishonest, she then disposed of the goods for the benefit of another person. But if D merely retains the goods for her own benefit she does not handle. The proper charge would be theft.[106]

(vi) Handling versus theft

Even though handling must occur after the original theft is completed,[107] virtually all handlings are themselves thefts.[108] Hence, in proving handling, the prosecution generally proves two different offences constituted by the same action. In principle, there is no objection to this, since not all thefts are handlings and the two offences have different maximum penalties. Moreover, they capture quite different modes of wrongdoing to another person's property interests. Where the facts establish that D received from a thief, therefore, the prosecution should charge handling rather than theft.

However, sometimes the facts may be uncertain, so that it is unclear which of the two offences has been committed by D. This often arises when D is found in possession of stolen goods and the prosecution cannot establish how D acquired possession of the goods (e.g. whether D stole them herself, or received them from the original thief). The doctrine of recent possession,[109] which often applies to such cases, supports a conviction for either theft or handling, without preference. Consequently, the jury or magistrates may be sure beyond reasonable doubt that D is either thief or handler, without knowing which of the two.

In such cases, it is permissible for the prosecution to charge D with alternative counts of theft[110] and handling. In *Stapylton* v. *O'Callaghan*,[111] the Divisional Court, dealing with an appeal by way of case stated from a magistrates' court, said that as D's handling (if that is what he had really done) would also have amounted to a theft, the bench should have convicted D of theft. In *Shelton*,[112] where a similar situation had arisen in the Crown Court, the Court of Appeal approved a direction by the judge which encouraged the jury to take a

---

[104] *Johnson* (1911) 6 Cr App R 218; *Matthews* [1950] 1 All ER 137, 138; *Smythe* (1980) 72 Cr App R 8, 13.

[105] Cf. *Pitchley* (1973) 57 Cr App R 30; *Smythe* (1980) 72 Cr App R 8, 13.

[106] *Matthews* [1950] 1 All ER 137, 138.

[107] Cf. s. 22(1): "otherwise than in the course of stealing".

[108] See above, § 14.1(i)(f).

[109] Above, § 14.1(iii)(c).

[110] Or robbery or burglary, as the case may be, depending on the circumstances of the original theft.

[111] [1973] 2 All ER 782.

[112] (1986) 83 Cr App R 384.

similar approach.[113] Given that, of the two possible offences, it is theft that carries the lower maximum penalty, the result is not unjust to the defendant.

§ 14.2 Laundering

Sections 327, 328, and 329 of the Proceeds of Crime Act (POCA) 2002 create three related offences of laundering "criminal property".[114] By section 327 it is an offence to conceal, disguise, convert, transfer or remove criminal property. By section 328 a person "commits an offence if he enters into or becomes concerned in an arrangement which he knows or suspects facilitates (by whatever means) the acquisition, retention, use or control of criminal property by or on behalf of another person". And by section 329 a person commits an offence if he acquires criminal property, uses it, or has it in possession.

These offences are aimed at those who help major criminals disguise the proceeds of large-scale criminal activities: for example, the property developer whose activities are financed by a drug baron; the people trafficker who is rewarded for his contribution by shares in the property company, on which large dividends are later paid; and where the "criminal property" which everyone had in mind was money, in large quantities. However, the offences themselves are not so limited, and in consequence duplicate to a very large extent the offence of handling stolen goods—and indeed some other criminal offences too.

(i) Criminal property

A central requirement in all three of these offences is that D's behaviour should relate to "criminal property". This is defined, in a back-to-front way, by section 340(2), which is as follows:

(2) Criminal conduct is conduct which—
(a) constitutes an offence in any part of the United Kingdom, or
(b) would constitute an offence in any part of the United Kingdom if it occurred there.
(3) Property is criminal property if—
(a) it constitutes a person's benefit from criminal conduct or it represents such a benefit (in whole or part and whether directly or indirectly), and
(b) the alleged offender knows or suspects that it constitutes or represents such a benefit.
(4) It is immaterial—
(a) who carried out the conduct;
(b) who benefited from it;
(c) whether the conduct occurred before or after the passing of this Act.
(5) A person benefits from conduct if he obtains property as a result of or in connection with the conduct.[115]

---

[113] The Court provided that, "in the unlikely event of the jury not agreeing amongst themselves whether theft or handling has been proved, they should be discharged".

[114] These offences replace with one single set of offences a messy situation under the previous law, which deployed two sets of offences, one under the Criminal Justice Act 1988 and another under the Drug Trafficking Act 1994.

[115] The definition is continued in subsections (6)–(10); subsection (9) provides that "property" includes all property, real or personal, tangible or intangible.

This definition is extremely wide. If taken at face value, it would make D potentially guilty of money-laundering by reason of the simple fact of committing a crime from which he derived a financial benefit: including theft, or fraud, obviously—and less obviously, tax evasion, drug dealing, and a range of other acquisitive offences. Plainly, such duplication would be undesirable and fortunately the courts have avoided it (at least to some extent) by interpreting section 340 as requiring the benefit to arise from some crime *other* than any crime which D incidentally commits when he carries out the act(s) in relation to the property that constitute the offence under sections 327, 328, or 329.

In *Geary*,[116] D was prosecuted under section 328 in respect of an "arrangement" to facilitate another person to acquire, retain, or control criminal property. The prosecution case was that D had received a large sum of money which X had earlier obtained by fraud. D's story, however, was that X had given him the money to look after in order to hide it from X's wife, whom X was divorcing in proceedings in which he wanted to present himself to the court as poorer than he really was. If this was true, then D and X were guilty of a conspiracy to pervert the course of justice. But this, said the Court of Appeal, was not enough to make D guilty of the section 328 offence because, even if the money acquired the status of "criminal property" when it was handed over in pursuit of the conspiracy, it did not have that status before it was handed over. In so holding, the Court followed the same line as had been taken, in the context of a prosecution under section 327, in the earlier case of *Loizou*.[117] And in *Akhtar*,[118] the Court of Appeal later said, as might be expected, that the same limitation applied to "criminal property" in the context of all three of the laundering offences.

This limit on the scope of criminal property is sometimes expressed by saying that the subject-matter of the laundering offence must represent the benefit of a crime committed *before* the conduct by D in respect of which he stands accused of money-laundering. But although the crime which turns the subject-matter of the offence into "criminal property" will usually take place before the acts alleged as laundering, it need not do so, and in some cases it will be committed at the same time. Believing that the "predicate offence" (as it is usually called) must be committed earlier in time, in *GH*[119] the Court of Appeal held that D was not guilty of money-laundering by "arranging" (under section 328) when he made his bank account available to B, who made a dishonest living by selling non-existent motor-insurance to credulous motorists, as a receptacle into which the victims of B's frauds could be directed to pay their premiums. But in the Supreme Court this ruling was reversed. Distinguishing *Geary*, it said the issue was not whether the subject-matter of the laundering offence was somebody's benefit from a crime committed earlier in time, but whether it was somebody's benefit from a crime committed *independently* of the acts in respect of which D now stood accused of money-laundering. Here, D was accused of money-laundering by reason of the arrangement he had made with B to enable B to receive and store the money which B extracted from the victims of his frauds. And this money "became criminal property in the hands of B, not by reason of the arrangement made between B and [D] but by reason of the fact that it was obtained through fraud perpetrated on the victims."[120]

---

[116] [2010] EWCA Crim 1925, [2011] 1 Cr App R 8.
[117] [2004] EWCA Crim 1579, [2005] 2 Cr App R 37.
[118] [2011] EWCA Crim 146, [2011] 1 Cr App R 37.
[119] [2015] UKSC 24, [2015] 1 WLR 2126; on appeal from [2013] EWCA Crim 2237.
[120] The need for a distinct "predicate offence" appears to have been overlooked in *Ogden*: below, § 14.2(ii)(c).

If "criminal property" presupposes the existence of a separate "predicate offence", it does not presuppose the existence of a separate offender who committed it. Indeed, when defining "criminal property" section 340 expressly provides that it is immaterial "who carried out the [criminal] conduct" and "who benefited from it". It follows that, in principle, the criminal who committed the offences which gave rise to the existence of "criminal property" can then commit offences of money-laundering by reason of what he or she does with it thereafter. Thus a drug-dealer who by his illicit trade builds up a fortune commits an offence under section 327 if he hides it away somewhere, or uses it to buy a luxury apartment, or spirits it off to South America; and a person who steals a BMW commits a further offence under section 329 if he "uses" it by driving it around, or even if he merely keeps it to gloat over in the privacy of his garage.[121] In this respect, these two money-laundering offences differ significantly from the offence of handling, which, as we saw earlier, is carefully constructed to make it impossible for the original thief to commit an offence of handling by reason of what she does with the property afterwards. But if a second person is not required for the section 327 and 329 offences, a second person *is* required for the commission of an offence under section 328—the "arranging" offence—because this section specifically states that the arrangement must one which facilitates "the acquisition, retention, use or control of criminal property *by or on behalf of another person."*

Additionally, if "criminal property" presupposes the existence of a separate "predicate offence", there is no need, according to the case law, for the prosecution to identify it, or to show who committed it. In *Craig*,[122] the Court of Appeal held, in the context of a prosecution under section 329, that D's guilt can be established by circumstantial evidence suggesting that he has acquired or possessed "criminal property" the nature and source of which are not identified. In this case the prosecution produced evidence that D had "used quantities of cash, expensive motor vehicles and jet skis, which could not be justified on the wages that he had earned", and at a time when "his income was declared as nil". Taken with D's failure to provide any convincing explanation of where the money came from, this, said the prosecution, showed that he had been profiting from crime; but neither the prosecution nor the judge in his direction to the jury sought to identify the crimes or types of crime from which the profit came. On such evidence, said the Court of Appeal, the jury was entitled to convict D of money-laundering.[123] Although the decision was trenchantly criticised,[124] in the later case of *Anwoir* the Court of Appeal took the view that it was rightly decided:[125]

> "there are two ways in which the Crown can prove the property derives from crime, (a) by showing that it derives from conduct of a specific kind or kinds and that conduct of that kind or those kinds is unlawful, or (b) by evidence of the circumstances in which the property is handled which are such as to give rise to the irresistible inference that it can only be derived from crime."

So, to borrow the title of a chapter from Thackeray's *Vanity Fair*, a defendant is liable to be convicted of money-laundering on evidence that shows no more than that he is a person

---

[121] Conduct which would seem to be an offence under s. 329(c).

[122] [2007] EWCA Crim 2913.

[123] But the conviction was quashed on another ground—the judge's failure to put D's defence to the jury adequately.

[124] By Richardson, [2008] 7 *Criminal Law Week*, No. 5.

[125] [2008] EWCA Crim 1354, [2009] 1 WLR 980; Walters, "Prosecuting Money Launderers: Do the Prosecution Have to Prove the Predicate Offence?" [2009] *Crim LR* 571.

who apparently knows "how to live well on nothing a year". This is contentious, as the Court of Appeal itself recognised in *Anwoir*, where it certified a point public importance for the purpose of an appeal to the House of Lords; but leave to appeal was refused, and for now that is where the matter rests.[126]

(ii) The three offences: further details

(a) Actus reus

By section 327, an offence is committed where a person "(a) conceals criminal property, (b) disguises criminal property, (c) converts criminal property, (d) transfers criminal property", or "(e) removes criminal property from England and Wales or from Scotland or from Northern Ireland". The range of behaviour covered by these expressions, which are largely self-explanatory, is clearly very wide; and the case-law shows no inclination to narrow it. In *Fazal*,[127] the Court of Appeal held that a person is guilty of "converting" criminal property where he allowed another person the use of his bank account as a depositary for the proceeds of his crimes, even though he himself took no positive action in relation to the money. This conduct was, of course, more obviously covered by the section 328 offence of making an arrangement that facilitates another person's acquisition, retention, use, or control. But the Court said that the statutory provisions are not mutually exclusive.

By section 328, an offence is committed where a person "enters into or becomes concerned in an arrangement which he knows or suspects facilitates (by whatever means) the acquisition, retention, use or control of criminal property by or on behalf of another person". The key phrase here is "an arrangement". Though wide, its breadth is not infinite. Thus in *Dare v. CPS*,[128] the Administrative Court held that, although the offence would be committed by a potential purchaser who made an agreement with another person to buy a stolen car, it was not committed where the buyer and seller had only got as far as the preliminary discussions. However, if there is a firm agreement, there is no reason why the section 329 offence should not be committed where the arrangement relates to something which, though not yet "criminal property", will have become so by the time the arrangement is carried out: as where D makes a definite arrangement with X to buy a car (or a series of cars) which X has not yet stolen, but plans to steal to order; or where D agrees to allow X to use his bank account to store the proceeds of crimes yet to be committed.[129]

By section 329, an offence is committed where a person "(a) acquires criminal property, (b) uses criminal property", or "(c) has possession of criminal property".[130] These phrases, which once again are largely self-explanatory, also cover a wide range of behaviour. However, the section 329 offence differs from the previous two offences in one important

---

[126] See *Kuchadia* [2015] EWCA Crim 1252, [2015] 1 WLR 4895, and the vigorous criticism by Richardson, [2015] 34 *Criminal Law Week*, No. 6.

[127] [2009] EWCA Crim 1697, [2010] 1 WLR 694.

[128] [2012] EWHC 2074 (Admin), (2013) 177 JP 37.

[129] On this, see *Smith and Hogan*, 1138.

[130] In 1996, as part of the hurried legislative response to *Preddy* (see § 15.1 below), s. 24A was added to the Theft Act 1968 to create a new offence of "dishonestly retaining a wrongful credit". A "wrongful credit" is defined in s. 24(2A) to mean a credit which derives from theft, blackmail, fraud, or stolen goods. Though the offence is now largely duplicated by POCA s. 329, it remains in force.

respect, because it is subject to a specific defence which does not apply to the others. By section 329(2)(c), D avoids criminal liability under section 329 if "he acquired or used or had possession of the property for adequate consideration". In *Hogan v. DPP*,[131] the Court of Appeal held that what amounts to "adequate consideration" is ultimately a question of fact, and an issue on which D is entitled to the benefit of the doubt; and further, if D did acquire the property for adequate consideration, he is not guilty of the section 329 offence[132] even if he knew full well the property was stolen, and whether or not the court thinks he was dishonest.

For all three of these offences, however, D incurs no liability if any one of a list of other conditions is met. Thus D is exempt if, before he did the act, he made a "disclosure" to "a constable, a customs officer or a nominated officer",[133] or intended to do so and had a reasonable excuse for leaving it until afterwards, and in certain other more specific circumstances.[134]

(b) Mens rea

In the offence of handling, as we saw, the mens rea requirements are exacting; D must "know or believe" that the goods were stolen, and in addition his conduct must be "dishonest". For the money-laundering offences the mens rea requirement is much less exacting. For all three offences it is sufficient that D "knows or suspects" that the property is "criminal property".[135]

(c) The relationship between money-laundering and other property offences

The money-laundering offences are aimed at those who help major criminals disguise the proceeds of large-scale criminal activities. As was noted earlier, the "criminal property" which the lawmakers had in mind was money, in large quantities. However, the offences themselves are much broader than that. Most obviously, the "acquisition" offence created by section 329 clearly covers handling by receiving. Stolen goods fall within the definition of "criminal property" set out in section 340(3), and having received them D will "have possession" of them, and may have "acquired" them too. This will be so not only if the property in question is the proceeds of a major bank robbery, but equally if it is (say) a stolen CD player that D bought from a shady character at a car boot sale or in the local pub.

From the prosecutor's point of view, a charge of laundering under section 329 of POCA 2002 has a number of practical advantages over a charge of handling under section 22 of the Theft Act 1968. First, whereas handling only applies where the goods were obtained by theft, blackmail, or fraud,[136] "criminal property" for the purpose of the laundering offences means property obtained by any crime at all. Secondly, as we saw in § 14.1(iii), the mens rea

---

[131] [2007] EWHC 978 (Admin), [2007] 1 WLR 2944.

[132] Though possibly to charges under ss. 327 or 328.

[133] Section 338.

[134] Other conditions include the fact that the property was obtained abroad by conduct which was legal there and, where the person who received or otherwise dealt with the property was a bank or similar, that the property was a sum of money less than £250.

[135] By virtue of s. 340(2)(b), which (rather oddly) incorporates this requirement into the definition of "criminal property", and again, and more specifically, by virtue of s. 328(1) in relation to that offence.

[136] Theft Act 1968, s. 24(4).

requirement for handling is exacting, because D is guilty of handling only where he acted "knowing or believing" that the goods were stolen. For the section 329 offence, by contrast, it is enough that D merely *suspected* that the goods were "criminal property".[137] Thirdly, an ingredient in the offence of handling is "dishonesty", which means that D is not guilty if the tribunal of fact accepts that his behaviour was in accordance with accepted standards in society or, failing that, that D genuinely believed it was.[138] There is no such let-out for D where he is charged under section 329. Lastly, the section 329 offence can be established by evidence that is more general and less specific than the evidence needed to support a charge of handling. To convict D of handling, the prosecution must produce evidence to show that, acting with the necessary mens rea, D received or otherwise dealt with an item of stolen property that is identified—which, as we have seen, is not necessary for money-laundering.

As against this, the section 329 offence has two disadvantages for prosecutors compared with handling: D is exempt from liability if, first, D acquired or used or had possession of the property for adequate consideration;[139] and secondly, and much less plausibly, if D had notified the relevant authorities as to what was going on. Despite this, prosecutors are understandably tempted to use section 329 in cases where, on the face of it, handling would be the obvious charge. In *Wilkinson* v. *DPP*,[140] for example, a defendant was found riding a stolen mini motorcycle in circumstances suggesting he had either stolen it himself or acquired it from the person who had done so. For this he was prosecuted under section 329 rather than for theft, burglary, or handling. Thinking the choice of charge was most unfair, he sought to challenge the decision of the Crown Prosecution Service to prosecute him for this offence by way of judicial review. The Divisional Court expressed disquiet about the choice of charge, but the application for judicial review was rejected. Similar disquiet was expressed by the Court of Appeal in the later and almost identical case of *Rose*.[141] But expressions of judicial disquiet such as these do not, of course, curtail the scope of the offence. At present the only thing that keeps section 329 of POCA 2002 in check is the sense of proportion and fair play within the CPS,[142] which, as cases such as *Rose* and *ex parte Wilkinson* show, occasionally deserts them.[143] This overlap would not exist if "criminal property" in section 340(2) were read in a restrictive sense, so that the phrase "constitutes a person's benefit from criminal conduct" means "constitutes a person's benefit from *another*

---

[137] POCA 2002, s. 340(3)(b). On an expansive reading of s. 328 (though not ss. 327 or 329), D could commit an offence of money laundering by "arranging" if he wrongly *suspects* that the property which is the subject-matter of the arrangement is "criminal property" (where in fact it is not). But it seems unlikely that the courts would so construe it—both on grounds of principle, and in the light of the decision in *Montila* [2004] UKHL 50, [2004] 1 WLR 3141, where the House of Lords refused to give such an interpretation to a similar offence under the previous law.

[138] Above, § 14.1(iv).

[139] Section 329(2)(c).

[140] [2006] EWHC 3012 (Admin); noted by Rule, [2007] 1 *Archbold News*, 5.

[141] [2008] EWCA Crim 239, [2008] 1 WLR 2113.

[142] The CPS's official Legal Guidance in respect of money-laundering contains the following: "A careful judgement will need to be made as to whether it is in the public interest to proceed with the money laundering offence in the event of a plea to the underlying criminality by a defendant who is also indicted for laundering his *own* proceeds. The prosecutor should take into account whether the laundering activity involves such a significant attempt to conceal ill-gotten gains that a court may consider a consecutive sentence." (Emphasis in original.) This document is published on the CPS website at http://www.cps.gov.uk/legal/p_to_r/proceeds_of_crime_money_laundering/#

[143] In *Rose* [2008] EWCA Crim 239, [2008] 1 WLR 2113, para. 18, the Court of Appeal quoted statistics furnished by the CPS to rebut the claim that they were routinely using s. 329 as a substitute for handling; in 2007 there were 1,856 charges under s. 329, as against 19,931 of handling.

person's criminal conduct"—but this is impossible, given that section 340(3) expressly says "it is immaterial ... who carried out the conduct". In 2005, Parliament amended POCA 2002[144] to limit the offences in various ways, *inter alia* by providing that where a bank is the potential defendant and the conduct alleged to constitute laundering is a transaction with an existing bank account, the transaction must involve more than £250. A further and more general threshold limit is surely called for, to avoid the obvious problems of fair labelling that can otherwise arise.[145]

Neither is this the only possible overlap. In *Ogden*,[146] members of a family of drug-dealers were prosecuted for a range of offences, among them conspiracy to convert criminal property contrary to section 327. The Court of Appeal upheld the convictions for this offence. Dealing in goods, it said, is one method of converting them; and as "illegal drugs by their nature always represent 'criminal property'",[147] any person who sells illegal drugs is automatically guilty of the additional offence of money-laundering. Disputing this analysis, the defence argued that if it were correct, a person who bought illegal drugs, or merely possessed them for his own personal use, would automatically commit an offence of money-laundering under section 329 (acquisition, or possession). The Court of Appeal accepted this but brushed the point aside, saying "We have no doubt that good sense will prevail ...". The mistake the Court made here, surely, was to forget that by section 340 "criminal property" means (in essence) the profit generated by another crime, and to interpret it as meaning any property that it is a criminal offence to possess. If "criminal property" is read in this extended sense, then money-laundering duplicates an even wider range of other criminal offences: to name but a few, downloading, storing, or distributing child pornography,[148] unlawfully possessing a prohibited weapon,[149] or taking eggs from a wild bird's nest.[150]

§ 14.3 Robbery

Robbery was originally an offence at common law, later defined by statute.[151] In its current form the offence is criminalised by section 8 of the Theft Act 1968:

(1) A person is guilty of robbery if he steals, and immediately before or at the time of doing so, and in order to do so, he uses force on any person or puts or seeks to put any person in fear of being then and there subjected to force.
(2) A person guilty of robbery, or of an assault with intent to rob, shall on conviction on indictment be liable to imprisonment for life.

Simply put, robbery is a species of theft which is aggravated by assault. Thus it is to some extent unusual, in that it combines a property offence with an offence of violence against the person, with penalties more severe than the punishments for those individual offences.

---

[144] By the Serious Organised Crime and Police Act 2005, amending ss. 327, 328, and 329 of POCA 2002.
[145] Above, § 2.4.
[146] [2016] EWCA Crim 6.
[147] *Ibid.*, para. 52.
[148] Protection of Children Act 1978, s. 1.
[149] Firearms Act 1968, s. 5
[150] Wild Life and Countryside Act 1981, s. 1.
[151] Larceny Act 1916, s. 23 (re-enacting a provision of the Larceny Act 1861).

Partly, this is because the introduction of force makes theft more likely to succeed and, conversely, the object of theft makes the assault more highly motivated, arguably exposing the victim to a greater risk of injury.[152] More importantly, however, the use of force to complete a theft changes the moral character of D's action, such that it is legitimate to criminalise D's wrong specifically by the "combined" offence of robbery. What is significant about robbery is not merely that D usurps V's property rights, but how she does so. The expectations of personal and property security are preconditions of a stable, meaningful life; for both individuals and society. Robbery undermines *both* of these expectations. Unlike theft, the victim of a robbery cannot resort to any reassuring knowledge that at least her interest in personal integrity was not attacked. Thus it is perhaps misleading to suggest that robbery is a species of aggravated theft. The difference is not merely one of degree.[153]

Nonetheless, characterising robbery as a species of "theft" does reflect the law, in that the offence of robbery presupposes one of theft. The elements of robbery are as follows:

(i)   theft;

(ii)   accompanied by the use or threat of force;

(iii)   which occurs immediately before or at the time of the theft; and

(iv)   where the force is used or threatened in order to commit theft.

(i) Theft

The offence of theft must be proved before there can be any question of robbery.[154]

Hence, if the defendant is not dishonest, no robbery is committed. The case of *Skivington*,[155] discussed in § 13.8(i), is instructive. D held up a wages clerk and demanded his wife's wages: though this was an assault, it was held there was no larceny (and would now be no theft) and therefore no robbery, since he believed he had a lawful claim to the wages. This amounted to a belief that he had a right to deprive the clerk of the money; therefore D was not dishonest, and would not now be dishonest within the meaning of section 2(1)(a).

Note that the claim of right asserted by D in *Skivington* will operate solely in respect of the theft element. Where theft of the property cannot be proved, it is irrelevant—for the purposes of robbery—whether D believes he has a right to use force.[156] However, the

---

[152] Note, "A Rationale of the Law of Aggravated Theft" (1954) 54 *Columbia LR* 84, 102.

[153] Simester and Sullivan, "On the Nature and Rationale of Property Offences" in Duff and Green (eds.), *Defining Crimes: Essays on the Criminal Law's Special Part* (2005) 168, 194–5.

[154] *Guy* (1990) 93 Cr App R 108 (CA). The uncertainty expressed on this point by the Court of Appeal in *Forrester* [1992] Crim LR 792 was, it is submitted, unwarranted—as the note on the case observes: [1992] Crim LR 792, 794–5.

[155] [1968] 1 QB 166 (decided prior to the Theft Act 1968); cf. *Robinson* [1977] Crim LR 173; *Hemmings* (1864) 4 F & F 50, 176 ER 462.

[156] Cf. *Langham* (1984) 36 SASR 48. Contrast, in the United States, *People v. Reid* 508 NE (2d) 661 (1987); Model Penal Code, § 222.1; ruling that a claim of right that would negate a simple theft would not *ipso facto* negate robbery. Arguably, the American approach is to be preferred. In theft, the claim of right under s. 2(1)(a) implies that D did not realise he was wrongly usurping V's property rights. In *Skivington*, the claim of right was invoked by D for a more complex purpose: effectively, to justify D's forcible self-help by extra-judicial means. Arguably, where excessive force is used, a mere claim of right should not automatically exculpate D from a charge of robbery. See Note, "A Rationale of the Law of Aggravated Theft" (1954) 54 *Columbia LR* 84, 98.

absence of justification in respect of the force used will mean that D is independently guilty of an offence against the person.[157]

Similarly, no robbery is committed if D took the property with no intent permanently to deprive. Thus in *Mitchell*,[158] D violently hijacked V's BMW, abandoning it a few miles away on the road with its hazard lights flashing. The Court of Appeal quashed D's robbery conviction on the ground that there was no underlying theft because it was clear from the evidence that D did not intend V to lose her car permanently. The same result was reached in *Vinall*,[159] where the subject-matter of the hijack was a cycle rather than a luxury car.

(ii) Use or threat of force

Whether or not force is used is a question of fact for the jury to decide.[160] The main difficulty that may arise is where D exerts only a slight and non-violent pressure. In *Dawson*, D1 jostled V, causing V to lose his balance and giving D2 an opportunity to relieve V of his wallet. The Court of Appeal held this was sufficient evidence of force to go to the jury.

The trial judge in *Dawson* had directed that the force used had to be "substantial". However, the Court of Appeal refused to endorse that qualification, preferring to leave the question open. There are difficult issues here, and they remain unresolved. A mere touching, involving very slight pressure that in no way interferes with V's freedom of movement, certainly should not count as force for the purposes of robbery:[161] but it is, from the perspective of physics, an application of force. What seems to be required is that the force be *significant* (rather than substantial), in that it in some way modifies V's movement or freedom of movement. A test along these lines would adequately explain *Dawson* (which was surely rightly decided). It would also explain the decision in *Hale*,[162] where D put his hand over V's mouth in order to stop V from shouting for help. The Court of Appeal affirmed D's conviction for robbery.

One upshot of this is that the crime of robbery has a very broad range, encompassing within the same label both a theft accompanied by a minor push and a theft committed using weapons and serious violence.[163] As such, the crime appears to violate principles of fair labelling, since a conviction for "robbery" does not clearly indicate the seriousness of D's wrongdoing.[164] There is a case here for law reform; in particular, for dividing the existing single crime of robbery into two or three more narrowly defined categories, according to whether the theft was accompanied merely by significant force, by the use of weapons, or by serious violence.[165]

---

[157] Cf. *Wilson* [1984] AC 242, where D was convicted of assault occasioning actual bodily harm as an alternative to burglary.

[158] [2008] EWCA Crim 850; discussed above, § 13.7(ii).

[159] [2011] EWCA Crim 2652, [2012] 1 Cr App R.

[160] *Dawson and James* (1976) 64 Cr App R 170.

[161] Analogously, opening an unlocked door in the normal way does not count as a forcible entry: cf. *Ryan* v. *Shilcock* (1851) 7 Exch 72, 75, 155 ER 861, 862.

[162] (1978) 68 Cr App R 415.

[163] For a sense of the variety, compare O'Donnell and Morrison, "Armed and Dangerous? The Use of Firearms in Robbery" (1997) 36 *Howard J Crim Justice* 305; Gill, *Commercial Robbery: Offenders' Perspectives on Security and Crime Prevention* (2000); and Smith, *The Nature of Personal Robbery* (2003).

[164] See above, § 2.4; Ashworth, "Robbery Re-assessed" [2002] *Crim LR* 851.

[165] Compare in this context the crime of burglary, discussed below in § 14.4.

(a) Force against the person or against the property?

Suppose D violently snatches V's bag, without touching V herself. Is this robbery? In other words, must force be applied directly to the person, or is it sufficient that the appropriation be "by force", directed at the stolen property but impacting indirectly on V? At common law, the rule was that the force had to be directed at the person.[166] A snatching was not enough, unless the victim was thereby injured.[167]

It appears, however, that this distinction is not preserved in section 8(1)—contrary to the intentions of those who framed the Act.[168] In *Clouden*,[169] D tore a basket from V's grasp and ran off with it. Because D approached her from behind, V had no opportunity to resist and D offered no force directly to her person. At common law this was not robbery but, said the Court of Appeal, "the old distinctions have gone".[170] D's appeal against conviction was dismissed. Force against property, which causes force to be applied to the person, is sufficient.

The decision in *Clouden* has been criticised for muddying the clear waters distinguishing robbery from theft. As Sir John Smith commented, the case looks more akin to that of the pickpocket than the bank robber.[171] In *P and Others*,[172] however, the Divisional Court, having considered *Clouden*, stressed that a *substantial* degree of force is a necessary ingredient in the offence of robbery, whether applied to V's body or to the property. In so holding, it quashed convictions for robbery imposed for snatching a cigarette out of another person's hand. In such a case the force used, they suggested, must be a degree of force which would potentially have been painful if V had sought to resist it.[173]

(b) Threats of force

The actual application of force is not required. Under section 8(1), it is sufficient if D "puts or seeks to put any person in fear of being then and there subjected to force". This is consistent with the law of assault, which includes threats to apply force as well as its actual application.[174] The victim must apprehend being subjected "there and then" to force: threatening to disclose embarrassing details about someone's past, or to apply force at a later date, unless she hands over property may be blackmail,[175] but not robbery.

---

[166] *Gnosil* (1824) 1 C & P 304, 171 ER 1206: "The mere act of taking, being forcible, will not make this offence a highway robbery: to constitute the crime of highway robbery, the force must be … of such a nature, as to shew that it was intended to overpower the party robbed, and prevent his resisting, and not merely to get possession of the property stolen. Thus, if a man walking after a woman in the street, were by violence to pull her shawl from her shoulders, though he might use considerable violence, it would not, in my opinion, be highway robbery." See also *Baker* (1783) 1 Leach 290, 168 ER 247; *Steward* 2 East PC 702.

[167] As in *Moore* (1784) 1 Leach 335, 168 ER 270, where D snatched a diamond pin fastened to V's hair, tearing away part of her hair in the process.

[168] Report of the Criminal Law Revision Committee, *Theft and Related Offences* Cmnd. 2977 (1966) para. 65.

[169] [1987] Crim LR 56.

[170] Citing *Dawson and James* (1976) 64 Cr App R 170.

[171] [1987] Crim LR 56, 57.

[172] *P and Others* v. *Director of Public Prosecutions* [2012] EWHC 1657 (Admin), [2013] 1 WLR 2337; noted by Ormerod, [2013] Crim LR 151.

[173] A observation that Ormerod (*ibid.*) suggests ought to be read with caution: "There need not be 'pain', merely use of force on any person. Wrenching a shoe from a prosthetic leg would surely be robbery from the wearer even if no pain was felt by him."

[174] Above, Chapter 11.

[175] Theft Act 1968, s. 21.

Although by section 8(1) part of the definition of the offence is that D "puts or seeks to put [V] in fear of being ... subjected to force", this means only that D must cause or try to cause V to anticipate the use of force upon him. It does not mean that the prosecution have to prove that V was frightened, or that D sought to frighten him. So, where a gang of youths surrounded V, who submitted to their emptying his pockets because he foresaw that force would be used on him if he resisted, they were rightly convicted of robbery even though in evidence V denied feeling "scared" or "particularly threatened".[176]

(c) Third persons

The force need not be used or threatened against the victim of the theft.[177] If D points a gun at V's colleague, T, in order to obtain money from V, D commits robbery (of V). Note, however, that if force is merely threatened rather than applied, it is the person against whom force is threatened who must be "put in fear of being then and there subjected to force". Suppose, for example, that D threatens V that she will shoot V's friend, T, unless V hands money over to D. T is out of earshot, or hears but fails to understand the threat. Somewhat surprisingly, on these facts, D does not commit robbery.[178] V is not put in fear of being subjected to force, since the force is threatened against T. T is not put in fear of being subjected to force, since the threat is directed to V and T does not hear it. This could only be a case of blackmail.[179]

(iii) Immediately before or at the time of the theft

Suppose the following example:

D picks V's pocket, extracting V's wallet. V realises what D has done and immediately accosts her. D violently strikes V and runs off.

Has D committed robbery, or is she guilty of separate offences of theft and battery?[180] The answer depends on whether the battery occurs "at the time of the theft". If the theft is completed and D's use of force is merely in order to escape, she is not guilty of robbery.[181] This analysis is reinforced by the requirement, to be discussed in § 14.3(iv), that the force be used or threatened in order to *commit* theft, rather than (say) to escape from it.

What time-frame does "at the time of the theft" import? This question arises elsewhere in the Theft Act, and was considered in §§ 13.6(iv) and 14.1(i)(f). Prima facie, robbery cannot be committed if the force is used or threatened after the offence of theft is completed. The difficulty with this restriction is that, under the interpretation of appropriation established in *Morris* and *Gomez*,[182] the wallet is stolen by D as soon as it is touched.

---

[176] *R v. DPP* [2007] EWHC 739 (Admin), (2007) 171 JP 404.

[177] See Andrews, "Robbery" [1966] *Crim LR* 524, 524–6.

[178] Section 8(1) appears in this respect to be slightly narrower than the common law. Previously, it was robbery if D took property by threatening immediately to kill the victim's child: *Donally* (1799) 2 East PC 715, 718; *Reane* (1794) 2 Leach 616, 619, 168 ER 410, 412 n. 1.

[179] Theft Act 1968, s. 21.

[180] Above, Chapter 11.

[181] As was intended: see the Report of the Criminal Law Revision Committee, *Theft and Related Offences* Cmnd. 2977 (1966) para. 66.

[182] Above, § 13.6, 13.6(ii).

Thereafter, D cannot become guilty of robbery. One example of this analysis is the decision by the Court of Appeal in *Pitham and Hehl*,[183] a handling case. M had offered to sell P and H some furniture that did not belong to him. P and H were convicted of handling and appealed on the ground that the handling occurred "in the course of" the theft by M, and so was excluded by the proviso in section 22.[184] However, the Court upheld the convictions, diagnosing that M, the thief:[185]

> "took the two appellants to 20 Parry Road, showed them the property and invited them to buy what they wanted. He was then, in the words of [s. 3(1)], 'assuming the rights of the owner.' The moment he did that he appropriated [the owner's] goods to himself. The appropriation was complete. After this appropriation had been completed there was no question of these two appellants taking part, in the words of section 22, in dealing with the goods 'in the course of stealing.'"

As a general rule, this seems too extreme.[186] It would mean that, were V to accost D—and be met with violence—while D was still extracting the wallet from V's pocket, D could not commit robbery.

The obvious solution to this difficulty is to accept that robbery cannot be committed after the theft is complete, but to describe D's appropriation of the wallet as a "continuing act", i.e. to regard the act of appropriation as continuing after D has touched the wallet. The balance of the case law supports this analysis. In *Hale*, for example, the Court of Appeal stated that:[187]

> "the act of appropriation does not suddenly cease. It is a continuous act and it is a matter for the jury to decide whether or not the act of appropriation has finished."

If, as seems most likely, the continuing act analysis ultimately prevails, robbery will be possible after D's act of appropriation begins but not after it ends; the determination of when the appropriation ends will depend on the facts of each case. (In the example given, it would no doubt be after D has withdrawn her hand from V's pocket, and perhaps when she begins to walk away.)

An alternative solution would be to disengage the phrase "at the time of the theft" from the technical question when the theft is committed, and interpret that phrase as referring to D's theftuous activity or escapade, viewed in its wider context. Hence, one might say "the offence of theft is established" for the purposes of section 1 as soon as D's hand touches the wallet; but that it was still "at the time of the theft" for the purposes of section 8 until D began, say, to escape.[188] One advantage of this interpretation is that it requires no manipulating of the definition of theft in order to satisfy the demands of robbery—it avoids having the cart drive the horse.

---

[183] (1976) 65 Cr App R 45. Cf. *Corcoran* v. *Anderton* (1980) 71 Cr App R 104.

[184] See above, § 14.1(i)(f).

[185] (1977) 65 Cr App R 45, 49.

[186] Indeed, the Court in *Pitham and Hehl* was careful not to foreclose the possibility of an alternative conclusion in different fact situations.

[187] (1978) 68 Cr App R 415, 418. Note that this case was decided before *Gomez*; see also *Donaghy* v. *Marshall* [1981] Crim LR 644. In *Lockley* [1995] Crim LR 656, the Court of Appeal endorsed a continuing act analysis and thought that *Hale* was unaffected by *Gomez*; but *Hale* and *Gomez* were said by the same court to be difficult to reconcile in *Atakpu and Abraham* [1994] QB 69, 80. More recently, the possibility of a continuing act has been acknowledged in *Bowden* [2002] EWCA Crim 1279.

[188] Cf. the suggestion in *Atakpu and Abraham* [1994] QB 69, 80: was D still "on the job"?

(iv) In order to commit theft

The mere coincidence of theft and force is insufficient for robbery. Force must be used, or threatened, *in order* to steal.[189] The motive counts. If D assaults V and then, while V is unconscious, decides to take V's watch, D commits assault and theft but not robbery.

Implicitly, the element of motive imports an associated requirement that D's use of force must itself be intentional. If D accidentally knocks V over while trying to pick his pocket, she cannot be guilty of robbery since she does not mean to use force in order to relieve V of his wallet.[190] Similarly, suppose that D inadvertently frightens V who, in fear, offers her money. D may commit theft should she dishonestly take advantage of V's fear and accept the money, but she does not rob.[191]

(v) Assault with intent to rob

Section 8(2) creates a supplementary offence of assault with intent to rob, which is punishable to the same extent as the completed offence. In practice, the existence of this offence means that it will rarely be necessary to charge D with attempted robbery, as most attempted robberies will also constitute assault with intent to rob.

§ 14.4 Burglary

Burglary has been a serious offence since the earliest days of the common law. By the second half of the twentieth century the law relating to burglary, and the related offence of housebreaking, had become technical and complicated, and it was thought that simplification and rationalisation was needed. With that in mind, the Theft Act rolled the two offences into one to create a single new offence of burglary. As we shall see, however, the new law is neither entirely simple nor completely rational. It is not one of the major successes of the 1968 reform.

The offence of burglary is now to be found in section 9 of the Theft Act 1968. So far as is immediately relevant, the section provides:

(1) A person is guilty of burglary if—
(a) he enters any building or part of a building as a trespasser and with intent to commit any such offence as is mentioned in subsection (2) below; or
(b) having entered any building or part of a building as a trespasser he steals or attempts to steal anything in the building or that part of it or inflicts or attempts to inflict on any person therein any grievous bodily harm.
(2) The offences referred to in subsection (1)(a) above are offences of stealing anything in the building or part of a building in question, of inflicting on any person therein any grievous bodily harm, and of doing unlawful damage to the building or anything therein.

The offence carries a maximum penalty of 10 years, or 14 years if the building is a dwelling. Section 10 goes on to create a further offence of "aggravated burglary", which is

---

[189] Cf. *Shendley* [1970] Crim LR 49; *James* [1997] Crim LR 598.
[190] Cf. *Edwards* (1843) 1 Cox CC 32.
[191] *Bruce* [1975] 3 All ER 277, 279H–J.

burglary when in possession of "any firearm, imitation firearm, any weapon of offence or any explosive". For aggravated burglary the maximum penalty is imprisonment for life.[192]

In distinguishing between paragraphs (a) and (b) of section 9(1), the section creates two types of offence of simple burglary, one committed at the time of entry and one that is committed inside the building. The elements of the offence under section 9(1)(a) are as follows:

(a) entry by D;
(b) as a knowing or reckless trespasser;
(c) into a building or part of a building;
(d1) with intent, at the time of entry, to commit one of the following ("ulterior") crimes: stealing, inflicting grievous bodily harm, or doing unlawful damage.

Under section 9(1)(b), the required elements are:

(a) entry by D;
(b) as a knowing or reckless trespasser;
(c) into a building or part of a building; and
(d2) while in the building, D commits one of the following (ulterior) crimes: stealing, attempting to steal, inflicting grievous bodily harm, or attempting to inflict grievous bodily harm.

In either case, by virtue of section 9(3), for the purposes of sentencing for simple burglary the court must also determine whether the building is a dwelling.[193] Technically, by enacting different maximum penalties for dwellings as opposed to other buildings,[194] the effect of section 9(3) is to create different offences, corresponding to the different maximum penalties.[195] There are, therefore, four types of offence in all: two for section 9(1)(a)[196] and two for section 9(1)(b).

The resulting offence is peculiarly lop-sided, in that the lists of other offences which turn a trespassory entry into a burglary differ as between the section 9(1)(a) offence and the offence created by section 9(1)(b).[197] As originally designed by the Criminal Law Revision Committee, the lists would have been the same, which would have made the offence much simpler; but the original plan was modified as the legislation passed through Parliament. Originally, the list of intended crimes in section 9(1)(a) included one additional crime. It

---

[192] The Court of Appeal has held that aggravated offence is not committed by an armed accessory to a burglary who waits outside while his unarmed colleague is at work within: *Klass* [1998] 1 Cr App R 453; affirmed in *Wiggins* [2012] EWCA Crim 885, (2012) 176 JP 305. The reason for this seeming generosity is that the aggravated offence exists to discourage burglars from entering property when bearing arms—rather than to discourage them from setting out to burgle when "tooled up".

[193] At common law, a dwelling is a place that is regularly slept in: *Lyons* (1778) 1 Leach 185, 168 ER 195; *Thompson* (1796) 2 Leach 771, 168 ER 485.

[194] See too s. 111 of the Powers of Criminal Courts (Sentencing) Act 2000 (prescribing a minimum sentence of three years' imprisonment for a third domestic burglary conviction).

[195] See *Courtie* [1984] AC 463, 471 (Lord Diplock).

[196] That is, trespassory entry of a dwelling with intent to commit, etc.; and trespassory entry of a building not being a dwelling with intent to commit, etc.

[197] Under the earlier law, the offences of burglary and housebreaking depended on the commission of, or intention to commit, a *felony*. See further below, § 14.4(iv).

was also burglary to enter as a trespasser with intent to commit rape (as will be seen when discussing the notorious case of *Collins*,[198] below). However, that version of burglary was deleted by the Sexual Offences Act 2003, which introduced a separate and wider offence of trespass with intent to commit a sexual offence.[199]

(i) Entry

Entry is a physical activity rather than an instantaneous event.[200] Consequently, it can be difficult to draw the line between a completed entry, for the purposes of burglary, and an incomplete attempt. At common law, it was sufficient if any part whatsoever of the body protruded inside the building. Thus, for example, inserting a fingertip beyond the line of the window frame[201] or grasping the inner sill of a window[202] would amount to an entry. This test has the advantage of at least being reasonably straightforward to apply, even if it turns "entry" into rather a technical concept. The Theft Act 1968, which was enacted against the background of this law, makes no reference itself to what constitutes an entry, and it seems to have been assumed during the passage of the Act that the common law rules would continue to apply.[203]

Since enactment of the Act, however, modern cases have sought to qualify the common law test. In *Collins*,[204] Edmund Davies LJ stated that the entry must be "effective and substantial" to satisfy section 9. In *Brown*,[205] however, the Court of Appeal rejected "substantial" as a requirement and said that the entry need only be "effective". D had been seen standing outside, but with the top half of his body inside, a shop's display window. He was apparently rummaging inside the window for goods. While, ultimately, entry is a question of fact for the jury, the Court ruled there was no need for D's whole body to be inside the building and that, on these facts, there had clearly been an entry.

Notwithstanding *Brown*, it is unclear how important is the requirement for "effective" entry. In *Ryan*,[206] only D's head and arm entered the building before D became stuck, so that he was never in a position to steal. The Court of Appeal held that it was irrelevant whether his entry had been sufficiently effective to put D in a position to steal. This seems right, but it raises the question: can "effective" or "substantial" be given any meaningful role in qualifying the requirement for entry? If an arm and head suffice, where is the line to be drawn? How can *Ryan* be distinguished from the fingertip entry?

It is submitted that no useful line can be drawn, and that the "effective" (or "substantial") test advanced in these cases should be either disregarded or understood as a *de minimis* rule: a trivial or practically negligible entry, e.g. by the tip of a finger, is insufficient for section 9; but any significant intrusion inside the space of the building qualifies as an entry.

---

[198] § 14.4(ii).
[199] Contrary to s. 63 of the Sexual Offences Act 2003.
[200] Smith, *Property Offences* (1994) § 28-27.
[201] *Davis* (1823) Russ & Ry 499, 168 ER 917. Cf. *Bailey* (1818) Russ & Ry 341, 168 ER 835, and cases cited there; *Perkes* (1824) 1 C & P 300, 171 ER 1204.
[202] *Parkin* [1950] 1 KB 155.
[203] HL Debs., vol. 290, cols. 85–6.
[204] [1973] 1 QB 100, 106. The facts of the case are set out below, in § 14.3(ii).
[205] [1985] Crim LR 212.
[206] (1995) 160 JP 610, noted [1996] Crim LR 320.

(a) Instruments

At common law, entry may be done by an instrument, unless the instrument was intruded solely to enable D to enter in person. For example, casting hooks through a window in order to drag carpets out of the building was sufficient for burglary,[207] but inserting a jemmy in order to lever open a door (and thereby enter oneself) was not.[208] Presumably, the rule that entry by instrument is sufficient will continue to apply under section 9. It is less clear, however, that the exception should be preserved for jemmies and the like which are used to secure entry. The exception arose out of the requirement at common law that there be both a "breaking" and an "entry"; it was thought that where an instrument entered the building in the activity of breaking, that could not by itself also constitute the entry.[209] Since the 1968 Act removes the element of "breaking" from burglary, this rationale no longer applies.

(ii) As a trespasser

The actus reus of the earlier law was "breaking and entering". The concept of breaking, like entering, had collected a body of case law around it, and it was in the hope of simplifying matters that the new law replaced the requirement of "breaking" with a requirement that D should be a trespasser when he enters the building. But the concept of entry *as a trespass*er has not proved to be an easy one, as we shall see.

Trespass is a tort, and whether D is a trespasser is a question purely of civil law, of which only a summary can be given here. Apart from situations where entry is specifically authorised by law,[210] the main criterion is whether D has received consent to enter from someone authorised to give that consent. The most striking case on trespassory entry under the 1968 Act is *Collins*.[211] The facts of the case were as follows:

> D, naked in all material respects,[212] had climbed up to a bedroom window with intent to commit rape when he was seen by the occupier's daughter, who was in bed at the time. Mistaking D for her boyfriend, the daughter invited D to climb through the window for the purpose of having sexual intercourse. This he did, and it was only while they were in the throes of intercourse that the daughter realised her mistake; whereupon she slapped him in the face, bit him, and retired to the bathroom.

The facts disclose two possible moments at which D might have become guilty of burglary. The first possibility turned on whether D had already effected an entry through the window, onto the inner sill, when he was invited in. If so, a conviction for burglary would be

---

[207] Case determined Hilary Term, 26 Eliz; (1583) 1 Anderson 114, 123 ER 383. Cf. *Richardson and Brown* [1998] 2 Cr App R (S) 87 (using a JCB digger to ram the wall of a bank and to scoop out the cash dispenser installed there).

[208] Cf. *Hughes* (1785) 1 Leach 406, 168 ER 305.

[209] This is the best explanation of *Tucker* (1844) 1 Cox CC 73, where insertion of a knife in order to lever open a window latch was held to be an entry. D had already committed a breaking by first smashing the window pane (cf. 2 East PC, chap xv § 3).

[210] E.g. where police officers act in execution of a search warrant, or where a landlord distrains for rent.

[211] [1973] 1 QB 100. As was noted earlier, rape is no longer a qualifying offence within s. 9(1)(a).

[212] According to the Court of Appeal (*per* Edmund Davies LJ at 102–3), D had "stripped off all his clothes, with the exception of his socks, because apparently he took the view that if the girl's mother entered the bedroom it would be easier to effect a rapid escape if he had his socks on than if he was in his bare feet. That is a matter about which we are not called upon to express any view, and would in any event find ourselves unable to express one."

straightforward and the later invitation irrelevant, since the offence under section 9(1)(a) was by then complete.

On the first question there was insufficient evidence to support D's conviction. Alternatively, therefore, assuming D entered only after he was invited in, it was necessary to decide whether he was a trespasser at that later moment. The Court of Appeal ruled that D committed no burglary. Prima facie, D had received permission to enter from a person authorised to give it. As we shall see below, although the mistake vitiated that permission and D was in law a trespasser,[213] the apparent invitation prevented his entry from being a knowing or reckless trespass.[214]

(a) Authority to enter

The person who permits D's entry must be authorised to do so. Apart from the occupier of the property (usually the owner or leaseholder), any other member of the household has a general authority to invite persons on to the premises for lawful purposes,[215] although this invitation can be revoked or overridden by the occupier.[216]

D will also be a trespasser if the terms of his authority to enter are exceeded. In *Jones and Smith*,[217] D had a general licence to enter his father's house. One night, he went to the house and stole two television sets. His conviction for burglary was upheld by the Court of Appeal. D's licence did not extend so far as to permit entry for an unlawful purpose such as theft.[218]

Glanville Williams has criticised the decision in *Jones and Smith*,[219] suggesting that it forces the issue of trespass to depend on D's mental state (i.e. his criminal purpose) rather than upon any objective facts, such as the express terms of D's licence. Apart from causing burglary to look like a thoughtcrime, the possibility that D's mental state may make his entry unauthorised requires, in turn, that the courts draw lines which are not at all obvious in advance. This is contrary to the aspiration that the law should give fair warning to defendants of their potential crimes. Additionally, if it is the intent to commit theft that makes D a trespasser, the range of burglary is considerably expanded—on this view, if D enters a shop intending to shoplift, D is a burglar. It is to be hoped that the rule in *Jones and Smith* will not be extended to buildings that are open generally to the public. Otherwise, a person who writes a graffito on the wall of a public lavatory would appear to be a burglar.

Notwithstanding these criticisms of *Jones and Smith*, the current law appears to be that D is a trespasser if he enters with an intention to exceed the terms of his licence while on the property.[220] Those terms may be explicit: in *Taylor v. Jackson*,[221] for example, V gave D

---

[213] Below, § 14.4(ii)(b).

[214] Below, § 14.4(ii)(c).

[215] E.g. *Robson v. Hallett* [1967] 2 QB 939 (police officers were not trespassers when invited onto the premises by the occupier's son); *Collins* [1973] QB 100, 107.

[216] As it was in *Robson v. Hallett* [1967] 2 QB 939.

[217] [1976] 3 All ER 54.

[218] Arguably, the decision is better justified on the ground that D came with an accomplice, who had no authority to enter at all, and whom D abetted. For discussion, see Smith, *Property Offences* (1994) § 28-12f.

[219] *TBCL* 847ff. See Pace, "Burglarious Trespass" [1985] *Crim LR* 716.

[220] Of course, D may become a trespasser after entering, if his subsequent actions exceed the terms of his licence. But this does not help us here, since for burglary D must be a trespasser at the moment when he enters. The civil law doctrine of trespass *ab initio* has no application to the criminal law: *Collins* [1973] QB 100, 107.

[221] (1898) 78 LT 555.

permission to enter his land and hunt for rabbits. Instead, D went onto the land in order to hunt for hares. This was held to be evidence of trespass.

Alternatively, the terms of the licence may be implicit. Typically, there will be implicit restrictions which (i) exclude entry in order to commit a tort or a criminal offence.[222] They probably (ii) also exclude other activities which are wrongful or dangerous:[223] "When you invite a person into your house to use the staircase you do not invite him to slide down the banisters".[224] Similarly, (iii) entry with an intention which is contrary to or undermines the purpose for which the licence was granted is likely also to be trespass.[225] These categories may well overlap; as in *Barker*,[226] an Australian case, where D had been asked by V, his neighbour, to keep an eye on V's house while V was away. Instead, D entered and stole some furniture. D's conviction for burglary was upheld by the High Court.

(b) Mistaken authorisation

In *Collins* (above), the daughter's invitation to enter was invalidated by a fundamental mistake regarding D's identity.[227] Hence, D did not have a genuine authorisation to enter, and did so as a trespasser. (The case turned therefore on whether D knew of the mistake, and so entered knowing he was or might be trespassing.) Where the occupier's mistake is not fundamental, authorisation to enter will nonetheless be invalid if it is obtained by deception or fraud. Presumably, by analogy with pre-Act law,[228] D's entry under these circumstances would be as a trespasser.

(c) Mental element in criminal trespass

Under civil law, an action for trespass to land lay even though the defendant had no idea that he was not entitled to enter the property. If D enters a neighbour's house, thinking by mistake it is his own, D commits a tort.[229] This rule of strict liability does not apply in the criminal law. To be guilty of burglary, D must know or be subjectively reckless about the facts that make his entry a trespass. As Edmund-Davies LJ stated in *Collins*:[230]

> "there cannot be a conviction for entering premises 'as a trespasser' within the meaning of section 9 of the Theft Act unless the person entering does so knowing that he is a trespasser and nevertheless deliberately enters, or, at the very least, is reckless as to whether or not he is entering the premises of another without the other party's consent."

---

[222] Cf. *Jones and Smith* [1976] 3 All ER 54.

[223] *Hillen and Pettigrew* v. *ICI (Alkali) Ltd* [1936] AC 65, 69.

[224] *The Calgarth, the Otarama* [1927] P 93, 110. Cited by Lord Atkin in *Hillen and Pettigrew* v. *ICI (Alkali) Ltd* [1936] AC 65, 69.

[225] "So far as he sets foot on so much as the premises as lie outside the invitation or uses them for purposes which are alien to the invitation he is not an invitee but a trespasser": *Hillen and Pettigrew* v. *ICI (Alkali) Ltd* [1936] AC 65, 69. Cf. *Savoy Hotel* v. *BBC* (1983) 133 NLJ 105, though contrast *Byrne* v. *Kinematograph Renters Society Ltd* [1958] 2 All ER 579 for a different result on analogous facts.

[226] (1983) 153 CLR 338.

[227] Cf. the discussion of mistakes, above, § 13.4(iv)(c).

[228] In *Boyle* [1954] 2 QB 292, D tricked V into permitting D to enter by pretending he was an employee of the BBC sent to investigate problems with local radio transmissions. On these facts, D was held guilty of housebreaking.

[229] *Basely* v. *Clarkson* (1682) 3 Lev 37, 83 ER 565; *Conway* v. *Wimpey & Co (No 2)* [1951] 2 KB 266, 273–4.

[230] [1973] QB 100, 105.

This is not to require that D knows he is, *in law*, a trespasser; rather that he knows or recognises the possible existence of the *facts*, i.e. those facts which make him a trespasser. Thus in *Collins* (above), where D entered through the window at the mistaken invitation of the lady inside, D's appeal against conviction was allowed "on the basis that the jury were never invited to consider the vital question whether this young man did enter the premises as a trespasser, that is to say knowing perfectly well that he had no invitation to enter or reckless of whether or not his entry was with permission". Thus, had D been aware of the woman's mistake about D's identity, he would have been guilty of burglary.

(iii) A building or part of a building

What counts as a building cannot be stated with precision. According to Byles J, it is "a structure of considerable size and intended to be permanent or at least to endure for a considerable time";[231] although these words were intended to be elucidatory rather than definitive. Byles J's test would exclude a tent[232] or a Portaloo, and probably a telephone box. On the other hand, it seems the building need not be affixed to the soil. In *B and S* v. *Leathley*,[233] the Carlisle Crown Court, applying the statement of Byles J, ruled that a large freezer container, which was sitting on railway sleepers and could be moved by crane, was a building. The Court took into account that the container had lockable doors, was connected to an independent electricity supply, and was intended by its owner to remain *in situ* for the foreseeable future. Implicit in *B and S* v. *Leathley* is that detached outbuildings are also buildings for the purposes of burglary. Hence, a trespassory entry into a garage would be capable of constituting burglary.[234]

Prima facie, the definition of a building excludes vehicles.[235] However, where vehicles or vessels are inhabited, the scope of burglary is specifically extended by section 9(4), which provides:

> References in subsection (1) and (2) above to a building and the reference in subsection (3) above to a building which is also a dwelling, shall apply also to an inhabited vehicle or vessel, and shall apply to any such vehicle or vessel at times when the person having a habitation in it is not there as well as at times when he is.

Thus breaking into a caravan or houseboat would be burglary while the vehicle or boat is being used as a residence, even if the resident is away at the time. A caravan that is used only for holidays, however, would be "inhabited" only during the holiday and probably, therefore, could not be burgled at other times.[236]

---

[231] *Stevens* v. *Gourlay* (1859) 7 CBNS 99, 112, 141 ER 752, 757.

[232] Cf. Criminal Law Revision Committee, *Theft and Related Offences* Cmnd. 2977 (1966) para. 78.

[233] [1979] Crim LR 314.

[234] Cf. *Whitmore* v. *Bedford* (1843) 5 Man & G 9, 134 ER 460.

[235] E.g. an articulated lorry trailer: *Norfolk Constabulary* v. *Seekings and Gould* [1986] Crim LR 167, differing from *B and S* v. *Leathley* [1979] Crim LR 314 in that the trailer still rested on its own wheels. Compare s. 292(4) of the Canadian Criminal Code, which specifically includes railway stock, trailers, and aircraft.

[236] Cf. the common law definition of a dwelling as a place that is regularly slept in: *Lyons* (1778) 1 Leach 185, 168 ER 195; *Thompson* (1796) 2 Leach 771, 168 ER 485.

(a) Part of a building

The phrase "part of a building" is included because of the possibility that D may have permission to enter a building, without being allowed access to the whole of the interior. In such cases, D can commit burglary by intruding into that part of the building where her entry is disallowed. A hotel guest, for example, commits burglary by entering another guest's room with intent to steal, even though she has permission to be in the hotel. Similarly, in *Walkington*,[237] D's general permission to enter a shop did not save her from conviction for burglary when she went behind the counter in order to plunder the till. The counter effectively bounded an area from which customers were excluded.

It is not clear whether a building can be severed into "parts" without some sort of physical division, such as the barrier that was created by the sales counter in *Walkington*. Certainly, any physical division need not be permanent, since in *Walkington* itself the counter was a movable one. In principle, it ought to be sufficient for the purposes of establishing a trespassory entry that the area is clearly demarcated, even if this is done merely by drawing lines on the floor. However, the point remains undecided.

(iv) With intent to commit, or committing, the ulterior offence

Burglary, whether under section 9(1)(a) or under (9(1)(b), presupposes an "ulterior offence". In the first variety of the offence D must enter with intent to commit a listed crime, and in the second he must actually do so. This reflects, albeit a little dimly, the structure of the earlier law, in which an ingredient in the offence was either the intent to commit, or the actual commission of, a *felony*, felonies being a class of grave offences which the law at one time singled out for special treatment. The "ulterior offences" set out in section 9 are a selection of crimes which amounted to felonies before felonies were abolished as a separate category of offence.[238]

Under section 9(1)(a), the offence of burglarious entry, the prosecution must prove that *at the time he entered* D intended[239] therein to commit one of the following offences: stealing, inflicting grievous bodily harm, or doing unlawful damage. The offence is committed at point of entry; if, having entered, D then changes his mind and leaves without committing the offence, it is too late. The offence is committed and cannot be undone.

As with all future-intent offences, difficult questions sometimes arise if D's intent is conditional. Suppose that D enters a building intending to steal only if he finds something worth stealing. In principle, cases of conditional intention should be treated as ones of intention, so that D is guilty of burglary in this example.[240] Conditional intention is discussed further in the context of theft, above, in § 13.7(i)(f).[241] In the context of the difficulties there discussed, however, notice that whereas one cannot *steal* something that does not exist, one can *intend* to do so; hence D can be guilty of burglary when he enters V's house

---

[237] [1979] 2 All ER 716.
[238] By the Criminal Law Act 1967, s. 1.
[239] As the terms of s. 9(1)(a) makes clear, recklessness is insufficient: *A* v. *DPP* [2003] All ER (D) 393. For the purposes of the intoxication rules (below, § 18.3), the offence is one of specific intent: *Durante* [1972] 1 WLR 1612.
[240] *A-G's References (Nos. 1 and 2 of 1979)* [1980] QB 180.
[241] See also the general discussion above, § 5.1(viii).

with conditional intent to steal a diamond (should it be there), even though there is no diamond.

Under section 9(1)(b), burglary is constituted by committing, or attempting, the offences either of theft or of inflicting grievous bodily harm, *after* D has entered the building as a trespasser. Thus the time at which burglary is committed is when D commits, or attempts to commit, the ulterior offence once inside the building.

Note that, under both paragraphs of section 9(1), the intended, committed or attempted offence must be within the building (or part-building) that D has entered as a trespasser. Hence if D enters V's flat without permission, solely in order to access his own adjacent flat where, for insurance purposes, he intends to stage a "theft" of electronic equipment, he does not commit burglary. His trespassory entry into V's flat was without intent to steal "therein".

(a) Stealing

For the purposes of burglary, "stealing" connotes theft, contrary to section 1, and does not refer to obtaining by fraud or blackmail.[242] Wherever "steal" carries a wider meaning than "theft", the Act makes this clear by express provision,[243] and no such provision is made for burglary. Note, however, that in the wake of *Gomez*[244] any obtaining by fraud is likely anyway to be theft; thus the apparently narrow meaning of "stealing" in section 9(1) imposes few practical restrictions.[245]

(b) Inflicting grievous bodily harm

For section 9(1)(a), the relevant offence is section 18 of the OAPA 1861; for section 9(1)(b), the relevant offences are sections 18, 20, and 23 of the OAPA 1861. Those offences are discussed in Chapter 11 and will not be traversed here. One rather odd decision must, however, be mentioned. In *Wilson and Jenkins*,[246] the defendants entered a house and committed a serious assault on the occupants. They were charged with burglary under section 9(1)(b). On appeal, the Court of Appeal stated that there was no requirement in section 9(1)(b) that D's action actually be an *offence*:[247]

> "It seems unlikely that in this context Parliament intended to restrict the expression 'inflict grievous bodily harm' to the narrow area of assault. To test this proposition it may be helpful to consider a set of circumstance that could not be described as fanciful. An intruder gains access to the house without breaking in (where there is an open window, for instance). He is on the premises as a trespasser, and his intrusion is observed by someone in the house of whom he may not even be aware, and as a result that person suffers severe shock, with a resulting stroke. In such a case it is difficult to see how an assault could be alleged; but nevertheless

---

[242] Cf. *Low* v. *Blease* [1975] Crim LR 513 (entry with intent dishonestly to use electricity, although contrary to s. 13, was not burglary, since using electricity was not theft within s. 1).

[243] E.g. in the case of handling: above, § 14.1(ii)(a).

[244] [1993] AC 442. See above, § 13.6(ii).

[245] Bearing in mind the discussion of *Jones and Smith* [1976] 3 All ER 54 above, in § 14.4(ii)(a), this appears to suggest that someone entering a social security office intending fraudulently to claim an unemployment benefit would commit burglary. It is to be hoped that such a case would not be treated as involving a trespass.

[246] [1984] AC 242 (HL); *sub nom. Jenkins and Jenkins* [1983] 1 All ER 1000 (CA).

[247] [1983] 1 All ER 1000, 1004. No comment was made on this point by the House of Lords, which reversed the Court of Appeal's decision on other grounds.

his presence would have been a direct cause of the stroke,[248] which must amount to grievous bodily harm. Should such an event fall outside the provisions of s 9, when causing some damage to the property falls fairly within it?"

Thus, the Court concluded, whatever the proper interpretation of the words "to inflict grievous bodily harm" in the OAPA 1861, "we would be of the opinion that they have the wider meaning in section 9(1)(b) of the 1968 Act".[249]

With respect to the Court of Appeal, this conclusion—and the example given by the Court—is bizarre. While it is true that section 9(1)(a) includes, and section 9(1)(b) omits, the word "offence", in fact that omission was a mere error of drafting.[250] The Court's interpretation of section 9(1)(b) makes it possible to commit burglary by accident—turning the offence into one of strict liability.[251] There is no question but that this was not the intention of Parliament.[252] Burglary is a very serious offence which carries a substantial penalty, and it is extraordinary that it may be committed without mens rea (save to enter as a trespasser, which is a wholly different type of wrongdoing). It is to be hoped that, in the future, the Court's view will not be followed.

(c) Unlawful damage

Damage is unlawful when it is contrary to the Criminal Damage Act 1971 (below, § 14.5–6). In particular, it is an offence under section 1 of that Act intentionally or recklessly to destroy or damage any property belonging to another. Note that unlawful damage is a relevant offence only for the purposes of burglarious *entry*, contrary to section 9(1)(a). Thus a trespasser who vandalises the interior of a building does not commit burglary unless she entered the building intending to do so.

(v) The rationale of burglary

Some writers have expressed scepticism as to whether burglary deserves its status as a separate and serious offence. Robinson asks:[253]

> "One may wonder, then, why burglary is retained as an offense in modern codes. Conviction for criminal intrusion and for attempt to commit the intended offense would seem adequately and properly to punish the conduct constituting burglary."

On this view, it is all the more puzzling, one may add, that burglary carries a maximum sentence greater than theft itself. The crime is, in Robinson's view, explicable only by historical tradition.

In our view, however, a separate and serious offence of burglary is in principle fully justified. In the first place, it involves a separate and distinct evil from the "ulterior offences"

---

[248] But surely not an infliction: see Gardner, "Rationality and the Rule of Law in Offences Against the Person" [1994] *CLJ* 502, 504–6.

[249] [1983] 1 All ER 1000, 1005.

[250] Smith, "Burglary under the Theft Bill" [1968] *Crim LR* 367.

[251] Strict, rather than constructive, liability, because the further element of the offence is not a mere consequence but a *novus actus* by D. See above, Chapter 6.

[252] See the commentary on *Jenkins and Jenkins* at [1983] Crim LR 386.

[253] *Criminal Law* (1997) 778.

upon which it in a sense depends: the violation of personal space. As such, it is a wrong in its own right. The trespassory entry by D not only exposes V to risk of a serious ulterior crime; in so doing, it also violates V's private life—an important protected interest under Article 8 of the ECHR.

The strongest case of this—subject under section 9(3) to distinctive sentencing provisions—is where the premises are a dwelling-house.[254] Interaction with and exposure to other members of society is integral to public life; conversely, our sense of identity and well-being as individuals depends upon our being able to reserve private space, from which other persons can be excluded. It is through controlling our private environment that we are able to have 'breathing space' from interactions with other people. Burglary compromises that space. It is hardly surprising that house burglary, in particular, causes victims great distress even if they were absent at the material time. The victim of such a burglary cannot be sure of the peaceable and secure enjoyment even of her own home. For most people, when the integrity of their private space cannot be taken for granted, one of the foundations of their well-being is destroyed.

An analogous if less powerful claim can be made for burglary of other buildings. One of the main functions of structures such as warehouses, offices, and the like is to help safeguard people and property by establishing a physical separation from the public environment. Within that secured space, people can relax at least some of the precautions they may take when in public, by putting down their handbags, remaining late to work, and the like. Conversely, if that space is not perceived to be fully secure, such practices become disrupted. Even in these non-domestic contexts, the existence and control of a realm of quasi-private space affects the manner in which we live.

The existence of secured private space also influences how we organise our property. Just as at home, goods in warehouses and offices can be arrayed or stocked without securing each individually. Thus a related harm of burglary is that it gives D unparalleled access to take (or damage) a whole range of V's goods, whether domestic or commercial, in a way that, say, pickpocketing does not. Here too, the case of a domestic burglary is an aggravated one: the goods to which D has access tend to include our highly personal things (underclothes, private letters, and the like) as well as things with high sentimental value—something that reinforces the sense of 'violation' experienced by burglary victims.

The "personal space" argument is supplemented by consequentialist considerations. Entry into a building is a significant physical step by which D commits herself to carrying out the ulterior crime. In effect, it ups the stakes, making it more likely that the ulterior offence will be committed. Moreover, because the activity occurs inside a building, it increases the probability that incidental violence will ensue should D be chanced upon by someone else:[255]

> "Frequently a person discovered in the course of committing a crime [in public] is in a position where he realizes that resistance is useless and that he must flee or surrender. Again, the person who discovers the criminal does not always have a sufficient interest to offer forcible intervention. Both of these factual situations are conducive to the non-occurrence of incidental crimes. Neither is likely to result when a trespasser is discovered while committing a crime

---

[254] Indeed, this was originally the only variety of burglary known to the common law. See 3 Coke Inst. 63.
[255] Note, "A Rationale of the Law of Burglary" (1951) 51 *Col LR* 1009, 1026.

in a dwelling;[256] rather, resistance to the criminal and consequent injury to occupants, seems probable."

To these two arguments there is a third and practical one that can be added. Burglary in its section 9(1)(a) version is a convenient offence for prosecuting those who have, in a literal and non-legal sense, attempted to commit a crime, in circumstances where a charge of attempt might run into difficulties because, as the law stands, an attempt must involve behaviour that is "more than merely preparatory to the commission of the offence".[257]

(vi) A case for reform

However, if there are good reasons for the existence of a crime of burglary in general, the particular offence that is created by section 9 of the Theft Act is open to the criticism that it is doubly inept. If the rationale for the offence is as we have described it, the section 9 offence is too wide in some respects, and other respects too narrow. It is too wide because it covers any building, including a public one. Whose personal space is violated, one wonders, if D enters a railway station with a view to picking pockets? It is also too wide because the concept of "entry as a trespasser", as interpreted in *Jones and Smith*, potentially extends the offence of burglary to behaviour that can only with difficulty be seen as a "violation" of a private area: for example, entering a supermarket during opening hours with the intention not of purchasing but of shoplifting. And the offence is too narrow because it fails to cover a range of violations of personal space which are extremely serious: for example, breaking into a person's home in order to seek private information or to plant bugging devices; or bursting into a neighbour's house in order to verbally abuse him in the presence of his wife and family.

In the codes of continental Europe the equivalent of burglary commonly consists of two offences. First, theft when committed in an inhabited building is an aggravated form of theft, to which a higher penalty attaches.[258] Secondly, there is a general offence of trespassing into other people's homes.[259] Yet oddly, UK governments, though prepared to create limited offences of aggravated trespass[260] and ever-ready to back the creation of new offences of trespassing upon state property,[261] have been resistant to the idea of making it a criminal offence to trespass into people's homes. When in 1991 the Calcutt Committee[262] proposed criminal offences of trespass into private property to obtain information, the Government eventually rejected the idea as likely to "prevent responsible journalism".[263] Regrettably, it seems probable that the real reason for this resistance was that the Home Office feared such legislation would inhibit covert policing and the activities of the secret service. About the time this public discussion was taking place, it came to light that the Home Secretary had

---

[256] It is submitted that this is true, to a lesser extent, of any other building.

[257] For a graphic illustration of the problem see *Geddes* [1996] Crim LR 894; above, §9.4.

[258] *Code pénal*, art. 311-4 para. 6 (France); *Codice penale*, art. 625 (Italy); StGB § 243 (Germany).

[259] *Code pénal*, art. 226-4 (France); *Codice penale*, art. 633 (Italy); StGB §§ 123–4 (Germany).

[260] Criminal Justice and Public Order Act 1994, Part V; and now a further offence of squatting in residential property, created by s. 144 of the Legal Aid, Sentencing and Punishment of Offenders Act 2012.

[261] For a lengthy list, see Williams, *TBCL*, 916–17, who concludes "One day, no doubt, we shall have some more sensible and general provision for criminal trespass".

[262] *Report of the Committee on Privacy and Related Matters* Cm. 1102 (1990).

[263] *Privacy and Media Intrusion—the Government's Response* Cm. 2918 (1995), §3.26.

issued a circular to the police, encouraging them to use Watergate-style break-ins to plant listening devices, even though to do so amounted to a civil trespass.[264]

§ 14.5 Criminal damage

This area of the law has a tangled history. Originally, arson was a felony at common law, and to this specific form of criminal damage other crimes of damage were added piecemeal over the years. In 1861 this muddle was consolidated by an Act of Parliament,[265] a statute similar in style and spirit to the Offences Against the Person Act.[266] But unlike offences against the person, the law relating to criminal damage was later recast in a simpler and more rational form by a major reforming statute, the Criminal Damage Act, in 1971.[267]

The core offence of criminal damage is contained in section 1(1) of the Criminal Damage Act:

> A person who without lawful excuse destroys or damages property belonging to another intending to destroy or damage any such property or being reckless whether any such property would be destroyed or damaged shall be guilty of an offence.

The offence, which is punishable by imprisonment for a maximum of 10 years, contains six main elements. The actus reus is:

(i)   that D destroys or damages
(ii) property; and
(iii) the property belongs to another.

The mens rea components are:

(iv) D intends or is reckless about destroying or damaging the property; and
(v)   D is (at least) reckless whether the property belongs to another.

Finally, the section provides for a defence:

(vi) D's conduct is without lawful excuse.

We shall consider these elements in turn.

(i) Destroys or damages

There must be some actual, physical damage to the property. We will focus here on the meaning of "damages" rather than "destroys", since the latter term seems to add nothing to the former, save in that it is apt to comprehend many of the more extreme or comprehensive instances of damage.

---

[264] *Khan* [1997] AC 558; noted [1997] CLJ 6. The sequel to this case was *Khan v UK* (2001) EHRR 45, in which the United Kingdom was condemned for failure to respect Article 8 of the ECHR, and the enactment of Part II of the Police Act 1997, giving the police the legal right to do this sort of thing in certain circumstances, and provided the procedure laid down by the Act is followed.

[265] The Malicious Damage Act 1861.

[266] See Chapter 11.

[267] The 1971 Act was based on a Report from the Law Commission: *Criminal Law: Offences of Damage to Property*, Law Com. No. 29 (1970).

What counts as damage is a question of fact and degree for the jury, and requires evaluation of the particular circumstances of the case.[268] There is no requirement that the damage be severe. One who walks across another's lawn may damage it by flattening the grass.[269] Neither is there any requirement that the damage be permanent or irreparable. Smearing mud graffiti on the wall of a police cell, which cost £7 to clean off, has been ruled capable of being criminal damage.[270] Similarly, it has been held that erasing a computer program can be criminal damage. In *Cox* v. *Riley*,[271] D intentionally deleted the program from a printed circuit card that operated a computerised saw, rendering the saw inoperable. He was convicted of criminal damage, a conviction upheld on appeal on the ground that deletion of the program constituted damage to the circuit card, since it necessitated expending time, labour and money to reprogram the card. The Divisional Court cited a helpful discussion from the unreported case of *Henderson* v. *Battley*, in which D was charged with damaging a development land site in the Isle of Dogs. The site, which had been cleared, was flat except for one pile of crushed concrete kept for use in the laying of temporary roads during the development. Without authority, D dumped 30 lorry loads of soil and rubble and mud on the site, effectively using it as a tip. The Court of Appeal held that, even though the underlying land was not itself altered, dumping rubbish could constitute criminal damage:[272]

> "if as here there is evidence that the owner of the land reasonably found it necessary to spend about £2,000 to remove the results of the appellant's operations it is not irrelevant to the question of whether this land, as a building site, was damaged. Ultimately whether damage was done to this land was a question of fact and degree for the jury. Damage can be of various kinds. In the Concise Oxford Dictionary 'damage' is defined as 'injury impairing value or usefulness.' That is a definition which would fit in very well with doing something to a cleared building site which at any rate for the time being impairs its usefulness as such. In addition, as it necessitates work and the expenditure of a large sum of money to restore it to its former state, it reduces its present value as a building site. This land was a perfectly good building site which did not need £2,000 spending on it in order to sell or use it as such until the appellants began their operations."

The Court also relied upon early authority in *Fisher*,[273] where D inserted an object into a machine and made other alterations that temporarily rendered the machine useless. This was held capable of constituting damage, on the basis that it took two hours' labour (albeit no additional materials) to restore the machine to proper working order.

Overall, what emerges from the cases is a two-part test: any significant alteration to property can count as damage, provided it requires more than a trivial expenditure of time, effort, or money to undo. In respect of undoing the alteration, we may contrast the smearing of mud on a wall with a scenario in which D affixes a "Post-it" note to V's door. The

---

[268] *Roe* v. *Kingerlee* [1986] Crim LR 735 (DC); *Samuels* v. *Stubbs* [1972] 4 SASR 200, 203; *Hardman* v. *Chief Constable of Avon and Somerset* [1986] Crim LR 331 (CC).
[269] *Gayford* v. *Chouler* [1898] 1 QB 316 (DC).
[270] *Roe* v. *Kingerlee* [1986] Crim LR 735 (DC).
[271] (1986) 83 Cr App R 54 (DC).
[272] Court of Appeal, Criminal Division, 29/11/84, at 3B; quoted in *Cox* v. *Riley* (1986) 83 Cr App R 54, 57 (DC).
[273] (1865) LR 1 CCR 7.

note can simply be lifted off, and it is submitted that D's act does not damage the door. In similar vein, spitting on a policeman's raincoat was ruled not to be damage in so far as the spittle could be removed simply by wiping it with a damp cloth.[274] Painting silhouettes on a pavement using soluble paint, on the other hand, was rightly held to be criminal damage after the local authority washed the markings away with high-pressure jets, even though they would eventually have been dissolved by rain.[275] Rainwater would not have removed the damage forthwith.

But that still leaves the question of when there is a significant alteration. Standard *indicia* are if the property is rendered either less usable[276] or less valuable.[277] To illustrate by counterexample, in *Morphitis* v. *Salmon* D removed a scaffolding bar from a barrier that was blocking an access road. The bar was subsequently found to be scratched. Even if D had caused the scratching, however, the Court ruled that this would not be criminal damage since it impaired neither the value nor the usefulness of the bar, scratching being a normal incident of scaffolding components.[278]

More difficult are the car-clamping cases. The courts have ruled that wheel clamping does not, in itself, damage the car, seemingly because it is a removable appendage that does not physically harm the vehicle. According to Laws J, in *Drake* v. *DPP*:[279]

> "But one way or another, whatever the example one chooses, there must be some intrusion into what, in the course of argument, Mann LJ described as the 'integrity of the object in question.' There was no such intrusion here. There was nothing which, as matter of ordinary language, could sensibly be regarded as damage to the car. Certainly the wheel clamp was applied to it. I do not, for my part, believe that a court could properly have held that this application amounted to 'damage.'"

It is submitted that these cases are wrongly decided. Admittedly, one may more readily think of them as involving detention rather than damage. But in light of the foregoing case law, the better view must be that clamping involves detention *by* damage. Contrast a scenario in which D erects a fence or other barrier around a car in order to prevent its departure, without affixing the barrier to the car. D does not damage the car. But if D applies a clamp directly to the car he does physically interfere so as to affect its "integrity"—no less than dumping rubbish on a land site or adding mud graffiti to a wall. Notwithstanding the assertion by Laws J, there is no necessity for any "intrusion into" the interior of the object. Surely the requirement for a physical alteration can be satisfied either internally or externally.[280]

---

[274] *A (A Juvenile)* v. *R* [1978] Crim LR 689 (CC).

[275] *Hardman* v. *Chief Constable of Avon and Somerset* [1986] Crim LR 331 (CC); distinguishing *A (A Juvenile)* v. *R* [1978] Crim LR 689 (CC) (above).

[276] *Roper* v. *Knott* [1898] 1 QB 868 (DC) (spoiling milk by adulterating it with water).

[277] *Foster* (1852) 6 Cox CC 25.

[278] [1990] Crim LR 48 (DC). The Court noted, *obiter*, that while D was not guilty of damaging the bar itself, he could have been convicted of criminal damage to the barrier as a whole—had he been so charged.

[279] [1994] RTR 411, 418 (DC); cf. *Lloyd* v. *DPP* [1992] 1 All ER 982 (DC).

[280] The clamping (or otherwise immobilising) of motor vehicles without lawful authority is now made a specific criminal offence by s. 54 of the Protection of Freedoms Act 2012. By s. 54(2), the express or implied consent of the owner of the vehicle (as might be argued to exist from a warning about clamping on a notice-board or the back of ticket) does not count as "lawful authority" for the purpose of this offence.

(ii) Property

Most tangible things can be damaged. According to section 10(1) of the 1971 Act:

> In this Act "property" means property of a tangible nature, whether real or personal, including money and—
>
> (a)   including wild creatures which have been tamed or are ordinarily kept in captivity, and any other wild creatures or their carcasses if, but only if, they have been reduced into possession which has not been lost or abandoned or are in the course of being reduced into possession; but
>
> (b)   not including mushrooms growing wild on any land or flowers, fruit or foliage of a plant growing wild on any land.
>
> For the purposes of this subsection "mushroom" includes any fungus and "plant" includes any shrub or tree.

As with the law of theft, the scope of the offence is wide-ranging and includes most forms of tangible property known to the common law. Indeed, like the definition in section 4(1) of the Theft Act 1968, "property" is not here statutorily defined; we must begin with that concept as it is understood in the civil law,[281] and section 10(1) simply operates to modify the underlying civil law concept.

The most important difference from theft is that criminal damage requires the property to be *tangible*, something that reflects the physical nature of the concept of damage within the 1971 Act. Hence extinguishing a debt (owed to V) by appropriating V's bank account cannot be criminal damage, even though it might be said to "destroy" V's chose in action, because choses in action are intangible property and fall outwith the scope of section 10(1).

A second point of difference is that land can be damaged, without being subject to the restrictions applicable in the context of theft.[282] Additionally, things growing wild cannot be damaged, whereas they can be stolen if picked for a commercial purpose.[283]

(iii) Belonging to another

Under section 1(1), the core offence of criminal damage can be committed only when the property damaged "belongs" to someone other than V. (The aggravated offence does not require this: see below, § 14.6.) This means that, for the core offence, some other person must have an interest in the subject matter of the damage. As with theft, this does not preclude D's being the owner of the item, so long as her ownership is not absolute; as when V, say, has a lien over the property, or is a joint owner, or has some other interest in the property. In such a case the property can be criminally damaged by D (or by anyone else, including V). But if D is absolute owner of the property, she cannot commit the offence under section 1(1). It does not "belong to another" for the purposes of the Act.

---

[281] For general discussion, see above, § 13.3.
[282] Theft Act 1968, s. 4(2); above, § 13.3(ii)(a).
[283] Theft Act 1968, s. 4(3); above, § 13.3(ii)(b).

The meaning of "belonging to another" is elaborated in section 10:

(2) Property shall be treated for the purposes of this Act as belonging to any person—

(a) having the custody or control of it;

(b) having in it any proprietary right or interest (not being an equitable interest arising only from an agreement to transfer or grant an interest); or

(c) having a charge on it.

(3) Where property is subject to a trust, the persons to whom it belongs shall be so treated as including any person having a right to enforce the trust.

(4) Property of a corporation sole shall be so treated as belonging to the corporation notwithstanding a vacancy in the corporation.

As with the corresponding provisions in section 5 of the Theft Act, the scope of the section is effective to protect virtually any form of proprietary interest, whether of ownership or possession, and whether at common law or equity. Although the section mentions "custody *or* control", it is not clear that the latter term adds anything much. Physical control would in any event also constitute a form of custody, and any other right of control would presumably only qualify if it were enforceable *in rem*, i.e. if it were a proprietary interest. Similarly, the inclusion of a "charge" in section 10(2)(c) is probably superfluous, since charges are normally a form of proprietary interest.

On the other hand, where there is no custody or control there *must* be a proprietary interest. Thus the section does not protect interests that may arise when D enters into an agreement to sell goods to V on some future date. Section 10(2)(b) makes it clear that the latter sort of interest is not protected, by contrast with contracts of sale that transfer ownership immediately. Hence if, before the agreed date of the future transfer, D were to destroy the goods, D would not commit criminal damage. Similarly, neither is D guilty of an offence under section 1(1) if he sets fire to his car intending to claim the insurance, because an insurer has no proprietary interest in the subject matter of the policy.[284]

(iv) Intentional or reckless damage

The *damage* (or destruction) must be done either intentionally or (subjectively) recklessly. If D throws a stone at V and misses, he does not become guilty of criminal damage when the stone misses V but goes on to break V's window, unless the risk of its doing so was foreseen by D.[285] The subjective nature of this recklessness requirement is authoritatively reasserted by the House of Lords in *G*,[286] overruling the decision in *Caldwell*[287] which was for a time authority that failing to foresee an obvious and serious risk of the actus reus could also constitute recklessness. These decisions are discussed in detail in § 5.2(i) above. In gist, the law now requires that D either intends to damage the property,[288] or actually foresees a risk that the property will be damaged by her conduct.

---

[284] Cf. *Denton* [1981] 1 WLR 1446, 1448–9 (CA).

[285] Cf. *Pembliton* (1874) LR 2 CCC 119.

[286] [2004] AC 1034.

[287] [1982] AC 341 (HL).

[288] Above, § 5.1.

As with recklessness generally, in the latter case the risk she foresees must also be an unreasonable one to run.[289] No doubt, for example, by hitting a six at the village cricket ground D creates a slight risk of causing damage to a neighbouring house. Suppose that, although he does not intend such damage, he is aware of the risk. Typically, nonetheless, the risk he creates is a reasonable one and, if a window should be broken, D will not be accounted reckless.[290]

(v) Intention or recklessness whether the property belongs to another

In respect of the core offence in section 1(1), the general requirement of intention or recklessness extends to the actus reus element that the property *belongs to another*. To count as "intention" when applied to circumstances,[291] D would need either to hope, know, or believe that the property belongs to someone else.[292] But this is not especially important, since it is anyway sufficient that D is reckless about the ownership of the property. Given the meaning of the latter term in the context of circumstances,[293] D will be reckless whether the property belongs to another if she either recognises a risk that the property is not absolutely hers; or if, in the extensional case allowed for by the House of Lords in *B (a minor)* v. *DPP*,[294] she acts without believing that the property belongs to her (i.e. if she has no belief either way).

The importance of this mens rea element is emphasised in *Smith (David)*.[295] D, a tenant, with permission installed stereo wiring in his flat which he covered by mounting covering panels and other materials. Upon termination of the tenancy, D damaged the panels in order to remove the wiring. By operation of law, the panels had became part of the flat when installed and so belonged to the owner. Nonetheless, although D was certainly civilly liable for the damage, his conviction of criminal damage was quashed, since D honestly believed that the panels were his. In the Court's analysis:[296]

> "Construing the language of section 1(1) we have no doubt that the actus reus is 'destroying or damaging any property belonging to another.' It is not possible to exclude the words 'belonging to another' which describes the 'property'. Applying the ordinary principles of mens rea, the intention and recklessness and the absence of lawful excuse required to constitute the offence have reference to property belonging to another. It follows that in our judgment no offence is committed under this section if a person destroys or causes damage to property belonging to another if he does so in the honest though mistaken belief that the property is his own, and provided that the belief is honestly held it is irrelevant to consider whether or not it is a justifiable belief."

---

[289] This proviso is noted above, § 5.2.
[290] Famously, neither is he negligent in tort law: *Miller* v. *Jackson* [1977] QB 966; *Bolton* v. *Stone* [1951] AC 850.
[291] Above, § 5.1(v).
[292] In the wider sense of belonging to another defined by s. 10; above, § 14.5(iii).
[293] Above, § 5.2(iii).
[294] [2000] 2 AC 428, 459 (Lord Mackay), 466 (Lord Nicholls).
[295] [1974] QB 354 (CA).
[296] *Ibid.*, 360.

(vi) Without lawful excuse

As with other offences, the offence of criminal damage is only prima facie established by proof of the foregoing actus reus and mens rea elements. D may still have a defence; for example, if he acted in self-defence or in circumstances of necessity. Unusually, however, the Act offers its own lengthy supplementary definition of "lawful excuse" in section 5:

(1) This section applies to any offence under section 1(1) above and any offence under section 2 or 3 above other than one involving a threat by the person charged to destroy or damage property in a way which he knows is likely to endanger the life of another or involving an intent by the person charged to use or cause or permit the use of something in his custody or under his control so to destroy or damage property.

(2) A person charged with an offence to which this section applies shall, whether or not he would be treated for the purposes of this Act as having a lawful excuse apart from this subsection, be treated for those purposes as having a lawful excuse—

(a)   if at the time of the act or acts alleged to constitute the offence he believed that the person or persons whom he believed to be entitled to consent to the destruction of or damage to the property in question had so consented, or would have so consented to it if he or they had known of the destruction or damage and its circumstances; or

(b)   if he destroyed or damaged or threatened to destroy or damage the property in question or, in the case of a charge of an offence under section 3 above, intended to use or cause or permit the use of something to destroy or damage it, in order to protect property belonging to himself or another or a right or interest in property which was or which he believed to be vested in himself or another, and at the time of the act or acts alleged to constitute the offence he believed—

(i)   that the property, right or interest was in immediate need of protection; and

(ii)   that the means of protection adopted or proposed to be adopted were or would be reasonable having regard to all the circumstances.

(3) For the purposes of this section it is immaterial whether a belief is justified or not if it is honestly held.

(4) For the purposes of subsection (2) above a right or interest in property includes any right or privilege in or over land, whether created by grant, licence or otherwise.

(5) This section shall not be construed as casting doubt on any defence recognised by law as a defence to criminal charges.

Section 5(2) lays down two statutory grounds of lawful excuse: consent and defence of property. For both versions, section 5(3) makes clear that the test is subjective: the availability of the defence depends on what D *believed*, rather than the actual fact of the matter or even whether D's belief was reasonable. Unusually, this is so even if D makes a mistake due to intoxication.[297] We consider the two versions in turn.

(a) Consent

Section 5(2)(a) establishes a defence of lawful excuse if D believes that the owner (or other person entitled to consent, such as the owner's representative) has consented to

---

[297] *Jaggard* v. *Dickinson* [1981] QB 527 (DC). D had been given permission to treat her friend's house as her own. She broke into the wrong house one evening, drunkenly thinking it was her friend's. D's conviction was quashed on the footing that she genuinely believed she had consent to break in; and s. 5(3) stipulates a subjective rather than objective test. See below, § 18.3(iii)(a).

the damage's being inflicted, or would have done so had she known about it.[298] A striking illustration is *Denton*,[299] in which D set fire to his employer's cotton mill, causing some £40,000 worth of damage. He acted purportedly in the belief that his employer had encouraged him to do so, since the business was in difficulty and a fire would "help its financial circumstances". On these facts, the Court of Appeal quashed D's conviction. The underlying fraudulent motive was irrelevant, at least to a charge of criminal damage: D's belief that he had consent, from someone he thought entitled to give such consent,[300] was sufficient to establish a lawful excuse.

(b) Defence of property

Frequently this defence will overlap with the defence of prevention of crime in section 3 of the Criminal Law Act 1967 (discussed in § 21.2). However, it is available even when the threat to property is not itself criminal.[301] In *Chamberlain* v. *Lindon*,[302] for example, following a dispute about the extent of D's right of way over part of V's land, V built a wall restricting D's vehicular access. D demolished the wall. The Divisional Court affirmed his acquittal of criminal damage, because D had acted in order to protect his right of way, which was a "right or interest in property" falling within section 5(2)(b).

In order to qualify for the defence, D must subjectively believe (i) that the property (or interest therein) belonged to himself or another; (ii) that it was in *immediate* need of protection; and (iii) that conduct was a *reasonable* means of protecting the property. D's conduct must also be undertaken (iv) *in order to* protect the property. These elements deserve separate consideration.

Belonging to himself or another.
Interestingly, there is nothing in the section to suggest that "another" cannot be the very owner of the damaged property, as when D breaks into V's house in order to put out a fire there. Section 5(2)(b) seems to require only that the property or interest being protected was thought by D to belong to *someone*, and not to be abandoned or otherwise ownerless. The point was important in *Cresswell* v. *DPP*,[303] where the defendants went onto farmland and destroyed badger traps in order to protect wild badgers. Because the badgers had not been reduced into possession they were ownerless and not property, so fell outside the scope of section 5. The defendants' convictions were upheld.

Immediate need of protection.
Whether D believes the property is in need of protection is a subjective question. But the courts have held that whether the perceived need counts as "immediate" is an *objective* question to be determined by the jury (or judge, as the case may be), in light of the facts and circumstances that D believes to exist. This point was decisive in *Hill*,[304] where D was

---

[298] Compare s. 2(1)(b) of the Theft Act 1968; above, § 13.8(ii).
[299] [1981] 1 WLR 1446 (CA).
[300] Not including God: *Blake* v. *DPP* [1993] Crim LR 586 (DC). Consent is discussed in § 21.1 below.
[301] But, unlike the defence of prevention of crime, there must be a threat to *property*: cf. *Cresswell* v. *DPP* [2006] EWHC 3379, [2007] Env LR D8; *Kelleher* [2003] EWCA Crim 3525, (2003) 147 SJLB 1395; *Baker* [1997] Crim LR 497.
[302] [1998] 1 WLR 1252 (QB).
[303] [2006] EWHC 3379, [2007] Env LR D8.
[304] *Hill and Hall* (1989) 89 Cr App R 74 (CA Crim Div).

charged with possessing articles (namely hacksaw blades) with intent to damage the perimeter fence of a naval base.[305] She claimed that her purpose was to bring about the abandonment of the base which, in the even of international hostilities breaking out, she believed would be the target of a nuclear strike with consequential damage to surrounding property, including hers. Even accepting her view of the facts, however, the Court of Appeal ruled that the perceived threat was not immediate. The defence requires "that she believed that immediate action had to be taken to do something which would otherwise be a crime in order to prevent the immediate risk of something worse happening".[306] On D's own account, there was no "immediate" risk at hand. It seems that this will turn, in part, on whether the perceived threat has crystallised or remains as yet conjectural. *Hill* was distinguished on this basis in *Chamberlain v. Lindon* (above), where D had demolished V's wall to preserve a right of way:[307]

> "The appellants in [Hill] had professed to be concerned as to the potential consequences of a possible nuclear attack in the future. Here, on the facts, as believed by the defendant, his right of way was actually being obstructed.... it was not a case of there being a risk of an obstruction at some future speculative date—there was a present need to remove the obstruction. The defendant was not destroying or damaging property as some sort of pre-emptive strike to prevent some future obstruction."

A reasonable means of protection.

Somewhat surprisingly, the statute makes it clear that what counts is D's own belief that her response is reasonable; the matter is not one for objective assessment by the court:[308]

> "[T]he question is not whether the means of protection adopted by the defendant were objectively reasonable having regard to all the circumstances, but whether the defendant believed them to be so. By virtue of section 5(3) it is immaterial whether his belief was justified, provided it was honestly held."

In this respect, the section 5 defence is more generous than other, more general, justificatory defences found in the criminal law, where the courts have—rightly—held that the defendant's response must be *objectively* reasonable or proportionate, regardless of D's own views on the question.[309] As we shall see in the next paragraph, the generosity of section 5 to defendants makes the courts uneasy, and in some cases they have sought to limit it.

In order to protect the property.

D must actually have the purpose of protecting property, although that need not be her only reason for acting.[310] Purpose is a subjective concept—it turns on *why* D acted, what she was trying to achieve. However, the courts have bent the wording by purporting to add an objective gloss to the interpretation of "in order to protect property" in section 5(2)(b). In *Hunt*,[311] D was assisting his wife who was deputy warden in a block of old persons'

---

[305] Contrary to s. 3 of the Criminal Damage Act 1971.

[306] (1989) 89 Cr App R 74, 79–80.

[307] [1998] 1 WLR 1252, 1260. The Court also pointed to the defendant's viewpoint that, the longer the wall remained, the more urgent the need to remove it, to avoid any suggestion of acquiescence in the obstruction.

[308] *Chamberlain v. Lindon* [1998] 1 WLR 1252, 1262.

[309] Below, § 21.2(ii), (iv).

[310] *Chamberlain v. Lindon* [1998] 1 WLR 1252, 1259.

[311] (1978) 66 Cr App R 105 (CA Crim Div).

flats. He discovered that the fire alarm was not working; apparently the Council had been informed but had not repaired the alarm. D subsequently set fire to some bedding in a relatively isolated part of the block of flats in order (i) to draw attention to the defective alarm and thereby (ii) to protect the block of flats from the risks posed by the defective alarm. Affirming his conviction, the Court of Appeal accepted the first purpose but rejected the second:[312]

> "The question whether or not a particular act of destruction or damage or threat of destruction or damage was done or made in order to protect property belonging to another must be, on the true construction of the statute, an objective test. Therefore we have to ask ourselves whether, whatever the state of this man's mind and assuming an honest belief, that which he admittedly did was done in order to protect this particular property, namely the old people's home in Hertfordshire?
>
> If one formulates the question in that way, in the view of each member of this Court, for the reason Slynn J gave during the argument, it admits of only one answer: this was not done in order to protect property; it was done in order to draw attention to the defective state of the fire alarm. It was not an act which *in itself* did protect or was capable of protecting property."

But purpose is a subjective, not objective concept. What this gloss amounts to is a new requirement, not found in the statute: that D's immediate action must "in itself" be capable of protecting property. But this requirement is simply not part of section 5(2), which requires that D's purpose in acting be to protect property, and that D actually believe his immediate action is a reasonable way of seeking to achieve that purpose. There is no requirement that his action should achieve the purpose *directly*.[313] Suppose that D breaks into V's house in order to telephone the fire brigade because T's house, next door, is ablaze. Breaking into the house is not "in itself" capable of protecting T's property. Yet no-one would or should deny that D has a lawful excuse under section 5(2)(b).

It is submitted that the better explanation of *Hunt* is that, notwithstanding his genuine purpose to bolster the protection mechanisms in the block of flats, the lawful excuse within section 5 was unavailable because the threat was not immediate.

Undeterred by *Hunt*, protestors often seek to invoke section 5 in situations which that decision would probably exclude—and in practice juries are often sympathetic. Thus in 2000 a jury famously acquitted 27 protesters accused of destroying genetically modified maize, whose defence was that they believed their act was necessary to protect other crops and plants in the surrounding area.[314] Similarly, in 2008 another jury acquitted a group of Greenpeace activists who had painted the word "Gordon" on the chimney of Kingsnorth power station, whose defence was that they believed their act was necessary to prevent climate change from damaging property all over the world.[315] But less successful with his jury was the man who decapitated a statue of Mrs Thatcher, allegedly causing £150,000 of damage, who sought to invoke section 5 on the ground that he believed his

---

[312] *Ibid.*, 108 (emphasis added).
[313] A similar requirement of proximity is suggested in *Hill* (1989) 89 Cr App R 74, 79.
[314] "GM Chaos as Melchett is Freed", *The Times*, 21 September 2000.
[315] "Protesters Cleared over Damage to Power Plant", *The Times*, 11 September 2008.

act was necessary to prevent the destruction of the world by globalisation and the spread of materialistic values.[316]

(vii) Criminal damage—a distinctive wrong

Similarly to offences such as robbery and burglary, criminal damage resembles theft in that it is intrinsically bound up with the violation of another person's property rights. Indeed, to deprive the owner of a chattel by destroying it can be the actus reus of a theft.[317] Like those other offences, however, criminal damage merits separate criminalisation because of the distinctive manner in which V's rights are violated. Many typical instances of vandalism involve the infliction of damage using percussive force, fire, or explosions, conduct that may well endanger others, or cause alarm and concern even to bystanders lacking any proprietary interest in the property being damaged. (Hence, as we see in § 14.6, the enactment of aggravated criminal damage offences.) To that extent, the offence becomes part of the family of offences concerned with restraining violence and disorder—concerns generally outside the ambit of theft *simpliciter*, save for lootings in circumstances of civil tumult. And, to the extent that it is associated with these different forms of wrongful conduct, criminal damage is a proprietary wrong different in kind from theft. Vandalism frequently has an expressive dimension, communicating a contempt for society, and for the victim, which goes beyond a mere appropriation of property rights; that further wrong, in turn, warrants a label distinct from theft.

Not all types of vandalism involve violence. But all cases of vandalism share a second, intrinsic feature: criminal damage is concerned with the item of property *per se*, and not just with another's rights over that item. When D steals V's book, she does not attack the item itself but, rather, pre-empts V's rights to use and exchange the book. The book itself remains usable and exchangeable; indeed, it is simply the subject of an involuntary exchange. By contrast, when E destroys V's book he attacks the use- and exchange-value of the item in anyone's hands and not merely V's. Its value is lost *tout court*, not just to V; society's store of wealth is diminished. In this respect, the harm of criminal damage differs from that of theft.

§ 14.6 Aggravated criminal damage and arson

Section 1(2) of the Criminal Damage Act 1971 creates an aggravated offence of intentionally or recklessly destroying or damaging property and thereby endangering life:

> A person who without lawful excuse destroys or damages any property, whether belonging to himself or another—
> (a) intending to destroy or damage any property or being reckless as to whether any property would be destroyed or damaged; and
> (b) intending by the destruction or damage to endanger the life of another or being reckless as to whether the life of another would be thereby endangered;
> shall be guilty of an offence.

---

[316] *Kelleher* [2003] EWCA Crim 3525. The trial judge directed the jury in accordance with *Hunt*, and the Court of Appeal upheld the conviction, reaffirming the objective test set out in that decision. The defendant in this case was sentenced to three months' imprisonment.

[317] *Cabbage* (1815) Russ & Ry 292, 168 ER 809.

There are three main elements to the offence, which is punishable by life imprisonment.[318] The actus reus is:

(i)   that D destroys or damages property belonging to *someone*.

The law on this is the same as for the section 1(1) offence, and is discussed above in § 14.5(i)–(iii); except that there is no requirement in section 1(2) that the property belong to someone other than D.[319] This reflects the fact that the aggravated offence is not truly a property offence at all, but rather an endangerment-based offence against the person.[320] For the same reason, the lawful excuse defence in section 5 is unavailable to a charge under section 1(2).[321] However, other general defences, such as self-defence, are available in the normal way.[322]

The mens rea components of the aggravated offence are:

(i)   D intends or is reckless about destroying or damaging the property (as above, § 14.5(iv); and

(ii)   D intends thereby to endanger the life of another, or is (at least) reckless whether the life of another will thereby be endangered.

Section 1(2) might be termed an ulterior mens rea offence.[323] There is no actus reus requirement that anyone's life in fact be endangered; all that is required is that property is damaged with the intent or in the (subjective)[324] belief that life may be endangered thereby. This point is illustrated in *Parker*,[325] where D set fire to his semi-detached house, realising that his neighbours' lives may be endangered. His conviction was upheld notwithstanding that the neighbours turned out to be away.

The language of section 1(2)(b) stipulates that the endangerment must be *by* (or "thereby") the damage or destruction. It is not enough that D's act happens to cause both property damage and personal danger: the former must be (foreseen or intended as) a route to the latter. In *Steer*, D fired a rifle at the windows of V's house, both intending to cause damage and being reckless whether life would be endangered. His conviction under section 1(2) was nonetheless quashed. He was reckless whether life would be

---

[318] *Per* s. 4.

[319] Cf. *A-G's Reference (No. 98 of 2001)* [2001] EWCA Crim 3068, [2002] 2 Cr App R(S) 25; *Parker* [1993] Crim LR 856 (CA).

[320] Cf. *Merrick* [1996] 1 Cr App R 130 (CA), and the critical discussion in Elliott, "Endangering Life by Destroying or Damaging Property" [1997] *Crim LR* 382, 388–9.

[321] *Per* s. 5(1), set out above in § 14.5(vi).

[322] This is made clear by the express retention of the phrase, "without lawful excuse" in the opening line of s. 1(2) notwithstanding that the supplementary definition in s. 5 is inapplicable to s. 1(2).

[323] Cf. Horder, "Crimes of Ulterior Intent" in Simester and Smith (eds.), *Harm and Culpability* (1996) 153.

[324] *Cooper* [2004] EWCA Crim 1382; following *G* [2003] UK HL 50, above, § 5.2(i). The Court in *Cooper* opined at para. 12 that "[i]t is now, in the light of *G*, incumbent on a trial judge to direct a jury, in a case of this kind, that the risk of danger to life was obvious and significant to the defendant. In other words, a subjective element is essential before the jury can convict of this offence." *Quaere* however whether the risk now need even be obvious, as opposed to foreseen (and, as foreseen, an unreasonable risk to run).

[325] [1993] Crim LR 856 (CA). Note that Parker was decided prior to *G* and *Cooper* (see preceding footnote) and applied an objective standard of recklessness.

endangered *by the bullets*, not by the damage to the house. The crucial nexus, "thereby", was missing:[326]

> "To be guilty under subsection (2) he must additionally have intended to endanger life or been reckless as to whether life would be endangered 'by the damage' to property which he caused. This is the context in which the words must be construed and it seems to me impossible to read the words 'by the damage' as meaning 'by the damage or by the act which caused the damage'."

On the other hand, D would have been guilty of the offence had he foreseen danger to life caused by the spray of glass from the broken windows.

Relatedly, there is no requirement that the damage caused must be the same as that which was contemplated by D. It is enough that D intends or foresees endangering life by the property damage that he contemplates will follow from his actions; and that, by acting as he does, D causes *some* property damage:[327]

> "Thus, if a defendant throws a brick at the windscreen of a moving vehicle, given that he causes some damage to the vehicle, whether he is guilty under section 1(2) does not depend on whether the brick hits or misses the windscreen, but whether he intended to hit it and intended that the damage therefrom should endanger life or whether he was reckless as to that outcome."

Implicitly, it is not necessary that the property damage that ultimately results from D's actions should itself endanger life.

(i) Arson

By virtue of section 1(3),[328] in cases where the criminal damage in section 1(1) or 1(2) is caused by fire, the offence is called *arson* (or arson with intent to endanger life, etc., as the case may be) and is punishable by life imprisonment.[329] The mens rea requirement is correspondingly modified: D must intend, or foresee, causing damage *by fire*. It is not enough that the contemplated damage happens unexpectedly to cause a fire, even if that fire then endangers the lives of others.[330]

§ 14.7 Preliminary offences

As with sexual offences[331] and with fraud,[332] criminal damage and arson are backed up by a range of preliminary offences in "inchoate mode". Section 2 of the Criminal Damage Act creates an offence of uttering threats to damage or destroy property, and section 3 an offence of possessing anything with intent to do so. This policy is taken further by the

---

[326] [1988] AC 111, 117 (Lord Bridge). Cf. *Webster* [1995] 2 All ER 168 (CA).

[327] *Webster, ibid.,* 497; approving *Dudley* [1989] Crim LR 57.

[328] "An offence committed under this section by destroying or damaging property by fire shall be charged as arson." Section 1(3) effectively rejects the Law Commission's recommendation that there should be no separate offence of arson (although criminal damage should incur a greater maximum penalty when caused by fire): Law Com. No. 29, *Report on Offences of Damage to Property* (1970) paras. 28–33.

[329] *Per* s. 4.

[330] Cf. *Cooper (G) and Cooper (Y)* [1991] Crim LR 524 (CA).

[331] Above, § 12.

[332] See below, § 15.6.

Explosive Substances Act 1883. In addition to an offence of "unlawfully and maliciously" causing an explosion likely to endanger life or cause serious damage to property,[333] the 1883 Act creates an offence of making or possessing an explosive substance with intent to do this.[334] And to make doubly sure, it creates yet a further offence of making or possessing an explosive substance "under such circumstances as to give rise to a reasonable suspicion that he is not making it or does not have it in his possession or under his control for a lawful object",[335] of which the defendant, where such circumstances are shown, is guilty "unless he can show that he made it or had it in his possession or under his control for a lawful object".[336] The first two of these three offences are punishable with life imprisonment, the third with 14 years.

---

[333] Explosive Substances Act 1883, s. 2.

[334] *Ibid.*, s. 3(1)(a).

[335] *Ibid.*, s. 4.

[336] The case law to date assumes that the burden so placed on the defendant is a legal one: see *Attorney-General's Reference (No. 2 of 1983)* [1984] QB 456; *Berry* [1985] AC 246. But in the light of Art. 6(2) of the ECHR and the decision *Sheldrake and Attorney-General's Reference (No. 4 of 2002)* [2004] UKHL 43, [2005] 1 AC 264, the courts may in future reconsider the matter and interpret it as imposing an evidential burden only. See above, § 3.2.

15

FRAUD

Theft is not the only way of usurping another's property rights. Sometimes, the wrongfulness of the defendant's behaviour may be more subtle. It may, for example, lie in the fact that D duped V into transferring ownership consensually[1] or into performing services for D, or in the fact that she fraudulently gained from the use of V's assets even though V suffered no loss. In common with theftuous offences, wrongdoing of this sort involves dishonest behaviour by D regarding the property of another. However, its prevention often requires the enactment of offences which differ substantially from traditional forms of theft.

The extent to which such offences are necessary has sometimes been questioned.[2] For example, although acquisition by deception may not give rise to tortious claims in trespass or conversion,[3] other civil law remedies, such as deceit, are usually available to the aggrieved party. In addition, much commercial wrongdoing is controlled by administrative regulation of the marketplace, buttressed by the civil sanctions available to professional bodies. Given such existing sanctions, and the commitment in this country to a broadly liberal economic philosophy, is it really essential to fence in the marketplace with criminal law?

The answer is yes. Our rights to private property are part of the very fabric of the modern United Kingdom.[4] Property relations are shared elements which help to structure our interpersonal relations within the community. As such, they are integral to our membership of society, and to the understanding we have of our own lives. In particular, one feature of our participation in a broadly liberal society is the autonomy we have in respect of our property—the freedom to use, control, and dispose of that property as we wish.

As was noted above, in Chapter 13, there are limitations to our autonomy as proprietors. Even the freedoms of contract and testament are substantially constrained by law. Neither may we use our assets to fund criminal activities, and we are compelled by the State to contribute through taxation to certain communal goals which may not be of direct personal benefit to us. Nonetheless, the importance of individualism to the UK polity means that personal property rights have attracted better protection from the criminal law than many more abstract social or community values, such as an unpolluted environment or a well-educated populace. By contrast with these examples, the occurrence of harms is more readily criminalised and prosecuted when there is an identifiable victim whose concrete individual rights have been transgressed.

---

[1] Although, following *Gomez* and *Hinks*, this case would now also be theft. See above, § 13.6(ii).
[2] See, e.g., *Jones* (1703) 2 Ld Raymond 1013, 92 ER 174; *Goodhall* (1821) Russ & Ry 461, 168 ER 898.
[3] Since possession and/or title will normally have passed, at least prima facie.
[4] Cf. Waldron, *The Right to Private Property* (1988); Ryan, *Property and Political Theory* (1986); Nozick, *Anarchy, State and Utopia* (1974); Epstein, "Property as a Fundamental Civil Right" (1992) 29 *Cal West LR* 187; Harris, *Property and Justice* (1996).

This imbalance may be reason for complaint, but not on the basis that property rights deserve reduced protection. Indeed, the harms involved in property offences shade into those addressed by offences against the person, and any suggestion that offences against property are concerned solely with material loss would be misleading. The violation of our homes by a burglary, for example, may cause psychological injury and distress quite independent of the quantum of loss. Offences such as theft, fraud, and blackmail are generally categorised as property offences, and understandably so, for they involve wrongful acquisition of property. But they are also, in a very real sense, offences against the person. In each case, the conduct prohibited can be seen as an attack upon the victim's entitlement to dispose of his property by his own full and informed choice. Thus, the conduct represents an attack upon the victim's rights of free will and autonomy, and upon his freedom to exercise control over his own situation. Blackmail, for instance, involves D infringing V's legitimate control over his own affairs by imposing her free will in place of his. This subjugation of V resembles an assault as much as it does a "property" wrong. Fraud by false representation, understood in this sense, is a crime partly because it entails the manipulation or exploitation of another. Unlike the corresponding civil law remedies, property offences, in differing ways, protect the individual's entitlement to respect as an autonomous member of our society.

§ 15.1 Statutory fraud—general

The major measure for criminalising fraudulent conduct is the Fraud Act 2006,[5] which came into force on 15 January 2007;[6] and it is with the offences created by this legislation that this chapter will be mainly concerned. For the details of the law of fraud as it stood before that date, readers should refer to earlier editions. A thumbnail account of it is given here, however, to put the new law into context and explain the thinking behind the reform.

The recent history[7] of the law of fraud is that, together with the law of theft, it was recast in the Theft Act 1968, the new law consisting of a principal offence of obtaining property by deception,[8] flanked by subsidiary offences that included procuring the execution of a valuable security by deception[9] and an opaquely drafted offence called "obtaining a pecuniary advantage by deception".[10] The 1968 makeover of fraud was less successful than the reform of theft,[11] and in 1978 it was necessary to pass a further Theft Act, creating three

---

[5] For helpful analysis of the key provisions, see Ormerod, "The Fraud Act 2006: Criminalising Lying?" [2007] *Crim LR* 193. See also Ormerod and Williams, *Smith's Law of Theft* (9th ed., 2007).

[6] The Fraud Act 2006 (Commencement) Order 2006 (SI 2006/3200).

[7] The early history of the matter is that from the Middle Ages there was a general common law offence of cheating, which was supplemented from an early date by a range of specific statutory offences. For a list, see Blackstone, *Commentaries* (1765–9), Book IV, chap. 12, § 9. The usual penalty for the various forms of cheating was the pillory, the rationale, in the days before newspapers and easy travel, in part being the need to warn the public of a fellow citizen who was not to be trusted to do business with.

[8] Theft Act 1968, s. 15.

[9] *Ibid.*, s. 20; the typical example was telling lies to persuade someone to write a cheque.

[10] *Ibid.*, s. 16.

[11] This was not entirely the fault of the Criminal Law Revision Committee, whose proposals were in this case departed from when the Bill that became the Theft Act 1968 was prepared and enacted.

further fraud offences: obtaining services by deception,[12] evading liability by deception,[13] and making off without payment.[14] In 1996 the House of Lords, in a spirit completely opposite to the one which three years earlier had animated their decision on the scope of theft in *Gomez*,[15] gave the offence of obtaining property by deception a narrow and technical interpretation, holding that it did not cover the person who by deception caused a bank or building society to transfer money to his bank account,[16] in response to which it was necessary to create a further new offence of obtaining a money transfer by deception.[17] In the background to this clutter of narrowly drawn offences lurked the protean common law offence of conspiracy to defraud, ready to be invoked by prosecutors against any customers who proved particularly difficult. The resulting law was complicated and its fragmented state provided ample means for defendants to wrong-foot prosecutors by arguing that, dishonest though they were, they had been charged with the wrong offence. In the light of this, the government referred the law of fraud to the Law Commission, whose proposals were largely accepted in the Fraud Act 2006.[18]

The Fraud Act 2006 abolished a swathe of specific fraud offences[19] and replaced them with a new general fraud offence that can be committed in one of three ways, namely by false representation, by failing to disclose information, and by abuse of position. As there is but one offence, as a matter of substantive law it would not matter if the evidence establishes that fraud was committed in another fashion to that initially alleged by the prosecution. The prosecution may base their case on a false representation which they fail to prove, yet nonetheless establish that a fraud was perpetrated by D's failure to disclose information to V that he was under a legal duty to divulge. As a matter of practice, however, the prosecution should set out the case against D as clearly as possible,[20] and any trial must be fair within the terms of Article 6 of the ECHR.[21] A further innovation is that, unlike the previous offences, the actus reus of the new fraud offence is "minimalist". An essential ingredient in the new offence, like the old ones, is dishonesty. But whereas the old offences required D by his dishonesty to have obtained something, or to have caused something to happen, under the new law it is enough that D behaved dishonestly with this aim in mind. Each form of the offence of fraud is a conduct crime, not a result crime. In effect, fraud is an inchoate offence, although, since technically it is a substantive crime in its own right,

---

[12] Theft Act 1978, s. 1.

[13] *Ibid.*, s. 2.

[14] *Ibid.*, s. 3.

[15] [1993] AC 442; above, § 13.6(ii)(a).

[16] *Preddy* [1996] AC 815; surprisingly, the panel contained two of the judges who formed part of the majority in *Gomez*.

[17] Theft Act 1968, ss. 15A and 15B, hastily added by the Theft (Amendment) Act 1996.

[18] LCCP No. 155, *Legislating the Criminal Code: Fraud and Deception*; Law Com. No. 276, *Fraud* (on which see Sullivan, "Fraud: the Latest Law Commission Proposals" (2003) 52 *Journal of Criminal Law* 139); Home Office, *Fraud Law Reform: Consultation on Proposals for Legislation* (2004).

[19] Obtaining property by deception (Theft Act 1968, s.15); obtaining a money transfer by deception (*ibid.*, s. 15A); obtaining a pecuniary advantage by deception (*ibid.*, s. 16); procuring the execution of a valuable security by deception (*ibid.*, s. 20); obtaining services by deception (Theft Act 1978, s. 1); evading liability by deception (*ibid.*, s. 2).

[20] *Maxwell* [1978] 3 All ER 1140, 1142.

[21] It is an important principle of criminal procedure that, where the prosecution has advanced the case against a defendant on one basis, the court may not be invited to convict him on a different basis which he has had no chance to contest. For an example of this principle in action see *Falconer-Attlee* (1974) 58 Cr App R 348.

a further layer of inchoate liability will attach.[22] Much conduct that would formerly be regarded as preliminary to fraudulent conduct—and even beyond the scope of inchoate offences—will now constitute criminal offences. The general effect of this, of course, is to move the stage at which D incurs criminal liability to an earlier point in time. A practical illustration is the case of *Jeevarajah*:[23]

> D1 and D1 ran a corner shop, at which lottery tickets were sold. V would regularly buy tickets there, and each time he bought new tickets he would ask the Ds if any of his last tickets had won. When one day he did have a winning ticket, they falsely told him that he had as usual lost, and then sought unsuccessfully to claim to the money for themselves.

For this, they were prosecuted for fraud under the Fraud Act, to which they pleaded guilty.[24] Under the earlier law, this would have been at most an attempt—with room for argument about proximity, as is always a possibility with attempt.[25] Under the new law the defendants committed the full offence of fraud at the point when they told their lie to V, let alone when they then tried to claim the money.

This effect is accentuated by the Act's also creating two new offences of possession of articles for use in fraud, and making or supplying articles for use in frauds. The slide towards redefining offences in "inchoate mode" appears to be a general trend, as we have seen from the earlier chapters of this book: in recent years the law on sexual offences has been reshaped in this direction,[26] the common law offence of incitement has been replaced by a statutory regime the reach of which is considerably wider,[27] and other parts of the law have been similarly widened too.[28] Helpful as this is to prosecutors, it raises serious questions in relation to the Harm Principle, which we discuss in the next chapter.

Before analysing the ingredients of the offence of fraud, a word should be said about legislative technique. Whatever one may think about the way in which the Fraud Act 2006 extends the reach of criminal liability, this law does have the merit of being clearly drafted, and the resulting law is much simpler and more accessible than it was before. Six complicated offences have been replaced by one single new offence, plus three supplementary offences; together with the parts of the earlier law that remain, the general law of criminal fraud now consists of some eight offences.[29] This is in sharp contrast to the new law on sexual offences: as we saw in Chapter 12, to cover the central ground of sexual violence and the sexual abuse of children, the Sexual Offences Act 2003 creates no fewer than 21 separate offences, and the total number of sexual offences it contains is some 50. Moreover, whereas the provisions of the Fraud Act are short and simple, many of those of Sexual Offences Act are long and complicated. It is possible to envisage the provisions of the Fraud Act forming part of an eventual criminal code, but not those of the Sexual Offences Act.

---

[22] As is the case for the statutory offence of aiding and abetting suicide: *McCann* (1971) 56 Cr App R 359.

[23] [2012] EWCA Crim 1299.

[24] They were sentenced to 14 months' imprisonment, against which they unsuccessfully appealed.

[25] The possibility arises because whether D's behaviour was sufficiently proximate to the completed crime is ultimately a question of fact, not law; see above, § 9.4.

[26] See above, Chapter 12.

[27] Serious Crime Act 2007, Part 2 (offences of assisting or encouraging crime); above, § 9.2.

[28] Another example is the law on terrorism, which has been widely expanded by the creation of new preliminary offences, e.g. by s. 5 of the Terrorism Act 2006.

[29] Fraud; possession of articles for use in frauds; making or supplying articles for use in frauds; obtaining services dishonestly; making off without payment; forgery; false accounting; conspiracy to defraud.

Mention should be made of a provision that the Fraud Act 2006 does not contain. Despite the consistent view of the Law Commission that any new fraud act should mark the abolition of conspiracy to defraud,[30] the Government refused to abolish this "indefensible anomaly".[31] The refusal was based exclusively on pragmatism: the risk of gaps in the coverage of fraudulent conduct.[32] It seems a safe bet that any future editions of this work will continue to have a section on conspiracy to defraud.[33] In an attempt to prevent the over-use of this offence, the Attorney General has issued official guidance to prosecutors concerning when conspiracy to defraud should be charged instead of a substantive offence.[34] Despite this official move to restrict its use, however, it remains very much alive.[35]

Below we analyse the three forms of the fraud offence. Before we descend to detail the different ways of committing fraud, we shall first examine the features that are common to all three forms of the offence. There must be proof of dishonesty, and there must be an intent to gain or to cause loss or risk of loss in money or property. We shall deal with those elements in full before examining in further detail the three branches of the offence: (i) fraud by false representation; (ii) fraud by failing to disclose information; and (iii) fraud by abuse of position.

§ 15.2 Common elements: "dishonesty", and "intent to make a gain or cause a loss"

(i) Intent to make a gain or cause a loss

The false representation must be made with an intent to make a gain for oneself or another, or with an intent to cause loss to another, or an intent to expose another to a risk of loss. Section 5 of the Fraud Act is as follows:

5 "Gain" and "loss"
(1) The references to gain and loss in sections 2 to 4 are to be read in accordance with this section.
(2) "Gain" and "loss"—
(a)   extend only to gain or loss in money or other property;
(b)   include any such gain or loss whether temporary or permanent;
and "property" means any property whether real or personal (including things in action and other intangible property).
(3) "Gain" includes a gain by keeping what one has, as well as a gain by getting what one does not have.
(4) "Loss" includes a loss by not getting what one might get, as well as a loss by parting with what one has.

Confining gains and losses to money and property reins in what remains a very wide offence. To make a false pretence to obtain confidential information about a forthcoming takeover

---

[30] Most recently Law Com. No. 276, para. 1.4.
[31] *Ibid.*
[32] HL Debate, cols. 1113–16, 14 March 2006: Lord Goldsmith, Attorney General.
[33] In this edition it is treated below in § 15.9.
[34] Available online at https://www.gov.uk/guidance/use-of-the-common-law-offence-of-conspiracy-to-defraud--6
[35] Some examples of its recent use are given in § 15.9(v) below.

bid may fall foul of insider trading legislation but it will not be fraud by false pretences, as confidential information without more is not a form of intangible property.[36] To be sure, D may intend to make a gain by using the information to buy shares in the target company at the pre-bid price but the gain will be made by the subsequent sale of the shares to the bidder. Some very important gains which are not directly economic are thereby excluded from the scope of fraud, as when D gains entry to a prestigious university by inflating his grades (and causes the loss of a vital opportunity to the better-qualified candidate he displaces)—or when, having got there, he cheats in his exams to improve the quality of his degree; but regulation of such things as university entry procedures is best done by offences targeted on specific abuses.

That said, the fact that the offence covers frauds intended to cause loss as well as gains, and that "loss" includes a loss by not getting what one might get as well as a loss by parting with what one has, means that frauds committed to obtain something that does not count as "property" will fall within the offence if they enable D to get a free benefit for which he would otherwise have had to pay. Thus, in principle, telling lies to obtain sexual favours falls outside the scope of the offence of fraud because sexual favours are not property; thus, it would not catch someone like the defendant in *Jheeta*,[37] who persuaded his gullible girl-friend to continue their relationship by producing false evidence that he was suicidal. How-ever, if V had been a prostitute and D had persuaded her to have sex with him on the basis of a promise to pay which he did not intend to keep, his fraud would have been intended to cause her a loss, and an offence under the Fraud Act would have been committed.

In the usual case where D makes a false pretence in order to gain, the intent involved will almost invariably be the natural, core sense of the term;[38] as when D tells a deliberate lie in order dishonestly to obtain money from V. However, it is also possible to envisage circumstances where D's intent to make a gain will be of the non-core, foresight-of-moral-certainty variety.[39] Suppose that D goes to Lord's cricket ground wearing an MCC tie. His principal objective in doing so is to pass himself off as a member of the MCC among his friends and acquaintances but he knows that, as on previous occasions, he will be charged the lower admission price payable by members of the MCC. He commits fraud by false pretences.

Where the allegation is that D intended to cause loss to another, the intent will typically be of the non-core variety, unless V is motivated by malice. So, if D borrows £50 from V, assuring her that he will pay her on Sunday but knowing that in his foreseeable financial circumstances he has no chance of doing so, he commits fraud. That still holds even if he intends to buy a lottery ticket with part of the money and fervently hopes he will be a mil-lionaire following the draw on Saturday night. He knows it is virtually certain that V will not be paid on Sunday.

Note that it is enough to expose another to a *risk* of loss.[40] In other words, D is potentially guilty of the offence where he is reckless whether V will lose out, as well as where he believes

---

[36] See the discussion above, § 13.3(i)(a).
[37] [2007] EWCA Crim 1699, [2008] 1 WLR 2582; above, § 12.3(iii)(b).
[38] Above, § 5.1(i)–(iii).
[39] Above, § 5.1(iv).
[40] Sections 2(1)(b)(ii), 3(b)(ii), and 4(1)(c)(ii). Such an intention also suffices for conspiracy to defraud: *Allsop* (1976) 64 Cr App R 29; below, § 15.9(iii)(a), (iv).

this consequence is certain. This is a considerable extension of the reach of statutory fraud, applying to each of the three ways of committing the offence. Suppose that, in a variant of the £50 loan example, D expects to be able to repay V on Sunday because he anticipates payment of a debt he is owed on Friday. However, he is aware of a risk that repayment may not happen until some time later. D knows that he has exposed V to the risk of loss which, the Act stipulates,[41] includes temporary losses. Many times each day, individuals and organisations will enter time-bounded repayment commitments aware that contingencies of various kinds may preclude the timely meeting of their obligation to repay. If D is aware of a non-minimal risk of time default in repaying V, he intends to expose V to the risk of loss. Making a binding commitment to pay on time will be a false pretence if D is aware of the possibility of default unless V has been made aware of and accepts the risk of untimely payment. It is submitted that much, if not most, conduct of this kind should be responded to by the renegotiation of credit terms against a backdrop of civil law enforcement of bad debts, and not remedied by the criminal law. However, whether particular incidents of this sort constitute fraud will depend now upon the vagaries of dishonesty, and the application of the *Ghosh* test.

(a) Intending to generate a gain or loss by means of the fraud

The intent must go together with the fraud. So, for an offence of fraud by false representation, D must intend to make the gain *by making the representation*.[42] Suppose that D enters a conversation with V and at some point falsely claims to be an Old Etonian, merely intending to raise his status in the eyes of V. At some later point in the conversation D, having forgotten his earlier lie, successfully asks V for a loan of £200. Even if V would not have made this loan but for his assumption about the reliability of Old Etonians, D commits no offence. At the time he made his false representation he did not intend to make money by lying. It would be different if, when asking for money, D thought his earlier lie about his schooling might favourably influence V. The false representation still has effect and now it is being deployed by D to make a gain for himself.

Under the previous law of fraud, the main offences required not only that D acted fraudulently, but that he obtained something by doing so. This gave rise to problems of causation and remoteness. On the whole, the case law took the line that the fraudulent act must be the direct and immediate cause of the obtaining, and not merely create the setting in which a more immediate cause could operate. Thus, where a man told lies that enabled him to place a bet on credit, and the horse he had backed then won, he was held not guilty of obtaining the winnings by false pretences, because the immediate cause of his gain was the fact that the horse had won;[43] and in another case it was held (at first instance) that a woman who obtained a teaching post by means of a forged certificate was not guilty of obtaining her salary by false pretences, because the immediate cause was her doing her job.[44] In other cases, however, a more robust line was taken. In *Button*,[45] a conviction was upheld for obtaining a

---

[41] Section 5(2)(b).
[42] Section 2(1)(b).
[43] *Clucas* [1949] 2 KB 226.
[44] *Lewis* (1922) Russell (12th ed.) Vol. II, 1186 n. 66, discussed in *King* [1987] QB 547.
[45] [1900[2 QB 597.

prize by false pretences where a runner had lied to obtain a handicap advantage, the court rejecting the argument that the immediate cause of the obtaining was that he had won the race; in *King*,[46] a conviction for attempting to obtain money by deception was upheld where fraudulent contractors had lied to persuade a householder to allow them to cut down her trees, in the hope of getting her to pay for the work, the court rejecting the argument that the deception merely provided the opportunity to earn the money by cutting down the trees; and a similar reasoning was applied in *Miller*,[47] where a dishonest motorist extracted exorbitant fares for driving foreigners from airports, whom he had persuaded to enter his vehicle by pretending to be a licensed taxi driver. In order to circumvent this problem, section 16 of the Theft Act 1968—now repealed—created specific offences of using deception in order to obtain insurance, to obtain the opportunity to earn money in employment, or to win money by betting.

Although the new offence of fraud is in "inchoate mode" and it is no longer necessary to prove that as a result of the fraud D actually obtained anything, the problem discussed in the previous paragraph has not completely gone away. Although D is guilty even where nothing was obtained, the prosecution must still show that D *intended* to make a gain or cause a loss *by means of* the fraud he has practised. Under section 2, D is guilty of fraud where he "intends, by making the representation" to make a gain or cause a loss; under section 3, D is guilty of fraud where he "intends, by failing to disclose the information" to make a gain or cause a loss; and by section 4, D is guilty of fraud where he "intends, by means of the abuse of that position" to make a gain or cause a loss. In consequence, causal speculation may still be necessary. If a gain has been made (or loss caused, etc.), it will provide a useful focus for determining whether the gain was made by making the representation. If no gain is actually made, the question must be along the lines of asking whether the gain that D intended would, if realised, have been made *by* making the representation. A point of particular difficulty is the case where D lies to get a job. Clearly any salary that would have been made would constitute a gain—but would it have been made by way of the false pretence? Formerly, D could be charged with the specific offence under the then section 16 of the Theft Act 1968, but that is no longer an option. As this point is one of some practical importance, it is surprising that Fraud Act fails to deal with it explicitly.[48] Another topical example is "phishing": sending fraudulent emails, purporting to come from legitimate sources, designed to persuade the recipients to reveal their personal details—which the sender hopes to use later to extract money by practising identity fraud.

The point of principle at issue here arose in *Gilbert*,[49] in which D had told lies to a bank in order to persuade it to open an account, which she and others planned to use in

---

[46] [1987] QB 547.

[47] (1992) 95 Cr App R 421. This case is criticised by A.T.H. Smith, *Property Offences* (1994) §17.125.

[48] Prosecutions under the Fraud Act have been brought for doing this, but the point remains to be tested on appeal because all those prosecuted seem to have pleaded guilty—e.g. Rhiannon Mackay, whose case attracted media coverage: *Daily Mail* 27 March 2010, Those who tell lies to obtain jobs will often commit other offences. Fortunately for their potential patients, it is a criminal offence for unqualified persons to practice as doctors (Medical Act 1983, s. 49) or as dentists (Dentists Act 1984, s. 38). For the possible application of the offence of forgery, see below, § 15.11.

[49] [2012] EWCA Crim 2392.

connection with property deals out of which they were hoping to make money. The Court of Appeal quashed the conviction, apparently[50] because it thought the profits of the eventual deals, if they materialised, would been too remote from the lies by which D persuaded the bank to open the account.

In a number of recurrent situations, possible difficulties of this sort are circumvented by the existence of specific offences: for example, section 42 of the Gambling Act 2005, whereby a person commits a criminal offence if she cheats at gambling "or does anything to enable another person to cheat at gambling"—cheating including, for these purposes, improper improvement of the chance of winning.[51]

(ii) Dishonesty

Following in the footsteps of the legislation it replaced, the Fraud Act 2006 contains no definition of the key element of dishonesty. Of course, in run-of-the-mill cases this will cause no difficulty, as when D tells V he is collecting a debt that V owes to E, D lacking any intention to pay the money to E. If the prosecution proves these facts they will normally also have proved D's dishonesty. But suppose that E owes D money to the same value as V's debt to E, and D thinks the only way he will ever be paid is to intercept the payment that V is due to make to E? Imagine further that, after receiving the money from V by claiming he is collecting it for E, D then informs V why he did so and advises V not to make any further payment to E. If D were to be charged with *theft* of the money received from V, the issue of dishonesty would be resolved with the aid of the claim of right provision to be found in section 2(1)(a) of the Theft Act 1968.[52] As there is no similar guidance in the Fraud Act 2006, the judge or magistrates at D's trial for fraud by false representation can only have recourse to the test for dishonesty in disputable cases set down in *Ghosh*:[53]

(i)   Was what was done dishonest according to the ordinary standards of reasonable and honest people?

(ii)   Did the defendant realise that reasonable and honest people would regard what he did as dishonest?

This failure in the 2006 Act to make special provision for recurring cases is in principle regrettable. The case of the D–V–E debt triangle is not straightforward in terms of moral evaluation—what, for juror X, may be an example of legitimate self-help may be, for juror Y, a disreputable machination—and the law needs to set a standard for such divisive cases. The fact that the Fraud Act 2006 neglects to set any standard leaves the matter at

---

[50] The judgment was given unreserved and it is not entirely clear whether the conviction was quashed because of this, or simply because the Court of Appeal thought the judge had not explained the issue with sufficient clarity to the jury.

[51] By s. 42(2), "it is immaterial whether a person who cheats improves his chances of winning anything, or wins anything". This offence, among others, featured in the high-profile prosecution of members of the Pakistani cricket team for match-fixing: see *Majeed* [2012] EWCA Crim 1186, [2012] 2 Cr App R 18.

[52] See the discussion above, § 13(8)(i).

[53] [1982] QB 1053, 1064. For discussion, see above, § 13(8)(iii).

large, with *Ghosh* the only, and uncertain, guide.[54] We will return to this lack of clarity that the absence of even a partial definition of dishonesty engenders when examining the other mens rea elements.

§ 15.3 Fraud by false representation: section 2

(i) *The actus reus*

This form of the fraud offence is defined by section 2 of the Fraud Act 2006, which is as follows:

> **2 Fraud by false representation**
> (1) A person is in breach of this section if he—
> (a) dishonestly makes a false representation, and
> (b) intends, by making the representation—
>   (i) to make a gain for himself or another, or
>   (ii) to cause loss to another or to expose another to a risk of loss.
> (2) A representation is false if—
> (a) it is untrue or misleading, and
> (b) the person making it knows that it is, or might be, untrue or misleading.
> (3) "Representation" means any representation as to fact or law, including a representation as to the state of mind of—
> (a) the person making the representation, or
> (b) any other person.
> (4) A representation may be express or implied.
> (5) For the purposes of this section a representation may be regarded as made if it (or anything implying it) is submitted in any form to any system or device designed to receive, convey or respond to communications (with or without human intervention).

The conduct element of this form of fraud is the making of a false representation. This generates three points of inquiry: (a) what counts as a representation; (b) when is the representation false; and (c) when is the representation "made"? We consider each of these points in turn.

(a) A representation

As under the previous law,[55] this may be a representation as to fact or law, and it may be as to a person's state of mind—typically, D's intention to pay for something, but potentially it could be about anybody's intention to do anything. Also as under the previous law, the representation may be express, or implied. Under the old law the courts had decided, in relation to various recurrent situations in everyday life, that certain implied representations are made, and the same approach is likely to be taken with the new. Thus writing a cheque

---

[54] Although there is no control over perverse applications of the *Ghosh* test by juries, the Divisional Court is willing to intervene when it disapproves of the way in which magistrates have applied it. For an example see *Gohill* v. *DPP* [2007] EWHC 239 (Admin).

[55] Theft Act 1968 s. 15(4): "For the purposes of this section 'deception' means any deception (whether deliberate or reckless) by words or conduct as to fact or as to law, including a deception as to the present intentions of the person using the deception or any other person".

implies a representation that it will be honoured when presented for payment.[56] As Robert Goff LJ said in *Gilmartin*,[57]

> "by the simple giving of a cheque, whether postdated or not, the drawer impliedly represents that the state of facts existing at the date of delivery of the cheque is such that in the ordinary course the cheque will on presentation for payment on or after the date specified in the cheque, be met."

Since this is a prediction of future events, a further representation must be implied from it that the drawer of the cheque presently intends and expects that it will be honoured when presented. Another common situation is the use of a credit card or bank card, which involves a representation that the person using it has authority to do so.[58] When a person fills in a withdrawal form at a bank, she makes an implied representation that the bank is indebted to her in that amount[59]—unless, presumably, overdraft facilities have been arranged. Where D purports to sell goods to V, there is usually an implied representation that D has the capacity to pass ownership of the goods,[60] and that the goods are genuine.[61] Conversely, where D buys or orders goods, she impliedly represents her present intention to pay for them;[62] and where payment on the spot is expected (e.g. at a restaurant or service station), she impliedly represents also that she has the ability to pay.[63] So, for instance, where D takes a taxi, she implies by her conduct that she has money for the fare.[64] Furthermore, D is also sometimes treated as making an implied representation when, having made a statement that was true at the time, it is later falsified by events, and D thereafter acquiesces in V's continuing to act on the basis that the situation is still as it was. Thus in *Rai*,[65] D obtained a grant from the Birmingham City Council to install a bathroom in his house for the use of his aged and infirm mother. Before work was commenced, D's mother died. D refrained from notifying the council of his mother's death, and the council subsequently commissioned builders to install the bathroom. D's conviction for obtaining the building services by deception was upheld by the Court of Appeal, on the ground that allowing the

---

[56] *DPP v. Turner* [1974] AC 357, 367 (Lord Reid). (Note that this representation encompasses the implied representations stated in the old case of *Hazelton* (1874) LR 2 CCR 134. It is submitted that the earlier case may now be disregarded.) See also the discussion in Smith, *Property Offences* (1994) § 17.52.

[57] [1983] QB 953, 962.

[58] *MPC v. Charles* [1977] AC 177; *Lambie* [1982] AC 449. These decisions, however, fail to address the causation point—that the vendor accepting the card may rely only upon the minimum representation required to validate the charge transaction, i.e. that the customer is the person named on the face of the card (itself an implied representation: *Abdullah* [1982] Crim LR 122). See Smith, "The Idea of Criminal Deception" [1982] *Crim LR* 721.

[59] *Hamilton* (1991) 92 Cr App R 54.

[60] *Sampson* (1885) 52 LT (NS) 772. Cf. *Eichholz v. Bannister* (1864) 17 CB (NS) 708, 723, 144 ER 284, 290: "in almost all the transactions of sale in common life the seller by the very act of selling holds out to the buyer that he is the owner of the article he offers for sale".

[61] *Jean Jacques Williams* [1980] Crim LR 589.

[62] *DPP v. Ray* [1974] AC 370.

[63] *Ibid.*, 379, 382.

[64] *Waterfall* [1970] 1 QB 148, 150 (Lord Parker).

[65] [2000] 1 Cr App R 242. Contrast, in Australia, *Nelson v R.* [1987] WAR 57, 60 (Burt CJ), where it was said that the rule of equity, that a person has a duty to disclose in a pre-contractual situation where a statement inducing a contract becomes false prior to conclusion of the contract, "is not a rule which has anything to do with the criminal offence of obtaining something by a false pretence". The application of the equitable rule was also rejected by Lord Hodson in *DPP v. Ray* [1974] AC 370, 389. However, his Lordship was in the minority and the point was not taken up by the majority.

works to be done in his house without explaining the change of circumstances amounted to deception.

A different result eventuated on the facts in *United Arab Emirates* v. *Allen*.[66] In that case, the Administrative Court held that, where a person gave a lender an undated cheque as security for a loan, she was not required to seek the lending institution out and warn it when her bank balance dwindled to the point that the cheque would no longer be honoured if presented. The result might have been different, one suspects, if instead of all the money being handed over at the outset the loan was handed over in instalments—and by accepting an instalment the borrower, like the defendant in *Rai*, had allowed the alleged victim of the fraud to confer a benefit on her after she knew that the situation had changed.

A false representation will normally be made by words, but it can equally be made by conduct: as in the celebrated nineteenth-century case in which a person who was not a member of the university obtained credit from a tradesman by entering his shop dressed in an Oxford cap and gown.[67]

(b) False

By section 2(2)(b) a representation is false "if it is untrue *or misleading*". Clearly some representations may be literally true but are nonetheless to be regarded as false because, although true, they are misleading. When will this be? Take a hypothetical case discussed in *Hinks*:[68] a situation where D and V are negotiating the sale of D's garage. V enquires of D what the turnover of the business was, as per the latest set of accounts, and receives in response the true figures. V's subsequent offer price reflects a valuation based on the assumption that the figures were a useful guide to future profitability. D knows this, but is also aware that a bypass road to be constructed in the near future will take away practically all the passing trade. Just as the House of Lords contemplated that D's accepting V's purchase price could be theft of V's money, we must take seriously the prospect that D might now also be guilty of fraud by false representation when he gives V the accurate figures: the offence does not require the actual making of the gain or loss. Were the figures misleading? In the context of V's query, it is submitted that the answer must be yes. One problem with this answer is that it takes the criminal law beyond what constitutes a misrepresentation for the purposes of the law of contract, where the boundaries of the concept are mediated by the principle of *caveat emptor*. A related issue is the dishonest trader who, sensing that his customer is gullible, quotes an excessive price for goods to be supplied or work to be done, which the customer foolishly accepts. Absent any positive misrepresentation, the resulting contract would be binding; but could his statement be misleading, in the sense that his figures falsely implied that he was quoting the going rate?[69] Extending the notion of falsity

---

[66] [2012] EWHC 1712 (Admin), [2012] 1 WLR 3419. In this case the lender's extradition was sought by the United Arab Emirates, where the transaction had taken place and where her behaviour apparently did constitute a criminal offence. The issue arose because the UK only extradites to that country where the behaviour in question would also have constituted a crime in the UK.

[67] *Barnard* (1837) 7 C & P 784, 173 ER 342; cf. *Parker and Bulteel* (1916) 25 Cox CC 145: a banker who keeps his doors open and continues to trade may thereby represent that he is solvent.

[68] [2001] 2 AC 241, 251–2 (Lord Steyn).

[69] Overcharging gullible customers in this way can in principle be theft: as in *Williams* [2001] 1 Cr App R 362; see above, § 13.6(c)(vi). If the trader is someone with whom the gullible customer deals regularly and has come to trust, he could possibly be guilty of fraud by abuse of position: see below, § 15.5.

to representations that are misleading yet true could lead to further incoherence at the interface of criminal and civil law.

(c) Made

A final point about fraud by false representation is a basic one about the actus reus. Although the offence of fraud is now inchoate in the sense that the defendant who makes a false representation commits an offence of fraud whether or not any gain or loss results, it is still necessary for the representation to be "made"; but when, as a matter of law, does this happen? If D writes a begging letter that contains a false representation, it could be made when he writes it, when he sends it, or when it actually comes to the attention of the sender. Although in a sense the representation was "made" when the letter was written, we suggest this interpretation is too wide; apart from any other consideration, sections 6 and 7 of the Fraud Act create specific offences of possessing and making articles for use in frauds, which this interpretation of the main offence would make redundant. At the other end of the scale, if the false representation has been uttered, there seems no particularly good reason to require the prosecutor to prove that it came to anyone's attention. It is therefore suggested that a false representation is made when it is uttered.[70] In the case of an oral representation, this means when the maker spoke it, whether or not it was heard; in the case of a letter, it would be when it was posted; and in the case of an email, it would be "made" when it was sent. Although a representation, by its nature, must be intended to reach someone, there seems to be no reason why in law a "false representation" must be made to an identified individual, and we suggest that the offence potentially covers acquisitive lies uttered to the world in general: for example, by a fraudulent advertisement in a newspaper,[71] or in the following situation with which most readers are likely to be familiar.

> David, having acquired a list of 20,000 email addresses, sends them all a "spam" falsely informing them that they have won a lottery, and that they can claim their prize by sending an "administrative fee", by Western Union, to D's address in Tobleronia.

(d) False representations made to systems and devices

Under the former law of deception, only persons could be deceived.[72] However commonsensical this may seem, it left some serious gaps in the control of fraudulent conduct. For instance, in Re Holmes,[73] where D's extradition was sought for a multi-million dollar bank fraud committed in Germany, the Court of Appeal pointed out, with regret, that D would have committed no deception offences in England if, without telling any lies, he had dishonestly secured a bank transfer by using wholly automated processes. To plug this gap, section 2(5) provides:

> For the purposes of this section a representation may be regarded as made if it (or anything implying it) is submitted in any form to any system or device designed to receive, convey or respond to communications (with or without human intervention).

---

[70] This view is also taken by Smith and Hogan 1004 and by the editors of Archbold (2016 edition) § 21.327.
[71] As in the old case of Silverlock [1894] 2 QB 766.
[72] See further, 3rd edition, § 15.4(iii)(c).
[73] [2004] EWHC 2020; [2005] 1 WLR 1857; the Court of Appeal also discussed the issue of whether D was guilty here of theft: see above, § 13.5(i)(b).

The language seems well adapted to its purposes and will help to ensure justice in a case such as *Re Holmes*.

(ii) Mens rea

There are three elements to the mens rea: the false representation must be made dishonestly;[74] it must be made with intent to gain or cause loss, or to expose another to the risk of loss;[75] and it must be made with knowledge that the representation either is untrue or misleading, or that it might be untrue or misleading.[76] We considered the first two of these elements above, in § 15.2.

(a) Knowledge that the representation is or might be untrue or misleading

This mens rea element is imported into the definition of a "false representation" by section 2(2)(b). The plainest and least problematic case will be where D knows that his representation is untrue. If D says he is just about to come into a considerable inheritance when he knows that he will receive just £100 from the deceased, he is camped in the territory of fraud when he tells this lie to induce a large loan from V. Also well within the notion of fraudulent behaviour is when D says to V, "I am sure this painting is a genuine Constable", when in reality he is not sure, because he is aware of the distinct possibility that it might be an expert copy.

Yet one soon reaches territory where there is genuine doubt about the propriety of criminalising aspects of D's conduct. It is well known, for instance, that the attribution of paintings to artists long departed can be a matter of fine judgement on which experts of equal standing may disagree. Go back to the assurance that D gives to V about the attribution of a painting to Constable. After claiming that he is so convinced, D adds, "Professor Jones, perhaps our leading Constable scholar, is of that view too". All manner of nuances may be in play here. Professor Jones may well be a leading Constable scholar, but he may be notorious within his scholarly community for his willingness to make positive attributions, particularly when used as a consultant to a leading dealer with a painting of contested provenance to sell. And what if D knows that Professor Jones's positive attribution was a probabilistic, "on the balance of evidence", conclusion and he also knows that Professor Smith, regarded by his peers as *the* Constable scholar, was dismissive of the painting, convinced that it was a copy. As V dithers about spending what for him is a vast sum of money, D remarks that there has been great interest from the United States, a statement based on a tentative email from a US client. And what of V? Is it in point that he is an experienced purchaser of high-value art who will essentially make his own judgement about the value of the painting? Does the analysis change if he is a first-time buyer of high-value art, trusting of and guided by D? Does the fact that fraud by false pretences may be proved without proof that anyone was deceived, or that any gain or loss occurred, have any relevance to what constitutes

---

[74] Section 2(1)(a); above, § 15.2(ii).

[75] Section 2(1)(b); above, § 15.2(i).

[76] Section 2(2). To be guilty, D must of course be subjectively aware that the statement was untrue or misleading. So it is a serious misdirection to tell a jury that D is guilty if he ought to have been aware of this: *Augunas* [2013] EWCA Crim 2046, [2014] 1 Cr App R 241.

a false representation? Must D's representation be misleading in some general, objective sense or is it enough that D knew it might mislead V? If the painting is subsequently shown to be a copy, bought by V at a price well in excess of its true value, a potential prosecutor of D for the offence of fraud by false pretences will have much to ponder. (The answer to these problems may be that the representation must be known by its maker to be capable of misleading the person to whom it is made.)[77]

§ 15.4 Fraud by failing to disclose information: section 3

Section 3 of the Fraud Act 2006 makes D liable for statutory fraud if he dishonestly fails to disclose information that he is under a legal duty to disclose, intending by failing to disclose the information to gain for himself or cause loss to another, or to expose another to the risk of loss. The section provides as follows:

3 Fraud by failing to disclose information
A person is in breach of this section if he—
(a) dishonestly fails to disclose to another person information which he is under a legal duty to disclose, and
(b) intends, by failing to disclose the information—
(i) to make a gain for himself or another, or
(ii) to cause loss to another or to expose another to a risk of loss.

The core element of this variant of fraud is the breach of a *legal* duty to disclose information. The Law Commission, and at first the government, initially envisaged this limb of the new fraud offence as going wider, and covering not only failure to disclose information that the civil law requires to be disclosed but also any failure to disclose information which D knows V is trusting him to disclose.[78] This proposed second limb was criticised as liable to bring the criminal law into collision with the civil law, and in particular, the *caveat emptor* rule: the basic rule of English civil law that when a person sells something he is under no obligation to disclose its defects, and it is the buyer's business to discover them. Thus, when a person sells a house, for example, he need not tell the buyer that it is full of woodworm or dry rot, or that the house next door is occupied by the "neighbour from Hell", whose presence is the reason for the sale. This rule comes as a surprise to many people who think that honest sellers would reveal such things; and the proposed second limb could easily have resulted in sellers being successfully prosecuted for fraud for sales the completion of which, in civil law, they would be entitled to enforce.[79] In the light of this objection the government changed its mind, and introduced a Fraud Bill in which the "failure to disclose" limb of the offence was limited to cases where D was under a legal duty to disclose.

---

[77] We are grateful to Mr Peter Glazebrook for this suggestion.

[78] Law Com No. 276 (2002); Home Office, *Fraud Law Reform: Consultation on Proposals for Legislation* (2004) § 20.

[79] The *caveat emptor* rule is subject to certain important exceptions—particularly in respect of chattels, when sold in the course of trade or business. In such a sale the seller impliedly guarantees that they are of "satisfactory quality" and, where the buyer's purpose is known to the seller, that they are "fit for purpose": Sale of Good Act 1979, s. 14, and for consumer sales, Consumer Rights Act 2015, ss. 9 and 10.

So to what sort of legal duties does section 3 apply? The following passage from the Law Commission's report is a useful guide:[80]

"Such a duty may derive from statute (such as provisions governing company prospectuses), from the fact that the transaction in question is one of the utmost good faith (such as a contract for insurance), from the express or implied terms of a contract, from the customs of a particular trade or market, or from the existence of a fiduciary relationship between the parties (such as agent and principal). For this purpose [the fraud offence] there is a legal duty to disclose information not only if the defendant's failure to disclose it gives the victim a cause of action for damages, but also if the law gives the victim the right to set aside any change in his or her legal position to which he or she may consent as a result of non-disclosure. For example, a person in a fiduciary position has a duty to disclose material information when entering into a contract with his or her beneficiary, in the sense that a failure to make such disclosure will entitle the beneficiary to rescind the contract and to reclaim any property transferred under it."

Statutory duties to disclose are very common; but where a duty to disclose is imposed by a statute, that statute usually makes it a criminal offence to fail to comply with it.[81] So, in practice, a failure to fulfil a statutory duty to disclose is likely to be prosecuted as an offence under the legislation that created it, rather than as an offence of fraud, even where it is done with intent to make a gain or cause a loss. In practice, most failures to disclose that result in prosecutions for the offence of fraud are likely to arise from contracts. A legal duty to disclose can arise from a contract in a number of different ways.

First, and most obviously, D may be bound by a contract to V which imposes on him an ongoing obligation to disclose certain matters as and when they happen. For example, a supervisor in a supermarket might be required by his contract of employment to report thefts or other pieces of grave misconduct by the other staff. If D noticed an assistant commit a theft, and because she was his girlfriend deliberately failed to report it, his failure to disclose might make him guilty of an offence of fraud.[82]

Secondly, some contracts are entered into on the basis that one party has disclosed all material matters to the other. With certain types of contract, notably contracts of insurance, this is the rule unless the parties have agreed otherwise; such contracts are known as contracts of "utmost good faith" or, to lawyers who like Latin, contracts *uberrimae fidei*.[83] Even outside these specific types of contract, it is open to the parties to make any kind of contract on this basis. An employer, for example, could make it a condition of an employment contract that the person appointed must reveal his criminal convictions (if any). In either of these situations there would clearly be a legal duty to disclose, and a non-disclosure could potentially result in criminal liability for fraud if the other elements of the offence—in particular, dishonesty and a sufficient causal link[84]—were present.

---

[80] Law Com. No. 276, para. 7.28.

[81] For example, Regulations made under the Public Health (Control of Disease) Act 1984 impose duties on various people to notify the public authorities about a range of dangerous diseases; and by s. 15 of the Act a failure to notify as required is made a criminal offence.

[82] Though probably not done with the intention to cause loss in the sense of a *desire* to do so, D would presumably have "oblique intention", which would be sufficient; see above, § 15.2(i); also § 5.1(iv).

[83] For a detailed review, see Beale and others (eds.), *Chitty on Contracts* (23nd ed., 2015) §7.155ff. Though insurance contracts fall into this category, contracts with mortgage suppliers do not: as was recognised in *White* [2014] EWCA Crim 1781, where the Court quashed D's conviction under s. 3 of the Fraud Act for failing to disclose, when obtaining a mortgage, that he was unemployed.

[84] See above, § 15.2(a).

Another case of "legal duty to disclose" arising in the field of contract is where a person induces a contract by making a representation that is true at the time, but which, by the time the contract is carried out, has been falsified by events. In this situation the law treats the original representation as "continuing"; the deliberate failure to correct it then constitutes a misrepresentation, which—like any other misrepresentation—gives the innocent party the right to rescind the contract.[85] Here a fraudulent failure to point out the true position could presumably also ground a prosecution for fraud under section 3 of the Fraud Act; and in a case like *Rai*[86] there is a possible overlap with fraud by false representation contrary to section 2.

A "legal duty" to disclose could also arise by operation of the law of tort. If D hired V a piece of equipment, intentionally failing to point out that it is electrically unsafe, and V accidentally electrocuted himself when using it, V's tortious claim against D would involve the argument that D owed V, in general terms, a "duty of care", and, in specific terms, a "duty to warn"—which would presumably count as a "legal duty to disclose" for the purpose of triggering criminal liability under section 3, if the other ingredients of the offence were present.[87] Some other cases are less clear-cut. One is the situation where, under an exception to the *caveat emptor* rule, a seller impliedly guarantees the quality of the goods she sells. In this situation the seller is civilly liable to the buyer if, unknown to the buyer, the goods contain a hidden defect. But does that mean that the seller is under a "legal duty" to disclose it? A defendant prosecuted for fraud in such a case would presumably argue that she was under a legal duty to deliver goods of satisfactory quality, but that is not the same thing as being under a legal duty to disclose defects. In response, the prosecutor might try to argue that the seller in such a situation impliedly represents that the goods are of satisfactory quality, so making the seller criminally liability for fraud by false representation under section 2. Undeniably, the full enforcement of this form of fraud will involve in-depth consideration of civil law issues. This is entirely appropriate in the context of a modern law of fraud. Here criminal courts will have to address the civil law and the criminal law from a perspective of unity[88] and set aside their reluctance to investigate difficult civil law questions.[89]

From the fact that it is an ingredient in section 3 that D's failure to disclose should be committed with the aim of making a gain or causing a loss it necessarily follows that the failure must be an intentional one. However, section 3 does not tell us whether, in addition to knowing that he has kept quiet about something, D must also be aware that the information was something which the law required him to reveal. Here two well-known principles pull in opposite directions. One is the principle that, where a statute creating an offence consisting of an actus reus is silent on whether mens rea is required, the existence of a mens rea requirement is presumed.[90] The other is that "ignorance of the law is no defence".[91] How this conflict is to be resolved here is not easy. In general, the "ignorance of law is no defence"

---

[85] *With v O'Flanagan* [1936] Ch 575.

[86] [2000] 1 Cr App R 242; see above, § 15.3(i)(a).

[87] If the defect in the equipment makes it dangerous to the user and D provides it in the course of business, it is more likely that he would be prosecuted for an offence under s. 3 of the Health and Safety at Work Act 1974.

[88] Avoiding the incoherence exemplified by the decision in *Hinks* [2001] 2 AC 241; see above, § 13.6(ii)(c).

[89] As in *Morris* [1984] AC 320, 334; above, § 13.6(ii).

[90] *Sweet v. Parsley* [1970] AC 132; above, § 6.1.

[91] Below, § 18.2.

rule is limited to mistakes about the criminal law—that is, whether a given type of act is a criminal offence—and it does not apply to a mistake of civil law "at one remove" upon which the existence of criminal liability depends. As those legal duties to disclose which trigger criminal liability under section 3 of the Fraud Act are likely to be predominantly imposed by civil law, this would suggest that in this case the mens rea principle prevails. On the other hand, the courts might reason that, as D is protected by a requirement that his behaviour be "dishonest", he does not need the further protection of being guilty only where he knew the law required him to disclose. "OK, I knew it was dishonest not to mention it, but I thought it was legal" is not, after all, a line of defence that is likely to engage much judicial sympathy.

§ 15.5 Fraud by abuse of position

Section 4 of the Fraud Act is as follows:

4 Fraud by abuse of position
(1) A person is in breach of this section if he—
(a)   occupies a position in which he is expected to safeguard, or not to act against, the financial interests of another person,
(b)   dishonestly abuses that position, and
(c)   intends, by means of the abuse of that position—
(i)   to make a gain for himself or another, or
(ii)   to cause loss to another or to expose another to a risk of loss.
(2) A person may be regarded as having abused his position even though his conduct consisted of an omission rather than an act.

According to the Law Commission, this offence is intended for the situation in which D is in a position in which she "is expected" to act in a certain kind of way, and abuses it by acting otherwise. Unlike the offence of fraud by failure to disclose, there is no requirement here that the "expectation" that D behave in a particular kind of way should have any legal teeth attached to it. The offence applies, obviously, where the obligation D is under to safeguard V's financial interests is one imposed by the civil law, but in principle it equally applies where his obligation is a purely moral one. It is enough that D, in the position that he occupies, "is expected" to safeguard V's financial interests.

The Act does not identify the person who should do the expecting. The Law Commission clearly envisaged that this person was V. Thus in their Report they said that

> "The essence of the kind of relationship which in our view should be a prerequisite of this form of the offence is that *the victim* has voluntarily put the defendant in a privileged position, by virtue of which the defendant is expected to safeguard the victim's financial interests or given power to damage those interests."[92]

However, the requirement that the relationship be one that V has voluntarily created is not reflected in the way that section 4 is drafted; in consequence, the offence is also committed where D is placed in the position that he abuses not by V, but by operation of the law. Thus it potentially applies not only where (for example) V has chosen to empower D to

---

[92] Law Com. No. 276, § 7.37 (emphasis added).

act on his behalf by an enduring power of attorney, but also where X has died nominating D as executor of a will of which V is a beneficiary, and in the situation where V is mentally incapable and a civil court, without V being aware of this, has made an order authorising D to manage V's affairs. This, we believe, is right, because, although a person who abuses either of these positions will often in the process commit fraud by failure to disclose, or even theft, situations could arise in which D's dishonest abuse of one of these positions would otherwise fall outside the reach of the criminal law.[93]

In these two cases, and in many others, D's obligation to safeguard V's financial position will be a legal one. Indeed, very often D will owe V what the law calls a "fiduciary duty",[94] though a fiduciary relationship, at least in its traditional forms, will not be necessary. In a passage from its Report later reprinted in the government's Explanatory Notes, the Law Commission gave the following thumbnail sketch of the range of relationships it had in mind when devising the offence.

> "The necessary relationship will be present between trustee and beneficiary, director and company, professional person and client, agent and principal, employee and employer, or between partners. It may arise otherwise, for example within a family, or in the context of voluntary work, or in any context where the parties are not at arm's length. In nearly all cases where it arises, it will be recognised by the civil law as importing fiduciary duties, and any relationship that is so recognised will suffice. We see no reason, however, why the existence of such duties should be essential. This does not of course mean that it would be entirely a matter for the fact-finders whether the necessary relationship exists. The question whether the particular facts alleged can properly be described as giving rise to that relationship will be an issue capable of being ruled upon by the judge and, if the case goes to the jury, of being the subject of directions."[95]

It will be clear from this that the offence of fraud by abuse of position provides a relatively straightforward means of deterring and punishing a number of forms of dishonesty that are worthy of the attention of the criminal law, but which can be brought within the scope of other offences of dishonesty only with difficulty, if at all. One such group comprises employees who take bribes, make secret profits, or otherwise dishonestly enrich themselves at the expense of their employers.[96] Another comprises acquisitive family members, neighbours, or acquaintances who batten on vulnerable people who have lost their wits, or who never had any, and relieve them of their money or other property by inducing them to make them gifts or exorbitant payments for minor services, or otherwise financially abuse them. As we saw earlier, the House of Lords contrived to bring one example of this behaviour within the ambit of the crime of theft—albeit at the cost of a rupture of legal principle—in *Hinks*;[97] but other cases, similar in principle, can be imagined which could not be brought within the scope of theft—for example, if instead of persuading a vulnerable person to give him money, D induced him to allow D to use or occupy his property without payment. Another unscrupulous person who would seem to be caught by section 4 is the tradesman who regularly supplies V with goods or services, building up over the

---

[93] For example, if under s. 18 of the Mental Capacity Act 2005 the court made an order authorising D to run V's business, and D then deliberately ran V's business down by diverting V's customers to his own.

[94] See above, § 13.5.

[95] Law Com. No. 276, para. 738.

[96] See above, § 13.5(i)(b) and (c).

[97] [2001] 2 AC 241; see above, § 13.6(ii)(c).

course of time a relationship in which V comes to trust him but then abuses V's trust by charging him prices that are far above the going rate. In *Silverman*,[98] the Court of Appeal said that a defendant who had grossly overcharged two elderly spinsters for rewiring and redecorating a house could be guilty of the (now abolished) offence of obtaining property by deception:[99] given the situation of mutual trust, which had built up over a number of years, D had impliedly represented that his firm would derive more than a modest profit from the work. We suggest that, should these facts occur again, such a defendant would now be guilty of the offence of fraud by abuse of position.

The outer limits of the section 4 offence were explored in *Valujevs*.[100] Here D was an unlicensed[101] gangmaster whose business was providing labourers for Fenland farmers. He was accused, among other things, of fraud by abuse of position, on the basis of his having undertaken the payment of the labourers' wages, from which he had been making exorbitant deductions. In interlocutory proceedings, the Court of Appeal ruled that the proceedings on this count could properly proceed. The key ingredient in section 4 is an "expectation" that D would safeguard and not act against the financial interests of another. Such an expectation exists, the Court said, if a reasonable third person, viewing the arrangement from outside, would expect D so to behave: "It would be untenable to suggest that the expectation should be that of either the potential victim (the test would, in all likelihood, be too low) or the defendant (the test is likely to be set too high)." In a jury trial, it added, the judge should first decide whether the defendant's position could potentially satisfy this test; if so, it was then for the jury to decide if it does.

The Court further qualified its remarks by saying that, although the section 4 offence does not require a "fiduciary duty" in the strict legal sense,[102] it does require "an obligation that is akin" to one. So section 4 "does not apply to those who simply supply accommodation, goods, services or labour, whether on favourable or unfavourable terms and whether or not they have a stronger bargaining position."

If fraud by abuse of position has the advantage of flexibility, it also has the corresponding disadvantage of being distinctly vague. As put forward by the Law Commission, the offence would have been limited to an abuse of position that was carried out covertly: in the Draft Bill attached to Law Commission's Report, an ingredient in the proposed offence was that the defendant "dishonestly *and secretly* abuses that position". But even this modest limitation did not appeal to the government,[103] and it is not reflected in the drafting of the Act. Apart from those discussed above, the only limiting requirement in the definition of the offence appears to be that D must have entered into, or been placed in, a relationship with V that is more than merely transitory. The result is that, as so often with the Fraud Act 2006, the only real limit to the offence are the two questions on dishonesty put in *Ghosh*.[104]

---

[98] (1988) 86 Cr App R 213; also *Stevens* (1844) 1 Cox CC 83.

[99] Theft Act 1968, s. 15.

[100] [2014] EWCA Crim 2888, [2015] 3 WLR 109.

[101] The Gangmasters (Licensing) Act 2004 imposes a compulsory licensing regime, with the aim of controlling abuses of the type seen here.

[102] For an explanation, see § 13.5(i)(c) above.

[103] Having floated the idea of including this requirement in *Fraud Law Reform—Consultation on Proposals for Legislation* (May 2004), the government eventually rejected it lest it "lead to technical arguments in court", concluding that "the value-laden concepts of 'dishonesty' and 'abuse' were sufficient in themselves to set the parameters for the offence". *Fraud Law Reform, Government Response to Consultations* (2004) §§ 28–9.

[104] [1982] QB 1053; above, §§ 15.2 and 13.8.

If this variety of the offence of fraud has the potential to catch a range of unscrupulously acquisitive people who in moral terms deserve the attention of the criminal law, it could also potentially catch a range of people whom there is no pressing need to bring within the criminal law at all—and even some whose behaviour, if improper, falls far outside the scope of what most people would regard as fraud: for example, the employee who is persistently late for work, or persistently shirks when he gets there;[105] an employee "occupies a position in which he is expected to safeguard, or not act against, the financial interests" of his employer, and by behaving in this way he is acting against them.[106] It is therefore reassuring, at least to some limited extent, that the official guidance issued to the CPS on the exercise of the discretion to prosecute under the Fraud Act 2006[107] says that "Prosecutors should guard against the criminal law being used as a debt collection agency or to protect the commercial interests of companies and organisations".

§ 15.6 Possessing, making and supplying articles for use in frauds

By turning the main offence of fraud into a "conduct offence" instead of a "result offence", the Fraud Act 2006 widened the net of criminal liability, in particular by pushing backwards the point in time at which a move in the direction of a crime turns into a completed criminal offence. This effect is accentuated by the fact that the Act also creates two backup offences: possessing articles for use in frauds and making or supplying articles for use in frauds. These two offences were the brainchild not of the Law Commission, which devised the new tripartite offence of fraud, but of the Home Office. It justified them by referring to the existing offence of "going equipped"—that is to say, being out and about carrying the necessary equipment—to commit various offences under the Theft Act,[108] which it said "merits reconsideration".[109] By "reconsideration" it meant "major extension", and a major extension of this form of inchoate liability is what these two new offences have achieved.

The possession offence is created by section 6(1):

> A person is guilty of an offence if he has in his possession or under his control any article for use in the course of or in connection with any fraud.

This offence goes far beyond the "going equipped" provision in section 25 of the Theft Act from which it supposedly derived, because it applies where D possesses or controls the article anywhere, including in the privacy of his home. It is also very broad, because it covers the possession of "any article for use in the course of or in connection with any fraud". So it includes not only articles that have been made or adapted for this purpose, but also, potentially, articles whose normal use is innocent.[110] Taken to the limit, it would seem to cover

---

[105] Ormerod, "The Fraud Act 2006: Criminalising Lying?" [2007] *Crim LR* 193, 209.

[106] If prosecuted for fraud, he might argue that he acted without the necessary intention to make a gain or cause a loss; though this argument might fail, because, as we saw in § 15.2, an oblique intention appears to be enough.

[107] Published on the website of the Crown Prosecution Service; online at http://www.cps.gov.uk/legal/d_to_g/fraud_act/#a10

[108] Theft Act 1968, s. 25. In its original form the offence was going equipped for any "burglary, theft or cheat"; as amended by the Fraud Act 2006, it is now limited to going equipped for any "burglary or theft".

[109] Home Office, *Fraud Law Reform—Consultation on Proposals for Legislation* (2004).

[110] In *Sakalauskas* [2013] EWCA Crim 2278, [2014] 1 WLR 1204, the article in question was the jerry-can which D was carrying in his car, allegedly for storing petrol obtained from fuel-stations using fraudulently obtained bank-cards.

the possession (or control) of a pencil or a pen, which D—or even someone else—intends to use to complete a form making a fraudulent insurance claim, or to write a begging letter with a lie in it.

In the light of this, it was a welcome development when the Court of Appeal in *Sakalauskas*[111] made it clear that a person is only guilty of the possession offence when the article is intended for the commission of an offence and he is actually aware of this. In this case the narrow point before the Court was whether the section 6 offence is limited to the possession of articles meant for future use in fraud, or covers the possession of articles used to commit frauds in the past. In deciding that it is limited to articles for future use, the Court approved and applied the interpretation previously given to the (supposedly) precursor offence under section 25 of the Theft Act of "going equipped". In *Ellames*[112] the Court had said that a person is only guilty of "going equipped" if he has the item with him intending that it should be used—either by himself or by another person—for the commission of a future offence.

Less worrying on grounds of possible overbreadth is the new offence of making or supplying articles for use in frauds. So far as is relevant, section 7 of the Fraud Act 2006 is as follows:

> (1) A person is guilty of an offence if he makes, adapts, supplies or offers to supply any article—
> (a) knowing that it is designed or adapted for use in the course of or in connection with fraud, or
> (b) intending it to be used to commit, or assist in the commission of, fraud.

As an example of the sort of behaviour this offence is aimed at, the official Explanatory Notes mention the person who makes and markets "black boxes" which dishonest householders can fit to electricity meters, causing them to run slow or backwards.[113] This is conduct which the House of Lords in *Hollinshead*[114] managed, with some difficulty, to squeeze into the offence of conspiracy to defraud, but it obviously extends to catch those who produce equipment that is capable of causing damage that is much more extensive. Section 8(1) makes it clear that "article" includes "any program or data held in electronic form". So it would cover, for example, computer equipment for cloning credit cards.

Unlike the possession offence, section 7 is drafted so as to impose clear outer limits upon its scope. The actus reus requires positive conduct in the form of "making, adapting, supplying or offering", and there is a strong mens rea requirement too: to be guilty, D must either know that the equipment is designed or adapted for use in fraud, or intend that it be so used.

§ 15.7 Dishonestly obtaining services

The Theft Act 1968 gave ample protection to owners against dishonest invasions or acquisitions of their property rights, but provided little, if any, protection against dishonesty for those who provided services. In 1978 this problem was addressed by the creation of

---

[111] *Ibid.*
[112] [1974] 1 WLR 1391.
[113] Explanatory Notes, § 28.
[114] [1985] AC 975.

a new offence of obtaining services by deception.[115] However, that offence was limited to obtaining services by telling lies and did not cover the situation where, without deception, a dishonest person simply helped himself to them. Though this difficulty was partly met by various specific offences, like the offence under the Railway Regulation Act 1889 of travelling on trains without payment of the fare,[116] this was thought to be an undesirable gap in the law. Therefore, the Fraud Act 2006 abolished the offence of obtaining services by deception, and section 11 created in its place a wider offence of obtaining services dishonestly.

The section 11 offence is committed where a person "obtains services for himself or another by a dishonest act".[117] It is limited, however, to services which are provided in the expectation that they will be paid for or have been paid for, and the person who obtains them knows that they are (or might be) provided on this basis and intends to get them without payment, or without paying the full price.[118] Unlike the offence of making off without payment, which is discussed in the next section, the offence is not restricted to services the payment for which is legally enforceable. Thus it is an offence under section 11 of the Fraud Act to obtain the sexual services of a prostitute dishonestly, although it is not the offence of making off without payment if, having obtained them without dishonesty, the customer runs off without paying.

The offence of dishonestly obtaining services is not committed, however, by dishonestly obtaining services which are rendered, and meant to be rendered, free of charge. Thus a dishonest householder who, by falsely claiming to have injured his back, persuades his gullible neighbour to carry his furniture downstairs as a good turn would not be guilty of the offence; and it would make no difference if the neighbour were by trade a furniture remover, who normally charged for his work.[119] A fortiori there would be no criminal liability under section 11 in a case like *Jheeta*,[120] where, by an elaborate fraud, D persuaded his girlfriend V to continue having sexual intercourse with him.

§ 15.8 Making off without payment

Section 3 of the Theft Act 1978 is as follows:

Making off without payment.
(1) Subject to subsection (3) below, a person who, knowing that payment on the spot for any goods supplied or service done is required or expected from him, dishonestly makes off without having paid as required or expected and with intent to avoid payment of the amount due shall be guilty of an offence.

---

[115] Theft Act 1978, s. 1, enacted in response to the Thirteenth Report of the Criminal Law Revision Committee: *Section 16 of the Theft Act 1968* Cmnd. 6733 (1977).

[116] Railway Regulation Act 1889, s. 5(3); cf. art. 143 of the Air Navigation Order 2009/3015, which makes it a criminal offence to stow oneself away upon an aircraft.

[117] Fraud Act 2006, s. 11(1).

[118] *Ibid.*, s. 11(2).

[119] Though in such a case D would commit the offence of fraud by false representation; under s. 5(4), a "loss" includes a loss "by not getting what one might get"; so the false representation causes the neighbour a loss if he would otherwise have charged for what he did.

[120] [2007] EWCA Crim 1699, [2008] 1 WLR 2582; see above, § 12.3(iii)(b).

(2) For purposes of this section "payment on the spot" includes payment at the time of collecting goods on which work has been done or in respect of which service has been provided.
(3) Subsection (1) above shall not apply where the supply of the goods or the doing of the service is contrary to law, or where the service done is such that payment is not legally enforceable.

This offence was created to deal with the specific problem of the person who runs off without paying. If she was dishonest from the outset and obtained the goods or services when she never had any intention of paying for them, she is likely to be guilty of a range of other offences, including fraud by false representation; if she actually obtains property or services, then the offences she is guilty of are theft or dishonestly obtaining services. However, there is a problem if D was initially honest but changed her mind only after the property or services had been obtained. If, for example, D intends to pay for a meal in a restaurant at the time she orders it, she does not commit an offence of fraud by false representation when she places the order. If she still intends to pay for it when it is served and she eats it, she is not then dishonest and she commits no offence of theft. Furthermore, when she eats the food it becomes her property, and if she later decides to run away without paying she commits no theft because, although she is now dishonest, she does not appropriate "property belonging to another". The half-digested meal now in her stomach belongs in law to her and her alone. Unlike the case where V gives D money which D pays into her bank account, there is no room for argument here that the restaurateur retains some form of residual ownership, in respect of which he can be regarded as the victim of a theft. Unlike dishonest savers, dishonest diners cannot be made to disgorge *in specie* their ill-gotten gains. It was to fill this gap in the law that this offence was created.[121]

Though this provision is clearly drafted, it leaves open two points of doubt, both of which have been answered in the case law. The first is whether the phrase "with intent to avoid payment" means with the intention of avoiding it permanently or whether—subject to the requirement of dishonesty—D is also guilty if she intends to pay later. In *Allen*,[122] the House of Lords held that D is guilty only where she intends to avoid payment permanently. The second is the scope of the phrase "makes off". This clearly covers sneaking away or running away (and, indeed, strolling away, eye-balling the restaurateur as she goes, where D is bigger and more muscular than V). But does it cover the case where D tells V a lie that persuades V to consent to her leaving? In *Vincent*,[123] the Court of Appeal held that it does not. Unlike in the case of theft, the courts have declined to interpret this offence extensively, and have resolved its ambiguities in favour of the defendant.

§ 15.9 Conspiracy to defraud

Prior to the Fraud Act 2006, there was no general criminal offence of fraud. The defrauding of one individual by another did not *per se* constitute a crime.[124] For the most part, fraud

---

[121] Criminal Law Revision Committee, Thirteenth Report, *Section 16 of the Theft Act 1968* Cmnd. 6733 (1977). Spencer, "The Theft Act 1978" [1979] *Crim LR* 24. Other legal systems have also found it necessary to create a special offence to deal with this form of dishonesty; see art. 313-5 of the French *Code pénal* ("*filouterie*").

[122] [1985] AC 1029.

[123] [2001] 2 Cr App R 150.

[124] *Wheatly* (1761) 2 Burr 1125, 97 ER 746. An exception was the old offence of cheat, which was confined to fraud "in a subject concerning the public, which, as between subject and subject, would only be actionable by a civil action": *Bembridge* (1783) 22 St Tr 1, 99 ER 679 (Lord Mansfield).

was criminalised historically through more specific offences, which addressed particular forms of economic activity when done with a fraudulent intent.[125]

However, the common law does recognise an offence of *conspiracy* to defraud, operative where the fraud involves two or more persons acting together.[126] The essence of the offence is an agreement to practise a fraud on somebody.[127] In *Scott*,[128] the House of Lords thought it "clearly the law" that:

> "an agreement by two or more by dishonesty to deprive a person of something which is his or to which he is or would be or might be entitled and an agreement by two or more by dishonesty to injure some proprietary right of his, suffices to constitute the offence of conspiracy to defraud."

Although its importance has diminished with the enactment of various statutory offences, especially the Fraud Act 2006, conspiracy to defraud remains a catch-all offence covering conduct that does not fall under other substantive fraud offences. The scope of the crime is extremely wide, because of the broad definition of fraud; especially the fact that the conspiracy need not be to commit an offence, but may also be to commit a civil wrong;[129] and according to some of the authorities, perhaps certain kinds of moral wrongs.[130] For these reasons, the offence might be thought prima facie objectionable and one to be used sparingly. Its broad language offers little guidance to prospective offenders—by contrast, a series of offences each of which specifies an actus reus more narrowly offers better guidance to citizens, by warning clearly that proposed conduct falls within the reach of the criminal law.[131]

Furthermore, the offence makes illegal conduct by two defendants that may not be criminal when done by only one. It is hard to see how that distinction between individual and group, and its very serious consequences, are justified. Why does the moral character of an ordinary civil or moral wrong change, *so much so that it becomes a crime*, simply because it is perpetrated by two rather than one?[132] The anomaly created by conspiracy to defraud is, moreover, difficult to reconcile with the ordinary crime of conspiracy *per se*,[133] which requires that the conduct conspired at should itself be an offence.

---

[125] See Smith, *Property Offences* (1994), especially chap. 22; *Arlidge and Parry on Fraud* (2nd ed, 1996).

[126] *Hevey* (1782) 1 Leach 232, 168 ER 218. See Hadden, "Conspiracy to Defraud" [1966] *CLJ* 248; Gillies, "The Offence of Conspiracy to Defraud" (1977) 51 *ALJ* 247.

[127] *Wai Yu-tsang* v. *R.* [1991] 4 All ER 664.

[128] *Scott* v. *Metropolitan Police Commissioner* [1975] AC 819, 840 (Viscount Dilhorne).

[129] *Warburton* (1870) LR 1 CCR 274; *Weaver* (1931) 45 CLR 321, 334. In *Potter* [1953] 1 All ER 296, a recalcitrant debenture-holder entered into an agreement whereby he was guaranteed an additional 7 shillings in the pound on his debentures from an outside source, in return for his agreement to a scheme whereby all debenture holders were to agree to a composition of 8 shillings in the pound. D's counsel argued that the private agreement was merely unenforceable or void as a fraudulent preference, and did not constitute an indictable offence. Cassells J disagreed, holding that there was an indictable offence of conspiracy, although at trial both defendants were acquitted.

[130] *Timothy* (1858) 1 F & F 39, 175 ER 616; *Heymann* v. *R.* (1873) LR 8 QB 102, 105; cf. *Weaver* (1931) 45 CLR 321, 346–7 (but see at 349). These authorities might not be followed after *Norris* v *US* [2008] UKHL 16, [2008] AC 920 and *Goldshield plc* [2008] UKHL 17, [2009] 1 WLR 458; see below.

[131] See the discussion of fair warning, above, § 2.3.

[132] For an argument that the moral character of the wrong changes when there is conspiracy, see Dennis, "The Rationale of Criminal Conspiracy" (1977) 93 *LQR* 39. But Dennis does not suggest that the moral character of the defendants' activities changes so drastically that a conspiracy to do a mere civil wrong (let alone lawful acts) should be criminalised.

[133] Contrary to s. 1(1) of the Criminal Law Act 1977. See above, § 9.3.

Aggravating these problems is the difficulty of drawing a boundary between mere sharp practice in the commercial sphere and criminal dishonesty. The two shade into each other,[134] and in practice it may be the element of conspiracy that redesignates a transaction from unscrupulous to illegal. Perhaps as a consequence of this, in the public mind fraud has tended to lack the graphic moral character of theft or receiving, and there is a continuing debate whether commercial malpractice is a proper subject for "public law", or whether it should primarily be dealt with by civil law mechanisms; particularly since such wrongdoing is often perceived to be victimless, in that there may be no identifiable individual who is directly and immediately out of pocket as a result of the defendant's activities.[135] Even where the activities are regulated by criminal law, the law's control mechanisms are different from those for street crime, in terms of the social standing of the suspects, and in terms of the comparative immunity of "white-collar crimes" from police surveillance or normal criminal prosecution.[136] Nonetheless, serious commercial fraud has increased considerably, and is extremely costly to society in economic terms. No doubt this is attributable to the evolution of commercial practices.[137] Modern credit economies enable fraudsters to manipulate wealth in large denominations, without being constrained by having to deal with its physical manifestation. The techniques of wrongdoing multiply as the variety and complexity of financial transactions increases, requiring specialist knowledge to initiate, process, and, above all, monitor. This changing nature of commercial and financial life presents at least one reason for retention of a fall-back crime such as conspiracy to defraud, since it may be impossible for specific legislation constantly to keep up with the mutating ways in which fraud may be committed, especially given modern communications and computing innovations, and the globalisation of securities and other markets.[138]

The elements of conspiracy to defraud are:

(i)   an agreement between two or more persons;
(ii)   that contemplates using fraudulent means;
(iii) to prejudice the rights of another person, or to induce another to act contrary to her public duty; and
(iv)   mens rea.

We consider these elements in turn.

(i) Agreement with another person

The law on this point is the same as for ordinary conspiracy.[139] There must be an act of agreement, constituting a joint decision to commit the fraud. Preliminary negotiations

---

[134] According to the Law Commission, *Fraud* Law Com. No. 276 (2002) § 1.6, "the common law offence of conspiracy is so wide that it offers little guidance on the difference between fraudulent and lawful conduct".

[135] See the general discussion at the beginning of this chapter.

[136] Levi, *Regulating Fraud: White-collar Crime and the Criminal Process* (1987) 15. See also Hadden, "Fraud in the City: The Role of the Criminal Law" [1983] *Crim LR* 500.

[137] Cf. Hall, *Theft, Law and Society* (2nd ed., 1952) 300.

[138] See Sullivan, "Fraud and the Efficacy of the Criminal Law: A Proposal for a Wide Residual Offence" [1985] *Crim LR* 616; McBarnet and Whelan, "The Elusive Spirit of the Law: Formalism and the Struggle for Legal Control" (1991) 54 *MLR* 848; Smith, "Conspiracy to Defraud: Some Comments on the Law Commission's Report" [1995] *Crim LR* 209.

[139] See the more detailed discussion above, in § 9.2(ii); also Orchard, "'Agreement' in Criminal Conspiracy" [1974] *Crim LR* 297 and 335.

or discussions regarding the possibility of doing something fraudulent, which do not crystallise into any firm decision, are insufficient.[140] Neither is there a conspiracy where the parties each have the same thought or intention, but have not communicated this to each other: a concurrence between two people of "mere wicked thoughts not intended to be acted upon"[141] will not do. The joint decision required for conspiracy exists only if there is a genuine agreement to defraud between the parties.

In general, there are three kinds of conspiratorial agreement. The simplest variety is where each conspirator is aware of the existence of all the others and knows that they are parties to the agreement. The second, more complex, case is the "wheel" (or "cartwheel") conspiracy, where A, B, and C (the spokes) are all individually in contact with D (the hub), but have never met each other.[142] The third variant is the "chain" conspiracy, where A contacts B, who contacts C, who contacts D, and so on.[143] However, it is important not to roll up a number of separate transactions in one conspiracy charge. This point is made in *Griffiths*,[144] where a lime supplier (Griffiths), his accountant, and seven farmers whom Griffiths supplied were charged with conspiracy to defraud the government of subsidies. Their convictions were quashed on appeal, as there was no evidence of any collusion between the farmers, either directly or through the intermediation of Griffiths, but only of separate conspiracies between the supplier and individual farmers.[145]

Like statutory conspiracy, a conspiracy to defraud, once formed, does not admit of withdrawal. After an agreement is reached, and the other elements are established, the crime of conspiracy to defraud is complete and it is irrelevant that subsequently one or all of the parties decide to abandon the agreement.[146]

(ii) By fraudulent means

The conspiracy must involve the use of fraudulent or dishonest means.[147] To illustrate the importance of this requirement, suppose that a solicitor acting in her professional

---

[140] This is the explanation of *Walker* [1962] Crim LR 458. D had participated in discussions about a planned payroll robbery, but later withdrew. His conviction was quashed as it was not proven that the discussions had progressed beyond the stage of negotiation before his withdrawal. See above, § 9.3(ii)(c); also *Barnard* (1980) 70 Cr App R 28.

[141] *Banks* (1873) 12 Cox CC 393, 399.

[142] Cf. *Ex p Coffey, Re Evans* [1971] NSWLR 434.

[143] *Ardalan* [1972] 2 All ER 257. Note, however, the cautionary words of Roskill LJ (at 262) that "words or phrases such as 'wheels', 'cartwheels', 'chain', 'sub-conspiracies' and so on are used only to illustrate and clarify the principle and for no other purpose".

[144] [1966] 1 QB 589.

[145] [1966] 1 QB 589, 599: "It is right and proper to say that the judge correctly pointed out the principle, saying that the Crown had to prove that the conspirators put their heads together to defraud the Ministry. The trouble is that it never seems to have been considered ... whether or not in this case each farmer put his head together with Griffiths' head without any thought of a general conspiracy." Hence, although each defendant may have conspired separately with Griffiths, the convictions were unsafe since the defendants should not have been joined in a conglomerate charge.

[146] Above, § 9.3(ii)(d). Cf. *O'Brien* (1955) 2 DLR 311, 314 (Taschereau J): "If a person, with one or several others, agrees to commit an unlawful act, and later, after having had the intention to carry it through, refuses to put the plan into effect, that person is nevertheless guilty".

[147] In *Scott* [1975] AC 819, 840, this criterion is encapsulated in the phrase "by dishonesty", operating as an actus reus element; see the passage quoted above in the text at § 15.9. In order clearly to distinguish it from the mens rea component of dishonesty (below, § 15.9(iv)), we refer to this element as "by fraudulent means". Early

capacity agrees to perform certain services for her client which will cause loss to another party. These facts disclose no conspiracy to defraud unless the services go beyond her ordinary duties as a solicitor.[148] Similarly, many business decisions do—and are meant to—prejudice the economic interests of rivals, yet one is entitled to neglect those rival interests provided the decision involves a legitimate course of action. Thus in *Zemmel*,[149] the defendants' agreement to delay paying a creditor was held not to be a conspiracy to defraud.

On the other hand, the requirement of fraudulent *modus operandi* is quite easily satisfied. Obviously, the use of deceit or falsehood is sufficient (although it would now anyway fall within the scope of section 1 of the Fraud Act 2006). In *Lewis*,[150] for example, it was held that an arrangement made for mock bidding at an auction could be a conspiracy to defraud, since the scheme was intended, through a deception, to induce innocent buyers to bid more than necessary. Similarly, in *A-G's Reference (No. 1 of 1982)*,[151] manufacturing fake whisky was held to be a conspiracy to defraud unknowing purchasers. These are cases where the agreement involved a false representation, express or implied. But conspiracy to defraud has a much wider scope than this. In *Weaver*,[152] the High Court of Australia said that the offence embraces "every kind and description of fraudulent statement, conduct, trick, or device", including "false accounts, fabricated shares, false representations or conduct".[153] Even if there is no representation, many cases will involve deceit; as in *Hollinshead*, where the defendants agreed to manufacture and sell "black box" devices whose only purpose was to cause electricity meters to produce erroneous readings.

Moreover, there is no *requirement* that there be either a falsehood or that anyone must be deceived.[154] In *Scott*,[155] for example, the defendants bribed cinema employees to let them borrow films, which were then copied in breach of copyright. Their behaviour was certainly fraudulent, even though it involved neither falsehood nor deceit.

(iii) The object of the conspiracy

Conspiracy to defraud may be committed in either of two general forms: by conspiring to prejudice the rights of another person, or to induce another to act contrary to her public duty.

---

cases express it in the requirement that a common law conspiracy be either to do an unlawful act or to do a lawful act *by unlawful means: Jones* (1832) 4 B & Ad 345, 349, 110 ER 485, 487.

[148] *Tighe and Maher* (1926) 26 SR (NSW) 94.
[149] (1985) 81 Cr App R 279.
[150] (1869) 11 Cox CC 404.
[151] [1983] QB 751.
[152] (1931) 45 CLR 321.
[153] *Ibid.*, 334.
[154] Contrast the definition by Buckley J in *Re London & Globe Finance Corp Ltd* [1903] 1 Ch 728, 732, which (wrongly) suggests that deceit is necessary for fraud: "To deceive is, I apprehend, to induce a man to believe that a thing is true which is false, and which the person practising the deceit knows or believes to be false. To defraud is to deprive by deceit: it is by deceit to induce a man to act to his injury. More tersely it may be put, that to deceive is by falsehood to induce a state of mind; to defraud is by deceit to induce a course of action."
[155] [1975] AC 819. See also *Sinclair* [1968] 1 WLR 1246; *Hollinshead* [1985] AC 975.

(a) To prejudice the rights of another

The paradigm case of conspiracy to defraud is where D conspires to obtain a benefit at the expense of another's assets. In many cases this can, and should, be charged under ordinary conspiracy principles; as either conspiracy to steal, or conspiracy to commit the statutory offence of fraud under section 1 of the Fraud Act 2006. However, conspiracy to defraud, unlike theft, is not limited to the case where D's plan is to obtain something that is recognised as "property" for the purposes of that offence: thus it encompasses depriving someone of land, or exploiting another's confidential information.

It is possible that the offence may even extend to dishonest plans to interfere with "interests" of a kind that the civil law would not recognise as "property" at all. It has been suggested, for example, that it might cover using dishonest means to persuade a testatrix to change her will in favour of the defendants.[156] This would not be theft even of an equitable interest, since the (erstwhile) potential beneficiaries under a will have merely a *spes successionis*, and are not deprived of any proprietary right. However, such an extensive interpretation of interests was rejected by Hickinbottom J in *Evans*.[157] In that case, D and others were directors of a company formed to carry out open-cast coal-mining in South Wales. This operation required licences from various public authorities, which were granted on condition that the land be restored after the coal had been extracted. Hoping to evade this obligation, they allegedly concocted a scheme to transfer the freehold of the sites—together, they hoped, with the obligation to restore the sites—to dummy companies in the British Virgin Islands against whom the public authorities would find it impossible to enforce the conditions of the licences. Hickinbottom J ruled that this conduct did not constitute a conspiracy to defraud the public authorities, because their statutory powers to enforce the conditions of the licence did not count as a proprietary interest. As a precedent, the authority of this case is limited, both because it was a ruling at first instance which for procedural reasons the Crown was unable to appeal,[158] and because it was doubted, *obiter*, by the Court of Appeal in a later case.[159] But like the *Norris* case, which is discussed below, it demonstrates a growing unwillingness in the courts to extend the boundaries of the offence.[160]

---

[156] See the commentary by J.C. Smith on *Tillings and Tillings* [1985] Crim LR 393.

[157] [2014] 1 WLR 2817; discussed by Jarvis, "Conspiracy to Defraud: A Siren to Lure Unwary Prosecutors" [2014] Crim LR 738.

[158] The judge's ruling was made in response to a defence application, under the Crime and Disorder Act 1998, to dismiss the charges on the ground that the evidence the Crown proposed to call would not justify a conviction. As the law currently stands there is no right of appeal against such a ruling—anomalously, given that a judge's ruling of "no case to answer" when made after the evidence has been called is subject to appeal. The only step open to the Crown in *Evans* was to try to relaunch the proceedings by persuading a High Court Judge to issue a voluntary bill of indictment. This the Crown attempted to do, but without success: see [2015] EWHC 283, [2015] 1 WLR 3595, and further comment by Jarvis, [2015] Crim LR 704.

[159] *H* [2015] EWCA Crim 46, an interlocutory appeal in the prosecution that resulted in *Hayes* [2015] EWCA Crim 1944 (above, § 13.8(iv)).

[160] As part of its case, the Crown alleged that the defendants had, by fraud, induced the company's auditors to release funds which the company had set aside to pay for the restoration—some of which then found its way, via other shell companies, into their own pockets. If proved, these allegations would have supported convictions for a number of other offences, including conspiracy to defraud the company.

The core of defrauding is disadvantage to others: usually, deprivation of or prejudice to a victim's interests. So it is not necessary that the purpose of the conspiracy should be to benefit anyone.[161] In *Welham* v. *DPP*, Lord Radcliffe pointed out that:[162]

> "Although in the nature of things [defrauding] is almost invariably associated with the obtaining of an advantage for the person who commits the fraud, it is the effect upon the person who is the object of the fraud that ultimately determines its meaning."

The law thus looks at the effect of the fraud on the victim, irrespective of whether the defendants sought thereby to make a gain.

Further, if we concentrate upon the victim, we find that she may be defrauded even if she suffers no loss. It is sufficient that the conspiracy *puts at risk* the economic, or property, interests or rights of the victim.[163] In *Scott* (above, § 15.9(ii)), a conspiracy to defraud was established notwithstanding that the breach of copyright caused no direct pecuniary loss to the cinema owners, and simply had the potential to deprive them of profits. Similarly, in *Adams* v. *R.* it was said that there may be a conspiracy to defraud based upon an agreement dishonestly to conceal information, where the conspirator is under a duty to disclose it, or upon an agreement dishonestly to withhold information from persons entitled to require its disclosure[164]—whether or not those persons suffer financial harm as a result.

The victim need not be a particular person, and in the past the offence has been applied to conspiracies to rig markets.[165] In *Norris* v. *Government of the United States of America*,[166] however, the House of Lords held that it does not. A cartel agreement, it said, does not amount to a conspiracy to defraud in the absence of some aggravating factor, such as "fraud, misrepresentation, violence, intimidation or inducement of a breach of contract".[167] In reaching this decision it was influenced by the notion that, in order to comply with Article 7 of the European Convention on Human Rights, a prohibition imposed by the criminal law must be sufficiently clear and certain, and in this connection it referred to its previous decisions in *Rimmington*[168] and *Jones*.[169] No previous cartel agreement, said the Law Lords, had been held to amount to a conspiracy to defraud where no such aggravating factor was present, and they did not think it right to extend the boundaries of the offence to cover such a situation. In the past, conspiracy to defraud has been a protean offence, often extended by the courts to cover new situations, but from

---

[161] Cf. *Cope* (1719) 1 Str 144, 93 ER 438.

[162] [1961] AC 103, 123. (D was charged with uttering forged documents with intent to defraud, contrary to s. 6 of the Forgery Act 1912.) Cf. Viscount Dilhorne in *Scott* v. *MPC* [1975] AC 819, 839: "'to defraud' ordinarily means, in my opinion, to deprive a person dishonestly of something which is his or of something to which he is or would or might but for the perpetration of the fraud be entitled."

[163] *Allsop* (1976) 64 Cr App R 29; *Wai Yu-tsang* v. *R* [1992] 1 AC 269.

[164] [1995] 1 WLR 52, 65. The Privy Council held that a conspiracy to defraud existed where company directors dishonestly agreed to conceal information relating to secret profits, so as to impede action by the company to recover those profits. However, there must still be an intention to act to the prejudice of some extant right: "A person is not prejudiced if he is hindered in inquiring into the source of moneys in which he has no interest. He can only suffer prejudice in relation to some right or interest which he possesses."

[165] Early authorities include *De Berenger* (1814) 3 M & S 67, 105 ER 536; *Burch* (1865) 4 F & F 407, 176 ER 622; *Aspinall* (1876) 1 QBD 730, affirmed 35 LT 738, 741n; *Scott* v. *Brown, Doering, McNab & Co* (1892) 2 QB 724.

[166] [2008] UKHL 16, [2008] AC 920.

[167] Per Lord Bingham at para. 17.

[168] [2005] UKHL 63, [2006] 2 AC 459; and see above, § 2.2.

[169] [2006] UKHL 16, [2007] 1 AC 136.

Norris v. *USA* (and from *Goldshield Group plc*,[170] which followed and applied it) it seems that its expansive days are past. In 2002, Parliament created a statutory offence of price-fixing, punishable with up to five years' imprisonment,[171] and it is for that offence that those who conspire to rig the market should now be prosecuted.

(b) To induce another to act contrary to her public duty

In addition to defrauding particular persons and unascertained persons through the marketplace, the fraud may also be on the "public" at large, where no individual's particular interests (actual or potential) are jeopardised. "Where the intended victim of a 'conspiracy to defraud' is a person performing public duties as distinct from a private individual it is sufficient if the purpose is to cause him to act contrary to his duty."[172] Consequently, there may be a conspiracy fraudulently to obtain a driving licence,[173] National Insurance number,[174] confidential information,[175] or membership of a society.[176] But for this head of conspiracy to defraud it seems that the public official must be caused to *act*, rather than prevented from doing so. In *Evans* (discussed in § 15.9(iii)(a) above), the Crown also failed in an attempt to argue that the defendants were guilty of this alternative form of conspiracy to defraud: their scheme, if intended to prevent the authorities from enforcing the planning conditions, was not intended to cause them to *act* contrary to their duties.

There is some authority that cases involving public officials are not distinctive, but rather illustrations of a more general proposition that conspiracy to defraud does not require an intention to cause loss, so that cases of "public duty" fraud might extend to victims not occupying a public office: "the expression 'intent to defraud' is not to be given a narrow meaning, involving an intention to cause economic loss to another. In broad terms, it means simply an intention to practise a fraud on another, or an intention to act to the prejudice of another man's right."[177] However, that authority should be understood as establishing no more than the proposition set out in the foregoing subsection (§ 15.9(iii)(a)), that it is ordinarily sufficient in conspiracy to defraud that the victim's rights or interests are deliberately put at risk and that there is no need for the conspirators to aim at causing loss.[178] Any wider interpretation should be doubted, since it would further extend an already vague and overbroad offence. Moreover, it would be contrary to House of Lords authority that the

---

[170] [2008] UKHL 17, [2009] 1 WLR 458.

[171] Enterprise Act 2002, Part 6. For an account of the first prosecution under the Act (*Whittle and others* [2008] EWCA Crim 2560), see Lucraft, Payne, and Rawlings, "The Dunlop Three: the Cartel Offence Makes its Debut" [2006] 1 *Archbold News* 7. In order to make it easier to secure convictions, in 2013 Parliament amended s. 188 of the Enterprise Act 2002 to remove "dishonesty" as an element.

[172] *Scott* v. *MPC* [1975] AC 819, 841 (Lord Diplock).

[173] *Potter* [1958] 2 All ER 51.

[174] *Moses & Ansbro* [1991] Crim LR 617.

[175] *DPP* v. *Withers* [1975] AC 842.

[176] Cf. *Bassey* (1931) 22 Cr App R 160, where an unqualified student acting alone, who attempted to gain admission to the Inner Temple by the use of forged references and degree certificates, was held to have defrauded the Benchers of that Inn.

[177] *Wai Yu-tsang* v. *R* [1992] 1 AC 269, 276; citing Lord Denning's judgment in *Welham* v. *DPP* [1961] AC 103, 133.

[178] This analysis would explain the rejection of Lord Diplock's separate categorisation in *Scott* v. *Metropolitan Police Commissioner* [1975] AC 819, 841 by the Privy Council in *Wai Yu-tsang* v. *R* [1992] 1 AC 269.

public duty cases are a "special line of cases",[179] a separate category,[180] perhaps a surviving variety of the now-rejected generic wrong of conspiracy to effect a public mischief.[181] Lord Kilbrandon asserts, and defends, the distinctiveness of defrauding a public official most clearly in *Withers* v. *DPP*:[182]

> "Moreover, as regards the first count, I am not prepared to accept that 'officials of banks and building societies' are public officers within the meaning of *Welham* v. *Director of Public Prosecutions* [1961] AC 103. The fact that very many people have bank accounts and some deal with building societies does not change the relationship between institution and customer from a private to a public one. It would be dangerous to use analogy for the purpose of extending a meaning of fraud which has already, for the purposes of the law of conspiracy, gone beyond its common content of prejudice to proprietary rights."

Quite so.

(c) Illegality of object?

As was pointed out earlier (§ 15.9), and unlike ordinary conspiracy,[183] the object of a conspiracy to defraud need not itself constitute an offence when done. This, perhaps, is an inevitable consequence of finding a conspiracy to defraud where V's interests are merely put at risk—in the absence of a crystallised loss or gain, the contemplated activities may well be insufficiently harmful to attract the wrath of criminalisation. Nonetheless, it is submitted that the scope of conspiracy to defraud should be confined to conspiracies at least to commit a legal wrong, and that conspiracy to commit a moral wrong, *simpliciter*, should not fall within the criminal law.[184]

(d) Impossibility

What happens where the means chosen by the conspirators fail to work, e.g. because the intended victims were already aware of the facts and could not be deceived? By contrast with the modern statutory offence of conspiracy, impossibility is a defence to conspiracies at common law[185] and therefore remains a defence to the charge of conspiracy to defraud.

---

[179] *Welham* v. *DPP* [1961] AC 103, 124 (Lord Radcliffe); cf. also *Withers* v. *DPP* [1975] AC 842, 873 (Lord Simon).

[180] *Scott* v. *MPC* [1975] AC 819, 841, *per* Lord Diplock: "(2) Where the intended victim of a 'conspiracy to defraud' is a private individual the purpose of the conspirators must be to cause the victim economic loss by depriving him of some property or right, corporeal or incorporeal, to which he is or would or might become entitled. The intended means by which the purpose is to be achieved must be dishonest. They need not involve fraudulent misrepresentation such as is needed to constitute the civil tort of deceit. Dishonesty of any kind is enough. (3) Where the intended victim of a 'conspiracy to defraud' is a person performing public duties as distinct from a private individual it is sufficient if the purpose is to cause him to act contrary to his public duty, and the intended means of achieving this purpose are dishonest. The purpose need not involve causing economic loss to anyone." Although Lord Diplock's categorisation was disapproved by the Privy Council in *Wai Yu-tsang* v. *R* [1992] 1 AC 269, 277, the disagreement was motivated by rejection of his Lordship's analysis of category (2), in particular of the requirement that actual loss be intended.

[181] Held to disclose no offence known to law in *Withers* v. *DPP* [1975] AC 842 (HL).

[182] [1975] AC 842, 877. Unfortunately, the decision was not considered by the Privy Council in *Wai Yu-tsang* v. *R* [1992] 1 AC 269.

[183] See above, § 9.3(i).

[184] Cf. Williams, *CLGP* §§ 222, 226.

[185] *DPP* v. *Nock* [1978] AC 979.

Thus, in general, no offence is committed when the conspiracy necessarily cannot achieve its objective because of legal or physical impossibility.[186] The defence of impossibility is discussed in more detail above, in § 9.5.

(iv) Mens rea

The mens rea of conspiracy to defraud is sometimes described as an "intent to defraud". In fact, the mens rea components are more specific than this:

(i)   dishonesty; and
(ii)   intention to carry out the agreement.

The first element, dishonesty, bears the same meaning as it does for theft.[187] Although, at one time, it was suggested that the meanings were different,[188] this possibility was expressly negated by the Court of Appeal in *Ghosh*.[189] *Ghosh* is now the leading case on dishonesty for both offences.

Secondly, there must be an intention on the part of the alleged conspirator to carry out her part of the agreement.[190] Thus there is no conspiracy by D if he appears to agree, but secretly intends to frustrate the execution of the plan;[191] nor if D has no intention of playing his allocated role.[192] As with all crimes where motive is not part of the mens rea, a benign motive or purpose will not of itself foreclose an agreement to defraud from constituting a conspiracy. It is sufficient that the agreement exists and that D intends to carry it out.[193]

It might be thought that conspiracy to defraud requires, perhaps in addition to the above two elements, a separate intent to defraud. Not so. Proof of an intention to carry out the agreement to defraud is, of itself, sufficient to establish an intent to defraud; thus, in the context of conspiracy, the requirement of an intent to defraud adds nothing to the two elements identified here. In particular, since fraud may be committed simply by placing another's rights or interests in jeopardy, an "intent to defraud" means simply a (dishonest) intention to act to the potential prejudice of another person's rights[194]—i.e. to carry out the agreement. This includes deliberately putting V's rights at risk, whether or not actual loss is intended. As the Court of Appeal stated in *Sinclair*:[195]

"To cheat and defraud is to act with deliberate dishonesty to the prejudice of another person's proprietary right. In the context of this case the alleged conspiracy to cheat and defraud is an

---

[186] Cf. *Bennett* (1979) 68 Cr App R 168, distinguishing cases where the means employed were physically incapable of achieving the purpose from an agreement which might have worked, but which failed because of the behaviour of some person external to the agreement.

[187] See above, § 13.8.

[188] In that the test of dishonesty was subjective for conspiracy to defraud, but objective for theft: *McIvor* [1982] 1 All ER 491, 497; *Landy* [1981] 1 All ER 1172, 1181.

[189] [1982] QB 1053, 1059–61.

[190] Cf. *Gemmell* [1985] 2 NZLR 740; *O'Brien* [1955] 2 DLR 311.

[191] *Anderson* [1986] AC 27, 38ff.

[192] Cf. *Thomson* (1965) 50 Cr App R 1.

[193] *Wai Yu-tsang* [1992] 1 AC 269; *Hagan* [1985] Crim LR 598. See also the discussion of *Smith* [1960] 2 QB 423, above, § 5. However, as Smith notes in his commentary on *Hagan* [1985] Crim LR 598, 599, D's motive may sometimes raise issues relevant to the question of dishonesty, e.g. when D believes he has a claim of right.

[194] *Wai Yu-tsang* [1992] 1 AC 269, 276 (Lord Goff).

[195] [1968] 1 WLR 1246, 1250. See also *Olan, Hudsson & Hartnett* (1978) 41 CCC (2d) 145.

agreement by a director of a company and others dishonestly to take a risk with the assets of the company by using them in a manner which was known to be not in the best interests of the company and to be prejudicial to the minority shareholders."

Similarly, in *Allsop*, the Court of Appeal remarked:[196]

"If the deceit which is employed imperils the economic interest of the person deceived, this is sufficient to constitute fraud even though in the event no actual loss is suffered and notwithstanding that the deceiver did not desire to bring about an actual loss.... Interests which are imperilled are less valuable in terms of money than those same interests when they are secure and protected. Where a person intends by deceit to induce a course of conduct in another which puts that other's economic interests in jeopardy he is guilty of fraud even though he does not intend or desire that actual loss should ultimately be suffered by that other in this context."

(v) Conspiracy to defraud, statutory fraud, and clarity of law

In its protean form, as it existed before the House of Lords decided in *Norris v. USA*[197] that it was not to be further extended, it was questionable whether conspiracy to defraud met the standards of clarity required for a system of criminal law fit for a liberal democracy. The offence had an enormous, non-particularised scope, with its crucial reliance on the notion of dishonesty. In the *Fourteenth Report* of the Joint Parliamentary Committee on Human Rights, the compatibility of conspiracy to defraud with Article 7 of the ECHR was doubted,[198] because of its over-reliance on jury findings of dishonesty.[199] It was widely anticipated that the Fraud Act 2006 would abolish conspiracy to defraud but, as we have seen, it did not. Conspiracy to defraud continues to operate in tandem with statutory fraud and in recent years there have been some high-profile prosecutions for the offence.[200] Surprisingly, perhaps, the view was taken in the *Fourteenth Report* that the Bill which in substance became the 2006 Act was compatible with Article 7. The offence of statutory fraud proposed in the Bill was taken to have a more substantial conduct element than conspiracy to defraud, making less objectionable the recourse to dishonesty.[201] But, as we have seen in our discussion of fraud by false representation[202] and, particularly, fraud by abuse of position,[203] reliance on a judgment of dishonesty is pervasive. Recall too the hollowing-out of the actus reus in theft by the decisions in *Gomez*[204] and *Hinks*,[205] which considerably increases the role of dishonesty in that offence.[206] It was once said

---

[196] (1976) 64 Cr App R 29, 31–2.

[197] [2008] UKHL 16, [2008] AC 920; see above, § 15.9(iii)(a).

[198] Art. 7, which proscribes retroactive criminal law, has been interpreted as requiring minimum standards of clarity for criminal offences: above, § 2.2.

[199] Session 2004–05, para. 2.12.

[200] Among them the LIBOR rate-fixing prosecutions which produced *Hayes* [2015] EWCA Crim 1944, discussed in § 13.8(iv) above; the prosecution in relation to open-cast mining in South Wales which produced *Evans* [2014] 1 WLR 2817, discussed in § 15.9.(iii)(a) above; and a prosecution for conspiracy to defraud brought in respect of a large-scale motor-insurance fraud in County Durham, part of which later reached the Court of Appeal as *Mckenzie* [2013] EWCA Crim 1544, [2014] 1 Cr App R (S) 68.

[201] *Ibid.*, para. 2.14.

[202] Above, § 15.3.

[203] Above, § 15.5.

[204] [1993] AC 442.

[205] [2001] AC 241.

[206] See above, § 13.6(ii)(a)–(c).

that you could communicate the substance of property offences and offences against the person with the precept, "be honest and refrain from violence".[207] Certainly the first part of that advice is the best that can be offered by way of advance guidance about the content of large parts of the modern law of fraud and theft.

§ 15.10 Specific offences of fraud

The general offences of fraud described in this chapter are supplemented by a great many specific statutory ones. Thus it is, for example, a specific statutory offence to cheat at gambling,[208] to make a false statement to obtain a driving licence (or to prevent someone from obtaining one),[209] and also to make a false statement to obtain a passport.[210] A battery of highly specific offences criminalises the making of false statements in connection with applications for various types of grant.[211] At the head of these in terms of practical importance is the offence of making a false statement or representation with a view to obtaining a social security benefit, which results each year in more convictions than the whole of the law of sexual offences.[212] It is also a statutory offence to fraudulently evade income tax[213] and VAT,[214] and here the statutory offences are backed up by an ancient and far-reaching common law offence of "cheating the public revenue", for which life imprisonment could in theory be imposed.[215] Many (though not all) of these offences cover misbehaviour that could equally be prosecuted as fraud under section 1 of the Fraud Act 2006, but the investigation and prosecution of these offences is usually in the hands of the government departments responsible for the area of public business to which they relate, whose officials are familiar with the specific offences and prefer to use them.

§ 15.11 Forgery and false accounting

The law of fraud is also buttressed by two other general offences: forgery and false accounting. Though both are practically important, here they will be described in outline only.[216]

---

[207] Quoted by Glanville Williams, in the preface to his *Textbook of Criminal Law* (1st ed., 1978).

[208] Gaming Act 2005, s. 42.

[209] Road Traffic Act 1988, s. 174.

[210] Criminal Justice Act 1925, s. 36.

[211] See, for example, s. 51 of the Agriculture Act 1993.

[212] Social Security Administration Act 1992, s. 111A; in answer to a parliamentary question on 14 July 2009, the Minister said that 13,393 persons had been convicted of offences of social security fraud in the previous year. This is approximately double the number of persons convicted of all sex offences.

[213] Taxes Management Act 1970, s. 106A.

[214] Value Added Tax Act 1994, s. 72.

[215] For the details, see *Archbold* (2016 edition) § 25.409ff. The offence covers, inter alia, defrauding the revenue by omission: *Redford* (1989) 89 Cr App R 1; and in *Hunt* [1994] Crim LR 747 the Court of Appeal interpreted it as a "conduct crime", of which a person can be guilty even though no loss to the Revenue has actually occurred. Cheating the Revenue was originally just one aspect of an even broader common law offence of cheating, which was abolished except as regards frauds on the revenue by the Theft Act 1968, s. 32(1). In *Dosanjh* [2013] EWCA Crim 2366, [2014] 1 WLR 1780, the Court of Appeal said that, for a serious instance of VAT fraud, it was appropriate to prosecute the defendant for the common law offence and for him then to be sentenced more severely than would have been possible under the statutory regime.

[216] For a fuller account of forgery see *Archbold* (2016) chap. 22 and *Smith and Hogan* chap. 28; for false accounting, see *Archbold* § 21.177ff and *Smith and Hogan* chap. 24.

Forgery is a crime with a long and colourful history; it was originally a crime at common law and at one time some forms of it carried the death penalty and others mutilation.[217] In its present form it derives from the Forgery and Counterfeiting Act 1981, a reforming and codifying statute based on a report by the Law Commission.[218] The basic definition of the offence is set out in section 1 of this Act, which is as follows:

> A person is guilty of forgery if he makes a false instrument, with the intention that he or another shall use it to induce somebody to accept it as genuine, and by reason of so accepting it to do or not to do some act to his own or any other person's prejudice.

As with previous versions of the offence, the essential element of the offence of forgery is the making of an "instrument" which purports to be something it is not. Thus, as is often said, "a forgery is a document which not only tells a lie, but tells a lie about itself".[219] Although most forgeries comprise false documents, the offence can be committed in relation to anything that counts as an "instrument" within the definition set out in section 8, which includes not only documents of all types, but also postage stamps and Inland Revenue stamps, and "any disc, tape, sound track or other device on or in which information is recorded or stored by mechanical, electronic or other means". Banknotes are specifically excluded from this definition; the creation of false money, whether in coin or paper form, and of whatever country,[220] is specifically covered by separate provisions of the Act.[221] The concept of "falsity" is elaborated in some detail by section 9 of the Act, and section 10 provides an extensive (and exhaustive) definition of intending to induce a person to act to his "prejudice". Among the cases listed is enabling a person to "earn remuneration or greater remuneration" from that person. So, if doubt exists as to whether a person who tells lies to get a job commits an offence under the Fraud Act,[222] he is clearly guilty of forgery if, to support his lie, he fabricates a bogus reference or degree certificate. The basic offence of forgery is flanked by back-up offences of knowingly possessing forgeries[223] and knowingly making use of them.[224] So the fraudulent job-seeker is also guilty if he obtains these documents from a friend whose literary or artistic skills are superior to his own. Unlike most of the other offences of fraud, it is not an ingredient in the offence of forgery that D's behaviour be "dishonest". So although the Fraud Act 2006 contemplates the possibility of the "honest liar", the Forgery and Counterfeiting Act 1981 gives no quarter to his friend the "honest forger".

---

[217] And hence it led to the execution at Tyburn, in 1777, of the fashionable clergyman and author Dr William Dodd. This was a *cause célèbre* which attracted much attention at the time. Some 23,000 members of the Universities of Oxford and Cambridge signed a petition begging the King for mercy—pressure which is said to have been counter-productive (Philip Rawlings, *Dictionary of National Biography*). By a statute of Elizabeth I, certain forms of the offence were also at one time punished by "standing in the pillory, and having both his ears cut off, and his nostrils slit and seared" (Blackstone, *Commentaries*, Book IV, chap. 17, III).

[218] Law Com. No. 55, *Report on Forgery and Counterfeit Currency* (1973).

[219] Kenny, *Outlines of Criminal Law* (14th ed., 1932) 264.

[220] So the provision covers the manufacture of false euros.

[221] In particular, Forgery and Counterfeiting Act 1981, s. 27.

[222] See above, § 15.2(i)(a).

[223] Forgery and Counterfeiting Act 1981, s. 5.

[224] *Ibid.*, ss. 3 and 4.

The requirement that a forgery purport to be something it is not means that the crooked accountant who "cooks the books" does not commit a forgery; even if the firm's books as cooked contain entries that are false, the books are still their books. To meet this and other difficulties, section 17 of the Theft Act 1968 creates an offence of false accounting.[225] It is as follows:

(1) Where a person dishonestly, with a view to gain for himself or another or with intent to cause loss to another,—

(a)   destroys, defaces, conceals or falsifies any account or any record or document made or required for any accounting purpose; or

(b)   in furnishing information for any purpose produces or makes use of any account, or any such record or document as aforesaid, which to his knowledge is or may be misleading, false or deceptive in a material particular;

he shall, on conviction on indictment, be liable to imprisonment for a term not exceeding seven years.

(2) For purposes of this section a person who makes or concurs in making in an account or other document an entry which is or may be misleading, false or deceptive in a material particular, or who omits or concurs in omitting a material particular from an account or other document, is to be treated as falsifying the account or document.

This offence is more generous to defendants than forgery, because here an essential ingredient is dishonesty, as understood in *Ghosh*. However, although a defendant who thought his false accounting was in accordance with accepted standards in society has a defence—at any rate, if the tribunal of fact believes him—it seems that he has no defence if he was unaware that the document he falsified or destroyed was required for accounting purposes. Surprisingly, the Court of Appeal in *Graham*[226] suggested that in this respect section 17 is an offence of strict liability.

---

[225] There were precursor offences, dating from the nineteenth century, of falsification of accounts. See the Criminal Law Revision Committee, Eighth Report, *Theft and Related Offences* (Cmnd. 2977, 1966), § 102ff.

[226] [1997] 1 Cr App R 302, 314.

16

THE MORAL LIMITS OF CRIMINALISATION

Over the past few chapters we have investigated some of the better-known common law and statutory offences. There are, of course, many other offences, both minor and serious, known to the law. Beyond that, however, there are many forms of wrongdoing that are not offences at all—and rightly so. The criminal law is not a tool to be deployed wherever someone may do wrong. As a regulatory device, it is a bluntly coercive and morally loaded tool, something to be used sparingly and with care. This generates a problem of *criminalisation*: although it may frequently be appropriate, indeed necessary, to have criminal prohibitions, we should always be careful of overextending the reach of the criminal law, and of infringing too far upon citizens' rights of free choice and individual liberty. We *should* use the criminal law to prohibit conduct—but we should not over-prohibit.

The question becomes, therefore, *when* should we extend the criminal law to regulate conduct? Suppose that a responsible legislature seeks to enact an appropriate, morally justifiable, range of criminal prohibitions. What criteria should it apply when deciding whether to proscribe something? The decision whether a particular action or state of affairs is sufficiently serious to warrant criminalisation always involves difficult judgements, and will be affected by the political values, state of development, and social structure of a society. There is no sphere of industrial, commercial, or administrative activity untouched by the criminal law. As criminal lawyers, however, we must enquire whether conduct made criminal merits that designation.

A useful starting point is that there should be parsimony in criminalisation: offences "should be created only when absolutely necessary".[1] The criminal sanction is the most drastic of the State's standard tools for regulating the conduct of individuals. It represents the most severe infringement of a person's liberty and, as such, should be available only where there is a clear social justification.

Broadly speaking, we can identify two types of criteria that must be met if the creation of an offence is to be morally legitimate. There must, first, be a prima facie *positive* case for State regulation, in that the activity at issue must be sufficiently serious to warrant intervention. In general, as we shall argue, this requires that the conduct leads directly or (under certain conditions) indirectly to significant levels of harm or offence being suffered by others.

Secondly, certain *negative* constraints must also be met. In particular, it must be shown that the *criminal* law offers the best method of regulation, being preferable to alternative methods of legal control that are available to the State; and the practicalities must be considered of drawing up an offence in terms that are effective, enforceable, and meet rule of law and other concerns. It may be, if these negative constraints cannot be met, that the State

---

[1] *Per* Lord Williams of Mostyn, HL Deb., vol. 602, col. WA 58; June 18, 1999.

ought not to criminalise certain types of conduct notwithstanding that initially there is a positive case for doing so.

In this chapter, we will focus mainly on the competing *positive* grounds for state intervention: the main types of reasons why the state might validly choose to intervene and criminalise some action. Later, we will briefly discuss some of the constraints that might nonetheless make the criminal law an inappropriate response.

When is behaviour, prima facie, sufficiently serious to warrant criminalisation? This question is highly controversial, because it raises squarely the issue of the limits of the state's moral authority over individuals. Joel Feinberg's classic discussion of the problem identifies four possible grounds of justifiable intervention: harm to others, offence to others, immorality, and harm to self.[2] As we shall see, liberal philosophers (including Feinberg himself) tend to endorse only the first two of those grounds, rejecting the case for criminalising conduct on purely moralistic or paternalistic grounds. Below we offer a short introduction to these four grounds of state intervention.

§ 16.1 The Harm Principle

At the core of liberalism is the proposition that the State is justified in intervening to regulate conduct only when that conduct causes or risks *harm to others*. Conduct that merely harms oneself, or which is thought to be immoral but otherwise harmless, is on this account ineligible for prohibition. Famously, the Harm Principle was first articulated by John Stuart Mill:[3]

> "The principle is, that the sole end for which mankind are warranted, individually or collectively, in interfering with the liberty of action of any of their number is self-protection. That the only purpose for which power can rightfully be exercised over any member of a civilised community against his will is to prevent harm to others. His own good, either physical or moral, is not a sufficient warrant."

Expressed in this way, the Harm Principle is a negative constraint: in the absence of harm or risk of harm, the State is not morally entitled to intervene. It does not follow that, conversely, the State *is* justified in intervening whenever D's conduct causes or risks harm to others. That conclusion can only be reached after further factors are considered, such as those to be discussed below. Perhaps more importantly, Mill offers no definition of what counts as a *harm*; without which, the application of the Harm Principle is indeterminate.

Liberal philosophers have built on Mill's analysis in an attempt to eradicate these problems. The most extensive exposition is now offered by Feinberg, who summarises the principle as follows:[4]

> "It is always a good reason in support of penal legislation that it would be effective in preventing (eliminating, reducing) harm to persons other than the actor (the one prohibited from acting) and there is no other means that is equally effective at no greater cost to other values."

---

[2] *The Moral Limits of the Criminal Law* (1984–87): vol. 1, *Harm to Others* (1984); vol. 2, *Offense to Others* (1985); vol. 3, *Harm to Self* (1986); vol. 4, *Harmless Wrongdoing* (1988).

[3] *On Liberty* chap. 1, para. 9.

[4] *Harm to Others* (1984) 26. See also Simester and von Hirsch, *Crimes, Harms, and Wrongs: On the Principles of Criminalisation* (2011) chap. 3.

Notice that this is formulated as a positive claim. On Feinberg's account, if creating a criminal offence would prevent harm to others, there is a positive reason in favour of criminalisation. This leaves it possible for Feinberg, and us, to accept the legitimacy of other, supplementary, grounds for criminalisation (such as offence) where the conduct is not likely to be harmful.

A second feature of Feinberg's version of the Harm Principle is that it is *instrumental* rather than *act*-centred. There is nothing in his principle that requires the prohibited act *itself* to be harmful, or even that it risks causing harm. Gardner and Shute embrace this instrumental version:[5]

> "It is no objection under the harm principle that a harmless action was criminalized, nor even that an action with no tendency to cause harm was criminalized. It is enough to meet the demands of the harm principle that, if the action were not criminalized, *that* would be harmful."

What matters for Gardner and Shute, in other words, is not the question, "is this act (potentially) harmful?" but, rather, "what if this act were permitted?" For example, the *prospect* that I might be burgled may lead me to avoid taking lengthy holidays, to take out insurance, to install an alarm in my house, and so forth. Suppose it were made an offence for postal workers to inform third parties that a householder was away from home. The offence could be justified under this version of the harm principle if there were reason to think that it would be at least partially effective in reducing such precautionary costs.

Hence there are multiple versions of the Harm Principle to choose from.[6] On instrumental versions of the Harm Principle, it need not be objectionable that certain *per se* harmless acts are criminalised.[7] And one might prefer a version of the Principle (whether instrumental or act-centred) in which harm is an *essential* condition of criminalising, or a version in which it is merely one ground for doing so. In principle, one might subscribe to Feinberg's articulation of the Harm Principle and at the same time consistently accept that the State is also justified in criminalising some conduct on the grounds that it is immoral. That would, however, be inconsistent with the principle espoused by Mill. Especially for political liberal theory, part of the point of the Harm Principle is that it forces an enquiry into the consequences of conduct and its prohibition—does it lead to harm to anyone other than the actor? According to the Harm Principle, proponents of a particular criminal offence cannot simply allege that the relevant conduct is immoral. Rather, they must identify precisely what are the particular effects of that conduct,[8] and of its prohibition: the distinct way in which it involves damage to the lives of other persons. That claim can then be subjected to public debate. Empirical evidence of a link to the alleged harm can be demanded and scrutinised.

Consider, for example, the decision by the House of Lords in *Brown*[9] that, in the context of sadomasochistic sexual activity, it is an offence to inflict actual bodily harm on another person notwithstanding that the "victim" consents. One justification offered for this act

---

[5] "The Wrongness of Rape" in Horder (ed.), *Oxford Essays in Jurisprudence* (4th series, 2000) 193, 216.

[6] This point is helpfully brought out by Edwards, "Harm Principles" (2014) 20 *Legal Theory* 253. Indirect harm of the sort Gardner and Shute contemplate is, however, subject to remoteness constraints: see below, § 16.1(v).

[7] Contra, e.g., Ripstein, "Beyond the Harm Principle" (2006) 34 *Phil and Public Affairs* 216; Duff, *Answering for Crime* (2007) chap. 6.

[8] Packer, *The Limits of the Criminal Sanction* (1968) 262.

[9] [1994] 1 AC 212. See also §§ 21.1(iv).

of judicial criminalisation was that the legalisation of such activities might encourage the seduction and "corruption of young men".[10] But would it? It is a cheap claim to make when no supporting evidence is offered. Given the presumption against criminalisation, the onus is on its proponents to bring clear evidence that creating a new offence *will* prevent harm from occurring.

This onus is all too often ignored. A particularly bad example is the enactment of an offence of possessing "non-photographic pornographic images of children", i.e. porno-graphic cartoons and the like. No children need be involved in the making of such images. Nonetheless, claimed the Home Office, such images were potentially harmful, both because they might be used to "groom" children and because they might "fuel abuse of real children by reinforcing potential abusers' inappropriate feelings toward children", and presumably tend to increase the incidences of actual abuse.[11] Not only was no evidence offered to sup-port these claimed effects, but such evidence was expressly disclaimed:[12]

> "We are unaware of any specific research into whether there is a link between accessing these fantasy images of child sex abuse and the commission of offences against children, but it is *felt* by police and children's welfare organisations that the possession and circulation of these images serves to legitimize and reinforce highly inappropriate views about children."

So, notwithstanding the seriousness of any decision to criminalise, the government was willing to legislate on the basis of no more than a bare assertion, made by those to whom it listens most. This is a straightforward abandonment of the obligation to justify any prohibition in terms of the Harm Principle.

In the following paragraphs we consider aspects of the Harm Principle in more detail.

(i) What counts as a harm?

A harm, on Feinberg's account, is a "thwarting, setting back, or defeating of an interest".[13] When we are harmed, one or more of our interests is left in a worse state than it was before-hand. In turn, a person's *interests* comprise the things that make his life go well;[14] thus we are harmed when our lives are changed for the worse. Harm involves the impairment of a person's opportunities to engage in worthwhile activities and relationships, and to pur-sue valuable, self-chosen, goals. In this sense, harm is prospective rather than backward-looking: it involves a diminution of one's opportunities to enjoy or pursue a good life.

---

[10] *Ibid.*, 246 (Lord Jauncey).

[11] Home Office, *Consultation on the Possession of Non-photographic Visual Depictions of Child Sexual Abuse* (2007) 5. See the sensitive discussion by Ost, "Criminalising Fabricated Images of Child Pornography: A Matter of Harm or Morality?" (2010) 30 *Legal Studies* 230. The upshot was s. 62 of the Coroners and Justice Act 2009.

[12] Home Office, *ibid.*, 1 (emphasis added).

[13] *Harm to Others* (1984) 33.

[14] In Feinberg's account, "One's interests ... consist of all those things in which one has a stake.... These inter-ests, or perhaps more accurately, the things these interests are *in*, are distinguishable components of a person's well-being: he flourishes or languishes as they flourish or languish. What promotes them is to his advantage or *in his interest*; what thwarts them is to his detriment or *against his interest*" (*Harm to Others* (1984) 34). See, too, his "Harm to Others: a Rejoinder" (1986) *Criminal Justice Ethics* 16, 26, where Feinberg recapitulates: "I argued that to harm a person was to set back his interest and violate his right. To have an interest, in turn, is to have a stake in some outcome, just as if one had 'invested' some of one's own good in it, thus assuming the risk of personal harm or setback."

Characteristically, harm is brought about though the impairment of V's personal or proprietary resources. However, as Feinberg observes, what makes such impairment harmful is not the impairment *per se* but its implication for V's well-being:[15]

> "A broken arm is an impaired arm, one which has (temporarily) lost its capacity to serve a person's needs effectively, and in virtue of that impairment, its possessor's welfare interest is harmed."

Similarly, in the context of property crimes, one can say that "any harm to a person by denying him the use or the value of his property is a harm to him precisely because it diminishes his opportunities".[16]

Clearly, people have interests in their property and in their personal integrity. But we also have other interests that are capable of being harmed. Hyman Gross suggests that, before it can be said that a person has an interest in something (X), the thing must "be of sufficient value to [the person] that the assertion of a claim by or on behalf of [that person] based on the loss or significant impairment of X is not unreasonable".[17] He offers a four-part categorisation of the types of cases where one's interests are harmed: (i) "violations of interest in retaining or maintaining what one is entitled to have" (e.g. theft); (ii) "offences to sensibility" (e.g. obscenity); (iii) "impairment of collective welfare" (e.g. counterfeiting, which undermines the economy); and (iv) "violations of governmental interests" (e.g. contempt of court).[18]

We consider offences to sensibility in § 16.2 below, under the rubric of the Offence Principle. But categories (iii) and (iv) show that we can be harmed without directly being the victim; and, indeed, when there is no victim at all. Hence, on occasion, it may be appropriate to enact "victimless" crimes. Tax evasion is rightly a crime notwithstanding that there is no particular victim who is deprived of assets directly. Perhaps it is not the same sort of wrong as is theft. But if T illegitimately reduces his tax burden, T effectively takes from, and wrongs, his fellow taxpayers. The money must come from somewhere: if not from T, then from others. The obligation to pay tax is a collective duty, one that each person owes to his fellow citizens and not merely to the State.

Similarly, attacks on the integrity of the currency (e.g. large-scale counterfeiting) or on the operation of the judicial systems (e.g. contempt of court) matter in part because they tend to undermine State-implemented regimes that exist for the benefit of us all. State intervention is warranted because the community as a whole would also suffer harm were these general regimes to be undermined. Undermining the currency, for instance, would lead to losses of value stored as currency and tend to destabilise the systems that co-ordinate a nation's economic activity;[19] which, in turn, would deprive people of many opportunities

---

[15] *Harm to Others* (1984) 53. Cf. Kleinig's claim that, in the case of a temporary hurt or an abduction that has no lasting effects upon its victim, there may be interference with a welfare interest but no harm: Kleinig, "Crime and the Concept of Harm" (1978) 15 *Am Phil Q* 27, 32; Feinberg, *Harm to Others* (1984) 52–3.

[16] Raz, "Autonomy, Toleration, and the Harm Principle" in Gavison (ed.), *Issues in Contemporary Legal Philosophy* (1987) 313, 327. Cf. Perry, "Corrective v. Distributive Justice" in Horder (ed.), *Oxford Essays in Jurisprudence* (4th series, 2000) 237, 256: "The main reason that personal injury constitutes harm is that it interferes with personal autonomy. It interferes, that is to say, with the set of opportunities and options from which one is able to choose what to do in one's life."

[17] *A Theory of Criminal Justice* (1979) 116.

[18] *Ibid.*, 119–21.

[19] Cf. *St Margaret's Trust Ltd* [1958] 1 WLR 522, 527.

for personal and social advancement. Minimising or preventing that sort of indirect, prospective harm to our interests is rightly the business of the State.

(ii) Seriousness

Indeed, once the nature of the harm is identified, we can see why some apparently victimless crimes, such as counterfeiting, are regarded as very serious indeed. This is one of the payoffs of the Harm Principle: in forcing us to consider more precisely why we are concerned about the activity that is to be criminalised, it gives us tools with which to rank the seriousness of offences and thus decide what level of punishment, if any, is appropriate.

Von Hirsch and Jareborg have developed this point in the context of victim-oriented crimes.[20] In their seminal paper, the authors identify four generic interests that we all have directly: (i) physical integrity (health, safety, avoidance of physical pain); (ii) material support and amenity (nutrition, shelter, basic amenities); (iii) freedom from humiliation or degrading treatment; and (iv) privacy and autonomy. The justification of any existing or prospective crime can then be assessed in two steps, as follows.

First, one should identify which category of interest the crime is designed to protect. Secondly, it is necessary to assess the degree to which standard instances of that crime will adversely affect the living standard—the opportunities for V to live a good life—of a typical victim. Von Hirsch and Jareborg divide the severity of these effects into four bands: (a) subsistence (simple survival with only basic human functions); (b) minimal well-being (maintaining minimal levels of comfort and dignity); (c) adequate well-being (maintaining adequate levels of comfort and dignity); and (d) significant enhancement (above-adequate quality of life).

On this approach, we can see that homicide attacks physical integrity in such a way as to undermine even subsistence; it is, thus, more serious than a typical robbery and much more serious than petty theft or a minor assault. On the other hand, road traffic regulations become extremely important, since they too are concerned with saving lives and thus protect our fundamental interests. It may be that, because less culpable, dangerous driving should be punished less severely than murder. But, like murder, the existence of an offence of dangerous driving is justified within the Harm Principle by the desirability of saving lives.

(iii) Harms as wrongs

In Feinberg's words,[21]

> "One person wrongs another when his indefensible (unjustifiable and inexcusable) conduct violates the other's right, and in all but certain very special cases such conduct will also invade the other's interest and thus be harmful in the sense [of a setback to interests]."

---

[20] "Gauging Criminal Harm: A Living-Standard Analysis" (1991) 11 *OJLS* 1.
[21] *Harm to Others* (1984) 34.

In order to fall within the scope of the Harm Principle and be a prima facie candidate for criminalisation, the harm must also be a wrong.[22] Suppose, for example, that a judge sentences P to imprisonment for life following P's conviction of murder. P's interests will be set back by such a sentence. He will lose his freedom and many opportunities to advance his life and prospects. Nonetheless, the judge does no wrong in depriving P of his freedom in this way. Her act of sentencing falls outside the Harm Principle because, although P's situation is worsened when he is deprived of his liberty, P has lost nothing to which he had a right.

The example illustrates that our interests can be set back without our being wronged. Indeed, this is something that often occurs in economic transactions. In a broadly free market, individuals are entitled to pursue their own interests. In so doing, they wrong no one even if their self-advancing conduct has deleterious side-effects for others. Side-effects are a natural feature of competitive interaction: if D tenders successfully for a contract, D may know that in so doing she will deprive others of that contract and, in turn, weaken their commercial viability, cause employees to be laid off, and so forth. Yet D does no wrong and the case falls outside the scope of the Harm Principle.

(iv) Balancing requirements

Even if the harm *is* wrongful, it should not necessarily be criminalised. The Harm Principle provides for a balancing of interests, one that considers the extent and likelihood of the harm involved and weighs that against the implications of criminalisation. Feinberg's account presents a number of factors to be taken into account at this stage:[23]

> "(a) the greater the gravity of a possible harm, the less probable its occurrence need be to justify prohibition of the conduct that threatens to produce it;
> (b) the greater the probability of harm, the less grave the harm need be to justify coercion;
> (c) the greater the magnitude of the risk of harm, itself compounded out of gravity and probability, the less reasonable it is to accept the risk;
> (d) the more valuable (useful) the dangerous conduct, both to the actor and to others, the more reasonable it is to take the risk of harmful consequences, and for extremely valuable conduct it is reasonable run risks up to the point of clear and present danger;
> (e) the more reasonable a risk of harm (the danger), the weaker is the case for prohibiting the conduct that creates it."

A responsible legislator should, therefore, consider the gravity and likelihood of the wrongful harm and weigh that against the social value of the conduct to be prohibited and the degree of intrusion upon citizens' lives that criminalisation would involve. The greater the gravity and likelihood of the harm, the stronger the case for criminalisation; conversely, the more valuable the conduct is, or the more the prohibition would limit liberty, the stronger the case against criminalisation. In addition, other rights that a citizen may have, for

---

[22] Cf. Raz, "Autonomy, Toleration, and the Harm Principle" in Gavison (ed.), *Issues in Contemporary Legal Philosophy* (1987) 313, 328: "Since 'causing harm' by its very meaning demands that the action is prima facie wrong it is a normative concept acquiring its specific meaning from the moral theory within which it is embedded". The requirement for a wrong is particularly important in the special case where the harm is "reactive": Simester and von Hirsch, *Crimes, Harms, and Wrongs: On the Principles of Criminalisation* (2011) § 3.2(c).
[23] *Harm to Others* (1984) 216.

example to free speech or privacy, should be respected.[24] These rights may militate against creating certain types of crimes, especially (as we shall see below) in the context of offensive behaviour.

It is a calculation of this sort that justifies the setting of speed limits. In the United Kingdom, for example, it is prohibited to drive on the highway at speeds in excess of 70 miles per hour. Is this a legitimate criminal law? The answer is, yes. Driving at 75 miles per hour may not be inherently immoral or wrong. But the faster one drives, the higher the probability that if something goes wrong, serious injury and property damage will result. Hence the case for setting speed limits is capable of falling within the scope of the Harm Principle, and is amenable to criminal regulation. On the other hand, even though setting the speed limit at (say) 20 miles per hour would save more lives, the social costs, in terms of inefficient transportation systems, would be too great. Decisions of this sort require a balancing of factors, such as the effect on public mobility of setting the limit too low, against the costs, in terms of scale and likelihood of injuries, of setting the limit too high.

Resolution of that balancing process will depend on reference to standard cases. The Harm Principle is in play here because speeding *standardly* causes or creates a risk of harm, even if not in every instance. Inevitably, the criminal law is a blunt instrument, regulating in terms of average cases and incapable of reflecting the myriad variations upon those cases that real life delivers.

To a large extent, this constraint is a matter of resources, and of their efficient use—it is simply uneconomic to frame and administer laws that take into account the particularities of every person's situation. Hence, criminal law tends to prohibit actions on the basis of their typical risks and consequences, leaving further refinement, if any, to the realm of exceptions. It is an offence, we have said, to drive faster than 70 miles per hour. This is so notwithstanding that there is no intrinsic significance to that speed. Depending on the circumstances (perhaps the road is empty) and on the particular driver (perhaps he is Lewis Hamilton), there may on occasion be no significant risk when a driver travels at a faster clip than 70. Nonetheless, specifying a precise limit is a convenient and enforceable means by which to regulate dangerous driving; and the limit itself is determined by reference to risks in standard cases.

(v) Remote harms

Many actions are not immediately harmful but may lead to harm *remotely*.[25] My selling you a handgun, for example, does not in itself harm you but rather puts you in a position where subsequently you may harm another person. This possibility is an implicit feature of inchoate offences, such as incitement to murder; and of what are sometimes called "substantive inchoate" offences, such as the offence of "going equipped". It is a crime to be on the street at night when in possession of an article, such as a jemmy (or "crowbar"), for use in connection with a burglary.[26] The justification for this offence is not that I have the jemmy, but rather that I may use it.

---

[24] This general approach may be termed the "standard harms analysis": Simester and von Hirsch, *Crimes, Harms, and Wrongs: On the Principles of Criminalisation* (2011) § 4.2.

[25] *Ibid*, chap. 4.

[26] Theft Act 1968, s. 25.

Remote harms present a particular challenge for the Harm Principle, a challenge additional to the kinds of evidential issues noted earlier, in the contexts of *Brown* and non-photographic pornographic images of children.[27] While it may sometimes be appropriate, very often there are difficulties about basing criminalisation on remote harms, especially those predicated on the eventual criminal choices of third persons. Consider the following hypothetical situation. Suppose that, as Murray has argued, there is evidence that unregulated premarital sex yields higher rates of illegitimate births, leading to more children growing up in impoverished households with weakened parental control; and that, in turn, this generates higher crime rates by these offspring.[28] If we concede the empirical links, we can conclude that unregulated premarital sex leads to harm. But it does not follow that there is even a prima facie case for criminalising premarital sex. The harm is produced not by D's own conduct but by the subsequent choices of third parties (in this case, offspring) whom D does not control. That being so, it is not clear why the harm should be D's lookout: why should D be accountable, through the criminal law, for the freely chosen subsequent actions of others?[29] Why, in other words, should D lose an otherwise harmless option just because of the subsequent independent choices that others may make?

On occasion it is apt to prohibit an activity because of a remote harm. This may occur where D's act in some way underwrites or facilitates the later wrongdoing by others. For example, it may be appropriate to prohibit D from publishing a book detailing various ways of killing one's enemies, because the link between D's activity and murders by others influenced or helped by D's book is sufficiently close that the remote harm can fairly be imputed back to D. But in the absence of special reasons for imputing remote harms to D, the mere existence of such harms supplies no reason for criminalising D's otherwise innocent conduct.

To invoke the Harm Principle, we have noted, an action must not only be conducive to harm; it must also be a wrong. This constraint is particularly apposite to remote harm. The criminal law embodies, by its nature, an element of blame or censure. But in remote harm cases, it still needs to be shown why D should be condemned for her non-harmful action, just because that action happens to be linked, through chains of complex social interaction, to the subsequent injurious behaviour of some separate and autonomous person, E. Prima facie, it seems unjust to impose penal censure on D, at least where D has no power to control the harmful choices of E, and where D has not sought to assist or encourage those choices. This challenge is especially pertinent with the increasing deployment of pre-emptive or "prophylactic" crimes designed to safeguard against terrorist and other threats to collective security.[30]

---

[27] Above, § 16.1.

[28] See Murray, *The Emerging British Underclass* (London 1990); also Murray, *Underclass: The Crisis Deepens* (London 1994). Cf. Simester and von Hirsch, *Crimes, Harms, and Wrongs: On the Principles of Criminalisation* (2011) § 4.4(a).

[29] *Ibid.*, 61: "An actor may properly be held responsible if he brings about a harmful result himself, or if he brings it about through another person, e.g. by inducement or persuasion. But to hold him liable merely because (say) another person chooses voluntarily to follow his example, in a manner that causes or risks harm, infringes basic notions of the separateness of persons as choosing agents. It is that other person who has made the culpable choice of bringing about harm, not the original actor."

[30] For discussion, see Horder, "Harmless Wrongdoing and the Anticipatory Perspective on Criminalisation" in Sullivan and Dennis (eds.), *Seeking Security: Pre-empting the Commission of Criminal Harms* (2012) 79; also, in the same volume, Simester, "Prophylactic Crimes", 59.

§ 16.2 The Offence Principle

Suppose that, one day, D and E catch a bus into town. While riding on the bus, they decide to have sexual intercourse, notwithstanding the presence of the other passengers. Their conduct may not harm anyone else, and seems to fall outside the scope of the Harm Principle. Yet it will cause great offence, no doubt, to many others on the bus who are forced to witness their activity. Should conduct of that sort be criminalised?

Feinberg certainly thinks so:[31]

> "It is always a good reason in support of a proposed criminal prohibition that it would probably be an effective way of preventing serious offense (as opposed to injury or harm) to persons other than the actor, and that it is probably a necessary means to that end."

Many, probably most, liberals agree that actions may sometimes be prohibited on the grounds of their offensiveness, and there is widespread acceptance of the Offence Principle as a secondary principle of criminalisation, one that supplements the Harm Principle.

When is the Offence Principle in play? Merely showing that D's conduct is disgusting or unpleasant will not invoke the Offence Principle. For Feinberg, conduct is offensive when it affronts other people's sensibilities, i.e. when it causes them involuntarily to undergo an unpleasant and disliked psychological experience, by way of reaction to the conduct. Causing any such affront, in his view, constitutes prima facie grounds for invoking the criminal law, provided the matter is sufficiently serious.

There must, however, be *serious* offence to others. Moreover, on Feinberg's account, the case for criminalisation must satisfy a sophisticated balancing test that is designed to criminalise offence more sparingly. First, a responsible legislator should consider the impact of the conduct on its audience, by examining the magnitude of the affront to see how pervasively and intensely it is felt. As part of that examination, a standard of "reasonable avoidability" is imposed: the easier it is for members of the public to avoid settings where the conduct occurs, the less serious the offence is. Pornography may cause affront to many when viewed involuntarily or unexpectedly, but V cannot reasonably complain if he has specifically visited an adult cinema to see it.

Secondly, the importance of the offending conduct should be examined from the actor's perspective. The more central the conduct is to an actor's way of life, the greater is the claim not to have the conduct prohibited. As part of this examination, a standard of "alternative opportunities" is applied: restrictions on the conduct become more acceptable if there are satisfactory alternative times and places at which the actor could perform the conduct with less offence (say by showing pornography only at home or in adult cinemas and not more generally).

The broader social impact of the conduct needs also to be considered. The more independent general usefulness the supposedly offending conduct has, the less the claim to prohibition. For this purpose, free expression of opinion is, following Mill, deemed to have its own social value, "in virtue of the great social utility of free expression and discussion generally, as well as the vital personal interest most people have in being able to speak their minds fearlessly".[32] I may cause considerable and widespread offence when I advocate the

---

[31] *Offense to Others* (1985) 1. See also the collection of essays in von Hirsch and Simester (eds.), *Incivilities: Regulating Offensive Behaviour* (2006).
[32] Feinberg, *Offense to Others* (1985) 44.

legalization of, say, necrophilia; but the importance of preserving free political debate is such as to outweigh any case for criminalisation that the offence may generate.

(i) Offensive conduct as a wrong

The application of these considerations means that, on Feinberg's account, some conduct that widely offends should still be legally permissible, e.g. when committed in settings readily avoidable by others. Thus, although nudity may legitimately be criminalised when practised on city streets, similar exposure might nonetheless be permitted at designated beaches, at which those not so inclined need not bathe.

Even so, however, Feinberg underplays a further consideration: the need for the affront to be wrongful. It is not affront *per se* to the sensibilities of others—even widespread affront—that should justify possible state intervention, but affront *plus* valid reasons for objecting to the conduct.[33] Suppose, for example, that the sight of an interracial or gay couple holding hands causes enormous affront in a particular community. It seems to us that, regardless of the scale of the reaction, there is no case for invoking the Offence Principle here, because there is nothing wrong with that couple's behaviour.

This point is particularly important in the criminal law, which *punishes*, and censures, the offender for having done wrong. That being the case, the criminalisation of conduct should require a plausible claim of wrongdoing. With conduct that supposedly is offensive, one must therefore ask: why does the actor deserve censure? If the essence of offence is merely that the conduct displeases many people, then it is not clear that wrongdoing has occurred at all. "I don't like it" should never suffice as a basis for criminalisation, regardless of the numbers who say it. Better reasons need to be provided why there is something reprehensible about the behaviour that deserves a censuring response.

What makes offensive conduct wrong, generally speaking, is the manner in which it treats other persons. Racial insults are a paradigm of this class of case: they tend both to cause affront in the audience and to do so by communicating contempt for that audience. Another variety of offence is exhibitionism. Suppose that D is sitting peaceably in the park, but cannot concentrate on his newspaper because E and F are copulating noisily on the grass nearby. D may rightly complain. He has a legitimate claim not to have the intimate facts of E and F's relationship forced upon him. This may be singularly in point in locations like parks, which we value, *inter alia*, as places to interact with other persons who are not intimates, and where, consequently, such offensive activities are likely to cause much greater discomfort than they would in more private contexts.

(ii) A communicative and conventional wrong

In so far as offensive conduct is something that communicates to V, the person experiencing the conduct, a lack of respect and consideration, it is characteristically a form of expressive action. As such, even if one accepts the Offence Principle as a legitimate ground of criminalisation, such cases should be criminalised sparingly because of the importance of allowing free expression in a society. The need to accommodate diverse and sometimes inconsistent

---

[33] Simester and von Hirsch, *Crimes, Harms, and Wrongs: On the Principles of Criminalisation* (2011) chap. 6.

styles of life, which may depend for their success on being publicly manifested, militates in favour of a "thick skin" approach to the regulation of expressive acts, even when those acts are offensive to others. Friction is a characteristic of social interaction, at least in a pluralistic society. Such societies require of their members a certain robustness of sensibility, so that incivility may be tolerated for the sake of personal and cultural diversity.

A second reason for caution with the Offence Principle is how close its application can resemble that of the next principle we shall discuss, Legal Moralism.[34] Some of the most uncontroversial examples of offence involve sexual activity in public places. The examples are uncontroversial because there remains a strong moral consensus disapproving of such conduct, a consensus which underpins the convention that it should not be done. What counts for the Offence Principle may be the convention, but what generates the convention is the widespread moral view.

At the same time, the convention is not *merely* the articulation of a moral view. Legal Moralism is concerned with regulating actions that are morally wrong: the Offence Principle, by contrast, is concerned with how we treat each other. Conventions such as those governing acceptable conduct in public places thus serve an important instrumental purpose, by helping to delineate the boundaries between personal and public, and setting the terms of our interaction with strangers. D's respect for V implies respect for the terms under which they (usually, by convention) interact. This holds independently of the particular terms of the convention. When D exposes himself, uninvited, to V, he both violates the applicable social convention and, further, wrongs V by failing to respect the socially agreed terms under which she interacts with others.

§ 16.3 Legal Moralism

According to the legal moralist, it is legitimate to use the criminal law to prohibit immorality *per se*—conduct that is wrong independently of any adverse effect it may have on other people. As Feinberg explains, the legal moralist holds that it "can be morally legitimate to prohibit conduct on the ground that it is inherently immoral, even though it causes neither harm nor offense to the actor or to others".[35] Legal moralism finds it justifiable to criminalise acts that may be termed free-floating evils, in that they neither infringe the rights of, nor harm, any other person.

Most obviously, such acts might include private, self-regarding, or consensual immorality, and the violation of religious norms.[36] A good example is *Brown*, mentioned earlier,[37] where the House of Lords held that, in the context of sadomasochistic sexual activity, the

---

[34] The potential for overlap may be seen in *DPP* v. *Collins* [2006] UKHL 40, [2006] 1 WLR 2223; noted [2007] Crim LR 98, (2006) 17 Ent LR 236: in the context of sending a grossly offensive message by means of a public electronic communications network, contrary to s. 127(1)(a) of the Communications Act 2003, what counts as "grossly offensive" is an objective question, based on the standards of an "open and just" society (at para. 9). As the commentators observe, even a private, adult chat-line call might therefore be illegal.

[35] *Harm to Others* (1984) 27. By the time he wrote *Harmless Wrongdoing* (1988), Feinberg himself had come to think that the State has *some* reason to regulate wrongs which float free of human interests; although he maintained that such reasons were likely to be insufficient to justify criminalisation. See *ibid.*, 321–3.

[36] See, e.g., Feinberg, *Harmless Wrongdoing* (1988) 20–5. Cf. *R* (*on the application of Stephen Green*) v. *The City of Westminster Magistrates' Court* [2007] EWHC 2785, (2008) 19 Ent LR 54 (blasphemy, an offence since repealed).

[37] [1994] 1 AC 212; above, § 16.1; also §§ 21.1, 21.1(v).

infliction of actual bodily harm upon a consenting adult "victim" was an offence. From the perspective of the Harm Principle, there is no wrong to V since the activity occurs with V's consent. But from the perspective of legal moralism, D's conduct may be regarded as inherently wrong—and therefore legitimately proscribed. (Indeed, V's consent simply makes V, too, a participant in the offence.) Another illustration is *Shaw* v. *DPP*,[38] in which the defendant was charged with an offence of conspiring to corrupt public morals.[39] On appeal, the count in the indictment charging this offence was upheld by the House of Lords. According to Lord Simonds, "there remains in the courts of law a residual power to enforce the supreme and fundamental purpose of the law, to conserve not only the safety and order but also the moral welfare of the state".[40]

Lord Devlin controversially argued for legal moralism on the ground that a society's moral values are an indispensable part of its structural framework.[41] In turn, if harmless immoralities were permitted, this would tend to undermine the social fabric, dissolving the moral consensus underpinning society and leading, ultimately, to social disintegration and anarchy. Strictly speaking, Devlin's argument is not an argument in favour of pure legal moralism. Rather, it rests implicitly on the Harm Principle. Social disintegration, if it occurred, would certainly be a bad thing for the lives and interests of citizens. Further, if permitting some immoral act would lead to social disintegration then, subject to the problem of remote harms noted in § 16.1(i)(e), the state has prima facie reason to criminalise the act. To do so would not violate the liberal precepts of the Harm Principle.

The main problem with Devlin's social harm argument is the need to establish an empirical link between mere immorality and social disintegration. It may be that certain specific, immoral acts will tend to threaten the continuance of the social structure, but that possibility needs to be investigated for *each* specific act, and cannot simply be asserted as a general truth for *all* immoral acts, however minor.

More generally, pure legal moralism shares with Lord Devlin's version the characteristic of entrenching the *status quo ante*. By its nature, legal moralism is conservative, in that immorality is measured against the prevailing social mores of the time: difference in moral value is, by that standard, immoral and may therefore be suppressed. One objection to this approach, therefore, is that not all change is bad. The abolition of slavery was a good thing; so, too, it is desirable that mixed-race couples may now publicise their association, even in communities where segregation formerly was enforced. Especially in a heterogeneous society containing a wide variety of subcultures, moral stagnation enforced by the criminal law seems unattractive. Difference, even conflict, between the lives and values of citizens can be a dynamic force for the evolution of a vigorous, thriving, and valuable culture.

A related difficulty with legal moralism is the problem of identifying a stable classification of immoral acts. Is homosexuality immoral (wherefore it may be prohibited)? It depends who, when, and where one asks. Criminalisation merely on the basis of immorality leaves a great deal to the whims and fashions of the times (and, indeed, of the prevailing location or culture: adultery, not proscribed at all in many countries, is a capital

---

[38] [1962] AC 220.
[39] Until then unknown: see above, §§ 2.2–3.
[40] [1962] AC 220, 267.
[41] Devlin, *The Enforcement of Morals* (1965) 8–14.

offence in others). The nature of modern secularism is such that it is increasingly unclear what moral frameworks are available, or agreed upon, by which to gauge whether an act is immoral and therefore eligible for proscription. As Alldridge has pointed out, some activities that once were regarded as *malum in se* are now entirely permissible, whereas some commercial activities that formerly were permitted are now regarded as very serious wrongs.[42] Thus a private, consenting homosexual act used to be a serious crime and now is none whatsoever[43]—yet the essential nature of the conduct has not changed in the interim.

Perhaps surprisingly, this *ad hoc* view of morality is celebrated as a virtue by Lord Devlin: "*Shaw's* case settles for the purpose of the law that morality in England means what twelve men and women think it means—in other words it is to be ascertained as a question of fact".[44] Yet many areas of morality are open to honest and reasoned disagreement. Abortion and obscenity, for example, present situations where different juries may reach opposite conclusions over what is moral and what is immoral. And criminal lawyers know all too well the difficulty of applying a homogeneous standard of "dishonesty" in theft.[45] This suggests that it will not do to criminalise conduct merely on the assumption that there is for each moral dispute an "objective" resolution.[46]

Were England and Wales a uniform society comprised of citizens with identical values, Lord Devlin's approach might present few problems. But that is not the case. Ours is a multicultural environment, incorporating diverse ethnic, religious, moral and philosophical perspectives. The law regulates in order to assist in the smooth functioning of our society, yet a multicultural society also needs tolerance. The guidance provided by the Harm and Offence Principles are important aids in ensuring that tolerance, by ruling out criminal censure for mere immorality.[47] Prohibition on grounds of immorality exposes even legislators to the charge that, in truth, they are simply imposing their own moral values upon the nation.

There are better versions of legal moralism in the more recent literature.[48] Those versions tend to invoke critical ("objective") morality, rather than conventional morality, as the ground for criminalisation; and to claim that preventing immorality gives us *some* reason in favour of criminalising, a reason that need not be decisive—so it does not follow on such versions that we should *always* criminalise immoral conduct.

It seems plausible that immorality is at least a condition of criminalisation. In Chapter 1 we emphasised the condemnatory nature of the criminal law. Criminal convictions articulate public judgements of wrongful behaviour by the defendant: that she has acted reprehensibly.[49] She is labelled as a wrongdoer who is eligible for punishment. When the state

---

[42] Alldridge, "Making Criminal Law Known" in Shute and Simester (eds.), *Criminal Law Theory: Essays on the General Part* (2002) 103, 107ff.

[43] Cf. amendment of s. 12 of the Sexual Offences Act 1956 by s. 1 of the Sexual Offences Act 1967.

[44] "Law, Democracy and Morality" (1962) 110 Pa L Rev 635, 648.

[45] Above, § 13.8(iv)(a).

[46] For this reason, it is to be welcomed that acting *contra bonos mores* has been ruled too vague to count as criminal: *Hashman and Harrup v. United Kingdom* (1999) 30 EHRR 241.

[47] See generally Feinberg, *Harmless Wrongdoing* (1988).

[48] See, e.g., Moore, *Placing Blame* (1997) chap. 16; Duff, "Towards a Modest Legal Moralism" (2014) 8 *Crim Law and Phil* 217; also the essays in Renzo (ed.), *Symposium on Law, Liberty and Morality: Fifty Years On* (2013) 7 *Crim Law and Phil* 417–548.

[49] Above, § 1.1(iii).

makes such pronouncements, it ought to tell the truth. In turn, this means that the prohibited act should actually *be* morally wrongful.[50]

Legal moralism, however, goes beyond that. It claims that immorality supplies a positive reason to criminalise. Indeed, for most legal moralists, immorality can in principle justify criminalisation without appeal to considerations such as harm or offence. At this point, the argument becomes more controversial. The difficulty lies in the potential for legal moralism to clash with the liberal ideal of autonomy. Criminalisation takes options away from people. It is an intrusive and condemnatory form of coercion. Accepting the general case for criminalising mere immorality will, inevitably, lead to restrictions of autonomy, especially because the criminal law is very coarse grained, so that its prohibitions are typically framed in broad rather than narrow terms. Given the diversity of human needs and preferences, criminal prohibitions will inevitably deprive some individuals of freedoms that are valuable to them: such persons will, in effect, be harmed by the prohibitions.

The strongest cases for depriving people of opportunities in this way arise where D's activity is likely to diminish the opportunities for others to live good lives. In these cases, a condition of D's well-being (her autonomy) is weighed against a condition of V's well-being: like is compared with like. But in these very cases, D's conduct is by definition harmful. Where, by contrast, the conduct is merely immoral, the interests of persons (such as D) are being weighed only against abstract judgements of morality. There is no well-being or autonomy-based reason *for* criminalisation, only against: like is not being compared with like. In a liberal society, the interests of persons should take priority at this point. Thus it is arguable that mere immorality is, by itself, insufficient for criminalisation.

§ 16.4 Paternalism

Feinberg summarises the Paternalistic justification of criminalisation as follows:[51]

> "It is always a good reason in support of a prohibition that it is probably necessary to prevent harm (physical, psychological, or economic) to the actor himself and there is probably no other means that is equally effective at no greater cost to other values."

Like the Harm Principle, paternalism demands harm. But it goes beyond the Harm Principle in that it warrants the criminalisation of self-harm: D may be prohibited, *for her own sake*, from performing certain acts. A standard legal example of such prohibitions is the criminal law duty to wear seat belts when driving a car.[52] The duty is imposed for D's own benefit, on the grounds that persons who fail to wear a seat belt are likely to suffer much more severe injuries in an accident than are those who wear one.[53]

---

[50] Often, especially in crimes *mala prohibita*, the conduct is wrongful only *in light of the law*. For accounts of how this can be legitimate, see, e.g., Duff and Marshall, "'Remote Harms' and the Two Harm Principles" in Simester, du Bois-Pedain, and Neumann (eds.), *Liberal Criminal Theory: Essays for Andreas von Hirsch* (2014) 205, 214ff; Simester and von Hirsch, *Crimes, Harms, and Wrongs: On the Principles of Criminalisation* (2011) 24ff.

[51] *Harm to Others* (1984) 26–7.

[52] We concentrate here on the driver on the ground that back-seat passengers who fail to wear seat belts may harm not only themselves but also those seated in front of them.

[53] It is sometimes argued that there is harm to others in such cases, since the State is likely to incur greater costs in providing healthcare to drivers who are more seriously injured after failing to wear a seat belt. This argument is not straightforward, however, since the State's intervention is voluntary; it is open to the State to refuse to treat such persons, or to require them to take out private insurance.

Prima facie, there seems little that is objectionable about a law requiring persons to wear seat belts when in a car. But this is one of the strongest cases for paternalistic intervention. The obligation is a minor one, which does not hinder the activity of driving. It is a burden easily discharged, while the harm at risk and the costs of treatment are substantial. The state's insistence that D wear a seat belt is not destructive of her style of life. Thus the case is one where the disvalue attached to the infringement of D's autonomy is minor, and arguably outweighed by the interest in D's welfare that is advanced.

Paternalistic intervention may be appropriate more generally in cases where D's choice to harm herself cannot be said to be considered or responsible. Children and the mentally defective have extensive restrictions imposed upon their ability to engage in sexual intercourse, on the grounds that their choice to do so may not be fully understood.

But even if this argument be accepted in respect of seat belts and irresponsible actors, it cannot be generalised very far. In *Harm to Self*, Feinberg considers the theory of a broadly based paternalism in detail—and rejects it:[54]

> "The cases for and against legal paternalism then can be summed up as follows. In favor of the principle is the fact that there are many laws now on the books that *seem* to have had paternalism as an essential part of their implicit rationales, and that some of these at least, seem to most of us to be sensible and legitimate restrictions. It is also a consideration in favor of paternalism that preventable personal harm (set-back interest) is universally thought to be a great evil, and that such harm is no less harmful when self-caused than when caused by others. If society can substantially diminish the net amount of harm to interests caused from *all* sources, that would be a great social gain. If that prospect provides the moral basis underlying the harm to others principle, why should it not have application as well to self-caused harm and thus support equally the principle of legal paternalism?
>
> On the other side, it is argued that a consistent application of legal paternalism would lead to the creation of new crimes that would be odious and offensive to common sense, leading to the general punishment of risk-takers, the enforcement of prudence, and the interference with saints and heroes. Moreover, hard paternalistic justification of any restriction of personal liberty is especially offensive morally, because it invades the realm of personal autonomy where each competent, responsible, adult human being should reign supreme."

The obligation is on the legal paternalist to show why it is justified to coerce D and promote her welfare at the expense of her autonomy.

One way of approaching that challenge is by arguing that autonomy is only of instrumental value: having options is valuable, that is to say, only in so far as the options themselves are valuable. On this view, there is no value in permitting self-maiming, say by cutting one's arm off, because there is no value in the activity that is being permitted. However, this argument establishes only that there is no obligation on the State positively to foster or support such activities. It does not follow that the State has the right to *prohibit* valueless activities. Justified proscription through the criminal law requires something stronger: positive reasons why we should coerce, threaten, and impose sanctions upon a wrongdoer. The paternalistic legislative assertion, "We are sending you to jail for your own good", makes very little sense when addressed to responsible, autonomous, citizens in a mature liberal democracy. It amounts to saying, "we shall harm you lest you harm

---

[54] *Harm to Self* (1986) 25.

yourself". And punishing the choices of one autonomous agent as a deterrent to others is equally objectionable.

A moment's reflection, moreover, reveals that the potential for invasive paternalism is enormous. So many features of modern life are not especially good for us—getting drunk, playing dangerous sports, smoking, eating fatty foods, failing to take regular exercise. A consistent paternalist should seek to eliminate them all. But freedom includes the freedom to go wrong. Respect for persons as autonomous agents involves respect for individuals as deliberating agents who have the capacity independently to pursue goals and values which they have themselves adopted. If we are not allowed to choose badly then, in effect, our choices are no longer determined by our own goals and values. A paternalistic legal system which made people's choices for them may well end up alienating people from their own conduct:[55]

> "Why not interfere with someone else's shaping of his own life? ... I conjecture that the answer is connected with that elusive and difficult notion: the meaning of life. A person's shaping his life in accordance with some overall plan is his way of giving meaning to his life; only a being with the capacity to so shape his life can have or strive for a meaningful life."

Our well-being does not just require the successful pursuit of valuable goals; it requires also that we identify and engage with those goals—that they be *our* goals. Paternalism, by contrast, imposes the state's goals and values upon us. In the criminal law, moreover, it does so coercively. When a person's choices are pre-empted by the law, she does not shape her own life.[56] And to live a meaningful life, one must shape it oneself.[57]

§ 16.5 Negative grounds for intervention: regulatory alternatives

Perhaps we can establish a positive case for regulating some candidate activity through the criminal law. But we need also to consider whether, nonetheless, there are reasons *not* to criminalise. The next stage of the enquiry involves considering whether the criminal law is the most appropriate tool for regulating the activity. In particular, the advantages and disadvantages of using the criminal law should be measured against those accruing to alternative regulatory mechanisms. As a general rule, if some other form of State intervention falling short of criminalisation would be effective to regulate the conduct at issue, that alternative should be preferred. The criminal prohibition should be deployed only as a last resort.

(i) Tax

On occasions in the past, Western governments have attempted to regulate alcohol by criminal prohibition. The results were disastrous; sales and consumption simply went

---

[55] Nozick, *Anarchy, State and Utopia* (1974) 50.

[56] Raz, *The Morality of Freedom* (1986) 382.

[57] For a more confined defence of paternalism, advocating the continuing use and development of civil law methods to prevent (in particular) teenage and young adult suicides and serious self-harm, see Sullivan, "Liberalism and Constraining Choice: the Cases of Death and Serious Bodily Harm" in Smith and Deazley (eds.), *The Legal, Medical and Cultural Regulation of the Body* (2009) 205.

underground, creating a black market ripe for extortion and racketeering. Nowadays, control is exercised via licensing arrangements and tax. One of the standard modern functions of the tax system is to regulate behaviour by manipulating the cost of products in order to reduce (or sometimes, increase)[58] demand. The mechanism of tax is one means by which the State can influence, without prohibiting outright, the behaviour of citizens. Part of the overt rationale for tobacco and alcohol duties is to deter consumers from smoking and drinking and, at least in part, to help ensure that the price of cigarettes and alcohol reflects the true cost to society (including healthcare costs) of these products.

Consumption taxes of this sort do, of course, affect options. If the price of his cigarettes is increased, D will have less money left for other activities. In the absence of offsetting income tax rebates, such measures tend to have a regressive effect on the poor. As such, tax measures are both an improvement on criminalisation in so far as they are less coercive and preserve more options for citizens and, at the same time, less equitable than criminalisation in so far as they are likely to affect different socio-economic classes asymmetrically.

(ii) Tort law

A second option is for the State to regulate an activity by means of a statutory or common law tort. Intervention through the civil law involves a substantial intrusion of the legal process, but remains less coercive than the criminal justice process: there is no arrest, no imprisonment, and no record of a criminal conviction. In some situations, therefore, the creation of a statutory tort may be an excellent alternative to criminal sanctions. This is especially so when considering compliance incentives for large corporations. An industrial accident costing many lives might lead to a company facing fines without limits if the accident was caused by gross failures of senior management;[59] yet that same company may be far more concerned by the millions of pounds it might incur in tort damages on account of simple negligence.

It is not a complete alternative. Tort law effectively prices rather than prohibits; it lacks the mandatory character of the criminal law, and requires a claimant with adequate resources to bring a legal action. Moreover, in many instances tortfeasors may be able to defray the costs of liability by means of insurance.

(iii) Other mechanisms

There is a variety of other methods for addressing harmful or odious behaviour, including advertising and licensing. A classic example of the former is the campaign against drink-driving, which has been instrumental in bringing about a sea-change in public attitudes toward the wrongfulness of driving while drunk. Although not appropriate to all varieties of wrong (for example, there is normally no need to polemicise against performing acts that are already widely perceived as *mala in se*), education and advertising can in some instances raise awareness of the potential harmfulness of an activity, in circumstances where that harmfulness had previously gone unremarked.

---

[58] For example, in the case of children. One reason for providing benefits and/or tax credits to parents is that children are, *inter alia*, public goods; hence the State has reason to subsidise part of the cost of their upbringing.
[59] Corporate Manslaughter and Homicide Act 2007, s. 1.

Licensing is also a familiar form of modern regulation. The performance of many activities—e.g. running a public house, possessing a firearm, and even driving—requires a licence. All of these activities import risks of harm, either direct or remote. But each is valuable, and it may be inappropriate, because of the social costs, to criminalise the activity altogether. So the activities are permitted, but only under conditions that are regulated by means of licensing systems. The criminal law, in turn, sits in the background to prohibit persons from carrying out each activity without, or in breach of, the licence. Licensing systems represent a significant limitation of individual liberty, but fall a long way short of outright prohibition. Moreover, they offer a more flexible tool than do generalised criminal laws, since the terms of each licence can be adapted to specific cases by the magistrates or authority responsible for administering that licence.

Another modern-day mechanism for monitoring specialist commercial activities is the establishment of activity-specific regulatory agencies equipped with powers to impose sanctions, including disqualifications and financial penalties, for norm-violating behaviour. According to the Law Commission, "There are now over 60 national regulators with the power, subject to certain limitations or checks, to make (criminal) law".[60] These kinds of agencies are particularly familiar in the financial services industry and the delivery of public utilities. There are certainly dangers in these kinds of regulation,[61] not least of which is the risk of having a punitive system without the protections embedded in the criminal law. As a means of administering standards of conduct for commercial actors, however, they can offer a useful alternative to the use of strict-liability criminal offences, while not displacing the role of the criminal law in more serious forms of wrongdoing.[62]

(iv) Contra: some advantages of using the criminal law

Even though alternative methods of regulation, if practical, should normally be preferred to the criminal law, it is worth noting that there are sometimes advantages in resorting to criminalisation. Unlike any other area of law, the criminal law systematically stigmatises activities (through prohibition) and persons (though conviction and punishment). But sometimes that stigmatisation is appropriate. The symbolic significance of enacting that some activity is a criminal offence can be a reason *in favour* of criminalisation, at least where stigmatisation of the activity is desirable. If used selectively, the creation of a criminal law can be a tool for communicating to the public that the prohibited activity is a serious wrong that *must* not be done.

There are also some practical considerations. Given that the State pays the costs of investigating, prosecuting, and punishing criminal conduct, it may be better placed to regulate wrongs than are, say, private individuals through the law of tort. Suppose that my next-door

---

[60] LCCP No. 195, *Criminal Liability in Regulatory Contexts* (2010) para. 1.21.

[61] See, e.g., Braithwaite, *Regulatory Capitalism: How it Works, Ideas for Making it Work Better* (2008) 4: "the reciprocal relationship between corporatization and regulation creates a world in which there is more governance of all kinds. *1984* did arrive."

[62] See Macrory, *Regulatory Justice: Sanctioning in a Post-Hampton World* (2006). See also LCCP No. 195, *Criminal Liability in Regulatory Contexts* (2010). The Macrory Review recommends introducing into English law a civil-law regime of non-fault monetary administrative penalties. The difficulty any regulatory system of this kind faces, of course, is to avoid issuing judgments involving censorious hard treatment—in which case, the process becomes in-substance criminal: cf. *Öztürk v. Germany* (1984) 6 EHRR 409.

neighbour throws a stone through one of the panes in my greenhouse, which it will cost some £20 to replace. It is likely to be impractical for me to pursue her through the law of tort. But a criminal prosecution will cost me only my time. In this respect, criminal regulation by the State may augment the rule of law, through increasing the consistency with which legal rights are enforced in like cases, rather than leaving the matter to irregular administration by individual claimants.

§ 16.6 Negative grounds for intervention: the rule of law

If the criminal law *is* to be used, its deployment should comply with a variety of constraints, both rule of law and pragmatic. The former, which we outline here, are discussed more fully in chapter 2.

(i) Rule of law constraints on criminalisation

First, it is desirable that the form of the criminal law proposed meets rule of law constraints, which were considered in §§ 2.1–4. In particular, the law should be prospective not retrospective (§ 2.2).[63] Secondly, the law should give fair warning, by defining the prohibited activity with sufficient certainty (§ 2.3). It needs to be understandable, predictable, and not vague. The more clearly defined the offence, the less potential there is for injustice with respect to those whose conduct falls close to its limits. Further, the more certainty there is in the drafting, the more confident society can be that an individual convicted under that offence is fairly labelled (§ 2.4). The law must make clear what sort of criminal each offender is—what the conviction is for. The criminal law speaks to society as well as wrongdoers when it convicts them, and it should communicate its judgment with precision, by accurately naming and describing the crime of which they are convicted.

Specificity of drafting has an additional dimension, in that more narrowly defined crimes are less likely to lead to discretionary enforcement. If an offence is too broadly drafted, so that it requires selective prosecution, the liability of defendants is, in effect, remaindered to the decisions of officials—creating the risk of unfair, inappropriate, or potentially even discriminatory prosecutions.[64] It is not unknown for defendants to be found guilty of offences even though, in the view of the court, a prosecution should not have been brought.[65] This possibility should be minimised.

---

[63] Cf. Art. 7(1) of the ECHR: "no one shall be held guilty of any criminal offence on account of any act or omission which did not constitute a criminal offence under national or international law at the time when it was committed. Nor shall a heavier penalty be imposed than the one that was applicable at the time the criminal offence was committed." This rule is also a common law principle of statutory interpretation: "in the absence of express words or a truly necessary implication, Parliament must be presumed to legislate on the assumption that the principle of legality will supplement the text." *B (a minor)* v. *DPP* [2000] AC 428, 470 (Lord Steyn).

[64] Compare the use, not intended by the legislature, of Anti-Social Behaviour Orders against prostitutes and beggars: Burney, "'No Spitting': Regulation of Offensive Behaviour in England and Wales" in von Hirsch and Simester (eds.), *Incivilities: Regulating Offensive Behaviour* (2006) 195, 206.

[65] E.g. *Smedleys Ltd* v. *Breed* [1974] AC 839; *Hart* v. *Bex* [1957] Crim LR 622; cf. *James & Son* v. *Smee* [1955] 1 QB 78.

(ii) The individuation of offences

How many offences do we need? Do we really need to distinguish theft from deception, rape from sexual assault, and sections 18 from 20 in the OAPA 1861? Or would it be enough just to have just a few generic crimes including, say, violation of another's property right; violation of another's person; damaging the environment; and so on? The answer to the last question is no. While the law may sometimes draw unnecessary distinctions, broad category offences would be inappropriate. Enacting only generic crimes would tend to suppress the fact that, within each field of harmful wrongdoing, each of our existing offences may involve a different wrong, a different harm, or both. It is for this reason that they are rightly separate offences.

In looking to explain and justify the existence of any offence, it is necessary to identify what harm, and what wrong, is addressed by that crime. Obtaining by deception may, for example, lead to much the same immediate harm as does theft—a straightforward diminution of V's resources—but the wrong is different. The thief bypasses ordinary mechanisms for allocating and transferring property. The deceiver exploits them, and induces V to make the transfer herself. Thus deception is not inconsistent with V's proprietary rights in the same manner as is theft. As such, the two are rightly distinguished by criminal law.[66]

This claim, about the importance of drawing distinctions, is an extension of the principles of fair warning (§ 2.3) and fair labelling (§ 2.4). *Ex ante*, citizens need to know where they stand. They need advance warning concerning their actions; in particular, about whether what they are going to do is a crime and, if so, what sort of crime it is. *Ex post*, offenders ought to be labelled with an adequate degree of precision, in order that the criminal record identifies the gist of D's criminal wrongdoing. Both principles require that each offence is labelled and defined in such a way that it conveys to citizens an accurate moral picture of the prohibited conduct, one that is neither misleading nor unduly vague or overgeneralised. Offences should, so far as is practical, reflect meaningful distinctions in the public mind between different types of culpable wrongdoing. This mandates that they are drawn up in such a way that they capture, and differentiate, significant differences in the harmfulness, wrongfulness, and/or culpability of various types of action.

By way of illustration, the distinctions between murder, maiming, and criminal damage are significant because the harms (and indeed the wrongs) at stake are quite different. Their differences are sufficient to warrant enacting separate offences, since the meaning and moral significance of each action is clearly distinguished in the public mind. Attempted murder, too, is rightly distinguished from murder because of the difference in resulting harm. Likewise, although the harms of theft and of criminal damage are similar, the manners in which they are inflicted involve two different forms of wrongdoing; forms that are sufficiently distinct in the public mind to warrant independent recognition by the criminal law.

Occasionally, too, there may be a case for distinguishing between two harmful activities on the grounds of culpability. An assault being negligent with regard to any consequential risks to life would typically lack the same culpability as an assault being reckless about those

---

[66] Cf. Simester and Sullivan, "On the Nature and Rationale of Property Offences" in Duff and Green (eds.), *Defining Crimes: Essays on the Special Part of the Criminal Law* (2005) 168, 188–90; Chalmers and Leverick, "Fair Labelling in Criminal Law" (2008) 71 *MLR* 217, 239–40.

same risks—and, if ever worthy of being criminalised as form of a homicide (which we doubt), ought surely to be a separate offence and not lumped in with murder or reckless manslaughter.

Not every difference is worthy of capture. Even though many US states follow the old common law in drawing a rudimentary distinction between petty and grand larceny, nobody would suggest that there should be a much more refined series of theft offences, graded in minute detail (say, theft of less than £50 value; theft of less than £100 value; theft of less than £200 value; and so on). Excessively specific offences risk clogging the trial process with unmeritorious technical argument, and obfuscating the moral clarity of the law's communications. At least in the context of non-specialist activities such as property offences, people (both *ex ante* and *ex post*) need to know the law's requirements in gist and not precisely. As such, meaning is better conveyed through publicly shared moral distinctions that are broadly rather than narrowly significant, provided those broader distinctions communicate an adequately nuanced statement of the prohibited wrongdoing. The degree of specificity that the law should adopt when distinguishing various harms and wrongs is, therefore, a trade-off that depends in part on the range of moral differentiations informing the public imagination. The fragmentation of the particular must be balanced against the vagueness of the general.

§ 16.7 Negative grounds for intervention: practical constraints

Finally, in addition to rule of law constraints, a variety of other considerations must be taken into account before concluding that criminalisation through the proposed offence is the right response.

(i) What side-effects will criminalisation have?

Suppose a clearly drafted law is proposed that criminalises the failure to disclose one's HIV-positive status to a sexual partner. One thing to consider before enacting such a law is whether it will have the effect of deterring those persons who are most at risk of contracting HIV from being tested. By not knowing their status, they keep themselves outside the scope of the offence—but without advancing the underlying aim of the offence, which is to protect their partners. In these sorts of cases, the legislator should consider whether, in effect, enacting the proposed law will do more harm than good.

It has not escaped judicial notice that one of the concerns about the use of drugs is consequential criminality: the prospect that drug users will steal, deal in drugs, enter into prostitution, or commit other crimes in order to finance their habit.[67] But a responsible legislator might also think that these considerations argue for *de* criminalisation. The price of illegal drugs is high because the drugs are illegal—if not illegal, no doubt users will need less money to pay for their habits, leading (it may be thought) to a significant reduction in consequential crime. Compare, too, the eras of alcohol prohibition, which led to an upsurge in violent conflict between gangs involved in the black market that arose to replace the licit

---

[67] Cf. *R v. Aramah* (1982) 4 Crim App R (S) 407, 408–9 (Lord Lane CJ). See more generally Alldridge, "Dealing with Drug Dealing" in Simester and Smith (eds.), *Harm and Culpability* (1996) 239.

trade. If criminalisation of an activity is likely to produce such undesirable consequences as these, that is a powerful reason not to prohibit.

(ii) Pragmatics of the criminal justice system

A proposed offence might also be rejected for reasons of implementation. In particular, the offence needs to be capable of being administered, by enforcement authorities and prosecutors. Ideally, it will be specified in clear and unambiguous terms, so that (as well as giving fair warning to citizens) those responsible for its administration will be confident of their ability to use the new law with predictable outcomes. Further, the terms it uses will cohere with and not reinvent existing legal concepts, facilitating understanding by professionals within the criminal justice system and avoiding the need for costly retraining exercises.

Another consideration is policing. The detection of some proposed crimes may be too difficult: this is one reason not to criminalise, say, unmarried sexual intercourse in private. Alternatively, crimes may be detectable only by invasive methods of surveillance; it needs to be considered to what extent the power to use such methods is desirable. There is also the question of cost: how expensive are the means of investigation? Will enforcement agencies be able to afford to monitor the new offence? Will effective policing of the offence require additional resources and legal powers?

There are many other issues that must be resolved when a new offence is created (mode of trial, evidential requirements, sentencing options, etc.). We cannot do justice to them all here. The key point is that, even though a prima facie case can be made in favour of criminalising an activity, e.g. because it is harmful to others, it does not follow that criminal legislation is the best response. Other forms of intervention need to be considered; sometimes, it may be best not to legislate at all. The criminal law is a powerful, expensive, and invasive tool. It should not be used lightly.

17

DEFENCES: AN OVERVIEW

In Chapters 10–15 we have outlined the elements of a number of different offences in English criminal law, such as murder, rape, and theft. In Chapters 18–21 we will discuss a range of defences that a defendant may invoke when charged with those offences. The division made in this book relies on a basic distinction in the criminal law between offences and defences. Typically, if D brings about the actus reus of an offence with the requisite mens rea, then, prima facie, she has committed that offence. But for most writers, these are not the only components of criminal liability. Conduct which is prima facie an offence will not lead to a conviction if the defendant has a recognised defence:[1]

> "[A]s a matter of analysis we can think of a crime as being made up of three ingredients, actus reus, mens rea and (a negative element) absence of a valid defence."

To illustrate this distinction, consider the following scenario:

> Imagine that you are watching a videotape showing D striking V in the face with his fist. From the film, it seems that D's conduct was deliberate. There is no indication that D was in a state of automatism[2] or that the blow was in any way accidental. You are instructed to give an account of what, if any, criminal offences D may have committed.

Taking what has been seen at face value, it appears that D has committed battery.[3] The elements of that offence, set out above in § 11.3, are satisfied. Indeed, if V has suffered any degree of injury, other more serious offences may also come into play.[4]

Before we attribute any criminal liability to D, however, certain questions must be put. Why was D striking V? D and V may have agreed to fight. We must enquire whether they were fighting in anger or in sport and, in either case, whether and to what extent V has been injured. Alternatively, D may have hit V to pre-empt what he took to be an imminent attack. If his assumptions were correct and his response proportionate to the danger posed

---

[1] Lanham, "Larsonneur Revisited" [1976] *Crim LR* 276, 276; see also Smith, *Justification and Excuse in the Criminal Law* (1989) 1. On the distinction between "offence elements" and "defence elements" see generally Campbell, "Offence and Defence" in Dennis (ed.), *Criminal Law and Criminal Justice* (1987) 73; Williams, "Offences and Defences" (1982) 2 *LS* 233; above, § 1.3.

[2] Above, § 4.3.

[3] The choice of term may seem pedantry; it would be more natural to speak of D's assaulting V. But since the decision in *DPP v. Little* [1992] QB 645, we must distinguish between frightening V (assault) and hitting V (battery), save in statutory contexts where it is accepted that the term assault may be used in the sense of battery. See above, § 11.1. In *Nelson* [2013] WLR (D) 10, the term "assault by beating" is used as a synonym for battery but the Court of Appeal confirmed that an allegation of assault by beating did not include an allegation of common assault.

[4] OAPA 1861, ss. 47, 20, 18.

by V, D's conduct would be justified.[5] But D may have misconstrued V's wholly peaceable intentions. Even then, D may be excused any liability provided he genuinely believed he was under attack and made a proportionate response to that perceived danger.[6] Before coming to any firm conclusion on that, we should inquire whether D acted under the influence of drink or drugs. If he did, any mistake induced by his intoxicated condition will not necessarily afford him an excuse.[7] What if D had not perceived any threat from V and struck him out of pure aggression? Even now, we should not jump to conclusions. D's aggressive behaviour may have stemmed from a psychotic condition which renders him legally insane.[8]

D's deliberate punching of V confronts us with evidence of a prima facie crime unless there is some *explanation* why, despite appearances, D has not committed that crime. Such explanations, only some of which have been canvassed above, can be described, in the broadest of terms, as defences. These explanations—defences—may take very different forms but generally fall into one of two groups. First, the explanation D offers may sustain a claim that the prosecution has failed to prove the elements of the prima facie offence charged. Alternatively, his explanation may concede that the definitional elements of the crime charged are present but contend that, nonetheless, liability should not be imposed because his conduct was justifiable or excusable.

§ 17.1 "Failure of proof" versus "substantive" defences

Strictly speaking, "defences" falling within the first group are not defences at all; they are denials of proof. For instance, the "defence" of voluntary intoxication is germane only to the question whether it can be proved that D possessed the intent required to commit a particular crime.[9] However, it is convenient to follow conventional usage, and from now on we will drop the quotation marks and speak of these failure of proof explanations as defences. To illustrate:

> Suppose, in our example above, that D's punch broke V's jaw. D has been charged with causing grievous bodily harm with intent to cause grievous bodily harm.[10] In a case of direct attack, a finding that D intended seriously to hurt V may be inferred from the primary facts unless D can cast doubt on the reliability of the inference.[11] He may seek to do this, for example, by adducing evidence that he was intoxicated and thus did not form the intent the crime requires.[12]

If D does raise a reasonable doubt on the issue of his intent, his defence of intoxication will have succeeded. Analytically, the role of this defence is to deny mens rea.

By contrast with such failure or proof defences, the second group comprises what may be termed supervening or true defences. Proof of the elements of the prima facie offence

---

[5] Below, § 21.2.
[6] Below, § 18.1(iii).
[7] Below, § 18.3.
[8] Below, § 19.1.
[9] Simester, "Intoxication is Never a Defence" [2009] *Crim LR* 3.
[10] OAPA 1861, s. 18.
[11] *Moloney* [1985] AC 905; *Beeson* [1994] Crim LR 190.
[12] *Beard* [1920] AC 479 (HL); *Sheehan* [1975] 2 All ER 960 (CA).

is established, but a conviction would be unjust because justificatory or excusatory circumstances were present.[13] For instance:

> Assume that D struck V in order to defend himself, because V was about to attack him with a knife. D's proportionate response to the danger he was in entails that what would otherwise be unlawful is lawful. There was an intentional infliction of force on another, but a finding of battery is deflected by the justifiable nature of D's actions.

The demarcation between failure of proof defences and supervening defences is clear in principle but is shifting and unstable in practice. This is well illustrated by the defence of mistake. For many years, when raising a claim of mistaken belief that force was necessary in self-defence, the mistake had to be based on reasonable grounds.[14] During that time, if D were to raise mistaken self-defence in answer to a charge of battery, it was natural to separate what were seen as the definitional elements of battery—the intentional or reckless infliction of force—from the question whether that infliction of force was *lawful*. So if the prosecution proved that D had intentionally struck V (the prima facie offence), D would be excused only if he *reasonably* believed it was necessary to strike V in self-defence. The defence, even if it succeeded, still left in place the definitional elements of battery. Accordingly, mistake was a true or supervening defence. However, the position changed with the decision of the Court of Appeal in *Williams (Gladstone)*.[15] The actus reus of battery was taken to be the application of *unlawful* force, and the mens rea to be intentionally or recklessly inflicting unlawful force. By packing unlawfulness into the actus reus, D would lack mens rea—intent or recklessness about the actus reus of battery—if he believed, reasonably or otherwise, in the presence of circumstances which would have made his conduct lawful. Following *Williams* the defence of mistake is now, predominantly, a failure of proof defence.[16]

For many offences, whether a particular element is characterised as a constituent of the offence or as something external to it is a matter of convention, not of principle.[17] And judges will adopt different conventions. For example, in *Brown*,[18] the House of Lords had to decide, *inter alia*, whether consent by V to the force applied by D was compatible with proof of *assault* occasioning actual bodily harm.[19] For the minority,[20] lack of consent was an integral part of the actus reus of assault; the presence of consent precluded proof of assault. For the majority,[21] the application of force constituted the actus reus of the offence and consent was something to be raised by way of substantive defence.

---

[13] *Per* Smith, "On Actus Reus and Mens Rea" in Glazebrook (ed.), *Reshaping the Criminal Law* (1978) 95, 98: "they do not negative either traditional *mens rea* or *actus reus*, but operate in some way independently".

[14] *Rose* (1884) 15 Cox CC 540; *Chisham* (1963) 47 Cr App R 130 (CCA).

[15] [1987] 3 All ER 411.

[16] See too *Beckford v. R.* [1988] AC 130 (PC) and, for criticism, Simester, "Mistakes in Defence" (1992) 12 *OJLS* 295.

[17] But not always. For instance, lack of consent is integral to the conception of rape and must be part of its offence definition. A strong case can be made that the same applies to assaults and batteries that do not threaten any physical harm as when D makes what would otherwise be a threatening gesture to V as part of a game. V's consent takes D's conduct outside the prohibitory norm of assault; it becomes conduct in which the criminal law has no regulatory interest.

[18] [1994] AC 212. See below, § 21.1(iv)(a).

[19] The term "assault" in s. 47 of the OAPA 1861 comprehends battery as well as "pure" assault; see above, § 11.4.

[20] Lord Mustill and Lord Slynn.

[21] Lords Templeman, Jauncey, and Lowry.

In practice, this conceptual inconsistency is not a major concern because the issues to be resolved at trial remain essentially the same irrespective of whether a particular defence is conceptualised as a failure of proof defence or a supervening defence. Take a case where D punches V at V's request. The minority in *Brown* would say that in those circumstances there was no battery, because the absence of consent is a defining element of battery; the conduct falls beyond the defining elements of the offence. The majority, by contrast, would regard the issue of consent as raising a defence to a case of battery. Either way, the dynamics of the trial would remain the same. If the prosecution adduces convincing evidence that D deliberately struck V, a conviction for battery will ensue unless D offers some explanation to avoid conviction. Whether his explanation (V consented) is conceptualised as throwing doubt on the prosecution's prima facie case or as raising a supervening defence in response to the prima facie case, either way, an evidential onus effectively rests on D to raise the issue. If D's evidence raises the possibility of V's consent, the prosecution then has the probative burden of disproving the reality of V's consent.[22]

This holds true for cases whenever the ultimate probative burden is on the prosecution, even though an evidential onus might have passed at some point to the defence. There are some defences where a probative onus is placed on the defence (e.g. insanity at common law and many statutory defences).[23] In the main, these are supervening defences: they assume that the prosecution has proved its case unless D can establish the defence on the balance of probabilities.[24]

In general, success on the basis of a failure of proof defence or a substantive defence secures an acquittal. If we put aside the special case of acquittals on the ground of insanity,[25] an acquittal is an acquittal; no distinctions are drawn between acquittals afforded by different defences. Arguably, this undiscriminating approach suppresses an important distinction. D may be acquitted in circumstances where his putatively criminal conduct may be said to be wholly *justified* (e.g. proportionate response to a deadly threat). Or he may be acquitted in circumstances where he is *excused* because his conduct was insufficiently culpable for a conviction but where his actions remain an intrusion upon V's legally protected interests (e.g. where D punched V because he unreasonably assumed that V was about to attack him).[26] Suggestions have been made that a formal legal distinction should be drawn

---

[22] Above, § 3.2. The same analysis holds for mistake even in its "failure of proof" version: "mistake is a defence … in the sense that it is raised as an issue by the accused. The Crown is rarely possessed of the knowledge of the subjective factors which may have caused an accused to entertain a belief in a fallacious set of facts": *Pappajohn* v. *R.* (1980) 52 CCC (2d) 481, 494 (Dickson J).

[23] See above, § 3.2(i).

[24] For example, the statutory partial defence of diminished responsibility is in point only where the constituent elements of the crime of murder have been proved or admitted. This was an important consideration for the Court of Appeal in *Lambert* [2002] 2 QB 981, when ruling that placing the burden of proof on D to prove the elements of diminished responsibility did not contravene the presumption of innocence guaranteed by Art. 6(2) of the ECHR. But it is not invariably the case that a probative burden is imposed on D only when the prosecution has established the constituent elements of the offence charged. For instance, where D raises insanity on the basis that because of a disease of the mind he did not understand the nature and quality of his acts, in substance he must prove that he lacked mens rea for the offence charged. The Law Commission has taken the view that this contravenes Art. 6(2): Law Commission, *Insanity and Automatism: A Discussion Paper* (2013) para. 5.59.

[25] Criminal Procedure (Insanity) Act 1964, s. 1.

[26] As in *Ashley* v. *Chief Constable for Sussex* [2008] UKHL 25, where the House of Lords accepted that D did not commit any crime when he used force on V because he believed, albeit unreasonably, that force was necessary to prevent crime, yet held that D's conduct was tortious.

between justified conduct and excusable conduct, a distinction to be reflected by differ-ent forms of acquittal and in the taxonomy of criminal defences.[27] We shall not use the distinction as an organising principle in the following chapters (save for the special case of necessity). Nonetheless, in light of the frequent arguments that have been made in favour of using the distinction to classify defences, it is necessary to explain why we have not deployed it here.

§ 17.2 Justification and excuse[28]

At one time, English law distinguished justifiable homicide from excusable homicide. A justified killer could retain his possessions whereas a person merely excused had to forfeit his possessions to the Crown. However, in 1828 forfeiture was abolished, and since then this jurisdiction has not distinguished between justification and excuse on the formal plane. Paul Robinson, for one, would reinstate a formal distinction between cases of justifica-tion and cases of excuse. For Robinson, if D is merely excused, he should receive a verdict in the form "not guilty by reason of excuse". Although D would be acquitted, civil coercive measures may be taken to further the goals of special deterrence and rehabilitation. If D's conduct is found to be justified then, according to Robinson, the verdict should be "justi-fied" and D would be free from any form of coercive measures.[29]

Clearly, if the distinction between justification and excuse is to be as salient as Robinson proposes, a clear and usable differentiation is required between cases of justification and cases of excuse. How does Robinson mark the difference? For him, the justification of con-duct does *not* require investigating the motivation and practical reasoning of the actor. Justification arises, in a utilitarian fashion, from the consequences that D's conduct brings about. If those consequences are beneficial for society, the conduct is justified. For excuses, on the other hand, the consequences of D's conduct may violate legally protected interests, but D may nonetheless be excused provided that, in all the circumstances, he is insuffi-ciently blameworthy to merit conviction. As Robinson succinctly puts it, "an actor's *conduct* is justified; an actor is excused".[30]

Robinson's position is vividly illustrated by his view of the case of Motti Ashkenazi, an Israeli who, with dishonest intent, took a backpack he saw lying on a crowded beach. Unknown to Ashkenazi, the bag contained a terrorist bomb; inadvertently, he had saved many lives. Because of this, Robinson would deny that Ashkenazi committed any theft.[31]

---

[27] Robinson, "Criminal Law Defenses: A Systematic Analysis" (1982) 82 *Columbia LR* 199.
[28] Fletcher, *Rethinking Criminal Law* (1989) chap. 10; Dressler, "New Thoughts about the Concept of Justifica-tion in the Criminal Law: A Critique of Fletcher's Thinking and Rethinking" (1984) 32 *UCLA LR* 61; Corrado (ed.), *Justification and Excuse in the Criminal Law* (1994); Horder, *Excusing Crime* (2004); Williams, "The Theory of Excuses" [1982] *Crim LR* 732; Greenawalt, "The Perplexing Borders of Justification and Excuse" (1984) 84 *Col LR* 1897; Smith, *Justification and Excuse in the Criminal Law* (1989); Simester, "On Justifications and Excuses" in Zedner and Roberts (eds.), *Principles and Values in Criminal Law and Criminal Justice: Essays in Honour of Andrew Ashworth* (2012) 95; Dressler, "Reflections on *Dudley and Stephens* and Killing the Innocent: Taking the Wrong Conceptual Path" in Baker and Horder (eds.), *The Sanctity of Life and the Criminal Law: The Legacy of Glanville Williams* (2013) 126.
[29] Robinson, "Criminal Law Defenses: A Systematic Analysis" (1982) 82 *Col LR* 199, 245–7.
[30] Robinson, *Fundamentals of Criminal Law* (1988) 664.
[31] Indeed, according to Robinson, Ashkenazi had a "right" to take the bag, in that anyone who knew the true facts would not be allowed to interfere with Ashkenazi's taking of the bag.

He argues that such conduct would not fall within the prohibitory norm of theft, because the criminal law is not concerned to punish beneficent outcomes. This principle, which exempts a person such as Ashkenazi, provides a derogation from the prohibitory norm of the offence in question. Following his acquittal, a law-making precedent would be established to the effect that property belonging to others may lawfully be removed if lives are thereby saved. This is a general norm about legally justified conduct, not specific to any particular actor. On Robinson's view, to be within the exemption, D need not be aware that his conduct will achieve a good outcome; indeed, as in Ashkenazi's case, his motive may be reprehensible.

Contrast a situation where D is merely excused; a case, say, where D misconstrues the peaceable intention of V and strikes a pre-emptive blow because he erroneously assumes that V was about to attack. D's striking V violates V's right not to be unlawfully harmed, something that remains a cause for concern even if we excuse D from criminal liability. In this case, when we assess D's responsibility for that harm, the focus is on his state of mind and disposition. It is because D *thought* he was under attack and therefore was not acting in an aggressive or predatory manner that we may excuse him.[32] Whether an excuse is granted requires an estimate of blameworthiness. If the mistake was an unreasonable one, arguably he should still be punished for the intrusion on V's rights; although, currently, English law merely requires that D's mistake be genuine.[33] According to Robinson, when D is excused we make a finding that in *these* circumstances it would be unjust to convict D. The judgment is personal to D; it generates no law-making precedent to guide the conduct of others in the future.[34]

Robinson's theorisation of the excuse/justification distinction has been highly influential and, if correct, it should be deployed as a central organising principle in any account of defences. Ultimately, however, his theorisation is unconvincing.[35] Robinson's view that questions going to D's motivation and practical reasoning should be excluded from findings of justification is not a necessary truth, merely a position that Robinson adopts. English law, for instance, does not take the view that good outcomes, *by themselves*, entail justification. In the famous case of *Dadson*,[36] D shot and wounded V, an escaping felon. The court accepted that (at that time) a person was justified in shooting to prevent the escape of fleeing felons. But D did not know V was a felon and, because of that, he was convicted of unlawful wounding with intent to do grievous bodily harm. As one would expect, Robinson has argued that *Dadson* is wrongly decided,[37] yet even he concedes that a conviction for *attempted* unlawful wounding would have been in order in the case.[38]

---

[32] Which is why, according to Robinson, someone apprised of the true facts would commit an offence against V if she assists D's attack.

[33] See below, § 18.1(iii).

[34] See also Fletcher, "The Individualisation of Excusing Conditions" (1974) 47 *So Cal LR* 1269.

[35] For penetrating critique of an "objectivist" view of justification, see Greenawalt, "The Perplexing Boundaries of Justification and Excuse" (1984) 84 *Col LR* 1897.

[36] (1850) 4 Cox CC 358.

[37] "Competing Theories of Justification: Deeds v. Reasons" in Simester and Smith (eds.), *Harm and Culpability* (1996) 45. But see too, from *Harm and Culpability*, Gardner, "Justifications and Reasons", 103 and Simester, "Why Distinguish Intention from Foresight?", 71, 87ff; also Sullivan, "Bad Thoughts and Bad Acts" [1990] *Crim LR* 559.

[38] This is a considerable concession by Robinson to the objectivist rigour of his position since, if attempt liability remains possible, the beneficent outcome does not preclude criminal liability. Robinson's theory, in allowing this concession, effectively takes a particular view on what constitutes "harm" in the context of substantive offences. The harm, in Robinson's account, is not "wounding" but "unjustified wounding"; in turn, Dadson attempted but failed to inflict an unjustified wound.

Moreover, once we allow, as English law does, evaluations of personal motivation and blameworthiness to enter into the question of justification, it is even possible for a bad outcome to be the result of *justified* conduct:

> Suppose, for instance, that D, an armed police officer, receives an order to kill V instantly. He has been informed by his superiors (and has no reason to doubt the information) that V is a terrorist on the point of detonating a bomb in a crowded street. D follows his orders and shoots V dead. Unfortunately, those instructing D had made a tragic error; V was going about her lawful business.

We know that according to Robinson, D should receive a verdict of "not guilty by reason of excuse" and should potentially also be subject to civil deterrent or remedial measures. But why merely excused? D's motivation was impeccable—to prevent widespread loss of life. There was no flaw in his practical reasoning—he shot the person identified as a terrorist and had no reason to think the information he was given was false. Should he receive the same order in like circumstances in the future, he should carry out the order. He would be justified in doing so and in breach of his duty as a police officer should he decline, *irrespective of whether D was a terrorist* (provided D was unaware that V was no terrorist and had no reason to think that the order received was based on an erroneous risk assessment). Moreover, just as in the case of Ashkenazi, we can generalise the grounds of D's acquittal into a law-making precedent. The case would inform us that a person intending to use proportionate means to save lives will commit no offence, notwithstanding that he causes the death of an innocent person if he had good reason to believe that the means he employed were necessary and proportionate means.[39]

Of course, from V's perspective everything depends on his status. If he is a terrorist, any resort to force to pre-empt D's lawful use of force upon him would be an offence against D. But if V is innocent, he should be allowed to defend himself even when he knows that D has made a reasonable mistake and is doing his duty as a law enforcement official. As an innocent person, V is in full possession of his right to life.[40] Admittedly, the fact that in such circumstances D and V are both entitled to use force against the other is not tidy. Indeed, for policy reasons, there is something to be said for denying V any right to use force against D, if D is a policeman or other official acting in the legitimate execution of his duty.[41] Yet such a restriction would effectively sacrifice V's right to life in favour of greater safety for law enforcers.[42] Irrespective of the soundness or otherwise of such a policy, there is no logical or moral *imperative* requiring self-sacrifice.[43]

---

[39] Even if Robinson insists, as he would, that the bad outcome makes this a case of excuse, it is an excuse very different in structure from, say, that afforded by duress. The reasons for affording the excuse can be formulated as a guide for future conduct.

[40] Contrast, for example, the situation where V launches an unlawful and deadly attack on D which D can only repel by using deadly force on V.

[41] The issue is inconclusively discussed in *Kenlin* v. Gardiner [1967] 2 QB 510. There is a lengthy discussion of this matter in *Lawson* v. *Forsythe* [1986] VR 515, with a majority favouring the view that the fact that D is acting lawfully in the execution of his duty should not categorically deny the right of V to defend himself against the officers.

[42] See further Sullivan, "The Hard Treatment of Innocent Persons in State Responses to the Threat of Large Scale and Imminent Terrorist Violence: Examining the Legal Constraints" in Sullivan and Dennis (eds.), *Seeking Security: Pre-empting Criminal Harms* (2012) 293, 300–5.

[43] The conclusion that in these circumstances both D and V may be said to be justified in using force against each other has been criticised as a logical contradiction. It is true that a reasons rather than deeds account of justification may entail that circumstances arise where the criminal law cannot give priority to one right-holder

Whatever the position for V, if D should find himself on a criminal charge in respect of V's death, the reasonableness of his conduct entitles D to an unqualified acquittal.[44] On the other hand, the same is not necessarily true if D has made an unreasonable mistake about the danger V poses. In that case, D does not have the same moral entitlement to an acquittal. Nonetheless, the view may be taken that D's conduct should not be punished on the ground that negligence is insufficient culpability for serious offences against the person—as it has in England and Wales.[45]

Of course, we need not employ Robinson's version of the justification/excuse divide. We could adopt a model which would consider not merely outcomes but also the nature and quality of D's motivation and practical reasoning.[46] But we will not follow that course here, for several reasons. First, there may be situations where exemption from liability is clearly warranted but where neither the head of justification nor that of excuse seems adequately to capture D's non-liability. Suppose, for example, that D is a paranoid schizophrenic who believes that V is an agent of the Devil and must be killed at all costs. It would be conventional to say that his killing V is excusable on the grounds of his insanity. (Clearly, it is not justified by his insanity.) But should we really *excuse* people such as D? When we excuse, we condescend. The excused defendant could and should have done better, yet, in all the circumstances, our judgement of her conduct is not sufficiently adverse to warrant sanctions. But an insane person's conduct does not constitute a condonable lapse from the standards of self-control we might reasonably expect of him. It is not that D's action is understandable and insufficiently culpable. Rather, D is not responsible, as a deliberative agent, for her action at all. We exempt D because her mental condition places her outside that scheme of reference whereby moral judgements—distinctions between justification and excuse—derive their meaning.[47]

Secondly, particular defences may straddle the boundaries of justification and excuse, however those terms are defined. For instance, duress is typically characterised as an excuse. Frequently, it is. In *Hudson and Taylor*,[48] we may have preferred D to be a witness of truth at a criminal trial and not to commit perjury. (Indeed, in the light of *Hasan*,[49] as applied in *Batchelor*,[50] duress is now unavailable on similar facts.)[51] We would like witnesses to pass

---

over another when each lawfully resorts to the use of force. However, this is not contradiction. It merely illustrates that if the focus is on grounds for blame and punishment we may encounter persons who in moral terms are in the same case. Of course, the fact that D is justified in killing the innocent V does not qualify or limit V's innocent status—something that should be reflected in compensatory entitlements at civil law. See further Husak, "Conflicts of Justifications" (1999) 18 *Law and Phil* 41; Husak, "On the Supposed Priority of Justification to Excuse" (2005) 24 *Law and Phil* 557.

[44] If the conduct of his superiors was grossly negligent, no doubt they may be liable for manslaughter.

[45] For unreasonable mistakes and exculpation, see further § 18.1. For discussion of whether law enforcement officials should be absolved from criminal liability on the basis of unreasonable mistakes, see § 21.2 (ix); see also Simester, "On Justifications and Excuses" in Zedner and Roberts (eds.), *Principles and Values in Criminal Law and Criminal Justice: Essays in Honour of Andrew Ashworth* (2012) 95, 108–10.

[46] For instance, Uniake uses the term "agent-perspectivally justified" for this approach: *Permissible Killing* (1994) 48–9.

[47] Moore, *Law and Psychiatry* (1984) 197–8, 244–5.

[48] [1971] 2 QB 202; below, § 19.1(i)(a).

[49] [2005] 2 AC 467 (HL).

[50] [2013] EWCA Crim 2638.

[51] For further discussion, see below, § 20.1(i)(b).

the test of courage when threatened with death or serious bodily harm. Still, D was, at the time of *Hudson and Taylor*, exempted when she failed that test. In the realm of excuse, the focus was on the fear she must have experienced and how difficult it must have been in the circumstances to do her duty as a witness. By contrast, there have been a series of cases where the defence of "duress by circumstances" has been successfully invoked in answer to motoring offences. For example, in *Willer*,[52] D drove his car in a pedestrianised precinct in order to avoid a threat of death or serious bodily harm. Now, understandably, D was in very great fear and that fear, of itself, would have allowed him exemption within the terms of the defence of duress. But to focus on the fear alone is to distort D's story. If driving through the precinct was without risk to others, then it was far better that D did so rather than be killed or badly hurt. His action was justified.[53] And even if not experiencing any of the pressures of fear—he may be icily calm—his justification is sufficient of itself.

Finally, there may be situations where there is agreement that D should not be convicted but disagreement whether, on the same facts, his conduct was justifiable or excusable. Take a case where D is charged with the battery of his son, V. D claims the defence of reasonable chastisement.[54] One strand of opinion holds that certain forms of physical punishment are fully justifiable in the case of serious misbehaviour of children. Alternatively, one may hold the view that chastisement of children is never appropriate, however serious the child's misconduct, but, given the diversity and strength of the differing views of reasonable people on this topic, think that persons of a different persuasion should not be convicted for beating their children (provided the chastisement does not exceed certain limits). Accordingly, there may be consensus among a group of individuals that a defence of reasonable chastisement should be available but a diversity of views about the nature of this defence. The spectrum may range from firm belief in the justifiable nature of corporal punishment, through persons who respect cultural diversity, to persons who think chastisement is wrong and should be punishable but consider that the time is not yet ripe for change in the law.[55]

Because the heads of justification and excuse do not cover the entire range of defences and because there are uncertainties about the definition and application of those terms, in the following chapters we will not classify defences under these rubrics.[56] This is subject to an exception for what may be termed non-coerced necessity. Non-coerced necessity comprises situations where D decides to contravene the letter of the law in order to achieve

---

[52] (1986) 83 Cr App R 225 (CA).

[53] And see *Pipe* [2012] EWHC 1821 (Admin); [2012] All ER (D) 238, where the Divisional Court ruled that D should have been allowed to argue that driving in excess of the speed limit was justified when driving to hospital with his injured son (who had a suspected broken leg), following the failure of an ambulance to arrive. The case cited in support of that view was *Conway* [1989] QB 290, a case resolved under the rubric of duress of circumstances. In *Pipe*, however, the injury had already occurred and there was no risk of death. Given that duress is confined to immediate threats of death, serious bodily injury, or rape, the applicable defence would seem to be necessity.

[54] Below, § 21.4.

[55] Arguably, the current law reflects a compromise between these various views, in allowing parents to chastise children but not to cause actual bodily harm or worse: see § 21.4.

[56] For argument that dividing the territory of defences under a binary system of justification and excuse leads to oversimplification, see Duff, *Answering for Crime* (2007) 264–84; for the view that preoccupation with whether conduct is justified or excused can distract from the central question of whether conduct is sufficiently culpable to be punished, see Alexander and Ferzan, *Crime and Culpability: A Theory of Criminal Law* (2009) 88–93; for some general scepticism about the utility of the distinction between justification and excuse, see Dennis, "On Necessity as a Defence to Crime: Possibilities, Problems and the Limits of Justification and Excuse" (2009) 3 *Crim Law and Phil* 29.

an outcome of greater social benefit than would accrue through compliance with law. We may speak of such a decision as "non-coerced" if D's personal interests are not at stake: for example, where D, a doctor, decides that the mentally incompetent V's best interests would be served by a sterilisation operation. A defence of necessity may be allowed in such circumstances.[57] It is a claim of justification, not of excuse. For such a defence to be afforded, D's calculation must be right; if her cost–benefit analysis is found wanting, her defence of necessity will fail.[58]

§ 17.3 The defences to be considered—an outline scheme

The present state of English law does not permit a logically derived scheme for presenting defences. In the following chapters, all that can be done is to organise our account of defences under broad and to some extent overlapping categories.

First, in Chapter 18 we will consider *failure of proof defences*, namely the defences of mistake and intoxication. In its current form, the defence of mistake of fact is mainly used to raise doubt whether D had the mens rea element of the offence charged. But here, as elsewhere, there is inconsistency and, on occasion, a claim to have made a mistake of fact will take the form of a true or supervening defence.[59] To the extent that mistake of law provides a defence, it too operates predominantly as a failure of proof defence. Intoxication, whether voluntary or involuntary, is always a failure of proof defence; its only relevance pertains to proof of the mens rea element of the crime charged.

Secondly, we will turn in Chapter 19 to *mental condition defences*. These defences concern circumstances where, in the light of some mental condition of D that arises from an internal disorder, it would be unjust to convict D either (i) for any crime, or (ii) for the crime with which she has been charged. A mental condition that exempts conviction from any crime is a condition which satisfies the criteria of insanity within the *M'Naghten* Rules. A mental condition defence that offers merely partial exemption from criminal liability is the statutory defence of diminished responsibility; murder will be reduced to manslaughter if D can demonstrate that her responsibility for a prima facie murder was substantially impaired by some internally derived mental condition that falls within section 2 of the Homicide Act 1957. Finally in Chapter 19, we will consider the defence of infancy, which can also be characterised as a form of deliberative incapacity defence.[60] Although it is a defence of status (no one under 10 years of age can commit a crime), the status is predicated on assumptions concerning such a person's mental development and consequent moral irresponsibility for her actions.

---

[57] Below, § 21.3.

[58] It would be possible for D's conduct to remain within the realm of necessity (on a non-Robinsonian account) if she has made a *reasonable* mistake of fact, provided the cost–benefit analysis was appropriate to the facts she reasonably assumed.

[59] As is the case where D claims that he thought, albeit mistakenly, that he was under duress: as we shall see, such a claim must be based on reasonable grounds: *Graham* [1982] 1 All ER 801 (CA).

[60] We would be rebuked in this by Stephen: "The one is healthy immaturity, the other diseased maturity and between these there is no sort of resemblance": *A History of the Criminal Law of England* (1883) vol. II, 150–1.

Thirdly, we will turn in Chapter 20 to what we term *defences of circumstantial pressure*. These defences are available to persons who have the capacity to obey the law but are allowed exemption from liability by virtue of the pressure imposed by particular contexts. The defence of duress is the core member of this class of defence. We will also consider here the defences of superior orders and entrapment, although in each of these cases factors additional to the pressure placed on D are relevant to the grounds for exemption. Included too is the defence (if such a defence exists) of impossibility. A defence of impossibility, in the pure and literal sense, is a claim by D that compliance with law was physically (as opposed to morally) impossible. Strictly speaking, such a defence is *sui generis*; we include it in this section because of its focus on surrounding circumstances that affect D's non-compliance with the law.

Finally, Chapter 21 considers what will be called *defences of permissible conduct*. These are defences which permit contravention of the letter of the law provided D has acted for a qualifying reason. Unlike, say, insanity, these defences incorporate reasons in favour of acting in a particular way and, to an extent, allow a measure of planning and prediction: "I hope he will not attack but, if he does, I can defend myself". Such defences include consent, defence of self and others, prevention of crime and unlawful escapes, necessity, and reasonable chastisement. In many circumstances covered by these defences, D may find herself under considerable pressure: for example, where she is attacked by V and fears for her life. If D then kills V in self-defence, she is permitted that defence provided her actions were a proportionate response to the danger. Unlike duress, however, any understandable fear would play no direct part in her acquittal were she to be charged with V's murder (indeed duress, controversially, is not an available defence to murder). What counts for self-defence is the reasonableness of her response: it matters not whether she defended herself in a state of terror or in a state of calm resolution.[61]

---

[61] However, some allowance is made for the frightening circumstances typical of self-defence situations when assessing the proportionality of D's response to D's attack: below, § 21.2(iv).

18

FAILURE OF PROOF: MISTAKE AND INTOXICATION

Any mistake that D makes when committing an offence will have no bearing on her criminal liability unless it causes her to lack mens rea or provides her with a legally recognised excuse. She may take valuable property thinking that it belongs to X, a wealthy person against whom she has a grudge. In fact the property belongs to V, D's best friend. But for that mistake, D would not have appropriated the property. Her mistake is quite irrelevant for her liability. All the elements of theft are present and D lacks any legally recognised excuse.

With one exception, where mistakes are legally relevant, they are relevant only to questions of exculpation. Mistakes have no inculpatory effect, even should the mistake reveal a propensity to commit criminal acts. For example, in *Taaffe*,[1] D concealed a sealed packet when entering the United Kingdom. The packet was found to contain drugs. The prosecution accepted D's claim that he thought the packet contained foreign currency. He concealed the packet because he thought it was an offence to import money from overseas. That was not so; it is perfectly legal, with the abolition of exchange control, to bring in foreign money. The prosecution argued that D's belief that he was acting illegally, together with the fact that he was in possession of drugs, entailed liability for the offence of knowingly importing goods subject to import control. The House of Lords quashed his conviction. His mere belief that he was committing a crime did not suffice to constitute the mens rea for the offence charged.

Taaffe must be carefully distinguished from the famous case of *Dadson*.[2] Taking foreign currency into the UK is now something intrinsically lawful. No justificatory or excusatory explanation is required: if D wants to bring currency into the country, he can. In *Dadson*, D shot and wounded V to stop him from making off with wood that he had stolen. V had previous convictions for stealing wood which made him an escaping felon and, at that time, a felon could be shot if that was the only way of preventing escape. But D was unaware of V's previous convictions and consequently was convicted of a wounding offence. Unlike in *Taaffe*, Dadson did have mens rea. The underlying difference, moreover, is that to wound someone by shooting does require an excuse or justification. It was therefore open to the Court to rule that D was not justified in shooting V unless aware of the circumstances on which the claim to be justified had to be based.[3]

---

[1] *Taaffe* [1984] AC 539.
[2] (1850) 4 Cox 358.
[3] For further discussion see above § 17.2.

There is one exception to the general principle that mistakes are relevant only to exculpation. It applies in the law of attempts. Facts may exist which render a particular crime impossible to commit. For example, suppose that X sells a cheap video recorder to D. Because the price is so low, D is sure that she is acquiring a stolen item. Were that assumption correct, she would commit the offence of handling stolen goods. If her assumption turns out to be incorrect, liability for that offence is precluded. However, since the Criminal Attempts Act 1981, she is guilty of attempting to handle stolen goods. The impossibility of committing the full offence no longer affords a defence to a charge of attempt. To that limited extent, a mistake may have an inculpatory effect.[4]

§ 18.1 Mistake of fact, mens rea, and the decision in *Morgan*

The House of Lords decision in *Morgan*[5] provides the starting point for an analysis of the defence of mistake of fact in English law. Prior to that decision, there was authority that, to afford a defence, any mistake of fact had to be a *reasonable* one.[6] This requirement gave rise to a contradiction. With the passing of section 8 of the Criminal Justice Act 1967, proof of any intention or foresight required to establish liability for an offence had to be proof of the subjective intention or foresight *possessed by the defendant*. Section 8 disallows drawing inferences of intent or foresight of a particular result solely on the basis that such a result was the natural and probable consequence of D's conduct.[7] Consequently, if D did not apprehend that his conduct would bring about a likely consequence, he could not be taken to have intended or foreseen that consequence, however foolish or indifferent his lack of awareness showed him to be. A wholly unreasonable mistake of fact may well negate intention or foresight. How then could there be an insistence, *post* section 8, that a mistake, to provide exemption, must be based on reasonable grounds if D's mistake precluded either intent or foresight with respect to a definitional element of the offence?

(i) Subjective mens rea and mistake

The matter came to a head in *Morgan*. At trial, and before the Court of Appeal,[8] it was ruled that to afford a defence to a charge of rape, a belief in the victim's consent had to be based on reasonable grounds. In the Court of Appeal, Bridge LJ finessed the contradiction between this reasonableness requirement and the terms of section 8 by asserting that unless a mistake was based on reasonable grounds there would be an insufficient basis, as a matter of evidence, on which to raise a defence of mistake.[9] The House of Lords rejected this evidential analysis. Their Lordships accepted that a reasonable mistake would typically have more credibility with a jury, yet unreasonable mistakes could be made and evidence to that

---

[4] See above, § 9.4(iii).
[5] [1976] AC 182 (HL).
[6] *Rose* (1884) 15 Cox CC 540; *Chisham* [1963] 47 Cr App R 130 (CA).
[7] Above, § 5.1(ix).
[8] [1975] 1 All ER 8.
[9] *Ibid.*, 14.

effect could be adduced. Such a mistake might avoid liability for an offence because, as Lord Hailsham explained, in the context of rape:[10]

> "Once one has accepted, what seems to me abundantly clear, that the prohibited act in rape is non-consensual sexual intercourse, and that the guilty state of mind is an intention to commit it, it seems to me to follow as a matter of inexorable logic that there is no room either for a 'defence' of honest belief or mistake, or of a defence of honest and reasonable belief or mistake. Either the prosecution proves that the accused had the requisite intent, or it does not. In the former case it succeeds, and in the latter it fails."

This passage makes clear that where the issue is proof of a subjective form of mens rea it is, strictly, a misnomer to speak of a "defence" of mistake of fact. The issue is whether mens rea has been established. Thus, in rape at the time of *Morgan* D had to know or be reckless whether V has consented to sexual intercourse.[11] If D is mistaken about this, he does not claim a "defence" of mistaken belief—rather, he denies mens rea.

Yet it remains a natural usage to speak in terms of a defence of mistake. If, say, the prosecution were to prove the actus reus of rape, an inference that D has mens rea would normally be straightforward from those proved facts. Accordingly, if he is to avoid the drawing of that inference, D would normally be expected to suggest some reason why it should not be drawn.[12] It is perfectly acceptable to say that D is defending himself when he attempts to raise a doubt about his mens rea. The terminology will not mislead, provided it is well understood that the burden of proving mens rea rests with the prosecution. Very often, the prosecution will discharge that task in the course of proving the actus reus, since the inference drawn from proof of the facts surrounding V's non-consent is likely to be sufficient unless D offers some explanation of his conduct.[13] If his explanation raises an evidential issue, the prosecution's probative task is joined again.

(ii) Application of Morgan to definitional elements

The approach to mistake elucidated in *Morgan* will apply straightforwardly where the mens rea required for the offence is coincident with the actus reus. One would hope that such a coincidence could be taken for granted, particularly for serious offences. Unfortunately, the "correspondence principle"[14] is of uneven application in English law. If the mens rea required for a particular offence does not correspond or embrace the entirety of the actus reus, what would otherwise be a mistake germane to liability may turn out to be

---

[10] [1976] AC 182, 214. Cf. *Smith* [1974] 1 QB 354, 360.

[11] Since the Sexual Offences Act 2003, D must have reasonable grounds for his belief that V is consenting. Above, § 12.5.

[12] In this situation, a *tactical*—not *evidential*—burden rests on D. For explanation of the difference see above, § 3.2 n. 42.

[13] Section 35 of the Criminal Justice and Public Order Act 1994 allows the court or jury to draw such inferences as appear proper from the failure of D to give evidence or from a refusal, without good cause, to answer any question. Although s. 38(3) provides that failure to testify is not by itself to constitute a basis for conviction, in the situation under discussion, the prosecution have proved that V did not consent to intercourse with D. On the general approach to s. 35, see *Cowan* [1996] QB 373 (CA).

[14] Above, § 6.5.

immaterial. In *Ellis*,[15] for example, D was charged with knowingly evading a restriction on the importation of a Class A drug—an offence in its own right and not a mere instance of a more general offence concerned with the importation of controlled items.[16] D claimed to believe that he was bringing pornography rather than heroin into the country. The Court of Appeal ruled that the mens rea required was knowledge that the item in possession was an item subject to import control.[17] It was unnecessary that D should know the nature of the item in question. Accordingly, his conviction for evading the restriction of Class A drugs was confirmed. The logic of *Morgan* does not apply to the actus reus of the offence in such a case, save to this extent: D could offer a defence of mistake if he genuinely believed, however unreasonably, that he was not carrying any form of contraband.

Morgan offers welcome clarification. Yet two areas of difficulty remain. First, cognisance was taken by their Lordships of a line of authority which required that any mistake relating to a belief in a need to use defensive force had to be based on reasonable grounds if it were to have an exculpatory effect.[18] Secondly, note was also taken of the well-known and long-standing decision in *Tolson*[19] which decided, in the context of the offence of bigamy, that any belief in a capacity to enter into a valid form of marriage had to be reasonable if it was to provide an excuse. The House indicated that its decision in *Morgan* should not be read as undermining *Tolson*.[20]

We must now examine each of these reservations from the subjective approach.

(iii) Mistake of fact and defences

In *Albert* v. *Lavin*,[21] D assumed that he was under restraint by a passer-by; in fact, V was a plain-clothes police officer attempting to restrain D from queue-jumping at a bus-stop. V had intervened because he feared that D's conduct would lead to a breach of the peace in the light of the irate responses of fellow passengers.

It was argued on D's behalf that, although it may have been unreasonable for D to believe that V was not a policeman, he was entitled to a defence of mistake.[22] The Divisional Court confirmed the magistrate's ruling that such a belief, to afford a defence, had to be reasonable. *Morgan*, it was explained, concerned the *definitional* elements of offences. Here, by contrast, the definitional elements were present—D had intentionally inflicted force on V.

---

[15] (1986) 84 Cr Appr R 235. See too *Forbes* [2001] UKHL 40, [2002] 2 AC 512.

[16] Following the decision of the House of Lords in *Courtie* [1984] AC 463, if a statute provides that particular facts or circumstances increase the maximum penalty for an offence, a discrete offence is created incorporating those facts or circumstances as defining elements. This rule applies in the case of drugs, since greater penalties are provided for Class A drugs than for non-Class-A drugs.

[17] D was charged under s. 170(2) of the Customs and Excise Management Act 1979 which requires, *inter alia*, that D be "knowingly concerned" in the importation of a controlled drug. The requirement of knowledge relates to the item in possession. D could not have known he was in possession of pornography because he had no pornographic items in his possession. At most, he believed that he did. Whereas *true* beliefs may be accounted in law as knowledge (above, § 5.4), it strains credulity to breaking-point to classify a false belief as a form of knowledge.

[18] *Rose* (1884) 15 Cox CC 540; *Chisham* [1963] 47 Cr App R 130 (CA).

[19] (1889) 23 QBD 168 (CCR).

[20] [1976] AC 182, 201–2 (Lord Cross), 214–15 (Lord Hailsham).

[21] [1981] 1 All ER 628 (DC); affirmed on other grounds [1982] AC 546 (HL).

[22] The Divisional Court assumed that only police officers could physically restrain persons to prevent a breach of the peace. The House of Lords subsequently held that all subjects have this right. On that view, D's mistake, unreasonable or otherwise, was immaterial.

The question for the court was not whether there had been an assault but whether the assault was an *unlawful* assault.[23] The Divisional Court approved previous authority which ruled that force based on an unreasonable belief in justificatory facts was unlawful force.[24]

The analysis applied in *Albert* v. *Lavin* was successfully challenged in *Gladstone Williams*.[25] The Court of Appeal rejected the notion that the requirement of unlawfulness was something that stood apart from the offence itself. The unlawfulness was integral to the offence and, on that view, the mens rea for assault was an intent to apply unlawful violence. Consequently, a person who believed that force was necessary to protect another from violence would lack an intent to inflict unlawful force. The approach in *Gladstone Williams* was endorsed by the Privy Council in *Beckford*[26] and may be regarded as authoritative for cases involving beliefs in the need for preventive or defensive force.

However, this wholly subjective approach does not apply to all mistakes. In *Graham*,[27] the Court of Appeal considered that a mistaken belief in the existence of circumstances constituting legally adequate duress must be based on reasonable grounds if it is to constitute a defence, an approach endorsed by the House of Lords in *Howe*[28] and again in *Hasan*.[29] The latter case in particular bases its refusal to endorse an subjective approach on a concern to tighten the conditions of a defence easily fabricated and abused. That kind of policy-based reasoning could be applied to claims to have acted in self-defence, when such claims are unsupported by objective fact. For many years prior to *Gladstone Williams*, English law insisted that any claim of self-defence be based on reasonable grounds. However, in the case of mistaken self-defence statute has intervened decisively, and the subjective approach prevails.[30] The trial judge made an egregious error in *Yaman*[31] in directing the jury to consider the reasonableness of D's belief that the gas fitters and inspector, who had broken into his shop in his absence to disconnect the gas supply, were burglars. As the Court of Appeal admonished, it was clear beyond question that D's forceful response to this intrusion had to be evaluated on the basis of his genuine belief that he was confronting burglars.[32]

Clarkson and Keating offer a principled explanation for the current divergence of approach between cases of duress and cases of self-defence. For them, the difference may be explained on the basis that a belief in the need to use preventive force is a belief that one's conduct is justified whereas a belief that one may be subjected to duress amounts to a claim merely to be excused.[33] They rationalise this divergence on the grounds that, in the former

---

[23] [1981] 1 All ER 628, 639 (Hodgson J).

[24] *Weston* (1879) 14 Cox CC 346; *Rose* (1884) 15 Cox CC 540; *Owens* v. *HM Advocate* 1946 JC 119; *Chisham* (1963) 47 Cr App R 130.

[25] [1987] 3 All ER 411.

[26] [1988] AC 130. For critical commentary see Simester, "Mistakes in Defence" (1992) 12 *OJLS* 295.

[27] [1982] 1 All ER 801.

[28] [1987] AC 417.

[29] [2005] 2 AC 467.

[30] Criminal Justice and Immigration Act 2008, s. 76(4).

[31] [2012] EWCA Crim 1075

[32] Surprisingly, perhaps, the Court of Appeal were satisfied that a properly directed jury would have found D's spontaneous act of hitting V on the head with a hammer disproportionate. Given that D assumed that he was confronting a three-man burglary team, the issue of proportionality might have been best resolved by a jury on a retrial.

[33] *Criminal Law: Text and Materials* (6th ed., 2007) 197–8. It is of some interest to note that, writing alone, Clarkson has proposed that duress, self-defence, and necessity should be integrated within a unified defence—a proposal that contradicts the division jointly argued for. See Clarkson, "Necessary Action: a New Defence" [2004] *Crim LR* 81; contra, Chan and Simester, "Duress, Necessity: How Many Defences?" (2005) 16 *King's College LJ* 121.

case, a defendant believes he is acting in a lawful and justified—i.e. blameless—manner; by contrast with the latter case, where even if D were right his conduct would be neither lawful nor justified. This view implies the claim that if D1 attacks V because he unreasonably assumes that V is about to attack him, he is in better moral standing than, say, D2, who drives his car through a pedestrianised area to escape V whom he unreasonably assumed was about to kill him. D1's mistake relates to self-defence (justification) and D2's to duress of circumstances (excuse). But it is far from obvious that they are different moral cases.[34]

The reason for the different approaches appears to be the happenstance that typifies our uncodified criminal law. The element of unlawfulness which must, axiomatically, be present for the commission of any offence may, as in *Gladstone Williams*, be treated as something integral to the definition of the offence. Where that analysis is employed, the wholly subjective approach taken in *Morgan* will prevail and any genuine belief in facts which would have rendered D's conduct lawful will provide an excuse. However, if the matter is not covered by authority, a court minded not to follow the subjectivism of *Morgan* may, as in *Graham*, treat the defence in question as something extraneous to the defining elements of the offence. If that analysis is employed, a court may require, as in *Graham*, that mistakes must be based on reasonable grounds to afford a defence. It has been persuasively argued that resolving such issues by reference to the categories of defining elements or defence elements is to elevate legalism over substantive moral assessment.[35] For instance, lack of consent is clearly a defining element of rape. Yet there are good reasons why a belief in V's consent to sex should be based on reasonable grounds to afford a defence, a position now achieved under the Sexual Offences Act 2003 for rape and other non-consensual sexual offences.[36]

Similarly, while the legislature has adopted objective standards for definitional features of serious crimes in measures such the Sexual Offences Act 2003 and the Proceeds of Crime Act 2002, at the same time the House of Lords in *G*[37] gave a ringing and general endorsement to the subjective approach to central elements of serious offences when abolishing *Caldwell* recklessness.[38] Ironically, in a later decision of the same name,[39] the House of Lords upheld the imposition of strict liability for an offence carrying a maximum penalty of life imprisonment—despite previous authority of its own[40] that (had the Court been strongly minded to do so) could have been deployed to require subjective mens rea for the element in question (the age of the victim) and hence makes available a defence of mistake, even where based on unreasonable grounds.[41] English law lacks any general theory of exculpation to guide decision-making on the nature and range of the defence of mistake. A settled theory could only come by way of a criminal code, a remote prospect indeed.[42]

---

[34] As argued earlier, assigning defences to the categories of either justification or excuse will run up against the difficulty that defences may operate over the two categories: § 17.2.

[35] Tur, "Subjectivism and Objectivism: Towards Synthesis" in Shute, Gardner and Horder (eds.), *Action and Value in Criminal Law* (1993) 213.

[36] Above, §§ 12.6–9.

[37] [2003] UKHL 50; [2004] 1 AC 1034.

[38] Above § 5.2(i).

[39] *G* [2008] UKHL 37.

[40] *B (a minor)* v. *DPP* [2000] 2 AC 428; *K* [2002] 1 AC 462. See further above, § 6.1(i).

[41] See above, § 12.11(i). In fact the defendant in *G* (a boy of 16) was found to have a reasonable belief that V, a 12-year-old girl, was aged 15.

[42] The Law Commission for England and Wales announced the abandonment of the criminal law codification project in 2008: Law Com. No. 311, *Tenth Programme of Law Reform* (2008).

The need for general principle is underscored by the confusion and uncertainty engendered by a series of cases relating to mistake and defences. In *Martin (David)*,[43] the Court of Appeal ruled that it was a misdirection for the trial judge to direct that D should have had reasonable grounds to believe that his mother's life was in danger before excusing on the ground of mistaken duress. Instead, the jury should have been directed that a genuine belief, reasonable or otherwise, should suffice. While the decision has the virtue of concordance with the cases involving mistaken self-defence, confusion is shown by the cavalier treatment of the previous authority dealing with mistaken duress, where a reasonable mistake is insisted upon. In the light of the endorsement of a reasonable mistake requirement by the House of Lords in *Hasan*,[44] we can put *Martin (David)* to one side as an aberration in the case law on mistaken duress, albeit one indicative of the instability in general terms of the approach to mistake.

In *Martin (Anthony)*,[45] a case of self-defence, the Court of Appeal confirmed that a belief in a need to defend oneself need not be based on reasonable grounds: a genuine belief sufficed. However, the Court of Appeal introduced a surprising, and untenable, distinction between (i) the facts on which D's perception that he was under attack was based and (ii) the danger presented by those facts. In relation to (ii), D had claimed that his personality disorder, exacerbated by depression, induced him to perceive a greater threat to his safety arising from a burglary at his isolated farmhouse than would have been perceived by a normal person. The Court held that, whereas in relation to (i) the facts must be presumed to be as D saw them, (ii) the danger presented by those facts must be evaluated *objectively*. D's plea of mistaken self-defence therefore failed, because his response to the objectively ascertained danger (rather than his imagined danger) was excessive.

The distinction drawn by the Court of Appeal between the facts *per se* and the danger arising from the facts is spurious. Suppose that V reaches into the inside of his jacket to extract a cigarette lighter; D assumes he is reaching for a gun. According to *Martin (Anthony)*, we are to allow D the benefit of his belief that V was reaching for a gun, however unreasonable D's belief, but must make an objective appraisal of the danger arising from these presumed facts. But what is it for a person to believe self-defence is required? It is to think that something dangerous is happening or about to happen. That is a belief about the facts: in the realm of *mistaken* beliefs, there is no division between the facts themselves and the danger to which the facts give rise.

This was perceived very clearly by the Privy Council in *Shaw v. R*,[46] a case decided shortly before *Martin (Anthony)* and not cited in the latter case. In *Shaw*, the appellants were appealing against a direction which invited the jury to assess the reasonableness of D's self-defence on the basis of the facts as they were rather than the facts as D believed them to be. The Privy Council expressed the proper test for self-defence as follows:[47]

"In the opinion of the Board it was necessary for the trial judge to ask two essential questions (however expressed) for the jury's consideration. (1) Did the appellant honestly believe or may

---

[43] [2000] 2 Cr App R 42.
[44] [2005] 2 AC 467; approving the requirement therefore stated in *Graham* [1982] 1 All ER 801.
[45] [2001] EWCA Crim 2245, [2002] 2 WLR 1.
[46] [2001] 1 WLR 1519.
[47] [2001] 1 WLR 1519, 1527 (emphasis added).

be honestly have believed that it was necessary to defend himself? (2) If so, and taking the circumstances *and the danger* as the appellant honestly believed them to be, was the amount of force which he used reasonable?"

Much the better view, then, in conceptual terms, is that D must be assessed on the basis of the danger he took to be present—a fully subjective test. As we shall see directly, D's response to that perceived danger must be reasonably proportionate (to the facts as D perceived them to be).

However, the force of the policy consideration that led to the forced distinction between belief in the need to defend oneself (subjective test) and the danger presented by the supposed attack (objective test) should be acknowledged. In *Martin (Anthony)*, the manufacturing of this distinction meant that self-defence was disallowed, whereas D's plea of diminished responsibility succeeded. In terms of the public interest that may be seen as a more balanced result than unqualified acquittal for a man who was psychologically disposed to over-react. Such a concern was very much to the mind of the Court of Appeal in *Oye*,[48] where D, because he was experiencing a psychotic episode, attacked policemen whom he took to be evil spirits. Both (mistaken) self-defence and insanity were put to the jury—and rejected.[49] On appeal, the Court of Appeal substituted D's convictions for affray and grievous bodily harm with a verdict of not guilty by reason of insanity. No place was found for mistaken self-defence: "An insane person cannot set the standards of reasonableness as to the degree of force used by reference to his own insanity."[50]

By contrast, in *Press*,[51] D was allowed to raise mistaken self-defence by claiming that his condition of post-traumatic stress disorder led him to believe that it was necessary to use force of the gravity he employed. The Court of Appeal found that his mental condition could be referenced to support his defence: *Oye* was distinguished on the basis that the expert evidence in the instant case fell short of establishing an insane delusion. It is submitted that this distinction is inadequate even in its own terms.[52] Either way, however, the case law needs to be resolved. In particular, what requires resolution at appellate level is the scope of the rule that a belief in the need to use defensive force need only be genuine rather than reasonable. Should the rule be modified in the case of persons whose belief in the requirement to use force is influenced by an abnormal mental condition likely to recur?

The situation is different in cases where a mistake must be based on reasonable grounds, where any mistake influenced by a mental or personality disorder would seem irrelevant. Suppose that D, a paranoid schizophrenic, misconstrues an impatient remark by P about D's delay in repaying a loan as a threat to kill him unless the debt is repaid by stealing from V. As a result, D steals from V. If he wished to raise mistaken duress as a defence to theft, there

---

[48] [2013] EWCA Crim 1725, [2014] 1 WLR 3354.

[49] For an argument that only the defence of insanity should have been considered by the jury on these facts, see Child and Sullivan, "When Does the Insanity Defence Apply? Some Recent Cases" [2014] *Crim LR* 788; also below, § 19.1(ii)(c).

[50] [2013] EWCA Crim 1725, para. 47.

[51] [2013] EWCA Crim 1849.

[52] It is not obvious why D's PSTD was not a disease of the mind for the purposes of an insanity defence, if it led to his belief that the force used was justified and therefore not "wrong" within the meaning of the *M'Naghten* Rules: below, 19.1(ii)(c).

would seem no scope for D to bring his condition into play when evaluating whether his belief in a death threat was reasonable. The fact that the belief is attributable to his mental disorder undermines any claim that it was reasonable.

Similarly, in B,[53] D, a schizophrenic believed he had sexual healing powers. V, his wife, submitted but did not consent to intercourse with him. It was optimistically argued for D at his trial for rape that, in assessing whether D's belief in V's consent was reasonable,[54] the question should be whether it was reasonable in the particular circumstances of D, circumstances which should include his disability which gave rise to the false belief. Hughes LJ curtly dismissed the submission: "A delusional belief in consent, if entertained, would be by definition irrational and thus unreasonable".[55] He went on to suggest a possible distinction between delusional beliefs and beliefs which were not necessarily irrational but which, nonetheless, were beliefs that ordinary people would not hold; referencing, in particular, persons of "less than ordinary intelligence" or with an "inability to recognise behavioural cues". His Lordship considered that beliefs attributable to those conditions were not necessarily irrational and hence unreasonable.[56] Drawing lines between delusional beliefs on the one hand and obtuse yet reasonable beliefs on the other will not be easy.

(iv) The rule in Tolson

In *Tolson*,[57] the Court of Crown Cases Reserved resolved, by a majority, that there would be a defence to a charge of bigamy if D had reasonable grounds to believe that she was free to enter into marriage. Accordingly, on the facts of *Tolson*, a reasonable belief that one's husband had drowned at sea would suffice, but a belief, however strongly held, based on inadequate grounds would not. How is this approach compatible with *Morgan*?

According to Lord Cross, the explanation lies in the definition of the offence of bigamy. Bigamy penalises "whosoever, being married, shall marry another person during the life of the former husband or wife". It may be noted that there is no indication of what mental element, if any, is required for this offence. For Lord Cross, this was crucial:[58]

> "If the words defining an offence provide either expressly or impliedly that a man is not to be guilty of it if he believes something to be true, then he cannot be found guilty if the jury think that he may have believed it to be true, however inadequate were his reasons for doing so. But, if the definition of the offence is on the face of it 'absolute' and the defendant is seeking to escape his prima facie liability by a defence of mistaken belief, I can see no hardship to him in requiring the mistake—if it is to afford him a defence—to be based on reasonable grounds."

Lord Cross's account provides a cogent distinction between rape (the offence at issue in *Morgan*), which has an explicit mental element, and the crime of bigamy. Indeed, there are many offences which make no reference to a mental element. As a matter of judicial interpretation, however, the approach outlined by Lord Cross has rarely been taken. More

---

[53] [2013] EWCA Crim 3; above, § 5.5(ii).
[54] As is required by s.1(2) of the Sexual Offences Act 2003.
[55] [2013] EWCA Crim 3, para. 35.
[56] *Ibid.*, para. 41.
[57] (1889) 23 QBD 168 (CCR).
[58] [1976] AC 182, 202–3.

typically, courts have either found an implication of mens rea from the statutory context or determined that the offence is one of strict liability. Strict liability tempered by a defence of reasonable mistake is an option not considered.[59] Such an approach has taken hold only in bigamy[60] and in the now-rarely prosecuted offence of taking a girl under the age of 16 from the possession of her parents or guardian.[61] As the House of Lords has now confirmed,[62] the rule in *Tolson* lacks any generality.

(v) Mistake of fact and mistake as to an applicable standard

It is customary to draw a distinction between mistakes of fact on the one hand and mistakes of law on the other, with only the former kind of mistake allowed an exculpatory effect. We shall address the fact/law divide in the next section. Before we do, it is necessary to consider another distinction which is more easily confused: the distinction between facts and standards.

Not all applicable standards are reduced to specific rules of law. For instance, section 3 of the Criminal Law Act 1967 allows force to be used in the prevention of crime provided it is "reasonable in the circumstances". What constitutes reasonable force in the particular circumstances is a question of fact. By the very nature of the reasonableness standard, it is a matter for objective appraisal. But if the matter is one of fact rather than law, arguably a person who has used unreasonable force may claim to have made a mistake of fact if she believed the force employed was appropriate to the circumstances. Such an argument was accepted by the Court of Appeal in *Scarlett*,[63] where D, a pub landlord, was found guilty of constructive manslaughter at trial on the basis of having committed battery against V, a customer, whom he used excessive force to eject. On appeal, his conviction was quashed on the basis that, if D believed the circumstances called for the degree of force he used, he was entitled to a defence of mistake of fact even if his belief was unreasonable.[64]

It is submitted that *Scarlett* is wrongly decided and should not be followed. The judgment of the Court of Appeal confuses the category of fact (data concerning surrounding circumstances) with the category of standards (evaluation) which, juridically, are likened to questions of fact only because the matter is left to the jury rather than the judge to adjudicate upon. Despite their classification as matters of fact, such standards are normative, requiring an objective assessment which may well be at variance with D's own evaluation of her conduct. In *Scarlett* the court took itself to be applying the decision in *Gladstone*

---

[59] Lord Devlin has claimed, extra-judicially, that as a matter of statutory construction the choice, in practical terms, is between implying a mens rea term or reading a provision literally, thereby imposing strict liability: *Samples of Law Making* (1963) 76. Lord Devlin has in mind construction of the defining elements of the *offence*, whereas the *Tolson* approach provides a *defence* which precludes punishment of the blameless. It would have been possible for the judiciary to extend this approach beyond bigamy and kindred offences. For instance, in other Commonwealth jurisdictions, due diligence defences have been judicially created to mitigate strict liability in the regulatory sphere: see above, § 6.4.

[60] *King* [1964] 1 QB 285 (CA); *Gould* [1968] 2 QB 65 (CA).

[61] *Hibbert* (1869) LR 1 CCR 184.

[62] *B (a minor) v. DPP* [2000] 2 AC 428. The decision in *Tolson* was given no salience in the review of approaches to mens rea by the House of Lords in *G* [2003] UKHL 50; [2004] 1 AC 1034.

[63] [1993] 4 All ER 629 (CA).

[64] *Ibid.*, 636 (Beldam LJ).

Williams.[65] That decision, as we have noted, merely decides that if a person mistakenly assumes that she or another is about to be attacked, her actions are to be judged as if that assumption were true. There is nothing in the case which obliges subsequent courts to accept a defendant's own view of what constitutes *a reasonable* response to the situation that she perceived herself to be in. The approach in *Scarlett* undermines section 3 of the Criminal Law Act 1967, which mandates *reasonable* force in the prevention of crime. A police officer, for instance, acting excessively but with a genuine zeal in the cause of crime prevention may, if *Scarlett* is correct, claim a defence of mistake of fact. Fortunately, in *Owino*,[66] where there was a gross disproportion between D's violent response and the threat he claimed to be facing from V, the Court of Appeal confirmed D's conviction for malicious wounding and stated that should there be any conflict between its previous decisions in *Gladstone Williams* and *Scarlett*, it was the former decision that should prevail. A similar view was expressed in *Armstrong-Braun*.[67] *Dicta* that D's response to the danger he took to exist must be reasonable and proportionate can be found in the post-*Scarlett* cases of *Armstrong-Braun*, Shaw v. R.,[68] *Martin (David)*,[69] *Leckey*,[70] and *Rashford*.[71] The matter is now put beyond doubt by the Criminal Justice and Immigration Act 2008 for cases involving force used by way of self-defence or the prevention of crime. The degree of force used by D is not to be regarded as having been reasonable in the circumstances as D believed them to be if it was a disproportionate response to those circumstances.[72]

Accordingly, the defence of mistake of fact is confined to facts in the sense of data about the world, misperceptions on the part of D concerning the circumstances in which she acted. Examples would be mistakes about the intentions of another, or D's taking V's umbrella mistakenly assuming that it was her own. Questions of normative standards fall outside the scope of the defence.

§ 18.2 Ignorance and mistake of law

"Ignorance of law is no excuse" is a saying widely disseminated in our culture and, as generalisations go, it has a large core of truth.[73] In *Esop*,[74] D, a subject of the Ottoman Empire, was accused of committing buggery while aboard a ship docked in an English port. Such conduct was not an offence in his place of domicile and the court accepted that D, as a complete stranger to this country and its ways, had no reason to think that he was breaking the law. These factors were held irrelevant to the issue of liability.[75]

---

[65] [1987] 3 All ER 411 (CA).
[66] (1996) 2 Cr App R 128 (CA).
[67] [1999] Crim LR 416.
[68] [2001] 1 WLR 1519.
[69] [2000] 2 Cr App R 42.
[70] [2005] NICA 26.
[71] [2005] EWCA Crim 3377.
[72] Section 76(6).
[73] Ashworth, "Excusable Mistake of Law" [1974] *Crim LR* 652; Husak and von Hirsch, "Culpability and Mistake of Law" in Shute, Gardner, and Horder (eds.), *Action and Value in Criminal Law* (1993) 157; Smith, "Error and Mistake of Law in Anglo-American Criminal Law" (1984) 14 *Anglo-American LR* 3.
[74] (1836) 7 C & P 456, 173 ER 203.
[75] In *Christian v. R* [2006] 2 AC 400, the Privy Council confirmed that it was irrelevant to liability for various sexual offences, including rape, that the defendants (Pitcairn islanders) were unaware that they were subject to

From *Bailey*,[76] it appears that ignorance of law will not afford an excuse even if D was in a situation where it was impossible for him to learn that the relevant law applied to him: accordingly, it did not avail D to demonstrate that the statutory provision in question had been extended to British vessels while his ship was at sea and beyond communication with England. Neither will a positive belief, based on legal advice, that one's conduct is lawful give grounds for exemption. In *Cooper* v. *Simmons*,[77] D, an apprentice, received misleading legal advice that he was no longer bound by his indentures following the death of his master. Nevertheless, he was convicted of unlawfully absenting himself from his apprenticeship.

It may seem perfectly reasonable that D's legal position should be determined by the law as it actually is and not how he has assumed it to be. However, that holds true only provided the law is readily ascertainable—which may be far from the case, particularly for areas of activity extensively and frequently regulated. Typically, the regulatory scheme is a patchwork of primary and secondary legislation of considerable volume. There is no statute law database with hyperlinks, a lack of provision criticised by the English Law Commission.[78] Even experienced lawyers practising in a particular regulatory domain may be unaware of significant changes in the law within that domain. In *Chambers*,[79] changes in the law relating to the confiscation of the proceeds of crime which were favourable to defendants were known neither to the Customs and Excise prosecutors nor, seemingly, to defence lawyers, despite those changes having occurred some five years before the confiscation proceedings. In fairness to the lawyers involved, the public and private sector databases used by the profession did not register the changes. There arose the disturbing possibility that prison sentences were being served by persons who had failed to comply with the terms of a confiscation order lacking any valid legal basis.[80] To date, this lamentable state of affairs has not prompted the courts to modify the maxim that ignorance of law is no excuse.

However, it would be a mistake to assert that D's state of legal knowledge is invariably irrelevant to the question whether D has committed an offence. Such knowledge will, of course, be relevant where a statutory offence expressly provides that particular forms of knowledge or beliefs about legal questions are germane. Further, courts occasionally construe statutory offences as requiring, by implication, knowledge or beliefs concerning questions of law. Additionally, the expanding discretionary jurisdiction to stay criminal proceedings as an "abuse or process"[81] may well require consideration of the defendant's legal knowledge or beliefs. The importance of this jurisdiction is likely to increase with the incorporation into English law of Article 6 of the ECHR, granting to defendants a right of fair trial. Consideration must be given also to Article 7 of the ECHR, which proscribes retroactive laws. In certain circumstances, application of the maxim that ignorance of the law does not excuse will be tantamount to imposing liability on a retroactive basis.

English criminal law. See further Power, "Pitcairn Island: Sexual Offending, Cultural Difference, and Ignorance of the Law" [2007] *Crim LR* 609.

[76] (1800) Russ & Ry 1, 168 ER 651 (CCR).

[77] (1862) 26 JP 486.

[78] *Post-Legislative Scrutiny* Law Com. No. 302 (2006).

[79] [2008] EWCA Crim 2467.

[80] Customs and Excise gave an undertaking to the Court of Appeal to review past cases in the light of the newly discovered change in the law.

[81] Choo, *Abuse of Process and Judicial Stays of Criminal Proceedings* (2nd ed., 2008).

(i) Construing offences and mistake or ignorance of law

Statutes may make explicit reference to the defendant's legal knowledge or beliefs. For instance, section 2(1)(a) of the Theft Act 1968 provides that D's appropriation of property belonging to another is not to be regarded as dishonest if she believes she has, in law, the right to deprive the other of it. Alternatively, even if the statute is not explicit, a court may conclude that the mens rea for a particular offence is negated by a mistake of law made by D. In *Smith*,[82] D damaged V's speakers when removing them from fixed positions. D assumed that he was removing his own speakers but, unawares, by fixing them to a wall in his rented flat he had made the items, in legal terms, fixtures and, hence, the property of the landlord V. On one view, D's conviction at trial for criminal damage is uncontroversial. He was reckless about damaging the speakers, as he anticipated that the manner of removal which he employed might damage them. He was aware of the facts that made the speakers V's property—he himself had fixed them to the wall. That D was unaware of the property-transferring effect of his conduct was regarded by the trial judge as a mistake of law, relevant to mitigation but not to liability for the offence.

The Court of Appeal quashed D's conviction. It took the gravamen of criminal damage to be the destruction or damage of property that was known or suspected by D to belong to another. The court discussed the matter in terms of mens rea, which is entirely appropriate. The point is that mens rea in the context of *Smith* required a degree of awareness on the part of D of the legal consequences of his conduct.

Another way of categorising the appellate ruling in *Smith* is to say that a mistake of civil law was in issue and questions of civil law are equivalent to questions of fact. But while it is true that courts are far readier to allow mistakes of civil law to exempt than they are to exculpate for mistakes of substantive criminal law, there is no hard and fast rule. The effect of the master's death on the legal relationship of master and apprentice is clearly a matter of civil law. Yet, as we saw in *Cooper v. Simmons*,[83] D's mistaken belief that the death of his master had freed him from the obligations of service did not provide a defence to a criminal charge of unlawfully absenting himself from his apprenticeship. Conversely, there are cases, albeit rare, where courts have inferred that Parliament intended that ignorance of a rule of criminal law should excuse. For instance, in *Secretary of State for Trade and Industry v. Hart*,[84] D acted as auditor of a company of which he was a director. In so doing, he appeared to be in breach of the terms of section 13(5) of the Companies Act 1976, which prohibits any person from acting as auditor of a company if "he knows that he is disqualified for appointment to that office". D knew all the facts (i.e. that he was a director of the company) that made for his disqualification.[85] Yet the Divisional Court held that something further was required to satisfy the requirement of knowledge: knowledge of the statutory disqualification rules was a prerequisite of liability. D's mistake was clearly a mistake of criminal law. Nonetheless, Ormrod LJ stated:[86]

> "If that means that he is entitled to rely on ignorance of the law as a defence, in contrast to the usual practice and the usual rule, the answer is that the section gives him that right."

---

[82] [1974] QB 354 (CA).
[83] (1862) 26 JP 486; above, § 18.2.
[84] [1982] 1 All ER 817.
[85] By virtue of s. 161(2) of the Companies Act 1948.
[86] [1982] 1 All ER 817, 822.

There is no settled jurisprudence to guide us as to when the approach taken in *Hart* will be adopted. Contrast the decision in *Johnson* v. *Youden*,[87] where P built a house under the authority of a building licence that was subject to a condition limiting the price for which the house might subsequently be sold. P sold the house for a net price in excess of the limit, thereby contravening section 7 of the Building Materials and Housing Act 1945. D, P's solicitor, was charged as an accomplice to P's offence. It was accepted that, as an accomplice, the required mens rea was knowledge of the essential elements of the offence. Despite the fact that D had read the Act and had formed the opinion that the transaction, as structured, was lawful, the Divisional Court directed the first instance justices to convict. Knowledge was satisfied on the basis of D's awareness of the terms of the licence and of the terms of the sale; the Court held it was not necessary to know that the transaction was in breach of the Act, since to require such knowledge would be to excuse D on the basis of ignorance of law.

It may seem perfectly reasonable to expect solicitors to apprise themselves of law applicable to their professional involvement. Equally, however, one would suppose that a company director should appreciate that the essence of a company audit is independent scrutiny of the financial situation of the company. All that can be said with any measure of confidence is that the line taken in *Johnson* v. *Youden* is more typical than that adopted in *Hart*. It can also be said that, generally, courts will be more receptive to claims of excuse founded on mistake or ignorance of the civil law than of the criminal law. What is signally lacking in English law is any discussion of what general principles should be invoked when determining whether, if at all, mistake or ignorance of law should provide a defence.

(ii) Mistake or ignorance of law, abuse of process, and the right to fair trial

In *Arrowsmith*,[88] D distributed leaflets to soldiers eligible to serve in Northern Ireland, urging them to desist from serving in that province. She was prosecuted under the Incitement to Disaffection Act 1934. *Inter alia*, she defended herself on the basis that a letter she received from the Director of Public Prosecutions would have led any reasonable person, including the defendant, to believe that distribution of the leaflets did not contravene the Act. Accordingly, she claimed a defence of excusable mistake of law, a claim rejected both at trial and on appeal.[89]

The case raises some difficult questions. Clearly, prosecuting authorities should not be disadvantaged by offering bona fide advice to persons seeking to stay on the right side of the law. Such advice may be optimistically interpreted or disingenuously construed, and the prosecutorial task should not be stymied through such contingencies. Yet, if the nature and extent of D's proposed conduct has been clearly understood by a person in authority of appropriate standing who goes on to give an unequivocal assurance that no prosecution will ensue, there is a strong ethical case for allowing a defence of reasonable or excusable mistake of law.

---

[87] [1950] 1 KB 544 (DC).

[88] [1975] QB 678 (CA).

[89] The facts of *Arrowsmith* were not conducive to recognition of an excusable mistake of law defence arising from official advice. D had received a letter from the Director of Public Prosecutions (whose consent was required) indicating that he would not be consenting to a prosecution in respect of earlier distributions of the pamphlet, a weak basis from which to infer that the DPP took D's conduct to be lawful. The Court of Appeal gave no indication of what the position would have been on stronger facts.

An argument in favour of the unyielding stance in *Arrowsmith* is that advice, even advice reasonably relied upon, should not pre-empt the Court's right, and duty, to determine the law. Not infrequently, persons will receive legal advice to the effect, say, that premises which they own meet requirements of the Health and Safety at Work Act 1974 or that their factory emissions comply with environmental legislation. It may well be in the public interest that such advice should be judicially scrutinised and appropriate standards imposed.

Even so, there remains room for an appropriate procedural defence. An important distinction should be drawn between advice about the law and official assurances that *particular conduct* will not be prosecuted. As Ashworth has argued, in the latter case something akin to estoppel should be seen to arise where the assurance has been given by an official of sufficient authority and has been relied upon by the person subsequently prosecuted.[90] The distinction is best observed, perhaps, not by a defence of reasonable mistake of law but by reference to notions of due process and fair trial. In *R. v. Croydon Justices, ex parte Dean*,[91] it was found to be an abuse of process to instigate criminal proceedings against a person who had agreed to give evidence in return for an assurance that he would not be prosecuted. The same reasoning would apply to a person assured that her planned conduct conforms with law, should the assurance be given by an official of appropriate standing.[92] Any trial which would constitute an abuse of process is, further, likely to contravene Article 6 of the ECHR, which secures the defendant's right to a fair trial.

(a) A right to receive guidance in ECHR-protected activities: and a right to rely on guidance received generally?

The argument that an assurance, by an appropriate public official, that conduct will not be prosecuted should preclude a subsequent prosecution for an offence which is based on that conduct is boosted by the decision of the House of Lords in *Purdy*.[93] This was not a case where a relevant official had given an assurance to D that he would not be prosecuted. The applicants were seeking information from the Director of Prosecutions concerning the circumstances in which the Director would be likely to authorise a prosecution should D assist V's suicide by acts done in England enabling V to travel to a country where suicide was lawful.[94] There was public knowledge of over 150 previous cases of facilitating travel abroad for the purpose of suicide and none of these cases had resulted in a prosecution. The Director's legal and policy analysis of such cases was not known; all that he had said

---

[90] "Testing Fidelity to Legal Values: Official Involvement and Criminal Justice" in Shute and Simester (eds.), *Criminal Law Theory: Doctrines of the General Part* (2002) 299. Jerome Hall has objected to providing a mistake of law defence in such circumstances, on the grounds that it would give the advice greater legal potency than the view of the law taken by the court and thus contravene the principle of legality: *General Principles of Criminal Law* (2nd ed., 1960) 380–3. But such a defence would operate *in personam*. The law, in terms of its general application, would be the law as determined by the Court. The defence would merely recognise that it would be unfair to convict D *on this particular occasion* and could no more subvert the definition and interpretation of law than would, say, allowing duress to be raised in response to a charge of theft.

[91] [1993] Crim LR 758.

[92] One argument in favour of treating these cases as a matter of abuse of process is that it underscores the fact that these cases involve dimensions not merely of personal injustice but also of due process and institutional propriety. A disadvantage is the discretionary nature of the abuse of process jurisdiction.

[93] [2009] UKHL 45.

[94] Under s. 2(4) of the Suicide Act 1961, the Director must give consent for any prosecution brought for assisting suicide contrary to s. 1(2).

officially was that it should not be assumed that assistance of the kind D had in mind would not be prosecuted.

The House of Lords ruled unanimously that the state of uncertainty regarding any possible prosecution engaged the right of D and V to a protected private life as guaranteed by Article 8(1) of the ECHR. If the State is to interfere with the right to private life then, among other things, it must do so in "accordance with the law", as is required by Article 8(2). In giving the leading opinion of the Appellate Committee, Lord Rodger held that in the context of Article 8 (2) the term "law" embraced the decision-making of the Director of Public Prosecutions relating to his consent to prosecutions for the offence of assisting suicide.[95] Lord Rodger concluded that the Director's decision-making concerning assisted suicide lacked the foreseeability and accessibility that the European Convention requires. To remedy those deficiencies, the Director was obliged to draft and publicly disseminate a sufficiently informative policy document regarding the giving of his consent to prosecutions for assisting suicide.[96]

To be sure, *Purdy* is a very particular and poignant case, but it is not devoid of significance for our discussion. By no means will every case where there is uncertainty about future prosecution engage Article 8. However, Lord Rodger's analysis of the requirements of legality in the context of the ECHR has clear relevance for Article 7. As we have seen (and will consider further below),[97] this Article, as interpreted, goes further than proscribing retroactive penal law. The criminal law must achieve minimum standards of clarity and consistency, must satisfy what is termed a "quality of law" test. It is clear from *Purdy* that the DPP would act in breach of Article 8 in the very unlikely future event of consenting to a prosecution for assisting suicide in circumstances where his published policy indicated that no prosecution would be brought. Yet it should also follow that the Director would breach Article 7. That conclusion should also hold for any case where a prosecutor, acting within the terms of his office, has given an assurance that a prosecution will not be brought, whether that assurance is conveyed in a public policy document or by way of a verifiable undertaking to a specific individual, and whether or not there was an ECHR-based right to receive such guidance.

When reflecting on the general import of *Purdy*, one matter must be kept in mind. All members of the Appellate Committee considered it likely that the assistance D contemplated giving V would breach the letter of the law, either as an offence of assisting suicide (Lord Hope; Lord Neuberger; Baroness Hale) or for complicity in murder (Lord Phillips; Lord Brown).[98] Remarkably, however, they held that D and V had a *legal* right to a sufficiency of information about the likelihood of D's prosecution. Our major concern in this section has been with persons confronted with legal uncertainty who, following official advice or assurances, reasonably assumed that their acts were in compliance with the substantive law. They were thus not merely entitled to assurance and clarification: they received

---

[95] [2009] UKHL 45, para. 44.

[96] *Ibid.*, paras. 54–9.

[97] For the earlier discussion, see § 2.3.

[98] For a convincing argument that the assistance that D contemplated giving V would not have founded a charge of complicity in murder, see Hirst, "Assisted Suicide after Purdy: The Unresolved Issue" [2009] *Crim LR* 870.

it. From the perspective of due process values, persons in that class have an even more compelling entitlement not to be embarrassed by a subsequent prosecution.

(iii) Ignorance of law and Article 7 of the ECHR

As well as affecting prosecution decisions, Article 7-type arguments may also become in point during the trial itself. Consider the facts of *Lim Chin Aik*,[99] where D was prosecuted for being an unregistered alien present in Singapore. A registration requirement had been imposed on aliens present in Singapore by an unpublished ordinance which had not been notified to persons affected by its terms. The Privy Council construed the offence as requiring mens rea and advised that D lacked mens rea as he was unaware of any duty to register.

In its own terms, the decision is entirely satisfactory. Yet by characterising the matter as one of mens rea, the broader question of when ignorance of law may excuse is not addressed. Neither is the tension with earlier authority such as *Bailey*.[100] Broader considerations may nowadays be encouraged by Article 7 of the ECHR, which proscribes retroactive penal law. Of course, the mischief at work in cases such as *Lim Chin Aik* and *Bailey* is not, strictly, retroactivity: the laws under which the respective defendants were prosecuted existed at the time of their conduct. Yet from the perspective of fairness to the defendant, no distinction can be drawn between retroactive law and law which cannot be known to the defendant at the time of her conduct.[101] Article 7 protection should be extended to such cases.

It is doubtful if Article 7 protection will be extended to laws that may not be widely known by the public yet are passed directly by Parliament (rather than regulation by statutory instrument) and are published and accessible online. But as Ashworth, in a valuable article,[102] observes, such is the volume of recent criminal law that the substance of serious criminal offences in core areas of the criminal law, such as sexual offences, may be completely unknown to those who breach their terms. He instances *Thomas*,[103] where D contravened section 25 of the Sexual Offences Act 2003 (sex with a family member) by having sexual intercourse with V, aged 17, who had been fostered by D and his wife. Fostering had ended two years before the intercourse, when V left D's care to live in other accommodation. Had V been 18 years of age there would have been no offence. It was accepted that D was wholly unaware that his conduct was criminal, yet he was sentenced to imprisonment for four years, reduced on appeal to two years in the light of unawareness that he was committing an offence.

Ashworth argues strongly that English law should provide a defence of excusable ignorance of criminal law in cases such *Thomas*. He accepts that adult citizens are under a duty to obtain a reasonable knowledge of the criminal law, but insists that the duty should be pitched at a reasonable level of expectation. He argues for far more proactivity from the government in disseminating knowledge of the criminal law. The moral sentiment behind

---

[99] [1963] AC 160. See too *Chambers* [2008] EWCA Crim 2467.

[100] (1800) Russ and Ry 1, 168 ER 651 (CCR).

[101] See above, §§ 2.2–3.

[102] "Ignorance of the Criminal Law, and Duties to Avoid it" (2011) 74 *MLR* 1; see further Ashworth, *Positive Obligations in Criminal Law* (2013) chap. 3.

[103] [2006] 1 Cr App R (S) 602.

Ashworth's proposals is powerful,[104] but the detail of any such new defence is likely to be difficult to resolve.[105] Even with will and commitment, there will be limits to the state's capacity to inculcate knowledge of the criminal law. Obedience to the strictures imposed upon conduct is highly dependent on cultural norms and values rather than the letter of the law, even for serious offences. Consider section 25 of the Sexual offences Act 2003: the idea informing the variant of the offence at issue in *Thomas* appears to be that a sexual relationship between a carer and a sometime-cared-for child is not lawful until the child has reached 18. Is that restriction aligned with reasonable expectations? Such questions may be very difficult to adjudicate.

§ 18.3 Intoxication

The voluntary consumption of alcohol is closely associated with the subsequent commission of crimes—particularly crimes of violence and vandalism.[106] Intoxication, even involuntary intoxication,[107] will never provide a defence in its own terms. It is never enough to claim, however convincingly, that the offending behaviour in issue would not have occurred but for one's intoxicated condition. The adage "a drunken intent is still an intent"[108] reflects an unyielding resistance to the proposition that an intoxicated condition of itself gives rise to any form of exculpation. Indeed, for many hundreds of years, the fact of intoxication was regarded as something which aggravated rather than mitigated the commission of a crime.[109] Although that is no longer the case, there remains an understandable reluctance to allow voluntary intoxication to afford any form of advantage to D. In *Dowds*,[110] there was a refusal to accept that voluntary intoxication even to an extreme degree could be a "recognized medical condition" for the purposes of section 2 of the Homicide Act 1957.[111] Likewise in *Asmelash*,[112] self-induced intoxication was not to be included in "the circumstances

---

[104] Such a defence is available in France. Article 122-3 of the Code pénal provides: "N'est pas pénalement responsable la personne qui justifie avoir cru, par une erreur sur le droit qu'elle n'était pas en mesure d'éviter, pouvoir légitimement accomplir l'acte."

[105] For arguments against a mistake of law defence see Azmat, "What Mistake of Law Just Might Be: Legal Moralism, Liberal Positivism, and the Mistake of Law Doctrine" (2015) 18 *New Criminal LR* 369. Azmat's chief concern is that a mistake of law defence will provide a "safe harbour" for those who should have made a greater effort to ascertain the applicable law, thereby undermining the duty to know the law and creating inefficiencies by shifting the burden of rebuttal onto prosecutors and courts.

[106] "Alcohol is a cortical depressant. Since it is the higher and most recently evolved brain functions which are first affected by depressants, the immediate effect of a dose of alcohol is to inhibit those cerebral functions which are associated with orderly community behaviour and with finer critical judgments": Mason, *Forensic Medicine for Lawyers* (3rd ed., 1995) 351. Numerous studies have indicated that many violent offenders have taken significant amounts of drink or drugs at the time of the offence. There is, of course, no straightforward causal link: personal, gender, and cultural factors will strongly influence how intoxicated persons behave. See further Hodge, "Alcohol and Violence" in Taylor (ed.), *Violence in Society* (1993) 127; Dingwall, *Alcohol and Crime* (2005).

[107] Below, § 18.3(v).

[108] *Sheehan* [1975] 2 All ER 960, 963 (CA); *Kingston* [1995] 2 AC 355.

[109] Barlow, "Drug Intoxication and the Principle of *Capacitas Rationalis*" (1984) 100 *LQR* 639.

[110] [2012] EWCA Crim 281.

[111] Section 2 allows the plea of diminished responsibility to a charge of murder, which if successful reduces the offence to manslaughter. See further below, § 19.2(ii)(b).

[112] [2013] EWCA Crim 157.

of D" when evaluating D's response to V's conduct for the purposes of the loss of control defence.[113]

Intoxication may, however, form the evidential basis for claims of lack of mens rea. D may assert that because of his drunken condition he did not intend to kill or seriously hurt V when he attacked him and, accordingly, he should not be found guilty of murder. Additionally, D may argue that because of confusion induced by his condition, he thought that V was about to attack him and, on that basis, be allowed a defence of mistake of fact. The extent and frequency of such claims expand if questions relating to proof of mens rea and pleas of mistake are resolved by way of a subjective test. Section 8 of the Criminal Justice Act 1967, it will be recalled,[114] requires proof of what D intended or foresaw to be established by reference to what D *himself* intended or foresaw. The fact that a particular result was a natural and probable result of D's conduct is merely evidence that D *may* have intended or foreseen that result; it will not establish *ipso facto* that he did have intent or foresight. Recall too the decisions in *Gladstone Williams* and *Beckford*:[115] mistaken beliefs in the need for defensive or preventive force are to be judged on the basis of what D himself believed and are not subject to any requirement of reasonableness.

Consequently, if intoxicated wrongdoers were tried on the basis of the subjective principles outlined above, those principles might pave the way for many acquittals. For instance, a claim that D thought she was under attack might gain a vestige of credibility only because of D's assertion that her intoxicated state led to confusion and misperception.

Unsurprisingly, the courts have proved reluctant to give full rein to a subjective approach when dealing with pleas supported evidentially by a state of voluntary intoxication. What has emerged is an uneasy compromise between the standard account of mens rea and the requirements of deterrence and social protection. Using the language that has evolved in this area of law, for offences which are designated crimes of *specific intent*, the normal principles of mens rea obtain. A state of intoxication may be adduced as evidence in order to rebut an inference of intent that otherwise would be drawn. If D may have been too drunk to intend the outcome, he will be acquitted of the offence. By contrast, for offences of *basic intent*, evidence of intoxication will not negate an inference of basic intent. Indeed, far from rebutting such an inference, on one account of the law, the state of intoxication will *constitute* the culpability required for the crime.[116]

These matters will be addressed in more detail below. First, however, a brief discussion of what constitutes a state of "intoxication" may be helpful. No definition of intoxication exists in the case law. There is no statement concerning what level of disinhibition or confusion induced by drink or drugs is sufficient for legal purposes. For cases of specific intent, no such definition is required. The question will be whether the impact of any drink or drugs taken by D makes it reasonably possible that he did not form the intent the offence requires. The same should apply for crimes of basic intent were it the law that evidence of the voluntary consumption of drink or drugs is simply disregarded when determining whether a basic intent has been proved. However, it may be that such evidence, far from

---

[113] Coroners and Justice Act 2009, s. 54 (partial defence to murder).
[114] Above, § 5.1(ix).
[115] Above, § 18.1(iii).
[116] See further Simester, "Intoxication is Never a Defence" [2009] *Crim LR* 3.

being disregarded, provides the very culpability required for the crime.[117] If that be so, then some minimum threshold of intoxication should be required; for a crime of basic intent, the prosecution should not be relieved from its burden of proof by establishing that D had taken *some* quantity of drink or drugs prior to the conduct alleged.[118] The matter is obscure and will be revisited when analysing the leading case of *Majewski*.[119]

In deeming when an issue of intoxication arises, no distinction is drawn between alcohol and drugs such as heroin, cocaine, cannabis, and LSD.[120] Drugs such as Librium and Valium, and compounds such as insulin, when taken for therapeutic reasons, are in different case. If drugs are taken to treat the symptoms of some underlying condition of D, the normal principles of mens rea will apply and the special rules relating to voluntary intoxication will not be relevant.[121]

(i) Voluntary intoxication and crimes of specific intent

For crimes of specific intent, the position is straightforward. In *Beard*,[122] the House of Lords ruled that on a charge of murder (a crime of specific intent), evidence of D's drunkenness *was* relevant to whether D had intended to kill or seriously hurt V. Lord Birkenhead's leading judgment caused some confusion for later courts by stating that evidence of drunkenness would be relevant in crimes of specific intent if it "showed that [D] was *incapable* of forming a specific intent".[123] In *Sheehan*,[124] however, the Court of Appeal ruled that language of Lord Birkenhead should be read in the light of the decision in *Woolmington*[125] regarding the burden of proof in criminal cases. Accordingly, the question in specific intent cases is not whether D was capable of forming the required specific intent but *whether D in fact formed the intent*. Evidence of intoxication may throw a reasonable doubt on the prosecution's case just like any other evidence germane to the issue of intent.

Accordingly, *if* a crime is a crime of specific intent, the position is clear. What is less clear is *when* a crime is one of specific rather than basic intent. The leading case on this issue is the House of Lords decision in *Majewski*.[126]

Lord Elwyn-Jones, giving the judgment of the House, considered that a crime of specific intent was a crime where the mens rea extends beyond the actus reus[127]—i.e. crimes of *ulterior* intent.[128] The idea is certainly intelligible. Burglary, for instance, must be considered a crime of specific intent because all that is required by way of an actus reus is an entry as a trespasser into a building. The offence is complete on entry if it can be proved that D

---

[117] *Ibid.*

[118] There is an *obiter* remark in *Stubbs* (1989) 88 Cr App R 53, 54 that the intoxication needed to be "very extreme".

[119] [1977] AC 443 (HL).

[120] *Lipman* [1970] 1 QB 152 (CA).

[121] See below, § 18.3(iv).

[122] [1920] AC 479. See Handler, "Intoxication and Criminal Responsibility in England, 1819–1920" (2013) 33 *OJLS* 243.

[123] *Ibid.*, 501–2 (emphasis added).

[124] [1975] 2 All ER 960.

[125] [1935] AC 462; above, § 3.2.

[126] [1977] AC 443.

[127] *Ibid.*, 471, citing Lord Simon's speech in *Morgan* [1976] AC 182, 216.

[128] See above, § 5.1(vii).

intended to steal.[129] Moreover, according to the Court of Appeal in *Heard*,[130] a crime is a crime of specific intent even if recklessness is sufficient for an element going beyond the actus reus. The court used as an example the intentional or reckless causing of criminal damage being reckless as to whether life was endangered.[131] As the offence does not require that life actually be endangered but merely an act of criminal damage which is believed to carry that risk, on the analysis in *Heard* the crime is one of specific intent,[132] endorsing the view of Lord Edmund Davies in *Caldwell*.[133] At least, that is the position for now.[134]

Despite the intelligibility of this definition, it nevertheless fails to explain the case law. It is well established that murder is a crime of specific intent.[135] Yet in murder, the mens rea need not extend to the entirety of the actus reus, let alone beyond it, because an intent to cause grievous bodily harm will suffice.[136] Further, on Lord Elwyn-Jones's definition the same crime could be of either specific intent or basic intent, depending on how it is committed. Section 18 of the OAPA 1861 penalises wounding with intent to cause grievous bodily harm and, additionally, causing grievous bodily harm with intent to cause grievous bodily harm. Where the actus reus of the offence takes the form of a wound insufficiently serious to constitute grievous bodily harm, the intent to be provided is a specific intent of the form indicated by Lord Elwyn-Jones. But where the actus reus has taken the form of grievous bodily harm, the intent to be proved need only correspond to the actus reus and does not go beyond it. It is no longer a specific intent crime in his Lordship's terms. Yet it is accepted that section 18 is a crime of specific intent whatever form its takes.[137]

Alternatively, Lord Simon, giving judgment in *Majewski*, considered that an offence of specific intent was a crime where the mens rea required proof of a "purposive element",[138] a view also endorsed in *Heard*.[139] There the court seemingly took the view that the whole territory of specific intent could be mapped by reference to crimes of ulterior intent, as just discussed, and crimes requiring proof of intent in the sense of purpose. But this will not do either. Murder may be committed in a fashion which fits neither category because the mental element for this offence can be established without proof of purpose: foresight of virtual certainty suffices. Furthermore, where an offence contrary to section 18 of the OAPA 1861 takes the form of causing grievous bodily harm with intent to do grievous bodily harm, foresight of the virtual certainty of causing harm of that gravity suffices.[140] But there is no doubt that an offence under section 18 is always a crime of specific intent.

In the light of this confusion, the only safe course is to follow relevant precedents. On that basis, a list of established specific intent crimes can be drawn up. Murder, wounding

---

[129] Theft Act 1968, s. 9; above, § 14.3.

[130] [2007] EWCA Crim 125; above, § 12.4.

[131] Criminal Damage Act 1971, s. 1(2)(b).

[132] [2007] EWCA Crim 125, para. 31.

[133] [1982] AC 341.

[134] In *Coley* [2013] EWCA Crim 223, para. 57, the Court acknowledged *Heard* but noted that the decision was *obiter* on this point and suggested that the matter may need to be revisited on a future occasion.

[135] *Beard* [1920] AC 479; *Gallagher* [1963] AC 349; *Sheehan* [1975] 2 All ER 960.

[136] Above, § 10.3(i)(a).

[137] *Bratty v. A-G for Northern Ireland* [1973] AC 386; *Pordage* [1975] Crim LR 575; *Davies* [1991] Crim LR 469.

[138] [1977] AC 443.

[139] [2007] EWCA Crim 125, para. 31.

[140] Above, § 11.6(ii).

or causing grievous bodily harm with intent to cause grievous bodily harm, theft,[141] burglary,[142] and handling stolen goods[143] are crimes of specific intent. Most other crimes requiring proof of mens rea are crimes of basic intent. To the extent that this area of law can be explained in conceptual terms, we offer the following generalisation: crimes designated crimes of specific intent are crimes where the mens rea is exclusively (as in murder) or predominantly (as in burglary) expressed in terms of intent. Where intent is the exclusive or predominant form of culpability, on the basis of precedent we can say that the offence is a crime of specific intent even if the intent is not ulterior or purposive, despite the *dicta* in *Majewski* and *Heard* which would lead one to suppose that for an intent to be a specific intent it must be of the ulterior or purposive kind. The fact that one element of an offence requires intent will not of itself make for a crime of specific intent (unless the intent is an ulterior or purposive intent; in which case the offence will be a crime of specific intent at least for that element) if predominantly the offence does not require proof of intent.

In *Heard*,[144] the court considered the offence of sexual assault.[145] To prove the offence, an intentional touching (*inter alia*) is required, but intention is not required for the other elements of the offence. As the Court of Appeal considered the intent for the touching need not be purposive, the offence was concluded to be a crime of basic intent. The difficulty with this analysis is, as noted previously, that the intent for murder need not be of the purposive kind; so clearly the analysis in *Heard* is not universally applicable. In the light of precedent, particularly the House of Lords decision in *Majewski*,[146] all we can say is that, where an intent is of the purposive or ulterior kind, the intent is a specific intent; where the intent is of a non-purposive or non-ulterior kind, it may or may not be a basic intent. Where recklessness, or something lesser than intent or recklessness, suffices as the predominant form of culpability for the offence, it is a crime of basic intent.

Despite these complexities, the basic intent/specific intent divide has worked tolerably well in practice. In the area of violent offences where intoxication is frequently a background factor, it is well established that assault, battery, assault occasioning bodily harm, malicious wounding or inflicting grievous bodily harm, and involuntary manslaughter are crimes of basic intent, allowing convictions for these offences despite D's intoxicated condition. By contrast, murder and wounding or causing grievous bodily harm with intent are specific intent offences, where D may seek to deflect an inference of intent by reference to his intoxicated condition. Likewise, generalising from the decision in *Heard*,[147] we can say that as well as sexual assault (the offence at issue in the case), rape, assault by penetration, and causing a person to engage in sexual activity are all crimes of basic intent, since the structure of those offences sufficiently parallels sexual assault to fall within the analysis in *Heard*.[148]

That said, the structure is rickety. Crimes divide into the camps of specific intent or basic intent but the logic of the analysis in *Heard* should lead to the conclusion that one element

---

[141] *Ruse v. Read* [1949] 1 KB 377 (DC).
[142] *Durante* [1972] 1 WLR 1612 (CA).
[143] *Ibid*.
[144] [2007] EWCA Crim 125.
[145] Contrary to s. 3 of the Sexual Offences Act 2003; above, § 12.8.
[146] [1977] AC 443.
[147] [2007] EWCA Crim 125.
[148] §§ 12.1–4.

of an offence may be a specific intent element and another element a basic intent element with the relevance of intoxication dependent upon which element is in question. Indeed, it seems that the same element may be one of basic intent or specific intent according to the facts of the case. In the crime of sexual assault whether the assault is "sexual" depends on whether it is objectively sexual or, where the act is equivocal, by reference to the purpose of the actor.[149] Where the act alleged is objectively sexual, evidence of drunkenness will not be relevant to deflect any inference that would otherwise be made that the touching was intentional. If the act is equivocal, as in *Court*,[150] in principle evidence of intoxication should be relevant to the question whether D's purpose was sexual. But whether such an approach will be taken by the courts is conjectural. It may be that a court will take a coarse-grained approach and rule that, because sexual assault has been designated a crime of basic intent, evidence of intoxication is not to be used to deflect any finding of mens rea in respect of *any* element of the offence.

Equally conjectural is the position where the prosecution seeks to prove that an offence able to be committed intentionally or recklessly was, in fact, committed intentionally. Consider the offence of causing criminal damage with intent or recklessness.[151] A prosecutor may decide to charge the offence exclusively in terms of intent in order to obtain a jury finding that the damage was done intentionally. In those circumstances, is a crime (otherwise) of basic intent to be treated as a crime of specific intent? The uncertainty that exists on these issues indicates the need for legislative intervention in this area.

(ii) Voluntary intoxication and crimes of basic intent [152]

In *Majewski*,[153] D was charged with assault, an offence that can be committed recklessly or intentionally and which is therefore a crime of basic intent. D had consumed large quantities of drink and drugs. He attacked V in circumstances which, from an external perspective, indicated a deliberate assault. He claimed neither to have intended nor foreseen that he would inflict any force upon V; at the time of the incident he claimed he was "a drunken automaton", not conscious of what he was doing. It was argued for D that section 8 of the Criminal Justice Act 1967 requires that proof of D's intention or foresight must be established by reference "to all the evidence", including evidence of his intoxicated condition.

Lord Elwyn-Jones, for a unanimous House of Lords, rejected this argument. He noted that a distinction between specific intent crimes and basic intent crimes had been created long before the enactment of section 8. His Lordship observed that there was a longstanding principle of substantive law that evidence of intoxication was relevant only where the offence charged was one of specific intent. Accordingly, the statutory phrase "by reference to all the evidence" should be read as a reference to "all the *relevant* evidence".[154]

---

[149] Sexual Offences Act 2003, s. 78.

[150] [1989] 1 AC 28. See the discussion above, § 12.5.

[151] Criminal Damage Act 1971, s. 1.

[152] Ward, "Making Sense of Self-induced Intoxication" [1986] *CLJ* 247; Smith, "Intoxication and the Mental Element in Crime" in Wallington and Merkin (eds.), Essays in Memory of Professor F.H. Lawson (1986) 119; Gardner, "The Importance of Majewski" (1994) 14 *OJLS* 279; Williams, "Voluntary Intoxication—A Lost Cause?" (2013) 129 *LQR* 264.

[153] [1977] AC 443.

[154] *Ibid.*, 476.

The evidence of intoxication was irrelevant and, consequently, the conviction for assault could be confirmed.

That was enough to decide the case, and if matters had rested there the position for basic intent offences would have been relatively straightforward. In a case of a seemingly deliberate assault like *Majewski*,[155] a defendant would not be permitted to assert a lack of mens rea on the basis of intoxication. In formal terms, the prosecution would still have to establish the intention or recklessness that a conviction for assault requires; but that would typically be straightforward if, as on the facts of *Majewski*, the only conceivable explanation accounting for an absence of mens rea was the intoxicated condition of the defendant. That said, if D were a drunken automaton, his seemingly intentional assault would have been no such thing. In that sense, the finding of intention or recklessness on which a conviction for assault must necessarily rest is a fiction. By disregarding the evidence of intoxication we do not turn automatic conduct into purposeful conduct unless we presuppose an event that did not occur.[156]

At one point in his judgment, Lord Elwyn-Jones presents the issue simply as a matter of disregarding evidence of intoxication, but later his explanation for affirming the conviction changes. The condition of intoxication is taken to *constitute* the culpability required for the offence:[157]

> "If a man of his own volition takes a substance which causes him to cast off the restraints of reason and conscience, no wrong is done to him by holding him answerable criminally for any injury he may do while in that condition. His course of conduct in reducing himself by drugs and drink to that condition in my view supplies the evidence of mens rea, of guilty mind certainly sufficient for crimes of basic intent. It is a reckless course of conduct and recklessness is enough to constitute the necessary mens rea in assault cases."

It will readily be appreciated that the recklessness involved is not the recklessness that would otherwise be required to establish assault. There is no need to prove that D foresaw any threat of force inflicted on V. The essence of this form of recklessness appears to be that D, by taking drugs or alcohol, has "cast off the constraints of reason and conscience". On one interpretation, this could mean that whenever the prosecution can establish that D would not have perpetrated the actus reus of a basic intent offence but for the taking of drink or drugs, it is relieved from any obligation to establish the mens rea that it would otherwise have to prove. The inculpatory sweep of such a principle could be very broad. To date, the outer limits of this form of "recklessness" have not been explored in the case law. The reported cases deal with defendants significantly affected by the substances taken. In such cases, the practical difference between merely excluding evidence of intoxication when determining D's mens rea and treating intoxication as a form of culpability is small, even indiscernible. Clearly, the defence cannot raise intoxication to throw doubt on the presence of intent or recklessness when the crime charged is a crime of basic intent. It remains possible, however, that under current law the prosecution can adduce evidence of

---

[155] D had quarrelled with V, had verbally indicated that he would hit V and, indeed, went on to hit him.
[156] See further Simester, "Intoxication is Never a Defence" [2009] *Crim LR* 3, 5–7.
[157] [1977] AC 443, 474–5.

intoxication, which, for Lord Elwyn-Jones, of itself establishes the culpability for crimes of basic intent.[158]

(iii) Mistake, accident, and intoxication

(a) Basic intent offences

Majewski was not a case that involved any form of mistake. D claimed that his mind was blank, not that he had formed any false view of his circumstances induced by drink and drugs. Accordingly, it would have been possible to read *Majewski* as inapplicable to mistake cases, an approach adopted by Mustill J (as he then was) in *Jaggard* v. *Dickinson*.[159] D had caused damage to a house in order to gain entry. In her intoxicated state she entered a house believing it to be the house of a friend, who would have consented to her unusual method of gaining access. Section 5(2) of the Criminal Damage Act 1971 provides a defence to a charge of criminal damage if D "believes" the owner of the property would have consented to her actions. In allowing her appeal, Mustill J denied that quashing her conviction was to allow voluntary intoxication to preclude mens rea in crime of basic intent. Her intoxication merely lent credence to her belief. Her conviction was quashed because she *believed* she had the owner's consent and not because she was drunk. As such, she fell within the literal terms of the section 5(2) defence.

Jaggard is in line with the standard approach to the exculpatory effect of mistakes taken in modern English criminal law. As we saw in § 18.1(iii), typically a genuine even if unreasonable mistake will exempt the defendant should it negate a definitional element of the offence or generate a belief that the elements of a recognised defence are present. Drunken mistakes could be regarded as within the class of unreasonable mistakes. However, Mustill J's approach has not been generally accepted.[160] Working against it has been a concern over the propensity of intoxicated persons to make mistakes leading to violent or forceful conduct. This has led the appellate courts to treat cases of intoxicated mistakes as being within the mischief addressed by the House of Lords in *Majewski*. Doing so accords with the view, expressed by Lord Elwyn-Jones in that case, that intoxication, in the context of basic intent offences, is a form of culpability.

How far does the exclusion extend? The matter is undecided. Potentially, for basic intent offences, any mistake made by D should be disregarded if it is established that D was intoxicated at the material time. But that would go too far. Rather, the mistake should be disregarded if the prosecution can establish that, but for D's intoxicated condition, his mistake would not have been made. That is the position under section 6(5) of the Public

---

[158] It is not known whether a prosecution has taken this course at trial. Certainly the *dicta* of Lord Elwyn-Jones suggests that it can. See also Lord Simon's judgment, at 478: "There is no juristic reason why mental incapacity (short of *M'Naghten* insanity), brought about by self-induced intoxication, to realise what one is doing or its probable consequences should not be such a state of mind stigmatised as wrongful by the criminal law; and there is every practical reason why it should be". But contrast Lord Salmon who emphasised, appositely, that the House was deciding whether intoxication could be relied upon by way of *defence*.

[159] [1981] QB 527 (DC).

[160] See the authorities discussed in § 18.3(iii)(b) below, which disallow mistaken beliefs as to defences; also *Woods* (1982) 74 Cr App R 312 (CA) and *Fotheringham* (1988) 88 Cr App R 206 (CA), which disfavour intoxicated beliefs in consent as valid defences. *Jaggard* is thus anomalous.

Order Act 1986 for offences under that Act. The principle should be regarded as of general application.[161]

What should be the case for accidents? What if D accidentally bumps into V when intoxicated? If the accident would have occurred in any event—V rushed round a blind corner—a battery should not be attributed to D merely because he was intoxicated. Thus a key question for the court in any basic intent case is whether the intoxication made a difference, in as much as D would have foreseen the relevant risk if sober.[162] But what if the intoxication *was* part of the explanation, as in *Brady*,[163] where D climbed a balcony above a dance floor, stood on the balcony rail, and fell onto a dancer below, causing permanent disabling injury? Neither the climb nor the fall would have occurred but for D's intoxication. Because of the way the matter was argued at trial, the Court of Appeal was limited to considering whether D's fall could be regarded as a malicious act for the purposes of maliciously inflicting grievous bodily harm within section 20 of the OAPA 1861. It was ruled that the fall did not come within the ruling in *Majewski*:[164] it was an accident, not an attack. The outcome might have been different had the court been able to consider the precursor to the fall, the non-accidental climb, which was considered, entirely reasonably, to be a cause of D's injury. Then the issue would have been whether D would have foreseen the risk of falling and injuring someone had he made the climb sober. If that would have been the case, he would be liable for maliciously inflicting grievous bodily harm.

That accidents, even if attributable to a state of intoxication, fall outside the scope of *Majewski* receives strong if *obiter* support from *Heard*,[165] where, in considered remarks, the view was taken that any accidental touching would not be treated as a deliberate touching even if D would not have made the contact with V but for his inebriated state. Even in such circumstances, "the mind must go with the body" if the touching is to be regarded as deliberate.[166] Intriguingly, the Court of Appeal felt that the element of deliberateness would be lacking in a case such as *Lipman*,[167] where D, in an LSD-induced trance, took himself to be grappling with a snake whereas in reality he was strangling V. But the killing in *Lipman* was not an accident; it was the product of conduct actively performed by D, albeit in a state of hallucination. There is no reason to doubt that the verdict of manslaughter reached in that case would not be repeated on similar facts.

(b) Specific intent offences

In respect of specific intent crimes, one might confidently expect that intoxication would be treated as evidence relevant to any exculpatory claim based on a mistake. So far as any mistake concerns the definitional elements of such an offence, that is certainly the position. Unfortunately, however, in two cases, *O'Grady*[168] and *O'Connor*,[169] the Court of Appeal has

---

[161] As the Law Commission has recommended. A provision to apply this principle to non-fatal offences against the person is made in the Home Office Bill: see further below, § 18.3(viii).

[162] *Richardson and Irwin* [1999] 1 Cr App R 392; *Aitken, Bennett and Barson* [1992] 1 WLR 1066.

[163] [2006] EWCA Crim 2413.

[164] [1977] AC 443.

[165] [2007] EWCA Crim 125.

[166] *Ibid.*, para. 17.

[167] (1969) 55 Cr App R 600.

[168] [1987] QB 995; see the note by Milgate at [1987] *CLJ* 381.

[169] [1991] Crim LR 135.

taken the view that mistakes which relate to defences are to be disregarded if the mistakes are induced by D's intoxicated state even where the crime is one of specific intent. In *O'Grady*, D's conviction for manslaughter was confirmed on the basis that his drunken belief that he was being attacked by V would not found a defence of mistake. As manslaughter is a crime of basic intent, the ruling is unexceptionable. However, the court, in considered *dicta*, stated that his drunken belief would be disregarded even on a charge of murder. In *O'Connor*, this view was taken to be binding even though the remarks made about murder in *O'Grady* were clearly *obiter*. *O'Connor* involved an appeal against murder: in the event, the appeal succeeded on the ground that evidence of his intoxicated state was relevant to the question whether D intended to kill or cause grievous bodily harm. So, again, remarks about the irrelevance of drunken mistakes relating to elements of defences were *obiter*.

Unfortunately, these *dicta* were approved and applied in *Hatton*,[170] where D was not permitted to raise a drink-induced belief that he was under attack by way of defence to murder. Although this must now be accepted as the state of the law, when D claims a belief that force was necessary in self-defence or to prevent a crime,[171] absurd distinctions arise. Take the facts of *Lipman*.[172] D, under the influence of LSD, thought he was under attack from a snake and in that deluded condition strangled V. He was acquitted of murder (although guilty of manslaughter) on the ground that he lacked an intent to kill or cause serious harm to a human being. If his delusion had taken the form of an attack by a human being, then, according to *O'Grady*, *O'Connor*, and now conclusively *Hatton*, he should have been found guilty of murder. Recall that, in *Gladstone Williams*[173] and *Beckford*,[174] the Court of Appeal and the Privy Council refused to treat mistakes going to defences any differently from mistakes going to definitional elements. That approach is equally in point for intoxicated mistakes when raised on a charge involving a specific intent offence.

(iv) Intoxication arising from drugs taken for therapeutic reasons

In *Bailey*,[175] D, a diabetic, took insulin for his condition, but neglected to follow the dietary regime his doctor prescribed. In *Hardie*,[176] D, upset and agitated, took an excessive quantity of Librium belonging to someone else in an attempt to pacify himself. In the former case, D became hypoglycaemic (a condition regarded as one of automatism) and attacked V. In the latter case, D set fire to V's flat. He claimed that the drugs disorientated him, rendering him incapable of appreciating the destructive nature of his conduct.

In both cases, the Court of Appeal ruled that the trial judges had erred in directing that *Majewski* applied. Instead, the normal principles of mens rea were taken to be the applicable standard.

---

[170] [2005] EWCA Crim 2951. For incisive critical commentary see Spencer, "Drunken Defence" [2006] *CLJ* 267; Dingwall, "Intoxicated Mistakes about the Need for Self-defence" (2007) 70 *MLR* 127.

[171] Section 76(5) of the Criminal Justice and Immigration Act 2008 provides that D cannot rely on any mistaken belief attributable to voluntary intoxication when claiming to have acted in self-defence or the prevention of crime.

[172] [1970] 1 QB 152 (CA).

[173] [1987] 3 All ER 411 (CA). See above, § 18.1(iii).

[174] [1988] AC 130 (PC).

[175] [1983] 2 All ER 503 (CA).

[176] [1984] 3 All ER 848 (CA).

The key to both decisions is a commendable reluctance to subject persons taking drugs for therapeutic benefit to the regime of social protection endorsed by the House of Lords in *Majewski. Bailey*, in particular, is instructive on this point. In *Bailey*, D was not immune from criticism; his hypoglycaemic condition would have been avoided had he followed his doctor's instructions. Yet the court took appropriate and compassionate cognisance of the fact that, for a diabetic, the taking of insulin and the management of its destabilising effects is a lifetime burden. In *Hardie*, there are some distracting *dicta* to the effect that tranquilising drugs such as Librium and Valium differ in their pharmacological properties from alcohol: the former drugs are of "soporific effect" whereas the latter gives rise to "aggression and violence".[177] But this is a false distinction. The physiological properties of tranquillising drugs and alcohol are similar; their effects ensue from depressing the central nervous system. The essential point about *Hardie* is that D was taking the drug to calm his nerves, the reason why the drug is prescribed. Had the very same drugs been consumed "on the street" in order to enjoy their disinhibiting effects, then the *Majewski* regime would surely have been invoked. Of course, alcohol is often taken to "calm the nerves". But it is not a therapeutic drug. Rest assured, alcohol will incur *Majewski* for whatever reason it is consumed.

(v) Involuntary intoxication

Potentially, the largest group of persons who may claim that their intoxication is involuntary are those addicted to alcohol or other intoxicants. In *Tandy*,[178] the exculpatory potential of alcoholism was discussed in the context of the statutory defence of diminished responsibility. The view was taken that alcoholism might reduce culpability, but only if it produced involuntary drinking, a condition where D had no choice when to take her first drink of the day and was unable to refrain from drinking thereafter. If D's dependency on alcohol reached these extremes, it should follow that D should not be treated as voluntarily intoxicated in any context. The restrictions are so stringent that few, if any, alcoholics could satisfy them. Their stringency was remarked upon in *Wood*[179] and in *Stewart*,[180] with a recognition that even alcoholics do not drink incessantly. Yet the barrier remains very high: "an irresistible craving for or compulsion to drink".[181]

An involuntary state of intoxication does not come within the *Majewski* regime.[182] A firm view is taken of what constitutes "involuntary" intoxication. If D is aware that she is taking intoxicating substances any subsequent inebriation will be taken to be voluntary even if a mistake has been made about the strength of the item taken.[183]

There are, however, some settled cases of involuntary intoxication. A medically prescribed drug taken for therapeutic reasons may give rise to involuntary intoxication if

---

[177] *Ibid.*, 853 (Parker LJ).
[178] [1989] 1 All ER 267 (CA).
[179] [2008] EWCA Crim 1305.
[180] [2009] EWCA Crim 593, [2009] Crim LR 807; [2010] EWCA Crim 2159.
[181] [2009] EWCA Crim 593, [2009] Crim LR 807, para. 31; [2010] EWCA Crim 2159, para. 7.
[182] In the case of offences under the Public Order Act 1986, the *Majewski* principles are clearly disapplied where the state of intoxication is not self-induced: s. 6(5).
[183] *Allen* [1988] Crim LR 698 (CA).

no warning is given as to any destabilising properties of the drug. The same applies if D suffers an unpredictable, aberrant reaction to the drug[184] or if, without her knowledge, she is slipped a destabilising drug.[185]

(a) No discrete defence

In *Kingston*,[186] D took himself to be drinking a normal cup of coffee which in fact had been laced with destabilising drugs by a malevolent third party. D, a person with paedophile inclinations, became disinhibited and performed non-penetrative sexual acts on an unconscious (drugged) teenage boy. The House of Lords confirmed his conviction for indecent assault. At trial, it was found that, notwithstanding the disinhibiting effects of the drugs, he intended his sexual actions. Therefore, said their Lordships, he was guilty of the offence. The only concession to the fact that he was involuntarily intoxicated took the form of not presuming mens rea on the basis of *Majewski*. It was irrelevant to proof of mens rea that the fault for D's condition lay with others. The term mens rea was treated as a technical expression denoting nothing more than the mental element specified for the offence in question, a mental element which was present on the facts.[187]

A more expansive view of the exculpatory effect of a state of involuntary intoxication had been taken by the Court of Appeal.[188] They were prepared to allow a defence to any crime for a person involuntarily intoxicated if it were the case that the crime committed by D would not have been perpetrated by him had he not been intoxicated. The breadth of this newly created, and short-lived, defence was alarmingly wide. Nonetheless, there is something to be said for the principle. A person who commits a crime (perhaps one less heinous than intentional killing, intentional causing of serious bodily harm, or non-consensual penetrative sex) arguably should be allowed a defence if a state of involuntary intoxication induced conduct on his part which otherwise would not have occurred and which was not characteristic of him.[189] Be that as it may, however, the House of Lords in *Kingston* took the view that any development along those or other lines was a matter for the legislature and not for the courts. The Law Commission has recommended that the current position should remain; involuntary intoxication may be adduced as evidence to rebut an inference of mens rea or support a claim of mistake for all crimes of mens rea, but should not constitute any form of substantive defence.[190]

(vi) Intoxication and mental condition defences

Suppose that D is intoxicated. Should another mental state supervene, it need not follow that her intoxication should preclude reliance on any defence that may arise from the

---

[184] In principle this should apply to the condition known as "pathological intoxication", where relatively small quantities of alcohol may activate a form of latent epilepsy or other conditions. However, such a phenomenon may be regarded as a form of insanity: Mackay, *Mental Condition Defences in the Criminal Law* (1995) 165–9; and see below, Chapter 19.

[185] Cf. *Kingston* [1995] 2 AC 355, 369ff (HL).

[186] *Ibid.*

[187] *Ibid.*, 366.

[188] [1994] QB 81.

[189] Sullivan, "Making Excuses" in Simester and Smith (eds.), *Harm and Culpability* (1996) 131; Sullivan, "Involuntary Intoxication and Beyond" [1994] *Crim LR* 272; below, § 21.2(i)(b).

[190] Law Com. No.314, *Intoxication and Criminal Liability* (2009) part 4.

subsequent mental condition. In *Stripp*,[191] D, while intoxicated, fell over and sustained concussion. It was held that if the dominant cause of his automatous state was concussion rather than alcohol, he would be able to raise a plea of automatism and would not fall foul of the *Majewski* principles. A similar approach was taken in *Burns*,[192] where the cumulative effects of brain damage, alcohol, and medication rendered D an automaton. He was permitted to defend himself on the basis of automatism because his condition was primarily due to the effects of his medication. By contrast, in *Lipman*,[193] D's state of automatism was attributable to the drug LSD; consequently, the mens rea and the actus reus elements of manslaughter were attributed to him on the basis that he was voluntarily intoxicated at the material time.

D's condition in *Lipman* was far from the slurred speech and unsteady gait long associated with too much alcohol. The LSD produced a trance-like condition with hallucinations. Yet as that condition came about directly from the consumption of a voluntarily taken drug, a plea of non-insane automatism will not be entertained. A similar approach is taken in *Coley*,[194] where D, aged 17, who had spent the day playing video games and smoking strong cannabis, took himself to bed, then got up in the early hours, entered the house next door (to which he had free access), and repeatedly stabbed V. D claimed no recollection of this incident at his trial for attempted murder. The Court of Appeal, confirming D's conviction for this offence, regarded D's condition as one of voluntary intoxication. There was expert evidence to the effect that the cannabis consumption might have caused a "brief psychotic episode";[195] since, however, any such condition was attributable to the drug there was no disease of the mind. Neither would there be any basis for a plea of non-insane automatism, as it is a long-established proposition in law "that a self-induced incapacity will not excuse".[196]

The analysis changes if D's state of mind comes about from the withdrawal symptoms which arise from abstinence from a drug. In *Davis*,[197] Stephen J considered delirium tremens (hallucinosis), a condition arising from the reaction of the brain and nerve receptors to the withdrawal of alcohol, to be a disease of the mind.[198] Likewise in *Harris*,[199] the voices and hallucinations that D heard and saw were withdrawal symptoms following abstinence after a period of heavy drinking. Six days after his last alcoholic drink, the voices instructed him to burn down his house. These symptoms constituted a disease of the mind in the eye of the law. Although a defence of insanity was not available (even if he had wanted it) because he understood the nature and wrongfulness of his actions and therefore was guilty of simple arson, his condition was questionably ruled admissible

---

[191] (1978) 69 Cr App R 318 (CA).
[192] (1973) 58 Cr App R 364 (CA).
[193] [1970] 1 QB 152 (CA).
[194] [2013] EWCA Crim 223.
[195] *Ibid.*, para. 9.
[196] *Ibid.*, para. 19, quoting from the decision of the Court of Appeal in *Quick* [1973] QB 910. Strictly speaking, the possibility of non-insane automatism did not arise in *Coley* because the jury found that D had a specific intent to kill.
[197] (1881) 14 Cox CC 563.
[198] A conclusion endorsed by Lord Birkenhead in *Beard* [1920] AC 479.
[199] [2013] EWCA Crim 223.

to throw doubt on whether he possessed the ulterior mens rea required to be guilty of aggravated arson.[200]

(vii) Intoxication, negligence, and strict liability

As we have seen, intoxication may preclude or, in cases of basic intent, effectively provide the culpability required for an offence. Where an offence does not require any form of intent or foresight to be proved, voluntary intoxication is effectively irrelevant to any objective standard of culpability. If an offence provides for conviction on the basis of negligence, D's intoxication may explain why she did not attain the standard to be expected of a reasonable person.[201] In such cases there is no point in D drawing attention to her condition of intoxication; it will merely strengthen the case against her. The reasonable person is not voluntarily drunk.

Possibly, a different view may be taken regarding involuntary intoxication. As we have seen, "a drunken intent is still an intent" and no concession to that rule is made for involuntary intoxication.[202] However, negligence is a term of moral evaluation, a dimension absent from the word "intent". The fact that her state of intoxication was involuntary may deflect the grounds of criticism inherent in negligence. The standard applied should be the reasonable, involuntarily intoxicated person. The law, however, is uncertain. The case of *Elliott* v. *C*[203] suggests that these concessions will not necessarily be made. *Hardie*,[204] on the other hand, offers *sub silentio* support for the position argued for here.

For crimes of strict liability, there is no elbow room even for a plea of involuntary intoxication; liability is imposed on the basis of commission of the actus reus. Should involuntary intoxication lead to a condition of automatism, however, an actus reus should not be attributed to D because her conduct would not have been a voluntary act or omission.[205]

(viii) Reform

The law relating to intoxication is complex and replete with uncertainties of conception and ambit. It need not be so. In *O'Connor*,[206] the High Court of Australia was unimpressed with the English law on this topic. In a refreshingly straightforward approach, the Court decided that intoxicated defendants could be dealt with under the ordinary principles of

---

[200] Which requires D to intend or be reckless whether the life of another would be endangered by the damage or destruction of the property: Criminal Damage Act 1971, s. 1(2). It would seem on accepted principles that he was raising a defence of insanity rather than a simple plea of lack of mens rea for the aggravated version of the defence too: see further § 19.1(ii)(d).

[201] Above, § 5.5(i).

[202] Above, § 18.3(v).

[203] [1983] 2 All ER 1005 (CA). The Court of Appeal disregarded D's learning disability when applying the *Caldwell* recklessness test; see above, §§ 5.2(i), 5.5(ii).

[204] [1984] 3 All ER 848. The Court of Appeal quashed D's conviction for criminal damage as the trial judge had ruled inadmissible evidence that D had not foreseen the consequences of his conduct because of medication he had taken in order to clam himself. However, the Court of Appeal's decision could alternatively be explained on the basis of an oversight that *Caldwell* recklessness was the applicable standard.

[205] Above, § 4.3(iii)(d). See also the recommendation to this effect in Law Com. No. 229, *Intoxication and Criminal Liability* (1995) para. 8.36.

[206] (1980) 146 CLR 64; Orchard, "Surviving without *Majewski* Down Under" [1993] *Crim LR* 426.

mens rea. Intoxication, preponderantly, is raised in the contexts of violence and vandalism. The mens rea requirements for crimes such as assault, malicious wounding, and criminal damage are hardly sophisticated mental states and are well within the capacities even of persons in advanced states of intoxication. The High Court was content to trust juries to come to appropriate decisions in cases involving intoxicated defendants and a similar approach has been taken by the Supreme Court of Canada.[207]

In England and Wales, the *Majewski* principle, or some statutory adaptation of it, seems set to remain for the indefinite future. No law reform body has recommended the abolition of the intoxication rules: the return to first principles that has occurred in Canada and Australia seems most unlikely here.

The latest suggestions for placing the intoxication rules on a statutory footing come from the Law Commission.[208] In a complex set of proposals,[209] the Law Commission broadly retains the essential features of the current position regarding criminal liability and intoxication, although, commendably, the Commission rejects the confusing division of offences into crimes of specific and basic intent.

To summarise: where an offence contains one or more fault elements defined in terms of intent or knowledge, evidence of voluntary intoxication can be called in determining whether or not intent or knowledge is proved. Where the fault element is recklessness, a person voluntarily intoxicated will be attributed the foresight of consequences and the knowledge of circumstances he would have had if sober. Where there is a claim by an intoxicated person to have mistakenly believed that facts existed which, if true, would give rise to a right to use force in self-defence or the prevention of crime, any defence of mistaken belief will fail (whatever the crime charged) if the true facts would have been apparent to a sober person.

Although this summary omits some of the detail of the Commission's recommendations, it captures the essentials. To date there is no indication of when, if ever, these proposals may be enacted. Given that they more or less confirm the current position, the matter would seem to lack urgency.

---

[207] In *Daviault* (1994) 118 DLR (4th) 469, the Supreme Court of Canada ruled that to depart from ordinary principles of mens rea (as *Majewski* does) would violate the Canadian Charter of Rights and Freedoms. However, it seems that dispensing with *Majewski* has not been without its difficulties in Australia and Canada: Gough, "Surviving without *Majewski*?" [2002] *Crim LR* 719.

[208] Law Com. No. 314, *Intoxication and Criminal Liability* (2009). For a discussion of earlier proposals, see Home Office, *Violence: Reforming the Offences against the Person Act 1861* (1998) Draft Bill, cl. 19.

[209] See the draft bill and explanatory notes at Appendix A. Cf. also Child, "Drink, Drugs and Law Reform: a Review of Law Commission Report No. 314" [2009] *Crim LR* 488.

19

MENTAL CONDITION DEFENCES

§ 19.1 Insanity

A defence of insanity[1] is a long-established feature of English law, of considerable symbolic importance. It signals that the rules of the criminal law are addressed to rational persons who have the capacity to understand and comply with rules.[2] Persons lacking such capacity may need to be restrained and confined, but there is a long-held sentiment that they should not be designated criminals.[3]

The defence is rarely deployed, for several reasons. First, in English law, insanity is narrowly interpreted. Many persons with medical conditions commonly held to be forms of insanity fall outside the scope of the defence, although, paradoxically, the defence can also embrace persons who are in no sense medically insane. Secondly, an insanity plea does not result in an unqualified acquittal. The acquittal conferred as a result of a successful plea is the special verdict of "not guilty by reason of insanity",[4] which leaves the defendant under the control of the court. Prior to the Criminal Procedure (Insanity and Unfitness to Plead) Act 1991, the disposal outcome was mandatory—a period of indefinite detention in a special hospital unless and until the Home Secretary ordered release. This inflexibility has now been changed by legislation: a range of non-penal measures is available to the judge at her discretion, ranging from a a supervision order to a hospital order with or without restriction of time.[5] In theory, the availability of disposal outcomes such as supervision and time-limited hospital orders should increase recourse to the insanity defence and there is some evidence of a modest increase in the number of insanity pleas raised by the defence.[6] Nonetheless, the label "insane" remains profoundly unattractive to persons afflicted with mental illness, as is any prospect of an indefinite stay in a special hospital. Accordingly, many defendants whose mental condition may undercut any culpability for the offence charged choose to plead guilty or defend themselves on other grounds.

---

[1] Mackay, *Mental Condition Defences in the Criminal Law* (1995) chap. 2; Moore, *Law and Psychiatry* (1984) chap. 6; Morris, *Madness and the Criminal Law* (1982); Morse, "Excusing the Crazy: The Insanity Defence Reconsidered" (1985) 58 *So Cal LR* 777.

[2] Bonnie, "The Moral Basis of the Insanity Defence" (1983) 69 *ABAJ* 194.

[3] The first recorded case of outright acquittal by reason of insanity in England was in 1505: Walker, *Crime and Insanity in England* (1968) 26. It seems the defendant was set free.

[4] Trial of Lunatics Act 1883, s. 2(1).

[5] Criminal Procedure (Insanity) Act 1964 as amended by the Criminal Procedure (Insanity and Unfitness to Plead) Act 1991 and Domestic Violence, Crimes and Victims Act 2004. For a short description of the steps by which reform proceeded, see below, § 19.1(i)(b).

[6] Mackay and Kearns, "More Facts about the Insanity Defence" [1999] *Crim LR* 714; Mackay, "Ten More Years of the Insanity Defence" [2012] *Crim LR* 946.

The position is hardly satisfactory. The high incidence of mentally disordered persons in the prison population who should be receiving treatment for their condition[7] demonstrates that, for mentally disordered offenders, the criminal justice system is failing both in terms of justice to individual defendants and in terms of health and social policy. Yet the marginalisation of the insanity defence does not mean that it can be ignored or considered only cursorily. The minimum standard of rationality demanded by law to warrant inclusion in the class of persons who are subject to punishment is a topic of intrinsic importance for the legitimacy of state punishment. Further, even the most practically minded criminal lawyer needs to be aware of what constitutes an insanity plea. Because of the public interest in subjecting dangerous persons to restraint, not only the defendant but also the judge and even the prosecution may raise the issue of insanity if the facts of the case indicate that grounds for the defence are present. Accordingly, a defendant seeking to plead automatism or a lack of mens rea may find that her plea is treated as a plea of insanity.[8] Theoretically, the same switch may occur if she pleads diminished responsibility to a charge of murder.[9]

(i) Mental condition of defendant prior to trial

Before considering the insanity defence, a full appreciation of the relevance of any abnormality of mind on the part of D to the criminal justice process requires consideration of two situations where an evaluation of D's mental condition may postpone or terminate the trial itself.

(a) Removal to a mental hospital by order of Home Secretary

Under the provisions of the Mental Health Act 1983, the Home Secretary, if satisfied on the basis of reports from at least two medical practitioners that D is suffering from mental illness or severe mental impairment, may order that D be detained in hospital if the minister is of the opinion that it is in the public interest to do so.[10]

On the face of it, this is an extremely wide power that, it seems, is exercised with restraint. It is, in practice, reserved for cases of profound derangement or disability, situations where it is obvious that any trial would serve no useful purpose given the current condition of D. Should D make a sufficient recovery, the practice is for D then to be brought to trial.[11]

(b) Unfitness to plead

Under sections 4 and 4A of the Criminal Procedure (Insanity) Act 1964,[12] a finding may be made, on the initiative of the defence, prosecution, or judge, that D is unfit to plead.[13] Normally the matter will be dealt with on arraignment—before the trial begins and a plea is

---

[7] HO/DHSS, *Interdepartmental Working Group into Mentally Disturbed Offenders in the Prison System* (1987). Bradley, *The Bradley Report: Lord Bradley's Review of People with Mental Health Problems or Learning Disabilities in the Criminal Justice System* (2009).

[8] *Kemp* [1957] 1 QB 399; *Sullivan* [1984] AC 156.

[9] Criminal Procedure (Insanity) Act 1964, s. 6. It seems the provision is not used.

[10] Mental Health Act 1983, ss. 47, 48.

[11] *Report of the Committee on Mentally Disordered Offenders* Cmnd. 6244 (1975) para. 3.38.

[12] As amended by the Criminal Procedure (Insanity and Unfitness to Plead) Act 1991 and the Domestic Violence, Crimes and Victims Act 2004.

[13] See generally Mackay, *Mental Condition Defences in the Criminal Law* (1995) chap. 5.

entered. If the judge makes a finding at this stage that D is fit to stand trial, a jury is empanelled for the trial itself. However, the judge may consider that the strength of the prosecution case should be tested before the issue of fitness is resolved: should that be the case, the judge may postpone the issue until the opening of the defence case. If, at that later stage, the judge finds that D has no case to answer, D is acquitted. Should there be a case to answer, however, the court will then determine whether D is fit to plead before hearing the defence.

Criteria of unfitness are left unspecified in the Criminal Procedure (Insanity) Act 1964, which leaves the test of unfitness to the determination of the courts. From the early nineteenth century, the test has been narrowly cognitive, and focused on D's capacity to "plead to the indictment" and to be "of sufficient intellect to comprehend the course of the proceedings in the trial so as to make a proper defence, to challenge a juror to whom he may wish to object and comprehend the details of the evidence".[14] What this test, still approved in the twenty-first century,[15] does not do is test whether D has genuine "decisional competence"— the wherewithal to reflect with a degree of insight where his best interests lie.[16] For instance, the test will not assist a defendant who, because of his affliction, irrationally refuses to have presented an otherwise relevant line of defence or to testify to a particular matter. Does a person who is found fit to plead but is otherwise lacking in decisional competence receive a fair trial as guaranteed by Article 6 of the ECHR? Although much will depend on the impact of the disability at the trial itself, there is, it is suggested, one useful general principle that should be applied. If, as a result of the impact of D's disability on the course of the trial, there may be reason to think that a verdict of guilty would not have been returned had D been possessed of adequate decisional competence, the trial should be adjudged unfair. Better still would be for English law to adopt the test propounded by the US Supreme Court when determining fitness to plead: whether D has "sufficient present ability to consult his lawyer with a reasonable degree of rational understanding—and whether he has a rational as well as factual understanding of the proceedings against him".[17] Such hopes seem ill-founded in the light of the recent decision in *Moyle*.[18] D suffered from paranoid delusions and as a consequence believed that the court and even his own lawyers were united in a conspiracy against him. The Court of Appeal accepted that his circumstances were far from ideal in terms of seeking his own best interests on a rational basis but it refused to budge from the narrow cognitive test hitherto applied, and on that basis confirmed that D was fit to plead.

The unfitness to plead procedures have recently been reviewed by the Law Commission.[19] The Commission's overarching principle is that D "should be able to participate effectively in the proceedings on the offence or offences charged".[20] When addressing that question, the following matters should be considered: the assistance available to D in the proceedings;[21] an understanding of what the charges mean and their nature, and an

---

[14] *Pritchard* (1836) 7 C & P 303.

[15] *M* [2003] EWCA Crim 3452; *Robertson* [1968] 3 All ER 557.

[16] For very persuasive advocacy of a test of decisional competence, see Mackay, "On Being Insane in Jersey Part 3: the Case of the *Attorney General v O'Driscoll*" [2004] *Crim LR* 219.

[17] *Dusky* v. *US* 362 US 402 (1960).

[18] [2009] Crim LR 586.

[19] Law Com 364, Unfitness *to Plead* (2016).

[20] *Ibid.*, para. 3.35.

[21] *Ibid.*, para. 3.61.

understanding of the evidence, the trial process, and the consequences of conviction;[22] the ability to give instructions to a legal representative, to follow the proceedings and give evidence; the abilities to decide how to plead, whether to give evidence, and whether to elect a Crown Court trial;[23] and, finally, "the ability to make any other decision that may need to be made in connection with the trial".[24]

A reformulation, along these lines, of the criteria that should be used when deciding whether D is fit to plead would be very welcome. The questions to be asked go deeper than the current law, probing the matter of whether D has any mental grasp on how his interests might be served. For instance, it seems likely that in the circumstances obtaining in *Moyle* (above) D would not be found fit to plead. But the test is still solely (and properly) confined to D's capacity to understand the trial process. Disadvantages stemming from circumstance outside the trial process, which have no bearing on his understanding of that process, will not prevent a trial, even if they place D in a difficult position at the trial itself. To illustrate: in *Podola*,[25] D claimed he had no recollection of the circumstances or the reasons for his killing of V because of his "hysterical amnesia" concerning the incident. Because D was otherwise perfectly normal at the time of his trial, he was judged fit to plead. It is considered that *Podola* was correctly decided and should still apply even if the Law Commission proposal is implemented. Of course, D might be under a disadvantage at his trial. It may be that he killed in self-defence and could explain why that was necessary if only he could remember. But his lack of recall does not affect his decisional competence. Once decisional competence is established, it is appropriate that a trial should be held, where such matters as the nature and causes of hysterical amnesia can be tested properly before a jury.

Prior to 1991, a person found unfit to plead was held at the disposal of the Home Secretary without any determination of the evidence against them. Consequently, there were cases of persons being detained for substantial periods of time despite considerable doubt over the basis of the allegations made against them. A significant and welcome reform introduced by the Criminal Procedure (Insanity and Unfitness to Plead) Act 1991 provides that, upon there being a finding of unfitness to plead, the jury shall then decide on such evidence already given (if any) and such evidence introduced by the prosecution or defence whether D "did the act or made the omission" charged against him as the offence.[26] If they are not satisfied that D did the act or omission constituting the actus reus of the offence, D is to be acquitted and therefore not subject to any disposal or future prosecution.[27]

Although clearly an advance on the previous position, this reform is not without its difficulties. Inevitably, a person unfit to plead may experience difficulty in effectively participating in the proceedings. As the proceedings are not a criminal trial, the full protection of Article 6 of the ECHR is not engaged and a finding that D did the act or made the omission will not be disturbed despite D's difficulties in comprehending (and refuting) the evidence called against him.[28] The focus is solely on whether D "did the act or made the omission", and this has been held in the context of murder charges to rule out evidence suggesting

---

[22] *Ibid.*, para. 3.85-3.86.
[23] *Ibid.*, para. 3.107–3.116.
[24] *Ibid.*, para. 3.117.
[25] [1960] 1 QB 325.
[26] Criminal Procedure Insanity Act 1964, s. 4A.
[27] *Ibid.*, s. 4A(4).
[28] *Kerr* [2002] Crim LR 57; affirmed in *H* [2003] UKHL 1.

diminished responsibility or provocation, on the basis that this would take the hearing into questions of D's mental state whereas the legislative provision confines the enquiry into whether the actus reus of the offence can be attributed to D.[29]

Prima facie, this approach would rule out any consideration of defences that might have been available to D. However, an exception exists if the possibility of a defence can be established by "objective evidence" rather than by reference to D's "state of knowledge".[30] The matter of objective evidence arose in *Wells and others*,[31] where it was taken to include CCTV, cell site evidence of location, scene-of-crime, and expert forensic evidence. It did not include any assertions made by D as to whether he was suffering from a mental disorder that undermined his reliability.[32]

The spirit of such attempts by the courts to mitigate the potential injustice to D of disposal orders—which might involve long-term confinement—based on mere proof of act or omission has been carried over to the question whether there are any circumstances in which the fault element can be considered in the context of proof of the act or omission. In *B (M)*,[33] the Court of Appeal found that for the offence of voyeurism the "act" (of "voyeurism") imported the purpose of obtaining sexual gratification. On the other hand, it did not involve any consideration of D's awareness regarding V's non-consent to being watched, because such awareness went only to the fault element of the offence.[34] Similarly in *Young*,[35] in the context of an offence requiring proof of the dishonest concealment of a material fact,[36] the intention to conceal was found to be an integral part of the act of concealment but the purpose of the concealment and any related dishonesty were not for the jury's consideration.

Obviously, the current position is not ideal. Yet any critique of these cases is rather beside the point. Clearly, the Court in each of these cases was trying to do what it could to afford justice to D, within the constraints of an inquiry limited to proof of the external elements of the offence charged. The Law Commission has recently addressed the question of whether this constraint should apply.[37] In direct and clear terms, the Commission proposes that the prosecution be required to prove all the elements of the offence beyond a reasonable doubt against a defendant found unfit to stand trial. If the prosecution can do this, D will be subject to the orders of the court: otherwise D will be acquitted.[38]

Upon a finding of unfitness to plead, together with a finding that D did the act or omission alleged, D becomes subject to the disposal of the court. Following enactment of the Criminal Procedure (Insanity and Unfitness to Plead) Act 1991, the range of disposal options is now considerable, although at first this flexibility was not extended where the charge was murder. There is a range of non-punitive court orders (including involuntary confinement in a special hospital) geared to the needs of the defendant and the protection of the public.

---

[29] *Antoine* [2000] UKHL 20, [2001] 1 AC 340.
[30] *Ibid.*, 376.
[31] [2015] EWCA Crim 2, [2015] 1 WLR 2797.
[32] *Ibid.*, para. 15.
[33] [2012] EWCA Crim 770, [2013] 1 WLR 499.
[34] *Ibid.*, paras. 63–6.
[35] *R (Young)* v. *Central Criminal Court* [2002] EWHC 548 (Admin), [2002] 2 Cr App R 178.
[36] An offence under what is now the Financial Services Act 2012, s. 89.
[37] Law Com. No. 364, *Unfitness to Plead* (2016).
[38] *Ibid.*, para. 5.85.

Where the charge was murder, however, the 1991 Act permitted only one outcome: indefinite detention in a special hospital until released with the permission of the Home Secretary or by order of a Mental Health Review Tribunal.[39] Happily, this discrepancy was addressed following the case of *Grant*,[40] in which the Court of Appeal expressed doubt whether the 1991 regime for persons charged with murder would comply with Article 5 of the ECHR (protection of liberty) and associated jurisprudence, which allows the detention of the mentally ill only if necessary for treatment or protection of the patient and others. Those criteria are not addressed in the determination of whether D did the act or made the omission. As a consequence of subsequent amending legislation,[41] section 5 of the Criminal Procedure (Insanity) Act 1964 now provides the full range of disposal options for murder cases but also provides that if the grounds for a hospital order with restriction are present in such a case, then such an order must be made.

(ii) The M'Naghten Rules

In England and Wales, the insanity defence is based on the *M'Naghten* Rules.[42] These rules comprise a series of answers given by judges of the Queen's Bench in 1843 to questions put by members of the House of Lords. The occasion was prompted by the public outcry which followed the acquittal, on grounds of insanity, of Daniel M'Naghten, who had killed Sir Edmund Drummond in an attempt to murder Sir Robert Peel.[43]

Strictly speaking, the answers given were, in formal terms, of no binding effect. However, they are regarded as an authoritative and comprehensive statement of the law, a status endorsed by the House of Lords in *Sullivan*.[44] The Rules provide that:

(i)   there is a rebuttable presumption that everyone is sane;
(ii)   proof of insanity requires proof of a defect of reason;
(iii)   the defect of reason must emanate from a disease of the mind;
(iv)   it must be proved that the defect of reason *either*
        (a) caused D to be unaware of the nature and quality of his act *or*
        (b) caused D not to know that his act was wrong.[45]

We will consider these elements in turn.

(a) Burden of proof

The presumption of sanity requires D to prove her defence of insanity.[46] Proof is discharged on a balance of probabilities and not beyond any reasonable doubt.[47] As the cases below

---

[39] Pursuant to the underlying Act: Criminal Procedure (Insanity) Act 1964, s. 5(2).
[40] [2002] Crim LR 403.
[41] Domestic Violence, Crime and Violence Act 2004.
[42] (1843) 10 C & F 200, 8 ER 718.
[43] West and Walk, *Daniel McNaughton: His Trial and the Aftermath* (1977). (There is uncertainly over the correct spelling of the defendant's name: "M'Naghten" is the most common version.)
[44] [1984] AC 156, 171.
[45] The Rules also contain a provision relating to insane delusions. It is generally agreed that the provision adds nothing of substance to the main body of the Rules and it will not be considered here.
[46] *Bratty v. A-G for Northern Ireland* [1963] AC 386 (HL).
[47] *Carr-Briant* [1943] KB 607 (CCA).

on "disease of the mind" will illustrate, the line between a claim to have lacked mens rea (or, in cases of unconsciousness, to have lacked voluntary responsibility for the actus reus) and a plea of insanity may be extremely fine. It is unsatisfactory to have different standards of proof in respect of closely analogous issues. Nonetheless, that is the current law.[48] As we noted in § 2.5(i), reverse burdens of proof may be vulnerable to scrutiny under the terms of Article 6(2) of the ECHR (presumption of innocence) and may, on occasion, be "read down" to merely an evidential burden. In *Lambert*,[49] however, the Court of Appeal ruled that there was no contravention of Article 6(2) in placing the onus of proof on D to establish his diminished responsibility in response to a charge of murder. Influential upon the Court's finding was the fact that the prosecution had to prove the elements of murder before the burden was imposed on D. As we shall see below, when D claims that he did not perceive the "the nature and quality" of his act because of a disease of the mind, the applicable case law effectively requires D to prove the lack of a voluntary act and/or a lack of mens rea. In such cases, the prosecution is in effect relieved of its burden of proof on vital elements of the offence charged and in those cases it seems entirely appropriate that D's burden be reduced to an evidential one. It is worth noting that, in its recent discussion paper on the law of insanity, the Law Commission considered that to impose a persuasive burden on D on matters which go to core elements of the offence contravenes the presumption of innocence guaranteed by Article 6(2). It has proposed that D should produce evidence sufficient to raise the issue if he seeks an acquittal on the ground of a recognised medical condition; but upon his doing that, the prosecution must then disprove the defence.[50]

Even if the burden was reduced to the production of evidence sufficient to raise the issue, D would still need to produce some medical evidence indicative of the possibility of insanity: section 1 of the Criminal Procedure (Insanity and Unfitness to Plead) Act 1991 provides that a verdict of not guilty by reason of insanity is not to be returned unless evidence has been given by two or more medical practitioners, including at least one medical witness duly approved as having expertise in mental health.

As things stand, no English court has addressed the tension between the burden of proof in insanity and the usual requirement for the prosecution to prove a voluntary act and mens rea attributable to D. Under section 2(1) of the Trial of Lunatics Act 1883, where insanity is proved, the special verdict follows provided the jury is satisfied that D "did the act or made the omission charged, but was insane". The confirms that, if D is found to be insane, the prosecution need only prove beyond reasonable doubt the actus reus of the offence; the special verdict requires no proof of any mens rea required for the crime with which D is charged.[51]

(b) Defect of reason

It is appropriate to define insanity in terms of failures of rationality. We do not regard persons whose foundational beliefs or practical reasoning are radically defective as accountable moral agents if their bizarre beliefs or deranged reasoning appear to arise from some

---

[48] For an excellent critique of the current position, see Jones, "Insanity, Automatism and the Burden of Proof on the Accused" (1995) 111 *LQR* 475.

[49] [2001] 1 Cr App R 205 (CA).

[50] Law Commission, *Insanity and Automatism: A Discussion Paper* (2013) paras. 8.9–8.45.

[51] *A-G's Reference (No. 3 of 1998)* [1999] 3 All ER 40 (CA).

internal pathology. If, under the influence of drink or drugs, D believes she can execute some dangerous manoeuvre, we may, other things being equal, hold her morally responsible for any harm that follows her attempt to do so. Should the same belief arise from schizophrenic delusion, talk of moral responsibility would seem to miss the mark.

For the purposes of the insanity defence, the defect of reason may arise for a brief period of time and need not constitute an aspect of D's character. A temporary blackout is sufficient.[52] In *Clarke*,[53] "defect of reason" was taken to imply the cessation of a relevant deliberative faculty for however brief a period of time. The details of the case were as follows:

> D, in a depressed state, had inadvertently taken an item from a supermarket shelf and placed it in her shopping bag. In response to a charge of theft, she claimed an absence of dishonesty but was held to be raising a plea of insanity. The Court of Appeal ruled that she had not put her sanity in issue. She was not asserting a defect of reason arising from a disease of the mind. Rather, because of absent-mindedness associated with depression, she had failed to exercise a faculty she still possessed.

The reasoning is unconvincing. It would have been entirely apt to say that her mental processes were defective. Nonetheless, the disapplication of the insanity defence in *Clarke* is appropriate. It is submitted that a better way of achieving that outcome would have been to accept that D was suffering from a cognitive defect but to deny that it arose from a "disease of the mind". This would require defining the latter phrase in terms which exclude conditions such as depression. We turn now to the definition of that phrase.

(c) Disease of the mind

It needs to be stressed at the outset that what constitutes a disease of the mind within the scope of the Rules is a legal, not a medical, question. Although section 1 of the Criminal Procedure (Insanity and Unfitness to Plead) Act 1991 requires evidence to be given by two or more medical practitioners before the special verdict of acquittal on the ground of insanity may be returned, the medical witnesses will be giving evidence in response to criteria set down by law. It may be that, on a particular occasion, medical witnesses are satisfied that D is insane or not insane according to medical criteria (in so far as that term is known to medical practice). But what matters is whether the evidence demonstrates that D was within the legal conception of insanity at the time the actus reus occurred.

The well-known judgment of Devlin J in *Kemp*[54] illustrates the policy considerations which influence the legal meaning of insanity. D, by all accounts a loving husband, made a sudden and violent attack on V, his wife. He claimed to have acted in a state of automatism: evidence was given that his arteriosclerosis could produce an automatous state by cutting off the blood supply to the brain. Devlin J ruled that a plea of non-insane automatism was unavailable. A disease of the mind, for the purpose of the Rules, was any internal disorder which affected the faculties of memory, reason, or understanding. Accordingly, the evidence raised on D's behalf put his sanity in issue. It was irrelevant that such a notion of insanity might be greeted with incredulity outside a courtroom, nor did it matter that the episode of insanity was, as in the case itself, of brief duration. Devlin J's approach has been consistently

---

[52] Provided, of course, that it arises from a disease of the mind: see below, § 19.1(ii)(c).
[53] [1972] 1 All ER 219 (CA).
[54] [1957] 1 QB 399.

followed by appellate courts and received conclusive endorsement by the House of Lords in *Sullivan*,[55] where a state of automatism arising from an epileptic fit was ruled to be a condition falling within the Rules.

The explicit policy that has driven this capacious definition of a disease of the mind is the legitimate concern that certain persons likely to be involved in repeated episodes of dangerous behaviour should be subject to restraint rather than be given an unqualified acquittal on the basis of automatism or lack of mens rea. Lord Denning forcefully expressed the view that any mental disorder which had manifested itself in violence and which was prone to recur should be classified as a disease of the mind.[56] It is submitted, however, that the legitimate concern for public safety should be resolved through civil rather than criminal procedures.[57] As things stand, persons of good character, such as the defendants in *Kemp* and *Sullivan*, may prefer to plead guilty to offences they did not commit rather than pursue an insanity plea with all its pejorative overtones.

Within the terms of this (flawed) public protection rationale, the insanity plea has an exclusionary character. In the typical case such as *Sullivan*, D leads evidence suggestive of lack of mens rea or automatism. If the explanation for this state of affairs rests on some internal disorder, D is denied access to these simple denials of responsibility and must plead insanity to avoid conviction. Whatever the merits or otherwise of this "trumping" effect of the insanity plea,[58] in terms of equality of treatment it should be consistently applied. Yet it is inconsistently applied. So, in *C*,[59] D was acquitted of aggravated arson on the basis of a reasonable doubt over whether, in setting fire to his own flat, he foresaw that it might spread to other properties, even though his failure to consider this risk stemmed from an internal disorder.[60] In *Oye*,[61] because of an internal disorder, D thought he was under attack by evil spirits, taking the form of police officers. He was allowed to raise the defence of mistaken self-defence as well as insanity.[62] Whether or not one agrees with the nature and

---

[55] [1984] AC 156.

[56] *Bratty v. A-G for Northern Ireland* [1963] AC 386, 410.

[57] The Mental Health Act 1983 provides for the civil commitment of persons suffering from mental disorder, severe mental impairment, mental impairment, and psychopathic disorder if such persons constitute a danger to themselves or to others.

[58] What may be the unwelcome intrusion of this defence into D's case is recognised by provision for an appeal against a ruling that insanity is the applicable defence: Criminal Appeal Act 1968, s. 12.

[59] [2013] EWCA Crim 923.

[60] D heard voices and hallucinated after abruptly ceasing heavy drinking. The condition was ruled by the Court of Appeal to be a state of insanity, a defence which according to the court would have failed on the charge of simple arson if put at his trial because he was aware of the nature and quality of his act when he set fire to his flat. However, the court considered he could have successfully raised insanity to the charge of aggravated arson because his mental condition made him unaware that the fire would spread to other properties. See too *Stephenson* [1979] QB 695, where D's acquittal of arson was upheld on the basis of lack of recklessness because his schizophrenia prevented him from realising that the fire he set would spread. The leading case of *Sullivan* [1984] AC 156 makes no separation between the act and its consequences when determining whether D was aware of the nature and quality of his act. For criticism of *C* and other cases to like effect, see Child and Sullivan, "When Does the Insanity Defence Apply? Some Recent Cases" [2014] *Crim LR* 788.

[61] [2013] EWCA Crim 1725.

[62] At trial, the jury were first directed on mistaken self-defence and then insanity. If the jury had found in favour of mistaken self-defence it would have lacked any jurisdiction to consider insanity as D was entitled to an unqualified acquittal, a matter not considered by the presiding judge when giving his directions. The jury found him guilty: the Court of Appeal substituted a verdict of insanity.

consequences of the insanity plea, while it remains in play it should be applied predictably to defendants in like case.

The cardinal limiting factor on what constitutes a disease of the mind is that, to be classified as a form of insanity, the condition must arise from some psychosis, organic or functional disorder, injury, or other inherent condition; or, to use the summary expression used by the courts, from some factor "internal" to the defendant. Conversely, a state of destabilisation engendered by "external" factors is not, legally, a disease of the mind. Accordingly, in *Quick*,[63] where D became hypoglycaemic as a consequence of the insulin he had taken for his diabetic condition, the Court of Appeal ruled that the was entitled to raise a plea of non-insane automatism. By contrast, in *Hennessy*,[64] D, a diabetic, had *failed* to take his insulin. Consequently, he became *hyper*glycaemic. But he was denied a defence of non-insane automatism because his condition was a symptom of his diabetes. Each defendant had in common mismanagement of his illness and dangerousness after entering into an automatous condition. What is remarkable is their differing treatment at the hands of the law. In a case such as *Quick*, if D raises the possibility that he was an automaton at the time of the conduct alleged to constitute an offence, the burden of disproof is on the prosecution and D will receive an unqualified acquittal should that burden not be discharged. In a case like *Hennessy*, D must prove his automatism and will receive a special verdict of acquittal by reason of insanity if he does.[65]

If the court is satisfied that D's claim to have been an automaton or to have lacked mens rea stems from some form of internal disorder, he will be taken to have raised a plea of insanity even if the form of disorder afflicting D has not been identified. In *Burgess*,[66] D performed a violent act apparently while sleep. The medical evidence failed to identify any underlying cause of the incident but testimony was given that violent somnambulism was abnormal and must, in the absence of any evidence of an external cause, arise from some internal condition.[67] Accordingly, the explanation—whatever it was—constituted a disease of the mind.[68]

The approach in *Burgess* mirrors that taken by the Supreme Court of Canada in the well-known case of *Rabey*,[69] where D claimed that the shock of his girlfriend V's rejection had induced a state of disassociation at the time of his attack upon her, rendering him incapable of forming mens rea. D claimed that this condition was induced by an external factor—V's rejection of him—and should be regarded as a state of non-insane

---

[63] [1973] QB 910 (CA).

[64] [1989] 1 WLR 287 (CA).

[65] See the remarks above, § 19.1(ii)(a).

[66] [1991] 2 All ER 769 (CA).

[67] For a very useful account of the aetiology of sleep disorders and the appropriate legal responses to sleep disordered behaviours, see Wilson *et al.*, "Violence, Sleepwalking and the Criminal Law" [2005] *Crim LR* 624.

[68] Mackay has criticised the decision on the ground that the somnambulism did not lead to the cessation of the faculties of memory, reason, and understanding; that was caused by the preceding condition of sleep, a normal condition: *Mental Condition Defences* (1995) 45–51, citing the Supreme Court of Canada's decision in *Parks* (1992) 95 DLR (4th) 27. Perhaps, in defence of *Burgess*, D's bodily movements may be said to combine with the condition of sleep, producing a discrete, disordered state, a compound of sleep and the internal disorder which leads to the ambulatory activity. Such an answer is not an argument of principle for classifying sleepwalking as a form of insanity, merely acknowledgement that it is somewhat forced to maintain a separation between somnambulism and sleep when the states are, as they must be, coincident. However, for criticism of this rationalisation of the decision in *Burgess*, see Mackay, "Sleepwalking, Automatism and Insanity" [2006] *Crim LR* 901.

[69] (1980) 114 DLR (3d) 193.

automatism. The Supreme Court held that because D's reaction was so abnormal and extreme, it must have been the product of some internal predisposing factor which was merely *triggered*, not *caused*, by V's rejection. Accordingly, insanity was the only defence available on such facts.

In *Rabey*, it was suggested, *obiter*, that if an external event is so traumatic in its impact as to cause a state of disassociation in persons of normal sensibility, a defence of non-insane automatism might be available.[70] This suggestion was followed in the trial case of *T*,[71] where D, acting in a state of disassociation induced by the effects of being raped three days earlier, was held entitled to plead non-insane automatism to a charge of robbery.

To summarise this section: under English law, the source of a defect of reasoning will generally be regarded as a disease of the mind if either (i) it is "internal" to the defendant (*Kemp, Sullivan, Hennessy, Burgess*); or (ii) it is an "external" trigger that would not normally produce such a result in ordinary persons (*Rabey*), so that by inference it discloses an internal cause. Where the source is external *and* the sort of event likely to cause a defect of reasoning even in normal persons (*Quick, T*), the case is not one of insanity. Finally, there may be "mixed" cases where the state of automation is a product of internal and external causes; as in *Roach*,[72] where personality disorder, prescription drugs, alcohol, and fatigue all seemingly played a part in bringing about D's automatic state. The Court of Appeal took what may be termed a "predominant cause" approach: because the predominant causes were external factors, the correct classification was therefore non-insane automatism.

(d) The nature and quality of D's act

If the defect of reason induced by the disease of the mind causes D not to perceive the nature and quality of her act, she will be entitled to an acquittal on the grounds of insanity. A person such as the defendant in *Sullivan* does not apprehend the nature and quality of his conduct if he is in a state of automatism induced by an epileptic fit. Neither, to take Stephen's example, would a person who cut off a sleeping man's head because it would be great fun to see him look for it when he woke up.[73]

The expression "nature and quality" has been construed narrowly. It has been taken to mean nothing more than the *physical* aspects of the circumstances and consequences attending D's conduct.[74] Many persons who are radically psychotic will, notwithstanding, appreciate the nature and quality of their acts in the limited sense adopted by English law. Suppose that, because of her schizophrenic delusions, D thinks she has been ordered to kill V. If she is aware that V is a person, she will fall outside this limb of the Rules. This narrow approach has been criticised and contrasts with interpretations adopted in some US jurisdictions, where the phrase "nature and quality" has been interpreted in a more liberal

---

[70] *Ibid.*, 199, quoting from the decision by the Ontario Court of Appeal (1977) 79 DLR (3d) 414, 435. It is of interest that the High Court of Australia in *Falconer* (1990) 65 ALJR 20, another "psychic blow" case, has rejected the internal/external factor analysis favoured in England and Canada. A state of disassociation caused by the shock of an event is to be regarded as a form of non-insane automatism unless there is identification of some underlying disability afflicting D which is suggestive of future dangerousness.

[71] [1990] Crim LR 256; and see now *Huckerby* [2004] EWCA Crim 3251.

[72] [2001] EWCA 2698.

[73] *History of the Criminal Law* (1883) vol. II, 166.

[74] *Codère* (1916) 12 Cr App R 21 (CCA).

fashion to take into account D's full understanding of the impact and moral dimensions of her conduct.[75]

At the same time, there has been a reaction in the United States against expansive interpretations of the *M'Naghten* Rules.[76] Wider interpretation of the phrase has, in practice, led to extended testimony from expert witnesses of a speculative and impalpable character. The trial of John Hinckley for the shooting of President Reagan gave rise to a widespread sentiment, reflected in legislative initiatives in many jurisdictions,[77] that acquittals on the ground of insanity could be won by chequebook recruitment of malleable experts. Clearly, the criminal conviction of persons afflicted with grave mental illness is unjust. Yet the way forward may not be best delivered by adopting a freer interpretation of the Rules.

(e) Knowledge that D's act is wrong

Should D appreciate the nature and quality of his acts, he may still receive a verdict of insanity should it be the case that he did not know that his act was wrong. As interpreted by English courts, this is *not* a test of *moral* wrongness. D will know that his conduct is "wrong", and thereby fail this limb of the insanity test, if:

(i)   D knows that his conduct contravenes the law;[78] or

(ii) D knows that his conduct transgresses "the ordinary standards adopted by reasonable men".[79]

Again, it is obviously the case that seriously deranged persons will fall outside the insanity defence because they will be aware that their conduct is "wrong" in the sense stipulated by English law.[80] In *Sutcliffe*,[81] D took it as his divinely endorsed mission to kill prostitutes. He doubtless knew his conduct was contrary to law (and that it would be disapproved of by persons of his acquaintance). He was, in fact, schizophrenic to a severe degree but still quite sane within the terms of the English law of insanity.[82] This narrow conception of the meaning of "wrong" was confirmed by the Court of Appeal in *Johnson*.[83] There was some sympathy for the view that the interpretation of this limb of the insanity test is too

---

[75] Goldstein, *The Insanity Defence* (1967) 49–51.

[76] Mackay, "Post-Hinkley Insanity in the USA" [1988] *Crim LR* 88.

[77] Low, Jeffries, and Bonnie, *Criminal Law: Cases and Materials* (2nd ed., 1986) 663–4.

[78] *Windle* [1952] 2 QB 826 (CCA); *M'Naghten* (1843) 10 Cl & F 200, 209, 8 ER 718, 722.

[79] *Codère* (1916) 12 Cr App R 21, 27; *M'Naghten* (1843) 10 Cl & F 200, 210, 8 ER 718, 723. The relevance of this second variety of "wrongness" was doubted in *Windle* [1952] 2 QB 826, 834; but the remarks on this point were *obiter* only.

[80] In *Stapleton v. R.* (1952) 86 CLR 358, the High Court of Australia was of the view that the *M'Naghten* Rules were too narrowly construed in *Windle* (above, n. 46), and that a defence of insanity should be available to D if he believes that his act was right by the standards of reasonable men notwithstanding his awareness of the illegality of his conduct. For contrasting views of the decision, see Morris at (1953) 16 *MLR* 435 and Montrose at (1954) 17 *MLR* 383. There is no sign of the Australian view being adopted here. See n. 59 below and associated text.

[81] *The Times*, 30 April 1981.

[82] The defence of insanity is narrower in 2000 than in 1800. In *Hadfield* (1800) 27 St Tr 1281, D shot at the King in order that he, D, should hang and thereby escape the imminent destruction of the world by God. He was found insane. As Williams observes, D clearly knew his act was contrary to law, thereby establishing his sanity: *CLGP* 493–4.

[83] [2007] EWCA Crim 1978, [2008] Crim LR 132.

confined; nonetheless, the court refused the invitation to adopt any wider conception of the meaning of wrong.[84]

(f) Insane delusions

There is a passage in the *M'Naghten* Rules that deals specifically with persons who are afflicted with a "partial delusion only" but who are not in other respects insane. The responsibility of such a person is to be considered as if the facts with respect to which the delusion exists were real. This express provision for partial delusions does not appear to add anything to the substance of the Rules; the illustrations provided (such as a supposed need for self-defence) indicate that the effect of the delusion must be to prevent D from knowing the nature and quality of his actions or from knowing that his actions were wrong. The superfluity of this aspect of the *M'Naghten* Rules is borne out by the lack of case law arising thereunder. A rare and recent case is *Oye*,[85] where a deluded D believed that police officers were evil spirits, set on killing him: the delusion limb of the rules was explicitly referenced by the Court of Appeal when substituting D's conviction for a verdict of not guilty by reason of insanity. This was unnecessary. D would not have known that his conduct was wrong, and if he believed that the officers were non-earthly beings (albeit adopting human form) he would not have been aware of the nature and quality of his acts. That said, there was an exact fit between the facts of the case and the self-defence example posited in the part of the Rules dealing with partial delusion. Moreover, apart from the very violent conduct that led to criminal proceedings, there was no evidence of mental disturbance before or shortly after the incident.[86] Apart from his delusional episode, D was in other respects sane. Though not strictly necessary, it is understandable why the little-used provision was invoked.

(g) The scope of the M'Naghten Rules

The Rules lay down criteria for a general defence of insanity applicable to all offences. However, that was not the view of the Divisional Court in *DPP* v. *H*,[87] which ruled that a defence of insanity had no application to an offence of strict liability. The ruling was based on an error, namely that a successful plea of insanity established a lack of mens rea. But as we have seen, this is true only of the "nature and quality" limb of the Rules: the "knowledge that the act is wrong" limb provides for a defence applicable in circumstances where D has mens rea. An important rationale of the insanity defence is to protect mentally disordered persons from punishment. This concern is engaged for all criminal offences.

(iii) The defence of insanity and the ECHR

In our earlier discussion of the burden of proof in insanity, it was noted that imposing a persuasive burden on D to show that her conduct was not voluntary or done with mens rea

---

[84] For an argument that it was open to the Court of Appeal to adopt a wider test, see Mackay, "Righting the Wrong?—Some Observations on the Second Limb of the M'Naghten Rules" [2009] *Crim LR* 80.

[85] [2013] EWCA Crim 1725.

[86] There was some speculation among the expert witnesses that the delusional episode was induced by smoking strong cannabis; later, however, there was agreement between them that it was a psychotic episode caused by some unspecified internal condition.

[87] [1997] 1 WLR 1406; above, § 6.2.

is arguably in breach of Article 6(2) of the ECHR.[88] The problems of aligning the English law of insanity with the minimum standards required by the European Convention for the Protection of Human Rights do not end there, however.

Article 5(1) of the ECHR allows, "in accordance with a procedure prescribed by law", "the lawful detention of persons of unsound mind". Under the jurisprudence interpreting Article 5, there is a requirement that the question of unsoundness of mind must be resolved by reference to "objective medical expertise".[89] Thus the detention on grounds of insanity of anyone who, by good practice standards of the medical profession,[90] is not considered to be of unsound mind will contravene Article 5. While section 1 of the Criminal Procedure (Insanity and Unfitness to Plead) Act 1991 requires evidence from two medical practitioners before a special verdict can be returned by a jury, as Sutherland and Gearty have noted, this provision does not address the point that the category of insanity in English law allows detention of persons who are not of unsound mind in any acceptable medical sense.[91] If a medical expert witness were to testify that D's automatism stems from, say, his underlying diabetes, the common law will designate the condition as insanity.[92] Such a classification would be rejected by any reputable body of "objective medical expertise".

Decisions such as *Sullivan* and *Kemp*, where defendants who were in no sense mentally ill faced a choice between pleading guilty to crimes they did not commit or pleading insanity, therefore involve fundamental contraventions of human rights. Such persons should be allowed to contest their guilt without risk of detention under a classification of insanity.[93]

These arguments can be put directly in domestic law following implementation of the Human Rights Act 1998.[94] By virtue of section 6, a court will be obliged to apply what is required under the Convention even if that requires departing from previous decisions of the highest authority such as the House of Lords decision in *Sullivan*. In criminal law contexts, findings of insanity which are compatible with objective medical expertise would be greatly facilitated if courts would use, as a benchmark, those mental conditions which permit compulsory civil commitment.[95]

(iv) Reform of insanity law

In normative and conceptual terms, the English law of insanity is open to significant criticism. Yet the law of insanity has remained essentially unchanged since the mid-nineteenth

---

[88] § 19.1(ii)(a).

[89] Harris, O'Boyle and Warbrick, *Law of the European Convention on Human Rights* (2nd ed., 2009) 133–7, 153–9.

[90] *Winterwerp* v. *Netherlands* (1979) 2 EHRR 387. The European Court of Human Rights laid down three conditions: (i) the individual detained must be reliably shown by objective medical expertise to be of unsound mind; (ii) the individual's mental disorder must be of a kind or degree warranting compulsory confinement; and (iii) the disorder must persist throughout the period of detention.

[91] "Insanity and the European Court of Human Rights" [1992] *Crim LR* 418, 420–1; see too Baker, "Human Rights, *M'Naghten* and the 1991 Act" [1994] *Crim LR* 84; Mackay and Gearty, "On Being Insane in Jersey" [2001] *Crim LR* 560; Mackay, "On Being Insane in Jersey Part Two" [2002] *Crim LR* 728.

[92] *Hennessy* [1989] 1 WLR 287 (CA).

[93] It may be that, if a particular person can reliably be predicted to be a danger to others, a form of non-punitive civil commitment may be permissible. On the difficulty of reliable prediction see Floud and Young, *Dangerousness and Criminal Justice* (1981); Palmstierna, "One in Thirty Predictions of Assault by Discharged Psychiatric Patients will be Correct" [1999] *BMJ* 1270.

[94] See above, § 2.5.

[95] Mental Health Act 1983.

century.[96] The Law Commission has started a new reform initiative with a scoping paper followed by a discussion paper focused on identifying the way in which the law of insanity and its perceived difficulties impacts on the day-to-day operation of criminal justice system.[97] It seems exactly the right priority to ascertain the practical need for reform. Recent legislative reforms relating to the disposal options that a judge has following a verdict of not guilty by reason of insanity have removed a lot of the sting from the criticisms of the current law: now, even following a special verdict on a charge of murder, D does not face the prospect of indefinite detention until a government minister decides it is safe for him to be released. Yet even the most practically minded and cost-conscious reform initiative must also address fundamental questions. And for the insanity defence the most fundamental question is, when does D's mental condition exempt him from blame and censure?

As interpreted in England and Wales, the *M'Naghten* Rules provide an exclusively cognitive test for determining insanity. A person who may be unequivocally "mad" in terms of diagnostic criteria may yet know the nature and quality of her act in the narrow sense of the term used in English law and know that it was contrary to law. Lord Devlin defended this emphasis on cognition on the grounds that the faculty of cognition was the main distinguishing feature between man and animals.[98] Yet in matters of criminal punishment, the key question is whether the defendant has manifested sufficient culpability to warrant being *punished* (as distinct from restrained). Questions which focus on cognition alone[99] will not capture all the dimensions of culpability. A schizophrenic under the delusion that he has divinely ordained killings to commit might find it difficult to resist the voices he hears in his head when they enjoin such killings. The clinical literature contains many examples of behaviour strongly influenced by delusions or obsessions arising from pathological states.[100] English law has not been receptive to such learning: in response to an argument that a defendant should be adjudged insane if his conduct was driven by pathological impulses, Lord Hewart described it as "a fantastical theory ... which if it were to become part of our criminal law would be merely subversive".[101]

Conversely, when the interests of social control have appeared to judges to be best served by the insanity defence, an expansive approach has been taken to the notion of disease of the mind, leaving special verdicts the only exculpatory route for persons such as diabetics or epileptics who are sane under any non-legal meaning of that term.[102] So: a schizophrenic may not be insane, but a diabetic is. It is a conclusion only a lawyer could reach.

---

[96] As the insanity defence was most important in the context of capital murder, the introduction of the defence of diminished responsibility in 1957 reduced the practical importance of insanity and in that sense can be regarded as a significant reform in the provision of mental disorder defences.

[97] *Insanity and Automatism: A Scoping Paper* (2012); Peay, "Insanity and Automatism: Questions from and about the Law Commission Scoping Paper" [2012] *Crim LR* 927; Law Commission, *Criminal Liability: Insanity and Automatism. A Discussion Paper* (2013).

[98] "Mental Abnormality and the Criminal Law" in Macdonald (ed.), *Changing Legal Objectives* (1963) 71.

[99] This is particularly true where the matters that D must know are as narrowly conceived as they are under English law. An emphasis on questions of cognition rather than volition has been extolled as one of the virtues of the *M'Naghten* Rules in US jurisprudence, but there the interpretation of what D must know is more liberal: Livermore and Meehl, "The Virtues of *M'Naghten*" (1967) 51 *Minn LR* 789.

[100] Goldberg and Huxley, *Common Mental Disorders: A Biosocial Model* (1992).

[101] *Kopsch* (1925) 19 Cr App R 50, 51 (CCA).

[102] To compound the problem, while protection of the public from the recurrence of violent episodes has been the nominated policy behind this expansive approach, there is little evidence that diabetics and epileptics who have been involved in such incidents constitute an ongoing danger: Fenwick, *Automatism, Medicine and the Law* (1990) 10.

The narrow interpretation of the two principal limbs of the *M'Naghten* Rules is one of the main reasons why the insanity defence is not more frequently employed. The Criminal Procedure (Insanity and Unfitness to Plead Act) 1991 allows a variety of disposal outcomes after a special verdict,[103] but this has not, to date, encouraged significantly more insanity pleas.[104] Arguably a more expansive mental disorder defence is required to address the needs of mentally ill persons who become defendants in criminal trials.

Such a proposal would be opposed by those who advocate the abolition of the insanity defence. Abolitionists may be sceptics such as Thomas Szasz, who in his voluminous writings time and again refers to mental illness as a convenient myth exploited by the "ill" and their carers.[105] However, the Szasz viewpoint founders against the advances made in the reliable identification of mental disorders.[106] More telling is the abolitionist proposal made by Norval Morris.[107] He asserts that a cohort of mentally disordered persons comprising a statistically significant number and representative of the main kinds of mental disorder will contain no greater incidence of persons with offending behaviour than an equivalent sized cohort made up of randomly selected persons. Yet if we were to compare both those groups with an equivalent cohort of males between the ages of 14 and 22, living in socially deprived circumstances in inner-city areas, we would find a much greater incidence of offenders in the last group.[108]

As Morris observes, one response to these findings is to advocate a defence of social deprivation.[109] He does not support that but instead argues that all three groups should receive the same treatment, subject to the relevance of other legally recognised defences. Personal and social circumstances should be relevant to sentencing but not to liability. Accordingly, if, for a mentally disordered person, her mental condition precluded mens rea, she should receive an unqualified acquittal like anyone else. If she is considered dangerous, then civil commitment should be considered; that job should not be done through the insanity defence. If she has mens rea, she should be convicted and her disorder considered when determining what sentence or treatment she should receive.

Morris makes a powerful case. He buttresses his arguments from principle with well-founded observations of how the insanity defence operates in the US context. The majority of disordered offenders are processed through plea bargains and guilty pleas, as with other non-disordered offenders. Insanity, in practice, is confined to very serious offences, particularly capital murder. Significant advantages accrue to those offenders who can afford

---

[103] Including a hospital order (with or without restriction), a guardianship order, supervision and treatment order, and an absolute discharge.

[104] Mackay and Kearns, "More Fact(s) about the Insanity Defence" [1999] *Crim LR* 714

[105] *The Manufacture of Madness* (1970); *The Myth of Mental Illness* (1961).

[106] American Medical Association, DSM (IV) (2013).

[107] "The Criminal Responsibility of the Mentally Ill" (1982) 33 *Syracuse LR* 477.

[108] Significant research carried out after Morris's article indicates that certain diagnoses, notably schizophrenia, are predictive of violence but not strongly predictive: Bowden, "Violence and Mental Disorder" in Walker (ed.), *Dangerous People* (1996) 13. However, the point remains that age, gender, and social circumstances are more highly correlated with crime, including violent crime.

[109] Bazelon, "The Morality of the Criminal Law" (1976) 49 *So Cal LR* 385; Delgado, "Rotten Social Background: Should the Criminal Law Recognise a Defense of Severe Environmental Deprivation?" (1985) 3 *J Law and Inequality* 9.

eminent expert witnesses—the more the better—whose evidence is frequently of a prolix and speculative character.

On the other hand, Morris's argument underplays the fact that there *are* persons so disordered or so deficient in cognitive capacities that the presence, in formal terms, of mens rea would not entail any measure of culpability.[110] For those persons, any form of conviction is wrong: an injustice is done to persons severely psychotic if thereby deprived of any capacity for sequential thought and practical reasoning, as would also be the case for profoundly learning-disabled persons or those afflicted with advanced dementia. These extreme conditions are capable of satisfactory definition; persons with such conditions should not be found guilty of crimes because they are so irrational or mentally disabled as to be beyond any moral scheme of reference.

Outside these categories, the Morris position has considerable force, since there is less diagnostic precision and more scope for debate concerning culpability. A case in point is that of Anders Breivik,[111] who displayed considerable cunning when exploding a car bomb, causing eight deaths, and then killing a further sixty-nine persons with an automatic weapon.[112] Breivik was found guilty of murder but not before two court-appointed psychiatrists reported that he was psychotic[113] because of his schizophrenia and therefore not criminally responsible under Norwegian law. That report was superseded by a second psychiatric report which found the Breivik was not psychotic, clearing the path to a criminal trial.[114] What is not in dispute is that Breivik was a fervent admirer of Adolf Hitler and believed that his violent acts and the promulgation of his racist views would prove inspirational and, as in the case of Hitler, culminate in an authoritarian regime replacing effete democracy. In the first psychiatric report his world view and the atrocity it led to were the product of schizophrenia. In the second report,[115] he is a political extremist responsible for his thoughts and deeds.

(a) The Law Commission

Of course, irrational beliefs are held by many sane persons. But assume that the first psychiatric report in the Breivik case was the more convincing, that his political views were

---

[110] Bonnie, "The Moral Basis of the Insanity Defense" (1983) 69 *ABAJ* 194; Brady, "Abolish the Insanity Defense? No!" (1971) 8 *Houston LR* 629.

[111] Moore, "The Quest for a Responsible Responsibility Test: Norwegian Insanity Law after Breivik" (2015) 9 *Crim Law and Phil* 645.

[112] When setting his car bomb adjacent to a government building, Breivik placed a sign ("Sewer cleaning in progress") to explain the smell of sulphur. Later, he dressed in police uniform to gain access to the summer camp where he killed his further victims. For a brief yet informative account of Breivik's crimes and his mental condition at the time they were committed, see Wessely, "Anders Breivik, the Public and Psychiatry" (2012) 379 *The Lancet* 1563.

[113] Under the Norwegian Criminal Code, s. 44, any person who was psychotic or unconscious at the time of his or her otherwise criminal act is deemed irresponsible.

[114] If an insanity plea is raised in Norway, D is examined by two psychiatrists who report to the Commission of Forensic Medicine. If that report is passed on to the trial court, the matter of D's mental condition is almost invariably determined according to the findings in the report. It is unusual for the Commission to order a second report: see further Moore, "The Quest for a Responsible Responsibility Test: Norwegian Insanity Law after Breivik" (2015) 9 *Crim Law and Phil* 645, 646–7.

[115] This was accepted by the trial court, which found that his beliefs were intelligible in the context of an extremist political culture. The court also took into account that, although a paranoid loner, Breivik could function efficiently in a range of areas: Oslo District Court Judgment, TOSLO-2011-188627-24E (24 August 2012) 59–66.

symptomatic of a mental disorder rather than those of a "normal" person succumbing to extremism. Such an assumption provides a useful perspective from which to assess the proposed reforms of English insanity law put out for discussion by the Law Commission.[116] The Commission would abolish the current law and replace it by a statutory defence. Under its terms, if D had a "qualifying recognised medical condition"[117] which wholly deprived her of the capacity (1) to make a judgment rationally; or (2) to understand she was doing something wrong or (3) to control her actions, she would be found "not criminally responsible by reason of a qualifying, recognised medical condition".

On the assumption that Breivik's beliefs stemmed from a mental pathology, they would seem (1) not to arise from a rational judgement. Additionally, since under the Commission's proposals the understanding of wrongness goes beyond knowledge that one's actions are contrary to law and into the question of whether one could understand that the conduct was something that should not be done,[118] Breivik would seem (2) to have believed, due to his (assumed) mental disorder, that he had done the right thing. On top of that, because he saw himself as a man of destiny, he may well have found it obligatory to act and was arguably, in that sense, (3) unable to control his actions. Notice that any one of these findings is sufficient to pre-empt conviction. Seemingly then, Breivik would not be guilty of murder.

The acquittal of persons such as Breivik would be disquieting. Wherever his views came from, they were appalling and led to a horror that he conceived, planned and executed. Reflection on this case inclines one to the view that a defence based on mental disorder should be narrower than the Law Commission proposes. It is submitted that the position of mentally disordered persons whose condition falls short of severe psychosis or profound cognitive impairment should be the same as that of any other defendant and, importantly, they should be taken out of the criminal justice system if the elements of the offence with which they have been charged are not made out.

Accordingly, under any reformed law, a defence of mental disorder with a special verdict allowing control of the defendant should be available for any person with a serious mental disorder incompatible with moral agency or severe learning disability whose conduct and state of mind satisfies the definitional elements of a crime.[119] For dangerous, mentally disordered persons who do not fulfil these criteria, restraint should be a civil and not a

---

[116] *Criminal Liability: Insanity and Automatism. A Discussion Paper* (2013). See paras. 4.123–4.130 for the terms of the defence.

[117] What is a qualifying, medical condition will be based on medical testimony but is a legal concept to be decided by the court. Excluded at the outset will be anti-social personality disorder and acute intoxication: *ibid.,* paras. 4.55–4.84.

[118] *Ibid.,* paras. 4.19–4.33.

[119] This is in line with the Report of the Committee on Mentally Abnormal Offenders (Cmnd. 6244, 1975), which recommended allowing a defence of mental disorder if D suffered from severe mental illness or severe subnormality. Persons in that class would receive a special verdict and remain within the jurisdiction of the court if the elements of the offence are proved and any defence such as a genuine belief in the need for self-defence disproved. Note, however, the further constraint in the Draft Criminal Code (Law Com. No. 177, 1989), cl. 35(2), which refuses a defence to persons in that category if it is proved beyond reasonable doubt "that the offence was not attributable to the severe mental illness or severe mental handicap". Contrast the view of Moore, who has long held that the best version of an insanity defence should take the form of a status defence, confined to those persons comparable in terms of moral agency to "infants, animals and trees": "The Quest for a Responsible Responsibility Test: Norwegian Insanity Law after Breivik" (2015) 9 *Crim Law and Phil* 645, 680–1; see too Moore, *Law and Psychiatry* (1984) chap. 6.

criminal process.[120] For convenience and public safety it may be necessary to conjoin civil commitment with criminal proceedings in certain cases.

§ 19.2 Diminished responsibility

Diminished responsibility is a statutory defence, first introduced into English law by section 2 of the Homicide Act 1957. A reformulated version of subsection (1) of section 2 has been introduced by section 52 of the Coroners and Justice Act 2009, as follows:[121]

> (1) A person ("D") who kills or is a party to the killing of another is not to be convicted of murder if D was suffering from an abnormality of mental functioning which—
> (a)   arose from a recognised medical condition,
> (b)   substantially impaired D's ability to do one or more of the things mentioned in subsection (1A), and
> (c)   provides an explanation for D's acts and omissions in doing or being a party to the killing.
> (1A) Those things are—
> (a)   to understand the nature of D's conduct;
> (b)   to form a rational judgement;
> (c)   to exercise self-control.
> (1B) For the purposes of subsection (1)(c), an abnormality of mental functioning provides an explanation for D's conduct if it causes, or is a significant contributory factor in causing, D to carry out that conduct.

Unlike an insanity plea, a successful defence of diminished responsibility does not secure an acquittal. The effect is to reduce the grade of offence from murder to manslaughter.[122] For offences other than murder, there is no defence of diminished responsibility, and matters which would fall within section 2 in the context of murder become matters of mitigation, not defence.[123] The *raison d'être* of section 2 is to avoid the fixed penalty for murder and to afford the sentencing judge the complete discretion that a verdict of manslaughter allows. A large range of culpability falls within the provision; one defendant may successfully plead the defence yet receive a light sentence or even a hospital order without restriction, whereas another defendant may receive a very substantial term of imprisonment: each outcome may be justifiable in its own terms. Recently, the courts have prioritised public safety over questions of culpability and the best interests of D, even where D clearly is in need of hospital treatment. In *Vowles*,[124] the Court of Appeal stressed what it saw as the virtue of section 45A of the Mental Health Act 1983, relative to other forms of disposal. Section 45A empowers a court to hand down a sentence of imprisonment but direct that the prisoner goes first to hospital for treatment. Under the section 45A regime, D remains a prisoner rather than a

---

[120] Institutional arrangements would have to be made to ensure that the civil process should be initiated immediately for persons acquitted but reasonably taken to be dangerous to others or themselves. The important thing is that if an offence has not been proved, any confinement should satisfy the terms of mental health legislation concerned with therapy and personal and public safety.

[121] Mackay, "The New Diminished Responsibility Plea" [2010] *Crim LR* 290.

[122] Homicide Act 1957, s. 2(3).

[123] For a proposal that a defence of diminished responsibility be more widely available, see Horder, "Pleading Involuntary Lack of Capacity" [1993] *CLJ* 298.

[124] [2015] EWCA Crim 45.

patient and any release is a matter for the Parole Board whose decisions are based on public safety rather than the interests of D.[125]

(i) The burden of proof

Section 2(2) places the burden of proof on the defence.[126] On general principles, any burden placed on the defence is discharged on a balance of probabilities. The burden was placed on the defence as it was thought that it would be anomalous to arrange the matter any differently from the position prevailing for insanity. It is unfortunate that the opportunity has not been taken to change the position for insanity and to provide, in either case, that the burden of disproof should ultimately fall to the prosecution should the defence discharge the evidential onus of raising insanity or diminished responsibility as a live issue. There is no reason in principle why insanity and diminished responsibility should be treated any differently from defences such as self-defence or duress in the matter of proof. The determining factor has been the presumption of sanity, but that presumption could surely have been displaced on a basis of evidential onus rather than the imposition of a full probative burden.[127] Be that as it may, the Court of Appeal has held that there is no breach of Article 6(2) of the ECHR in placing the burden of proof on D, ruling it not to be disproportionate principally because the burden did not fall to D until the prosecution had proved the elements of murder.[128] The same facts may, on occasion, raise both an issue of diminished responsibility and an issue under the loss of control defence. In the case of the latter, a burden of disproof falls to the prosecution.[129] It cannot be easy for juries to assess the same facts raising two separate but overlapping issues under different standards of proof.[130]

(ii) The elements of the defence

There are four elements to the defence: there must be an abnormality of mental functioning; the abnormality must arise from a recognised medical condition; the abnormality must give rise to a substantial impairment of mental ability; and this must provide an explanation for D's acts or omissions in doing or being a party to the killing. By contrast with the insanity defence, there is no requirement that medical evidence must be submitted as a condition of raising the defence, but it can be readily appreciated that expert medical evidence is a practical necessity if the defence is to be successfully raised.[131] Prior to the 2009 reformulation, the ultimate question was whether D's *responsibility* for the killing of V was substantially impaired, essentially a matter for the moral sense of the jury—a judgment

---

[125] For criticism of *Vowles* see Peay, "Responsibility, Culpability and the Sentencing of Mentally Disordered Offenders: Objectives in Conflict" [2016] *Crim LR* 152.

[126] Homicide Act 1957, s. 2(2).

[127] See above, § 19.1(ii)(a).

[128] *Lambert* [2001] 1 Cr App R 205.

[129] Coroners and Justice Act 2009, s. 54(5).

[130] Mackay, "Pleading Provocation and Diminished Responsibility Together" [1988] *Crim LR* 411. Although the article discusses the earlier version of diminished responsibility and the old defence of provocation which is now replaced by the statutory defence of loss of control, the difficulties analysed by Mackay in large part carry over to the new law.

[131] In *Bunch* [2013] EWCA Crim 2498, the practical necessity for medical witnesses supporting the defence was affirmed.

informed but not compelled by the medical evidence. The ultimate question is now more fact specific: did the recognised medical condition (which must substantially impair either D's understanding of the nature of his conduct, or D's ability to form a rational judgment, or D's ability to exercise self-control) provide an *explanation* for D's acts or omissions? That is a question amenable to psychiatric testimony. In *Brennan*,[132] Davis LJ accepted the legitimacy of hearing expert testimony concerning whether D's mental condition was explanatory of D's conduct.[133] D had been convicted of murder despite unchallenged evidence from the expert witnesses that all the elements supporting a finding of diminished responsibility were present. The Court of Appeal ruled that, in the light of this, the trial judge should have withdrawn the charge of murder from the jury.

(a) An abnormality of mental functioning

The phrase "abnormality of mental functioning"[134] replaces "abnormality of the mind" in the original version of the defence. Reviewing that predecessor phrase, Lord Parker CJ defined "abnormality" as "a state of mind so different from that of ordinary human beings that the reasonable man would term it abnormal", which does not really take the matter forward.[135] Abnormality of mental functioning is in formal terms a free-standing element of the defence but, as will be examined below, there must also be proof that there was a substantial impairment of one or more of D's capacities to understand the nature of his conduct, to form a rational judgement, or to exercise self-control.[136] In cases where there is diminished capacity to understand one's conduct or to make rational judgements, that of itself will very likely establish abnormality of mental functioning. Less obvious will be cases where D claims that his ability to exercise self-control was substantially impaired due to psycopathy or forms of personality disorder, but where he lacks any delusional beliefs and is not afflicted by auditory or visual hallucinations. The objects of D's desires may be reprehensible, but that does not entail that they arise from an abnormality of mental functioning. In such cases the line between a radically reduced capacity to control oneself and a non-condonable failure to control oneself may be very fine,[137] and a jury's perception that D is abnormal and by that token not fully responsible for his acts may be significant. In *Byrne*,[138] D strangled a young women and mutilated her corpse. Evidence was given that he was subject to perverted sexual desires which were much harder to resist than normal sexual desires and the verdict in his favour must imply a jury finding of "abnormality of mind" under the previous law. Contrast *Sutcliffe*,[139] where D had killed a large number of sex workers, claiming that he had orders from God to do so. Although there was cogent evidence that D was a schizophrenic,[140] his defence under the original version of diminished

---

[132] [2014] EWCA Crim 2387.

[133] *Ibid.*, para 51.

[134] Homicide Act 1957, s. 2(1).

[135] *Byrne* [1960] 2 QB 396, 403.

[136] Homicide Act 1957, s. 2(1A).

[137] Wootton, "Diminished Responsibility: A Layman's View" (1960) *LQR* 224. Although the article deals with the previous version of the defence, the same problem of differentiating between the difficulties of self-control that can beset anyone and those failures of self-control that partially excuse are present in the current law.

[138] [1960] 2 QB 396.

[139] *The Times*, 30 April 1981.

[140] D was transferred to a special hospital early in his life sentence for murder.

responsibility failed. Although D, under the new version, could raise a lack of capacity to make a rational judgement[141] in addition to substantially impaired ability to exercise self-control,[142] a jury might yet be reluctant to find in his favour given the gruesome facts of the case. The final verdict is with the jury, however strong the evidence of abnormality of mental functioning.

(b) A recognised medical condition

The abnormality of mental functioning must arise from a recognised medical condition.[143] Although the defence of diminished responsibility most readily brings to mind forms of mental diseases such as schizophrenia or bipolar disorder, transient disorders of the mind brought about by conditions such as diabetes and arteriosclerosis should also readily fall within the category of medical condition. Mere stress brought about by, say, the protracted suffering of a gravely ill partner will not suffice unless the stress induces a recognised medical condition. Again, this requirement underscores the practical necessity for expert medical evidence.

There is no approved list of recognised medical conditions. The matter is left at large, allowing the defence to be sensitive to advances in the expert consensus as to what amounts to a medical condition. Of course, there may be disputes among experts as to what amounts to a medical condition. In resolving those disputes, reference will no doubt be made to the World Health Organization's *International Statistical Classification of Diseases and Related Health Problems* (ICD 10) and the American Medical Association's *Diagnostic and Statistical Manual* (DSM). Given the prestige of these glossaries, it would be tempting for courts to assume that if a particular condition relating to D is described in one or both of these compilations as a medical condition, then it is a recognised medical condition for the purposes of the diminished responsibility defence. The temptation should be resisted. The term "recognised medical condition" is a statutory term and is ultimately a question of law to be resolved by the judge. For instance, DSM lists "intermittent explosive disorder" as a medical condition.[144] It is far from obvious whether this should be accepted as a recognised medical condition for the purposes of the law. As Hughes LJ observed of this particular medical condition in *Dowds*, "any suggestion it could give rise to a defence because it amounted to an impairment of mental functioning would to say the least, demand extremely careful attention".[145]

The important decision of *Dowds* demonstrates that ICD 10 and the DSM are merely indicative and not conclusive as to what in law makes for a recognised medical condition. D had killed his wife when he was acutely intoxicated. He was a binge drinker but not alcohol dependent. It was argued for D that a state of acute intoxication was of itself a recognised medical condition because it was listed as such in both ICD 10 and DSM.[146] The Court of Appeal ruled that the new diminished responsibility defence had to be read

---

[141] It may be rational for a believer in God to follow His orders, but it is surely irrational to believe He has issued a personal mandate to kill sex workers.

[142] Presumably D thought that orders from God must be obeyed.

[143] Homicide Act 1957, s. 2(1)(a).

[144] DSM IV 663/667. Also listed are other crimogenic conditions such as kleptomania and sexual sadism.

[145] *Dowds* [2012] EWCA Crim 281, para. 31.

[146] *Ibid.*, para. 33.

against the well-established principle that voluntary intoxication did not constitute any form of excuse but was only relevant to proof of mens rea.[147] There was nothing in the legislation or its history to indicate any departure from that principle. Consequently, any form of voluntary intoxication was not a recognised medical condition for the purposes of the law.[148]

In substance, *Dowds* confirms the position taken by the House of Lords in *Dietschmann*[149] for the old law of diminished responsibility: voluntary intoxication will neither assist nor deny a defence of diminished responsibility. The question is, putting the state of intoxication to one side, whether the elements of the defence are made out.[150] Does the position alter if D is alcohol-dependent or addicted to any other form of drug? Addiction is indisputably a medical condition. In the light of *Dowds* and previous authoriy the answer seems to be negative, provided the addiction is compatible with what the law considers to be the voluntary taking of the drug. As we have examined previously, the conditions for involuntariness are set very high,[151] and there is no indication that this is about to change.[152]

Although inclusion as a medical condition in DSM or ICD 10 does not guarantee that any particular condition relating to D will be regarded as a recognised medical condition, neither should the absence of the condition from the lists entail the dismissal of the condition as a medical condition. If satisfied that a reputable body of medical experts considers D's condition to be a medical condition, the judge can classify it as a recognised medical condition.[153] That said, there will be some facets of D's psychological dispositions or state of development which may have a bearing on her responsibility for her acts but which cannot be plausibly medicalised so as to bring it within the parameters of the defence. Under the previous law, provision was made for "arrested or retarded development of mind" and the Law Commission recommended that any reformulated version of the defence should make provision for developmental immaturity for persons under the age of 18.[154] That proposal was explicitly rejected by the government, which was of the view that conditions such as autism and learning disabilities were sufficiently accommodated within the term recognised medical condition.[155] Because of this determination, the fact that D is, say, eleven years old, immature for her age, and therefore suggestible will not assist her. There are striking examples of young persons convicted for murder under the joint enterprise doctrine whose involvement in the killing was peripheral to say the least and who were clearly under

---

[147] Simester, "Intoxication is Never a Defence" [2009] *Criminal Law Review* 3.

[148] *Dowds* [2012] EWCA Crim 281, paras. 34–5.

[149] [2003] 1 AC 209.

[150] Sullivan, "Intoxicants and Diminished Responsibility" [1994] *Crim LR* 156; cf. Gibson, "Intoxicants and Diminished Responsibility: The Impact of the Coroners and Justice Act 2009" [2011] *Crim LR* 909.

[151] § 18.3(v).

[152] Apart from the decisions in *Tandy* [1989] 1 All ER 267, *Wood* [2008] EWCA Crim 1305, and *Stewart* [2009] EWCA Crim 593 (which insist, in the context of diminished responsibility, on a compulsion to drink), there is also the refusal to accept that voluntary intoxication can form part of D's "circumstances" for the purposes of the loss-of-control partial defence in *Asmelash* [2013] EWCA Crim 157; and rejection of temporary drug-induced psychosis as a disease of the mind in *Coley* [2013] EWCA Crim 223.

[153] Criminal courts would find guidance on what may be considered a reputable if minority medical opinion from the tort cases of *Bolam v. Friern Hospital Management Committee* [1957] 2 All ER 118 and *Bolitho v. City and Hackney Health Authority* [1998] AC 232.

[154] Law Com. No. 304, *Murder, Manslaughter and Infanticide* (2006) paras. 5.125–5.137.

[155] Ministry of Justice, *Murder, Manslaughter and Infanticide: Proposals for Reform of the Law. Summary of Responses and Government Position*, Response to Consultation, CP(R) 19/08 (2009).

the influence of the older protagonists.[156] The exclusion of developmental immaturity is regrettable.

(c) Substantial impairment of mental functioning

Prior to 2009, the law required proof of a *substantial* impairment of D's *responsibility* for his acts or omissions in doing the killing. By contrast, the current law requires a substantial impairment of D's ability to do one or more of three things: (i) to understand the nature of her conduct; (ii) to form a rational judgement; or (iii) to exercise self-control.[157] (It is important to bear in mind that the defence is not made out even if one or more of these abilities is found to be substantially impaired. D must further show that his mental disability provided an explanation for his conduct, a matter analysed below.)

Substantial.

At first, there was no reason to suppose that the meaning of "substantial" has changed from the old law. In R,[158] Judge LCJ considered that the meaning of substantial could not really be further explained but usefully added that use of the word indicated that conditions which were "trivial and insignificant" could be set aside. He also added that the "defence should be available without the defendant having to show that his mental responsibility for his actions was so grossly impaired as to be extinguished". Adapting his words to the new provision, D must show a significant diminution of her ability to understand her conduct, to form a rational judgement, or to exercise self-control, but her disability need not be wholly destructive of all capacity in those aspects of mental functioning. In the absence of definitive expert testimony, it should be for the jury to find whether any impairment of one or more of the relevant faculties passed the threshold of the "trivial and insignificant" and was weighty enough to be a substantial impairment. That, of course, leaves open the possibility that an impairment which is more than trivial and insignificant may, nonetheless, be found not to be substantial.

More recently, some doubt has been cast on the analysis of Judge LCJ in R. In *Golds*,[159] Elias LJ was astute to notice a tension between two cases decided under the old law, namely *Lloyd*[160] and *Simcox*.[161] On his Honour's reading of these cases, there remains an unresolved question: is it the case that any impairment that is more than trivial and insignificant should by that very token be treated as "substantial", or is it the case that something more than trivial and insignificant might still be less than "substantial"? For Elias LJ the way forward was for judges to direct juries in the terms of the statute and offer no guidance on the meaning of substantial. But now the matter has been raised, defence counsel will surely argue that any finding that an impairment was more than trivial or insignificant entails a finding that it was substantial. A further appellate decision is necessary.

---

[156] The campaigning group Justice for Families has an informative database giving details of the many convictions for murder of young people based on joint enterprise: see http//www.justice-for-families.org.uk.

[157] Homicide Act 1957, s. 2(1A).

[158] [2010] EWCA Crim 194, para. 15.

[159] [2014] EWCA Crim 748.

[160] [1967] 1 QB 75.

[161] [1964] Crim LR 402.

Three categories of mental functioning.
The first disability, an impaired capacity to understand the nature of her conduct, is uncomfortably reminiscent of the fist limb of the *M'Naghten* Rules, which, as we have seen, has received a very narrow interpretation.[162] Indeed, the example the Law Commission gave to illustrate an impairment of this ability is of a boy of 10 who does not really understand the physical nature of his conduct.[163] The ability to form a rational judgement offers on its face a more rounded approach by comparison with the insanity defence and it is clear that the Law Commission intended the impairment of this ability to be found in cases which go beyond the insanity defence.[164] Finally, impairment of the ability to exercise self-control clearly covers territory beyond the insanity defence, which makes no accommodation for volitional incapacity. In *Byrne*,[165] a successful defence under the old law of diminished responsibility was founded on evidence of perverted sexual urges which, according to expert testimony, were more difficult to control than normal sexual desires. Such a case would go to the jury under the new law if there were expert testimony that his perverted sexual urges arose from a recognised medical condition and were substantially more difficult to control than more normal sexual desires.

It can be concluded with some confidence that, in determining whether D has a substantial impairment of mental functioning, the courts will give an interpretation attuned to the rationale of this partial defence—which is not concerned with defendants who lack culpability but with defendants who may lack the culpability for murder. Moreover, it must always be borne in mind, when assessing whether D has a substantial impairment of mental functioning, that the impairment of mental functioning of itself does not ground the defence. The final question is whether the impairment provides an explanation for D's acts and omissions in doing (or being a party to) the killing.

(d) An abnormality of mental functioning that provides an explanation for D's conduct

The requirements of the new defence are, in an important sense, less accommodating than its *M'Naghten* counterpart. In the case of a plea of insanity, D's defence will succeed if he proves that he did not know his conduct was wrong or that he did not understand the nature and quality of his actions. In the case of diminished responsibility, however, it will not suffice to prove that a recognised medical condition undermined D's rationality or powers of understanding, even if those faculties are radically affected. The disability alone does not suffice: the disability must provide an explanation for the acts or omissions related to D's killing of V.[166] That explanation, it seems, must establish, on the balance of probabilities, that D's abnormality of mental functioning "causes, or is a significant contributory factor in causing, D to carry out the conduct".[167]

---

[162] § 19.1(ii)(d).

[163] In the example, the boy has been left to play violent video games for much of his life and he loses his temper and kills another child who attempts to steal his game. He assumes that his victim can be later revived, as happens in the game: Law Com. No. 304, *Murder, Manslaughter and Infanticide* (2006) para. 5.121(1)(a).

[164] As an example of an impairment to make a rational judgement, the Law Commission instanced a depressed man who has been a long-term carer for his terminally ill wife. She has requested many times that he kill her and he finally complies because "I felt that I would never think straight again until I had given her what she wanted" (*ibid.*, para. 5.121(2)(c)). It is doubtful whether a defence of insanity could be raised on those facts.

[165] [1960] 2 QB 396.

[166] Homicide Act 1957, s. 2(1)(c).

[167] Homicide Act 1957, s. 2(1B).

On the face of it, the statutory language provides that the linkage between the substantial impairment of mental functioning and the killing has to be of this causal nature: "provides an explanation if it causes or is a significant contributory factor in causing" the killing. That was the view of the government[168] and is the natural reading of the provision. However, there could have been more explicitness on this important matter. The provision contains no locution such as "if and only if". *Smith and Hogan* argues that the provision merely states that a causal linkage provides an explanation without precluding non-causal explanations.[169] But a statement that an explanation of the killing is provided by a causal link is a statement of the obvious; as such, one would expect explicit mention of non-causal explanations were they included too. Their omission suggests that a causal linkage is necessary.

In terms of causal doctrine, no distinction of principle should be drawn between a cause of an event and a significant contributory factor in causing an event. A significant contributory factor is clearly some input into bringing about the event which is more than *de minimis* and is therefore a cause of the event in the eye of the law even if more dominant causal features are also in play.[170] The event in question is the killing of V and the most direct causal agent in the history of that event is, of course, D. This causal element in the partial defence must be premised on the idea that the lack of ability to understand one's conduct, to make a rational judgement, or to exercise self-control must be one of a set of necessary conditions which together are sufficient to cause V's death. Normally, it would be said that the reasons which motivated D to kill V (say, D wanted V's money) explain rather than "cause" D's killing, as voluntary human conduct is regarded as uncaused.[171] However, because, under the terms of section 2, the explanation must take a causal form, it seems that if the motivation arises from an abnormality of mental functioning it is to be regarded in this context as a cause of as well as supplying a reason for the killing.

To test this conclusion, recall the decision of the House of Lords in *Kennedy (No. 2)*.[172] V died because he took heroin and he took heroin because he was a heroin addict. Addiction is clearly a medical condition. But recall that his taking of the drug was regarded as entirely his own voluntary act. Suppose that D is a heroin addict desperate for the drug and he kills V because the only way he can get access to the drug at this point in time is to kill V and seize V's heroin. D's craving for the drug arises from his addiction, a medical condition. It could be argued on his behalf that the condition of heroin addiction brought about an abnormality of mental functioning which substantially affected his ability to form a rational judgement and to exercise self-control. Does the decision in *Kennedy* impede this line of argument? The answer must be no. We know the taking of the drug in *Kennedy* was found to be voluntary. It must follow, therefore, that D's killing of V in our example was voluntary. In turn, for the purposes of this partial defence, a voluntary act of killing can be caused and not merely explained by the reasons that motivated D to kill. In the light of our

---

[168] "We do not believe that this partial defence should succeed when random coincidence has brought together the activity of the person and the recognised medical condition ... there must have been at least a significant contributory factor in causing the defendant to act as he did. We do not require the defence to prove that it was the only cause or the main cause or the most important factor, but there must be something that is more than a merely trivial factor." *Hansard*, HC, 4 March 2009, col. 416.

[169] *Smith and Hogan* 616.

[170] See above, § 4.2(ii)(c).

[171] Above, § 4.2(iii)(b).

[172] [2008] 1 AC 269.

previous discussion, we know that the law will not afford addiction the status of a *recognised* medical condition unless the consumption of the drug is considered involuntary by standards which even confirmed addicts are unlikely to reach.[173] However, in cases of acting in response to the promptings of schizophrenic delusions or violent sexual urges, the defence may well go to the jury on the ground that the abnormality of mental functioning was a causal part of the explanation of D's act of killing.

This insistence on a causal link between the abnormality of mental functioning and the killing of V is likely to narrow the scope of the defence. Under the former version of section 2, no linkage was required between D's abnormality of mind and the killing of V: the only question was whether the abnormality of mind substantially impaired D's responsibility for it. For instance, in *Dietschmann*,[174] D would not have killed V had he not been disinhibited by drink. The House of Lords confirmed that the fact that D would not have killed but for drink did not disentitle him from putting forward his extreme grief reaction to a recent bereavement as a factor diminishing D's responsibility for the killing. As things stand now, D would have to prove that his grief reaction was a causal factor in the killing.

The extent and nature of this change can be seen from a sample of cases collected as part of a study of diminished responsibility conducted for the Law Commission.[175] For instance, in Case 50, D is reported to have killed his lover V in a fit of jealousy because V had formed a romantic relationship with a third party. D had a history of schizophrenia and the prosecution accepted D's plea of guilty to manslaughter on the grounds of diminished responsibility. Essentially, the prosecution did this because of a firm diagnosis of schizophrenia. There was no finding or even a suggestion that D's schizophrenia in any way explained the killing and, of course, many killings done in jealous rage are perpetrated by persons unafflicted with any medical disability. But the admittedly awkward wording of the previous defence allowed a reading whereby one's state of schizophrenia of itself diminished one's moral responsibility, analogous to states such as infancy. Under the reformulated section 2, an account would have to be given of *how* the disease caused the killing. Unless there is a causal connection with a symptom—for example, Peter Sutcliffe's killing of prostitutes because of his psychotic belief that God had ordered him to do so—the defence is unavailable.

The case for introducing a formal requirement of this sort is not clear-cut. The position for schizophrenics is troubling. The condition raises the risk of violence by sufferers, but only to a small degree.[176] The new section 2 is undoubtedly a more clearly worded, more schematic provision than the earlier version. There is now a much clearer divide between the loss-of-control partial defence (as a partial condonation for persons in stressful circumstances) and diminished responsibility which looks to D's abnormal functioning.[177] Yet if that new tidiness comes at the price of murder convictions and mandatory life

---

[173] Above, § 19.2(ii)(b).

[174] [2003] 1 AC 1209.

[175] Law Com. No. 290, *Partial Defences to Murder* (2004) Appendix B.

[176] Walsh *et al.*, "Violence and Schizophrenia: Examining the Evidence" (2002) 180 *British Journal of Psychiatry* 490. There are significantly higher risks of violence on the part of persons diagnosed with depression, bipolar disorder, and, in particular, substance abuse disorders and personality disorders.

[177] As a matter of practice, under the previous law the line between the two defences was blurred. In over 70% of cases where diminished responsibility was raised, the plea was accepted without argument by the prosecution, often in cases of mercy killings and violent family relationships where the drivers of the killings were circumstantial rather than pathological. For discussion and references, see the fourth edition of this work at § 19.2(iv).

sentences for schizophrenics and others in like case, who may never receive adequate treatment for their symptoms in a prison setting, it is hardly an exercise in liberal and humane law reform.

§ 19.3 Infanticide

Conceptually, infanticide[178] is not a defence but a category of homicide. The offence of infanticide under the Infanticide Act 1938 is committed if D, the mother of V, a child under the age of 12 months, kills V when the balance of her mind is disturbed by reason of her not having fully recovered from the effect of giving birth to the child, or by reason of the effect of lactation consequent upon birth of the child. The offence provides, within its limited terms of reference, a more accommodating ground of mitigation than diminished responsibility in its original or new form. There is no requirement that the balance of D's mind should be disturbed by a condition amounting to a clinical disorder.[179] The jury may return a verdict of infanticide as an alternative to a finding of murder or of manslaughter,[180] or the offence may be charged in its own right. If the issue is contested, it seems that D need not prove that the balance of her mind was disturbed but must merely raise an evidential issue.[181] Most verdicts of infanticide arise from a plea of guilty to the offence. The scale of punishment is the same as manslaughter. The most frequent outcome is a probation order.

Studies of the working of the Infanticide Act 1938 indicate that a plea of guilty to infanticide will readily be accepted in cases where a mother kills her child when the child is under the age of 12 months if there is evidence of emotional disturbance at the time of the killing.[182] This liberal approach in practice contrasts with the restrictive terms of the Act. According to the statute, D's mind must be disturbed by (i) not having fully recovered from the effect of giving birth or (ii) by reason of the effect of lactation consequent upon the birth of the child. The latter condition is medically controversial[183] and we may focus attention on the first. It will be noted that, strictly, D's disturbance must be the result of the birth process and not owing to pressures, economic or emotional, arising from the introduction of a new child into D's domestic environment. In the informal world of guilty pleas, it would appear that such fine discriminations are not made.

---

[178] Mackay, *Mental Condition Defences in the Criminal Law* (1995) 207–14; Maier-Katkin and Ogle, "A Rationale for Infanticide Laws" [1993] *Crim LR* 903; Loughnan, "The 'Strange' Case of the Infanticide Doctrine (2012) 32 *OJLS* 685.

[179] From a study of 23 persons convicted of infanticide, only two could be considered mentally ill: d'Orban, "Women who Kill their Children" (1974) 134 *British Journal of Psychiatry* 560.

[180] Infanticide Act 1938, s. 1(2), as amended by the Coroners and Justice Act 2009.

[181] The Act makes no reference to a burden of proof on D.

[182] Mackay, "The Consequences of Killing Very Young Children" [1993] *Crim LR* 21.

[183] Bluglass, "Infanticide" [1978] *Bulletin of the Royal College of Psychiatrists* 14. In Law Com. No. 304, para. 826, reference is made to a yet-unpublished study reporting a link between lactation and dopamine sensitivity which may trigger psychosis. Maier-Katkin and Ogle note that childbirth itself can give rise to mental disturbance, although social and familial pressures are more important causes of subsequent instability: "A Rationale for Infanticide Laws" [1993] *Crim LR* 903.

It would be better if the law were redrafted to bring it closer to practice. The Law Commission's proposed Criminal Code would have amended infanticide with the formulation:[184]

> "A woman who, but for this section, would be guilty of murder or manslaughter of her child is not guilty of murder or manslaughter, but is guilty of infanticide, if her act is done when the child is under the age of twelve months and when the balance of her mind was disturbed by reason of the effect of giving birth or circumstances consequent upon that birth."

Even under that formulation, however, restrictions would remain which could operate with arbitrary effect. The offence would still require that the child killed be under 12 months of age and would be confined to women. It is perhaps no surprise therefore that, more recently, the Law Commission has recommended that the offence should remain as it is.[185]

§ 19.4 Infancy

(i) Children below the age of 10 years

At common law, any child under the age of 7 was *doli incapax*: deemed incapable of committing a crime.[186] The qualifying age has been raised by statute to 10 years.[187] Although provision was made at one time to raise the age further to 14,[188] it was never put into effect. In fact, legislative policy has now gone into reverse, with greater emphasis on punitive responses to wrongdoing by children and young people.[189]

Whatever a child under the age of 10 does, with whatever state of mind, it cannot constitute a crime; although it may lead to the imposition of a civil care order.[190] The incapacity of the child may well affect the legal position of persons associated with the conduct perpetrated by the infant. If D, a person above the age of criminal responsibility, were to instruct C, an infant under the age of 10, to take property from V, this, all other things being equal, would constitute a theft by D through the innocent agency of C. If C were to take V's property on his own initiative and hand it on to D, D's dishonest acceptance of the property would be theft rather than handling.[191]

(ii) Children between the age of 10 and 14 years

At common law, there was a presumption that a child aged above nine years and below 14 was *doli incapax*, a presumption rebutted if the prosecution could prove a "mischievous

---

[184] Law Com. No. 177, *A Criminal Code for England and Wales* (1989) cl. 64(1); Law Com. No. 304, *Murder, Manslaughter and Infanticide* (2006) Part 8.

[185] Law Com No. 304, para. 8.23.

[186] Kean, "The History of the Criminal Liability of Children" (1937) 53 *LQR* 364.

[187] Children and Young Persons Act 1933, s. 50, as amended by the Children and Young Persons Act 1963, s. 16. The age of criminal responsibility is low compared, for instance, to France (13), Germany (14), and Spain (16); it has been criticised as too low by the UN Committee on the Rights of the Child, *Concluding Observations: Great Britain and Northern Ireland* (2008). See further, Ashworth, *Positive Obligations in Criminal Law* (2013) 177.

[188] Children and Young Persons Act 1969, s. 4.

[189] Criminal Justice and Public Order Act 1994; Crime and Disorder Act 1998.

[190] Children Act 1989, s. 25.

[191] *Walters v. Lunt* [1951] 2 All ER 645 (CCA).

discretion" on the part of D—i.e. the capacity to differentiate between right and wrong.[192] The need to establish mischievous discretion was something additional to the mens rea required for the offence with which the infant was charged. This presumption of *doli inca-pax* came under attack predominantly on the ground that it excused those infants most in need of reformative or corrective measures.[193] It was abolished by section 34 of the Crime and Disorder Act 1998, which provides:

> The rebuttable presumption of criminal law that a child aged 10 or over is incapable of com-mitting an offence is hereby abolished.

On the face of it, the meaning of this provision seems clear. It abolishes a presumption. Accordingly, it remains open for a child under 14 to raise the defence of *doli incapax*.[194] On general principles of proof, the child should present evidence suggestive of an incapacity to make judgements of right and wrong and then the onus will be on the prosecution to prove that the child possessed a sufficient sense of right and wrong to warrant a criminal conviction.[195] That was the view of the Solicitor General on the second reading of the Bill. He envisaged a child raising the defence if he has "genuine learning difficulties and … is genuinely at sea on the question of right and wrong".[196]

Yet, despite the seeming clarity of section 34, a view has been taken that the abolition of the presumption entails the abolition of the defence of *doli incapax* altogether for children aged 10 years and over, an interpretation endorsed in a Home Office circular on the Act.[197] This view accords with the attitude expressed by judges and politicians that the defence of *doli incapax* was an indulgence incompatible with an effective response to juvenile offend-ing. The case law on *doli incapax* is confined to situations where the prosecution seeks to demonstrate the presence of mischievous discretion; there is no jurisprudence on rais-ing the defence. Conditioned by that background, it is understandable, perhaps, that the abolition of the presumption has been taken to mean the abolition of the infancy defence altogether in the case of children between the ages of 10 and 14. Yet the presumption of an incapacity and the incapacity itself are clearly different things. The abolition of a long-standing defence requires language expressed in the clearest of terms.

Unfortunately, however, that was not the view taken by the House of Lords in *R v. JTB*.[198] The Appellate Committee accepted that the presumption of *doli incapax* and the defence of *doli incapax* were two different things, and that to hold that section 34 abolished the pre-sumption while leaving intact the defence was a tenable reading of the section. But, ques-tionably invoking the interpretive latitude permitted by *Pepper v. Hart*,[199] Lord Phillips, in

---

[192] *Owen* (1830) 4 C & P 236, 172 ER 685; *Manley* (1844) 1 Cox CC 104; *Gorrie* (1919) 83 JP 136.

[193] See, especially, *C* [1996] AC 1.

[194] As is cogently argued in Walker, "The End of an Old Song" (1999) 149 *NLJ* 64.

[195] *Woolmington* [1935] AC 462 (HL).

[196] *Hansard*, Lords, 16 December 1997, col. 596.

[197] As cited in *Walker*, "The End of an Old Song" (1999) 149 *NLJ* 64, the circular reads: "children who are over the age of criminal responsibility (10- to 13-year-olds) will be treated in the same way as other juveniles when deciding whether or not prosecution is appropriate".

[198] [2009] UKHL 20.

[199] [1993] AC 593. *JTB* was a very questionable application of this already controversial decision. On the face of it, the terms of s. 34 are not ambiguous. It abolishes the presumption but not the defence itself. *Pepper v. Hart* is used by Lord Phillips to go behind the text and subvert its meaning; and, moreover, to do so against the interests of D. In its original conception, *Pepper v. Hart* conferred an exceptional and rare permission to consult Hansard

his majority judgment, perused the parliamentary debates on section 34 and was satisfied that ministers used the term *doli incapax* to include both the defence and the presumption, and that they intended the measure to abolish *doli incapax* in both dimensions.[200] On that basis, the defence was taken to have been abolished by section 34.

When the presumption was operative, the prosecution could experience considerable difficulty in demonstrating sufficient moral awareness on the part of the child by reference to evidence that went beyond establishing the mens rea for the offence. The need for such evidence was confirmed in *C*,[201] where it was held that the presumption of *doli incapax* was not rebutted by evidence of intentional damage of property. To convict D of criminal damage, it had to be proved that he knew it was *wrong* to damage other people's property. But, with the decision in *JTB*, all the prosecution need do now is to prove mens rea.

England and Wales does make certain other allowances for defendants of a young age. When sentencing a defendant under the age of 18, the court is obliged to consider the welfare of D in addition to the prevention of youth offending,[202] and typically any trial will be held in the Youth Court rather than the Crown Court. However, if the offending is serious (most notably murder) the venue may still be the Crown Court although Article 6 (fair trial) of the European Convention for the Protection of Human Rights requires special measures to allow effective participation in the proceedings for children and young people.[203] The defences of duress and self-defence, as interpreted, can take into account the age of D and so too can the partial defences to murder of diminished responsibility and loss of self-control. The Law Commission has recently proposed a defence for persons who cannot "understand that the conduct was something he or she ought not to do". However, if enacted in its current form it will only apply if the failure of understanding is based on a "recognised medical condition" so it would not assist, say, a developmentally immature 13-year-old.[204] There would still be cases such as *Wilson*,[205] where the 13-year-old D participated in a murder instigated and predominantly carried out by his father, but under duress. That defence is not, of course, available in murder and, although "swept along" by his father, D was found to have the requisite intent and was therefore guilty of murder. In the words of Ashworth, "A child of 13 would only have a hazy and under-developed of the social meaning of serious injury and death ... a child of that age cannot really understand the significance of such acts and their consequences."[206] But under the current law: no matter.

---

for ministerial statements in support of an interpretation of an otherwise ambiguous provision in a manner which would not disturb settled and reasonable expectations. See further Bennion, "Mens Rea and Defendants below the Age of Discretion" [2009] *Crim LR* 757.

[200] Even though he referenced the remarks of the Solicitor General, cited in the text above.
[201] [1996] AC 1.
[202] Criminal Justice Act 2003, s. 142A, as inserted by s. 9 of the Criminal Justice and Immigration Act 2008.
[203] *T and V v. United Kingdom* (2000) 30 EHRR 121; *SC v. United Kingdom* (2005) 40 EHRR 226.
[204] *Criminal Liability: Insanity and Automatism. A Discussion Paper* (2013) para. 4.126.
[205] [2007] EWCA Crim 1251.
[206] Ashworth, *Positive Obligations in Criminal Law* (2013) 193.

20

DEFENCES OF CIRCUMSTANTIAL PRESSURE

§ 20.1 Duress

The common law has long conceded that if crimes (excluding murder, attempted murder, and probably treason) are committed under threat of immediate or almost immediate death or serious bodily harm, D may be exonerated. The rationale for this concession is debated. One argument has been that the deterrent force of the criminal law is ineffective when competing with countervailing threats of imminent death or serious injury. It is sound utilitarian theory to confine the imposition of sanctions to circumstances where they will secure some benefit. Why make an uncertain threat of future imprisonment or fine in the face of an unyielding and certain threat of death or serious bodily harm?[1] The point is well made in respect of individual deterrence. In terms of general deterrence, however, it may be thought particularly appropriate for the criminal law to be at its most unyielding when privately organised violence undermines the official sanctions of the criminal law, an argument not without force in a time of terrorist organisations and violent gangs.[2] Nonetheless, it is possible to subscribe to general deterrence as a justifying principle for state punishment, while insisting that the infliction of a sanction on a particular individual should satisfy the requirements of justice.[3] Those who reject utilitarianism will insist that the convictions of individuals comply with the requirements of justice. From the perspective of just deserts, it would be unacceptably Draconian to punish persons who have acted to avoid catastrophic harm to themselves, to those to whom they are attached or feel responsible.[4] For the most part, this last sentiment reflects the current state of English law.

Duress is commonly regarded as the quintessential excuse, a concession to human frailty: a conception of the defence recently endorsed by the House of Lords in *Hasan*.[5] On most occasions, it does indeed operate in the realm of excuse, which is to say that we would make D a subject of praise were he to resist the coercion and merely excuse him were he to submit to the pressure. Yet this analysis is not always appropriate. Suppose that D, a

---

[1] For this reason Bentham approved the provision of a defence of duress: *Introduction to the Principles of Morals and Legislation* (1789) chap. xiv, para. 11.

[2] "Criminal law is itself a system of compulsion on the widest scale. It is a collection of threats of injury to life, liberty, and property if people do commit crimes. Are such threats to be withdrawn as soon as they are encountered by opposing threats?": Stephen, *History of the Criminal Law of England* (1883) vol. II, 107–8.

[3] Hart, *Punishment and Responsibility* (1968) chap. vii.

[4] Some theorists, such as Schopp, believe that a conviction should be recorded against D; but not even he requires D to be punished. Schopp's views are discussed below, § 20.1(iv).

[5] [2005] UKHL 22, para. 18; [2005] 2 AC 467, 489 (Lord Bingham).

taxi-driver, is carrying in his cab P, an armed man. P instructs him to park the vehicle outside a tobacconist's so that he may purchase cigarettes. D observes that parking is prohibited on the road adjacent to the shop; P responds he will blow D's brains out unless he does as he is told. It would be perverse to say that we *excuse* D for parking in the wrong place. He would have done the right thing, such is the disparity of the respective harms.[6] Where the balance of harms is more even, the pressure exerted on D is largely why we exonerate him. But where the discrepancy between the cost of complying with the letter of the law and the value of yielding to the threat is of the magnitude of our taxi-driver example, the focus is on the justifiability of his act. It may be that D has had a very bad day and to some degree welcomes the end of it all; still, if he decides after all to carry on living and parks his vehicle on the lines in order to do so, we should grant him the defence of duress.

Regardless whether, in particular cases, the emphasis is on excusatory pressure or on justifiable choice, duress operates in either context as a "pure" supervening defence. A valid plea of duress leaves intact the definitional elements of the offence charged. It is only when those elements have been proved against D that she need turn to duress as a way of avoiding the conviction that would otherwise follow. While, on occasion, attempts have been made to explain the defence of duress on the ground that, to be successful, it must negate actus reus or mens rea, we concur with the observation by Lord Bingham, in his wide-ranging review of the defence in *Hasan*, that "where duress is established it does not ordinarily operate to negative any legal ingredient of the crime".[7]

For centuries, duress traditionally involved situations where D committed a crime nominated by X, the person issuing the threat. Recently, the boundaries of the defence have been significantly enlarged, accommodating situations now known as "duress of circumstances".[8] These are cases where D (or another) is threatened with death or serious harm and, in order to avoid the harm, D, on his own initiative, commits what ordinarily would be a crime. The ramifications of this development are a work in progress, yet it is safe to say that duress by circumstances is now established as a discrete subdivision of the defence. In turn, this has helped prepare the way for an unequivocal recognition of a defence of necessity in English law. In this chapter we will examine the borderland between duress of circumstances and necessity, but we will defer a full consideration of the defence of necessity to Chapter 21.

(i) Duress by threat

First, we will examine duress in its traditional sense: a threat by P which will be lifted only if D commits a crime nominated by P.

---

[6] Under the rubric of duress (unlike that of necessity) we do not acquit D *for* doing the right thing: we acquit because he was under threat of death and acted in response to that threat. But where the disparity between what the duressor requires and what the duressor threatens is great, it seems right to conclude that D was justified in acting as he did unless we accord some transcendental value to compliance with the letter of the law. See further above, § 17.2.

[7] [2005] UKHL 22, para. 18. However, his Lordship took the view that duress always operates in the realm of excuse; contrasting with the view expressed here that, according to circumstances, duress may be variously excusatory or justificatory. We discuss the nature and rationale of duress further below, § 20.1(iv).

[8] Below, § 20.1(ii).

(a) The seriousness of the threat

The threat must be to inflict immediate or almost immediate death or serious bodily harm,[9] or rape.[10] Nothing below threats of death, serious harm, or rape is regarded, in law, as having sufficient coercive effect.[11] It is easy to envisage how other kinds of threat, e.g. to destroy a thriving business, or to expose details of a person's personal life, might be extremely effective in undermining resistance. Nonetheless, as a matter of policy, a threat of physical harm is insisted upon. Contrast the law of offences against the person, where psychological harm is regarded as bodily harm and serious psychological harm is regarded as grievous bodily harm.[12] Despite this, in *Baker*,[13] the Court of Appeal insisted that in the context of the defence of duress, a threat of physical harm was required.

There seems little immediate prospect of a more liberal approach. In *Quayle*,[14] the Court of Appeal refused to enlarge the notion of physical, bodily harm to accommodate physical *pain*, even extreme physical pain.[15] Moreover, in *Hasan* the House of Lords took judicial notice of the increasing recourse to duress as a defence, especially in relation to drug dealing and associated offences, and of the difficulty experienced by prosecutors in rebutting this defence (particularly when raised late in the day). These considerations have prompted an overt policy to confine the defence within narrow limits.[16] In this climate, we may assume that a rigid requirement, for threats of death or serious physical harm in the most literal sense, will remain an essential condition of duress for the foreseeable future.

(b) A "present" threat: immediate or almost immediate and unavoidable

The immediacy of the threatened harm is an important requirement. At one time, the courts showed a degree of sensitivity and realism in applying this criterion. In *Hudson*,[17] D gave false testimony when she observed P, who had earlier threatened to "cut her up", staring at her intently as she was about to give evidence in a criminal trial involving defendants with a well-founded reputation for serious violence. She knew P was associated with the defendants. On appeal against D's conviction for perjury, the Court of Appeal ruled that a defence of duress should have been left to the jury. The Court took the view that a threat may be "present" or operative despite a delay in its implementation. Whereas the trial judge had been of the view that the defence must fail as D was safe in court when giving her

---

[9] There are many authorities which insist that only death or serious harm will suffice; they are confirmed in an authoritative review of the defence by *Hasan* [2005] UKHL 22.

[10] The Court of Appeal accepted in *A(RJ)* [2012] EWCA Crim 434 and *CS* [2012] EWCA Crim 389 that in principle a threat of rape could raise the defence.

[11] In *Steane* [1947] KB 997, 1005, Goddard LCJ spoke, *obiter*, in terms of false imprisonment constituting adequate duress but in *Dao* [2012] EWCA Crim 1717, false imprisonment was not considered sufficient to raise duress. In *Valderrama-Vega* [1985] Crim LR 220 (CA), financial pressures and sexual blackmail were thought not to constitute legally adequate duress.

[12] *Burstow* [1998] AC 147 (HL); above, § 11.5(i)(a).

[13] [1997] Crim LR 497 (CA).

[14] [2005] EWCA Crim 1415; [2006] 1 All ER 988.

[15] The Court of Appeal required "extraneous circumstances capable of objective scrutiny by judge and jury" (*ibid.*, para. 75).

[16] [2005] UKHL 22, para. 21.

[17] [1971] 2 QB 202.

perjured testimony, for the Court of Appeal it was enough that the threats could have been implemented later that day on the streets of Salford.[18]

In *Abdul-Hussain*,[19] the Court of Appeal suggested that "imminent" was a more appropriate term than immediate and, certainly, an imminent rather than an immediate harm was at issue in *Hudson*. At the same time, "imminence" must still be understood as referring to something due to happen in the very near future. In *Cole*,[20] the Court of Appeal was, it is submitted, right to reject a defence of duress to robbery when D robbed building societies in order to pay debts on a due date and thereby avoid violence on that later date. Indeed, *Abdul-Hussain* itself was questionable on its facts. D and others hijacked a plane in order to travel to England from Sudan. They had good reason to fear that the Sudanese authorities might deport them to Iraq (where they were likely to be tortured and killed) at some time yet to be resolved. The Court of Appeal ruled that the trial judge was wrong to remove the issue of duress from the jury on the grounds of lack of immediately threatened harm. Arguably, a stricter view of imminence should be taken if the defence is to be kept within manageable bounds. That concern was very much to the mind of the House of Lords in *Hasan*. Although the matter did not fall for decision, Lord Bingham in his majority judgment specifically approved of the approach in *Cole* and disapproved of what he felt was a lax approach to the immediacy requirement in *Hudson* and particularly *Abdul-Hussain*.[21] In the view of their Lordships, the implementation of the threat must follow "immediately or almost immediately".[22]

So it seems that "imminence" is not enough. But perhaps there is still some limited room for manoeuvre. It is possible, even in the light of Lord Bingham's stricter approach, to distinguish between *Hudson* and *Abdul-Hussain*. In the latter case, the prospect of return to Iraq at the time of the hijack in Sudan was real but subject to contingencies and an uncertain time line. In *Hudson*, by contrast, P was present in court looking intently at D as she gave evidence. Furthermore, it was accepted that there was a real possibility that P and others would inflict serious violence on D later that same day. It is noteworthy that Baroness Hale, in a separate judgment, considered that the other members of the Court were overly concerned with denying the defence to criminals and their associates and insufficiently sensitive to the awful dilemmas that may confront vulnerable and innocent people caught up in the violence of others and beyond effective protection from the police and other agencies. Unfortunately, the more accommodating approach of Baroness Hale has not attracted support. In *Batchelor*,[23] Lord Bingham's reservations concerning the decision in *Hudson* were adopted and reinforced: "The teen-aged girls were no doubt in genuine and real fear

---

[18] By way of corollary, the Court of Appeal insisted that a realistic view should be taken of the degree of police protection available to D.

[19] [1999] Crim LR 570.

[20] [1994] Crim LR 582; below, § 20.1(i)(c).

[21] Baroness Hale was the only other member of the Court who gave a judgment on the duress aspect of *Hasan* and she favoured a rather less strict attitude to the defining conditions of the defence than did the other members of the bench (who concurred with Lord Bingham). The matter was *obiter* since, as will be discussed in § 20.1(i)(g), the House concurred unanimously that duress should be unavailable because D had voluntarily exposed himself to the risk of being coerced to commit offences.

[22] [2005] UKHL 22, para. 28.

[23] [2013] EWCA Crim 2638.

of their safety in *Hudson* but that was not a justification for applying the defence of duress, because they had the opportunity to avoid complying with the threat."[24] In *Batchelor*, D had not reported his difficulties to the police, because he had been told that his children would be tortured should he do so. His failure to contact the authorities precluded any reliance on the defence of duress.[25]

In addition to being immediate or almost immediate, the threat must also be unavoidable.[26] The exculpatory force of duress is based on the lack of viable alternatives: commit the offence or be killed (or seriously hurt). If there is a "safe avenue of escape", that should surely be taken.[27] Similarly, if effective protection is available to D, the threat is unlikely to constitute legally adequate duress.[28]

In practice, immediacy will in most circumstances be strongly linked with unavoidability. But they are not inseparable: as when P points a knife at D and threatens to stab her forthwith unless she hands over the keys to the bank's safe, but D makes her escape through a side door. If the threat is not of almost immediate application, then, as Lord Bingham put it, "there may be little if any room for doubt that [D] could have taken evasive action, whether by going to the police or in some other way".[29] But on particular facts, a less than completely immediate threat may nonetheless be in substance unavoidable: as the Court of Appeal recognised on the facts of *Hudson*.[30] Yet, from the negative attitude to that decision on the part of the majority in *Hasan*, it seems that a threat must be unavoidable *and* almost immediate. The fact that D acted as she did because she believed, entirely reasonably, that she would die or be very seriously hurt if she did not will not suffice. One can only hope that in deserving cases, courts will take what elbow room is needed from the qualification, *almost* immediate.

(c) Nomination of the crime

As currently interpreted, duress by threats involves an explicit or implicit requirement from X that D commits a *particular* crime. By contrast, in *Cole*,[31] D was ordered by X to make timely repayment of a debt or suffer serious harm. Consequently, he robbed a branch of a building society in order to obtain money for repayment. He was refused a defence of duress, *inter alia* because X had not *nominated*, expressly or impliedly, the crime D should

---

[24] *Ibid.*, para. 15.

[25] It seems that any physical opportunity to contact the police must be taken, regardless of the consequences. In the Australian case of *Taiapa* [2009] HCA 53, D drove to collect drugs on the order of P after he, his pregnant wife, and his mother had been threatened at gunpoint by P. Despite the fact that his wife and mother were placed in great and immediate danger, his failure to drive to the police rather than collect the drugs entailed the failure of his plea of duress: "an unparticularised concern that police protection may not be a guarantee of safety cannot without more supply reasonable grounds for a belief that there is no option other than to break the law in order to escape the execution of a threat" (para. 40).

[26] "No one could question that if a person can avoid the effects of duress by escaping from the threats, without damage to himself, he must do so": *Sharp* [1987] QB 853, 857 (Lord Lane CJ).

[27] *Gill* [1963] 2 All ER 688 (CA); *Hurley and Murray* [1967] VR 526; *N* [2007] EWCA Crim 3479.

[28] *Hudson* [1971] 2 QB 202; *Baker* [1999] 2 Cr App R 335 (CA). The need for imminence is separate from the question of protection: D may lose the defence of duress if she fails to seek effective protection even from an imminent threat. Conversely, if the threat (however real) is not imminent, the issue of effective protection does not arise.

[29] [2005] UKHL 22, para. 28. Cf., in Australia, *Taiapa v. R* [2009] HCA 53, para. 31ff.

[30] [1971] 2 QB 202.

[31] [1994] Crim LR 582 (CA); discussed above, § 20.1(i)(b).

commit. Robbing a building society was, rather, D's response to the predicament posed by X.

Historically, *Cole* is in line with the common law on duress by threats. Yet it is hard to discern what normative significance nomination has. Moreover, any requirement of nomination would appear now to be superseded by the evolution of the new subcategory of duress known as duress of circumstances (below, § 20.1 (ii)). Under that head, it is enough that D commits the offence (short of murder or attempted murder) as an avoiding response to an imminent threat of death or serious violence.[32] From D's perspective, the moral and legal issues at stake in duress by threats and duress of circumstances are essentially the same. "Nomination" is irrelevant. It is therefore submitted that nomination should not be a requirement for any form of duress. *Cole* is best explained on the basis of the finding that, in any event, the threat was insufficiently immediate.

(d) Resistance to the threat

In *Graham*, the Court of Appeal ruled that the threat made by X must, in all the circumstances, have been enough to overcome the resistance of a "sober person of reasonable firmness".[33] Recall that the threat must be a threat of imminent death or serious bodily harm. One might consider that most persons of reasonable firmness would succumb to pressure of that extreme kind. However, *Graham*, which was approved by the House of Lords in *Howe*,[34] makes clear that a balancing exercise must be done on each occasion between the threat and the crime that X requires D to commit. The more serious the offence and the greater its impact on innocent third parties, the more that is to be expected of D by way of resistance. As Lords Wilberforce and Edmund-Davies remarked in *Abbott*, "the more dreadful the circumstances of the [crime], ... the stronger and more irresistible the duress needed before it could be regarded as affording any defence".[35]

Indeed, for murder or attempted murder, resistance to the threat must be unwavering. In *Howe*[36] the House of Lords ruled that duress could not be invoked as a defence to murder; further, it was immaterial whether D's involvement was as a principal or an accomplice.[37] In *Gotts*,[38] the House of Lords held that the rule in *Howe* extended to cases of attempted murder. On the other hand, in *Ness*,[39] there was a ruling at trial that duress could be raised as a defence to conspiracy to murder. This seems sensible. Excluding the defence from murder and attempted murder is arguably harsh, but at least for those crimes D would be doing

---

[32] The Court of Appeal discussed some duress of circumstance cases but considered that the offences which fell to be excused under that head were, unlike the robberies in *Cole*, "spontaneous" reactions to the threats. The adjective is unhelpful. In every case they were *chosen* reactions, offences committed under the volition of the defendants and unnominated by anyone else.

[33] [1982] 1 All ER 801, 806.

[34] [1987] AC 417.

[35] [1976] 3 All ER 140, 152 (PC) (dissenting). The comments are made in the context of murder (and, as we shall see, are no longer applicable to that offence), but remain in point for other offences.

[36] [1987] AC 417.

[37] *Howe* overruled *Lynch* [1975] AC 653, where the House of Lords had permitted duress to be raised to *complicity* in murder, and confirmed *Abbott* [1976] 3 All ER 140, where the Privy Council had denied a defence of duress to murder as a principal.

[38] [1992] 2 AC 412.

[39] [2011] Crim LR 645.

or near to doing the ultimate harm to V. It would be even harsher to deny the offence to conduct prior to the stage of attempt.

The exclusion of murder and attempted murder from the defence of duress is too rigid.[40] Lord Hailsham, arguing in favour of the current law, stated that to rule otherwise would be to vindicate "the coward and the poltroon".[41] Heroism is a quality to be praised, but it does not follow that its absence is reason for censure. There will be occasions where we would expect even a person of reasonable firmness to be coerced into participating in murder, for example if a taxi-driver were to find his cab commandeered by armed terrorists and himself ordered at gunpoint to be the driver for a terrorist operation. It cannot be right that the cab-driver will receive the same mandatory sentence as those who threatened him and who carried out the killings. Yet the same inflexibility applies to youngsters. In *Wilson*,[42] a boy of 13 was pressurized by his father to assist in the killing of V. The exclusion of the defence was confirmed by the Court of Appeal despite its recognition that D was unable to resist his violent and overbearing father. The position is all the more anomalous given that a person who intentionally causes grievous bodily harm (which is a sufficient mens rea for murder) would be able to raise a defence of duress if his victim should survive the attack. It is noteworthy that in the context of a case where he was seeking to narrow the defence of duress, Lord Bingham stated that the argument for the extension of the defence to murder was, in logic "irresistible".[43] The Law Commission has since recommended extension of the defence to murder.[44]

(e) A sober person of reasonable firmness

What characteristics constitute the sober person of reasonable firmness, the standard of fortitude required by *Graham* and approved in *Howe*? This notional person may be attributed the age and sex of the defendant and must be assumed to be sober.[45] If the defendant is pregnant, so too is the notional person.[46] Unsurprisingly, timidity and pliancy were held in *Graham* to be non-attributable: to attribute them would have been to contradict the yardstick of reasonable firmness.[47]

In *Emery*,[48] the Court of Appeal considered *obiter* that a recognised psychiatric syndrome or mental illness could be attributed to the person of reasonable firmness. The Court envisaged that a jury could properly be asked what degree of resistance should have been shown by a woman suffering from post-traumatic stress disorder which had resulted in

---

[40] Treason may also fall outside the defence.

[41] *Howe* [1987] AC 417, 432.

[42] [2007] QB 960.

[43] *Hasan* [2005] UKHL 22, para. 21.

[44] *Murder, Manslaughter and Infanticide*, Law Com. No. 304 (2006) part 6. The Law Commission's proposal places the burden of proof on D and insists that there must be an immediate threat of fatal harm.

[45] In *Graham* [1982] 1 All ER 801, 806, Lane LCJ drew a direct (and questionable) analogy with provocation and aligned the "characteristics" applicable to pleas of provocation with characteristics allowed when applying the defence of duress.

[46] *Bowen* [1996] 4 All ER 837, 844 (CA), where there is added fear for the unborn child.

[47] Confirmed in *Bowen*, *ibid.*: "The mere fact that the accused is more pliable, vulnerable, timid, or susceptible to threats than a normal person are not characteristics [*sic*] with which it is legitimate to invest the reasonable/ordinary person for the purpose of considering the objective test".

[48] (1993) 14 Cr App R (S) 394 (CA).

a condition of learned helplessness. Yet, even if D's condition is a product of psychiatric disorder,[49] there seems to be an element of contradiction in attributing learned helplessness to "a woman of reasonable firmness". A possible way of reconciling this with an objective test is to allow such a condition to be attributed if a woman of reasonable firmness would have been afflicted with learned helplessness had she been subjected to the same experiences as D. However, this rationalisation, which is not made explicit in *Emery*, leads to singularly unattractive distinctions. Why should a state of learned helplessness generated by life's vicissitudes be treated more favourably than a similar condition which arises from a person's genetic endowment?[50] Ideally, such cases should be dealt with within a liberally drafted defence of diminished responsibility unconfined to cases of murder,[51] rather than by undermining the coherence of the reasonable firmness standard.[52]

What *is* clear, at least, is that any condition which does not amount to a mental illness or psychiatric disorder will not be attributed. The case law excludes personal characteristics such as "grossly elevated neurotic state",[53] unusual vulnerability to pressure,[54] and lack of firmness arising from sexual abuse.[55]

(f) Impact of the threat

Even if a threat of death or serious harm has been made which would have moved to action a person of reasonable firmness, it does not follow that D will be allowed a defence of duress. She *herself* must be influenced by that threat to commit the crime. If the commission of the crime is something she would have done anyway, a defence is not available. On the other hand, provided the threat was a material reason why D committed the crime, it need not have been the sole or even the dominant reason. In *Valderrama-Vega*,[56] D was confronted with threats of financial loss, exposure of his homosexuality, and physical violence. Only the last, of course, qualifies as legal duress. The Court of Appeal considered that D was entitled to raise a defence of duress if he would not have committed the crime but for threats of violence. If so, it was immaterial that other pressures were operating at the same time.

(g) Voluntary exposure to threats

Duress may not be available as a defence if D voluntarily consorts with persons who resort to violence when committing offences or joins an organisation aware that the infliction

---

[49] Moreover, the condition must explain why D was, subjectively, unable to resist the oppressor. In *GAC* [2013] EWCA Crim 1472, for example, D's claim that her battered women syndrome should have been taken into account when considering duress as a defence to dealing in Class A drugs was treated with great circumspection. For Hallett LJ, the condition would only assist the defence if it were predicated upon serious violence to such a degree that the defendant "had lost her free will" (*ibid.*, para. 51).

[50] For a telling critique of applying an objective standard in duress, see Smith, "Duress and Steadfastness: In Pursuit of the Unintelligible" [1999] *Crim LR* 363.

[51] See Horder, "Pleading Involuntary Lack of Capacity" (1993) 52 *CLJ* 298; Horder, *Excusing Crime* (2004) 183–5.

[52] Recall the similar difficulties which undermined the reasonable man standard in provocation, now resolved by reverting to an objective standard tempered only by the sex and age of D: *A-G for Jersey v. Holley* [2005] UKPC 23, [2005] 2 AC 580; Coroners and Justice Act 2009, s. 54.

[53] *Hegarty* [1994] Crim LR 353 (CA).

[54] *Horne* [1994] Crim LR 584 (CA).

[55] *Hirst* [1995] 1 Cr App R 82 (CA).

[56] [1985] Crim LR 220 (CA).

of violence is one of its organising principles. So, if D joins a terrorist organisation or an organised criminal gang, it will not avail him that he was later faced with a choice between offending and suffering "discipline" involving serious physical harm.[57] This is a salutary principle, an important limitation on the capacity of intrinsically violent organisations to provide its membership with immunity from wrongdoing. Nonetheless, it should be open for D to show that he has left the organisation, or dissociated himself from his acquaintances, of his own volition; thereafter, he should not be precluded from raising the defence. Additionally, he should not lose the defence if he was made to join the gang by a threat of imminent violence which continued thereafter.

This exclusionary principle was bolstered by the decision of the House of Lords in *Hasan*.[58] D had worked as driver and minder for E, who ran an escort agency. After P, a drug dealer and a man of violence, became E's boyfriend, D was ousted from his role in working for E. Nonetheless, as the jury found, D and P had remained in contact. Subsequently, P ordered D to carry out a burglary in the company of another person, F, informing D that F would kill him unless the crime was carried out. On these facts, the House of Lords ruled that any claim of duress must fail. In the words of Lord Bingham:[59]

> "The policy of the law must be to discourage association with known criminals, and it should be slow to excuse the criminal conduct of those who do so. If a person voluntarily becomes or remains associated with others engaged in criminal activity in a situation where he knows or ought reasonably to know that he may be the subject of compulsion by them or their associates, he cannot rely on the defence of duress to excuse any act which he is thereafter compelled to do by them."

The width of this statement should be emphasised. The fact of association is enough; D's association with P need not involve any joint criminal activity. Presumably D must know that P is a criminal although Lord Bingham does not explicitly state this. Once the fact of association is proved, D will be denied access to the defence of duress if he ought reasonably to have known that P might subject him to compulsion. Note the fact that D ought to have realised that D might be violent to him is enough. It is not necessary that he should have reasonably anticipated that P might coerce him into the commission of a crime.

This is tough law, too tough for Baroness Hale. She expressed an understandable fear that women in relationships with criminal men might be denied the defence merely on the basis that they should have foreseen that P might be violent to them in the course of the relationship. She would insist that D should have foreseen that P would coerce her into committing a crime, a condition which she considered would have been fulfilled on the facts of *Hasan*. The majority disavowed that limitation, confirming the decision in *Harmer*.[60] In *Harmer*, D was coerced by E into smuggling Class A drugs. D was a drug addict and was aware of the risk that E might be violent to him should he fail to pay on time for drugs supplied by E. D had not anticipated that E would coerce him into committing criminal acts to clear his indebtedness. Nonetheless, the Court of Appeal upheld the ruling of the trial

---

[57] *Sharp* [1987] QB 853 (CA). (An organised criminal gang. D was threatened with being shot when seeking to withdraw from a robbery; a defence of duress was denied.)

[58] [2005] UKHL 22; [2005] 2 AC 467.

[59] *Ibid.*, para. 38.

[60] [2002] Crim LR 401.

judge in refusing D a defence of duress. The fact that D was aware of the risk of violence from E should he form an association with him precluded any reliance on E's threats as a form of duress.

(h) Threats to persons other than D

The paradigm situation in duress is where X threatens D with immediate death or grievous bodily harm unless she promptly commits a crime nominated by X. As we have seen, the essence of the defence is the pressure that the threat exerts on D herself, a threat sufficient to sway a person of reasonable firmness. The pressure on D may be equally or even more intense should the threat be made against E, the husband or daughter or any other person closely connected with D. There is authority that the defence of duress will accommodate such situations[61] and every reason in principle why it should. D may be able to resist a threat to herself yet be unable to allow her resistance to initiate death or serious harm to a loved one. Indeed, the defence of duress should not be constrained by any closed list of relationships. Suppose that X, a bank robber, threatens to shoot a customer unless D, a bank employee, hands over the key to the safe. It is easy to imagine how D may feel constrained to comply.[62] In *Hasan* Lord Bingham stated that the threat could be to D, his immediate family, and to any "person for whose safety the defendant would reasonably regard himself as responsible".[63]

(ii) Duress of circumstances

In a sequence of cases—*Willer*,[64] *Conway*,[65] and *Martin*[66]—the Court of Appeal has laid the foundation for a "duress of circumstances" defence. The first two cases involved driving offences; it was ruled on both occasions that a defence of duress should have been left to the jury in the light of evidence that the vehicles had been driven as they had in order to escape threats of serious violence. These rulings were confirmed in *Martin*, where the Court of Appeal ruled that D should have been allowed to raise a defence of duress in answer to a charge of driving while disqualified. D's wife had threatened to kill herself unless D drove their son to his place of work.

    Martin can be explained in terms of duress by threats. It is true that the threat was not directed at D, but it was (self-)directed to his wife and there is authority that a threat to one's wife will suffice.[67] Furthermore, the crime that D had to commit was implicit in the

---

[61] *Hurley and Murray* [1967] VR 526 (Victoria SC) (threats to *de facto* wife); *Ortiz* (1986) 83 Cr App R 173 (CA) (assumption that threats to wife and daughter would suffice); *Martin* [1989] 1 All ER 652 (CA) (offending to ward off a threat of suicide by wife). In *CS* [2012] EWCA Crim 389, a threat of sexual abuse to a daughter was considered capable of raising a defence of duress provided the abuse would constitute rape. The defence failed for other reasons.

[62] It is noteworthy that in *Conway* [1989] QB 290 (CA), the threat constituting duress of circumstances was to D's passenger rather than D. The Court did not investigate the nature of the relationship between D and the passenger. The Draft Criminal Code (Law Com. No. 177), cl. 42, refers to threats "to cause death or serious personal harm to himself *or another*".

[63] [2005] UKHL 22, para. 21(3).

[64] (1986) 83 Cr App R (CA).

[65] [1989] QB 290 (CA).

[66] [1989] 1 All ER 652 (CA).

[67] *Hurley and Murray* [1967] VR 526 (Victoria SC); *Ortiz* (1986) 83 Cr App R 173 (CA).

terms of the threat. *Conway* and *Willer*, however, do enter new territory. In these cases, D responded to the threat by committing a crime of his own choosing. It was certainly not a case of X's directing D to do something. X, on the account offered by D, would have preferred D to do nothing; to stay where he was so that X could inflict violence on him.

Interestingly, there is no suggestion by the Court of Appeal in either decision that any extension of the law has occurred. Prior to these cases, the predominant view was that committing a crime of one's own initiative in order to avoid harm founded, if anything, a plea of necessity rather than duress unless the circumstances fell within self-defence.[68] Further, it is thought that conduct covered by necessity must be justified conduct; conduct that is merely excused cannot be said to have been necessary. Accordingly, *Willer* and *Conway* advance the law of excuse-based defences. Properly so. A threat of death or serious bodily harm was present in each case. The crimes were committed under the pressure of such threats. It is clearly established that if X tells D to drive his car on the pavement or be shot, D would have a defence of duress were he to do as he was told. There seems little justification for treating the circumstances that arose in *Willer* differently merely because D drove on his own initiative onto the pavement to escape being shot. By analogy with duress by threats, it will be sufficient that a person of reasonable firmness would have responded to the pressure in a manner similar to D, provided D's response did not take the form of committing or attempting murder. Further, if we allow cases like *Willer* and *Conway* to fall within the law of duress, we should allow pressures arising from natural forces within the defence too. If D drives on to the pavement to avoid a herd of charging bulls he should be able to raise the defence.[69]

One important limitation on the range of threats that D can invoke by way of defence is that the threat must emanate from an external source. D cannot, for example, raise duress of circumstance in answer to a charge of prison escape by reference to the suicidal urges to which his confinement gave rise.[70]

(a) Duress of circumstances distinguished from necessity

The cases under discussion above were found relevant on the facts of *Pommell*.[71] D was arrested late at night in his bed in possession of a sub-machine gun. On his account, he came to have the gun because he had persuaded X, who was planning "to shoot some geezer with it", to hand it over to him. D, so his story went, had taken it into his custody in order to hand it to his brother who would turn it over to the police and would have done so in the morning but for the inconvenience of his arrest. The trial judge had ruled that no defence issue arose on these facts, even assuming them to be true.[72] The Court of Appeal overruled him. Authorities such as *Willer* required his story, if supported by any evidence, to be put to the jury.

---

[68] Elliot, "Necessity, Duress and Self-Defence" [1989] *Crim LR* 611; Horder, "Self-Defence, Necessity and Duress: Understanding the Relationship" (1998) 1 *Canadian J Law & Juris* 143.

[69] *Smith and Hogan* 362.

[70] *Rogers and Rose* (1998) 1 Cr App R 143 (CA).

[71] [1995] 2 Cr App R 607 (CA).

[72] Remarkably, Mr. Pommell subsequently came into possession of a gun for the second time and again was frustrated from handing it into police custody by premature arrest. This time he successfully raised an interesting point in the law of evidence: *Pommell* [1999] *Crim LR* 576 (CA).

It should be noted that *Pommell* is a different kind of case from any of those discussed so far in this section. According to his version of events, D himself was never under any immediate threat or pressure from X. The "geezer" whom X intended to kill was not nearby when D persuaded him to hand over the weapon. What D was doing amounted to a responsible exercise in citizenship, unconstrained by any danger or pressure. Here we are dealing with a case of necessity rather than duress. This is in some sense acknowledged by the Court, which uses the expressions "duress" and "necessity" indifferently in its judgment. D seems clearly to have been justified in what he did. Surely it is better to be in possession of a firearm without a licence than to permit X to follow his murderous path? But where D acts in such a fashion, not under coercion himself, he *must* be justified; whereas duress may be allowed to excuse. Accordingly, *Pommell* may be regarded, at least *sub silentio*, as a case of necessity, a defence to be discussed more fully below.[73] The same vacillation between necessity and duress occurred in *CS*.[74] D was charged with the abduction of a child contrary to s. 1 of the Child Abduction Act 1984. D claimed that it was necessary to take the child V to Spain as she reasonably believed that, in the UK, V was in imminent danger of serious harm arising from sexual abuse by V's father. At the pre-trial hearing and on appeal reference was made predominantly to the defence of necessity but also to duress of circumstances: the Court of Appeal found it unnecessary to determine whether there was any difference between the two defences.[75]

But differentiation was desirable. Both defences were rejected, firstly on the ground that D lacked any reasonable belief that V was imminently threatened with serious bodily harm. A second ground of rejection was that, even if there was a well-founded belief that V was imminently threatened with serious harm, the 1984 Act provided defences of consent and reasonable belief in consent by the parties entitled to access to the child.[76] In the eyes of the Court, the existence of the statutory defences, together with D's right to bring her concerns to a child protection hearing, removed any need for V to resort to self-help. This conflation of duress and necessity obscures recognition of matters which relate to one defence rather than the other. What other solutions were available to D (other than taking the law into her own hand hands) were clearly relevant to a plea of necessity,[77] a defence which can be raised not only for immediate emergencies but also to ongoing states of affairs and non-imminent dangers. But in cases where there is a true or reasonable belief in a threat of immediate death or serious harm, there is no realistic recourse to anything other than self-help.

The lack of understanding of the differences between necessity and duress in *CS* is evident from the court's opinion that for either defence to apply there must be an immediate threat of death or serious bodily harm. To be sure, there may well arise circumstances of dire emergency where both defences will be in play. But their respective rationales differ. For duress, essentially one is asking whether a person of reasonable firmness and stability

---

[73] § 21. 3 4.

[74] [2012] EWCA Crim 389. And see too *S and L* [2009] EWCA Crim 85 for the treatment of necessity and duress as interchangeable terms and the insistence on an immediate threat of death or serious harm.

[75] *Ibid.*, para 15. Reference could more appropriately have been made to duress by threats because, as discussed above, that form of the defence extends to threats made against persons to whom D feels a sense of responsibility.

[76] Subsections 1(4), 1(5). These defences were hardly in point for D given the state of her relationship with V's father.

[77] The Court of Appeal cited decisively *Quayle* [2005] EWCA Crim 1415 on this further ground of rejection, a necessity not a duress case. See further § 21.3(iv).

would have succumbed to the threat too. For necessity, there is a broader question. In the circumstances that D was in (or reasonably believed herself to be in), was departing from the letter of the law a legitimate option? That last question does not always require an emergency involving an immediate threat.[78] Moreover, it can properly be put in cases such as where D acted to save the learning disabled V from becoming pregnant,[79] or to protect the vulnerable V from the dangers that would arise if V were free to come and go as he pleased,[80] in addition to the avoidance of death and serious bodily harm.[81]

(iii) Mistaken duress

In *Graham*,[82] the Court of Appeal considered that if D *reasonably* believed in the existence of circumstances that would have given a sober person of reasonable firmness good cause to fear death or serious injury, then he was entitled to raise the defence as if his belief were true. The Court's insistence on a reasonable mistake draws on an analogy with the erstwhile defence of provocation, which was also based on a reasonable person standard. However, in provocation, the cases of *Letenock*[83] and *Wardrope*[84] go further. They allow an intoxicated belief in the existence of a provocative incident to provide a ground of excuse. This went unremarked in *Graham*. Confusingly, in *Martin (David)*,[85] the Court of Appeal endorsed a subjective approach to mistaken duress and seemed of the same view in *Safi*.[86] In *Hasan*, however, the requirement for a reasonable mistake was reaffirmed by the House of Lords.[87] Although the affirmation was *obiter*, it was in the course of a wide-ranging review of the defence and should be regarded as settling the issue.

It will be recalled that beliefs relating to self-defence and the prevention of crime need only be genuine and need not be based on reasonable grounds,[88] whereas belief in the existence of duress, like consent in sexual offences, must be based on reasonable grounds.[89] It may well be that these differences are appropriate in their respective fields of application, but these discrepancies have not been addressed in the case law, which offers no persuasive general account. For cases of self-defence and force used in the prevention of crime, the matter is now resolved by statute: a genuine if unreasonable belief may form the basis of a defence provided the force used was proportionate to the circumstances that D believed to exist.[90]

---

[78] Cf. *Re A (Children)* [2001] Fam 147; below, § 21.3.(ii)(e).

[79] *F v. West Berkshire Health Authority* [1990] 2 AC 1.

[80] *Re L, R v. Bournewood Community and NHS Trust, ex parte L* [1999] 1 AC 458.

[81] In *Pipe v DPP* [2012] EWHC 1821 (Admin); [2012] All ER D 238, the Court ruled that the magistrates should have allowed D to raise the defence of necessity when speeding to take his partner's son to hospital following the failure of the ambulance service to respond to an emergency call. The boy was in great pain following a broken leg but was not in danger of any other serious harm.

[82] [1982] 1 All ER 801, 806; see too *Cairns* [1999] 2 Cr App R 137 (CA).

[83] (1917) 12 Cr App R 221 (CCA).

[84] [1960] Crim LR 770 (CCA).

[85] *Martin* [2000] 2 Cr App R 42. The favouring of an objective approach in *Graham* had been approved, *obiter*, by the House of Lords in *Howe* [1987] AC 417.

[86] [2003] Crim LR 721.

[87] [2005] UKHL 22, para. 23.

[88] Above, § 18.1(iii).

[89] See above, § 12.5.

[90] Criminal Justice and Immigration Act, s. 76(4), (6); below, § 21.2.

(iv) A rationale of duress

There has been considerable doctrinal uncertainty concerning why duress should provide a defence. The claim has been made that threats as extreme as death or serious bodily harm induce conduct which is involuntary and, consequently, not fairly attributable to the person coerced.[91] On this view, duress may even negate the actus reus of the offence. Yet this explanation does not convince. The involuntariness in question in cases of duress is of a less fundamental kind than the physical involuntariness of conduct occurring in a state of automatism or as a consequence of a reflex response.[92] When D commits a crime rather than be killed, she is making a choice, albeit in circumstances not of her own making.[93] Of course, a person choosing between death or committing a crime is making a choice of a different order from that involved in choosing, say, between a winter or summer holiday. Yet the decision to commit the crime is a product of deliberation. It is *her* choice, albeit a constrained choice. Even the most coercive of threats is compatible with proof of actus reus, as English law implicitly recognises when denying the defence of duress to anyone charged with murder.

Alternatively, it has been asserted that duress of sufficient potency is incompatible with a finding of mens rea.[94] Unfortunately, this is equally unconvincing, at least in English law. The term mens rea is a technical expression, a reference to the mental element required for the offence in question.[95] Sometimes the presence of duress may negate particular forms of mens rea: a manner of driving that would be accounted reckless may not deserve that description if driving as D did was the only way of escaping a threat of death or grievous bodily harm.[96] Yet there will be many occasions where the presence of duress is compatible with proof of mens rea. Indeed, this is the norm. If D commits crime X rather than be killed, she does so deliberately. D intends the wrong she commits, even if she regrets having to do so. The regrettable exclusion of duress as a defence to murder underscores this point. Findings that D possessed the mens rea for murder, despite the psychological impact on D of an immediate threat of death, have been made in several cases.[97] As duress frequently will not defeat proof of any mental element required for the crime, it should logically follows that duress is an applicable defence for strict liability offences.[98]

---

[91] *Per* Widgery LJ in *Hudson* [1971] 2 QB 202, 206, "It is clearly established that duress provides a defence ... if the will of the accused has been overborne by threats of death or serious personal injury so that the commission of the alleged offence was no longer the voluntary act of the accused".

[92] § 4.3(i).

[93] "A criminal walking to execution is under compulsion if any man can be said to be so, but his motions are just as much voluntary as if he [were] going to leave his place of confinement and regain his liberty. He walks to his death because he prefers it to being carried": Stephen, *History of the Criminal Law of England* (1883) vol. II, 102.

[94] *Paquette* (1997) 70 DLR (3d) 129 (Supreme Court of Canada); criticised by Colvin, *Principles of Criminal Law* (2nd ed., 1991) 236–8.

[95] *Yip Chiu-cheung* [1995] AC 111 (PC); *Kingston* [1995] 2 AC 355 (HL).

[96] *Harris* [1995] 1 Cr App R 170 (CA). But see *Backshall* [1999] 1 Cr App R 35, where the Court of Appeal held, on a charge of driving without due care and attention, that the issue of necessity or duress of circumstances would be more clearly resolved by invoking those defences, rather than by assessing whether the driving was done with due care and attention.

[97] See for example *Abbott* [1977] AC 755.

[98] But note the decision of the Divisional Court in *Hampshire County Council* v. *E* [2007] EWHC 2584 (Admin), where the defence of duress was considered to be inapplicable to the strict liability/status offence based on child truancy from school. Yet there are decisions, like *Martin*, where duress has been found applicable to a strict liability offence (driving without a valid licence). In *E*, the particular nature of the offence charged was stressed: namely,

Thus duress is generally compatible with the definitional elements of the offence with which the defendant is charged. Schopp has argued that the presence of these elements should entail a conviction because duress does not provide any plausible ground of excuse or justification.[99] Contrasting duress with mistake-based and disability defences, Schopp observes that defendants pleading duress possess the capacities of responsible agents and possess the knowledge with which to exercise these capacities. As he puts it, defendants raising duress "act on action plans that include the acts exemplifying the objective offence elements as intended components".[100] The choice to offend is theirs. Schopp acknowledges that duress may have considerable mitigating force and concedes that in many cases no punishment whatever would be warranted. In order to allow for such cases, he proposes a special verdict to be available, "a purely vindicating conviction" from which no penal consequences would flow. For him, recording a conviction of this special kind will reflect the general community condemnation of conduct which breaches the rules of the criminal law by an agent free from disability and lacking any deficiencies in knowledge or perception.[101]

Schopp radically underestimates the stigmatic impact of a conviction for a serious offence. Allowing duress, in appropriate circumstances, to provide complete exculpation signals that the criminal law, which is a system of *blame* as well as punishment,[102] withholds its censure from conduct that merely demonstrates a failure of virtue. The criminal law does not demand perfection. The essence of duress is a pressure to conform to the will of the duressor which not even a person of reasonable firmness could have resisted. When that condition is met, it is defamatory to impose a conviction, and a form of hypocrisy that is best avoided.

The defence is based on a moral evaluation of D's conduct: can we be sure that an ordinary person of reasonable firmness would have done better than D? It is not a disability defence; as Ashworth observes, it is available to D even though she may have been "cool as a cucumber" when responding to the threat of death or serious personal injury.[103] Sometimes, the jury's task will be easy. Surely it is better that D gives a burglar the keys to V's house rather than be instantly shot? At other times, intractable decisions may arise: it must be a dreadful thing to be under threat of death at the hands of an oppressive political regime, but it is also dreadful to hijack an aeroplane, spreading insecurity and terror.[104] Either way, in resolving such questions, we can only employ the normative standard of an ordinary person of reasonable firmness with reference to the values and interests at stake in the instant case. It should not, outside the realm of defences based on disability, be enough for a defendant to claim that she, from weakness of will or timidity, could not have done

---

to be a parent of a child of compulsory school age failing to attend school regularly contrary to s. 444(1) of the Education Act 1996. According to the Court, liability did not require any voluntary act or omission on the part of a defendant parent; the fact of non-attendance sufficed for liability. On that impoverished view of the sufficient conditions for criminal liability there is a certain logic in excluding duress as a defence for absolute(as interpreted) status offences. For further criticism of this Draconian style of interpretation see below, § 20.5.

[99] Schopp, *Justification Defenses and Just Convictions* (1998) chap. 5.
[100] *Ibid.*, 141.
[101] *Ibid.*, 142–6.
[102] Above, § 1.1(iii).
[103] *Principles of Criminal Law* (3rd ed., 1999) 231.
[104] *Abdul-Hussain* [1999] Crim LR 570.

better. It *should* be enough for her to answer that only persons of special virtue could have done better.

It has recently been argued that the key to the defence of duress is that D must act out of necessity and that duress along with self-defence and necessity should be conjoined into a single defence of "necessary action".[105] But there are salient differences between these separate defences. In its pure form, a plea of necessity is a claim that D has done more good than harm by non-compliance with the law. A plausible claim that the world was left a better place is no part of the rationale of duress. It is neither a necessary nor sufficient condition. Duress differs from self-defence in that the victim of any harmful act done by D will not be the duressor whereas self-defence is directed at the source of the danger (or a person who, inadvertently or otherwise, is assisting or impeding an effective response to the danger).[106] These differences underscore the distinctiveness of duress as a defence. The threshold is set very high: an immediate threat of death or serious bodily harm with a controversial exclusion of the offence of murder. To insist on steadfast compliance with the letter of the law in the face of such immediate peril is to ask for too much, even in the case of a person of reasonable firmness. Duress is a concession allowed on a more limited basis than the permissions that may be granted within the terms of self-defence and necessity.

§ 20.2 Marital coercion

The defence of marital coercion was abolished by section 177 of the Anti-Social Behaviour, Crime and Policing Act 2014, which came into force on 13 May 2014. The defence was rarely raised in any event,[107] and it may well be that no remnant cases will come before the courts.

§ 20.3 Superior orders

Criminal conduct cannot be justified or excused on the basis of the order of a superior, be that superior a public or private official. This is an important constitutional principle, founded on the lack of any dispensing power in English law.[108] A superior order may preclude liability on another ground: if D is ordered to destroy property and is instructed that it is the property of his employer, he will lack mens rea for the crime of criminal damage.[109] In general, however, in the absence of a defence of reasonable mistake of law,[110] a belief that conduct is lawful merely because of the order of a superior will not avail if the mens rea of the offence is present. Accordingly, an undercover police officer committed the offence of drug-trafficking when he took drugs from Hong Kong to Sydney because he knew the

---

[105] Clarkson, "Necessary Action: A New Defence" [2004] *Crim LR* 81; contrast Chan and Simester, "Duress, Necessity: How Many Defences?" (2005) 16 *King's College LJ* 121.

[106] *Richens* [2011] EWCA Crim 1626

[107] For discussion of the former defence, see the fifth edition of this work.

[108] *Entick v. Carrington* (1765) 19 St Tr 1029, 95 ER 807.

[109] *James* (1837) 8 C & P 131, 173 ER 429.

[110] Above, § 18.2.

item transported to be drugs—the fact that he was part of a police operation to expose and convict drug-traffickers was held to be irrelevant.[111]

The lack of any power on the part of officials to suspend the operation of law is an admirable constitutional principle. However, in the context of criminal trials, it may produce harsh results. In *Kelly* v. *Minister of Defence*,[112] a civil action, a soldier shot and killed V, a person whom he took to be a terrorist. V in fact was a joy-rider. *Inter alia*, the soldier was seeking to prevent V from committing terrorist crimes in the future, a permissible justification according to the Court of Appeal of Northern Ireland. That decision is open to serious criticism and may well be reconsidered.[113] Envisage a situation where, in circumstances such as those in *Kelly*, D received an order from E, his commanding officer, to shoot to kill V. D's options in such circumstances are unenviable: if he refused the order he might well be court-martialled for disobeying a lawful order, whereas obedience to an unlawful order may lead to a mandatory life sentence. Under the current, uncertain, state of the law if is not clear whether the order is lawful, so either outcome is possible. A junior soldier is surely in no position to decide these issues. Resolving the important and competing principles at stake in such cases is not easy, particularly as cases such as *Kelly* tend to arise in highly charged political contexts. Accommodation of the competing interests would be a great deal easier were there no mandatory penalty for murder.

§ 20.4 Entrapment

Not infrequently, police and other law enforcement officials resort to forms of encouragement, pressure, or persuasion in order to obtain evidence of criminal activity.[114] For instance, E, a plain-clothes policeman, may present himself as a person anxious to acquire illegal drugs. D may be an unsuspecting drug dealer and supply drugs in response to a first request by E. Alternatively, D may not be a drug dealer but may nonetheless obtain drugs to supply E because E has offered a large sum of money for this service, or because E has frightened him into doing so by some form of threat. There may well arise situations where we can be sure that D would not have committed the offence with which he was charged but for the machinations of E.

What kinds of machinations by the police or other officials[115] can properly be said to amount to entrapment is debatable. If E has coerced or deceived D into committing a crime which, prior to E's intervention, D had no intention to commit, it seems appropriate to say that D was entrapped, even if the coercion fell short of legal duress and the deception did not preclude D forming the mens rea for the crime. There may be less certainty

---

[111] *Yip Chiu-cheung* [1995] 1 AC 111 (PC). The House of Lords in *Clegg* [1995] 1 AC 482 confirmed, *obiter*, that military orders would not afford a defence.

[112] [1989] NI 341.

[113] Below, § 20.2(v).

[114] Redmayne, "Exploring Entrapment" in Zedner and Roberts (eds.) *Principles and Values in Criminal Law and Criminal Justice: Essays in Honour of Andrew Ashworth* (2012) 157; Ho, "State Entrapment" (2010) 31 *Legal Studies* 71; Squires, "The Problem with Entrapment" (2006) 26 *OJLS* 351.

[115] D cannot raise entrapment to exclude evidence or stay the proceedings unless officials or persons acting at the behest of officials were the entrappers: *Shannon* v. *UK* [2005] Crim LR 133; Hofmeyr, "The Problem of Private Entrapment [2006] *Crim LR* 133.

about inducements and opportunities laid on by E to which D succumbs. In *Williams and O'Hare*,[116] D helped himself to cartons of cigarettes from the back of a van which E, by way of temptation, had parked with the back doors open. The Court of Appeal, finding E's conduct unexceptionable, drew a distinction between "providing temptation" and "entrapment", a distinction approved in subsequent litigation by the House of Lords.[117] Professor Ashworth disagrees: "Leaving cartons of cigarettes unattended is little different from leaving a wallet on a park bench: neither is normal behaviour and both represent extraordinary temptation".[118] But where the temptation is to commit theft it should surely be resisted. Although such exercises in "virtue testing" are not attractive, they fall well short of abusive police practice.

A greater degree of sympathy for D seems in order on the facts of *Sang*,[119] where D was charged with dealing in counterfeit currency. He argued that he was inveigled into obtaining and supplying forged notes by the constant persuasion and insistence of E, an undercover police officer. Entrapment by an *agent provocateur*, it was claimed, should provide a complete defence to the charge in circumstances where commission of the offence was the consequence of acts of entrapment of law enforcement officials.[120] The House of Lords, however, rejected any defence of entrapment. Entrapping conduct may involve offences (as principals or accomplices) by police officers, but would not normally provide a ground of exemption for the person entrapped. This rejection of a substantive personal defence of entrapment seems correct. The persistence of the undercover officer is clearly a factor in D's offending yet neither justifies nor excuses it. But what is different here from *Williams* is that D's initial resistance to offending was worn down by the officer's persistence. This goes beyond pro-active policing to oppressive policing. If such policing is to be curbed, the further ruling in *Sang* that any evidence obtained by entrapment was admissible at trial is to be regretted. The exclusion of evidence may be extremely advantageous for D but that is a by-product of discouraging the police from using such methods to obtain evidence.

The rejection of an entrapment defence personal to D has been criticised. Choo, for instance argues for the recognition of a substantive defence of entrapment on the basis that entrapment:[121]

> "causes, in a broad sense, the commission of a crime.... The actual commission of the crime can be regarded as having been a fruit of the impropriety.... There is no justification for conviction of an entrapped defendant."

In terms of the personal culpability of the offender, this argument is wanting. Choo is using "cause" in a very broad sense indeed; unless the mode of entrapment is destructive of D's autonomy, a decision by D, say, to supply drugs to E will be the act of an autono-

---

[116] (1994) 98 Cr App R 209.

[117] *Loosely* [2001] UKHL 53, [2001] 1 WLR 2060. In *Palmer and Others* [2014] EWCA Crim 1681, police set up a shop which rapidly became known as a no-questions-asked buyer of anything on offer. This was judged acceptable virtue-testing rather than oppressive entrapment.

[118] Ashworth, "Redrawing the Boundaries of Entrapment" [2002] *Crim LR* 161,175.

[119] [1980] AC 402 (HL).

[120] The defence is allowed to a number of non-violent crimes in the United States, although there is division as to the rationale of the defence: contrast *Sorrells* v. *US* (1932) 287 US 435 (emphasising reduced culpability of offender) with *Sherman* v. *US* 356 US 369 (1958) (focussing on unacceptable police methods).

[121] *Abuse of Process and Judicial Stays of Criminal Proceedings* (1993) 167.

mous person, however persistent or persuasive the conduct of E. If E were simply an eager customer for drugs, any claim to exonerate D on account of E's persistence would be risible. The fact that E is an undercover policeman does not alter D's normative position. What attracts attention here is the normative position of E. To be sure, certain methods of entrapment go too far. The question then arises whether correcting such excesses is best done by providing an entrapment defence for D, notwithstanding the lack of any excuse personal to her, or by procedural means that impact directly on police methods. The latter seems a preferable route.[122]

To date, English law has taken that latter route. It has stopped short of reversing *Sang*, while taking some steps to discourage police malpractice. There are two main mechanisms. First, section 78 of the Police and Criminal Evidence Act 1984 grants a discretion to the court to exclude evidence if, in all the circumstances, including the circumstances in which the evidence was obtained, it would have such an adverse effect on the fairness of the proceedings that the court ought not to admit it. In *Smurthwaite*,[123] the Court of Appeal considered that the phrase "fairness of the proceedings" could accommodate not only consideration of the position of the accused but also matters of "fairness to the public". In certain circumstances, evidence obtained by entrapping manœuvres could be excluded. Lord Taylor CJ laid particular emphasis on whether D would have committed the offence but for the enticement of the undercover officer, and on whether the role of the officer was active or passive.

Secondly, in *Latif*,[124] the House of Lords took the view that evidence obtained by entrapment could be excluded as an abuse of the process of the court. The House drew a comparison with exclusion under section 78 and emphasised that the judicial discretion to exclude on abuse of process grounds was focused on the public interest in the integrity of the criminal process rather than on unfairness to the individual defendant. This jurisdiction is discretionary, involving a balancing exercise between the nature and gravity of the crime and public interest in effective enforcement, on the one hand, and the nature and seriousness of the misconduct by law enforcement officers on the other.

In addition to the exclusion of evidence, the practical effect of raising the issue of entrapment may also be to obtain a reduction in sentence.[125]

The question whether English law may be obliged to go further and provide more protection for D from police entrapment arose following the decision of the European Court of Human Rights in *Teixeira de Castro* v. *Portugal*.[126] D, a person with no criminal record and unknown to the police, was introduced to two undercover police officers. At their request, he bought heroin on their behalf. He was convicted of drug dealing on the evidence of the officers and sentenced to six years' imprisonment. The European Court, in a strong

---

[122] Similarly, and contrary to the arguments put forward in Dyer, "The Problem of Media Entrapment" [2015] *Crim LR* 311, the machinations of the press should not provide any defence for persons manipulated into crime unless the methods used provide a recognised defence. The answer lies in the proper regulation of the press, a vast and problematic topic. Undercover reporters may easily slip into assisting and encouraging crime, complicity, and indeed offending in their own right (e.g. by making corrupt payments).

[123] (1994) 98 Cr App R 437 (CA).

[124] [1996] 1 All ER 353 (HL).

[125] e.g. *Springer* [1999] 1 Cr App R (S) 217 (CA).

[126] [1998] Crim LR 751.

judgment, ruled that resort to incitement on the part of the officers had deprived D of a fair trial, within the terms of Article 6 of the ECHR, "from the outset". A balancing exercise of the kind employed in the English abuse of process cases is notably absent from the Court's reasoning. Evidence obtained by police incitement entailed, without more, a breach of Article 6. Even in the context of drug-trafficking, the right to a fair trial could not be sacrificed in the interests of effective law enforcement.

In the conjoined appeals of *Loosely* and *A-G's Reference (No. 3 of 2000)*,[127] the House of Lords declined to find that the decision in *Teixeira* required provision of a substantive defence of entrapment in English law. To that extent its previous decision in *Sang* is confirmed. Yet the decision in *Teixeira* was not without impact. The House of Lords accepted that the guarantee of fair trial under Article 6 might require examination of the entirety of the prosecution process. Their Lordships considered that it was possible for the fairness of a trial to be compromised by unacceptable forms of entrapment. In their view, the best way to emphasise this focus on the integrity of the trial process (rather than on any personal injustice to D) would be to make a finding of abuse of process, which operates as a complete bar to the prosecution. Where the issue of entrapment first arises during the course of the trial, the House considered that issues of fairness to D could be adequately addressed by exercising the discretion to exclude evidence allowed under section 78 of the Police and Criminal Evidence Act 1984.[128]

What guidance does the House of Lords provide on what might be considered excessive methods of entrapment? Unsurprisingly, nothing approaching an exact formula is provided. Much will depend on the nature of the offence, the propensities of the offender, and the difficulties of enforcement. In the broadest of terms, a distinction is drawn between providing D with an opportunity to offend—an opportunity freely taken—and conduct that unconscionably pressures or entices D into committing an offence he would not otherwise have committed.

Certainly, the police have considerable latitude under the present dispensation. In *Jones*,[129] D had left graffiti messages seeking contact with under-age girls for sex. These were followed up by undercover police officers, who finally secured a rendezvous with D, after he initially failed to appear, by sending him a series of explicit text messages. The Court of Appeal held the police conduct appropriate: it did not, the Court asserted, amount to inciting D to commit under-age sex offences. With respect, this reasoning must be doubted, in light of the readiness to find incitement by persons who merely respond positively to unsolicited offers to supply pornographic services.[130]

(i) Delineation

Given the very broad nature of the evaluations at stake, and the complex normative issues involved, further precision seems at present unobtainable. Future litigation exploring the

---

[127] [2001] UKHL 53; *Loosely* [2001] 1 WLR 2060; Ashworth, "Redrawing the Boundaries of Entrapment" [2002] *Crim LR* 161.
[128] [2001] UKHL 53, paras. 42–4.
[129] [2007] EWCA Crim 1118.
[130] *Goldman* [2001] Crim LR 822.

borderland between acceptable and unacceptable entrapping procedures seems inevitable. Attempts have been made at clarification. Ho considers the essential question to be whether D would have committed the same or a similar offence at some future time had there been no intervention from E.[131] For Redmayne, the major consideration is whether D was already committing the same or similar offences prior to the entrapment.[132] The question Ho poses is unavoidably conjectural. Redmayne's question may be difficult to verify: D may be a consistent offender but he might have steered clear of detection.

The heart of the matter seems to be a balance between the difficulties of enforcing the law, the seriousness of the offence, and the form of the entrapment. Take the enforcement of the law relating to the possession and supply of drugs against addicts. Addicts will often share supplies with other addicts. But they will be wary of supplying to persons unknown to them because use of entrapment to enforce the law is well known. It is submitted that, when evaluating the legitimacy of entrapment methods in this sphere of law enforcement the focus should be on police methods rather than on D's past or future drug crimes. In M,[133] an undercover officer (P) befriended D, a drug addict, bought him alcohol (D was banned from local off licences), and persuaded him to obtain drugs from M. The Court of Appeal considered that P's conduct was acceptable in that it went no further than typical interactions between addicts who were friends and acquaintances. Contrast an example given by Lord Nichols in *Loosely* where P wears down D's resistance by offering more and more significant sums of money, a case of state-created crime.[134]

Whether D has offended in the past or may do so in the future seems particularly beside the point where the police trap ensnares a particularly dangerous offender. An example provided by Redmayne himself may be used to make this point.[135] Suppose that there have been rapes in the local park and the rapist has eluded capture. E, a plain clothes policewoman, goes to the park at a late hour as a rape target. D attempts to rape her. DNA analysis shows that D is not the rapist the police were anxious to arrest. Nothing further than the fact of his attempted rape of E is known about D's criminal tendencies. It seems beside the point to try to discover if D had already raped or tried to rape and equally beside the point to conjecture whether the incident with E was something of the kind very likely to happen in any event. What matters is that the police initiative is non-oppressive and the crime highly serious. Surely any attempt to stay the trial of D for the attempted rape of V on the grounds of entrapment must fail.

§ 20.5 Impossibility

As the majority of duties imposed by the criminal law are negative duties—things we must not do—the defence of impossibility[136] has a limited scope. Save for quite exceptional

---

[131] Ho, "State Entrapment" (2010) 31 *Legal Studies* 71.

[132] Redmayne, "Exploring Entrapment" in Zedner and Roberts (eds.) *Principles and Values in Criminal Law and Criminal Justice: Essays in Honour of Andrew Ashworth* (2012) 157.

[133] [2011] EWCA Crim 648.

[134] [2001] UKHL 53, para. 4.

[135] Redmayne, "Exploring Entrapment" in Zedner and Roberts (eds.) *Principles and Values in Criminal Law and Criminal Justice: Essays in Honour of Andrew Ashworth* (2012) 157, 168.

[136] Smart, "Criminal Responsibility for Failing to do the Impossible" (1987) 103 *LQR* 532; *CLGP* 746–8.

circumstances, which would in any event be covered by other doctrines, it is always possible to refrain from some action. It is different with offences which consist of an omission to do something or with the acquisition of some proscribed status. Circumstances may arise where the law requires an act that cannot be performed by D or where the acquisition of the proscribed status was impossible for D to avoid. If, in either case, D was not at fault in bringing about the impossibility, he should not be liable for any offence.

On rare occasions, English law has allowed an impossibility defence, though without any real consistency.[137] The courts have tended to approach questions of impossibility on the basis of interpreting the terms of a particular statute, rather than from the perspective of any general principle. It is submitted, however, that the best approach is not necessarily to recognise a defence of impossibility. Rather than being a matter of defence, impossibility raises an issue going to the very suppositions of criminal liability. If D is not responsible for the impossibility, then he may properly claim that the omission he is charged with, or the status he is blamed for acquiring, is not something which is linked to any voluntary conduct ascribable to him. That is to say: impossibility is a species of *involuntariness*. For this reason, the cases on impossibility are discussed above, in § 4.3(ii).

Criminal liability, properly understood, must always be associated with some voluntary act or omission on the part of D.[138] If, say, D is unable to discharge some legal obligation because he chose to go to bed and was asleep at the time the duty fell to be done, he may properly be convicted in respect of his failure of duty.[139] But if he cannot perform his duty because, through no fault of his own, someone has unforeseeably tied him to a bed, there is nothing on which any form of *criminal* liability can be based. It is remarkable that this simple and fundamental restraint on criminal liability is not consistently respected.[140] Remarkable or otherwise, English law remains impervious to the injustice of liability in such cases. In *Hampshire County Council* v. *E*,[141] D was charged with being the parent of a child of compulsory school age, a child who "fails to attend school regularly".[142] The Divisional Court was adamant that liability could be imposed on an utterly blameless parent who could not have ensured attendance by any means, whenever a literal reading of this statutory provision covered the facts at hand. By contrast, In *Robinson-Pierre*,[143] we find a rare instance of reading the plain terms of a statutory provision in light of a principle that it ought to comport with the minimal requirements necessary for any coherent finding of criminal liability. It is an offence for D to be an owner of a dog that is out of control in a public place and the offence is aggravated if the dog should injure V while out of control.[144] D's dog did attack and injure V in public, but only because police officers had, without warning, battered his front door down, allowing the animal to run out of the house. D was

---

[137] See the cases discussed above, § 4.3(ii)(a)–(d).

[138] Above, § 4.3(ii).

[139] Antecedent fault is discussed above, § 4.3(iii).

[140] Although recognition of this principle would prevent certain forms of injustice, the principle is still compatible with the existence of very bad laws. For instance, respect for the principle would disallow, say, criminal liability for the mere fact of having curly hair; yet it would not forestall a law which required those with curly hair to shave their heads. See above, § 4.1(ii)(a).

[141] [2007] EWHC 2584 (Admin).

[142] Contrary to s. 441 of the Education Act 1996.

[143] [2013] EWCA Crim 2396, [2014] 1 WLR 2638.

[144] Dangerous Dogs Act 1991, s. 3.

convicted at first instance: he was the owner of the dog, a dog that had attacked and injured V in public, while out of control; there was nothing more to prove in terms of the explicit elements of the offence. The Court of Appeal thought otherwise. It saw no sense in convicting D for an incident which was the product of a third party intervention which D could not prevent, and held that Parliament could not have intended that the offence could be committed in such circumstances. It would be pleasant to think that *Robinson-Pierre* might presage a less literal approach than has prevailed in so many other cases, but the possibility that it will be confined to the particular offence at issue cannot be discounted.

Constitutions which disallow "cruel and unusual punishments" proscribe liability in such circumstances.[145] A principled and consistent recognition that voluntary conduct is a prerequisite of any form of criminal liability would obviate the need for any defence of impossibility.[146] That recognition, which, as we suggested in Chapter 4, can be found in the common law, is entrenched by Article 6 of the ECHR, and even by Article 3, which proscribes inhuman and degrading punishment.[147]

---

[145] *Robinson* v. *California* (1962) 370 US 660; but contrast *Powell* v. *Texas* (1968) 392 US 514.

[146] Above, § 4.3. If preferred, this could be expressed as an insistence on confining criminal punishment to events within D's *control*: cf. Simester, "On the So-called Requirement for Voluntary Action" (1998) 1 *Buffalo Crim LR* 403; Husak, "Does Criminal Liability Require an Act" in Duff (ed.), *Philosophy and Criminal Law* (1998) 60; Duff, *Answering for Crime* (2007) § 5.5.

[147] For fuller argument see Sullivan, "Conduct and Proof of Conduct: Minimum Conditions for Criminal Liability" in Kaikobad and Bohlander (eds.), *International Law and Power, Perspectives on Legal Order and Justice: Essays in Honour of Colin Warbrick* (2009) 235.

21

PERMISSIBLE CONDUCT

§ 21.1 Consent[1]

Normally, it would be straightforwardly harmful, wrongful, and criminal for D to hit V. Suppose, however, that V has agreed with D to enter a boxing ring to box a few rounds. As the law stands at present, neither D nor V commits an offence in hitting the other because each has consented to such contact, a consent that current law regards as effective.[2]

If English law consistently followed the precepts of classic liberalism, V's consent to conduct by D, which otherwise violates a protected interest of V (and V alone), would negate any criminal liability on the part of D. This liberal tradition[3] makes personal autonomy a key value[4] and disavows coercion through the criminal law as a means of furthering an individual's best interests.[5] The acceptable scope of the criminal law, on the classical liberal view, is to prevent harm (and some would add offence)[6] to others.[7] Of course, what constitutes harm or offence may itself be disputed. But, in principle, if the harm in question is self-regarding and freely consented to, state intervention is unjustified. Provided V

---

[1] Law Com. Consultation Paper No. 139, *Consent in the Criminal Law* (1995), especially Appendix C (contributed by Roberts); Roberts, "The Philosophical Foundations of Consent in the Criminal Law" (1997) 17 *OJLS* 389; Shute, "Something Old, Something New, Something Borrowed: Three Aspects of the Project" [1996] *Crim LR* 684; Westen, *The Logic of Consent* (2004). See also above, § 12.3.

[2] There would be general agreement among criminal lawyers that organised boxing as sport is legal but, such is the chaotic state of English law on when effective consent may be given to the infliction of physical harm, it is impossible to give a satisfactory *legal* account of the legality of boxing; as Lord Mustill recognised in *Brown* [1994] 1 AC 212. See further Gunn and Ormerod, "The Legality of Boxing" (1995) 15 *LS* 181.

[3] Classically expounded in Mill, *On Liberty* (1859).

[4] Raz, *The Morality of Freedom* (1986).

[5] Attempts have been made to find space for a measure of paternalism—or better, perhaps, communitarian concern—within a liberal framework (Hart, *Law, Liberty and Morality* (1963)) and liberal theorists such as Raz, who allow a State interest in the worth of subjects' lives, concede, in theory, coercive interventions by the State to enhance the *worthwhile* autonomy of subjects. For a recent attempt to justify selective, coercive interventions as a way of advancing the welfare of adult, competent subjects, see Sullivan, "Liberalism and Constraining Choice: The Cases of Death and Serious Bodily Harm" in Smith and Deazley (eds.), *The Legal, Medical and Cultural Regulation of the Body: Transformation and Transgression* (2009) 205. Classic liberalism, by contrast, protects "the right to go wrong." For a comprehensive elaboration of the classic liberal position see Feinberg, *The Moral Limits of the Criminal Law*: vol. 1, *Harm to Others* (1984); vol. 2, *Offence to Others* (1985); vol. 3, *Harm to Self* (1986); vol. 4, *Harmless Wrongdoing* (1988). For discussion of paternalism, see Dworkin, "Paternalism" (1972) 56 *Monist* 65; Dworkin, *The Theory and Practice of Autonomy* (1988) chap. 8; Glover, *Causing Death and Saving Lives* (1977) chap. 5; Kleinig, *Paternalism* (1983); above, § 1.2(i)(b).

[6] Feinberg, *Offence to Others* (1985). Feinberg allows the criminalisation of offensive conduct but only under strict conditions, the most important of which is that the offensive conduct must be something that takes place in public—such as open sexual intercourse in the view of persons who do not wish to witness the spectacle but cannot avoid doing so. See above, §1.2(i)(b).

[7] Above, § 1.2(i).

has the capacity and opportunity to make a free and informed decision, the State should not interfere with V's autonomous choices. Even if, from the perspective of a reasonable bystander, what V has consented to constitutes a harm—a blow on the face, say—if V has fully consented, from the liberal perspective he has not been *wronged*. If V is of the age of consent, and is of normal mental capacity, it is for her and not the state to resolve what things she may legitimately do. In theory, this sovereignty of choice for D should hold good provided her choices are self-regarding.[8] If this condition is satisfied and D has V's full consent, he would not commit an offence against V whatever it was that he did to V's person or property:[9]

> "[F]ully valid consent ought to be a defence to all the crimes that are defined in terms of individuals acting on other individuals, including battery [causing serious injury] and murder.... Collaborative behaviour ought never to be criminal when the collaboration is fully voluntary on both sides and no interests other than those of the collaborative parties are directly or substantially affected."

English criminal law frequently departs from the liberal stance just outlined. In the sphere of harms against the person, the law allows very little scope for autonomy. Unless special considerations apply, V's consent shields D from criminal liability only if the harm inflicted did not amount to actual bodily harm or worse. Determining when special considerations apply is not easy. As we shall see, English law is internally inconsistent and, on occasion, irrational, when determining whether consent to the risk of significant harm is effective.

The leading case is *Brown*.[10] By a three-to-two majority, the House of Lords ruled that consensual sadomasochistic activity does not fall within any recognised exception to the general legal principle that V's consent affords no defence to D should the harm inflicted be actual bodily harm or worse. That was clearly the majority decision, yet none of the judgments of the majority satisfactorily explains why consent should be irrelevant in these circumstances. In the judgments, one can discern two different principles justifying state intervention in matters of sexual preference. First, there is a strand of legal moralism: the view that if conduct is sufficiently immoral or degrading, that *of itself* merits the punishing of persons who engage in such conduct, despite the consensual nature and self-regarding quality of the acts concerned.[11] Secondly, we find an attitude of paternalism: the view that the criminal law may be used to protect persons from themselves. These two principles are sometimes expressed in the same judgment.[12] While not contradictory principles, they tend to support differing conclusions, something the majority judgments do not address: if intervention in personal preferences is based on paternalism, one may well differentiate, in

---

[8] The boundaries of self-regard are, of course, contestable: for example, should V's choice be restricted because ex- posing herself to danger may impose legal duties of treatment or rescue on others?

[9] Feinberg, *Harmless Wrongdoing* (1988) 165.

[10] [1994] 1 AC 212.

[11] "Pleasure derived from the infliction of pain is an evil thing. Cruelty is uncivilised": [1994] 1 AC 212, 237 (Lord Templeman).

[12] "There were obvious dangers of serious personal injury or blood infection.... It is fortunate that there were no permanent injuries to a victim.... Such violence is injurious to the participants and unpredictably dangerous": *ibid.*, 236 (Lord Templeman).

the context of the facts arising in *Brown*, between those who endure the pain and those who inflict it;[13] whereas legal moralism would draw no distinction.[14]

The parameters of legally valid consent are unstable and contestable. There are, nonetheless, clear cases where it can be said that a freely given and sufficiently informed consent by V will preclude any finding of liability against D. Conversely, there are clear cases where consent is legally irrelevant. It is in the middle ground that the lack of guiding principles is exposed.

(i) Consent: offence or defence?

The normative and legal significance of consent may operate in one of three ways, according to the nature of the particular offence.

First, consent may preclude the harm that is the subject matter of the offence. The essence of rape, for example, is intercourse without consent. There is nothing wrong or harmful about sexual intercourse: freely given consent (given by persons of the age of consent) takes sexual activity outside the concerns of the criminal law. The same is true of those commonplace touchings that occur in the course of ordinary life—the tap on the shoulder for attention, the playful push. Here, typically, consent may be assumed. It is only when the consent is withdrawn—"Don't tap me on the shoulder again"—that the prospect of a harm, the breach of privacy; the threat of further physical interference, constituted by the lack of consent arises.[15] In these situations, non-consent is an integral part of the actus reus of the offence. If there is consent to such things, there is no event or state of affairs to concern the criminal law.

Secondly, there are situations where a harm does occur but consent precludes any liability from following. Take a situation where D and V have agreed to fight. D punches V in the face without causing him any physical injury. There is a form of harm here; ordinarily, being punched in the face is unwelcome and unsettling. However, no offence of battery has been committed, because D consented. Although D inflicts the sort of harm that is normally a battery, his conduct is permissible and outside the criminal law. On liberal principles, even if there is harm, there is no wrong. It is unclear whether, in legal terms, consent operates here as an element of the offence (i.e. is part of the actus reus) or as a defence. According to the minority in *Brown*, the actus reus of battery is the infliction of force on V *without the consent of V*. Although the majority treated consent as something external to the offence of battery, a defence that might justify it, that analysis was in the context of cases where the battery occasions actual bodily harm.

---

[13] A paternalist might respond by saying that punishing those masochists who may be exploited by sadists reduces the number of people who submit to sadists, thereby advancing welfare overall. But even in its own terms, the response is problematic. It would be very difficult to measure what further increments of deterrence are achieved by punishing masochists in addition to sadists. Further, the punishment of a member of the protected class is a disvalue to be set against any advance in welfare achieved for that individual and in the quantum of welfare generally.

[14] In *Gnango* [2011] UKSC 59, paras. 44–53, Lord Phillips considered that in the case of "willing" victims, only where the offence charged was for the protection of a defined class of vulnerable persons, such as underage sex offences (the *Tyrrell* principle: above, § 7.6(iv)(a)), would the victim not be implicated as an accessory in the crime of the perpetrator. For his Lordship, both the sadists and the masochists in *Brown* [1994] 1 AC 212 should be treated as guilty of the offences charged.

[15] Above, § 11.2(i)(a).

The position certainly changes if D's punch causes V actual bodily harm or worse. Under English law, that degree of injury cannot be consented to unless special circumstances apply. Establishing special circumstances that render V's consent effective in law involves raising a *defence* of consent. However, as we shall see in § 21.1(v), the scope of this defence is uncertain. In our fighting example, D will not incur liability if he inflicts actual bodily harm or worse, provided he is fighting V in an organised boxing tournament or sparring in a gym, but he will be liable for criminal offences if fighting with his bare fists in a public or private place.[16] There are many other situations where the legality of consensual fighting which may cause injury—free-fighting; Thai boxing; full contact karate—is entirely unclear.[17] Conceptually, we can, as indicated, distinguish between lack of consent as a constituent of the offence or as raising an issue of consent by way of defence. The distinction may impinge on matters of proof. When lack of consent is a constituent of the actus reus, the prosecution must prove a lack of consent of its own motion. When the presence of consent operates as a defence, an evidential onus will lie on the defence to raise the issue. If it can do that, a probative onus to disprove the presence of consent will fall to the prosecution.[18] On occasion, this difference may affect the dynamics and shape of a trial. Suppose that D throws what appears to be a friendly arm over D's shoulder. If it was indeed a friendly arm, no offence, no actus reus, has occurred. To make a battery of it the prosecution would have to show that, for example, D was a stranger to V and his action was sudden and threatening. Contrast the case where D walks up to V and punches him hard on the nose. Prove that and the prosecution has proved its case unless the defence can plausibly suggest some exonerating explanation (perhaps it was a film stunt that miscarried). Only if the defence can come up with something plausible must the prosecution then rebut it.

(ii) The definition of consent

There is no general, analytical definition of consent in English law. Conceptual tidiness and predictability of outcome would be furthered if such a definition could be successfully formulated, a definition that would descend from the realm of concepts to marshal the messier world of facts and value. But it is hard to fashion an analytical/conceptual definition that would be serviceable in all the contexts where consent may arise as an issue. The truth of the matter is that whether a valid consent has been given frequently involves normative as well as analytical questions, and the normative issues may change according to context.[19] The closest thing that we have to a general definition is section 74 of the Sexual Offences Act 2003 which, for sexual offences based on the absence of consent, provides that a person "consents if he agrees by choice and has the freedom and capacity to make that choice". As we saw in the context of sexual offences, however, section 74 does not help in the difficult case.[20] In cases where the presence or absence of consent is contestable it merely poses questions for the debate.

---

[16] *A-G's Reference (No. 6 of 1980)* [1981] QB 715 (CA).

[17] See Law Com. Consultation Paper No. 139, *Consent in the Criminal Law* (1995) Appendix D.

[18] *Woolmington* [1935] AC 462 (HL); above, § 3.2.

[19] Wertheimer, *Coercion* (1987); Dripps, "For a Negative, Normative Model of Consent, with a Comment on Preference Skepticism" (1996) 2 *Legal Theory* 113.

[20] § 12.3(iii).

There are many straightforward cases of non-consent, where D simply overrides V's decision-making capacities. If D forces himself sexually upon V by using violence, we can say categorically that V does not consent to sex with D. The same applies where D overcomes V's resistance to sexual contact by threats of violence.[21] She cannot be said to be exercising her autonomy; she is merely mitigating some of the features of her appalling situation. In law, submission is not consent.

More room for argument arises where V does not encounter a prospect of physical violence but is confronted with a choice of unwelcome options presented by D. For example, D may threaten to inform her employer of her past criminal record or refuse her access to her children unless she agrees to sexual intercourse. In *Olugboja*,[22] the Court of Appeal drew a distinction between consent, albeit reluctant consent, on the one hand and mere submission on the other. The Court provided no criteria with which to draw this distinction, indicating that it would be for the jury to use their common sense. This approach has been criticised for vacuity and, indeed, it merely states the problem without providing any resources with which to solve it.[23] Yet, in fairness, the constituents of consent are elusive and cannot be reduced to any simple test, particularly when we move beyond violence and the threat of violence.

Any inquiry into whether V has consented to an interaction with D must, in the case of persons of normal mental capacities,[24] of necessity be limited to matters of cognition, volition, and the nature and purpose of D's interaction with V. If V was aware of the essential features of what she was consenting to, and was not deceived or coerced by D, a finding of valid consent should normally follow, unless the conduct involved is, in the eye of the law, something that even a competent adult cannot choose to do.[25] Whether the consent was something that was conducive to V's well-being or something she might later regret would not be relevant, unless the setback to well-being was so serious as to raise questions as to whether she made a sufficiently free and informed choice.

This shallow take on consent, which we consider appropriate for questions of crime and punishment, has been challenged by Michelle Madden Dempsey. For her, the well-being of V should be at the centre of any inquiry into the presence or absence of consent.[26] She argues that, when V gives a free and informed consent to her interaction with D, it is usually safe for D to assume that he is acting in V's best interests: V will typically know better than anyone else what suits best for her. But not always. Suppose, for example, that D knows V has a long-standing wish to become a nun. He also knows that she is sexually attracted to him and he has sex with her at her request, although aware that later she will be greatly

---

[21] Surprisingly, s. 75(2) of the Sexual Offences Act 2003 merely creates a rebuttable presumption of lack of consent to sexual conduct where D uses or threatens force immediately beforehand. Perhaps, in a sexual context, the participants' preferences may accommodate some violence in the course of the activity but, where violence or the threat of violence is used to overcome resistance, we can surely speak in categorical terms about a lack of consent.

[22] [1982] QB 320.

[23] For further discussion of *Olugboja* see above, § 12.3(iii)(b) and Gardner, "Appreciating *Olugboja*" (1996) 16 *LS* 275.

[24] In cases where V lacks normal mental capacities criminal courts may be influenced by s. 1 of the Mental Capacity Act 2005 which provides, "a person lacks capacity in relation to a matter if at the material time he is unable to make a decision for himself in relation to the matter because of an impairment, or a disturbance in the functioning of, the mind or brain".

[25] See below, §21.1(iv).

[26] Dempsey, "Victimless Conduct and the Volenti Maxim: How Consent Works" (2013) 7 *Crim Law and Phil* 11.

troubled by her weakness of will.[27] The suggestion is that D has not obtained V's true consent because he knows that, in going along with her wish to have sex with him, he is damaging her long-term interests. There is something in this. One might reasonably think there is some ground for criticism of D's conduct. However, even if we assume a lack of virtue on D's part,[28] it should not be confused with the kind of serious wrongdoing that warrants a criminal conviction and punishment.

(iii) Factors that may vitiate consent

(a) Force and fear of force

That force or the fear of force vitiates consent is uncontroversial. If force or the threat of force is explicitly present at the time of D's act, one can readily conclude that V lacks freedom to choose. The same applies if the threat of force is in the background but still to the mind of V. In *C v. R.*,[29] V had been sexually abused by her stepfather D since the age of 5. Between the ages of 16 and 25 there was evidence, photographic and textual, suggesting that V enjoyed and consented to sex with D. But the dominion and control reinforced by threats, including threats to kill her and her boyfriend, continued to hold her in thrall to D. He was aware that the appearance of pleasure and consent were feigned in order to appease him. The Court of Appeal confirmed that this apparent consent was non-consent.

The force or threat of force need not involve serious bodily harm. D rapes V if he obtains sex by threatening to punch her in the face; it need not be the case that the blow, if struck, would cause V serious hurt. In principle, force should also comprehend any extreme fears or phobias with which V is afflicted. If D threatens to leave V in a locked car, knowing her to be claustrophobic, that should constitute force sufficient to vitiate consent.[30]

(b) Non-physical coercion

There is authority that pressure falling short of physical harm or the threat of such harm is insufficiently coercive to render a hard choice a case of submission rather than consent. In *Latter v. Braddell*,[31] a civil case, V, a maid, was ordered to submit to an intimate medical examination to check for pregnancy as a condition of further employment. V underwent the test under tearful protest. It was held that V had consented to this procedure and could not succeed in her action for assault. In an unreported decision,[32] Winn J ruled that a policeman charged with rape on the basis of obtaining sexual intercourse with V by threatening to make false reports against her had no case to answer. Glanville Williams has

---

[27] The example is given by Jonathan Herring, who agrees with Dempsey's conception of consent: "Consent in the Criminal Law: The Importance of Relationality and Responsibility" in Reed and Bohlander (eds.), *General Defences in Criminal Law: Domestic and Comparative Perspectives* (2014) 63, 69.

[28] And even that much would be controversial. One cannot assert confidently that there will be consensus on whether D has done wrong, and if so, what kind of wrong it is. For a confirmed atheist, life in a nunnery would be a wasted life based on a delusion. Such disputation should not be part of the business of a criminal court.

[29] [2012] EWCA Crim 2034.

[30] Cf. s. 75(2) of the Sexual Offences Act 2003; above, § 12.3(ii).

[31] (1881) 50 LJQB 166.

[32] The decision is referred to in *Olugboja* [1982] QB 320 (see above, § 12.3(iii)(b)) and Gardner, "Appreciating *Olugboja*" (1996) 16 *LS* 275.

supported the line taken in these two cases. His view, taken with particular reference to the appropriate scope of the offence of rape, is that once beyond violence or the threat of violence, the line between reluctant consent and mere submission is unacceptably vague and should not be used to determine liability for serious offences. He is not averse to penalising the policeman's conduct in the case above, but advises creating offences which do not employ consent as a constituent element.[33]

Arguably, the restrictive approach advocated by Williams is no longer tenable following the decision in *Olugboja*.[34] V had been driven to a house and raped there by X. D then informed her that he was going to have sex with her and ordered her to remove her trousers. V complied with his wishes and did not physically resist D. Confirming D's conviction for rape, the Court of Appeal held, as we noted in § 21.1(ii), that it is for the jury to distinguish on the facts before it between consent and mere submission. Importantly, the Court did not require a direction to the effect that consent would be absent only if V complied under threat of violence from D. It should be noted, however, that in the factual circumstances of *Olugboja*, V was in an inherently threatening situation; indeed, she had already been raped by someone still present in the house. If the direction to the jury is read against these facts, arguably no extension of the law beyond the point advocated by Williams was involved.

In the Rhodesian case of *McCoy*,[35] a more expansive approach was adopted unequivocally. V, an airline hostess, had broken company rules and was anticipating a period of "grounding" with consequent loss of pay. D, her manager, offered to cancel her grounding order if she would submit to a caning on her bottom. He was convicted of indecent assault, affirmed on appeal, on the basis that V's compliance with his wishes was a coerced submission and not a product of her consent. Similarly, in *Wellard*,[36] when discussing D's appeal against sentence, the Court of Appeal made no adverse comment on the propriety of his previous conviction for rape, a conviction sustained on the basis of obtaining sexual intercourse by threatening, in his capacity as a security guard, to report aspects of V's sexual conduct. The idea that coercion can embrace pressures going beyond violence and the threat of violence is supported by the Court of Appeal's decision in *Kirk*.[37] In a brief judgment, it upheld the trial judge in allowing a charge of rape to be put before the jury in circumstances where V, a homeless and hungry 13-year-old girl, allowed D, an adult male, sexual intercourse in return for a small sum of money to buy food. The case provides little if any guidance beyond its facts. Essentially, the jury were left to themselves to decide whether D had the freedom and capacity to choose to have sex with D.[38]

The better view, it is submitted, is that there is no categorical rule that only violence or the threat of violence has sufficient coercive effect to negate consent. As a matter of principle, threats of a non-physical kind are surely capable of inducing submission rather than

---

[33] *TBCL* 551–8.
[34] [1982] QB 320.
[35] 1953 (2) SA 4 (Rhodesian CA).
[36] (1978) 67 Cr App R 364, 368 (CA).
[37] [2008] EWCA Crim 434.
[38] V had sought D out at his workplace and waited with him until they were left alone there. They had previously been in a relationship where D had been abusive. Beyond doubt, D was an unpleasant and exploitative man prepared to have sex with an underage and very vulnerable girl. One may surmise that these factors weighed heavily in his conviction for rape, in addition to any jury discourse on the meaning of consent.

consent. Whether the threat at issue in the instant case has the necessary weight should, ultimately, be a question of fact for the jury. Because it is so difficult to frame a stable meaning for consent serviceable in all contexts, one simply has to tolerate the lack of precision that this approach entails. But judges should not allow too much latitude; they should robustly exercise their jurisdiction to remove cases from a jury if of the view that no reasonable jury could find a lack of consent on the evidence. Such an approach is open on the state of the authorities and, arguably, is endorsed by *Olugboja*. In the context of non-consensual sexual offences, the test is now framed in terms of whether V had the "freedom and capacity to choose".[39] This is in effect another way of asking a jury to choose between submission and consent, a normative as much as an analytical question.

(c) Threats and opportunities

In the case of non-physical threats, a helpful distinction should be borne in mind, namely the distinction between threats and opportunities. The latter may involve agonising choices for the agent but it is typically only the former that constrain and vitiate consent. The distinction may be elaborated by contrasting the facts of *Wellard*[40] with *McCoy*.[41]

In *Wellard*, D, by threatening to report his observations of V unless she submitted to intercourse with him, confronted V with two awful alternatives. She was faced with two entirely negative choices because of D's actions and can truly be said to have submitted rather than consented to one fate rather than the other; or, in the language of section 75(2) of the Sexual Offences Act, she lacked freedom and capacity to choose in respect of each alternative, merely submitting as to one unchosen outcome rather than the other.

In *McCoy*, V broke her rules of employment and faced a sanction. D, in making his proposal, however unsavoury, was increasing V's options from the starting-point of V's self-created baseline. *Pace* the Court of Appeal of Rhodesia, it is hard to understand how V was constrained by D's proposal.[42] She appears to have accepted it because it offered, all things considered, a new and better way forward from her current situation.

In distinguishing between threats and opportunities, it is important to keep in mind V's existing rights and legitimate expectations. V, an actor, is entitled to be considered for the part on her thespian merits. If the casting-couch is an obligatory way-station for auditioning for the part it constitutes a threat; if it is a way of stealing a march on her competitors, it is an opportunity. The threat/opportunity divide should only be used for guidance; it is not a "bright-line" rule. There may arise situations where V's baseline situation is so unenviable and the stakes so high that the price for an opportunity may be paid without true consent.[43]

---

[39] Section 75(2) Sexual Offences Act 2003.

[40] *Ibid.*

[41] 1953 (2) SA 4.

[42] Perhaps, as Lamond argues, the threat/opportunity distinction depends also on D's reasons for implementing the unwelcome alternative: "Coercion, Threats, and the Puzzle of Blackmail" in Simester and Smith (eds.), *Harm and Culpability* (1996) 215.

[43] The facts of *Latter* v. *Bradell* (above, § 21.1(iii)(b)) illustrate this limitation of the threat/opportunity distinction. V had no legal right to further employment; accordingly, D's offer of further employment on condition of an intimate examination to check for pregnancy was, strictly, an opportunity. Yet the available options for a Victorian domestic servant were likely to be exceedingly limited, arguably rendering D's proposal a coercive act (despite the finding of the Court in that case).

(d) Mistake or ignorance on the part of V regarding D's conduct or its consequences

In the famous case of *Clarence*,[44] D had sexual intercourse with V, his wife, neglecting to inform her that he was infected with gonorrhoea. Consequently, V contracted this disease and D was charged with a number of offences against the person. A central issue in the case was whether V, given her ignorance of D's dangerous condition, had given an effective consent to intercourse. The Court for Crown Cases Reserved held that his failure to disclose his infection did not vitiate V's consent. According to the court, she understood the *nature* of the act she consented to. Her ignorance related to a mere *attribute* of D's conduct, its propensity to pass on infection.

Essentially, the analysis in *Clarence* was confirmed by the Court of Appeal in *EB*,[45] with its ruling that D's failure to disclose his HIV-positive status did not entail that he had raped V when he had intercourse with her without disclosing his condition. That rape had not occurred might at first seem surprising, because V would not have agreed to sex had she known of his infected condition. Yet the same opinion was also expressed, *obiter* in *Dica*[46] and in *Konzani*.[47] We now seem to have a well-established rule that failure to disclose a sexually transmitted disease (STD), however serious the condition is, does not vitiate the consent to the sex act *in the dimension of sexual activity*.

The position changes if there is an active deception by D. The fact that the foregoing cases involved non-disclosure was stressed by the Court of Appeal in *Assange* v. *Swedish Judicial Authority*.[48] V agreed to have sex with D on condition that he used a condom. Deceptively, he did not use a condom. It was accepted that this deceptive omission did not deceive V as to the nature and purpose of the sexual activity.[49] But the effect of his deception was to vitiate V's freedom to choose to have sex with D.[50] The logic of this ruling must carry over to deception by D as to the state of his sexual health. If V stipulates a condition on which she will have sex, any deceitful breach of this condition by D will negate a free choice to have sex on the part of V. At the same time, it seems that non-disclosure falling short of deception will neither negate V's understanding of the nature of the sex act nor negate a free choice to participate in the sexual activity.[51]

Non-disclosure (or indeed deception) may in any event generate liability for a different offence. Thus, in *Konzani* it was ruled that, by passing on HIV to V without fully informing her of his positive status, D had maliciously inflicted grievous bodily harm contrary to section 20 of the OAPA 1861, a conclusion anticipated in *Dica*.[52] So now we have a situation

---

[44] (1888) 22 QBD 23 (CCR).

[45] [2006] EWCA Crim 2945.

[46] [2004] QB 1257 (CA).

[47] [2005] 2 Cr App R 14 (CA).

[48] [2011] EWHC 2849 (Admin).

[49] *Ibid.*, para. 87.

[50] Cf. rulings to the same effect in *McNally* [2013] EWCA Crim 1051 (D, a woman pretending to be a man) and *R(F)* [2013] EWHC 945 (Admin) (D breaking promise not to ejaculate inside V's vagina).

[51] Cf. *ibid.*, para. 90, at least in the context of HIV status. The line between non-disclosure and deception may be fine. Suppose that D has an intimate, long-term relationship with V but neglects to inform her that he has contracted an STD after a one-night stand with P. Does he deceive V when he has unprotected sex (as is their usual practice) with V?

[52] In *Clarence* the wording of s. 20 was taken to preclude any liability unless the harm was inflicted by way of battery, a view now superseded; above, § 11.5(i). That caveat aside, several members of the court in *Clarence* took STDs to be a form of grievous bodily harm, a position confirmed in *Konzani* and *Dica*. The Law Commission

where, in law, it may be possible for V to consent to D's act in one dimension but not consent to other facets of the act that, for the purposes of the criminal law, belong in a different dimension. This is the case even if V would have refused D's act *tout court* had she known the true position.

A further level of complexity is introduced by the insistence in *Konzani* that any valid consent by V to D's act in the dimension of risk of infection had to be a "fully informed" consent, a condition only satisfied if, prior to sexual intercourse, V was aware of his HIV-positive status. This is a more demanding test of consent than is required for the act of intercourse *qua* sex. It is simply not the case that valid consent is given to sexual conduct in the dimension of sexual activity only if the nature of the conduct is understood in all its aspects by V before it occurs. But it now seems to be the case that different tests for consent may be in play with respect to different aspects of the same act.[53]

It would be possible to regulate cases of mistake and ignorance much more straightforwardly than this. Jonathan Herring proposes a beguilingly simple test for sexual offences:[54]

"If at the time of the sexual activity a person:
(i)   is mistaken as to a fact; and
(ii)   had s/he known the truth about that fact would not have consented to it
then s/he did not consent to the sexual activity."

This is a much more sweeping principle of vitiation than currently applies. Adopting such a principle would entail a conviction for rape on facts such as *Konzani*, in addition to liability under section 20 of the OAPA 1861. While on balance we do not favour liability for rape in those circumstances, a finding of rape is in no sense outlandish where the matter undisclosed is of such vital importance and so tightly bound to the act of sexual intercourse.[55] But a conviction for rape would also follow if D, say, has sexual intercourse with his partner after deceitfully agreeing to her proposal to visit relatives at the weekend, without disclosing his plans instead to be travelling in the opposite direction to watch a rugby match. He may have told his lie not with sex in mind but to postpone the inevitable row they will have when he reveals that his plans for the weekend are different from hers. Yet later that evening, when they have fully mutual and enjoyable sex, under a Herring dispensation, he will be in the process of raping V if, according to Herring, he knew or ought to have known that she would not have agreed to sex on that occasion had she known the truth about his plans for the weekend.[56]

---

has published a consultation paper on whether there should be specific offences relating to STDs: LCCP No. 217 (2014) chap. 6.

[53] For strong criticism of this aspect of *Konzani* see Weait, "Knowledge, Autonomy and Consent" [2005] *Crim LR* 673. In our view, contra Weait, the approach in *Konzani* employing different standards of consent for different aspects of conduct is defensible. Whereas consent to sexual conduct may be dynamic and evolving during an episode of conduct, and be expressed solely in deeds, consent as to latent physical dangers must have a firm knowledge base. It is not unreasonable to set the knowledge standard at actual awareness of the danger rather than an appreciation of a risk of the danger if the focus is exclusively on the harm done to V. In the broader picture of public health, it is far from obvious that vigorous enforcement of the law against the reckless spread of infection will encourage disclosure of sexual contacts and the seeking out of treatment.

[54] Herring, "Mistaken Sex" [2005] *Crim LR* 511, 517.

[55] The Supreme Court of Canada has upheld a conviction for rape on such facts: *Currier* [1998] SCR 371.

[56] [2005] *Crim LR* 511, 517.

A finding that D had raped V in those circumstances would be unsettling.[57] Yet, from the perspective of findings of full consent, with its focus on the state of knowledge and disposition of V, there is considerable force in Herring's position. There is force to the proposition that consent to some activity is vitiated if an agent would not have permitted the activity but for a mistake or ignorance of a fact that, if disclosed, would have resulted in the agent's not consenting. The difficulty is that if we allow full sway to that proposition, we will in some cases, even in cases where lack of consent is placed at the heart of the offence, find D liable for wrongs that he did not commit.

To avoid such outcomes, we must set aside the cut-and-dried method of Herring and try a more nuanced approach. In *Clarence*,[58] an attempt to do this was made in terms of a distinction between the core nature of an act and the mere attributes of an act. For the Court in *Clarence*, if V understood the nature of the act notwithstanding any ignorance or mistake about some of its aspects, she would give a valid consent. The risk of serious infection was seen as merely a concomitant, not part of the defining core of sexual intercourse with an infected person. On this analysis, only when a sexually motivated act is passed off as something non-sexual is there non-consent to sex.[59] But one difficulty with this approach is that a purportedly analytical distinction between the core nature and the mere attributes of an act may have little bearing on the facts that matter to *V*, the things that count for her in deciding to consent to an act. For V1 the fact that the act is sexual may outweigh any other consideration; even being the unwitting victim of a plausible subterfuge which inveigles her into sexual activity may entail a devastating loss of status in her cultural community. For V2, sex not fully chosen may constitute a matter for anger and regret but on a different and lesser plane to the harm of a life-threatening infection. We can see how a preoccupation with the consent of V in circumstances where she is mistaken or ignorant of facts relevant to her decision-making may deflect attention from the more salient issue of what *wrong* D does to V when he exploits her mistake or ignorance to induce a consent that would not have been obtained had V been apprised of the full picture.

A focus on the wrong D has done to V underlies some recent decisions involving ignorance or mistake on the part of V as to facts relevant to consent. In *Dica*[60] and *Konzani*,[61] the Court of Appeal entertained no doubt that V may give a valid consent to sexual activity with D despite a failure by D to disclose his HIV-positive status. The gravamen of D's wrong in such circumstances was taken to be the infection of V. On balance this seems correct, although from V's perspective the harm might not have been confined to infection, serious though that was. If a relationship was involved, the breach of trust may well put a retrospective blight on the sexual aspects of the relationship. Accordingly, conviction for an offence against the person may not capture all aspects of Ds wrongdoing against V. But attempting to bring V fully to book by conjoining charges of rape to charges based on causing physical

---

[57] See Gross, "Rape, Moralism and Human Rights" [2007] *Crim LR* 220; Herring, "Human Rights and Rape: A Reply to Hyman Gross" [2007] *Crim LR* 228; Laird, "Rapist or Rogue? Deception, Consent and the Sexual Offences Act 2003" [2014] *Crim LR* 491; Rubenfeld "The Riddle of Rape-by-Deception and the Myth of Sexual Autonomy" (2013) 122 *Yale LJ* 1372.

[58] (1888) 22 QBD 23.

[59] As in *Rosinski* (1824) 1 Lew CC 11.

[60] [2004] QB 1257.

[61] [2005] 2 Cr App R 14.

harm arguably takes us too far beyond current legal and cultural understandings of rape. Less uncertainty may be had about the decision in *Linekar*,[62] where D had sex with V, a prostitute, and then ran off without paying. The Court of Appeal rightly held that D had not raped V. The wrong that is rape had not occurred. If V regularly made herself available for sex for payment and, all other things equal, her decisions about providing sexual services were based purely on economics, she was not sexually violated. She was conned into providing sexual services and, at the time, D could have been better charged with obtaining sexual intercourse by false pretences.[63] That offence was abolished by the Sexual Offences Act 2003. Even in the absence of a suitable charge,[64] courts should resist stretching the boundaries of offences based on sexual violation to reach such conduct.

We may now understand better the role of consent in cases where V is mistaken or ignorant as to aspects or the consequences of D's conduct. The focus is exclusively on V only when we ask the threshold question of whether the mistake or ignorance at issue was material in terms of her decision to consent to what D proposed to do. So, if on facts similar to *Linekar* it should turn out that V was only hoping to be paid by D, that she would have had sex with him with or without payment, consent is present and there is no offence of any kind by D. But if, as in the case itself, payment was the condition of consent, then it is logical to conclude that there was no full consent to sexual intercourse. Staying in the realm of logic, it would then be possible to conclude that V had been raped by D. Deflecting that logic entails going beyond questions that are exclusively concerned with V's knowledge and understanding of D's conduct, and addressing why he exploited V's mistake, or ignorance, as to some aspect of the conduct or its consequences. When evaluating the wrong D did to V, we may have to return to V's understanding of D's act. She may, despite any mistake or ignorance affecting her decision-making, have sufficient understanding of D's act in one of its dimensions to rule out any wrongdoing by D *in that regard*; but may still be wronged by D in respect of other matters of which she was insufficiently aware. Additionally, there will be occasions where V's ignorance or mistake precludes a sufficient understanding of D's conduct as a whole: as when sexual intercourse is passed off as a form of necessary therapy;[65] or, conversely, when what V thinks is a shared sex act is in fact a malign practical joke designed by D to humiliate V.[66] Where V so profoundly misunderstands the context and significance of the activity, effective consent is precluded.

(e) Mistake or ignorance on the part of V regarding D's identity or status

Whether a mistake by V about D's identity vitiates her consent very much depends on the nature of the conduct at issue. In the case of non-commercial sexual activity, one might suppose that the identity of one's partner is crucial and any mistake on that matter destructive of consent. Surprisingly, in *Barrow*,[67] it was held not to be a case of rape where D impersonated V's husband. Subsequently, however, it was enacted that a man commits rape

---

[62] [1995] QB 250.
[63] Sexual Offences Act 1956, s. 3.
[64] Such conduct should fall within the offence of dishonestly obtaining services by deception, contrary to s. 11 of the Fraud Act 2006.
[65] *Williams* [1923] 1 KB 340.
[66] *Devonald* [2008] EWCA Crim 527; above, § 12.3(i)(b).
[67] (1868) LR 1 CCR 81.

if he obtains a woman's consent by representing himself as her husband. The narrow terms of this legislative reversal allowed the view that if the impersonation was of someone other than a husband, the general principle in *Barrow* still stood—that mistake as to personal identity of a sexual partner does not vitiate one's essential understanding of the act consented to. That argument, thankfully, did not impress the Court of Appeal in *Elbekkay*,[68] which ruled that the question of personality went to the heart of consent in sexual matters. Consequently, D was guilty of raping V when obtaining sexual intercourse with her by passing himself off as her boyfriend. For non-consensual sexual offences the matter is now placed on a secure statutory footing by section 76(2) of the Sexual Offences Act 2003, which applies an irrebuttable presumption of non-consent where D impersonates "a person known personally to the complainant".

Matters relating to the status or qualifications of D may also be germane to consent. In *Richardson*,[69] at trial it was held that V had made the equivalent to a mistake of identity when she submitted to dental treatment by D, assuming him to be a qualified dentist, whereas he was suspended from practice. The conviction was quashed on the ground that the finding below unduly distorted the natural meaning of "identity". *Richardson* must be contrasted with *Tabassum*,[70] where the conviction of D for indecent assault was confirmed following D's intimate examination of women in what may (or may not)[71] have been genuine research into the incidence of breast cancer. D had been aware that the subjects of the examinations wrongly assumed him to be medically qualified (although he did have academic qualifications useful for the research he claimed to be conducting). The reconciliation of *Tabassum* with *Richardson* is not obvious. To the extent that the decisions can be squared, the answer does not lie in any claim that a mistake of identity was made in *Tabassum*. The answer, if there is one, is that in the case of intimate examinations, the procedure when carried out by a doctor is something fundamentally different from the procedure when carried out by a lay-person.

For less intimate forms of contact, the importance of D's identity will very much depend on the circumstances. In the case of forcible contact in the sphere of sport, for example, identity should only be an issue if V has made it clear that her participation is dependent on D's identity.

(f) The age of understanding for effective consent

In order to give an effective consent, V must possess a sufficiently mature capacity to understand the nature of the interaction that D proposes. For certain acts, legislation designates an age under which consent will be ineffective, such as 16 for sexual activity. For medical treatment, consent given at the age of 16 is taken to be effective, other things being equal.[72] It does not follow that the consent of a younger person will be ineffective. As the House of Lords explained in *Gillick*,[73] a person under that age may nonetheless give consent to

---

[68] [1995] Crim LR 163.

[69] [1999] QB 444.

[70] [2000] 2 Cr App R 328.

[71] Bearing in mind the burden of proof on the prosecution, D should be given the benefit of any doubt as to his true purpose.

[72] Family Law Reform Act 1969, s. 8.

[73] [1986] AC 112.

treatment which is in her best interests if she has sufficient maturity and understanding to assess her interests.

It was widely assumed that a "*Gillick*-competent" young person could refuse as well as consent to treatment. Donaldson MR thought differently in *Re R*,[74] when he ordered treatment for a 15-year-old girl with an eating disorder, even though he accepted that her refusal of treatment was a refusal on the part of a *Gillick*-competent person. He introduced the notion of "joint key-holders"; she could unlock the door, making her treatment lawful by virtue of her consent, but so too could other competent persons, such as the court exercising its wardship jurisdiction, on her behalf.

This asymmetry between refusal of treatment and consent to treatment has been widely attacked and, indeed, it would be hard to follow if the sole value informing *Gillick*-competence were personal autonomy.[75] But it is not. *Gillick* was, *inter alia*, a case concerned to ensure that treatment in the best interests of a patient is delivered. The leading consideration in *Gillick* was ensuring that sexually active girls under the age of 16 received contraception even in circumstances where parents or guardians would not be involved in the decision-making. In *Re R*, again the underlying concern was that a patient with volatile mood swings would receive therapy which would (and did) save her life. The cases reflect the fact that the consequences of accepting treatment are typically beneficent, whereas the outcomes ensuing from the refusal of treatment may be catastrophic. In that sense, the decisions in *Gillick* and *Re R* have a greater affinity than may at first appear.[76]

If, on policy or moral grounds, the court disapproves of the interaction between D and V, it may be astute to find a lack of competence on the ground of age. That appears to have been the case in *Burrell v. Harmer*,[77] where D tattooed V, a 13-year-old boy, for payment. According to the Divisional Court, this constituted an assault on V, based on the questionable finding that he did not understand the nature of the act that D had performed upon him.[78]

(iv) The limits of consent

(a) The general rule

As we have seen, V's consent will generally be ineffective if D's conduct causes actual bodily harm or worse. Actual bodily harm need not involve any injury of any significance; it consists of harm which "need not be permanent, but must, no doubt, be more than transient or trifling".[79] Cuts, bruises, and bloody noses fall within the category. In *A-G's Reference (No. 6 of 1980)*, a case where D and V fought by agreement in a public street, Lord Lane CJ put the position as follows:[80]

> "it is not in the public interest that people should try to cause, or should cause, each other actual bodily harm for no good reason … it is an assault if actual bodily harm is *intended and/or caused*."

---

[74] [1992] Fam 11 (CA).
[75] Grubb, "Treatment Decisions" in Grubb (ed.), *Choices and Decisions in Health Care* (1993) 54–68.
[76] See further Teff, *Reasonable Care* (1994) 146–52.
[77] [1967] Crim LR 169.
[78] D's conduct would now be more straightforwardly dealt with under the Tattooing of Minors Act 1969.
[79] *Donovan* [1934] 2 KB 498, 509.
[80] [1981] QB 715, 719 (emphasis added).

These remarks were approved by the House of Lords in *Brown*.[81] The most obvious feature of the current law is the extremely limited scope for effective consent. It will be noted that consent is taken to be ineffective not merely when D *intends* to cause V actual bodily harm but also when he *in fact* causes actual bodily harm. In *Boyea*,[82] D, with V's consent, indulged in "vigorous sex"; so vigorous that it was considered likely to cause actual bodily harm. It was accepted that it was not D's intention to cause V harm, neither did he foresee that he would. If harm had *not* been caused, the sexual interchange between D and V would have been entirely lawful. The Court of Appeal ruled that the fact that harm was caused rendered V's consent ineffectual, applying the *dictum* of Lord Lane (above) in *A-G's Reference (No. 6 of 1980)*.

Boyea may be contrasted with *Kimber*,[83] where the Court of Appeal ruled that lack of consent was a definitional requirement of assault and that, consequently, D would lack the mens rea for assault if he mistakenly believed that he had V's consent. *Kimber* supports the view that the essence of assault (as with rape) is the lack of consent. Where significant bodily harm occurs, other forms of criminal liability may ensue but it would remain the case that, if V consented to D's act, V would not have been *assaulted*. *Boyea* holds otherwise. A consensual act may yet be an assault if D intends actual bodily harm (or worse) or inadvertently causes actual bodily harm.

In summary: under current law, the general rule is that what would otherwise be an offence against the person such as assault and battery can be consented to, provided actual bodily harm (or worse) is neither intended nor in fact caused. More serious offences, such as assault occasioning actual bodily harm, cannot be consented to.

(b) Exceptions to the general rule

Exception 1: Organised sports.

It was accepted in *Brown*, confirming earlier authority, that in the course of "properly organised sports" V could lawfully take the risk of being *seriously* hurt by D. The extent of this exception is far from clear. Obviously well-established sports with rule-making bodies such as association football, rugby football, hockey, and cricket fall within this exception. In a very useful review of the sports exception,[84] Lord Woolf emphasised the importance of open public performance, rules of the game, and disciplinary and governing bodies. The better regulated the "zone of toleration", the more secure the participants from interference under the general law. Yet, as the Law Commission observed, the position of minority sports such as Thai boxing and full contact karate is less secure.[85]

The case law on sports injuries and criminal liability also draws a distinction between injuries, including foreseen injuries, which are a by-product of play and intentionally inflicted injury. In *Bradshaw*,[86] it was said that an act intended to cause serious injury would be unlawful even if it complied with the rules of the game. But provided there is no intent to cause injury, there may be effective consent to injuries inflicted outside the rules of the

---

[81] [1994] 1 AC 212.
[82] [1992] Crim LR 574.
[83] [1983] 3 All ER 316. See also the trial case of *Slingsby* [1995] Crim LR 570.
[84] *Barnes* [2005] 1 WLR 910.
[85] Law Com. Consultation Paper No. 139, *Consent in the Criminal Law* (1995) Part XII.
[86] (1878) Cox CC 83.

game. In *Barnes*,[87] the Court of Appeal confirmed the category of what may be called the conventional foul, the kind of thing that players should expect and thereby consent to when they participate in a particular kind of game.

Intent seems to be the key. If the move by D is intended to cause V injury, it may well constitute an offence against the person irrespective of whether D's play is within or outside the rules of the game. If what D did is within the rules of the game, it is submitted that the intent in question should be direct or core intent.[88] This is because it is possible that forms of well accepted conduct—well-timed, full-impact tackles in rugby—might, on a particular occasion, satisfy a *Woollin*-based[89] test of intentionally causing injury. It is not appropriate that participants in well-recognised sports should be liable for serious offences for conduct which is consistent with the rules of the sport. In this context, a parallel may be drawn with the constriction of intent to core intent in medical contexts.[90]

Notoriously, the sport of boxing does not fit the picture just sketched. The causing of serious injury with a direct intent to cause such injury seems to be at the heart of the sport, notwithstanding pious references to the "noble art of self-defence". Lord Mustill, a dissentient in *Brown*, was at a loss to understand how intentionally causing serious injury for financial gain could be considered lawful, whereas inflicting painful but non-serious injury for sexual gratification, as in *Brown*, was illegal.[91] The legality of boxing, if such it is, does not rest on any statute or well-regarded appellate case. In favour of the legality of boxing is its openness, its rule book, its governing bodies—factors given salience for sport generally in *Barnes*—and, above all, the generally held assumption of legality that has stood for many years. Were boxing suddenly to be regarded as illegal in the course of criminal litigation, there would be a real question of retroactive law and grounds for challenge under Article 7 of the ECHR. But just as with the former immunity granted to husbands who raped their wives,[92] the legality of boxing could crumble without the need for legislation should public and judicial opinion turn decisively against the sport as an acceptable form of activity within the moral framework of current society. There is no indication that that stage has been reached.

We tentatively offer the following summary:

(i)   In games which do not involve fighting as the defining activity: where the injury is intentionally inflicted, criminal liability may arise even if the incident falls within the rules of the particular game. If the incident does fall within the rules of a long-accepted, publicly open and properly organised game, the intention to cause injury should be a direct intention before criminal liability may ensue.

(ii)   In games which do not involve fighting as the defining activity: where the injury is non-intentional and a foreseeable consequence of playing the game, the rules of the game may be considered very strong evidence of what risks are consented to

---

[87] [2005] 1 WLR 910.

[88] See above, § 5.1.

[89] [1999] 1 AC 82. For a wide-ranging discussion of the legality of boxing see Gunn and Ormerod, "The Legality of Boxing" (1995) 15 *LS* 181.

[90] Ashworth, "Criminal Liability in a Medical Context; The Treatment of Good Intentions" in Simester and Smith, *Harm and Culpability* (1996) 173.

[91] [1994] 1 AC 212.

[92] *R v. R.* [1992] 1AC 599; above, § 2.2.

by the players. Further, incidents falling beyond the rules of the game but within its bounds of tolerance—e.g. marginally late tackles in rugby or football—will also fall within the boundaries of effective consent.

(iii)   In the anomalous case of sports that involve rule-governed fighting, all manner of injury, up to and including death, would seem to be within the purview of effective consent, provided the injury is inflicted within the rules of the sport. (This rule is offered with confidence only for fighting sports long tolerated and openly presented and organised, such as boxing and wrestling, when conducted under the auspices of the relevant controlling bodies. New fighting sports or fighting sports new to this jurisdiction, e.g. free- or cage-fighting and Thai boxing, are of doubtful legality notwithstanding their public performance and extensive media coverage.)

(iv)   Intentionally inflicted injuries falling outside the rules of any game should lead straightforwardly to criminal liability. The intention may be either direct or oblique (i.e. virtually certain).

Exception 2: Horseplay.
In addition to organised sport, "rough, undisciplined play" allows scope for consent even to the risk of serious harm of the kind that occurred in *Aitken*,[93] where air force officers in an after-dinner mess game amused themselves, *inter alia*, by dousing each other with fuel and setting it alight. The idea, apparently, was to test the fire-resistance properties of their flying-suits. As all concerned had consented to this exceedingly dangerous activity, it was held that no offence had been committed against V, a participant, who suffered horrendous burns. The activity must constitute "play": if injury is intentionally inflicted, the conduct will lose its character as play.

Other exceptions.
Beyond the categories of sport and play, the exceptions from the general rule are eclectic and of uncertain scope. Therapeutic surgery is clearly lawful. So too, it seems, are non-therapeutic plastic surgery, contraceptive surgery, and sex-change operations.[94] Body piercing and tattooing of non-minors are now prevalent and apparently lawful,[95] including the fearsome "do-it-yourself" branding by hot knife that occurred in *Wilson*.[96] Female circumcision is clearly unlawful because of legislative intervention[97] though we must still assume that religiously ordained male circumcision is lawful.[98] The legality of customary and tribal scarifications and markings is debatable, particularly in the case of minors. We may bring this confusing and miscellaneous list to a close by mentioning "dangerous exhibitions": there is high authority that such displays, whatever precisely they are, are lawful.[99]

---

[93]   *Aitken, Bennett and Barson* [1992] 1 WLR 1066 (CA). See too *Jones* (1986) 83 Cr App R 375.
[94]   Discussed in Law Com. Consultation Paper No. 139, *Consent in the Criminal Law* (1995) Part VIII.
[95]   *Ibid.*, Part IX.
[96]   [1997] QB 47 (CA); below, § 21.1(v).
[97]   The Prohibition of Female Circumcision Act 1985.
[98]   Law Com. Consultation Paper No. 139, *Consent in the Criminal Law* (1995) para. 9.2.
[99]   *A-G's Reference (No. 6 of 1980)* [1981] QB 715 (CA).

(v) The limits of consent—critique

Any account of consent which seeks an acceptable degree of consistent principle and policy is confounded by the *ad hoc* nature of the legal materials to hand.[100] The confusing nature of the current situation can best be exemplified by contrasting the decision of the House of Lords in *Brown*[101] with the subsequent Court of Appeal decision in *Wilson*.[102] In the former case, an organised group of homosexual men had devised elaborate and ritualised methods of inflicting pain on consenting group members. Although bodily harm was inflicted, no member of the group required medical assistance as a consequence of these bizarre activities. In the latter case, a wife requested that her husband brand his initials on her buttocks. She required medical treatment to salve the burns that he inflicted with her consent. In *Brown*, there were convictions for occasioning actual bodily harm and malicious wounding: in *Wilson*, the defendant was acquitted. Why the difference?

The decision in *Brown*, though controversial in policy terms, at least can be expressed straightforwardly. The House of Lords confirmed the general rule that effective consent could not be given if the harm amounted to actual bodily harm or worse. The value of free sexual expression between consenting adults did not weigh sufficiently to displace the general rule. The rule was characterised as a rule about the control of violence and the infliction of harm to that degree was considered a token of violence. The sexual motivation of the defendants did not supervene on the violence and change its nature to private sexual conduct; an opinion confirmed by the European Court of Human Rights in finding that the conviction of the defendants did not infringe the right to privacy under Article 8 of the ECHR.[103] The Court of Appeal in *Wilson* found three grounds of differentiation with *Brown*.[104] First, in *Wilson*, there was no "aggressive intent", as had been present in *Brown*. The distinction is spurious. If a person were to be branded without consent, it would be a violent act. In both *Brown* and *Wilson* there was no aggressive intent because of consent. Secondly, the Court of Appeal described *Brown* as a "truly extreme" case, involving "physical torture". Yet only in *Wilson* was medical attention needed. Finally, the branding procedure was characterised as a form of tattooing and not, like the various acts in *Brown*, as acts of violence. At this point, we must abandon any attempt at classification and analysis. Why violence perpetrated for sport, horseplay, or ornamentation has an acceptability denied to sexual fulfilment lies beyond reason.[105] All that can be done is to note and docket the decisions of the courts as and when they arise. In *Emmett*,[106] D and V, a couple soon to be married,[107] indulged in two episodes of consensual sexual risk-taking which miscarried,

---

[100] Kell, "Social Disutility and the Law of Consent" (1994) 14 *OJLS* 121.

[101] [1994] 1 AC 212.

[102] [1997] QB 47.

[103] *Laskey et al* v. *United Kingdom* (1997) 24 EHRR 39.

[104] *Ibid.*, 50.

[105] "The position is unprincipled and incoherent.... [R]ecognition of individual autonomy [concerns] the right of individuals of sufficient understanding to make their own decisions about what is good for them. In principle, this should apply to people's sexual preferences. Indeed, it is hard to see how the interest (whether public or private) in allowing people to express their sexuality, which forms a fundamental part of people's personality, could be less important than the interest in allowing people to play sports": Feldman, *Civil Liberties and Human Rights* (1993) 517.

[106] *Emmett (Stephen Roy)*, *The Times*, 15 October 1999 (CA).

[107] They were married at the time of D's trial.

causing actual bodily harm on each occasion. The harm, unlike the harm in *Brown*, was not intended, though the risk of harm was clearly present. The Court of Appeal confirmed D's conviction for assault occasioning actual bodily harm. *Wilson* was distinguished as a tattooing case. In the light of the ruling in *Dica*[108] and the considered dicta in *Konzani*[109] which allow that, if fully informed, V may give a valid consent to the risk of contracting an STD (again, *Brown* was distinguished as a case concerned with violence) we can now say that consent may be given in sexual contexts even to a risk of death, if the risk arises from a potential infection; but there will be zero tolerance for all other forms of risk that arise in the course of sexual activity.

A law which employs such distinctions is a law ripe for change. The Law Commission's Second Consultation Paper on the role of consent in the criminal law provides a useful agenda for reform. The core suggestion of the Commission's Report is that consent to harm on the part of competent persons should be effective in all spheres of activity provided the harm consented-to falls short of serious injury.[110] This strikes a balance between the values of paternalism and autonomy, allowing greater weight to the latter but denying validity to choices that favour the infliction of serious injury on the basis that an agent opting for harm of that gravity can be assumed not to be acting in her own best interests.

The Law Commission's recommendation has been attacked as a muddled and unstable compromise. Paul Roberts, for instance, has argued that the only principled stance for a modern, heterogeneous democracy is thorough-going liberalism, a liberalism that would enjoin respect and freedom for *any* self-regarding choice made by a competent agent.[111] Certainly the liberal position in its pure form is cut and dried. In terms of individual choice, the freedom to choose is maximised and the shadow of the criminal law removed. The self-regarding choice of a competent agent precludes any finding of a wrong done to the agent and, in the absence of any wrong, with it any ground of intervention for the consistent liberal. Yet if persons are to be allowed complete freedom to choose, inevitably some very dark choices will be made; such as the choices of Bernd Brandes and Armin Miewes, that the latter should make a meal of parts of the former's body, some parts to be mutually consumed while Brandes was being hacked by Miewes to his inevitable death, the rest for Miewes later.[112] Given that neither Miewes nor Brandes were incompetent decision-makers in terms of their mental capacities,[113] the sentence of life imprisonment for manslaughter handed down by a German court was a great injustice to Miewes from the classic liberal perspective. From that vantage, the consent of Brandes entailed that no wrong had been done to him and that should have entailed that Miews had committed no crime.

Yet even many liberals, on learning of Miewes's sentence, will not experience the sense of indignation that is the typical reaction on encountering an injustice. Indeed, the real and

---

[108] [2004] QB 1257.

[109] [2005] 2 Cr App R 14.

[110] Law Com. Consultation Paper No. 139, *Consent in the Criminal Law* (1995) paras. 4.46–53.

[111] Roberts, "The Philosophical Foundations of Consent in the Criminal Law" (1997) 17 *OJLS* 389.

[112] This macabre case is discussed by Bergelson, "The Right to be Hurt; Testing the Boundaries of Consent" (2007) 75 *George Washington LR* 165, 167.

[113] Consistent liberalism is constantly threatened by reading back from bizarre choices an inference that the chooser in making such a choice has demonstrated his mental incapacity and hence his ineligibility for autonomous agency. If that temptation is avoided in the cases of Brandes and Miewes, there was nothing to cast doubt on their mental capacities.

imagined horrors that may flow from unrestrained choice led Joel Feinberg, the leading philosopher on the application of liberal principles to the criminal law, to concede that the criminal law could intervene to suppress what he terms "free floating evils".[114] One token of such an evil acknowledged by Feinberg was a commercially sponsored gladiatorial contest to the death. If such a contest is to be regarded as evil, then for Feinberg it is of the free floating kind, as the consent of the contestants entails that no one has been wronged. But he allows that a society that permits such public events debases itself, loses civic virtue, and that it may be permissible to depart from the liberal framework to suppress such evils in the general societal interest. Other commentators have striven to bring proscription of extreme choices within the liberal paradigm by challenging the claim that a freely chosen harm by an autonomous agent can never constitute a wrong to the agent.

Duff maintains that the gladiatorial contestants have been wronged, their interests as human subjects have been set back, as even chosen participation degrades and dehumanises those involved. For a state not to intervene to prevent the degradation of the participants would be a wrong by that state. Preventing such contests advances the interests of those who would otherwise have participated.[115] In similar vein, Dan-Cohen maintains that to allow participation in such spectacles is to disrespect the participants, to regard them as lacking moral worth.[116] Whether the liberal framework is left intact after such adjustments is doubtful. When read in full, it is clear that Duff and Dan-Cohen would deploy their arguments for interventions overriding consent sparingly, yet differences emerge between them; with Dan-Cohen, for instance, more receptive to respecting the choices of sadomasochists than is Duff.[117] If we turn from differences between liberally minded philosophers to the state of public opinion, there will be a signal lack of consensus over what freely chosen activities dehumanise, degrade, or disrespect the moral worth of the participants. If we opt for liberalism all the way down, we have a clear-cut basis for intervention but are likely to end up with more "free floating evils" than public opinion is prepared to tolerate. If we allow intervention on the back of such culturally contestable criteria as degradation and disrespect, we may give too much elbow room to pressures for conformity and intolerance.

The radically different cultural, social, and religious groups present within the jurisdiction of England and Wales renders impossible any large and stable consensus on the limits of consent. Indeed, because of the lack of any consensus emerging from its consultation exercise and the absence of any political enthusiasm to liberalise the current law to any degree, the Law Commission has dropped the consent project.[118] However realistic, this is a matter for regret for anyone wishing to move on from the chaotic and overly punitive condition of the current law. Allowing effective consent to any harm falling short of serious harm would have significantly advanced tolerance and freedom. Considerable scope would still have been left for paternalism or, if you will, authoritarian communitarianism, a political necessity it seems. If scope is to be allowed to paternalism, it is important that

---

[114] *Harmless Wrongdoing* (1988) 3–33.

[115] Duff, "Harms and Wrongs" (2001) 5 *Buffalo Crim LR* 13, 39.

[116] "Basic Values and the Victim's State of Mind" (2000) 88 *California LR* 759.

[117] Duff subsequently changed his position on sadomasochistic sex in *Answering for Crime* (2007) 131: "we should realise that this way of finding sexual gratification is, within that sub-culture, a way in which the participants express their love and respect for each other".

[118] Law Commission, *Eighth Programme (2001–02)* HC 227, para. 44.

the ground of intervention should be a genuine concern for the interests of the harmed agent and not mere moralism.[119] For that to be the case, only the person inflicting the harm should be subject to penal sanctions. The person harmed should not also be liable as a joint principal or accomplice. Currently, outside the narrow scope of the *Tyrrell*[120] principle, no distinction is drawn in terms of exposure to criminal liability between the person harmed and the person causing the harm. This is difficult to square with a paternalistic concern for the interests of the harmed agent. Apologists for the current dispensation, under which those who harm and those who submit to harm are eligible for punishment, will invoke deterrence to defend the status quo in terms of paternalism. But what increments of deterrence are added by punishing both camps is entirely conjectural and to be set against conjectured gains is the palpable damage that convictions and punishments do to those who endure them. The present dispensation sits best with legal moralism. And legal moralism is not a proper basis for the deployment of criminal law in a modern, plural democracy.

§ 21.2 Self-defence and the prevention of crime[121]

Section 3 of the Criminal Law Act 1967 provides:

> (1) A person may use such force as is reasonable in the circumstances in the prevention of crime, or in effecting or assisting in the lawful arrest of offenders or suspected offenders or of persons unlawfully at large.
> (2) Subsection (1) above shall replace the rules of the common law on the question when force used for a purpose mentioned in the subsection is justified by that purpose.

If force is employed in circumstances which are within subsection (1), then, as indicated by subsection (2), the old common law no longer applies: the lawfulness or otherwise of the force will be determined by reference to the very broad standard of reasonableness prescribed in subsection (1). There will be circumstances where recourse to force by D is justified to prevent crime, but where D is not preventing a crime on the part of V; as when force against V is necessary to prevent a crime by P. For instance, D, a policeman bundles V out of the way to get at P who is carrying an explosive he intends to detonate. Such incidents will be covered by section 3(1).[122] Contrast a situation where V, though attacking D, is not committing a crime on account of his infancy or mental disorder. In such circumstances, D's right to use proportionate force to protect himself must rest on the long-established common-law entitlement to use force by way of self-defence.

The application of both the statutory and common-law defences is now complicated by the enactment of section 76 of the Criminal Justice and Immigration Act 2008. That section sets down various criteria for resolving whether force used within the terms

---

[119] For an attempt to argue in favour of a limited range of coercive measures to advance the best interests of those coerced, see Sullivan, "Liberalism and Constraining Choice: The Cases of Death and Serious Bodily Harm" in Smith and Deazley (eds.), *The Legal Medical and Cultural Regulation of the Body* (2009) 205, 225–33.

[120] [1894] 1 QB 710; above, § 7.6(ii)(a).

[121] Smith, *Justification and Excuse in the Criminal Law* (1989) chap. 4; Leverick, *Killing in Self-Defence* (2006).

[122] The example is taken from *Hichens* [2011] EWCA Crim 1626, [2011] 2 Cr App R 26, para. 30; below, § 21.2(vii). The Court of Appeal accepted in principle that D would have been entitled to use some degree of force on V to stop her from opening their front door to the angry and violent P if that had been the only way to prevent P's entry. The finding at trial that there were non-violent means to achieve the same result was confirmed.

of section 3 of the Criminal Law Act 1967 or by way of common law self-defence is to be considered reasonable:

76 Reasonable force for purposes of self-defence etc.

(1) This section applies where in proceedings for an offence—

(a)   an issue arises as to whether a person charged with the offence ("D") is entitled to rely on a defence within subsection (2), and

(b)   the question arises whether the degree of force used by D against a person ("V") was reasonable in the circumstances.

(2) The defences are—

(a)   the common law defence of self-defence;

(aa) the common law defence of defence of property; and

(b)   the defences provided by section 3(1) of the Criminal Law Act 1967 (c. 58) or section 3(1) of the Criminal Law Act (Northern Ireland) 1967 (c. 18 (N.I.)) (use of force in prevention of crime or making arrest).

(3) The question whether the degree of force used by D was reasonable in the circumstances is to be decided by reference to the circumstances as D believed them to be, and subsections (4) to (8) also apply in connection with deciding that question.

(4) If D claims to have held a particular belief as regards the existence of any circumstances—

(a)   the reasonableness or otherwise of that belief is relevant to the question whether D genuinely held it; but

(b)   if it is determined that D did genuinely hold it, D is entitled to rely on it for the purposes of subsection (3), whether or not—

(i) it was mistaken, or

(ii) (if it was mistaken) the mistake was a reasonable one to have made.

(5) But subsection (4)(b) does not enable D to rely on any mistaken belief attributable to intoxication that was voluntarily induced.

(5A) In a householder case, the degree of force used by D is not to be regarded as having been reasonable in the circumstances as D believed them to be if it was grossly disproportionate in those circumstances.

(6) In a case other than a householder case, the degree of force used by D is not to be regarded as having been reasonable in the circumstances as D believed them to be if it was disproportionate in those circumstances.

(6A) In deciding the question mentioned in subsection (3), a possibility that D could have retreated is to be considered (so far as relevant) as a factor to be taken into account, rather than as giving rise to a duty to retreat.

(7) In deciding the question mentioned in subsection (3) the following considerations are to be taken into account (so far as relevant in the circumstances of the case)—

(a) that a person acting for a legitimate purpose may not be able to weigh to a nicety the exact measure of any necessary action; and

(b) that evidence of a person's having only done what the person honestly and instinctively thought was necessary for a legitimate purpose constitutes strong evidence that only reasonable action was taken by that person for that purpose.

(8) Subsections (6A) and (7) are not to be read as preventing other matters from being taken into account where they are relevant to deciding the question mentioned in subsection (3).

(8A) For the purposes of this section "a householder case" is a case where—

(a)   the defence concerned is the common law defence of self-defence,

(b)   the force concerned is force used by D while in or partly in a building, or part of a building, that is a dwelling or is forces accommodation (or is both),

(c)   D is not a trespasser at the time the force is used, and

(d)   at that time D believed V to be in, or entering, the building or part as a trespasser.

(8B) Where—

(a)   a part of a building is a dwelling where D dwells,

(b)   another part of the building is a place of work for D or another person who dwells in the first part, and

(c)   that other part is internally accessible from the first part, that other part, and any internal means of access between the two parts, are each treated for the purposes of subsection (8A) as a part of a building that is a dwelling.

(8C) Where—

(a)   a part of a building is forces accommodation that is living or sleeping accommodation for D,

(b)   another part of the building is a place of work for D or another person for whom the first part is living or sleeping accommodation, and

(c)   that other part is internally accessible from the first part, that other part, and any internal means of access between the two parts, are each treated for the purposes of subsection (8A) as a part of a building that is forces accommodation.

(8D) Subsections (4) and (5) apply for the purposes of subsection (8A)(d) as they apply for the purposes of subsection (3).

(8E) The fact that a person derives title from a trespasser, or has the permission of a trespasser, does not prevent the person from being a trespasser for the purposes of subsection (8A).

(8F) In subsections (8A) to (8C)—

"*building*" includes a vehicle or vessel, and

"*forces accommodation*" means service living accommodation for the purposes of Part 3 of the Armed Forces Act 2006 by virtue of section 96(1)(a) or (b) of that Act.

(9) This section, except so far as making different provision for householder cases, is intended to clarify the operation of the existing defences mentioned in subsection (2).

(10) In this section—

(a)   "*legitimate purpose*" means—

    (i) the purpose of self-defence under the common law,

    (ia) the purpose of defence of property under the common law, or

    (ii) the prevention of crime or effecting or assisting in the lawful arrest of persons mentioned in the provisions referred to in subsection (2)(b);

(b)   references to self-defence include acting in defence of another person; and

(c)   references to the degree of force used are to the type and amount of force used.

Usually, such a provision would supersede the existing law and make for a new page, if not a blank slate. But section 76 has produced a more nuanced outcome: it is stated in subsection (9) that the section "except so far as making different provision for householder cases" is intended only to "to clarify the operation of the existing defences."

What, then, in practical terms, is the import of section 76? One would assume that section 76 will be the first point of reference when any dispute arises as to the legitimacy of any token of force based on a claim of crime prevention or self-defence. In situations where the section confirms D's contention that the use of force and/or the degree of force used was legitimate, that should resolve the argument, save for any claim that section 76 is more permissive in the particular circumstances than allowed for by Article 2 of the ECHR. But what of the situation when D claims to have used legitimate force yet there can be argument whether such force is plainly endorsed by the language of section 76? Two situations must be distinguished, though in practice there may well be disputation as to which situation applies.

First, there may be circumstances where D's claim to have used legitimate force seems plainly at odds with the relevant language of section 76 but where the claim to legitimacy is supported by authority decided before the Criminal Justice and Immigration Act 2008. It is submitted that in those cases the statutory language should prevail. The process of clarification encompasses the resolution of what could previously be considered moot points. For circumstances where the statutory language fails to provide clear guidance, however, the parties are back to arguing the correct interpretation of section 3 of the Criminal Law Act 1967 or the common law of self-defence, as the case may be, subject to any relevant input from the ECHR and its jurisprudence.[123]

There is old authority that self-defence has a more restrictive field of application than is allowed for by a general right to use reasonable force within the terms set out in section 3,[124] but now the idea of *reasonable* response to violence or the imminent threat of violence must be at the heart of both defences. Where the conduct of V is violent or threatens violence, it will, almost invariably, constitute a criminal act on the part of V. Should D defend himself against V, his reaction is aptly characterised as an act of self-defence but it is, at one and the same time, something done to prevent V from committing or continuing a crime even though D's primary purpose is to protect himself. It would be most unsatisfactory if the criteria against which D's defensive conduct is judged were to differ according to whether we describe it as self-defence or crime prevention. Indeed, it would be pointless to conceive of the common law of self-defence as more narrow than section 3, should both defences be applicable on the facts. Accordingly, where V's violent or threatening conduct constitutes an offence, it is submitted that the legality of D's defensive response should be assessed solely in terms of the reasonableness standard set by the Criminal Law Act 1967 and as explicated by section 76 of the Criminal Justice and Immigration Act 2008.[125]

There will, however, be some exceptional situations where D may act in justifiable self-defence against V even though V's conduct does not constitute a crime. D may fend off an attack launched by an insane person, or by an infant, or by a person who has mistakenly assumed that D was about to attack him. In these cases, section 3 of the Criminal Law Act 1967 will not apply and it is possible to argue that the traditional, more restrictive, law of self-defence still governs. This is no authority directly in point. Particularly given the intervention of the Criminal Justice and Immigration Act 2008, which draws no distinction between the defences, it would be anomalous if the legality of D's conduct were to be judged by different standards in these kinds of cases. Whether English law should be resolving all issues that may arise when evaluating the legitimacy of defensive force merely by reference to a standard of reasonableness is debatable.[126] Yet this approach prevails at the present time and all defendants raising an issue of defensive force should be treated alike unless there is

---

[123] On which see below, § 21.2(viii).

[124] Cf. the rule that D must take any safe avenue of retreat before responding violently to the threat posed by V: below, § 21.2(iii).

[125] For further discussion of the interplay between s. 3 and the common law see Harlow, "Self-Defence: Public Right or Private Privilege" [1974] *Crim LR* 528.

[126] Ashworth, "Self-Defence and the Right to Life" [1975] *CLJ* 272.

good reason to do otherwise. We conclude that a plain reasonableness standard obtains for all cases of self-defence, whether or not the assailant is committing a criminal act.[127]

In one obvious way, force used in the prevention of crime is wider than self-defence in that crimes may be prevented by recourse to reasonable force even where no threat to life or limb is present. D may be about to break into an empty building to commit theft and can lawfully be prevented from doing so by forcible means if necessary. However, it seems that the crime to be prevented must at least be a crime triable in England or Wales. In *Jones*,[128] the defendants claimed that various forms of damage inflicted on RAF property were instances of reasonable force used to prevent crimes of aggression to be committed by Her Majesty's Government in Iraq. It was ruled that section 3 was not engaged because its application is restricted to crimes triable in England and Wales, whereas crimes of aggression are crimes contrary to international law and not crimes contrary to English law. The Court noted that there is nothing in the legislative history of section 3 suggestive of an extra-territorial reach.

(i) Force

A claim to have used force in self-defence or prevention of crime is a claim to have used legitimate force. The term "force" is used in section 3 and is employed at common law. Clearly, "force" comprehends any violence that D has resorted to and, additionally, covers such conduct as the breaking of a window or the battering down of a door. The term, as a matter of ordinary language, will not cover any acts that lack a violent or percussive character. Accordingly, in *Blake*,[129] it was held that D could not raise a defence within the terms of section 3 where his conduct took the form of writing on V's property with a felt-tip pen. Likewise, in *Hutchinson* v. *Newbury Magistrate's Court*,[130] it was held that wire-cutting a perimeter fence did not constitute "force".

These decisions are unexceptionable in terms of the literal meaning of the word force, but may have unfortunate consequences. Suppose that D's only way of warning X that X's life is in danger is to write a message on V's whitewashed wall. D could not raise a section 3 defence to a charge of criminal damage if he painted his message on V's wall—but he could raise the issue if he brought a hammer and chisel to the task. On the principle that the "greater includes the lesser", if D can justify an act of force as a response to particular circumstances, *a fortiori* justification should be accorded to a lesser, non-forceful response to the same situation.[131] Yet the decision in *Blake* indicates the contrary, and it is notable that in the cases of *Conway*[132] and *Willer*,[133] where, in each case, D escaped unlawful serious violence by committing a driving offence, the Court of Appeal chose to extend the

---

[127] The assumption appears warranted by *McInnes* [1971] 3 All ER 295 and *Devlin* v. *Armstrong* [1971] NI 13: it was assumed in each of these decisions that, with the passing of s. 3 of the Criminal Law Act 1967, failure to retreat before resorting to violence was merely a factor to be considered when assessing the reasonableness of D's conduct.

[128] [2005] QB 259; but note the reservation in the text below, § 21.3(iv).

[129] [1993] Crim LR 586 (DC). See also the discussion of force in the context of robbery: above, § 14.2(ii).

[130] *The Independent*, 20 November 2000 (QBD).

[131] Perhaps such a case could now be defended on the basis of necessity: below, § 21.3.

[132] [1989] QB 290 (CA).

[133] (1986) 83 Cr App R 225 (CA).

defence of duress (to accommodate circumstances where the crime was not nominated by the duressor) rather than gloss the term "force" in order to bring the cases within self-defence or the prevention of crime. It will be recalled that a defence of duress is available only if the harm threatened is death or serious bodily harm and cannot be raised to a charge of murder. Further, mistaken duress must, if it is to afford a defence, be based on reasonable grounds.[134] These restrictions do not apply to the use of defensive force or to the mistaken belief in the need for such force.[135] To have a stricter regime for non-violent responses seems insupportable. In *Bayer*,[136] the Divisional Court expressed sympathy for the view that all forms of conduct directed at preventing crime should be appraised within the terms of section 3 of the Criminal Law Act 1967 and that conduct otherwise criminal but not involving force should not lead to liability if it was a reasonable measure to prevent the commission of a crime.

(ii) Reasonable force—a question of fact

Force used in self-defence or the prevention of crime must be "such force as is reason-able in the circumstances" if it is to be lawful. Difficult issues may arise when apprais-ing a particular incident involving force. Broadly, they will involve questions concerning the *necessity* to use force at all and whether the amount of force used was a *proportionate* response to the circumstances. Whether the force used by D was reasonable in the circum-stances is a question of fact to be determined by the jury. As with any question of fact, guidance, including strong guidance, may be given by the presiding judge. The jury should be advised that the judgment of reasonableness should be on broad and liberal grounds—jewellers' scales are not required.[137] Or, as it is put in the Criminal Justice and Immigration Act 2008, "a person acting for a legitimate purpose may not be able to weigh to a nicety the exact measure of any necessary action".[138] That said, if a judge should come to the view that, even on the most favourable view of the evidence, no reasonable jury could find that the force D employed was either necessary or proportionate, the correct course is to withdraw the issue from the jury.

This conclusion is at odds with the decision in *Scarlett*,[139] where D caused the death of V, a trespasser, by using what the jury found to be excessive force when ejecting him from the premises. On appeal, D's conviction for manslaughter was quashed on the basis that if D thought the force he employed was reasonable (even though it was found to be excessive), he was entitled to a defence of mistake. The decision in *Scarlett* is based on a misreading of *Gladstone Williams*,[140] where it was decided that if D makes a mistake of fact concerning the need for force, his conduct is to be evaluated as if his mistaken assumption were a true assumption. *Williams*, however, does not require D to be given the benefit of his mistaken view about what constitutes reasonable force. *Williams* involved a mistake of circumstan-tial fact, a mistaken assumption that V was an aggressor whereas in truth he was a police

---

[134] Above, § 20.1(iii).
[135] Above, § 18.1(iii).
[136] [2004] Crim LR 663.
[137] *Reed v. Wastie* [1972] Crim LR 221 (DC).
[138] Section 76(7)(a).
[139] [1993] 4 All ER 629 (CA).
[140] [1987] 3 All ER 411 (CA).

officer making an arrest; *Scarlett* involves a mistake of normative evaluation.[141] This was clearly perceived in two subsequent decisions of the Court of Appeal, namely *Owino*[142] and *Armstrong-Braun*.[143] In neither case was *Scarlett* said to be wrong but the "correct" reading of *Gladstone Williams* was emphasised. The clarification provided for by section 76(6) of the Criminal Justice and Immigration Act 2008 is helpful: "In a case other than a householder case, the degree of force used by D is not to be regarded as having been reasonable in the circumstances as D believed them to be if it was disproportionate in those circumstances." This is clearly an objective test.[144] It seems safe to conclude that *Scarlett* will not be followed.

(iii) Force as a necessary means

Force cannot be justified to prevent a crime or to defend against an attack unless it was a necessary means of doing so. If D is aware that a safe alternative to the use of force is available, ordinarily he should take it. So, if D can prevent the entry of V, a burglar, by locking a door, she should do that rather than allow V to enter and then subject him to force.

The common law of self-defence required D to take any safe avenue of retreat.[145] On one view, this is a sensible rule entailed by the necessity principle. A deliberate failure to retreat rendered the subsequent use of force something that was avoidable. Andrew Ashworth is a firm advocate of a rule of retreat, particularly for cases where in order to stand his ground D would have to use fatal force against V. Ashworth contends that if D is obliged to retreat to a place of safety in such cases then there is full compliance with the right to life guaranteed by Article 2 of the ECHR: D lives and V lives.[146] However, the Court of Appeal in *Julien*[147] held that, with the passing of section 3 of the Criminal Law Act 1967, the question is now simply whether D's use of force was reasonable: a failure to retreat is merely a factor to be taken into account when determining the reasonableness of D's conduct. Of course, Article 2 and its jurisprudence is also a factor to be taken into account within the terms of the Human Rights Act 1998.

The approach in *Julien*, since codified (save for householders) in section 76(6A) of the Criminal Justice and Immigration Act, is welcome in that it allows due weight to be given to D's right to autonomy. If D is behaving in a non-threatening, law-abiding manner in a place where she has a right to be, she should be under no duty to exert herself at the unlawful behest of V. The question of necessity to use force should normally take, as its baseline, D's right to the peaceful enjoyment of her autonomous choices. This is supported in the important case of *Field*,[148] which rules that D may remain at a place of lawful resort notwithstanding his knowledge that V may attack him should he stay there. By electing to

---

[141] Although the reasonableness of D's force is a question of "fact" in the sense that it is for the jury rather than the judge to resolve, it is not the same type of fact as the circumstantial facts mistaken by the defendant in *Williams*. For further discussion of the distinction see above, § 18.1(v).

[142] (1996) 2 Cr App R 128 (CA).

[143] [1999] Crim LR 416.

[144] Even in householder cases, the ultimate question is whether the householder used such force as was reasonable in the circumstances: see § 21.2(iv) below.

[145] Turner, *Kenny's Outlines of Criminal Law* (16th ed., 1952) 113–14.

[146] Ashworth, *Principles* (6th edn, 2009) 120–4.

[147] [1969] 1 WLR 839 (CA). See too the discussion above, § 21.2.

[148] [1972] Crim LR 435 (CA).

visit a place of known danger, he does not forfeit his right to defend himself should he elect to stay where he is despite the threat of imminent violence. The right to maintain a lawful presence would be particularly in point where D's presence is objected to by V on racist or other disreputable grounds. To maintain for such cases that the preservation of V's life should trump the enjoyment of D's civil rights is too rigid a stance. Of course, a different set of considerations would apply for a case where, say, V is infuriated because D is sitting in V's favourite chair in the pub and D knows he could restore V to calm simply by sitting in another chair. Here it may well be thought unreasonable for D to resort to fatal force in order to remain *in situ* even if that was the only way he could do so.

In cases falling short of fatal force, it seems clear there is no duty to make a safe departure from the scene, if one's presence at the scene is a lawful presence. In *Redmond-Bate*,[149] the Divisional Court had to decide whether D and others had legitimately been arrested for breach of the peace. D had been preaching, quite lawfully, on cathedral steps. A crowd of about 100 gathered, some of whom showed hostility to D. D was arrested when she refused to desist from preaching. In finding the arrest unlawful, the Court held that citizens could not be called upon to desist from lawful conduct. Only when lawful conduct gives rise to a reasonable apprehension that it will, *by interfering with the rights or liberties of others*, provoke violence, is a police officer empowered to take steps to prevent it.

Accordingly, it may be concluded that D will not lose the right to defend himself by maintaining a lawful voluntary presence. Note, however, that we are dealing with *defensive* force. If D deliberately provokes V in order that he, D, may then be able to fight with V, D will not ordinarily be afforded a right of self-defence.[150] In such circumstances, it may readily be found that D was the true aggressor. However, it does not follow that D will lose the right to defend himself even if he is the first to provoke or initiate violence. Self-defence has been found to be available to D in a number of cases despite the fact that D was initially the aggressor.[151] It will not always be easy to pinpoint that moment when D's status changes from aggressor to defender. This and other difficulties were thoughtfully reviewed in *Keane* by Hughes LJ,[152] who advised that merely because V "turns the tables" on the aggressor D does not mean that D becomes a defender at that turning point.[153] The key consideration is whether V's response to D's attack took a disproportionate form.[154] There will be easy cases, as when V immediately responds with a knife to D's unarmed aggression. In less clear-cut cases, there may be fine lines for the jury to draw between D's unlawfully participating in a fight that he started and the moment it became justifiable for him to use force in defending himself from V. Because of these difficulties, it may be tempting to disqualify from self-defence anyone who is the initial antagonist, particularly anyone seeking a fight. Yet even the most disagreeable of persons may legitimately defend themselves. Imagine that D, who is unarmed, pushes V and abuses him in racist terms: V, furious, then rushes at D with a knife. D is entitled to defend himself, provided he uses proportionate means, however disreputable his provoking conduct and character. D has not forfeited his right to life.[155]

---

[149] [1999] Crim LR 998.

[150] *Mason* (1756) 1 East PC 239; *Browne* [1973] NI 96, 107.

[151] *Rashford* [2005] EWCA Crim 3377; *Burns v HM Advocate* (1995) SLT 1090; *Harvey* [2009] EWCA Crim 469.

[152] [2010] EWCA Crim 2514.

[153] *Ibid.*, para. 6.

[154] *Ibid.*, para. 17.

[155] It has been argued that self-defence should not be made available to D if D deliberately provokes a violent response from V in order to have the opportunity to be violent to V: Robinson, "Causing the Conditions of One's

(iv) Force and proportionality

Force which is disproportionate to the needs of the occasion is unreasonable force. As remarked already, questions of proportionality need to be resolved in a broad and liberal manner, eschewing the benefits of hindsight. Only in the plainest case should a judge, after finding that some force was necessary, remove a defence from the jury on the grounds of disproportionality:[156]

> "If there has been an attack so that defence is reasonably necessary it will be recognised that a person defending himself cannot weigh to a nicety the exact measure of his necessary defensive action. If a jury thought that in a moment of unexpected anguish a person attacked had only done what he honestly and instinctively thought was necessary, that would be the most potent evidence that only reasonable defensive action had been taken."

That this is a presumption of evidence, however strong a presumption, rather than a rule of law is confirmed by the Criminal Justice and Immigration Act 2008: "evidence of a person having only done what the person honestly and instinctively thought was necessary for a legitimate purpose constitutes strong evidence that only reasonable action was taken by that person for that purpose." If there is cogent evidence that D, through excessive fear and anxiety, clearly went "over the top", the presiding judge would be entitled to rule out any claim of legitimate force. The 2008 Act clearly states that the force used by D is not to be regarded as having been reasonable in the circumstances as D believed them to be if it was disproportionate in those circumstances.[157] But there is a strong presumption that the jury rather than the judge should resolve the issue.

(a) Householders

One would think that a requirement that defensive force must be proportionate force would be above controversy. However, there have been a number of cases where householders have been prosecuted for offences arising from force used against burglars who have entered their home. Several of these cases received wide press coverage sympathetic to the householder under prosecution or the threat of prosecution.[158] Section 76[159] now provides that, in a "householder case",[160] the degree of force used by D in self-defence "is not to be regarded as

---

Own Defence: A Study of the Limits of Theory in Criminal Law Doctrine" (1985) 71 *Virginia LR* 1. However, V's conduct must be assessed too. Even if D has provoked the violent encounter, at any given point in the fight the question must be put whether V is justified or excused in using force of the kind and degree V is using. If the answer is negative, then D is permitted to defend himself. See Alexander, "Causing the Conditions of One's Own Defense: A Theoretical Non-Problem" (2013) 7 *Crim Law and Phil* 623.

[156] *Palmer* [1971] 1 AC 814 (PC) (Lord Morris).

[157] Section 76(6).

[158] Perhaps the best-known of these cases is the case of Tony Martin, who was charged with murder as a consequence of fatally shooting a burglar who was on the point of entering his isolated farmhouse: *Martin (Anthony)* [2001] EWCA Crim 2245, [2002] 2 WLR 1; above, § 18.1(iii). Despite the concerns raised by cases such as Martin's, such prosecutions are rare. A survey by the Crime Prosecution Service of cases between 1990 and 2005 found only 11 prosecutions. Almost without exception these cases involved disproportionate force often inflicted past the point of danger: Lipscombe, *Householders and the Criminal Law of Self-Defence* (2013).

[159] As inserted by s. 43 of the Crime and Courts Act 2013.

[160] The phrase covers the use of force against persons who have entered a dwelling house or part of a dwelling house or accommodation for the armed forces and who are believed by non-trespassers present in the household to be trespassers.

reasonable in the circumstances as D believed them to be if it was grossly disproportionate to those circumstances".[161] And while it remains the case that disproportionate force is not to be regarded as reasonable force, the latest version of that stipulation is now confined to cases "other than a householder case".[162] Similarly, the subsection advising that the purpose of section 76 is merely to clarify the operation of existing defences, now contains the caveat "except so far as making provision for householder cases".[163] The implication of this legislative development appears to be that disproportionate force (falling short of *grossly* disproportionate force) in self-defence by householders in dwellings should be condoned. Such a reading is borne out by a Ministry of Justice circular stating that the objective of the revision is "to strengthen the law in favour of householders who use force in self-defence", providing "greater latitude in extreme cases".[164] Yet the same publication also advises that the householder provisions must be read in conjunction with the rest of section 76 of the Criminal Justice and Immigration Act 2008, which requires any force used to be reasonable in the circumstances as the defendant believed them to be.[165]

This conundrum was tested in *Denby Collins*.[166] In that case, D had restrained V, a trespasser in his home, with a headlock for some six minutes before the police arrived. V suffered extreme brain damage. The Crown Prosecution Service (CPS) decided not to prosecute D, taking the view that disproportionate force on the part of householders was condonable and therefore a conviction was not a realistic prospect on the facts of the case. V, the claimant, accepted that this decision was based on a correct view of the law and argued that a law of self-defence in those terms contravened Article 2 of the European Convention, which restricted lethal or life-threatening force in self-defence to force that was absolutely necessary.

However, Levenson LJ ruled that the CPS had misunderstood the applicable law. The householder provisions did not permit the use of disproportionate force by house-holders *tout court*. Force of that degree might or might not be considered reasonable force by a jury. The test to be applied at common law, and under the terms of section 76(3), was whether the force used by D was reasonable in the circumstances as D believed them to be. Properly understood, the householder provisions were compliant with the Convention: the jurisprudence firmly established that restricting defensive force to force that was reasonable in the circumstances was an acceptable standard to employ.[167]

Many will welcome this minimalist reading of the controversial householder provisions. Yet there is an undeniable tension here. As we have seen, when a jury is deciding whether D might have used disproportionate force, it must give careful attention to whether D acted in a manner that he honestly and instinctively thought was necessary.[168] A finding that force, despite this latitude allowed to D, was nevertheless disproportionate rather argues

---

[161] Section 76(5A).

[162] Section 76(6).

[163] Section 76(9).

[164] Ministry of Justice Circular 2013/02, paras. 8, 11. The circular gives one factual example of the kind of case where s. 43 might be decisive (para. 20). The ordeal described would be terrifying for a householder, but the response of the householder seems far from extreme (one blow to the back of the violent intruder's head as he departs through the shattered door of the premises that he has forcefully entered) and something one would expect to be within the law of self-defence in any event in terms of sending the intruder on his way.

[165] Section 76(3).

[166] *R (Denby Collins)* v. *Secretary of State for of Justice* [2016] EWHC 33 (Admin).

[167] A matter considered very fully in the case: *ibid.*, paras. 35–64.

[168] Section 76(7)(b).

against any finding that the force was reasonable. Levenson LJ gives one situation where such a finding might occur. He instances a case where a householder declines an opportunity for safe retreat. The learned judge considered that while such failure to retreat might undermine a plea of self-defence in a non-householder case, in a householder case the jury might allow the defence even though they considered that a failure to retreat rendered the force used disproportionate. This, with respect, is very puzzling. The question of retreat is normally considered to go to the question of the necessity to use any force at all rather than to an evaluation of the degree of force used.[169]

It is worth emphasising that the qualifying circumstances, where a householder may claim whatever latitude these ill-advised changes may permit, are limited to self-defence and the defence of others.[170] Any act that focuses exclusively on the defence or recovery of property, or on detaining the intruder (as when D uses force to prevent the trespasser V from leaving the house), is subject to the normal proportionality requirement. Should V, in such circumstances, manage to escape from the house and hide in D's garden, once outside the household,[171] then any force that D may use against V in self-defence must be proportionate force.

(b) Excessive force

If a jury should find that the force was excessive, the defence of self-defence will fail *in toto*. If there was an entitlement to use *some* force, this may be thought to attenuate culpability to an extent. Where the sentence is subject to the discretion of the judge, any diminution of culpability can be reflected in the sentence passed. That is, of course, not possible where the sentence is fixed by law, as it is for the crime of murder. In certain states of Australia, a form of manslaughter was judicially created to allow for such a verdict where D had killed with the mens rea for murder but in circumstances where he was entitled to use a degree of force, albeit a lesser degree than the force he used.[172] A similar judicial initiative has been consistently rejected in England and Wales, most recently by the House of Lords in *Clegg*.[173] Indeed, the idea has been dropped in the land of its origin, on the ground that directions to juries required an excessive degree of complexity.[174] This seems unfortunate. As a matter of principle, a right to use a degree of violence towards the victim must surely, on occasion, diminish the culpability of D. A suitable direction to juries would appear no more intractable than for the cognate issues of provocation and diminished responsibility.[175]

---

[169] "In a householder case the failure [to retreat] and thus the use of force may be disproportionate but still reasonable": [2016] EWHC 33 (Admin) para. 23. The idea seems to be that because recourse to force was avoidable, its use was a disproportionate yet possibly reasonable response. But it is perfectly sensible to say that force was proportionate to the attack faced but nonetheless unreasonable because the attack could have been safely avoided. It does not make the same kind of sense to say that because an attack could have been but was not avoided, any force used to repel it is disproportionate.

[170] Section 76(8A)(a).

[171] Sections 76(8A)(b)–(d) and 76(8B)(a)–(c).

[172] *McKay* [1957] ALR 648; *Howe* (1958) 100 CLR 448.

[173] [1995] 1 AC 482; see *Palmer* [1971] 1 All ER 1077 (PC).

[174] *Zecevic* (1987) 61 ALJR 375.

[175] The Law Commission has recently recommended that a proposed offence of first-degree murder should be reduced to second-degree murder if D killed V because he was in fear of serious violence and a person of ordinary stability might have done the same or something similar in the circumstances: Law Com. No. 304, *Murder, Manslaughter and Infanticide* (2006).

Questions of proportionality may require difficult judgments by juries. The only guidance they have is their own sense of what is reasonable. A particular jury may find that it was permissible to kill to avoid serious bodily harm, for example, whereas another jury in a similar case may find such means excessive when compared to the threat. There is something to be said for more explicit guidance on commonly recurring situations, as is done, for example, in the Model Penal Code.[176] Judgments may be particularly difficult to make when incommensurable values are in play. It is often said that it can never be justified to kill in order to protect property.[177] Yet it is not obviously a categorical truth that any individual's life is of more intrinsic worth than any item of property. Is it necessarily unreasonable to kill a terrorist if such is the only means of preventing the destruction of priceless historic artefacts? The answer depends, in part, on one's core values. The lack of consensus on such issues suggests that the law should provide specific rules rather than leave such matters to *ad hoc* evaluations. To some extent that is now the case where the force used by D was fatal force. Article 2 of the ECHR allows certain derogations form V's right to life, but makes no provision for the protection of property.

(v) Pre-emptive force

The effective prevention of a crime or an attack may require pre-emptive force. There is no requirement within the terms of section 76 of the Criminal Justice and Immigration Act 2008, or from appellate authority, that D must wait until V actually attacks him before making a defensive response. It suffices that V's attack was imminent; thenceforth, D may defend himself.

Focusing on the prevention of crime rather than self-defence, there is authority that the time-frame for preventive responses is more generous. If D, a police officer, is sure that V will commit a serious offence in the future, arguably it is reasonable to use force to prevent that crime even though its commission is not yet imminent. Such a view was endorsed by the Court of Appeal of Northern Ireland in *Kelly*,[178] where D, a soldier, shot and killed V, the driver of a car. There was reason to think that V and his fellow passengers were terrorists and that, if allowed to escape, they would commit terrorist offences in the future. It was held that this (false)[179] belief justified the use of force, even though D was not firing to prevent V from committing some imminent, identified, offence; he was preventing non-specific crimes at some future time.

It is submitted that *Kelly* is unsustainable.[180] The criminal law contains significant restrictions on the use of force and restraint which are at odds with this decision. If we

---

[176] The Code has a number of provisions (3.04–08) which occupy several pages of close print dealing separately with self-protection; protection of other persons; protection of property; law enforcement; and persons with special responsibilities for care and safety of others. And see too Law Com. No. 177, *A Criminal Code for England and Wales* (1989) cl. 44.

[177] Killing to protect property is not one of the circumstances where life may be legitimately taken without contravening Article 2 of the ECHR. Were an English court to hold that it was lawful to use deadly force to protect any item of property, there would arguably be a breach of Article 2 however priceless in terms of culture and heritage the item that otherwise would have been destroyed.

[178] [1989] NI 341.

[179] In fact, V and his passengers were joyriders and not terrorists.

[180] Surprisingly, the decision was upheld by the European Commission of Human Rights (*Kelly v. UK* (1993) 74 DR 139), who found no contravention of Art. 2 of the ECHR on the basis that the force was used to effect a

turn to the law of arrest, a pre-emptive arrest is not possible until V is "about to" commit a crime.[181] The law of criminal attempt requires an act which is sufficiently proximate to the commission of the crime.[182] It is somewhat paradoxical that on facts such as *Kelly* D could not have used the slightest degree of restraint to make an arrest to prevent a crime yet to be committed but, nonetheless, was entitled to use fatal force for that end. This inconsistency cannot be tolerated. The laws of arrest and criminal attempt set parameters for the deployment of preventative force under section 3 of the Criminal Law Act 1967, parameters which were overlooked in *Kelly*.

However, without resiling from these points of criticism, it should be noted that the United Kingdom government does seem to take a view of the boundaries of legitimate, preventative force that is aligned with *Kelly*. It has used drones, controlled and directed by persons in the United Kingdom, to kill persons located abroad who are taken to be members of terrorist organisations hostile to the United Kingdom and its citizens.[183] These killings seek to prevent and deter terrorists from perpetrating acts of terror at some future time and place. The United Kingdom government has confidently asserted that these killings are lawful in terms of international law and domestic law.[184]

Although the use of force should be subjected to strict time restraints, more latitude may be allowed for pre-emptive measures which fall short of actual violence. In *Cousins*,[185] D presented a shotgun to V and threatened that he would use it at some future time unless X, a close relative of V, withdrew his threat to kill D. On appeal D's conviction for making threats to kill was quashed because, contrary to the ruling of the trial judge, D was entitled to raise a section 3 defence despite the fact that his life was not in imminent danger. The Court of Appeal emphasised that the case involved the threat of violence and not the use of force. In *A-G's Reference (No. 2 of 1983)*,[186] the Court of Appeal ruled that D's possession of petrol bombs was possession for a lawful purpose, the purpose being to defend his shop premises from ransack at a time of urban riots. The Court assumed that D would have been entitled to use petrol bombs to defend his premises should they come under attack. It followed that he was entitled to put himself in a position to use such means.

In both *Cousins* and *A-G's Reference*, the Court of Appeal considered that offences other than the offences charged *had* been committed: in the former case, unlawful possession of a firearm because of a lack of licence, and, in the latter, the unlawful manufacture and storing of explosives.[187] These *obiter dicta* need to be treated with some caution. If the firearm and

---

lawful arrest within the terms of Art. 2. As Professor Sir John Smith observes, how can a shooting carried out with an intent to kill be spoken of as an "arrest"? See Smith, "The Right to Life and the Right to Kill in Law Enforcement" (1994) 144 *NLJ* 354.

[181] Police and Criminal Evidence Act 1984, s. 24(7)(a).

[182] Above, § 9.3(i).

[183] As these killings are planned and initiated within the territory of the United Kingdom, they would be subject to the English law of homicide: see above, § 10.2(v).

[184] *Hansard*, HC cols. 25–7 (7 September 2015). For a useful discussion of the claim that these killings are lawful under domestic law, see Gardner, "The Domestic Criminal Legality of the RAF Drone Strike in Syria in August 2015" [2016] *Crim LR* 35.

[185] [1982] QB 26 (CA).

[186] [1984] QB 456 (CA).

[187] See too *Fegan* [1972] NI 80 (CA), where it was held that possession of a firearm to protect oneself against violence would be possession for a lawful object even though the possession was in itself unlawful for being unlicenced.

explosives, respectively, were obtained prior to the existence of the relevant threats, then liability for those offences ensues. Yet if the items were obtained by way of response to the threats, liability should not arise. If the use of a firearm as a threat is lawful in particular circumstances, it would be inconsistent to hold that acquiring a firearm to use lawfully in particular *identified* circumstances is unlawful. *Smith and Hogan* gives an example of V's threatening D with a gun, whereupon D wrests the gun from V and uses it to defend himself. If D's use of the weapon is lawful, the learned authors convincingly assert that to convict D of the unlawful possession of the weapon because he lacked a licence to possess a weapon would be absurd.[188] As we are dealing with conduct preliminary to the threat or use of force, prima facie it should not matter how items such as guns or explosives are acquired, provided they are acquired in order to respond to identified circumstances where the use or threatened use of such items would be lawful. (Contrast a scenario where D acquires a gun "just in case".) Of course, the longer D has possessed the gun, explosives, etc., the more difficult it will be to associate the acquisition of the item with a particular identifiable threat.

The imminence requirement may work harshly for D when she is subjected to episodes of violence by V, a more powerful person than D; D's only defensive option may be to take advantage of some moment of calm where D is unawares and vulnerable. The difficult is that providing a full defence, particularly for fatal violence inflicted pre-emptively, would be very difficult to confine to deserving circumstances. For instance, one would not want to legitimate anticipatory gangland killings, however real the "kill or be killed" dilemma that prompted them.[189] Some accommodation to what may be called the dilemma of powerlessness is now provided for by section 54 of the Coroners and Justice Act 2009. In the context of a charge of murder, if D has killed in response to a fear of serious violence (which need not be a fear of imminent violence) from V or another, she will be convicted of manslaughter rather than murder provided her fear of serious violence induced a lack of self-control at the time of the killing.[190]

(vi) Force and non-criminal threats

If D defends himself against conduct of V's which is not criminal, section 3 of the Criminal Law Act 1967 will not be in play since any defensive force by D will not prevent a crime on the part of V. Nonetheless, as we noted earlier,[191] it is probable that the legitimacy of his defensive response will be assessed according to the same standard of reasonableness.

It is generally accepted that D may defend himself against unjustified force even if she knows that the force in question does not constitute a criminal act. Suppose that D, a nurse in a mental health hospital, is attacked by V, a patient she knows to be insane. It is submitted that she can take all reasonable steps to defend herself including, should it be necessary, the use of fatal force. Were this incident assessed from the perspective of the right to life, it

---

[188] *Smith and Hogan* 396.

[189] A useful comparison may be drawn with Lord Bingham's restatement of the law of duress in *Hasan* [2005] UKHL 22, [2005] 2 AC 467, where he was very concerned to exclude from the defence threats made by D's criminal associates.

[190] Sections 54, 55(1)–(4).

[191] Above, § 21.2, 21.2(iii).

could be argued that V, if sufficiently deranged to be within the defence of insanity, has not forfeited any of his rights by making this attack. From a right-to-life perspective, there is no obvious reason why it should be V rather than D who dies. Yet, though D and V have rights to life of equal standing, it is V, albeit blamelessly, who has violated D's right to autonomy. D is under no obligation to surrender her life for the benefit of V's life. Her right to autonomy allows self-preference, the sustaining of her own life with its responsibilities to those close to her, provided she does not actively violate the right to autonomy of others.[192]

The logic of this analysis flows to any situation where V's conduct constitutes an encroachment of D's autonomy and a threat to her security of person. It is not necessary that V's conduct should take the form of an attack on D. Take a situation that arose in the course of the Zeebrugge ferry disaster.[193] D and others were seeking to climb a rope ladder in order to leave the hold of a ship that was filling with seawater. The way was barred by V who, immobilised by fear, clung to the ladder despite urgent requests to climb it. D, in order to save himself and others from drowning, tore V from the ladder. Consequently, V died from drowning; D and others climbed to safety. It may be objected that D's act was not done in self-defence or in defence of others because V was not attacking anyone. Yet V's behaviour constituted an immediate threat of death to others and encroached on their autonomy by restricting, without justification, their freedom of movement. There seems no difference of principle between this situation and being attacked by a mad person. It may be said that the ferry disaster situation is a case of duress by circumstances and, possibly, of necessity. Conceptually, such a classification is possible (though not exhaustive). The drawback of rejecting the equally plausible characterisation of D's conduct as self-defence is that duress and (generally) necessity are not available defences to a charge of murder.[194] It is important to repeat that the right to self-defence will arise only if V's conduct is a threat to D's security of person *and* an encroachment on her autonomy. To take a famous example, suppose that in open seas V is first to a wooden plank, sufficient to support her but nobody else. D will drown unless he is able to take sole occupancy of it.[195] In a sense, V's possession of the plank is an immediate threat to D's life. Yet D should not be permitted to remove her from it. By taking possession of the plank, V exercised her own autonomy without violating D's.

In *Re A (Children)*,[196] Ward LJ justified a separation operation that entailed the survival of one conjoined twin J and the certain death of the other twin M. M's own heart and lungs were inadequate to sustain M's life. While joined to J, M survived only by relying on J's heart to pump the blood oxygenated by J. It was estimated that J's heart would fail under the strain within three to six months, with the inevitable consequence that both J and M would die. If a successful separation operation were to be carried out, J's prospects for a healthy life were good.

Ward LJ equated M's life-sapping dependence on J's heart and lungs as tantamount to an attack upon J, an attack from which J was entitled to be defended. In resolving that the killing of M would be lawful self-defence, he stressed J's prospects for a normal life, by contrast with M who was "self-designated" for death. On first impression this reference to

---

[192] See further Uniacke, *Permissible Killing—The Self-defence Justification of Homicide* (1994) 158–93.
[193] Discussed in Smith, *Justification and Excuse in the Criminal Law* (1989) 73–4.
[194] See §§ 20.1(ii)(b), 21.3(ii)(e).
[195] Cicero, *De Officiis* iii, 23.
[196] [2001] Fam 147.

"self-designation" sits oddly with a right of self-defence.[197] If V launches an unlawful attack on D that, of itself, gives D an entitlement to defend himself, even if D is an old man with a terminal illness and V a young, healthy man. Yet in the context of *Re A* the drawing of a contrast between the life prospects of M, on the one hand, and J, on the other, is understandable. It was the fact that M's dependence radically cut down J's life expectancy that made their coexistence a threat to J; it would have been quite otherwise had J's outlook have been as dire as M's.

It would be unwise to hazard any generalisation concerning the scope of self-defence from facts so specific as those in *Re A (Children)*, particularly as only Ward LJ based his judgment on this ground. Moreover, there is a considerable technical difficulty in subsuming the facts of the case under self-defence, namely the imminence requirement. J, at the time of the operation, was estimated to have three to six months to live, yet it would have been grotesque to delay the intervention until she was at death's door. Nonetheless, the case gives support for the view that facts such as those discussed above arising in the course of Zeebrugge tragedy would fall within the purview of self-defence.

(vii) Harming innocent persons to prevent crimes to others

The police and the military (and sometimes private citizens) may be involved in situations where the prevention of crime can only be done by subjecting innocent persons to harm. *Hichens*[198] endorses the view that proportionate force can be used against innocent, non-threatening persons if that is the only way to prevent a crime by P. The examples given in that case are untroubling: no-one can object to D, a policeman, "bundling" V out of his path in order to engage with P, who is carrying a live explosive. More troubling examples, however, abound. The violent and armed P clasps V to his body as a human shield and breaks cover while firing at the surrounding police. His fire is returned by the officers and V is killed by a police bullet. Very likely the police response would be found justifiable.[199]

One limitation on using crime preventative force against innocent persons would be the general acceptance that serious injury or death cannot be intentionally inflicted as a means to prevent P's crime. Suppose that P and his fellow hostage-takers threaten to kill the hostages unless V is handed over to them. D, who is supervising the police response, is aware that the threat to the hostages is very serious but is also aware that P wishes to get his hands on V in order to kill him. The better view is that V cannot lawfully be handed over to P.[200]

What, then, of the much discussed case of the passenger plane, hijacked by terrorists, flying towards the high, densely populated building? The dilemma facing D, the Ministry of Defence decision-taker, is that, although the building and the persons present inside can only be saved by the destroying the plane while in flight, ordering the destruction of the plane is to order the intentional killing of its passengers. That is why the German Supreme

---

[197] Quite apart from the difficulty of characterising M as an innocent attacker, since she was not *acting* at all: cf. Chan and Simester, "Duress, Necessity: How Many Defences?" (2005) 16 *King's College LJ* 121, 128–9.

[198] [2011] EWCA Crim 1626, [2011] 2 Cr App R 26.

[199] The shooting scenario in the text is the facts of *Pagett* (1983) 76 Cr App R 279, where the causal agent was found to be P in that he created a situation where the police were duty bound to use force to prevent his escape.

[200] Simester, "Moral Certainty and the Boundaries of Intention" (1996) 16 *OJLS* 445.

Court, addressing this situation as a scenario rather than an *ex post* reality, ruled that legislation authorising the destruction of the plane in such cases was unconstitutional.[201] For the Court, the taking of innocent life could not be condoned by legislation because it would violate the right to dignity (Article 1 of the German Constitution) and the right to life (Article 2 of the German Constitution). The UK Select Committee on Defence takes a different view and advises destruction of the plane.[202] The latter position takes a hard but in many ways attractive line. On the facts available to D, the passengers will die in any event. Better then that the people in the building should live.[203]

But what if D acted on a miscalculation with terrible consequences? Let us say that the plane destroyed on the orders of D had strayed from its flight path and was flying low over London, doing so to avoid severe turbulence. Because of a fault in air-to-ground communications, no messages were exchanged between the pilot and air traffic control. D assumed a terrorist hijack and the imminent destruction of a high-rise building. When discussing mistakes concerning circumstances giving rise to defences, we saw that, as things stand, an unreasonable mistake as to the need to use force in the prevention of crime could yet be an excusing mistake even in the case of public officials.[204] There is much to be said for a reasonableness standard where the intentional taking of innocent lives is involved.

(viii) The defence of others

Clearly, under section 3 of the Criminal Law Act 1967, if D intervenes to defend E from the commission of a crime against E, intervention will be justified provided reasonable force is used. There is every reason to adopt the same rule for circumstances where D intervenes to prevent V from inflicting non-criminal but unjustified force on E (D, a nurse, intervenes to prevent V, a patient afflicted with insanity, from attacking another patient). A right to intervene on behalf of others is recognised at common law[205] and still applies to situations where intervention is warranted to protect another from unjustified force. As the Criminal Justice and Immigration Act 2008 confirms, "references to self-defence include acting in defence of another person".[206]

---

[201] Judgment of the German Federal Constitutional Court of 15 February 2006, 1 BvR 357/05; invalidating § 114 III of the Air-Transport Security Act (2005). For discussion of this case see Bohlander, "*In extremis?* Hijacked Airplanes, 'Collateral Damage' and the Limits of the Criminal Law" [2006] *Crim LR* 579.

[202] House of Commons Defence Committee, *Defence and Security in the UK: Sixth Report of Session 2001–02* (Volume I: Report and Proceedings of the Committee) HC 518-I (2002) paras. 8–9. The general legal justification here is necessity. More straightforwardly, justification can be found within the statutory authority under s. 3 of the Criminal Law Act 1967 to use reasonable force in the prevention of crime. Clearly the destruction of the building will be a crime, and it is well established that fatal force can be used to prevent crime if proportionate to the occasion whereas doubts remain whether innocent life can be taken under the rubric of necessity.

[203] For further discussion, see Hörnle, "Hijacked Planes: May they Be Shot Down?" (2007) 10 *New Criminal Law Review* 582; Sullivan, "The Hard Treatment of Innocent Persons in State Responses to the Threat of Large Scale and Imminent Terrorist Violence: Examining the Legal Restraints" in Sullivan and Dennis (eds.), *Seeking Security: Pre-empting the Commission of Criminal Harms* (2012) 293, 305–309.

[204] § 18.1(iii).

[205] Smith and Hogan, *Criminal Law* (1965) 235.

[206] Section 76(10)(b).

(ix) Fatal force and Article 2 of the ECHR

Article 2 of the ECHR provides that everyone's right to life shall be protected by law. Deprivation of life will not contravene Article 2 if, *inter alia*, it results from the use of force which is no more than *absolutely necessary*:

(a)   in defence of any person from unlawful violence; or

(b)   in order to effect a lawful arrest or to prevent the escape of a person lawfully detained.

Should the action of a State official, such as a police officer or soldier, contravene Convention standards, that conduct will directly implicate the United Kingdom. Through its official, the State itself has breached the Convention. Accordingly, post-incorporation, when concerned with acts by state officials the English courts should construe the broad terms of section 3 of the Criminal Law Act 1967 to conform with Article 2.[207] Although the Convention standard of "absolute necessity" contrasts with the reasonableness standard prescribed by section 3, the Convention jurisprudence does not take the phrase literally—a *reasonable* belief in the need for force will comply with Article 2.[208] As we have seen, an unreasonable belief in the need for force will ground a defence of mistake in English law.[209] Under the Convention, however, it has been suggested that for law enforcement officials a reasonable belief may now be required.[210] Certainly, a state law enforcement official who causes death while acting unreasonably may well incur a liability on the part of the UK to pay compensation under the provisions of the European Convention for the Protection of Human Rights. Yet it does not follow from that that the UK is obliged to amend its law of homicide to create a special offence of negligent homicide for its officials.[211] The question would be whether a State obligation to pay compensation if its officials negligently cause deaths,[212] coupled with liability for manslaughter for state agents of officials who have caused death while acting with gross negligence, suffices for compliance with Article 2 of the ECHR.[213] In our view, it does.

Where a private individual uses force against another individual, the State is not directly implicated in any wrong that may have arisen. The State may be in breach of Article 2,

---

[207]   This includes taking into account any settled jurisprudence of the ECHR relating to Art. 2: Human Rights Act 1998, s. 2.

[208]   *McCann and others* v. *UK* (1996) 21 EHRR 97; *Andronicou* v. *Cyprus* (1998) 25 EHRR 491. In *Juozaitene, Bikulius v Lithunia* (2008) 47 EHRR 55, it was strongly emphasised that state officials must act reasonably when resorting to fatal force. For a full and learned account of the Convention jurisprudence on force used in crime prevention and self-defence, and its compatibility with the law of England and Wales, see the judgment of Levenson LJ in *Denby Collins* [2016] EWHC 33 (Admin) paras. 35–71.

[209]   Above, § 18.1(iii).

[210]   See, e.g., Leverick, *Killing in Self Defence* (2006).

[211]   After all, when a policeman, like anyone else, is tried for a crime, that person is tried in their capacity of individual citizen, not *qua* state official. The conviction is personal, not official. There are, to be sure, some crimes that can only be committed by a state official such as misconduct in public office. In such cases the role is partly constitutive of the wrong. This does not apply in cases of self-defence. That is less obviously the case when the official is using force in the prevention of crime; but even in those cases, the official will be empowered under the terms of s. 3 of the Criminal Law Act 1967, which confers on *everyone* a power to use reasonable force in the prevention of crime.

[212]   Confirmed in *Ashley* v. *Chief Constable of Sussex* [2008] UKHL 25, [2008] 1 AC 962 (unreasonable mistake by police no answer in tort).

[213]   Cf. Rogers, "Applying the Doctrine of Positive Obligations in the European Convention on Human Rights to Domestic Substantive Criminal Law in Domestic Proceedings" [2003] *Crim LR* 690.

however, if the current law provides inadequate protection for the lives of its citizens.[214] The question then arises whether allowing private individuals a defence of unreasonable mistake, in cases involving death, insufficiently protects the right to life of persons overall. Here an issue of balance arises: the protection of the public may need to be reconciled with the degree of culpability required for just punishment. Empirical questions surface too: how much more dangerous is a society that allows a defence of unreasonable mistake in homicide contexts? One would need also to note that not all unreasonable mistakes excuse. A grossly negligent mistake will allow a conviction for manslaughter. A belief that force was proportionate will not avail if the force is found to be excessive.[215] On balance, it is submitted that allowing some latitude to unreasonable mistakes for homicides perpetrated by private individuals does not bring the United Kingdom into breach of Article 2.[216]

Article 2 permits the use of fatal force to prevent unlawful violence. There is no reference to the defence of property and, because Article 2 is regarded as a fundamental provision to be construed strictly, use of fatal force to protect property surely contravenes the Convention. It seems very likely that any law of permitting force to prevent crime which allowed private citizens to take life in order to protect property will therefore be found wanting. Earlier in this chapter (§ 21.2(iv)), we questioned whether it would always be unreasonable to take life to defend property but, under the Convention, that appears to be the position.

§ 21.3 Necessity[217]

Suppose D is driving a modern, safe, car on an uncrowded motorway with his pregnant wife as passenger. Her contractions, and associated pain, indicate that the birth process has begun sooner than expected. Were D to refrain from driving any faster than 70mph, we would likely find his rigid compliance with the letter of the law a mistaken priority. If his refusal to go any faster were to result in tragedy it might be argued against him that his duty of care for his wife trumped any duty to comply with speed limits on that occasion. Had he acted differently and driven at a speed beyond the legal limit, but not to dangerous excess, surely his duties to wife and unborn child would prevail over his duty to drive no faster than 70mph?

---

[214] As was found in respect of the defence of "reasonable chastisement" that English law affords to parents of children: *A v. UK* [1998] Crim LR 892; below, § 21.4.

[215] *Clegg* [1995] 1 AC 482.

[216] For differing view of this question see Leverick, "Is English Self-defence Law Incompatible with Art 2 of the ECHR?" [2002] *Crim LR* 347; Smith, "The Use of Force in Public or Private Defence and Article 2" [2002] *Crim LR* 958; Leverick, "The Use of Force in Public and Private Defence and Article 2: A Reply to Professor Smith" [2002] *Crim LR* 963. Notwithstanding the view expressed here in the text, the Joint Parliamentary Committee on Human Rights, in reviewing the retention of the subjective test in what became s. 76 of the Criminal Justice and Immigration Act 2008, considered that the retention of this test might put the UK in breach of Article 2, particularly in cases involving the use of force by public law enforcement officials: *Fifteenth Report of Session 2007/2008 Legislation* HL paper No. 81; HC paper No. 440, paras. 2.26–2.28.

[217] Fletcher, *Rethinking Criminal Law* (1978) 759–97, 818–35, 855–75; Smith, *Justification and Excuse in the Criminal Law* (1989) chap. 3; Schopp, *Justification Defences and Just Convictions* (1998) chap. 6; Brudner, "A Theory of Necessity" (1987) 7 *OJLS* 338; Gardner, "Necessity's Newest Inventions" (1991) 11 *OJLS* 125; Dennis, "On Necessity as a Defence to Crime: Possibilities, Problems and the Limits of Justification and Excuse" (2009) 3 *Crim L and Phil* 29.

In the event of a prosecution for speeding, D might be better advised to concede that it was his duty to comply with the speed limit but that, in the circumstances in which he found himself, his breach of duty should be excused. In other words, he should plead duress of circumstances rather than justificatory necessity as a matter of legal tactics.[218] English case law contains some vigorous rejections of any notion that necessity may be invoked as an excuse or justification for a crime. In *Kitson*, D,[219] who was asleep on the back seat of a car, awoke to find the car was moving down the hill on which it was parked. To avert catastrophe, he assumed control of the vehicle and steered it safely to a stationary position on the side of the road. The fact that he was responding to an emergency and refrained from driving any further once the situation was resolved did not exempt him from liability for driving a car when unfit due to drink. In *Buckoke* v. *GLC*,[220] the Court of Appeal had to decide whether a driver of a fire-engine on an emergency call could elect to go past a red traffic light. The answer was a resounding no, an answer to be given even if the road was clear and a person some 50 yards from the now stationary vehicles required immediate life-saving rescue from the fire service. A final example is afforded by *Southwark LBC* v. *Williams*,[221] where the Court of Appeal rejected an argument that homeless people could take temporary refuge in vacant council premises without committing acts of trespass.

These are older cases. Yet the intransigent approach taken in them still surfaces. In *R (Nicklinson)* v. *Ministry of Justice*, an ambitious argument that voluntary euthanasia and assisted suicide could be justified as a necessary and proportionate response to the suffering of the applicants was raised before the Court of Appeal.[222] One ground for rejection given by the court was that English law knows no general defence of necessity.[223] It is notable that no attempt was made by the applicants to revive a necessity argument before the Supreme Court.[224]

As will be demonstrated below, the Court of Appeal was wrong to assert that English law does not recognise a necessity defence. But before we consider the relevant cases, we should recognise the central concerns which even now lead to claims that the defence is unknown and which will always and properly limit the defence to a modest and supplementary role. There is an understandable reluctance to allow individuals to be the judge of when to dispense with the letter of the law:[225]

> "The law regards with the deepest suspicion any remedies of self-help, and permits these remedies to be resorted to only in very special circumstances. The reason for such circumspection is clear—necessity can very easily become simply a mask for anarchy."

---

[218] In *Pipe* v. *DPP* [2012] EWHC 1821 (Admin); [2012] All ER (D) 238, D exceeded the speed limit in order to get his injured son who was suffering severe pain to hospital, after waiting in vain for an ambulance. He was convicted of speeding by magistrates. The Divisional Court ruled that he should have been allowed to put forward a defence of necessity, citing *Conway* [1989] QB 290. That case, which involved a victimless traffic offence, was decided on the basis of duress of circumstances, a defence now well established, and applies to situations where the person under threat is a third party for whom D feels responsible. See above, § 20.1(ii).

[219] (1955) 39 Cr App R 66 (CCA).

[220] [1971] 1 Ch 655 (CA).

[221] [1971] 1 Ch 734 (CA).

[222] [2014] EWCA Civ 961. See Stark, "Necessity and Nicklinson" [2013] *Crim LR* 949.

[223] [2014] EWCA Civ 961, para. 28.

[224] [2014] UKSC 38. In the Supreme Court, the applicants made no argument for the permissibility of voluntary euthanasia but made some headway with the claim that the right to private life guaranteed under Article 8 of the ECHR could permit assistance in suicide for persons in the dire circumstances of the applicants.

[225] *Southwark London Borough* v. *Williams* [1971] Ch 734, 740 (Edmund Davies LJ). Cf. Brudner, "A Theory of Necessity" (1987) 7 *OJLS* 338, 342–4.

This is a Rule of Law argument. The legal system will simply not work if its authority is optional. Derogation from its rules is not permitted save in specific, confined circumstances. It is clearly in the public interest that traffic signals be rigidly obeyed: general security would be much diminished if overriding discretions were allowed. The use of vacant council properties is best resolved by the local political decision-making processes, implemented by consistent administration rather than *ad hoc* self-help. And so on. The drawback produced by this unyielding stance is that it exposes to criminal liability persons whose conduct may have brought about significant benefit and whose motivation may have been impeccable. This is a powerful consideration and warrants the admissibility of a necessity plea. Yet it is a plea that imports considerable difficulties of definition and ambit.

(i) Recognition of a necessity defence in modern case law

In large part, the re-emergence of a defence of necessity did not arise from any considered reflection but by way of extending the defence of duress to embrace duress of circumstances. By removing the requirement of a crime nominated by the duressor, and allowing the defence to be raised where D responds to immediate threats of death or serious harm on his own initiative, cases such as *Conway*[226] and *Willer*[227] allowed the ground thereby covered by duress to encroach on territory which, if within the realm of defences at all, could only be accommodated by referencing necessity. Nonetheless, those cases adhere to the informing idea of duress, namely that the defendant's act was coerced by a fear of immediate death or serious bodily harm. Essentially, the content of the legal norm violated is not being challenged by claiming the priority of a competing value;[228] rather, the argument is that compliance with law cannot reasonably be expected from a person under such pressure. Further, the crime of murder remains outside the scope of the duress defence; so too do wrongs committed in response to any lesser threat than immediate death or serious harm.[229] By contrast, neither of those strictures apply on those rare occasions where a defence of necessity is permitted to address the ethical quality of D's intervention rather than the pressure that D was under when he acted.

Duress of circumstances was extended to a very different situation in the case of *Pommel*.[230] Recall that D took possession of a sub-machine gun from a person who had it in mind "to kill some geezer". D himself was not that "geezer" and was under no threat. Essentially, his reasoning was that it was better to take possession of the gun, despite the lack of a licence, rather than to allow it to remain in the hands of a person intending to use it to kill. D was asserting the value of saving life over the letter of the gun-control laws while at the same time furthering the ultimate goals of gun laws, namely keeping weapons out of the

---

[226] [1989] QB 290 (CA).

[227] (1986) 83 Cr App R 225 (CA).

[228] Because such claims are so troubling to the coherence of the legal order, the Supreme Court of Canada (save for Wilson J) was of the opinion in *Perka* (1984) 13 DLR (4th) 1 that necessity claims must operate in the realm of excuse. But as we shall see, necessity pleas will be raised in circumstances where D herself is unpressurised; as, for example, where D, a surgeon, decides that V's best interests as a severely learning disabled person who is sexually active will be served by a sterilisation operation. It should not be enough to excuse D for carrying out such a radical intervention without V's consent: the operation must be, all things considered, the right thing to do.

[229] See above, § 20.1(i)(d).

[230] [1995] 2 Cr App R 607 (CA); above, § 20.1(ii)(a).

wrong hands. This is a defence of necessity; as seems implicitly to have been recognised by the Court of Appeal, which used the terms necessity and duress interchangeably.[231]

A more considered recognition of a defence of necessity was given by the House of Lords in two cases involving incompetent patients. In the first, *F v. West Berkshire Health Authority*,[232] the legality of a sterilisation operation on a sexually active but learning-disabled patient was in issue. Pregnancy was judged to be something which it was in the interests of the patient to avoid at all costs; measures short of sterilisation were assessed as ineffective or impracticable. Lords Brandon and Goff premised the legality of the operation on ground of necessity. In *R v. Bournewood Community and Mental Health NHS Trust*,[233] the legality of the detention and treatment of an informally admitted mentally incompetent patient whose detention fell outside the regime provided by the Mental Health Act 1983 was held, unanimously, to be justified by necessity. Cases of considerable antiquity[234] were restored to memory to ground the ruling that a defence of necessity is known to English law.[235] What the decision (and previous decisions) lacks, however, is any considered discussion of the rationale and ambit of the defence.[236]

(ii) The rationale and ambit of necessity

Discussion of necessity inevitably contains a large measure of conjecture. The idea behind the defence is simple and beguiling: achieve the greater good rather than slavishly follow the letter of the law. There will be occasions where following this injunction will produce incontrovertible gains in welfare and an absence of countervailing harms. Yet an absence of countervailing harms is not a necessary condition for raising the defence. A balance of harms test may be allowed in some circumstances. In other situations, vested legal rights take priority, and prevent D from justifying the harm done to V on a balance of harms test.

There is no unitary rationale of the necessity defence.[237] Rather, within the general rubric of "necessity", the defence cloaks a number of intertwined justificatory reasons. What they have in common is at least a degree of urgency, which may fall short of immediate emergency. Sometimes it may be possible to seek the assistance of the courts *ex ante* to determine the legality of a proposed course of action. In medical cases, the courts have shown a commendable degree of procedural flexibility in advising on the legality of proposed surgery, surgery that would constitute a criminal (and tortious) act unless warranted by necessity. Where prior guidance of the courts is feasible, the Rule of Law concerns discussed above are less pressing. Yet there will be occasions where immediate action is called for—E will die, say, unless D drives to hospital in excess of the speed limit. Nowadays, a court may rule, *ex post facto*, that D was entitled to drive in excess of the limit. As the threatened danger

---

[231] In *Quayle* [2005] EWCA Crim 1415, paras. 41 and 42, there is recognition that *Pommel* is in different case from the other duress by circumstances authorities.

[232] [1990] 2 AC 1.

[233] [1998] 3 All ER 289 (HL).

[234] *Mouse's Case* (1608) 12 Co Rep 63.

[235] In *Hasan* [2005] 2 AC 467 and *Quayle* [2005] EWCA Crim 1415, one can find *dicta* sceptical about whether talk of a general defence of necessity is grounded in legal reality but at the same time a recognition that cases such as *Re F* and *Bournewood* cannot really be placed under the rubric of duress of circumstances.

[236] [1998] 3 All ER 673 (CA).

[237] Cf. Chan and Simester, "Duress, Necessity: How Many Defences?" (2005) 16 *King's College LJ* 121.

was death, a court minded to find D not guilty may prefer to achieve that result by way of excusatory duress rather than justificatory necessity. If D was speeding to hospital because E was in excruciating pain, the duress option would not be available,[238] and the difficulties that the necessity plea brings would have to be faced.

What must be present in every case if a defence of necessity is to succeed is an identifiable harm which can only be avoided if, in the near future, the letter of the law is breached. If the harm is more remote than that (particularly where the harm has a degree of conjecture and imprecision), D cannot take the law into her own hands and must address her concerns in some other fashion. In *Shayler*,[239] D, a civil servant employed in MI5, was concerned that the kind of covert actions supported by the service threatened rather than enhanced public security. He was held to be in breach of the Official Secrets Act 1989, consequent on sharing secret information with a newspaper. Even on the assumption that his concerns were warranted, he was not attempting to avert some imminent catastrophe by the only possible and proportionate means. There was no forthcoming event his actions were intended to avert, merely a fear that the covert operations of MI5 threatened public security generally.

Since necessity has such an uncertain scope, its frequent recognition could potentially undermine the authority of law. If defendants were permitted to break laws *whenever* there was, say, a lesser-evils justification (below), the generality of those laws would be undermined and their application would have to be reassessed on a case-by-case basis. It is for the legal system to determine when its prima facie laws may be broken. Ideally, in a democracy, the freedom of action that a perceived necessity requires should be afforded by legislative change. Yet constraints of time may preclude resort to legislation. In those circumstances, wherever possible, guidance from a court should be sought before the putatively illegal action is taken; as was done, for instance, in the conjoined twins separation case of *Re A (Children)*.[240] Where that is impossible and the only recourse is direct action by D, D may—exceptionally—be found to have been justified by necessity.

(a) A lesser-evils justification

The most obvious rationale for allowing necessity is a recognition that, on occasion, more welfare may ensue from breaking than from keeping the law. The defence looks to the consequences of particular episodes of conduct rather than to the desert of the actor. To be sure, on many occasions where a necessity defence may be invoked, the defendant is meritorious or blameless. Yet if, say, a driver of a fire-engine decides to pass a red light with complete safety on a clear road in order to effect a life-saving rescue, it misses the point to say that a conviction for a road traffic offence is not merited on retributivist grounds. The gain in welfare arising from saving a life rather than opting for pedantic compliance with regulatory law is so salient that it eclipses any issues of culpability and blame typically associated with law-breaking.

---

[238] *Quayle* [2005] EWCA Crim 1415 (pain, however severe, insufficient to raise duress). Cf. *Pipe v. DPP* [2012] EWHC 1821 (Admin); [2012] All ER (D) 238.

[239] [2001] 1 WLR 2206.

[240] [2001] Fam 147.

The fire-engine case is an easy example because the offence in question was a victimless offence; no one's rights or interests were overridden when making the rescue. Contrast the following case:

> D takes money from V to give to X so that X may have a life-saving operation only available to those who can travel abroad and pay for it. V is an elderly billionaire who lives alone in a large mansion full of cardboard boxes stuffed with money. He has no relatives, has made no will, and possesses no plans whatever for his money. Yet he resolutely refuses to give any of it away.

To take any of V's money should surely be theft, even if D is able to take the money in circumstances causing V no distress whatever (e.g. D takes one box from hundreds and V remains wholly unaware that it has gone). Where breaching the law involves harming an innocent person, there is a strong presumption against any claim that the wrong can be made right by reference to necessity. A balance of evils analysis cannot ordinarily abrogate the legally protected interests of persons who do not waive their rights. Outside specific situations, there is no principle of appropriation licensing the violation of another's rights merely on grounds of necessity.[241] In all probability, this limitation is unyielding in cases where the right violated relates to V's person,[242] but it may be, as discussed below, that a balance of harms test may still be applicable in a case where a proprietary right of V's is infringed in circumstances where adequate compensation can normally be given.

(b) Intervention in V's own interests where V is incompetent

This rights-based limitation on what would otherwise be an essentially utilitarian balancing exercise is always in point where the right-holder is competent to enforce or waive her rights. Matters are different where the right-holder is incompetent. In *West Berkshire*,[243] a compulsory sterilisation operation was lawfully carried out. In *Bournewood*,[244] a learning-disabled person was detained for compulsory treatment even though his adoptive family were anxious to bring him home. The rights overridden were of the most fundamental nature. Was it to the point that the persons whose rights were overridden were deemed incompetent to know their best interests and the procedures were carried out for the presumed benefit of these subjects? Probably; particularly in light of the Court of Appeal's decision in *St George's Healthcare NHS Trust v. S*,[245] which vindicated the right of a pregnant woman to refuse a caesarean operation, notwithstanding that the operation was required to preserve the life of the mother and of the unborn child. The judgement of the best interests of incompetent persons is a sensitive and troubling matter, something recognised particularly by Lord Steyn in *Bournewood*.[246]

---

[241] For instance, the Criminal Damage Act 1971 allows V's property to be destroyed or damaged if that is the only way of avoiding imminent and greater damage to D's property; but there are no general legal provisions permitting the use of other persons' property in circumstances of emergency.

[242] On the inability of certain "lesser-evil" considerations to override the rights of victims see Simester, "Necessity, Torture and the Rule of Law" in Ramraj (ed.), *Emergencies and the Limits of Legality* (2008) 289, §§ II, IV.

[243] [1990] 2 AC 1.

[244] [1998] 3 All ER 289.

[245] [1998] 3 All ER 673 (CA).

[246] [1998] 3 All ER 289, 307–9. In *HL v. UK* (2004) EHRR 761, the European Court of Human Rights held that detaining persons in hospitals under the common law of necessity contravened the right to liberty and security of the person guaranteed by Art. 5(1) of the Convention. The Mental Capacity Act 2005 (as amended by s. 50 of the Mental Health 2007) now makes it unlawful to deprive persons of liberty in hospitals or care homes for safety

(c) Violating rights of an autonomous innocent victim

The most important constraint on the necessity plea is that it cannot be invoked in circumstances where D overrides a legal right of a non-consenting person whose conduct constitutes no threat to the person or property of others. That is why D cannot take any money from V, the misanthropic billionaire, in the example discussed in § 21.2(a). It is why a person in a rare blood group cannot be forced to donate blood, however urgent the need for blood from this group. This fundamental limitation is not expressly stated in any English case. Yet its existence can be assumed with some assurance, particularly in the light to the decision in *St George's Healthcare NHS Trust* v *S*,[247] which, as we noted above, unequivocally upholds the right of a competent person to refuse any form of medical or surgical intervention however, pressing the need for assistance. Furthermore, the case decides that a life-saving procedure cannot be forced upon an unwilling person even if, at one and the same time, another significant interest—here the safe delivery of a late-term foetus—would be secured. If a person's legal rights cannot be overridden in order to treat her own medical needs, they cannot be violated in order to further the treatment of someone else.

(d) Violating property rights

This important limitation is subject to some *de minimis* exceptions. On occasion, the infringement of a right may be transitory and inflict no lasting setback to the interests of the right holder by comparison with the value being protected, e.g. where the infringement is required to preserve life. As Devlin J remarked in *Esso Petroleum Co Ltd* v. *Southport Corporation*, a tort case:[248]

> "The safety of human lives belongs to a different scale of values from the safety of property. The two are beyond comparison and the necessity for saving life has at all times been considered a proper ground for inflicting such damage as may be necessary upon another's property."

For example: it may be necessary to trespass across land to effect the rescue of X. Or it may be necessary to break into the absent V's house in order to telephone an ambulance required to take D to hospital for vital emergency treatment. In each of these cases, provided the situation is an emergency, such minor infringements of rights are compatible with allowing a necessity plea. Sufficient regard of V's interests will be offered if he is entitled to full compensation for any loss sustained.[249] Where the same conduct is both a tort and a crime, the courts have allowed compensation for the tort despite acquitting of the crime, as when a civil assault is committed because a reasonable belief in the need to use force was lacking but where D's genuine belief that the force was required to prevent a crime excused D from criminal liability.[250] Similarly, it would be possible to allow necessity in criminal proceedings for damaging or using property, but deny that defence when V demands compensation

---

or for treatment, unless an authorisation order is in place or under an order of the Court of Protection. For a review of the operational conditions for the making of these orders and their compliance with the Convention, see *P* [2014] UKSC 19.

[247] [1998] 3 All ER 673.
[248] [1956] AC 218, 228 (first instance judgment).
[249] Cf. the famous tort case of *Vincent* v. *Lake Erie Transportation Co.* 124 NW 221 (1910).
[250] *Ashley* v. *Chief Constable of Sussex Police* [2008] UKHL 25, [2008] AC 962.

for any financial loss. In such circumstances necessity would operate as a form of excuse as D's conduct is not fully justified in all legal dimensions.

What if V refuses or resists the use of his property by D? It seems that D may, say, pick up V's mobile phone from the table to alert emergency services even should V have declined D's request to use the phone. It may well be that D is entitled to use a reasonable degree of force should V attempt to take back the phone until the emergency call is made. But could D use a degree of force on V to access the phone in the first place? When, if ever, can V's right to personal integrity be violated in order to secure a greater good?

(e) Violating rights of personal integrity

Given the paramount importance of personal autonomy in a liberal democracy, it is difficult to imagine circumstances where the *de minimis* exception would ever permit the violation of an innocent (and competent) victim's *person*, in however minor a form. The view that the personal integrity of competent persons may never be violated is supported by the strong body of judicial opinion, most recently expressed by Lord McKay in *Howe*[251] (a duress case), that the famous case of *Dudley and Stephens*[252] precludes the raising of necessity as a defence to murder. In *Dudley*, D and others, survivors of a shipwreck, were adrift in an open boat in the South Atlantic. They killed and consumed without his consent the youngest and weakest member of their party. But for this act, D and his companions would probably have died prior to rescue.[253] The case clearly decides that there is no defence to murder in such circumstances. Why the defence was unavailable does not emerge clearly from the judgment. In so far as D was arguing that the threat of imminent death excused his act, the denial of a defence can be understood; he was raising what we now would call a defence of duress of circumstances and, for better or worse, it is well established that a defence of duress is not available for murder.[254] Alternatively, we can read D's defence as a claim that he did the right thing: had this drastic step not been taken, all would have died including the victim of the killing. An emphasis on the value of the act raises the defence of necessity, giving weight to an interpretation of *Dudley* to the effect that necessity is not available as a defence to murder. Either way, it appears that current law refuses

---

[251] [1987] AC 417.

[252] (1884) 14 QBD 273 (CCR).

[253] A fascinating historical and socio-legal account of the case is given by Simpson, *Cannibalism and the Common Law* (1984). The jury, by special verdict, found that D and others would probably have died had they not killed and consumed V. The killing took place on the eighth day adrift and rescue came on the twentieth day. Legally speaking, therefore, D's act was necessary for survival, particularly in the light of the prosecution's burden of proof. Despite this, Coleridge LCJ queried the necessity of the act as an act of survival by noting that D might have been picked up next day or not picked up at all and, in either case, the killing would have been profitless. But D must be tried on the facts as they occurred and not on the basis of what might have been. To judge necessity on the basis of speculating on the range of possible worlds from a given baseline would be, effectively, to eliminate the defence.

[254] *Howe* [1987] AC 417. Joshua Dressler has argued that the failure in *Dudley* to focus exclusively on whether the defendants' conduct could be excused rather than justified has "misshaped the law of necessity and excuse" not merely in England but across the common law world: "Reflections on *Dudley and Stephens* and Killing the Innocent: Taking a Wrong Conceptual Path" in Baker and Horder (eds.), *The Sanctity of Life and the Criminal Law: The Legacy of Glanville Williams* (2013) 126, 129. A common reading of *Dudley* is that the killing of an innocent, non-threatening person can neither be justified nor excused: the judgment of Lord Coleridge uses the terms "justification" and "excuse" as synonyms for raising a defence.

to countenance a defence to murder unless the circumstances can be brought within the rubrics of self-defence or the prevention of crime (above, § 21.2).

There *may* be one exception to this rule: where V is the source of the danger faced by D. It is important to notice that *Dudley* was not concerned with that possibility. Coleridge LCJ referred to the victim as "a weak and unoffending boy". He was an autonomous individual and constituted no threat to anyone else. Because of this, he had a right to be left alone. It does not follow from *Dudley* that D may never cause personal injury to V. Consider the following case:

> D and others have survived a shipwreck. They are in a lifeboat on the open seas, which is filled to capacity. V, who is in the water, is holding on to the side of the boat. D realises that the weight of all the passengers, combined with V's actions, is causing the lifeboat to ship water. If V is allowed to continue holding on, the boat will ultimately sink entailing the death of everyone.

On these facts, D is presumably entitled to fend V off, even if that means V will drown more quickly. The case is similar to that which occurred during the Zeebrugge ferry disaster, described above in § 21.2(vi). Arguably, such situations should be accommodated within the defence of self-defence, which permits violence to the person extending even to murder. But if not self-defence,[255] then a defence of necessity should in principle be available. The prospects for the availability of such a defence are enhanced to a degree by the judgment of Brooke LJ in *Re A (Children)*.[256] As already discussed, the Court of Appeal permitted a separation operation to be carried out to allow a normal span of life for J even though the surgery inevitably entailed the death of her conjoined twin M. Alone of the three appellate judges, Brooke LJ squarely based his decision on the grounds of necessity (although it should be noted that Ward LJ expressed his agreement with Brooke LJ's decision). Brooke LJ found the operation to be justified on a straightforward application of the following three criteria, endorsed originally by Stephen:

(i)   the act is needed to avoid inevitable and irreparable evil;
(ii) no more should be done than is reasonably necessary for the purpose to be achieved; and
(iii) the evil inflicted must not be disproportionate to the evil avoided.

Taken at face value, these criteria are over-inclusive. They would allow extreme invasions of the personal integrity of autonomous, non-threatening persons whenever, on a consequentialist weighing of advantage, welfare overall would be increased. The facts of *Re A* should be stressed. Innocent though she indubitably was, M's demands on J's bodily resources were characterised as a direct threat to the life of J, a threat that would terminate an otherwise viable life within three to six months. From that perspective, the affinity with the emergency that arose in the context of the Zeebrugge ferry is reasonably close, M being the source of the threat. One factor informing these situations is that V's position is not significantly worsened by D's intervention. Either way, V will die. Even in *Re A*, the operation aside,

---

[255] If self-defence is confined to repulsing attacks, then fending off V may not fall with its purview.

[256] [2001] Fam 147. For discussion see Uniacke, "Was Mary's Death Murder?" (2001) 9 *Medical LR* 9; Huxtable, "Separation of the Conjoined Twins: Where Next for English Law?" [2002] *Crim LR* 549; Michalowski, "Sanctity of Life: Are Some Lives More Sacred Than Others?" [2002] *LS* 377; Chan and Simester, "Duress, Necessity: How Many Defences?" (2005) 16 *King's College LJ* 121.

M was "self-designated for a very early death". This consideration may well be crucial if personal injury is ever to be permitted under the guise of necessity. Suppose the following example:

> D, V, and others are speleologists. They are exploring a series of caves underground. Unfortunately, and through no one's fault, V becomes trapped in the mouth of one of the caves. The waters in the cave are rapidly rising, and the cave will soon be flooded. The trapped man is immovable. He is preventing the escape and survival not only of himself but also of his fellow speleologists. The only way of unblocking the exit is by cutting off his arm. Even though V objects, D does so and everyone survives.

Necessity would surely be available here as a defence to a charge of inflicting grievous bodily harm. Unlike the shipwreck example, this is not a case in which D is protecting his life against a threat posed by V's actions, so this is unlikely to be a case of self-defence. Rather, the speleologists face a common danger. It matters here not only (i) that like cases of self-defence, D's response is addressed to the source of the peril (and not to a third party), but also (ii) that V's interests are served as well as D's—D has not simply preferred his own interests to those of V. The latter condition is not a requirement of the defence of self-defence.

Condition (i) is also significant. Suppose that T, a terrorist, threatens to shoot D unless D, in turn, participates in a mission to murder V. If D does so, the case is neither self-defence nor necessity. It can only be argued as one of duress (and, as we saw, in § 20.1(i)(d), it would fail under the current law of duress). It would have been otherwise if D had responded by shooting T. Justification requires addressing the source of the danger, not deflecting it upon someone else.

Considerable caution is in order when assessing whether these conditions apply to circumstances going beyond the precise facts of the very few cases to hand. In the speleologist scenario discussed above, nobody died. What if the only way of allowing the escape of D and the others would inevitably have caused the death of V? A starting point would be the decision in Re A, where the innocent yet life-threatening M was killed as part of an operation intended to allow J a longer and better life. As we know, for Ward LJ it was a case of self-defence and for Brooke LJ a case of necessity. Although referencing these general defences, both judges were careful to say that nothing decided in the case had application beyond the particular circumstances of the case.[257] In Nicklinson, the Divisional Court[258] and the Court of Appeal[259] dismissed emphatically the notion that Re A had any bearing on the question of the permissibility of voluntary euthanasia. In terms of principle, one obvious point of difference between the facts of Nicklinson and Re A is that, in Re A, those responsible for the medical care of J and M owed competing duties of care to J and M and, in that sense, were in an unavoidable dilemma which only some authority set above them could resolve.[260]

---

[257] [2001] Fam 147, 204–5 (Ward LJ), 239 (Brooke LJ).

[258] R (on the application of Nicklinson) v. Ministry of Justice [2012] EWHC 2381 (Admin).

[259] [2013] EWCA Civ 961.

[260] No distinction was made between J and M in terms of their status as interest-bearing persons. On that basis, the unfortunate M had interests distinct from J's, interests not easy to specify and protect but which, none the less, were to some extent in tension with J's. As Stark argues, the Court in Nicklinson was therefore correct to rule that the necessity-based arguments in Re A had no relevance to the issues of euthanasia and suicide arising in that case: "Necessity and Nicklinson" [2013] Crim LR 949.

Could we say the same about D and his fellow, trapped speleologists? Although D's situation may not be as stringent in terms of the *duties* he owes to those immediately affected by his conduct, he too faces a scenario of vital competing interests. He too faces the dilemma of failing other(s) if he refuses to sacrifice the one. Thus the reasoning behind *Re A* is in point here.[261] However, the possibility that the case would be rigidly confined to its medical context cannot be discounted.

(iii) Necessity and legislative priority

Necessity is a common law principle. Accordingly, it should yield wherever statutory provision has been made for the emergency, crisis, or interest invoked to justify D's act. If, for example, as a consequence of the decision in *West Berkshire Health Authority*,[262] Parliament had enacted that sterilisation operations could not be carried out without the consent of the patient, necessity could never again be invoked in the circumstances of the *Berkshire* case. In *Bournewood*, the Court of Appeal took the view that the Mental Health Act 1983 provided a comprehensive regime for the detention and treatment of mentally incompetent patients.[263] V fell outside this scheme and, appropriately, on its view of the Act, the Court of Appeal ruled that necessity could not be invoked to allow V's continuing detention. By contrast, the House of Lords held (convincingly, in the light of the legislative history) that the scheme of the 1983 Act was not comprehensive and had designedly made no provision for patients such as V who were compliant and did not object to detention but who essentially lacked any means of volition to accept or reject detention and treatment. Accordingly, the immediate best interests of that class of patient could be addressed under the head of common law necessity.

Contrast the decision of the Court of Appeal in *Quayle*:[264] one aspect of the case concerned persons who had involved themselves in providing cannabis and various cannabis derivatives for other persons who, it appeared, could only find palliative relief for very painful symptoms by using these substances. Both possession and supply of these substances contravened provisions of the Misuse of Drugs Act 1971. That Act, as well as proscribing in general terms the possession, supply, etc., of controlled drugs, sets up an elaborate scheme for their lawful possession. The Court of Appeal took this scheme to be comprehensive and complete. It did not make general provision for doctors, let alone non-medically qualified persons, to supply cannabis for pain relief. Express provision was made for the medical use of opiates but no express provision was made for cannabis. Consequently, there was no space for a judicial ruling allowing the palliative use of cannabis on the ground of common law necessity. The area of concern was regulated by a statutory scheme.

Of course, D may well object that the statutory scheme found to be incompatible with raising necessity failed to meet her needs. For instance, in *CS*[265] D believed that her daughter V was in imminent danger of serious sexual abuse from her ex-partner. To protect V she took her to live in Spain, in breach of custody provisions regulating access to V by her and

---

[261] It is noteworthy that both Brooke LJ and Ward LJ approved the life-saving though life-taking action of the corporal in the Zeebrugge tragedy.

[262] [1996] 2 AC 1.

[263] [1998] 1 All ER 634.

[264] [2005] EWCA Crim 1415; [2006] 1 All ER 988.

[265] [2012] EWCA Crim 389.

her ex-partner, thereby committing the offence of child abduction. The Court of Appeal ruled that necessity could not be relied upon because her belief that her daughter was at risk of rape was unreasonable. The court went on to add that, even if the belief was well-founded, necessity would still not have been an available defence because there were statutory defences of consent or reasonable belief in consent by the other parties to the custody arrangements and also access to the family court to raise her concerns about her ex-partner. Yet, if D had a well-founded fear that her daughter might even be raped on the next visit to her father required under the custody arrangements, these defences and access to the court at some future point in time seem beside the point. Courts should not be too astute to clip the wings of necessity by finding that statutory schemes preclude its application.

As well as bowing out where the area of concern is already regulated, courts will be reluctant to intervene under the head of necessity where a claim of necessitous intervention is used to legitimate forms of direct action by way of protest or opposition to government actions or policies which involve criminal acts on the part of the protestors. In *Jones*,[266] D and others perpetrated acts of criminal damage at RAF airbases and claimed vindication on the ground that their otherwise criminal acts were reasonable force in the prevention of crime within the terms of section 3 of the Criminal Law Act 1967, the crime in question being the international law crime of aggression, committed, it was alleged, by the United Kingdom against Iraq. Entanglement in this issue was avoided by ruling that section 3 was only concerned with crimes justiciable within England and Wales. (One may wonder whether such a ruling would have been forthcoming against a person who used reasonable force in England against V, a French citizen, to prevent him from leaving England to carry out a murder in France.) An analogous upshot occurred in *Shayler*,[267] where D claimed it had been essential to breach official secrecy legislation to alert the public to the dangers they were in due to secret service incompetence. The Court of Appeal dismissed the necessity claim on the merits, as previously discussed: the House of Lords thought any discussion of necessity to be an irrelevancy.

Simon Gardner has argued that necessity claims cannot be avoided, however politically embarrassing a particular claim may be, if they raise a matter of legality and principle against Her Majesty's Government and not a mere difference of policy.[268] He turns to the ECHR as the major constraint on what the government may legitimately do and advocates the legal protection of forms of direct action which attempt to secure government compliance with the Convention. For instance, he envisages the courts protecting persons who have forcibly released prisoners whose detention is found to have been in breach of Article 5 of the ECHR. We anticipate that courts will rule, contra Gardner, that the only avenue of redress for unlawful detention is by way of legal challenge and not through the *ex post* vindication of forms of criminal conduct.

Necessity is a doctrine to be used sparingly in order to cover crises and gaps in provision which lead to an urgent need for remedial action; it is not a force for major changes to the laws of modern legal systems. This is particularly the case for the divisive issue of to what extent, if at all, voluntary euthanasia or assistance in suicide should be made available at the

---

[266] [2005] QB 259.
[267] [2001] 1 WLR 2206; above, § 21.3(ii).
[268] "Direct Action and the Defence of Necessity" [2005] *Crim LR* 371.

request of competent adults.[269] In England and Wales, arguments based on necessity that in circumstances of acute suffering medical assistance in dying should be legally permissible have failed to gain any traction.[270]

Where a social problem is structural and continuous, it is best addressed through the legislative and political process.[271] A homeless person cannot occupy an empty property as a home.[272] But anyone may take temporary shelter in such a property to avoid an immediate catastrophe.

(iv) Conclusion

Recent cases, particularly *Bournewood*,[273] have unequivocally recognised a defence of necessity. This defence must be carefully distinguished from the defence of duress of circumstances. Under the latter head, the primary focus is on the pressure that D was under, an excusatory claim premised on a threat of death or serious bodily harm. In the case of a necessity plea, attention is paid foremost to the value of D's act, the claim that by breaking the letter of the law more benefit was obtained than would have been the case with compliance. In principle, necessity should be available as a defence for all offences, including (sometimes) murder. Affording a necessity defence should not be at the expense of legal rights held by competent non-consenting persons. This principle is subject to a *de minimis* exception which will allow some infringements of rights by reason of necessity, albeit subject to full compensation to the right holder. Rarely, if ever, will this exception permit the violation of V's body. The bodies of non-competent persons may be violated on the ground of necessity but only where the necessitous intervention is for the benefit of the person violated.

It is inevitable that a defence with such a destabilising idea at its core should be ring-fenced by reference to legal rights which cannot be overridden in any circumstances or only

---

[269] "In a system governed by the rule of law, any such dispensing power requires great caution. It should not be used as a means of introducing major and controversial policy change": *R (on the application of Nicklinson)* v. *Ministry of Justice* [2012] EWHC 2381 (Admin) para. 74 (Toulson LJ).

[270] Where courts are performing their familiar task of interpreting cases and legislation, building on work already done, bold steps may be taken, even in controversial areas such as assistance in dying. As noted, in *Nicklinson*, necessity was considered to be an unsuitable basis for change; by contrast, arguments based on Art. 8 of the European Convention (right to private life) made in the Supreme Court persuaded Lady Hale and Lord Kerr that the denial of medical assistance in suicide to persons who found themselves in the circumstances of the applicants was a breach of Art. 8. Lord Neuberger, Lord Mance, and Lord Wilson accepted the force of the applicants' arguments but gave no rulings on the matter.

[271] This matter weighed heavily with the Court of Appeal in *Quayle*. The problem of pain relief was persistent and ongoing. See further, Lenckner, "The Principle of Interest Balancing as a General Basis of Justification" in Eser and Fletcher (eds.), *Justification and Excuse: Comparative Perspectives* (1987) vol. 1, 493. Arguably, the decision in *Bournewood* [1998] 3 All ER 289 is at odds with this limitation since, although the Court was faced with an emergency, the problem was systemic. It is not without interest that in two recent trial cases involving environmental protestors who committed acts of criminal damage against, respectively, GM crops and a coal-burning power station, successfully defended themselves on the basis that they were committing some damage to property to prevent greater damage to property at some future point and therefore were within the terms of s. 3 of the Criminal Damage Act 1971. It is doubtful whether the defendants should have been permitted to raise this defence: s. 3 is but a particularised version of a necessity defence and should be restricted by any restraints that apply to the general defence.

[272] *Southwark London Borough Council* v. *Williams* [1971] 1 Ch 734 (CA).

[273] [1998] 3 All ER 289 (HL).

in very exceptional cases. There is an understandable tendency for courts to resort to duress by circumstances rather than employ the idea of necessity even when the latter defence would seem more in point.[274] In practical terms, the coverage of the defence of necessity is extremely limited. The circumstances arising in *Re F* and *Bournewood* are now covered by legislation.[275] The most significant modern case is *Re A*, where what was otherwise murder was legitimated. Perhaps the most significant feature of that case was what might be termed the doctors' dilemma. They owed duties to each of J and M, duties that were to some extent incompatible, in as much as fulfilling J's best interests entailed the death of M. The law must come to the aid of persons who find themselves in circumstances where, whatever path is chosen, criminal liability beckons. Persons striving to do the right thing in stressful circumstances where the law may pull in different directions should be protected from such liability unless their choices are egregious.[276] Indeed, it has been suggested that justificatory necessity is confined to these conflict of duty situations.[277] That would be unfortunate because there may arise circumstances where necessitous interventions should be permitted for persons with a liberty to intervene rather than a duty. Either way, however, successful recourse to the defence of necessity will be a rare event.

§ 21.4 Chastisement[278]

At common law, disciplinary chastisement of an apprentice, servant, or child was permitted provided it was done by a person with the authority to do so and was of a "moderate, reasonable nature".[279] Nowadays, it may be asserted confidently that the age of legal corporal punishment for apprentices and junior employees has long gone. The social and legal substrata permitting force against persons in these categories have completely disappeared, and with them any colour of justification for disciplinary force.

Parents and persons *in loco parentis* are still allowed a common law power of reasonable and moderate chastisement.[280] A stepfather who frequently and severely beat his stepson with a garden cane was acquitted of battery by a jury on the ground of reasonable chastisement. An application on behalf of the boy was made to Strasbourg where the ECHR ruled

---

[274] In *Pommell* [1995] 2 Cr App R 607, D claimed to have taken possession of a gun to prevent P from shooting V. As D was not under threat at all and the threat to V was not immediate, the case would seem to be one of necessity rather than duress: the Court of Appeal referred to necessity and duress of circumstances interchangeably.

[275] See above, § 21.3(ii)(b). The Mental Capacity Act 2005 lays down procedures and guidance for deciding when incompetent persons over the age of 16 may be treated and/or detained in their best interests. Because persons detained under the Mental Health Act 1983 are not within the terms of the 2005 Act, a lacuna arises when a person detained under the 1983 Act requires medical treatment for reasons not relating to his or her mental health condition. In such circumstances the High Court can invoke its inherent jurisdiction to decide what course of action is in the best interests of the person within its protection: as in *Great Western Hospitals NHS Foundation Trust* v. *AA and others* [2014] EWHC 132 (Family).

[276] D should be judged on what risk assessment could be made in the circumstances, particularly where an immediate decision is necessary.

[277] "Justification must be premised on the need to fulfil a duty conflicting with the one which the accused is charged with having breached": *Perka* [1984] 2 SCR 232, 274 (Wilson J).

[278] Rogers, "A Criminal Lawyer's Response to Chastisement in the European Court of Human Rights" [2002] *Crim LR* 98.

[279] Kenny, *Outlines of Criminal Law* (1st ed., 1902) 108–9.

[280] *Hopley* (1860) 2 F & F 202, 175 ER 1024; *Clearly* v. *Booth* [1893] 1 QB 465.

that the common law provided insufficient protection for children, since it had exculpated (in that case) a degree of chastisement that constituted "inhuman and degrading treatment" within the terms of Article 3 of the Convention.[281] Under the Human Rights Act 1998, English courts are obliged to limit permissible chastisement to force not proscribed by Article 3. What degree of force falls outside Article 3 is unclear. Using a cane to sharp effect is clearly outlawed. Physical punishment *per se* is not banished.[282] But what physical punishment remains allowable under the Convention is a matter of conjecture. Neither does the Children Act 2004 proscribe physical chastisement, provided it is not cruel and does not cause actual bodily harm or worse to a child.[283] Parents cannot rely on any religious belief or practice to chastise beyond these limits.[284] The same must surely apply to reliance on any cultural norms or practices.

Schoolteachers are the largest class of persons who are regularly *in loco parentis* to children. Under pressure of earlier ECHR rulings, there has been legislation relating to the use of corporal punishment by teachers,[285] which has effectively revoked the right of teachers to use corporal punishment as a form of discipline. At one time it looked as if there might be a general revocation in the United Kingdom of the right to chastise, but the Government resiled from this step in the light of public consultations reporting that a majority of adults favoured a right to chastise children.[286] It seems that there is no cogent evidence that chastisement produces good parents or good children.[287] Fourteen European countries have abolished parental rights to chastise children, but it seems practice is set to continue here for the indefinite future.

§ 21.5 Defence of property

There is a long-standing common law right to protect property by reasonable force.[288] Very frequently this defence will add no further element to issues arising from force used in the prevention of crime or in self-defence. So, if V should break into D's home with intent to steal, D can use reasonable force to prevent V from appropriating his property, and the same applies to repelling any attack upon him that V might make. If V is merely a trespasser

---

[281] *A v. UK* [1998] Crim LR 892. The breach of Art. 3 by the United Kingdom was on the basis of allowing too broad a defence of chastisement which might allow the inhuman and degrading treatment of children. Exception was taken to the fact that it was for the prosecution to prove that the chastisement was not reasonable and moderate.

[282] *H* [2002] 1 Cr App R 59; Rogers, "A Criminal Lawyer's Response to Chastisement in the European Court of Human Rights" [2002] *Crim LR* 98.

[283] See s. 58, which provides that "reasonable punishment" cannot be a defence to any charge under ss. 18, 20, or 47 of the Offences against the Person Act 1861 or to a charge of child cruelty under s. 1 of the Children and Young Persons 1933.

[284] *R (Williamson) v. Secretary of State for Education* [2005] UKHL 15, [2005] 2 AC 246.

[285] Children and Young Persons Act 1933, s. 1; Education Act 1996, ss. 548, 549.

[286] See the discussion by Rogers, "A Criminal Lawyer's Response to Chastisement in the European Court of Human Rights" [2002] *Crim LR* 98.

[287] For a full legal and policy discussion see Keating "Protecting or Punishing Children: Physical Punishment, Human Rights and English Law Reform" (2006) 26 *LS* 394.

[288] *Green v. Goddard* (1704) 2 Salk 641.

and not a criminal,[289] D is still entitled to use force to eject him. However, D must start with peaceable means.[290] If V's trespass was non-forceful, D must, for instance, first tell V to leave and allow him time to do so before resorting to force to eject V.[291] A similar right to use force extends to moveable property as well as buildings and land: if V has taken D's moveable property by non-forceful means, D must give V the chance to hand back the property before using force to reclaim it.[292]

In *Hussey*,[293] the Court of Criminal Appeal gave forceful expression to D's right to defend his home. It was said that D could lawfully kill V if that was the only way that D could prevent V from unlawfully ejecting him from his home. It must be rare indeed for D to face the immediate and unlawful loss of his home to V without the threat of bodily harm, abduction, or false imprisonment. But where loss of possession of his home is the only thing that is threatened, it seems unlikely, *pace Hussey*, that D can resort to fatal force, even if that is the only way to keep possession. There are legal means of redress for unlawful eviction. It is doubtful, as was discussed in § 21.2(ix), whether Article 2 of the ECHR allows fatal force to protect property even where D faces the permanent loss of the property without any realistic legal redress. Where there is legal redress, the proscription of fatal force is even more rigid.

The right to use force to defend property against unlawful yet non-criminal usurpations is the subject of section 148 of the Legal Aid, Sentencing and Punishment of Offenders Act 2012 (amending section 76 of the Criminal Justice and Immigration Act 2008). This curious provision adds force used in the defence of property in addition to force used in self-defence and in the prevention of crime to the defences whose operation is to be "clarified" by the terms of section 76.[294] Retreat, prior to the use of force, to defend property is no longer a duty (if it ever was) but a factor to be taken into account.[295] It is difficult to see what, if anything, is changed by these legislative interventions. The right to defend property by force was well established and for a long time a failure to retreat has been subsumed into the question of whether resort to force was reasonable in the circumstances.

Where defence of property is the only defence available, D should be cautious about using force. Suppose that D has invited V to dinner at his home. V has outstayed his welcome and ignored several heavy hints that it is time for him to go. While reasonable force can be used to eject a trespasser, and V would become a trespasser if D finally lost patience and ordered him to leave, it must be doubtful whether he can enforce his order by force if V remains a bore rather than a threat. D would be best advised to take himself off to bed and tell V to let himself out. In *Burns*,[296] D picked up V, a sex worker, in his car and drove

---

[289] The scope of non-criminal trespass in residential property has been considerably reduced by s. 144 of the Legal Aid, Sentencing and Punishment of Offenders Act 2012, which makes squatting in residential premises, even if unoccupied, a criminal offence.

[290] Note that nothing in this requirement forecloses the possibility that an initially peaceable defence of property may be escalated, following a more violent response from V, into a situation requiring D to act in defence of her person.

[291] *Green v. Goddard* (1704) 2 Salk 641.

[292] *Bird v. Jones* (1845) 7 QB 742.

[293] (1924) 18 Cr App R 160.

[294] Sentencing and Punishment of Offenders Act 2012, s. 148(2).

[295] *Ibid.*, s. 148(3).

[296] [2010] EWCA Crim 1023.

to a secluded spot. On reaching the destination, D decided that he did not want sex with her. He paid her the amount agreed and ordered her to leave the car. Not unreasonably, V refused to leave as it was her understanding that after sex she would be driven back to where D had picked her up. D forcibly evicted her. The Court of Appeal confirmed D's conviction for assault occasioning actual bodily harm. Force was not necessary. D could restore quiet possession of his car by driving back to the pickup point.[297]

[297] Although the matter is not entirely clear from his judgment, it seems Lord Judge CJ considered that V became a trespasser in D's car upon being told to leave, but it was a trespass that could be terminated without resort to violence. A better view is that V was not a trespasser but was a passenger entitled to be taken back into town by D. On that view not even a presumptive right to use force against her would arise on the facts of the case.

22

DEFENCES AND BLAME: SOME OBSERVATIONS

In §§ 1.3 and 17, we discussed the structure of an offence. There, we noted that many questions of criminal liability can be resolved by deploying a threefold analysis along the following lines:

    (i)   Is there an actus reus?

    (ii)   Is there mens rea?

    (iii) Is there any supervening defence?

Employing this procedure will frequently be straightforward and useful. A negative answer to (i) or (ii) will preclude liability and it is appropriate to ascertain whether the definitional elements of a crime are present before turning, if necessary, to such matters as justification and excuse. If English law were more precise and consistent in its terminology, we might expect the term "defence" to be confined to issues arising under (iii), whereas matters contested within the terms of (i) or (ii) should go to questions of "definition" rather than defence. As we have seen, however, English law does not follow this pattern of usage. What are termed defences in the case law may arise under any of these headings. An ascription of an actus reus may be contested by raising a "defence" of automatism. Mens rea may be denied by claiming a "defence" of mistake. If what otherwise would be a crime is committed in response to an immediate threat of death, a defence of duress may be raised. Only this last case is a case of defence, within the terms of the threefold analysis.

It would be a mistake, however, to become preoccupied with correct usage. After all, it is perfectly natural to say that D is defending herself when she contests an issue on which her liability depends. So D may argue that to take V's new car without his permission and return it after driving 10,000 miles is not theft, because she lacked an intent to deprive V of his car permanently. Conceptually, whether she has an intent to deprive permanently is a question about the defining elements of theft but there is no vice in describing D's arguments as her defence to the charge of theft. What matters, substantively, is that the issues in dispute are clearly defined and the burden of proof is appropriately allocated. Provided these conditions are met, it is pedantry rather than rigour to insist on terminological exactitude.

Moreover, there is often an overlap between defences and elements of the offence. If D takes £10 from the absent V's wallet in an emergency (e.g. to pay for a taxi ride to hospital), she may not need to plead a defence of necessity or duress of circumstances, since she can plausibly deny that she was dishonest—which is part of the mens rea requirement for theft. Many mens rea terms, such as dishonesty, recklessness, and negligence, contain an evaluative as well as a cognitive element. It would be odd, for instance, to characterise the driver who justifiably mounts a pavement in order to avoid an out-of-control vehicle as driving "recklessly".[1]

Nonetheless, it is important to understand the nature and role of what we may term "true" or "supervening"[2] defences. These are defences which go to (iii), relating to pressures, exemptions, and permissions, rather than denials of actus reus or mens rea. When defining or interpreting the ambit of offences, legislatures and courts seek to identify particular types of wrongs. Delineation of these wrongs requires specification of the defining elements—actus reus and mens rea. To collide with someone accidentally is not to assault that person: an assault is something done intentionally or recklessly. The wrong that is murder has intentionality at its core. When identifying and individuating wrongs, we should seek as much clarity and precision as is feasible. In so far as possible, we must capture the essence of the wrong *ex ante*, in order to afford fair warning[3] and to avoid false labelling.[4] Inevitably, however, circumstances will arise when the defining elements of a particular offence are made out but where blame and punishment are unwarranted because of the presence of culpability-reducing factors present at the time of the offence. Supervening defences serve to ensure justice is done to defendants who would otherwise be convicted because their conduct fits the definition of an offence. Typically, when that definition is met, blame and punishment are merited. But not always: it is for those times when the move from liability to punishment should be blocked that we provide supervening defences.

§ 22.1 Some things defences cannot do

Broadly speaking, defences are provided to ensure that a person whose conduct does not exhibit sufficient culpability for conviction of an offence will not be convicted of that offence. A conviction, especially for a stigmatic criminal offence, is detrimental *per se*: D suffers a significant setback to her interests if she is convicted of a serious offence, even if she receives an absolute discharge. A conviction is a public act of blame and it must be warranted. Unfortunately, the defences currently allowed under English law provide inadequate protection. As things stand, persons may be convicted of offences despite the lack of sufficient—or indeed any—culpability.

This is for two sorts of reason. First, there are systemic limitations to the kind of exoneration that any criminal law system can recognise. Under the conventions of our criminal law, only a limited range of conditions may be taken into account when assessing whether, despite the presence of the definitional elements of an offence, D may nonetheless be exempted from liability. These limitations are intrinsic to a system reliant on the application of rules. They entail the conviction of certain defendants who may be morally blameless. At least at the formal level of adjudication, even the fairest systems of criminal law will convict some people who do not deserve to be blamed or punished for their conduct.

That melancholy fact provides no excuse for the second type of case. There are many situations where defences *could* be, but are not, made available to blameless persons despite

---

[1] *Harris* [1995] 1 Cr App R 170; but see *Backshall* [1999] 1 Cr App R 35.
[2] A term coined in Simester, "Mistakes in Defence" (1992) 12 *OJLS* 295.
[3] Above, § 2.3.
[4] Above, § 2.4.

the lack of any systemic need to exclude an excuse or justification of the kind that D raises. We shall discuss some of these situations below, in § 22.2. Before that, however, we begin by considering some of the systemic constraints on defences.

(i) Justifications and divergent values

Inevitably, any legal adjudication of blamelessness is constrained by the substantive values resident in the norms of the criminal law. What makes for a criminal wrong can vary enormously according to time and place. Within recent times, conduct such as adultery and consensual anal sex has been the subject of serious criminal offences in various Anglophone jurisdictions. Where such crimes remain in place, the conduct *must* be treated as wrongful in any criminal litigation. If D has an adulterous affair, then he is blameworthy within the conventions of that legal system. Any assessment of criminal culpability must accept as a *datum* the substantive morality contained in the norms of the criminal law.

This constraint is bound up with the authority of a legal system. Law works, *inter alia*, by coercing people, by imposing a standard of legally acceptable behaviour and demanding that they conform to that standard. If the norms that the law would have us observe were displaced, in each case, by those of the particular defendant, then the law would have no standard to impose.[5] Whatever one takes to be the purposes of law, their achievement requires the co-ordination of individuals' behaviour by ordering ("do not") rather than asking ("unless you want to"). Individuals cannot be legally justified in conducting themselves above or outside the compass of the law merely because they have different moral values—even if they are right. Any criminal legal system which aims to prevent wrongs must be able to determine wrongful behaviour by a standard independent of the defendant.

The claim to authority that legal norms exert has significant implications for the availability of particular defences. Consider the rule *ignorantia juris non excusat*: ignorance of the law does not excuse.[6] Suppose D is unaware of a prima facie offence that mandates behaviour she would not otherwise choose. The most difficult cases of this type arise in offences *mala prohibita*—when the defendant's action is to be avoided only because proscribed. For example, the only "wrong" about driving slightly but safely in excess of the speed limit is that one does so in breach of the law, rather than of the reasons for which that law was made. From D's perspective, even if she desires to comply with the law, no reason to modify her behaviour is generated by such offences unless D is aware of them. As such, D's ignorance is analogous to mistakes of fact and blameless when reasonable.[7] Yet the law may have

---

[5] "To permit one who knows but does not accede to the community valuation of interests to have an individual standard would at once destroy the law": Seavey, "Negligence—Subjective or Objective?" (1927) 41 *Harv LR* 1, 11. It is, of course, a further question whether the law's claim to authority is itself justified. In an unjust society, persons who receive few material advantages may have little attachment or regard for the prevailing social order, particularly if unequal outcomes track systemic divisions of race and gender. In such societies, defiance of aspects of the criminal law may be a warranted moral and political stance. Yet even then the reasons that ground morally legitimate defiance do not form any basis for exculpation *within* the terms of the criminal law itself. Intrinsically, the criminal law protects the status quo and criminal law defences must fall within that framework.

[6] Above, § 18.2.

[7] For discussion of what wrong, if any, is perpetrated when D breaches regulatory law in circumstances which do not engage with any underlying regulatory rationale see Duff, *Answering for Crime* (2007) 166–74; Schauer and Zeckhauser, "Regulation by Generalization", AEI-Brookings Joint Centre for Regulatory Studies Working Paper No

institutional reasons to disallow her defence. Sometimes, as in the driving example, D can be regarded as culpable for negligently failing to ascertain relevant law before embarking on a particular course of conduct. But the main arguments are instrumental; based, especially, upon the difficulty of proving the defendant ought to have known the law, and upon the need to provide incentives for citizens to become acquainted with law.[8] The literature on ignorance of law is vast[9] and we cannot conclude the debate here. The point is that these instrumental arguments depend on the need for the legal system to be effective even at some cost to countervailing moral constraints. Thus they point toward a rule governing mistakes of law that is, at least partly, disconnected from judgments of culpability.

In § 21.3, we noted that similar concerns about the authoritative status of law have, traditionally, hampered recognition of a defence of necessity. People are not permitted to choose for themselves whether some legal prohibition should be obeyed in particular circumstances; that, the courts have said, would be a recipe for anarchy.[10] This is a consideration that informs all justificatory defences. In general, individuals are not free to choose to break the law unless the situation is urgent, so that it cannot be resolved by recourse to the legal system. D cannot raze V's field to create a firebreak, thereby protecting the villagers against the realistic *prospect* of a forest fire, unless authorised by law. But she may do so if the fire is real and upon them.

(ii) Limiting excuses

Implicit in the claim to authority are further limitations. It is important that the practical scope of excusatory defences does not undermine the capacity of criminal law to sustain a system of order through rules.[11] Consequently, many episodes of blameless conduct which fall within the defining elements of offences must nonetheless be regarded as crimes, where they are the products of the normal and countless vicissitudes of life. Consider, for example, D, a man devastated by the recent departure of his partner. He drinks alcohol by way of solace and, being unaccustomed to alcohol, he rapidly becomes intoxicated. While in that condition, he is taunted by V and, in his disinhibited state, D lashes out at V with his fists. Even if D's life was exemplary up to that point, he must still be held liable for his assault. Were we to allow an excuse based on his current life situation, we would then be

---

05-16 (2005); Husak, "*Malum Prohibitum* and Retributivism" in Duff and Green (eds.), *Defining Crimes: Essays on the Special Part of the Criminal Law* (2005) 65.

[8] "The principle that ignorance of the law should not be a defence in criminal matters is not justified because it is fair, it is justified because it is necessary, even though it will sometimes produce an anomalous result": *Campbell* (1972) 21 CRNS 273, 280 (Kerans DCJ). Compare *People v. O'Brien* 31 Pac 45, 47 (1892). For an instrumental counter-argument, see *State v. O'Neil* (1910) 126 NW 454, 456.

[9] In the criminal context see, e.g., Ashworth, "Ignorance of the Criminal Law and Duties to Avoid It" (2011) 74 *MLR* 1; Ashworth, *Positive Obligations in Criminal Law* (2013) chap. 7; Azmat, "What Mistake of Law Just Might Be: Legal Moralism, Liberal Positivism, and the Mistake of Law Doctrine" (2015) 18 *New Criminal LR* 369. Brett, "Mistake of Law as a Criminal Defence" (1966) 5 *Melbourne ULR* 179; Hall and Seligman, "Mistake of Law and *Mens Rea*" (1940–41) 8 *U Chicago LR* 641; Keedy, "Ignorance and Mistake in the Criminal Law" (1908) 22 *Harv LR* 75; Williams, *TBCL*, 451–63; Fletcher, *Rethinking Criminal Law* (1978) 736–58; Hall, *General Principles of Criminal Law* (2nd ed., 1947) 376–92.

[10] *Southwark London Borough v. Williams* [1971] Ch 734, 740 (Edmund Davies LJ).

[11] For a thorough and nuanced discussion of the nature and limits of excusatory claims see Horder, *Excusing Crime* (2004).

committed to entertaining many other narratives of how "normal" life had dealt harshly with an accused. Yet, if we change our example to a situation where D did not know he was drinking alcohol because his soft drinks were surreptitiously laced, arguably he should have now a supervening defence. An excuse based on the fact of involuntary intoxication is exceptional, bounded, and forensically manageable. Were it to choose to do so, English law could, within certain limits, afford a defence of involuntary intoxication without undermining a system of ordering by rule.[12]

No doubt this conclusion would be attacked by critical theorists, who may regard a distinction between agents who drink while in thrall to strong emotions and agents who drink unwittingly as yet another of the arbitrary distinctions that undermine any claim of the criminal law to be based on consistent principles.[13] Norrie, for instance, has made much of the fact that we allow a defence of duress based on violence but disallow, as any excuse, the impact of poverty deprivation on conduct.[14] In some situations,[15] his critique has considerable force. Assessed in terms of culpability, there may be little difference if D shoplifts because she has been threatened with violence by her husband or shoplifts because she cannot face the disappointment of her children at Christmas. The short explanation for the variance is that we can sustain a law of theft even if we allow an excuse on the basis of violent coercion but not if we excuse on the grounds of economic deprivation. Maintenance of a law of theft in an unequal society may well entail the conviction of persons who must be held blameworthy within the terms of the criminal law but whose conduct does not merit punishment when judged by a wider frame of reference. Such judgments in favour of waiving punishment will tend to lack force outside the sphere of drastic deprivations relating to such necessities as food, shelter, and medical treatment: resentment at economic exclusion from the many other good things that money can buy is understandable but not mitigating. This intransigence can be parodied as the hard-nosed legal maintenance of economic inequality. But there is also equality of dignity and respect to which all citizens are entitled. That entitlement does not sit well with any claim that a person's disadvantaged position derogates from the responsibilities of citizenship unless one rejects on impersonal grounds the social order itself.[16]

The fact that the criminal law must employ a conception of blame that will, on occasion, include persons of good character suggests that the criminal law has little concern with the quality of a defendant's character. Its concern is with particular episodes of conduct

---

[12] See Sullivan, "Making Excuses" in Simester and Smith (eds.), *Harm and Culpability* (1996) 131, arguing that for some (but not all) crimes, a defence should be available if D would not have offended but for a state of disinhibition caused by involuntary intoxication. Contrast Moore, who would confine the defence to situations where involuntary intoxication "incapacitates to the point of insanity": "Stephen Morse on the Fundamental Psycho-Legal Error" (2016) 10 *Criminal Law and Philosophy* 45, 46.

[13] Kelman, "Interpretive Construction in the Substantive Criminal Law" (1981) 33 *Stanford LR* 591.

[14] *Crime, Reason and History* (2nd ed., 2001). See too Norrie, *Punishment, Responsibility and Justice* (2000), discussed in Sullivan, "Is Criminal Law Possible?" (2001) 22 *OJLS* 424.

[15] But not all. It is true that many criminal convictions are imposed on persons who lead lives of great social and economic deprivation. The association of such disadvantages with criminal behaviour is, statistically, irrefutable. That fact, as Norrie notes, has no bearing on whether a particular defendant from such a background is eligible for a criminal conviction. But it may also have little, if any, bearing on whether that defendant is eligible for moral blame. That D is poor does not entitle her to kill V.

[16] For a lucid account on the basic conditions and capacities for responsibility and accountability before the criminal law see Gardner, *Offences and Defences* (2007) chap. 9.

and whether a finding of blame, in the sense under discussion, can be made in respect of them.[17] The character of D is relevant to liability (as opposed to mitigation) only if it can be presented as afflicted by some form of pathology germane to a mental condition defence. D may be a firm believer in euthanasia, and, moved by compassion for V, she may bring about his death. The fact that D has led an impeccable life of selfless public service will have no bearing on her liability for murder. If, however, her concern for V has caused her to become extremely depressed, which has in turn led to her killing V, she may be able to raise a plea of diminished responsibility to a murder charge.[18]

The disassociation of background character from questions of liability is particularly poignant in cases where, for reasons beyond her control, D has undergone a radical change of character. Such was the claim of Patty Hearst, who was abducted and indoctrinated, as she claimed, by a cell of urban terrorists before participating in bank robberies and other criminal acts.[19] Yet, within the set of values that she had been induced to adopt, her acts were the product of her volition and comported with her practical reasoning. To allow Ms Hearst a defence on the basis that her criminogenic character was something unchosen by her would merely underscore the fact that, to a large extent, everyone's character is something beyond volitional control.[20] If, in our present circumstances, we are capable of practical reasoning and are physically and psychologically unconstrained, we are judged accountable for what we do. The test is always whether, as we are now and regardless of how we came to be what we are, we are capable of moral agency. If we satisfy that test, we are responsible and cannot evade *conviction*. It does not follow, however, that someone in the position of Patty Hearst should be *punished*, especially if she has been restored to her former law-abiding character by the time of her trial. These unusual circumstances ask searching questions concerning the foundational core of retributivism. As we have argued, the grounds for liability are present in this case. Does it follow that some measure of deserved punishment follows from that conclusion? In our view, punishment can be withheld in such an exceptional case without threat to the foundations and practice of criminal liability.

(iii) *Responsibility for one's character: free will and incapacity*

The case of Patty Hearst raises questions about the extent to which not only our actions, but also the motives that lie behind those actions, are free. As we saw in § 4.3, the criminal law exculpates conduct that is physically involuntary. Otherwise, however, the law assumes that all adult citizens are capable of understanding and complying with its rules, an assumption displaced only if D's transgression is attributable to a condition falling within the *M'Naghten* Rules. It does not, for instance, excuse to demonstrate that D was *psychologically* incapable of obeying the law on a particular occasion. D, a chronic alcoholic, is guilty of theft if he takes a bottle of spirits belonging to V, notwithstanding his craving for alcohol and lack of funds.[21]

---

[17] Moore, "Choice, Character and Excuse" in Paul, Miller, and Paul (eds.), *Crime, Culpability and Remedy* (1990) 29; but see also Arenella, "Character, Choice and Moral Agency" in *ibid.*, 59.

[18] Homicide Act 1957, s. 2(1)(c).

[19] See Alldridge, "Brainwashing as a Criminal Law Defence" [1984] *Crim LR* 726.

[20] Vuoso, "Background Responsibility and Excuse" (1987) 96 *Yale LJ* 1661.

[21] *Powell* v. *Texas* 392 US 514 (1968).

In light of these doctrinal strictures, it is frequently claimed that the criminal law assumes free will. In fact, it need make no commitment to free will, nor to determinism, nor to any compatibilist theory which mediates between these two positions.[22] Rather, the criminal law simply makes a categoric assumption that, save for special cases, D is responsible for her conduct. If particular conduct is in breach of the letter of the law, then, prima facie, D is taken to be at fault and a candidate for blame and sanction. It must then be resolved whether there is any reason not to make a finding of guilt. Criminal law legislation and adjudication cannot, on any long-term basis, stray too far from strong community sentiments concerning the immorality of particular forms of conduct.[23] If D stabs and injures V while in thrall to a psychotic delusion that V was an evil spirit about to kill him, there may be an acceptance that D should be confined in a place of safety but not be punished.[24] Contrast the feelings likely to be generated by the conduct of D, who has had penetrative sexual relations with young children. Even in the face of evidence that he has a form of psychological disorder which makes sexual control difficult, nonetheless there will be a strong demand for blame and punishment.[25]

The difference in likely popular reaction to these two cases is explained by what Strawson has famously called "reactive attitudes".[26] It may well be that the propensity to act upon psychotic delusions is of the same order of force as, say, the urges of a kleptomaniac to take property she covets. It is the "otherness" of a person afflicted with schizophrenia that attenuates the urge to blame and punish. But even in the case of persons with severe mental disorders such as schizophrenics, revulsion arising from any extreme conduct on D's part may supervene over any sympathy his condition might otherwise arouse, particularly where the conduct was sustained, and involved forethought and planning.[27] Indeed there is some evidence that "reactive attitudes" are hardening generally towards any anti-social conduct arising from mental pathology.[28]

---

[22] For an excellent account of the relevance of the free will/determinism debate to the form and practice of criminal liability, see Westen, "Getting the Fly out of the Bottle: The False Problem of Free Will and Determinism" (2005) 8 *Buffalo Crim LR* 101. The idea that academic criminal lawyers (unlike moral philosophers or neuroscientists) can bypass the free will/determinism debate has been challenged by Moore, "Stephen Morse on the Fundamental Psycho-Legal Error" (2016) 10 *Criminal Law and Philosophy* 45. Moore accepts that human conduct may be caused (insisting, correctly, that causation is not to be conflated with compulsion) and that D's choices may be determined by forces beyond the control of D. For him, this does not prevent soundly based judgments of culpability regarding the choices and associated conduct of D; however, the soundness of such judgments requires a philosophically convincing version of compatibilism. The position taken here is that useful doctrinal and theoretical work, internal to the criminal law, can be done from the agnostic position adopted by Westen. The resolution of the free will/determinism debate, and what that entails for the theory and practice of the criminal law, is a work in progress.

[23] Robinson and Darley, *Justice, Liability and Blame: Community Views and the Criminal Law* (1995).

[24] The facts of *Oye* [2013] EWCA Crim 1725. The jury convicted D of affray and offences against the person. Unusually, the Court of Appeal substituted a verdict of not guilty by reason of insanity.

[25] English law does make some accommodation to difficulties of self-control arising from mental disorder by way of the partial defence of diminished responsibility: as in *Byrne* [1960] QB 396. The Law Commission has proposed for discussion a defence of not guilty by reason of a recognised medical condition (to replace the defence of insanity) which includes a defence for persons whose condition causes a complete lack of self-control. This will most obviously cover persons in a state of automatism, though its terms do not include persons with anti-social personality disorders: Law Commission, *Criminal Liability: Insanity and Automatism: A Discussion Paper* (2013) para. 4.84. See further above, § 19.1(iv).

[26] "Freedom and Resentment" in *Freedom and Resentment* (1974) 1. See too Horder, "Criminal Law: Between Determinism, Liberalism, and Criminal Justice" (1996) 49 *Current Legal Problems* 159.

[27] As in *Sutcliffe*, The Times, 30 April, 1981.

[28] Sainsbury Centre for Mental Health, *Report on ASBOS and Mental Health* (2011); *Colohan* [2001] Crim LR 845.

Clearly, if a particular pathological condition does not impair a person's cognitive and reasoning capacities that person remains firmly within the community of blame. Consequently, even if a strong version of determinism were to be accepted as the best working hypothesis to explain and predict all forms of human behaviour, the institutions of state punishment are unlikely to wither away and be replaced by forms of preventive detention. Atrocious conduct would continue to elicit strong negative reactions. Those reactions will in part be expressed in a system of formal blame and sanction. The conventions of blame can withstand an acceptance that human beings are located in the natural order, an order constituted by causal regularities.

These are issues that arise prior to law. They affect our conceptions of humanity and morality. In particular, there are unanswerable questions about when a person's character is "normal" and, as Bernard Williams noted, disputes about the degree to which that should count.[29] Law, morality, and society each works with a concept of the "voluntary" that informs judgements of wrongdoing. But that concept is not profound. Even if D's action is done with mens rea and in a normal state of mind, there are deeper questions about why D is someone who wants to act as she does; whether it is within her choice or control to be such a person; whether her character is itself "voluntarily" chosen. One might then ask: is it fair that D should be subject to state punishment because she is the sort of person she is (when, one might say, that is not something D is responsible for)?

The concept of voluntariness offers no assistance with such questions. It shapes our analysis of physical conduct and casts no deeper light. Voluntariness may discern whether, given who and how she is, D deserves criminal sanctions, but cannot reveal whether D deserves to be that person she is.

(iv) Summary

Judgments about whether particular conduct is blameworthy must operate within the framework of substantive values contained in the norms of whatever criminal jurisdiction is in issue. Exemptions from blame cannot delve too deeply into the particularities of defendants' lives because the provision of defences must remain a matter of rule rather than discretion. Such constraints entail, from time to time, the blaming and punishment of persons who have not forfeited a claim to be of good character.

These constraints on findings of blamelessness are considerable and can lead some theorists to reject the criminal law as a system of principle rather than a system of coercion. But one must continue to strive for principle in a hostile social climate. Criminal law and criminal justice have often been highly politicised subjects in England and Wales; to gain electoral support, the main political parties have frequently resorted to proposals to extend criminal liability and increase punishments.[30] To some extent the Legal Aid, Sentencing and Punishment of Offenders Act 2012 brought in more temperate reforms, placing limitations on sentences for public protection and control orders. However, recent legislation that may

---

[29] "Moral Responsibility and Political Freedom" [1997] *CLJ* 96, 101–2. A reply by Duff and von Hirsch follows: "Responsibility, Retribution and the 'Voluntary': A Response to Williams" [1997] *CLJ* 103.

[30] For an instructive if depressing evaluation of the politicisation of criminal law and justice see Ashworth, "Is Criminal Law a Lost Cause?" (2000) 116 *LQR* 225.

yet allow householders the right to use disproportionate force in defence of persons and property indicates that the allure of populist headlines has not completely faded.[31]

§ 22.2 Some things the defences fail to do

Within its institutional limitations, one might reasonably anticipate that the defences afforded by the criminal law of England and Wales will, largely, ensure acquittals for the blameless. Broadly, supervening defences fall within two major categories. First, there are defences which focus on some aspect of D himself, an aspect which renders him morally irresponsible for the conduct forming the substance of the offence charged. Within that group are infancy, insanity, non-insane automatism, and, to an extent, diminished responsibility which merely requires responsibility to be attenuated rather than absent. Secondly, rather than picking out a particular quality of D's that pre-empts her moral responsibility for the offence,[32] there are defences which arise on the basis that any person, placed in the same set of circumstances or making the same factual assumptions as was D, could not fairly have been expected to comply with the letter of the law. This second category includes excuses[33] and justifications: indeed, falling within this latter group may be situations where, from a societal perspective, committing a prima facie offence is the preferred option.

Unfortunately, even where the constraints of institutional possibility do not apply, English law does not always exculpate the blameless.

(i) Irresponsibility defences

(a) Exemptions for infancy and insanity

Certain mental conditions may be incompatible with justified blame. Young children afford an obvious example. From an early age, children are capable of aggressive and predatory conduct. Such conduct may need to be restrained but a degree of maturity, a capacity for self-criticism, is required before formal pronouncements of blame and punishment are apt. English law takes the age of 10 as the threshold for criminal guilt. There must be considerable doubt whether pre-teenage children have, as a class, sufficient insight and maturity to be full candidates for blame and punishment. Some recognition that children of that age may lack the insight and maturity that should be a condition for full criminal responsibility was afforded by the defence of *doli incapax* for persons between 10 and 14. But, as we have discussed, that defence was swept away by the House of Lords as a consequence of a very contestable piece of statutory interpretation.[34] Not long before that decision, the European Commissioner for Human Rights had called for a raising of the age of criminal responsibility in England and Wales to bring that jurisdiction's treatment of children within

---

[31] See further above, § 21.2(iv).

[32] This generalisation is subject to any allowances made, within the "reasonable man" standards that operate in excuses such as duress and provocation, for weaknesses peculiar to the defendant: above, §§ 10.5(iii)(c), 20.1(i)(e). Thus the division we have made here is not clear-cut.

[33] Thus, as Gardner points out, excuses do not deny responsibility: "The Gist of Excuses" (1998) 1 *Buffalo Crim LR* 575, 588ff.

[34] *R v. JTB* [2009] UKHL 20; discussed above, § 19.5(ii).

the European mainstream.[35] Now the situation is even worse than the circumstances that informed his report.[36]

Particular concern arises where young children receive long terms of incarceration for a serious offence. In *R. v. Secretary of State for the Home Department, ex p Venables*, two 10-year-old boys were detained at Her Majesty's pleasure for murder.[37] Even if we assume a culpability commensurate with that gravest of crimes, the 15-year "tariff" the pair received raises a major issue of principle. All other things being equal, at the age of 18 they were to be transferred to young offender institutions and thereafter to prison. To what extent is a person of, say, 22 years the "same" person as he was at 10? Even if he is not in any perceptible sense a better person at 22, is there a sufficient link between his present self and his earlier conduct to justify a continuing expiation of it? The trial and punishment of young children raises questions concerning not only a sufficiency of culpability at the time of the crime but also the connection between past conduct and present punishment for that conduct during a period of continuous growth and change.

In addition to infancy, insanity has long been accepted in many cultures as incompatible with moral agency. The idea has not gone unchallenged. Szasz,[38] among others, has rejected the acceptance of insanity as an exculpating condition. For him, insanity is just another form of survival strategy, a chosen mode of existence. It is no disrespect to Szasz to say that his is, nowadays, almost a lone voice. The reality of insanity is a matter of vivid report in case histories and there are increasing prospects of identifying major mental pathologies with underlying physiological conditions. The "otherness" of persons afflicted with psychotic disorders—their profoundly disturbed sense of reality—places such persons beyond any community of blame constituted by a sufficient core of shared assumptions guiding practical reason.

Alas, the *M'Naghten* Rules exclude many profoundly disturbed people.[39] The class of psychotic persons outside the Rules may be said to constitute a body who should generally[40] be ineligible for blame and are victims of injustice when convicted and punished. One way of incrementally increasing the class of persons within the Rules would be to

---

[35] *Report by Mr Alvaro Gil-Robles, Commissioner for Human Rights on his Visit to the United Kingdom* (Com DH (2005) 6) paras. 105–7. For an informative survey and critique of the position of young defendants and the doctrines of the criminal law in England and Wales, see Ashworth, *Positive Obligations in Criminal Law* (2013) chap. 7.

[36] Undeniably, children as young as 10 and 11 can perpetrate appalling violence which gives rise to public anger and fear: cf. *The Guardian*, 21 January 2010, reporting crown court proceedings. But sustained non-punitive interventions in such cases may offer the only prospect of non-violent futures for such disturbed and dangerous young persons. Such interventions may be made in non-penal institutions but, where orders of indefinite detention are made (as they were in the case reported), one cannot rule out transfer to prison at some point in the future.

[37] [1998] AC 407. Ultimately, the boys were released on parole after spending eight years in custody.

[38] *The Manufacture of Madness* (1970); *The Myth of Mental Illness* (1961).

[39] § 19.1.

[40] There is, understandably, ambivalence about the moral responsibility of persons such as Anders Breivik who may suffer from a significant mental disorder but who are capable of conceiving and carrying out with skill and cunning large-scale and atrocious projects. Under current English law, "insanity" is confined to particular cognitive defects. There is force in the view that the insanity defence should be a pure status defence akin to infancy and confined to persons radically deficient in terms of their reasoning capacity: persons, in the words of Moore, akin to "Infants, animals and trees": "The Quest for a Responsible Responsibility Test: Norwegian Insanity Law after Breivik" (2015) 9 *Criminal Law and Philosophy* 645, 680. Beyond the scope of such a defence would be persons capable of forethought and sequential, rule-guided conduct, even where the conduct for which they are held responsible would not have occurred but for a mental disorder. See further above, § 19.1(iv).

interpret more expansively their key terms. But there seems no present judicial inclination to do that. Recently, the Court of Appeal declined to expand the concept of "wrong", as used in the Rules, to take in matters going beyond D's awareness that his conduct was in breach of law.[41] Even more restrictively, the courts have denied the applicability of the insanity defence to cases arguably falling within it. In *H*,[42] the Divisional Court ruled that the insanity defence had no application to offences of strict liability. In *Colohan*,[43] D's liability for the offence of harassment was not deflected by the fact that his behaviour stemmed directly from the disease of schizophrenia. One may contrast this parsimony in provision of this defence when it is raised by D to avoid conviction with the alacrity in which courts have found such conditions such as diabetes and epilepsy to be diseases of the mind when the alternative would be an unqualified acquittal on the basis of lack of mens rea.[44]

To some extent this situation was tempered by the partial statutory defence of diminished responsibility, albeit the remedy is confined to the offence of murder and diminishes but does not exclude blame and punishment. Under the original version of this defence, the majority of cases where diminished responsibility was raised proceeded by way of guilty plea with, on occasion, a humane if non-rigorous view taken concerning whether D's condition fell within the terms of s. 2 of the Homicide Act 1957. This may well change under the new version of s. 2. No longer do medical conditions which undermine D's rationality and capacity to understand his actions even partially exempt of their own accord. The condition must "explain" why D killed V. That requirement may not be met even in cases of profound disability such as schizophrenia.[45]

This partial defence, even in its narrower, reformulated version, continues to apply to persons whose cognitive and reasoning capacities are unimpaired but who may, because of a personality disorder, experience considerable difficulty in restraining criminogenic impulses. Peter Arenella[46] has argued forcefully argued that persons with profoundly disordered personalities, who are incapable of any degree of identification or sympathy with the interests of others, should be dealt with outside the framework of the criminal law. However, the concept of personality disorder or psychopathy is controversial medically and has gained no purchase in the realm of public sympathy or understanding. While it is possible to confine, without the need of a criminal conviction, persons with personality disorder on account of the danger they may present,[47] there are no proposals to exempt from conviction personality-disordered defendants who do perpetrate crimes.

---

[41] *Johnson* [2007] EWCA Crim 1978, [2008] Crim LR 132; above, § 19.1(g).

[42] [1997] 1 WLR 1406; criticised above, § 6.2.

[43] [2001] Crim LR 845.

[44] As in *Hennessy* [1989] 1 WLR 287 (CA); also *Sullivan* [1984] AC 156 (HL).

[45] See § 19.2(ii)(d).

[46] "Convicting the Morally Blameless: Reassessing the Relationship Between Legal and Moral Accountability" (1992) 39 *UCLA LR* 1511.

[47] In its original form, the Mental Health Act 1983 limited the class of persons who could be confined under the Act to persons whose mental disorder was "treatable". The Mental Health Act 2007 amends the 1983 Act by replacing the condition of treatability with one that "appropriate treatment" be available, i.e. procedures "to alleviate, or prevent the worsening of the disorder or one or more of its symptoms or manifestations". One intended effect of the change is to legitimise the confinement of persons with dangerous, anti-social, personality disorder.

(b) Destabilisation?

Persons who are not insane or personality-disordered may nonetheless find themselves in a destabilised condition and, in such a state, may perpetrate the actus reus of a crime. Where the condition is not self-induced and is incompatible with proof of mens rea, no conviction for the crime is possible. If, however, the definitional elements of a crime are present, liability will ensue. Recall *Kingston*,[48] where it is ruled that a "drunken intent is a criminal intent" even in circumstances where the drunken condition was involuntarily induced through the machinations of a third party. The House of Lords reversed the decision of the Court of Appeal,[49] which had allowed involuntary intoxication to serve as a defence to any crime provided the actus reus would not have been perpetrated but for the effects of the drink.

In correcting the generosity of the Court of Appeal, the House of Lords took an unduly formal view of the nature of criminal guilt. Guilt, for their Lordships, consisted merely of the presence of the definitional elements of the crime and the absence of any legally recognised justification or excuse. Even if the defendant were blameless, he would still be guilty of the offence. This approach completely disregards the reputational consequences of a conviction for a stigmatic offence: the public judgement of blame that inheres in the fact of conviction alone. It is submitted that if a court accepts D is blameless, the conditions that explain his blamelessness should provide, wherever systemically possible, the basis of a defence.

There are a number of personal conditions compatible with mens rea that preclude a sufficient moral culpability for conviction of that crime. Non-exhaustively, these include involuntary intoxication, confused states of consciousness induced by medication, the destabilising effects of post-traumatic stress disorder, premenstrual tension, epilepsy, arteriosclerosis, cerebral tumours, and diabetes. Such conditions may trigger outbursts of motiveless violence from persons who are otherwise morally well-disposed. The way that English law deals with these conditions at the present time is manifestly unsatisfactory.[50] Sometimes sympathy for a defendant may influence a court to find that the mental element for a crime is not made out—even though this may seem at variance with the facts of the case. If the mental element is held to be absent, either a straightforward acquittal or a qualified verdict of insanity will follow, depending on whether the court characterises the condition as arising from internal or external factors. If the mental element is found to be present then an acquittal cannot follow. Arguably, a general defence *should* be available for those afflicted with any of these conditions, notwithstanding the presence of mens rea. Of course, the availability of such a defence should be subject to a number of restrictive conditions.[51] But, where those conditions are met, it is submitted that this class of blameless persons could be excluded from liability without undermining the structure and cohesion of the criminal law.

---

[48] [1995] 2 AC 355; above, § 18.3(v)(a).

[49] [1993] 4 All ER 373.

[50] Sullivan, "Making Excuses" in Simester and Smith (eds.), *Harm and Culpability* (1996) 131, 145–50.

[51] In particular, provided (i) D would not have committed the offence but for being in a state of disequilibrium occasioned by his diabetes, post-traumatic stress, etc.; (ii) the offence at issue is not amongst the most serious of crimes, such as murder, rape, etc.; and (iii) D has not previously been convicted for a similar offence.

In our discussion of murder, we noted the terms of the partial defence of loss of control.[52] The defence allows the culpability-reducing factors of gross provocation and fear of serious violence to be taken into account at the trial stage. The introduction of such a partial defence is particularly in point for murder because of the mandatory penalty.[53] There is nothing, in principle, however, against the introduction of forms of legal mitigation (as opposed to sentencing discretion) for other offences. Jeremy Horder, for instance, has advocated the extension of diminished responsibility to offences other than murder.[54] If diminished responsibility were to be established in a non-homicide context, perhaps one could "cap" the maximum penalty that could be imposed to, say, half the maximum sentence provided for the offence. This form of mitigation would thus become a matter of *entitlement*, to be won in argument at trial or by concession on the part of the prosecution. There is merit in acknowledging the diminution of guilt in the realm of law rather than judicial discretion. Accordingly, forms of legal mitigation such as provocation and diminished responsibility which are currently confined to murder arguably should be available for offences generally.

(ii) When conformity with law cannot reasonably be expected

For defences in this second category, D's claim is, loosely, that in the circumstances any ethically well-disposed person could not reasonably have been expected to comply with the letter of the law. It is not that there is anything peculiar to himself which precludes liability. *Anyone*—or at least, anyone like D[55]—placed in similar circumstances could not reasonably have been expected to do differently. The emphasis is on the reasons or explanations why D acted as he did or found himself in the situation that he was, reasons or explanations potentially applicable to any actor.

Expectations of conformity with law may be pitched at unattainable levels. The most glaring situation of this kind is where, for reasons beyond the control of D and in circumstances that do not reveal any fault on her part, criminal liability is attached by way of an involuntarily acquired status, as in the notorious case of *Larsonneur*.[56] In principle, questions of involuntariness and control should be accommodated within the concept of actus reus.[57] Failing that, the blamelessness of defendants should be accommodated by way of a defence of impossibility.[58] But at present, English law tends to disregard principle in favour of *ad hoc* decisions, frequently tailored to the language of the particular offence.

Almost as fundamental in their unfairness are cases where liability will be incurred as an inevitable concomitant of carrying on a lawful trade or business. If peas are to be canned on an industrial scale, it is inevitable that some cans will contain foreign bodies, whatever reasonable checks and controls are put in place.[59] If "adult" videos, tobacco, or lottery tickets

---

[52] Above, § 10.5(vii).

[53] Under the Law Commission's scheme, first degree murder would be reduced to second degree murder, displacing the mandatory penalty.

[54] "Pleading Involuntary Lack of Capacity" [1993] *CLJ* 298, 316. See also Wasik, "Partial Excuses in the Criminal Law" (1982) 45 *MLR* 516, 522.

[55] Above, n. 23.

[56] (1933) 149 LT 542; above, 4.1(ii)(a).

[57] Above, § 4.3.

[58] Above, § 20.5.

[59] *Smedleys Ltd* v. *Breed* [1974] AC 839 (HL). See above, Chapter 6.

are allowed as items of commerce, then even careful shopkeepers and their assistants will sell or hire such items to persons who look older than they are, whatever precautions are taken.[60] To date, there seems no judicial inclination to mitigate the inherent unfairness of strict liability by way of a due diligence offence. Far from it. In *Chargot Ltd*,[61] the House of Lords considered the nature of the liability arising under the Health and Safety at Work etc. Act 1974, which requires employers "to ensure as far as is reasonably practicable, the health, safety and welfare at work." A fatal accident had occurred in the workplace. There was no evidence to suggest that the employer was in any way at fault for this. The Appellate Committee ruled that a workplace fatal accident *of itself* established a failure to ensure the health and safety of the deceased employee. When such a finding is made, the 1974 Act requires the employer to prove that the avoidance of the accident was not reasonably practicable.[62] Unsurprisingly, that could not be done given the absence of any discernible explanation for the accident.[63] The effect of the decision is to impose serious criminal liability on employers and associated management for any unexplained or unexplainable accident. If one starts from the premise that to run a lawful business is not a dubious activity, the decision in *Chargot* is harsh in the extreme. When faced with incidents that cannot be explained by way of reasonable investigation, it should surely suffice to exculpate that the employer and associated management can demonstrate due diligence in matters of health and safety. Suitably adapted, such a defence would also be relevant to a plea of excusable ignorance or mistake of law.

Less frequently encountered, but potentially productive of grave injustice when it arises, is the failure of English law to recognise any defence of superior orders. Consider a situation where D, an armed soldier, is ordered by his commanding officer, E, to shoot V. The reason for the order is, let us suppose, the belief that if V were allowed to escape, he will commit terrorist offences at some future time. It is probably the case that the order is unlawful; force used in the prevention of crime is likely to be found lawful only when the crime is imminent, although *Kelly*[64] favours a more expansive approach. The position of D is invidious. If he disobeys the order, adverse career and disciplinary consequences may well follow. Besides, D may believe, quite reasonably, that the order given by E is an order to do something which is lawful. Were he to be tried for murder consequent upon following the order, the prospect of a conviction on such facts would appear to be strong. Equally strong, it is submitted, is a plea for excuse on the part of D.

Currently, a defence of superior orders is uncountenanced even in circumstances where D's conduct is morally *justifiable*. In *Yip Chiu-cheung*,[65] D and E were charged with conspiring to traffic in controlled drugs. Their conviction depended on proof that F, who was not a defendant, was guilty of drug trafficking, in taking drugs from Hong Kong to Sydney. F was found to have committed the offence, notwithstanding that he was an undercover police officer whose only motivation was to bring D and E to justice, an endeavour for

---

[60] *Harrow LBC* v. *Shah* [1999] 1 WLR 83 (DC).

[61] [2008] UKHL73, [2009] 1 WLR 1.

[62] Section 40.

[63] The deceased had been driving a dumper truck which overturned, burying the driver under the load of soil it was transporting across the worksite.

[64] [1989] NI 341. See above, § 20.3.

[65] [1995] 1 AC 111.

which the Privy Council had only praise. The matter is put as one of high constitutional principle—the unconstitutionality of any dispensing power entailed that F was guilty. But this is a situation where F acted not to undermine but to reinforce the law's authority. It is legitimate to speculate whether that line of analysis would have held if F had actually been prosecuted for the offence.

In respect of the other defences recognised by English law, claims that blameless people are insufficiently accommodated are more controversial. The scope of the defence of duress has been criticised on the grounds that it is unavailable to a charge of murder.[66] Yet it is not *obviously* wrong to deny impunity for killing an innocent person in order to escape death or serious harm to oneself, and the counterarguments should be acknowledged even if one favours extending the defence to murder.[67] Similarly, whether the defences of mistaken self-defence or prevention of crime are under-inclusive of the blameless is a matter of controversy.[68] On the other hand, the law shows a meaner spirit when disallowing a defence where D kills an innocent person in order to avoid harm to innocent persons other than herself, particularly where she enjoys a close relationship with those whose welfare she prioritises. Arguably, too, English law is unduly restrictive in denying any form of mitigation to a person who was entitled to use some degree of force but who used force excessive for the occasion.[69] Certainly in the context of murder, the availability of a manslaughter verdict in such circumstances would be a welcome departure from the rigidity of the mandatory life sentence.

§ 22.3 Defence doctrine and judicial creativity

In principle, therefore, more could be done to exculpate blameless defendants. What chance is there of judicial innovation to meet these needs? In *Lynch*,[70] the House of Lords decided, by a majority, to extend the defence of duress to the crime of murder (a decision later reversed in *Howe*).[71] In the judgments two very different attitudes to enlarging the coverage of defences were expressed. For the majority, Lord Wilberforce said:[72]

> "I have no doubt that it is open to us, on normal judicial principles, to hold the defence admissible. We are here in the domain of the common law: our task is to fit what we can see as principle and authority to the facts before us, and it is no obstacle that these facts are new. The judges have always assumed responsibility for deciding questions of principle relating to criminal liability and guilt, and particularly for setting the standards by which the law expects normal men to act."

For the majority of the House, extending the defence of duress to acts of complicity in murder was an appropriate task for the highest appellate court, notwithstanding long-standing

---

[66] Smith, *Justification and Excuse in the Criminal Law* (1989) 92–5; above, §201(i)(d). The Law Commission has recently proposed the extension of duress to murder: Law Com. No. 304 (2006) part 6.

[67] For some thoughtful points, see Horder, "Occupying the Moral High Ground? The Law Commission on Duress" [1994] *Crim LR* 334, 335–6, 339–40.

[68] Simester, "Mistakes in Defence" (1992) 12 *OJLS* 295; above, § 18.1(iii).

[69] Above, § 21.2(iv).

[70] [1975] AC 653.

[71] [1987] AC 417.

[72] [1975] AC 653, 684.

institutional authority that the defence was not available in such circumstances. For the minority, this amounted to a usurpation of legislative authority. Lord Simon castigated the majority's approach:[73]

> "I can hardly conceive of circumstances less suitable than the instant for five members of an appellate committee of your Lordships' House to arrogate to ourselves so momentous a law-making initiative."

In the context of *defence* doctrine, the more expansive approach of Lord Wilberforce is to be preferred. The judicial role is well suited to expanding defence doctrine and even, when circumstances require so, the creation of a novel defence. In terms of the propriety of judicial law-making, one may distinguish between grounds of inculpation, on the one hand, and grounds of exculpation on the other.[74] In the former case, clarity and generality of application are important virtues when defining the prima facie offence. Further, any significant enlargement of a class of conduct which may be punished is a task for the legislature and not for an unelected judiciary. For exculpatory questions, however, it is possible to craft principled responses to the quiddity of a particular case without undermining the normative framework of the criminal law. The difference between questions of inculpation and exculpation was adverted to by Hughes LJ in *Dowds*, where his Lordship rejected the argument that the presumption of strict construction had any role when dealing with the availability of defences.[75] However, he had in mind the rejection or narrowing of defences rather than their expansion.[76] The late twentieth-century development of the defence of duress of circumstances and the overdue recognition of a defence of necessity indicate the willingness of some contemporary judges to give practical effect to findings of blamelessness.

But there are other judicial voices too. The House of Lords and Privy Council have each held that there may be a conviction for a serious stigmatic offence in circumstances where the defendant is blameless. Further, in *Clegg*,[77] the House of Lords expressed a reserved attitude to the judicial creation and extension of defences. In *C v. DPP*,[78] the House of Lords, in reinstating the then presumption of *doli incapax* for 10- to 14-year-olds,[79] spoke in general terms of the propriety of judicial law-making in criminal law. Speaking for the appellate committee, Lord Lowry laid down what he termed "aids of navigation". They are:[80]

> "(1) If the solution is doubtful, the judges should beware of imposing their own remedy. (2) Caution should prevail if Parliament has rejected opportunities of clearing up a known difficulty or has legislated, while leaving the difficulty untouched. (3) Disputed matters of social policy are less suitable areas for judicial intervention than purely legal problems. (4) Fundamental legal doctrines should not be lightly set aside. (5) Judges should not make a change unless they can achieve finality and certainty."

---

[73] *Ibid.*, 696.
[74] See, e.g., Smith, "Judicial Law Making in the Criminal Law" (1984) 100 *LQR* 46, esp. 63–7; cf. Stark, "*Howe* (1987)" in Handler, Mares and Williams (eds.), *Landmark Cases in Criminal Law* (2017).
[75] [2012] EWCA Crim 281, para. 35.
[76] Hughes LJ took the presumption to apply to the defining elements of offences, but it is equally in point where the ambit of criminal liability is expanded by limiting or rejecting defences.
[77] [1995] 1 AC 482.
[78] [1996] AC 1.
[79] Now abolished by the Crime and Disorder Act 1998, s. 34; above § 19.4.
[80] [1996] AC 1, 28.

These navigational aids are intended for general guidance. But, it is submitted, they are too restrictive when applied to the development of defence doctrine, by contrast with enlarging the scope of offences. At risk of repetition, what should drive the development of defence doctrine is a refusal to countenance the conviction of a blameless person for a serious criminal offence. We must accept that full expression of that principle is limited by the nature of the criminal law itself. But subject to that important proviso, what *can* be done by way of exempting of blameless persons, should be done. This may require a disregard for some of Lord Lowry's navigational aids, particularly the matter of finality and certainty. For example, consider the decision in *Bournewood*[81] which at long last recognised a defence of necessity. Beyond the facts of *Bournewood*, the limits of the defence are impossible to state with any assurance. That brings a degree of disvalue; but the disvalue is outweighed by the value of providing the defence. The primary norms of the criminal law remain intact as a guide to action and are not unduly undermined by allowing departures from the letter of law in cases of obvious necessity.

On the matter of sensitivity to the condition of blamelessness, it may be that we are set to enter a new judicial era. In an important extra-judicial lecture, Mrs Justice Arden (then Chairman of the Law Commission) gave her views on the centrality of the Human Rights Act 1998 to the substantive criminal law and, in particular, her view of the likely impact of Article 3 of the ECHR which proscribes torture and "inhuman and degrading treatment or punishment". The hypothetical case that she posed is so resonant of possibilities that it may be quoted in full:[82]

> "Suppose as a result of an accident, which was not the result of any negligence or intention, a factory owner pollutes the environment around his factory. He admits that the damage was caused by his factory and he pays a large sum of money to clear up the mess with a view to limiting the damage to his reputation. Suppose that he is then prosecuted for an environmental offence involving strict liability which carries an unlimited fine and he resists conviction on the ground that the accident had occurred accidentally and without fault. He contends that a conviction would cause him great loss of reputation. Can he successfully contend that for the law to impose strict liability, so that a person can show that the damage was not due to any negligence on his part, and that he has taken all the steps required to rectify the damage caused, has no defence, infringes his rights under Article 3?"

Mrs Justice Arden considered the likely answer to this question to be affirmative and envisaged a court creating a "due diligence and all reasonable steps to rectify" defence under the wide powers of construction provided by section 3 of the Human Rights Act 1998. She also adverted to Article 6(2), which provides that "everyone charged with a criminal offence shall be presumed innocent until proved guilty according to law", and queries the legitimacy of strict liability offences in the light of this presumption.

Strict liability has been judicially tolerated for a long time and has been confirmed at the appellate level.[83] Yet if other judges, in addition to Mrs Justice Arden, were to read the ECHR and the interpretative possibilities of the Human Rights Act 1998 as boldly as she does, the

---

[81] [1998] 3 All ER 289; above, § 21.3(i).

[82] "Criminal Law at the Crossroads: The Impact on Human Rights from the Law Commission's Perspective and the Need for a Code" [1999] *Crim LR* 439, 450; above, § 2.5(i).

[83] The House of Lords has recently confirmed the ECHR-compatibility of strict liability even in serious offences such as rape: *G* [2008] UKHL37, [2008] 1 WLR 1379.

lot of blameless defendants could significantly improve. Unfortunately, such speculation seems more optimistic than predictive. In *Barnfather* v. *London Borough of Islington and Secretary of State for Education and Skills*,[84] the Divisional Court had to consider whether D, a parent blameless in respect of her child's truanting from school, was guilty of an offence which in literal terms made parents guilty of an offence if the child "fails to attend regularly at the school".[85] In upholding D's conviction, the court confirmed authority finding the only constituent of the offence to be the child's truanting. Article 6(2) was of no assistance to D: the presumption of innocence was found to have no bearing on the substantive content of criminal offences. The same offence was at issue in *Hampshire County Council* v. *E*,[86] where the Divisional Court confirmed D's conviction even on the assumption that her drug-taking and -dealing 15-year-old son might have killed or seriously harmed her had she tried to ensure his school attendance. The court rejected the defence of duress on the ground that her liability was not founded on her own conduct.[87] Too often, judges fail to explore the resources of theory and doctrine in cases where conviction of a blameless person might thereby be avoided.[88]

There are, however, some recent examples of courts going beyond the all too literal interpretation of statutory provisions criticised here, in order to avoid conviction of the blameless. The *Hampshire* case can usefully be contrasted with *Robinson-Pierre*.[89] In the former case, that fact that D's liability was triggered by her unruly son's behaviour, rather than by any conduct of her own, was the pretext to neuter the defence of duress. In *Robinson-Pierre*, the fact that the escape of D's dog into a public place, uncontrolled and on the attack, was the result of its release by third parties, led the Court of Appeal to reason that Parliament could not have intended to punish the owner in such circumstances, as no public interest would be served and an unfair conviction imposed. Even though, on a literal interpretation, the offence in question was seemingly committed by the owner,[90] the Court of Appeal was prepared to interpret its terms in the light of fairness and proportionality. So simple and commonsensical is the reasoning, the temptation arises to treat *Robinson-Pierre* as a case of general importance. However, the decision in *Hampshire* forms part of a long-standing set of cases rigidly enforcing the school truanting offence and refusing any form of exemption save for those specifically referred to in the applicable legislation. Only time will tell how important *Robinson-Pierre* will be.[91]

On the face of it, *L and others*[92] could make for a major turning point in preventing the conviction and punishment of the blameless. Three of the appellants had been convicted of offences of producing and supplying cannabis. It was accepted that they had been

---

[84] [2003] EWHC 418 (Admin).

[85] Education Act 1996, s. 444.

[86] [2007] EWHC 2584 (Admin).

[87] See further Sullivan, "Parents and Their Truanting Children: an English Lesson in Liability without Responsibility" (2010) 12 *Otago LR* 285.

[88] For a particularly egregious example see *Rehman* v. *Woods* [2005] EWCA Crim 2056. For other examples of imprisonment of persons lacking any form of fault, see Ashworth, *Positive Obligations in Criminal Law* (2013) chap. 4, esp. 123–8.

[89] [2013] EWCA Crim 2396.

[90] Section 3 of the Dangerous Dogs Act 1991 on the face of it penalises any dog owner whose dog is in a public place and out of control. The offence is aggravated if the out-of-control dog attacks anyone.

[91] See further above, §§ 4.3(ii)(b), 20.5.

[92] [2013] EWCA Crim 991.

trafficked into the United Kingdom. There was considerable obscurity about the details of the trafficking and the respective ages of the appellants.[93] Be that as it may, the Court of Appeal found that being subjected to trafficking and the associated isolation and vulnerability "extinguished" any culpability for these offences. The Court of Appeal ruled that this lack of culpability should have led to a successful challenge to the prosecution at trial as an abuse of the process of the court. Accordingly, all the convictions were quashed.

Does all this mean that, whenever D can establish that he lacked any culpability in respect of any offence he has been charged with, he can claim that any further proceeding concerning that offence is an abuse of process? That would be a rash conclusion: there were special features surrounding L that inclined the court to be particularly averse to confirming the convictions.[94] Yet assuming that the abuse of process doctrine is more than "a wilderness of single instances",[95] there may be other successful challenges on that ground where the lack of culpability is particularly striking.

---

[93] *Ibid.*, paras. 45, 54, 67.

[94] As was suggested in § 3.1(ii)(c), it is possible to explain L on the more restrictive ground that it can be an abuse of process to prosecute defendants for conduct that the State was obliged under international law not to criminalise. The United Kingdom is party to the Council of Europe Convention on Preventing and Combating Trafficking of Human Beings and Protecting its Victims: Directive 2011/36/EU. Arguably, the Convention obliges the United Kingdom to legislate specific defences relating to the vulnerabilities of trafficked persons transported by persons organising criminal activities; this has not occurred. At the time of the appeal in L, the defendants had served their sentences; the appeals were consequent on interventions by the Child Protection Agency and the United Kingdom Borders Agency. It would seem that the audience addressed in the appeal was the Crown Prosecution Service who may now be more circumspect about proceeding against trafficked children and young persons: see further Sullivan, "Avoiding Criminal Liability and Excessive Punishment for Persons Who Lack Culpability" in Reed and Bohlander (eds.), *General Defences in Criminal Law: Domestic and Comparative Perspectives* (2014) 25, 26–9.

[95] Alfred, Lord Tennyson, *Aylmer's Field.*

BIBLIOGRAPHY

Adams, F., "Homicide and the Supposed Corpse" (1968) 1 *Otago LR* 278.

Advisory Council on the Penal System, *Sentences of Imprisonment: A Review of Maximum Penalties* (London: HMSO, 1978).

Advisory Group on the Law of Rape (Heilbron Committee), *Report of the Advisory Group on the Law of Rape* Cmnd. 6352 (London: HMSO, 1975).

Alexander, L., Alexander, "Causing the Conditions of One's Own Defense: a Theoretical Non-Problem" (2013) 7 *Criminal Law and Philosophy* 623.

——, "Criminal Liability for Omissions: An Inventory of Issues" in S. Shute and A.P. Simester (eds.), *Criminal Law Theory: Doctrines of the General Part* (Oxford: Oxford University Press, 2000) 121.

——, "The Moral Magic of Consent (II)" (1996) 2 *Legal Theory* 165.

Alexander, L. and Ferzan, K., *Crime and Culpability: a Theory of Criminal Law* (New York: Cambridge University Press, 2009).

Alldridge, P., "Common Sense, Innocent Agency, and Causation" (1992) 3 *Criminal Law Forum* 299.

——, "Dealing with Drug Dealing" in A.P. Simester and A.T.H. Smith (eds.), *Harm and Culpability* (Oxford: Oxford University Press, 1996) 239.

——, "Making Criminal Law Known" in S. Shute and A.P. Simester (eds.), *Criminal Law Theory: Doctrines of the General Part* (Oxford: Oxford University Press, 2002) 103.

——, "The Doctrine of Innocent Agency" (1990) 2 *Criminal Law Forum* 45.

——, "The Limits of Confiscation" [2011] *Criminal LR* 827.

——, *Money Laundering Law* (Oxford: Hart Publishing, 2003).

Allen, C., *Legal Duties and Other Essays in Jurisprudence* (Oxford: Oxford University Press, 1931).

Almond, P., "Public Perceptions of Work-related Fatality Cases: Reaching the Outer Limits of 'Populist Punitiveness'?" (2008) 48 *British Journal of Criminology* 448.

American Psychiatric Association, *Diagnostic and Statistical Manual of Mental Disorders* (Arlington: American Psychiatric Publishing, Inc., 4th ed., 2000).

Amirthalingam, K., "Caldwell Recklessness Is Dead, Long Live Mens Rea's Fecklessness" (2004) 67 *Modern LR* 491.

André, J., "Nagel, Williams and Moral Luck" (1983) 43 *Analysis* 202.

Andrews, L.B., "The Legal Status of the Embryo" (1986) 32 *Loyola LR* 257.

Andrews, J.A., "Robbery" [1966] *Criminal LR* 524.

——, "Wilfulness: a Lesson in Ambiguity" (1981) 1 *Legal Studies* 303.

Annas, J., "How Basic are Basic Actions?" (1977–78) 78 *Proceedings of the Aristotelian Society* 195.

Antrobus, S., "The Criminal Liability of Directors for Health and Safety Breaches and Manslaughter" [2013] *Criminal LR* 309.

Archibald, B.P., "The Constitutionalisation of the General Part of the Criminal Law" (1988) 67 *Canadian Bar Review* 403.

Arden, M., "Criminal Law at the Crossroads: The Impact on Human Rights from the Law Commission's Perspective and the Need for a Code" [1999] *Criminal LR* 439.

Arenella, P., "Character, Choice, and Moral Agency" in E.F. Paul, F.D. Miller, and J. Paul (eds.), *Crime, Culpability and Remedy* (Oxford: Blackwell, 1990) 59.

——, "Convicting the Morally Blameless: Reassessing the Relationship between Legal and Moral Accountability" (1992) 39 *UCLA LR* 1511.

Arlidge, A., "The Trial of Dr David Moor" [2000] *Criminal LR* 31.

Arlidge, A., Parry, J., and Gatt, I., *Arlidge and Parry on Fraud* (London: Sweet & Maxwell, 2nd ed., 1996).

Ashworth, A., "A Change of Normative Position: Determining the Contours of Culpability in Criminal Law" (2008) 11 *New Criminal LR* 232.

——, "A Decade of Human Rights in Criminal Justice" [2014] *Criminal LR* 325.

——, "Belief, Intent, and Criminal Liability" in J. Eekelaar and J. Bell (eds.), *Oxford Essays in Jurisprudence* (Oxford: Oxford University Press, 3rd Series, 1987) 1.

——, "Criminal Attempts and the Role of Resulting Harm under the Code and in the Common Law" (1988) 19 *Rutgers LJ* 725.

——, "Criminal Liability in a Medical Context: the Treatment of Good Intentions" in A.P. Simester and A.T.H. Smith (eds.), *Harm and Culpability* (Oxford: Oxford University Press, 1996) 173.

——, "Defining Criminal Offences without Harm" in P. Smith (ed.), *Criminal Law: Essays in Honour of J.C. Smith* (London: Butterworths, 1987) 7.

——, "Four Threats to the Presumption of Innocence" (2006) 10 *Evidence and Proof* 241.

——, "Ignorance of the Criminal Law, and Duties to Avoid it" (2011) 74 *Modern LR* 1.

——, "Interpreting Criminal Statutes: a Crisis of Legality?" (1991) 107 *Law Quarterly Review* 419.

——, "Is the Criminal Law a Lost Cause?" (2000) 116 *Law Quarterly Review* 225.

——, "Manslaughter by Omission and the Rule of Law" [2015] *Criminal LR* 563.

——, "Manslaughter: Generic or Nominate Offences?" in C. Clarkson and S. Cunningham (eds.), *Criminal Liability for Non-aggressive Deaths* (Aldershot: Ashgate, 2008).

——, "Preventive Orders and the Rule of Law" in D. Baker and J. Horder (eds.), *The Sanctity of Life and the Criminal Law: The Legacy of Glanville Williams* (Cambridge: Cambridge University Press, 2013) 45.

——, "Principles, Pragmatism and the Law Commission's Recommendations on Homicide Law Reform" [2007] *Criminal LR* 345.

——, "Public Duties and Criminal Omissions: Some Unresolved Questions" [2011] *J Commonwealth Criminal Law* 1.

——, "Reason, Logic and Criminal Liability" (1975) 91 *Law Quarterly Review* 102.

——, "Redrawing the Boundaries of Entrapment" [2002] *Criminal LR* 161.

——, "Robbery Re-assessed" [2002] *Criminal LR* 851.

——, "Self-defence and the Right to Life" [1975] *Cambridge LJ* 272.

——, "Taking the Consequences" in S. Shute, J. Gardner and J. Horder (eds.), *Action and Value in Criminal Law* (Oxford: Oxford University Press, 1993) 107.

——, "Testing Fidelity to Legal Values: Official Involvement and Criminal Justice" in S. Shute and A.P. Simester (eds.), *Criminal Law: Doctrines of the General Part* (Oxford: Oxford University Press, 2002) 299.

——, "The Doctrine of Provocation" [1976] *Cambridge LJ* 292.

——, "The Elasticity of Mens Rea" in C. Tapper (ed.), *Crime, Proof and Punishment: Essays in Memory of Sir Rupert Cross* (London: Butterworths, 1981) 45.

——, "The European Convention and Criminal Law" in Cambridge Centre for Public Law, *The Human Rights Act and the Criminal and Regulatory Process* (Oxford: Hart Publishing, 1999) 37.

——, "The Human Rights Act and the Substantive Criminal Law: A Non-minimalist View" [2000] *Criminal LR* 564.

——, "The Scope of Criminal Liability for Omissions" (1989) 105 *Law Quarterly Review* 424.

——, "Transferred Malice and Punishment for Unforeseen Consequences" in P. Glazebrook (ed.), *Reshaping the Criminal Law* (London: Sweet & Maxwell, 1978) 77.

——, *Positive Obligations in Criminal Law* (Oxford: Hart Publishing, 2013).

——, *Principles of Criminal Law* (Oxford: Oxford University Press, 2nd ed., 1995; 3rd ed., 1999).

Ashworth, A., Emmerson, B., and Macdonald, B., *Human Rights and Criminal Justice* (London: Sweet & Maxwell, 2nd ed., 2007).

Ashworth, A. and Horder, J., *Principles of Criminal Law* (Oxford: Oxford University Press, 7th ed., 2013).

Atiyah, P.S., "Common Law and Statute Law" (1985) 48 *Modern Law Review* 1.

——, *Vicarious Liability in the Law of Torts* (London: Butterworths, 1969).

Azmat, A.T., "What Mistake Of Law Just Might Be: Legal Moralism, Liberal Positivism, And The Mistake Of Law Doctrine" (2015) 18 *New Criminal LR* 369.

Bakalis, C., "Legislating Against Hatred: The Law Commission's Report on Hate Crime" [2015] *Criminal LR* 192.

Baker, B.M., "Mens Rea, Negligence and Criminal Law Reform" (1987) 6 *Law and Philosophy* 53.

Baker, E., "Human Rights, McNaghten and the 1991 Act" [1994] *Criminal LR* 84.

——, "Taking European Criminal Law Seriously" [1998] *Criminal LR* 361.

Bailey, V. and Blackburn, S., "The Punishment of Incest Act 1980: A Case Study in Law Creation" [1979] *Criminal LR* 708.

Bailin, A., "Criminalising Free Speech?" [2011] *Criminal LR* 705.

Bailin, A. and Craven, E., "Compensation for Miscarriages of Justice—Who Now Qualifies?" [2014] *Criminal LR* 511.

Baldwin, R., "Why Rules Don't Work" (1990) 53 *Modern Law Review* 321.

Bamforth, N., "The Application of the Human Rights Act 1998 to Public Authorities and Private Bodies" [1999] *Cambridge LJ* 159.

Barlow, N.L.A., "Drug Intoxication and the Principle of *Capacitas Rationalis*" (1984) 100 *Law Quarterly Review* 639.

Bayles, M., "Character, Purpose and Criminal Responsibility" (1982) 1 *Law and Philosophy* 5.

Bazelon, D., "The Morality of the Criminal Law" (1976) 49 *Southern California LR* 385.

Becker, B.C., "Human Being: The Boundaries of the Concept" (1974) 4 *Philosophy and Public Affairs* 334.

Bein, D., "The Theft of Use and the Element of 'Intent to Deprive Permanently' in Larceny" (1968) 3 *Israel LR* 368.

Bell, J. and Engle, G., *Cross on Statutory Interpretation* (London: Butterworths, 3rd ed., 1995).

Bennion, F., "Mens Rea and Defendants below the Age of Discretion [2009] *Criminal LR* 757.

Bennett, J., "Morality and Consequences" in S. McMurrin (ed.), *The Tanner Lectures in Human Values* (Cambridge: Cambridge University Press, 1981) 47.

——, *The Act Itself* (Oxford: Oxford University Press, 1995).

Bennion, F., "The Meaning of 'Sexual' in the Sexual Offences Bill" (2003) 167 *Justice of the Peace* 764.

——, "Mens Rea and Defendants below the Age of Discretion" [2009] *Criminal LR* 757.

Bentham, J., *An Introduction to the Principles of Morals and Legislation* (1789).

Bergelson, V., "The Right to Be Hurt; Testing the Boundaries of Consent" (2007) 75 *George Washington LR* 165.

Beynon, H., "Causation, Omissions and Complicity" [1987] *Criminal LR* 539.

——, "Doctors as Murderers" [1982] *Criminal LR* 17.

Birch, D., "Suffering in Silence: A Cost-benefit Analysis of Section 34 of the Criminal Justice and Public Order Act 1994" [1999] *Criminal LR* 769.

Birks, P., "Misdirected Funds: Restitution from the Recipient" (1980) *Lloyds Maritime and Commercial Law Quarterly* 296.

——, *An Introduction to the Law of Restitution* (Oxford: Oxford University Press, 1989).

Blake, L.W., "The Innocent Purchaser and Section 22 of the Theft Act" [1972] *Criminal LR* 494.

Blake, M., "Physician-assisted Suicide: A Criminal Offence or a Patient's Right?" (1997) 5 *Medical LR* 294.

Blake, M. and Ashworth, A., "The Presumption of Innocence in English Criminal Law" [1996] *Criminal LR* 306.

Blakey, G.R. and Goldsmith, M., "Criminal Redistribution of Stolen Property: The Need for Reform" (1976) 74 *Mich LR* 1512.

Blom-Cooper, L. and Morris, T., *Fine Lines and Distinctions: Murder, Manslaughter and the Unlawful Taking of Human Life* (Hook: Waterside Press, 2011).

——, *With Malice Aforethought: A Study of the Crime and Punishment for Homicide* (Oxford: Hart Publishing, 2004).

Bluglass, R., "Infanticide" [1978] *Bulletin of the Royal College of Psychiatrists* 14.

Bogart, J.H., "Commodification and Phenomenology: Evading Consent in Theory Regarding Rape" (1996) 2 *Legal Theory* 253.

Bogg, A. and Stanton-Ife, J., "Protecting the Vulnerable: Legality, Harm and Theft" (2003) 23 *Legal Studies* 402.

Bohlander, M., "*In extremis?* Hijacked Airplanes, 'Collateral Damage' and the Limits of the Criminal Law" [2006] *Criminal LR* 579.

——, "Mistaken Sex, Political Correctness and Correct Policy" (2007) 71 *Journal of Criminal Law* 412.

——, "Transferred Malice and Transferred Defenses: A Critique of the Traditional Doctrine and Arguments for a Change in Paradigm" (2010) 13 *New Criminal LR* 555.

——, "The Sexual Offences Act 2003 and the *Tyrrell* Principle—Criminalising the Victims" [2005] *Criminal LR* 701.

Bonnie, R.J., "The Moral Basis of the Insanity Defense" (1983) 69 *American Bar Assoc J* 194.

Bowden, P., "Violence and Mental Disorder" in N. Walker (ed.), *Dangerous People* (London: Blackstone Press, 1996) 13.

Bowley, M., "Talking about Sex" (1999) 149 *New LJ* 1739.

Bowsher, P., "Incest—should incest between consenting adults be a crime?" [2015] *Criminal LR* 208.

Bracton, *De Legibus et Consuetudinibus Angliae* (c. 1235).

Bradley, K., *The Bradley Report: Lord Bradley's Review of People with Mental Health Problems or Learning Disabilities in the Criminal Justice System* (London: Department of Health, 2009).

Brady, J.B., "Abolish the Insanity Defense? No!" (1971) 8 *Houston LR* 629.

Braithwaite, J., *Regulatory Capitalism: How it Works, Ideas for Making it Work Better* (Cheltenham: Edward Elgar, 2008).

Brett, P., "Mistake of Law as a Criminal Defence" (1966) 5 *Melbourne ULR* 179.

——, "Strict Responsibility: Possible Solutions" (1974) 37 *Modern Law Review* 417.

——, "The Physiology of Provocation" [1970] *Criminal LR* 640.

——, *Inquiry into Criminal Guilt* (London: Sweet & Maxwell, 1960).

Broderick, P.A., "Conditional Objectives of Conspiracies" (1985) 94 *Yale LJ* 895.

Bronitt, S., "Defending *Giorgianni*" (1993) 17 *Criminal LJ* 242 and 305.

——, "Spreading Disease and the Criminal Law" [1994] *Criminal LR* 21.

Brudner, A., "A Theory of Necessity" (1987) 7 *Oxford Journal of Legal Studies* 338.

——, "Guilt under the Charter: The Lure of Parliamentary Supremacy" (1998) 40 *Criminal Law Quarterly* 287.

Bruneau, D. and Taylor, A., "In Defence of *Pace and Rogers*" [2015] 8 *Archbold Review* 6.

Buard, J., "'Intent'" [1978] *Criminal LR* 5.

Burn, E.H., *Cheshire and Burn's Modern Law of Real Property* (London: Butterworths, 15th ed., 1994) 165.

Buckland, W., *A Text-book of Roman Law from Augustus to Justinian* (Cambridge: Cambridge University Press, 3d ed., 1963).

Buxton, R., "Being an Accessory to One's Own Murder" [2012] *Criminal LR* 275.

——, "By any Unlawful Act" (1966) 82 *Law Quarterly Review* 174.

——, "Complicity in the Criminal Code" (1969) 85 *Law Quarterly Review* 252.

——, "Joint Enterprise" [2009] *Criminal LR* 233.

——, "Some Simple Thoughts on Intention" [1988] *Criminal LR* 484.

——, "The Human Rights Act and the Substantive Criminal Law" [2000] *Criminal LR* 331.

Cambridge Centre for Public Law, *Constitutional Reform in the United Kingdom. Practice and Principles.* (Oxford: Hart Publishing, 1998).

——, *The Human Rights Act and the Criminal Justice and Regulatory Process* (Oxford: Hart Publishing, 1999).

Camp, P., "Section 69 of the Army Act 1955" [1999] *New LJ* 1736.

Campbell, K., "Conditional Intention" (1982) 2 *Legal Studies* 77.

——, "Offence and Defence" in I. Dennis (ed.), *Criminal Law and Criminal Justice* (London: Sweet & Maxwell, 1987) 73.

——, "The Test of Dishonesty in *R* v. *Ghosh*" [1984] *Cambridge LJ* 349.

Card, R., *Card, Cross and Jones: Criminal Law* (London: Butterworths, 20th ed., 2012).

Carlton, D.W. and Fischel, D.R., "The Regulation of Insider Trading" (1983) 35 *Stanford LR* 857.

Carson, W.G., "Symbolic and Instrumental Dimensions of Early Factory Legislation" in R. Hood (ed.), *Crime, Criminology and Public Policy: Essays in Honour of Sir Leon Radzinowicz* (London: Heinemann Educational, 1974).

——, "The Conventionalisation of Early Factory Crime" (1979) 7 *Int J Soc Law* 37.

Chalmers, J., "'Frenzied Law Making': Overcriminalization by Numbers" (2014) 67 *Current Legal Problems* 483.

Chalmers, J. and Leverick, F., "Fair Labelling in Criminal Law" (2008) 71 *Modern LR* 217.

——, "Quantifying Criminalization" in R.A. Duff *et al.* (eds.), *Criminalization: The Political Morality of the Criminal Law* (Oxford: Oxford University Press, 2015) 54.

——, "Tracking the Creation of Criminal Offences" [2013] *Criminal LR* 543.

Chalmers, J., Leverick, F., and Shaw, M., "Is Formal Criminalization Really on the Rise? Evidence from the 1950s" [2015] *Criminal LR* 177.

Chan, W. and Simester, A.P., "Duress, Necessity: How Many Defences?" (2005) 16 *King's College LJ* 121.

——, "Four Functions of Mens Rea" (2011) 70 *Cambridge LJ* 381.

Chappell, D. and Walsh, M., "'No Questions Asked,' A Consideration of the Crime of Criminal Receiving" (1974) 20 *Crime and Delinquency* 157.

——, "Receiving Stolen Property: The Need for a Systematic Inquiry into the Fencing Process" (1974) 11 *Criminology* 484.

Child, J., "Drink, Drugs and Law Reform: a Review of Law Commission Report No. 314" [2009] *Criminal LR* 488.

——, "The structure, coherence and limits of inchoate liability: the new *ulterior* element" (2014) 34 *Legal Studies* 537.

Child, J. and Sullivan, G.R., "When Does the Insanity Defence Apply? Some Recent Cases" [2014] *Criminal LR* 788.

Choo, A.L.-T., *Abuse of Process and Judicial Stays of Criminal Proceedings* (Oxford: Oxford University Press, 2nd ed., 2008).

Clarkson, C.M.V., "Attempt: The Conduct Requirement" (2009) 29 *Oxford Journal of Legal Studies* 25.

——, "Complicity, *Powell* and Manslaughter" [1998] *Criminal LR* 556.

——, "Corporate Manslaughter: Yet More Government Proposals" [2005] *Criminal LR* 677.

——, "Kicking Corporate Bodies and Damning Their Souls" (1996) 59 *Modern Law Review* 557.

——, "Necessary Action: A New Defence" [2004] *Criminal LR* 81.

——, "Theft and Fair Labelling" (1993) 56 *Modern Law Review* 554.

Clarkson, C.M.V., Cretney, S., Davis, G., and Shepherd, J., "Assaults: the Relationship between Seriousness, Criminalisation and Punishment" [1994] *Criminal LR* 4.

Clarkson, C.M.V. and Cunningham, S. (eds.), *Criminal Liability for Non-aggressive Deaths* (Aldershot: Ashgate, 2008).

—— and Keating, H., *Criminal Law: Text and Materials* (London: Sweet & Maxwell, 6th ed., 2007).

Cobb, N., "Property's Outlaws: Squatting, Land Use and Criminal Trespass" [2012] *Criminal LR* 114.

Coffee, J., "Does 'Unlawful' Mean 'Criminal'?: Reflections on the Disappearing Tort/Crime Distinction in American Law" (1991) 71 *Boston ULR* 193.

——, "No Soul to Damn: No Body to Kick: An Unscandalized Inquiry into the Problem of Corporate Punishment" (1981) 79 *Michigan LR* 386.

Cohen, M.D., "The 'Actus Reus' and Offences of 'Situation'" (1972) 7 *Israel LR* 186.

Coke, E., *Third Institute* (1641).

Coleman, K., Hird, C., and Povey, D., *Violent Crime Overview, Homicide and Gun Crime 2004/05* Home Office Statistical Bulletin 02/06 (London: Home Office, 2006).

Colvin, E., "Criminal Law and the Rule of Law" in P. Fitzgerald (ed.), *Crime, Justice and Codification: Essays in Commemoration of Jacques Fortin* (Toronto: Carswell, 1986) 125.

Committee on Mentally Abnormal Offenders, *Report of the Committee on Mentally Abnormal Offenders* Cmnd. 6244 (London: HMSO, 1975).

Committee on the Penalties for Homicide, *Report on the Penalties for Homicide* Cmnd. 5137 (Edinburgh: HMSO, 1972).

Cooke, R., *Turning Points of the Common Law* (London: Sweet & Maxwell, 1997).

Corrado, M. (ed.), *Justification and Excuse in the Criminal Law: An Anthology* (New York: Garland Publishing, 1994).

Council of Europe, *European Convention on Human Rights, Year: 1974* (Leiden: Martinus Nijhoff, 1976).

Cowan, S., "'Freedom and the Capacity to Make a Choice': a Feminist Analysis of Consent in the Criminal Law of Rape" in V. Munro and C. Stychin (eds.), *Sexuality and the Law: Feminist Engagements* (Abingdon: Routledge-Cavendish, 2007) 51.

Criminal Law Revision Committee, Eleventh Report, *Evidence (General)* Cmnd. 4991 (1971).

——, Fourteenth Report, *Offences Against the Person* Cmnd. 7844 (1980).

——, Fifteenth Report, *Sexual Offences* Cmnd. 9213 (1984).

——, Thirteenth Report, *Section 16 of the Theft Act 1968* Cmnd. 6733 (1977).

——, Eighth Report, *Theft and Related Offences* Cmnd. 2977 (1966).

——, *Working Paper on Section 16 of the Theft Act 1968* (1974).

Cripps, Y., "The Public Interest Defence to the Action for Breach of Confidence and the Law Commission's Proposals on Disclosure in the Public Interest" (1984) 4 *Oxford Journal of Legal Studies* 361.

Cross, J.T., "Protecting Confidential Information under the Criminal Law of Theft and Fraud" (1991) 11 *Oxford Journal of Legal Studies* 264.

Cross, R., "Duress and Aiding and Abetting (A Reply)" (1953) 69 *Law Quarterly Review* 354.

Cross, R. and Jones, P.A., *An Introduction to Criminal Law* (London: Butterworths, 3rd ed., 1953).

Cunningham, S., "Complicating Complicity: Aiding and Abetting Causing Death by Dangerous Driving in *R v Martin*" (2011) 74 *Modern LR* 767.

——, "Has Law Reform Policy been Driven in the Right Direction? How the New Causing Death by Driving Offences are Operating in Practice" [2013] *Criminal LR* 711.

Dan-Cohen, M., "Basic Values and the Victim's State of Mind" (2000) 88 *California LR* 759.

——, *Rights, Persons and Organisations: A Legal Theory for Bureaucratic Society* (Berkeley: University of California Press, 1986).

Davidson, D., *Essays on Actions and Events* (Oxford: Oxford University Press, 1980).

Davies, C.R., "Protection of Intellectual Property—a Myth?" [2004] *Journal of Criminal Law* 398.

Daw, R. and Solomon, A., "Assisted Suicide and Identifying the Public Interest in the Decision to Prosecute" [2010] *Criminal LR* 737.

Delgado, R., "Rotten Social Background: Should the Criminal Law Recognize a Defence of Severe Environmental Deprivation?" (1985) 3 *J Law and Inequality* 9.

Dell, S., *Murder into Manslaughter: The Diminished Responsibility Defence in Practice* (London: Institute of Psychiatry, 1984).

Dempsey, M., "Victimless Conduct and the Volenti Maxim: How Consent Works" (2013) 7 *Criminal Law and Philosophy* 11.

Dempsey, M. and Herring, J., "Why Sexual Penetration Requires Justification" (2007) 27 *Oxford Journal of Legal Studies* 467.

Denning, A.T., *Responsibility Before the Law: A Lecture* (Jerusalem: Magnes Press, 1961).

Dennis, I., "Intention and Complicity: A Reply" [1988] *Criminal LR* 649.

——, "On Necessity as a Defence to Crime: Possibilities, Problems and the Limits of Justification and Excuse" (2009) 3 *Criminal Law and Philosophy* 29.

——, "Reverse Onuses and the Presumption of Innocence: In Search of Principle" [2005] *Criminal LR* 901.

——, "Silence in the Police Station: The Marginalisation of Section 34" [2002] *Criminal LR* 25.

——, "The Criminal Justice and Public Order Act 1994: The Evidence Provisions" [1995] *Criminal LR* 4.

——, "The Law Commission and the Criminal Law: Reflections on the Codification Project" in M. Dyson, J. Lee and S. Stark (eds.), *Fifty Years of the Law Commissions: The Dynamics of Law Reform* (Oxford: Hart Publishing, 2016) 108.

——, "The Rationale of Criminal Conspiracy" (1977) 93 *Law Quarterly Review* 39.

——, "The Mental Element for Accessories" in P. Smith (ed.), *Criminal Law: Essays in Honour of J.C. Smith* (London: Butterworths, 1987) 40.

Department of Health, *Protecting Children, Supporting Parents: A Consultation Document on the Physical Punishment of Children* (London: Department of Health, 2000).

Department of Transport, *mv Herald of Free Enterprise: Report of Court No. 8074* (London: HMSO, 1987).

Devlin, P., "Law, Democracy and Morality" (1962) 110 *Pennsylvania LR* 635, 648.

——, "Mental Abnormality and the Criminal Law" in R.St.J. Macdonald (ed.), *Changing Legal Objectives* (Toronto: Toronto University Press, 1963) 71.

——, *Samples of Lawmaking* (London: Oxford University Press, 1962).

——, *The Enforcement of Morals* (Oxford: Oxford University Press, 1965).

Dickens, B., "Death" in I. Kennedy and A. Grubb (eds.), *Principles of Medical Law* (Oxford: Oxford University Press, 1998) 868.

Dillof, A.M., "Transferred Intent: an Enquiry into the Nature of Criminal Culpability" [1998] *Buffalo Criminal LR* 501.

Dingwall, G., *Alcohol and Crime* (London: Cavendish Publishing, 2005).

Dobson, A., "Shifting Sands: Multiple Counts in Prosecutions for Corporate Manslaughter" [2012] *Criminal LR* 200.

Dressler, J., "Battered Women Who Kill Their Sleeping Tormenters: Reflections on Maintaining Respect for Human Life while Killing Moral Monsters" in S. Shute and A.P. Simester (eds.), *Criminal Law Theory: Doctrines of the General Part* (Oxford: Oxford University Press, 2002) 259.

——, "New Thoughts about the Concept of Justification in the Criminal Law: A Critique of Fletcher's Thinking and Rethinking" (1984) 32 *UCLA LR* 61.

——, "Provocation: Partial Justification or Partial Excuse" (1988) 51 *Modern Law Review* 467.

——, "Reassessing the Theoretical Underpinnings of Accomplice Liability: New Solutions to an Old Problem" (1985) 37 *Hastings LJ* 91.

——, "Reflections on *Dudley and Stephens* and killing the innocent: taking the wrong conceptual path" in D. Baker and J. Horder (eds.), *The Sanctity of Life and the Criminal Law: The Legacy of Glanville Williams* (Cambridge: Cambridge University Press, 2013) 126.

——, "Rethinking Heat of Passion: A Defence in Search of a Rationale" (1982) 73 *J Criminal Law and Criminology*.

Dripps, D., "For a Negative, Normative Model of Consent, with a Comment on Preference-skepticism" (1996) 2 *Legal Theory* 113.

Dsouza, M., "Undermining Prima Facie Consent in the Criminal Law" (2014) 33 *Law and Philosophy* 489.

Dubber, M., "The Possession Paradigm: The Special Part and the Police Power Model of the Criminal Process" in R.A. Duff and S. Green (eds.), *Defining Crimes: Essays on the Special Part of the Criminal Law* (Oxford: Oxford University Press, 2005) 91.

Duff, R.A., "Attempted Homicide" (1995) 1 *Legal Theory* 149.

——, "'Can I Help You?' Accessorial Liability and the Intention to Assist" (1990) 10 *Legal Studies* 165.

——, "Choice, Character and Criminal Liability" (1993) 12 *Law and Philosophy* 345.

——, "Fitness to Plead and Fair Trials" [1994] *Criminal LR* 419.

——, "Harms and Wrongs" (2001) 5 *Buffalo Criminal LR* 13.

——, "Intention Revisited" in D. Baker and J. Horder (eds.), *The Sanctity of Life and the Criminal Law* (Cambridge: Cambridge University Press, 2013) 148.

——, "Intentionally Killing the Innocent" (1973) 34 *Analysis* 16.

——, "Intentions Legal and Philosophical" (1989) 9 *Oxford Journal of Legal Studies* 76.

——, "Professor Williams and Conditional Subjectivism" [1982] *Cambridge LJ* 273.

——, "Subjectivism, Objectivism and Criminal Attempts" in A.P. Simester and A.T.H. Smith (eds.), *Harm and Culpability* (Oxford: Oxford University Press, 1996) 19.

——, "The Circumstances of an Attempt" [1991] *Cambridge LJ* 100.

——, "The Obscure Intentions of the House of Lords" [1986] *Criminal LR* 771.

——, "Towards a Modest Legal Moralism" (2014) 8 *Criminal Law and Philosophy* 217.

——, *Answering for Crime: Responsibility and Liability in the Criminal Law* (Oxford: Hart Publishing, 2007).

——, *Criminal Attempts* (Oxford: Oxford University Press, 1996).

——, *Intention, Agency and Criminal Liability* (Oxford: Blackwell, 1990).

——, *Punishment, Communication and Community* (Oxford: Oxford University Press, 2001).

Duff, R.A. and Garland, D. (eds.), *A Reader on Punishment* (Oxford: Oxford University Press, 1994).

Duff, R.A. and Hirsch, A. von, "Responsibility, Retribution and the 'Voluntary': A Response to Williams" [1997] *Cambridge LJ* 103.

Duff, R.A. and Marshall, S.E., "'Remote Harms' and the Two Harm Principles" in A.P. Simester, A. du Bois-Pedain, and U. Neumann (eds.), *Liberal Criminal Theory: Essays for Andreas von Hirsch* (Oxford: Hart Publishing, 2014) 205.

Dworkin, G., "Paternalism" (1972) 56 *Monist* 65.

——, *The Theory and Practice of Autonomy* (Cambridge: Cambridge University Press, 1988).

Dworkin, R., "Hard Cases" in *Taking Rights Seriously* (London: Duckworth, 1977) 81.

——, *Law's Empire* (London: Fontana Press, 1986).

——, *Life's Dominion: An Argument About Abortion and Euthanasia* (London: HarperCollins, 1993).

Dyson, M., "Scrapping Khan" [2014] *Criminal LR* 445.

Edwards, J., "Duress and Aiding and Abetting" (1953) 69 *Law Quarterly Review* 226.

——, *Mens Rea in Statutory Offences* (London: MacMillan, 1955).

Edwards, J.R., "Harm Principles" (2014) 20 *Legal Theory* 253.

Edwards, S., "The Strangulation of Female Partners" [2015] *Criminal LR* 949.

Eldar, S., "The Limits of Transferred Malice" (2012) 32 *Oxford Journal of Legal Studies* 633.

Elliott, D.W., "Directors' Thefts and Dishonesty" [1991] *Criminal LR* 732.

——, "Dishonesty in Theft: A Dispensable Concept" [1982] *Criminal LR* 395.

——, "Dishonesty under the Theft Act" [1972] *Criminal LR* 625.

——, "Endangering Life by Destroying or Damaging Property" [1997] *Criminal LR* 382.

——, "Frightening a Person into Injuring Himself" [1974] *Criminal LR* 15.

——, "Mens Rea in Statutory Conspiracy" [1978] *Criminal LR* 202.

——, "Necessity, Duress and Self-defence" [1989] *Criminal LR* 611.

Elliott, I.D., "Responsibility for Involuntary Acts: *Ryan v. The Queen*" (1968) 41 *Australian LJ* 497.

Emmerson, B. and Ashworth, A., *Human Rights and Criminal Justice* (London: Sweet & Maxwell, 2001).

Emmerson, B., Ashworth, A., and Macdonald, A., *Human Rights and Criminal Justice* (London: Sweet & Maxwell, 2nd ed., 2007).

Engelhardt, H.T., "The Ontology of Abortion" (1973) 84 *Ethics* 217.

English, P., "What Did Section Three Do to the Law of Provocation?" [1970] *Criminal LR* 249.

Epstein, R., "Property as a Fundamental Civil Right" (1992) 29 *Cal West LR* 187.

Evans, J., *Statutory Interpretation* (Auckland: Oxford University Press, 1988).

Erens, B., McManus, S., Prescott, P., Field, J., Johnson, A., Wellings, K., Fenton, K., Mercer, C., Macdowall, W., Copas, A., and Nanchahal, K., *National Survey of Sexual Attitudes and Lifestyles II: Reference Tables and Summary Report* (London: National Centre for Social Research, 2003).

Farrier, M.D., "The Distinction between Murder and Manslaughter in its Procedural Context" (1976) 39 *Modern Law Review* 415

Fauconnet, P., *La Responsabilité: Étude de Sociologie* (Paris: F. Alcan, 1920).

Feinberg, J., "Action and Responsibility" in M. Black (ed.), *Philosophy in America* (Ithaca: Cornell University Press, 1965) 134.

——, "Harm to Others: A Rejoinder" (1986) *Criminal Justice Ethics* 16.

——, *Harm to Others* (New York: Oxford University Press, 1984).

——, *Harm to Self* (New York: Oxford University Press, 1986).

——, *Harmless Wrongdoing* (New York: Oxford University Press, 1988).

——, *Offense to Others* (New York: Oxford University Press, 1985).

Feldman, D., *Civil Liberties and Human Rights* (Oxford: Oxford University Press, 1993).

Fenwick, H., *Automatism, Medicine and the Law* (Cambridge: Cambridge University Press, Psychological Medicine Monograph 17: 1990).

Finch, E., "The Perfect Stalking Law: An Evaluation of the Efficacy of the Protection from Harassment Act 1997" [2002] *Criminal LR* 702.

——, *The Criminalisation of Stalking: Constructing the Problem and Evaluating the Solution* (London: Cavendish Publishing, 2001).

Finch, E. and Munro, V., "Intoxicated Consent and the Boundaries of Drug Assisted Rape" [2003] *Criminal LR* 773.

——, "The Demon Drink and the Demonized Woman: Socio-sexual Stereotypes and Responsibility Attribution in Rape Trials Involving Intoxicants" (2007) 16 *Social & Legal Studies* 591.

Finkel, N. *et al.*, "Lay Perspectives on Legal Conundrums: Impossible and Mistaken Act Cases" (1995) 19 *Law and Human Behaviour* 593.

Finkelstein, F., "Involuntary Crimes, Voluntarily Committed" in S. Shute and A.P. Simester (eds.), *Criminal Law Theory: Doctrines of the General Part* (Oxford: Oxford University Press, 2000) 143.

Finn, J., "Culpable Non-intervention: Reconsidering the Basis for Party Liability by Omission" (1994) 18 *Criminal LJ* 90.

Finn, P., *Fiduciary Obligations* (Sydney: Law Book Company, 1977).

Finnis, J., "*Bland*: Crossing the Rubicon?" (1993) 109 *Law Quarterly Review* 329.

——, "Intention and Side-effects" in R.G. Frey and C.W. Morris (eds.), *Liability and Responsibility* (Cambridge: Cambridge University Press, 1991) 32.

——, "The Rights and Wrongs of Abortion: a Reply to Judith Jarvis Thomson" (1973) 2 *Philosophy and Public Affairs* 117.

Fisse, B. and Braithwaite, J., "The Allocation of Responsibility for Corporate Crime: Individualism, Collectivism and Accountability" (1988) 11 *Sydney LR* 468.

——, *Corporations, Crime, and Accountability* (Cambridge: Cambridge University Press, 1993).

Fitzgerald, P.G. and Williams, G., "Carelessness, Indifference and Recklessness: Two Replies" (1962) 25 *Modern Law Review* 49.

Fleming, J., *The Law of Torts* (Sydney: Law Book Company, 7th ed., 1987; 8th ed., 1992).

Fletcher, G., "On the Moral Irrelevance of Bodily Movements" (1994) *U Pennsylvania LR* 1443.

——, "The Individualisation of Excusing Conditions" (1974) 47 *Southern California LR* 1269.

——, *Rethinking Criminal Law* (Boston: Little Brown, 1978).

Floud, J. and Young, W., *Dangerousness and Criminal Justice* (London: Heinemann, 1981).

Freckelton, I., "When Plight Makes Right: The Forensic Abuse Syndrome" (1994) 18 *Criminal LJ* 29.

Freedman, D., "Restoring Order to the Reasonable Person Test in the Reference of Provocation" [1998] *King's College LJ* 26.

French, P., "Fishing the Red Herrings out of a Sea of Moral Responsibility" in E. LePore and B.P. McLaughlin (eds.), *Actions and Events: Perspectives on the Philosophy of Donald Davidson* (Oxford: Blackwell, 1985) 73.

——, *Collective and Corporate Responsibility* (New York: Columbia University Press, 1984).

Furmston, M., *Cheshire, Fifoot and Furmston's Law of Contract* (London: Butterworths, 13th ed., 1996).

Galligan, D.J., "The Return to Retribution in Penal Theory" in C. Tapper (ed.), *Crime, Proof and Punishment* (London: Butterworths, 1981) 144.

——, "The Right to Silence Reconsidered" [1988] *Current Legal Problems* 69.

Gardner J., "Complicity and Causality" (2007) 1 *Criminal Law & Philosophy* 127.

——, "Justifications and Reasons" in A.P. Simester and A.T.H. Smith (eds.), *Harm and Culpability* (Oxford: Oxford University Press, 1996) 103.

——, "Rationality and the Rule of Law in Offences against the Person" (1994) 53 *Cambridge LJ* 502.

——, "The Gist of Excuses" (1998) 1 *Buffalo Criminal LR* 575.

——, "Wrongs and Faults" in A.P. Simester (ed.), *Appraising Strict Liability* (Oxford: Oxford University Press, 2005) 51.

——, *Offences and Defences: Selected Essays in the Philosophy of Criminal Law* (Oxford: Oxford University Press, 2007).

Gardner, J. and Macklem T., "Compassion without Respect? Nine Fallacies of *R v Smith*" [2001] *Criminal LR* 623.

——, "Provocation and Pluralism" (2001) 64 *Modern LR* 815.

Gardner, J. and Shute, S., "The Wrongness of Rape" in J. Horder (ed.), *Oxford Essays in Jurisprudence* (4th Series, Oxford: Oxford University Press, 2000) 193.

Gardner, S., "Appreciating *Olugboja*" (1996) 16 *Legal Studies* 275.

——, "Direct Action and the Defence of Necessity" [2005] *Criminal LR* 371.

——, "Is Theft a Rip-off?" (1990) 10 *Oxford Journal of Legal Studies* 441.

——, "Necessity's Newest Inventions" (1991) 11 *Oxford Journal of Legal Studies* 125.

——, "Property and Theft" [1998] *Criminal LR* 35.

——, "Reckless and Inconsiderate Rape" [1991] *Criminal LR* 172.

——, "Stalking" (1998) 114 *Law Quarterly Review* 33.

——, "The Domestic Criminal Legality of the RAF Drone Strike in Syria in August 2015" [2016] *Criminal LR* 35.

——, "The Importance of Majewski" (1994) 14 *Oxford Journal of Legal Studies* 279.

Gearty, C.A., "Reconciling Parliamentary Democracy and Human Rights" (2002) 118 *Law Quarterly Review* 248.

Geddes, L., "On the Intrinsic Wrongness of Killing Innocent People" (1973) 33 *Analysis* 93.

Gentle, S., "The Corporate Offence" [2011] *Criminal LR* 101.

Gibson, M., "Intoxicants and Diminished Responsibility: The Impact of the Coroners and Justice Act 2009" [2011] *Criminal LR* 909.

Giesen, D., *International Medical Malpractice Law* (London: Nijhoff, 1988).

Gill, M., *Commercial Robbery: Offenders' Perspectives on Security and Crime Prevention* (London: Blackstone Press, 2000).

Gillen, M., "Sanctions Against Insider Trading: A Proposal for Reform" (1991) 70 *Canadian Bar Review* 215.

Giles, M., "Judicial Law-making in the Criminal Courts: The Case of Marital Rape" [1992] *Criminal LR* 907.

Giles, M. and Uglow, S., "Appropriation and Manifest Criminality in Theft" (1992) 56 *J Criminal Law* 179.

Giliker, P., *Vicarious Liability in Tort* (Cambridge: Cambridge University Press, 2013).

Gillies, P., "The Offence of Conspiracy to Defraud" (1977) 51 *Australian LJ* 247.

Glaze, C.L., "Combatting Prenatal Substance Abuse: Court Ordered Protective Custody of the Fetus" (1997) 80 *Marquette LR* 793.

Glazebrook, P.R., "A Better Way of Convicting Business of Avoidable Deaths and Injuries" [2002] *Cambridge LJ* 405.

——, "Criminal Omissions: The Duty Requirement in Offences Against the Person" (1960) 76 *Law Quarterly Review* 386.

——, "How Old Did You Think She Was?" (2001) 60 *Cambridge LJ* 26.

——, "Revising the Theft Acts" [1993] *Cambridge LJ* 191.

——, "Situational Liability" in Glazebrook (ed.), *Reshaping the Criminal Law* (London: Sweet & Maxwell, 1978) 108.

——, "Structuring the Criminal Code: Functional Approaches to Complicity, Incomplete Offences and General Defences" in A.P. Simester and A.T.H. Smith (eds.), *Harm and Culpability* (Oxford: Oxford University Press, 1996) 195.

——, "Thief or Swindler: Who Cares?" [1991] *Cambridge LJ* 389.

——, (ed.), *Blackstone's Statutes on Criminal Law* (London: Blackstone Press, 9th ed., 1999).

——, (ed.), *Reshaping the Criminal Law: Essays in Honour of Glanville Williams* (London: Sweet & Maxwell, 1978).

Glover, J., *Causing Death and Saving Lives* (Harmondsworth: Penguin, 1977).

Glover, R., "Can Dishonesty be Salvaged? Theft and the Grounding of the *MSC Napoli*" (2010) 74 *Journal of Criminal Law* 53.

Gobert, J., "Corporate Criminality: New Crimes for the Times" [1994] *Criminal LR* 722.

Gobert, J. and Punch, M., *Rethinking Corporate Crime* (London: Butterworths, 2003).

Goff, R., "The Mental Element in the Crime of Murder" (1988) 104 *Law Quarterly Review* 30.

Goff, R. and Jones, G., *The Law of Restitution* (London: Sweet & Maxwell, 4th ed., 1993).

Goldberg, D. and Huxley, P., *Common Mental Disorders: A Biosocial Model* (London: Tavistock/ Routledge, 1992).

Goldstein, A.S., *The Insanity Defence* (New Haven: Yale University Press, 1967).

Goode, R., "Ownership and Obligation in Commercial Transactions" (1987) 103 *Law Quarterly Review* 433.

——, "Property and Unjust Enrichment" in A. Burrows (ed.), *Essays on the Law of Restitution* (Oxford: Oxford University Press, 1991) 215.

——, "The Right to Trace and Its Impact in Commercial Transactions" (1976) 92 *Law Quarterly Review* 360 and 528.

Goodhart, A.L., "The *Shaw* Case: The Law and Public Morals" (1961) 77 *Law Quarterly Review* 560.

Gordon, G.H., *The Criminal Law of Scotland* (Edinburgh: Green, 2nd ed., 1978).

Gough, S., "Surviving without *Majewski*?" [2002] *Criminal LR* 719.

Gray, K., "Property in Thin Air" [1991] 50 *Cambridge LJ* 252.

Gray, O., "The Standard of Care for Children Revisited" (1980) 45 *Missouri LR* 597.

Greaves, C.S., *The Criminal Law Consolidation and Amendment Acts of the 24 & 25 Vict. with Notes, Observations, and Forms for Summary Proceedings* (London: V. & R. Stevens, 2nd ed., 1862).

Green, S., "Theft and Conversion" (2012) 128 *Law Quarterly Review* 564.

Greenawalt, K., "The Perplexing Borders of Justification and Excuse" (1984) 84 *Columbia LR* 1897.

Grey, "The Disintegration of Property" in *NOMOS xxii: Property* (1980) 69.

Griew, E., "Consistency, Communication and Codification—Reflections on Two Mens Rea Words" in P.R. Glazebrook (ed.), *Reshaping the Criminal Law* (London: Sweet & Maxwell, 1978) 57.

——, "Dishonesty: The Objections to Feely and Ghosh" [1985] *Criminal LR* 341.

——, "Reckless Damage and Reckless Driving: Living with *Caldwell* and *Lawrence*" [1981] *Criminal LR* 743.

——, "Stealing and Obtaining Bank Credits" [1986] *Criminal LR* 356.

Gross, H., "Rape, Moralism and Human Rights" [2007] *Criminal LR* 220.

——, *A Theory of Criminal Justice* (New York: Oxford University Press, 1979).

Grubb, A., "Treatment Decisions: Keeping it in the Family" in A. Grubb (ed.), *Choices and Decisions in Health Care* (Chichester: Wiley, 1993) 37.

Grubb, A., Laing, J. and McHale, J.V. (eds.), *Principles of Medical Law* (Oxford: Oxford University Press, 3rd ed., 2010).

Grubin, D., "What Constitutes Fitness to Plead" [1998] *Criminal LR* 748.

Gunby C., et al, "Alcohol-related Rape Cases: Barristers Perspectives on the Sexual Offences Act 2003 and its Impact on Practice" (2010) 74 *Journal of Criminal Law* 579.

Gunn, M.J. and Ormerod, D., "The Legality of Boxing" (1995) 15 *Legal Studies* 181.

Hadden, T.B., "Conspiracy to Defraud" [1966] *Cambridge LJ* 248.

——, "Fraud in the City: The Role of the Criminal Law" [1983] *Criminal LR* 500.

Hall, J., "Negligent Behaviour Should Be Excluded from Penal Liability" (1963) 63 *Columbia LR* 632.

——, *General Principles of Criminal Law* (Indianapolis: Bobbs-Merrill, 2nd ed., 1960).

——, *Theft, Law and Society* (Indianapolis: Bobbs-Merrill, 2nd ed., 1952).

Hall, L., "Strict or Liberal Construction of Penal Statutes" (1935) 48 *Harvard LR* 748.

Hall, L. and Seligman, S.J., "Mistake of Law and Mens Rea" (1940–41) 8 *U Chicago LR* 641.

Halpin, A., "The Appropriate Appropriation" [1991] *Criminal LR* 426.

——, "The Test for Dishonesty" [1996] *Criminal LR* 283.

——, *Definition in the Criminal Law* (Oxford: Hart Publishing, 2004).

Hampton, J., "Mens Rea" in E.F. Paul, F.D. Miller, and J. Paul (eds.), *Crime, Culpability and Remedy* (Oxford: Blackwell, 1990) 1.

Handler, P., "Intoxication and Criminal Responsibility in England, 1819–1920" (2013) 33 *Oxford Journal of Legal Studies* 243.

Hanink, J.G., "Some Light on Double Effect" (1975) 35 *Analysis* 147.

Harlow, C., "Self-defence: Public Right or Private Privilege" [1974] *Criminal LR* 528.

Harris, D.J., O'Boyle, M., Bates, E., and Bockley, C., *Harris, O'Boyle, and Warbrick: Law of the European Convention on Human Rights* (Oxford: Oxford University Press, 3rd ed., 2014).

Harris, D.R., "The Concept of Possession in English Law" in A. Guest (ed.), *Oxford Essays in Jurisprudence* (Oxford: Oxford University Press, 1961) 69.

Harris, J., *Property and Justice* (Oxford: Oxford University Press, 1996).

Harris, J. and Grace, S., *A Question of Evidence? Investigating and Prosecuting Rape in the 1990's* Home Office Research Study No. 196 (London: Home Office, 1999).

Hart, H.L.A., "Definition and Theory in Jurisprudence" (1954) 70 *Law Quarterly Review* 37.

——, *Law, Liberty and Morality* (Oxford: Oxford University Press, 1963).

——, *Punishment and Responsibility* (Oxford: Oxford University Press, 1968); 2nd ed. edited by J. Gardner (Oxford: Oxford University Press, 2008).

Hart, H.L.A. and Honoré, A.M., *Causation in the Law* (Oxford: Oxford University Press, 2nd ed., 1985)

Hawkins, K., *Environment and Enforcement: Regulation and the Social Definition of Pollution* (Oxford: Oxford University Press, 1984).

——, *Law as Last Resort: Prosecution Decision-Making in a Regulating Agency* (Oxford: Oxford University Press, 2003).

Heaton, R., "Cheques and Balances" [2005] *Criminal LR* 747.

——, "Deceiving without Thieving" [2001] *Criminal LR* 712.

Herring, J., "Consent in the Criminal Law: The Importance of Relationality and Responsibility" in A. Reed and M. Bohlander (eds.), *General Defences in Criminal Law: Domestic and Comparative Perspectives* (Aldershot: Ashgate, 2014) 63.

——, "Familial Homicide, Failure to Protect and Domestic Violence—Who's the Victim?" [2007] *Criminal LR* 923.

——, "Human Rights and Rape: A Reply to Hyman Gross" [2007] *Criminal LR* 228.

——, "Mistaken Sex" [2005] *Criminal LR* 511.

——, Rape and the Definition of Consent" (2014) 26 *National Law School of India Review* 62.

——, "The Duty of Care in Gross Negligence Manslaughter" [2007] *Criminal LR* 24.

Heuston, R.F.V. and Buckley, R.A., *Salmond and Heuston on the Law of Torts* (London: Sweet & Maxwell, 20th ed., 1992).

Heydon, J.D., "The Corroboration of Accomplices" [1973] *Criminal LR* 264.

——, "The Problems of Entrapment" [1973] *Cambridge LJ* 268.

Hirsch, A. von, "Extending the Harm Principle: 'Remote' Harms and Fair Imputation" in A.P. Simester and A.T.H. Smith (eds.), *Harm and Culpability* (Oxford: Oxford University Press, 1996) 259.

——, "The Offence Principle in Criminal Law: Affront to Sensibility or Wrongdoing?" (2000) 11 *King's College LJ* 78.

——, *Censure and Sanctions* (Oxford: Oxford University Press, 1993).

——, *Doing Justice: the Choice of Punishments* (New York: Hill and Wang, 1976).

Hirsch, A. von and Ashworth, A. (eds.), *Principles of Sentencing: Readings on Theory and Policy* (Oxford: Hart Publishing, 2nd ed., 1998).

Hirsch, A. von, Garland, D. and Wakefield, A. (eds.), *Ethical and Social Perspectives on Situational Crime Prevention* (Oxford: Hart Publishing, 2004).

Hirsch, A. von and Jareborg, N., "Gauging Criminal Harm: A Living-sStandard Analysis" (1991) 11 *Oxford Journal of Legal Studies*, 1.

Hirsch, A. von and Simester, A.P. (eds.), *Incivilities: Regulating Offensive Behaviour* (Oxford: Hart Publishing, 2006).

Hirsch, A. von *et al.*, *Criminal Deterrence and Sentencing Severity: An Analysis of Recent Research* (Oxford: Hart Publishing, 1999).

Hirst, M., "Assault, Battery and Indirect Violence" [1999] *Criminal LR* 577.

——, "Causing Death by Driving and Other Offences" [2008] *Criminal LR* 339.

——, "Guilty; But of What?" (2000) 4 *International Journal of Evidence and Proof* 31.

Ho, H.L., "State Entrapment" (2010) 31 *Legal Studies* 71.

Hodge, J., "Alcohol and Violence" in P. Taylor (ed.), *Violence in Society* (London: Royal College of Physicians of London, 1993) 127.

Hofmeyr, K., "The Problem of Private Entrapment [2006] *Criminal LR* 133.

Hogan, B., "The Criminal Attempts Act and Attempting the Impossible" [1984] *Criminal LR* 584.

——, "Modernising the Law of Sexual Offences" in P. Glazebrook (ed.), *Reshaping the Criminal Law* (London: Sweet & Maxwell, 1978) 174.

——, "The *Dadson* Principle" [1989] *Criminal LR* 679.

——, "Victims as Parties to Crime" [1962] *Criminal LR* 683.

Hogg, P.W., *Constitutional Law of Canada* (Scarborough, Ontario: Carswell, 4th ed., 1997).

Hohfeld, W.N., *Fundamental Legal Conceptions as Applied in Judicial Reasoning* (New Haven: Yale University Press, 1919).

Home Office, *Consultation on the Possession of Non-photographic Visual Depictions of Child Sexual Abuse* (London: Home Office, 2007).

——, *Corporate Manslaughter: The Government's Draft Bill for Reform* Cmnd. 6497 (London: The Stationery Office, 2005).

——, *Criminal Statistics, England and Wales 1996* Cmnd. 3764 (London: Stationery Office, 1997).

——, *Fraud Law Reform: Consultation on Proposals for Legislation* (London: Home Office, 2004).

——, *Managing Dangerous People with Severe Personality Disorder: Proposals for Policy Development* (London: Home Office, 1999).

——, *Protecting the Public-Strengthening Protection against Sex Offenders and Reforming the Law on Sexual Offences* Cmnd. 5668 (London: Home Office, 2002).

——, *Racial Violence and Harassment: A Consultation Document* (London: Home Office, 1997).

——, *Reforming the Law on Involuntary Manslaughter: The Government's Proposals* (London: Home Office, 2000).

——, *Report of the Committee on Homosexual Offences and Prostitution* (Wolfenden Report) Cmnd. 247 (London: Home Office, 1957).

——, *Setting the Boundaries—Reforming the Law on Sex Offenders* (London: Home Office, 2000).

——, *Stalking the Solutions: A Consultation Paper* (London: Home Office, 1996).

——, *Violence: Reforming the Offences against the Person Act 1861* (London: Home Office, 1998).

Home Office and Department of Health and Social Security, *Interdepartmental Working Group into Mentally Disturbed Offenders in the Prison System* (London: Home Office, 1987).

Honoré, A.M., "Necessary and Sufficient Conditions in Tort Law" in D. Owen (ed.), *Philosophical Foundations of Tort Law* (Oxford: Oxford University Press, 1995) 363.

——, "Ownership" in A. Guest (ed.), *Oxford Essays in Jurisprudence* (Oxford: Oxford University Press, 1961) 107.

——, "Responsibility and Luck: The Moral Basis of Strict Liability" (1988) 104 *Law Quarterly Review* 530.

Hooper, M., "The Impact of the Human Rights Act on Judicial Decision-making" [1998] *European Human Rights Law Review* 676.

Hope, Lord, "Tailoring the Law on Vicarious Liability" (2013) 129 *Law Quarterly Review* 514.

Horder, J., "A Critique of the Correspondence Principle in Criminal Law" [1995] *Criminal LR* 759.

——, "Cognition, Emotion and Criminal Culpability" (1990) 106 *Law Quarterly Review* 469.

——, "Crimes of Ulterior Intent" in A.P. Simester and A.T.H. Smith (eds.), *Harm and Culpability* (Oxford: Oxford University Press, 1996) 153.

——, "Criminal Law: Between Determinism, Liberalism, and Criminal Justice" (1996) 49 *CLP* 159.

——, "Gross Negligence and Criminal Culpability" (1997) 47 *U Toronto LJ* 495.

——, "Harmless Wrongdoing and the Anticipatory Perspective on Criminalisation" in Sullivan and Dennis (eds.), *Seeking Security: Pre-empting the Commission of Criminal Harms* (2012) 79.

——, "How Culpability Can, and Cannot, Be Denied in Under-age Sex Crimes" [2001] *Criminal LR* 15.

——, "Occupying the Moral High Ground? The Law Commission on Duress" [1994] *Criminal LR* 343.

——, "Pleading Involuntary Lack of Capacity" [1993] *Cambridge LJ* 298.

——, "Questioning the Correspondence Principle—A Reply" [1999] *Criminal LR* 206.

——, "Reconsidering Psychic Assault" [1998] *Criminal LR* 392.

——, "Re-shaping the Subjective Element in the Provocation Defence" (2005) 25 *Oxford Journal of Legal Studies* 123.

——, "Rethinking Non-fatal Offences against the Person (1994) 14 *Oxford Journal of Legal Studies* 335.

——, "Strict Liability, Statutory Construction, and the Spirit of Liberty" (2002) 118 *Law Quarterly Review* 458.

——, "Transferred Malice and the Remoteness of Unexpected Outcomes from Intentions" [2006] *Criminal LR* 383.

——, "Two Histories and Four Hidden Principles of Mens Rea" (1997) 113 *Law Quarterly Review* 95.

——, "Whose Values Should Determine When Liability Is Strict?" in A.P. Simester (ed.), *Appraising Strict Liability* (Oxford: Oxford University Press, 2005) 105.

——, *Excusing Crime* (Oxford: Oxford University Press, 2004).

——, *Provocation and Responsibility* (Oxford: Oxford University Press, 1992).

Horder, J. and McGowan, L., "Manslaughter by Causing Another's Suicide" [2006] *Criminal LR* 1035.

Hörnle, T., "Hijacked Planes: May They Be Shot Down?" (2007) 10 *New Criminal LR* 582.

House of Commons Defence Committee, *Defence and Security in the UK: Sixth Report of Session 2001–02* HC 518 (London: TSO, 2002).

House of Lords, *Report of the Select Committee on Murder and Life Imprisonment* (Session 1988–89) HL Paper 78 (London: HMSO, 1989).

Howard, C., "Strict Responsibility in the High Court of Australia" (1960) 76 *Law Quarterly Review* 547.

——, *Strict Responsibility* (London: Sweet & Maxwell, 1963).

Howarth, W., "Handling Stolen Goods and Handling Salmon" [1987] *Criminal LR* 460.

Hudson, A.H., "Abandonment" in N. Palmer and E. McKendrick (eds.), *Interests in Goods* (London: LLP, 1993) 423.

——, "Is Divesting Abandonment Possible at Common Law?" (1984) 100 *Law Quarterly Review* 110.

Hughes, G., "Criminal Omissions" (1958) 67 *Yale LJ* 590.

Hume, D., *A Treatise of Human Nature* (Oxford: Oxford University Press, Selby-Bigge and Nidditch, eds., 2nd ed., 1978).

Hurd, H., "The Moral Magic of Consent" (1996) 2 *Legal Theory* 121, 165.

Husak, D.N., "Conflicts of Justifications" (1999) 18 *Law and Philosophy* 41.

——, "Does Criminal Liability Require an Act" in R.A. Duff (ed.), *Philosophy and Criminal Law* (Cambridge: Cambridge University Press, 1998) 60.

——, "*Malum Prohibitum* and Retributivism" in R.A. Duff and S. Green (eds.), *Defining Crimes: Essays on the Special Part of the Criminal Law* (Oxford: Oxford University Press, 2005) 65.

——, "On the Supposed Priority of Justification to Excuse" (2005) 24 *Law and Philosophy* 557.

——, "Recreational Drugs and Paternalism" (1989) 8 *Law and Philosophy* 353

——, "The Nature and Justifiability of Nonconsumate Offences" (1995) 37 *Arizona LR* 151.

——, "Transferred Intent" (1996) 10 *Notre Dame Journal of Legal Ethics and Public Policy* 65.

——, *Overcriminalization: The Limits of the Criminal Law* (New York: Oxford University Press, 2008).

——, *Philosophy of the Criminal Law* (New Jersey: Rowman and Littlefield, 1987).

Husak, D. and von Hirsch, A., "Culpability and Mistake of Law" in S. Shute, J. Gardner and J. Horder (eds.), *Action and Value in Criminal Law* (Oxford: Oxford University Press, 1993) 157.

Hutchinson, A.C., "Sault Ste. Marie, Mens Rea and the Halfway House: Public Welfare Offences Get a Home of Their Own" (1979) 17 *Osgoode Hall LJ* 415.

Hutter, B., *The Reasonable Arm of the Law Law? The Law Enforcement Procedures of Environmental Health Officers* (Oxford: Oxford University Press, 1988).

Huxtable, R., "Separation of the Conjoined Twin: Where Next for English Law?" [2002] *Criminal LR* 549.

Jackson, B.S., "*Storkwain*: A Case Study in Strict Liability and Self-regulation" [1991] *Criminal LR* 892.

Jackson, J., "Curtailing the Right to Silence: Lessons from Northern Ireland" [1991] *Criminal LR* 404.

James Jr, F., "The Qualities of the Reasonable Man in Negligence Cases" (1951) 16 *Missouri LR* 1.

Jareborg, N., "What Kind of Criminal Law Do We Want" in A. Snare (ed.), *Scandinavian Studies in Criminology* vol. 14 (Oslo: Pax Forlag A/S, 1995) 17.

Jarvis, P., "Conspiracy to defraud: a siren to lure unwary prosecutors" [2014] *Criminal LR* 738.

Jarvis, P. and Bisgrove, M., "The Use and Abuse of Conspiracy' [2014] *Criminal LR* 261.

Jeffries, J.C., "Legality, Vagueness, and the Construction of Penal Statutes" (1985) 71 *Virginia LR* 189.

Jeffries, J.C. and Stephan, P.B., "Defences, Presumptions, and Burden of Proof in the Criminal Law" (1979) 88 *Yale LJ* 1325.

Johnson, R., "The Unnecessary Crime of Conspiracy" (1973) 61 *California LR* 1137.

Jones, G., "Unjust Enrichment and the Fiduciary's Duty of Loyalty" (1968) 84 *Law Quarterly Review* 472.

Jones, T.H., "Causation, Homicide and the Supply of Drugs" (2006) 26 *Legal Studies* 139.

——, "Insanity, Automatism and the Burden of Proof on the Accused" (1995) 111 *Law Quarterly Review* 475.

Jos, P.H., Marshall, M.F., and Perlmutter, M., "The Charleston Policy on Cocaine Use during Pregnancy: A Cautionary Tale" (1995) 23 *J Law, Medicine and Ethics* 120.

JUSTICE, *Breaking the Rules: the Problem of Crimes and Contraventions* (London: JUSTICE, 1980).

Kadish, S., "Some Observations on the Use of Criminal Sanctions in Enforcing Economic Regulations" (1963) 30 *U Chicago LR* 423.

——, *Blame and Punishment* (New York: MacMillan, 1987).

Kant, *Groundwork of the Metaphysics of Morals* (1785).

Kaufman, R.M., "Legal Recognition of Independent Fetal Rights: The Trend towards Criminalizing Prenatal Maternal Conduct" (1997) 17 *Children's Legal Rights J* 20.

Kean, A.W.G., "The History of the Criminal Liability of Children" (1937) 53 *Law Quarterly Review* 364.

Keating, H., "Protecting or Punishing Children: Physical Punishment, Human Rights and English Law Reform" (2006) 26 *Legal Studies* 394.

Keedy, E.R., "Ignorance and Mistake in the Criminal Law" (1908) 22 *Harvard LR* 75.

Kell, D., "Social Disutility and the Law of Consent" (1994) 14 *Oxford Journal of Legal Studies* 121.

Kelman, M., "Interpretative Contraction in the Substantive Criminal Law" (1981) 33 *Stanford LR* 591.

Kennedy, I.M., "Switching Off Life Support Machines: The Legal Implications" [1977] *Criminal LR* 443.

Kenny, A., "Intention and Purpose in Law" in R.S. Summers (ed.), *Essays in Legal Philosophy* (London: Blackwells, 1968) 146.

Kenny, C.S., *Outlines of the Criminal Law* (Cambridge: Cambridge University Press, 1902; 2nd ed., 1904; 14th ed., 1932).

Kentridge, S., "The Incorporation of the European Convention on Human Rights" in Cambridge Centre for Public Law, *Constitutional Reform in the United Kingdom: Practice and Principles* (Oxford: Hart Publishing, 1998) 69.

Keown, J., "Restoring Moral and Intellectual Shape to the Law after *Bland*" (1997) 113 *Law Quarterly Review* 481.

Kleinig, J., "Crime and the Concept of Harm" (1978) *American Philosophical Quarterly* 27.

——, *Paternalism* (Manchester: Manchester University Press, 1983).

Klockars, C.B., *The Professional Fence* (New York: Free Press, 1974).

Koffman, L., "The Nature of Appropriation" [1982] *Criminal LR* 331.

——, "The Rise and Fall of Proportionality: The Failure of the Criminal Justice Act 1991" [2006] *Criminal LR* 281.

Krebs, B., "Joint Criminal Enterprise" [2010] 73 *Modern LR* 578.

Kremnitzer, M., "Interpretation in Criminal Law" [1986] 21 *Israel LR* 358.

Kugler, I., *Direct and Oblique Intention in the Criminal Law: An Inquiry into Degrees of Blameworthiness* (Aldershot: Ashgate, 2002).

Lacey, N., "Beset by Boundaries: The Home Office Review of Sex Offenders" [2001] *Criminal LR* 3.

Laird, K., "Rapist or Rogue? Deception, Consent and the Sexual Offences Act 2003" [2014] *Criminal LR* 492.

Lamond, G., "Coercion, Threats, and the Puzzle of Blackmail" in A.P. Simester and A.T.H. Smith (eds.), *Harm and Culpability* (Oxford: Oxford University Press, 1996) 215.

——, "What Is a Crime?" (2007) 27 *Oxford Journal of Legal Studies* 609.

Lanham, D.J., "Accomplices and Withdrawal" (1981) 97 *Law Quarterly Review* 575.

——, "Complicity, Concert and Conspiracy" (1980) 4 *Criminal LJ* 276.

——, "Drivers, Control, and Accomplices" [1982] *Criminal LR* 419.

——, "Duress and Void Contracts" (1966) 29 *Modern Law Review* 615.

——, "Larsonneur Revisited" [1976] *Criminal LR* 276.

——, "Primary and Derivative Criminal Liability: An Australian Perspective" [2000] *Criminal LR* 707.

——, "Wilful Blindness and the Criminal Law" (1985) 9 *Criminal LJ* 261.

Lavoie, J., "Ownership of Human Tissue: Life after *Moore* v. *Regents of the University of California*" [1989] 75 *Virginia LR* 1363.

Law Commission, No. 177, *A Criminal Code for England and Wales* (London: HMSO, 1989).

——, Consultation Paper No. 177, *A New Homicide Act for England and Wales?* (London: HMSO, 2006).

——, Consultation Paper No. 131, *Assisting and Encouraging Crime* (London: HMSO, 1993).

——, No. 102, *Attempt and Impossibility in Relation to Attempt, Conspiracy and Incitement* (London: HMSO, 1980).

——, No. 143, *Codification of the Criminal Law* (London: HMSO, 1985).

——, Consultation Paper No. 139, *Consent in the Criminal Law* (London: HMSO, 1995).

——, Consultation Paper No. 183, *Conspiracy and Attempts* (London: HMSO, 2007).

——, No. 318, *Conspiracy and Attempts* (London: HMSO, 2009).

——, No. 76, *Conspiracy and Criminal Law Reform* (London: HMSO, 1976).

——, Consultation Paper No. 195, *Criminal Liability in Regulatory Contexts* (London: HMSO, 2010).

——, *Criminal Liability: Insanity and Automatism. A Discussion Paper* (London: HMSO, 2013).

——, No. 83, *Defences of General Application* (London: HMSO, 1977).

——, No. 89, *Draft Criminal Liability (Mental Element) Bill* (London: HMSO, 1978).

——, No. 273, *Evidence of Bad Character in Criminal Proceedings* (London: HMSO, 2001).

——, No. 276, *Fraud* (London: HMSO, 2002)

——, Consultation Paper No. 155, *Fraud and Deception* (London: HMSO, 1999).

——, No. 348, *Hate Crime: Should the Current Offences be Extended?* (London: HMSO, 2014).

——, No. 10, *Imported Criminal Intent (Director of Public Prosecutions v. Smith)* (London: HMSO, 1967).

——, No. 300, *Inchoate Liability for Assisting and Encouraging Crime* (London: HMSO, 2006).

——, *Insanity and Automatism: A Discussion Paper* (London: HMSO, 2013).

——, *Insanity and Automatism: A Scoping Paper* (London: HMSO, 2012).

——, No. 314, *Intoxication and Criminal Liability* (London: HMSO, 2009).

——, No. 180, *Jurisdiction over Offences of Fraud and Dishonesty with a Foreign Element* (London: HMSO, 1989).

——, Consultation Paper No. 155, *Legislating the Criminal Code: Fraud and Deception* (London: HMSO, 1999).

——, No. 237, *Legislating the Criminal Code: Involuntary Manslaughter* (London: HMSO, 1996).

——, Consultation Paper No. 122, *Legislating the Criminal Code: Offences against the Person and General Principles* (London: HMSO, 1992).

——, No. 218, *Legislating the Criminal Code: Offences against the Person and General Principles* (London: HMSO, 1993).

——, Working Paper No. 23, "Malicious Damage" (London: HMSO, 1969).

——, No. 304, *Murder, Manslaughter and Infanticide* (London: HMSO, 2006).

——, No. 290, *Partial Defences to Murder* (London: HMSO, 2004).

——, No. 305, *Participation in Crime* (London: HMSO, 2007).

——, No. 302, *Post-legislative Scrutiny* Law Com. (London: HMSO, 2006).

——, No. 316, *Reform of Offences against the Person* (London: HMSO, 2015).

——, No. 55, *Report on Forgery and Counterfeit Currency* (London: HMSO, 1973).

——, No. 29, *Report on Offences of Damage to Property* (London: HMSO, 1970).

——, No. 364, *Unfitness to Plead* (London: HMSO, 2016).

——, Consultation Paper No. 197, *Unfitness to Plead* (London: HMSO, 2010).

Lazarus, L., "Positive Obligations and Criminal Justice: Duties to Protect or Coerce?" in L. Zedner and J. Roberts (eds.), *Principles and Values in Criminal Law and Criminal Justice: Essays in Honour of Andrew Ashworth* (Oxford: Oxford University Press, 2012) 135.

Leavens, A., "A Causative Approach to Omissions" (1988) 76 *California LR* 547.

Lederman, E., "Models for Imposing Corporate Criminal Liability: From Adaptation and Imitation Toward Aggregation and the Search for Self-identity" (2001) 4 *Buffalo Criminal LR* 642.

Leigh, L.H., "Some Remarks on Appropriation in the Law of Theft after *Morris*" (1985) 48 *Modern Law Review* 167.

——, *Strict and Vicarious Liability: A Study in Administrative Criminal Law* (London: Sweet & Maxwell, 1982).

Leipold, A., "A Case for Criminal Negligence" (2010) 29 *Law and Philosophy* 455.

Lenckner, T., "The Principle of Interest Balancing as a General Basis of Justification" in A. Eser and G. Fletcher (eds.), *Justification and Excuse: Comparative Perspectives* (Freiburg: Max Planck Institut, 1987) vol. 1, 493.

Leverick, F., "Is English Self-defence Law Incompatible with Article 2 of the ECHR?" [2002] *Criminal LR* 347.

——, "The Use of Force in Public and Private Defence and Article 2: A Reply to Professor Smith" [2002] *Criminal LR* 963.

——, *Killing in Self-defence* (Oxford: Oxford University Press, 2006).

Levi, M., "Fraud Trials in Perspective" [1984] *Criminal LR* 384.

——, *Regulating Fraud: White-collar Crime and the Criminal Process* (London: Tavistock, 1987) 15.

Lewis, D., "The Punishment that Leaves Something to Chance" (1989) 18 *Philosophy and Public Affairs* 53.

Lipscombe, S., *Householders and the Criminal Law of Self-defence* House of Commons Library Standard Note SN/HA/2959 (London, 2013).

List, C. and Pettit, P., *Group Agency: The Possibility, Design and Status of Corporate Agents* (Oxford: Oxford University Press, 2011).

Livermore, J.M. and Meehl, P.E., "The Virtues of M'Naghten" (1967) 51 *Minnesota LR* 789.

Locke, J., *Two Treatises of Civil Government* (New York: Dutton, 1924).

Loughnan, A., "The 'Strange' Case of the Infanticide Doctrine (2012) 32 *Oxford Journal of Legal Studies* 685.

Loveless, J., "*R v GAC*: Battered Woman 'Syndromization'" [2014] *Criminal LR* 655.

Low, P., Jeffries, J., and Bonnie, R., *Criminal Law: Cases and Materials* (New York: Foundation Press, 2nd ed., 1986).

Lowry, D.R., "The Blind and the Law of Tort" (1972) 20 *Chittys LJ* 253.

Lucas, J.R., "The Philosophy of the Reasonable Man" (1963) 13 *Philosophical Quarterly* 97.

Lucraft, M., Payne, T., and Rawlings, D., "The Dunlop Three: the Cartel Offence Makes its Debut" [2006] 1 *Archbold News* 7.

Lynch, A.C.E., "The Mental Element in the Actus Reus" (1982) 98 *Law Quarterly Review* 109.

McBain, G., "Abolishing Obsolete Legislation on Crimes and Criminal Procedure" (2011) 31 *Legal Studies* 96.

McColgan, A., "In Defence of Battered Women Who Kill" (1993) 130 *J Law and Society* 508.

MacCormick, D.N. and Summers, R.S. (eds.), *Interpreting Statutes: a Comparative Study* (Aldershot: Dartmouth, 1991).

Macdonald, S., "A Suicidal Woman, Roaming Pigs and a Noisy Trampolinist: Refining the ASBO's Definition of 'Anti-social Behaviour'" (2006) 69 *Modern LR* 183.

MacEwan, J., "Murder by Design: The Feel-good Factor and the Criminal Law" [2001] *Medical LR* 246.

MacEwan, N., "The New Stalking Offences in English Law: Will they Provide Effective Protection from Cyberstalking?" [2012] *Criminal LR* 767.

Macrory, R., *Regulatory Justice: Sanctioning in a Post-Hampton World* (London: Cabinet Office, 2006).

McGee, A., "Finding a Way through the Ethical and Legal Maze: Withdrawal of Medical Treatment and Euthanasia" [2005] *Medical LR* 357.

MacKay, R.D., "Intoxication as a Factor in Automatism" [1982] *Criminal LR* 146.

——, "On Being Insane in Jersey Part Two: The Appeal in *Jason Prior v Attorney General*" [2002] *Criminal LR* 728.

——, "On Being Insane in Jersey Part Three: The Case of the *Attorney General v O'Driscoll*" [2004] *Criminal LR* 219.

——, "Pleading Provocation and Diminished Responsibility Together" [1988] *Criminal LR* 411.

——, "Post-Hinkley Insanity in the USA" [1988] *Criminal LR* 88.

——, "Righting the Wrong?—Some Observations on the Second Limb of the M'Naghten Rules" [2009] *Criminal LR* 80.

——, "Sleepwalking, Automatism and Insanity" [2006] *Criminal LR* 901.

——, "Ten More Years of the Insanity Defence" [2012] *Criminal LR* 946.

——, "The Abnormality of Mind Factor in Diminished Responsibility" [1999] *Criminal LR* 117.

——, "The Consequences of Killing Very Young Children" [1993] *Criminal LR* 21.

——, "The New Diminished Responsibility Plea" [2010] *Criminal LR* 290.

——, "The Trial of the Facts and Unfitness to Plead" [1997] *Criminal LR* 644.

——, *Mental Condition Defences in the Criminal Law* (Oxford: Oxford University Press, 1995).

Mackay, R.D. and Gearty, C., "On Being Insane in Jersey: The Case of *Attorney General v Jason Prior*" [2001] *Criminal LR* 560.

Mackay, R.D. and Kearns, G., "More Fact(s) about the Insanity Defence" [1999] *Criminal LR* 714.

——, "The Continued Underuse of Unfitness to Plead and the Insanity Defence" [1994] *Criminal LR* 576.

Mackay, R.D. and Mitchell, B.J., "But Is this Provocation? Some Thoughts on the Law Commission's Report on Partial Defences to Murder" [2005] *Criminal LR* 44.

Mackie, J.L., "Causes and Conditions" in E. Sosa (ed.), *Causation and Conditionals* (London: Oxford University Press, 1975) 15.

Maclean, A.R., "Resurrection of the Body Snatchers" (2000) 150 *NLJ* 174.

Macklem, T. and Gardner J., "Provocation and Pluralism" (2001) 64 *Modern LR* 815.

Maier-Katkin, D. and Ogle, R., "A Rationale for Infanticide Laws" [1993] *Criminal LR* 903.

Manchester, C., "Knowledge, Due Diligence and Strict Liability in Regulatory Offences" [2006] *Criminal LR* 213.

Mandil, D.M., "Chance, Freedom and Criminal Liability" (1987) 87 *California LR* 125.

Mann, K., "Punitive Civil Sanctions: The Middle Ground between Criminal and Civil Law" (1992) 101 *Yale LJ* 1795.

Mannheim, H., "Mens Rea in German and English Criminal Law" (1935) 17 *J Comparative Legislation* 82, 236, and (1936) 18 *J Comparative Legislation* 78.

Marcus, P., "Criminal Conspiracy Law: Time to Turn Back from an Ever Expanding, Ever More Troubling Area" (1992) 1 *William and Mary Bill of Rights J* 1.

——, "The Criminal Agreement in Theory and in Practice (1977) 65 *Georgetown LJ* 925.

Marshall, A., *Principles of Economics* (New York: Macmillan, 8th ed., 1947).

Marshall, B., Webb, B., and Tilley, N., *Rationalisation of Current Research on Guns, Gangs and Other Weapons: Phase 1* (London: University College, 2005).

Marston, G., "Contemporaneity of Act and Intention in Crimes" [1970] 86 *Law Quarterly Review* 208.

Mason, J.K., *Forensic Medicine for Lawyers* (London: Butterworths, 3rd ed., 1995).

Mason, J.K. and Laurie, G.T., *Mason and McCall Smith's Law and Medical Ethics* (Oxford: Oxford University Press, 8th ed., 2010).

Matthews, P., "Whose Body? People and Property" (1983) 36 *Current Legal Problems* 193.

McAuley, F., "Anticipating the Past: The Defence of Provocation in Irish Law" (1987) 50 *Modern Law Review* 133.

McBarnet, D. and Whelan, C., "The Elusive Spirit of the Law: Formalism and the Struggle for Legal Control" (1991) 54 *Modern Law Review* 848.

McColgan, A., "Common Law and the Relevance of Sexual History Evidence" (1996) 15 *Oxford Journal of Legal Studies* 275.

——, "In Defence of Battered Women Who Kill" (1993) 130 *J Law and Soc* 508.

McEwan, J., "'I Thought She Consented': Defeat of the Rape Shield or the Defence that Shall Not Run?" [2006] *Criminal LR* 969.

McEwan, J. and Robilliard, St.J., "Recklessness: the House of Lords and the Criminal Law" (1981) 1 *Legal Studies* 267.

McHarg, A., "Reconciling Human Rights and the Public Interest: Conceptual Problems and Doctrinal Uncertainty in the Jurisprudence of the European Court of Human Rights" (1999) 62 *Modern Law Review* 671.

McKenna, B., "The Undefined Adverb in Criminal Statutes" [1966] *Criminal LR* 548.

Melissaris, E., "The Concept of Appropriation and the Offence of Theft" (2007) 70 *Modern Law Review* 581.

Mencken, H.L., *A New Dictionary of Quotations on Historical Principles from Ancient and Modern Sources* (New York: Alfred A. Knopf, 1942).

Mercer, C.H., et al, "Changes in Sexual Attitudes and Lifestyles in Britain through the Life Course and Over Time" (2013) 382 *The Lancet* 1781.

Merry, A. and McCall-Smith, A., *Errors, Medicine and the Law* (Cambridge: Cambridge University Press, 2001).

Michalowski, S., "Sanctity of Life: Are Some Lives More Sacred Than Others?" (2002) 22 *Legal Studies* 377.

Miles, J., "Sexual Offences: Consent, Capacity and Children" [2008] 10 *Archbold News* 6.

Mill, J.S., *On Liberty* (1859).

Milsom, S.F.C., *Historical Foundations of the Common Law* (London: Butterworths, 1969; 2nd ed., 1981).

Ministry of Justice, *Murder, Manslaughter and Infanticide: Proposals for Reform of the Law. Summary of Responses and Government Position* Response to Consultation, CP(R)19/08 (London: Ministry of Justice, 2009).

Mirfield, P., "Intention and Criminal Attempts" [2015] *Criminal LR* 142.

Mitchell, B., "In Defence of a Principle of Correspondence" [1999] *Criminal LR* 195.

——, "Multiple Wrongdoing and Offence Structure: A Plea for Consistency and Fair Labelling" (2001) 64 *Modern LR* 395.

Mitsilegas, V., *EU Criminal Law* (Oxford: Hart, 2009).

Moore, M.S., "Choice, Character, and Excuse" in E.F. Paul, F.D. Miller, and J. Paul (eds.), *Crime, Culpability and Remedy* (Oxford: Blackwell, 1990) 29.

——, "Intention as a Marker of Moral Culpability and Legal Punishability" in R.A. Duff and S. Green (eds.), *Philosophical Foundations of Criminal Law* (Oxford: Oxford University Press, 2011) 179.

——, "Stephen Morse on the Fundamental Psycho-Legal Error" (2016) 10 *Criminal Law and Philosophy* 45.

——, "The Quest for a Responsible Responsibility Test: Norwegian Insanity Law After Breivik" (2015) 9 *Criminal Law and Philosophy* 645.

——, *Act and Crime* (Oxford: Oxford University Press, 1993).

——, *Causation and Responsibility: An Essay in Law, Morals and Metaphysics* (Oxford: Oxford University Press, 2009).

——, *Law and Psychiatry: Rethinking the Relationship* (Cambridge: Cambridge University Press, 1984).

——, *Placing Blame: A Theory of Criminal Law* (Oxford: Clarendon Press, 1997).

Moore, M.S. and Hurd, H., "Punishing the Awkward, the Stupid, the Weak, and the Selfish: the Culpability of Negligence" (2011) 5 *Criminal Law and Philosophy* 147.

Morgan, P., "Vicarious Liability on the Move" (2013) 129 *Law Quarterly Review* 139.

Morris, N., "The Criminal Responsibility of the Mentally Ill" (1982) 33 *Syracuse LR* 477.

——, *Madness and the Criminal Law* (Chicago: University of Chicago Press, 1982).

Morrison, S.M., "Should there be a Domestic Violence Defence to the Offence of Familial Homicide?" [2013] *Criminal LR* 826.

Morse, S., "Excusing the Crazy: The Insanity Defence Reconsidered" (1985) 58 *Southern California LR* 777.

Moxon, D., *Sentencing Practice in the Crown Court*, Home Office Research Study No. 103 (London, HMSO: 1988).

Munday, R.J., "Handling the Evidential Exception" [1988] *Criminal LR* 345.

Murphy, J.G. and Hampton, J., *Forgiveness and Mercy* (Cambridge: Cambridge University Press, 1998).

Murray, C., *The Emerging British Underclass* (London: IEA Health and Welfare Unit, 1990).

——, *Underclass: The Crisis Deepens* (London: IEA Health and Welfare Unit, 1994).

Nagel, T., *Mortal Questions* (Cambridge: Cambridge University Press, 1979).

Nicholson, D., "Telling Tales: Gender Discrimination Gender Construction and Battered Women Who Kill" (1995) 3 *Feminist Leg Stud* 185.

——, "The Citizen's Duty to Assist the Police" [1992] *Criminal LR* 611.

Nicholson, D. and Sanghvi, R., "Battered Women and Provocation: The Implications of *R v. Ahluwalia*" [1993] *Criminal LR* 728.

Norrie, A., "A Critique of Criminal Causation" (1991) 54 *Modern Law Review* 685.

——, "After *Woollin*" [1999] *Criminal LR* 532.

——, "Between Orthodox Subjectivism and Moral Contextualism: Intention and the Consultation Paper" [2006] *Criminal LR* 486.

——, "From Criminal Law to Legal Theory: The Mysterious Case of the Reasonable Glue Sniffer" (2002) 65 *Modern LR* 38.

——, "'Simulacra of Morality?' Beyond the Ideal/Actual Antinomies of Criminal Justice" in Duff (ed.), *Philosophy and the Criminal Law* (Cambridge: Cambridge University Press, 1998) 101.

——, "The Coroners and Justice Act 2009—Partial Defences to Murder (1) Loss of Control" [2010] *Criminal LR* 275.

——, *Crime, Reason and History* (Cambridge: Cambridge University Press, 3rd ed., 2014).

——, *Punishment, Responsibility and Justice* (Oxford: Oxford University Press, 2000).

Note, "A Rationale of the Law of Aggravated Theft" (1954) 54 *Columbia LR* 84.

Note, "A Rationale of the Law of Burglary" (1951) 51 *Columbia LR* 1009.

Nourse, V., "Passion's Progress; Modern Law Reform and the Provocation Defence" (1997) 106 *Yale LJ* 1331.

Nozick, R., *Anarchy, State and Utopia* (Oxford: Oxford University Press, 1974).

O'Connor, D. and Fairall, P.A., *Criminal Defences* (Sydney: Butterworths, 2nd ed., 1988).

O'Donnell, I. and Morrison, S., "Armed and Dangerous? The Use of Firearms in Robbery" (1997) 36 *Howard J Criminal Justice* 305.

O'Donovan, K., "Defences for Battered Women Who Kill" (1991) 18 *J Law and Society* 219.

Oakley, A., *Constructive Trusts* (London: Sweet & Maxwell, 3rd ed., 1997).

Orchard, G., "'Agreement' in Criminal Conspiracy" [1974] *Criminal LR* 297 and 335.

——, "The Defence of Absence of Fault in Australasia and Canada" in P.F. Smith (ed.), *Criminal Law: Essays in Honour of J.C. Smith* (London: Butterworths, 1987) 114.

——, "Provocation—Recharacterisation of 'Characteristics'" (1996) 6 *Canterbury LR* 202.

——, "Surviving without Majewski—A View from Down Under" [1993] *Criminal LR* 426.

——, "The Golden Thread—Somewhat Frayed" (1988) 6 *Otago LR* 615.

——, "The Judicial Categorisation of Offences" (1983) 2 *Canterbury LR* 81.

Ormerod, D., "Cheating the Public Revenue" [1998] *Criminal LR* 627.

Ormerod, D. and Fortson, R., "Drug Suppliers as Manslaughterers (Again)" [2005] *Criminal LR* 819.

——, "Serious Crime Act 2007: The Part 2 Offences" [2009] *Criminal LR* 389.

Ormerod, D. and Taylor, R., "The Corporate Manslaughter and Corporate Homicide Act 2007" [2008] *Criminal LR* 589.

Ormerod, D. and Williams, D., *Smith: The Law of Theft* (Oxford: Oxford University Press, 9th ed., 2007).

d'Orban, P.T., "Women Who Kill their Children" (1979) 134 *British Journal of Psychiatry* 560.

Ost, S., "Criminalising Fabricated Images of Child Pornography: A Matter of Harm or Morality?" (2010) 30 *Legal Studies* 230.

O'Sullivan, J. and Hilliard, J., *The Law of Contract* (Oxford: Oxford University Press, 4th ed., 2010).

Ouyang, G. and Shiner, R.A., "Organisations and Agency" (1995) 1 *Legal Theory* 283.

Owusu-Bempah, A., "Prosecuting hate crime: procedural issues and the future of the aggravated offences" (2015) 35 *Legal Studies* 443.

——, "Silence in Suspicious Circumstances" [2014] *Criminal LR* 126.

Owusu-Bempah, A. and Walters, M., "Racially Aggravated Offences: When does Section 145 of the Criminal Justice Act 2003 apply?" [2016] *Criminal LR* 116.

Pace, P.J., "Burglarious Trespass" [1985] *Criminal LR* 716.

——, "Delegation: A Doctrine in Search of a Definition" [1982] *Criminal LR* 627.

Paciocco, D.W., "The Remedial Constructive Trust: A Principled Basis for Priorities over Creditors" (1989) 68 *Canadian Bar Review* 315.

Packer, H.L., *The Limits of the Criminal Sanction* (Stanford: Stanford University Press, 1968).

Padfield, N., "The High Price of Participation in Criminal Activities" [1993] *Cambridge LJ* 373.

Palmstierna, T., "One in Thirty Predictions of Assault by Discharged Psychiatric Patients Will Be Correct" [1999] *British Medical J* 1270.

Parry, D.L., "Judicial Approaches to Due Diligence" [1995] *Criminal LR* 695.

Patient, I., "Some Remarks about the Element of Voluntariness in Offences of Absolute Liability" [1968] *Criminal LR* 23.

Pearce, A.R., "Theft by False Promises" (1953) 101 *U Pennsylvania LR* 967.

Peay, J., "Insanity and Automatism: Questions From and About the Law Commission Scoping Paper" [2012] *Criminal LR* 927.

——, "Responsibility, Culpability and the Sentencing of Mentally Disordered Offenders: Objectives in Conflict" [2016] *Criminal LR* 152.

Pedain, A., "Intention and the Terrorist Example" [2004] *Criminal LR* 284.

Peers, S., *EU Justice and Home Affairs Law* (Oxford: Oxford University Press, 2nd ed., 2006).

Perkins, R.M., "Parties to Crime" (1941) 89 *U Pennsylvania LR* 581.

——, "The Law of Homicide" (1946) 36 *J Criminal Law and Criminology* 391.

Perkins, R.M. and Boyle, R.N., *Criminal Law* (Mineola, N.Y.: Foundation Press, 3rd ed., 1982).

Perry, S., "Corrective Justice v. Distributive Justice" in J. Horder (ed.), *Oxford Essays in Jurisprudence* (4th Series, Oxford: Oxford University Press, 2000) 237.

Phillipson, G., "The Human Rights Act, 'Horizontal Effect' and the Common Law: A Bang or a Whimper" (1999) 62 *Modern Law Review* 824.

——, "(Mis)-Reading Section 3 of the Human Rights Act" (2003) 119 *Law Quarterly Review* 183.

Pickard, T., "Culpable Mistakes and Rape: Relating Mens Rea to the Crime" (1980) 30 *U Toronto LJ* 75.

Pieth, M. and Ivory, R. (eds.), *Corporate Criminal Liability: Emergence, Convergence and Risk* (Dordrecht: Springer, 2011).

Pollock, F. and Maitland, F.W. *The History of English Law Before the Time of Edward I* (Cambridge: Cambridge University Press, 2nd ed., 1911).

Popper, K., *The Poverty of Historicism* (London: Routledge and Kegan Paul, 1957).

Posner, R., *An Economic Theory of the Criminal Law* (1985) 85 *Columbia LR* 1193.

Pound, R., "Common Law and Legislation" (1907) 21 *Harvard LR* 383.

Power, H., "Pitcairn Island: Sexual Offending, Cultural Difference, and Ignorance of the Law" [2007] *Criminal LR* 609.

——, "Provocation and Culture" [2006] *Criminal LR* 871.

Price, D.P.T., "Assisted Suicide and Refusing Medical Treatment: Linguistics, Morals and Legal Contentions" (1996) 4 *Medical LR* 270.

Quick, O. and Wells, C. "Getting Tough with Defences" [2006] *Criminal LR* 514.

Quigley, M., "Property: The Future of Human Tissue?" (2009) 17 *Medical LR* 457.

Ramsay, P., "The Theory of Vulnerable Autonomy and the Legitimacy of Civil Preventative Orders" in B. McSherry, A. Norrie and S. Bronitt (eds.), *Regulating Deviance: The Redirection of Criminalisation and the Futures of Criminal Law* (2009) 109.

——, *The Insecurity State: Vulnerable Autonomy and the Right to Security in the Criminal Law* (Oxford: Oxford University Press, 2012).

Rawls, J., *A Theory of Justice* (Cambridge, Mass.: Harvard University Press, 1971; revised ed., 1999).

Raz, J., "Autonomy, Toleration, and the Harm Principle" in R. Gavison (ed.), *Issues in Contemporary Legal Philosophy* (Oxford: Clarendon Press, 1987; 2nd ed., 2009) 313.

——, *The Authority of Law* (Oxford: Oxford University Press, 1979).

——, *The Morality of Freedom* (Oxford: Oxford University Press, 1986).

Redmayne, M., "Exploring Entrapment" in Zedner and Roberts (eds.), *Principles and Values in Criminal Law and Criminal Justice: Essays in Honour of Andrew Ashworth* (Oxford: Oxford University Press, 2012) 157.

Reed, A. and Wake, N., "Sexual Infidelity Killings" in A. Reed and M. Bohlander (eds.), *Loss of Control and Diminished Responsibility: Domestic, Comparative and International Perspectives* (Aldershot: Ashgate, 2011) 117.

Reid, K., "Strict Liability: Some Principles for Parliament" (2008) 29 *Statute LR* 173.

Reiman, J. and van den Haag, E., "On the Common Saying that It Is Better that Ten Guilty Persons Escape than that One Innocent Suffer: *Pro* and *Con*" in E.F. Paul, F.D. Miller, and J. Paul (eds.), *Crime, Culpability and Remedy* (Oxford: Blackwell, 1990) 226.

Reid, K., "Strict Liability: Some Principles for Parliament" (2008) 29 *Statute LR* 173.

Reisman, D., "Possession and the Law of Finders" (1939) 52 *Harvard LR* 1105.

Reiss, A., "Selecting Strategies of Social Control over Organizational Life" in K. Hawkins and J.M. Thomas (eds.), *Enforcing Regulation* (Boston: Kluwer-Nijhoff, 1984) 25.

Richardson, G., "Strict Liability for Regulatory Crime: The Empirical Research" [1987] *Criminal LR* 295.

Richardson, G., Ogus, A., and Burrows, P., *Policing Pollution: A Study of Regulation and Enforcement* (Oxford: Oxford University Press, 1982).

Richardson, J., *Archbold: Criminal Pleading, Evidence and Practice* (London: Sweet and Maxwell, 2016).

Ripstein, A., "Beyond the Harm Principle" (2006) 34 *Philosophy and Public Affairs* 216.

Robbins, I.P., "Double Inchoate Crimes" (1989) 26 *Harvard J Legislation* 1.

Roberts, P., "Strict Liability and the Presumption of Innocence" in A.P. Simester (ed.), *Appraising Strict Liability* (Oxford: Oxford University Press, 2005) 151.

——, "Taking the Burden of Proof Seriously" [1995] *Criminal LR* 783.

——, "The Philosophical Foundations of Consent in the Criminal Law" (1997) 17 *Oxford Journal of Legal Studies* 389.

——, "The Presumption of Innocence Brought Home" (2002) 118 *Law Quarterly Review* 41.

Roberts, S., "More Lost Than Found" (1982) 45 *Modern Law Review* 683.

Robinson, P.H., "Causing the Conditions of One's Own Defence: A Study in the Limits of Theory in Criminal Law Doctrine" (1985) 71 *Virginia LR* 1.

——, "Competing Theories of Justification: Deeds v. Reasons" in A.P. Simester and A.T.H. Smith (eds.), *Harm and Culpability* (Oxford: Oxford University Press, 1996) 45.

——, "Criminal Law Defenses: A Systematic Analysis" (1982) 82 *Columbia LR* 199.

——, "The Criminal–Civil Distinction and the Utility of Desert" (1996) 76 *Boston ULR* 201.

——, *Criminal Law* (New York: Aspen Law and Business, 1997).

——, *Fundamentals of Criminal Law* (Boston: Little Brown, 1988).

Robinson, P.H. and Darley, J.M., "Objectivist versus Subjectivist View of Criminality: A Study in the Role of Social Science in Criminal Law Theory" (1998) 18 *Oxford Journal of Legal Studies* 409.

——, *Justice, Liability and Blame: Community Views and the Criminal Law* (1995).

Rock, P., *After Homicide: Practical and Political Responses to Bereavement* (Oxford: Clarendon Press, 1998).

Rogers, J., " A Criminal Lawyer's Response to Chastisement in the European Court of Human Rights" [2002] *Criminal LR* 98.

——, "Applying the Doctrine of Positive Obligations in the European Convention on Human Rights to Domestic Substantive Criminal Law in Domestic Proceedings" [2003] *Criminal LR* 690.

——, "Chastisement" [2002] *Criminal LR* 98.

——, "Further Developments under the Sexual Offences Act" [2013] 7 *Archbold Review* 7.

——, "Prosecutorial Policies, Prosecutorial Systems, and the Purdy Litigation" [2010] *Criminal LR* 543.

——, "Sexual Offences: Consent; 'Purpose' of Defendant" (2008) 72 *Journal of Criminal Law* 280.

——, "The Codification of Attempts and the Case for 'Preparation'" [2008] *Criminal LR* 937.

——, "The Effect of 'Deception' in the Sexual Offences Act 2003" [2013] 4 *Archbold Review* 7.

Rowe, P., "The Criminal Liability of a British Soldier Merely for Participating in the Iraq War 2003: a Response to Chilcot Evidence" [2010] *Criminal LR* 752.

Royal College of Physicians Working Group, "Criteria for the Diagnosis of Brain Stem Death" (1995) 29 *J Royal College of Physicians* 381.

Royal Commission on Capital Punishment, *Report of the Royal Commission on Capital Punishment, 1949–1953* Cmnd. 8932 (London: HMSO, 1953).

Rubenfeld J., "The Riddle of Rape-by-Deception and the Myth of Sexual Autonomy" (2013) 122 *Yale LJ* 1372.

Rumbold, J. and Wasik, M., "Diabetic drivers, hypoglycaemic unawareness, and automatism" [2011] *Criminal LR* 863.

Rumney, P., "Review of Sex Offenders and Rape and Law Reform: Another False Dawn?" [2001] 64 *Modern LR* 801.

Ryan, A., *Property and Political Theory* (Oxford: Blackwell, 1984).

Ryan, S., "Reckless Transmission of HIV: Knowledge and Culpability" [2006] *Criminal LR* 981.

Saunders, J.B., *Mozley & Whiteley's Law Dictionary* (London: Butterworths, 9th ed., 1977).

Sayre, F.B., "Criminal Responsibility for the Acts of Another" (1930) 43 *Harvard LR* 678.

——, "*Mens Rea*" (1932) 45 *Harvard LR* 974.

——, "Public Welfare Offences" (1933) 33 *Columbia LR* 55.

——, "The Present Significance of *Mens Rea* in the Criminal Law" in R. Pound (ed.), *Harvard Legal Essays Written in Honor of Joseph Henry Beale and Samuel Williston* (Harvard: Harvard University Press, 1934) 399.

Schauer, F. and Zeckhauser, R., "Regulation by Generalization" Working Paper No 05-16 (Washington D.C.: AEI-Brookings Joint Centre for Regulatory Studies, 2005).

Schopp, R.F., *Justification Defences and Just Convictions* (Cambridge: Cambridge University Press, 1998).

Schott, L., "Fetal Protection—An Overview of Recent State Legislative Responses" (1991) 22 *Memphis State University LR* 119.

Schulhofer, S.J., "Harm and Punishment: A Critique of Emphasis on the Results of Conduct in the Criminal Law" (1974) 122 *U Pennsylvania LR* 1497.

Searle, J.R., *The Construction of Social Reality* (London: Allen Lane, 1995).

Seavey, W., "Negligence—Subjective or Objective?" (1927) 41 *Harvard LR* 1.

Sharpe, A., "Criminalising Sexual Intimacy: Transgender defendants and the legal construction of non-consent" [2014] *Criminal LR* 207.

Shepherd, J.C., "Towards a Unified Concept of Fiduciary Relationships" (1981) 97 *Law Quarterly Review* 51.

Sherwin, E., "Constructive Trusts in Bankruptcy" (1989) *U Illinois LR* 297.

Shulman, H., "The Standard of Care Required of Children" (1928) 37 *Yale LJ* 618.

Shute, S., "Appropriation and the Law of Theft" [2002] *Criminal LR* 445.

——, "Knowledge and Belief in the Criminal Law" in S. Shute and A.P. Simester (eds.), *Criminal Law Theory: Doctrines of the General Part* (2002) 184.

——, "Something Old, Something New, Something Borrowed: Three Aspects of the Project" [1996] *Criminal LR* 684.

Shute, S. and Horder, J., "Thieving and Deceiving—What Is the Difference?" (1993) 56 *Modern Law Review* 548.

Shyllon, F.O., "The Corruption of 'Corruptly'" [1969] *Criminal LR* 250.

Simester, A.P., "A Disintegrated Theory of Culpability" in D. Baker and J. Horder (eds.), *The Sanctity of Life and the Criminal Law: The Legacy of Glanville Williams* (Cambridge: Cambridge University Press, 2013) 178.

——, "Can Negligence Be Culpable?" in J. Horder (ed.), *Oxford Essays in Jurisprudence* (4th Series, Oxford: Oxford University Press, 2000) 85.

——, "Intoxication Is Never a Defence" [2009] *Criminal LR* 3.

——, "Is Strict Liability Always Wrong?" in A.P. Simester (ed.), *Appraising Strict Liability* (Oxford: Oxford University Press, 2005) 21.

——, "Mistakes in Defence" (1992) 12 *Oxford Journal of Legal Studies* 295.

——, "Moral Certainty and the Boundaries of Intention" (1996) 16 *Oxford Journal of Legal Studies* 445.

——, "Murder, Mens Rea and the House of Lords—Again" (1999) 115 *Law Quarterly Review* 17.

——, "Necessity, Torture and the Rule of Law" in V. Ramraj (ed.), *Emergencies and the Limits of Legality* (Cambridge, Cambridge University Press: 2008) 289.

——, "On Justifications and Excuses" in L. Zedner and J. Roberts (eds.), *Principled Approaches to Criminal Law and Criminal Justice: Essays in Honour of Andrew Ashworth* (Oxford: Oxford University Press, 2012) 95.

——, "On the So-called Requirement for Voluntary Action" (1998) 1 *Buffalo Criminal LR* 403.

——, "Prophylactic Crimes" in G.R. Sullivan and I. Dennis (eds.), *Seeking Security: Pre-empting the Commission of Criminal Harms* (Oxford: Hart Publishing, 2012) 60.

——, "The Mental Element in Complicity" (2006) 122 *Law Quarterly Review* 578.

——, "Why Distinguish Intention from Foresight?" in A.P. Simester and A.T.H. Smith (eds.), *Harm and Culpability* (Oxford: Oxford University Press, 1996) 71.

——, "Why Omissions are Special" (1995) 1 *Legal Theory* 311.

—— (ed.), *Appraising Strict Liability* (Oxford: Oxford University Press, 2005).

Simester, A.P. and Chan, W., "Intention Thus Far" [1997] *Criminal LR* 704.

Simester, A.P. and Hirsch, A. von, "Regulating Offensive Conduct through Two-step Prohibitions" in A. von Hirsch and A.P. Simester (eds.), *Incivilities: Regulating Offensive Behaviour* (Oxford: Hart Publishing, 2006) 173.

——, "Rethinking the Offense Principle" (2002) 8 *Legal Theory* 269.

——, *Crimes, Harms, and Wrongs: On the Principles of Criminalisation* (Oxford: Hart Publishing, 2011).

Simester, A.P. and Roberts, P., "Strict Liability in UK Regulation" in R. Macrory, *Regulatory Justice: Sanctioning in a Post-Hampton World* Consultation Document (London: Cabinet Office, 2006) Annex E.

Simester, A.P. and Smith, A.T.H. (eds.), *Harm and Culpability* (Oxford: Oxford University Press, 1996).

Simester, A.P. and Sullivan, G.R., "On the Nature and Rationale of Property Offences" in R.A. Duff and S.P. Green (eds.), *Defining Crimes: Essays on the Criminal Law's Special Part* (Oxford: Oxford University Press, 2005) 168.

Simmonds, N., "The Possibility of Private Law" in J. Tasioulas (ed.), *Law, Values and Social Practices* (Aldershot: Dartmouth, 1997) 129.

Simons, K., "Is Strict Criminal Liability in the Grading of Offences Consistent with Retributive Desert?" (2012) 32 *Oxford Jounral of Legal Studies* 445.

Simpson, A.W.B., *Cannibalism and the Common Law* (Chicago: University of Chicago Press, 1984).

Singer, P., *Rethinking Life and Death: the Collapse of Our Traditional Ethics* (Oxford: Oxford University Press, 1995).

Singer, R., "The Resurgence of Mens Rea: III—The Rise and Fall of Strict Criminal Liability" (1989) 30 *Boston College LR* 337.

Sjolin, C., "Ten Years On: Consent under the Sexual Offences Act 2003" (2015) 79 *Journal of Criminal Law* 20.

Skegg, P., *Law, Ethics and Medicine: Studies in Medical Law* (Oxford: Oxford University Press, 1984).

Smart, A., "Criminal Responsibility for Failing to Do the Impossible" (1987) 103 *Law Quarterly Review* 532.

Smith, A.T.H., "Constructive Trusts in the Law of Theft" [1977] *Criminal LR* 395.

——, "Error and Mistake of Law in Anglo-American Criminal Law" (1984) 14 *Anglo-American LR* 3.

——, "Judicial Law Making in the Criminal Law" (1984) 100 *Law Quarterly Review* 46.

——, "On Actus Reus and Mens Rea" in P. Glazebrook (ed.), *Reshaping the Criminal Law* (London: Sweet & Maxwell, 1978) 95.

——, "Stealing the Body and its Parts" [1976] *Criminal LR* 622.

——, "The Human Rights Act and the Criminal Lawyer: The Constitutional Context" [1999] *Criminal LR* 251.

——, "The Idea of Deception" [1982] *Criminal LR* 721.

——, "The Use of Force in Public or Private Defence and Article 2" [2002] *Criminal LR* 958.

——, "Theft by Persons Required to Account" [1980] 1 *Canterbury LR* 15.

——, *Property Offences* (London: Sweet & Maxwell, 1994).

Smith, H., "Culpable Ignorance" (1983) 92 *The Philosophical Review* 543.

Smith, J., *The Nature of Personal Robbery* Home Office Research Study 254 (London: Home Office, 2003).

Smith, J.C., "A Note on 'Intention'" [1990] *Criminal LR* 85.

——, "Aid, Abet, Counsel, or Procure" in P. Glazebrook (ed.), *Reshaping the Criminal Law* (London: Sweet & Maxwell, 1978) 120.

——, "Burglary under the Theft Bill" [1968] *Criminal LR* 367.

——, "Civil Law Concepts in the Criminal Law" [1972B] *Cambridge LJ* 197.

——, "Codification of the Criminal Law" (1987) 2 *Denning LJ* 134.

——, "Conspiracy to Defraud: Some Comments on the Law Commission's Report" [1995] *Criminal LR* 209.

——, "Conspiracy under the Criminal Law Act 1977" [1977] *Criminal LR* 598 and 638.

——, "Criminal Liability of Accessories: Law and Law Reform" (1997) 113 *Law Quarterly Review* 453.

——, "Embezzlement and the Disobedient Servant" (1956) 19 *Modern Law Review* 39.

——, "'Intent': A Reply" [1978] *Criminal LR* 14.

——, "Intention in Criminal Law" (1974) 27 *Current Legal Problems* 93.

——, "Intoxication and the Mental Element in Crime" in P. Wallington and R. Merkin (eds.), *Essays in Memory of Professor F.H. Lawson* (London: Butterworths, 1986) 119.

——, "*Lister* v. *Stubbs* and the Criminal Law" (1994) 110 *Law Quarterly Review* 180.

——, "Mens Rea in Statutory Conspiracy: (3) Some Answers" [1978] *Criminal LR* 210.

——, "Obtaining Cheques by Deception or Theft" [1997] *Criminal LR* 396.

——, "Offences against the Person: the Home Office Consultation Paper" [1998] *Criminal LR* 317.

——, "Secondary Participation and Inchoate Offences" in C. Tapper (ed.), *Crime, Proof and Punishment* (London: Butterworths, 1981) 21.

——, "Secondary Participation in Crime—Can We Do Without It?" (1994) 144 *New LJ* 679.

——, "Stealing Tickets" [1998] *Criminal LR* 723.

——, "The Element of Chance in Criminal Liability" [1971] *Criminal LR* 63.

——, "The Presumption of Innocence" (1987) 38 *Northern Ireland Law Quarterly* 223.

——, "The Right to Life and the Right to Kill in Law Enforcement" (1994) 144 *New LJ* 354.

——, "The Scope of Fraudulent Conversion" [1961] *Criminal LR* 741 and 797.

——, "The Use of Force in Public or Private Defence and Article 2" [2002] *Criminal LR* 958.

——, "Theft and/or Handling" [1977] *Criminal LR* 517.

——, *Justification and Excuse in the Criminal Law* (London: Sweet & Maxwell, 1989).

Smith, J.C. and Hogan, B., *Criminal Law* (London: Butterworths, 1st ed., 1965; 4th ed., 1978; 5th ed., 1983; 7th ed., 1992; 8th ed., 1996, 10th ed., 2002).

Smith, K., Osborne, S., Lau, I., and Britton, A., *Homicides, Firearm Offences and Intimate Partner Violence 2010/2011: Supplementary Volume 2 to Crime in England and Wales* (London: Home Office, 2012).

Smith, K.J.M., "Duress and Steadfastness: In Pursuit of the Unintelligible" [1999] *Criminal LR* 363.

——, "Proximity in Attempt: Lord Lane's Midway Course" [1991] *Criminal LR* 576.

——, "Withdrawal in Complicity: A Restatement of Principles" [2001] *Criminal LR* 769.

——, *A Modern Treatise on the Law of Criminal Complicity* (Oxford: Oxford University Press, 1991).

Snelling, H.A., "The Alternative Verdict of Manslaughter" (1958) 32 *Australian LJ* 137.

Sparks, R.F., "Diminished Responsibility in Theory and Practice" (1964) 27 *Modern LR* 9.

Spencer, J.R., "Child and Family Offences" [2004] *Criminal LR* 347.

——, "Controlling the Discretion to Prosecute" (2012) 71 *Cambridge LJ* 27.

——, "Criminal Liability for Accidental Death: Back to the Middle Ages?" (2009) 68 *Cambridge LJ* 263.

——, "Criminal Liability for the Desecration of a Corpse" [2004] *Archbold News*, Issue 6, 7.

——, "EU Criminal Law" in C. Barnard and S. Peers (eds.), *European Union Law* (Oxford: Oxford University Press, 2014) 751.

——, "EU Criminal Law—the Present and the Future?" in A. Arnull, C. Barnard, M. Dougan and E. Spaventa (eds.), *A Constitutional Order of States? Essays in EU Law in Honour of Alan Dashwood* (Oxford: Hart Publishing, 2011) 341.

——, "Handling and Taking Risks—a Reply to Professor Williams" [1985] *Criminal LR* 440.

——, "Handling, Theft and the *Mala Fide* Purchaser" [1985] *Criminal LR* 92.

——, "Incest and Article 8 of the European Convention on Human Rights" (2013) 72 *Cambridge LJ* 5.

——, "International Law, People Trafficking and the Power to Stay Proceedings for Abuse of Process" (2014) 73 *Cambridge LJ* 11.

——, "People-trafficking: Some Reflections in the EU Legislation, and its Implementation in the UK" (2009) 11 *Cambridge Yearbook of European Legal Studies* 000.

——, "Sex by Deception" [2013] 9 *Archbold Review* 6.

——, "The European Arrest Warrant" (2003–4) 6 *Cambridge Yearbook of European Legal Studies* 201.

——, "The Metamorphosis of Section 6 of the Theft Act" [1977] *Criminal LR* 653.

——, "The Mishandling of Handling" [1981] *Criminal LR* 682.

——, "The Theft Act 1978" [1979] *Criminal LR* 24.

——, "Trying to Help another Person Commit a Crime" in P. Smith (ed.), *Criminal Law: Essays in Honour of J.C. Smith* (London: Butterworths, 1987) 148.

——, *Evidence of Bad Character* (Oxford: Hart Publishing, 3rd ed., 2016).

J.R. Spencer and A.-M.Brajeux, "Criminal Liability for Negligence—a Lesson from Across the Channel?" (2010) 59 *International and Comparative Law Quarterly* 1.

Spencer, J.R. and Pedain, A., "Approaches to Strict and Constructive Liability in Continental Criminal Law" in Simester (ed.), *Appraising Strict Liability* (2005) 237.

Spencer, J.R. and Virgo, G., "Encouraging and Assisting Crime: Legislate in Haste, Repent at Leisure" [2008] 9 *Archbold News* 7.

Spencer, S., "Assault with Intent to Rape—Dead or Alive?" [1986] *Criminal LR* 110.

Squires, D., "The Problem with Entrapment" (2006) 26 *Oxford Journal of Legal Studies* 351.

Stannard, J.E., "Making up for the Missing Element: A Sideways Look at Attempts" (1987) 7 *Legal Studies* 194.

Stark, F., "Encouraging or Assisting Clarity?" [2013] *Cambridge LJ* 497.

——, "*Howe* (1987)" in P. Handler, H. Mares and I. Williams (eds.), *Landmark Cases in Criminal Law* (Oxford: Oxford University Press, 2017).

——, "'It's Only Words': On Meaning and *Mens Rea*" (2013) 72 *Cambridge LJ* 155.

——, "Necessity and *Nicklinson*" [2013] *Criminal LR* 949.

——, "The Mens Rea of a Criminal Attempt" [2014] 3 *Archbold Review* 7.

Steel, A., "Describing Dishonest Means: The Implications of Seeing Dishonesty as a Course of Conduct or Mental Element and the Parallels with Indecency" (2010) 31 *Adelaide LR* 7.

——, "Problematic and Unnecessary? Issues with the Use of the Theft Offence to Protect Intangible Property" (2008) 30 *Sydney LR* 575.

——, "Taking Possession: The Defining Element of Theft?" (2008) 32 *Melbourne University LR* 1030.

——, "The Harms and Wrongs of Stealing: The Harm Principle and Dishonesty in Theft" (2008) 31 *University of New South Wales LJ* 712.

Stephen, J.F., *A History of the Criminal Law of England* (1883).

——, *Digest of the Criminal Law* (4th ed., 1887).

Stoop, D.F. de, "The Law in Australia Relating to the Transplantation of Organs from Cadavers" (1974) 48 *Australian LJ* 21.

Strawson, P., "Freedom and Resentment" in *Freedom and Resentment* (London: Methuen, 1974) 1.

Stuart, D., "The *Actus Reus* in Attempts" [1970] *Criminal LR* 505.

Stuckey, J.E., "The Equitable Action for Breach of Confidence: Is Information Ever Property?" (1981) 9 *Sydney LR* 402.

Sullivan, G.R., "Accessories and Principals after *Gnango*" in A. Reed and M. Bohlander (eds.), *Participation in Crime: Domestic and Comparative Perspectives* (Farnham: Ashgate, 2013) 37.

——, "Anger and Excuse: Reassessing Provocation" (1992) 12 *Oxford Journal of Legal Studies* 380.

——, "Avoiding Criminal Liability and Excessive Punishment for Persons Who Lack Culpability" in A. Reed and M. Bohlander (eds.), *General Defences in Criminal Law: Domestic and Comparative Perspectives* (Aldershot: Ashgate, 2014) 25.

——, "Bad Thoughts and Bad Acts" [1990] *Criminal LR* 559.

——, "Cause and the Contemporaneity of *Actus Reus* and *Mens Rea*" [1993] *Cambridge LJ* 487.

——, "Conduct and Complicity: Liability based on Omission and Risk" (2008) 39 *Cambrian LR* 687.

——, "Conduct and Proof of Conduct: Two Necessary Conditions for the Imposition of Criminal Liability" in K. Kaikobad and M. Bohlander (eds.), *International Law and Power: Perspectives on Legal Order and Justice* (Boston: Martinus Nijhoff, 2009) 235.

——, "Contemporaneity of Actus Reus and Mens Rea" [1993] *Cambridge LJ* 487.

——, "Corporate Killing—Some Government Proposals" [2001] *Cambridge LJ* 31.

——, "Crossing the Rubicon in Miami" (1978) 41 *Modern Law Review* 215.

——, "Doing Without Complicity" [2012] *Journal of Commonwealth Criminal Law* 199.

——, "Expressing Corporate Guilt" (1995) 15 *Oxford Journal of Legal Studies* 281.

——, "Fault Elements and Joint Enterprise" [1994] *Criminal LR* 252.

——, "First Degree Murder and Complicity" (2007) 1 *Criminal Law & Philosophy* 271.

——, "Fraud and the Efficacy of the Criminal Law: a Proposal for a Wide Residual Offence" [1985] *Criminal LR* 616.

——, "Fraud: the Latest Law Commission Proposals" (2003) 52 *Journal of Criminal Law* 139.

——, "Inchoate Liability for Assisting and Encouraging Crime—The Law Commission Report" [2006] *Criminal LR* 1047.

——, "Intent, Purpose and Complicity" [1988] *Criminal LR* 641.

——, "Intent, Subjective Recklessness and Culpability" (1992) 12 *Oxford Journal of Legal Studies* 380.

——, "Intoxicants and Diminished Responsibility" [1994] *Criminal LR* 156.

——, "Involuntary Intoxication and Beyond" [1994] *Criminal LR* 272.

——, "Is Criminal Law Possible?" (2001) 22 *Oxford Journal of Legal Studies* 424.

——, "Knowledge, Belief and Culpability" in S. Shute and A.P. Simester (eds.), *Criminal Law Theory: Doctrines of the General Part* (Oxford: Oxford University Press, 2002) 207.

——, "Liberalism and Constraining Choice: The Cases of Death and Serious Bodily Harm" in S. Smith and R. Deazley (eds.), *The Legal, Medical and Cultural Regulation of the Body: Transformation and Transgression* (Aldershot: Ashgate, 2009) 205.

——, "Making Excuses" in A.P. Simester and A.T.H. Smith (eds.), *Harm and Culpability* (Oxford: Oxford University Press, 1996) 131.

——, "Parents and Their Truanting Children: An English Lesson in Liability without Responsibility" (2010) 12 *Otago LR* 285.

——, "Strict Liability for Criminal Offences in England and Wales Following Incorporation into English Law of the ECHR" in A.P. Simester (ed.), *Appraising Strict Liability* (Oxford: Oxford University Press, 2005) 195.

——, "The Attribution of Culpability to Limited Companies" (1996) 55 *Cambridge LJ* 515.

——, "The Bribery Act 2010: An Overview" [2011] *Criminal LR* 87.

——, "The Hard Treatment of Innocent Persons in State Responses to the Threat of Large Scale and Imminent Terrorist Violence: Examining the Legal Constraints" in G.R. Sullivan and I. Dennis (eds.), *Seeking Security: Pre-empting Criminal Harms* (2012) 293.

——, "The Law Commission Consultation Paper on Complicity: Fault Elements and Joint Enterprise" [1994] *Criminal LR* 252.

——, "The Need for a Crime of Sexual Assault" [1989] *Criminal LR* 331.

——, "The Particularity of Serious Fraud" in P. Birks (ed.), *Pressing Problems in the Law. Vol. 1: Criminal Justice and Human Rights* (Oxford: Oxford University Press, 1995) 99.

——, "Violent Self-help" (1983) 46 *Modern Law Review* 78.

Sullivan, G.R. and Dennis, I. (eds.), *Seeking Security: Pre-empting Criminal Harms* (Oxford: Hart Publishing, 2012).

Sullivan, G.R. and Simester, A.P., "Causation without Limits: Causing Death while Driving without a Licence, while Disqualified, or without Insurance" [2012] *Criminal LR* 753.

Sullivan, G.R. and Warbrick, C., "Territoriality, Theft and *Atakpu*" (1994) *Criminal LR* 650.

Sutherland, P. and Gearty, C., "Insanity and the European Court of Human Rights" [1992] *Criminal LR* 418.

Sutton, M., Schneider, J. and Hetherington, S., *Tackling Theft with the Market Reduction Approach* Home Office Crime Reduction Research Series Paper 8 (London: Home Office, 2001).

Syrota, G., "A Radical Change in the Law of Recklessness?" [1982] *Criminal LR* 97.

Szasz, T., *The Manufacture of Madness: A Comparative Study of the Inquisition and the Mental Health Movement* (New York: Harper & Row, 1970).

——, *The Myth of Mental Illness* (New York: Harper & Row, 1961; 2nd ed., 1976).

Tadros, "A Human Right to a Fair Criminal Law" in J. Chalmers, F. Leverick and L. Farmer (eds.), *Essays in Criminal Law in Honour of Sir Gerald Gordon* (Edinburgh: Edinburgh University Press, 2010) 103.

——, "Fair Labelling and Social Solidarity" in Zedner and Roberts (eds.), *Principles and Values in Criminal Law and Criminal Justice: Essays in Honour of Andrew Ashworth* (2012) 67.

——, Tadros, "Rape without consent" (2006) 26 *Oxford Journal of Legal Studies* 515.

——, "The Homicide Ladder" (2006) 69 *Modern LR* 601.

——, "The Ideal of the Presumption of Innocence" (2014) 8 *Criminal Law and Philosophy* 449.

——, *Criminal Responsibility* (Oxford: Oxford University Press, 2005).

Tadros, V. and Tierney, S., "The Presumption of Innocence and the Human Rights Act" (2004) 67 *Modern Law Review* 402.

Tay, A., "Problems in the Law of Finding" (1964) 37 *Australian LJ* 350.

Taylor, R.D., "Complicity and Excuses" [1983] *Criminal LR* 656.

Taylor, R., "The Nature of 'Partial Defences' and the Coherence of Second Degree Murder" [2007] *Criminal LR* 345.

Teff, H., *Reasonable Care: Legal Perspectives on the Doctor–Patient Relationship* (Oxford: Oxford University Press, 1994).

Temkin, J., "Pre-natal Injury, Homicide and the Draft Criminal Code" [1986] *Cambridge LJ* 414.

——, "Sexual History Evidence—the Ravishment of Section 2" [1993] *Criminal LR* 3.

Temkin, J. and Ashworth, A., "The Sexual Offences Act 2003: Rape, Sexual Assaults and the Problems of Consent" [2004] *Criminal LR* 328.

Tigar, M., "The Right of Property and the Law of Theft" (1984) 62 *Texas LR* 1443.

Tur, R., "Legislative Technique and Human Rights: The Sad Case of Assisted Suicide" [2003] *Criminal LR* 3.

——, "Subjectivism and Objectivism: Towards Synthesis" in S. Shute, J. Gardner and J. Horder (eds.), *Action and Value in Criminal Law* (Oxford: Oxford University Press, 1993) 213.

Turner, J.W.C., "Larceny and Lucrum" (1941) 4 *Toronto LJ* 296.

——, "The Mental Element in Crimes at Common Law" in L. Radzinowicz and J.W.C. Turner (eds.), *The Modern Approach to Criminal Law* (London: Macmillan, 1948) 195.

——, "Two Cases of Larceny" in L. Radzinowicz and J.W.C. Turner (eds.), *The Modern Approach to Criminal Law* (London: Macmillan, 1948) 356.

——, *Kenny's Outlines of Criminal Law* (Cambridge: Cambridge University Press, 16th ed., 1952; 17th ed., 1958; 19th ed., 1965).

——, *Russell on Crime* (London: Stevens, 12th ed., 1964).

Ulph, J., "Confiscation Orders, Human Rights, and Penal Measures" (2010) 126 *Law Quarterly Review* 251.

Uniacke, S., "Was Mary's Death Murder?" (2001) 9 *Medical LR* 9.

——, *Permissible Killing—the Self-defence Justification of Homicide* (Cambridge: Cambridge University Press, 1994).

Virgo, G.J., "Criminal Attempts—The Law of Unintended Circumstances" [2014] *Cambridge LJ* 244.

——, "Encouraging or Assisting More than One Offence" (2012) 2 *Archbold Review* 6.

——, "Joint Enterprise is Dead: Long Live Accessorial Liability" [2012] *Criminal LR* 850.

——, "Making Sense of Section 46 of the Serious Crime Act 2007" (2013) 7 *Archbold Review* 4.

——, "Part 2 of the Serious Crime Act 2007—Enough is Enough" (2013) 3 *Archbold Review* 7.

——, "'We Do This in the Criminal Law and That in the Law of Tort': A New Fusion Debate" in S. Pitel, J. Neyers and E. Chamberlain (eds.), *Tort Law: Challenging Orthodoxy* (Oxford: Hart Publishing, 2013) 95.

——, *Principles of Equity and Trusts* (2nd ed., Oxford: Oxford University Press, 2016).

——, *The Principles of the Law of Restitution* (2nd ed., Oxford: Oxford University Press, 2006).

Vuoso, G., "Background Responsibility and Excuse" (1987) 96 *Yale LJ* 1661.

Wade, H.W.R., "The United Kingdom's Bill of Rights" in Cambridge Centre for Public Law, *Constitutional Reform in the United Kingdom: Practice and Principles* (Oxford: Hart Publishing, 1998) 59.

Waldron, J., *The Right to Private Property* (Oxford: Oxford University Press, 1988).

Walker, N., "The End of an Old Song" (1999) 149 *New LJ* 64.

——, *Crime and Insanity in England* (Edinburgh: Edinburgh University Press, 1968).

Walker, N. and Padfield, N., *Sentencing: Theory, Law and Practice* (London: Butterworths, 2nd ed., 1996).

Wall, J., "Sexual Offences and General Reasons Not to Have Sex" (2015) 35 *Oxford Journal of Legal Studies* 777.

——, "The Legal Status of Body Parts: A Framework" (2011) 31 *Oxford Journal of Legal Studies* 783.

Wallerstein, S., "'A Drunken Consent is Still Consent'—or is it? A Critical Analysis of a Drunken Consent Following *Bree*" (2009) 73 *Journal of Criminal Law* 318.

Walsh, E., *et al.*, "Violence and Schizophrenia: Examining the Evidence" (2002) 180 *British Journal of Psychiatry* 490.

Walters, M., "Conceptualizing Hostility for Hate Crime Law: Minding 'the Minutiae' when Interpreting Section 28(1)(a) of the Crime and Disorder Act 1998" (2014) 34 *Oxford Journal of Legal Studies* 47.

Walters, V., "Prosecuting Money Launderers: Do the Prosecution Have to Prove the Predicate Offence?" [2009] *Criminal LR* 571.

Warbrick, C. and Sullivan, G.R., "Ship Routeing Schemes and the Criminal Liability of the Master" [1984] *Lloyds Maritime and Commercial Law Quarterly* 23.

Ward, A.R., "Making Sense of Self-induced Intoxication" [1986] *Cambridge LJ* 247.

Ward, T., "Magistrates, Insanity and the Common Law" [1997] *Criminal LR* 796.

Warren, E.H., "Qualifying as Plaintiff in an Action for Conversion" (1936) 49 *Harvard LR* 1084.

Wasik, M., "A Learner's Careless Driving" [1982] *Criminal LR* 411.

——, "Abandoning Criminal Intent" [1980] *Criminal LR* 785.

——, "Mens Rea, Motive and the Problem of 'Dishonesty' in the Law of Theft" [1977] *Criminal LR* 543.

——, "Partial Excuses in the Criminal Law" (1982) 45 *Modern LR* 516.

Wasik, M. and Thompson, M.P., "Turning a Blind Eye as Constituting Mens Rea" (1981) 32 *Northern Ireland Law Quarterly* 328.

Waters, D., "Banks, Fiduciary Obligations and Unconscionable Transactions" (1986) 65 *Canadian Bar Review* 37.

Watkins, J.W.N., "Historical Explanation in the Social Sciences" (1957) 8 *British Journal for the Philosophy of Science* 104.

Weait, M., "Knowledge, Autonomy and Consent: *R v Konzani*" [2005] *Criminal LR* 763.

——, "Taking the Blame: Criminal Law, Social Responsibility and the Sexual Transmission of HIV" (2001) 23 *Journal of Social Welfare and Family Law* 441.

Weisiger, G.B., "Negligence of the Physically Infirm" (1946) 24 *North Carolina LR* 187.

Wellings, K., Field, J., Johnson, A., Wadsworth, J. and Bradshaw, S., *Sexual Behaviour in Britain: The National Survey of Sexual Attitudes and Lifestyles* (London: Penguin Books, 1994).

Wells, C., "Battered Women Syndrome and Defences to Homicide: Where Now?" (1994) 14 *Legal Studies* 266.

——, "Corporate criminal liability: a ten year review" [2014] *Criminal LR* 849.

——, "Stalking: the Criminal Law Response" [1997] *Criminal LR* 463.

——, *Corporations and Criminal Responsibility* (Oxford: Oxford University Press, 1993; 2nd ed 2001).

Wertheimer, A., *Coercion* (Princeton: Princeton University Press, 1987).

West, D.J. and Walk, A. (eds.), *Daniel McNaughton: His Trial and the Aftermath* (Ashford: Headley, 1977).

West, R., "A Comment on Consent, Sex, and Rape" (1996) 2 *Legal Theory* 233.

Westen, P., "Getting the Fly out of the Bottle: the False Problem of Free Will and Determinism" (2005) 8 *Buffalo Criminal LR* 101.

——, *The Logic of Consent: The Diversity and Deceptiveness of Consent As a Defense to Criminal Conduct* (Aldershot: Ashgate Dartmouth, 2004).

Wheat, K., "The Law's Treatment of the Suicidal" [2000] *Medical LR* 182.

White, A.R., "Intention, Purpose, Foresight and Desire" (1976) 92 *Law Quarterly Review* 569.

——, "The Identity and Time of the Actus Reus" [1977] *Criminal LR* 148.

——, "Trade Descriptions About the Future" (1974) 90 *Law Quarterly Review* 15.

White, R., "Civil Penalties: Oxymoron, Chimera and Stealth Sanction" (2010) 126 *Law Quarterly Review* 593.

White, S., "Continuing Representations in Criminal Law" (1986) 37 *Northern Ireland Law Quarterly* 255.

Williams, B., "Moral Luck" in *Moral Luck* (Cambridge: Cambridge University Press, 1981) 20.

——, "Moral Responsibility and Political Freedom" [1997] *Cambridge LJ* 96.

——, "The Actus Reus of Dr Caligari" (1994) 142 *U Pennsylvania LR* 1661.

——, *Ethics and the Limits of Philosophy* (London: Fontana, 1985).

Williams, Glanville, "Absolute Liability in Traffic Offences" [1967] *Criminal LR* 142 and 194.

——, "Appropriation: A Single or Continuous Act?" [1978] *Criminal LR* 69.

——, "Causation in Homicide" [1957] *Criminal LR* 429.

——, "Complicity, Purpose and the Draft Code" [1990] *Criminal LR* 4.

——, "Convictions and Fair Labelling" [1983] *Cambridge LJ* 85.

——, "Criminal Omissions—The Conventional View" (1991) 107 *Law Quarterly Review* 86.

——, "Evading Justice" [1975] *Criminal LR* 430.

——, "*Finis* for *Novus Actus*?" (1989) 48 *Cambridge LJ* 391.

——, "Handling, Theft and the Purchaser Who Takes a Chance" [1985] *Criminal LR* 432.

——, "Homicide and the Supernatural" (1949) 65 *Law Quarterly Review* 491.

——, "Innocent Agency and Causation" (1992) 3 *Criminal Law Forum* 289.

——, "Mistake as to Party in the Law of Contract" (1945) 23 *Canadian Bar Review* 271.

——, "Mistake in the Law of Theft" [1977] *Cambridge LJ* 62.

——, "Obedience to Law as a Crime" (1990) 53 *Modern Law Review* 445.

——, "Oblique Intention" (1987) 46 *Cambridge LJ* 417.

——, "Offences and Defences" (1982) 2 *Legal Studies* 233.

——, "Recklessness Redefined" [1981] *Cambridge LJ* 252.

——, "Temporary Appropriation Should Be Theft" [1981] *Criminal LR* 129.

——, "The Definition of Crime" (1955) *Current Legal Problems* 107.

——, "The Logic of 'Exceptions'" (1988) 47 *Cambridge LJ* 261.

——, "The Mens Rea for Murder: Leave it Alone" (1989) 105 *Law Quarterly Review* 387.

——, "The Theory of Excuses [1982] *Criminal LR* 732.

——, "The Unresolved Problem of Recklessness" (1988) 8 *Legal Studies* 74.

——, "Theft, Consent and Illegality" [1977] *Criminal LR* 127

——, "Three Rogues' Charters" [1980] *Criminal LR* 263.

——, "Venue and Ambit in the Criminal Law" (1961) 81 *Law Quarterly Review* 276, 395, 518.

——, "Victims and Other Exempt Parties in Crime" (1990) 10 *Legal Studies* 245.

——, "Victims as Parties to Crimes—A Further Comment" [1964] *Criminal LR* 686.

——, "What Should the Code Do about Omissions?" (1987) 7 *Legal Studies* 92.

——, *Criminal Law: The General Part* (London: Stevens, 2nd ed., 1961).

——, *Textbook of Criminal Law* (London: Stevens, 2nd ed., 1983).

——, *The Mental Element in Crime* (Jerusalem: Magnes Press, 1965).

——, *The Proof of Guilt: A Study of the English Criminal Trial* (London: Stevens, 2nd ed., 1958).

Williams, Glenys, "Gross Negligence Manslaughter and Duty of Care in 'Drugs' Cases: R. v Evans" [2009] *Criminal LR* 631.

Williams, R., "Deception, Mistake and Vitiation of the Victim's Consent" (2008) 124 *Law Quarterly Review* 132.

——, "Voluntary Intoxication—a Lost Cause?" (2013) 129 *Law Quarterly Review* 264.

Wilson, W., "A Plea for Rationality in the Law of Murder" (1990) 10 *Legal Studies* 307.

——, "The Structure of Criminal Homicide" [2006] *Criminal LR* 471.

Wilson, W. *et al.*, "Violence, Sleepwalking and the Criminal Law" [2005] *Criminal LR* 624.

Winfield, P.H., "Death as Affecting Liability in Tort" (1929) 29 *Columbia LR* 239.

——, "Quasi-contract Arising from Compulsion" (1944) 60 *Law Quarterly Review* 341.

Winslade, W.J., "Brady on Recklessness" (1972) 33 *Analysis* 31.

Withey, C., "Loss of Control: Loss of Opportunity?" [2011] *Criminal LR* 263.

Wolf, S., "The Legal and Moral Responsibility of Organisations" in J.R. Pennock and J.W. Chapman (eds.), *Criminal Justice* (New York: New York University Press, 1985).

Wolfram, S., "Eugenics and the Punishment of Incest Act 1908" [1983] *Criminal LR* 308.

Wootton, B., "Diminished Responsibility: A Layman's View" (1960) 76 *Law Quarterly Review* 224.

——, *Crime and the Criminal Law: Reflections of a Magistrate and a Social Scientist* (London: Sweet & Maxwell, 2nd ed., 1981).

World Health Organisation, *Diagnostic and Management Guidelines for Mental Disorders* (Geneva: World Health Organisation, 1996).

——, *International Statistical Classification of Diseases and Related Health Problems* ICD 10 (Geneva: World Health Organisation, 2010).

Wright, R.S., *Law of Criminal Conspiracies and Agreements* (London: Butterworths, 1873).

Yale, D.E.C., "A Year and a Day in Homicide" [1989] *Cambridge LJ* 202.

Yeo, S., "Sex, Ethnicity, Power of Self-control and Provocation Revisited" (1996) 18 *Sydney LR* 304.

Youdan, T.G. (ed.), *Equity, Fiduciaries and Trusts* (Toronto: Carswell, 1989).

Zedner, L. and Roberts, J. (eds.), *Principles and Values in Criminal Law and Criminal Justice: Essays in Honour of Andrew Ashworth* (Oxford: Oxford University Press, 2012).

INDEX